CW00802748

THE HORNBY COMPANION

Roger Beardsley

FRANK HORNBY
1863–1936

New Cavendish Books
LONDON

This book is dedicated to my darling Janet without whose forebearance and encouragement it would never have been completed.

Publishers' Note

In many instances, due to the rarity of the original documents, material has passed through several photographic processes and this may result in some diminution in quality. In addition, several enthusiastic past owners (in a time long before catalogues and ephemera were considered of historic value) have left their mark on the originals and these have been reproduced without amendment.

First edition published in Great Britain by New Cavendish Books – 1992.

Specification: 628 pages, over 900 illustrations including 265 in full colour.

The Hornby Companion Series

Design – John B. Cooper
Editorial Direction – Allen Levy
Editor – Narisa Chakra

Photosetting and mono illustrations by Wyvern Typesetting Ltd, Bristol.

Printed and bound in Hong Kong under the supervision of Mandarin Offset, London.

New Cavendish Books, 3 Denbigh Road, London W11 2SJ

ISBN 0 904568 95 4

Contents

Preface

I wrote in an introductory passage to Volume 6 that the Hornby Companion Series would be completed in 1988. I hope you will share my sentiment in that many of the best things in life are worth the wait.

At last in 1991 I commend you to Volume 8, the final book – the one that converts the series into a No. 10 Outfit! So much material remained that part of this work has been published as Volume 7a which with Volume 7 makes an attempt to do justice to *Meccano Magazine*, the best in-house magazine ever published.

If there is a bias towards Meccano material it is justified in terms of the longevity and importance of this product and its supporting literature. Few of the later products such as trains and diecast vehicles would have developed without the international fame of the pioneer product Meccano – for decades the world's finest constructional toy.

I was walking along a coastal path in southern Cornwall recently when my thoughts wandered to the subject of this series and what it was that united such a disparate bunch of people in their study and pursuit of pieces of coloured metal, diecast and tin made in Liverpool. Needless to say I was unable to encapsulate this phenomenon in a sentence let alone a word.

I have little doubt that if pressed we could all provide some explanation for the shared 'dementia' but suffice to say it has taken over a million words and thousands of illustrations to describe just the product without touching upon the sociological and psychological aspects of the subject. Perhaps a book entitled *'Meccanomania' – its Roots and Causes*, is waiting to be written.

I remember standing on a pavement seeing a boy clutching a green Hornby engine at the door of his house (the memory was clear enough to pin point an LNER 440). It was wartime and one only dreamt of such things. I still find Meccano products very special which has made the not entirely trouble free years of publishing this series totally worthwhile.

Allen Levy
London 1991

Introduction

This Volume, the last in the Hornby Companion Series, is for reasons of necessity more a celebration of the best of Meccano literature rather than an exhaustive work. To have attempted the latter would have been wellnigh impossible as well as being quite frankly undesirable. Fully covering the entire range over some 80 years would probably needed the space of the whole series and taken decades to complete. The result would have been extremely dull, unwieldy and in the main of interest only to a handful of collectors and Meccano academics.

For this reason, a great deal of condensing has had to take place giving rise to that age-old problem of what to leave out and therefore by inference what to include. Generally speaking the guiding principle has been that an item (or group of items) had to be of importance and interest in its own right or visually attractive to warrant inclusion. This has meant that much of the earliest material has not found a place. With really very few exceptions, items prior to the end of the First World War tend to be somewhat crude and lifeless. Important pieces from this era have been well covered in Volume 6 of the Hornby Companion Series and it would have been a waste of precious space to repeat them. Obviously one cannot deal with the outfit manuals without illustrating each main variety; omitting the earliest would have been wrong and would leave the reader without a full picture. Similarly it has been deemed pointless reproducing large numbers of manual pages which to all intents and purposes (for the majority of readers) are the same.

Other but similar considerations have ruled out much post-war literature, especially that from the late 1950s onwards. From then on, little of any real significance was produced and only a few visually interesting pieces relieve the boredom. In any case, literature of this period is in general very common and resides in large quantities on dealers' and collectors' disposal lists. This book had to be compiled with these factors in mind. Collectors do not want to purchase a volume which merely illustrates common material which they already have in profusion. Perhaps in fifty years some of it will benefit from antiquity, but age (and possible rarity) should not be the basis for treasuring otherwise undistinguished and charmless pieces of ephemera.

Another difficulty was that in selecting items, one kept coming back to the period 1920–1940, or, in other words, from the dawn of the first Hornby Trains to the wartime cessation of all production. So many items from this era cried out for inclusion on the grounds of both importance and artistic merit, often at the same time. It is also worth remembering that few collectors have the time, money or luck to be able to acquire more than a handful of the many desirable rarities from those years. Since it is this material which is the most sought-after, it was obvious that bias in that direction was essential.

Because of the wide range and types of literature, the chapters or sections of this volume differ one from another. For example, the importance of Meccano Standard Mechanisms and the Super Model Leaflets in the development of sophisticated modelling meant that some sort of analysis was necessary. The writing up of this material is therefore more in the nature of critical essays than commentaries. Catalogues and similar publicity or promotional material in the main require less comment and therefore little more than a straightforward historical introduction was necessary – they usually speak for themselves.

Printing Data

Collectors of Meccano literature have always counted themselves fortunate because of the existence of print references on most items from 1918 onwards. These detail the month and year of printing as well as the quantity printed in thousands. For example: 1 / 7 3 2 / 1 5

Thus 1 indicates the particular printer; 7 indicates July; 32 means 1932 and 15 indicates a run of 15,000 copies.

These codes can tell us a lot about an item's currency and are of great value to the researcher, although occasional misprints can lead to wild goose chases! They are also useful for those who wish to build-up collections of particular items. But it must not be forgotten that the majority of collectors only wish to keep items that are representative of a particular series. For example, whilst many will build-up a collection of one of each of the Super Model Leaflets, few will want, or be able to obtain, copies of all 85 or so print references actually issued. Similarly few would wish to acquire all the references for outfit instruction manuals printed between 1945 and 1953, which in total probably exceed 500. Most of those are members of large almost identical groups and such differences as there are must be extremely academic. Lists of printing references have therefore been given with circumspection – without attempting to be definitive. Collectors of one-inch pulleys, spanners and other minutiae have not held sway.

Foreign Editions

In the main this book deals with UK editions, although a Spanish edition of a 1959 Dinky Catalogue is reproduced in Chapter 9. Non-English versions of most items are known to exist in as many as six or more different languages. These have so far not been well documented and to have researched them fully would have been an almost impossible task within the timescale of this volume. Non-UK editions are therefore only mentioned where it is thought relevant.

By the very nature of things, this book is based on a personal choice. It has however been compiled with a view to making it appeal to as many collectors as possible. That there is a certain emphasis on literature which relates to Meccano as distinct from Hornby Trains or Dinky Toys is no accident. It was Meccano which was the fount and provided by far the largest volume of serious written material. In the end it has been Meccano which has lived on long after the last Hornby Train left the Test Room and the last real Dinky Toy the Paint Shop. Meccano has lasted nearly 90 years and looks well set for its century.

Acknowledgements

At this point in the proceedings it is usual to lapse into the Hollywood habit of thanking everybody from the office cleaner to the second cabin-boy's assistant's mate. The difference here is that so many people have given invaluable help. It is an invidious task to draw up a list, but the following have contributed much:

Geoff Anderton
Saul Bettinotti
Mick Burgess
Fred Gaisberg
Keith Cameron
Chris Graebe
The Gramophone Company
Tom McCallum
David Stokes
Clyde Suttle

Particular thanks must go to three people, Jim Gamble, Geoff Wright and Ken Ratcliff.

Jim has done so much towards what you see before you both with ideas and much material from his Nottingham Meccano Collection. Without his invaluable help Volume 8 would certainly never have been finished (or started for that matter!).

Geoff Wright of M W Models at Henley-on-Thames has put his own Meccano Library at my disposal, provided me with umpteen photocopies for research and been patient with my seemingly endless questions.

Ken Ratcliff had the unenviable task of photographing all the original documents. It is only when you start this type of work that you realise how difficult it is. The material is often of very variable quality, with the result that sometimes when the half-tone illustrations are clear and sharp, the printed word is otherwise. Compromise sometimes had to be the order of the day.

My thanks to all concerned.

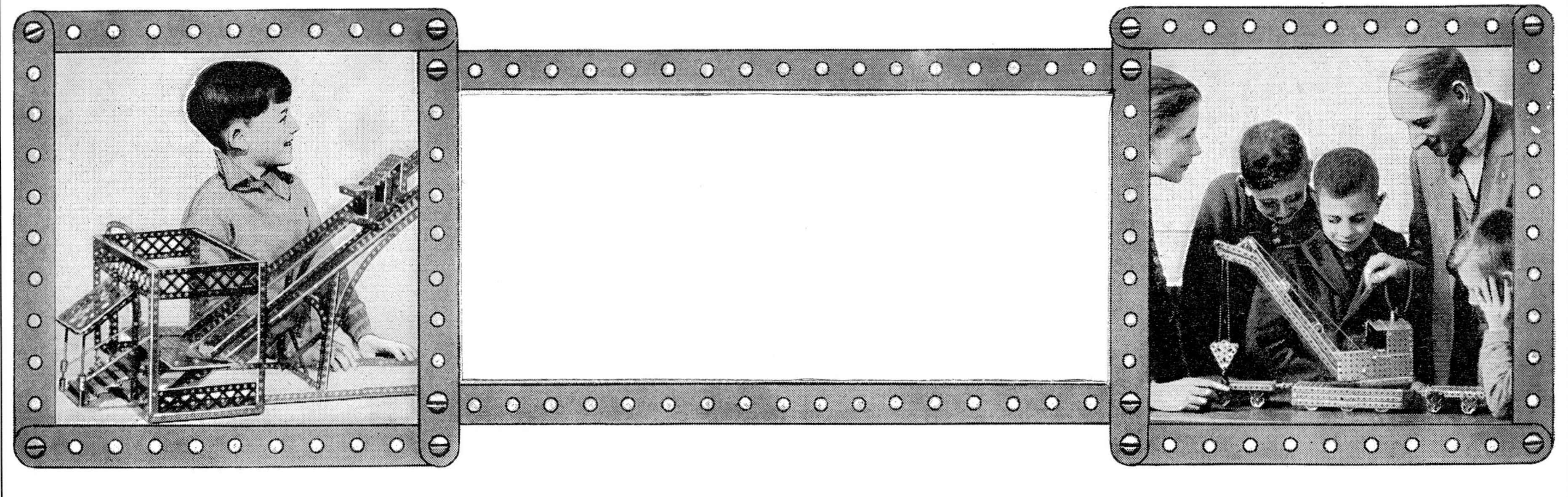

Prelude

For many years now, the various publications issued by Meccano Ltd during its long history, have been the subject of great interest for collectors of the products which emanated from Binns Road. They are avidly acquired as an adjunct to the toys which have thrilled many generations of boys both young and not-so-young. Why should this be so? The models shown in the early *Books of Instruction* rarely tax the abilities of the modern Meccano modeller and the locomotives so proudly displayed in the *Hornby Books of Trains* are long out of production. In fact to the casual observer, most Meccano literature would appear to be little more than a mine of useless, out-of-date information. In reality this is quite true, but then thankfully Meccano collectors have never bothered about such mundane good sense. (The author for one has no intention of ever giving up his Meccano Outfit whatever the Household Gods may say!) For those who bought Frank Hornby's creations first-hand, the literature was, and is, as the famous catalogue after which this volume is jacketed, a Magic Carpet to worlds of delight.

The historical value

It is certainly true that today most Meccano Products are collected and played with by adults – and the same is probably true for Meccano in its current French reincarnation. Meccano literature is currently appreciated not merely as commercial listings, however attractive, but as frozen moments of virtually every reader's past.

As with many collectables, the historic aspect of Meccano products is particularly strong and has been for many years. The depth to which some collectors will go to further their knowledge ranges from a passing curiosity to a quality of research which in academic fields would probably earn a PhD.

The paperwork issued by Meccano Ltd is of great importance as a source of historical information, although as we shall see later on great care needs to be exercised when formulating statements of fact based on this alone. However, when used intelligently, the literature enables us to build up a good picture, not only of the course of one or more particular products, but a pretty fair chart of the company's history. The products themselves can tell us little on their own but allied to the written word, the story can be deduced.

The literature can also convey something else, which is of great significance when considering the whole picture, namely the Meccano 'ethos' and by implication that of its 'deus ex Meccano' Frank Hornby (with apologies to my latin Master, Mr Minty, or Sid as he was known). Reference to the inside cover of most instruction manuals perhaps reveals most about this outlook which can be summarised as a realisation that the best traditions of British service can make good commercial sense:

'The service of Meccano does not end with the selling of an outfit and an instruction manual. When you want to know something more about engineering than is shown in our books, or when you strike a tough problem of any kind, write to us. The wonderful knowledge of engineering . . . gained only by years of hard earned experience, is at your service. *We want the Meccano boy to be the famous engineer of tomorrow*.' And they meant it. Just look at the short series of letters (fig 1) and consider the attention given.

The wealth of material published in support of Hornby's ideals and intentions is demonstrable proof they were not empty words. Reference to the whole range of literature issued shows that the high ideals to which Hornby and the company subscribed (though as intimated not completely altruistically) grew in the early years, peaked in the 1920s and 1930s and then after his death gradually declined. One could perhaps make the observation that it followed a similar curve to that which might be drawn to indicate the company's commercial success or otherwise. It would be wrong however to draw the conclusion that the one depended upon the other; in fact straightforward economics and the vagaries of fashion had a far greater and more damaging impact. It is worth considering that it was financial strength which enabled Hornby to run the company with such a benevolent eye.

To summarise, the literature provides us with a valuable tool without which it would be difficult or even impossible to chart Meccano's history. It also enables us to build up an historical picture of the way the company, as an entity, saw its role in the scheme of things.

It is of course not just for historical detail that collectors acquire the many and varied publications issued over three quarters of a century or more. In fact there are probably more collections which have been formed for other reasons. These 'other' reasons are highly subjective and frankly emotive, but we do need to examine them in order to understand what it is which drives an otherwise sane individual to hyperventilate at the discovery of some seemingly insignificant bit of paper or booklet that an outsider would have consigned to the dustbin long ago.

It is the generally accepted view that in terms of sheer quantity and quality, Meccano's golden age was the period from 1920 to 1940, or, in other words, from the dawn of the first Hornby Trains, via the greatly increased sophistication of Meccano

continued p. 10.

Telephone
Old Swan 701 (6 lines)

PLEASE ADDRESS ALL
COMMUNICATIONS TO
THE EDITOR

PUBLISHED MONTHLY IN THE INTERESTS
OF BOYS

Telegrams
Meccano Liverpool

EDITORIAL OFFICE
BINNS ROAD
LIVERPOOL

Master John Grieve,
Glasgow.

20th August,
1925.

Dear Grieve,

Many thanks for your letter. I quite understand why you could not write before, and I am very sorry indeed to learn of your Uncle's serious illness.

The drawing of the Watchstand which you enclosed is very interesting, and if you do not mind, I am keeping it to add to my collection.

I am glad that you have received a Meccano Clockwork Motor. Your parents are evidently good judges when it comes to presents, and I can quite imagine that this will make all the difference in your model-building. It is fine to build a model yourself and then to be able to work it by means of your motor.

I note that you require particulars of the "Eiffel Tower" model. Is it possible that you have not had a copy of the August Magazine? I simply cannot imagine any real Meccano enthusiast willingly missing this fine issue, and I am enclosing a copy herewith. On page 384 you will find the instructions that you require, and I shall be glad if you will enclose 3d in payment for this Magazine when next you write to me.

I am glad that you have ordered the "Hornby Book of Trains" as I am sure that this will interest you enormously.

With all good wishes,

Yours sincerely,

The Editor

FEC

Fig 1. *A fascinating series of letters from Meccano to an MM reader and Guild member from the mid-1920s.*

Telephone Old Swan 701 (6 lines)

Please address all communications to THE EDITOR

MECCANO MAGAZINE
PUBLISHED MONTHLY IN THE INTERESTS OF BOYS

Telegrams Meccano Liverpool

Editorial Office Binns Road Liverpool

Master J.D.Grieve,
Glasgow.

24th December,
1925.

Dear Grieve,

Many thanks for your letter from which I am sorry to learn that your uncle is dead and I trust you will accept my deepest sympathy.

Your remittance of 3d in stamps came safely to hand and a copy of the Motor Chassis leaflet has been sent you under separate cover, which I hope you will have received by now.

I think your Church Bazaar did wonderfully well in raising such a huge sum of money as £975. I note that you have sent up for a copy of the Magic Carpet booklet and no doubt when you receive this letter your booklet will have come to hand.

In regard to the Meccano Limousine, the body of it is fitted on to the Chassis, and you will find full particulars in the enclosed copy of the February 1924 issue of the "M.M."

With all good wishes for Christmas and the New Year.

I am,
Yours sincerely,
The Editor

Telephone Old Swan 701 (6 lines)

Please address all communications to THE EDITOR

MECCANO MAGAZINE

Telegrams Meccano, Liverpool

Editorial Office Binns Road Liverpool

Master John D. Grieve,
GLASGOW.

16th March, 1927

Dear Grieve,

Accept my best thanks for your letter received a few days ago, accompanied by two photographs of your latest model and yourself. They are very clear indeed, and I am very pleased to have had an opportunity of seeing your photograph, John. I should like to retain it for my "Picture Gallery" so perhaps you will let me know the next time you write if I may do so. The model looks very well indeed, and if I were you I should retain details of it for the next suitable model-building Contest, particulars of which will of course be given in the Magazine. I am returning the photograph of the model so that you will not need to prepare another.

I quite understand that you will not have much time for letter-writing if you have a great deal of homework, but the latter is necessary if you are anxious to do well at school, and I know that this is your aim. Work hard at school, John, and you will reap your reward later; I

MECCANO MAGAZINE — Continuation No. 1

Master John D. Grieve, Glasgow. 16th March, 1927

shall be interested in hearing how you have fared in the examination, so perhaps you will let me know when the results are ready.

I have heard that Rothesay is a very popular seaside resort in the north, and I am glad that you have had an opportunity of visiting it. The majority of boys show a keen interest in the engines on a ship, and quite a number of them make up their minds (on seeing the engines) that they will be engineers when they grow up! Engines seem to fascinate them; I know that when I was a boy I would stand for hours watching an engine working, but on looking back I am afraid I must have been a perfect nuisance to the engineers for I always had an unlimited number of questions to ask.

With all good wishes,

I am,
Yours sincerely,
The Editor

GB

Telephone: Old Swan 701

Please address all communications to THE SECRETARY

THE MECCANO GUILD
A FELLOWSHIP OF MECCANO BOYS

Telegrams: Meccano, Liverpool

Headquarters: Old Swan, Liverpool

Master John Duff Grieve,
GLASGOW.

May 13th
1925.

Dear Grieve,

I was pleased to have your very nicely written letter and as you intend to help the Guild I shall be delighted to assist you so I am sending some application forms and if you get a fair number of your pals and their friends to join, I see no reason why we should not soon have a really flourishing Meccano Club in Townhead.

With all good wishes,

I am,
Yours sincerely,
The Secretary

RM/WCB

Telephone: Old Swan 701

Please address all communications to THE SECRETARY

THE MECCANO GUILD
A FELLOWSHIP OF MECCANO BOYS

Telegrams: Meccano, Liverpool

Headquarters: Old Swan, Liverpool

Master John Duff Grieve,
GLASGOW.

May 28th
1925.

Dear Grieve,

I was pleased to receive your long and interesting letter and to know that you are of an inventive turn of mind and I am sure your Meccano outfit will provide very many more happy hours.

About the Magazine puzzles, if you read the page carefully you will see that for May the Puzzle Competition takes the form of making Palindromes and if you can devise one or two and send them on before Tuesday next they will be in time for a chance of winning a prize. The answers to the other puzzles are for your own interest and amusement this time.

I am extremely glad that you think you have passed your examinations and I hope you will always work hard, play hard, and laugh hard!

With all good wishes,

I am,
Yours sincerely,
The Secretary

RM/WCB.

Telephone Old Swan 701 (6 lines)

Please address all communications to THE EDITOR

MECCANO MAGAZINE
PUBLISHED MONTHLY IN THE INTERESTS OF BOYS

Telegrams Meccano Liverpool

Editorial Office Binns Road Liverpool

Master John Grieve,
Glasgow.

1st July
1925.

Dear Grieve,

Many thanks for your letter which I was very pleased to receive, and I am glad to note that you have won a first class certificate in a Bible Examination. I also note that your sister succeeded in winning two certificates, and you certainly appear to be a brainy family.

I shall be interested to see a drawing or snapshot of the model to which you refer, when next you write to me, and I shall always be pleased to hear about any models which you happen to build without aid.

With all good wishes and hoping to hear from you again shortly,

I am, Yours sincerely,
The Editor

BB.

Fig 1.

TELEPHONE: STONEYCROFT 2701 (8 LINES)

TELEGRAMS, MECCANO LIVERPOOL

MECCANO MAGAZINE

BINNS ROAD
LIVERPOOL 13

18th January 1952.

Mr.J.W.Beardsley,
Rosegarth,
20, Tewit Well Avenue,
HARROGATE, Yorkshire.

Dear Sir,

Thank you for your letter. We are very pleased to learn that your son is an enthusiastic model-builder, and we are glad to know that the "M.M." model-building articles have proved useful. We are always pleased to help model-builders with their problems, but you will appreciate that many different types of steering mechanisms can be made with Meccano and it is impossible to deal fully with the subject in a letter. If you will let us know the type of mechanism you have in mind and details of the model for which it is required, we will do our best to help you.

As you suggest it would be very difficult to deal with such a varied subject as general gearing in the limited space available in an "M.M." article, but we hope to deal with at least some aspects of gearing applied to Meccano models in future issues. The ratios between any two spur gears is easily found by dividing the number of teeth in the Pinion into the number of teeth in the Gear. Thus a Meccano ½" diameter 19-tooth Pinion meshed with a 57-tooth Gear gives a ratio of 3:1. The ratio of a Meccano Worm meshed with a Gear is always equivalent to the number of teeth in the Gear, and a Worm meshed with a ½" Pinion gives a ratio of 19:1. The correct ratio to be used in driving a particular model is largely a matter of experience. The Motor should always run at its maximum speed, and various ratios should be tried until the model is driven efficiently without any sign of labouring by the Motor.

We are not quite clear if your E20R Electric Motor failed to drive model No.10.20 completely, or if it was driven at a very slow speed. In the latter case the Motor may have sufficient power to enable you to cut out one stage of the reduction gearing while still driving the

p.t.o.

TELEPHONE: STONEYCROFT 2701 (8 LINES)

TELEGRAMS, MECCANO LIVERPOOL

MECCANO MAGAZINE

BINNS ROAD
LIVERPOOL 13

-2-

model satisfactorily. The original gearing employed in this model was based on the performance of the old E120 Electric Motor, and it would be advisable to experiment with the ratios to find a suitable reduction for the E20R Motor.

The enclosed sketch shows a modified steering arrangement for the Ambulance built with Outfit No.10. This makes use of a 57-tooth Gear in place of a Toothed Segment, and we hope it will be of some help to you.

A number of parts included in the No.10 Outfit are not actually used in the models shown in the Instructions Book, but your son will find there parts useful when he starts to build models to his own designs. We enclose cuttings describing the uses of some of the parts you mention. Spring Cord can be used to make small tension springs, or as the outer sheath of a Bowden cable control using thin wire as the inner core. The Cord can also be used as a driving belt in certain cases. The Centre Fork can be meshed with Sprocket Wheels in intermittent motion mechanisms, or used as the "knife edge" in bearings for models such as weighing machines and balances.

The Meccano publications you mention were printed many years ago, and we are afraid copies are no longer available. All stocks of the "Standard Mechanisms" and "How to Use Meccano Parts" Manuals, the New Models Books and the Super Model Leaflets are now exhausted.

Yours sincerely,
MECCANO MAGAZINE

N. G. Tudor

Editorial Department.

WJ/MM.

Fig 1.

parts and models in the 1920s, the enormous expansion of the product range in the early 1930s, up until the introduction and consolidation of the position of Hornby Dublo. Had it not been for a contemptible little man with a ridiculous moustache, things might have been very different and the era might have continued as before. But the war did happen and the post-war economic climate meant that there could never be a return to the pre-war levels of activity. There were some flashes of the old glory after 1945, but the world was a very different place, becoming further removed from those balmy (or so they now seem) pre-war days, as each year went by.

It is that view of pre-war days of a golden period, (whatever the realities) that gives literature of this period such an emotive pull.

Nostalgia

Nostalgia like the poor is always with us, but what exactly is it and what is its power?

The phrase 'It was much better in the good old days' has probably been used from time immemorial in relation to everything. Of course not everything was better 'in the good old days' – such claims are often the product of closed minds. However, in the case of Frank Hornby's creations, the general consensus is that they were better in those far off days before the war destroyed the benign Pax Britannica. (O tempora! O mores!)

The original meaning of nostalgia can be expressed as a desire, motivated by homesickness, to return to one's native land. Over the years this has been expanded to cover a longing for days gone by and a wish to relive the past. For the collector of Meccano products this naturally means reliving those carefree days when a Meccano Outfit or Hornby Train meant hours of oblivious pleasure.

Nostalgia for Binns Road toys is easy to understand – it was those things which were played with in youth. However with the exceptions of the *Meccano Magazine* and the various books of instruction, the literature did not have that kind of usage. What the paperwork (and especially the promotional ephemera) does do is to conjure up images which are as powerful today as they were several generations ago. Indeed, many of these publications describe their wares so alluringly that they only serve to inflame the desire of collectors to acquire more 'treasures'. That is of course exactly what they were intended to do in the first place. The fact that this can happen to people who never had any direct experience of Meccano toys shows just how potent was the particular magic which emanated from Binns Road.

The Magic

Meccano literature has been variously described as 'charming', 'appealing', 'alluring' and a host of other words expressing similar as well as complementary ideas. These are words which relate to concepts which are totally subjective and therefore impossible to define in absolute terms. No doubt psychologists could do this with wonderful theories involving childhood insecurity or deprivation.

Meccano Ltd's printed matter was in the main visually attractive. From a simple price list to a complete full colour catalogue the idea was the same – to make it look good and mouthwatering – rarely did they fail. As anyone involved in the printing or advertising industries will know, layout and artwork are of vital importance if the message is to be got across with any degree of success. This requires time, flair and above all, imagination. Even a cursory glance at the illustrations in this book will make it apparent that Meccano had no deficiencies in these departments.

Take for example the catalogue covers for 1930/31 illustrated on page 285. 'Toy Trains and Model Building for Pleasure' hits the eye straightaway. The bright red and black Royal Scot emerges from the frame, its apparent speed heightened by the use of plain white to the right of and below the locomotive. Then look at the cover produced by Halfords for their own shops. By comparison with the Meccano cover it seems dull and cluttered, the use of colour is poor and nothing stands out. A more serious problem is that it does not invite one to look inside. In fact the inside pages are identical, but what a difference a well-designed cover makes.

One device used particularly effectively was the mixing of pictures of different scales. Look at the 'Meccano' folder of 1933 (fig 2). Here we have an illustration of Super Model No. 19a, the Steam Excavator, but superimposed over it are photographs of two boys apparently operating the model. Note how the scales have been chosen to make it look 'right'. Now on its own, SML 19a is a most attractive model and quite suitable for the folder, but the addition of the two 'operators' makes it appear to be much larger and more imposing. Once again the designer's imagination has added to the overall effect and in the process transformed an otherwise ordinary picture of a model into what a boy might see in his mind's eye when playing with that excavator.

These are just two of the ways in which Meccano used design to achieve their objectives. Another was the care which they took with artwork and *continued p. 13.*

Fig 2. 1933 folder showing the mixing of scales.

DUKE'S MECCANO.

NURSERY DAYS RECALLED.

VISIT TO FAMOUS TOYWORKS.

ENGINE FOR PRINCESS ELIZABETH.

From Our Own Correspondent.

LIVERPOOL, Tuesday.

FOR half-an-hour this afternoon the Duke of York was transported back to the half-forgotten days of his boyhood to the time when he sat on the nursery floor and built toy bridges and cranes and engines.

He met the inventor of the most famous toy in the world—Mr. Frank Hornby, who, as a young engineer 30 years ago, made the first Meccano set.

When Mr. Hornby took the Duke over the great Mecanno factory in Binns-road, Liverpool, to-day, he recalled how he had played with the toy when he was young.

"Used to build all sorts of things," he told Mr. Hornby. "This is taking me back to boyhood." And when Mr. Hornby presented him with a beautiful little railway engine for Princess Elizabeth the Duke beamed.

"She'll be delighted with it," he *said.*

WORKING MODELS.

Very proudly Mr. Hornby led the Duke to a table where scores of models were working furiously. Brightly painted model trains ran dizzily round their narrow rails; a lift was ascending and descending an Eiffel Tower as tall as a man and tiny bulbs were winking at the top. Cranes jibbed and swung Overhead an aeroplane droned realistically.

The 1,200 girls who are employed in the works were obviously finding it difficult to maintain the instruction to "go on working as usual" during the Duke's visit. They sat demurely in front of endless moving platforms that carried their work from one to another, and only occasionally risked a quick, guilty glance at the Duke.

NERVOUS GIRL.

One girl whom he questioned was too nervous to answer, and the information had to be supplied by Mr. Hornby.

Discipline in the big factory suddenly snapped when somebody stopped the machinery and announced that the girls might go out and see the Duke leave.

In a body they jumped up and ran helter-skelter for the doors. The road outside was a mass of blue coats and brown overalls. As the girls pressed round the Duke's car, waving handkerchiefs and cheering frantically, the Duke smiled and waved his hand to them.

Fig 5. Press cutting from the Binns Road library relating to the Duke's visit. What happened to the train set?

Fig 3. The Duke of York at Binns Road, 20th May 1930.

Fig 4. The montage version of the same scene.

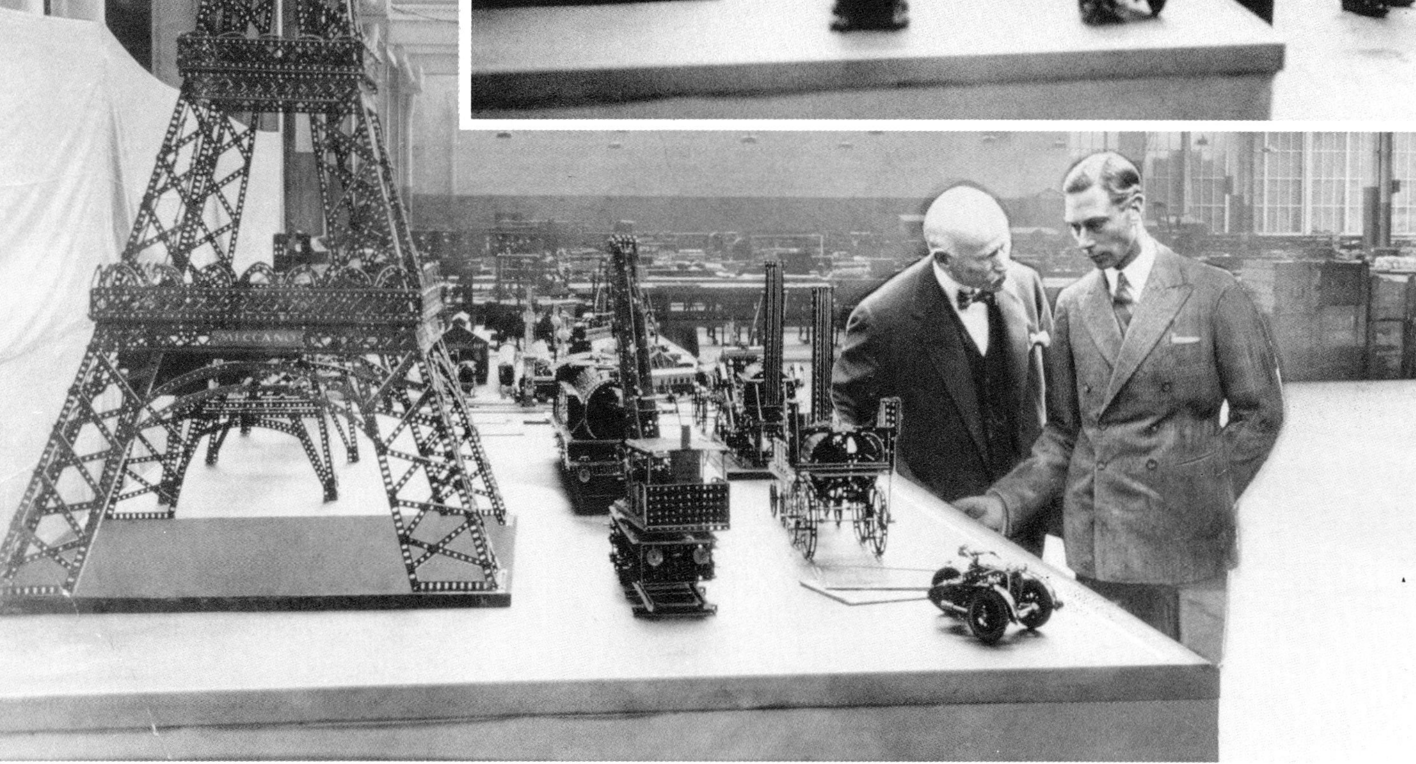

Fig 6. Original artwork for the illustration of the Bobigny factory and next to it the back page of a 1932 catalogue which used it.

MECCANO LTD.

Head Office and Factory :
OLD SWAN, LIVERPOOL, ENGLAND.

London Office and Warehouse :
Meccano Ltd.,
Walnut Tree Walk,
Kennington Road London. S.E.11.

Canadian Office and Warehouse :
Meccano Ltd.,
34 St. Patrick Street,
Toronto.

French Factory :
MECCANO (FRANCE) LTD., BOBIGNY.

Paris Office :
Meccano (France) Ltd.,
78/80 Rue Rébeval, Paris.

Meccano G.m.b.H.
Düsseldorf, Friedrich-Ebert-Strasse 18,
Berlin, S.W.42. Ritterstrasse 11.

Dick's Visit to Meccanoland

We weave beautifully coloured fabric with the Meccano Loom.

FROM 6 TO 60 THE CORRECT AGE

"About what age do boys usually take up Meccano, and when do they leave off building with it?"

"Tens of thousands of boys take it up at the age of four or five, practically as soon as they can use a screw-driver. As far as I can see, they give up building with Meccano only when they die! The most suitable age is anywhere between 6 and 60. Young boys play with it for the fun of building machines and seeing them operate. Boys from 14 to 20, who have reached the thinking age, find in Meccano something more than a hobby for their leisure hours. Through Meccano many of them have discovered that they have a natural gift and inclination for engineering work. They are making engineering their profession in life and solving the great question of their future career in the best way of all, that is by their own free choice and inclination. They take up real work, still encouraged and instructed by the hobby that they began as children.

"Even if a boy has never seen a machine in his life, he can build any of the hundreds of models shown in our Manuals of Instructions. I don't suppose that many boys start on the big models. They get loads of fun from the simpler ones, and while they are building these they are acquiring skill in putting the parts together and becoming familiar with the names and uses of all the various parts, so that when they come to the bigger models they have no trouble whatever."

"Then grown men—professors, draughtsmen and engineers—use Meccano for building scientific instruments, models of inventions, new devices and for trying out ideas. Here is a file of letters from men all over the world who have written to tell us that they are using Meccano every day of their lives for one thing or another,

11

Dick's Visit to Meccanoland

and by doing so are saving thousands of pounds that they would otherwise have to pay for models and patterns with which to try out their ideas."

A HUNDRED THOUSAND MODELS

"All this is very interesting indeed," I said, "and I am beginning to wonder why boys ever buy any toy other than Meccano. How many models do you think your biggest Outfit will make altogether?"

"That is a question," replied Mr. Hornby, "which I hope never to be able to answer. We show over 600 in our Manuals, and we have hundreds and hundreds of new ones, as yet unpublished, and each of them is as good as any we have ever had. New ideas for models reach us every day. Over a hundred thousand have been sent in for the Meccano Prize Contests by competitors—and I can tell you that as long as our staff of expert model-makers produce at their present rate, and as long as Meccano boys continue to show the same ingenuity in our many contests, the new models available will be unlimited in number. We describe new models in every issue of the *Meccano Magazine.*"

DON'T BUY AN IMITATION

"When Meccano was first invented it was possible to build only simple models with it, but as new engineering parts were added to the system, models of a much better type became possible, until now we claim that there is no mechanical movement known that cannot be worked out with Meccano. This is a strong claim, I know, but it is the fidelity of Meccano parts to engineering principles that has established the supremacy of the hobby, and given it a standing that competition cannot touch. The Meccano system is based on the laws of engineering and mechanics, and until these laws are superseded nothing can take its place. Take it from me, any other constructional toy that attempts to do the same thing in any other way is unscientific, and will do a boy more harm than good, distorting his mind instead of furnishing him with useful knowledge."

I felt that I wanted to interrupt Mr. Hornby to tell him how cordially I agreed with all he said, and how full of admiration I was for the great work that he and his Company were doing among boys like my own. His enthusiasm and earnestness were wonderful things to me, and I found myself beginning to

Mr. Hornby tells us how he came to invent Meccano.

12

Fig 7. Two pages from 'Dick's visit to Meccanoland'.

photographic material. In pre-war days, the company had at their disposal the expertise of a team of retouchers. Photographs from whatever source were carefully retouched to ensure maximum clarity when reproduced. A good example is the series of photographs of the Duke of York's visit to Binns Road in 1930. One of them (fig 3) shows the Duke and Hornby at a table filled with display models. The original 'snapshot' is fuzzy and totally unsuitable for reproduction. What the artwork department did was to take a 'studio' picture of the display table and to montage a picture of The Duke and Hornby taken from another photograph. To improve matters still further, the photograph of the display was retouched even to the extent of whitening the holes in the girders on the Eiffel Tower! The result can be seen in figs 4/5. The abilities of the artists at Binns Road are further demonstrated by the non-photographic illustration of the then new French Factory at Bobigny, almost photographic in its execution. This illustration was used on the reverse of many manuals and catalogues, one of which is shown in fig 6.

A word of caution. From the foregoing it will be clear that the expert attentions of the artwork department could (and do) give rise to a problem in relying upon the veracity of their illustrations. It cannot be over-emphasized how dangerous conclusions based on their evidence alone can be. Further examples of this problem occur later in the book.

Up until now we have only considered the visual element, but of course the written word played its part and Meccano had many talented writers, not least Hubert Lansley and Ellison Hawkes. Naturally the editorial style of Meccano publications varied according to type and did not conform to a rigid 'house style'. This would have been impossible given the wide range of printed matter issued by Meccano. It was also geared to the presumed age of the reader, so that we find simple straightforward language for younger readers but an adult approach for the older boy, this being especially important from the late 1920s onwards with the great increase in the sophistication and complexity of Meccano Models. To talk down to the adult reader of an article on epicyclic gear-boxes would have produced a somewhat negative response. Having said that, even the manuals for the smallest of outfits used basic engineering terms (albeit occasionally incorrectly in the early days).

Promotional material was naturally written in styles very different from that used in the technical and factual publications. Those which aimed at the prospective Meccano boy tended to assume that he would be of somewhat tender years. 'Dick's Visit to Meccanoland' (fig 7) is a typical example of this sort of booklet issued in the pre-war years. The picture of Dick shows a very young boy probably no more than seven or eight years of age. Oddly (to us at any rate) the writing which is in story-book style, contains some quite difficult words for a seven year old to negotiate e.g. '. . . and disclosed a neat mechanical contrivance with a little crank at one end and a wooden platform at the other.' The more one considers these booklets, the more one gains the impression that they were as much meant to be read aloud by a parent, as by the child itself. Perhaps dual targetting was the intention, after all if you can convince the purse strings. . .

One point never to be forgotten is the age in which much of this material was written. Whilst a seven year old today may well be virtually incapable of reading competently, standards of literacy were considerably higher in the 1920s and 1930s. In those days children were taught to read quickly using traditional methods, no phonetic absurdity then to make up for incompetent left-wing theorists amongst the would-be pedagogues. The era was also responsible for many of the expressions (and the seemingly patronising style) to be found in 'Dick's Visit' and others. 'Jolly good fun' and 'How topping' may seem quaint in the 1990s but they were in fashion 60 years ago.

Deep thinking social historians may find something profoundly significant in their use, but it should be remembered that the world was a much more civilised and mannered place in the days before social engineers got to work to 'do good' – speech as well as the written word reflected that.

For the older reader, the writing in promotional work was quite different as one would expect. One of the best examples is the 1928 *Meccano Book of Engineering* which was reproduced in its entirety in Volume 2 of this series. Here was a publication taking a serious look at the current state of engineering. Well written and beautifully produced, it concentrated on a small number of topics rather than trying to cover everything. What is interesting is that it not only deals with the physical details of the subject in question, but also its significance in a broader sense. For example, when discussing the irrigation system in Sind, it mentions not the technical detail, which had been covered earlier, but instead highlights what the project would achieve for the country involved. Something else which that publication deals with is the conservation of resources – a popular topic today but in 1928 an almost unheard-of and probably unwanted idea. But Meccano at that time always looked to the future, and the wisdom of this was proved by commercial success. It was its failure to move with the times which exacerbated the company's later downfall, but that is another story.

The range of styles and types of publication covered by the term 'Meccano Literature' is as this book demonstrates, very wide. However one publication included them all and more – the *Meccano Magazine.*

There are so many aspects to the *Meccano Magazine* that it gets a separate book to itself – Volume 7A. Not only that, Volume 7 of this series was devoted to reproducing all the covers, providing a subject index and giving its history extracted from Volume 6.

The *MM*'s importance in Meccano's history cannot be over-emphasised because of the commercial implications. Its value to the company was immense and in return Meccano Ltd accorded it high priority. This attention was amply rewarded and fully justified the investment. The *MM* soon became the 'Compleat' boys' magazine as Mr. Walton might have put it. Basically, it catered for its readers' natural thirst for knowledge in many fields of engineering. Add to that sections on Meccano, Hornby Trains, Dinky Toys, Hornby Dublo, Stamps, Railways and so forth, and you have the perfect magazine for boys of all ages.

Apart from its wide coverage, what else made the *Meccano Magazine*, especially in its peak years, so unique? What made it into something which even someone without any interest in old toys can pick up half a century or more later and find so engrossing? To find out one really needs to think back to Hornby's vision and Ellison Hawkes' genius and an excellent cross-section of this material is contained in Volume 7A. Suffice it to say that the *MM* was yet another example of the prodigious talents which inhabited Binns Road.

Conclusion

Dealing with and discussing Meccano literature is fraught with difficulty. Intangibles such as style, magic and visual attraction are all very subjective. What one may consider colourful another may think most vulgar. What rarely causes dissension though is the generally accepted view that in its finest years Meccano literature was something very special. This book is dedicated to that Golden Age.

Outfit Instruction Manuals

The most common items of Meccano literature are the ordinary instruction manuals supplied with each outfit. Bearing in mind the huge range and large print runs (100,000 was not uncommon), this is only to be expected. With the exception of material from the very earliest days and to a lesser extent the period 1934–1937, manuals for most years are still relatively easy to find. It remains possible for most collectors to build up a good representative collection.

Although the size and style of manuals varied throughout Meccano's history, most manuals within particular date-bands are very similar to each other and only the main styles and types will be covered here. The naturally occurring date-bands are as follows:

1. 1901–7. Mechanics Made Easy. Simplified Mechanics and the very first Meccano manuals.

2. 1908–35. First series of numbered outfits finally to No. 7.

3. 1934–37. Lettered series.

4. 1937–41. Second numerical series to outfit 10.

5. 1945–48. First post-war series.

6. 1948–53. Second post-war series (the famous W. H. Pinyon illustration).

7. 1954–56. Third post-war series (dragline in substitution for blocksetting crane).

8. 1956–62. Fourth series (completely revised dragline illustration).

9. 1962–69. The first 'exploded diagram' series.

10. 1970 onwards.

Before looking at each of these periods, a few words of caution. For those interested in the history of Meccano, the manuals can be something of a two-edged sword, in that they can tell us something about the development of the system, but only providing we already know the story in some detail. This somewhat contradictory statement stems from the fact that the manuals were frequently many years out of date. Sometimes artwork would be updated to show a part in its new form, but more often than not the illustration was left as it was. The only widespread exception to this was the cross-hatching added to plates from the mid 1930s to simulate those produced during the Blue/Gold era.

As an example, fig 1 shows a long out-of-date model no. G7 from the 1937 F-L manual, with the contrate wheel of the pattern which became obsolete in 1921! Fig 2 (model H23 from the same manual) shows the pawl as it was prior to 1926. Both these examples could be very misleading to the novice historian and indeed some of those who should know better have on occasions been guilty of ignoring the problems of anachronistic artwork.

Sometimes a set of illustrations would be extensively re-touched, for example, The Eiffel Tower, which was featured in many manuals. Fig 3 shows it as originally published and using the 1921–25 sidelever electric motor and braced girders. Fig 4 shows it retouched so as to appear to use strip plates.

Numerous similar anomalies and anachronisms can be found throughout the manuals of 70 or more years. The same difficulty arises with the parts list included in the manuals – frequently the illustrations were many years out of date and in some cases showed parts which were no longer obtainable.

All of this makes reliance on manuals for historical matters less than totally accurate. It is better, therefore, that they are enjoyed for what they are – delightful reminders of the past to be kept with the outfits to which they belong.

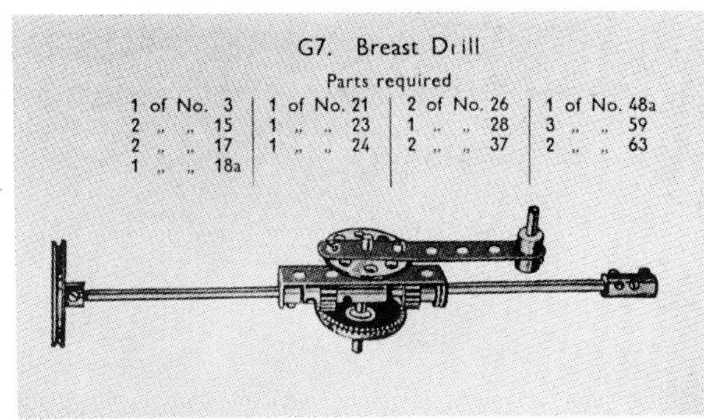

G7. Breast Drill
Parts required
1 of No. 3
2 „ „ 15
2 „ „ 17
1 „ „ 18a
1 of No. 21
1 „ „ 23
1 „ „ 24
2 of No. 26
1 „ „ 28
2 „ „ 37
1 of No. 48a
3 „ „ 59
2 „ „ 63

Fig 1. Note the obsolete contrate wheel (1937 Manual).

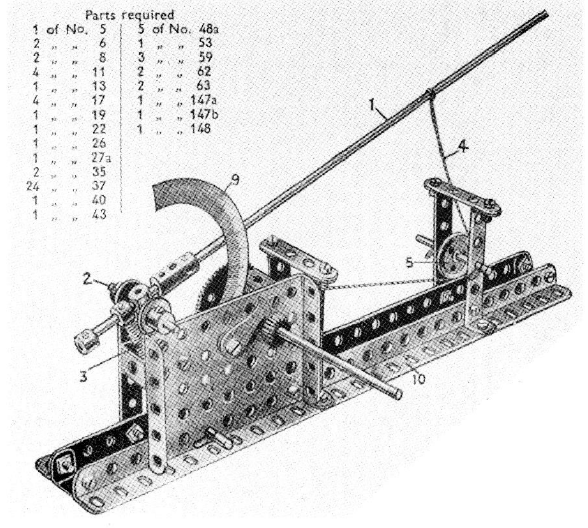

Parts required
1 of No. 5
2 „ „ 6
2 „ „ 8
4 „ „ 11
1 „ „ 13
4 „ „ 17
1 „ „ 19
1 „ „ 22
1 „ „ 26
1 „ „ 27a
2 „ „ 35
24 „ „ 37
1 „ „ 40
1 „ „ 43
5 of No. 48a
1 „ „ 53
3 „ „ 59
2 „ „ 62
2 „ „ 63
1 „ „ 147a
1 „ „ 147b
1 „ „ 148
1
2
3
4
5
9
10

Fig 2. Note the obsolete pawl (1937 Manual).

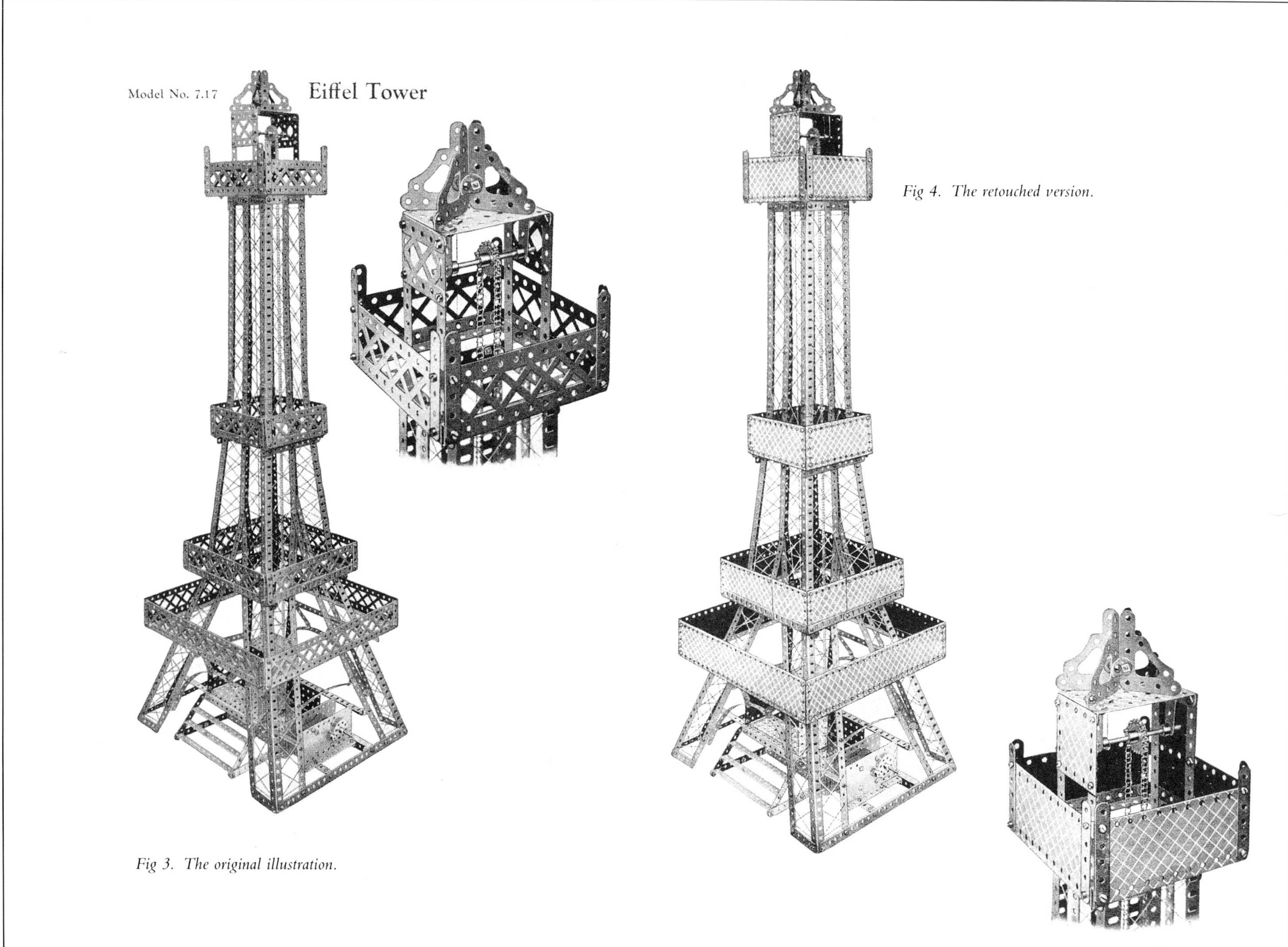

Fig 3. The original illustration.

Fig 4. The retouched version.

The Manual groups

1. 1901–1907. Figs 5–10. See also Volume 6.

The very earliest manuals were little more than booklets using in the main fairly crude line drawings. As the system progressed half-tone photographic blocks began to be used with a consequent improvement in clarity. Unfortunately this development was not fully continued and line drawings were not completely superceded until the late 1920s (they did in fact return in the 1960s and the reader can draw whatever conclusion he or she likes from this).

2. 1908–1935 (numerical series only). Figs 11–24.

1908 saw the introduction of a manual style which was to last for nearly 30 years. Obviously the models were subject to continuous revision with new ones regularly replacing outmoded or obsolete types, but the style changed surprisingly little. One major change concerned the principal manual which was supplied with most outfits (except for 1908 when individual books were supplied with each outfit). Up until 1927 the manual, frequently designated Book No. 1, covered models for outfits up to No. 7 (or No. 6 prior to the latter's introduction). 1928 saw the manuals split between outfits 00–3 and 4–7. This helped to prevent the manual from becoming too unwieldy, although bound editions containing both plus Meccano Standard Mechanisms were available (and supplied as standard with the largest outfits). By 1931 the split had changed to 00–4 and 5–7 although the last of the series, that for 1935, had reverted to 4–7. From 1921 onwards the instructions for the largest and most complex models were omitted from the manuals and instead separate leaflets were issued. (See chapter 4 'The Special and Super Model Leaflets').

Other manuals were issued during these years usually being additional to the main one. Thus the No. 2 manual containing details of what later became Super Models, was widely advertised in the early 1920s. At this point it is worth mentioning that from the early years of the First World War each manual was given a number (not print reference) which corresponded to the year of printing, e.g. No. 16 for 1916 and No. 20 for 1920. The smaller manuals for outfits 00–3 were usually numbered with the year plus an 'a' suffix i.e. No. 20a, etc. Those exclusively for smaller outfits were numbered thus: No 24.0 for a No. 0 outfit. These references are in addition to print references which appeared on most literature from 1918 onwards.

With the principal exceptions of 1915, 1917 and 1934, ordinary outfit manuals were produced annually. However, other manuals were issued especially for the smaller outfits, there being a whole series of 'A' manuals for outfits 00–3 which ran from just prior to the 1920s up until the introduction of the Blue/Gold colour scheme.

3. 1934–37 (the Blue-Gold lettered series of outfits). Figs 25–27

The introduction of the lettered outfits A-L for the new Blue/Gold colours necessitated a complete review of all manuals, although to say complete is an overstatement, for whilst the format was very different (a much larger size to begin with), much of the contents was not new. However, most existing illustrations were re-touched to show cross-hatching on plates thus matching the newly introduced parts.

The two main manuals issued were A-E and F-L, but many others were produced covering smaller and accessory outfits e.g. A-B, A-D, Ba & Ca etc. As with the previous series there was a bound manual which also included Standard Mechanisms and Meccano Parts and How to Use Them. Smaller manuals from this period are frequently found overprinted as being suitable for use with the later series of numbered outfits. This was wartime practice which used up obsolete stocks, thus saving valuable paper then in very short supply (principally one would imagine due to the Ministry of Information who must have been the originators of junk mail).

The lettered series manuals were very short-lived and although far more attractive than their predecessors were much less hardy, their flimsy paper covers suffering badly from the ravages of time. Copies in fine condition are hard to find.

4. 1937–1941. Figs 28–33

For the new numerical series of outfits the manuals really were completely revised. Virtually all the models were new and the format was altered. The new cover was one of the most attractive ever produced and the models were similarly pleasing to the eye (if not always to the heart of the engineer). The two main combinations of previous series were abandoned in favour of individual manuals i.e. 1, 1a, 2, 2a, 3, 3a, etc., up to 7/8 which like 9/10 were still combined.

During 1941 the various shortages caused a reversion to a cover similar to that of the lettered series but with a plain dark blue or orange background.

5. 1945–1948. Fig 34

Manuals issued during these years were largely reprints of the 1937–41 series but with the 1941 type cover in various colours such as green, blue, and orange.

6. 1948–1953. Figs 35–38

With the exception of the No. 10 manual which retained its pre-war models and cross-hatching, the whole range of manuals was revised with many new models and cross-hatching removed from earlier ones. Accessory outfit manuals retained their Blocksetter cover but the main series were given what must be one of the most evocative pieces of artwork ever produced by Meccano – the two boys, with father looking on, building the large version of the Giant Block-setting Crane.

7. 1954–1956. Figs 39–40 but see also section 8 below.

1954 marked the end of the line for the No. 10 manual. In its place a series of leaflets were issued giving building instructions for an initial 12 models. (These are fully dealt with in chapter 4.) For outfits 9 and below, revised manuals were produced featuring what was in effect a reworking of the 1948

Figs 5–6. Two of the earliest Meccano/Mechanics Made Easy manuals.

cover but showing a giant dragline rather than the blocksetter. The contents had in some cases been updated but there were still many older, though revised models. Accessory outfit manuals were also given a fresh cover which was to last until 1961. (Fig 42)

8. 1956–1961. Figs 41–48

Although retaining a dragline as its central feature, the 1956 cover was very different from its predecessors. Completely new artwork gave it a much brighter look, achieved by using a plain yellow background which highlighted the bright red and green of the model. Rear covers were also changed and no longer showed a parts list, but instead colour plates of sample models. These alterations were however the limit to the revision process since the contents were identical to the previous series.

The manuals for 1961 were the last of the traditional type which had served Meccano so well for over half a century. From here on, however, standards in all directions began to fall dramatically. It could be argued that the rot had already set in by 1954 with the loss of a No. 10 outfit manual, but then leaflet models were nothing new and in any case the remaining manuals were well up to standard and did not exhibit any of the depressing symptoms of their successors.

9. 1962–1969. Figs 49–53

1962 was heralded by a complete change of covers and contents. The front cover became a combination of photograph and drawing whilst the model instructions went over to 'exploded view' illustrations (in line drawing form) in an attempt to simplify the instructions and no doubt to economise in the matter of foreign editions. Removal of written instructions obviated the necessity for having every page reprinted in a foreign language.

Printed on poor quality paper, except for the earliest editions on art paper, this series is one of the least attractive visually and the contents were equally abysmal. There was a partial reversion to combined manuals rather than separate ones for each outfit. The No. 9 outfit manual was replaced by some quite awful leaflet models which are detailed in chapter 4.

10. 1970 onwards.

Manuals for 1970 were something of an improvement compared with those of the previous series. Much better quality paper allowed for the use of coloured line drawings which, as well as looking more attractive, made for greater clarity although they were less technical in style than the previous series. Some Multikit and other manuals used the older photographic system which should have been an improvement but poor and rather dim photographs ensured it was often otherwise. Examples of these manuals can be found on most dealers giveaway piles and are quite frankly not worth illustrating.

Fig 6.

Summary

The foregoing has looked at the basic manual types and styles. It has not attempted to evaluate the actual models themselves. This would be an impossible task within the confines of this volume and probably of interest to only a handful of collectors who would probably have their own opinions on the subject already.

Although representatives from each period (apart from 1970 onwards) have been illustrated, the author makes no apologies for bias in favour of quality. There is little doubt that the manuals were at their best between the late 1920s and the early 1950s. After this time, they are especially disappointing with few worthwhile models. In fact one could argue that the downward trend in overall quality paralleled Meccano Ltd's own demise. The position was summed-up very nicely, if sadly by a young model builder recently – 'The pictures and models in the later manuals don't make you want to build them.'

Sic transit . . .

Foreign Editions

As with most Meccano publications, foreign and other non-UK editions were produced but these are outside the scope of this book principally because apart from the language, they have usually been virtually identical to their UK counterparts.

Fig. No. 34. Swivelling and Luffing Jib Crane.

(Made with Meccano Outfit No. 3 or No. 2 and No. 2a)

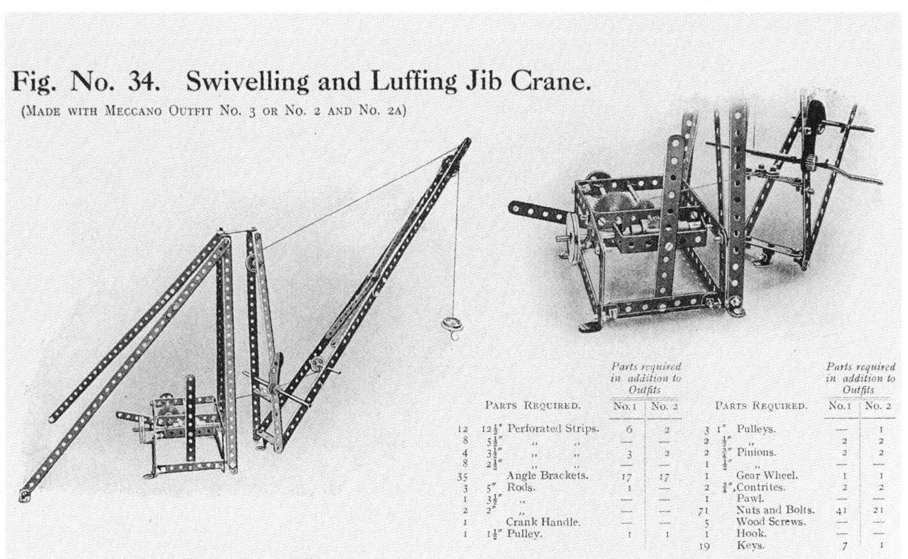

	Parts Required.	No. 1	No. 2
12	12½″ Perforated Strips.	6	2
8	5½″ ,, ,,	—	—
4	3½″ ,, ,,	3	2
8	2½″ ,, ,,	—	—
35	Angle Brackets.	17	17
3	5″ Rods.	1	—
1	3½″ ,,	—	—
2	2″ ,,	—	—
1	Crank Handle.	—	—
1	1½″ Pulley.	1	1
3	1″ Pulleys.	—	1
2	½″ ,,	2	2
2	¾″ Pinions.	2	2
1	½″ ,,	—	—
1	Gear Wheel.	1	1
2	¾″ Contrites.	2	2
1	Pawl.	—	—
71	Nuts and Bolts.	41	21
5	Wood Screws.	—	—
1	Hook.	—	—
19	Keys.	7	1

(No. 1 and No. 2 columns: *Parts required in addition to Outfits*)

This model is interesting as affording an example of a crane used to transport the load from, say, a ship's deck on to a quay, by "luffing" or altering the angle of the jib. The apparatus consists of two parts, a fixed frame and a swivelling and luffing jib. The construction of the fixed frame with the reversing frame and lever should present no difficulties.

The two 12½″ uprights are braced together as shown, and are held in vertical position by the two 12½″ connected to two 5½″ strips rearwardly sloping pieces, and from the structure so formed the reversing frame is carried.

..(27)..

Fig. No. 36. Level Crossing Gates.

(Made with Meccano Outfit No. 3 or No. 2 and No. 2a)

	Parts Required.	No. 1	No. 2
18	5½″ Perforated Strips.	8	—
4	3½″ ,, ,,	3	2
17	2½″ ,, ,,	5	1
6	Angle Girders.	6	2
32	,, Brackets.	14	14
4	1″ Pulley Wheels.	—	2
75	Nuts and Bolts.	45	25

(No. 1 and No. 2 columns: *Parts required in addition to Outfits*)

This model, if constructed with care, is a most admirable one, as the gates are opened simultaneously by the operation of one lever.

To construct it, commence by taking two angle girders and connecting them together in the second hole at each end with a 5½″ strip placed perpendicularly between them to form the supports of one pair of gates as shown in Figure A. The supports for the other pair of gates is arranged in a similar manner. These two structures are connected by two other angle girders, and braced by four 3½″ cross pieces as shown in the illustration.

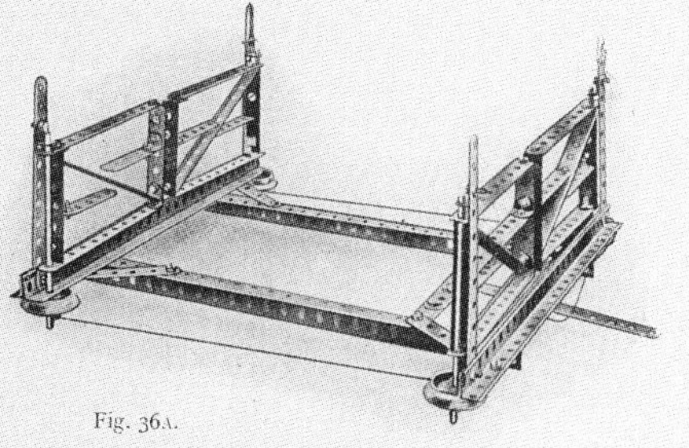

Fig. 36A.

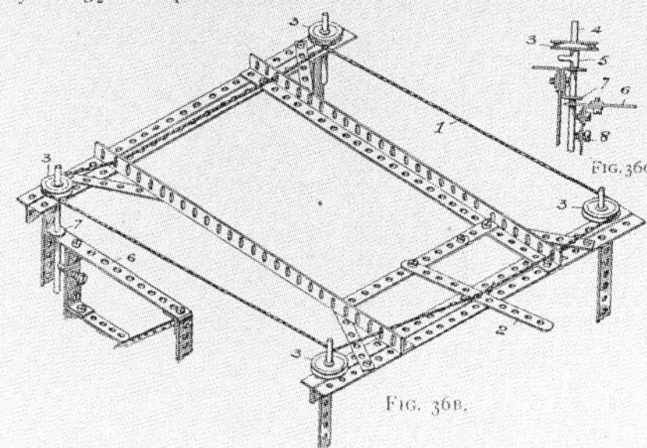

Fig. 36C.

Fig. 36B.

The gates are formed by connecting two 5½″ strips with a 2½″ strip and angle brackets in the end holes at one side. At the other side the 2½″ strip is connected in the second holes from the end to permit the axle rod to pass through upon which the gate swings.

Figure 36B is an inverted perspective view showing the arrangement of operating cord 1 which is passed from the operating lever 2, around the corner pulleys 3, and back to the lever 2. In order to obtain a better grip on the pulleys, it is desirable to wind the operating cord twice around them. It is to be noted that the cord 1 is wound in opposite directions around the diagonal pairs of pulleys 3.

Figure C is a side detail showing the method in which the operating pulley 3 is keyed upon the spindle 4 by the key 5. The gate 6 rests upon the angle bracket 7, and a pinching screw 8 is fitted in the inner side to grip it to the spindle 4, so that all rotate together.

..(25)..

Fig. No. 42. Travelling Crane.

(Made with Meccano Outfit No. 4 or No. 3 and No. 3a)

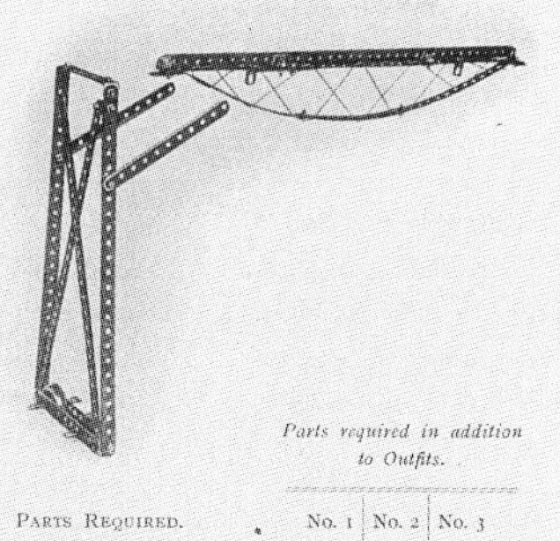

	Parts Required.	No. 1	No. 2	No. 3
18	12½″ Perforated Strips.	12	8	6
14	5½″ ,, ,,	4	—	—
2	3½″ ,, ,,	1	—	—
14	2½″ ,, ,,	2	—	—
40	Angle Brackets.	22	22	—
3	5″ Rods.	1	—	—
5	2″ ,,	3	3	2
2	Crank Handles.	1	1	—
8	Flanged Wheels.	8	4	4
2	1″ Pulleys.	—	—	—
2	¾″ Pinions.	2	2	—
1	½″ ,,	—	—	—
2	Gear Wheels.	2	2	1
1	Pawl.	—	—	—
88	Nuts and Bolts.	58	38	8
1	Hook.	—	—	—
20	Keys.	8	2	—

(No. 1, No. 2 and No. 3 columns: *Parts required in addition to Outfits.*)

..(31)..

Fig. No. 55. Coal Tip.

(Made with Meccano Outfit No. 5, or No. 4 and No. 4a)

	Parts Required.	No. 1	No. 2	No. 3	No. 4
2	12½″ Perforated Strips.	—	—	—	—
34	5½″ ,, ,,	24	16	13	6
8	3½″ ,, ,,	7	6	2	2
6	3″ ,, ,,	6	6	4	2
20	2½″ ,, ,,	8	4	—	—
6	Angle Girders.	6	2	—	—
53	,, Brackets.	35	35	8	—
4	6″ Rods.	4	4	3	2
3	5″ ,,	1	—	—	—
2	3½″ ,,	1	1	—	—
1	Crank Handle.	—	—	—	—
8	Flanged Wheels.	8	4	4	—
4	1″ Pulley ,,	—	2	1	—
2	¾″ Pinion ,,	2	2	—	—
1	½″ ,, ,,	—	—	—	—
1	Gear Wheel.	1	1	—	—
1	Pawl.	—	—	—	—
149	Nuts and Bolts.	119	99	69	27
23	Keys.	11	5	1	—

(No. 1 to No. 4 columns: *Parts required in addition to Outfits*)

..(42)..

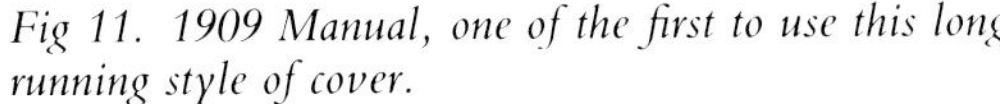

Fig 11. 1909 Manual, one of the first to use this long running style of cover.

MECCANO
(PATENTED)
INSTRUCTIONS
For the whole series of Models, comprising thirteen progressive outfits
9d. net
Copyright by MECCANO LIMITED, LIVERPOOL, throughout the World

Fig 14. 1913 Manual with aeroplane replacing the windmill. ↗

Fig 15. 1916 Manual and the appearance of the well-known → crane with clockwork motor.

Figs 7–10. Models from the 1907 Manual showing the ← mixture of Mechanics Made Easy and early Meccano models. Note the use of half-tone illustrations at this early date.

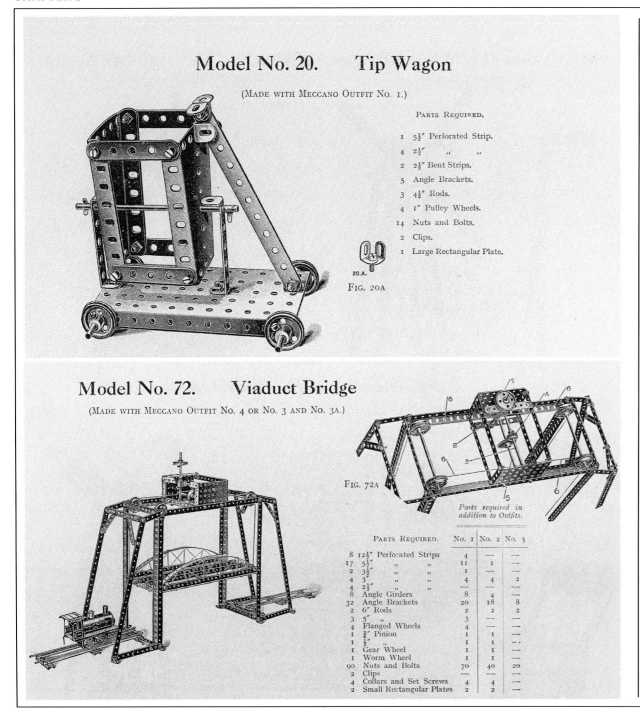

Model No. 20. Tip Wagon

(Made with Meccano Outfit No. 1.)

Parts Required.

1 5½" Perforated Strip.
4 2½" " "
2 2½" Bent Strips.
5 Angle Brackets.
3 4½" Rods.
4 1" Pulley Wheels.
14 Nuts and Bolts.
2 Clips.
1 Large Rectangular Plate.

Fig. 20A

Model No. 72. Viaduct Bridge

(Made with Meccano Outfit No. 4 or No. 3 and No. 3a.)

Fig. 72A

Parts required in addition to Outfits.

Parts Required.	No. 1	No. 2	No. 3
8 12½" Perforated Strips	4	—	—
17 5½" " "	11	1	—
2 3½" " "	1	—	—
4 3" " "	4	4	2
4 2½" " "	—	—	—
8 Angle Girders	8	4	—
32 Angle Brackets	20	18	8
2 6" Rods	2	2	2
3 5" "	3	—	—
4 Flanged Wheels	4	—	—
1 ¾" Pinion	1	1	—
1 ½" "	1	1	—
1 Gear Wheel	1	1	—
1 Worm Wheel	1	1	—
90 Nuts and Bolts	70	40	20
2 Clips	—	—	—
4 Collars and Set Screws	4	4	—
2 Small Rectangular Plates	2	2	—

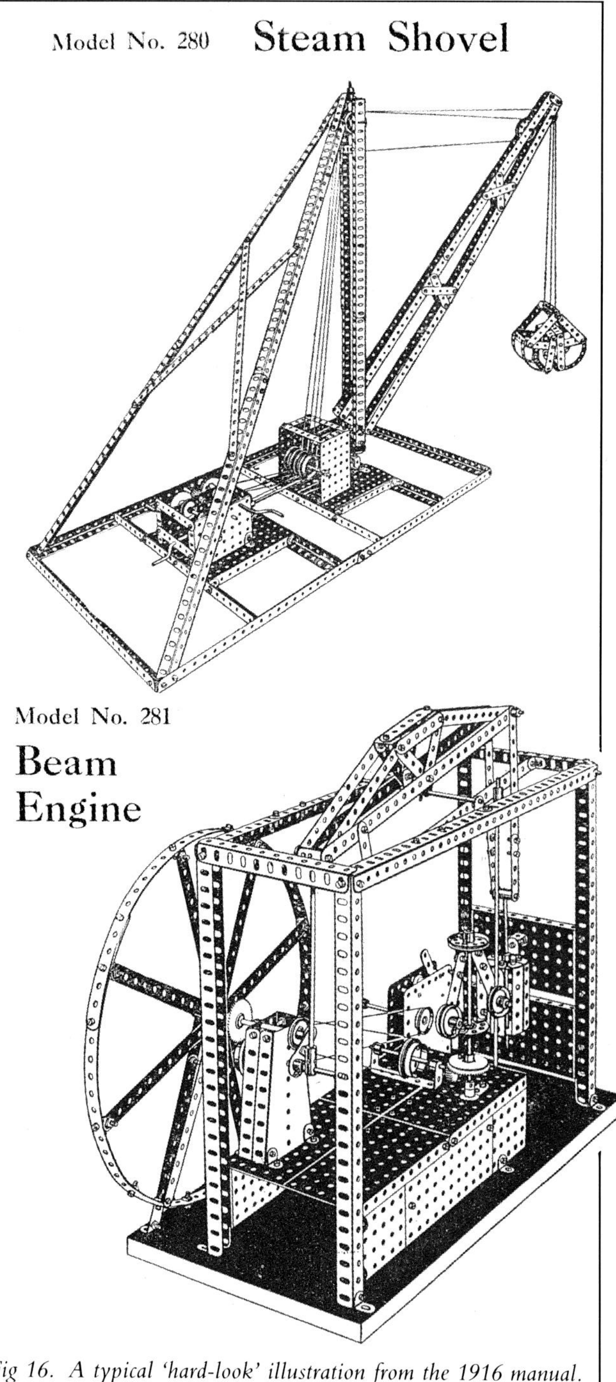

Fig 16. A typical 'hard-look' illustration from the 1916 manual.

Figs 12–13. Models from the 1913 Manual. The train was of course not Hornby!

Figs 17–19. The No. 0 Manual cover, introduction and page with 'sample' to whet the appetite. Note Mesopotamian Water Carriers! – the secret war time name for the then new tanks. This small manual has a most attractive picture much used on nut and bolt tins. It was subsequently used after the Second World War but without the legend 'Copyright 1920'.

A TALK WITH NEW MECCANO BOYS

Boys! This book is only the beginning of Meccano. You will get lots of fun building the models which it contains, but best of all it will show you what a fine hobby Meccano is, and how easy and delightful it is to build models with it.

Wouldn't you like to build all the splendid Meccano models which you have seen on exhibition in the toy-shops, and in our advertisements, and in the books and leaflets which we publish? Nothing could be easier; all the Meccano parts fit in with those you have in your No. 0 Outfit. This is the advantage of the standardisation of the whole Meccano system. Once you have got the idea of the equidistant holes, and the interchangeable parts, you can do anything with them. Take, for instance, one of the models which looks most complicated—the Meccano loom. It is just as easy for you to build it as it is for an engineer or a skilled mechanic.

Who shall play with the Helter-Skelter first?

That is what the Meccano system does—*the genius and skill and knowledge are in the parts*, and all you have to do is to screw them together. And when you have made a model such as the loom, you can do something with it. You can weave ties and belts in all colours and designs, just as good as the best you can buy in the shops. Our big Manual of Instructions shows you how to make this model, and it also shows you how to make the Helter-Skelter, and the big Cranes and Bridges, and all the prize models which have been sent in by expert Meccano boys, and which took big money prizes.

Remember, boys, that with Meccano you can make anything and everything which you can make with any other system, and that no other system can make the Meccano models.

THE NEW FULL MECCANO MANUAL OF INSTRUCTIONS CONTAINS HUNDREDS OF PRIZE-WINNING MODELS. GET YOUR COPY AT ONCE.

(3)

Fig 18.

YOU can build this Model of the wonderful British Tank with MECCANO

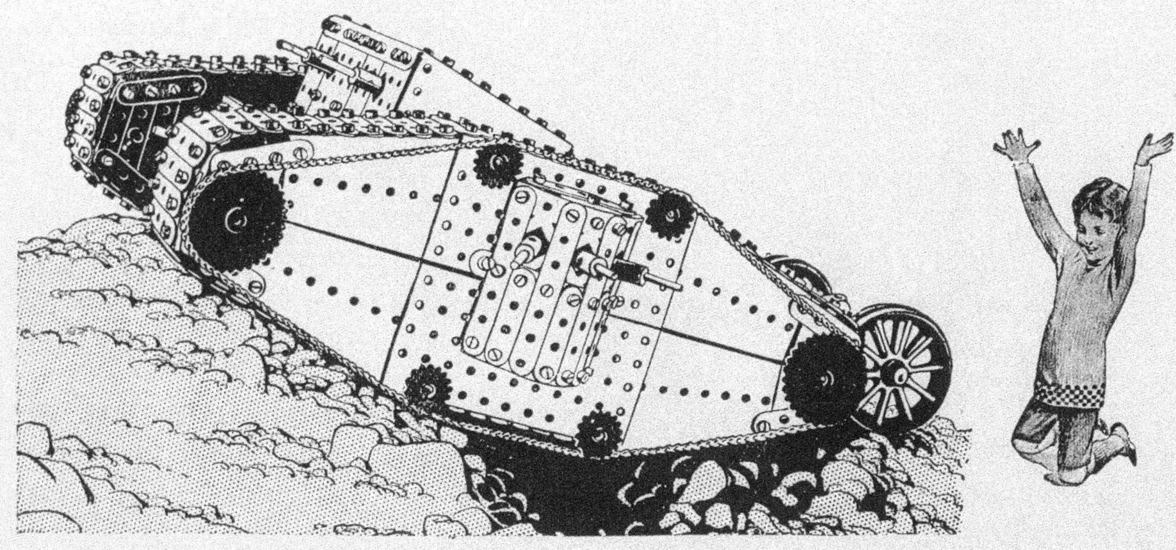

Meccano is Easy

Meccano is so easy, and our instructions are so complete, that we do not believe you will have any trouble; but if there is anything you do not quite understand, or if you have any suggestions to make, do not fail to write to us.

Boys! Build Bigger Models

When you have completed all the models in this book, your next purchase will be a No. 0a Accessory Outfit. This will convert your No. 0 Outfit into a No. 1. You will receive a large number of extra parts, and a big Manual of Instructions. You will be able to build scores of new and fascinating models, and will then realise what a wonderful hobby Meccano is.

The Meccano Magazine

This is a splendid Magazine, which is published for Meccano users. You will miss a lot of fun and pleasure if you do not become a regular reader. It contains articles on Meccano topics; essays by Meccano boys; tips to model-builders; replies to boys' queries by the Editor; announcements of new prize competitions which are running all the time, and which enable you to win valuable prizes; lists of prize-winners; and all kinds of useful information for boys. Write to the Editor, and he will send you your first copy FREE. If you wish to receive the Meccano Magazine regularly, you should send 2d. in stamps to cover postage on the next four issues. A double subscription of 4d. will, of course, ensure your receiving the next eight issues. Address your letters to the Editor, Meccano Works, Binns Road, Liverpool.

(4)

Fig 19.

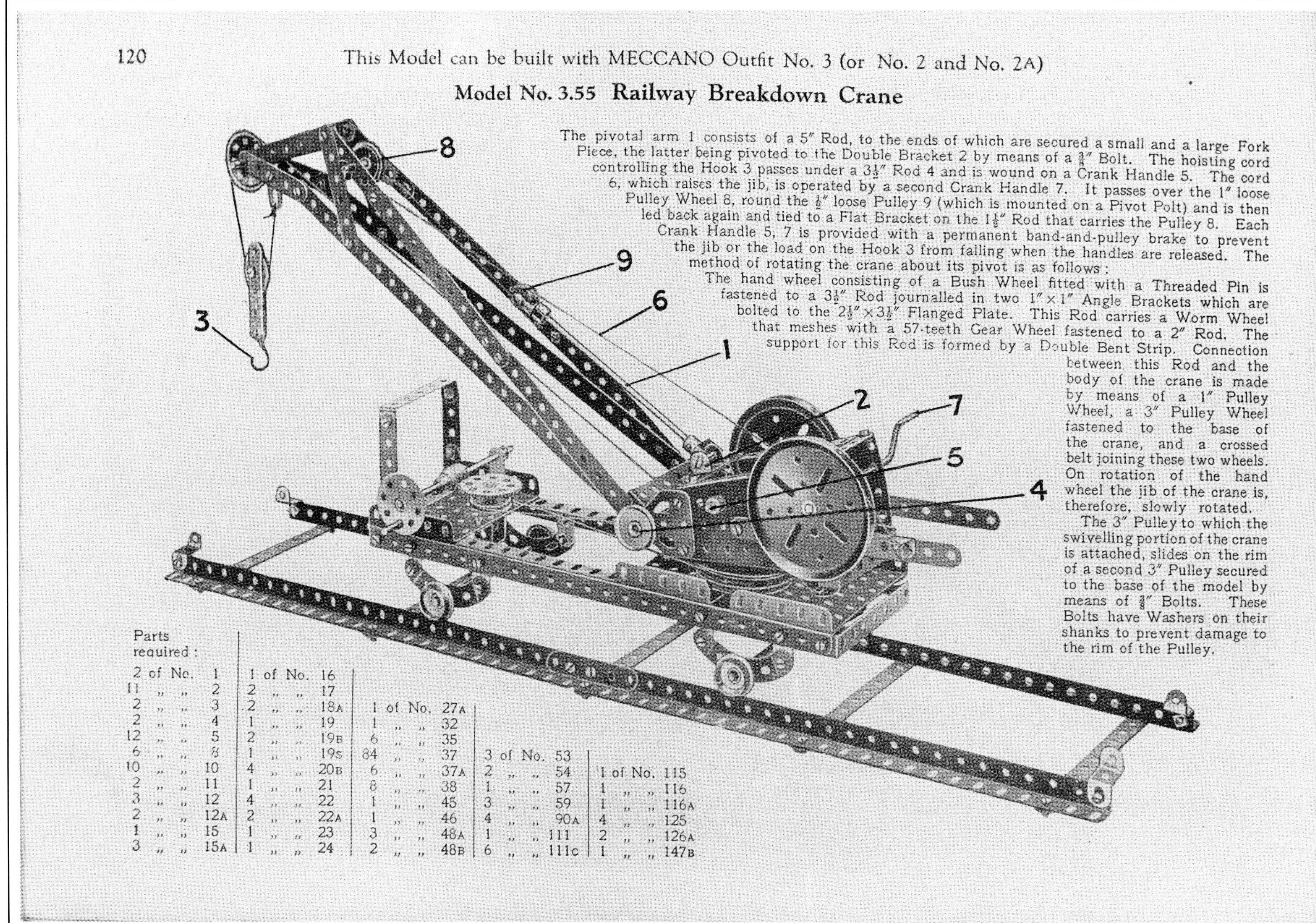

120 This Model can be built with MECCANO Outfit No. 3 (or No. 2 and No. 2A)

Model No. 3.55 Railway Breakdown Crane

The pivotal arm 1 consists of a 5″ Rod, to the ends of which are secured a small and a large Fork Piece, the latter being pivoted to the Double Bracket 2 by means of a 3/8″ Bolt. The hoisting cord controlling the Hook 3 passes under a 3½″ Rod 4 and is wound on a Crank Handle 5. The cord 6, which raises the jib, is operated by a second Crank Handle 7. It passes over the 1″ loose Pulley Wheel 8, round the ½″ loose Pulley 9 (which is mounted on a Pivot Polt) and is then led back again and tied to a Flat Bracket on the 1½″ Rod that carries the Pulley 8. Each Crank Handle 5, 7 is provided with a permanent band-and-pulley brake to prevent the jib or the load on the Hook 3 from falling when the handles are released. The method of rotating the crane about its pivot is as follows:

The hand wheel consisting of a Bush Wheel fitted with a Threaded Pin is fastened to a 3½″ Rod journalled in two 1″×1″ Angle Brackets which are bolted to the 2½″×3½″ Flanged Plate. This Rod carries a Worm Wheel that meshes with a 57-teeth Gear Wheel fastened to a 2″ Rod. The support for this Rod is formed by a Double Bent Strip. Connection between this Rod and the body of the crane is made by means of a 1″ Pulley Wheel, a 3″ Pulley Wheel fastened to the base of the crane, and a crossed belt joining these two wheels. On rotation of the hand wheel the jib of the crane is, therefore, slowly rotated.

The 3″ Pulley to which the swivelling portion of the crane is attached, slides on the rim of a second 3″ Pulley secured to the base of the model by means of 3/8″ Bolts. These Bolts have Washers on their shanks to prevent damage to the rim of the Pulley.

Parts required:

2 of No. 1	1 of No. 16			
11 „ „ 2	2 „ „ 17			
2 „ „ 3	2 „ „ 18A	1 of No. 27A		
2 „ „ 4	1 „ „ 19	1 „ „ 32		
12 „ „ 5	2 „ „ 19B	6 „ „ 35		
6 „ „ 8	1 „ „ 19S	84 „ „ 37	3 of No. 53	
10 „ „ 10	4 „ „ 20B	6 „ „ 37A	2 „ „ 54	1 of No. 115
2 „ „ 11	1 „ „ 21	8 „ „ 38	1 „ „ 57	1 „ „ 116
3 „ „ 12	4 „ „ 22	1 „ „ 45	3 „ „ 59	1 „ „ 116A
2 „ „ 12A	2 „ „ 22A	1 „ „ 46	4 „ „ 90A	4 „ „ 125
1 „ „ 15	1 „ „ 23	3 „ „ 48A	1 „ „ 111	2 „ „ 126A
3 „ „ 15A	1 „ „ 24	2 „ „ 48B	6 „ „ 111C	1 „ „ 147B

Fig 21. A typical model from the late 1920s.

Fig 20. Two 1930 Manual covers showing the way in which foreign editions were treated.

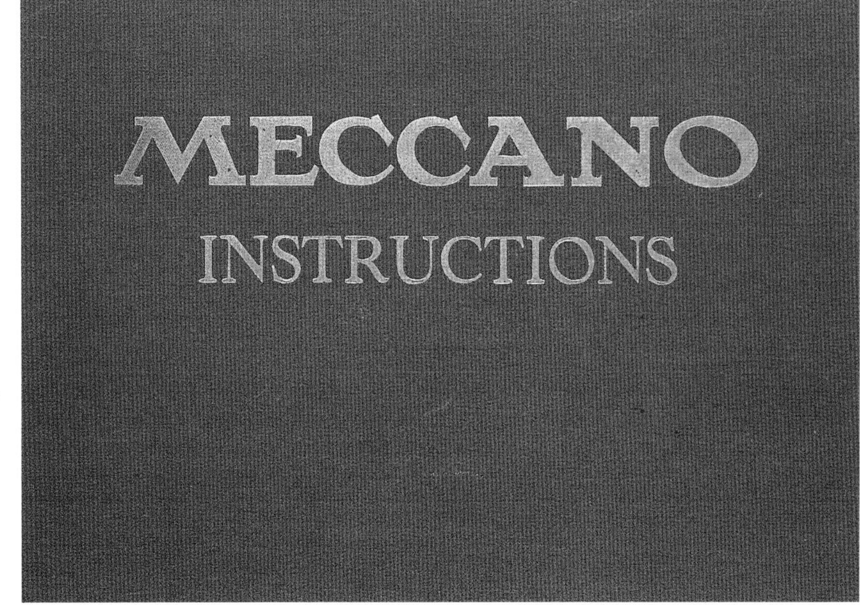

Fig 22. The 1929 bound manual containing manuals for outfits 00–3, 4–7 and Standard Mechanisms.

Fig 25. Cover of a typical manual for the first blue/gold (lettered series). The front cover was printed on very thin paper. →

Figs 23–24. The plain covers (and back) used in the early 1930s for smaller outfit manuals.

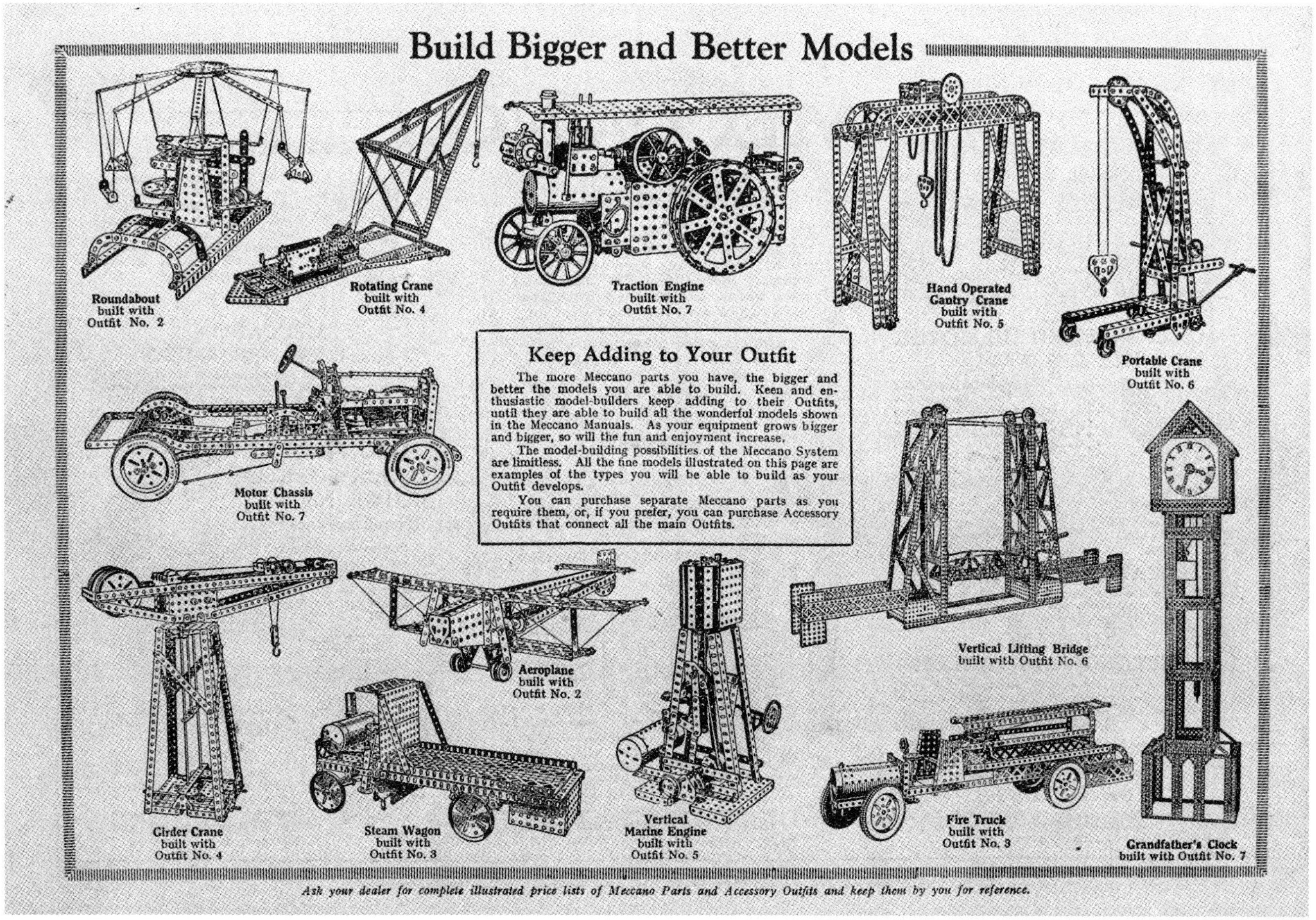

Build Bigger and Better Models

Roundabout built with Outfit No. 2

Rotating Crane built with Outfit No. 4

Traction Engine built with Outfit No. 7

Hand Operated Gantry Crane built with Outfit No. 5

Portable Crane built with Outfit No. 6

Motor Chassis built with Outfit No. 7

Keep Adding to Your Outfit

The more Meccano parts you have, the bigger and better the models you are able to build. Keen and enthusiastic model-builders keep adding to their Outfits, until they are able to build all the wonderful models shown in the Meccano Manuals. As your equipment grows bigger and bigger, so will the fun and enjoyment increase.

The model-building possibilities of the Meccano System are limitless. All the fine models illustrated on this page are examples of the types you will be able to build as your Outfit develops.

You can purchase separate Meccano parts as you require them, or, if you prefer, you can purchase Accessory Outfits that connect all the main Outfits.

Vertical Lifting Bridge built with Outfit No. 6

Aeroplane built with Outfit No. 2

Girder Crane built with Outfit No. 4

Steam Wagon built with Outfit No. 3

Vertical Marine Engine built with Outfit No. 5

Fire Truck built with Outfit No. 3

Grandfather's Clock built with Outfit No. 7

Ask your dealer for complete illustrated price lists of Meccano Parts and Accessory Outfits and keep them by you for reference.

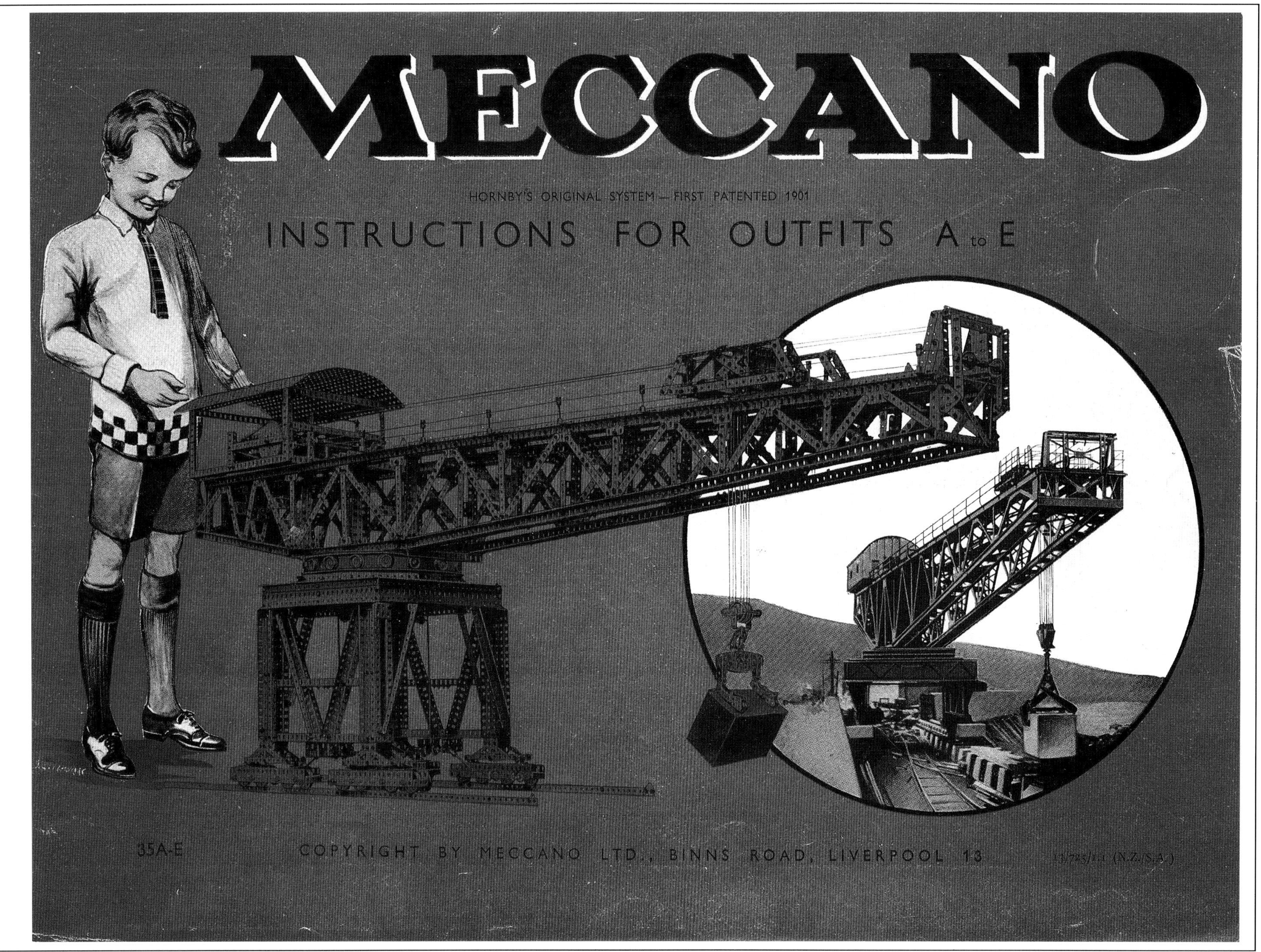
MECCANO
HORNBY'S ORIGINAL SYSTEM — FIRST PATENTED 1901
INSTRUCTIONS FOR OUTFITS A to E
35A-E
COPYRIGHT BY MECCANO LTD., BINNS ROAD, LIVERPOOL 13
(N.Z./S.A.)

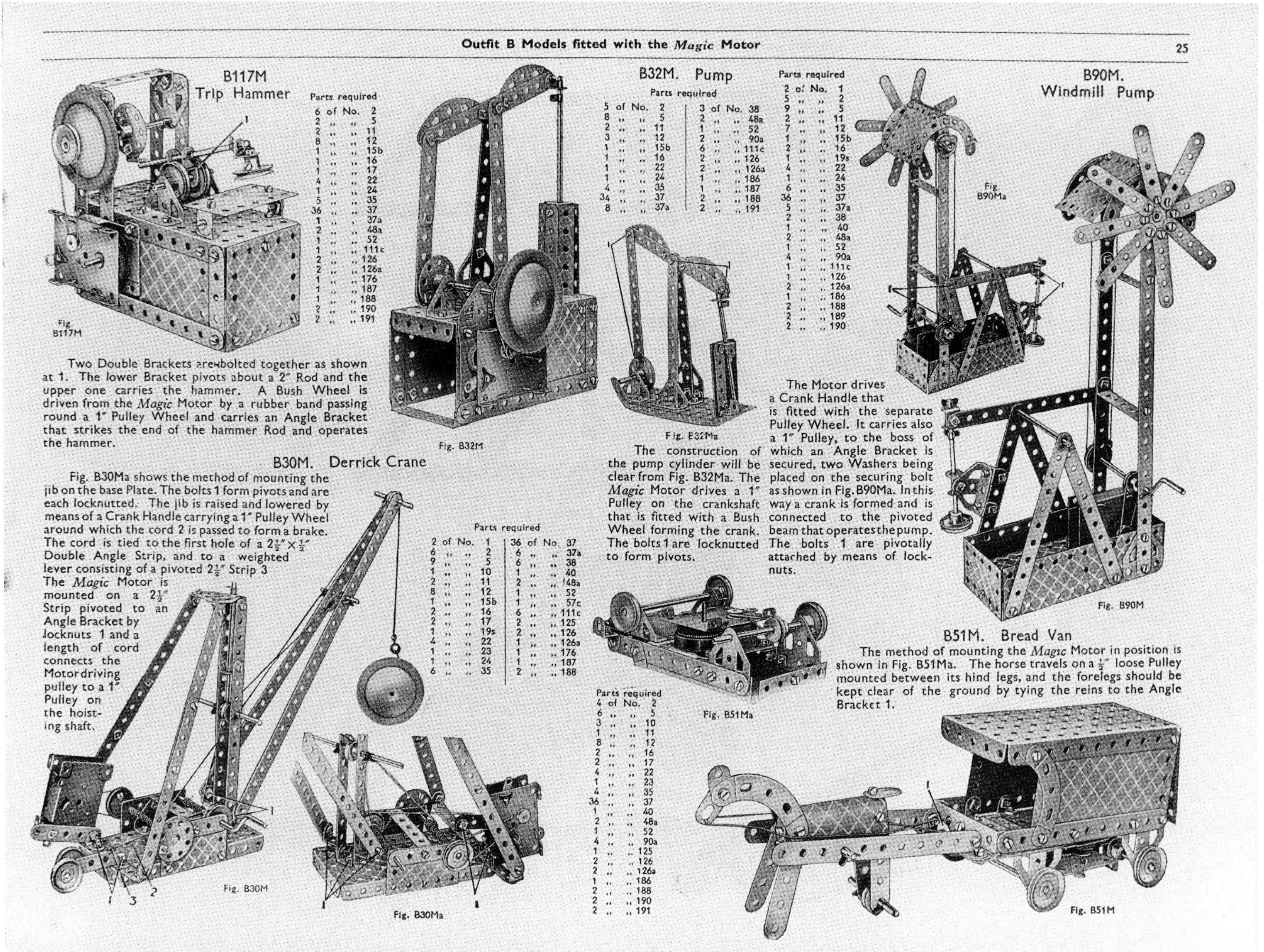

Outfit B Models fitted with the *Magic* Motor 25

B117M Trip Hammer

Parts required	
6 of No.	2
2 ,, ,,	5
2 ,, ,,	11
8 ,, ,,	12
1 ,, ,,	15b
1 ,, ,,	16
1 ,, ,,	17
4 ,, ,,	22
1 ,, ,,	24
5 ,, ,,	35
36 ,, ,,	37
1 ,, ,	37a
2 ,, ,,	48a
1 ,, ,,	52
1 ,, ,,	111c
2 ,, ,,	126
2 ,, ,,	126a
1 ,, ,,	176
1 ,, ,,	187
1 ,, ,,	188
2 ,, ,,	190
2 ,, ,,	191

Fig. B117M

Two Double Brackets are bolted together as shown at 1. The lower Bracket pivots about a 2" Rod and the upper one carries the hammer. A Bush Wheel is driven from the *Magic* Motor by a rubber band passing round a 1" Pulley Wheel and carries an Angle Bracket that strikes the end of the hammer Rod and operates the hammer.

B32M. Pump

Parts required			
5 of No.	2	3 of No.	38
8 ,, ,,	5	2 ,, ,,	48a
2 ,, ,,	11	1 ,, ,,	52
3 ,, ,,	12	2 ,, ,,	90a
1 ,, ,,	15b	6 ,, ,,	111c
1 ,, ,,	16	2 ,, ,,	126
1 ,, ,,	22	2 ,, ,,	126a
1 ,, ,,	24	1 ,, ,,	186
4 ,, ,,	35	1 ,, ,,	187
34 ,, ,,	37	2 ,, ,,	188
8 ,, ,,	37a	2 ,, ,,	191

Fig. B32M

Fig. B32Ma

The construction of the pump cylinder will be clear from Fig. B32Ma. The *Magic* Motor drives a 1" Pulley on the crankshaft that is fitted with a Bush Wheel forming the crank. The bolts 1 are locknutted to form pivots.

B90M. Windmill Pump

Parts required	
2 of No.	1
5 ,, ,,	2
9 ,, ,,	5
2 ,, ,,	11
7 ,, ,,	12
1 ,, ,,	15b
2 ,, ,,	16
1 ,, ,,	19s
4 ,, ,,	22
1 ,, ,,	24
6 ,, ,,	35
36 ,, ,,	37
5 ,, ,,	37a
2 ,, ,,	38
1 ,, ,,	40
2 ,, ,,	48a
1 ,, ,,	52
4 ,, ,,	90a
1 ,, ,,	111c
1 ,, ,,	126
2 ,, ,,	126a
1 ,, ,,	186
2 ,, ,,	188
2 ,, ,,	189
2 ,, ,,	190

Fig. B90Ma

The Motor drives a Crank Handle that is fitted with the separate Pulley Wheel. It carries also a 1" Pulley, to the boss of which an Angle Bracket is secured, two Washers being placed on the securing bolt as shown in Fig. B90Ma. In this way a crank is formed and is connected to the pivoted beam that operates the pump. The bolts 1 are pivotally attached by means of lock-nuts.

Fig. B90M

B30M. Derrick Crane

Fig. B30Ma shows the method of mounting the jib on the base Plate. The bolts 1 form pivots and are each locknutted. The jib is raised and lowered by means of a Crank Handle carrying a 1" Pulley Wheel around which the cord 2 is passed to form a brake. The cord is tied to the first hole of a $2\frac{1}{2}'' \times \frac{1}{2}''$ Double Angle Strip, and to a weighted lever consisting of a pivoted $2\frac{1}{2}''$ Strip 3 The *Magic* Motor is mounted on a $2\frac{1}{2}''$ Strip pivoted to an Angle Bracket by locknuts 1 and a length of cord connects the Motor driving pulley to a 1" Pulley on the hoisting shaft.

Parts required			
2 of No.	1	36 of No.	37
6 ,, ,,	2	6 ,, ,,	37a
9 ,, ,,	5	6 ,, ,,	38
1 ,, ,,	10	1 ,, ,,	40
2 ,, ,,	11	2 ,, ,,	48a
8 ,, ,,	12	1 ,, ,,	52
1 ,, ,,	15b	1 ,, ,,	57c
2 ,, ,,	16	6 ,, ,,	111c
2 ,, ,,	17	2 ,, ,,	125
1 ,, ,,	19s	2 ,, ,,	126
4 ,, ,,	22	1 ,, ,,	126a
1 ,, ,,	23	1 ,, ,,	176
1 ,, ,,	24	1 ,, ,,	187
6 ,, ,,	35	2 ,, ,,	188

Fig. B30M

Fig. B30Ma

B51M. Bread Van

Parts required	
4 of No.	2
6 ,, ,,	5
3 ,, ,,	10
1 ,, ,,	11
8 ,, ,,	12
2 ,, ,,	16
2 ,, ,,	17
4 ,, ,,	22
1 ,, ,,	23
4 ,, ,,	35
36 ,, ,,	37
1 ,, ,,	40
2 ,, ,,	48a
1 ,, ,,	52
4 ,, ,,	90a
1 ,, ,,	125
2 ,, ,,	126
2 ,, ,,	126a
1 ,, ,,	186
2 ,, ,,	188
2 ,, ,,	190
2 ,, ,,	191

Fig. B51Ma

The method of mounting the *Magic* Motor in position is shown in Fig. B51Ma. The horse travels on a $\frac{1}{2}''$ loose Pulley mounted between its hind legs, and the forelegs should be kept clear of the ground by tying the reins to the Angle Bracket 1.

Fig. B51M

Fig 26. A page from the 1935 Manual showing the new models. Many of the larger models were not new, but retouched versions of old ones.

MECCANO
HORNBY'S ORIGINAL SYSTEM — FIRST PATENTED 1901
INSTRUCTIONS FOR OUTFIT Oa
also
No. 1a ACCESSORY OUTFIT
PRICE
2d.
SPECIAL NOTICE
Owing to the acute paper shortage caused by the war we are unable to obtain further supplies of the Manual normally included with this Outfit. We are therefore obliged to make use of another Manual, which is slightly different. Most of the models illustrated in this Manual can be built exactly as shown ; a few others will require a certain amount of adaptation.
Please ignore all paragraphs headed "How to Continue." Your next purchase should be a No. 2a Accessory Outfit.
MECCANO LIMITED
ECCANO LTD., BINNS ROAD, LIVERPOOL 13
13/936/6 (U.K.) 2P

Fig 27. A lettered series manual overprinted so as to do duty for the later numerical series – a wartime emergency measure.

Figs 28–32. Covers for the 1937–1941 Manuals. The plain covers are from the early war years.

MECCANO
INSTRUCTIONS FOR
No. 3a ACCESSORY OUTFIT
No. 41.3a
COPYRIGHT BY MECCANO LIMITED, BINNS ROAD, LIVERPOOL 13, ENGLAND.

MECCANO
INSTRUCTIONS
FOR OUTFIT
No. 000
COPYRIGHT BY
No. 41.000
MECCANO LIMITED, LIVERPOOL 13, ENGLAND
ENG-UNIV

Figs 28–32.

MECCANO
Registered Trade Mark
THE WORLD'S FINEST HOBBY FOR BOYS

HOW TO BEGIN

With the Meccano Parts contained in this Outfit you will be able to build many different kinds of models — Cranes — Trucks — Roundabouts — and lots of other subjects that interest boys.

Each part in the Outfit is actually a real engineering part in miniature. The only tools required for fitting them together and making the splendid models illustrated in this Book are a Spanner and a Screwdriver, both of which you will find in the Outfit.

Make the simple models first. Choose the one you want to build and then lay out on the table all the parts mentioned in the 'Parts Required' list for that model. You will be able to identify the parts by looking at the pictures in the list below.

To help you to start building, we will describe how Model O.3, Garden Seat, is made. Begin by bolting to the Flanged Plate the 5½" Strips that form the back legs of the seat. Then attach the upper ends of these Strips to two further 5½" Strips to form the back. Two 2½" Strips are then bolted to the front flange of the Plate to form the front legs. The model is completed by fixing two 2½"×½" Double Angle Strips to the back to form arm rests.

In some models it is necessary to join certain parts together so that, although they cannot come apart, they are free to *pivot* or move in relation to one another. To do this the parts are bolted together as usual, ***but the nut is not screwed up tightly,*** so that the parts are not gripped. Then, to prevent the nut rom unscrewing, ***a second nut is screwed up tightly against it,*** the first nut meanwhile being held with a Spanner. This method of using a second nut is known as ***lock-nutting.***

THE MECCANO MAGIC MOTOR

The greatest thrill in Meccano model-building comes when a model is set to work by means of a Motor. The Meccano *Magic* Clockwork Motor is specially designed to drive the kind of models you can build with this Outfit.

The illustrations of

Models O.15, O.23 and O.26 show how the *Magic* Motor can be fitted to No. O Outfit models. One of these wonderful little Motors will add greatly to the fun you obtain from yourmodel-building.

The Meccano *Magic* Motor is not included in the Outfit.

A Rod is usually supported in a bearing, which is generally a hole in a Strip, Trunnion or Flat Trunnion, so that it is free to revolve. The Rod is then said to be *journalled* in the Strip, Trunnion or Flat Trunnion as the case may be.

When you have built all the models shown in this Book the fun is not over but is just beginning! Now comes the chance to make use of your own ideas. First of all rebuild some of the models making any small changes in construction that may occur to you; afterwards try building some simple models entirely to your own design. In doing this you will feel the thrill of the engineer and the inventor.

As you gain experience you will naturally wish to build bigger and better models. To do this you will need a larger Outfit containing a greater number and variety of parts. To convert your Outfit into the next larger one, the No. 1, you need a No. Oa Accessory Outfit.

If you ever meet with any small difficulty, or if you would like advice on any point connected with your model-building, write to ***Information Service, Meccano Ltd, Binns Road, Liverpool 13.***

CONTENTS OF MECCANO No. O OUTFIT

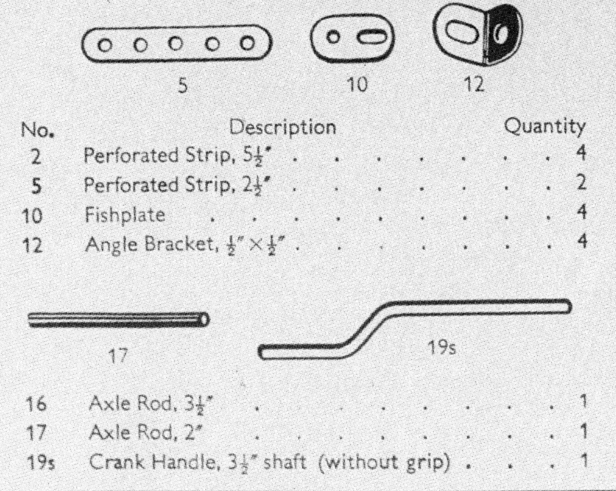

No.	Description	Quantity
2	Perforated Strip, 5½"	4
5	Perforated Strip, 2½"	2
10	Fishplate	4
12	Angle Bracket, ½"×½"	4
16	Axle Rod, 3½"	1
17	Axle Rod, 2"	1
19s	Crank Handle, 3½" shaft (without grip)	1

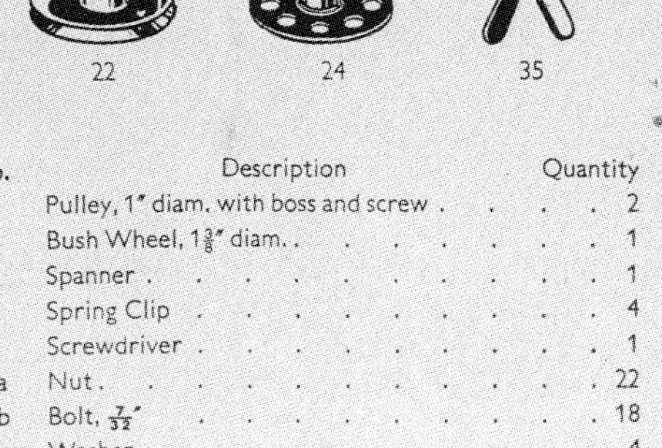

No.	Description	Quantity
22	Pulley, 1" diam. with boss and screw	2
24	Bush Wheel, 1⅜" diam.	1
34	Spanner	1
35	Spring Clip	4
36	Screwdriver	1
37a	Nut	22
37b	Bolt, $\frac{7}{32}$"	18
38	Washer	4

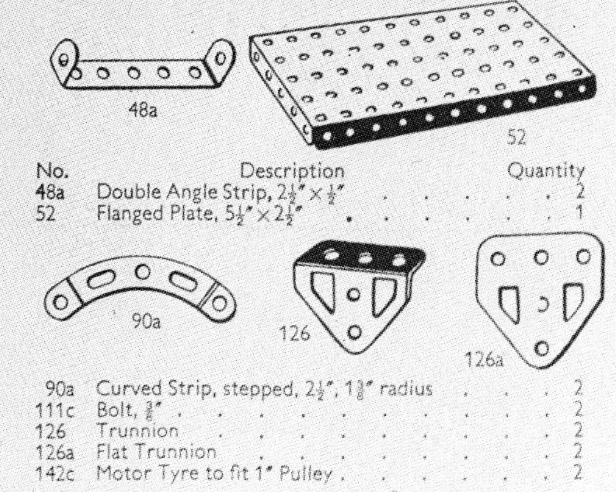

No.	Description	Quantity
48a	Double Angle Strip, 2½"×½"	2
52	Flanged Plate, 5½"×2½"	1
90a	Curved Strip, stepped, 2½", 1⅜" radius	2
111c	Bolt, ⅜"	2
126	Trunnion	2
126a	Flat Trunnion	2
142c	Motor Tyre to fit 1" Pulley	2

Fig 29. The inside cover of the 1941 No. 0 manual.

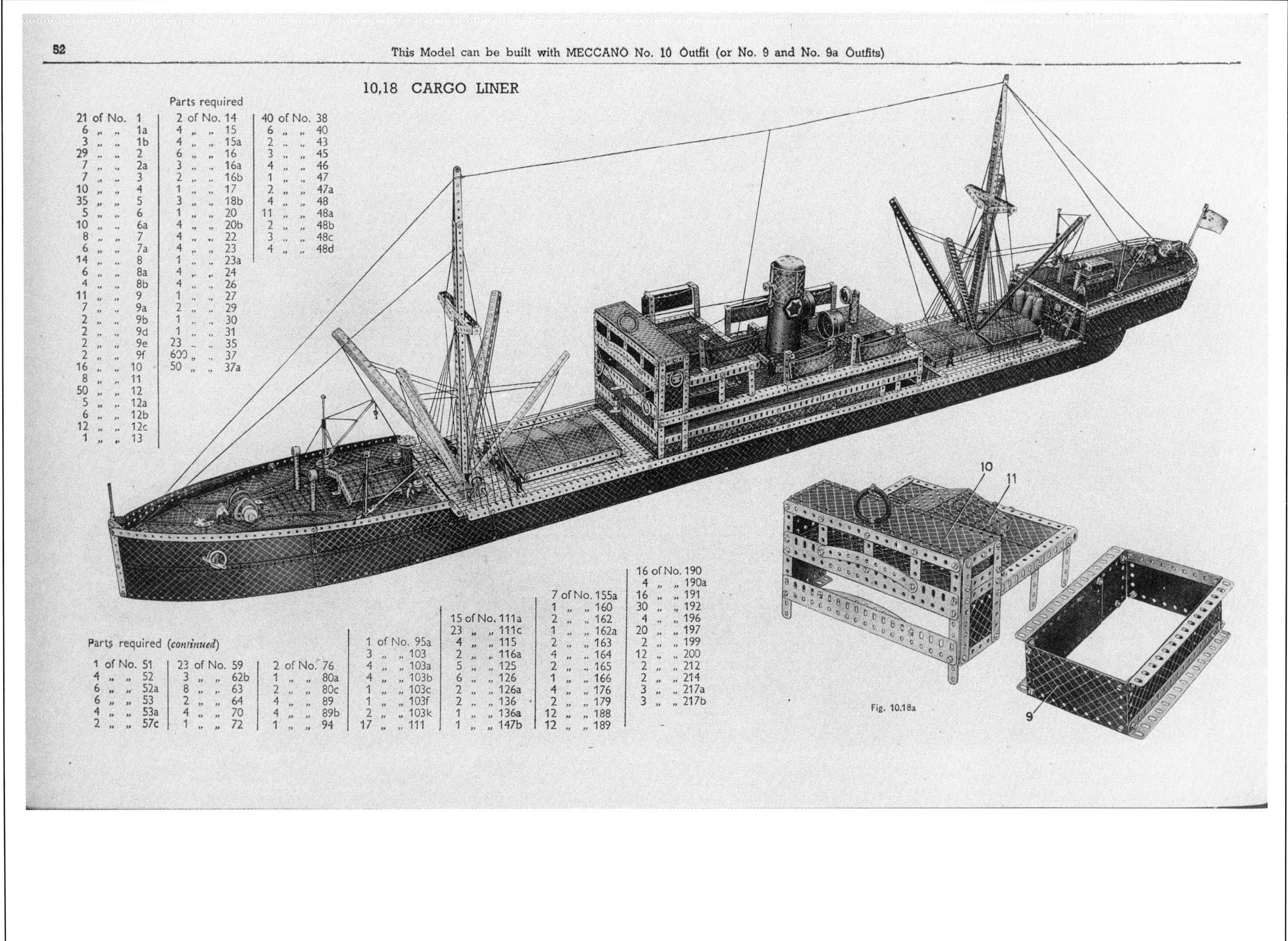

52 This Model can be built with MECCANO No. 10 Outfit (or No. 9 and No. 9a Outfits)

10,18 CARGO LINER

Parts required

21 of No. 1	2 of No. 14	40 of No. 38
6 „ „ 1a	4 „ „ 15	6 „ „ 40
3 „ „ 1b	4 „ „ 15a	2 „ „ 43
29 „ „ 2	6 „ „ 16	3 „ „ 45
7 „ „ 2a	3 „ „ 16a	4 „ „ 46
7 „ „ 3	2 „ „ 16b	1 „ „ 47
10 „ „ 4	1 „ „ 17	2 „ „ 47a
35 „ „ 5	3 „ „ 18b	4 „ „ 48
5 „ „ 6	1 „ „ 20	11 „ „ 48a
10 „ „ 6a	4 „ „ 20b	2 „ „ 48b
8 „ „ 7	4 „ „ 22	3 „ „ 48c
6 „ „ 7a	4 „ „ 23	4 „ „ 48d
14 „ „ 8	1 „ „ 23a	
6 „ „ 8a	4 „ „ 24	
4 „ „ 8b	4 „ „ 26	
11 „ „ 9	1 „ „ 27	
7 „ „ 9a	2 „ „ 29	
2 „ „ 9b	1 „ „ 30	
2 „ „ 9d	1 „ „ 31	
2 „ „ 9e	23 „ „ 35	
2 „ „ 9f	600 „ „ 37	
16 „ „ 10	50 „ „ 37a	
8 „ „ 11		
50 „ „ 12		
5 „ „ 12a		
6 „ „ 12b		
12 „ „ 12c		
1 „ „ 13		

Parts required (*continued*)

1 of No. 51	23 of No. 59	2 of No. 76	1 of No. 95a	15 of No. 111a	7 of No. 155a	16 of No. 190
4 „ „ 52	3 „ „ 62b	1 „ „ 80a	3 „ „ 103	23 „ „ 111c	1 „ „ 160	4 „ „ 190a
6 „ „ 52a	8 „ „ 63	2 „ „ 80c	4 „ „ 103a	4 „ „ 115	2 „ „ 162	16 „ „ 191
6 „ „ 53	2 „ „ 64	4 „ „ 89	4 „ „ 103b	2 „ „ 116a	1 „ „ 162a	30 „ „ 192
4 „ „ 53a	4 „ „ 70	4 „ „ 89b	1 „ „ 103c	5 „ „ 125	2 „ „ 163	4 „ „ 196
2 „ „ 57c	1 „ „ 72	1 „ „ 94	1 „ „ 103f	6 „ „ 126	4 „ „ 164	20 „ „ 197
			2 „ „ 103k	2 „ „ 126a	2 „ „ 165	2 „ „ 199
			17 „ „ 111	2 „ „ 136	1 „ „ 166	12 „ „ 200
				1 „ „ 136a	4 „ „ 176	2 „ „ 212
				1 „ „ 147b	2 „ „ 179	2 „ „ 214
					12 „ „ 188	3 „ „ 217a
					12 „ „ 189	3 „ „ 217b

Fig. 10.18a

10.5 SPORTS MOTOR CAR

This model is a realistic reproduction of a modern four-seater sports car and it incorporates all the main features of its prototype. It is designed on the unit construction principle, and the body can quickly be removed to reveal the various parts of the mechanism.

The chassis consists of two side members 1 each made by joining two compound angle girders together at each end by Flat Brackets to form a channel section girder. The compound angle girders consist of 12½" Angle Girders extended by a 3½" and a 4½" Angle Girder respectively. The side members are joined at the centre by a 5½" Angle Girder 2, which is braced by two 4½" Angle Girders bolted to the side members and to 1" Triangular Plates bolted to Angle Girder 2. Additional strength is supplied by 5½" Strip 3, to which a 2½" Strip is bolted but spaced from it by Washers. This serves also as a support for the driving unit. At the front end the side members are connected by a compound girder made by overlapping a 2½" and a 3½" Angle Girder by three holes.

At the rear the chassis is extended by a Formed Slotted Strip and two 2½" small radius Curved Strips. To these Strips are bolted a 3½" Angle Girder on one side, and two 2½" Angle Girders 4 overlapped by three holes on the other side. The Angle Girders on both sides are joined by a 5" compound girder. The front of the chassis is extended by two 5½" Curved Strips and a 5½" Strip, a 2" Strip being bolted to the latter to form the bumper supports.

The front springs 5 are of the semi-elliptic type and are built as follows. A 6½" compound strip, a 5½", a 4½", a 3½" and a 2½" Strip, are curved to shape and are joined together by passing a ¾" Bolt through their centre holes and through the end plain transverse bore of a Coupling, locking the Coupling in place by a Nut

(*Continued on next page*)

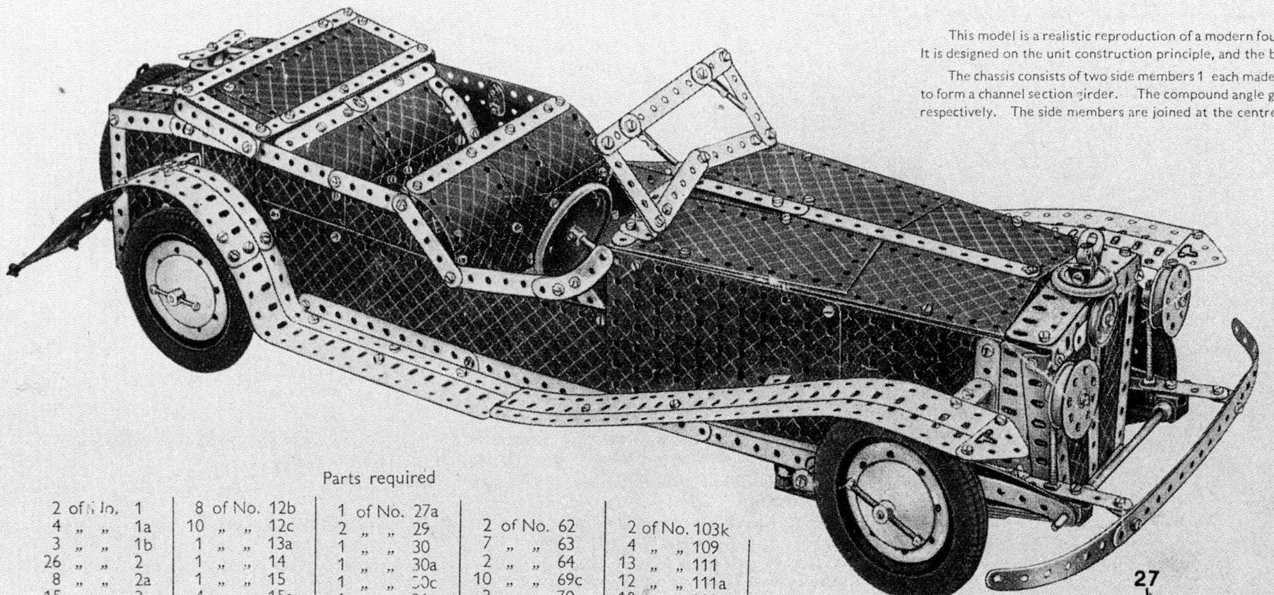

Parts required

2 of No. 1	8 of No. 12b	1 of No. 27a			
4 „ „ 1a	10 „ „ 12c	2 „ „ 29	2 of No. 62	2 of No. 103k	
3 „ „ 1b	1 „ „ 13a	1 „ „ 30	7 „ „ 63	4 „ „ 109	
26 „ „ 2	1 „ „ 14	1 „ „ 30a	2 „ „ 64	13 „ „ 111	
8 „ „ 2a	1 „ „ 15	1 „ „ 30c	10 „ „ 69c	12 „ „ 111a	
15 „ „ 3	4 „ „ 15a	1 „ „ 31	3 „ „ 70	18 „ „ 111c	
12 „ „ 4	3 „ „ 16	10 „ „ 35	2 „ „ 76	1 „ „ 115	
55 „ „ 5	6 „ „ 16a	429 „ „ 37	4 „ „ 77	1 „ „ 120b	
10 „ „ 6	1 „ „ 16b	50 „ „ 37a	2 „ „ 80c	2 „ „ 126a	10 of No. 188
8 „ „ 6a	3 „ „ 17	71 „ „ 38	1 „ „ 81	1 „ „ 128	8 „ „ 189
4 „ „ 8	3 „ „ 18a	1 „ „ 45	2 „ „ 82	4 „ „ 133	2 „ „ 190
4 „ „ 8b	4 „ „ 18b	1 „ „ 46	4 „ „ 89	2 „ „ 133a	2 „ „ 190a
10 „ „ 9	6 „ „ 19b	2 „ „ 47a	4 „ „ 89a	1 „ „ 136a	6 „ „ 192
6 „ „ 9a	4 „ „ 20	4 „ „ 48	2 „ „ 90	2 „ „ 137	2 „ „ 197
6 „ „ 9b	1 „ „ 21	10 „ „ 48a	6 „ „ 90a	2 „ „ 140	6 „ „ 199
3 „ „ 9c	1 „ „ 22	1 „ „ 48b	2 „ „ 103	6 „ „ 142b	12 „ „ 200
8 „ „ 9d	4 „ „ 22a	1 „ „ 48d	2 „ „ 103a	3 „ „ 155a	2 „ „ 212
2 „ „ 9e	1 „ „ 23	2 „ „ 51	4 „ „ 103b	6 „ „ 162a	2 „ „ 214
3 „ „ 9f	3 „ „ 24	2 „ „ 52	2 „ „ 103c	1 „ „ 163	2 „ „ 215
24 „ „ 10	4 „ „ 25	3 „ „ 52a	2 „ „ 103d	1 „ „ 164	5 „ „ 219
6 „ „ 11	6 „ „ 26	4 „ „ 53a	2 „ „ 103e	1 „ „ 171	1 „ „ P52
24 „ „ 12	1 „ „ 26b	1 „ „ 55a	3 „ „ 103f	1 „ „ 179	1E120 Electric
6 „ „ 12a	1 „ „ 27	20 „ „ 59	3 „ „ 103h	1 „ „ 187	Motor

30 27 31 28 29 18 15 16 13 12

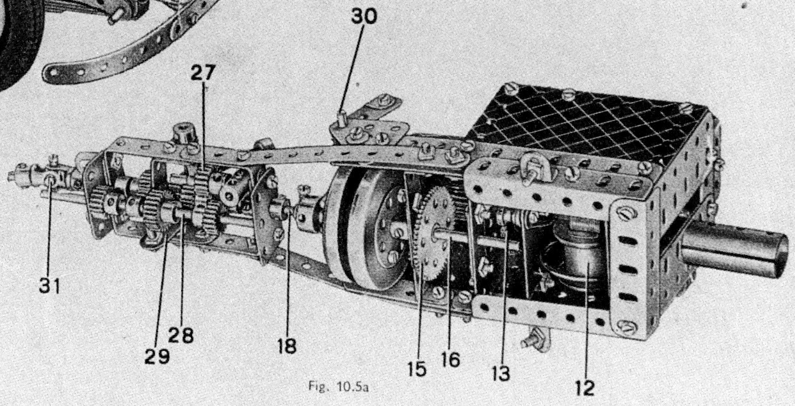

Fig. 10.5a

Figs 30–33. A selection of models from the numbered → blue/gold series manuals. Most were reproduced in early post-war manuals from which the illustration of the cargo ship is derived.

7.8 TELPHER RAILWAY AND ELEVATOR

Parts required

12 of No. 1	150 of No. 37	2 of No. 163
18 „ „ 2	6 „ „ 37a	1 „ „ 187
2 „ „ 3	14 „ „ 38	5 „ „ 188
2 „ „ 4	2 „ „ 40	5 „ „ 189
9 „ „ 5	1 „ „ 44	5 „ „ 190
4 „ „ 6a	1 „ „ 46	6 „ „ 192
8 „ „ 8	10 „ „ 48a	2 „ „ 197
18 „ „ 12	2 „ „ 48b	1 „ „ 198
3 „ „ 12a	1 „ „ 51	
6 „ „ 12c	2 „ „ 52	
2 „ „ 15	2 „ „ 53	
1 „ „ 15b	2 „ „ 54	
2 „ „ 16	1 „ „ 59	
1 „ „ 18a	2 „ „ 90	
1 „ „ 18b	1 „ „ 111	
1 „ „ 19h	4 „ „ 111c	
1 „ „ 20a	2 „ „ 125	
4 „ „ 20b	4 „ „ 126a	
2 „ „ 22		
2 „ „ 22a		
1 „ „ 23		
1 „ „ 23a		
1 „ „ 26		
1 „ „ 27a		
7 „ „ 35		

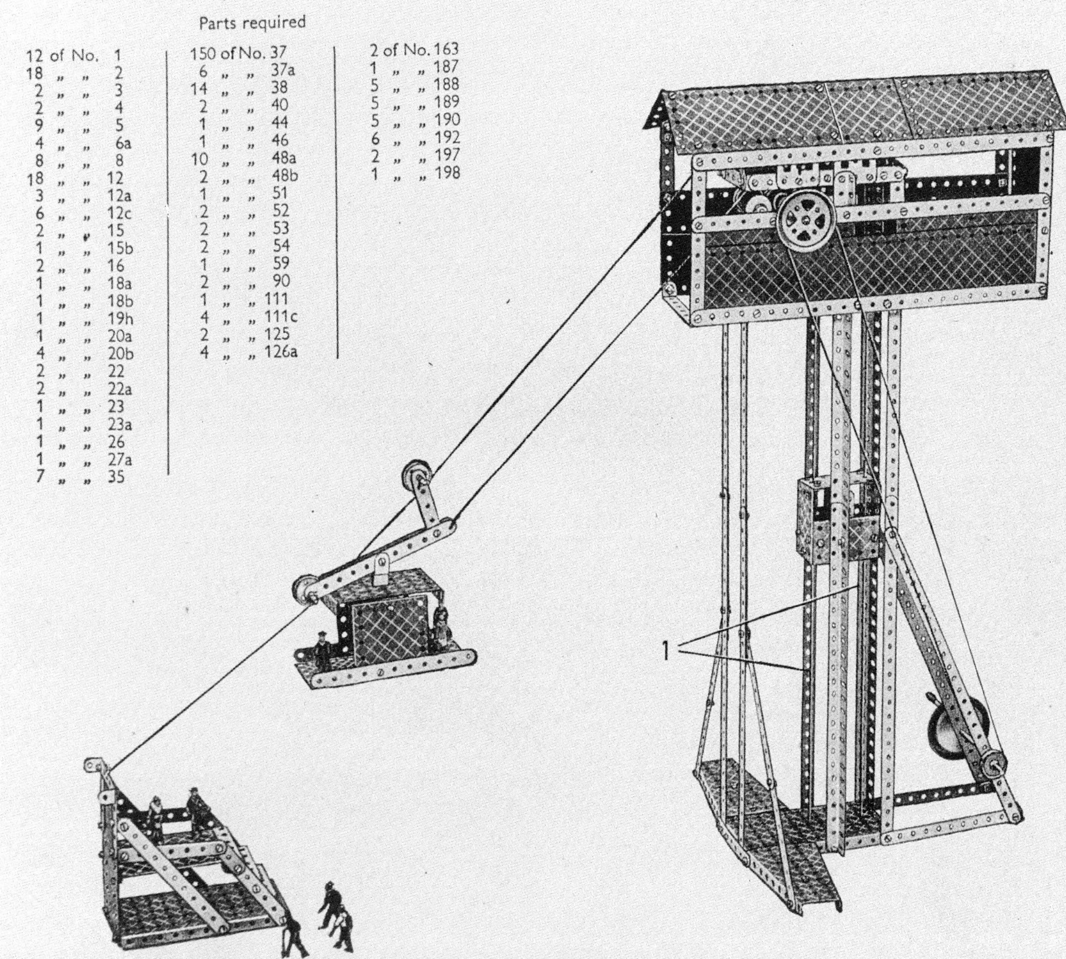

The control cabin is supported o four main pillars each made from two Angle Girders overlapped three holes. A ditional support is supplied by two compound strips made by overlapping two $12\frac{1}{2}$" Strips 11 holes, and bolting them to two $2\frac{1}{2}$" Strips overlapped three holes and attached by Angle Brackets to the base of the cabin. The supports are braced by $12\frac{1}{2}$" Strips and $9\frac{1}{2}$" compound strips.

The $12\frac{1}{2}" \times 2\frac{1}{2}"$ Strip Plates forming the sides of the cabin are attached to the rear pair of Angle Girders by Reversed Angle Brackets, and to the front pair of Angle Girders by Angle Brackets. The sides are spaced at the ends by $3\frac{1}{2}" \times \frac{1}{2}"$ Double Angle Strips.

The roof consists of a Hinged Flat Plate extended on each side by $5\frac{1}{2}" \times 2\frac{1}{2}"$ Flexible Plates, each of these overlapping the Hinged Flat Plate by two holes. The roof is attached to the sides by Obtuse Angle Brackets, and the back of the cabin, which consists of a $5\frac{1}{2}" \times 2\frac{1}{2}"$ and a $5\frac{1}{2}" \times 1\frac{1}{2}"$ Flexible Plate, is attached by two $1" \times 1"$ Angle Brackets.

The $5\frac{1}{2}$" Strips carrying the 1" Pulleys of the carriage are pivoted on a lock-nutted $\frac{3}{4}$" Bolt, which carries a Collar and two Washers for spacing purposes and is supported by a Stepped Bent Strip. The $\frac{3}{8}$" Bolt at the junction of the $2\frac{1}{2}$" Strips carries five Washers on its shank, to space the Strips apart.

Fig. 7.8a shows the cab with the roof removed to reveal the arrangement of the hoisting drums. The guide cords for the elevator are tied at 1, and the guide cord for the carriage is tied to an Obtuse Angle Bracket 2. Cord is tied around a $\frac{1}{2}$" loose Pulley fastened to a $1" \times 1"$ Angle Bracket on the lift, and then passes over a 1" fast Pulley and a $\frac{1}{2}$" fast Pulley at the top of the shaft and finally is wound around hoisting drum 3. A second Cord is tied to the carriage and is wound around hoisting drum 4.

A Crank Handle passed through holes in the $12\frac{1}{2}$" Strips bracing the Angle Girders carries a 1" fast Pulley that is connected by a belt of Cord to a 2" Pulley fastened on the 5" Rod carrying hoisting drum 3. A 57-teeth Gear on this Rod meshes with a $\frac{1}{2}$" Pinion on the 5" Rod of hoisting drum 4. In order to ensure that the lift reaches the top of the shaft at the same time as the carriage, the carriage Cord should be three times the length of the lift Cord.

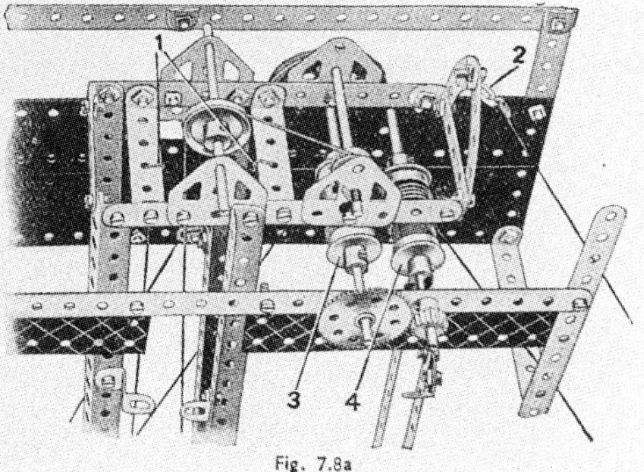

Fig. 7.8a

Figs 30–33.

6.14 PITHEAD GEAR

Each side of the lower framework of the model is made by bolting the vertical 12½" Angle Girders 1 and 12½" Strips 2 to the compound strips 3. The compound strips consist of a 12½" and a 5½" Strip joined together. The sides are connected by the 5½" Strips 4 and a 5½"×2½" Flanged Plate 5.

The tower consists of four 12½" Strips bolted to the lower framework and joined at the top by the 5½" Strips 6 and 5½"×1½" Flexible Plates 7, which are attached to the 12½" Strips by Angle Brackets. The 3" Pulleys 8 are held between Spring Clips on a 6½" Rod mounted in 2½" Strips bolted to the top of the tower.

Fig. 6.14a

One of the cages is formed by connecting together two 2½"×2½" Flexible Plates by means of 3½" Strips 9 and Angle Brackets. The second cage is made in a similar way, except that two 3½"×½" Double Angle Strips and two compound strips, each consisting of a 2½" Strip and a 1½" Strip, are used in place of the Strips 9. Guides for the cages are provided by four lengths of Cord. These are fastened at the top to Flat Trunnions (Fig. 6.14b) attached to the Strips 6 by Double Brackets, and at their lower ends to the 2½"×½" Double Angle Strips 11 and 1½"×½" Double Angle Strips 12. The Cords pass through Fishplates attached to top and bottom of the cages.

(Continued on next page)

Note: The Flanged Plate 18 and the winding shaft 17 should be assembled before the Motor is bolted in position. The length of the hoisting Cords can then be adjusted from the side of the model.

This Model can be built with MECCANO No. 6 Outfit (or No. 5 and No. 5a Outfits)

29

Fig 36.

10.6
PIT HEAD GEAR

Parts required

Qty	No.	Qty	No.
24 of No.	1	8 of No.	48b
5 „ „	1a	3 „ „	48c
1 „ „	1b	2 „ „	52
22 „ „	2	6 „ „	52a
10 „ „	2a	6 „ „	53
8 „ „	3	3 „ „	53a
8 „ „	4	10 „ „	59
30 „ „	5	2 „ „	62
8 „ „	7	4 „ „	62b
6 „ „	7a	1 „ „	63
16 „ „	8	4 „ „	70
6 „ „	8a	1 „ „	72
4 „ „	8b	2 „ „	76
12 „ „	9	2 „ „	94
8 „ „	9a	1 „ „	95
5 „ „	9b	1 „ „	96
4 „ „	9c	2 „ „	103
6 „ „	9d	1 „ „	103a
2 „ „	9e	2 „ „	103c
10 „ „	10	1 „ „	103e
4 „ „	12	1 „ „	103k
8 „ „	12a	2 „ „	109
4 „ „	12b	8 „ „	111
2 „ „	12c	4 „ „	111a
2 „ „	13	1 „ „	111c
2 „ „	13a	2 „ „	114
4 „ „	14	1 „ „	115
1 „ „	15	2 „ „	118
1 „ „	15a	1 „ „	126
1 „ „	15b	6 „ „	126a
1 „ „	17	2 „ „	136
3 „ „	19b	2 „ „	143
1 „ „	22	2 „ „	146
4 „ „	23	1 „ „	162b
2 „ „	24	2 „ „	167b
1 „ „	26	1 „ „	186
1 „ „	26b	8 „ „	189
1 „ „	27a	2 „ „	190
1 „ „	28	16 „ „	191
1 „ „	31	23 „ „	192
1 „ „	32	5 „ „	195
6 „ „	35	4 „ „	196
592 „ „	37	20 „ „	197
15 „ „	37a	1 E120 Electric Motor	
38 „ „	38		
6 „ „	40		
2 „ „	48		

This Model can be built with MECCANO No. 10 Outfit (or No. 9 and No. 9a Outfits)

18

Fig 38. *A model from a 1951 No. 10 Outfit manual. It is identical to its pre-war equivalent.*

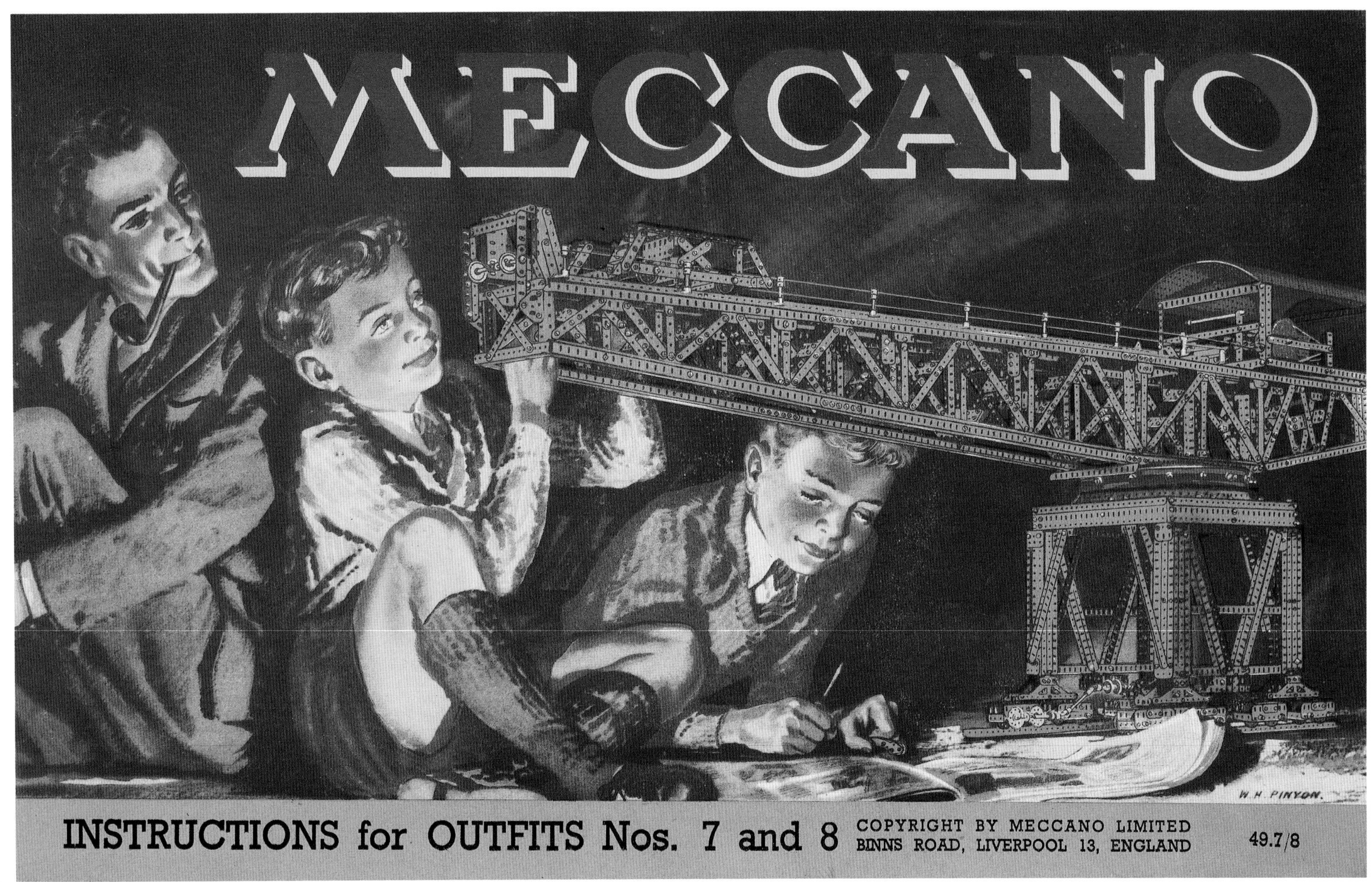

Fig 37. The classic W. H. Pinyon picture which is generally regarded as the finest of all manual-cover illustrations. It is especially warm and evokes wonderful memories in those who used them first-hand, and envy in those who did not.

Fig 39. Norman Tudor's file copies which he had marked → for revision.

1949 MANUALS 0 – 10
DESK. FILE.
MARKED FOR REVISION.
G. TUDOR.
No 9 Book THIS SERIES
No 9 AS PREVIOUS YEAR

MECCANO
Corrected to April 1952
BY MECCANO LIMITED
LIVERPOOL 13, ENGLAND
48.1
MECCANO
INSTRUCTIONS FOR No. O OUTFIT
No. 48.O
Out of Date
see later Edition
MARKED MANUAL 1948
COPYRIGHT BY MECCANO LTD. BINNS ROAD LIVERPOOL 13

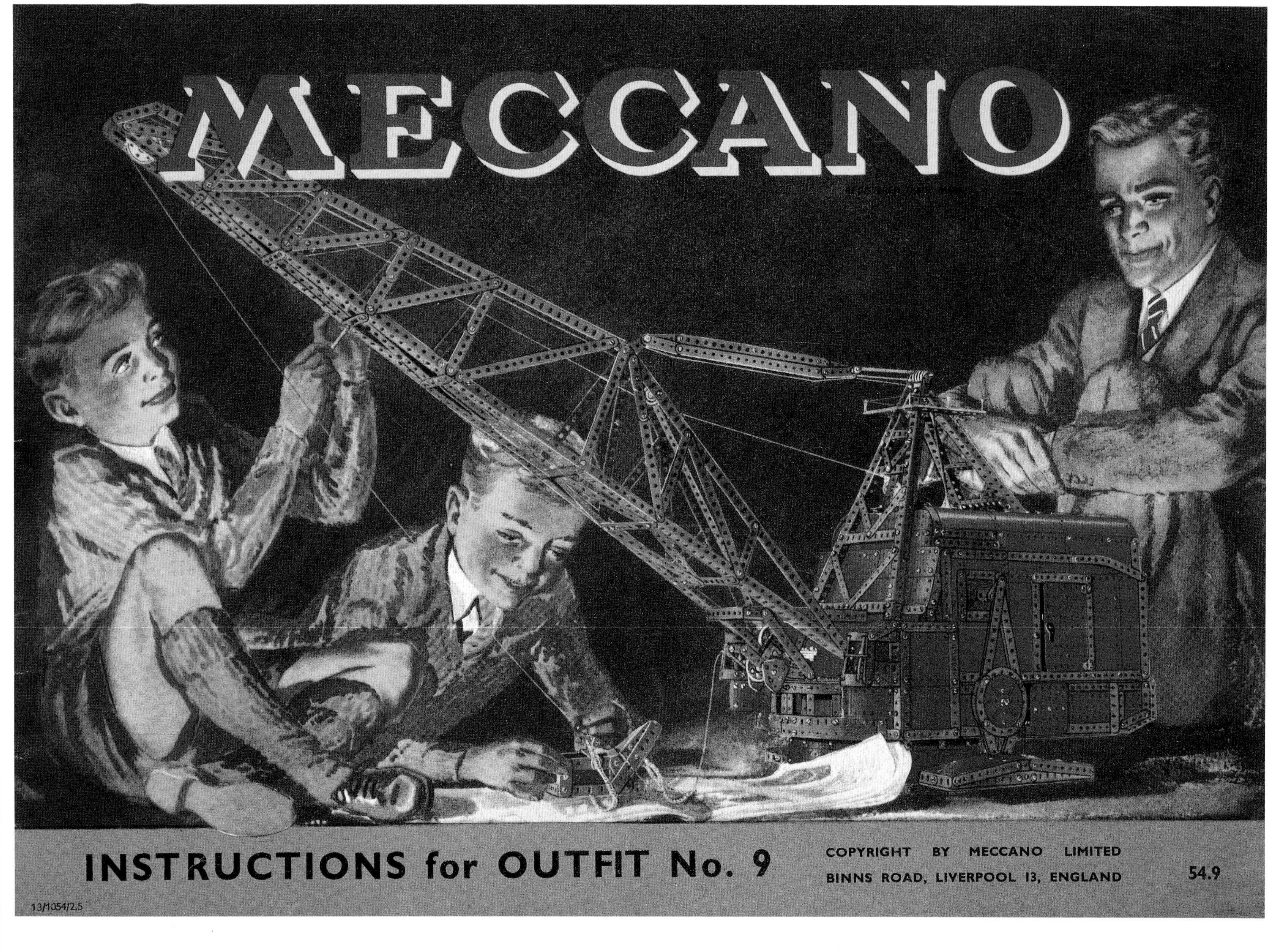
MECCANO
INSTRUCTIONS for OUTFIT No. 9
COPYRIGHT BY MECCANO LIMITED
BINNS ROAD, LIVERPOOL 13, ENGLAND
54.9
13/1054/2.5

←*Fig 40. A revised version of the Pinyon picture used after 1953.*

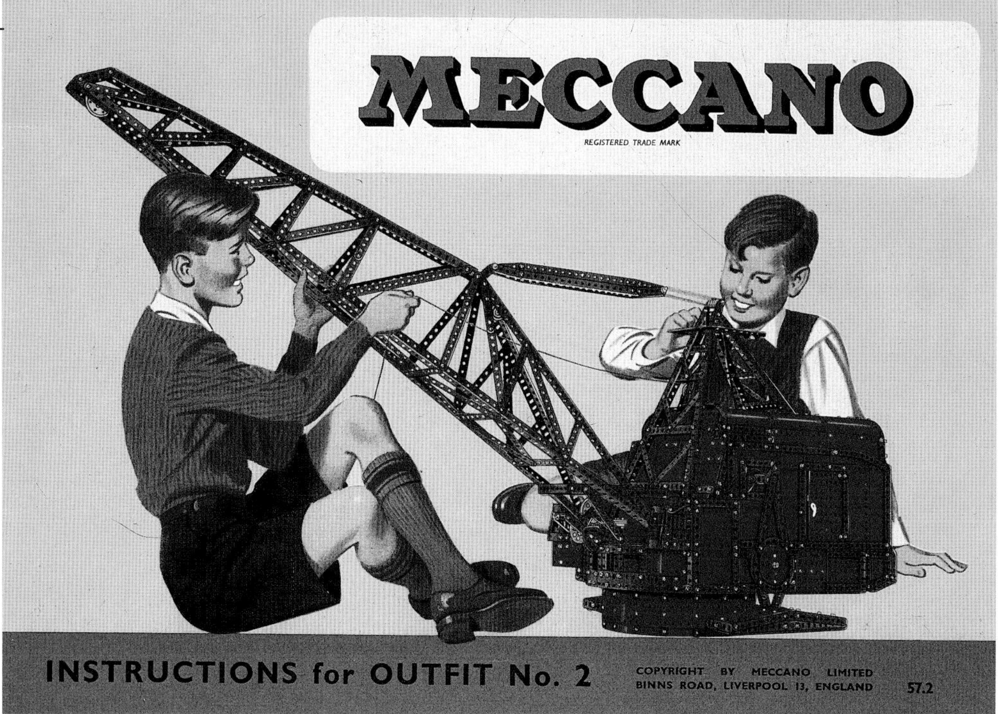

Fig 41. The 'modernised' version of the dragline cover. → *Though the models were the same, it marked the beginning of the end.*

Fig 42. The Accessory Outfit covers which did duty from 1953 up until 1962.

THESE MODELS CAN BE BUILT WITH MECCANO No. 2 OUTFIT (or No. 1 and No. 1A OUTFITS) 11

2.13 DRAGLINE EXCAVATOR

Parts Required

4 of No. 2	
6 „ „ 5	
2 „ „ 10	
8 „ „ 12	
1 „ „ 16	
2 „ „ 17	
1 „ „ 19g	
3 „ „ 22	
1 „ „ 24	2 of No. 111c
4 „ „ 35	2 „ „ 126
44 „ „ 37a	2 „ „ 126a
40 „ „ 37b	1 „ „ 176
1 „ „ 38	1 „ „ 187
1 „ „ 40	2 „ „ 188
1 „ „ 48a	2 „ „ 189
1 „ „ 52	2 „ „ 190
1 „ „ 57c	1 „ „ 199
2 „ „ 90a	2 „ „ 200

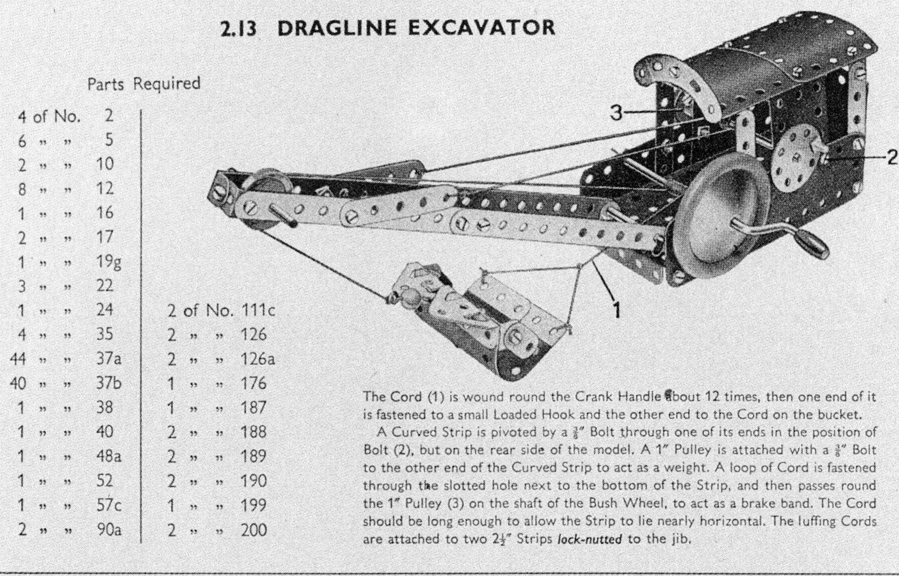

The Cord (1) is wound round the Crank Handle about 12 times, then one end of it is fastened to a small Loaded Hook and the other end to the Cord on the bucket.

A Curved Strip is pivoted by a ⅜" Bolt through one of its ends in the position of Bolt (2), but on the rear side of the model. A 1" Pulley is attached with a ⅜" Bolt to the other end of the Curved Strip to act as a weight. A loop of Cord is fastened through the slotted hole next to the bottom of the Strip, and then passes round the 1" Pulley (3) on the shaft of the Bush Wheel, to act as a brake band. The Cord should be long enough to allow the Strip to lie nearly horizontal. The luffing Cords are attached to two 2½" Strips *lock-nutted* to the jib.

2.14 RAILWAY SERVICE CRANE

The bearings (1) are Fishplates bolted to the Flanged Plate and the Flexible Plates respectively. The jib is fastened to two Trunnions (2), which are bolted to the Bush Wheel (3). A 2" Rod is secured in the boss of the Bush Wheel (3). It then passes through a hole in the Flanged Plate, and is held in position by a Spring Clip underneath the Plate.

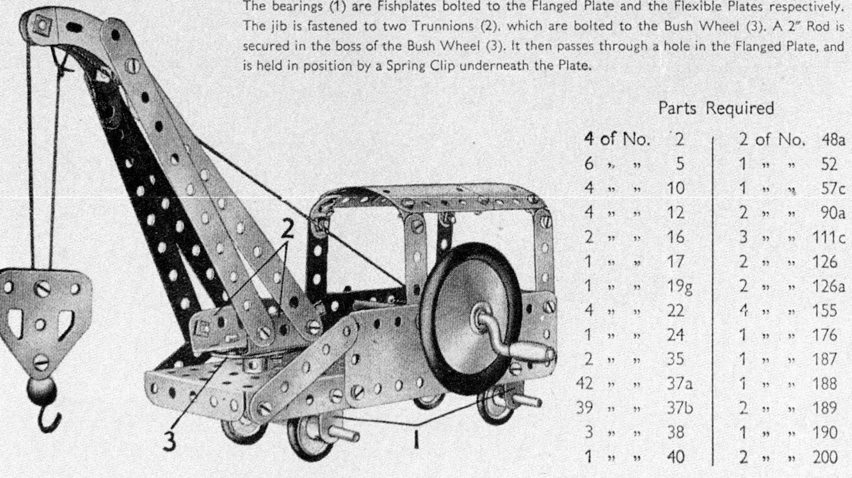

Parts Required

4 of No. 2	2 of No. 48a
6 „ „ 5	1 „ „ 52
4 „ „ 10	1 „ „ 57c
4 „ „ 12	2 „ „ 90a
2 „ „ 16	3 „ „ 111c
1 „ „ 17	1 „ „ 126
1 „ „ 19g	2 „ „ 126a
4 „ „ 22	4 „ „ 155
1 „ „ 24	1 „ „ 176
2 „ „ 35	1 „ „ 187
42 „ „ 37a	1 „ „ 188
39 „ „ 37b	2 „ „ 189
3 „ „ 38	1 „ „ 190
1 „ „ 40	2 „ „ 200

2.15 LETTER BALANCE

Each side of the model consists of a 5½"×1½" Flexible Plate edged by 5½" Strips (1). The sides are connected at the top by two 2½"×½" Double Angle Strips (2), and a 2½" Strip (3) is attached to one of them by Fishplates.

A 2½"×1½" Flexible Plate and a 2½"×2½" Flexible Plate bolted together are connected to the sides by Angle Brackets, to form the lower part of the front of the casing. A 2½"×1½" Flexible Plate (4) is used to fill in the upper section of the front, and it is connected to one of the Double Angle Strips (2) by an Angle Bracket. The casing is attached to the Flanged Plate forming the base by two Angle Brackets and a Trunnion (5).

The pointer consists of a 2½" Strip bolted to a Flat Trunnion, and it is gripped between two 1" Pulleys fitted with Rubber Rings. These Pulleys are fixed on a 3½" Rod (6) supported in the 2½" Strips (7) and (8).

A Rod and Strip Connector is attached to a 2" Rod (9), which is passed through Strip (3) and ½" Reversed Angle Bracket. The Rod and Strip Connector is attached by a *lock-nutted* bolt to a connecting bar (10), made from two 2½" Strips overlapped two holes. The lower end of the connecting bar is *lock-nutted* to a Bush Wheel, which is loose on a 3½" Rod (11).

A length of Cord from the connecting bar is passed several times round the Rod (6) and is tied to a Driving Band (12). The Driving Band is looped round the Rod (11).

A piece of cardboard is marked to form an indicator dial, which is then bolted to the front of the model.

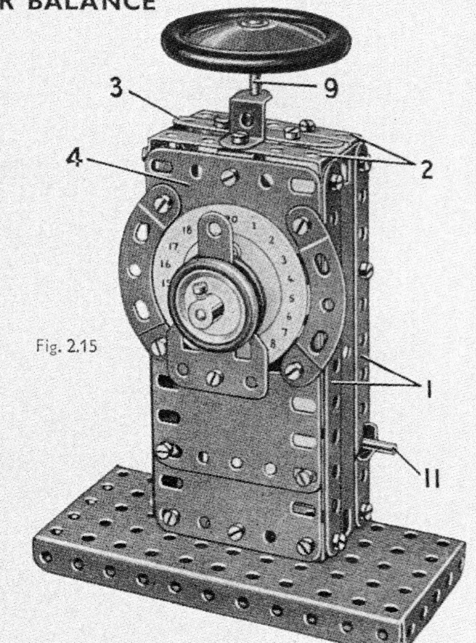

Fig. 2.15

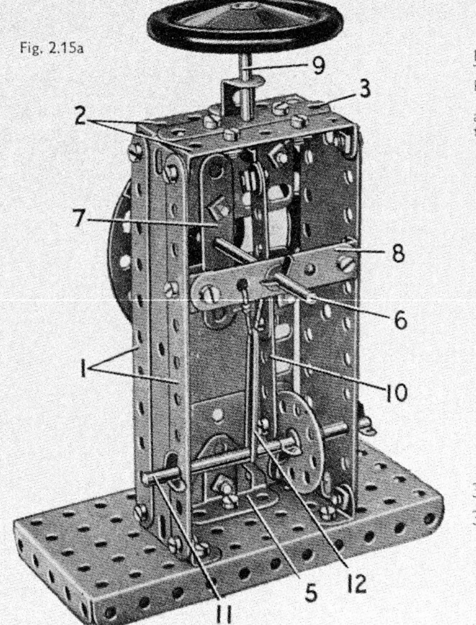

Fig. 2.15a

Parts Required

4 of No. 2	1 of No. 52
6 „ „ 5	2 „ „ 90a
2 „ „ 10	1 „ „ 111c
7 „ „ 12	1 „ „ 125
2 „ „ 16	1 „ „ 126
1 „ „ 17	1 „ „ 126a
2 „ „ 22	2 „ „ 155
1 „ „ 24	1 „ „ 186
4 „ „ 35	1 „ „ 187
36 „ „ 37a	1 „ „ 188
33 „ „ 37b	2 „ „ 189
2 „ „ 38	2 „ „ 190
1 „ „ 40	1 „ „ 212
2 „ „ 48a	

Fig 43.

Figs 43–45. Examples of models from the 1953–1961 period.

9.14 VERTICAL MILLING MACHINE

CONSTRUCTION OF THE BASE

The frame for the base consists of two 12½" Angle Girders (1) connected at the front by a built-up girder (2) made from two 12½" Strips. One of these Strips is connected to the Girders (1) by Angle Brackets. At the rear a 12½" Angle Girder (3) is attached to the Girders (1) by Angle Brackets, and a 12½" Strip (4) (Fig. 9.14a), is also fixed to Angle Brackets bolted to the Girders (1). Two 18½" Angle Girders (5) are bolted vertically to the Girder (3), and two 7½" Angle Girders (6) are fixed to the Girders (5) and to the flanges of a 3½" × 2½" Flanged Plate (11) bolted to the Strip (4).

The base is filled in as shown in Figs. 9.14 and 9.14a by Plates of various sizes supported by 12½" and 5½" Strips.

THE VERTICAL COLUMN

Two 5½" × 2½" Flexible Plates, extended upward by 2½" × 1½" Flexible Plates, are bolted to each end of the Girder (3) (Fig. 9.14c). The edge of the outer 5½" × 2½" Flexible Plate is strengthened by a 5½" Strip on the inside, and a 4½" × ½" Double Angle Strip is bolted along the top edges of the 2½" × 1½" Flexible Plates. The inner lugs of these Double Angle Strips are attached to the Girders (5). A 4½" × 2½" Flexible Plate (7) on each side is connected to the Plates at the rear by two Angle Brackets, and is edged at the front by a 12½" Angle Girder (8). A 5½" × 2½" Flat Plate at each end is attached to the base by an Angle Bracket, and is bolted at the top to the outer lug of the 4½" × ½" Double Angle Strip.

Two 12½" Angle Girders (9) are bolted vertically to the flange of a 3½" × 2½" Flanged Plate (10) (Fig. 9.14), which is fixed to the Girders (5) and to the centre of the Girder (8). The sides of the column are filled in by 12½" × 2½" Strip Plates, and the top is formed by a 3½" × 2½" Flanged Plate. The back is completed by two 5½" × 3½" Flat Plates and a 12½" × 2½" Strip Plate bolted between the Girders (5). At the upper end of the front of the column a 2½" × 2½" Flexible Plate is edged by two 3½" Strips and it is attached by an Angle Bracket to the 3½" × 2½" Flanged Plate that fills in the top.

(Continued on next page)

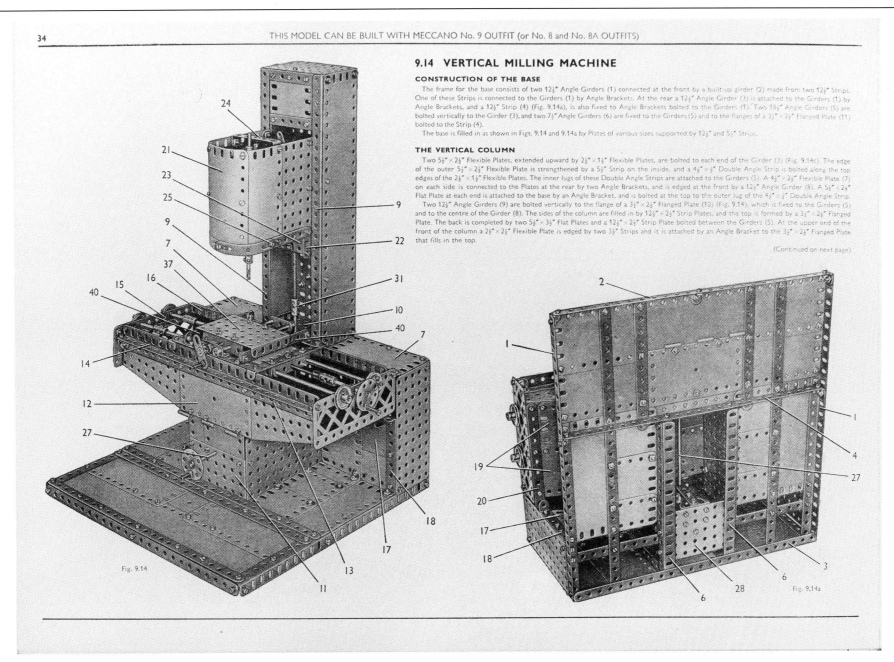

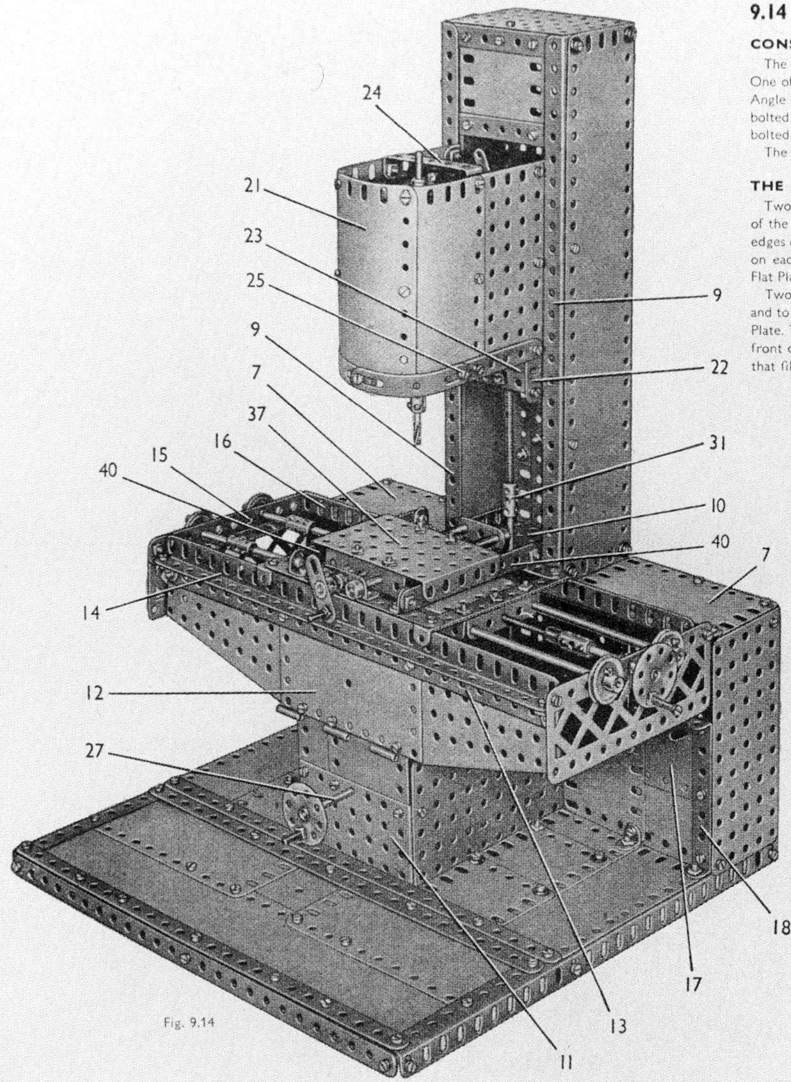

Fig. 9.14

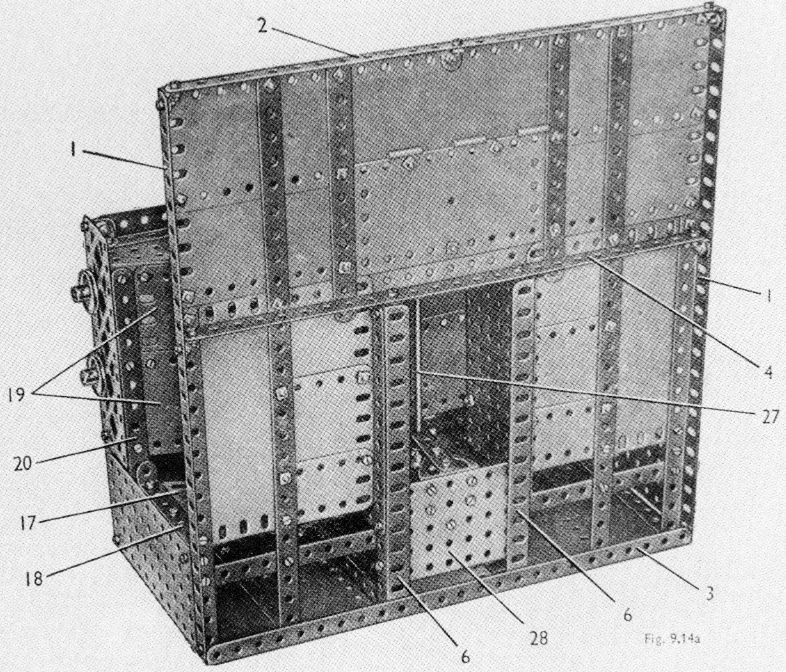

Fig. 9.14a

Fig 44.

MODEL 4.19 QUAYSIDE UNLOADER — Continued

Fig. 4.19a

The top edges of the Flexible Plates (1) are strengthened by 5½" Strips, and 2½"×1½" Triangular Plates (4) are bolted in position as shown.

Each leg of the gantry is a 5½" Strip braced to the gantry by a 2½" Strip (5). The legs are connected at their lower ends by Angle Brackets to 5½" Strips (6), and 1" Pulleys are held by their set-screws on ⅜" Bolts passed through these Strips.

The roof of the operating cabin consists of two 1$\frac{11}{16}$" radius Curved Plates edged as shown by three Formed Slotted Strips. The roof is attached by Obtuse Angle Brackets to four 2½" Strips bolted to the Flexible Plates (1). The back of the cabin is a 2½"×2½" Flexible Plate bolted to the 5½"×2½" Flanged Plate and connected to the sides by Angle Brackets.

A Flanged Sector Plate is attached to each side of the gantry by a Fishplate and a 2½"×1½" Triangular Flexible Plate (7). The Flanged Sector Plates are extended upward by 3½" Strips (8), which are braced by 2½" Stepped Curved Strips, and a 2½"×½" Double Angle Strip (9) is bolted between the Flanged Sector Plates.

The jib of the model consists of two 12½" Strips joined together by two 2½"×½" Double Angle Strips (10). The jib pivots on a Crank Handle (11) supported in the Flanged Sector Plates, and it can be luffed, or raised and lowered, by operating a Bush Wheel fixed on a 4" Rod (12). A length of Cord is tied to a Cord Anchoring Spring on the Rod, is led over a Rod (13) and is fastened to the front of the jib. The Rod (12) is free to slide about ¼" in its bearings, so that when the Bush Wheel is pushed in its set-screw catches on an Angle Bracket (14) bolted to the side of the cabin.

The crab or travelling carriage that carries the load-hoisting Cord is made by bolting two 2½"×½" Double Angle Strips to two Trunnions. The crab can be moved up or down the jib by turning the Crank Handle (11). A length of Cord is tied to the rear of the crab and is wound two or three times round the Crank Handle. The Cord is then taken round a ½" Pulley on a Rod (15) and is fastened to the front of the crab.

The hoisting Cord is tied to a Rod (16), is led over Rod (13) and a 1" Rod (17), and is fitted with a small Loaded Hook. A handle on Rod (16) is provided by an Angle Bracket fixed to a 1" Pulley (18) (Fig. 4.19a). Two Washers are slipped over a Bolt, which is then passed through the Angle Bracket and is screwed into the boss of the Pulley. A ⅜" Bolt is held by a nut in the Angle Bracket.

4.20 RACING CAR

The chassis is made by bolting two 12½" Strips to 2½"×½" Double Angle Strips (1) and (2). Each 12½" Strip is extended at its rear end by a 5½" Strip (3) that overlaps the 12½" Strip by five holes, and the ends of the 5½" Strips are bolted together to form the pointed tail. A 5½" Strip (4) is fixed to the chassis at each side, and these Strips are connected by a 2½"×½" Double Angle Strip (5).

The sides of the bonnet are formed by 5½"×1½" Flexible Plates (6) and 5½"×2½" Flexible Plates (7). The Plates (7) are curved and bolted together as shown, and their front edges are strengthened by Formed Slotted Strips. A 1½"×½" Double Angle Strip is fixed to the Plates (6) by a Bolt (8) on each side, and three 2½"×½" Double Angle Strips representing the radiator are bolted to the 1½"×½" Double Angle Strip. The rounded top of the radiator is formed by a Wheel Disc.

The sides of the driver's cockpit are 2½"×1½" Flexible Plates, and the tail is plated by a 1$\frac{11}{16}$" radius Curved Plate (9) on each side. The Curved Plates are connected at the top by a 'U'-section Curved Plate (10), and a second 'U'-section Curved Plate (11) is attached to the first by a Fishplate. Two 2½" Strips (12) are bolted to the Curved Plate (11), and they are connected to the Strips (3) by a Fishplate.

The rear wheels are each fixed on a 3½" Rod passed through a ½" Reversed Angle Bracket (13) and a Fishplate bolted to the Strip (3). The inner ends of the Rods are supported in Fishplates bolted to a Double Bracket that is fixed to the centre of Double Angle Strip (5). The front axle is a 4" and a 2" Rod joined by a Rod Connector.

The steering wheel is fixed on a 1" Rod held by a 1" Pulley in a Wheel Disc (14). The Wheel Disc and a 2½" Stepped Curved Strip (15) are attached to the bonnet by an Angle Bracket. The rear end of the exhaust pipe is supported as shown by two Obtuse Angle Brackets bolted together.

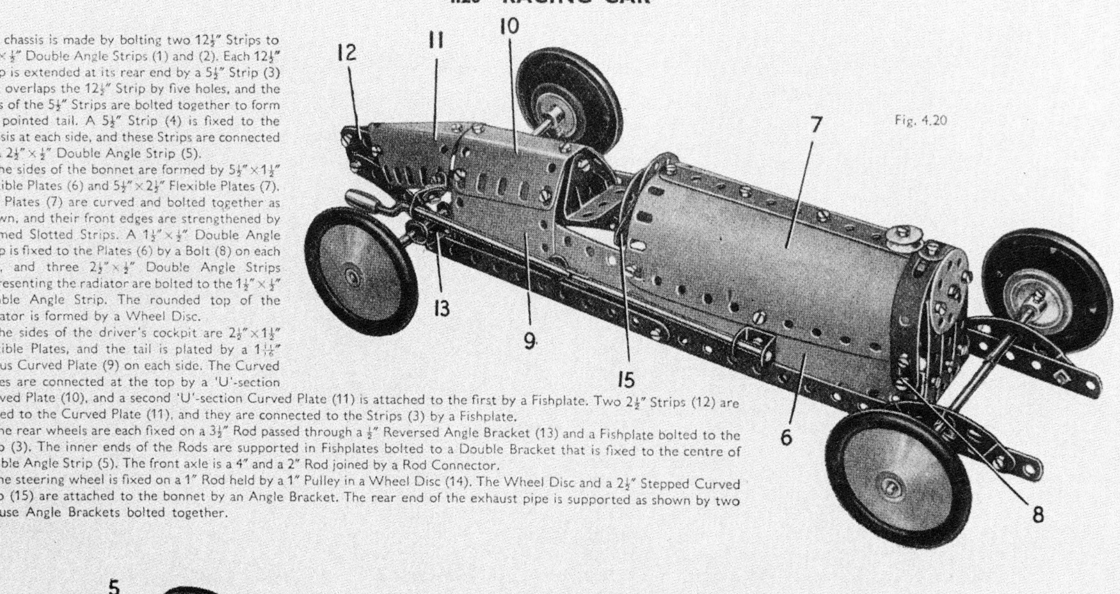

Fig. 4.20

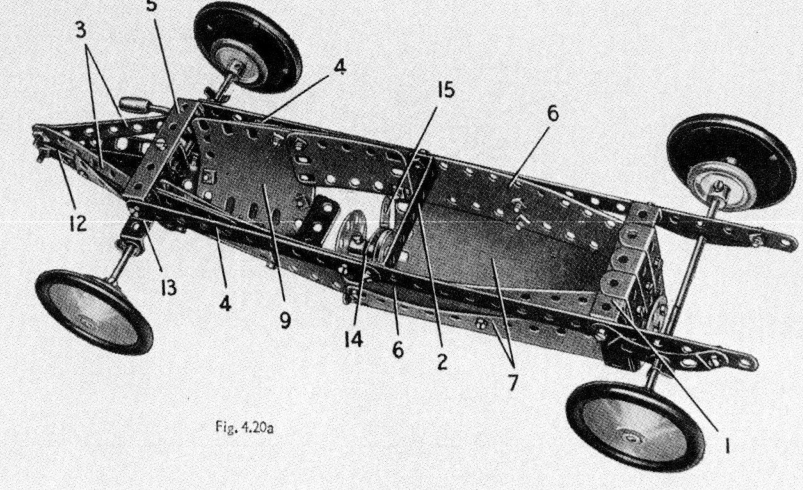

Fig. 4.20a

Parts Required

2 of No.	1	48 of No.	37b
5 " "	2	1 " "	48
3 " "	5	6 " "	48a
5 " "	10	3 " "	90a
2 " "	11	5 " "	111c
3 " "	12	2 " "	125
1 " "	12c	1 " "	126
2 " "	15b	4 " "	155
2 " "	16	4 " "	187
1 " "	17	2 " "	188
1 " "	18b	2 " "	189
1 " "	19g	2 " "	192
5 " "	22	2 " "	199
1 " "	23	2 " "	200
1 " "	24	1 " "	212
2 " "	24a	1 " "	213
6 " "	35	2 " "	215
53 " "	37a		

Fig 45.

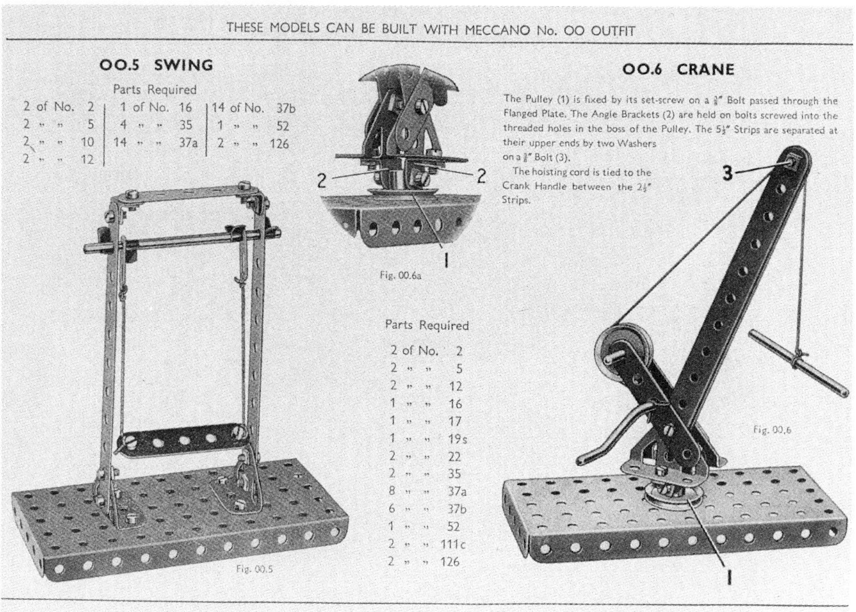

THESE MODELS CAN BE BUILT WITH MECCANO No. OO OUTFIT

OO.5 SWING

Parts Required

2 of No. 2	1 of No. 16	14 of No. 37b
2 " " 5	4 " " 35	1 " " 52
2 " " 10	14 " " 37a	2 " " 126
2 " " 12		

Fig. 00.5

OO.6 CRANE

The Pulley (1) is fixed by its set-screw on a ⅜" Bolt passed through the Flanged Plate. The Angle Brackets (2) are held on bolts screwed into the threaded holes in the boss of the Pulley. The 5½" Strips are separated at their upper ends by two Washers on a ⅜" Bolt (3).

The hoisting cord is tied to the Crank Handle between the 2½" Strips.

Fig. 00.6a

Parts Required

2 of No. 2
2 " " 5
2 " " 12
1 " " 16
1 " " 17
1 " " 19s
2 " " 22
2 " " 35
8 " " 37a
6 " " 37b
1 " " 52
2 " " 111c
2 " " 126

Fig. 00.6

Figs 46–47. The later 00 Outfit manual which continued ↑ the idea of a different cover for the more junior outfits.

Fig 48. A 1959 No. 0 Outfit cover – slightly less 'junior' → than that for the No. 0 manual.

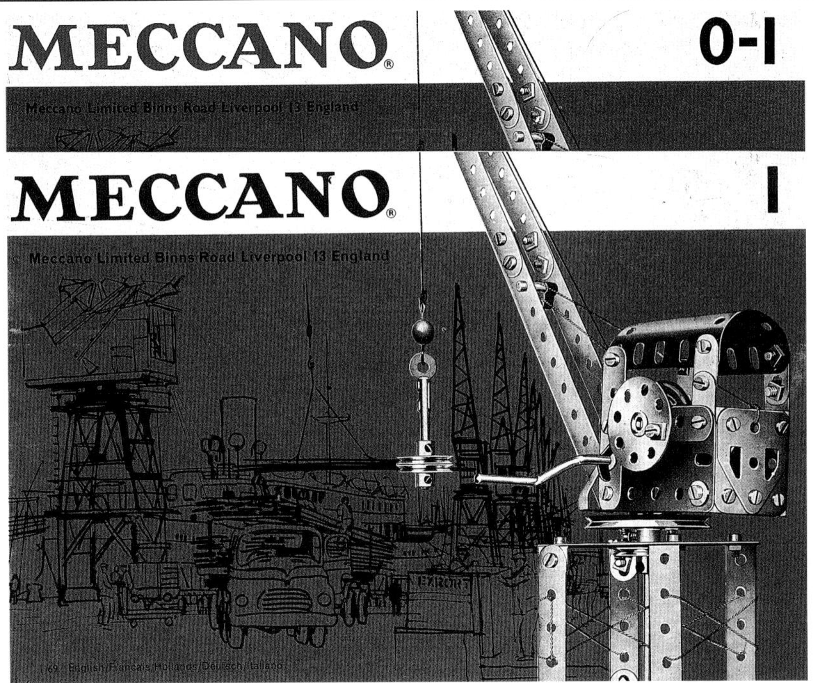

Figs 49–51. Covers from the period 1962–1969.

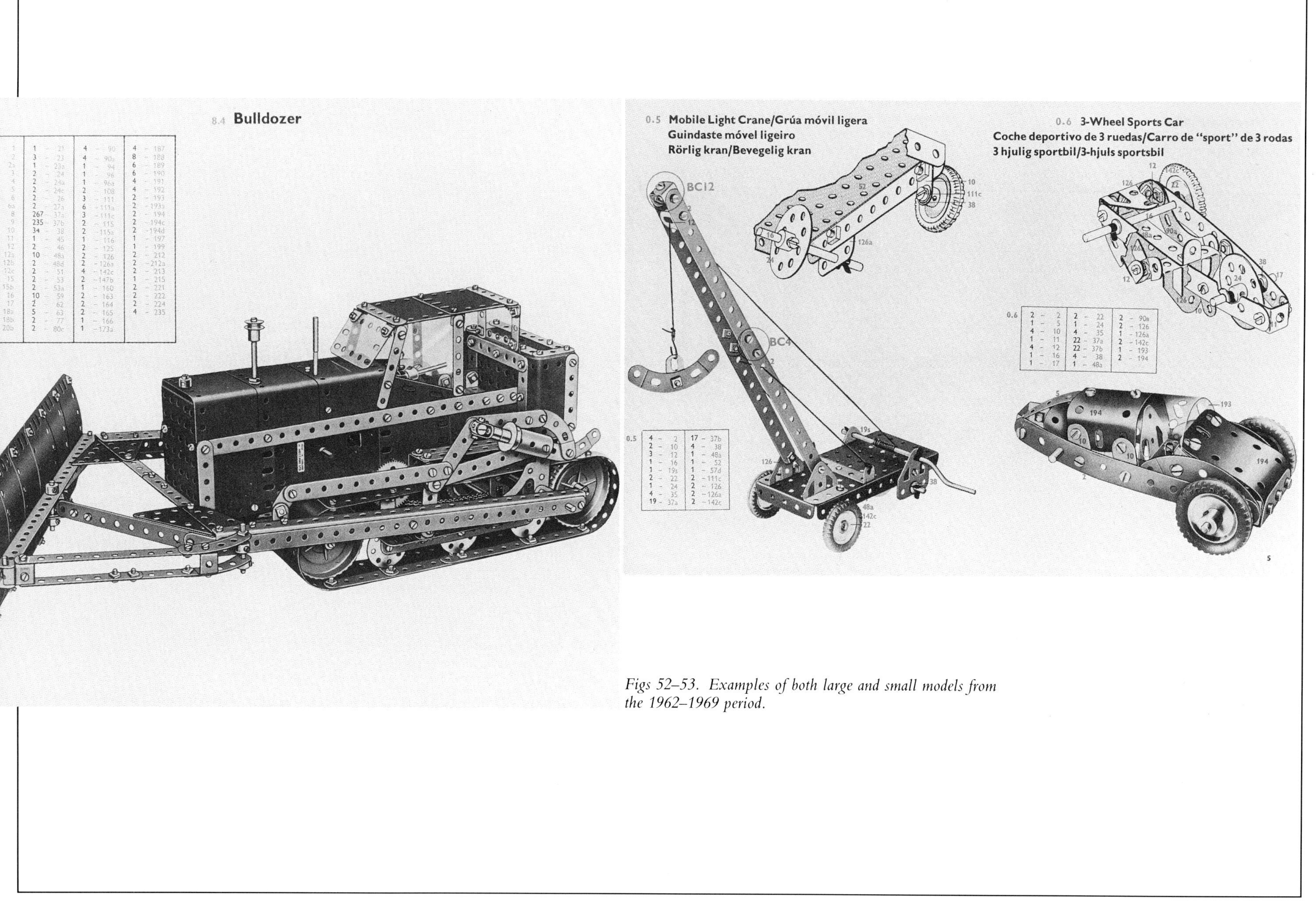

Figs 52–53. Examples of both large and small models from the 1962–1969 period.

Special Purpose Manuals

In addition to the standard outfits, Meccano produced at various times special outfits which necessitated appropriate manuals. Beginning with the Hornby System of Mechanical Demonstration they covered a very wide range indeed:

- Aeroplane Constructor Outfits
- Motor Car Constructor Outfits
- Mechanised Army
- Electrical Outfits
- Elektron
- Kemex
- Hornby System of Mechanical Demonstration
- Steam Engine (not an outfit)
- Dinky Builder
- X Series (including British Model Builder)

With the exception of Dinky Builder all of these were exclusively pre-war. Post-war publications include:

- Clock Kits
- Gears A and Gears B Outfits
- Mechanisms Outfits
- Elektrikit

For the sake of completeness one should perhaps mention the Multikit and Theme sets, but mention is really all they are worth.

The pre-war special purpose manuals were for the most part amongst the most attractive items produced by Meccano and what follows is a selection of the best. Little of the post-war material is shown. Gears A & B and Mechanisms are illustrated in chapter 6 and the Multikits/Theme set manuals are common but nevertheless, comparison is salutary.

All of the manuals in this section were of course available concurrently with the outfits to which they relate and for fuller details reference should be made to Volume 6 which covers all of them in detail. However, the following notes are relevant to the literature.

Aeroplane Constructor Outfits

(Figs 1–10)

These were the first of the special purpose outfits introduced during the great expansion of the product range in the first half of the 1930s. The first Aero Outfit appeared in 1931 and through a number of developments embracing ordinary as well as 'Special' outfits, continued right up until the general cessation of production in 1941. Although soon after their introduction changes in real aircraft had made the outfit models somewhat dated in appearance, they must have been a popular line since they continued to be available throughout the 1930s and indeed a modernised range of outfits was planned (and announced to dealers) for the 1940–41 season.

The manuals themselves were well produced with excellent illustrations, although as with most of the other special purpose manuals it would be more correct to term them booklets, for they give virtually no building instructions at all. Partly for this reason they (and their equivalents for the other special outfits) tend to be rather scarce especially in good condition.

Motor Car Constructor Outfits

(Figs 11–18)

The Motor Cars arrived a year after the Aeroplanes and were amongst the finest products ever to come out of the Binns Road factory. Design and finish were of a very high standard and they are all sought-after today. The manuals are distinctly rarer than the cars themselves probably because once they were made up, the box and remaining contents (no doubt including the manual) would more often than not have parted company with the car.

Mechanised Army

(Figs 19–22)

This was a very late introduction, appearing literally just before the outbreak of the Second World War. Only one version of the outfit was offered for sale, although two others were planned and even announced to dealers as being available later the following year, 1940. Two ARP outfits were also announced at this time but none was produced. Interestingly, the manual shown in the bulletin to dealers was simply an ordinary Mechanised Army instruction leaflet so it is highly unlikely that any ARP manual ever even reached the proof stage.

The actual Mechanised Army leaflet (it is little more than a folded broadsheet) is something of a disappointment with its rather poor quality illustrations, although this was perhaps only to be expected under the circumstances. They are not as scarce as one might expect. In fact, taking into account their short run of 18 months or so, they must have been a very popular line.

Electrical Outfits (first series 1920s)

(Figs 23–26)

In 1920, Meccano introduced 15 electrical parts (the 300 series) designed to be used with standard outfits. The range included such items as bobbins, terminals and contact screws as well as reels of wire and small bulbs. All these parts were included in the then current No. 7 Outfit but for those without such a luxury, two Electrical Accessory Outfits were introduced. That designated X1 contained all the 300 series electrical parts (in similar quantity to those in the No. 7) as well as a special manual. The X2 outfit contained an electric motor and 4 volt accumulator in addition to the parts.

Both outfits had a fairly short life, the X1 being last advertised in 1924 and the X2 notified as being withdrawn in a leaflet dated September 1929. The manual, however, was not deleted until 1930 when it also no longer formed part of the No. 7 Outfit. The parts did continue to be available (with some deletions in 1933) until the war-time shut down.

By today's standards the models in the Electrical Outfit Manual are somewhat primitive, but in their day they were up-to-date. By the time of its deletion much of the contents of the manual had been superseded by the relevant sections of Standard Mechanisms and How to Use Meccano Parts.

Elektron (Figs 27–28)

Some four years after the withdrawal of the Electrical Outfit X2, Meccano re-entered the market with Elektron in 1933. Unlike its predecessor, most of the parts were non-compatible with the standard system and thus designed to be used in isolation from standard Meccano. By this means the company no doubt hoped to break into markets which were already proving quite lucrative for other toy manufacturers. The manuals issued with the various Elektron outfits were well-produced booklets which like the actual outfits and their boxes have proved to be yet more examples of the quality of the Binns Road artwork department. They are understandably quite rare today, although they were produced (or at least available) until the wartime shutdown.

Kemex (Figs 29–30)

Introduced at the same time and for the same reasons as Elektron, Kemex was not quite the success which had been expected. Lotts Chemistry Sets were much too well entrenched for Kemex to make much of an impression in this field. Sales must have been reasonable, however, because they were not withdrawn until 1939. The manuals like those for Elektron were attractively presented and are rarely found today.

Hornby System of Mechanical Demonstration (Figs 31–33)

The Hornby System of Mechanical Demonstration which was available from 1909 until 1914 was Hornby's most determined effort to gain educational acceptance for Meccano as a serious scientific teaching aid. A very full description of the system is given in Volume 6 of this series, but, briefly, it comprised a number of outfits containing both standard and special Meccano parts together with a fairly thick manual detailing a large number of mechanical experiments which could be carried out with the parts provided. Unfortunately schools and other educational establishments did not flock to purchase the system and within five years it was withdrawn. The manual (there was only one covering all the outfits) is understandably quite rare, although it is found more often than the outfits. Very much in the style of the contemporary ordinary manuals, it does, however, make a fairly good attempt to explain the mechanical principles involved something conspicuously missing from its stablemates.

Steam Engine Manual (Figs 34–36)

Although there was never a Steam Engine Outfit, the manual supplied with the 1929 Steam Engine was much more than a set of instructions on how it was to be used. For as well as basic instructions on its operation and maintenance, the manual gives details of a good number of models adapted to use the Steam Engine as motive power. Most of these are very simple but two larger models are shown, although no instructions are given, reference being made instead to separate Super Model Leaflets. One of these, the Steam Shovel, was issued as leaflet No. 19a, but the other, a derrick crane based on SML 6 and given the number 6a was never issued. For further details see chapter 4. There were two known editions of the Steam Engine Manual, one for 1929 and a virtually identical one for 1930. Good copies of either of these are very scarce and usually, as might be expected, most have suffered from contact with water and being wedged into the box with the Steam Engine itself.

Dinky Builder (Figs 37–45)

To try to reach a younger market, Meccano brought out in 1934, a much simpler construction system using small coloured plates which were joined by what was in effect a series of hinges. Assembly was carried out by inserting rods into the castellated bent-over edges of the plates.

It was designed to appeal to both boys and girls, but though as a line it was successful it is not certain whether this aspect played a significant part. Dinky Builder was also unique amongst the pre-war special purpose outfits in that it was the only one to return after the war.

The manuals supplied with the outfits have a very particular charm about them and this was not lost after the war. Considering the number of outfits which must have been sold, pre-war Dinky Builder manuals are somewhat scarce, though this may be owing to the very nature of the product in that it was used by the youngest and perhaps least careful! It is also likely that it would have been discarded along with many other nursery toys having been fully worn-out or played-out.

X Series & British Model Builder (Figs 46–50)

A year before the introduction of Dinky Builder, Meccano decided to try to make inroads into the market which Trix had successfully developed, by producing a proper Meccano version of the Trix miniature construction system. At first sight there would appear to be little difference between the two, but closer inspection shows that the parts are made of steel instead of a light alloy/aluminium and that the holes are somewhat larger. In fact they turn out to be standard Meccano size. This made the X series parts compatible with the standard product, a feature duly noted in the *Meccano Magazine* articles of the time.

X series was not a success and had disappeared by 1936. Only the X Series clockwork motor (and two other small parts) survived and as the Magic

Motor remained current almost to the last. The system did, however, continue for a time (minus the clockwork motor), after the X series' demise, as The British Model Builder (which appeared in 1933 also) and was sold in shops other than Meccano dealers. In that respect it resembled The British Express train sets which were Hornby under another name.

The manuals for X series if that is what they can be called are little more than folding leaflets, although they are attractively set out. Not surprisingly they do not turn up that often.

The Post-War Years

Gears A, Gears B and Mechanisms Outfit. These are fully covered in chapter 6.

Elektrikit (Figs 51–54)

Originally a French-designed outfit, this was an improved and updated version of the two pre-war electrical outfits, although in reality it was infinitely superior and being more adaptable had a far wider range of uses. The date of introduction in the UK was 1963 and it lasted 14 years, seven of them with the designation 4EL rather than Elektrikit.

The manuals were well produced on good quality paper and in general made matters clear for the builder.

Clock Kits (Figs 55–56)

The No. 1 and No. 2 Clock Kits which came out in 1971 and 1972 respectively were something of an expensive disaster for the company. The No 1 kit was crude and the No 2 kit virtually, if not actually, a loss maker. They had both been withdrawn by 1979, although many a shop had stocks of them for years after that.

The instruction leaflets were single use only and served their purpose well if without any of the flair and charm of earlier productions.

In general the literature supplied with the pre-war special purpose outfits was of a high presentational standard and consequently is sought-after today. This cannot unfortunately be said of most of the post-war material, but then it would have been unreasonable to expect that a company increasingly under severe financial pressure from the late 1950s onwards would spend what it considered was unnecessary time and money on simple instruction booklets. Although not a cause of Meccano's troubles, perhaps it was a symptom of the malaise which appeared to be growing and which finally took hold.

MECCANO

AEROPLANE CONSTRUCTOR
INSTRUCTIONS
FOR OUTFIT
No. 2

Price 6d.

Copyright by MECCANO LIMITED, LIVERPOOL, throughout the world

No. 32-2AC

Figs 1–3. 1932 No. 2 Aero Constructor Outfit manual and pages.

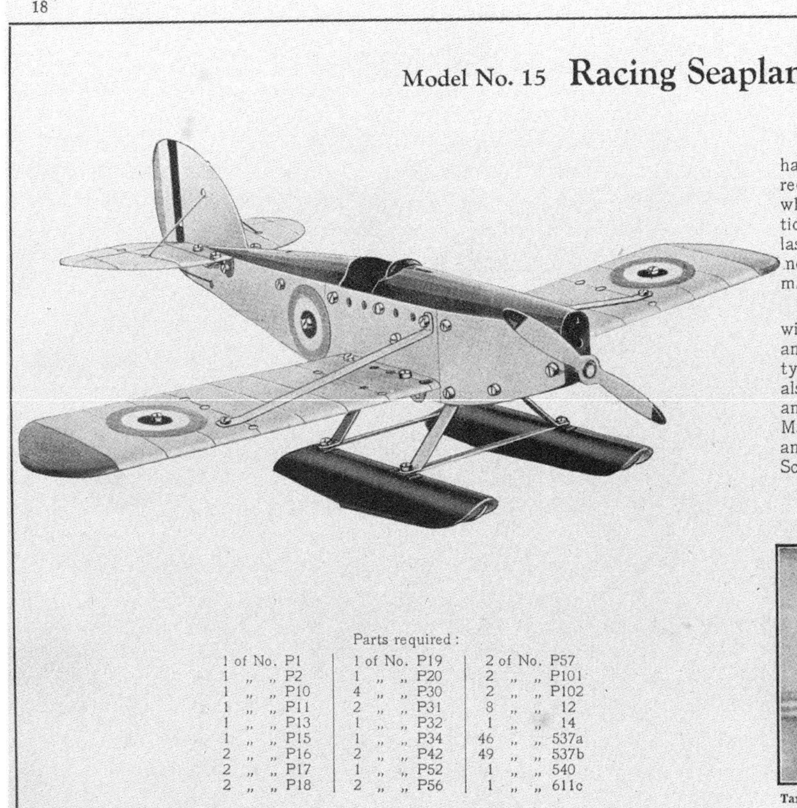
18

Model No. 15 **Racing Seaplane**

In recent years the low-wing monoplane seaplane has become the accepted type where high speeds are required, and even the Gloster Aircraft Co. Ltd., who for many years favoured the biplane construction for their Schneider Trophy machines, have at last abandoned it in favour of the monoplane. A model of the low-wing racing seaplane type of machine is shown on this page.

The Vickers-Supermarine Rolls-Royce S.6B, winner of the Schneider Trophy Contest in 1931, and holder of the world's air speed record, is of this type. The high-speed machines of other countries also are usually of the monoplane seaplane type, and a particularly interesting one is the Italian Macchi M-67. This machine, which is fitted with an Isotta-Fraschini engine, was produced for the Schneider Trophy Contest in 1929.

Parts required:

1 of No. P1	1 of No. P19	2 of No. P57
1 „ „ P2	1 „ „ P20	2 „ „ P101
1 „ „ P10	4 „ „ P30	2 „ „ P102
1 „ „ P11	2 „ „ P31	8 „ „ 12
1 „ „ P13	1 „ „ P32	1 „ „ 14
1 „ „ P15	1 „ „ P34	46 „ „ 537a
2 „ „ P16	2 „ „ P42	49 „ „ 537b
2 „ „ P17	1 „ „ P52	1 „ „ 540
2 „ „ P18	2 „ „ P56	1 „ „ 611c

Taxi-ing before taking off in the Vickers-Supermarine Rolls-Royce S.6B, on which a new record for the Schneider Trophy Contest was set up in 1931.

INSTRUCTIONS

How to Build Model Aeroplanes with Meccano Aeroplane Constructor Parts

Commence by building up the Fuselage, the details of which are clearly shown in the illustrations. The manner in which the propeller drive is arranged is shown in Fig. A. The Propeller is secured to one end of the 6½" Axle Rod 1, and the Rod is then pushed through the lower hole in the Fuselage Front. A ½" Pulley 2 is placed on the Rod together with the Rubber Driving Band 5. The end of the Axle Rod 1 is then pushed through the hole in the Propeller Shaft Bracket 3. The 6½" Axle Rod 1 is kept in place by means of the Collar 4. The 3¼" Axle Rod (part No. P62) is pushed through one Undercarriage Vee Strut and Wheel Shield and a ½" Fast Pulley 6 is placed on the Axle. A Rubber Tyre is now fitted to one Landing Wheel and the complete wheel is then placed in the Wheel Shield of the second Undercarriage Vee Strut. The end of the 3¼" Axle is then passed through the hole in the Undercarriage Vee Strut and through the centre hole in the Landing Wheel. A Rubber Tyre is next fitted to the second Landing Wheel and the complete wheel is placed in its Wheel Shield. To do this the 3¼" Axle is drawn slightly to one side and is then pushed back so that one end of the Axle passes into the centre hole of the Landing Wheel. Each Landing Wheel is locked in position on the Axle by rolling the Rubber Tyre to one side with the fingers so that the grub-screw is exposed and may then be rotated by the Screwdriver.

After the Landing Wheels have been secured in place the Driving Band may be placed round the groove in the ½" Pulley 2 and also round the groove of the Pulley 6. The Pulleys 2 and 6 may then be locked in position on their respective Rods by means of the grub-screws in their bosses.

Fig. A

Fig. B

Fitting the Radial Engine Units and Engine Casings. (Water-cooled type)

The method of fitting the Radial Engine to the wing is shown in Fig. C. The Engine Bracket 1 is first of all bolted to the wing. A Nut is screwed on to the projecting screwed shank 2 of the Radial Engine and the shank 2 is then passed through the hole in the Engine Bracket 1. The Nut 3 is now screwed into place thus locking the Engine in position.

When the water-cooled type of engine is to be represented, the Engine Casing unit is used separately. First bolt the Engine Casing Base to the wing by two Bolts. Next pass a Pivot Bolt through the boss of a small Propeller and screw a Nut on the end of it. Pass the projecting end of the Pivot Bolt through the hole in the front of the Engine Casing Base and lock the Bolt in place by another Nut. The Engine Casing Top is placed over the Base piece, and a 1" Screwed Rod is passed through the holes in the sides of the Top and through the perforated lugs in the Base. A Nut is screwed to each end of the Rod to hold it rigidly in position.

Assembling the Tail Planes and Rudder

The method of assembling the Tail Planes and Rudder will be followed from Fig. B. Two Angle Brackets are bolted to each Tail Plane, and the front Bracket 2 of each Tail Plane is secured to the fuselage by a 7/32" Bolt 3. A ⅜" Bolt 4 is passed through the rear Angle Bracket of one Tail Plane, through the Fuselage Side Rear sections, and through the rear Angle Bracket of the second Tail Plane. A Nut is placed upon the end of the Bolt and the Bolt is screwed up tightly so that the Tail Planes are locked rigidly to the rear of the fuselage of the model. The Tail Skid 5 of the machine is held in place between the Fuselage Side Rear sections by means of a 7/32" Bolt.

The Rudder is pushed into position between the ends of the Fuselage Side Rear sections, the lug on the front portion fitting into the slot in the Fuselage Top Rear section. It is held in place by the 7/32" Bolt 1.

When the Landing Wheels are mounted independently, a Pivot Bolt is first passed through the Wing Stay. A Landing Wheel with Rubber Tyre is placed in the Wheel Shield. The Pivot Bolt is then passed through the Wheel Shield and Landing Wheel and is held in position by means of two locknuts.

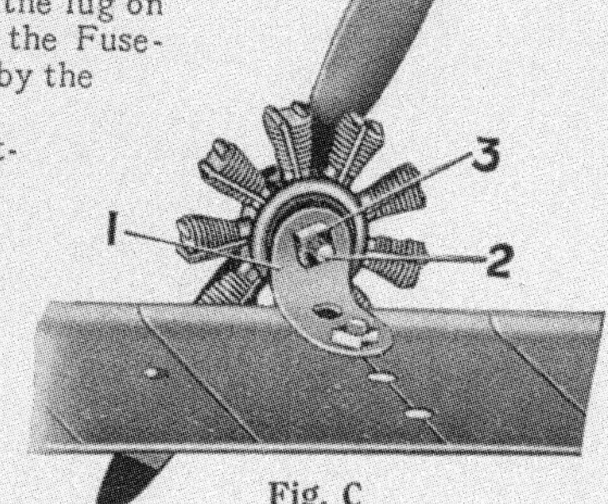

Fig. C

Fit a Meccano Aero Clockwork Motor into your Aeroplane Models. Ask your dealer for prices and full particulars.

AEROPLAN[E]

INSTR[UCTIONS]

FO[R]

N[o.]

SPECIAL NOTE.

The Military Identification Markings (P. 101 and P. 102) shown on the large Mainplanes and Fuselage of the models illustrated in this Manual are not now included in the Outfit. The large Mainplanes and the Fuselage Side Rear Sections now carry civil registration letters. The Military Rudder (P. 32) has been replaced in the Outfit by the Civil Rudder (P. 64).

The large Mainplanes (Parts Nos. P1 and P2) can be obtained without civil registration letters, for use with Military Markings, to special order.

Copyright by MECCANO LIMIT[ED]

2/433/15 (1P)

Figs 4–5. The No. 2 Manual with the special note regarding the new military markings.

22

Model No. 19 Italian Bomber

Sesquiplanes similar to Model No. 19 are not constructed in this country nor in many others, this type being favoured most particularly by the Italian Società Italiana Caproni, although not all the machines constructed by this firm are sesquiplanes. The most unusual feature of the type depicted in our model is that the longer wing is the lower and not the upper one. The machines of this design at present constructed by the Caproni firm are all bombers, and are fitted with anything up to six engines. The six-engined bomber is known as the Caproni Ca.90P.B. This machine is the largest bombing aeroplane at present in existence, and is the possessor of six world's records. It is equipped with six 1,000 h.p. Isotta-Fraschini "Asso-1,000" engines. This huge aeroplane has a loaded weight of about 66,000 lb., but in spite of this it has a maximum speed of 127.3 m.p.h. and a stalling speed of only 55.9 m.p.h.

Parts required:

1 of No. P1	1 of No. P19	1 of No. P55
1 „ „ P2	1 „ „ P20	1 „ „ P56
1 „ „ P3	2 „ „ P26	1 „ „ P60
1 „ „ P4	2 „ „ P27	6 „ „ 12
1 „ „ P10	4 „ „ P28	1 „ „ 16a
1 „ „ P11	1 „ „ P32	1 „ „ 82
1 „ „ P13	1 „ „ P35	49 „ „ 537a
1 „ „ P15	1 „ „ P40	47 „ „ 537b
2 „ „ P16	1 „ „ P41	1 „ „ 540
2 „ „ P17	2 „ „ P44	
2 „ „ P18	2 „ „ P53	

The realism of this model may be increased by fitting the Pilot No. P100 in the cockpit.

The six-engined Italian Caproni bomber, which is the world's largest bombing machine.

MECCANO AEROPLANE CONSTRUCTOR PARTS

No.		No.	
	Mainplanes	P52	Collar ... ...
‡P1	Large, Top, R.H. ‡P2 Top, L.H.	P53	Landing Wheel ... ...
P1a	„ Bottom, R.H. P2a Bottom, L.H.	P54	Rubber Driving Band ...
P3	Small—R.H. P4 L.H.	P55	Tail Skid ... ...
P7	Centre Section Plane ...	P56	Rear Bracket for Propeller Shaft ... ...
P8	Extension Plane	P57	Tie Rod for Floats ...
P10	Tail Plane—R.H.	P58	Undercarriage Vee Strut and Wheel Shield—R.H. ...
P11	„ „ L.H.	P59	Undercarriage Vee Strut and Wheel Shield—L.H. ...
	Fuselage Top	P60	Pivot Bolt with Two Nuts
P13	Front P14 Middle P15 Rear	P61	Engine Bracket ... ...
	Fuselage Sides	P62	Axle Rod, 3½" long ...
P16	Front P17 Middle P18 Rear, R.H. P18a Rear, L.H.	P63	Screwdriver ... ...
P19	Fuselage Underside P20 Fuselage Front	P64	Rudder (Civil) ... ...
	Interplane Struts	P65	Adjustable Tail Wheel ...
P24	Staggered—R.H. P25 L.H.	P75	No. 1 Aero Manual ...
P26	Angled—R.H. P27 L.H.	P76	No. 2 Aero Manual ...
P28	Interplane Strut—Straight	P100	Pilot ... ...
P29	Centre Section Strut—Straight	*P101	Identification Marking—Large
P30	Float and Centre Section Strut—Angled	*P102	„ „ Small
P31	Wing Stay P32 Rudder (Military)	12	Angle Bracket, ½" × ½" ...
P34	Propeller—Large	14	Axle Rod, 6½" long ...
P35	„ Small	16a	„ „ 2½" „ ...
P40	Base for Engine Casing ...	23a	Fast Pulley, ½" diameter ...
P41	Top for Engine Casing ...	34	Spanner ... ...
P42	Float, Complete	82	Screwed Rod, 1" long ...
P43	Radial Engine—Small ...	537a	Nuts 537b Bolts, 7/32" long
P44	Rubber Tyre for Landing Wheel	540	Hank of Cord ... ...
P46	Radial Engine—Large ...	611c	Bolts, ⅜" long ... ...

*The series includes identification markings in the correct colours of 16 different countries.
‡The large Mainplanes (Parts Nos. P1 and P2) can be obtained without civil registration letters, for use with Military Identification Markings, to special order.

CONTENTS OF MECCANO AEROPLANE CONSTRUCTOR OUTFIT No. 1

No.		Quantity	No.		Quantity
P1	Mainplane—Large, Top, R.H. ...	1	P52	Collar	1
P1a	„ „ Bottom, R.H.	1	P53	Landing Wheel	2
P2	„ „ Top, L.H.	1	P54	Rubber Driving Band ...	1
P2a	„ „ Bottom, L.H.	1	P55	Tail Skid	1
P8	Extension Plane	1	P56	Rear Bracket for Propeller Shaft	2
P10	Tail Plane—R.H.	1	P58	Undercarriage Vee Strut and Wheel Shield—R.H. ...	1
P11	„ „ L.H.	1	P59	Undercarriage Vee Strut and Wheel Shield—L.H. ...	1
	Fuselage Top		P62	Axle Rods, 3½" long ...	1
P13	Front ... 1 P15 Rear ...	1	P63	Screwdriver	1
	Fuselage Sides		P64	Rudder (Civil)	1
P16	Front...2 P17 Middle...2 P18 Rear, R.H.	1	P75	No. 1 Aero Manual ...	1
	P18a Rear, L.H.	1	P100	Pilot	1
P19	Fuselage Underside	1	12	Angle Brackets, ½"×½" ...	8
P20	„ Front	1	14	Axle Rod, 6½" long ...	1
P24	Interplane Strut—Staggered—R.H.	2	23a	Fast Pulley, ½" diameter ...	2
P25	„ „ „ L.H.	2	34	Spanner	1
P28	„ „ Straight ...	4	537a	Nuts	60
P29	Centre Section Strut—Straight	4	537b	Bolts, 7/32" long	58
P31	Wing Stay	2	540	Hank of Cord	1
P34	Propeller—Large	1	611c	Bolts, ⅜" long	2
P44	Rubber Tyre for Landing Wheel	2			

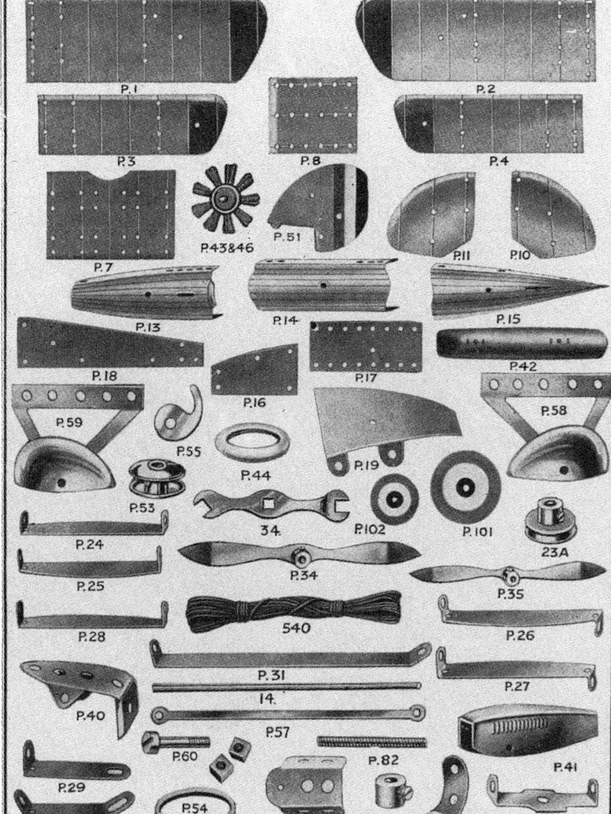

AEROPLANE CONSTRUCTOR OUTFITS

The aeroplane is rapidly taking its place as a regular means of high speed transport, and the time is not far distant when we shall use it as readily as today we employ the train, the steamship, and the motor car. Now is the time for every boy to learn how aeroplanes are designed and constructed, and to recognise at a glance the different types. The best way of doing this is to build aeroplanes for himself, and the Aeroplane Constructor Outfits have been designed specially for this purpose. This folder shows how to construct six different types of aeroplanes, but many other equally realistic models may be built by varying the positions of the parts.

How an Aeroplane flies

The fun of building with Aeroplane Constructor Outfits is greatly increased if you know something of the way in which a real aeroplane is controlled in flight. What strikes anyone examining an aeroplane for the first time is the simplicity of the manœuvring mechanism, everything being done by two levers. The first of these, the control column or "joy-stick," is not unlike the gear lever of a motor car, and is connected to two controls, the ailerons and the elevators. The ailerons are small movable flaps arranged along the trailing or rear edges of the wings, and the elevators form one of the two main parts of the tail unit. The other lever, the rudder bar, is near the floor of the cockpit and is operated by the feet. This bar controls the rudder, which is the second main portion of the tail unit.

Joy-Stick and Rudder

The joy-stick is the most fascinating factor in the control of an aeroplane. If you wish to fly level, you keep the stick in a central and vertical position. If you move it forward, the elevators are depressed and the machine promptly puts down its nose and tries to dive. If you pull the stick backward, the elevators are raised and the nose of the machine rises. Movement of the stick to left or right brings the ailerons into action. If you move it to the left, the left wings will go down; if you move it to the right, the right wings will drop. This raising and lowering of the wings is termed "banking."

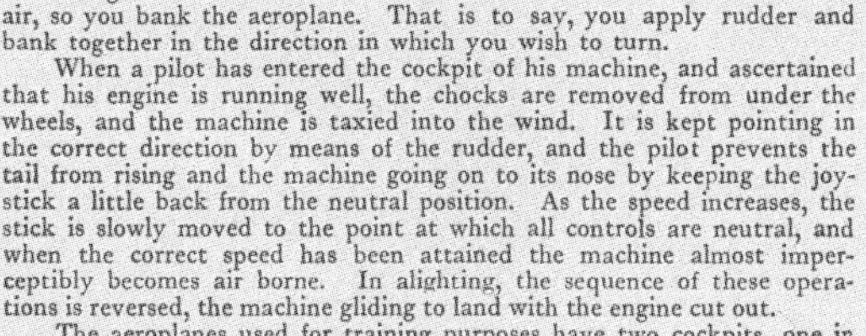

If you find that the aeroplane is veering to the left, you put on right rudder by moving the right foot gently forward; and similarly veering to the right is corrected by applying left rudder. If you wish to turn the aeroplane round, however, you must not attempt to do it by rudder alone, because in that case the machine would skid in a similar manner to a motor car racing round a bend on an unbanked road. You cannot bank the air, so you bank the aeroplane. That is to say, you apply rudder and bank together in the direction in which you wish to turn.

When a pilot has entered the cockpit of his machine, and ascertained that his engine is running well, the chocks are removed from under the wheels, and the machine is taxied into the wind. It is kept pointing in the correct direction by means of the rudder, and the pilot prevents the tail from rising and the machine going on to its nose by keeping the joy-stick a little back from the neutral position. As the speed increases, the stick is slowly moved to the point at which all controls are neutral, and when the correct speed has been attained the machine almost imperceptibly becomes air borne. In alighting, the sequence of these operations is reversed, the machine gliding to land with the engine cut out.

The aeroplanes used for training purposes have two cockpits, one in front of the other, the controls in each being exactly the same, and connected together. This arrangement enables the instructor, who sits in the front cockpit, to see exactly what manipulations are being made by the pupil behind, and to correct them accordingly. The instructor and his pupil communicate with each other by means of ear tubes attached to their helmets.

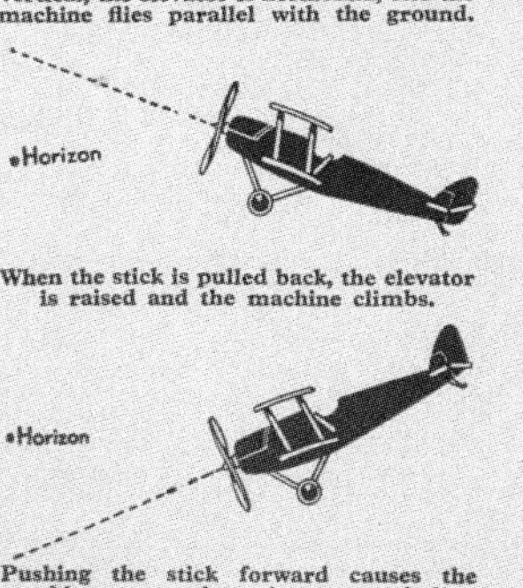

When the control column or "joy-stick" is vertical, the elevator is horizontal, and the machine flies parallel with the ground.

When the stick is pulled back, the elevator is raised and the machine climbs.

Pushing the stick forward causes the machine to put down its nose and dive.

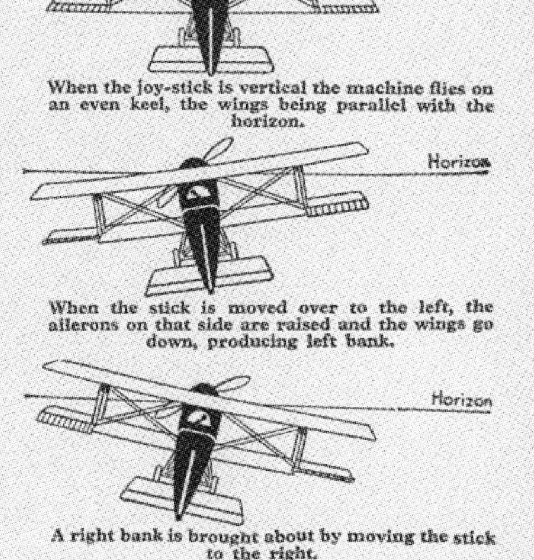

When the joy-stick is vertical the machine flies on an even keel, the wings being parallel with the horizon.

When the stick is moved over to the left, the ailerons on that side are raised and the wings go down, producing left bank.

A right bank is brought about by moving the stick to the right.

Figs 6–9. A No. 1 Manual from 1940 which showed how an aeroplane flew. An updated parts list was included as was a page of models designed to advance sales of the 1a Outfit.

MECCANO AEROPLANE CONSTRUCTOR ACCESSORY OUTFIT No. 1a

will enable you to build many additional models

Now that you have experienced the pleasure of building model aeroplanes you will be keen on proceeding further with this wonderful hobby. You may do this by purchasing a No. 1a Aeroplane Constructor Accessory Outfit, with which many additional models can be built, or you may increase the scope of your No. 1 Outfit by adding to it separate parts from time to time.

The four illustrations on this page show the types of machine you can build when you have a No. 1a Accessory Outfit. These include models of light aeroplanes, seaplanes and flying boats, and commercial air liners of both monoplane and biplane types.

Ask your dealer for a complete illustrated Price List.

A triple-engined biplane constructed with Aeroplane Constructor Outfit No. 2. This is an example of the many true-to-type biplanes that can be built with the No. 2 Outfit (or No. 1 and No. 1a Outfits combined).

Another interesting model that can be built with Aeroplane Constructor Outfit No. 2 (or No. 1 and No. 1a Outfits combined). Instructions for building three seaplanes are given, one of these being of similar design to the Italian Macchi machine that holds the world's speed record.

Many amphibians and flying boats can be built with Aeroplane Constructor Outfit No. 2 (or No. 1 and No. 1a Outfits combined). This illustration shows one of the most interesting of them. It is a model of a triple-engined amphibian.

Another fine model that can be built with Aeroplane Constructor Outfit No. 2 (or No. 1 and No. 1a Outfits combined). It is a triple-engined monoplane air liner and is similar in design to the famous "Southern Cross" flown by the late Sir Charles Kingsford Smith.

Printed in England

Fig 9.

Fig 10. Further flying lessons! →

Rolling consists of making the aeroplane roll round with its fuselage as the axis, and it is a very spectacular manoeuvre when carried out properly. There are two distinct types of roll, the slow and the " flick," and we will begin with the former. To do this we dive slightly with the engine partly off, and when we have gained enough speed we push the stick over to the right and bring the rudder into action as necessary, which causes the machine to bank and eventually to roll slowly over on to its back. In this position we are higher than when we entered the roll, and when we have completed it, and are right side up once more, we have climbed still further. The slow roll is usually carried out at a fairly good height, although it can be done quite close to the ground. Experienced pilots can even roll immediately upon taking off from the aerodrome and complete the manoeuvre without rising higher than the tops of the hangars.

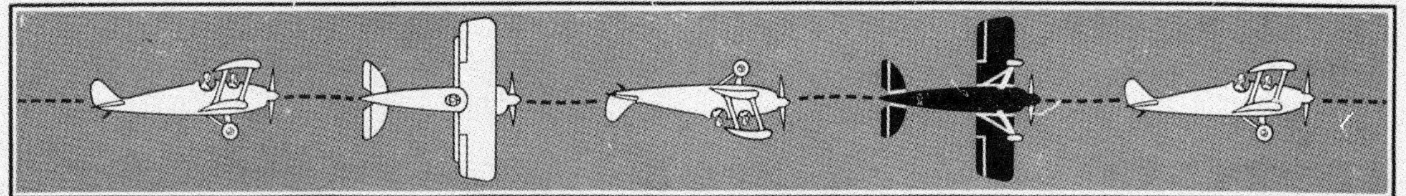

This sketch illustrates the various positions into which an aeroplane goes in course of one complete roll.

The flick roll is similar to the slow roll except that the machine rolls much more quickly. To begin with we fly at a speed some 30 or 40 m.p.h. less than our maximum. We now apply aileron in the direction of the roll and, increasing our speed, pull the stick back as far as possible and at the same time push the rudder bar hard over, causing the machine to roll very quickly. The roll is checked by centralising the stick and the rudder bar. It is difficult to make some aeroplanes perform this manoeuvre, as they try to fly round instead of rolling. Any difficulty of this kind can usually be overcome by moving the stick and the rudder bar quickly into their proper positions for the manoeuvre. Other aeroplanes will only do the roll properly in one direction.

The Half Roll and the Squadron Roll

The nature of the half roll is easily realised from its name. It is used by a pilot who wishes to fly upside down, for he flattens out when an ordinary roll is half completed. It is useful also when a half loop has been made, as it enables the machine to regain its proper flying position. This is described in the next column, in dealing with looping the loop.

The latest manoeuvre to be developed consists of a roll made by a number of machines flying in formation. This means that the complete flight, or squadron, as the case may be, rolls as one unit. The feat was first accomplished by pilots of the Royal Air Force and has been brought to great perfection. It is undoubtedly one of the most spectacular stunts that can be performed, and it has only been made possible by the production of such machines as the Hawker "Fury," and such engines as the Rolls-Royce "Kestrel" with which they are equipped. Striking exhibitions of the "squadron roll" are now usually given by the Royal Air Force at displays in which they take part.

Looping the loop is one of the most frequently performed aeroplane stunts, but although it appears very spectacular from the ground, it is in reality simple. It is generally stated that the manoeuvre was first executed by Pégoud, the famous French pioneer who was killed during the Great War, but it is sometimes claimed that the first person to loop was a Russian officer named Westoroff, who performed the feat in a Nieuport machine. It was certainly Pégoud who popularised the manoeuvre, however, and he gave exhibitions of it in this country on many occasions.

There are several kinds of loops, but we will start with what is known as a slow loop, probably the most graceful of all. First we glance at the altitude indicator to make sure that we have sufficient height, for as the speed of the machine during the manoeuvre is at times only a little above stalling point, engine failure might have serious results if we were not high enough to have room to regain control.

A Popular Manoeuvre—Looping the Loop

Before commencing the loop we fly level for a short time and then dive slightly, pushing the stick forward and keeping the rudder in the central position. We then slowly pull the stick backward, keeping the engine on until our machine has climbed on to its back and we can see the ground apparently above our heads, when we throttle back and ease the stick forward slightly as we come down in a steep dive. We must take care not to pull out of the dive too quickly for this imposes high stresses on the wings of the machine. In the early days of flying many fatal accidents were caused in this way, aeroplanes then not being as strong as modern machines.

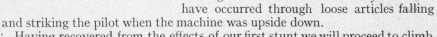

A Meccano Special aeroplane photographed in a rolling position.

During the manoeuvre the rudder must be applied to keep the machine straight, particularly when upside down at the top of the loop, for in this position there is a great tendency for the machine to fall to one side. When a pilot makes his first loop it is a common occurrence for him to forget to check his position by the horizon, the ground and the clouds, and then he may find himself coming out in a direction totally opposite to that which he expected. Another elementary mistake, caused by the slow speed at which the manoeuvre is executed, is to hang on top of the loop too long, causing the machine to stall. Many accidents have occurred through loose articles falling and striking the pilot when the machine was upside down.

Having recovered from the effects of our first stunt we will proceed to climb to gain height for an inverted or "outside" loop, which, as its name implies, is the reverse of the loop we have just described. We begin by flying more or less

MECCANO

TRADE MARKS 296321, 501113, 76, 12633, 10274, 55/13476, 569/13, 884/25, 2913, 80, 124, 336, 4174, 91637, 83171, 157149, 32822, 200639, 209733, 214061, 214062, 12892, 29094, 33316, 1818, 16737, 383/13, 5848, 50204, 10/12258, 22826, 18982, 20063/925, 9048, 5549, 2189, 16900, 72286, 2389, 41812, 5403, 7315, 18066, 139420, 494933–4–5–6, 29041, 26877,6595, 404718, 410379, 55096, 12240, 41234, 8223. 1855.

MOTOR CAR CONSTRUCTOR OUTFIT

INSTRUCTIONS

Price 3d.

Copyright by MECCANO LIMITED, LIVERPOOL, throughout the world.

No. 32 MC

ENGLISH EDITION.

16/732/25 (1P)

Model No. M1. Sports Tourer

Parts required:

1 of No. A1000	1 of No. A1041
1 „ „ A1004	1 „ „ A1042
1 „ „ A1006	1 „ „ A1043
1 „ „ A1008	1 „ „ A1045
1 „ „ A1010	1 „ „ A1046
1 „ „ A1012	1 „ „ A1050
1 „ „ A1014	2 „ „ A1051
1 „ „ A1015	2 „ „ A1052
2 „ „ A1021	3 „ „ A1055
2 „ „ A1023	1 „ „ A1056
4 „ „ A1024	2 „ „ A1057
1 „ „ A1026	5 „ „ A1058
1 „ „ A1027	1 „ „ A1060
1 „ „ A1028	1 „ „ A1061
1 „ „ A1029	1 „ „ A1063
1 „ „ A1030	1 „ „ A1064
1 „ „ A1031	2 „ „ A1065
1 „ „ A1032	1 „ „ A1066
1 „ „ A1033	1 „ „ A1070
1 „ „ A1034	2 „ „ A1071
2 „ „ A1035	1 „ „ A1072
1 „ „ A1036	2 „ „ A1073
3 „ „ A1037	1 „ „ A1074
1 „ „ A1038	1 „ „ A1075
1 „ „ A1039	43 „ „ A1076
1 „ „ A1040	54 „ „ A1077

Parts required:

1 of No. A1000	1 of No. A1041
1 „ „ A1004	1 „ „ A1042
1 „ „ A1006	1 „ „ A1043
1 „ „ A1008	1 „ „ A1045
1 „ „ A1010	1 „ „ A1046
1 „ „ A1012	1 „ „ A1050
1 „ „ A1015	2 „ „ A1051
2 „ „ A1020	2 „ „ A1052
2 „ „ A1022	3 „ „ A1055
4 „ „ A1024	1 „ „ A1056
2 „ „ A1025	2 „ „ A1057
1 „ „ A1026	5 „ „ A1058
1 „ „ A1027	1 „ „ A1060
1 „ „ A1028	1 „ „ A1061
1 „ „ A1029	1 „ „ A1063
1 „ „ A1030	1 „ „ A1064
1 „ „ A1031	2 „ „ A1065
1 „ „ A1032	1 „ „ A1066
1 „ „ A1033	1 „ „ A1070
1 „ „ A1034	2 „ „ A1071
2 „ „ A1035	1 „ „ A1072
1 „ „ A1036	2 „ „ A1073
3 „ „ A1037	1 „ „ A1074
1 „ „ A1038	1 „ „ A1075
1 „ „ A1039	39 „ „ A1076
1 „ „ A1040	50 „ „ A1077

Sports models are fascinating types of the modern motor vehicle, and the Meccano Motor Car Constructor enables fine examples of this type to be built. The term "sports" model covers a wide range of cars, including the well-known baby cars

The Romance

Figs 11–14. Part of an early Motor Car Outfit Instruction Book. Note the Supplementary Instructions.

INSTRUCTIONS

o build Model Motor Cars with Meccano Motor Car Constructor Parts

, and then pushed along the frame until 15 coincide with the pairs of holes close e frame sides. The Bonnet 8 complete ow placed over the Frame Members, so holes at each side of the front portion ncide with the holes in the Frame Side ediately behind the Front Mudguard g. 1). Four bolts are now passed through e and Steering Bracket members to lock sition.

Bar unit is assembled and attached to embers as shown in Fig. 1. First of all Bar 16 (see Fig. 4) flat on the table and umber Plate 17 in position. Next push ket 18 between the arms of the Bar 16 umber Plate 17 is clamped in position. mplete Bumper unit is now secured to ls of the Frame Members by means of lts (see Fig. 1).

e centre portion of the bodywork of the may e d e e e t ne vork the t, which Dash 19 e Bonnet 8

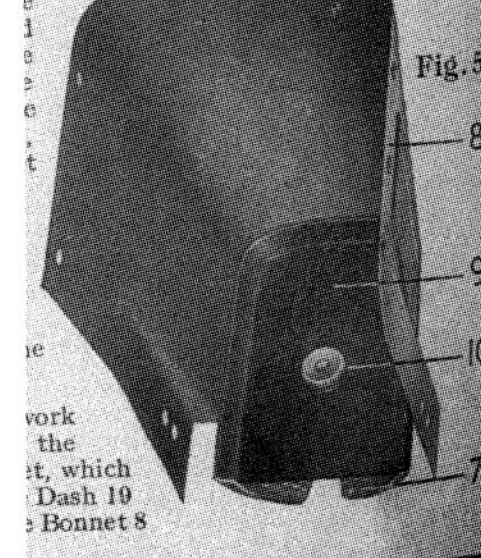

and bolts are passed through both sections and through the holes in the Frame 1 to hold the centre portion in position. The rear end of the Centre Section should not be bolted to the Frame at this stage.

Next take the Rounded Rear Section (No. A1015) and secure the Rear Number Plate 25 to it by means of two bolts fitted with nuts. Place the Rear Section over the ends of the Frame Members 1 and push it into position over the Centre Section 20. The Rear is held to the Centre Section by means of two bolts (see Fig. 1). Before bolting the Motor unit in place, secure the Rear Mudguard Brackets 26 to the Rear Mudguards 27 (see Fig. 6).

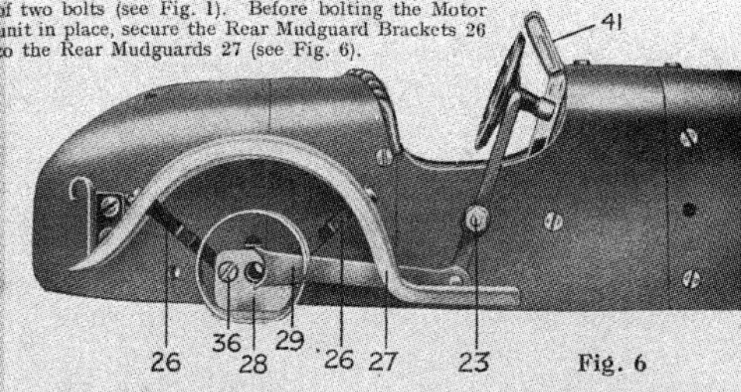

In order to fit the Motor unit, turn the car over and place the Motor casing in position so that the axle holes in the side lugs coincide with the holes in the Rear Section 24.

One pair of Mudguard Brackets 26 with Mudguard 27 attached are arranged in position at the left-hand side of the car looking from below, and on top of these the Brake Drum 28 is placed. Two bolts 36 are then passed through the Brake Drum, Mudguard Brackets, body, and Motor lugs, and are screwed up tightly so that everything is rigid. Two similar bolts are used to hold the Mudguard Brackets in position at the right-hand side of the car, but in this case the Brake Drum is omitted. To complete the internal-expanding brake mechanism, slip the Brake Rod 29 into the slot in the Brake Drum 28. The Brake Lever is mounted pivotally on the Stud 23, a nut being screwed on to the threaded end of the Stud in order to keep the Brake Lever in position. When the hand lever is in the forward position, as shown in Fig. 6, the brake is "off." When the lever is drawn back the cam portion of the Brake Rod 29 forces the split rim of the Brake Drum 28 outward against the flange in the road wheel and a powerful braking action results.

Fig. 7 (13, 12, 15, 11, 14)

The Rear Wheel 30 (fitted with grub-screw) is secured on one end of the Rear Axle 31 (see Fig. 9). In order to do this the Screwdriver is passed through the plain hole in the rim of the Wheel and the grub-screw in the boss rotated. Push the Axle 31 through the left-hand side of the Frame and place the Driving Pinion (part No. A1074) and the Collar 32 on the Axle. Then pass the free end of the Axle through the right-hand side of the Frame of the car, and place another Collar 33 on the Axle 31. Next push the Wheel 30 inward so that the Brake Drum 28 fits closely to the Wheel, and lock the Collars 32 and 33 in position against the sides of the Frame, a small amount of "play" being allowed to ensure free running. Next move the Driving Pinion into position so that it meshes with the teeth of the Contrate Wheel 34 of the Motor and secure it rigidly by means of its grub-screw. To complete the rear axle assembly, fix the second Rear Wheel 35 rigidly in place on the projecting end of the Axle 31.

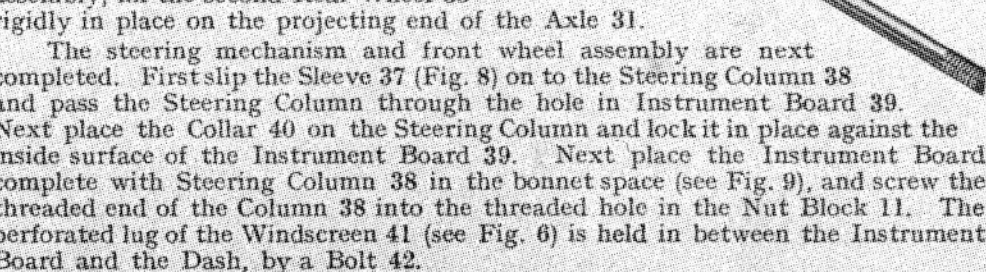

The steering mechanism and front wheel assembly are next completed. First slip the Sleeve 37 (Fig. 8) on to the Steering Column 38 and pass the Steering Column through the hole in Instrument Board 39. Next place the Collar 40 on the Steering Column and lock it in place against the inside surface of the Instrument Board 39. Next place the Instrument Board complete with Steering Column 38 in the bonnet space (see Fig. 9), and screw the threaded end of the Column 38 into the threaded hole in the Nut Block 11. The perforated lug of the Windscreen 41 (see Fig. 6) is held in between the Instrument Board and the Dash, by a Bolt 42.

Now mount the right- and left-hand Stub Axles 43 in position on the Stub Axle Pivots 44. Finally place the slotted portion of the Track Rod 45 over the pin of the Bell Crank 12 and secure the ends of the Track Rod to the Stub Axles 43 by means of the Track Rod Studs 46.

The Front and Rear Mudguards are coupled together by means of the Bolts 47 (see Fig. 9). Next secure the Spare Wheel by means of the special Bolt, after which the Front and Rear sections of the Undershield (parts Nos. A1063 and A1064) are overlapped and bolted together; the complete Undershield is then pushed into position. The slotted lugs of the Undershield sections fit in between the Frame Members and the inner sides of the bodywork, the Spanner being inserted through the D-shaped openings in order to lock the nuts. The Front Road Wheels are held in position on the Stub Axles 43 (see Fig. 9) by means of nuts.

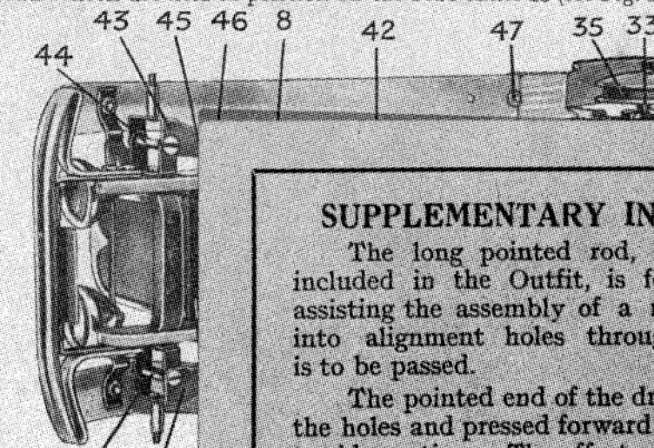

SUPPLEMENTARY INSTRUCTIONS

The long pointed rod, known as a drift, included in the Outfit, is for the purpose of assisting the assembly of a model by bringing into alignment holes through which a bolt is to be passed.

The pointed end of the drift is inserted into the holes and pressed forward with a slight, side-to-side motion. The effect of this is to pull the holes into alignment so that a bolt may be easily inserted.

MECCANO LIMITED, LIVERPOOL

1/833/25

The Romance of Automobile Engineering

The development of the motor car during the past 40 years is one of the greatest triumphs of engineering. To-day the motor vehicle is so widely used that it is difficult to realise that at the beginning of the century it was still looked upon as a curiosity. The authorities actually regarded it as a danger, and insisted that a man carrying a red flag should walk in front of every mechanically propelled road vehicle! The early cars were nothing more than modified horse-carriages fitted with single-cylinder petrol engines. They had chain drive, tiller steering, and rim brakes, and they ran on wooden carriage wheels shod with solid tyres. The bodywork was placed high above the roadway, and provided little or no protection for either driver or passenger. The pioneer motorists, therefore, were compelled to clothe themselves in heavy fur-lined storm-proof garments and sou'-westers as a protection against wind, rain and dust. In addition the engines fitted to the early vehicles were unreliable, and had an unpleasant habit of breaking down at the most inconvenient times and places. In short, a motor ride in those days was always liable to develop into a serious adventure. As time went on, however, the motor car gradually became more efficient and reliable, and its development has continued steadily until to-day it has reached an extremely high state of mechanical perfection.

A four-seater, three-wheel motor of 1888, with an engine of one-and-a-half horse power

A factor that has played an important part in the improvement of the motor-car is the experience obtained from high-speed motor racing. Motor racing has taken place almost from the inception of motoring, and many exciting duels were fought out on road and track in the early days. The famous Brooklands track, which was opened in 1907, provided a great stimulus to the testing of high-speed engines, while the gruelling test provided by the Grand Prix Road Races run over the Sarthe circuit in Northern France have had considerable influence on the design of the modern car. The early racing machines were clumsy and wasteful, very large engines being used to obtain quite low speeds; but it is from these cars that the modern highly efficient sports cars have been evolved.

An outstanding achievement of modern motor car engineering is the manner in which the world's land speed record has been raised through the skill and enterprise of such famous British motorists as Sir Malcolm Campbell, the late Sir Henry Segrave, and the late Mr. J. G. Parry-Thomas. During the past 10 years the record has been increased from just under 130 m.p.h. to the amazing figure of 254 m.p.h., this record being obtained by Sir Malcolm Campbell when driving a British "Bluebird" car at Daytona, U.S.A., in February, 1932. British automobile engineers have concentrated also upon obtaining the maximum efficiency from miniature engines, and the record recently set up by Mr. G. E. T. Eyston, in driving a tiny car with an engine having cylinders of only 750 c.c. capacity at a speed of 120 m.p.h., is proof of their success in this direction.

The range of modern motor vehicles covers a tremendous number of types, including small two-seater "baby" cars, saloon and open touring machines in a variety of sizes, racing cars, saloon coaches, buses, and a wide range of vehicles for industrial and commercial purposes. One of the most attractive types of cars is the sports model, which incorporates an engine having much of the high speed and rapid acceleration of a racing car, but is fitted with bodywork suitable for normal road travel and touring. The examples that can be built with the Meccano Motor Car Constructor are modelled on this type of car.

The high-speed car of the future probably will be driven either by an internal combustion turbine or by means of power transmitted by electric waves from a central source of supply.

Model motor-car building with the Meccano Motor Car Constructor is even more interesting if the working of the various mechanisms of an actual car is understood. The Motor Chassis assembled from standard Meccano parts is just the thing for providing this information, as it forms a complete demonstration of the various mechanisms in a real motor chassis. This model is fully described in Instruction Leaflet No. 1, which may be purchased from any Meccano dealer, or direct from Meccano, Ltd., Binns Road, Old Swan, Liverpool.

A Daimler dog-cart of 1896

A stream-lined super-car of the future

Fig 14.

BRITISH AND GUARANTEED

MOTOR CAR CONSTRUCTOR

MECCAUTO 538,189

INSTRUCTIONS FOR OUTFIT
No. 1

Price
United Kingdom 3d.
South Africa 5d.
Australia 6d.
New Zealand 5d.
Canada 10c

Copyright by
MECCANO LIMITED, LIVERPOOL, 13

13/538/6.5 (IP)

ENG - UNIV

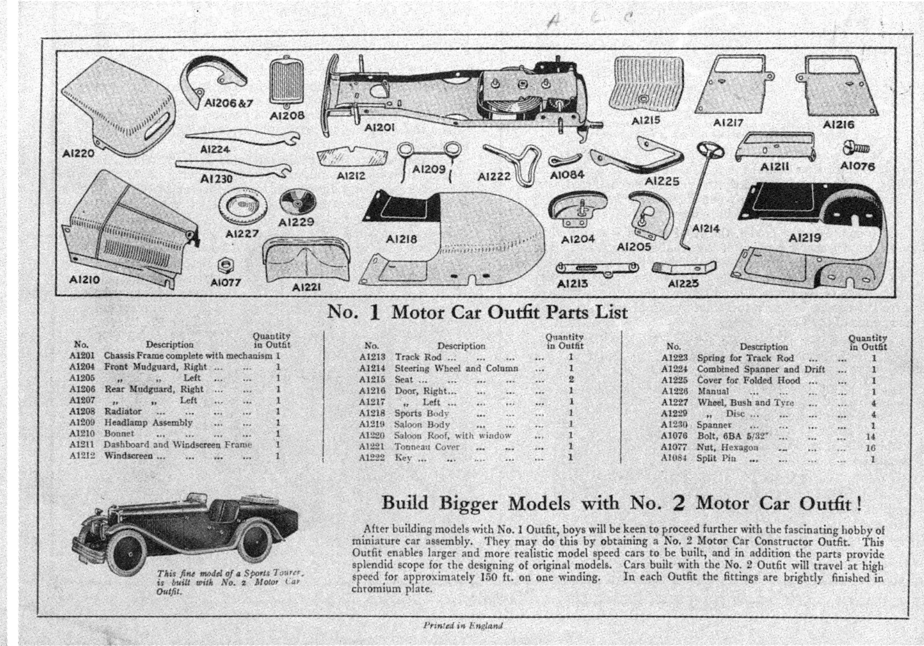

No. 1 Motor Car Outfit Parts List

No.	Description	Quantity in Outfit
A1201	Chassis Frame complete with mechanism	1
A1204	Front Mudguard, Right	1
A1205	„ „ Left	1
A1206	Rear Mudguard, Right	1
A1207	„ „ Left	1
A1208	Radiator	1
A1209	Headlamp Assembly	1
A1210	Bonnet	1
A1211	Dashboard and Windscreen Frame	1
A1212	Windscreen	1
A1213	Track Rod	1
A1214	Steering Wheel and Column ...	1
A1215	Seat	2
A1216	Door, Right...	1
A1217	„ Left	1
A1218	Sports Body	1
A1219	Saloon Body	1
A1220	Saloon Roof, with window ...	1
A1221	Tonneau Cover	1
A1222	Key	1
A1223	Spring for Track Rod	1
A1224	Combined Spanner and Drift ...	1
A1225	Cover for Folded Hood	1
A1226	Manual	1
A1227	Wheel, Bush and Tyre	4
A1229	„ Disc	4
A1230	Spanner	1
A1076	Bolt, 6BA 5/32"	14
A1077	Nut, Hexagon	16
A1084	Split Pin	1

This fine model of a Sports Tourer is built with No. 2 Motor Car Outfit.

Build Bigger Models with No. 2 Motor Car Outfit!

After building models with No. 1 Outfit, boys will be keen to proceed further with the fascinating hobby of miniature car assembly. They may do this by obtaining a No. 2 Motor Car Constructor Outfit. This Outfit enables larger and more realistic model speed cars to be built, and in addition the parts provide splendid scope for the designing of original models. Cars built with the No. 2 Outfit will travel at high speed for approximately 150 ft. on one winding. In each Outfit the fittings are brightly finished in chromium plate.

Printed in England

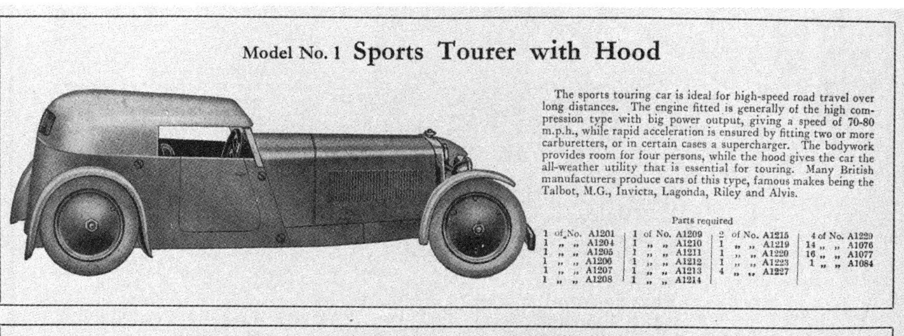

Model No. 1 Sports Tourer with Hood

The sports touring car is ideal for high-speed road travel over long distances. The engine fitted is generally of the high compression type with big power output, giving a speed of 70-80 m.p.h., while rapid acceleration is ensured by fitting two or more carburetters, or in certain cases a supercharger. The bodywork provides room for four persons, while the hood gives the car the all-weather utility that is essential for touring. Many British manufacturers produce cars of this type, famous makes being the Talbot, M.G., Invicta, Lagonda, Riley and Alvis.

Parts required

1 of No. A1201	1 of No. A1209	2 of No. A1215	4 of No. A1229
1 „ „ A1204	1 „ „ A1210	1 „ „ A1219	14 „ „ A1076
1 „ „ A1205	1 „ „ A1211	1 „ „ A1220	16 „ „ A1077
1 „ „ A1206	1 „ „ A1212	1 „ „ A1223	1 „ „ A1084
1 „ „ A1207	1 „ „ A1213	4 „ „ A1227	
1 „ „ A1208	1 „ „ A1214		

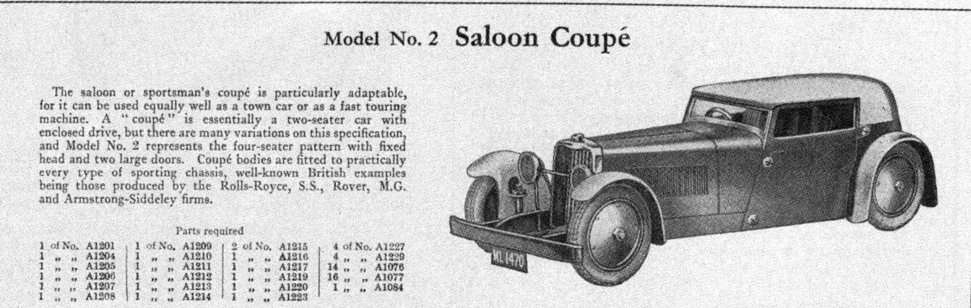

Model No. 2 Saloon Coupé

The saloon or sportsman's coupé is particularly adaptable, for it can be used equally well as a town car or as a fast touring machine. A "coupé" is essentially a two-seater car with enclosed drive, but there are many variations on this specification, and Model No. 2 represents the four-seater pattern with fixed head and two large doors. Coupé bodies are fitted to practically every type of sporting chassis, well-known British examples being those produced by the Rolls-Royce, S.S., Rover, M.G. and Armstrong-Siddeley firms.

Parts required

1 of No. A1201	1 of No. A1209	2 of No. A1215	4 of No. A1227
1 „ „ A1204	1 „ „ A1210	1 „ „ A1216	4 „ „ A1229
1 „ „ A1205	1 „ „ A1211	1 „ „ A1217	14 „ „ A1076
1 „ „ A1206	1 „ „ A1212	1 „ „ A1219	16 „ „ A1077
1 „ „ A1207	1 „ „ A1213	1 „ „ A1220	1 „ „ A1084
1 „ „ A1208	1 „ „ A1214	1 „ „ A1223	

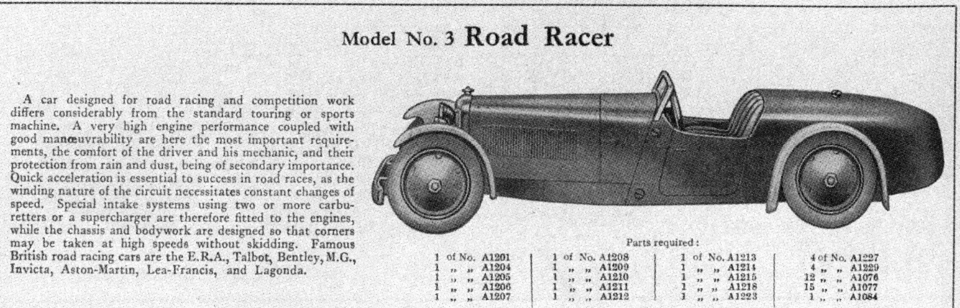

Model No. 3 Road Racer

A car designed for road racing and competition work differs considerably from the standard touring or sports machine. A very high engine performance coupled with good manœuvrability are here the most important requirements, the comfort of the driver and his mechanic, and their protection from rain and dust, being of secondary importance. Quick acceleration is essential to success in road races, as the winding nature of the circuit necessitates constant changes of speed. Special intake systems using two or more carburetters or a supercharger are therefore fitted to the engines, while the chassis and bodywork are designed so that corners may be taken at high speeds without skidding. Famous British road racing cars are the E.R.A., Talbot, Bentley, M.G., Invicta, Aston-Martin, Lea-Francis, and Lagonda.

Parts required:

1 of No. A1201	1 of No. A1208	1 of No. A1213	4 of No. A1227
1 „ „ A1204	1 „ „ A1209	1 „ „ A1214	4 „ „ A1229
1 „ „ A1205	1 „ „ A1210	1 „ „ A1215	12 „ „ A1076
1 „ „ A1206	1 „ „ A1211	1 „ „ A1218	15 „ „ A1077
1 „ „ A1207	1 „ „ A1212	1 „ „ A1223	1 „ „ A1084

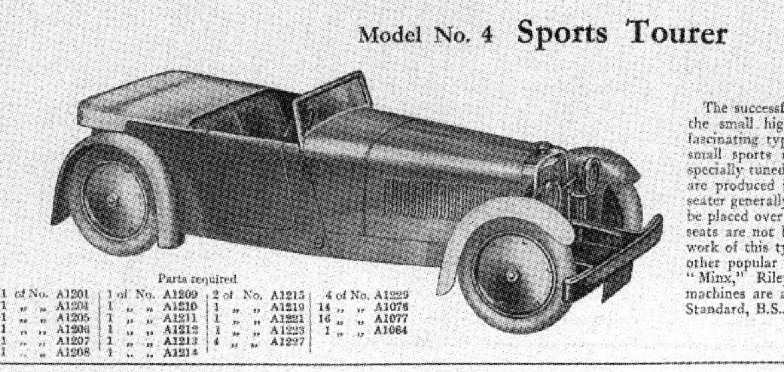

Model No. 4 Sports Tourer

The successful development by British motor engineers of the small high-efficiency engine has enabled a new and fascinating type of sports car to be produced. This is the small sports machine fitted with a "miniature" engine specially tuned to give a very high performance. These cars are produced in both two and four-seater types, the four-seater generally being provided with a canvas cover that can be placed over the rear section or "tonneau" when the rear seats are not being used. A chassis to which sports bodywork of this type is fitted is the Wolseley "Hornet," while other popular sports cars are the M.G. "Midget," Hillman "Minx," Riley "9" and Ford "Minor." Light sports machines are also produced by the Aston-Martin, Crossley, Standard, B.S.A. and Singer companies.

Parts required

1 of No. A1201	1 of No. A1209	2 of No. A1215	4 of No. A1229
1 „ „ A1204	1 „ „ A1210	1 „ „ A1219	14 „ „ A1076
1 „ „ A1205	1 „ „ A1211	1 „ „ A1221	16 „ „ A1077
1 „ „ A1206	1 „ „ A1212	1 „ „ A1223	1 „ „ A1084
1 „ „ A1207	1 „ „ A1213	4 „ „ A1227	
1 „ „ A1208	1 „ „ A1214		

Figs 15–18. A 1938 No. 1 Motor Car Constructor Manual.

MECCANO

INSTRUCTIONS

for building models

with the

MECHANISED ARMY OUTFIT

Prices
Great Britain 2d
South Africa 3d
Australia . . 4d
New Zealand 3d
Canada . 5c

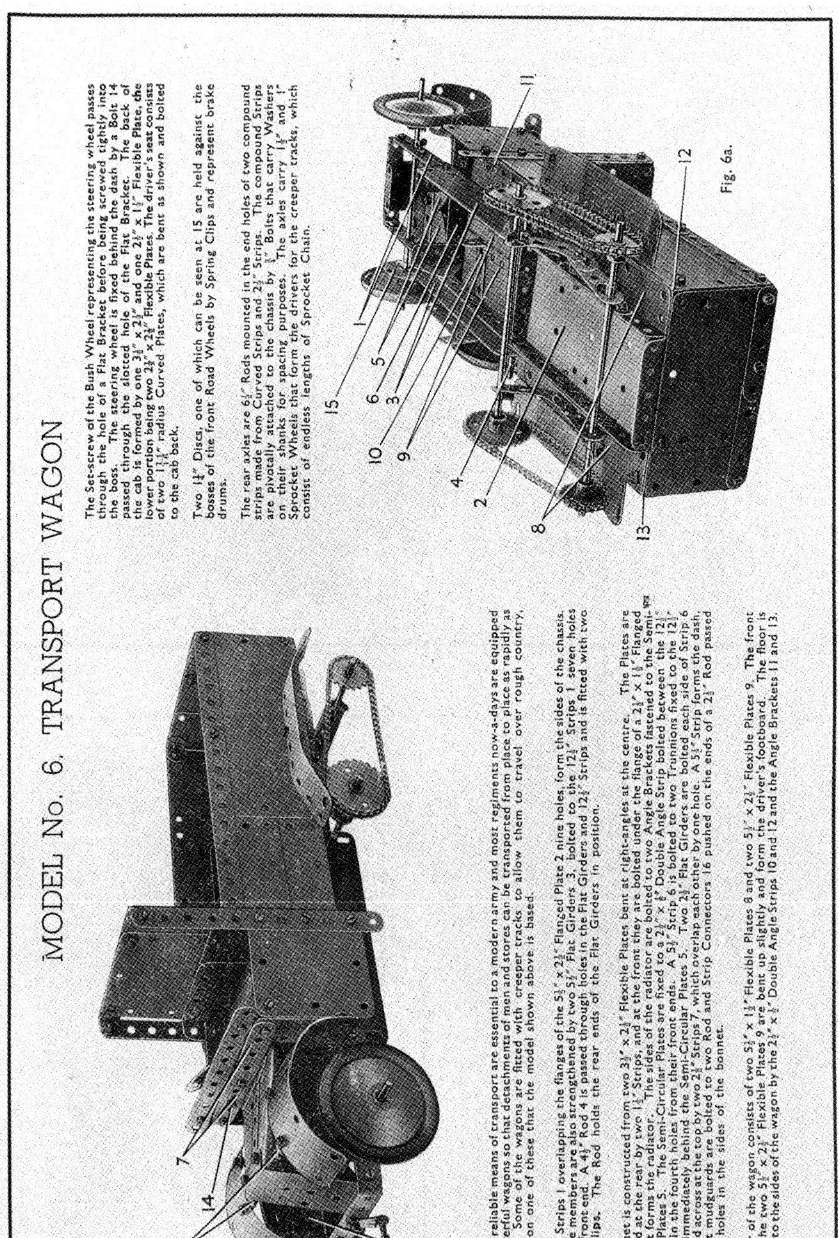

MODEL No. 6. TRANSPORT WAGON

Swift and reliable means of transport are essential to a modern army and most regiments now-a-days are equipped with powerful wagons so that detachments of men and stores can be transported from place to place as rapidly as possible. Some of the wagons are fitted with creeper tracks to allow them to travel over rough country, and it is on one of these that the model shown above is based.

Two 12½" Strips 1 overlapping the flanges of the 5½" x 2½" Flanged Plate 2 nine holes, form the sides of the chassis. These side members are also strengthened by two 5½" Flat Girders 3, bolted to the 12½" Strips 1 seven holes from the front end. A 4½" Rod 4 is passed through holes in the Flat Girders and 12½" Strips and is fitted with two Spring Clips. The Rod holds the rear ends of the Flat Girders in position.

The bonnet is constructed from two 3½" x 2½" Flexible Plates bent at right-angles at the centre. The Plates are connected at the rear by two 1½" Strips, and at the front they are bolted under the flange of a 2½" x 1½" Flanged Plate that forms the radiator. The sides of the radiator are bolted to two Angle Brackets fastened to the Semi-Circular Plates 5. The Semi-Circular Plates are fixed to a 2½" x ½" Double Angle Strip bolted between the 12½" Strips 1, in the fourth holes from their front ends. A 5½" Strip 6 is bolted to two Trunnions fixed to the 12½" Strips 1 immediately behind the Semi-Circular Plates 5. Two 2½" Flat Girders are bolted each side of Strip 6 and joined across at the top by two 2½" Strips 7, which overlap each other by one hole. A 5½" Strip forms the dash. The front mudguards are bolted to two Rod and Strip Connectors 16 pushed on the ends of a 2½" Rod passed through holes in the sides of the bonnet.

The floor of the wagon consists of two 5½" x 1½" Flexible Plates 8 and two 5½" x 2½" Flexible Plates 9. The front ends of the two 5½" x 2½" Flexible Plates 9 are bent up slightly and form the driver's footboard. The floor is attached to the sides of the wagon by the 2½" x ½" Double Angle Strips 10 and 12 and the Angle Brackets 11 and 13.

The Set-screw of the Bush Wheel representing the steering wheel passes through the hole of a Flat Bracket before being screwed tightly into the boss. The steering wheel is fixed behind the dash by a Bolt 14 passed through the slotted hole of the Flat Bracket. The back of the cab is formed by one 3½" x 2½" and one 2½" x 1½" Flexible Plate, the lower portion being two 2½" x 2½" Flexible Plates. The driver's seat consists of two 1 11/16" radius Curved Plates, which are bent as shown and bolted to the cab back.

Two 1½" Discs, one of which can be seen at 15 are held against the bosses of the front Road Wheels by Spring Clips and represent brake drums.

The rear axles are 6½" Rods mounted in the end holes of two compound strips made from Curved Strips and 2½" Strips. The compound Strips are pivotally attached to the chassis by ¾" Bolts that carry Washers on their shanks for spacing purposes. The axles carry 1½" and 1" Sprocket Wheels that form the drivers for the creeper tracks, which consist of endless lengths of Sprocket Chain.

Fig. 6a.

Figs 19–22. Mechanised Army instruction leaflet.

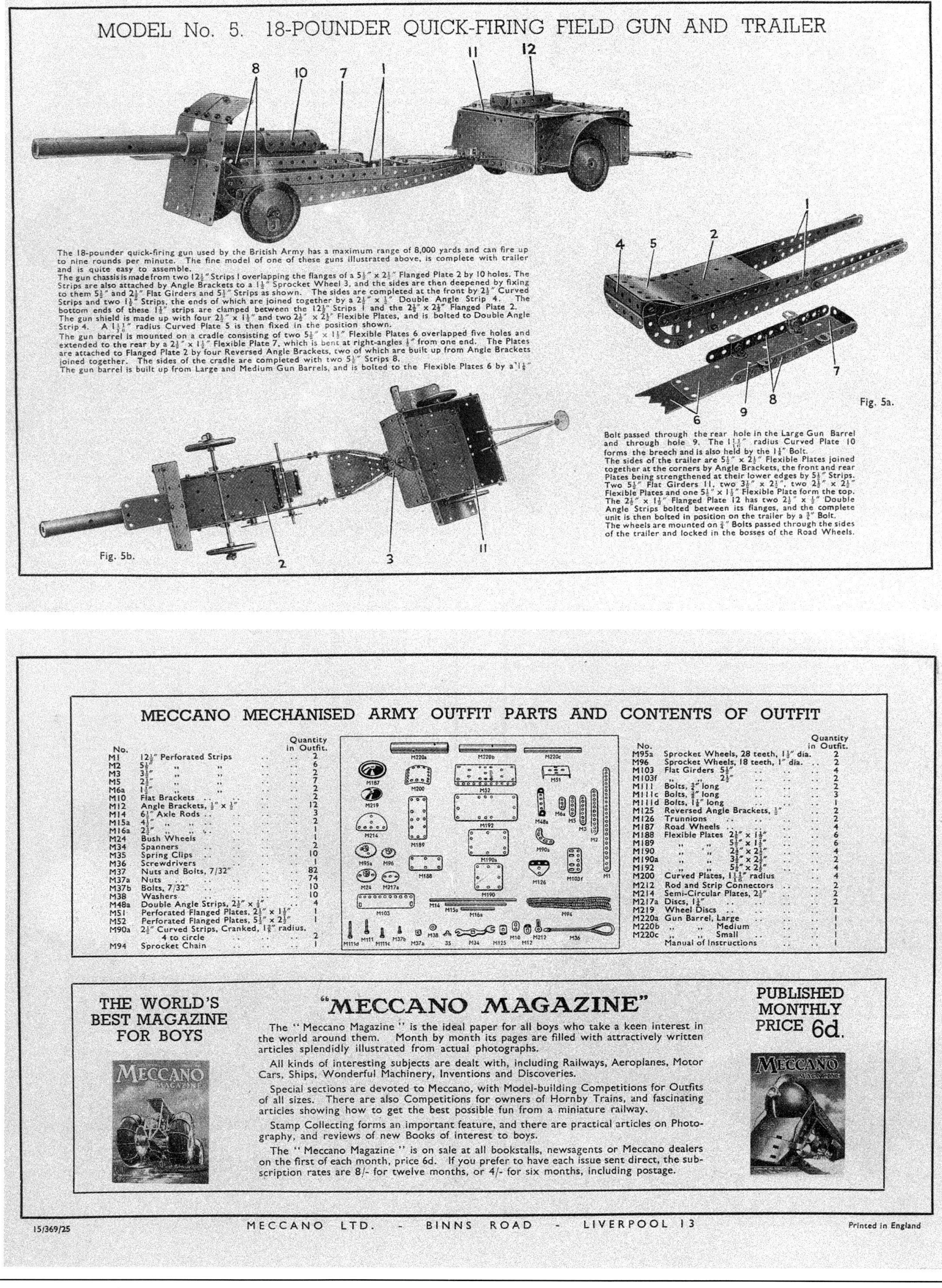

MODEL No. 5. 18-POUNDER QUICK-FIRING FIELD GUN AND TRAILER

The 18-pounder quick-firing gun used by the British Army has a maximum range of 8,000 yards and can fire up to nine rounds per minute. The fine model of one of these guns illustrated above, is complete with trailer and is quite easy to assemble.

The gun chassis is made from two 12½" Strips 1 overlapping the flanges of a 5½" x 2½" Flanged Plate 2 by 10 holes. The Strips are also attached by Angle Brackets to a 1½" Sprocket Wheel 3, and the sides are then deepened by fixing to them 5½" and 2½" Flat Girders and 5½" Strips as shown. The sides are completed at the front by 2½" Curved Strips and two 1½" Strips, the ends of which are joined together by a 2½" x ½" Double Angle Strip 4. The bottom ends of these 1½" strips are clamped between the 12½" Strips 1 and the 2½" x 2½" Flanged Plate 2.

The gun shield is made up with four 2½" x 1½" and two 2½" x 2½" Flexible Plates, and is bolted to Double Angle Strip 4. A 1 11/16" radius Curved Plate 5 is then fixed in the position shown.

The gun barrel is mounted on a cradle consisting of two 5½" x 1½" Flexible Plates 6 overlapped five holes and extended to the rear by a 2½" x 1½" Flexible Plate 7, which is bent at right-angles ½" from one end. The Plates are attached to Flanged Plate 2 by four Reversed Angle Brackets, two of which are built up from Angle Brackets joined together. The sides of the cradle are completed with two 5½" Strips 8.

The gun barrel is built up from Large and Medium Gun Barrels, and is bolted to the Flexible Plates 6 by a 1⅛" Bolt passed through the rear hole in the Large Gun Barrel and through hole 9. The 1 11/16" radius Curved Plate 10 forms the breech and is also held by the 1⅛" Bolt.

The sides of the trailer are 5½" x 2½" Flexible Plates joined together at the corners by Angle Brackets, the front and rear Plates being strengthened at their lower edges by 5½" Strips. Two 5½" Flat Girders 11, two 3½" x 2½", two 2½" x 2½" Flexible Plates and one 5½" x 1½" Flexible Plate form the top. The 2½" x 1½" Flanged Plate 12 has two 2½" x ½" Double Angle Strips bolted between its flanges, and the complete unit is then bolted in position on the trailer by a ¾" Bolt.

The wheels are mounted on ¾" Bolts passed through the sides of the trailer and locked in the bosses of the Road Wheels.

Fig. 5a.

Fig. 5b.

MECCANO MECHANISED ARMY OUTFIT PARTS AND CONTENTS OF OUTFIT

No.		Quantity in Outfit.
M1	12½" Perforated Strips	2
M2	5½" „ „	6
M3	3½" „ „	2
M5	2½" „ „	7
M6a	1½" „ „	2
M10	Flat Brackets	2
M12	Angle Brackets, ½" x ½"	12
M14	6½" Axle Rods	3
M15a	4½" „ „	2
M16a	2½" „ „	1
M24	Bush Wheels	1
M34	Spanners	2
M35	Spring Clips	10
M36	Screwdrivers	1
M37	Nuts and Bolts, 7/32"	82
M37a	Nuts	74
M37b	Bolts, 7/32"	10
M38	Washers	10
M48a	Double Angle Strips, 2½" x ½"	4
M51	Perforated Flanged Plates, 2½" x 1½"	1
M52	Perforated Flanged Plates, 5½" x 2½"	1
M90a	2½" Curved Strips, Cranked, 1⅜" radius, 4 to circle	2
M94	Sprocket Chain	1

No.		Quantity in Outfit.
M95a	Sprocket Wheels, 28 teeth, 1½" dia.	2
M96	Sprocket Wheels, 18 teeth, 1" dia.	2
M103	Flat Girders 5½"	4
M103f	„ „ 2½"	2
M111	Bolts, ¾" long	2
M111c	Bolts, ⅜" long	3
M111d	Bolts, 1⅛" long	1
M125	Reversed Angle Brackets, ½"	2
M126	Trunnions	2
M187	Road Wheels	4
M188	Flexible Plates 2½" x 1½"	6
M189	„ „ 5½" x 1½"	6
M190	„ „ 2½" x 2½"	4
M190a	„ „ 3½" x 2½"	2
M192	„ „ 5½" x 2½"	4
M200	Curved Plates, 1 11/16" radius	4
M212	Rod and Strip Connectors	2
M214	Semi-Circular Plates, 2½"	2
M217a	Discs, 1½"	2
M219	Wheel Discs	1
M220a	Gun Barrel, Large	1
M220b	„ „ Medium	1
M220c	„ „ Small	1
	Manual of Instructions	1

15/369/25

MECCANO LTD. - BINNS ROAD - LIVERPOOL 13

Printed in England

MECCANO

ELECTRICAL ACCESSORY OUTFIT

FOR MAKING ELECTRIC LOCOS : MAGNETIC CRANES
MORSE SIGNALLING APPARATUS : INDUCTION COIL
ELECTRIC LAMPS : MOTOR STARTER, Etc.

INSTRUCTIONS
1/6

Copyright by MECCANO LIMITED, LIVERPOOL, *throughout the World.*

TO SIGNAL IN BOTH DIRECTIONS OVER ONE PAIR OF WIRES MODEL No. 9

The Morse Key (Model 7) must be used to signal in either direction over one pair of wires. Full connections for two stations are given on the circuit drawing.

The wires passing through the dotted line may be extended to any length.

A Morse key, buzzer and accumulator are required at each station, using wire No. 23 for lines A and B.

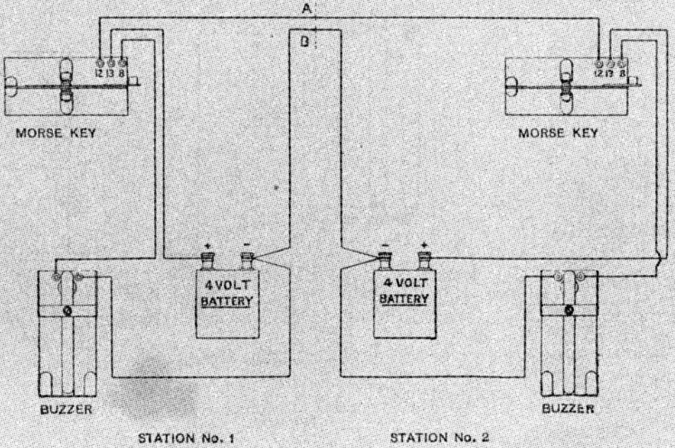

Fig. 9

On the Accumulator the terminal coloured red is positive and marked on the drawing with a cross + and the one coloured black is negative and marked with a dash — .

All wires should be tightly screwed to the terminals to make good connections.

Page 12

ELECTRIC SMOOTHING IRON MODEL No. 10

This is a departure from the models described previously, but it will be interesting to construct, and at the same time give some idea of electric heating.

All metals conduct electricity, some more readily than others. Those metals that do not conduct so well are said to offer a resistance to the flow of the current.

Wherever there is resistance in a circuit, heat is developed when a current passes through.

In this electric iron there is used two feet of bare iron wire, No. 27. This iron wire has a certain amount of resistance.

The bottom sector plate 1 or sole of the iron must first have two layers of brown paper nicely fitted inside. This is to insulate the bare wire from the metal plate.

Referring to Fig. 10A, one end of the iron wire is fastened with a Meccano nut and bolt 2 in hole 1 on the left hand side of the sector plate.

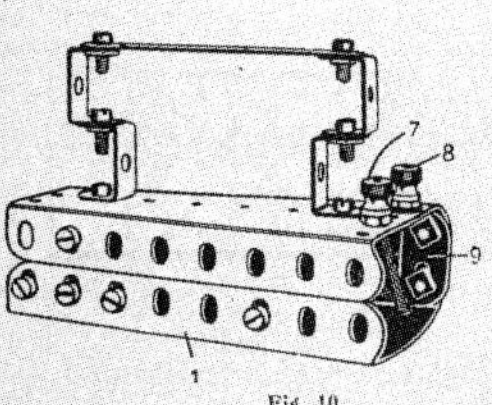

Fig. 10

Bend the wire 4 as shown in Fig. 10A and connect the other end to an insulated 6 B.A. bolt and nut 3 in hole 7 on the right-hand side. The iron wire should be made to lie flat and even on the brown paper after the ends have been connected.

On the insulated screw 3 another nut 5 is placed, and a short piece of insulated copper wire 6 fastened under this nut and then connected to the insulated terminal 8 on the top of the iron, Fig. 10.

Parts required.

1	No.	4
1	"	6
1	"	6A
2	"	10
4	"	11
4	"	12
15	"	37
2	"	54
2	"	302
2	"	303
3	"	304
4	"	305
2	"	306
24"	"	312
3"	"	314

Fig. 10A

To hold the iron wire 4 in position, cut two more layers of brown paper to fit in the sole and completely cover up the wire 4.

In the third and sixth holes on each side of the sole are bolted angle brackets and under these are placed strips which press down the top paper.

The top part of the iron should now be built. Fix two terminals, 7, 8, in the position shown, one, 8, is insulated, the other is not. The copper wire 6 from the sole is connected to the insulated terminal 8. The top is fastened to the sole by means of flat brackets 9 using the second hole on the left-hand side, and hole 8 on the right-hand side.

CONNECT THE TERMINALS 7, 8 TO YOUR 4-VOLT ACCUMULATOR, AND IN ABOUT TEN MINUTES THE IRON WILL BE WARM.

Page 13

MECCANO ELECTRIFIED

NOT many boys realise the tremendous part which electricity plays in our every-day life these days. We use the electric light, electric trams, telephone and telegraph, without thinking much of the wonderful power which gives us these great facilities, what this power is, or how it operates. The study of electricity is extremely fascinating, and it is our desire that all Meccano boys shall have a good insight into the subject and derive both pleasure and knowledge from it. A very large number of Meccano models may be operated by electricity, and in this Manual we show you how easily this may be done.

No one has yet been able to define electricity or tell us just what it is, and all we can say is that it is a natural force capable of unlimited uses. A long treatise might be written on the phenomena of electricity, but it is only necessary here to deal with it so far as it applies to engineering.

Before commencing to make the models in this Manual it is very necessary that a boy should know the meaning of the general terms used in Electricity, so that he may understand them whenever they are referred to.

VOLT. The practical unit of Electro-Motive Force (E.M.F.) is termed a Volt, and this represents the force of Electricity passing round a circuit. The more force there is the greater the voltage.

RESISTANCE OR OHMS. This means resistance to the current passing along a wire. Apart from silver, copper wire offers the least resistance to the current passing along it. If another class of wire were used, made from such metals as Zinc, Iron, Tin or Lead, which possess less conductivity, the resistance would be greater, consequently less current would be transmitted. The resistance of a Conductor increases as the length increases.

AMPERES. This means the rate at which Electricity flows around a circuit. The thicker the wire the more current may be transmitted.

WATT. This is the unit of Electrical Power and equals 0·7373 foot pounds per second, equal to 1/746 of a horse power. The number of watts is ascertained by multiplying the volts by the amperes. Thus, if the E.M.F. is four volts and the current two amperes, the power transmitted would be 8 watts.

Page 1

Figs 23–26. The Electrical Outfit Manual (1921 version labelled 'Accessory' outfit).

ELEKTRON
ELECTRICAL EXPERIMENTS

INSTRUCTIONS
FOR OUTFIT
No. 1

PRICE
1/-

No. 33-1EE

Fig 27. An Elektron Manual (1933).

principle : that opposite poles—one north and one south—attract one another, and that similar poles—two norths or two souths—repel each other.

One of the favourite experiments with a magnet is to suspend a chain of needles or Meccano Nuts from one of its poles, adding them slowly and carefully one by one to see how many the magnet will sustain. An interesting variation of this experiment is to make a loop of Nuts by suspending a chain of them from each pole of a magnet and gently bringing their ends into contact (Fig. 5). As the nuts used were not previously magnetised, these experiments show that the nut actually brought into contact with the magnet immediately becomes a magnet itself, and that the power of attraction is passed on to each nut added to the chain.

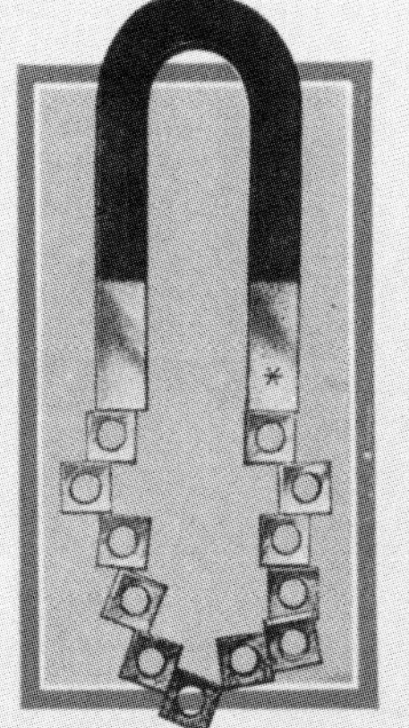

Fig. 5. A loop of Nuts held together by magnetic attraction.

Induced Magnetism

There is an easy way of testing this by suspending a large nail or a piece of soft iron from one end of the Bar Magnet, and dipping its lower end into a heap of filings, and then lifting it away. It will be found that a bunch of filings clings to it, showing that it has become a magnet (Fig. 6). If now we hold the nail in one hand and gently detach the magnet from it with the other, the filings immediately fall off, showing that the nail has lost its magnetic power. In the case of a chain of needles suspended from the end of a magnet, if we gently detach the first needle the remainder will fall away from it and from one another. This shows us that the magnetism induced in a needle by contact with a magnet is only temporary, since it ceases as soon as the magnet is taken away.

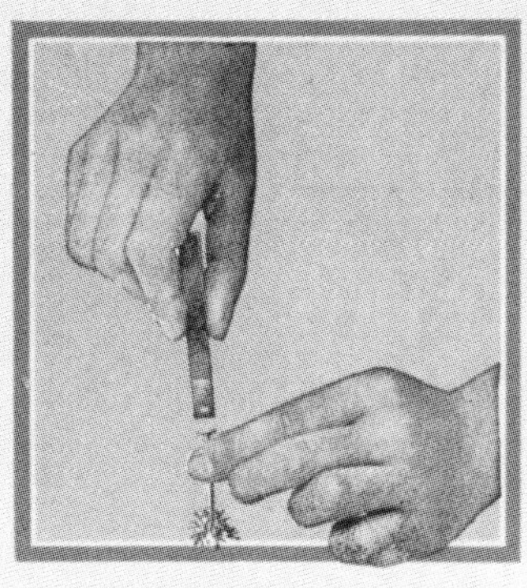

Fig. 6. A nail becomes a temporary magnet when held near a pole of a Bar Magnet.

If the iron filings used in our experiments become scattered, the natural thing to do is to pick them up with the magnet. This is quite easy, but trouble arises in persuading the magnet to part with them, and much scraping and pulling is necessary. This can be obviated by collecting the filings by means of a piece of soft iron hanging from a bar magnet, and therefore temporarily magnetised (Fig. 7). If the collected filings are then held over the container, they will be released and will fall neatly into it as soon as the magnet is taken away from the iron.

How to Make Magnets

Exactly as a piece of iron or steel may be turned into an artificial magnet by stroking it with a piece of lodestone, so may magnets be made with one of the Bar Magnets included in the Outfit. A medium-sized sewing needle makes a convenient piece of steel for the purpose, but it should first be tested with filings, to make sure that it is not already magnetic. Next, the needle is laid on the table and the north pole of the Bar Magnet is drawn slowly along it from eye to point (Fig. 8). This operation is repeated several times, care being taken to draw the magnet well beyond the point of the needle before bringing it back to the eye. Another test with filings will show that the needle has become a magnet.

It will be interesting now to find out which is the north and which the

Fig 28. A typical page from the Elektron Manual.

Kemex Chemical Experiments 15

the liquid a strip of Magnesium Ribbon (No. K116) half an inch in length. There is a violent action, and a gas is given off that burns with a blue flame when the mouth of the test tube is brought to the flame of the Spirit Lamp (Fig. 21). Similar results follow the use of Granulated Zinc (No. K134) or Iron Filings (No. K112) instead of Magnesium, but in these cases the action is less violent.

The name of the gas that burns so readily is hydrogen. It is colourless and has no smell. It is lighter than air, and may be collected in a test tube held above the mouth of the tube in which it is being produced. When collected in this manner the gas usually is mixed with a proportion of air, and there is a loud but harmless explosion when a light is applied to it.

Making Hydrogen in the Gas Generator

Hydrogen is more readily obtained if dilute sulphuric acid of accumulator strength is employed. In order to collect the gas for further experiments place half the Zinc included in the Outfit in the Wide-necked Flask (Part No. K10) and insert the Large Cork (Part No. K17), into the holes of which the Thistle Funnel (Part No. K11) and the small Right Angle Delivery Tube (Part No. K12) have been carefully worked. The lower end of the tube of the thistle funnel must be near the bottom of the wide-necked flask. This constitutes the gas generator, and in order to collect the hydrogen we may follow the plan adopted in the case of oxygen, using test tubes as well as jars as gasholders (Fig. 22).

Pour sufficient water down the thistle funnel to cover its lower end, and slowly add dilute sulphuric acid of accumulator strength until effervescence begins. Hydrogen then passes down the delivery tube and bubbles upward through the water in the large basin into the test tubes placed to receive it. As each test tube is filled, close it with the thumb and test its contents by bringing its mouth to the flame of the spirit lamp, which in this experiment must be kept as far away from the apparatus as possible. The gas first collected probably has a little air in it, and the mixture explodes with a loud noise, but harmlessly. When pure hydrogen is being collected the gas will burn quietly, a blue flame travelling up the test tube.

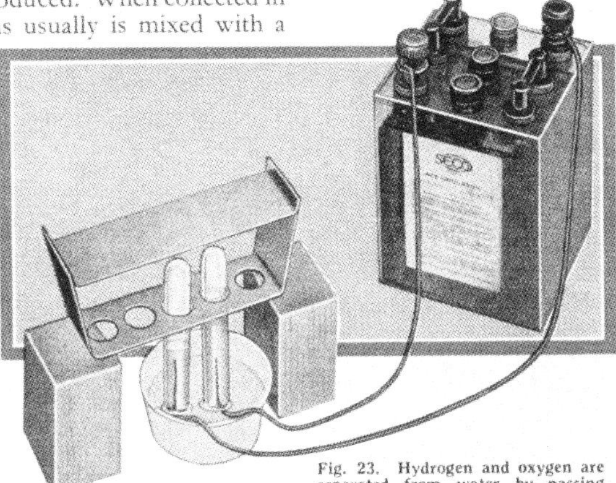

Fig. 23. Hydrogen and oxygen are separated from water by passing an electric current through it.

Pouring an Invisible Gas Upward

Pour more acid down the thistle funnel if necessary, and fill two test tubes with hydrogen. Hold these side by side with their mouths open, but with one inverted, and count 10 slowly. Then test each by means of a flame. No hydrogen is present in the test tube held with its mouth upward, but an explosion indicates that gas remains in the one that was inverted. This shows us that hydrogen is lighter than air.

A jar may be filled with hydrogen and the gas in it poured upward into a second jar as easily as the heavy gas carbon dioxide can be poured downward. Air is nearly 15 times as heavy as its own volume of hydrogen, and 1,000 cu. ft. of hydrogen give a lift in air of about 67 lb. Hydrogen therefore would seem to be ideal for use in airships, but is so readily inflammable that there is always danger of fire in envelopes filled with it.

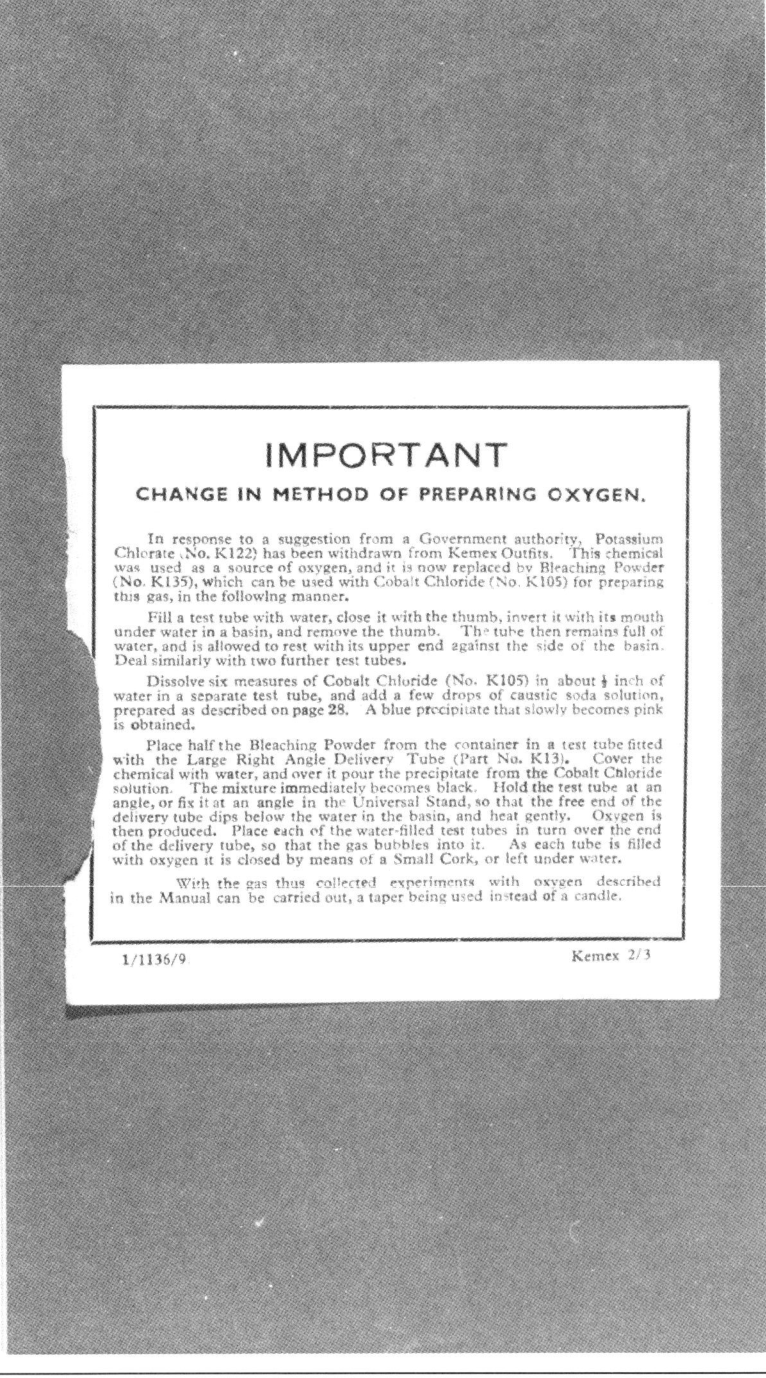

IMPORTANT

CHANGE IN METHOD OF PREPARING OXYGEN.

In response to a suggestion from a Government authority, Potassium Chlorate (No. K122) has been withdrawn from Kemex Outfits. This chemical was used as a source of oxygen, and it is now replaced by Bleaching Powder (No. K135), which can be used with Cobalt Chloride (No. K105) for preparing this gas, in the following manner.

Fill a test tube with water, close it with the thumb, invert it with its mouth under water in a basin, and remove the thumb. The tube then remains full of water, and is allowed to rest with its upper end against the side of the basin. Deal similarly with two further test tubes.

Dissolve six measures of Cobalt Chloride (No. K105) in about $\frac{1}{4}$ inch of water in a separate test tube, and add a few drops of caustic soda solution, prepared as described on page 28. A blue precipitate that slowly becomes pink is obtained.

Place half the Bleaching Powder from the container in a test tube fitted with the Large Right Angle Delivery Tube (Part No. K13). Cover the chemical with water, and over it pour the precipitate from the Cobalt Chloride solution. The mixture immediately becomes black. Hold the test tube at an angle, or fix it at an angle in the Universal Stand, so that the free end of the delivery tube dips below the water in the basin, and heat gently. Oxygen is then produced. Place each of the water-filled test tubes in turn over the end of the delivery tube, so that the gas bubbles into it. As each tube is filled with oxygen it is closed by means of a Small Cork, or left under water.

With the gas thus collected experiments with oxygen described in the Manual can be carried out, a taper being used instead of a candle.

1/1136/9 Kemex 2/3

THE HORNBY SYSTEM OF MECHANICAL DEMONSTRATION

Price 6d. nett.

Manufactured by

MECCANO, LTD.,
274, WEST DERBY ROAD,
LIVERPOOL.

Copyright.

SECTION C. MODEL 14

Epicycloidal Gear.

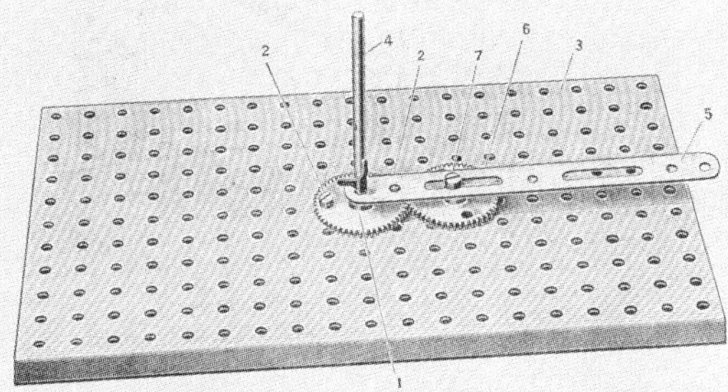

This model serves to illustrate the principle of an epicycloidal type of gearing. The main gear wheel 1 is bolted at 2 to the perforated plate 3, so that it is fixed to this plate; a short spindle 4 is loosely fitted in the bush of the fixed wheel 1, and a slotted strip 5 is mounted upon the spindle 4 and held in position axially on the strip by a key. At a suitable distance radially outward on the strip 5 a bolt 7 is fixed in one of the slots of the strip on the shank of which a gear wheel 6 is capable of rotating. As the arm 5 is rotated round the spindle 4 it will be noticed that the loose gear wheel 6, though of the same diameter as the fixed wheel 1, will make two complete revolutions about its axis 7 for every one complete revolution of the arm 5 about the fixed spindle 4.

This type of gear in which one wheel rotates outside another is called epicycloidal gear. Where a gear wheel or pinion rotates round a gear wheel, the teeth of which are formed on the inner face of the wheel, the gearing is called hypocycloidal.

39

SECTION C. MODEL 12

Forces Acting at the Cross Head.

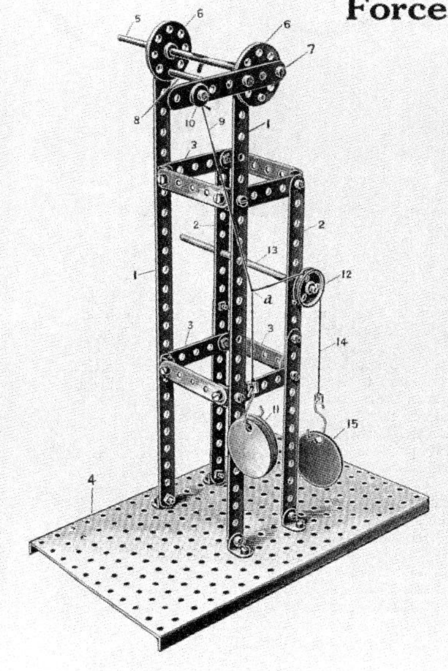

This is an example for determining the forces in an engine which act at the cross head, such as the pressure on the slides of the engine. The frame work is constructed of long strips 1 tied to shorter strips 2 by short cross pieces 3. These are all carried from the perforated plate 4. In the upper perforations of the upright strips 1 is mounted the shaft 5, upon which are keyed the bush wheels 6. To the nearer bush wheel is bolted a strip 7 which corresponds to the engine crank, a locking bar 8 being provided which is adapted to be inserted through the perforations in the strips 1 and the perforations in the bush wheels 6, thereby locking these bush wheels and consequently the crank 7 at any desired angle. A cord 9 is now connected to the small wheel 10, rotatably mounted on the crank, this cord carrying at its lower extremity a weight 11. A pulley 12 mounted upon a spindle 13 receives a second cord 14, at the end of which weights 15 are suspended. The junction *a* of the cord 14 and 9 corresponds to the cross head of an engine, the lower portion of the cord 9 representing the piston rod, and the upper inclined portion the connecting rod. The pull of the cord 14 will be a measure of the pressure exerted on the slides due to the angularity of the connecting rod. The junction *a* of the cords 14 and 9 should be kept in line with the centre of the perforations in the nearer strip 1 by adding weights at 15, and the crank 7 should be set at different angular positions round its path. The different weights required to be hung on the cord 14 to keep the point *a* central on the nearer strip 1 for a given weight 11 should be noted for the various positions of the crank 7, and it will be seen by so doing that the greater weight 15 is required when the crank 7 is at right angles to the direction of the piston, and decreases as the crank becomes more in line with the piston. From this it should be noted that the thrust on the slides of an engine increases from a minimum when the engine is at the end of the stroke to a maximum when it is in the middle of this stroke, the weight 15 being a measure of the thrust exerted by the cross head on the slides.

37

Figs 31–33. Cover and representative pages of the manual for the ill-fated Hornby System of Mechanical Demonstration.

← *Fig 30. A possibly dangerous page from the Kemex Manual together with a semi-government warning!*

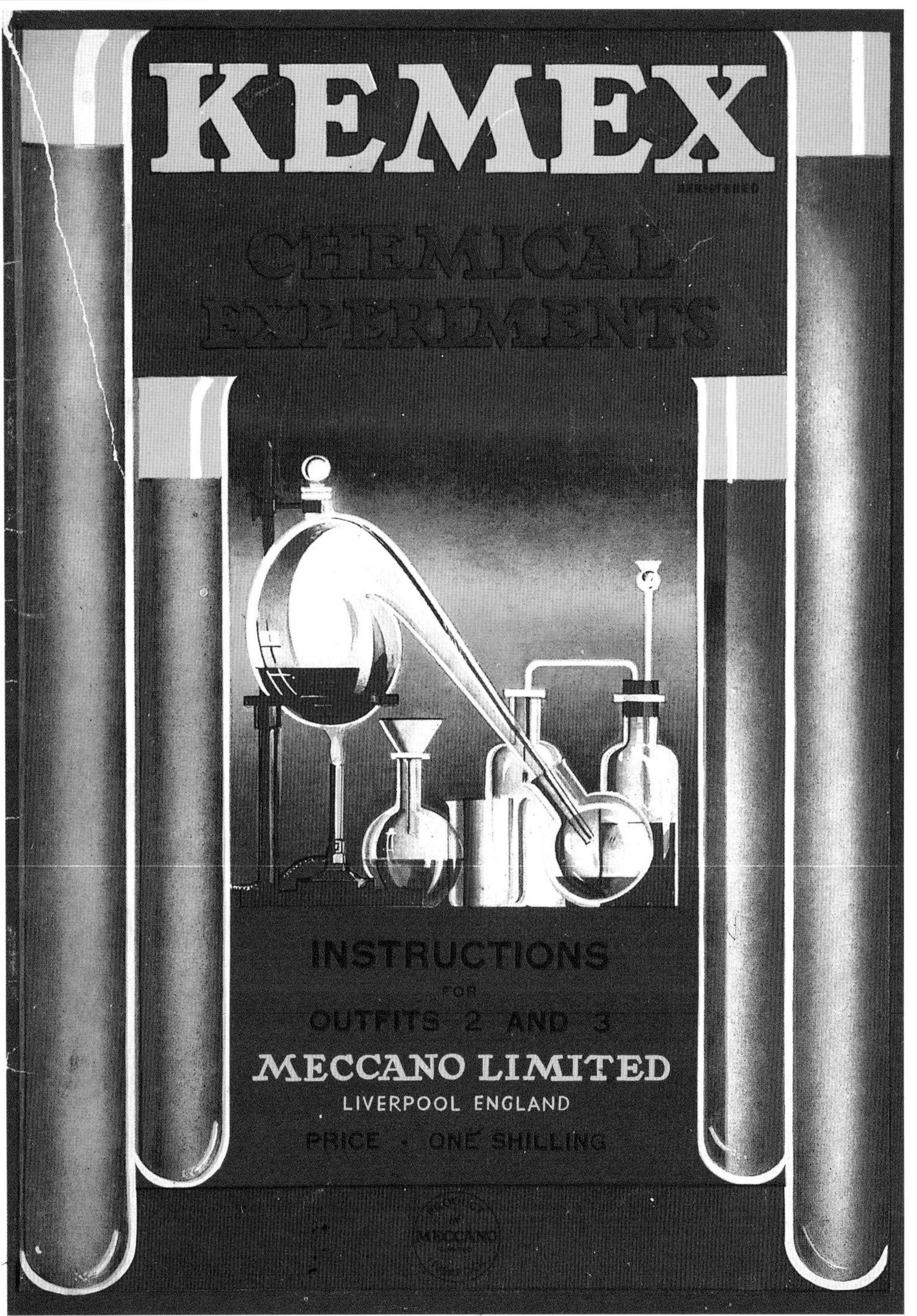

← *Fig 29. A most attractive Kemex Manual.*

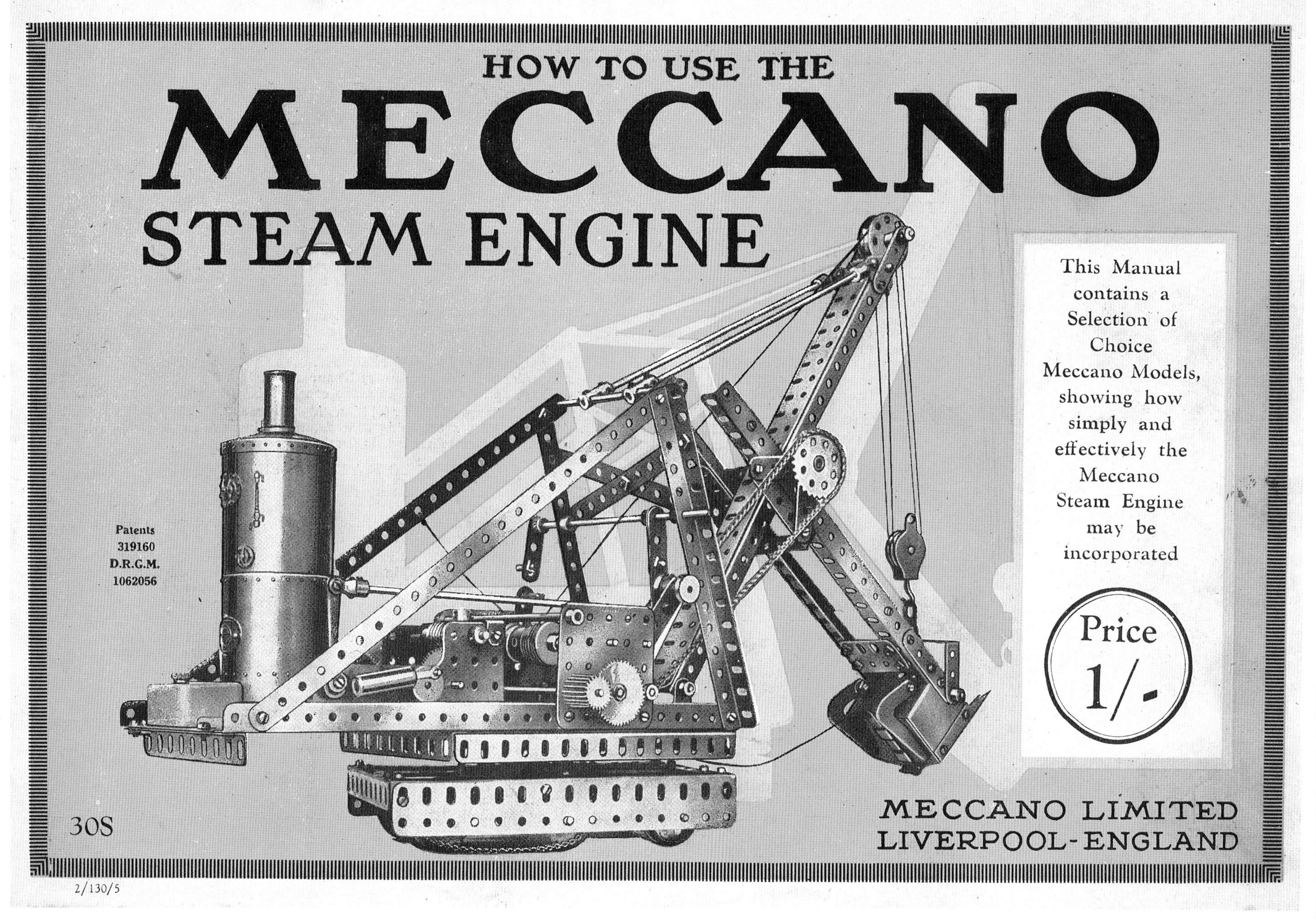

Fig 34. The 1930 edition of the Steam Engine Manual.

MECCANO STEAM-DRIVEN MODELS

Model No. S25 Steam Paddle Boat

The hull of the Paddle Boat should be proceeded with first; four 12½″ Braced Girders 1 and four 12½″ Strips 2 are connected to 5½″ × 2½″ Flanged Plates 3. The sides should then be stayed by two 4½″ × ½″ Double Angle Strips 4 and a 4½″ Strip 5 bolted in the fourth hole of the Flanged Plate 3 and spaced with two Washers. A 4½″ Angle Girder 6 is bolted to the two Flanged Plates 3 and a 5½″ Angle Girder 7 is secured to the top of each Plate. To the Angle Girders 7 are bolted two Flat Girders 8.

The 5″ Axle Rod 9 (Fig. S25a) carries two 1½″ Pulley Wheels 10 and a 1″ Sprocket Wheel 11. The vertical engine may now be secured in position by the bolts 18 (Fig. S25a) to the Strip 5 and the Double Angle Strip 4. A ½″ Pinion on the Rod 19 meshes with the Gear Wheel 20 on the 11½″ Rod 21. On the same Rod is a 1″ Sprocket Wheel 22 connected to the Sprocket Wheel 11 by means of Sprocket Chain. The paddle wheels may now be placed on the Rod 21. When the engine is set in motion the boat is caused to travel along the ground and the paddle wheels to rotate simultaneously. A Bush Wheel secured to a 3½″ Rod 23 forms the rear running wheel supporting the boat.

The upper structure is composed of two 3½″ × 2½″ Flanged Plates 24 bolted together and supported by 1½″ × ½″ Double Angle Strips 25 and 25a, the latter being bolted to a 4½″ Strip 26. A Coupling 27 mounted on a short Rod that passes through the Plate 24 and secured by a Collar and set-screw below, forms the bearing for the steering wheel 28. No. 29 is a 5½″ × ½″ Double Angle Strip connected to Angle Brackets secured to a 5½″ Flat Girder which, in turn, is bolted to the end Flanged Plates 24.

Fig. S25a

Parts required:

4 of No. 1	3 of No. 13	2 of No. 35	12 of No. 59
1 ,, ,, 2	1 ,, ,, 14	83 ,, ,, 37	1 ,, ,, 63
3 ,, ,, 2a	1 ,, ,, 15	7 ,, ,, 38	1 ,, ,, 89
5 ,, ,, 3	1 ,, ,, 16	2 ,, ,, 45	2 ,, ,, 90
1 ,, ,, 4	1 ,, ,, 16a	6 ,, ,, 48	9½″ ,, ,, 94
4 ,, ,, 5	2 ,, ,, 18a	8 ,, ,, 48a	1 ,, ,, 96
2 ,, ,, 6	4 ,, ,, 19b	2 ,, ,, 48c	1 ,, ,, 96a
2 ,, ,, 9	2 ,, ,, 21	1 ,, ,, 48d	4 ,, ,, 99
1 ,, ,, 9a	1 ,, ,, 24	2 ,, ,, 52	3 ,, ,, 103
2 ,, ,, 10	1 ,, ,, 26	2 ,, ,, 53	1 ,, ,, 126
18 ,, ,, 12	1 ,, ,, 27a		

These parts are all contained in the regular No. 4 Meccano Outfit with the exception of:—

2 of No. 6	2 of No. 48c
1 ,, ,, 9a	1 ,, ,, 89
1 ,, ,, 13	1 ,, ,, 96a
1 ,, ,, 16a	3 ,, ,, 103

which can be obtained from any Meccano dealer.

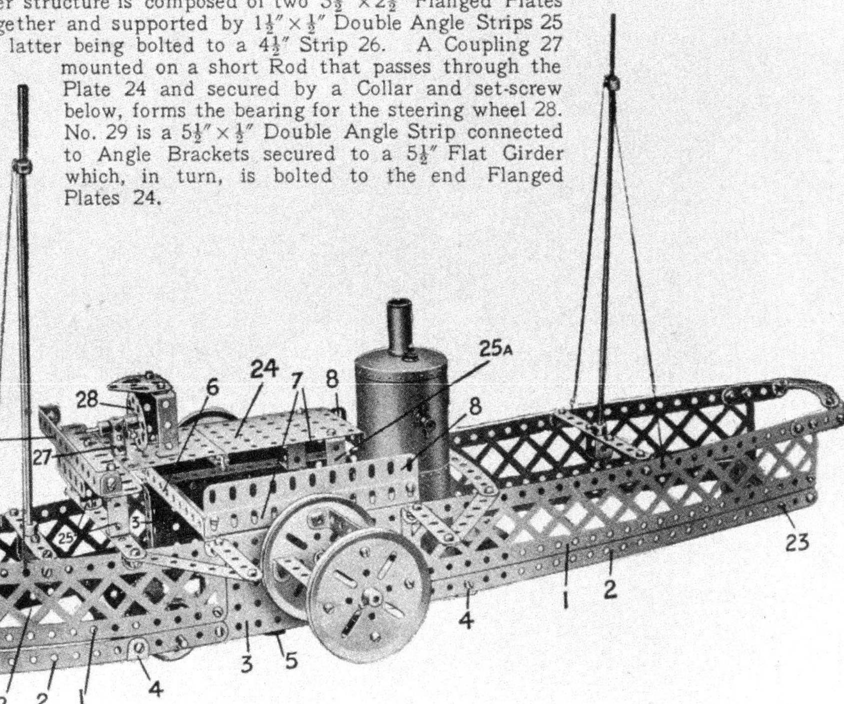

Figs 35–36. Two models from the Steam Engine Manual.

Model No. S27 Steam Wagon

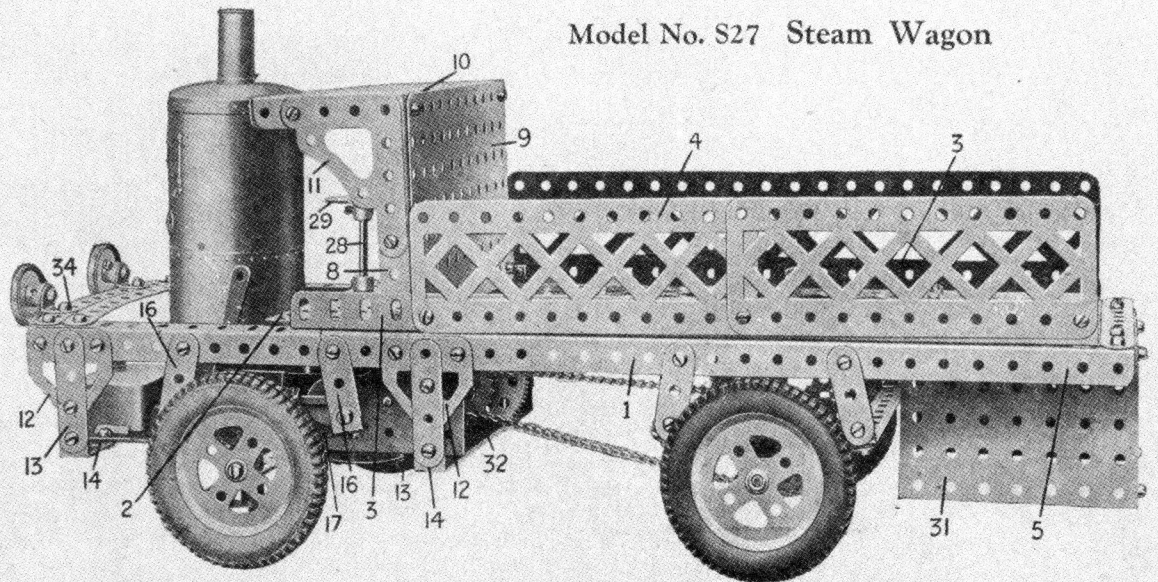

Parts required:

1 of No. 1		2 of No. 24
6 ,, ,, 2		1 ,, ,, 27A
2 ,, ,, 2A		106 ,, ,, 37
4 ,, ,, 3		12 ,, ,, 38
1 ,, ,, 4		2 ,, ,, 48D
1 ,, ,, 5		1 ,, ,, 52
5 ,, ,, 6		3 ,, ,, 53
8 ,, ,, 6A		6 ,, ,, 59
6 ,, ,, 8		2 ,, ,, 62
1 ,, ,, 9		1 ,, ,, 70
2 ,, ,, 9B		2 ,, ,, 89
2 ,, ,, 10		13″ ,, ,, 94
4 ,, ,, 11		1 ,, ,, 95A
12 ,, ,, 12		1 ,, ,, 96A
1 ,, ,, 14		2 ,, ,, 99
1 ,, ,, 15A		4 ,, ,, 100
1 ,, ,, 16B		2 ,, ,, 108
2 ,, ,, 18A		2 ,, ,, 111
4 ,, ,, 20A		4 ,, ,, 126A
2 ,, ,, 22		4 ,, ,, 142A

These parts are all contained in the regular No. 4 Meccano Outfit with the exception of the following, which can be obtained from any Meccano dealer:—

5 of No. 6	1 of No. 70
2 ,, ,, 9B	2 ,, ,, 89
1 ,, ,, 16B	1 ,, ,, 95A
4 ,, ,, 20A	1 ,, ,, 96A

4 of No. 142A

A 5½″ Angle Girder is secured across the 5½″ × 2½″ Flat Plate 2 by bolts 7 (Fig. S27A). At each end of this is bolted an upright 3½″ Angle Girder 8 to which is attached a 5½″ × 3½″ Flat Plate 9 to form the back of the cab and a 5½″ × 2½″ Flanged Plate 10 to form the hood. A 5½″ and a 2½″ Strip 15 (Fig. S27A) overlapped two holes and connected to the 5½″ Double Angle Strips 14 form a bearing for one end of the steering column 28. The steering gear is built up in the following manner. Two 1½″ Strips 16 are connected on each side of the members 1 as shown in Fig. S27. 3½″ Strips 17 (Fig. S27A) slightly curved to represent springs are attached by Angle Brackets to the Strips 16, Flat Brackets 18 being bolted in the centre holes of the Strips 17. The swivel supports for the stub axles of the wheels are each composed of a 1½″ Rod 19, a Double Bracket 20, a Collar 21 with two Washers above and below. The 1½″ Rods are held in position by a Collar 22 at the top and at the bottom by the Cranks 23 and 23a. A Strip 24 (formed of two 4½″ Strips overlapped fives holes) is connected pivotally at its ends to the Cranks 23 and 23a. The Crank 23 is also connected pivotally by a 2″ Strip 25 to a 3″ Strip 26 that is bolted to a Bush Wheel 27 mounted securely on the steering column 28. The stub axles of the front wheels are formed by passing a ¾″ Bolt through the boss of each wheel and screwing it into the Collar 21 until it pinches the Rod 19.

The spring bearings of the rear wheels are connected together at each end by 5½″ Strips 30. The carrier 31 is formed of three 3½″ × 2½″ Flanged Plates bolted together and secured to the bottom of the wagon by Angle Brackets.

The engine may now be placed in position and bolted to the Strips 14. The drive is taken by Sprocket Chain from the 1″ Sprocket Wheel 32 on the engine to the 1½″ Sprocket Wheel 33 on the back axle of the wagon.

Fig. S27A

Figs 39–40. Dinky Builder 'Super Models'! →

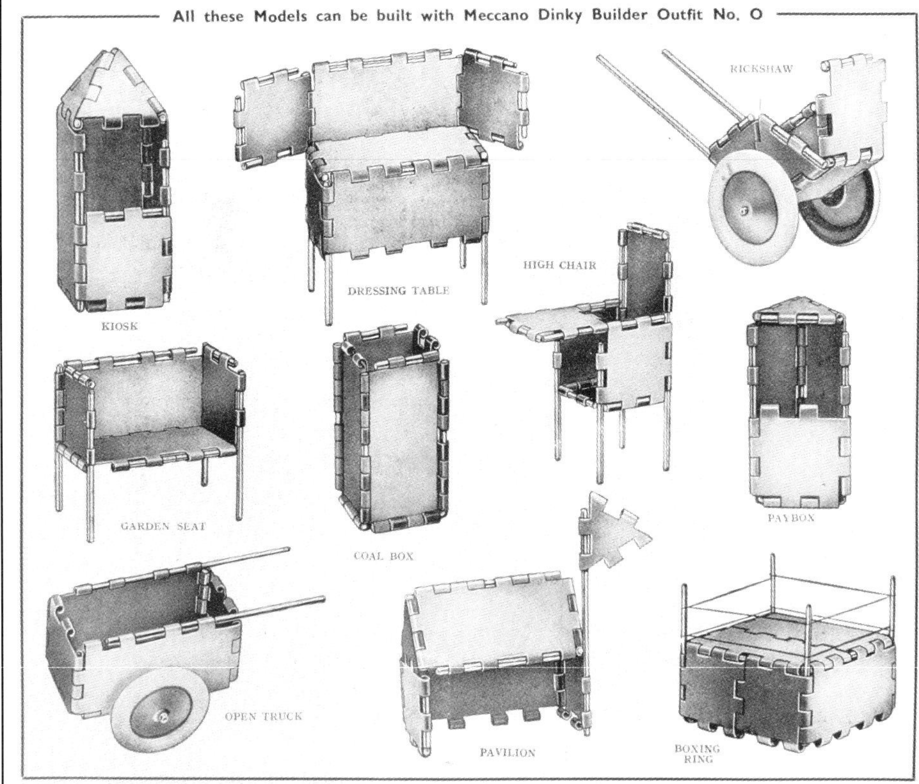

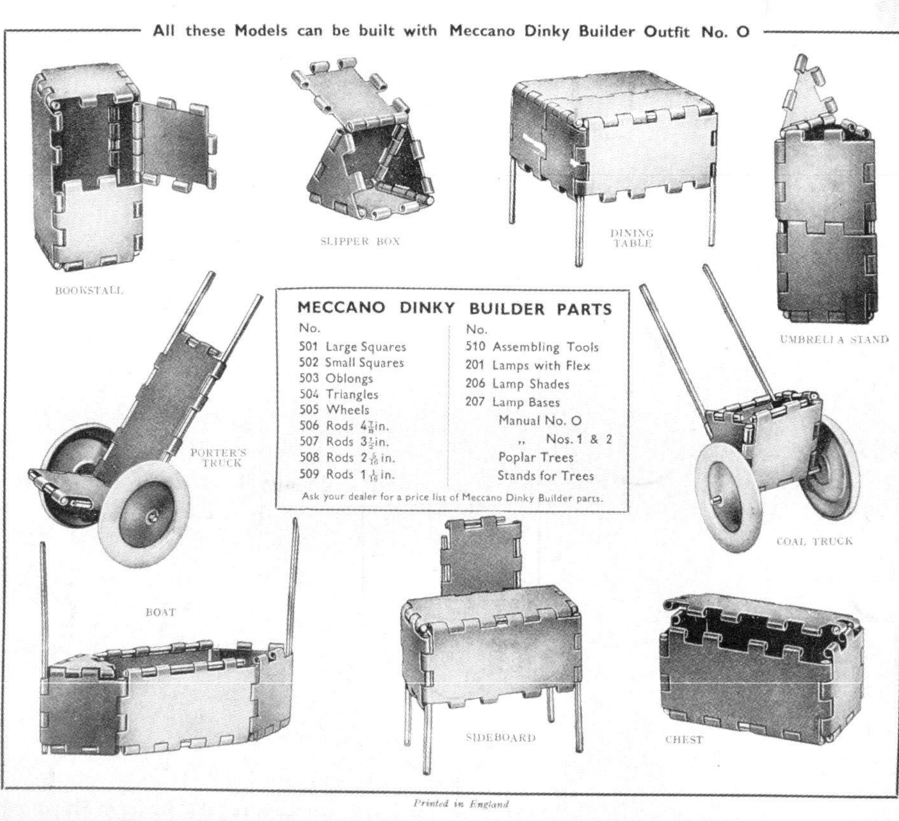

Figs 37–38. Basic Dinky Builder models.

PRODUCT of MECCANO LIMITED LIVERPOOL

DINKY BUILDER

SUPER MODELS

The splendid range of models illustrated in this special folder will give you some idea of the wonderful possibilities of the Dinky Builder system. When you have built all the models shown in your Instruction Folder, you will have become a really enthusiastic model-builder, and you can then buy Dinky Builder "A" Packets and build the magnificent super models described here. The number of Packets required additional to the contents of the respective outfits is indicated under the title of each model.

After you have built all our examples, you can start inventing new models for your own amusement. You will find this a most fascinating and absorbing pastime.

SHOP

No. 2 Outfit plus 4 "A" Packets.

A shelf is fitted behind the window and is made from an Oblong fitted at each end to a small Square. The door opens inward, and a Dinky Toy Customer is shown coming out of the shop. An air of activity is provided by other miniature figures and accessories from the Dinky Toy range.

CASTLE

No. 0 Outfit plus 8 "A" Packets.
No. 1 Outfit plus 7 "A" Packets.
No. 2 Outfit plus 2 "A" Packets

Large Squares and Oblongs are used for the main structure and an opening is left for the entrance. An Oblong forms the drawbridge, and is held up by two Triangles. Each of the towers is made from two Oblongs and four small Squares. The Poplar Trees add a finishing touch to the model.

BRIDGE

No. 0 Outfit plus 10 "A" Packets.
No. 1 Outfit plus 9 "A" Packets.
No. 2 Outfit plus 4 "A" Packets.

Meccano Dinky Toy Liners are shown passing under the bridge, and miniature Motor Vehicles can be made to travel to and fro along the roadway. Large Squares are used for the roadway and slopes, and Oblongs and small Squares form the towers.

CHAPEL

No. 0 Outfit plus 6 "A" Packets.
No. 1 Outfit plus 5 "A" Packets.
No. 2 Outfit

Large Squares are used for the lower portion of the building, and Oblongs form the roof of the main structure. The porch is made of four small Squares. The tree is from the No. 1 Outfit, and extra ones (obtainable separately) can be added to suggest natural surroundings.

SIX-WHEELED MOTOR LORRY

No. 0 Outfit plus 9 "A" Packets (and 4 wheels).
No. 1 Outfit plus 8 "A" Packets (and 2 wheels).
No. 2 Outfit plus 4 "A" Packets (and 2 wheels).

Details of the method of construction are shown in the underneath view of the model. The Rod for the rear Wheels is carried in two small Squares that are attached to Triangles and inserted in the floor of the Lorry, between an Oblong at each side, a small Square in front, and a large Square at the rear.

FACTORY

No. 0 Outfit plus 10 "A" Packets.
No. 1 Outfit plus 9 "A" Packets.
No. 2 Outfit plus 4 "A" Packets.

Squares are used for the walls and Oblongs for the roof, and the chimney is built up from Oblongs and small Squares. Dinky Toy Commercial Vehicles give a note of realism to the factory.

MOTOR LORRY

No. 0 Outfit plus 7 "A" Packets(and 2 wheels).
No. 1 Outfit plus 6 "A" Packets.
No. 2 Outfit plus 2 "A" Packets.

Four large and eight small Squares are used for the platform body, the sides of which are formed from Oblongs. Two Oblongs are fitted at the back of the cab. Miniature Loaded Sacks (Meccano Part No. 122) are used for the load.

Dinky Builder Outfits and Parts are manufactured by

MECCANO LTD., BINNS ROAD, LIVERPOOL 13, ENGLAND

13/735/40

Printed in England

DINKY BUILDER
Instructions for
No. O to No. 3 Outfits
Dinky Builder is one of the most fascinating building systems ever devised for the delight and pleasure of young children
COPYRIGHT BY MECCANO LTD. · BINNS ROAD · LIVERPOOL 13
13/1041/15
Eng-Univ.

DINKY BUILDER

Instructions

Dinky Builder plates are hinged on all sides, with intervening spaces, so that when two are placed side by side the hinged part of one plate fits into the corresponding space in the other. A rod can be pushed through the complete hinge, and in this manner any number of plates can be built up to form various geometrical shapes.

The simplest method of connecting a series of plates together to construct a model is first to lay out the necessary parts, hinges upward, on a flat surface, in the positions they will occupy in the completed model. (See Fig. 2.) The rods are then inserted, the special tool supplied with the Outfits being used to push them in. (See Fig. 1.)

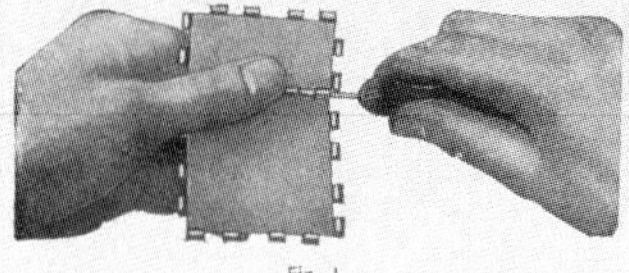
Fig. 1

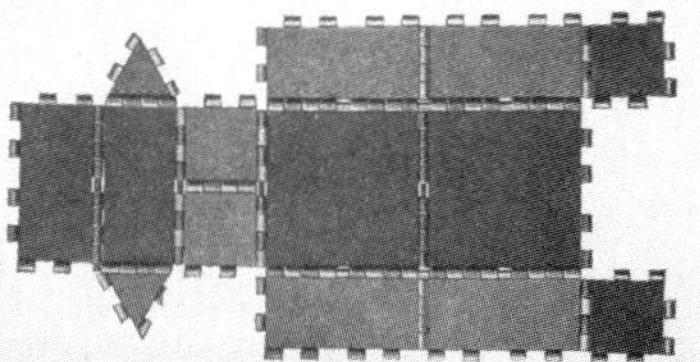
Fig. 2

Where a rod is inserted in the hinges of one plate only, it may occasionally be found that the rod is not gripped quite firmly enough to hold it in position. This may be easily adjusted by inserting the rod in the first hinge of the plate and gently bending this *very slightly* out of line with the other hinges (see Fig. 3). Then, when the rod is once more pushed through all the hinges, it will be held securely.

It is sometimes necessary to bring the hinges of two separate plates into line before the rod is inserted. In such cases the task of lining up will be greatly simplified by pushing the tool through the hinges so that they are brought into line, and then withdrawing it.

The tool must be used when disassembling the models. For this purpose it is pushed into the hinge forming the constructional connection, so that the rod is forced out. In this manner a model can be taken to pieces in a very short time.

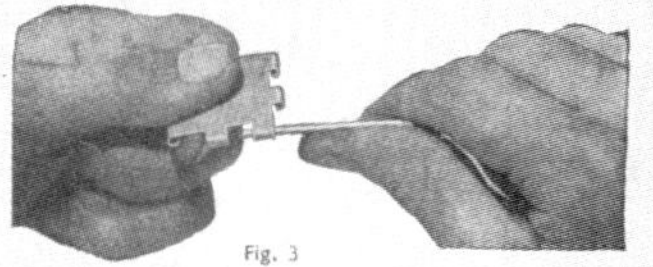
Fig. 3

PAGE TWO

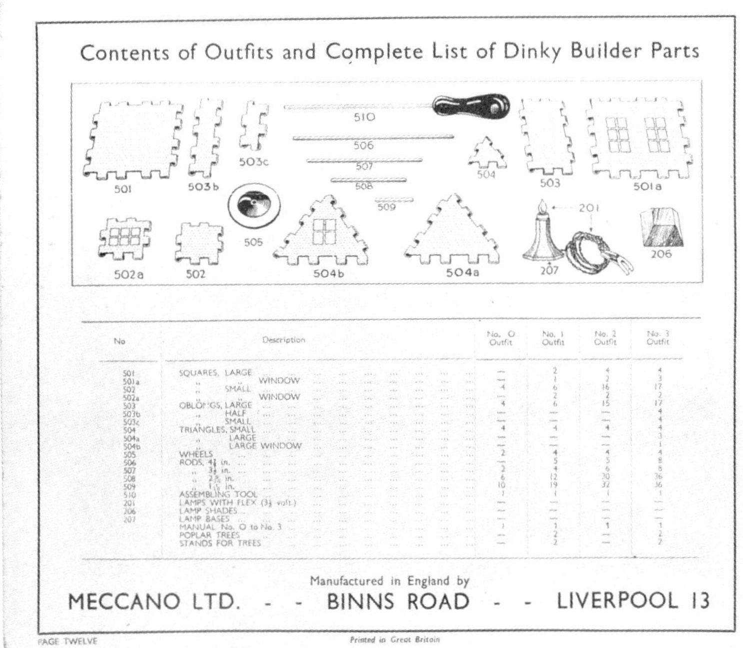
Contents of Outfits and Complete List of Dinky Builder Parts

No	Description	No. O Outfit	No. 1 Outfit	No. 2 Outfit	No. 3 Outfit
501	SQUARES, LARGE	—	2	4	4
501a	„ „ WINDOW	—	1	2	3
502	„ SMALL	4	6	16	17
502a	„ „ WINDOW	—	2	2	2
503	OBLONGS, LARGE	4	6	15	17
503b	„ HALF	—	—	—	4
503c	„ SMALL	—	—	—	4
504	TRIANGLES, SMALL	4	4	4	4
504a	„ LARGE	—	—	—	3
504b	„ LARGE WINDOW	—	—	—	1
505	WHEELS	2	4	4	4
506	RODS, 4½ in.	—	5	5	8
507	„ 3½ in.	2	4	6	8
508	„ [illegible] in.	6	12	30	36
509	„ [illegible] in.	10	19	32	36
510	ASSEMBLING TOOL	1	1	1	1
201	LAMPS WITH FLEX (3½ volt)	—	—	—	—
206	LAMP SHADES	—	—	—	—
207	LAMP BASES	—	—	—	—
	MANUAL No. O to No. 3	1	1	1	1
	POPLAR TREES	—	2	—	2
	STANDS FOR TREES	—	2	—	2

Manufactured in England by
MECCANO LTD. - - BINNS ROAD - - LIVERPOOL 13

PAGE TWELVE
Printed in Great Britain

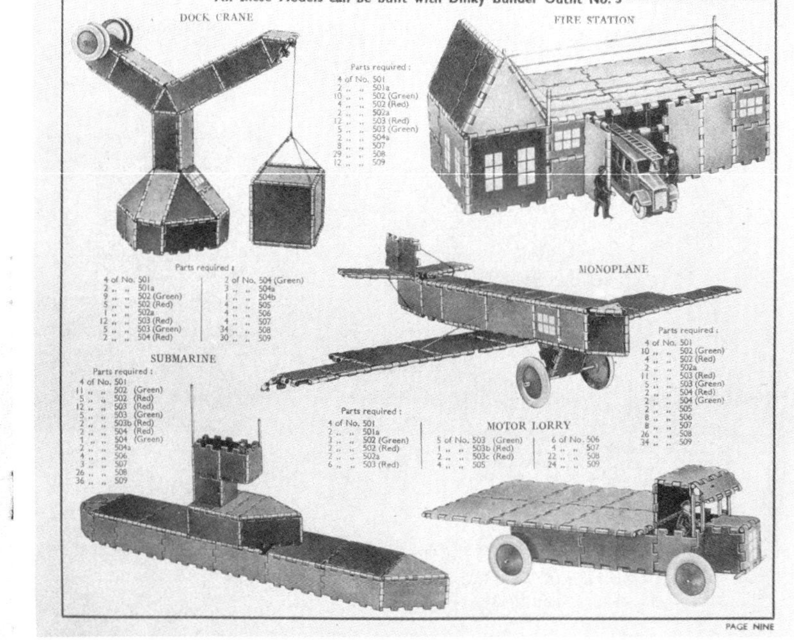

Figs 41–44. The 'Militarised' Dinky Builder of 1941.

←Fig 46.
An X series parts envelope.

Figs 47–48.
The X series No. 2 Outfit booklet and page of models.

Figs 49–50.
Similar pages from the British Model Builder No. 2 Outfit booklet for comparison. ↓

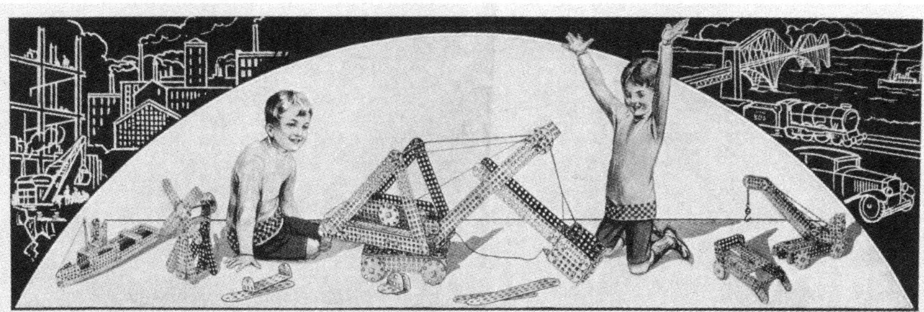

MECCANO

X SERIES OUTFIT No. 2

INSTRUCTIONS

The first step in constructing the models shown in this folder is to build the framework, afterwards tightening up the nuts and bolts.

Where Screwed Rods are used in addition to Double Angle Strips for spacing Strips apart, the latter should be secured first to ensure correct placing of the Rods. Any moving parts, such as wheel axles, etc., should next be fitted in position, and in arranging these care should be taken to leave a little play at the ends of the Rods to allow free movement.

The Discs are held on the Rods by a nut screwed up tightly on each side.

Pivoted joints are made by locking two nuts together on one bolt, so that the Strips, etc., are only held together loosely.

The greatest fun of all is to set your models to work by means of the Meccano X Clockwork Motor.

By adding more outfits you may build still larger and finer models and increase the interest of your hobby to an unlimited extent.

Meccano X parts may be used in conjunction with standard Meccano parts and accessories, thus opening up an entirely new field for model-building.

PRICE 1D.

Copyright by MECCANO LIMITED, LIVERPOOL, throughout the World.

7 532 65 (1P)

BRITISH MODEL BUILDER

OUTFIT No. 2

INSTRUCTIONS

The first step in constructing the models shown in this folder is to build the framework, afterwards tightening up the nuts and bolts.

Where Screwed Rods are used in addition to Double Angle Strips for spacing Strips apart, the latter should be secured first to ensure correct placing of the Rods. Any moving parts, such as wheel axles, etc., should next be fitted in position, and in arranging these, care should be taken to leave a little play at the ends of the Rods to allow free movement.

The Discs are held on the Rods by a nut screwed up tightly on each side.

Pivoted joints are made by locking two nuts together on one bolt, so that the Strips, etc., are only held together loosely.

By adding more Outfits you may build still larger and finer models and increase the interest of your hobby to an unlimited extent.

BRITISH MODEL BUILDER PARTS MAY BE USED IN CONJUNCTION WITH STANDARD MECCANO PARTS AND ACCESSORIES

13/634/3. Copyright

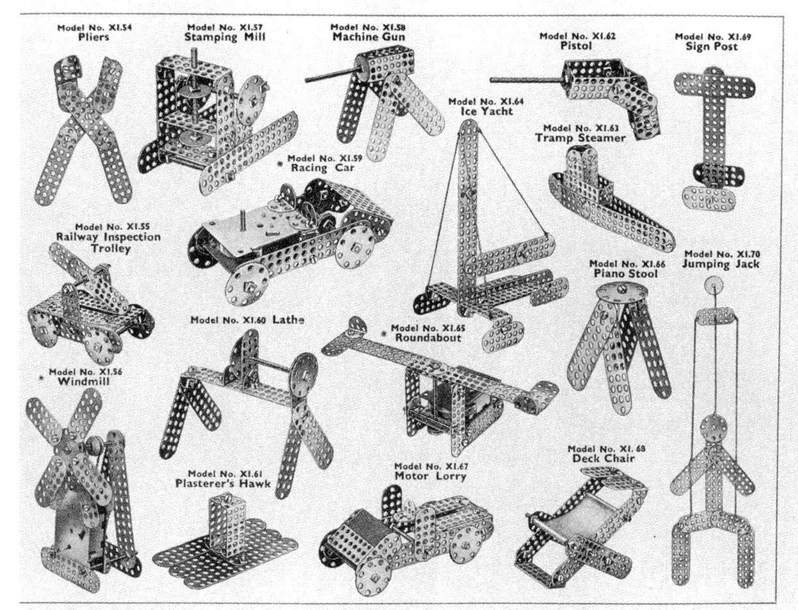

A Selection of Super Models made with British Model Builder parts
Mechanical Excavator
Monoplane
Tug Boat
KEEP ADDING TO YOUR OUTFIT
Boys, just look closely at the wonderful super models illustrated here. They are all made with British Model Builder parts and each one is a masterpiece. You will be keen to build fine models such as these, and you can do so by adding more Outfits, either No. 1 or No. 2, to the equipment you already possess. As your range of parts grows, so the model-building possibilities increase to a remarkable and unlimited extent. There is no fun to equal model-building with the British Model Builder.
Travelling Gantry Crane
Big Wheel
Planing Machine
Two-seater Car
Derrick Crane
Copyright
Printed in England

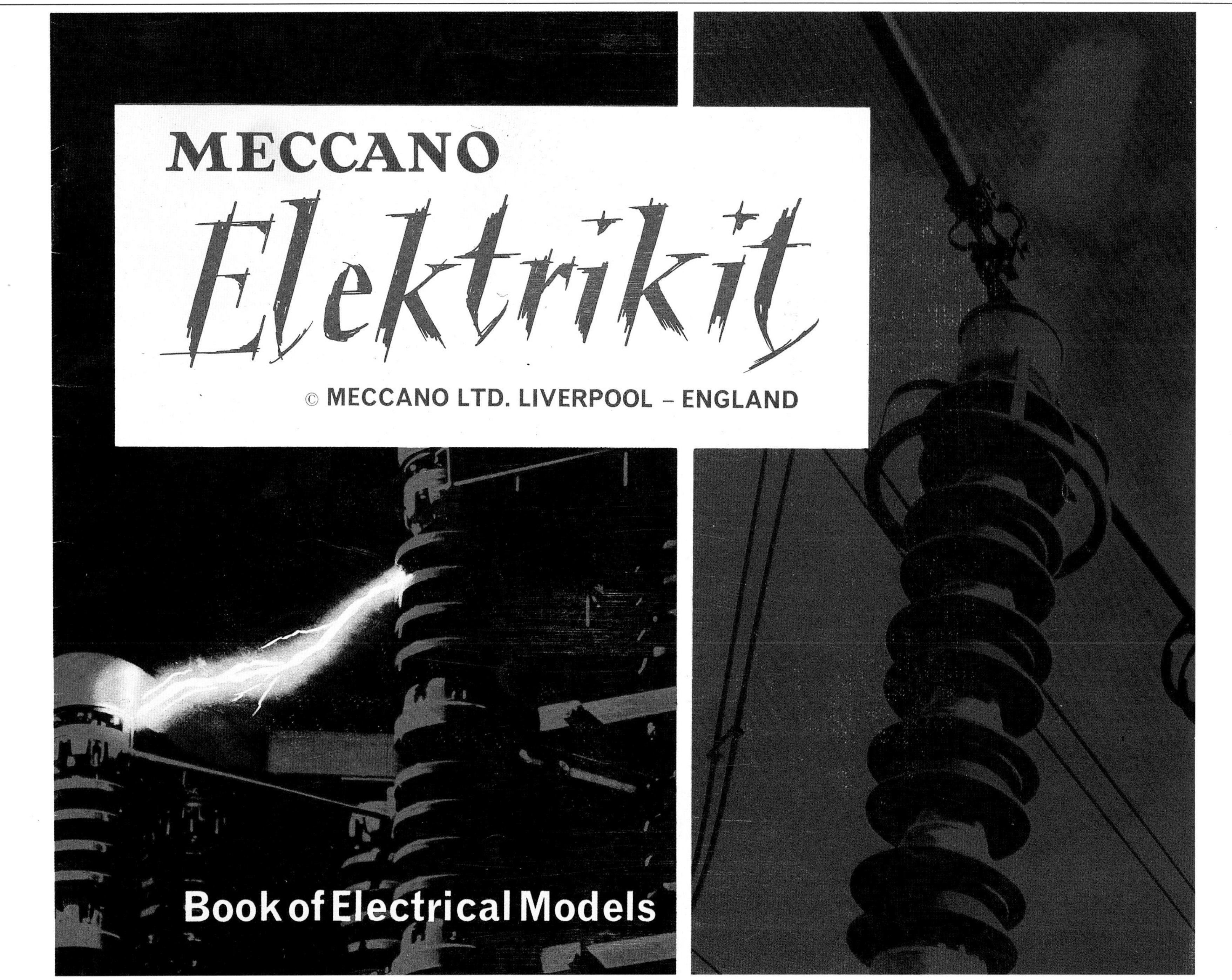

Fig 51. The Elektrikit Manual.

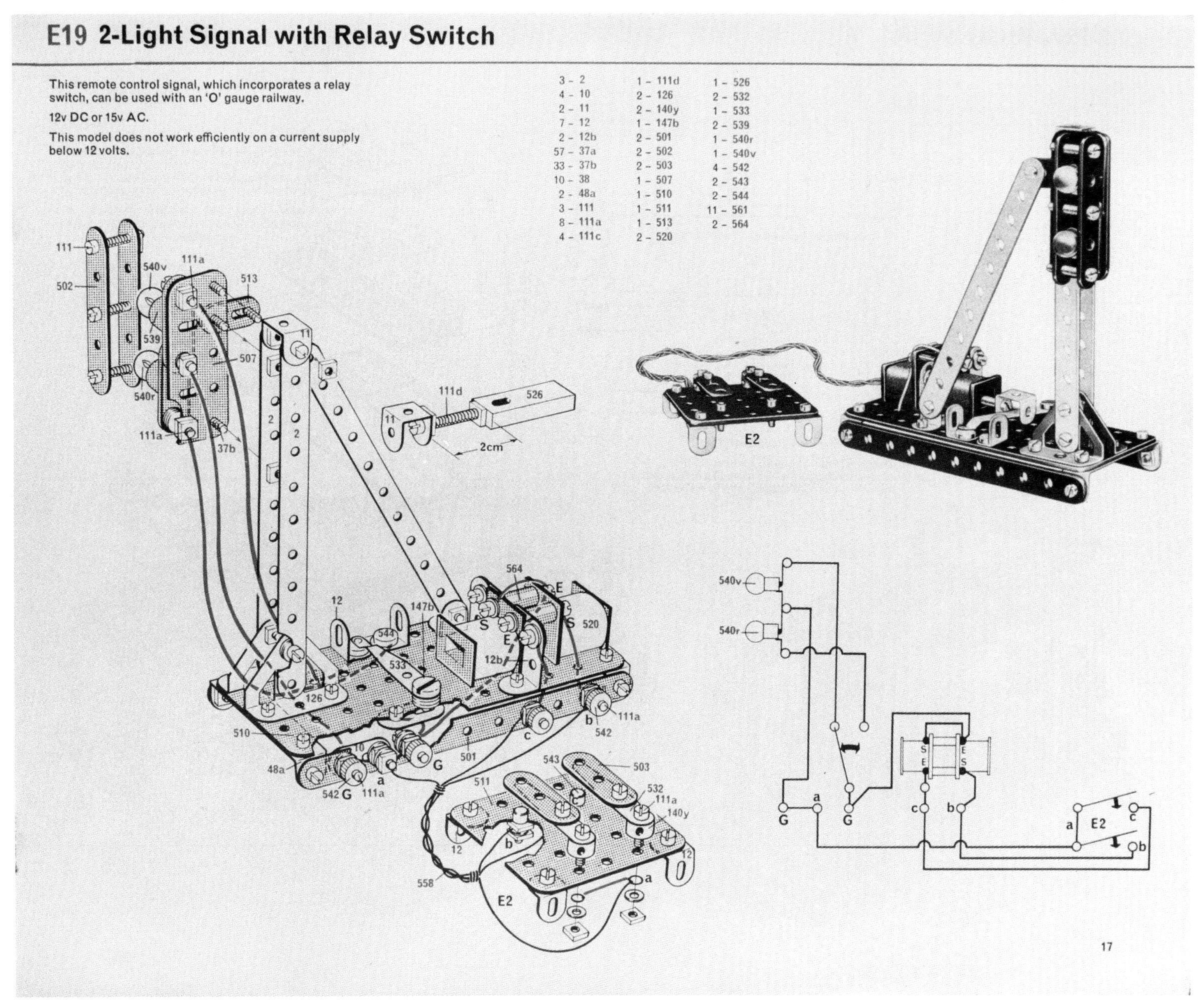

E19 2-Light Signal with Relay Switch

This remote control signal, which incorporates a relay switch, can be used with an 'O' gauge railway.

12v DC or 15v AC.

This model does not work efficiently on a current supply below 12 volts.

3 - 2	1 - 111d	1 - 526
4 - 10	2 - 126	2 - 532
2 - 11	2 - 140y	1 - 533
7 - 12	1 - 147b	2 - 539
2 - 12b	2 - 501	1 - 540r
57 - 37a	2 - 502	1 - 540v
33 - 37b	2 - 503	4 - 542
10 - 38	1 - 507	2 - 543
2 - 48a	1 - 510	2 - 544
3 - 111	1 - 511	11 - 561
8 - 111a	1 - 513	2 - 564
4 - 111c	2 - 520	

17

Figs 52–54. Three models from the Elektrikit Manual. Compare these with those from the 1920s Electrical Outfit Manual (Figs 23–26).

E34 Complete Morse Telegraph

In order to build this complete two-way telegraph system extra parts are required as detailed on page 2 of cover. Only two wires are required to connect the two telegraph posts and one of these can be connected through the domestic water pipes or some similar earth.

4·5v battery.

6–15v AC or DC.

R and **R2.** Same as in model E33.

Follow the wiring diagrams carefully when wiring up the models and make sure that the battery is connected the right way round.

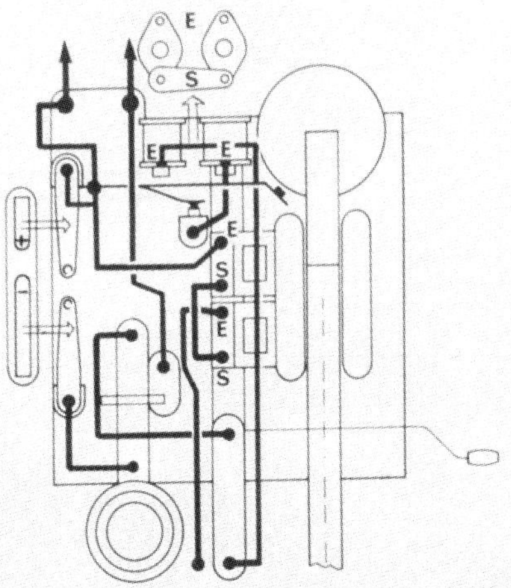

3 – 2	1 – 52	1 – 510	2 – 531
8 – 5	1 – 59	1 – 513	2 – 532
2 – 10	1 – 111	1 – 514	1 – 533
2 – 11	3 – 111a	1 – 516	2 – 534
11 – 12	9 – 111c	2 – 520	4 – 542
2 – 12b	1 – 111d	2 – 522	2 – 543
2 – 12c	1 – 115	4 – 525	5 – 544
1 – 17	1 – 120b	2 – 526	1 – 559
1 – 18a	2 – 126	1 – 527	10 – 561
1 – 18b	2 – 126a	2 – 528	1 – 562
1 – 19g	2 – 140y	2 – 529	1 – 563
1 – 22	1 – 147b	2 – 530	2 – 564
1 – 22a	2 – 155		
1 – 24	1 – 188		
2 – 35	1 – 213		
102 – 37a	1 – 214		
77 – 37b	2 – 502		
44 – 38	2 – 503		
1 – 38d	1 – 507		
2 – 48a	1 – 508		

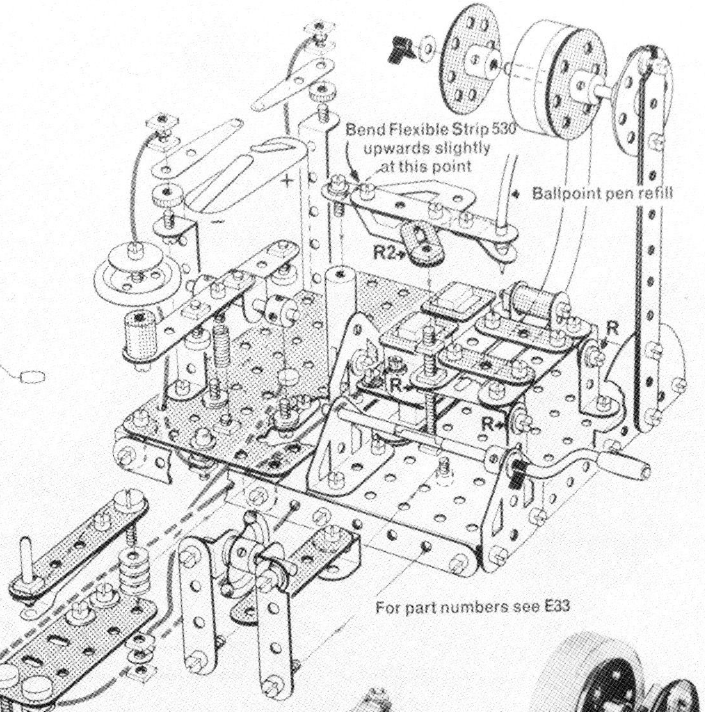

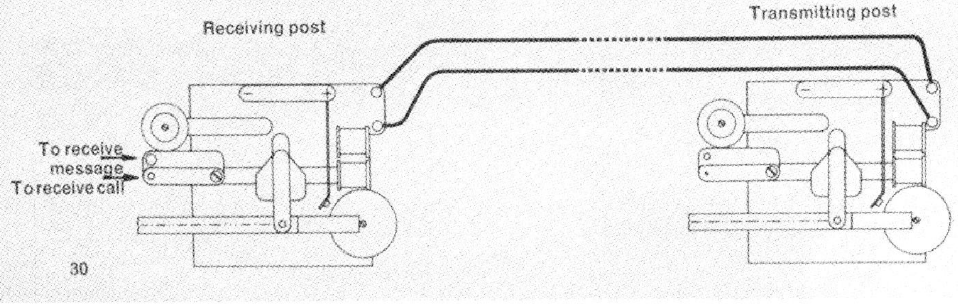

Bend Flexible Strip 530 upwards slightly at this point

Ballpoint pen refill

For part numbers see E33

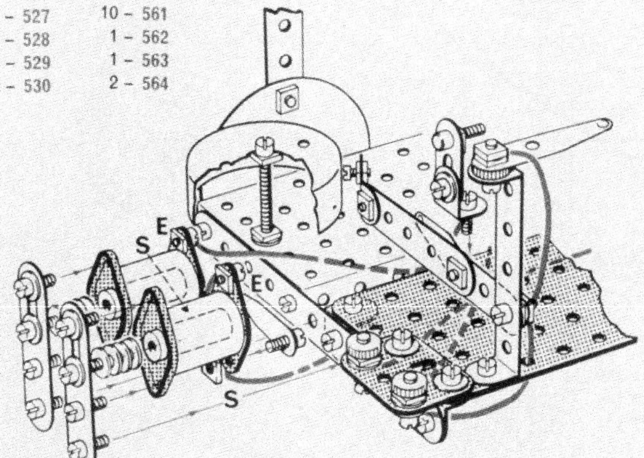

Receiving post

Transmitting post

To receive message

To receive call

30

Fig 53.

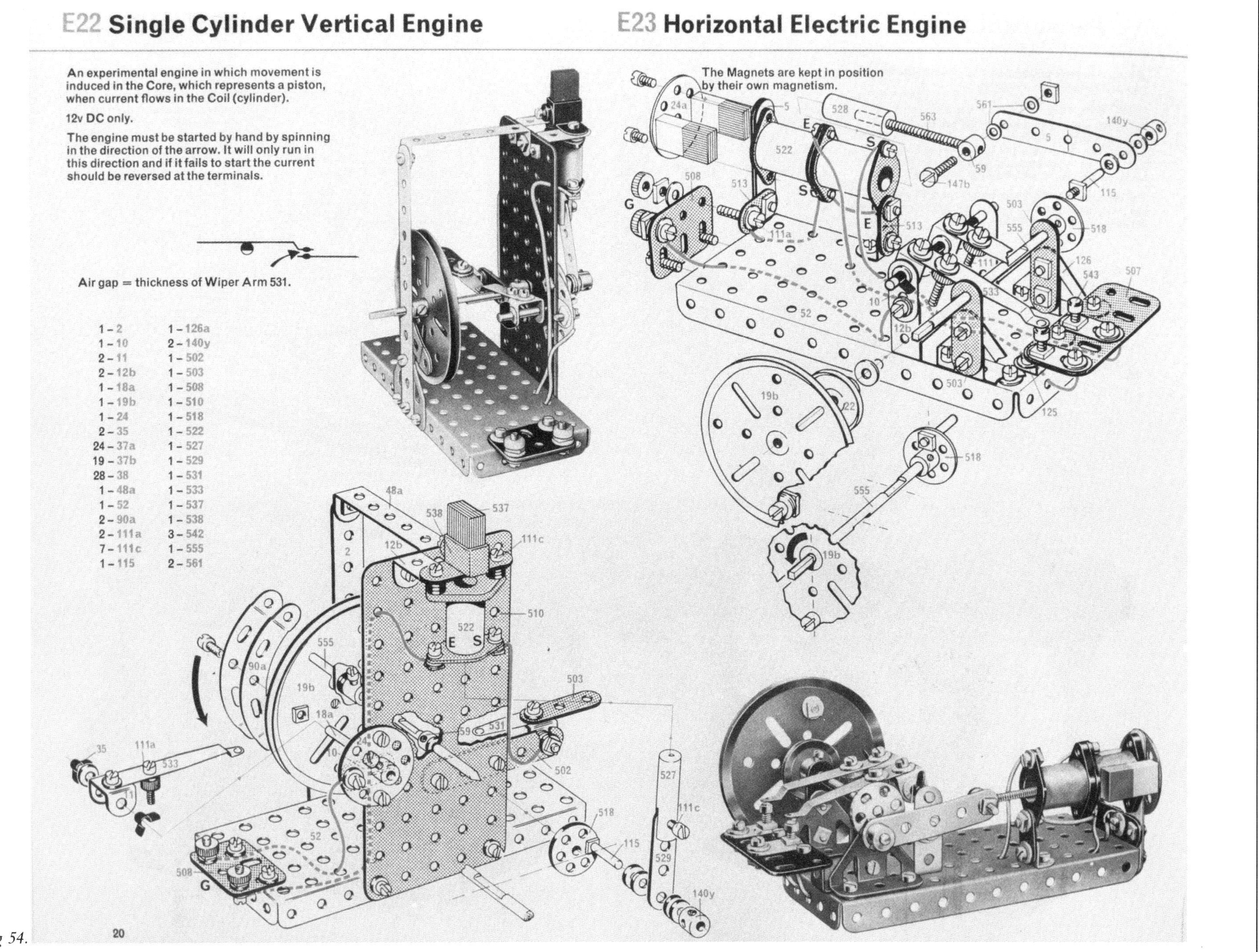

E22 Single Cylinder Vertical Engine

An experimental engine in which movement is induced in the Core, which represents a piston, when current flows in the Coil (cylinder).

12v DC only.

The engine must be started by hand by spinning in the direction of the arrow. It will only run in this direction and if it fails to start the current should be reversed at the terminals.

Air gap = thickness of Wiper Arm 531.

1 - 2	1 - 126a
1 - 10	2 - 140y
2 - 11	1 - 502
2 - 12b	1 - 503
1 - 18a	1 - 508
1 - 19b	1 - 510
1 - 24	1 - 518
2 - 35	1 - 522
24 - 37a	1 - 527
19 - 37b	1 - 529
28 - 38	1 - 531
1 - 48a	1 - 533
1 - 52	1 - 537
2 - 90a	1 - 538
2 - 111a	3 - 542
7 - 111c	1 - 555
1 - 115	2 - 561

E23 Horizontal Electric Engine

The Magnets are kept in position by their own magnetism.

20

Fig 54.

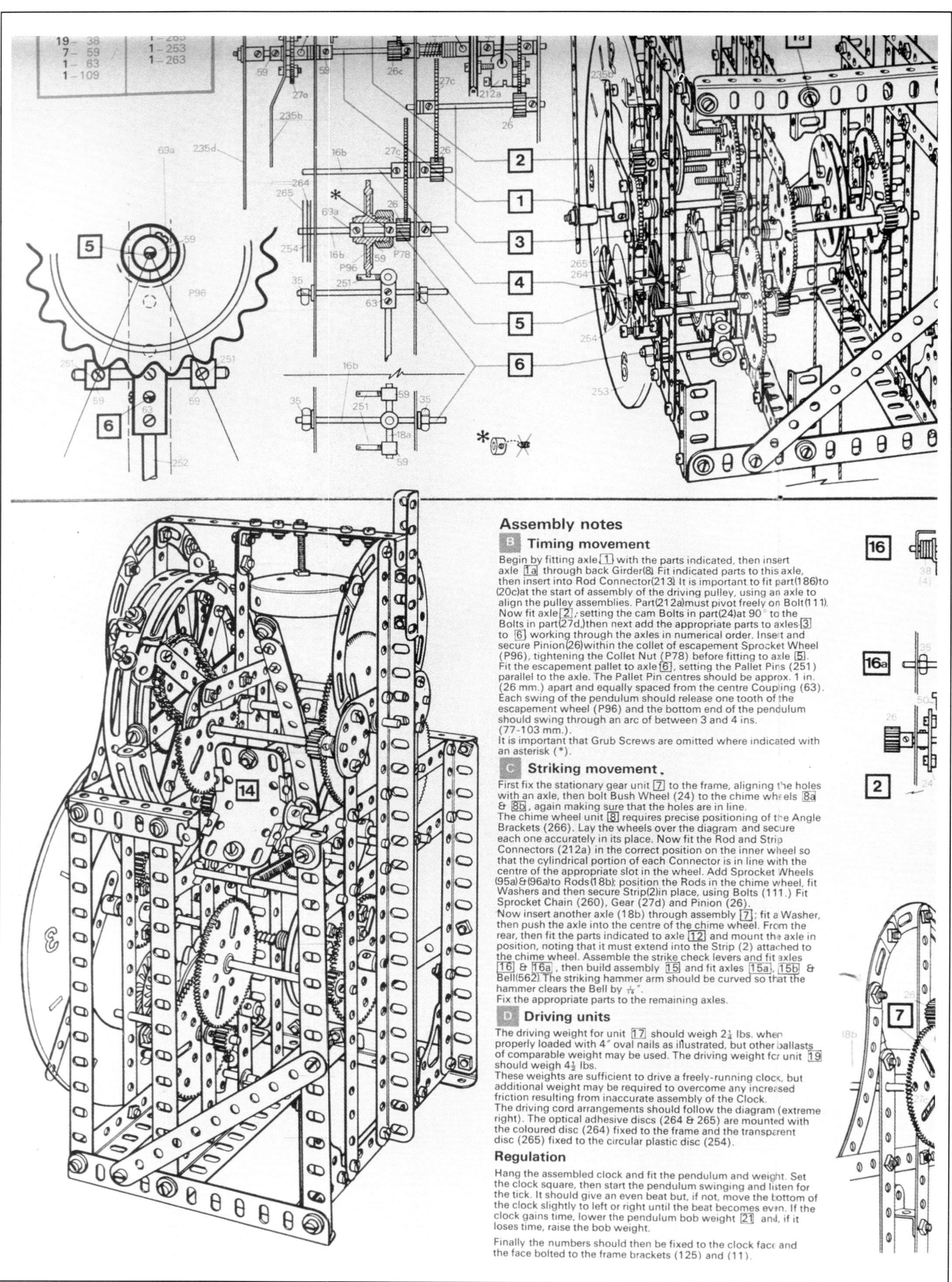

Assembly notes

B Timing movement

Begin by fitting axle [1] with the parts indicated, then insert axle [1a] through back Girder(8). Fit indicated parts to this axle, then insert into Rod Connector(213). It is important to fit part(186)to (20c)at the start of assembly of the driving pulley, using an axle to align the pulley assemblies. Part(212a)must pivot freely on Bolt(111). Now fit axle [2]; setting the cam Bolts in part(24)at 90° to the Bolts in part(27d,)then next add the appropriate parts to axles [3] to [6], working through the axles in numerical order. Insert and secure Pinion(26)within the collet of escapement Sprocket Wheel (P96), tightening the Collet Nut (P78) before fitting to axle [5]. Fit the escapement pallet to axle [6], setting the Pallet Pins (251) parallel to the axle. The Pallet Pin centres should be approx. 1 in. (26 mm.) apart and equally spaced from the centre Coupling (63). Each swing of the pendulum should release one tooth of the escapement wheel (P96) and the bottom end of the pendulum should swing through an arc of between 3 and 4 ins. (77-103 mm.).
It is important that Grub Screws are omitted where indicated with an asterisk (*).

C Striking movement.

First fix the stationary gear unit [7] to the frame, aligning the holes with an axle, then bolt Bush Wheel (24) to the chime wheels [8a] & [8b], again making sure that the holes are in line.
The chime wheel unit [8] requires precise positioning of the Angle Brackets (266). Lay the wheels over the diagram and secure each one accurately in its place. Now fit the Rod and Strip Connectors (212a) in the correct position on the inner wheel so that the cylindrical portion of each Connector is in line with the centre of the appropriate slot in the wheel. Add Sprocket Wheels (95a)&(96a)to Rods(18b); position the Rods in the chime wheel, fit Washers and then secure Strip(2)in place, using Bolts (111.) Fit Sprocket Chain (260), Gear (27d) and Pinion (26).
Now insert another axle (18b) through assembly [7]; fit a Washer, then push the axle into the centre of the chime wheel. From the rear, then fit the parts indicated to axle [12] and mount the axle in position, noting that it must extend into the Strip (2) attached to the chime wheel. Assemble the strike check levers and fit axles [16] & [16a], then build assembly [15] and fit axles [15a], [15b] & Bell(562). The striking hammer arm should be curved so that the hammer clears the Bell by $\frac{1}{16}$".
Fix the appropriate parts to the remaining axles.

D Driving units

The driving weight for unit [17] should weigh $2\frac{1}{4}$ lbs. when properly loaded with 4" oval nails as illustrated, but other ballasts of comparable weight may be used. The driving weight for unit [19] should weigh $4\frac{1}{2}$ lbs.
These weights are sufficient to drive a freely-running clock, but additional weight may be required to overcome any increased friction resulting from inaccurate assembly of the Clock.
The driving cord arrangements should follow the diagram (extreme right). The optical adhesive discs (264 & 265) are mounted with the coloured disc (264) fixed to the frame and the transparent disc (265) fixed to the circular plastic disc (254).

Regulation

Hang the assembled clock and fit the pendulum and weight. Set the clock square, then start the pendulum swinging and listen for the tick. It should give an even beat but, if not, move the bottom of the clock slightly to left or right until the beat becomes even. If the clock gains time, lower the pendulum bob weight [21] and, if it loses time, raise the bob weight.

Finally the numbers should then be fixed to the clock face and the face bolted to the frame brackets (125) and (11).

Fig 55.

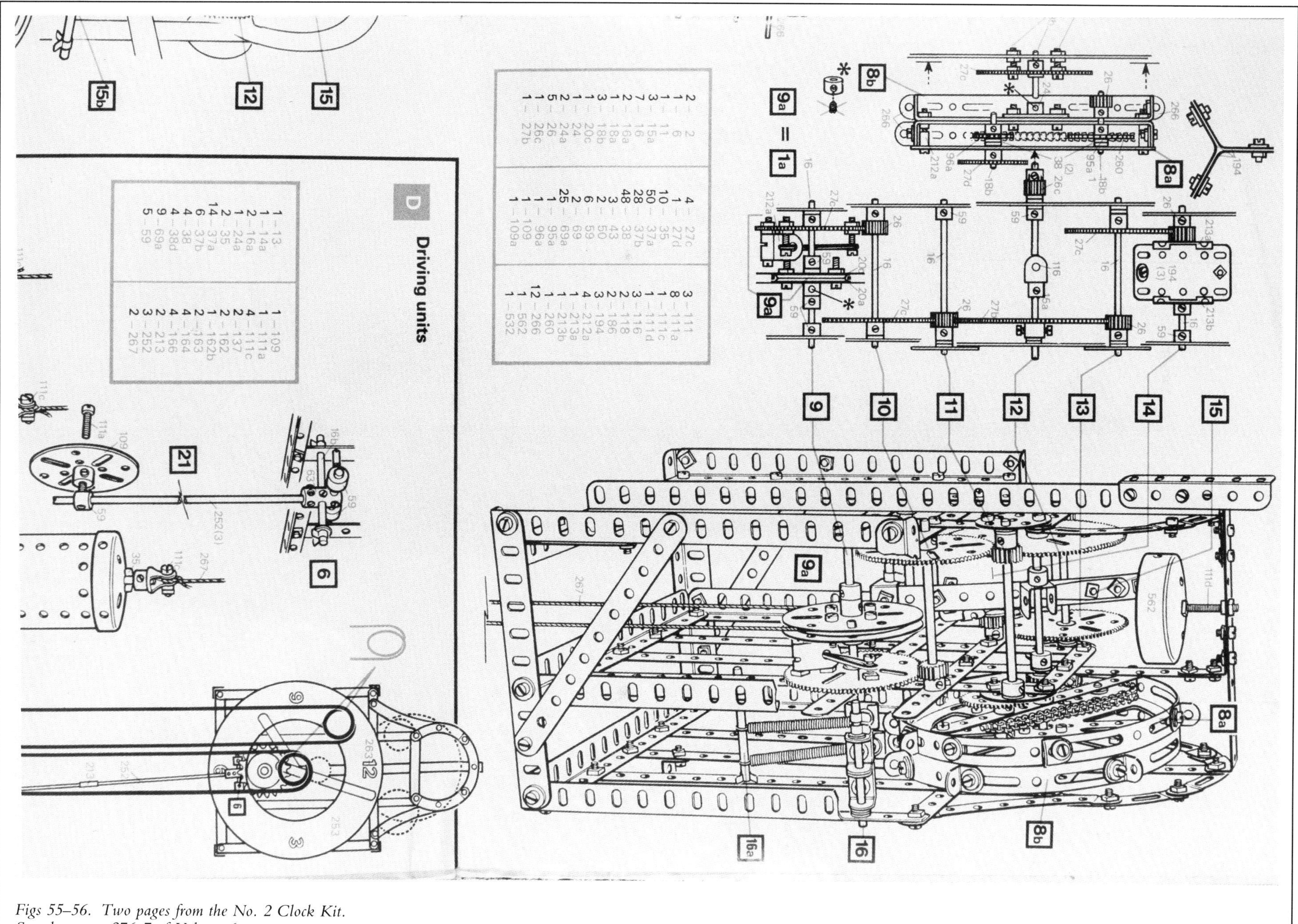

Figs 55–56. Two pages from the No. 2 Clock Kit.
See also pages 276–7 of Volume 6.

The Special and Super Model Leaflets

Origins

In the beginning and for quite a number of years, Meccano models were very simple and needed few if any written instructions. Indeed, many of even the largest in the pre-1920 models only needed one or perhaps two illustrations to enable the model to be built. A good example is the Funicular Railway (fig 1) which is quite a large model but needing little in the way of instructions.

Matters had begun to change in 1915 with the advent of the Gordon Crosby Motor Chassis and a year later the Meccanograph. In reality, the Meccanograph was not a complicated model but nevertheless it was accorded its own operating instructions which described in detail the way in which the various designs could be achieved, although the bulk of the space was devoted to completed patterns. The manual was therefore something of an extravagance.

The Gordon Crosby Motor Chassis was very different. It was originally designed as an entry for the 1914/5 Prize Model Building Competition which it proceeded to win. Its success was such that it was subsequently featured in the magazine *The Light Car*. It was this article in reprinted form which became what was in effect the first separate model building leaflet. (fig 2)

Strictly speaking it was not a model leaflet at all and would appear originally to have been more for publicity purposes than to enable reproduction of the model. There is, however, sufficient detail in both text and photographs to allow the chassis to be constructed without too much trouble.

Although simple by today's standards, the Gordon Crosby model marked an important stage in Meccano modelling. Compared with contemporary efforts it was revolutionary; which other model of the day could boast such features as a working clutch, two speed gearbox, semi-elliptic leaf springs and pedal operated brakes?

It is difficult to be sure of this leaflet's currency because so far all copies seen lack printing references. It was illustrated in manuals for at least five years and probably only became obsolete when Meccano Ltd's own Motor Chassis appeared. Distribution must have been encouraging because six years after it came into being, a more advanced Motor Chassis became the first subject in a series of Special Model Leaflets. Although this latter title was not official, it usefully differentiates between them and the 1928 series of Super Model Leaflets and the title will be used from hereonafter.

In the instruction manuals of 1921 two new models were featured, The Meccano Motor Chassis and The Meccano Loom. Both were considerably more advanced than previous versions and bore

continued p. 88.

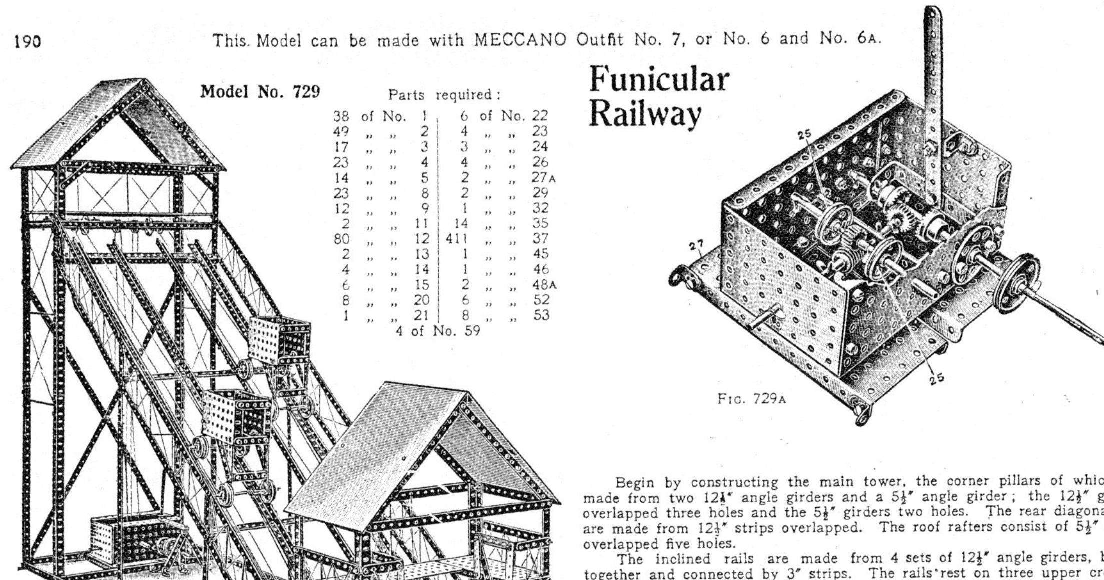

190 This Model can be made with MECCANO Outfit No. 7, or No. 6 and No. 6A.

Model No. 729

Funicular Railway

Parts required:

38 of No.	1	6 of No.	22
49 „ „	2	4 „ „	23
17 „ „	3	3 „ „	24
23 „ „	4	4 „ „	26
14 „ „	5	2 „ „	27A
23 „ „	8	2 „ „	29
12 „ „	9	1 „ „	32
2 „ „	11	14 „ „	35
80 „ „	12	411 „ „	37
2 „ „	13	1 „ „	45
4 „ „	14	1 „ „	46
6 „ „	15	2 „ „	48A
8 „ „	20	6 „ „	52
1 „ „	21	8 „ „	53

4 of No. 59

Fig. 729A

Begin by constructing the main tower, the corner pillars of which are made from two 12½" angle girders and a 5½" angle girder; the 12½" girders overlapped three holes and the 5½" girders two holes. The rear diagonal ties are made from 12½" strips overlapped. The roof rafters consist of 5½" strips overlapped five holes.

The inclined rails are made from 4 sets of 12½" angle girders, butted together and connected by 3" strips. The rails rest on three upper crossing 12½" angle girders, and a lower 12½" strip to the ends of which are bolted the latticed side rails supported by the vertical members. The loading platform is built up from 5½" girder strips to which are bolted side flanged plates which are again connected by two small flanged plates. The other constructional details of this loading tower should present no trouble.

The main tower, inclined rails, and loading platform are now coupled together by a series of horizontal 12½" strips overlapped as shown.

The wagons are made as follows: Two small flanged plates are connected top and bottom by 2½" strips. The journals for the front axle are made by two 3½" strips bolted inside the flanged plates, the axle being threaded through their lower projecting holes. The rear axle journals are made by carrying down two 3½" strips bolted in their upper holes to the flanged plates, and braced with the diagonal strips to the sides of the wagon. The axle is again threaded through the lowest holes. One end of the operating cord as shown in this view is secured to this rear axle; the other end, after passing round the pulleys is secured to the front axle. The gear box for operating the main hauling shaft is very fully shown in Fig. 729A, the operating cords from the pulleys 25 passing round the pulleys in the upper gear platform.

The Gear Box is mounted on two perforated plates 27, the angle brackets on which are bolted to the transverse strips at the base of the tower.

Fig 1. An example of a large but very simple model from the pre-1920 model range.

A Chassis built with Meccano

The following consists mainly of extracts which the Editor of "The Light Car" has courteously permitted us to make from an article appearing in the issue of July 7th, 1915

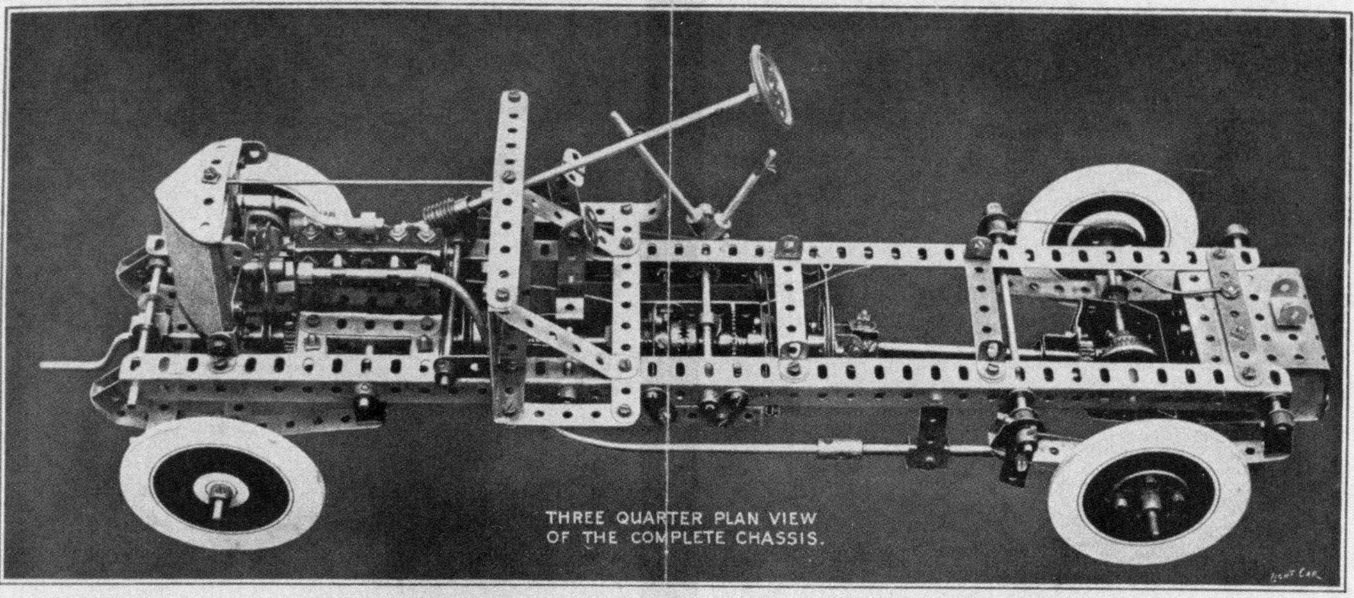

ABOUT six months ago, the makers of that instructive and interesting mechanical toy, Meccano, promoted a competition and offered £200 worth of prizes for the most ingenious mechanism constructed from Meccano parts. The regulations were that any number of these parts could be used in the construction of the mechanism submitted, but no outside assistance in the way of parts or material was to be employed. The lists closed last March, and the results have just been announced.

This interesting and very ingenious motor-car model, which has been awarded a divided second prize in the recent Meccano Competition, was designed and constructed entirely from Meccano parts by Mr. Gordon Crosby, of Leamington Spa. About 10,000 competitors submitted work from all over the world, and it is interesting to note that one of the prize-winners was M. Léon Bollée, the well-known motor-car manufacturer, of Paris, who sent in a model of a motor-car.

For the benefit of those readers who are not acquainted with Meccano parts, it is advisable to point out that each Meccano outfit comprises a number of flat and angular steel strips perforated with $\frac{3}{16}$in. holes at intervals of half an inch, $\frac{3}{16}$in. steel rods of varying lengths, small angle brackets, nuts, bolts,

The next item in the transmission is the clutch, which is built up of two disc-wheels—a bush wheel and a flanged-and-grooved wheel—and actuated by a pedal and clutch fork against the pressure of a small coil spring.

The change-speed gear is undoubtedly the most ingenious part of the model. It comprises two speeds of high and low-gear ratios, built into a frame which is bolted to the main frame. The high gear is a direct drive through "dog clutches" arranged by bringing into mesh two small contrate wheels, the teeth of the wheels forming the dogs. The change of speed is actuated by a cross-shaft connected to the change-speed lever, the sliding wheel being operated by a striking-fork cleverly constructed from a flat bracket attached to a collar which can be seen in the centre of the cross-shaft. The bracket is slotted, and the slot is made use of to encircle the gearshaft. When the change-speed lever is pushed over, away from the operator, the two dog clutches are thrown out of mesh, and the movement simultaneously brings the sliding gear wheel into mesh with the low-gear pinion carried on the layshaft. The drive is transmitted to the layshaft by means of a pinion on the main shaft with which a gear-wheel on the layshaft is in constant mesh.

Fig 2. The revolutionary 1915 Gordon Crosby motor chassis.

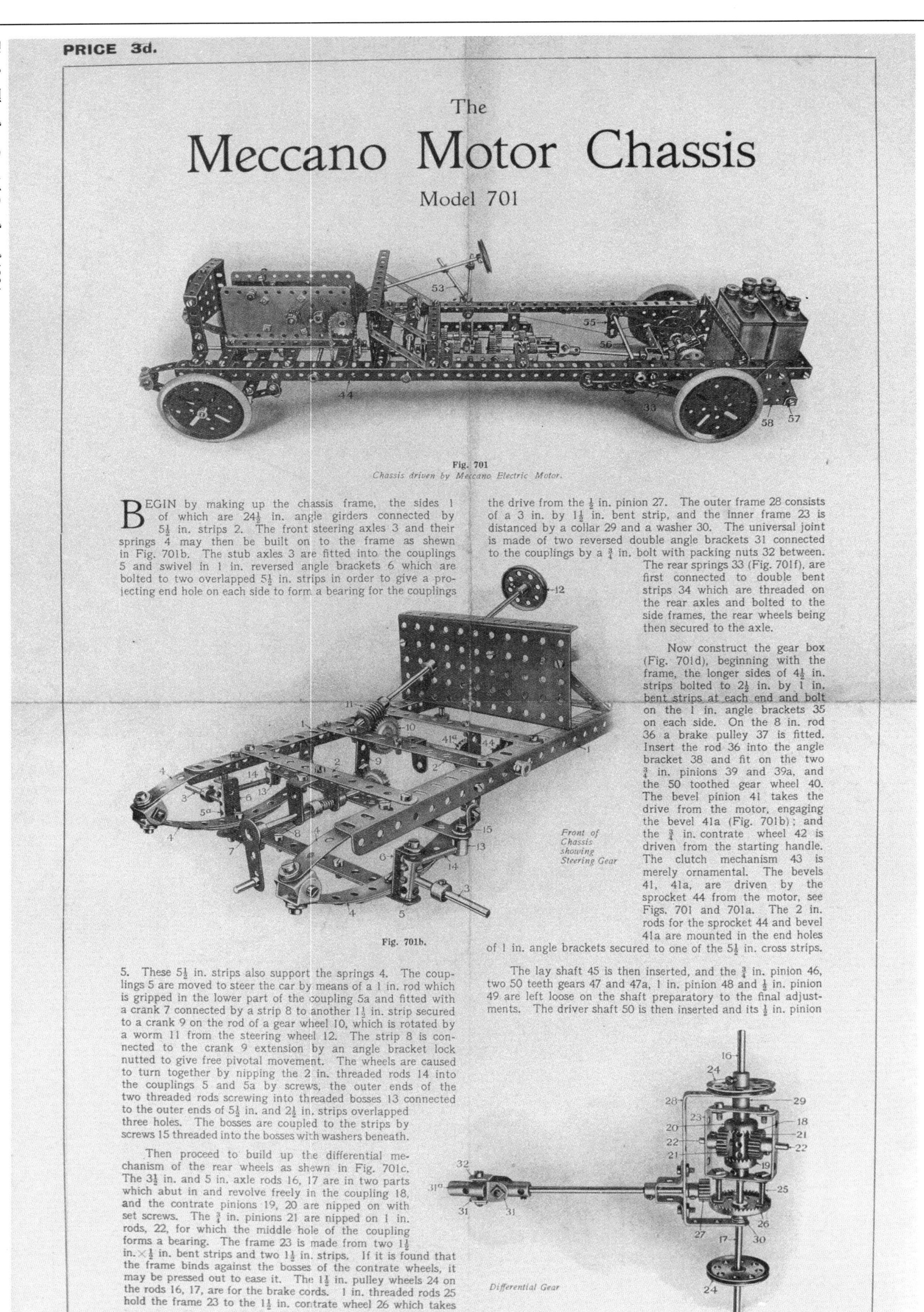

PRICE 3d.

The Meccano Motor Chassis

Model 701

Fig. 701
Chassis driven by Meccano Electric Motor.

BEGIN by making up the chassis frame, the sides 1 of which are $24\frac{1}{2}$ in. angle girders connected by $5\frac{1}{2}$ in. strips 2. The front steering axles 3 and their springs 4 may then be built on to the frame as shewn in Fig. 701b. The stub axles 3 are fitted into the couplings 5 and swivel in 1 in. reversed angle brackets 6 which are bolted to two overlapped $5\frac{1}{2}$ in. strips in order to give a projecting end hole on each side to form a bearing for the couplings 5. These $5\frac{1}{2}$ in. strips also support the springs 4. The couplings 5 are moved to steer the car by means of a 1 in. rod which is gripped in the lower part of the coupling 5a and fitted with a crank 7 connected by a strip 8 to another $1\frac{1}{2}$ in. strip secured to a crank 9 on the rod of a gear wheel 10, which is rotated by a worm 11 from the steering wheel 12. The strip 8 is connected to the crank 9 extension by an angle bracket lock nutted to give free pivotal movement. The wheels are caused to turn together by nipping the 2 in. threaded rods 14 into the couplings 5 and 5a by screws, the outer ends of the two threaded rods screwing into threaded bosses 13 connected to the outer ends of $5\frac{1}{2}$ in. and $2\frac{1}{2}$ in. strips overlapped three holes. The bosses are coupled to the strips by screws 15 threaded into the bosses with washers beneath.

Front of Chassis showing Steering Gear

Fig. 701b.

Then proceed to build up the differential mechanism of the rear wheels as shewn in Fig. 701c. The $3\frac{1}{2}$ in. and 5 in. axle rods 16, 17 are in two parts which abut in and revolve freely in the coupling 18, and the contrate pinions 19, 20 are nipped on with set screws. The $\frac{3}{4}$ in. pinions 21 are nipped on 1 in. rods, 22, for which the middle hole of the coupling forms a bearing. The frame 23 is made from two $1\frac{1}{2}$ in. $\times \frac{1}{2}$ in. bent strips and two $1\frac{1}{2}$ in. strips. If it is found that the frame binds against the bosses of the contrate wheels, it may be pressed out to ease it. The $1\frac{1}{2}$ in. pulley wheels 24 on the rods 16, 17, are for the brake cords. 1 in. threaded rods 25 hold the frame 23 to the $1\frac{1}{2}$ in. contrate wheel 26 which takes the drive from the $\frac{1}{2}$ in. pinion 27. The outer frame 28 consists of a 3 in. by $1\frac{1}{2}$ in. bent strip, and the inner frame 23 is distanced by a collar 29 and a washer 30. The universal joint is made of two reversed double angle brackets 31 connected to the couplings by a $\frac{3}{4}$ in. bolt with packing nuts 32 between. The rear springs 33 (Fig. 701f), are first connected to double bent strips 34 which are threaded on the rear axles and bolted to the side frames, the rear wheels being then secured to the axle.

Now construct the gear box (Fig. 701d), beginning with the frame, the longer sides of $4\frac{1}{2}$ in. strips bolted to $2\frac{1}{2}$ in. by 1 in. bent strips at each end and bolt on the 1 in. angle brackets 35 on each side. On the 8 in. rod 36 a brake pulley 37 is fitted. Insert the rod 36 into the angle bracket 38 and fit on the two $\frac{3}{4}$ in. pinions 39 and 39a, and the 50 toothed gear wheel 40. The bevel pinion 41 takes the drive from the motor, engaging the bevel 41a (Fig. 701b); and the $\frac{3}{4}$ in. contrate wheel 42 is driven from the starting handle. The clutch mechanism 43 is merely ornamental. The bevels 41, 41a, are driven by the sprocket 44 from the motor, see Figs. 701 and 701a. The 2 in. rods for the sprocket 44 and bevel 41a are mounted in the end holes of 1 in. angle brackets secured to one of the $5\frac{1}{2}$ in. cross strips.

The lay shaft 45 is then inserted, and the $\frac{3}{4}$ in. pinion 46, two 50 teeth gears 47 and 47a, 1 in. pinion 48 and $\frac{1}{2}$ in. pinion 49 are left loose on the shaft preparatory to the final adjustments. The driver shaft 50 is then inserted and its $\frac{1}{2}$ in. pinion

Differential Gear

Fig 3. The first Special Leaflet of 1921.

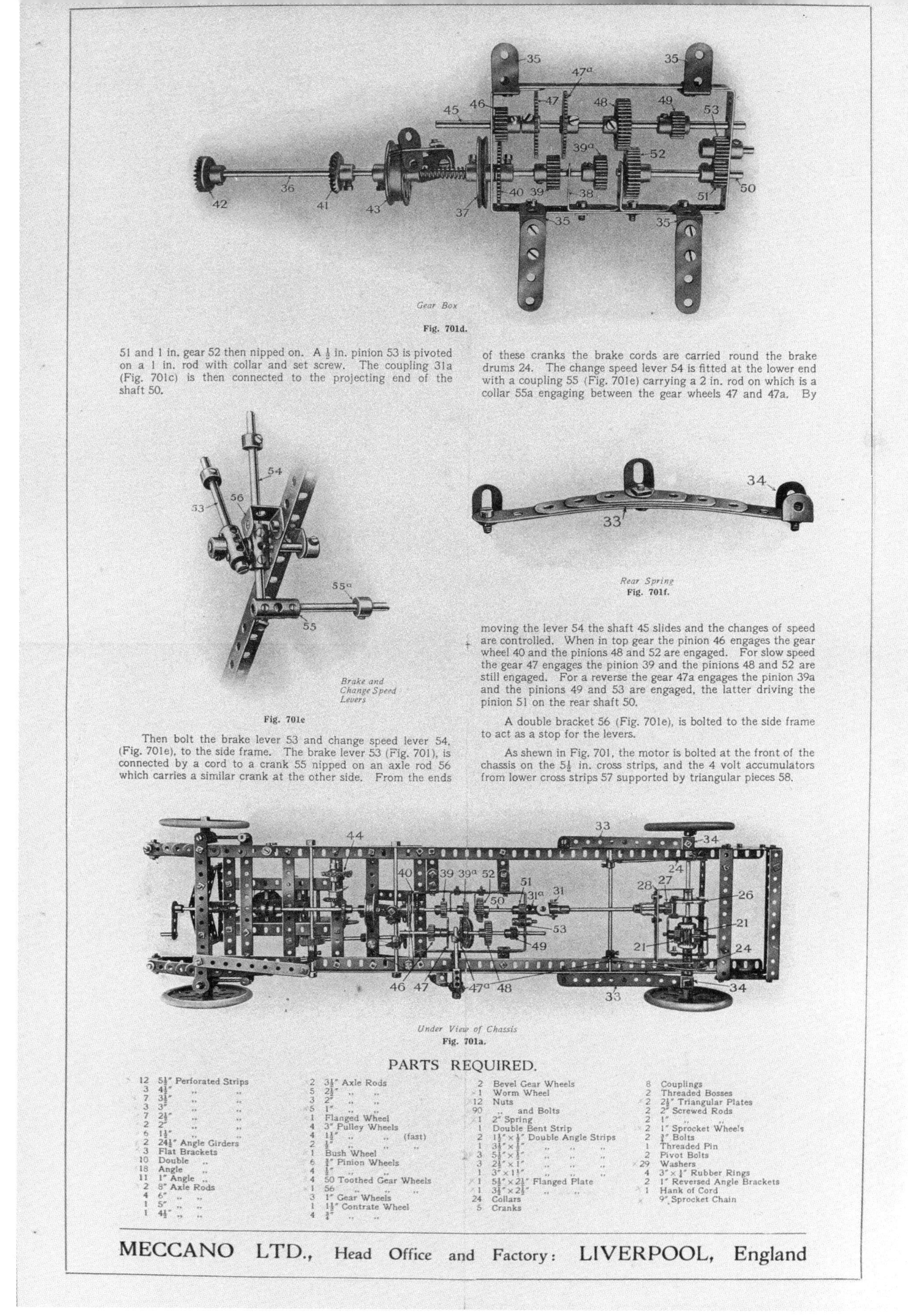

Gear Box

Fig. 701d.

51 and 1 in. gear 52 then nipped on. A ½ in. pinion 53 is pivoted on a 1 in. rod with collar and set screw. The coupling 31a (Fig. 701c) is then connected to the projecting end of the shaft 50.

of these cranks the brake cords are carried round the brake drums 24. The change speed lever 54 is fitted at the lower end with a coupling 55 (Fig. 701e) carrying a 2 in. rod on which is a collar 55a engaging between the gear wheels 47 and 47a. By

Brake and Change Speed Levers

Fig. 701e

Rear Spring

Fig. 701f.

moving the lever 54 the shaft 45 slides and the changes of speed are controlled. When in top gear the pinion 46 engages the gear wheel 40 and the pinions 48 and 52 are engaged. For slow speed the gear 47 engages the pinion 39 and the pinions 48 and 52 are still engaged. For a reverse the gear 47a engages the pinion 39a and the pinions 49 and 53 are engaged, the latter driving the pinion 51 on the rear shaft 50.

Then bolt the brake lever 53 and change speed lever 54, (Fig. 701e), to the side frame. The brake lever 53 (Fig. 701), is connected by a cord to a crank 55 nipped on an axle rod 56 which carries a similar crank at the other side. From the ends

A double bracket 56 (Fig. 701e), is bolted to the side frame to act as a stop for the levers.

As shewn in Fig. 701, the motor is bolted at the front of the chassis on the 5½ in. cross strips, and the 4 volt accumulators from lower cross strips 57 supported by triangular pieces 58.

Under View of Chassis

Fig. 701a.

PARTS REQUIRED.

12	5½" Perforated Strips	2	3½" Axle Rods	2	Bevel Gear Wheels	8	Couplings
3	4½" ,, ,,	5	2½" ,, ,,	1	Worm Wheel	2	Threaded Bosses
7	3½" ,, ,,	3	2" ,, ,,	12	Nuts	2	2½" Triangular Plates
3	3" ,, ,,	5	1" ,, ,,	90	,, and Bolts	2	2" Screwed Rods
7	2½" ,, ,,	1	Flanged Wheel	1	2" Spring	2	1" ,, ,,
2	2" ,, ,,	4	3" Pulley Wheels	1	Double Bent Strip	2	1" Sprocket Wheels
6	1½" ,, ,,	4	1½" ,, ,, (fast)	2	1½"×½" Double Angle Strips	2	¾" Bolts
2	24½" Angle Girders	2	1" ,, ,, ,,	1	3½"×½" ,, ,, ,,	1	Threaded Pin
3	Flat Brackets	1	Bush Wheel	3	5½"×½" ,, ,, ,,	2	Pivot Bolts
10	Double ,,	6	¾" Pinion Wheels	3	2½"×1" ,, ,, ,,	29	Washers
18	Angle ,,	4	½" ,, ,,	1	3"×1½" ,, ,, ,,	4	3"×¼" Rubber Rings
11	1" Angle ,,	4	50 Toothed Gear Wheels	1	5½"×2½" Flanged Plate	2	1" Reversed Angle Brackets
2	8" Axle Rods	1	56 ,, ,, ,,	1	3½"×2½" ,, ,,	1	Hank of Cord
4	6" ,, ,,	3	1" Gear Wheels	24	Collars		9" Sprocket Chain
1	5" ,, ,,	1	1½" Contrate Wheel	5	Cranks		
1	4½" ,, ,,	4	¾" ,, ,,				

MECCANO LTD., Head Office and Factory: LIVERPOOL, England

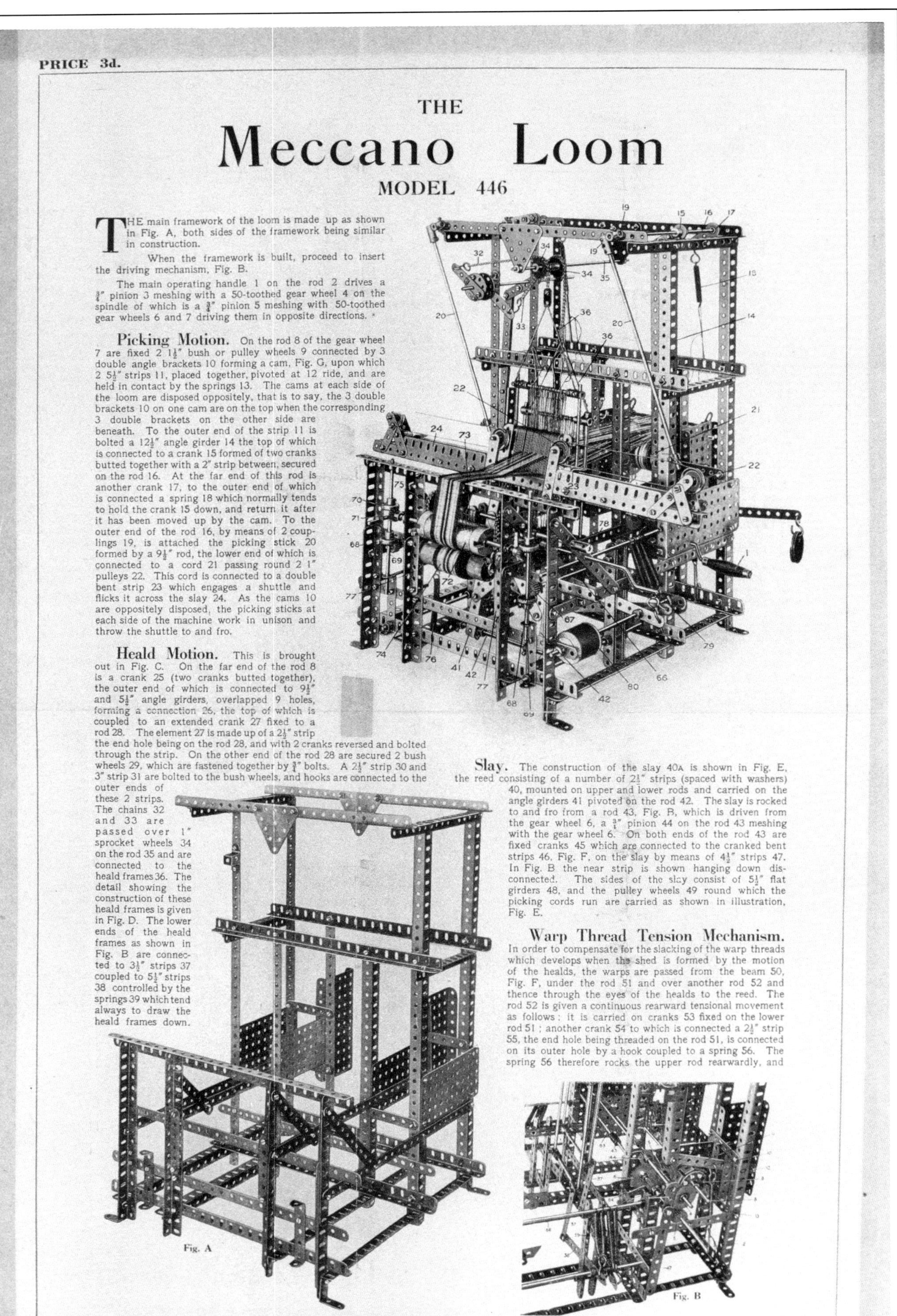

PRICE 3d.

THE Meccano Loom

MODEL 446

THE main framework of the loom is made up as shown in Fig. A, both sides of the framework being similar in construction.

When the framework is built, proceed to insert the driving mechanism, Fig. B.

The main operating handle 1 on the rod 2 drives a ¾" pinion 3 meshing with a 50-toothed gear wheel 4 on the spindle of which is a ⅜" pinion 5 meshing with 50-toothed gear wheels 6 and 7 driving them in opposite directions.

Picking Motion. On the rod 8 of the gear wheel 7 are fixed 2 1½" bush or pulley wheels 9 connected by 3 double angle brackets 10 forming a cam, Fig. G, upon which 2 5½" strips 11, placed together, pivoted at 12 ride, and are held in contact by the springs 13. The cams at each side of the loom are disposed oppositely, that is to say, the 3 double brackets 10 on one cam are on the top when the corresponding 3 double brackets on the other side are beneath. To the outer end of the strip 11 is bolted a 12½" angle girder 14 the top of which is connected to a crank 15 formed of two cranks butted together with a 2" strip between, secured on the rod 16. At the far end of this rod is another crank 17, to the outer end of which is connected a spring 18 which normally tends to hold the crank 15 down, and return it after it has been moved up by the cam. To the outer end of the rod 16, by means of 2 couplings 19, is attached the picking stick 20 formed by a 9½" rod, the lower end of which is connected to a cord 21 passing round 2 1" pulleys 22. This cord is connected to a double bent strip 23 which engages a shuttle and flicks it across the slay 24. As the cams 10 are oppositely disposed, the picking sticks at each side of the machine work in unison and throw the shuttle to and fro.

Heald Motion. This is brought out in Fig. C. On the far end of the rod 8 is a crank 25 (two cranks butted together), the outer end of which is connected to 9½" and 5½" angle girders, overlapped 9 holes, forming a connection 26, the top of which is coupled to an extended crank 27 fixed to a rod 28. The element 27 is made up of a 2½" strip the end hole being on the rod 28, and with 2 cranks reversed and bolted through the strip. On the other end of the rod 28 are secured 2 bush wheels 29, which are fastened together by ⅜" bolts. A 2½" strip 30 and 3" strip 31 are bolted to the bush wheels, and hooks are connected to the outer ends of these 2 strips. The chains 32 and 33 are passed over 1" sprocket wheels 34 on the rod 35 and are connected to the heald frames 36. The detail showing the construction of these heald frames is given in Fig. D. The lower ends of the heald frames as shown in Fig. B are connected to 3½" strips 37 coupled to 5½" strips 38 controlled by the springs 39 which tend always to draw the heald frames down.

Fig. A

Slay. The construction of the slay 40A is shown in Fig. E, the reed consisting of a number of 2½" strips (spaced with washers) 40, mounted on upper and lower rods and carried on the angle girders 41 pivoted on the rod 42. The slay is rocked to and fro from a rod 43, Fig. B, which is driven from the gear wheel 6, a ¾" pinion 44 on the rod 43 meshing with the gear wheel 6. On both ends of the rod 43 are fixed cranks 45 which are connected to the cranked bent strips 46, Fig. F, on the slay by means of 4½" strips 47. In Fig. B the near strip is shown hanging down disconnected. The sides of the slay consist of 5½" flat girders 48, and the pulley wheels 49 round which the picking cords run are carried as shown in illustration, Fig. E.

Warp Thread Tension Mechanism. In order to compensate for the slacking of the warp threads which develops when the shed is formed by the motion of the healds, the warps are passed from the beam 50, Fig. F, under the rod 51 and over another rod 52 and thence through the eyes of the healds to the reed. The rod 52 is given a continuous rearward tensional movement as follows: it is carried on cranks 53 fixed on the lower rod 51; another crank 54 to which is connected a 2½" strip 55, the end hole being threaded on the rod 51, is connected on its outer hole by a hook coupled to a spring 56. The spring 56 therefore rocks the upper rod rearwardly, and

Fig. B

Fig 4. The second in the series.

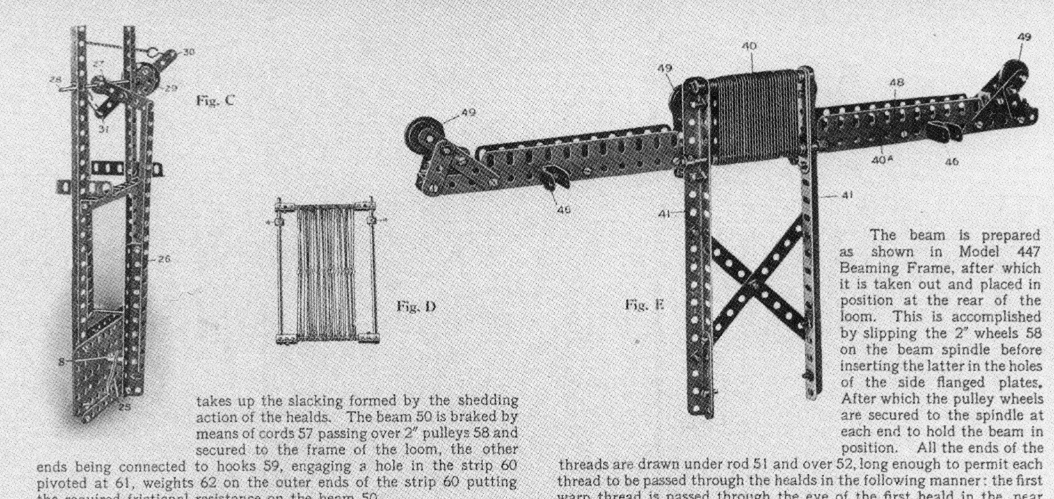

takes up the slacking formed by the shedding action of the healds. The beam 50 is braked by means of cords 57 passing over 2" pulleys 58 and secured to the frame of the loom, the other ends being connected to hooks 59, engaging a hole in the strip 60 pivoted at 61, weights 62 on the outer ends of the strip 60 putting the required frictional resistance on the beam 50.

Take up Motion. This is shown in Fig. B. On the rod 63 of the gear wheel 6 are also mounted 2 worms 64 which engage and drive 57-toothed wheels 65 on rods 66. ½" pinions 67 on which (Fig. 446) drive ¾" contrate wheels 68 on the vertical rods 69. It is to be noted that the contrate wheels 68 are reversed. Other ¾" contrate wheels 70 on the rods 69 engage and drive ½" pinions 71 on the sand roller 72. Owing to the gearing of the worm 64 and gear wheels 65 the necessary slow "take up" motion of the sand roller is imparted, and the woven material, after passing beneath the sand roller, passes over the rod 73 to the lower roller 74, on which the fabric is wound. The lower roller (74) is driven frictionally from the sand roller and is kept in frictional contact therewith by means of the chains 75 at either side, which are hooked on the rod of the roller 74 and are kept taut by springs 76 connected to the other end of the chains 75. The rod of the lower roller 74 is enabled to move away from the sand roller 72 so as to allow for the increasing diameter of the woven fabric thereon by causing the ends of its rod to engage between 2½" strips 77 and the frame of the machine at each side.

Fig. F

To Adjust Healds. To adjust the healds correctly set them so that the eyes of both heald frame sets are level when the cranks 45 are vertical and the strips 47 are horizontal.

A suitable material for use in this model is No. 8 Star Sylko for warp and No. 40 Sylko thread for weft. No thicker material should be used. Any drapery establishment will supply you.

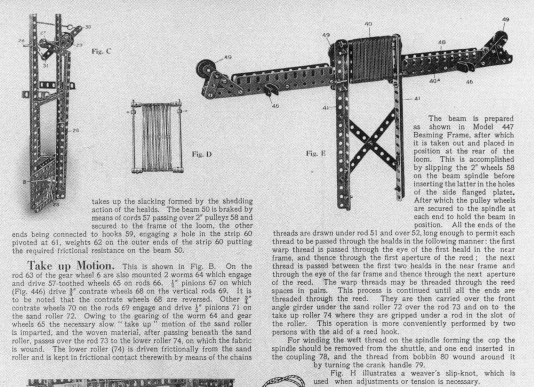

The beam is prepared as shown in Model 447 Beaming Frame, after which it is taken out and placed in position at the rear of the loom. This is accomplished by slipping the 2" wheels 58 on the beam spindle before inserting the latter in the holes of the side flanged plates. After which the pulley wheels are secured to the spindle at each end to hold the beam in position. All the ends of the threads are drawn under rod 51 and over 52, long enough to permit each thread to be passed through the healds in the following manner: the first warp thread is passed through the eye of the first heald in the near frame, and thence through the first aperture of the reed; the next thread is passed between the first two healds in the near frame and through the eye of the far frame and thence through the next aperture of the reed. The warp threads may be threaded through the reed spaces in pairs. This process is continued until all the ends are threaded through the reed. They are then carried over the front angle girder under the sand roller 72 over the rod 73 and on to the take up roller 74 where they are gripped under a rod in the slot of the roller. This operation is more conveniently performed by two persons with the aid of a reed hook.

For winding the weft thread on the spindle forming the cop the spindle should be removed from the shuttle, and one end inserted in the coupling 78, and the thread from bobbin 80 wound around it by turning the crank handle 79.

Fig. H illustrates a weaver's slip-knot, which is used when adjustments or tension is necessary.

Fig. H

BEAMING FRAME
(Model 447)

THE frame 1 upon which the warp threads are wound is built up of 12½" angle girders, 2 overlapped seven holes and bolted to a 5½" girder and 5½" strip crossed and connected to face plates 4 on the 11½" rod 5. Inside the frame, two 5½" angle girders are bolted nine holes from each end to form the inner bearings for the rods 5.

Another 5½" girder is bolted crosswise to these in the centre to form a stay. The warp threads are first wound upon the frame 1, and pass through the holes in a 24½" angle girder 6, and, converging together, pass between the 2½" strips 7 forming the reed, and so on to the beam 8. On the far side of the beam rod is a ½" pinion engaged by a pawl (not shown on the photograph) which prevents backward rotation of the beam as the warp threads are wound thereon by turning the 1½" pulley wheels 9. A brake mechanism for tensioning the frame 2 is provided by securing two 1" pulley wheels 10 at each end of the frame rod 5, cords 11, secured by hooks 12, passing over the pulleys 10 and being kept taut by the springs 12. A handle 13 is provided on the rod 5 by means of which the warp threads 14 are originally wound on the frame 2.

Fig. G

SHUTTLE

PARTS REQUIRED FOR LOOM

Qty	No.	Qty	No.	Qty	No.	Qty	No.	Qty	No.	Qty	No.
6 of No.	1	15 of No.	9	6 of No.	16	3 of No.	27A	2 of No.	52	12 of No	94
22	2	2	10	8	18A	4	29	17	57	4	96
8	3	8	11	2	19	2	32	55	59	42	101
9	4	4	12	2	20A	6	35	2	60	6	103
39	5	4	12A	4	21	195	37	15	62	1	104
4	6	4	13	4	22	33	37A	13	63	1	106
4	6A	13	13A	2	24	198	38	4	67	1	106A
6	7A	10	14	5	25	15	43	4	70	2	109
17	8	1	15	5	26	2	44	2	76	7	111
3	8A	1	15A	5	27	5	45	4	82		

PARTS REQUIRED FOR BEAMING FRAME

Qty	No.	Qty	No.
2 of No.	1	6 of No.	21
4	2	1	26
44	5	1	33
4	6	253	37
4	7	88	38
2	7A	4	43
12	8	8	57
10	9	10	59
8	12	1	63
2	13	1	103
3	14	4	109

MECCANO LTD. Head Office and Factory : LIVERPOOL, England

1121/2

little resemblance to them. The manuals showed an illustration of each but did not give any instructions, instead the reader was told that the space necessary for such detail was too great for the manual and reference should be made to the two special leaflets which contained building instructions.

The leaflets themselves were in large double-sided format measuring 11″ by 17″ and therefore somewhat smaller than the oversized 'Gordon Crosby' leaflet, which was some 12″ x 18½″.

The First of the New

The first one to have been prepared was the Motor Chassis (fig 3) and as can be seen, the model incorporated a two-speed and reverse gearbox, a back-axle differential, brakes, leaf springs and a fairly accurate representation of a car's steering mechanism. The gearbox although only two-speed, was a distinct improvement over the odd if ingenious one in the Gordon Crosby model. One feature of the earlier chassis not carried on was the working clutch – in the 1921 model it was purely for ornament.

The leaflet itself was a high-quality production with very clear illustrations. The gearbox is well shown in large scale as is the differential. Strangely, the leaf spring is shown upside down and continued to be so in future leaflets and Standard Mechanisms where it was also used. It was belatedly corrected in the 1933 edition of Standard Mechanisms before disappearing when the 1934 Blue/Gold edition of that manual appeared.

A further point to note is the lack of part numbers in the parts list – almost a hint of earlier days when they were frequently omitted.

Another Loom

The second leaflet to be issued, The Meccano Loom (fig 4) was quite the most complex model up until then and for sometime afterwards. It was a development of earlier loom models and was probably the first mechanical type to successfully and repetitively weave small pieces of cloth. However, the model was perfect not and in fact needs considerable strengthening and much modification if it is to operate for any length of time and even then the weave can be very erratic. Perfecting a Meccano Loom was to be many years away, but at least this one did work and could be built by any reasonably experienced modeller.

Unlike the Motor Chassis leaflet, the illustrations were not uniformly good nor were they as large a scale. Consequently there is a loss of clarity which is accentuated by some poor origination. As with most other leaflets there are some odd features and anomalies. For example, the view of the rear of the loom shows 50 grm weights of the usual 'triangular' section variety, but the main front view pictures much earlier 'disc' weights. The line drawings are earlier and that of the shuttle does not show the part in its usually known form. The handle used to operate the model was made of wood according to Meccano Ltd in the 1928 version of the same model, but no mention was made of this in the 1921 leaflet. Part numbers were used in the list unlike the Motor Chassis leaflet.

Both these first two Special Model Leaflets were supplied with the then new No. 7 outfit and could be built from the contents.

A New Clock

Matters remained at this stage until 1924 when the Meccano Grandfather Clock leaflet was added to the series (fig 5). It was an imposing model standing over 6 feet in height and was probably the first Meccano clock to keep reasonably good time. Although not perhaps very efficient mechanically, the 18 pound weight specified did drive the clock successfully. The weight was one of several parts required which were not in the Meccano system. The others were the face which would have been a simple matter to supply, the line for the weight and the brass spring connection for the pendulum. These last two were eventually added to the system.

The clock leaflet was not supplied with the No 7 outfit of the time because although the majority of the parts required were in the outfit, the huge number of braced girders (83 in all) was far outside the bounds of a No 7. However for the 1927/8 season the clock was being listed as in the outfit even though the number of braced girders was still woefully short of that required. This leaflet also went back to the system of not quoting part numbers and perhaps because of this, they are listed in a very strange order.

A Ship Coaler

The fourth and final Special Model Leaflet, The Ship Coaler, appeared in 1925 (fig 6). Unlike the Grandfather Clock, this one was supplied with and could be built from the contents of the No. 7 outfit. Although not a new subject, it was an improvement over previous versions. Building the model is not especially difficult but operating it is another matter altogether, and as described in the leaflet great manual dexterity is required to carry out the movements in sequence. When working fast it is rather spectacular if a little noisy.

There is possibly an earlier leaflet relating to the previous ship coaler model. The October 1922 manual only illustrates the model stating that instructions would be forwarded upon request. So far these instructions remain undiscovered or unrecognised.

Extras

There were two other leaflets in the same format which were not strictly model leaflets. These were the Charging Board and The Meccano Crystal Set. The Crystal Set Leaflet (fig 7), which was issued towards the end of 1922, was in reality the instruction leaflet for the RS2 set, the RS1 being the ready-built version. The Meccano Crystal Set was effectively a modified version of that produced by the Meccano Company in the United States (fig 8). Hornby had visited the US factory earlier that year and was so impressed with the set that he ordered production of a UK type.

The RS1 was extremely short-lived because of technical objections by the Postmaster General. Within a short time a very different ready-built set replaced the set shown in the leaflet (cf p. 314 HCS Vol 6) The original constructional type RS2 continued to be available, but to use it an 'experimental' licence was necessary. There was also a leaflet relating to the aerial for the sets (fig 9).

The other large format leaflet was for The Charging Board. This was supplied with the No. 7 outfit, and was a set of instructions for the construction of an electrical unit to enable 4 volt motors to be run direct from the mains and for accumulators to be charged in similar fashion. In both cases direct current was necessary, thus making it even more lethal. Indeed, the sight of the leaflet alone is enough to give an electrician apoplexy! (fig 10)

Print Data

The Motor Chassis, Ship Coaler and Loom leaflets are all known to have had more than one printing – see below for details. Apart from minor alterations such as model number designation, all the leaflets for each model so far examined appear to be identical. As was to be the case for many years, the Motor Chassis was by far the most popular. The second print for 1923 was probably in anticipation of the demand from its feature in the *Meccano Magazine* later that year.

So far no print for the Motor Chassis for 1927 has been unearthed which, in view of the illustration of the later Super Model Leaflet type in the April 1927 manual, is a pity. It must therefore remain speculation as to whether the 'New Meccano Motor Chassis' was issued as a large format leaflet prior to its appearance as a Super Model in 1928. There was however an SM-sized leaflet showing the new chassis printed in December 1927 and designated as Model No 701.

There were US versions of some, if not all, the Special Model Leaflets with the probable exception of the Charging Board. The question of foreign language editions has still to be resolved.

U.K. Print Data	(known to the author)		
Motor Chassis	621/2.5	1021/3	223/1
	423/1	1124/1	326/1
	1126/1	1227/5 (see text)	
Loom	1121/2	1124/1	326/1
	927/1		
Ship Coaler	125/1	427/1	
Clock	124/1		
Crystal Set	1022/1	423/1	
Charging Board	1121/2.5		

Fig 8. The US version of the Crystal Set upon which the UK was based.

Price List of Parts used in Radio Set

(12A) (45)

Part No.		Price
5	Perforated Strips, 2½" long.....½ doz.	.15
12	Angle Brackets ......1 doz.	.12
12A	Angle Brackets, 1" ......each	.05
16	Axle Rods, 3½" long ......each	.05
34	Spanners ......each	.10
36	Screw Drivers ......each	.10
37A	Nuts ......1 doz.	.05
37B	Bolts ......1 doz.	.10
38	Washers ......1 doz.	.05
45	Double Bent Strips ......each	.05
53	Perf. Flanged Plates, 3½"x2½"..each	.20
60	Double Angle Strips, 2½"x½"...each	.05
63	Couplings ......each	.15
63C	Couplings, Threaded ......each	.20

(63) (63C) (76) (302) (125) (303)

Part No.		Price
76	Triangular Plates, 2½" ......each	.05
81	Screwed Rods, 2" long ......each	.10
102	Single Bent Strips ......each	.05
111	Bolts, ¾" long ......each	.02
125	Reversed Angle Brackets, ½"...½ doz.	.20
202	Insulating Bushes ......1 doz.	.16
303	Insulating Washers ......1 doz.	.08
304	6 B. A. Screws ......1 doz.	.15
305	6 B. A. Nuts ......1 doz.	.10

These and any other Meccano parts can be purchased at any time in any quantities. If your dealer cannot supply you, we will ship your order direct on receipt of price. We prepay postage on orders over $1.00 only.

(306) (404) (410) (411)

Part No.		Price
306	Terminals ......each	.05
403	Insulating Triangular Plates, 2½"..each	.03
404	Insulating Handles ......each	.15
405	Brass Washers, $\frac{1}{16}$" ......1 doz.	.10
406	Hook-up Wire ......length	.05
407	Inductance Discs, wound ......pair	2.00
409	Detector Arm, complete ......each (This Arm includes the last five items listed under "Detector" above.)	.45
410	"Meccolite" (All-sensitive crystal) ......each	.30
411	Crystal Cup ......each	.10
412	Polished Mounting Boards ......each	1.25
412A	Brass Wood Screws ......1 doz.	.10
412B	Wire Staples ......1 doz.	.05
	Instruction Leaflets ......each	.05

RS 1. Meccano Crystal Radio Receiving Set, assembled. Complete as illustrated on Page 1, (without phones or aerial) ......Price $12.50

RS 2. Outfit containing parts to make Meccano Crystal Radio Receiving Set, with tools and instructions (without phones or aerial) ......Price $10.00

MECCANO COMPANY
INCORPORATED
ELIZABETH, NEW JERSEY

Fresh discoveries are being made from time to time and therefore the above list should only be taken as a guide to those leaflets known to exist at the time of writing.

Conclusion

The four basic model leaflets – Loom, Motor Chassis, Clock and Ship Coaler marked an important stage in the development of Meccano modelling. All four were technically much more advanced than anything which had gone before and set the seal on the direction which model building would take for some 15 years. They were not perfect models, but then which are? In any case, it can be argued that Hornby himself did not necessarily believe that a published design should remain inviolate. Improvements and developments were always welcomed.

continued p. 99.

Price 3d.

THE MECCANO CLOCK

THE following instructions will enable any Meccano boy to build a "grandfather's clock" with Meccano. This clock stands well over 6 ft. in height and keeps perfect time. With the exception of the 18 lb. weight, the wire by which it hangs, the dial plate and the light spring (80 Fig. E), the model is made entirely of Meccano. The clock keeps perfect time, and is the outcome of experiments conducted in the Meccano model-building department. A large number of these clocks have been constructed, and have been tested-out very thoroughly. With careful adjustment every clock has been made to keep perfect time.

CONSTRUCTING THE FRAME

Commence by making the frame to carry the gear trains. This frame (shown in Fig. D) consists of vertical 12½" angle girders (1), connected by 5½" angle girders (2) and 5½" strips (3). Bolt three 5½" × 2½" flat plates (4) to the 5½" double angle strips (5) above and below, and two 2½" × 2½" flat plates (6) to the plates (4) but on the other sides of the lower double angle strips (5) and overlapped two holes with the larger plates (4). Cranks (7) bolted to flanged trunnions (8) on the top of the frame form the

Fig. B

pivotal bearings for the pendulum. A 12" strip (9) is bolted vertically to one of the trunnions and to the 5½" strips (10) to form bearings for the main gear train. A double bent strip (11) and a 1½" strip behind are bolted on the left side of the frame to form a bearing for the winding handle (65 Fig. E). A second double bent strip (12) is provided, to form a bearing for the shift gear that disconnects the driving train from the gearing of the hands, when the fingers are being set.

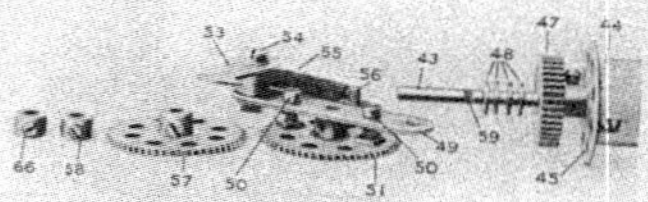

A flat trunnion (13 Fig. D) is bolted below the left perforated plate (6) to form a bearing for the lowest 3" rod of the clock train (18 Fig. E). The position of the other perforated strips will be easily seen from Fig. D.

THE MAIN GEAR TRAIN

When the frame has been constructed, proceed to build the main driving gear train, as shown in Fig. E. This consists of three ½" pinions (14) connected with 57-toothed gear wheels (15) and three ¾" pinions (16) connected with 50-toothed gear wheels (17). These are secured on the rods 18, the top rod being 3½" long and the remainder 3" long. They pass through holes in the left-hand plates (4 and 6) and the strip 9, collars (10A) being fitted on each rod on each side of the strip 9. No collars are necessary at the other ends of the rods.

On the end of the 3½" rod (19) is a ¾" pinion (20), which is seen more clearly in Fig. G. This pinion gears with a 50-toothed gear wheel (21) fixed on a 2" rod (22) which is able to slide in the plates (6). On this rod also is a ½" pinion (23) geared with a 57-toothed wheel (24) on a 4½" rod (25) carrying the minute hand (26 Fig. E). The web of a crank (27 Fig. G), engages the 2" rod (22), the crank being bolted to a 3½" rod (28) carrying a double bracket bolted to a bell crank (29) and pivoted on a rod (30) in the double bent strip (12).

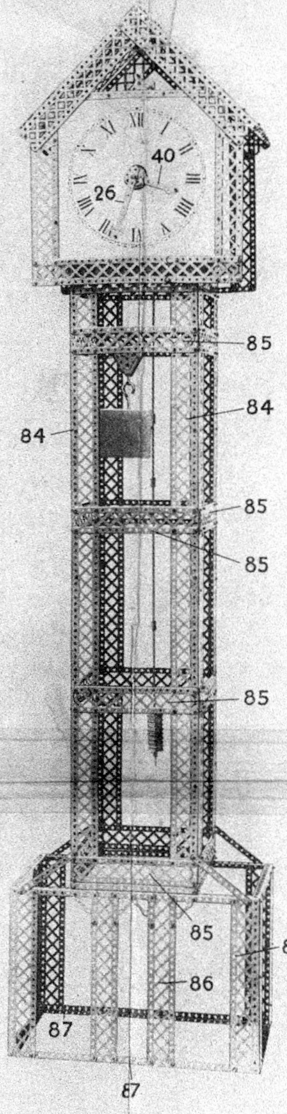

ADJUSTING THE HANDS

A cord (31) is connected to the bell crank (29) and by pulling on this cord, the rod (28) is caused to slide and move the gear (21) in or out of engagement with the pinion (20). This releases the driving train from the clock hands and enables the hands to be freely adjusted.

In order to drive the hour hand from the minute hand rod (25), a ½" pinion (32) on this rod drives a 57-toothed gear (33) mounted on a 2" rod. This engages a second 57-toothed gear (34 Fig. E), the ¾" pinion (35) on the same 2" rod driving a 50-toothed gear (36). Another ¾" pinion (see Fig. E) on this rod drives a 50-toothed gear (37). On the 2½" rod of this last wheel is a 1½" sprocket wheel (38 Fig. E and Fig. J) which is coupled to a similar sprocket (39) loose on the rod 25. The hour hand (40 Fig. J) consists of a 2½" strip and is connected by

Fig. C

a ½" reversed angle bracket (41) to a 1½" strip (42). This is bolted to the sprocket wheel (39) and spaced by two washers to give clearance for the sprocket chain. The reversed angle bracket (41) is necessary to enable the hour hand 40 to be brought clear of the dial plate.

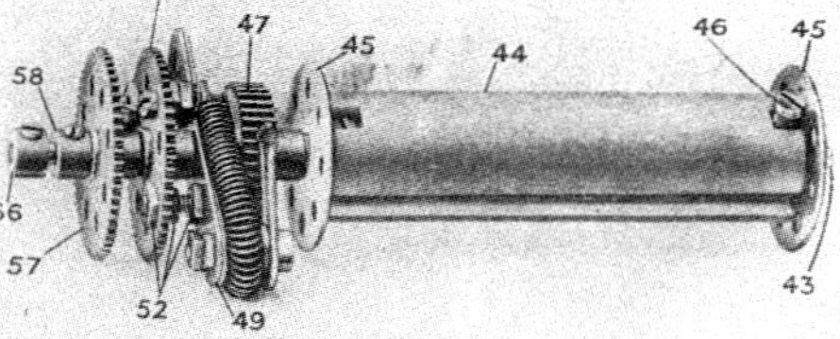

RATCHET WINDING MECHANISM

The ratchet mechanism permitting the winding of the weight is built up as shown in Figs. B, C and F. As will be seen from the two first-mentioned, the complete ratchet element is made by passing a 6" rod (43 Fig. B) through a wood roller (44), the ends of which are clamped between two bush wheels (45) secured on the rod. The bosses of the bush wheels are entered into the ends of the wood roller and the bolts (46) engage in the end notches of the wood roller to key the roller to the bush wheel (45).

A 1" gear wheel (47) is then bolted on the rod (43) with its boss close against the end bush wheel (45). Four washers (48) are then threaded on the rod.

The element shown in the centre of Fig. B is next passed over the rod. This element is made as follows: Two 2½" strips (49) are bolted by ¾" bolts (50) to a 57-toothed gear wheel (51), lock-nuts (52 Fig. C) being fitted on the bolts on each side of the gear wheel (51) and also beneath the strips (49). A pawl (53) is pivoted at (54) in the end hole of the strips (49) and a spring (55) is connected to the pawl boss by a screw, and also to a ¾" bolt (56) on the gear

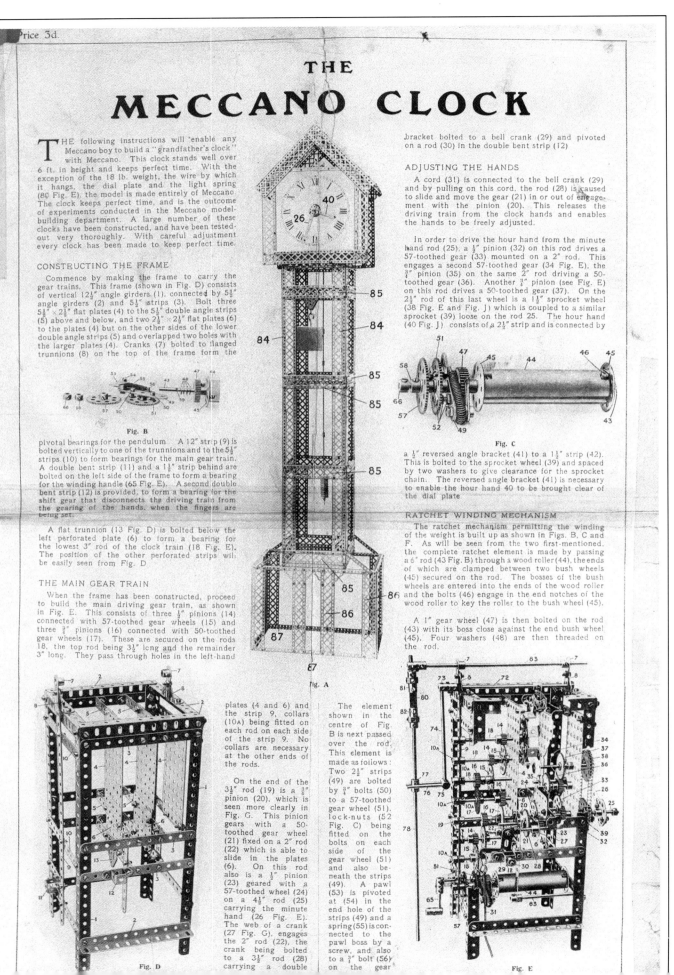

Fig. A

Fig. D

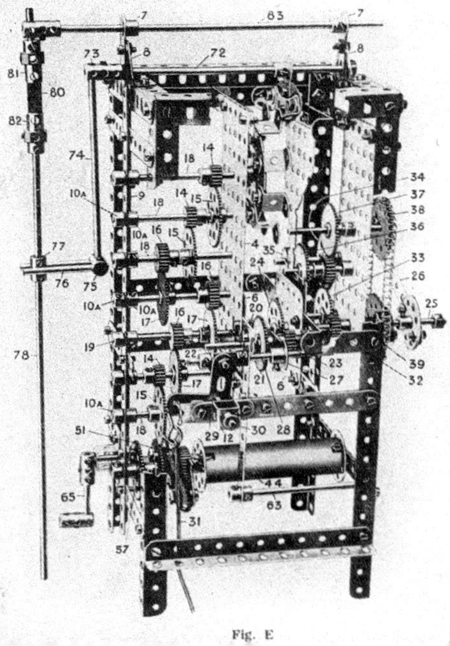

Fig. E

Fig 5. *The third leaflet to be issued.*

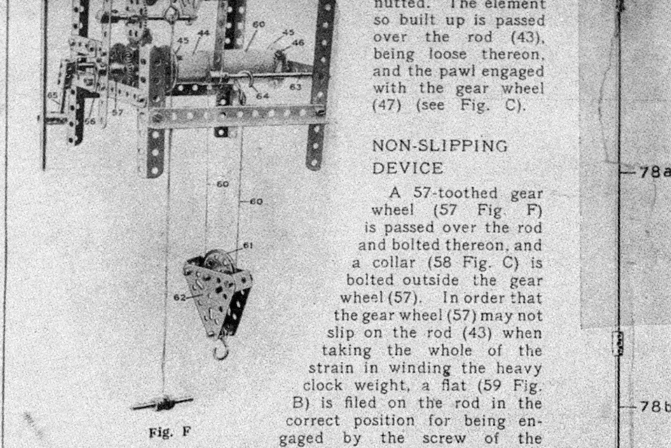
Fig. F

nutted. The element so built up is passed over the rod (43), being loose thereon, and the pawl engaged with the gear wheel (47) (see Fig. C).

NON-SLIPPING DEVICE

A 57-toothed gear wheel (57 Fig. F) is passed over the rod and bolted thereon, and a collar (58 Fig. C) is bolted outside the gear wheel (57). In order that the gear wheel (57) may not slip on the rod (43) when taking the whole of the strain in winding the heavy clock weight, a flat (59 Fig. B) is filed on the rod in the correct position for being engaged by the screw of the gear wheel (57). This gives the wheel a secure grip on the rod.

WINDING THE CLOCK

A stranded wire cord (60) is wound on the wood roller (44) and passes round a pulley (61) in the pulley block (62). This is made up of two $2\frac{1}{2}''$ triangular plates bolted together with double brackets, and carries the $1\frac{1}{2}''$ pulley wheel (61). The other end of the cord (60) is hooked (at 64) over the rod (63).

After the wood roller (44) has been inserted in place, another collar (66) is secured on the extreme end of rod (43 Fig. F). The clock is wound by a crank handle (65) provided with a $\frac{1}{2}''$ pinion (not visible in the photograph), which engages the gear wheel (57). The roller (44) drives the main gear train, by reason of its gear wheel (51) engaging the first gear (15) of the train.

THE ESCAPEMENT WHEEL AND PALLET

Next, proceed to construct the escapement, which consists of an escapement wheel and a pallet mechanism. The former (Fig. K) consists of a face plate (66a) to which are attached eight $\frac{1}{2}''$ reversed angle brackets (67). In order that these shall not move, they are pressed hard against the circular edge of the plate, and then bolted in position with washers (68) beneath the bolt-heads.

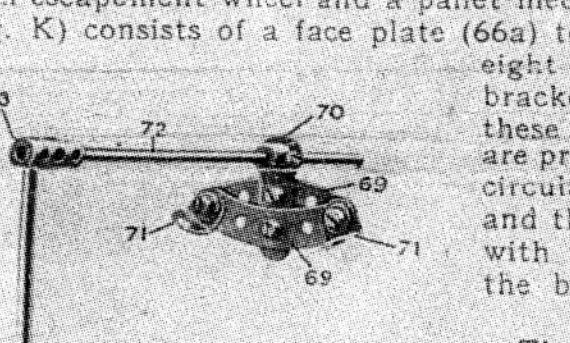
Fig. I

The pallet mechanism (Fig. I) consists of two $2\frac{1}{2}''$ reversed curved strips (69) with the web of a crank (70) bolted between. Angle brackets (71) are bolted in the end holes of the curved strips which form the pallets. The crank (70) is bolted on a 6" rod (72, see Fig. E) and a 5" rod (74) is secured to a coupling (73) on the end of the rod (72). At the lower end of this is a coupling (75) carrying two 2" rods (76) which engage against two collars (77) on the pendulum rod (78).

THE PENDULUM

As shown in Fig. H, the pendulum consists of four $11\frac{1}{2}''$ (78, 78a, 78c, and 78d) and a 5" rod (78b) connected by couplings. As also shown in Fig. H, the pendulum is connected to the lower end of the $11\frac{1}{2}''$ rod (78) (see Fig. E).

The pendulum weight (79) is made up of ten flanged wheels. A light spring (80) connects the strip couplings (81 and 82), the coupling (81) being connected to the 8" rod (83) which is secured in the bosses of the cranks (7). The spring (80) is necessary in order to provide for an easy escapement movement of the pendulum.

CONSTRUCTING THE MAIN FRAME

The main frame may now be built. This consists of two $24\frac{1}{2}''$ angle girders at each vertical corner, overlapped three holes. To these are secured $12\frac{1}{2}''$ braced girders (84) connected by $9\frac{1}{2}''$ horizontal braced girders (85). The base consists of $12\frac{1}{2}''$ vertical braced girders (86) and horizontal $18\frac{1}{2}''$ angle girders (87), at the front and back.

The construction of the head of the clock will be clearly seen from Fig. L. It is

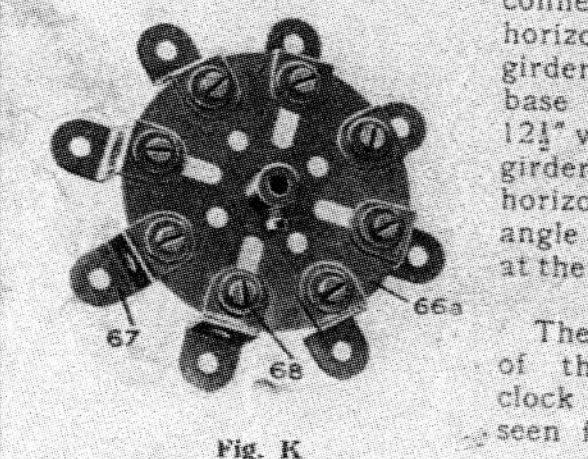
Fig. K

Fig. H

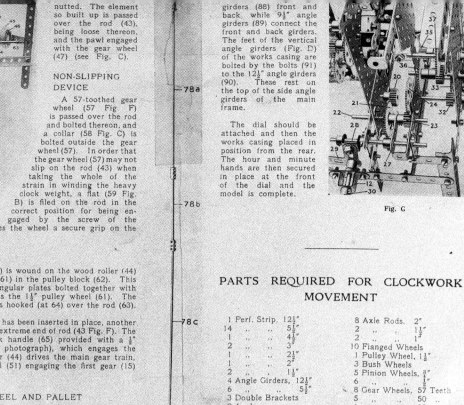

girders (88) front and back, while $9\frac{1}{2}''$ angle girders (89) connect the front and back girders. The feet of the vertical angle girders (Fig. D) of the works casing are bolted by the bolts (91) to the $12\frac{1}{2}''$ angle girders (90). These rest on the top of the side angle girders of the main frame.

The dial should be attached and then the works casing placed in position from the rear. The hour and minute hands are then secured in place at the front of the dial and the model is complete.

Fig. G

PARTS REQUIRED FOR CLOCKWORK MOVEMENT

- 1 Perf. Strip, $12\frac{1}{2}''$
- 14 ,, ,, $5\frac{1}{2}''$
- 1 ,, ,, $4\frac{1}{2}''$
- 2 ,, ,, 3"
- 1 ,, ,, $2\frac{1}{2}''$
- 1 ,, ,, 2"
- 2 ,, ,, $1\frac{1}{2}''$
- 4 Angle Girders, $12\frac{1}{2}''$
- 6 ,, ,, $5\frac{1}{2}''$
- 3 Double Brackets
- 2 Angle ,,
- 4 Axle Rods, $11\frac{1}{2}''$
- 1 ,, ,, 8"
- 2 ,, ,, 6"
- 3 ,, ,, $4\frac{1}{2}''$
- 9 ,, ,, $3\frac{1}{2}''$
- 1 ,, ,, 3"
- 1 ,, ,, $2\frac{1}{2}''$
- 6 Double Angle Strips, $5\frac{1}{2}'' \times \frac{1}{2}''$
- 4 Cranks
- 9 Couplings
- 2 Strip Couplings
- 3 Flat Plates, $5\frac{1}{2}'' \times 2\frac{1}{2}''$
- 2 Flat Plates, $2\frac{1}{2}'' \times 2\frac{1}{2}$
- 2 Triangular Plates, $2\frac{1}{2}''$
- 2 Triangular Plates, 1"
- 2 Curved Strips, $2\frac{1}{2}''$
- 8 Axle Rods, 2"
- 2 ,, ,, $1\frac{1}{2}''$
- 2 ,, ,, 1"
- 10 Flanged Wheels
- 1 Pulley Wheel, $1\frac{1}{2}''$
- 3 Bush Wheels
- 5 Pinion Wheels, $\frac{3}{4}''$
- 6 ,, ,, $\frac{1}{2}''$
- 8 Gear Wheels, 57 Teeth
- 5 ,, ,, 50 ,,
- 1 ,, ,, 38 ,,
- 1 Pawl
- 106 Nuts and Bolts
- 20 Washers
- 1 Spring
- 2 Double Bent Strips
- 3 Hooks
- 35 Collars

Fig. J

- 10" Sprocket Chain
- 2 Sprocket Wheels, $1\frac{1}{2}''$
- 1 Wood Roller
- 1 Face Plate
- 2 Bolts, $\frac{3}{4}''$
- 9 Reversed Angle Brackets, $\frac{1}{2}'' \times \frac{1}{2}''$
- 2 Trunnions
- 1 Flat Trunnion
- 1 Boss Bell Crank
- 10 ft. Flexible Steel Wire
- 1 Face

Fig. L

PARTS REQUIRED FOR CLOCK CASE AND FRAME

- 51 Braced Girders, $12\frac{1}{2}''$
- 24 ,, ,, $9\frac{1}{2}''$
- 8 ,, ,, $3\frac{1}{2}''$
- 8 Angle Girders, $24\frac{1}{2}''$
- 4 ,, ,, $18\frac{1}{2}''$
- 14 ,, ,, $12\frac{1}{2}''$
- 14 ,, ,, $9\frac{1}{2}''$
- 4 Perforated Strips, $5\frac{1}{2}''$
- 2 ,, $3\frac{1}{2}''$
- 4 Architraves
- 329 Nuts and Bolts
- 8 Washers
- 10 Angle Brackets
- 1 18lb. Weight

MECCANO LTD. BINNS ROAD LIVERPOOL

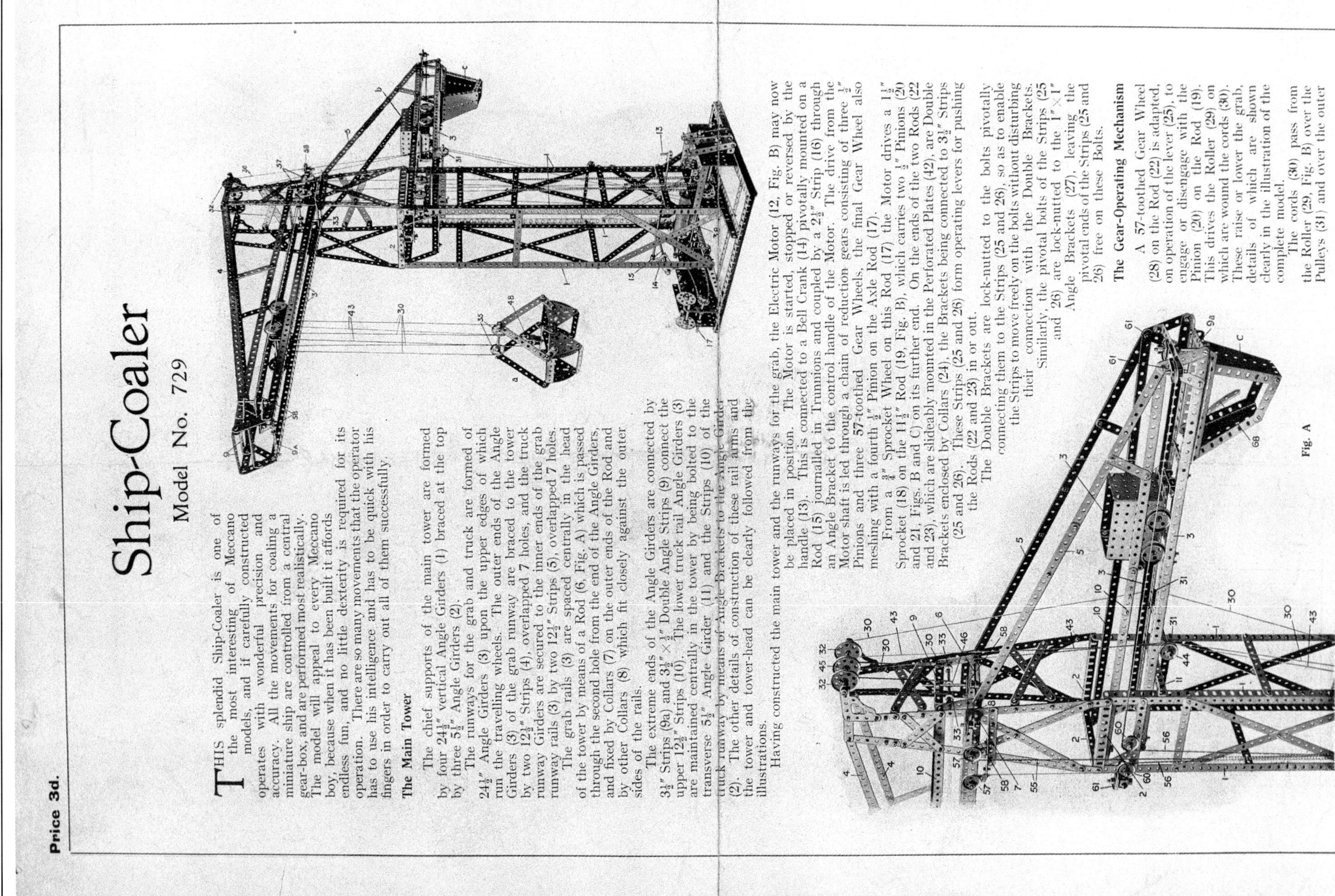

Price 3d.

Ship-Coaler

Model No. 729

THIS splendid Ship-Coaler is one of the most interesting of Meccano models, and if carefully constructed operates with wonderful precision and accuracy. All the movements for coaling a miniature ship are controlled from a central gear-box, and are performed most realistically. The model will appeal to every Meccano boy, because when it has been built it affords endless fun, and no little dexterity is required for its operation. There are so many movements that the operator has to use his intelligence and has to be quick with his fingers in order to carry out all of them successfully.

The Main Tower

The chief supports of the main tower are formed by four $24\frac{1}{2}''$ vertical Angle Girders (1) braced at the top by three $5\frac{1}{2}''$ Angle Girders (2).

The runways for the grab and truck are formed of $24\frac{1}{2}''$ Angle Girders (3) upon the upper edges of which run the travelling wheels. The outer ends of the Angle Girders (3) of the grab runway are braced to the tower by two $12\frac{1}{2}''$ Strips (4), overlapped 7 holes, and the truck runway Girders are secured to the inner ends of the grab runway rails (3) by two $12\frac{1}{2}''$ Strips (5), overlapped 7 holes.

The grab rails (3) are spaced centrally in the head of the tower by means of a Rod (6, Fig. A) which is passed through the second hole from the end of the Angle Girders, and fixed by Collars (7) on the outer ends of the Rod and by other Collars (8) which fit closely against the outer sides of the rails.

The extreme ends of the Angle Girders are connected by $3\frac{1}{2}''$ Strips (9a) and $3\frac{1}{2}'' \times \frac{1}{2}''$ Double Angle Strips (9) connect the upper $12\frac{1}{2}''$ Strips (10). The lower truck rail Angle Girders (3) are maintained centrally in the tower by being bolted to the transverse $5\frac{1}{2}''$ Angle Girder (11) and the Strips (10) of the truck runway by means of Angle Brackets to the Angle Girder (2). The other details of construction of these rail arms and the tower and tower-head can be clearly followed from the illustrations.

Having constructed the main tower and the runways for the grab, the Electric Motor (12, Fig. B) may now be placed in position. The Motor is started, stopped or reversed by the handle (13). This is connected to a Bell Crank (14) pivotally mounted on a Rod (15) journalled in Trunnions and coupled by a $2\frac{1}{2}''$ Strip (16) through an Angle Bracket to the control handle of the Motor. The drive from the Motor shaft is led through a chain of reduction gears consisting of three $\frac{1}{2}''$ Pinions and three 57-toothed Gear Wheels, the final Gear Wheel also meshing with a fourth $\frac{1}{2}''$ Pinion on the Axle Rod (17).

From a $\frac{3}{4}''$ Sprocket Wheel on this Rod (17) the Motor drives a $1\frac{1}{2}''$ Sprocket (18) on the $11\frac{1}{2}''$ Rod (19, Fig. B), which carries two $\frac{1}{2}''$ Pinions (20 and 21, Figs. B and C) on its further end. On the ends of the two Rods (22 and 23), which are slideably mounted in the Perforated Plates (42), are Double Brackets enclosed by Collars (24), the Brackets being connected to $3\frac{1}{2}''$ Strips (25 and 26). These Strips (25 and 26) form operating levers for pushing the Rods (22 and 23) in or out.

The Double Brackets are lock-nutted to the bolts pivotally connecting them to the Strips (25 and 26), so as to enable the Strips to move freely on the bolts without disturbing their connection with the Double Brackets. Similarly, the pivotal bolts of the Strips (25 and 26) are lock-nutted to the $1'' \times 1''$ Angle Brackets (27), leaving the pivotal ends of the Strips (25 and 26) free on these Bolts.

The Gear-Operating Mechanism

A 57-toothed Gear Wheel (28) on the Rod (22) is adapted, on operation of the lever (25), to engage or disengage with the Pinion (20) on the Rod (19). This drives the Roller (29) on which are wound the cords (30). These raise or lower the grab, details of which are shown clearly in the illustration of the complete model.

The cords (30) pass from the Roller (29, Fig. B) over the Pulleys (31) and over the outer

Fig. A

Fig 6. The last of the large format model leaflets.

top Pulleys (32, Fig. A), returning down and passing around ½" Pulleys (33) on to other ½" Pulleys (34) on the trolley (Fig. D). From thence the cords pass down and around 1" Pulleys (35) on the grab, and returning up around ½" Pulleys (36) on the trolley, are made fast in the 3½"×½" Double Angle Strip (37). As the Roller (29) is caused to rotate by the Motor in one or other direction, the grab will be raised or lowered.

Another Roller (38, Figs. B and C) is mounted on the 11½" Rod (39). This Rod slides in the Plates (42) directly above the 11½" Rod (19) carrying the Pinion (21, Figs. B and C). A 57-toothed Gear Wheel (40) on the Rod (39) is engaged or disengaged with the Pinion (21) by the operation of the 3½" Strip (41). This Strip acts as a control handle in a similar manner to the Strips (25 and 26) and is lock-nutted to the pivotal bolts as previously described.

Fig. B

Opening and Closing the Grab

When the Gear Wheel (40) is engaged with the Pinion (21), which is on the Rod (19) driven by the Motor, the Roller (38) rotates and the cord (43) on that Roller is wound up. This cord passes over an outer 1" Pulley (44, Fig. A), over a central 1½" Pulley (45) at the extreme top, down and around a ½" Pulley (46) to the trolley and over a ½" Pulley (47) thereon, (Fig. D). It passes around a 1" Pulley (48) on the grab below, returning up to and over a ½" Pulley (49) on the trolley, and from there it is made fast to the Double Angle Strip (37). Consequently by manipulating the handle (41) the grab may be opened or closed if it is stationary. When both the handles (41 and 25) throw the Rods (39 and 22) in gear with the main driving Rod (19), the grab is hoisted or lowered in an open or closed condition.

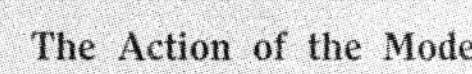

The Action of the Model

A Spring (50, Fig. B) is engaged over the end of the Rod (39) carrying the Roller (38) and another Spring (51) on the end of the Rod (22). These act as frictional drags or brakes on these Rods, preventing the load in the grab running away when the gears are out of mesh.

The mechanism is designed so that a load may be picked up by the grab at the outer end of the trolley arm. The load is then raised and the grab travels inwards on the rails (3). Meanwhile, the truck simultaneously travels inwards until, when the grab is over the truck, it (the grab) is opened and the load deposited in the truck.

Both the truck and the grab then travel outwards, the movement being completed by the truck depositing its load down the chute.

The Travelling Grab

This inward and outward travelling action of the grab and the truck is effected from the third handle (26, Fig. C). This controls the Rod (23) on which a 57-toothed Gear Wheel (52), when engaged with the Pinion (20), causes the Rod (23) to be rotated.

Fig. C

The Rod (23) carries two ¾" Sprocket Wheels (53 and 54) which are engaged by Sprocket Chains connected to cords (55 and 56, Fig. A). The cords (55) pass over 1" Pulley Wheels (57) and end Pulley Wheels (58, Figs. A and D) disposed horizontally at either extremity of the grab runway, being finally connected to the Flat Brackets (59) on the trolley of the grab. Consequently as the Chain on the Sprocket Wheel (53) is wound in one or other direction, according to the direction of rotation of the main driving Rod (19), so will the grab and its trolley be caused to travel in or out along the rails (3).

Simultaneous Action of Grab and Truck

Similarly the cords (56, Fig. A) connected to the Chain meshing with the other Sprocket (54) pass over 1" Pulleys (60, Fig. A) around the horizontally-arranged 1" Pulleys (61), the ends of the cord being connected to Brackets (62) at each end of the truck (61, Fig. E). As the Sprocket Chains (53 and 54) rotate together, both the grab and the truck travel at the same time, but in order to ensure that they travel in opposite directions, so that they both move inwards or outwards together, the cords (56) are crossed before they pass over the Pulleys (60), while the cords (55) are left open.

Fig. D

As the truck approaches the outer end of its travel, it discharges its contents down the chute as previously mentioned. To enable this to take place, the bottom of the truck (63) is pivoted (as shown in Fig. E) on a 3" Rod (64). At the other end of the bottom Plate (63) is a ½" Pulley (65), carried on a 1½" Rod (66) mounted in a 1½" Double Angle Strip (67) secured to the base and spaced by five Washers (69).

In the centre of the rails (3) on the truck runway a central Strip (68) is provided on which the ½" Pulley (65) runs. This Strip (68) is bent downward at the mouth of the chute. Consequently, as the base of the truck reaches the chute, the wheel (65) rides down the bent end (68) and permits the bottom of the truck to open and the load to be discharged.

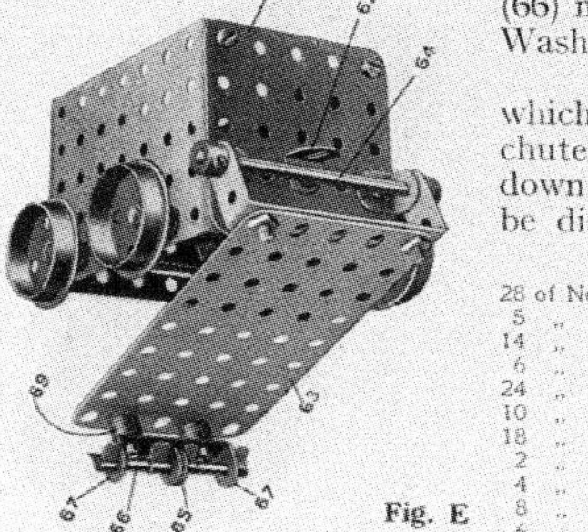

Fig. E

PARTS REQUIRED:

28 of No. 1						1 of No. 95A
5 " " 1A	6 of No. 9	6 of No. 16	10 of No. 23	3 of No. 44	1 of No. 53A	2 " " 96A
14 " " 2	1 " " 9A	2 " " 16A	4 " " 24	2 " " 45	1 " " 54	2 " " 103D
6 " " 2A	4 " " 10	2 " " 16B	3 " " 26	1 " " 46	50 " " 59	2 " " 106
24 " " 3	6 " " 11	2 " " 17	4 " " 27A	1 " " 48	3 " " 63	2 " " 108
10 " " 4	18 " " 12	2 " " 18A	12 " " 35	7 " " 48A	2 " " 70	2 " " 111
18 " " 5	5 " " 12A	3 " " 18B	280 " " 37	11 " " 48B	2 " " 72	8 " " 115
2 " " 6	3 " " 13	8 " " 20	16 " " 37A	1 " " 48C	4 " " 76	1 " " 124
4 " " 6A	3 " " 14	3 " " 21	30 " " 38	1 " " 48D	2 " " 77	2 " " 125
8 " " 7	2 " " 15	5 " " 22	1 " " 40	1 " " 52	4 " " 90	4 " " 126
6 " " 8	3 " " 15A	14 " " 22A	2 " " 43	2 " " 53	48" " " 94	1 " " 128

Meccano Ltd. Binns Road Liverpool England

427/1

Price 2d.

The Meccano Crystal Receiving Set

FIG. A. THE MECCANO CRYSTAL RECEIVING SET

THE MECCANO CRYSTAL RECEIVING SET is the result of much study and experiment to produce an apparatus that is both easy to make and efficient in operation. It is constructed entirely of standard Meccano parts, with the addition of one or two Radio fittings, such as electrical terminals, crystals, and telephone receiver.

The crystal used in the receiver is Meccolite, a new highly sensitive substance the formula of which has been developed by our scientific staff. Meccolite is made in our own laboratories and we have proved by experiments that it gives far better results for radio purposes than any other crystal. Not only is the range of the apparatus increased, enabling signals to be received from greater distances, but the signals are also very much clearer and stronger than those obtained when other crystals are used.

Some of the Meccano parts are made of Specially Prepared Fibre instead of steel, in order to provide insulation. This Special Fibre is a preparation to be obtained only from Meccano Limited, and has been found to give perfect insulation. The fact that it is made in strips of different lengths and plates of varying sizes, enables it to be used for a variety of purposes in the construction of Radio apparatus, the equidistant holes of the Meccano system greatly adding to its value. Every part in the Meccano Receiving Set is standardised and any part may be obtained from your dealer, or direct from Meccano Limited.

The Meccano Receiving apparatus is as easy to construct as any of the hundreds of Meccano models that boys all over the world build every day. Any boy who builds the apparatus will obtain not only great pleasure but also a sound knowledge of the wonderful new science of Radio. All Meccano boys should set to work and make this wonderful Receiving Set. There is a delightful experience in store for them and many a thrill when they hear concerts, speeches lectures and other entertainments by means of an instrument which they themselves have assembled and installed in their own homes.

Do not consider that you have exhausted the possibilities of Radio with your Meccano Crystal Set. Take a real interest in the subject and try experiments. With Meccano parts you have a wonderful means of testing-out, in an easy and rapid manner, any new ideas that may occur to you. We want Meccano boys to be foremost in invention and discovery and Radio presents an unlimited field in which great opportunities are ever present, waiting only to be grasped by persistent, imaginative and inventive boys and men.

Radio tests are being made and experiments conducted in the Meccano factories every day by special staffs of highly-trained experts, and we shall have much to say regarding the results of their work in the future. Already a number of valuable discoveries have been made in the direction of obtaining improved results in Radio receiving with the aid of Meccano parts. Discoveries and improvements will be announced in the *Meccano Magazine*. We strongly advise every Meccano boy to take this Magazine regularly in the future, for its pages include a special Radio section in addition to many other articles of general interest to all boys. A specimen copy will be sent free on request.

The Meccano Receiving Set consists of three distinct sections:—The Tuning Condenser, the Detector and the Inductances.

CONDENSER

Proceed by securing to the board a 5½" × 3½" perforated metal plate (2, Fig. A) with four corner bolts, after which the fixed portion of the condenser (Fig. B) may be constructed. This is formed by connecting eight 2½" triangular plates together at the lower end by a 2" threaded rod (14) and at the same time spacing them by two nickel washers between each plate, afterwards clamping them at each end by a washer and a nut. At the upper end a 2" threaded rod (14A) is used. Before threading the rod through the plates two Triangular Fibre Plates should be placed between each pair, and spaced apart by a nickel and brass washer, so as to make the upper spacing uniform with the lower, clamping them together in the same manner as the lower end. It will be noticed that in these Triangular Fibre Plates one of the corner holes is cut out; this is intended to clear the washers on the rod (14) in order to make a better electrical contact. The fixed portion may now be fastened in position between two 2½" × 1½" angle strips (5 and 5A) and a 2½" strip (17) is bolted at the top with a spacing washer at each end and extra nuts (15) are threaded to both ends of the rods (14 and 14A) to centralise them. The strips (5 and 5A) are then secured to the plate (2) at 6 and 6A by two No. 6 B.A. bolts with an insulating fibre bush between each angle strip and the plate. The movable portion (Fig. C) is composed of seven triangular plates threaded in a similar manner to those in the fixed portion with two nickel spacing washers at the top and bottom, but no Triangular Fibre Plates are used. This movable portion is then passed between the apertures of the fixed portion and connected to the 1" × ½" brackets (7, Fig. A) and lock nutted on the outside of the same brackets. The insulating handles (19) may now be screwed on; these are intended to prevent interference with the signals or telephony received by the apparatus.

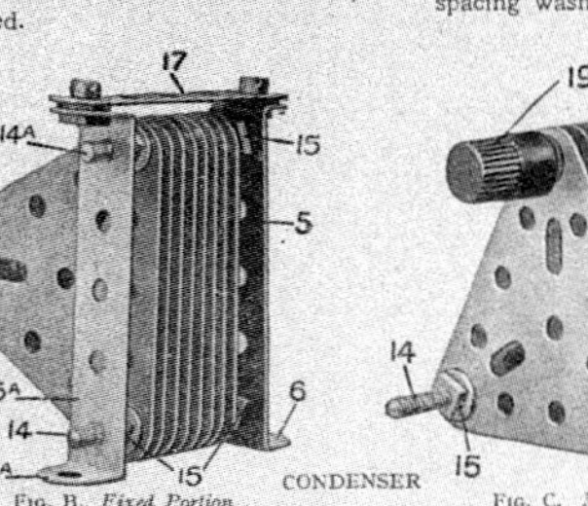

FIG. B. *Fixed Portion* — CONDENSER — FIG. C. *Movable Portion*

THE MECCOLITE CRYSTAL DETECTOR

A 4½" × 2½" Special Fibre plate (20, Fig. A) is attached in a similar manner to the plate (2). A single bent strip (23) is secured along with a flat bracket (24) to the plate (20); this forms the bearing for the detector arm (29). A 1" angle bracket (26) and a 1½" strip (27) are bolted to the same plate as shown. To the upper end of the angle bracket (26) is bolted a cup (4) holding the Meccolite Crystal. The detector arm (29) is then placed between the faces of the bent strip (23) with which it forms a universal joint to enable the best position to be found on the crystal for the fine contact wire called the "cat-whisker."

The vibrating currents so induced in the discs 38 and 39 are rectified, or only allowed to pass in one direction through the Meccolite Crystal, thus enabling the telephone to make the signals audible.

INDUCTANCES

To one corner of a 2½" × 2½" Special Fibre Plate (30, Figs. A and D) are attached two trunnions (31) on each side of the plate (30) as shown, and at the upper corresponding corner of the same plate are attached the inductance discs (38 and 39). It will be noted that the hinges are arranged so that the discs may be brought together as closely as possible. Two terminals (33 and 34) are connected in the two top holes of the outer corner of the plate (30), and a further two terminals (35 and 36) are connected lower down.

Fig 7. The first type crystal set leaflet.

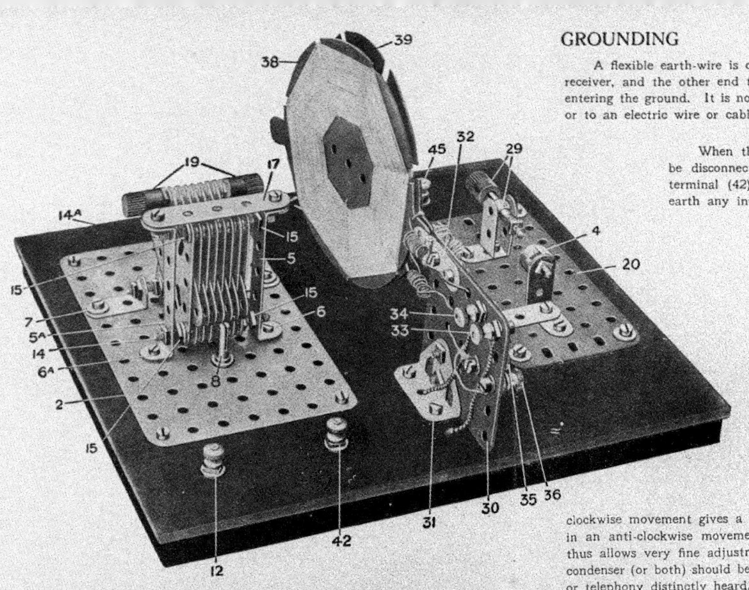

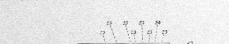

Fig. D. REVERSE SIDE OF MECCANO CRYSTAL RECEIVING SET

GROUNDING

A flexible earth-wire is connected to the earth terminal (42, Fig. D) on the receiver, and the other end to a water-pipe or other suitable metallic conductor entering the ground. It is not desirable to connect the ground wire to a gas pipe or to an electric wire or cable.

When the apparatus is not in use, the lead-in wire should be disconnected from terminal (12) and the ground wire from terminal (42) and the two wires connected together, so as to earth any influence picked up by the aerial.

OPERATING THE RECEIVER

Before the apparatus, is adjusted the phone should be held to the ear and the inductance discs (38 and 39) brought closely together. The condenser should then be placed about the centre of its arc of movement. At the same time the detector arm should be gently moved on the face of the crystal, so as to select its most sensitive point.

A light degree of pressure on the crystal is required and the insulated handle of the detector arm controls the pressure. Turning the handle to the right in a clockwise movement gives a light contact whereas turning the handle to the left in an anti-clockwise movement results in a heavier contact. The detector arm thus allows very fine adjustment. When this point is reached, the discs or the condenser (or both) should be moved until the sound is magnified, and the signals or telephony distinctly heard.

WIRING

The wiring will be made clear by reference to Figs. D and E and by remembering that Fig. E is an underneath view of Fig. D. From aerial terminal (12) the 3½" steel strip (10, Fig. E) carries the impulses to the connection (6A) and through the condenser to the terminal on (7), thence by wire (41) to terminal (35) to which is also attached one end (46) of the winding on the disc (38), thence through the coil and the other end (47) to terminal (36) and thence by wire (43) to the earth terminal (42). The impulses are induced by the winding of the disc (39) and pass to the terminals (33 and 34). Another wire (51) is also connected to the terminal (34) carrying the impulses to the telephone terminal on (44). An additional wire (54) is also connected to terminals (33 and 28) through which the impulses also pass, and thence through the detector and by a 2" metal strip (40) connected to terminal (25) to the other telephone terminal (45).

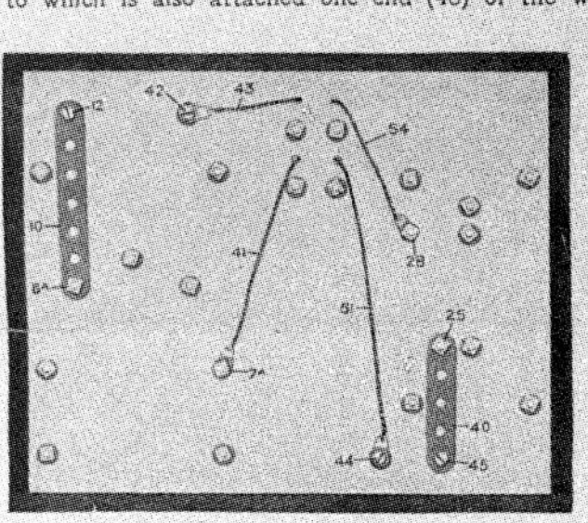

Fig. E.
UNDERNEATH VIEW OF MOUNTING BOARD

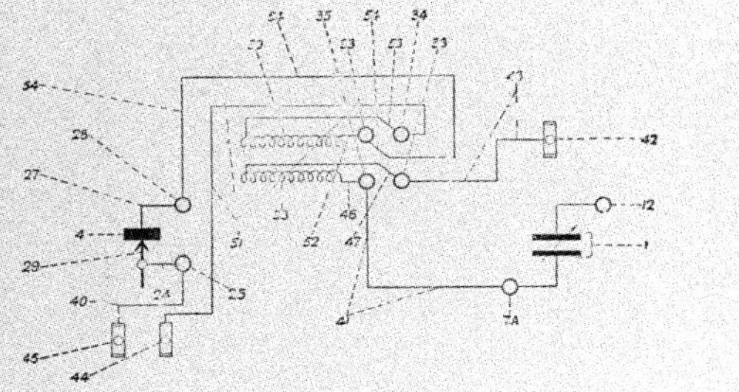

Fig. G. WIRING DIAGRAM

1. Condenser.
7A. Condenser terminal.
12. Aerial terminal.
24. 1½" connecting strip.
25. Detector-arm terminal.
27. Connecting strip to detector crystal.
28. Detector terminal.
29. Detector arm.
4. Crystal and cup.
33., 34. Terminals for inductance disc 39 and connections.
35., 36. Terminals for inductance disc 38 and connections.
38., 39. Inductance discs.
40. Wire, connecting detector terminal 25 to telephone terminal 45.
41. Wire connecting condenser and inductance discs.
42. Earth terminal.
43. Wire connecting terminal (36) to earth terminal.
44., 45. Telephone terminals.
46., 47. Winding of inductance disc 38 connected to terminals 35 and 36.
51. Wire connecting terminal 34 to telephone terminal 44.
52., 53. Winding of inductance disc 39 connected to terminals 33 and 34.
54. Wire connecting terminal 33 to detector terminal 28.

AERIAL

This is a single copper wire suspended between two insulated points in an elevated position. It receives the impulses which are conducted by the lead-in wire to the receiver. A length of up to 100 ft. is permitted for a single wire,

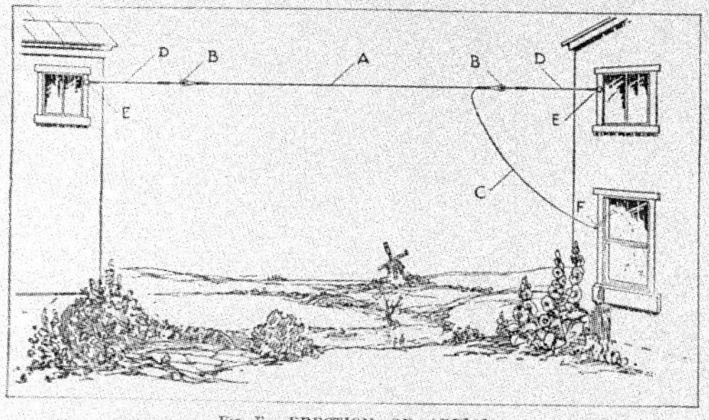

Fig. F. ERECTION OF AERIAL.

A. Antenna. B. Insulators (porcelain). C. Lead-in wire.
D. Rope. E. Staples or screwed eyes. F. Aperture.

including the lead-in. If the distance between the two points to which it is intended to fix the aerial be greater than is necessary, the insulators may be attached to a rope or line which is fastened to the points chosen. The lead-in wire should, however, be as close as possible to the receiver, and should be soldered to the antenna to make a good connection. Fig. F shows how the aerial should be erected.

No. 16 gauge bare copper wire is used for the antenna, each end of which is connected with porcelain insulators by being passed through one of the holes and twisted. This portion, apart from the lead-in should be about 65 to 75 ft. in length, the length of the antenna being governed by the local conditions, according to the space available for erecting an aerial. A long antenna is an advantage, though excellent results may be obtained on short antenna if it is well insulated.

The lead-in (C) should be passed through an aperture (F) insulated with rubber-coated wire, as supplied with the Meccano aerial.

PRICES OF MECCANO RADIO RECEIVING AND AERIAL SETS AND SPECIAL RADIO PARTS.

RS1. Meccano Crystal Receiving Set, complete. Efficiency tested. Packed in strong carton ... ... price 55/–

RS2. Outfit containing parts to make Meccano Crystal Receiving Set, in strong carton ... ... price 45/–

AS1. Aerial Set, complete, and ready for connecting to receiver (including earth wire) ... ... price 12/6

Meccano Radio Parts.

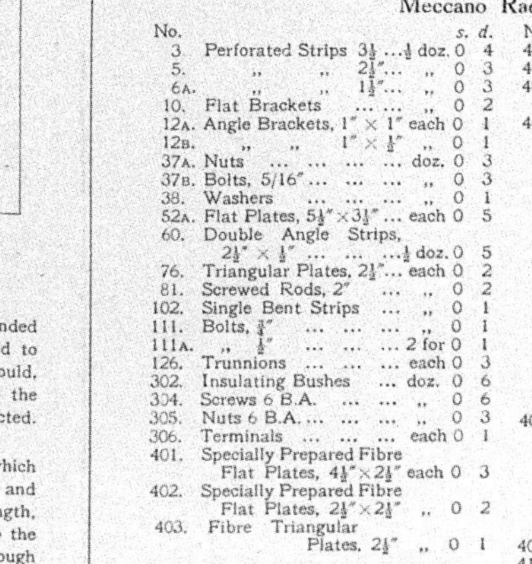

No.			s.	d.
3.	Perforated Strips 3½	... ½ doz.	0	4
5.	" " 2½"	... "	0	3
6A.	" " 1½"	... "	0	3
10.	Flat Brackets	... "	0	2
12A.	Angle Brackets, 1" × 1"	each	0	1
12B.	" " 1" × ½"	"	0	1
37A.	Nuts	... doz.	0	3
37B.	Bolts, 5/16"	... "	0	3
38.	Washers	... "	0	1
52A.	Flat Plates, 5½" × 3½"	... each	0	5
60.	Double Angle Strips, 2½" × ½"	... ½ doz.	0	5
76.	Triangular Plates, 2½"	... each	0	2
81.	Screwed Rods, 2"	... "	0	2
102.	Single Bent Strips	... "	0	1
111.	Bolts, ¾"	... "	0	1
111A.	" ½"	... 2 for	0	1
126.	Trunnions	... each	0	3
302.	Insulating Bushes	... doz.	0	6
304.	Screws 6 B.A.	... "	0	6
305.	Nuts 6 B.A.	... "	0	3
306.	Terminals	... each	0	1
401.	Specially Prepared Fibre Flat Plates, 4½" × 2½"	each	0	3
402.	Specially Prepared Fibre Flat Plates, 2½" × 2½"	"	0	2
403.	Fibre Triangular Plates, 2½"	"	0	1

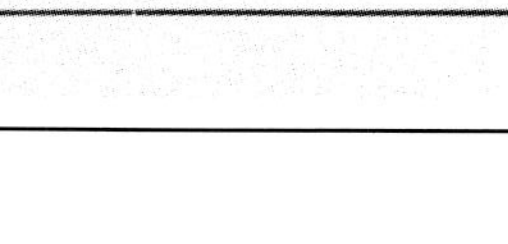

(No. 404) (No. 410) (No. 411)

No.			s.	d.
404.	Insulating Handles	... each	0	3
405.	Brass Washers, 1/32"	... doz.	0	4
406.	9" Lengths 22s Bell-wire with Tags	... each	0	2
407.	Inductance Discs (wave length approximately 500 metres)	... per pair	6	0
408.	Single Telephone Receivers (2000 ohms)	each	18	6
409.	Detector Arms, complete,	each	1	0
410.	Meccolite Crystals Mounted (Complete with Clips, No. 411)	... each	2	6
411.	Clips for Crystals	... "	0	3
412.	Mounting Boards	... "	5	0
	Instruction Leaflets	... "	0	2

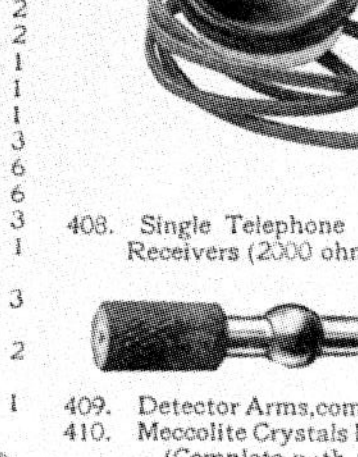

MECCANO LTD. LIVERPOOL

INSTRUCTIONS.

The Meccano Single Aerial

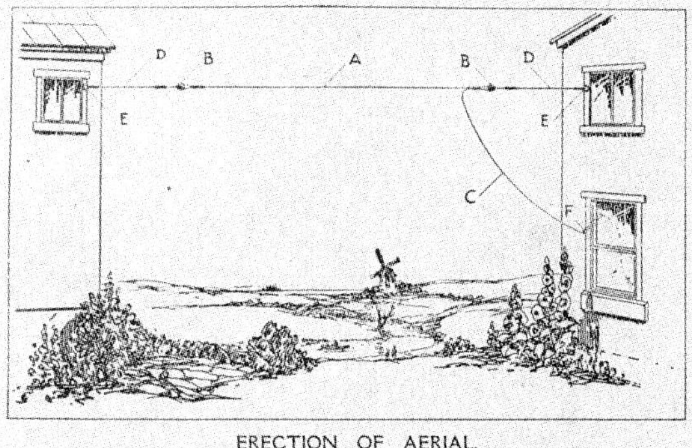

ERECTION OF AERIAL.

A. Antenna. B. Insulators (porcelain). C. Lead-in Wire.
D. Rope. E. Staples or Screwed Eyes. F. Aperture.

THE Antenna (A) consisting of about 100 ft. of No. 16 gauge bare copper wire, receives the radio impulses, which are conducted to the receiver by an insulated lead-in wire (C).

The antenna is suspended between two porcelain insulators (BB), the purpose of which is to prevent the antenna from touching anything that is capable of conducting an electric current. If this occurs the radio impulse will be conducted to earth, instead of to the receiving apparatus.

The results obtained depend very largely on the aerial, which should be as high up as possible. One end of the aerial may be fastened to the window-frame of an attic or an upper room, and the other end to a window-frame opposite, or to a clothes post or garden fence.

If the distance between two convenient points is greater than the length of aerial wire available, the insulators may be attached to a rope or line (DD), itself fastened to the points chosen (EE). The lead-in wire (C) should be passed through a hole in the window frame (F) or an open window to the Receiving Apparatus, which should be as near to the aerial as possible.

One end of the earth wire is connected to the Receiver terminal marked "Earth," the other to a water-pipe or other suitable metallic conductor that enters the ground. Before connecting the earth-wire to the water-pipe, the latter should be carefully scraped and any paint or dirt removed, to ensure perfect connection.

MECCANO LIMITED BINNS ROAD LIVERPOOL

2122/2·5

INSTRUCTIONS.

The Meccano Radio Receiving Set

CONNECT the insulated lead-in wire from the aerial to the terminal marked "Aerial" on the receiving apparatus, and one end of the bare earth wire to the terminal marked "Earth," the other end being connected to a water pipe or other metallic conductor entering the ground.

The detector-arm is adjusted so that the fine copper wire, or "cat-whisker," lightly touches the crystal. The most sensitive spot on the crystal should be selected by moving the cat-whisker, which should lightly touch, but not press upon, the crystal.

The slideable tuner is moved slowly along its slide until it reaches a point at which Morse or telephony is heard. Fine adjustment is then made until the best result is obtained. With P.M.G. aerial broadcasting will usually be found with the indicator at about "30" on the scale, the figures on which will be found useful for indicating the positions on the cylinder for picking up any desired transmitting stations once they have been found and noted.

It is by the careful operation of the detector-arm and the sliding tuner that the best results are obtained.

The winding on the Meccano Receiving Set allows for reception on wave lengths from zero to about 1,000 metres. By sliding the tuner to the left, the wave length will be increased, and Morse signals from ships at sea and from land stations may be received.

If the receiver is left connected to the lead-in wire when not in use, the cat-whisker should be moved from the face of the crystal, as otherwise the latter may become "tired." When receiving is finished the apparatus should be disconnected from earth and lead-in wires, which should then be connected together so as to earth any influences picked up by the aerial.

If you are in any difficulty in regard to Radio, write to the Radio Editor of the *Meccano Magazine*, who will be pleased to help you.

MECCANO LIMITED BINNS ROAD LIVERPOOL

1222/2·5

Fig 9. The Aerial leaflet.

PRICE 2d.

The Meccano Charging Board

and How to Make It.

TO meet the requirements of many Meccano boys, who wish to run their Meccano Motors direct from the main in their own homes, we have designed a simple type of apparatus which is safe and easy to use. This is the Meccano Charging Board, which may be obtained through any Meccano dealer, price 50/– complete (except for two 60-watt lamps). It is important to note, however, that the *Charging Board can be used only in those towns where the source of supply is direct current.* In the case of the supply being an alternating current, other methods are necessary.

In addition to enabling the Meccano Motor to be run direct from the main, the Meccano Charging Board may also be used for charging accumulators, and in this connection it is very economical in use. To recharge an accumulator (after the first charge, which requires approximately 40 hours) it is necessary to leave it on charge for about 10 hours. If a direct current of, say, 200 volts be used, the cost of charging a cell would amount to about 4d. Several accumulators may be charged at the same time at no extra cost.

(4, Fig. C) in the "off" position. Next insert the 60-watt lamps in the two batten lamp holders (6 and 6A) on the Board and switch on the current from the main supply. Place the plug in the socket (7) and throw on the double-pole switch (4). The two lamps on the panel should then light up if the bare ends of the flexible wire (2, Fig. A), from the plug are placed together.

FINDING POSITIVE AND NEGATIVE WIRES.—Before connecting the accumulator to these flexible wires, the positive and negative wires must be identified. This is accomplished by the use of pole-finding paper, as follows:—

A piece of the paper is damped with water and then placed on wood or cardboard. The ends of the wires from the plug (7) are then pressed lightly on the paper about half an inch apart, with the switches "on." The positive wire will leave a dark mark on the paper and the wire should then be plainly marked or labelled for future reference. After once finding the correct polarity the adapter (1) and plug (7) should not be removed. (*Note.*—Some pole-finding paper shows a red mark from the negative wire, and enquiry should be made when purchasing as to the type of paper supplied.)

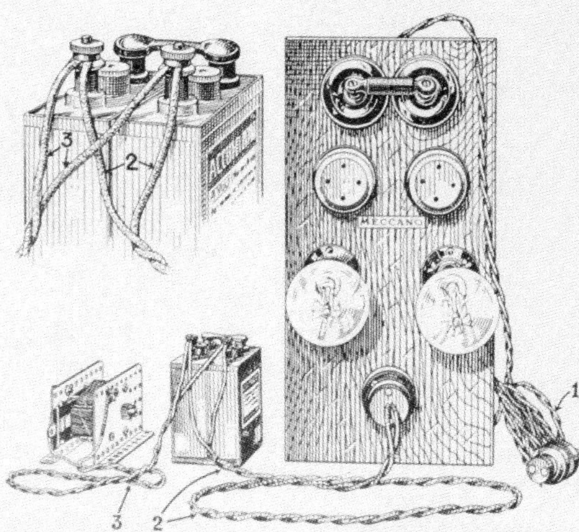

FIG. A.—RUNNING THE MECCANO MOTOR DIRECT FROM THE MAIN BY MEANS OF THE CHARGING BOARD.

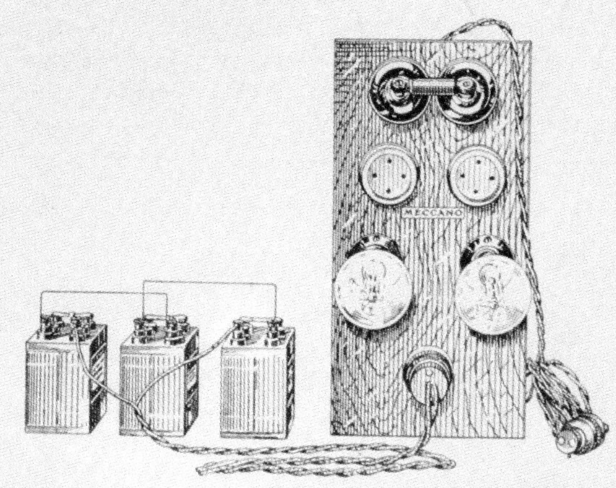

FIG. B.—CHARGING ACCUMULATORS FROM THE MAIN BY MEANS OF CHARGING BOARD.

Fig 10. The lethal Charging Board.

The Meccano Charging Board is not difficult to construct, and those boys who are interested in electricity and who are handy with their tools can easily make it themselves at a reduced cost, by means of the instructions given below. The following list shows the apparatus required, and this may be obtained from any Electrician.

1 5-ampere coupled tumbler switch, or two separate tumbler switches.
2 circular 5-ampere singe pole fuses.
2 batten lamp holders.
1 5-ampere wall socket and plug.
1 adapter (if connection is to be made to an existing lamp holder).
4 yards No. 14/36 flexible wire.
3 yards No. 20 vulcanised india-rubber and braided wire.
1 small piece of pole-finding paper.
12 inches of 1-ampere fuse wire.
2 60-watt lamps (or 1 ½-watt, taking ½ ampere).

In addition to the above, a piece of board is required, measuring approximately 14" × 8" × ⅞".

It is recommended that the Charging Board be fixed to a wall, and if this suggestion is adopted it will be necessary to affix a batten on each side to allow space for the wires at the back of the board when so fixed. The front of the board may be varnished or polished, as desired.

The covers should first be taken off the switches (4), fuses (5), lamp holders (6 and 6A), and wall-socket (7), Fig. C. and the wire-clamping screws of the terminals unscrewed. The switches, etc., should be then symmetrically arranged, on the board and the wire holes and fixing holes marked out with a thin bradawl. The holes should be drilled with a ⅜" drill, and the switches, etc., screwed down in position. The No. 20 vulcanised india-rubber and braided wire should be used to wire the board, and the circuit diagram shown in Fig. C should be followed. A little loose wire should be left in each case at the rear of the Board, and the ends of the wire secured in the terminals by their clamping screws.

In cutting away the insulation and baring the wires for the connection, it is important to remember not to cut away more than necessary. In every case insulation should enter the holes in the porcelain bases on which the connections are made.

It will be noticed that on one lamp holder (6A, Fig. C.) two wires are connected to each terminal. This connection should present no difficulty, however, if a reasonable amount of care is exercised. To wire the adapter (1, Fig. A), remove the cover, unscrew the terminal screws, and thread the bare ends of the flexible wire into the holes of the terminals. Tighten up the screws and replace the cover. Measure off the amount of flexible necessary to reach the lamp holder which will be used, and connect the opposite ends of the flexible wire from the adapter to the two outside terminals of the double pole switch (Fig. C, 4). The plug which fits into the socket (7) should also be wired to a short length of the flexible. Remove the cover of the plug (7) and connect the ends of the flexible to the terminal of this socket, and, having done this, replace the cover.

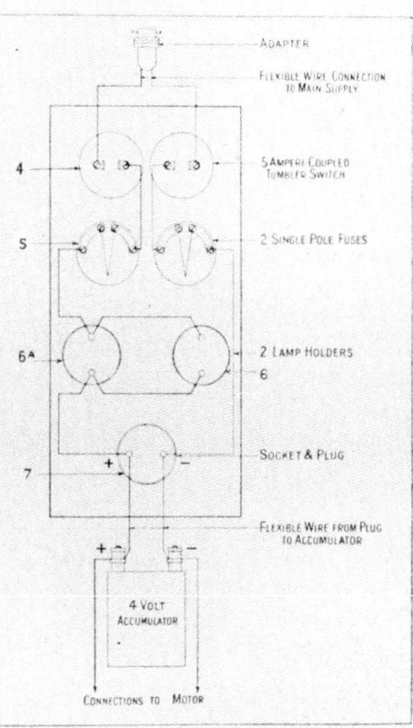

FIG. C.—WIRING DIAGRAM FOR CHARGING BOARD.

A piece of fuse wire should now be inserted in each fuse (5), care being taken that the wire is screwed tightly under the small screws and washers of the terminals.

To make connection with the main supply, remove the lamp from the holder which is to be used, and insert the adapter (1), already connected to the panel. Before doing this it is important to place the double-pole switch

It is interesting to observe in passing that the full force of the current which flows to the accumulator through the Board does not travel along the wires (3) to the motor. As the main current seeks the line of least resistance, it discharges itself into the accumulator, and the two wires (3) carry only 4 volts.

If the wires (2) were connected directly to the motor no damage would occur, nor would any result be obtained except that the two lamps would light, for the motor is of low resistance and the current passes through its windings, without, however, causing it to work.

FIRST CHARGE.—The accumulators which we send out require to be charged before they can be used. The first charge requires a little more care and attention than do subsequent charges. Before the accumulator can be charged it must be filled with brimstone sulphuric acid diluted to the specific gravity of 1·150, which may be obtained through any Chemist. After the accumulator has been filled it should be allowed to stand for about three hours before charging is attempted, to enable the glass wool between the plates to absorb a quantity of acid and so render the accumulator active. Before charging is attempted, a fresh quantity of acid should be added so that the plates are just covered. It may then be connected with the Charging Board in the method already described, and allowed to remain on charge for about 40 hours. When fully charged the acid will give off gas and froth from the vent holes at the top of the cell.

It is important to remove all traces of acid at all times from the outside of the accumulator, for sulphuric acid is a powerful corrosive.

RE-CHARGING.—To re-charge the accumulator it is necessary first to ascertain that there is sufficient acid in it to cover the plates. It may then be connected up with the Charging Board and placed on charge, as in the first case. About 10 hours are required for this and subsequent charges.

CHARGING MORE THAN ONE ACCUMULATOR.—When more than one accumulator is to be charged, the accumulators should be placed in a row near the Charging Board and the connection made as follows: The positive wire from the Board should be connected with the positive terminal of one of the end cells, and the negative wire to the negative terminal of the cell at the other end. The intermediate accumulators should be connected by wires from the negative terminal of one to the positive terminal of the other (see Fig. B).

COST OF CHARGING.—The Charging Board provides only ½ ampere, and the first charge takes 30 to 40 hours, 10 hours only being required for each subsequent charge. If a direct current of, say, 200 volts be used, this multiplied by ½ or ·50 ampere would represent 100 watts. As the Board of Trade unit is 1,000-watt hours, the cost of a cell remaining on charge for 10 hours would be 10 times 100, equal to 1 unit. Assuming the price per unit to be, say, 4d., this figure would represent the cost of charging one cell. As the current passing through a combination of cells is no more than that passing through one (see Fig. B), it will be clear that several accumulators may be charged at one time with no extra cost.

1121/2.5

MECCANO LTD. Head Office and Factory: LIVERPOOL, ENGLAND.

Fig 10.

The Super Model and other leaflets

The 1921–1927 series of Special Model Leaflets paved the way for further sets of instructions for the increasingly more complex models being designed. The large vertical format of the earlier leaflets was unwieldy and the decision was taken to reduce the size to something more manageable. The pages were halved in size, becoming horizontal in format; the result was a leaflet with an 11″ × 8″ page size capable of expansion when necessary, something not possible with the earlier type.

The new series of leaflets were given the heading 'Special Instruction Leaflets for Building Meccano Super Models' and issue commenced in 1928. The Super Model Leaflets or SMLs as they are usually known form the subject of Volume 2 of the Hornby Companion Series. In it, the author, Geoff Wright, has given a very full history. However for the sake of completeness a short resumé and a few notes are not out of place.

The original series of SMLs comprised 37 leaflets. 29 were issued in 1928, five in 1929 and the remaining three in 1930. There were a further five 'a' designated leaflets issued between 1929 and 1936 (1a, 11a, 14a, 16a and 19a), as well as two wholesale revisions in 1936 (nos 28 and 29) making a total of 44. Despite the words of the Meccano publicity machine, out of the 29 published in 1928 only nine were 'new', the remainder being earlier manual models given a separate leaflet (this assumes that No. 1, The Motor Chassis was not issued as a large format leaflet in 1927). Those published in 1929 and 1930, as well as the 'a' leaflets, were new with the exception of 11a which was really a reworking of No. 11 using strip plates instead of braced girders.

Not all the models in the series justified the title 'Super Model', nor indeed a separate leaflet although most of the new ones did. The obvious exception is No. 8, the Roundabout which was issued as part of the campaign to sell the then newly-introduced Geared Roller Bearing.

Many of the leaflet models, particularly the existing ones, were capable of being built from the contents of either the No. 6 or No. 7 outfits (or K and L respectively from 1934) and were supplied with them. As with the earlier series the outfit manuals simply showed a picture of the model and referred the reader to the leaflet.

Since quite a number of the existing models required little in the way of expanded text, the remaining space was used to discuss the real versions of the models concerned, in some cases the last page was used to publicise the SML series.

Most of the SMLs ran to more than one edition and many had some form of updating. In 1931 a whole series of addenda slips were printed which referred in the main to the withdrawal of either the High Voltage Motor or the 4 volt motor (fig 11). In 1934 a large number of new editions partially superceded the slips and also referred to the change from Red/Green to Blue/Gold, although it was not until 1936 that cross-hatching was added (to those reprinted in that year). During their currency, many leaflets had minor alterations to the text and parts lists which in particular were frequently wrong.

Up until 1936 the series remained intact, except where 'a' leaflets replaced previous versions. That year however saw many deletions which reduced the list to 19, 15 of which had a reprint of 500 copies each during the latter part of the year. These were all 'outfit' models and the implication is that they were to see the company through until the following year when the new numerical series outfits with their self-contained manuals appeared. At this point the SMLs became obsolete and were finally deleted.

Whilst it would not be practical to fully discuss the Super Models, the following notes should prove relevant. UK print references are given after each note. (NR followed by a date means there is leaflet

SPECIAL NOTE TO LEAFLET No. 6

STIFF LEG DERRICK

Since the publication of this leaflet the manufacture of the High Voltage Motor has been discontinued, and a 6-volt Motor introduced in its place. This 6-volt Motor will work the model quite satisfactorily, and no alteration to the reduction gearing or to the gear itself will be found necessary. Current for operating the new Motor may be obtained from the Meccano 6-volt 20 amp. hour Accumulator.

1/331/2·55

SPECIAL NOTE TO LEAFLET No. 19

STEAM SHOVEL

The diameter of the Circular Strip has recently been increased ½ in., and therefore it is necessary to modify slightly the construction of the roller race on which the model slews. This is done most easily by reversing the ½ in. fast Pulleys forming the rollers, so that their bosses come up against the Double Brackets in which are journalled the Rods carrying the ½ in. fast Pulleys. This method makes it unnecessary to use extra parts.

1/331/10

SPECIAL NOTE TO LEAFLET No. 15

BALTIC TANK LOCOMOTIVE

The 4-volt Motor used for driving this model is no longer manufactured, and its place has been taken by a 6-volt Motor. The bunker of the locomotive was originally designed to house the 4-volt 20 amp. hour Accumulator. The 6-volt 20 amp. hour Accumulator, from which the new 6-volt Motor draws its current, is too large to fit inside the bunker, and therefore it is necessary to remove the back of the cab in order to accommodate it. This modification does not materially affect the appearance of the model.

1/331/18

SPECIAL NOTE TO LEAFLET No. 2

SHIP COALER

Since the publication of this leaflet the manufacture of the High Voltage Motor and the 4-volt Motor has been discontinued; and these Motors have been replaced by a 6-volt Motor. No difficulty should be experienced in incorporating the 6-volt Motor in this model, as it is secured in place in a similar manner to that shown in Fig. 1. No alteration need be made to the gearing.

1/331/4·2

Fig 11. A group of supplementary leaflets of the type used to update the SMLs.

without a print code: the date given is that most likely.)

No. 1 The Motor Chassis. (Fig 12)

As a model it showed many advances in building techniques and featured a 3-speed and reverse gear-box, differential, Ackermann steering, internal expanding brakes, torque rods and a radiator fan. Its success can be judged by the fact that it became one of the company's flagships and perhaps the best known demonstration model. A No. 7 Outfit model.

328/5 528/5 2/430/5 1/432/2.5

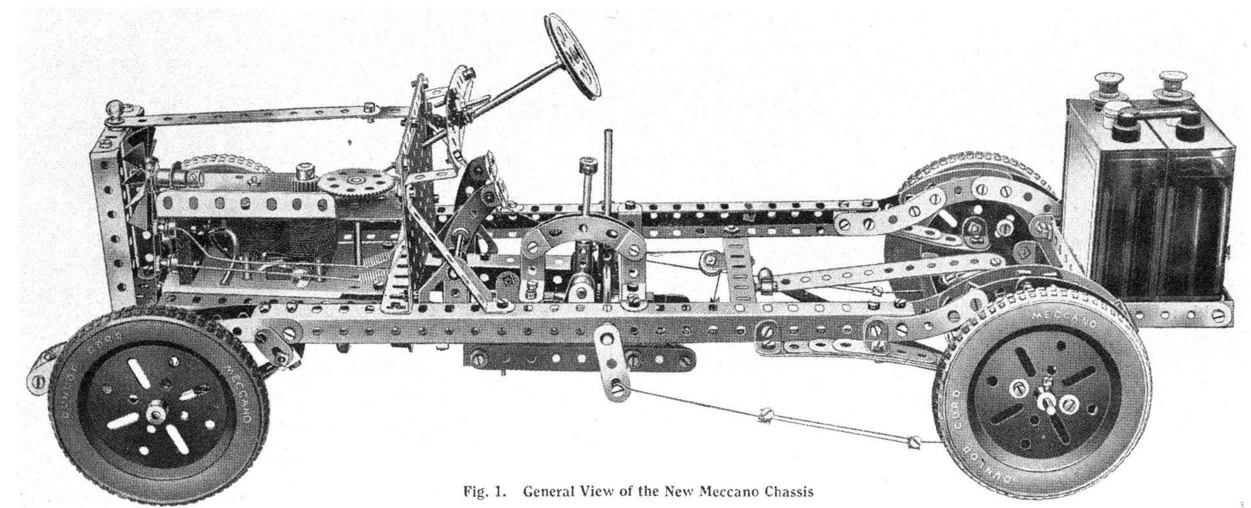

Fig. 1. General View of the New Meccano Chassis

Fig 12. SML 1.

Fig 13. SML 1A.

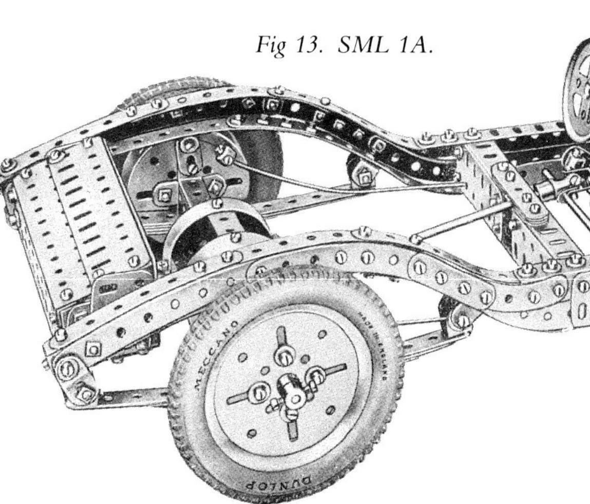

No. 1a The Motor Chassis. (Fig 13)

The replacement motor chassis was published at the end of 1934 to coincide with the introduction of the Blue/Gold Meccano. It was based on the Bentley chassis of the time and featured a power-unit 'block' which enclosed the advanced 4-speed and reverse gearbox, E1/6 motor and clutch. Although rather tricky to build, it is an excellent model which can be made to work well. An L Outfit model although the E1/6 motor was not the type supplied with the outfit.

21/1134/5

Fig 14. SML 2.

No. 2 High Speed Ship Coaler. (Fig 14)

A modified though similar version of the earlier Special Model Leaflet of 1925 and the same comments apply. A No. 7 Outfit model.

428/5 1228/5 1/636/.5 (Supplementary leaflet 1/331/4.2)

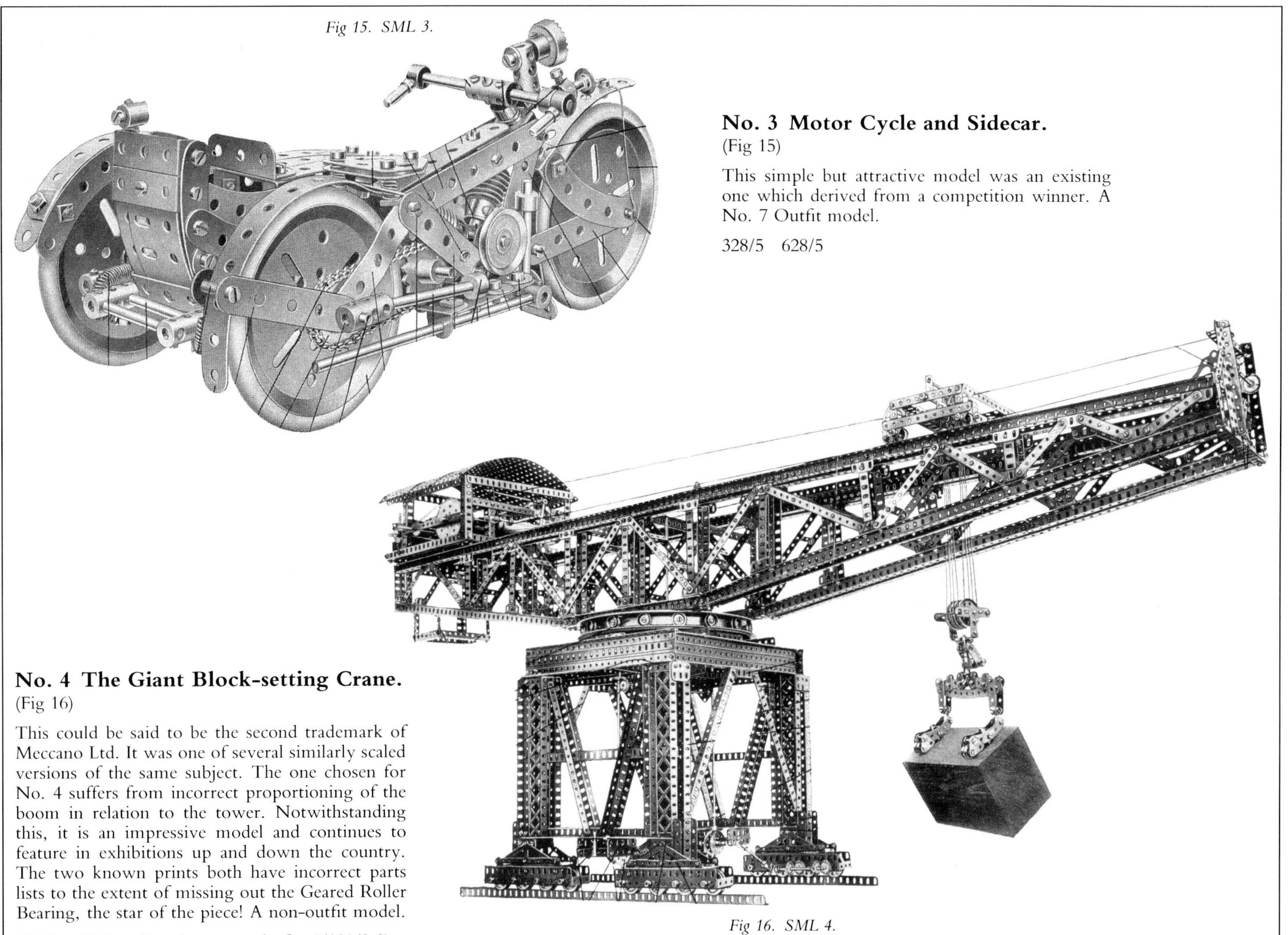

Fig 15. SML 3.

No. 3 Motor Cycle and Sidecar.

(Fig 15)

This simple but attractive model was an existing one which derived from a competition winner. A No. 7 Outfit model.

328/5 628/5

No. 4 The Giant Block-setting Crane.

(Fig 16)

This could be said to be the second trademark of Meccano Ltd. It was one of several similarly scaled versions of the same subject. The one chosen for No. 4 suffers from incorrect proportioning of the boom in relation to the tower. Notwithstanding this, it is an impressive model and continues to feature in exhibitions up and down the country. The two known prints both have incorrect parts lists to the extent of missing out the Geared Roller Bearing, the star of the piece! A non-outfit model.

428/5 628/5 (Supplementary leaflet 1/331/3.2)

Fig 16. SML 4.

No. 5 Travelling Bucket Dredger.

(Fig 17)

An existing model which was given the benefit of photographic enhancement to bring it up-to-date. Although not difficult to build, it is one of the best operators especially if you have a good line of Hornby trucks to load! A No. 7 Outfit model.

528/5 828/5 1/736/.5

Fig 17. SML 5.

Fig 18. SML 6.

No. 6 Stiff Leg Derrick. (Fig 18)

An earlier manual model which itself was derived from a previous version. Although simple and hardly a Super Model, SML 6 was to have been a vehicle for the 1929 Steam Engine and a number, 6a, was allocated. The leaflet was advertised but never actually appeared as Meccano Ltd explained to an enquirer in 1933. (fig 19/20) A No. 7 Outfit model.

628/5 828/5 6/432/1 1/836/.5
(Supplementary leaflet 1/331/2.55)

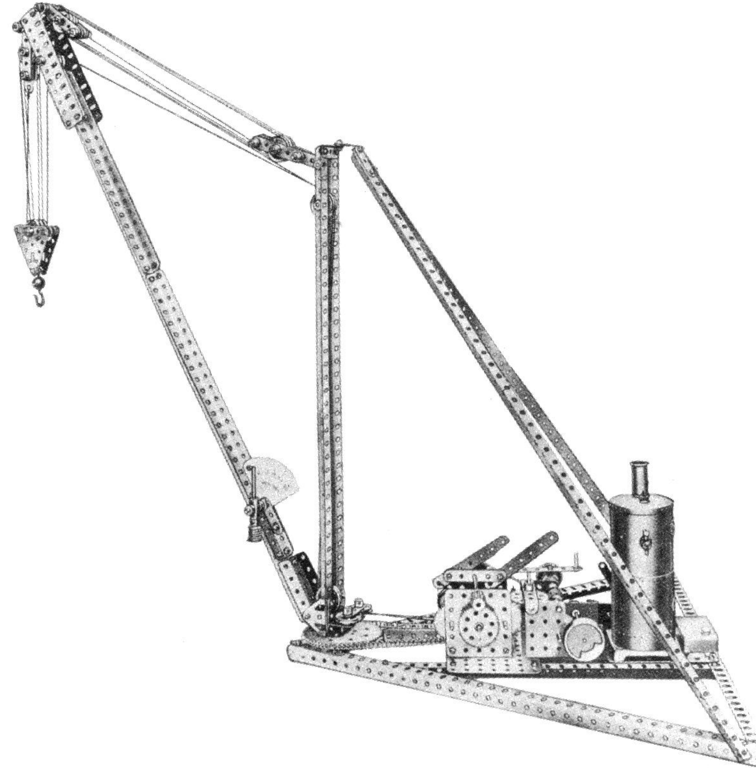

Fig 19. (The non-existant SML 6a).

Fig 20. Letter from Meccano explaining the non-appearance of leaflet No. 6A.

MECCANO L^TD TORONTO.
MECCANO (FRANCE) L^TD PARIS.
MECCANO G.M.B.H. DUSSELDORF.

MECCANO AGENCIES.

AMSTERDAM. ASUNCION. AUCKLAND. BARCELONA. BASLE. BATAVIA. BOGOTA. BOMBAY. BRUSSELS. BUENOS AIRES. CALCUTTA. CAPE TOWN. CARACAS. COLOMBO. DURBAN. GENOA. GUAYAQUIL. HELSINGFORS. HONG KONG. IQUITOS. ISTANBUL. JERUSALEM. JOHANNESBURG. KARACHI. MEXICO. MONTE VIDEO. OSLO. RIO DE JANEIRO. SANTIAGO. SAO PAULO. SHANGHAI. STOCKHOLM. SYDNEY. TRINIDAD. VIENNA.

MECCANO L^TD
LIVERPOOL

TELEPHONE: OLD SWAN 701 (6 LINES)
TELEGRAMS: MECCANO, LIVERPOOL.

LONDON OFFICE & WAREHOUSE.
WALNUT TREE WALK.
KENNINGTON ROAD. S.E. II.

HEAD OFFICE AND FACTORY,
BINNS ROAD, OLD SWAN,
LIVERPOOL.

Master William Wilson,
B I R M I N G H A M, 6.

22nd April, 1933.

Dear Sir,

We thank you for your remittance received to-day, and in reply to your request we write to inform you that we have never published Special Instruction Leaflet No. 6A. It was announced in the "Meccano Magazine" some time ago that it was proposed to build the Stiff-Leg Derrick to be operated by steam, and that a leaflet No. 6A would be published; on investigation it was found that it would not be practicable to drive the Derrick by steam. We are sending you the instructions for building the electrically-driven Stiff-Leg Derrick, which we trust will suit your requirements.

Yours faithfully,

MECCANO LIMITED

R. Ashtroll

RH/-

Correspondence Dept.

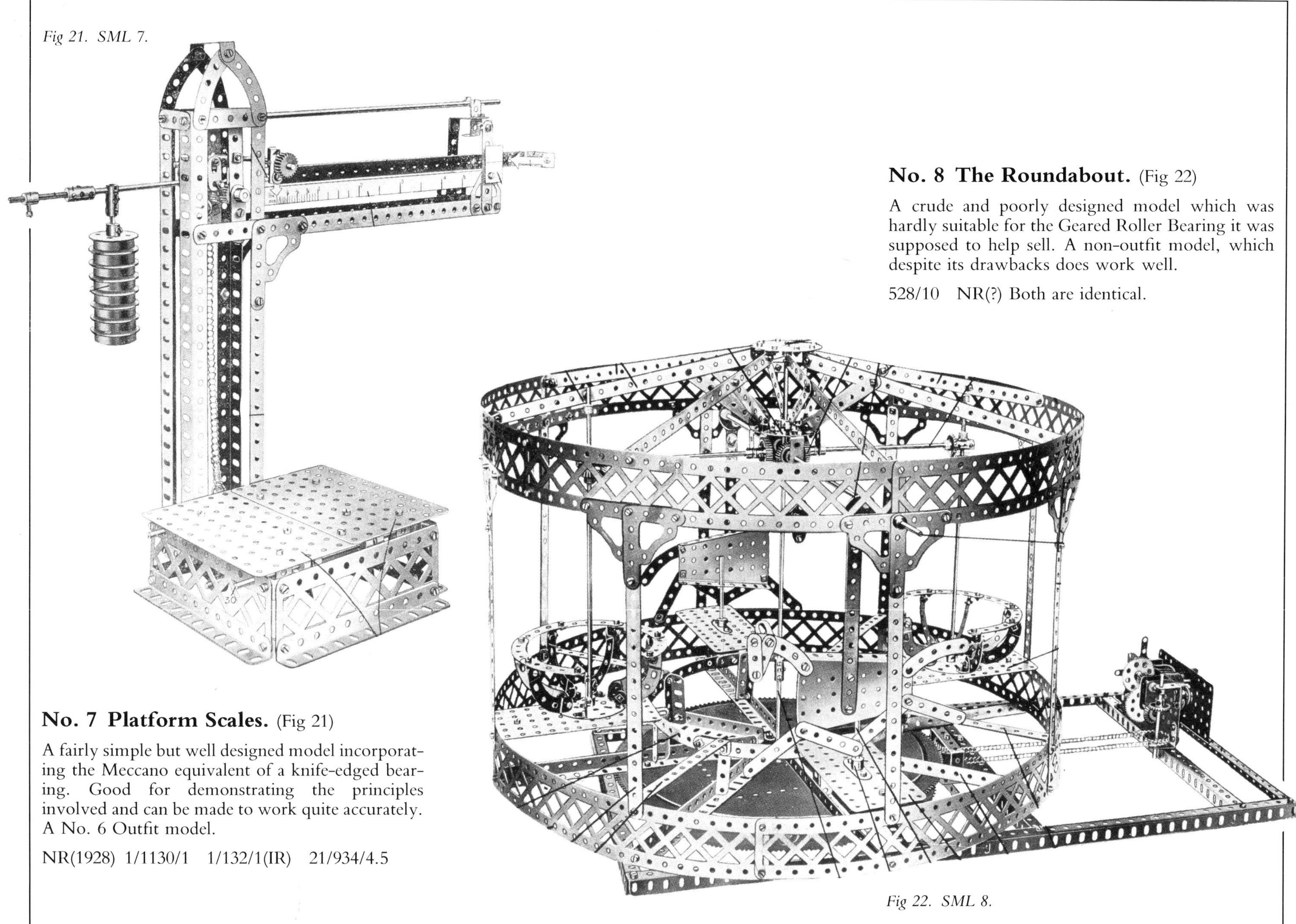

Fig 21. SML 7.

No. 8 The Roundabout. (Fig 22)

A crude and poorly designed model which was hardly suitable for the Geared Roller Bearing it was supposed to help sell. A non-outfit model, which despite its drawbacks does work well.

528/10 NR(?) Both are identical.

No. 7 Platform Scales. (Fig 21)

A fairly simple but well designed model incorporating the Meccano equivalent of a knife-edged bearing. Good for demonstrating the principles involved and can be made to work quite accurately. A No. 6 Outfit model.

NR(1928) 1/1130/1 1/132/1(IR) 21/934/4.5

Fig 22. SML 8.

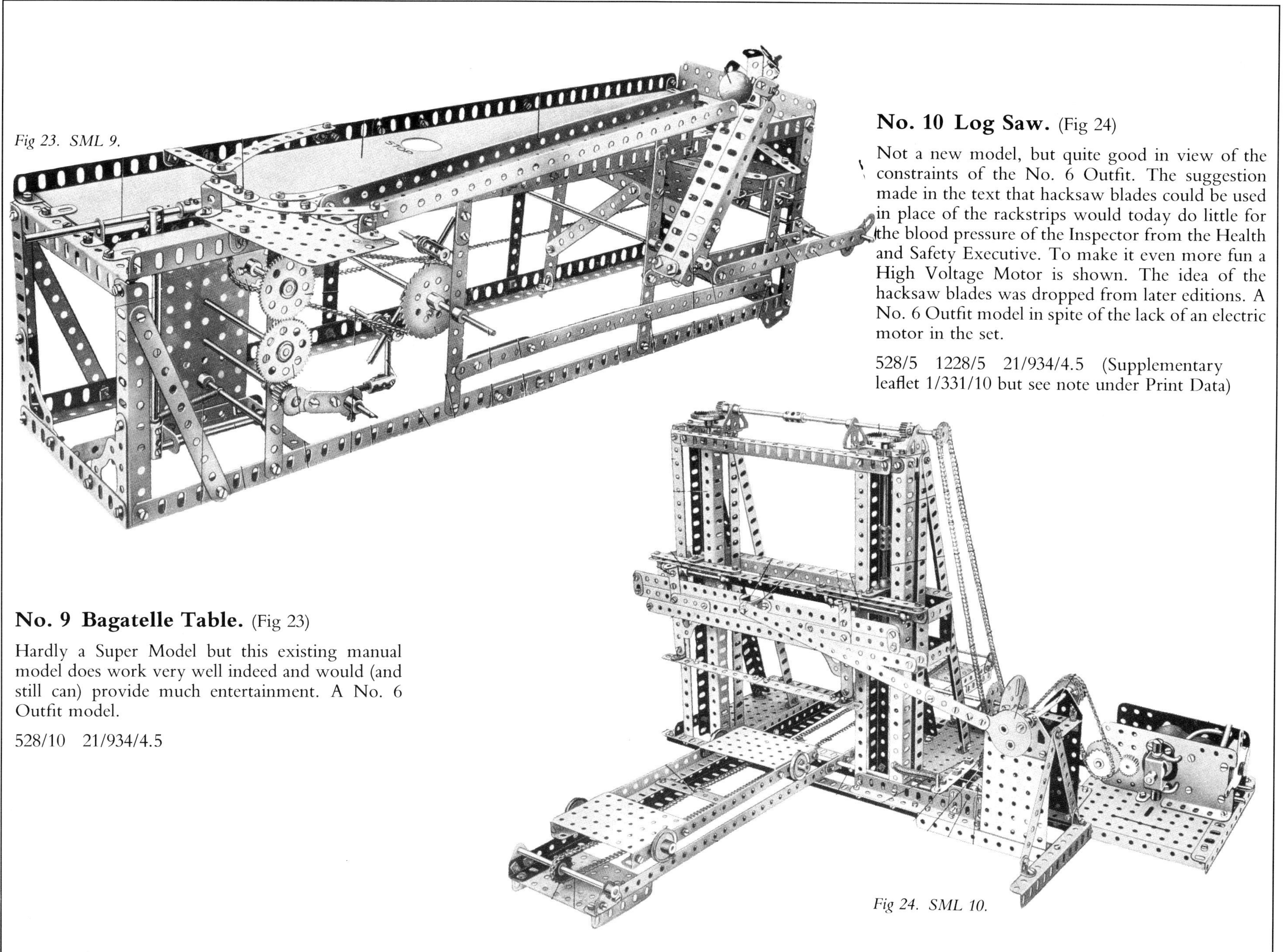

Fig 23. SML 9.

No. 10 Log Saw. (Fig 24)

Not a new model, but quite good in view of the constraints of the No. 6 Outfit. The suggestion made in the text that hacksaw blades could be used in place of the rackstrips would today do little for the blood pressure of the Inspector from the Health and Safety Executive. To make it even more fun a High Voltage Motor is shown. The idea of the hacksaw blades was dropped from later editions. A No. 6 Outfit model in spite of the lack of an electric motor in the set.

528/5 1228/5 21/934/4.5 (Supplementary leaflet 1/331/10 but see note under Print Data)

No. 9 Bagatelle Table. (Fig 23)

Hardly a Super Model but this existing manual model does work very well indeed and would (and still can) provide much entertainment. A No. 6 Outfit model.

528/10 21/934/4.5

Fig 24. SML 10.

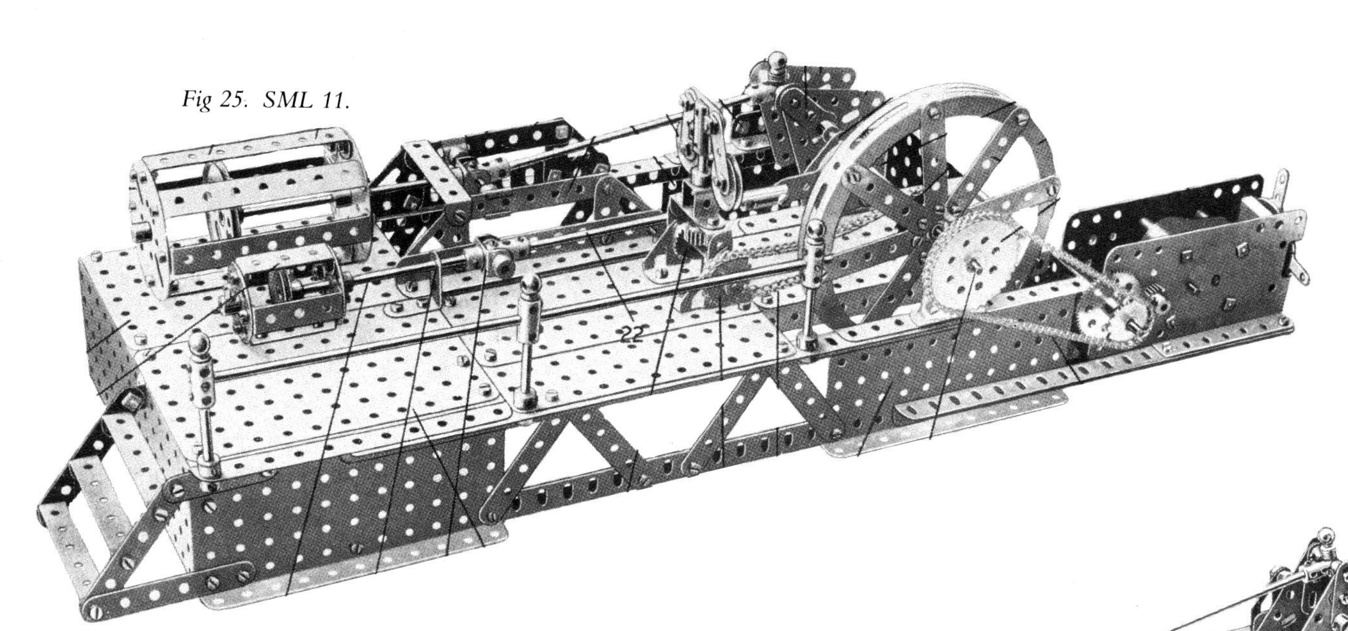

Fig 25. SML 11.

Fig 26. SML 11A.

No. 11 Single Cylinder Horizontal Steam Engine. (Fig 25)

Another earlier manual model but obviously a popular one because it ran to five editions. The original used the 1920 sidelever motor but for the SML the photograph was retouched to make it look like the then current version of the 1925 type. Although simple it is good for demonstration purposes and when the crankshaft is made properly it will run all day without attention. A No. 6 model although an electric motor was not included in the outfit.

528/10 7/1130/1 7/931/1 6/432/1.5 21/934/4

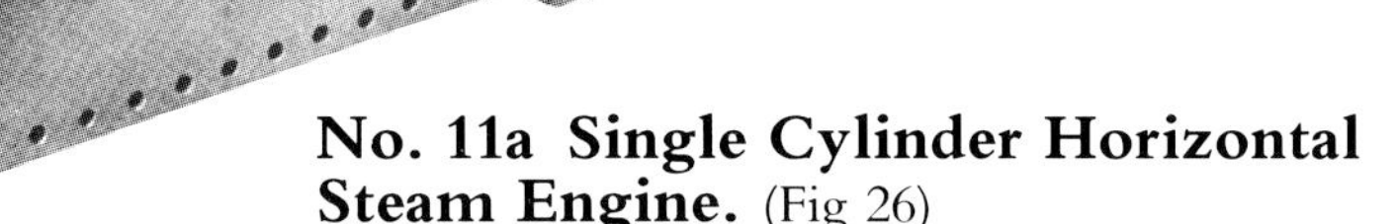

No. 11a Single Cylinder Horizontal Steam Engine. (Fig 26)

This was in effect No. 11 but reworked to use the new strip plates which were introduced with the Blue/Gold Meccano. Three of the illustrations are the same as in the previous leaflet. So far only one print (for 1936) has been confirmed although the inference from the manuals is that it was available from 1935 onwards.

1/836/.5

No. 14 Grandfather Clock. (Fig 29)

Basically a reprint of the earlier Special Model Leaflet and the same remarks apply. A No. 7 Outfit model despite the lack of anywhere near the number of braced girders needed for the case.

428/5

No. 14a Grandfather Clock. (Fig 30)

An improved version of No. 14 but without any change to the escapement which still left a lot to be desired. Not quite as expensive in braced girders but still needing far more than the No. 7 Outfit provided.

1/331/3

Fig 27. SML 12.

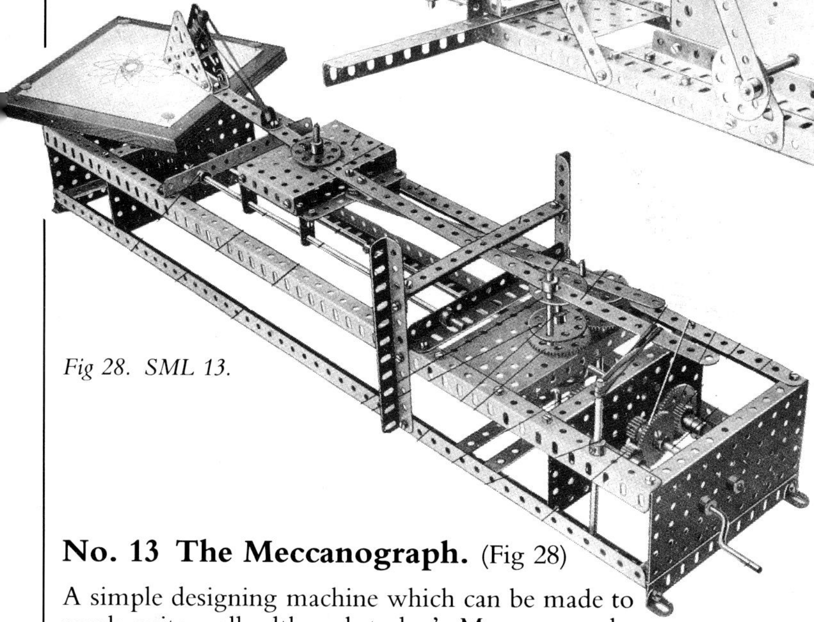

No. 12 Stone Sawing Machine. (Fig 27)

The last of the No. 6 Outfit models in the 1st series of leaflets issued. Again the title of Super Model is difficult to justify and this has less claim than the other No. 6 models. Having said that, it ran to five printings so it cannot have been a failure. As with the Log Saw, hacksaw blades were suggested: most unsuitable except for those interested in kitchen table surgery!

528/5 1028/5 7/1130/1 6/432/1.5 21/934/4

Fig 28. SML 13.

No. 13 The Meccanograph. (Fig 28)

A simple designing machine which can be made to work quite well, although today's Meccanographs are in a totally different class. This particular one had been around for sometime and 12 years before a similar machine was accorded the honour of a separate manual to describe its operation. A No. 7 Outfit model.

628/10 1/636/.5

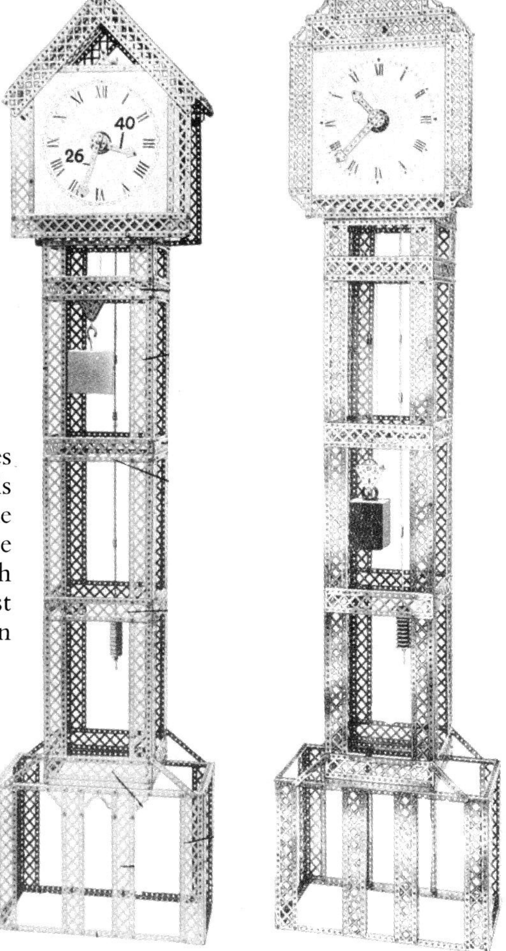

Fig 29. SML 14. *Fig 30. SML 14A.*

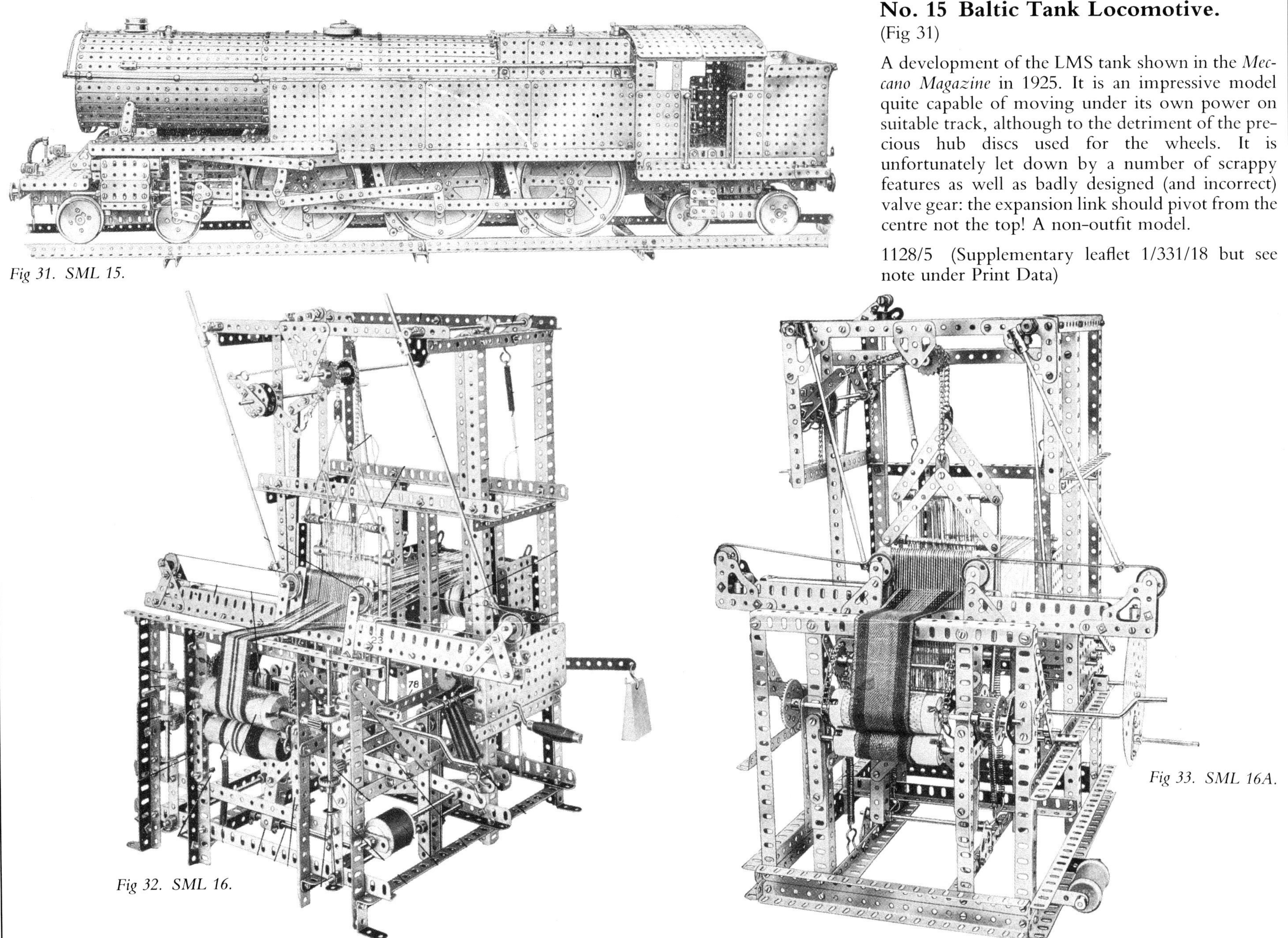

Fig 31. SML 15.

No. 15 Baltic Tank Locomotive.

(Fig 31)

A development of the LMS tank shown in the *Meccano Magazine* in 1925. It is an impressive model quite capable of moving under its own power on suitable track, although to the detriment of the precious hub discs used for the wheels. It is unfortunately let down by a number of scrappy features as well as badly designed (and incorrect) valve gear: the expansion link should pivot from the centre not the top! A non-outfit model.

1128/5 (Supplementary leaflet 1/331/18 but see note under Print Data)

Fig 32. SML 16.

Fig 33. SML 16A.

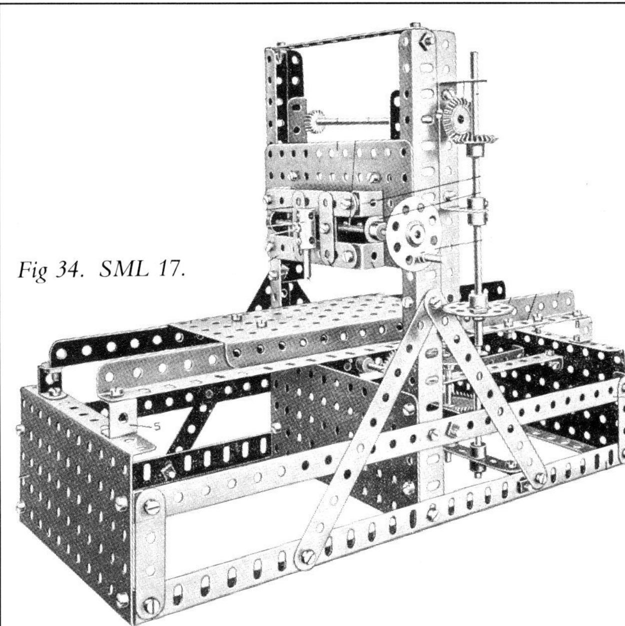

Fig 34. SML 17.

No. 17 Planing Machine. (Fig 34)

A small simple existing model the instructions for which take up barely $1\frac{1}{2}$ sides of the 4 in the leaflet. There was only one known print which was sufficient to supply Outfits 7 and L from 1928 to 1935; an indication of its popularity perhaps.

928/5

←

No. 16 The Loom. (Fig 32)

Like the Grandfather Clock, this is similar to its Special Model Leaflet predecessor but with expanded text. A No. 7 Outfit model.

628/5 928/5

←

No. 16a The Loom. (Fig 33)

An improved version of No. 16 which dates from about 1930. Marginally better than the earlier model but still similar enough to have many of its faults. A No. 7 outfit model.

NR (1930)

No. 18 Revolving Crane. (Fig 35)→

Another much older model which did not justify the title Super Model. According to the instructions, however, 'many hours can be passed happily by using the Revolving Crane to lift loads of sand . . .': possibly. There may well be a supplementary leaflet relating to the withdrawal of the 4-volt motor.

1028/5 1/736/.5

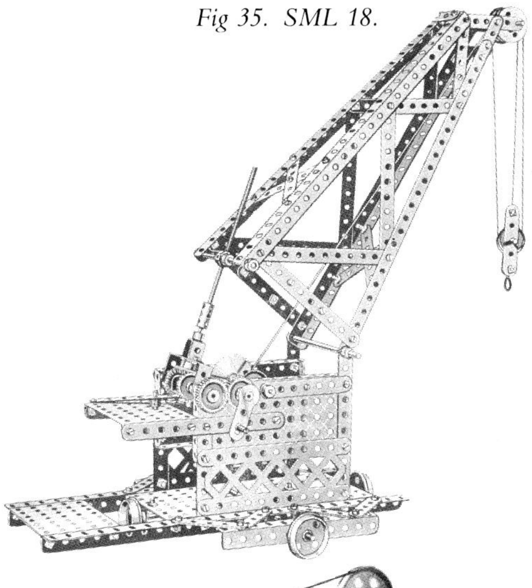

No. 19 Steam Shovel. (Fig 36) ↓

An earlier model but an excellent one nonetheless. A number of its features including the base and digger bucket were used as examples in Standard Mechanisms. The base as shown in Standard Mechanisms uses a 7″ circular strip, but the SML illustration shows the pre-production size of $6\frac{1}{2}''$. Fuller details are given in the chapter on Standard Mechanisms. A No. 7 Outfit model.

828/5 21/934/4 (Supplementary leaflet 1/331/10 – see note in print data)

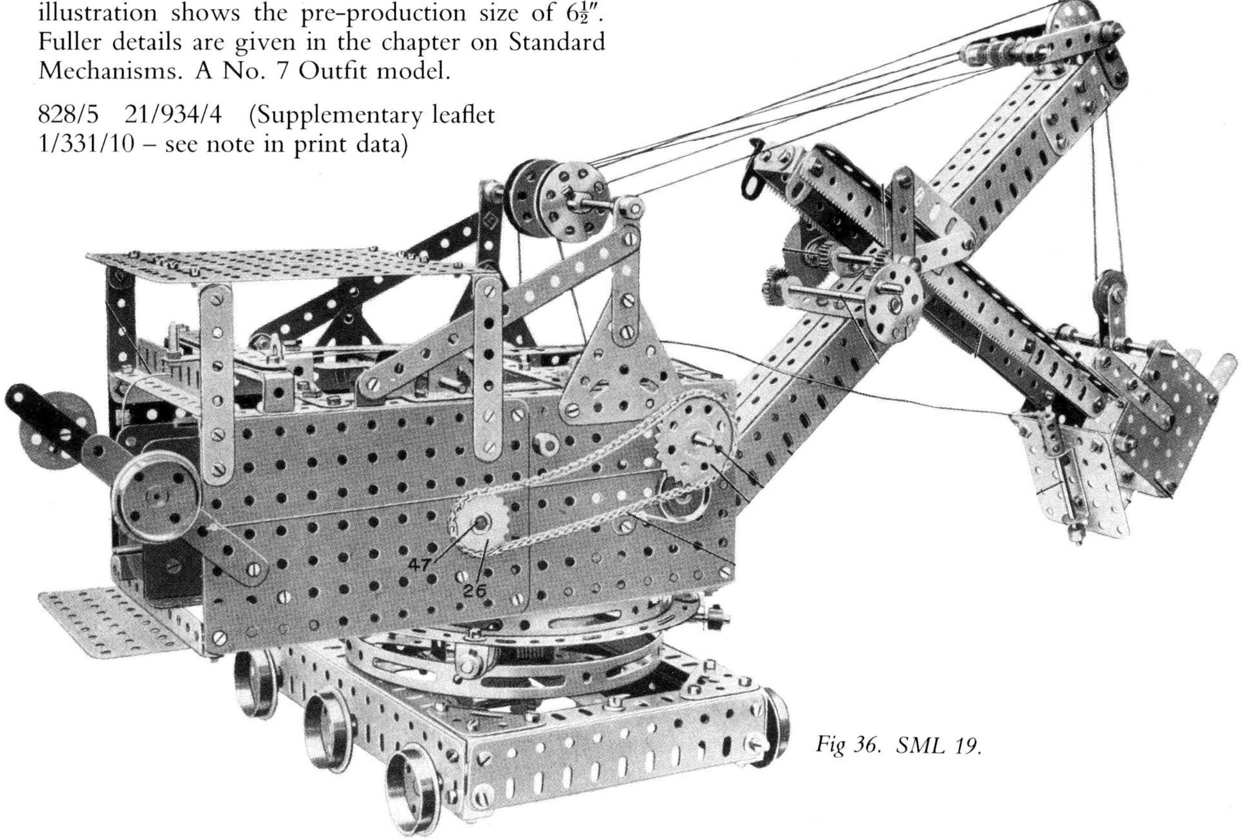

Fig 35. SML 18.

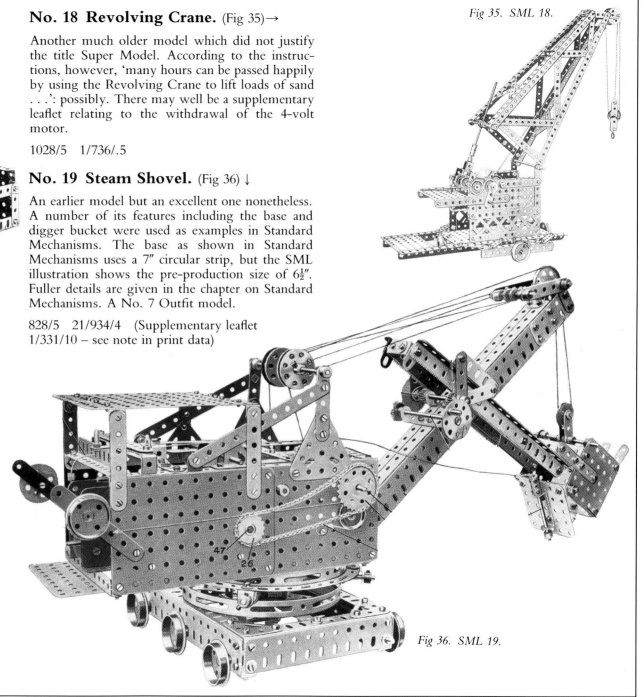

Fig 36. SML 19.

No. 19a The Steam Excavator. (Fig 37)

The main and really only worthwhile model to use the 1929 Steam Engine. A good design spoilt by a sloppy gear change and poorly thought-out ratios. With a little more thought it could have been much better, although today it is an easy enough matter to make the minor modifications necessary. Was originally to have been numbered SML 35. A non-outfit model. See also the chapter on Standard Mechanisms.

7/1229/5

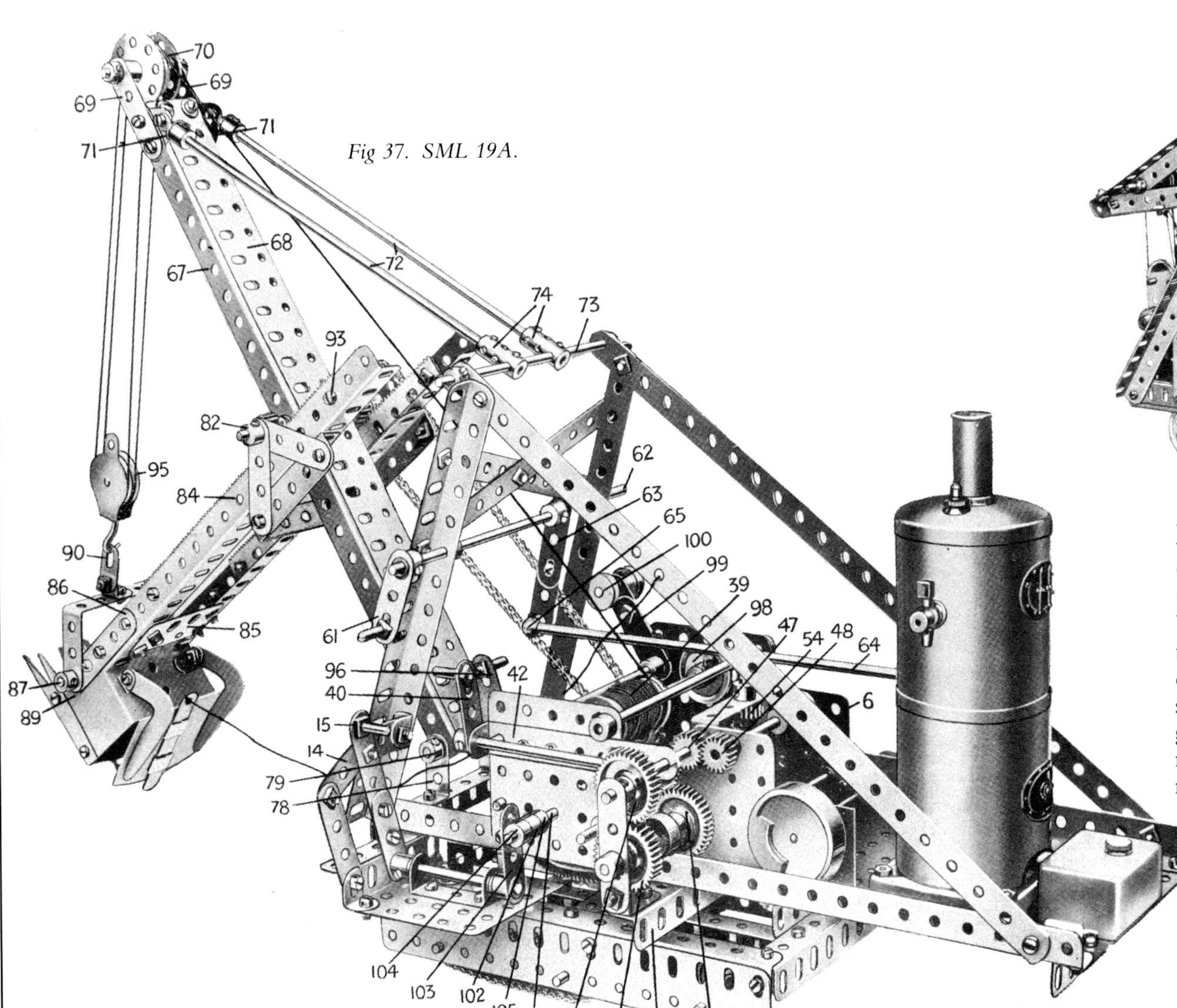

Fig 37. SML 19A.

Fig 38. SML 20 as published.

No. 20 Electric Mobile Crane. (Fig 38)

Originally No. 20 was to have been The Aeroscope (fig 39), but for some reason it was never published. When the leaflet finally appeared a year later it was this small but neat model of a petrol/electric mobile crane. Two minor faults easily corrected are, a sloppy castor mechanism and an out-of-vertical gearbox sideplate which is very noticeable in the main front cover illustration. A No. 7 Outfit model.

7/1229/5 1/836/.5

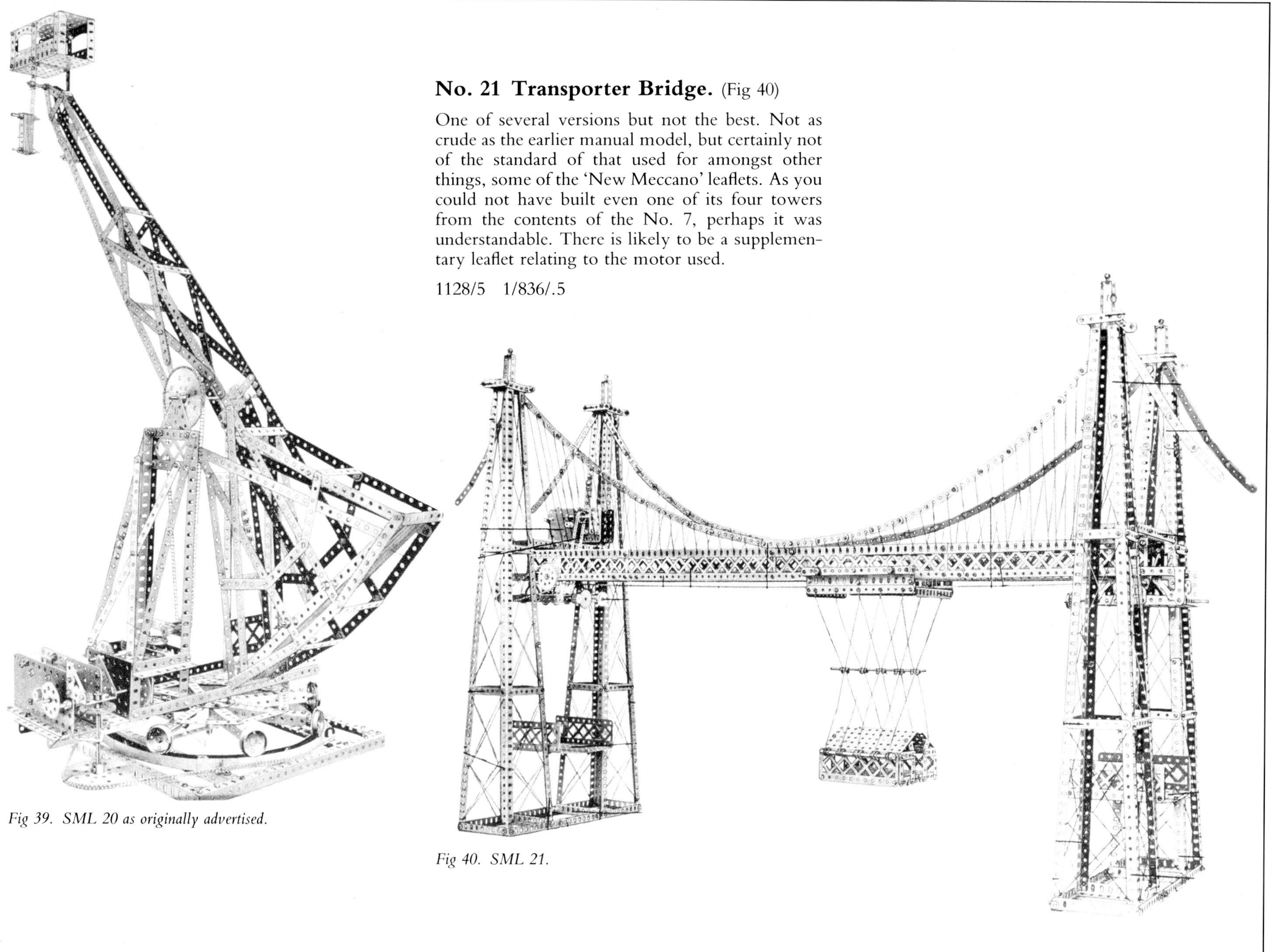

Fig 39. SML 20 as originally advertised.

No. 21 Transporter Bridge. (Fig 40)

One of several versions but not the best. Not as crude as the earlier manual model, but certainly not of the standard of that used for amongst other things, some of the 'New Meccano' leaflets. As you could not have built even one of its four towers from the contents of the No. 7, perhaps it was understandable. There is likely to be a supplementary leaflet relating to the motor used.

1128/5 1/836/.5

Fig 40. SML 21.

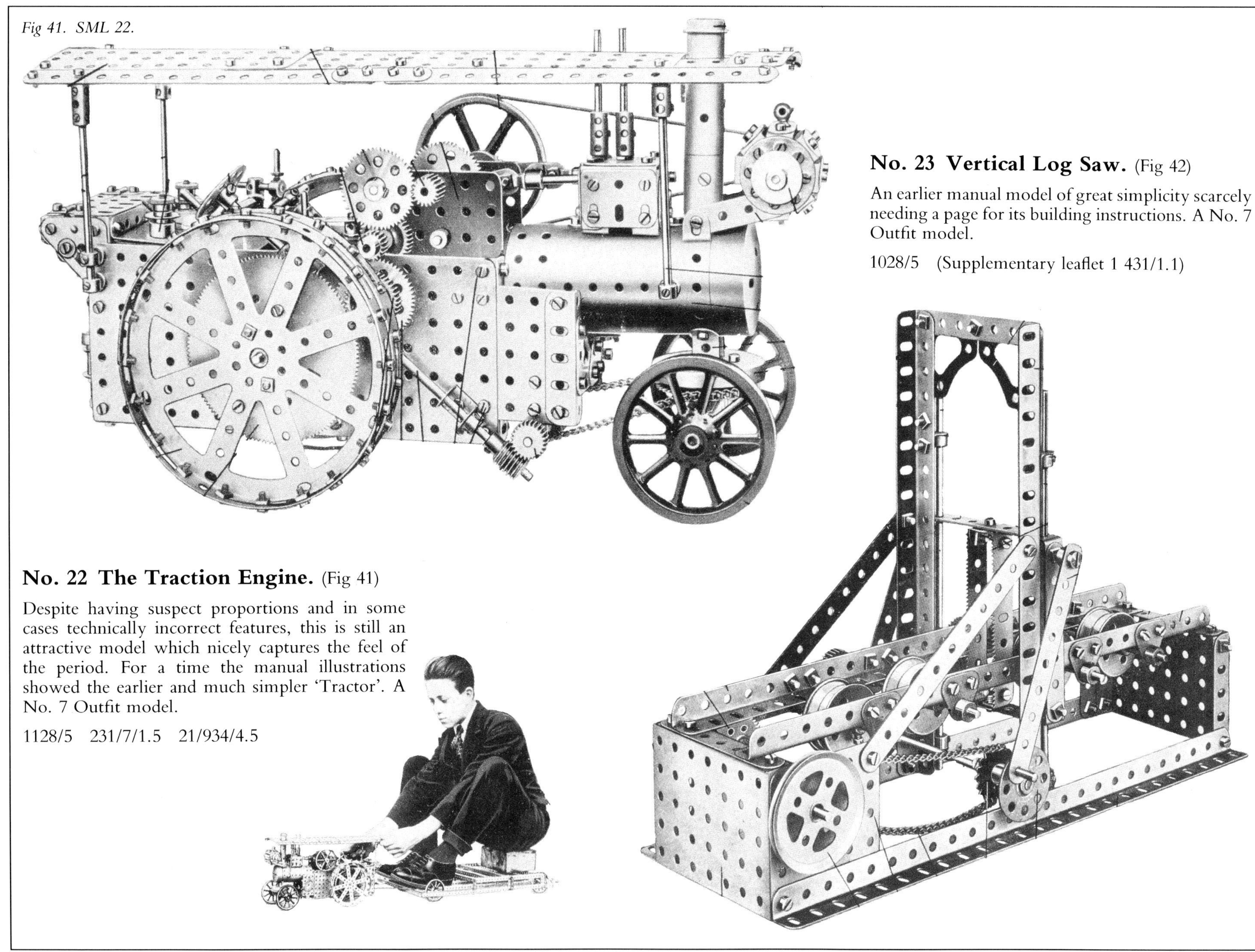

Fig 41. SML 22.

No. 23 Vertical Log Saw. (Fig 42)

An earlier manual model of great simplicity scarcely needing a page for its building instructions. A No. 7 Outfit model.

1028/5 (Supplementary leaflet 1 431/1.1)

No. 22 The Traction Engine. (Fig 41)

Despite having suspect proportions and in some cases technically incorrect features, this is still an attractive model which nicely captures the feel of the period. For a time the manual illustrations showed the earlier and much simpler 'Tractor'. A No. 7 Outfit model.

1128/5 231/7/1.5 21/934/4.5

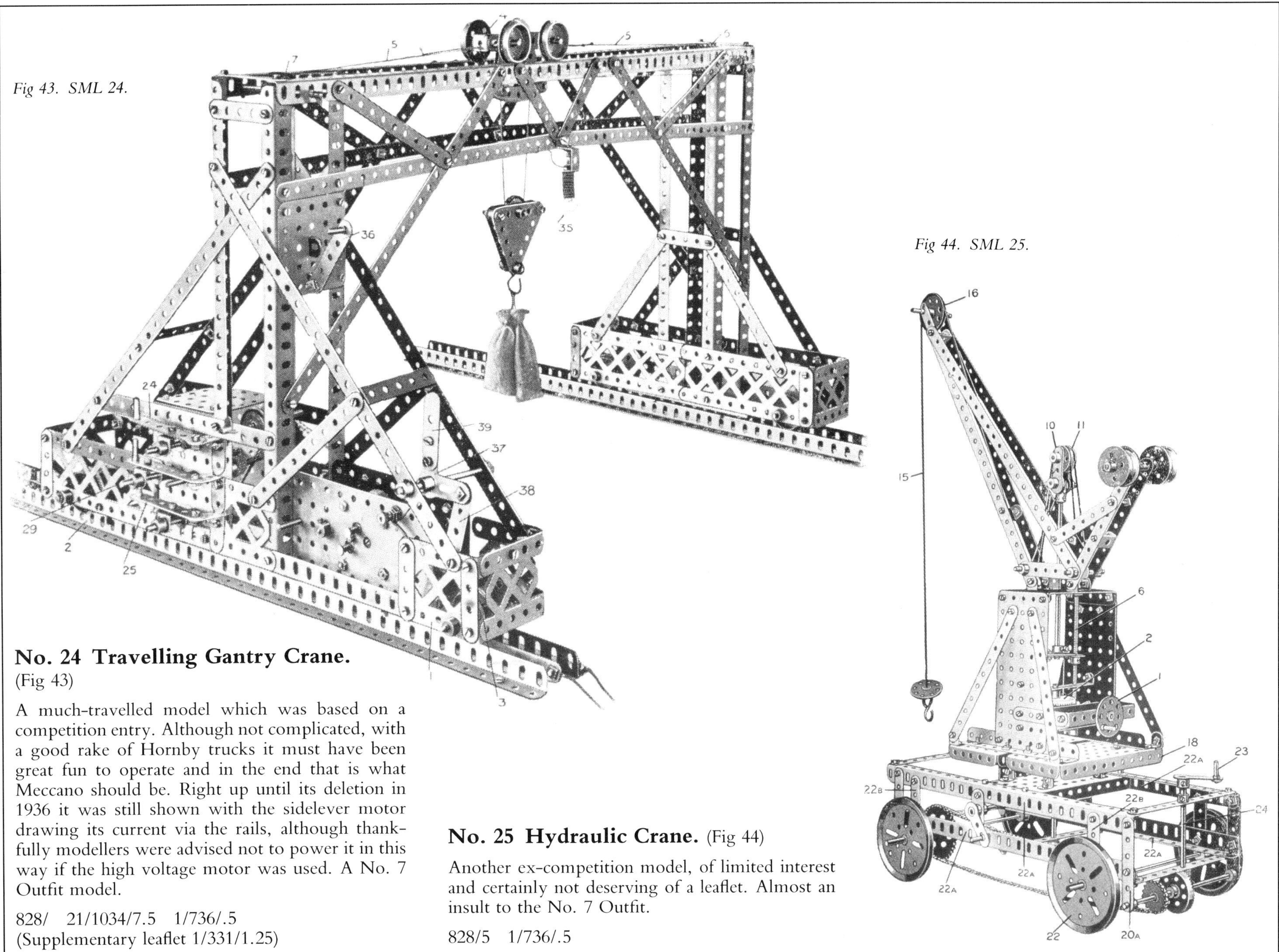

Fig 43. SML 24.

Fig 44. SML 25.

No. 24 Travelling Gantry Crane.
(Fig 43)

A much-travelled model which was based on a competition entry. Although not complicated, with a good rake of Hornby trucks it must have been great fun to operate and in the end that is what Meccano should be. Right up until its deletion in 1936 it was still shown with the sidelever motor drawing its current via the rails, although thankfully modellers were advised not to power it in this way if the high voltage motor was used. A No. 7 Outfit model.

828/ 21/1034/7.5 1/736/.5
(Supplementary leaflet 1/331/1.25)

No. 25 Hydraulic Crane. (Fig 44)

Another ex-competition model, of limited interest and certainly not deserving of a leaflet. Almost an insult to the No. 7 Outfit.

828/5 1/736/.5

No. 26 Twin Elliptic Harmonograph.
(Fig 45)

A quite fascinating random 'designing machine' more properly called a harmonic motion recorder. It is capable of producing extremely intricate patterns no two of which are ever likely to be identical. A No. 7 Outfit model.

1228/5

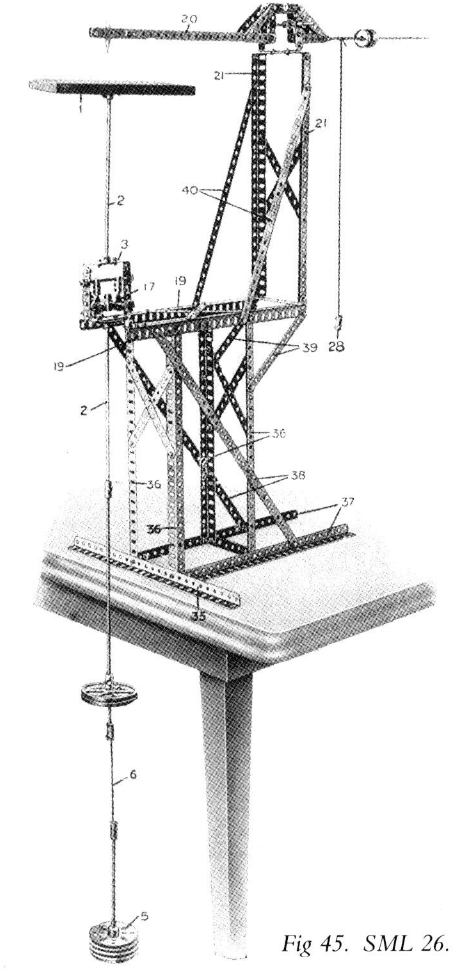

Fig 45. SML 26.

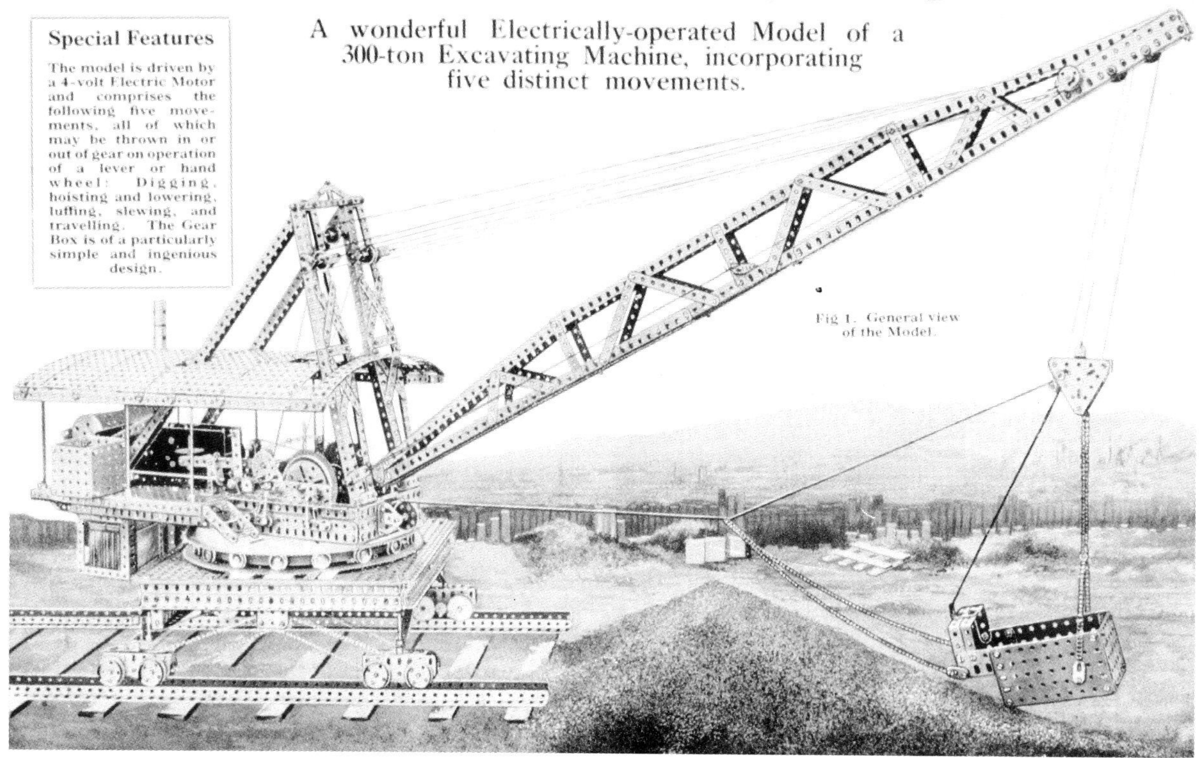

Meccano Giant Dragline
A wonderful Electrically-operated Model of a 300-ton Excavating Machine, incorporating five distinct movements.
Special Features
The model is driven by a 4-volt Electric Motor and comprises the following five movements, all of which may be thrown in or out of gear on operation of a lever or hand wheel: Digging, hoisting and lowering, luffing, slewing, and travelling. The Gear Box is of a particularly simple and ingenious design.
Fig 1. General view of the Model.

Fig 46. SML 27.

No. 27 Giant Dragline. (Fig 46)

A large model with many good features, although the suggestion that a hole for the chimney be cut out of a $5\frac{1}{2} \times 3\frac{1}{2}$ plate is not one of them. As with many of the large models of the day, strengthening in places pays dividends. It is the gearbox which lets it down, but in fairness one must say that even after 60 years a truly satisfactory dragline gearbox has not made an appearance. The problem is that dynamics do not scale down in the same way as mechanical structures and the dragline operation is much affected by dynamics. Despite its drawbacks, it is still a fine model which will no doubt continue to be built and exhibited for many years to come. A non-outfit model.

There was an earlier version of the Dragline using channel segments for the roller bearing. For some years Standard Mechanisms used an illustration of the base of this model to show the use of that particular part. This early Dragline (which appeared in 1924 following a competition) had a rather different gearbox to that in SML 27 and also lacked a roof.

1228/5 (Supplementary leaflet 1/331/3)

No. 28 The Pontoon Crane. (Fig 47)

Another much earlier manual model and one which achieved additional fame by appearing on the front covers of Standard Mechanisms 1934–6 and Meccano Parts and How to Use Them. (See Ch. 6) It was the only SML to use two electric motors and when first published showed the 1920 type motor with side lever. When the SML was issued the motors had been photographically retouched to look like 1925 types, hence the rather distorted appearance of the reversing levers. Single motor operation was mentioned but with no great enthusiasm.

Although the Geared Roller Bearing had just been introduced, the Pontoon Crane still used the built-up roller bearing with channel segments, which was odd as it would have publicised the new part much better than the Roundabout. Although reference was made in the text to its existence no real attempt was made to sell it.

All of this makes even less sense when it is realised that a fresh model of the Pontoon Crane using the GRB (and only one motor) had been designed within a few months (fig 48 and see also chapter 6). In fact it was not until 1936 when the SMLs had a last half-hearted fling that a GRB version was published (fig 49) and then a different one again. A No. 7 Outfit model despite the shortage of one electric motor.

1128/5 1/936/.5 (using part no. 167)

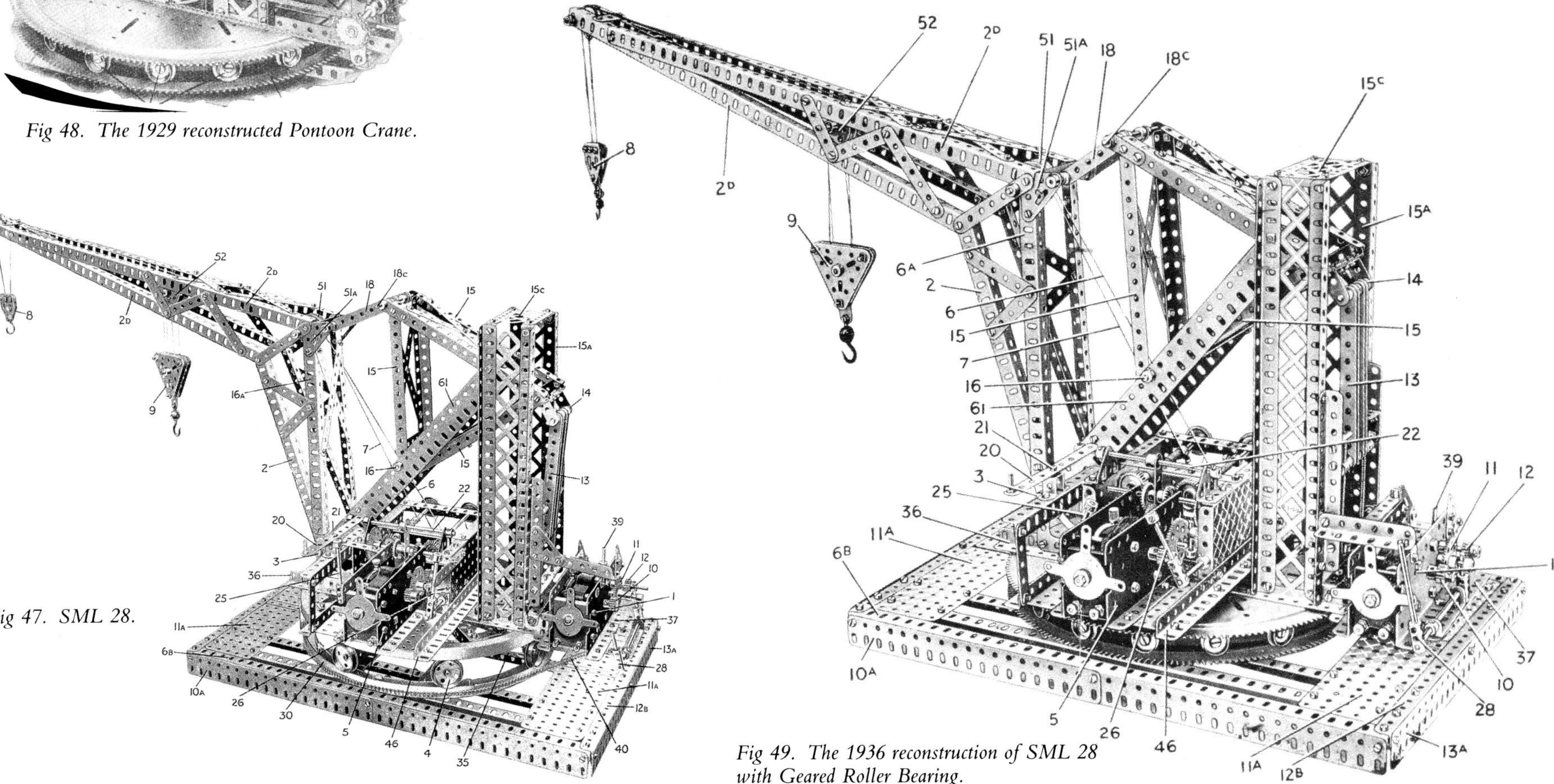

Fig 48. *The 1929 reconstructed Pontoon Crane.*

Fig 47. *SML 28.*

Fig 49. The 1936 reconstruction of SML 28 with Geared Roller Bearing.

No. 29 The Hammerhead Crane.

(Fig 50)

Again a much earlier manual model and one frequently used in publicity material. In 'Jackie Coogan visits a Meccano factory' it is shown apparently built from the contents of what looks like a No. 4 Outfit. A very special No. 4 for young master Coogan! (fig 51) The original model used the 1922/3 experimental High Voltage Motor (see Standard Mechanisms chapter 6) but when it appeared as an SML the artwork department had changed it to the 1925 type HV; this time with much greater success than with the Pontoon Crane. Like that model the built-up roller bearing with channel segments was used and similarly a revised leaflet using the GRB was published in 1936 (fig 52). A No. 7 Outfit model.

1228/5 1/1136/.5

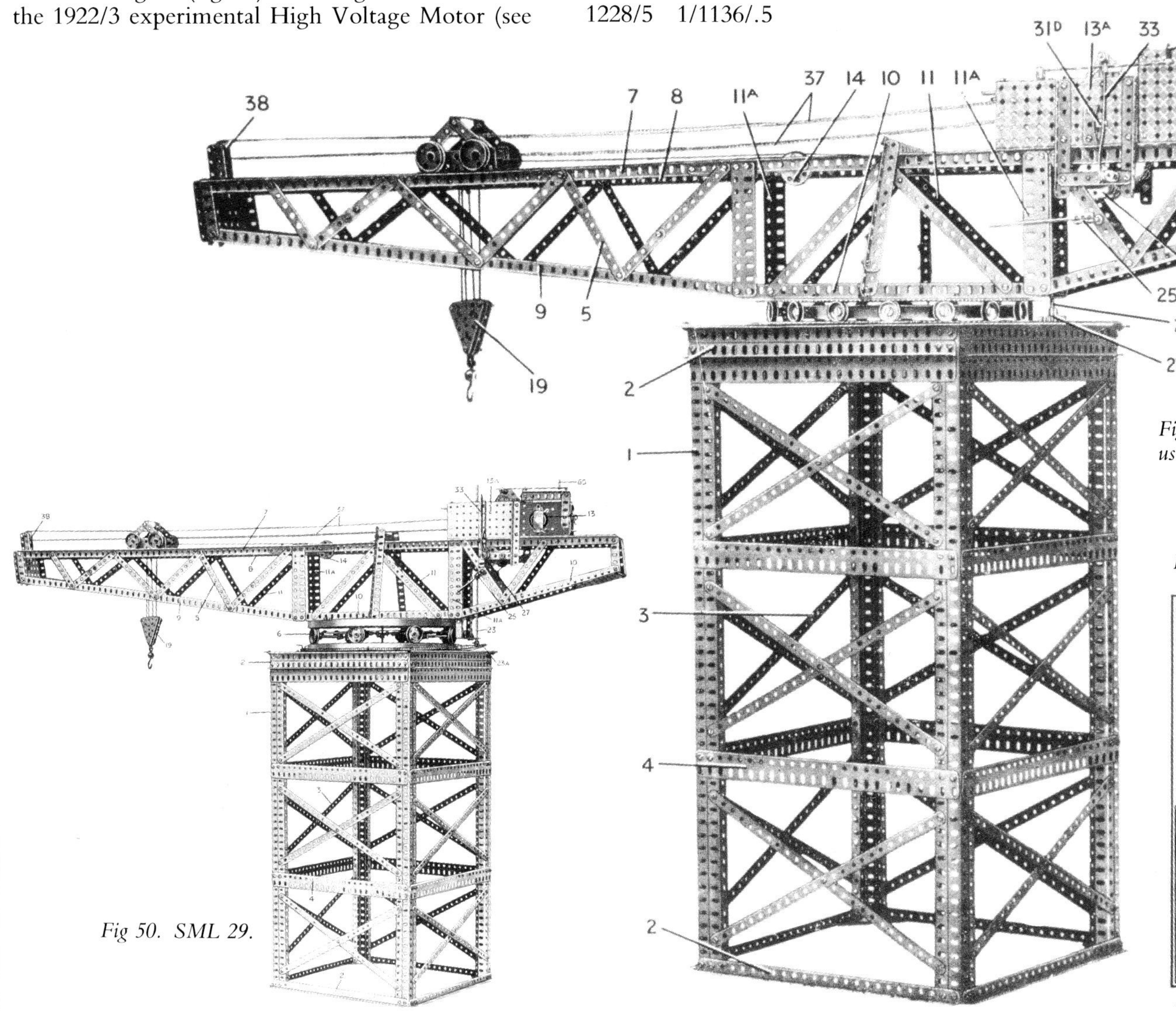

Fig 52. The revised Hammerhead Crane leaflet using the Geared Roller Bearing.

Fig 51. Jackie Coogan's Special No. 4 Outfit?

Jackie Coogan at work on his Hammerhead Crane. The pulley block, apparently, calls for some serious thinking

Fig 50. SML 29.

No. 31 Goods Warehouse with Electric Elevators. (Fig 55)

An improved version of the older manual model but still nowhere near the standard of the early 1930s competition winner by Keith Cameron which was a push-button operated model of very advanced design. Nevertheless SML 31 can be made to work quite well and is not difficult to construct. A No. 7 Outfit model.

3/729/5 1/836.5

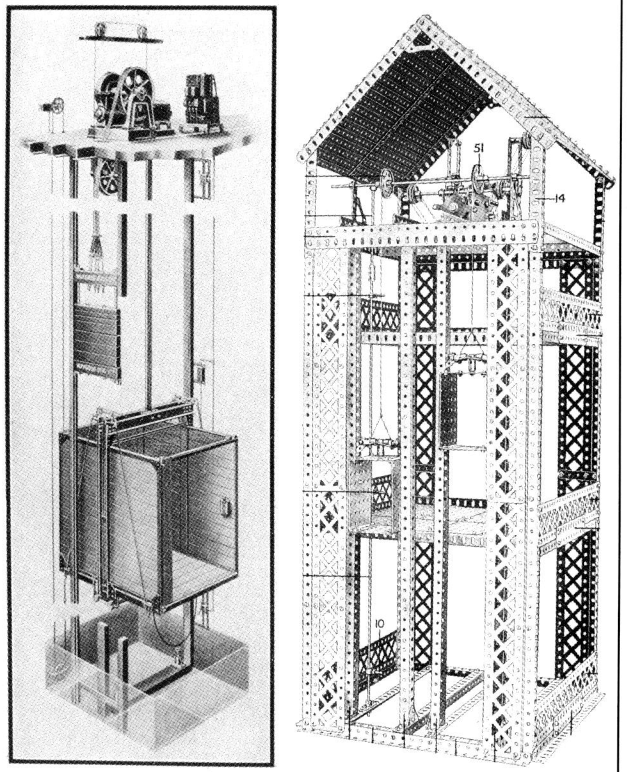

Fig 55. SML 31.

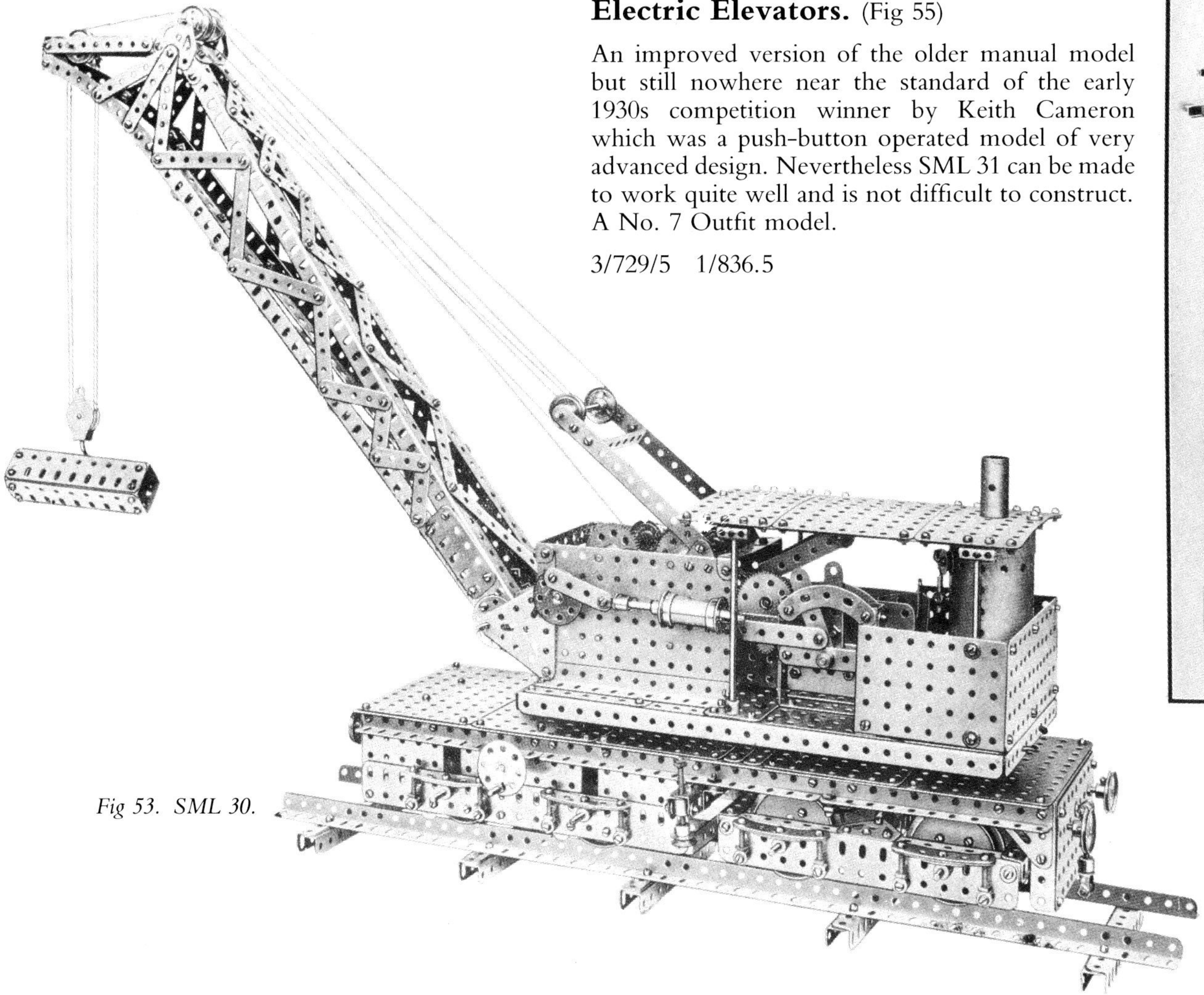

Fig 53. SML 30.

No. 30 Railway Breakdown Crane.
(Fig 53)

Despite not being quite right in its proportions and lacking a match truck, SML 30 is one of the most attractive and successful models in the series. It has a neat, well-designed gearbox which is only let down by the lack of a long pivot bolt in the radial gear change system. Such a part is now available and so the problem of too much play in the pinion mounted on the ordinary bolt is a thing of the past. Motor control is by way of a very compact stud contact resistance controller (fig 54) a feature which could have been more widely used to good effect. A No. 7 Outfit model.

7/929/5 1/736/.5

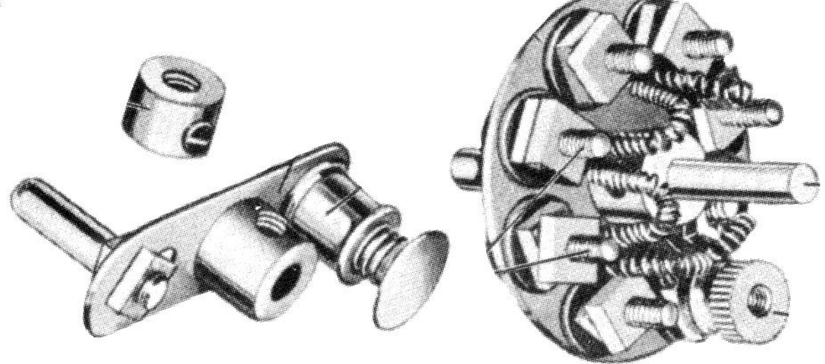

Fig 54. Motor controller used in SML 30.

No. 32 Twin Cylinder Horizontal Steam Engine. (Fig 56)

A large and good-looking model which operates very well indeed. Its main drawback is the need for 32 channel segments and the consequent cost of obtaining these rare obsolete parts. Ring frames can be used and there is a view of a reconstructed model showing how to use these (fig 57) in the 1935 edition of Meccano Parts and How to Use Them. A complete picture has not so far been traced and it does not seem likely that an updated leaflet was ever issued. Instead remaining stocks were overprinted with a note (fig 58) concerning the withdrawal of channel segments (which took place in 1935). A non-outfit model.

729/5

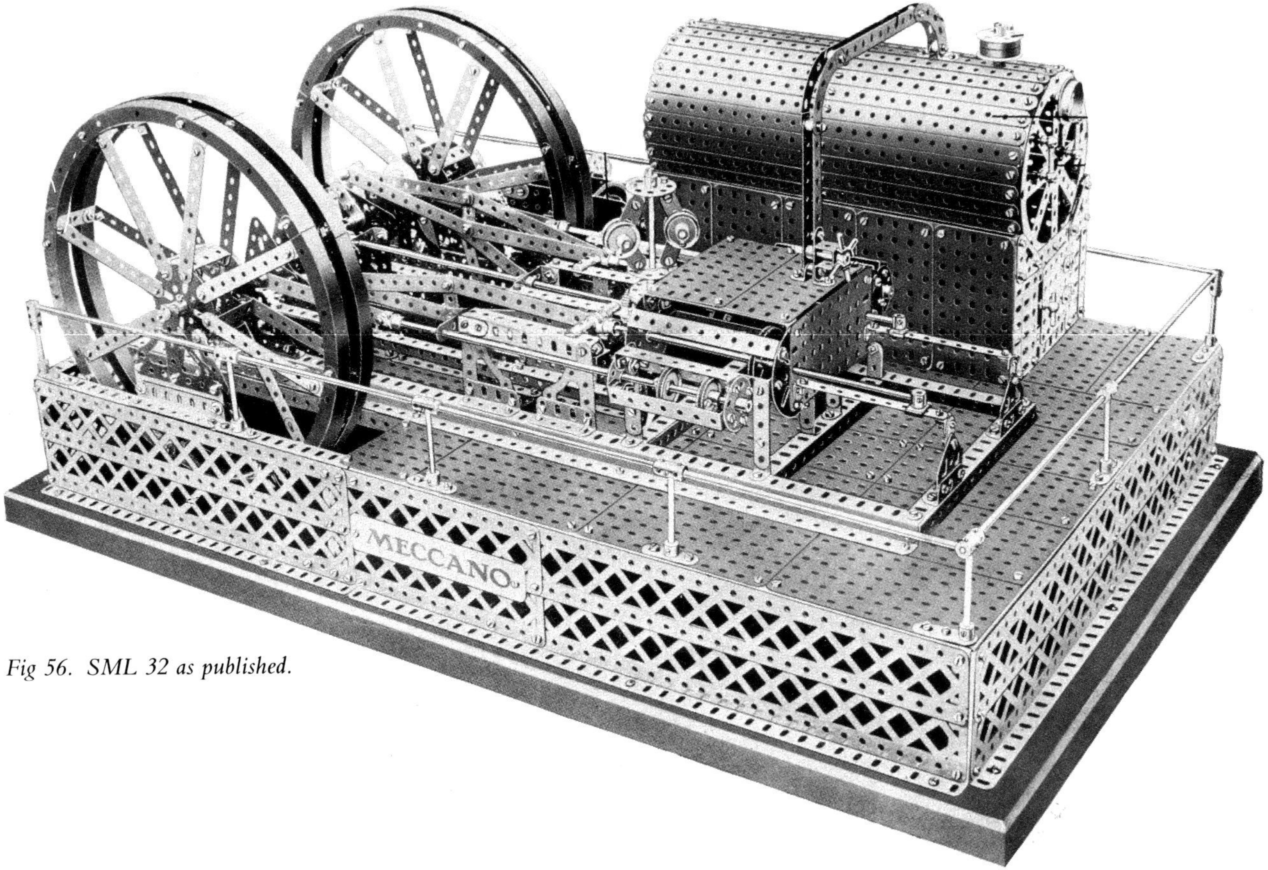

Fig 56. SML 32 as published.

Fig 57. SML 32 using ring frames instead of channel segments.

Fig 58. The 1935 overprint on SML 32.

Part No. 119, Channel Segment, has been withdrawn. It is replaced by Part No. 167b, Ring Frame, which is a complete unit. A few small changes will be involved, including altering the length of the spokes or inner bracing members, and the position of the securing nuts and bolts used for the old parts.

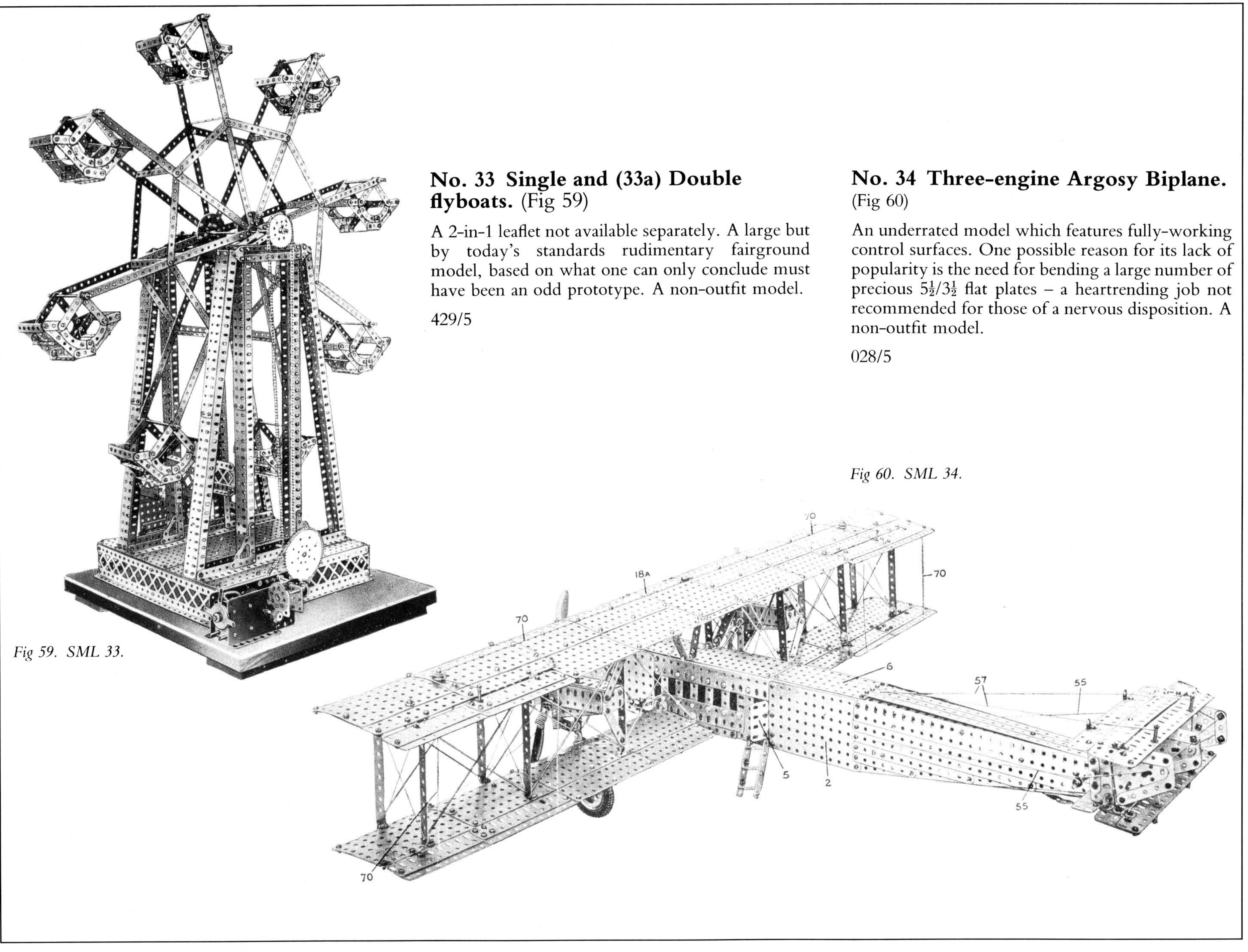

Fig 59. SML 33.

No. 33 Single and (33a) Double flyboats. (Fig 59)

A 2-in-1 leaflet not available separately. A large but by today's standards rudimentary fairground model, based on what one can only conclude must have been an odd prototype. A non-outfit model.

429/5

No. 34 Three-engine Argosy Biplane. (Fig 60)

An underrated model which features fully-working control surfaces. One possible reason for its lack of popularity is the need for bending a large number of precious $5\frac{1}{2}/3\frac{1}{2}$ flat plates – a heartrending job not recommended for those of a nervous disposition. A non-outfit model.

028/5

Fig 60. SML 34.

Fig 61. SML 35.

No. 35 Automatic Grabbing Crane.
(Fig 61)

Another potentially good model which was spoilt by being built-down to the contents of a particular outfit, in this case the No. 7, although the GRB which is specified was not included in the outfit. Tower and superstructure especially required more thought for the prototype and somehow one feels that a better job could have been done even within the bounds of the No. 7. A pity because the subject is good.

7/730/5 1/836/.5

No. 36 Electric Derrick Crane. (Fig 62)

A large and fairly accurate model although by no means complicated. It could have been improved by using the jib construction system for the rear tie-members, but this would have taken it out of the scope of the No. 7 Outfit from which it could be built.

3/130/5

No. 37 6″ Howitzer, Limber and Tractor. (Fig 63)

The last of the basic series and a No. 6 Outfit model although the electric motor was not included in that set. A good small-scale model notwithstanding the constraints of the outfit. The tractor unit can be steered by its caterpiller tracks and the howitzer fires washers quite some way. An attractive representation of the original and one which would have afforded much pleasure.

7/830/5

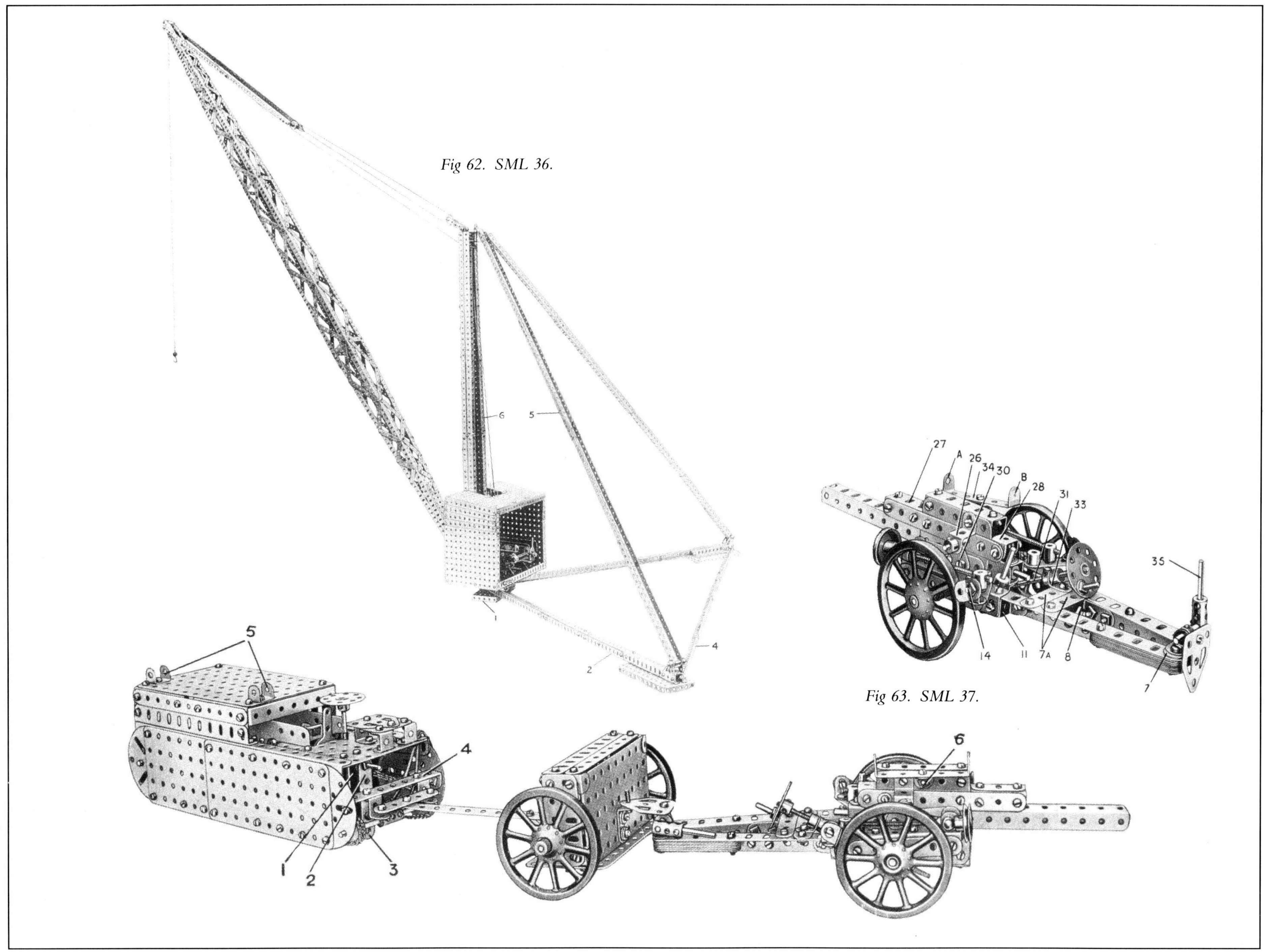

Fig 62. SML 36.

Fig 63. SML 37.

Print Data

All known UK print references have been listed after the model description for each SML. With the exception of the 1936 print for No. 24, all those listed are in the author's collection. That particular edition for the Travelling Gantry Crane has been reported but so far has not been seen in the flesh. However since that leaflet was amongst those included in the final 'L' outfit of 1937 most of which had a 1936 print it is quite likely that it is correct.

A free gift!

In December 1934 a free sample leaflet was given away with the *Meccano Magazine*. The September and October printings of Nos. 7, 9, 10, 11, 12, 19, 22 and 24 (totalling 37,500) would appear to have been for this purpose. All these leaflets have a reference to the change from Red/Green to Blue/Gold (fig 64) and an opportunity was also taken to update the text with regard to obsolete motors, parts, etc.

This special print run gives us a possible clue as to the circulation of the *Meccano Magazine* at the time i.e. some 40,000. The peak of 70,000 in 1930 must have been very difficult to sustain in the early years of the depression and we do know that Meccano Ltd were frequently left with many unsold copies. It would not be unreasonable therefore to presume that the leaflet print was based on the circulation of the time. Any shortfall would no doubt have been made up from stocks of less popular leaflets. Indeed, from the number of these 1934 leaflets found trimmed to size (to fit the *Meccano Magazine* format), it appears that older leaflets were used first. It is these which are more often found cut to size.

The illustrations to this leaflet show the model built in Red-Green Meccano parts. Its construction in the Blue-Gold Meccano parts is exactly the same, except that Strip Plates should be used wherever Braced Girders are shown, as the latter parts have been withdrawn from the Meccano Outfits. If preferred, however, Braced Girders may be purchased separately.

Fig 64. Detail from a leaflet (SML 12) referring to the changes of 1934.

Examination of the printing data of the Supplementary Leaflets or 'special notes' also gives rise to some rather interesting theories.

The numbers printed are very exact indeed e.g. 2,550 for No. 6, 1,250 for No. 24 and 1,100 for No. 23. Because of the insignificant cost of printing the small slips which were produced in-house (the '1' as the first digit of the print code signifies this) those figures must represent the stocks of individual SMLs at that date.

Looking further, and taking No. 23 as an example, it appears that 1,100 leaflets were sufficient to supply the company's needs from 1931 until 1936 when No. 23 was deleted. Since it was a No. 7 outfit model (or 'L') it would follow that production of the largest outfits cannot have been more than that figure. Sales of no more than 200/250 per year for Nos. 6a and 7 (or Ka and L) would not seem out of line and the supposition probably not far from the truth.

Three of the Supplementary Leaflet references would seem to be incorrect. That for No. 15 is almost certainly 1.8 not 18 since only 5,000 of the

No. 19. Precio Argentina $0.10 España Pts. 0.30

INSTRUCCIONES para construir Super-Modelos

EXCAVADORA MECÁNICA

Un modelo de grandisimo interés que reproduce fielmente todas las operaciones de su prototipo en la mecánica moderna

Caracteristicas Especiales:

Mecanismo de traslación y rotación—Tren de engranajes para subir y bajar el brazo, actuado por motor electrico—Los ajustes del brazo dragador se efectuan, mediante una disposición de cremallera con piñon. La estructura superior gira sobre un rodamiento de rodillos.

La edificación moderna cuenta con muchas disposiciones ingeniosas para ahorrar mano de obra, y entre los más salientes y de más utilidad, se halla la excavadora mecánica que actualmente tratamos.

No puede dudarse de la verdad de lo espuesto, por que una máquina de ésta clase puede quebrantar y separar en un día más cantidad de tierra que pudieran hacerlo dos mil obreros armados con picos y palas. Nos faltan palabras para describir el alboroto que produciría ésta multitud durante su trabajo. Y como describir la confusión ocasionada al llegar la hora del descanso y cuando estos mismos obreros deben prepararse la comida y tambien debe calcularse el perimetro ocupado para poder comer con relativa comodidad. La pérdida de la mano de obra es muy importante, comparada con la de este obrero rival, esa Excavadora Mecánica, que sin cansancio alguno diariamente y a todas horas está en condiciones

No. 19. Prijs Holland f. 0.15

Speciale Aanwijzingsbladen voor den bouw van schitterende Meccano modellen

DE MECCANO STOOMSCHOP

Een model van onbegrensd belang en toepassing dat alle werkzaamheden verricht van een werkelijke stoomschop of mechanische excavateur

Speciale bijzonderheden

Het model omvat zij- en draaimechanisme, en drijfwerk om de arm op te hijschen of te laten zakken, door een Electrische Motor aangedreven. De schoparm is verstelbaar door tandstrook en rondsel drijfwerk. De bovenbouw draait op een speciaal rollager.

Vele arbeidsbesparende middelen zijn beschikbaar voor hedendaagsche ingenieurs, en hieronder is er waarschijnlijk geen een nuttiger dan de stoomschop of mechanische excavateur, zooals hij soms genoemd wordt.

De waarheid van deze mededeeling zal worden beseft wanneer men verneemt, dat een groote stoomschop in één dag net zooveel materiaal kan verwijderen als zou kunnen worden uitgegraven door 2000 man met houweelen en schoppen!

Stel U voor een oogenblik 2000 man voor, aan het werk op een bouwterrein. Stel U de beweging voor van zulk een menigte, 2000 houweelen en schoppen hanteerend.

Denk dan ook aan het stoppen om "even op adem te komen" of om zich van de eene plaats naar de andere te verplaatsen. Wat een schaftuur zou het zijn—2000 kannen

Nr. 19. Pris Danmark Kr. 0.20 Norge Kr. 0.20

Særlige Oplysninger om Bygning af Meccano Super Modeller

MECCANO DAMP-SKOVL

En Model af ubegrænset Interesse og Anvendelse, som udfører al en virkelig Dampskovls eller mekanisk Jordarbejders Arbejde

Særligt fremhæves:

Modellen omfatter vandrende og roterende Mekanisme, Kranløftning og Kransænkning og drives ved Elektromotor. Skovlarmen er indstillelig ved Hjælp af Tandhjul og Drev. Overbygningen roterer paa et specielt Rulleskaalsleje.

Mange arbejdsbesparende Opfindelser staar nutildags til Ingeniørens Disposition, og blandt disse er næppe nogen mere brugbar end Dampskovlen eller—som den undertiden kaldes: Den mekaniske Jordarbejder.

Sandheden heraf kan man bedst forestille sig, naar man erfarer, at en stor Dampskovl paa en Dag kan grave og flytte lige saa meget Materiale som 2000 Mand med Hakker og Skovle. Forestil Dem en Gang 2000 Mand i Arbejde! Tænk Dem Synet af disse 2000 arbejdende Hakker og Skovle i Bevægelse!

Tænk Dem endvidere alle de smaa Afbrydelser for at "puste lidt" eller for at bevæge sig fra et Sted til et andet! Tænk paa en Middagstime, hvor der skal aabnes for 2000 Madpakker og laves 2000 Kopper Kaffe!

Nr. 19. Preis Schweiz Frk. 0.20

Spezial-Instruktionshefte zum Bau grösserer Meccano Modelle

MECCANO DAMPFSCHAUFEL

Ein Modell von unbegrenztem Interesse und Anwendungsmöglichkeiten, die alle Betätigungen einer richtigen Dampfschaufel erlauben.

Besondere Eigenschaften:

Das Modell umfasst fahrbare und drehbare Mechanismen, Auslieger-getriebe zum heben und senken, die durch elektrischen Motor bewerkstelligt werden. Der Schaufelarm ist durch Sperr- und Trieblinggetriebe justierbar. Die Oberstruktur dreht sich auf einer besonderen Kugellaufbahn.

Ingenieure von heute haben sich vieler, Arbeit sparender Entwürfe bedient, und unter diesen ist vielleicht keiner so nützlich wie die Dampfschaufel oder der "mechanische Erdarbeiter," wie sie manchmal genannt wird.

Die Wahrheit dieser Behauptung wird voll erkannt werden, wenn man lernt, dass eine Dampfschaufel in einem Tage soviel Material ausgraben kann wie 2,000 Männer mit Axt und Spaten. Stellt Euch mal einen Moment 2,000 Mann bei der Arbeit vor. Denkt Euch den Tumult, den solch eine Menge mit den 2,000 Spaten verursachen würde.

Dann wieder denkt an die vielen Aufenthalte, "einen Luftzug einzuatmen," oder sich von einem Punkte zum anderen zu bequemen. Was für eine Mittagsstunde würde das sein, 2,000 Kannen Kaffees müssten gekocht werden und 2,000 Esskörbe geöffnet.

Dies ist sicher ein Bild verschwendeter Energie und Zeit wenn man das mechan-

Fig 66. An example of one of the four language leaflets issued to extend the adaptability of the SMLs.

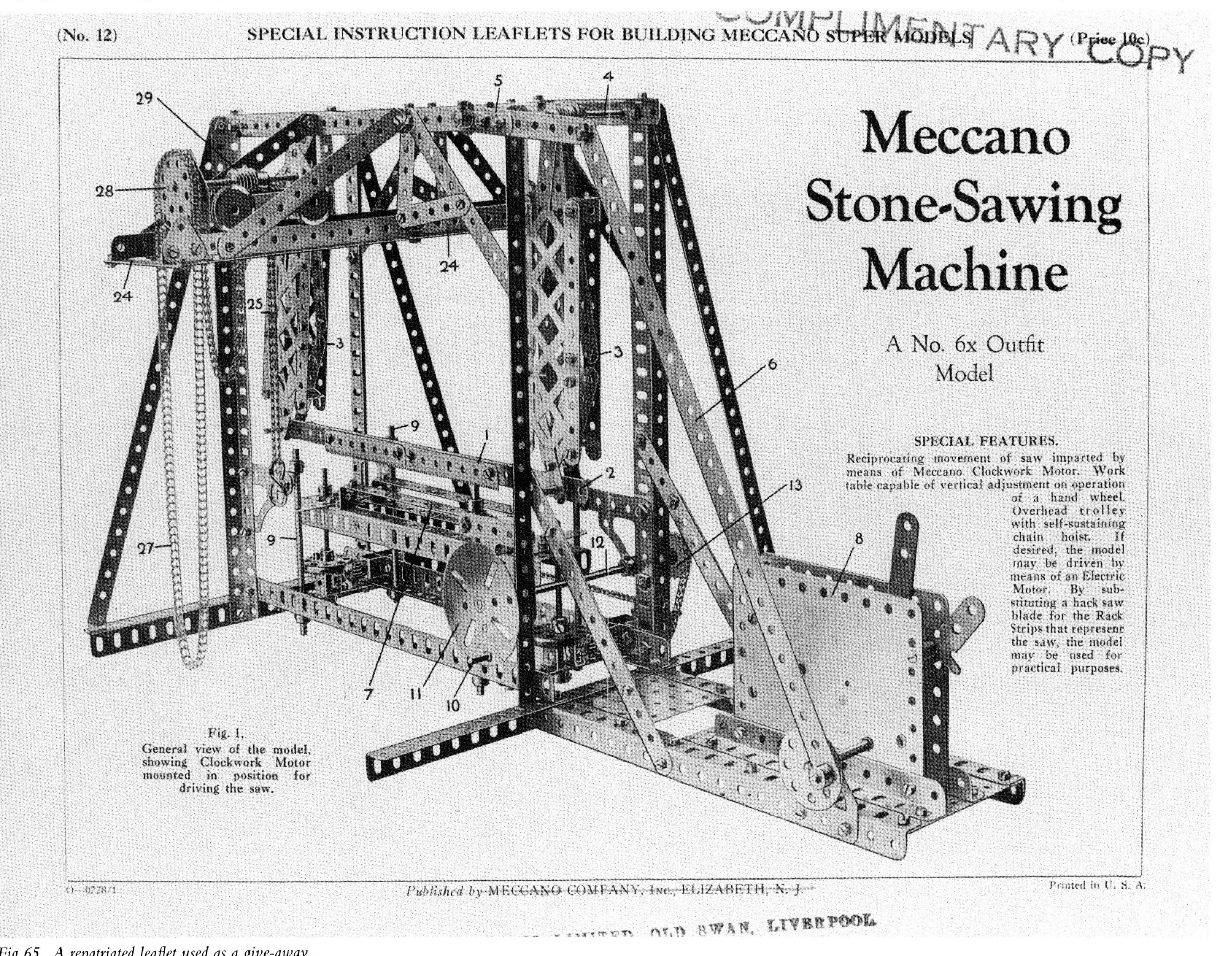
(No. 12)
SPECIAL INSTRUCTION LEAFLETS FOR BUILDING MECCANO SUPER MODELS
(Price 10c)
COMPLIMENTARY COPY
Meccano Stone-Sawing Machine
A No. 6x Outfit Model
SPECIAL FEATURES.
Reciprocating movement of saw imparted by means of Meccano Clockwork Motor. Work table capable of vertical adjustment on operation of a hand wheel. Overhead trolley with self-sustaining chain hoist. If desired, the model may be driven by means of an Electric Motor. By substituting a hack saw blade for the Rack Strips that represent the saw, the model may be used for practical purposes.
Fig. 1, General view of the model, showing Clockwork Motor mounted in position for driving the saw.
O—0728/1
Published by MECCANO COMPANY, Inc., ELIZABETH, N. J.
Printed in U. S. A.
OLD SWAN, LIVERPOOL

Fig 65. A repatriated leaflet used as a give-away.

Meccano Leaflets in Six Languages

Many readers no doubt will be interested to know that the Special Instruction Leaflets describing the well-known Meccano Super Models are printed in several languages. These include French, German, Spanish, Dutch and Danish. The French leaflets are printed and issued in exactly the same manner as those in English, but in the four remaining languages special editions without illustrations have been prepared. These are intended for use in conjunction with the English edition.

As an illustration we may take the Motor Chassis leaflet. A Meccano enthusiast living in Germany, Spain, Holland, Norway, or Denmark, who wishes to build this wonderful model may obtain the four-language leaflet describing this model by writing to Meccano Ltd., Liverpool. With it is sent the English leaflet, which contains the illustrations, and to these he may refer while reading the instructions in his own language.

Meccano boys in this country who are learning one or more of the languages referred to will find the leaflets of great assistance. They may read the versions in English and in the foreign language side by side, or may follow the more interesting and useful plan of reading the instructions in the foreign language and referring to the English leaflet only for confirmation, or for assistance when unknown words are encountered.

The appropriate four-language leaflet will be sent free of charge to every purchaser of a special Instruction Leaflet who expresses the desire to have it. The leaflets are published at various prices. From time to time complete lists appear in the pages of the "*M.M.*," and full information regarding the leaflets published in all six languages will be forwarded to any reader who applies to Meccano Limited, Binns Road, Liverpool.

Fig 67. Announcement in the November 1930 MM.

original leaflet were ever printed in the first place. The same problem with a decimal point is likely to have happened with Nos. 10 and 19. Again only 5,000 of the original leaflets each were printed prior to 1931, and 10,000 should probably read 1,000.

Foreign Editions

The only special English-language editions of the SMLs were those for the USA. Most of these state that they were printed in America but there are very few differences between them and their UK counterparts except for spelling and prices. No. 8 did however become the Merry-go-Round. The US editions were for Nos. 1 to 14 plus No. 16 (correct at time of writing) and with the exception of No. 1 only appear to have had one print each.

The US editions had a very short life because of the sale of the Meccano Company in America to Gilbert in 1929. Some may well have found their way to Canada, but many were repatriated to the UK and used as complimentary copies. (Fig 65)

There were French editions of virtually all the SMLs with the possible exceptions of 11a and 32 together with GRB versions of Nos. 28 and 29. Nos. 1 and 14 were also printed in Spanish and German; the latter in two editions, one for Germany and one for Switzerland both identical except for the price and details of the publisher. No. 16 was also printed in German despite the four-language leaflet already in existence (see below). The Loom must have been a good seller in Germany.

The four-language leaflets just mentioned first appeared in 1928. To save printing leaflets in many different languages, it was decided to publish text-only translations to go with the English versions of the leaflets. These covered Spanish, Dutch, Danish and German (fig 66 shows a typical leaflet). At least 28 of the SMLs were given 4 language texts in this way and it is likely that more remain to be discovered. The November edition of the *Meccano Magazine* rather belatedly advertised these leaflets showing once again how an opportunity for selling a Meccano product was lost through lack of publicity in the *MM* (fig 67).

The following are the print references of all 4-language leaflets so far known:

Four-language leaflets – text only

SML	Printing Reference	SML	Printing Reference
1	NR 7/631/1(R)	17	529/2.5
2	NR	18	129/2.5
3	728/2.5	19	1228/2.5
5	NR	20	1/332/1
6	329/2.5	21	7/729/2.5
7	NR	22	6/532/1
8	828/2.5	23	629/2.5
9	NR & 7/631/1(R)	24	129/2.5
10	NR	25	1228/2.5
11	NR & 7/31/6/1(R)	26	1/731/1
12	NR & 7/631/1(R)	29	6/132/1
13	1028/2.5	30	NR
14	1028/2.5	37	1/632/1
16	1128/2.5		

Sundries

When issued with either a No. 6, 6a or No. 7 Outfit (or K, Ka or L), the Super Model leaflets were enclosed in a special envelope. There are a number of slightly different types one of which is shown in fig 68.

At various times single-page leaflets were issued advertising the whole SML series. Two have so far seen the light of day:

1128/2.5 (illustrated in fig 69) 2/1029/5

Conclusion

If anything in Meccano could be described as being like the curate's egg, it is the 1928–36 series of Super Models, although to be fair there is far more good than bad. As pieces of Meccano literature they are beautiful productions with extensively retouched photographs making for great clarity. It would be prohibitively expensive to produce them today but in the 1920s and 1930s labour was cheap.

As to the models themselves, that is where opinion will always be divided. It must be remembered that many of the leaflet models had to come within the bounds of a particular outfit so as to justify and probably subsidise those which did not. It should also be borne in mind that the SMLs were not designed to satisfy the requirements of a sophisticated adult enthusiast of 60 years later. The fact that many of them still do so is something of a tribute to their designers.

Out of the 41 separate models, six were for the No. 6 Outfit (or 'K') and naturally were severely limited by the available parts. However to the proud possessor of a new No. 6, they would have been quite wonderful and no doubt whet the appetite for bigger things. From that point of view their inclusion was fully justified. A further 27 were No. 7 or 'L' outfit models of which probably 10 do not warrant the title because of poor design or extreme simplicity; better could have been produced from the contents of the outfits.

Of the eight remaining (which did not have the restriction as to numbers of parts) only one really deserves to be left out – the Roundabout. Ignoring the No. 6 outfit models which are a different case,

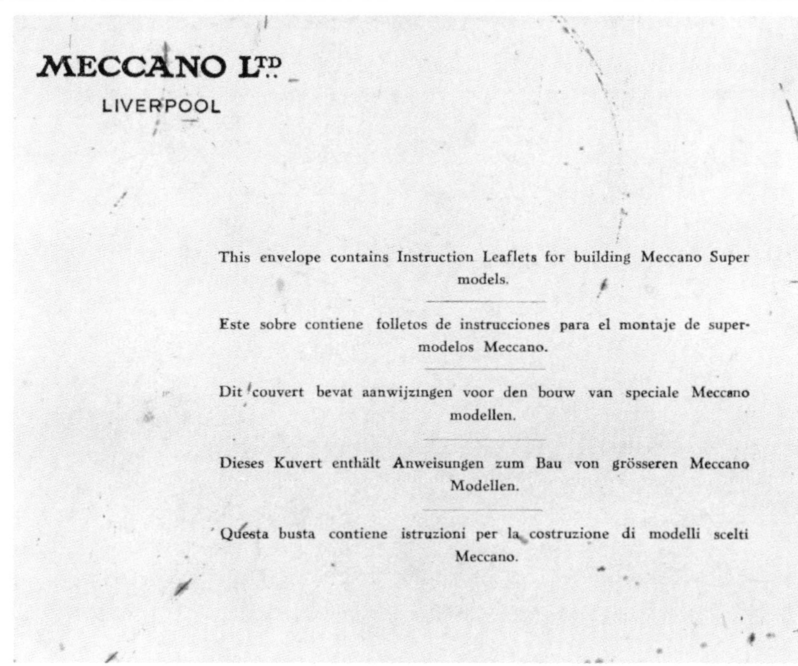
MECCANO L^TD
LIVERPOOL

This envelope contains Instruction Leaflets for building Meccano Super models.

Este sobre contiene folletos de instrucciones para el montaje de super-modelos Meccano.

Dit couvert bevat aanwijzingen voor den bouw van speciale Meccano modellen.

Dieses Kuvert enthält Anweisungen zum Bau von grösseren Meccano Modellen.

Questa busta contiene istruzioni per la costruzione di modelli scelti Meccano.

Fig 68. The envelope used to hold the Super Model Leaflets supplied with an outfit.

one is therefore drawn to the conclusion that some two thirds of the SMLs, quite a fair proportion, were worthy of the title. One further point is that all the SMLs can be made to work, most of them very successfully. The same cannot be said for too many of their successors.

The only regret with the SML series is that it was not carried on to include models such as the Automatic Printing Machine, the MRS Lorry and the Master Clock. These were featured in the *Meccano Magazine* but would have benefited from being published as a leaflet. Perhaps the sales of non-outfit model leaflets were simply not good enough; one thing is obvious, not enough publicity was given to the series. Having said that, Hornby's death in 1936 would have still sounded the knell whatever had transpired.

continued p. 129.

Fig 69. A publicity leaflet detailing the SMLs available. Note that No. 20 is missing (see text) and Nos 30, 31, 32 and 33 were not available until well into the following year.

MECCANO

SUPER MODELS

Our expert designers have produced for us 34 super models that reach the highest pinnacle ever attained in Meccano construction. Each model in this series is a masterpiece and there is not a boy who will not be eager to build them all.

These models are so important that we have engaged expert engineers to describe them and a special leaflet with beautiful half-tone illustrations has been written for each of them. A selection of the leaflets is illustrated on this page.

A brief description of each model in the series is given below and the number and price of the special Instruction Leaflet are indicated. Copies of the leaflets may be obtained from any Meccano dealer or direct from us, post free, at the prices shown.

No. 1 MOTOR CHASSIS. This model runs perfectly under its own power. It has Ackermann Steering, Differential, Gear Box and Clutch, etc.
Price of special Instruction Leaflet 3d.

No. 2 SHIP COALER. All the movements of a real ship-coaler are reproduced in this model.
Price of special Instruction Leaflet 3d.

No. 3 MOTORCYCLE AND SIDE-CAR. The sidecar is of stream-line design and is mounted on springs. The motorcycle is complete with lamps, horn, exhaust pipes, etc.
Price of special Instruction Leaflet 2d.

No. 4 GIANT BLOCK-SETTING CRANE. This realistic model is fitted with an accurate reproduction of Fidler's blocksetting gear.
Price of special Instruction Leaflet 6d.

No. 5 TRAVELLING BUCKET DREDGER. In this model trucks and wagons can run underneath the chute through which falls the material raised by the dredger buckets.
Price of special Instruction Leaflet 2d.

No. 6 STIFF-LEG DERRICK. This model has many interesting movements, including hoisting, luffing and swivelling, which are controlled by suitable levers.
Price of special Instruction Leaflet 2d.

No. 7 PLATFORM SCALES. This model will weigh articles up to 4½ lbs. with remarkable accuracy.
Price of special Instruction Leaflet 2d.

No. 8 ROUNDABOUT. This model is most attractive when in motion. As the roundabout rotates the cars spin round and the horses rise and fall.
Price of special Instruction Leaflet 2d.

No. 9 BAGATELLE TABLE. This is an interesting model that will give hours of fun to the players.
Price of special Instruction Leaflet 2d.

No. 10 LOG SAW. In this model the saw is driven rapidly to and fro while the work table travels beneath it.
Price of special Instruction Leaflet 2d.

No. 11 SINGLE-CYLINDER HORIZONTAL STEAM ENGINE. Fitted with balanced crankshaft, crosshead, and centrifugal governor.
Price of special Instruction Leaflet 2d.

No. 12 STONE SAWING MACHINE. The model is equipped with adjustable work table and overhead trolley with self-sustaining chain hoist.
Price of special Instruction Leaflet 2d.

No. 13 MECCANOGRAPH. This wonderful model will draw hundreds of beautiful designs.
Price of special Instruction Leaflet 3d.

No. 14 GRANDFATHER CLOCK. A practical example of Meccano model-building. The model keeps accurate time.
Price of special Instruction Leaflet 3d.

No. 15 BALTIC TANK LOCOMOTIVE. The driving wheels are operated by an Electric Motor. An accurate reproduction of Walschaerts' Valve Gear is fitted.
Price of special Instruction Leaflet 3d.

No. 16 LOOM. This is perhaps the greatest Meccano success. The model weaves beautiful material.
Price of special Instruction Leaflet 3d.

No. 17 PLANING MACHINE. Fitted with quick-return motion.
Price of special Instruction Leaflet 2d.

No. 18 REVOLVING CRANE. This model is fitted with screw-operated luffing gear.
Price of special Instruction Leaflet 2d.

No. 19 STEAM SHOVEL. This model embodies travelling and rotating mechanisms and jib hoisting and lowering gear.
Price of special Instruction Leaflet 2d.

No. 21 TRANSPORTER BRIDGE. The carriage automatically travels to and fro for as long as the motor is driven, pausing for a few seconds at each end of its travel.
Price of special Instruction Leaflet 2d.

No. 22 TRACTION ENGINE. A remarkably realistic model that will pull a boy of average weight. Fitted with two speeds.
Price of special Instruction Leaflet 2d.

No. 23 VERTICAL LOG SAW. While the saws are in motion, the logs are fed slowly to them.
Price of special Instruction Leaflet 2d.

No. 24 TRAVELLING GANTRY CRANE. The movements of this model comprise the traversing of the entire gantry, hoisting and lowering, and the traversing of the crane trolley.
Price of special Instruction Leaflet 2d.

No. 25 HYDRAULIC CRANE. The hydraulic ram is represented realistically by a powerful screw mechanism.
Price of special Instruction Leaflet 2d.

No. 26 TWIN ELLIPTIC HARMONOGRAPH. Some beautiful designs may be produced with this model.
Price of special Instruction Leaflet 2d.

No. 27 DRAGLINE. This imposing model of a giant excavator is fitted with travelling, luffing, slewing, and dragging movements.
Price of special Instruction Leaflet 3d.

No. 28 PONTOON CRANE. The movements of this model include the operation of the two hoisting blocks, slewing of the entire crane, and luffing.
Price of special Instruction Leaflet 2d.

No. 29 HAMMERHEAD CRANE. This is a very realistic and powerful model, comprising traversing, hoisting and slewing motions.
Price of special Instruction Leaflet 2d.

No. 30 BREAKDOWN CRANE. This model is equipped with travelling, slewing, luffing, and hoisting motions, and also is fitted with laminated springs, brakes, out-riggers, etc.
Price of special Instruction Leaflet 3d.

No. 31 WAREHOUSE WITH ELEVATORS. The two cages are driven automatically and work alternately, pausing at top and bottom positions.
Price of special Instruction Leaflet 3d.

No. 32 TWO-CYLINDER STEAM ENGINE AND BOILER. This is a realistic working model of a complete steam plant, equipped with valve gear, governor, balanced cranks, etc.
Price of special Instruction Leaflet 3d.

No. 33 SINGLE AND DOUBLE FLYBOATS. These two models represent popular pleasure-fair attractions.
Price of special Instruction Leaflet 3d.

No. 34 THREE-ENGINE BIPLANE. This is a realistic model of an "Argosy" machine, and is fitted with ailerons, elevators and rudders.
Price of special Instruction Leaflet 3d.

Giant Block-setting Crane

No. 4 Leaflet. Price 6d.

No. 11 Leaflet. Price 2d.

No. 7 Leaflet. Price 2d.

No. 1 Leaflet. Price 3d.

No. 25 Leaflet. Price 2d.

No. 5 Leaflet. Price 2d.

No. 3 Leaflet. Price 2d.

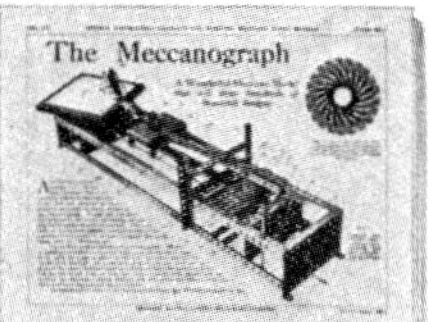

No. 13 Leaflet. Price 3d.

No. 10 Leaflet. Price 2d.

No. 17 Leaflet. Price 2d.

No. 6 Leaflet. Price 2d.

No. 19 Leaflet. Price 2d.

MECCANO LIMITED

OLD SWAN, LIVERPOOL

THIS MODEL CAN BE BUILT WITH MECCANO OUTFIT No. 10

Leaflet No. 7

MECCANO

Block-setting Crane

(MODEL No. 10.7)

15

21

17

19

SPECIAL FEATURES

This fine model represents one of the giant cranes used for laying concrete blocks in the building of harbours and breakwaters. It is powered by a Meccano E20R type 20-volt Electric Motor, and carries out all the movements of the actual crane.

The impressive model described and illustrated in this Leaflet is a reproduction of one of the massive cranes used for lifting and placing in position the huge blocks of concrete required in the building of sea breakwaters and harbour walls. Often these blocks weigh as much as 50 tons, and some of the cranes that are specially made to handle them are among the largest in existence. Cranes of this kind, which are known as block-setting cranes, are splendid subjects for the Meccano model-builder, and the fine model dealt with in this Leaflet incorporates as many details of an actual crane as possible. It has four movements, all of which are powered by an E20R type Electric Motor and controlled from levers in the driving cab.

FIG. 1
The Meccano Block-setting Crane described in this Leaflet

COPYRIGHT BY MECCANO LTD., LIVERPOOL, ENGLAND

Fig 70. A poor model from the 1954 series of leaflets.

THIS MODEL CAN BE BUILT WITH MECCANO OUTFIT No. 10

Leaflet No. 1

MECCANO
Railway Service Crane

(MODEL No. 10.1)

SPECIAL FEATURES

The hoisting, lowering and luffing movements of the model are all driven by a Meccano 20-volt Motor through gearing, and the crane will lift considerable loads. The crane truck is strongly built and is mounted on eight wheels carried in swivelling bogies. Other details include outriggers and sliding doors in the cab.

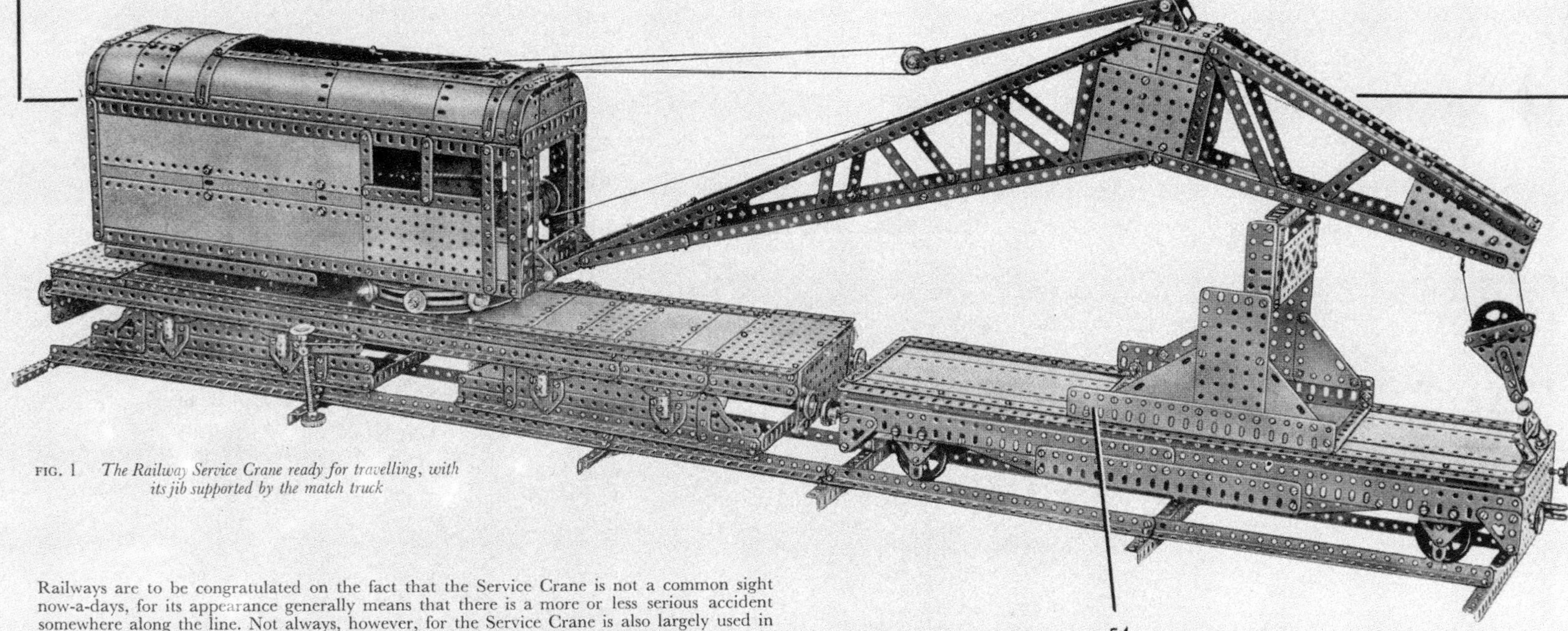

FIG. 1 *The Railway Service Crane ready for travelling, with its jib supported by the match truck*

Railways are to be congratulated on the fact that the Service Crane is not a common sight now-a-days, for its appearance generally means that there is a more or less serious accident somewhere along the line. Not always, however, for the Service Crane is also largely used in track laying operations and other constructional or maintenance work on the railways.

The Service train is usually made up of several vehicles in addition to the locomotive. These comprise vans containing tools, first-aid appliances, and accommodation for the train staff, and — most important from the Meccano boy's point of view — the crane itself. The latter is usually provided with a 'match truck', on which the jib rests when it is in the lowered position for travelling.

The Meccano model described in this leaflet is a faithful representation of a typical modern Service Crane. It reproduces the principal movements of its prototype and is fitted with outriggers and swivelling bogies. The crane is driven by a Meccano 20-volt Electric Motor and will lift considerable loads. The crane truck is about 30″ in overall length and the match truck is approximately 24″ long.

Crane Truck Underframe (Fig. 3)

Each side-member of the underframe consists of two built-up girders. One of these is a 24½″ Angle Girder extended at each end by a 3½″ Angle Girder and the other consists of a 24½″ Angle Girder lengthened at one end by two 3½″ Angle Girders. The built-up girders are connected together at the centre by a 2½″ Flat Girder, and at each end by Fishplates.

The side-members are connected by two 5½″ Angle Girders (1) and at each end a 5½″×2½″ Flat Plate is attached to the side-members by Angle Brackets. The Flat Plates are edged by 2½″ and 5½″ Strips, with a Stepped Bent Strip bolted to one of them to form a coupling between the crane truck and the match truck.

Fig 71. Another disaster!

THIS MODEL CAN BE BUILT WITH MECCANO OUTFIT No. 10

Leaflet No. 13

MECCANO

Combine Harvester

(MODEL No. 10.13)

SPECIAL FEATURES

This model represents one of the many mechanical appliances used on modern farms. A two-speed and reverse gear-box gives different traction speeds, and other features include workable steering gear and a power-driven reel or beater.

FIG. 1
This fine model of a Combine Harvester includes a wealth of detail that makes it an attractive subject for the advanced model-builder

The model described in this Leaflet represents a typical harvesting machine used on many farms. It is a most interesting model to construct and operate and power for driving it is supplied by a Meccano E20R Electric Motor.

Fig 72. The Combine Harvester – one of the few good models from the 1954 series.

To the present day

Why is it that over 60 years after the first Super Model Leaflets were published they are still enjoyed, collected and the models rebuilt? There is no one reason, although many are simply good models to make and offer scope for improvement (let us not forget that Hornby wanted boys to improve upon models). The inherent quality of the leaflets themselves must also be part of their allure but one cannot help but think that once again that special charm which Binns Road imparted to so many things during the great days, continues to make itself felt after nearly a lifetime. The great popularity of Volume 2 the Hornby Companion Series bears witness to this.

Post War Leaflets

The demise of the 'L' outfit in 1937 and the introduction of the much smaller No. 10 Outfit meant that the SMLs were no longer required. The No. 10 Outfit models were all new, and used strip and flexible plates extensively in their construction. More importantly, the instructions were all contained in the manual.

This state of affairs continued until 1954 when the No. 10 manual and its models were scrapped in favour of separate leaflets each describing a new model. Initially there were 12 but subsequently a further eight were issued, although these were not supplied with the No. 10 (they could be built from it). In size and style they were very similar to the pre-war SMLs, but there the similarity ends.

The most striking difference is not, as one might expect, one of size or scope but in the new models' almost total lack of elegance and visual attraction. Many are downright ugly. There is an old engineering saying that 'if it looks right then it is right'. How true in the case of the 1954 series of leaflet models. The Railway Breakdown Crane and the Giant Block-Setting Crane are typical, (figs 70–71) although to be fair, a few, such as the Combine Harvester (fig 72), were quite good. A common problem with these 1954 models is that many simply do not work because of poor or inadequate design. The result is that few if any of this series are ever revived today. Far better models can be built from the contents of a No. 10 and Meccano threw away a golden opportunity to produce a good, modern series of Super Models which would have surely been a much better advertisement than the poor things which were issued.

If the No. 10 leaflets are bad enough then there is worse to come. Some time later further additions were made to the series of 20. These were culled from the No. 9 Outfit models and went back to the partial use of line drawings instead of photographs. This was partly because of the use of 'exploded' diagrams which obviated the need for written text. To say that these models were crude is to seriously understate the case. It is not beyond the imagination to believe that such 'models' would have precipitated a strike in the 1930s model room. Fig 73 is as good a reason as any.

A sad end to what started with such promise.

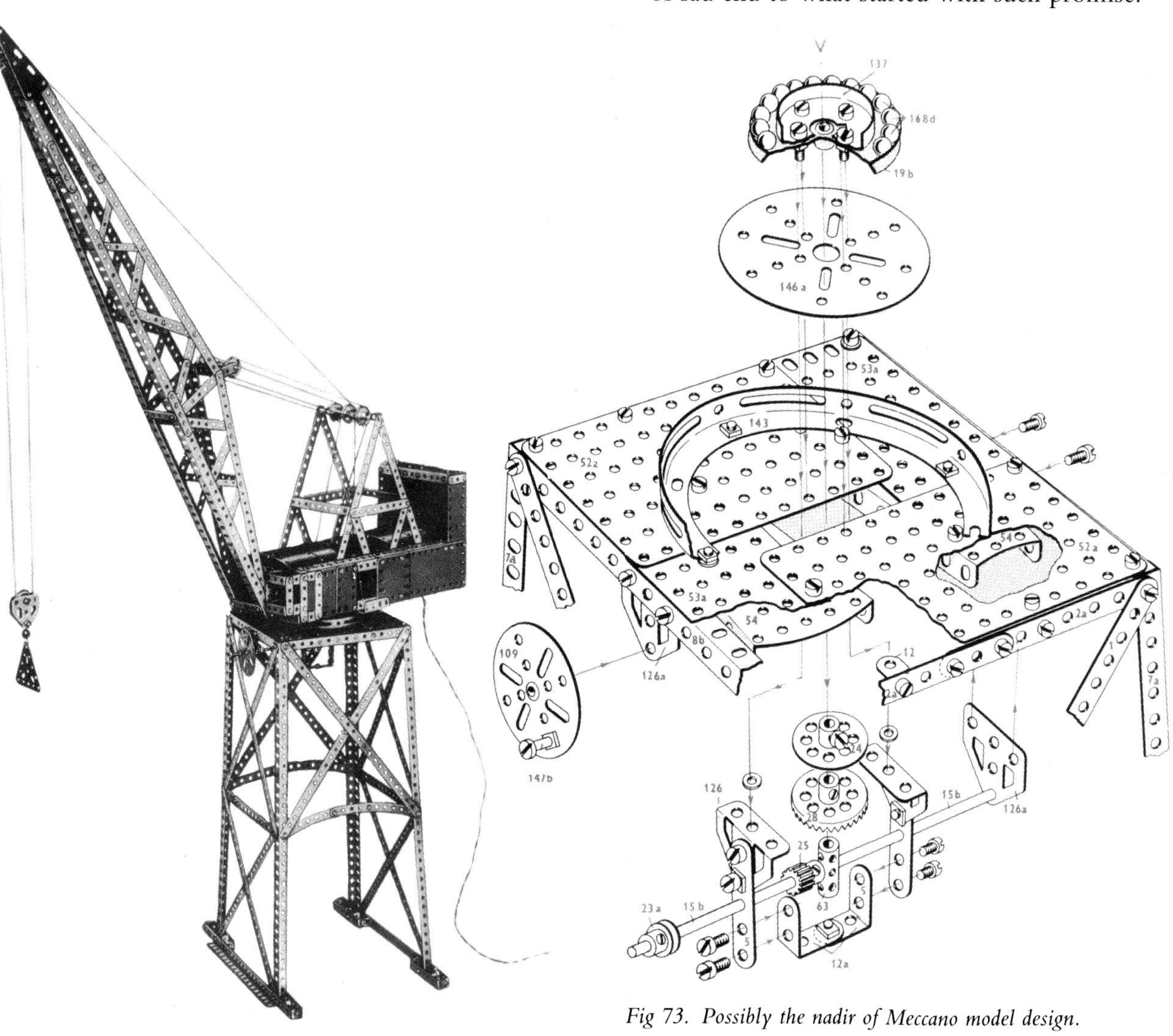

Fig 73. Possibly the nadir of Meccano model design.

CHAPTER 5

Books of New and Prize Models

Almost from the beginning, competitions were a feature of the Meccano world. The earliest was probably a Mechanics Made Easy competition announced in October 1903, only two years after the system was introduced. The reasons for such competitions are not hard to find – publicity, encouragement and ideas for new models. It is the latter which was probably the most valuable result of a model-building competition. In effect the time and money needed to design new models for the manuals was drastically reduced by what could be described as sub-contracting on the cheap. The tens of thousands of drawings and photographs submitted were copyright-free and available at any time.

The publicity gained from such competitions was, until the advent of the *Meccano Magazine*, somewhat doubtful. Announcements and results had to be made by way of journals like *The Model Engineer* and trade catalogues, and this was obviously not the best way to get the most out of the exercise. The 1914–15 Prize Model Competition (which was the biggest up until then) changed all that, with the issue of a small manual-sized booklet which published photographs and details of the winning entries (figs 1, 2 & 3). A more lacklustre cover is hard to imagine and the rather primitive models (by today's standards) are hardly much better. It really is only the Gordon Crosby motor chassis (see Special/Super Models Chapter, fig 2) which stands out. The manual, which does not bear any print reference, was circulated extensively and was included, it is believed, in many outfits most notably with the first Special Inventor's Outfit.

The following Prize Model Competition for 1915–16 also resulted in a special manual which, despite having a similar cover to the earlier one, contained somewhat better models. A special booklet was also published giving details of all the prize winners (figs 4A–D). Since no ordinary manual was produced in 1915 the Prize Model Book was the only source of new models.

After 1915 the First World War began to take its toll and no further Prize Model Books were produced. In fact it was to be another 12 years or so before a similar publication appeared and then in a very different format.

1928 was an important year in Meccano history. The Geared Roller Bearing, Digger Bucket, Super Model Leaflets and the *Meccano Book of Engineering* were all introduced that year and the No. 7 Outfit reached its zenith. On top of all that came a fresh 'Book of New Models' described on its cover as being 'Prize winning models, movements and ideas of the year'. The bright orange cover (fig 5) illustrated the largest of many versions of the Block-setting Crane as well as an impressive prototype, although it was not quite the same as the advertised cover (fig 6).

continued p. 135.

Fig 1. The first Meccano Book of Prize Models.

PROGRESS
CERTIFICATE
OF
MERIT
Awarded to
For excellence of design and construction, in connection with the Meccano Model Building Competition
Famous Engineers
STEPHENSON
WATT
BRINDLEY
BRUNEL
SMEATON
RENNIE
Famous Inventors
ARKWRIGHT
NASMYTH
HUNTSMAN
BRAMAH
DIESEL
PARSONS
Chairman
Meccano Ltd.

Fig 0. An unused certificate of the type awarded to winners in model building competitions. Note the early nickel-plate model crane still shown.

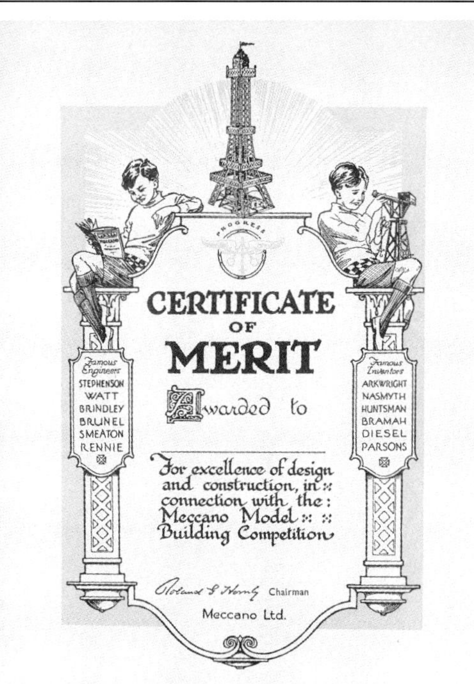

Automatic Escapement.
B. S. Fuess, 204, McDonough Street, Brooklyn, New York.
Horizontal Slide Valve Engine.
A. P. Rollett, 36, Balfour Street, Gainsborough, Lincs.
There are seven regular Meccano outfits costing from 3s. to 100s. Each one is complete, but you can always add new outfits and parts to it, in order to build bigger and better models.
Double-action Windmill Pump.
J. Carter, 4855, Berenice Avenue, Chicago, Ill., U.S.A.
Disappearing Gun.
C. Winthrop, Junr., 830, Carter Avenue, Wichita, Kans., U.S.A.
Passenger Elevator.
H. Puckett, Chickasha, Okla, U.S.A.
Motor Tricycle and Gun.
Bombardier Thornely, 2/1. S.M. War R.G.A., 14, Louise Road, Northampton.
Mowing Machine.
J. Mould, 307, Gidlow Lane, Wigan.
Lima Bean Thresher.
James B. Anderson, 619, Canyon Drive, Beverly Hills, Cal., U.S.A.
Page 12

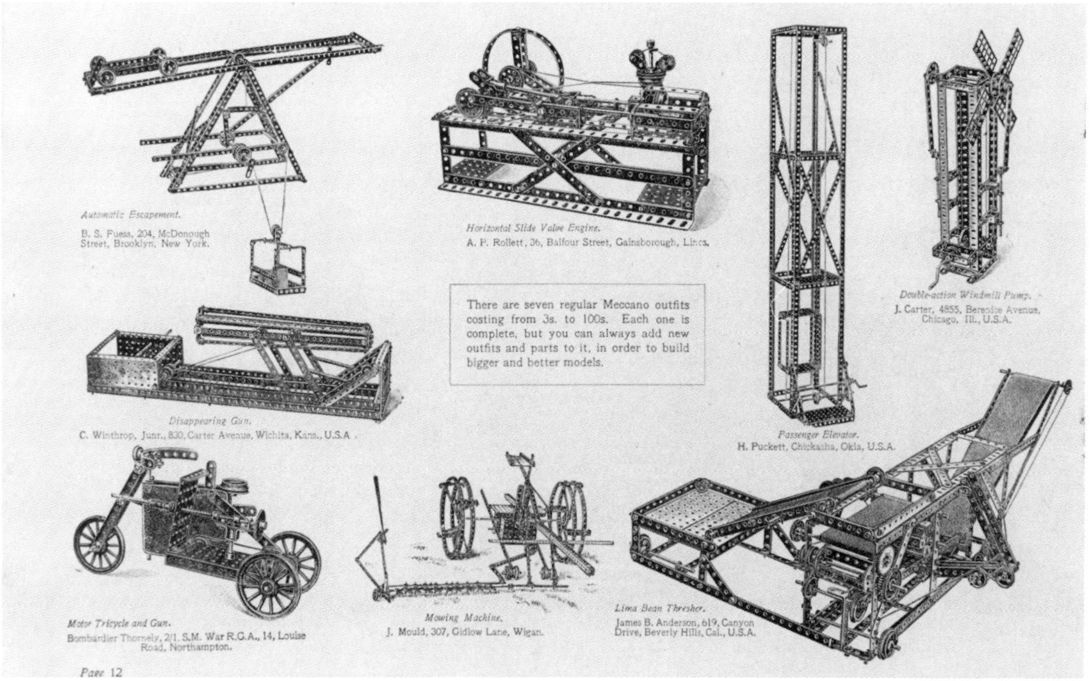

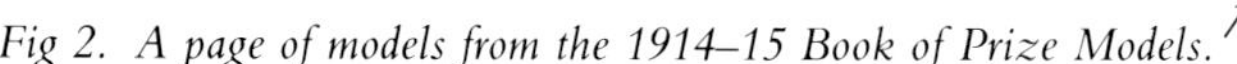

Fig 2. A page of models from the 1914–15 Book of Prize Models. ↗

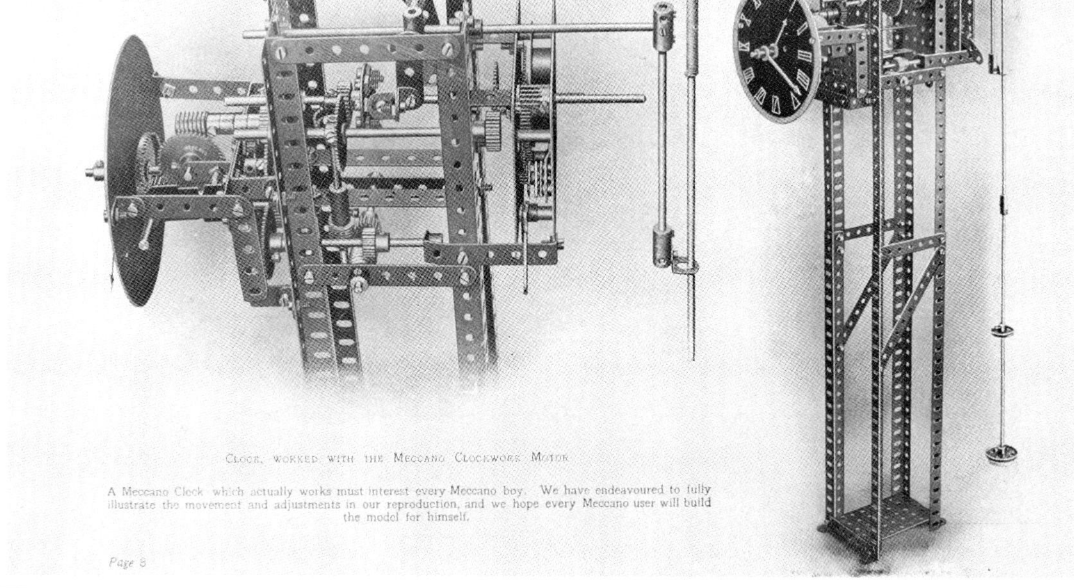

Sent in by E. Lawrence Wood Albany House, Bognor, Eng.
Clock, worked with the Meccano Clockwork Motor
A Meccano Clock which actually works must interest every Meccano boy. We have endeavoured to fully illustrate the movement and adjustments in our reproduction, and we hope every Meccano user will build the model for himself.
Page 8

Fig 3. A crude clock from the 1914–15 Book of Prize Models. →

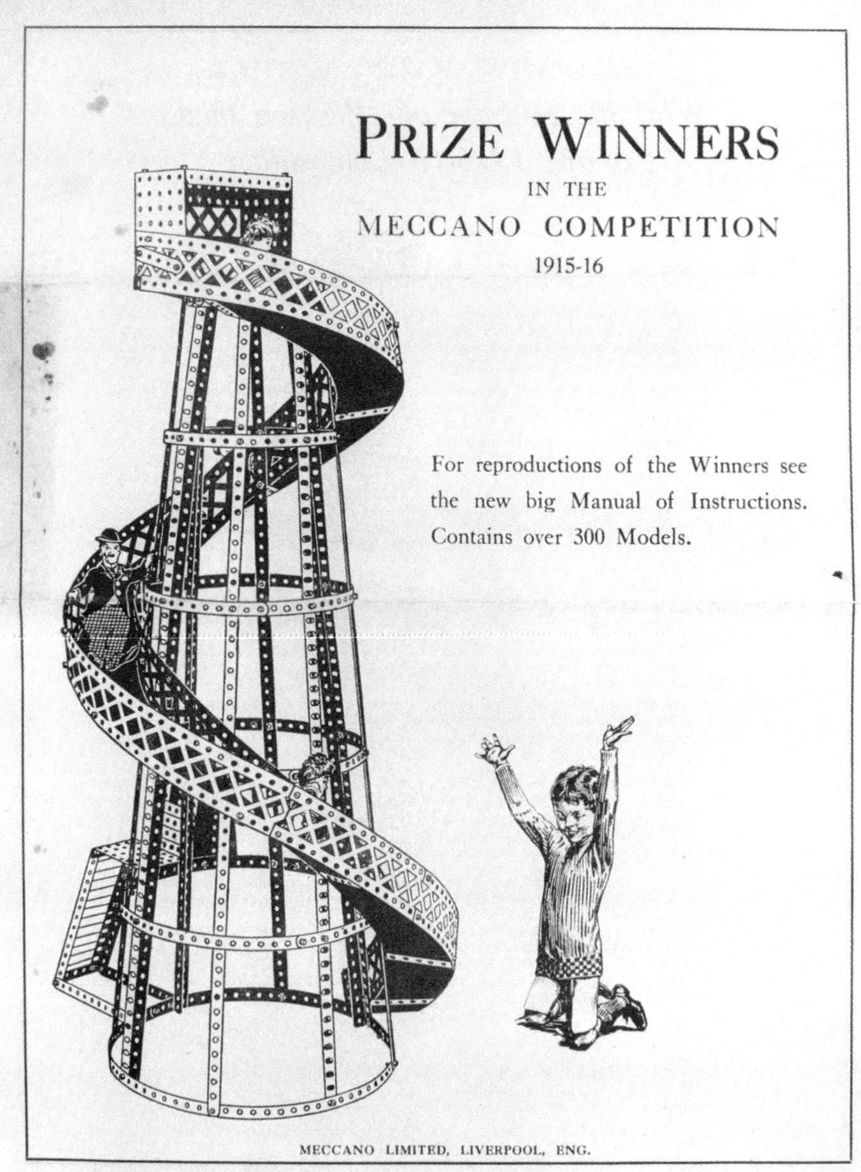

PRIZE WINNERS
IN THE
MECCANO COMPETITION
1915-16
For reproductions of the Winners see the new big Manual of Instructions. Contains over 300 Models.
MECCANO LIMITED, LIVERPOOL, ENG.

Fig 4A.

What the Inventor of Meccano thinks of the 1915-16 Competition

THE feature of the Meccano Competitions which pleases me best is that it brings me in close contact with so many thousands of ardent users of Meccano. During the last few weeks I have examined thousands and thousands of models sent in to me from every corner of the earth, and have been amazed and delighted by the ingenuity and resourcefulness of Meccano boys.

This competition has been much more successful than the last one; the entries have been more numerous, and an altogether higher standard of merit has been attained. So many excellent models have been sent in that I have decided to increase both the value and number of the prizes. This will account for the prize list being such a long one.

Letters have come to me in all languages, containing expressions of warmth and gratitude towards Meccano and myself, which have touched me to the heart. Letters from bright, sturdy, intelligent boys with brains to grasp the genius in Meccano and enterprise to break fresh ground, and send in something new and different. Hundreds of letters from boys in homes and hospitals, lying on beds of sickness from which many of them, unhappily, will never rise again, charged with touching words of gratitude for the pleasure and happy hours which Meccano has given to them. Letters from lonely boys in the Western States of America, in the heart of Africa, India, Australia, and far away points of the earth which I had never heard of before, telling me how Meccano has come as a boon to them to brighten up their long winter evenings. Letters from brave young boys on the battle-front, who are living with their parents within sound and reach of the enemy's guns, sending me models of cannon, armoured trains, or of aeroplanes which fly over their heads for the purpose of either destroying or defending them.

This world-tribute to the Meccano hobby has touched me deeply, and I should like to have the happiness of meeting all my Meccano boys, to thank them and encourage them, and talk over their Meccano problems and experiences with them.

I have been reluctantly compelled to reject a number of very excellent models sent in by boys who have shown an amount of ingenuity which is truly remarkable, owing in some cases to the fact that the models are too intricate and costly for most boys; in others, because the models, although distinctly clever, represent specialised movements which would not appeal strongly to Meccano boys; and in others because too much outside material other than Meccano has been employed, which would have to be manufactured specially. We may be able to reproduce shortly some of these models, as they indicate the extraordinary uses to which Meccano parts may be applied.

I hope that competitors who have not had the good fortune to win prizes will not feel in the least discouraged. A very large number of them show great cleverness and inventiveness, and I have no doubt whatever that many of the losing competitors in this competition will be winners in the next. The 1916-7 competition will start at once, and entry forms will be available very shortly. I hope to see all the old Meccano competitors and many new ones making a serious attempt for the big money prizes.

Just as we did last year, we shall issue a special prize model book, containing illustrations of a large number of winning models, and I know that it will please you all to see what a magnificent lot they are.

I want you specially this year to get the new Manual of Instructions, which will be ready in July. In addition to some of the best models which have been invented during the past fifteen years, I have this time included a large number of the winning models in the 1914-5 competition, and as many as I can crowd in from the 1915-6 competition. Such a book, teeming with new and wonderful things, has never been issued before. There is enjoyment and fun in every page of it, which I want each of you to share.

Managing Director of Meccano, Ltd.

Fig 4B.

Fig 4A–D. Details of the 1915–16 prize winners.

LIST of PRIZE WINNERS

1st Cash Prize - - £50 0 0
Divided amongst three competitors.

J. Yoxall, 76, Carleton St., Nelson, Lancs.................... *Loom*
William H. Maple, 857, Manida St., Bronx., New York, U.S.A. *Designing Machine*
Pierre Attinger, 17, Pertuis du Sault, Neuchâtel, Switzerland. . *Crane*

2nd & 3rd Cash Prizes - £35 0 0
Divided amongst four competitors.

Brian B. Gardner, 9, St. Michael's Villas, Headingley, Leeds *Helter Skelter*
Chas. B. Allen, Loretto School, Musselburgh, Scotland, *Billiard Player*
Herbert E. Volckmann, 111, So. 9th St., Brooklyn, N.Y., U.S.A. *Aeroscope*
R. F. Wilson, "Nithsdale," Swallowbeck, Lincoln............ *Crane*

4th Cash Prize - - £7 10 0

Ian F. Ferguson, 77, Elsham Rd., Kensington, London, W. . . *Escalator*

5th Cash Prize - - £5 0 0

R. J. Hankinson, 2, West Cliff Mansions, Eastbourne. . . . *Radial Crane*

6th Cash Prize - - £2 10 0

Sydney F. Martin, 18, Avon Rd., Walthamstow, Essex *Weighing Machine*

8 No. 5 MECCANO OUTFITS

A. Kempton, 31, Mandeville St., Liverpool, N....... *Purchase Block*
J. B. Scott, 14, Ivydale Rd., Higher Tranmere, Birkenhead *Stone Sawing Machine*
N. W. Lee, "Ardennes," Staindrop Rd., Darlington...... *Beam Scales*
W. J. Linggood, 11, London Rd., Crayford, Kent. . . . *Bowling Alley*
V. Price, 1, Horsford Rd., Brixton, London, S.W. . . *Tunnelling Machine*
A. R. Jefferson, 57, Auckland Rd., Doncaster, Yorks. . . *Pit Headgear*
Jas. Clark, 60, Regent St., Greenock...................... *Derrick*
Edward W. Sawyer, River Hall, Biddenden, Kent. . *Profiling Machine*

15 No. 4 MECCANO OUTFITS

Geo. W. Gunn, 73, Castle Rd., Cathcart, Glasgow. . . . *Mechanical Navvy*
Robert Brun, 29, Rue du Commerce, Rion (Puy de Dôme), France *Distance Measuring Machine*
F. Gordon Crosby, 2, York Rd., Leamington Spa. . *Tank Locomotive*
M. Gheury, 40, Westmount Rd., Eltham, S.E. . . . *Modern Windmill*
Th. Guyon, 82, Bis Avenue du Chemin de Fer, Le Raincy (Seine-et-Oise), France...................... *Rolling Bridge with Pivoting Crane*
A. Ussher, Gownbogs, Charterhouse, Godalming, Surrey *Electric Locomotive*
Arthur N. Moore, 6, Buckingham Place, Cambridge, Mass., U.S.A. *Hay Stacker*
Hubert Lloyd, 139, Marlborough Rd., Cheetham Hill, Manchester *Automatic Weighing Machine*
Alfred J. Hunt, Leighton Mount, 117, Waverley Rd., Reading *Caterpillar and Gun*
Marc Reyniers, 45, Rue Saint Ferdinand, Paris, France. . *Skein Winder*
A. Claymore, 2, Clerks Lane, Kilmarnock............. *Fret Saw*
John A. Brough, 43, Ray St., Heanor, Derby. . . . . . *Sighting Rule*
Ernest A. Seeley, 57, Avenell Rd., Highbury, N., *Automatic Machine*
E. G. Cullwick, 153, Tettenhall Rd., Wolverhampton . . *Dental Chair*
Ronald Pardey, Trinity Florence Rd., Shanklin, I. of W. *Armed Motor Cycle*

50 No. 3 MECCANO OUTFITS

W. C. Cunnington, Helpston Heath, Peterborough.......... *Elevator*
Harold W. Collins, 40, Elsinore Rd., Forest Hill, S. E. . . . . *Field Gun*
George S. Reid, 54, Marchmont Rd., Edinburgh...... *Maxim Gun*
Fredk. R. Black, Mount Carmel, 289, Cavehill Rd., Belfast *Linen Rolling Machine*
S. Camusat, 39, Rue des Aubépines, Bois-Colombes (Seine), France *Distance Indicator*
F. Bruce Newby, junr., 2812, West Av., Newport News, Va., U.S.A., *Two-storey Saw Mill*
Robt. K. Jeffrey, Bexley, Columbus, Ohio, U.S.A. *Excavating Machine*
Francis Pottenger, Monrovia, California, U.S.A. . . *Swinging Bridge*
Norman Springall, 24, Westmoreland Rd., Urmston, Nr. Manchester *Carpet Sweeper*
Conrad Groth, Saint Ausgar, Iowa, U.S.A....... *Manure Spreader*
Jos. G. Price, 21, Church Av., Drumcondra, Dublin. . . . *Jaunting Car*
W. W. Jacques, 97, Whalley Rd., Accrington, Lancs . . . . *Joy Wheel*
G. Proctor, 81, Water Street, Accrington, Lancs. . . . . . . *Joy Wheel*
Ian F. Ferguson, 77, Elsham Rd., Kensington, W. . . *Express Delivery*

Truda Widdowson, The Hall House, Bulwell, Notts., *Delivery Cart*
Raymond Morot, 35, Rue St. Laurent, Beauvais (Oise), France *Needlework Basket*
Henry Osbourne, 12, Clive Av., Hastings, Sussex. . *Searchlight Tower*
Edwin T. Porter, 422, South Harrison St., Shelbyville, Indiana, U.S.A. .... *Swing Saw*
Samuel Weatherby, 1017, Ind St., Lawrence Kan, U.S.A. . . *Hand Car*
Louis Gordon, Agent-Voyer, Bergerac (Dordogne), France, *Catapult*
E. Smedley, junr., 20, Vergette St., Peterborough. . *Timber Carriage*
Geoffrey Heath, Castle Gresley, Burton-on-Trent. . *Windmill Scare*
Neville Arnold, West End Cottage, Whittlesford, Cambs., *Horse Hoe*
Rene Govaert, 8, St. Paul's Terrace, Norton, Malton, Yorks. *Belgian Water Wheel*
Albert Wroe, Four Lane Ends, Mapplewell, Barnsley, *Sledge Velocipede*
Percy Winterbone, 7, Marine Terrace, Margate. . . . *Chocolate Mixer*
Raymond Eichner, 1541, Mulberry St., Reading, Pa., U.S.A. *Direct-lift Bridge*
R. Hugot, Rue Meurdrac, Les Andelys, France, *Platform Anti-aircraft Gun*
Irving H. Roland, 409, Academy St., So. Orange, New Jersey, U.S.A. *Cutting Machine*
Ellwood K. Lewis, junr., 6112, Jefferson St., Philadelphia, Pa., U.S.A. *Electric Truck*
Kenneth Shaw Safe, Ocean Lawn, Newport, R.I., U.S.A., *Weather Vane*
Calvin Hosmer, Box 567, Sharon, Mass. U.S.A.......... *Punch Press*
Wilson Robinson Gaythwaite, 66, High St., Cleator Moor, Cumb. *Wallpaper Cutter*
Maurice Dartville, 12, Rue des Granges, Besançon (Doubs), France *Drop Hammer*
C. R. H. Simpson, Towcester, Northamptonshire. . . . . . *Field Kitchen*
Joe Carter, 4855, Berenice Ave., Chicago, Illinois, U.S.A. *Washing Machine*
Maurice Jacquin, Perception, Maclas (Loire), France *Winnowing Machine*
H. D. Krug, 7323, Kelly Street, Homewood, Pittsburgh, Pa., U.S.A. *Tape Machine*
P. Hood Bennett, 48, Godolphin Rd., Shepherd's Bush, London *Workshop*
E. Stanley Flanagan, 2030, Broadway, New York, U.S.A., *Lawn Mower*
F. S. Matthes, 97, Washington St., Long Branch, N.J., U.S.A. *Farm Tractor*
Jas. Fraser, 4, Lethamill Terrace, Millerston, by Glasgow *Marble Polishing Machine*
Alfred E. Cope, 11, Norton St., Old Trafford, Manchester, *Model Theatre*
E. Lang, 102, Barton Terrace, North Adelaide, S. Australia. . *Periscope*
Eric A. Jones, 238, Willow Av., Edgbaston, Birmingham *Drop the Nigger*
F. M. Vaughan, 7, Ferncroft Av., Hampstead, N.W. . . . . . *Hand Cart*
J. Hartemann, 122, Rue de Toul, Nancy, France . . . . *Land Boat*
T. E. Brown, 55, Mosley St., Barrow-in-Furness. . . . . . *Kitchen Range*
A. Binnall Grosvenor, 145, Bank St., Heath Hayes, Cannock *Measuring Machine*
A. P. Rollett, 36, Balfour St., Gainsborough, Lincs., *Platform Scales*

45 No. 2 MECCANO OUTFITS

Lewis E. Moore, 270, Mill St., Newtonville, Mass., U.S.A., *Stone Crusher*
Chas. D. Cathart, 78, Judson St., Albany, New York, U.S.A. *Fire Extension Ladder*
R. G. Torrens, 85, North Main St., Youghal co. Cork. . . . *Praxinscope*

Fig 4C.

List of Prize Winners—*continued*

45 No. 2 MECCANO OUTFITS—*Continued*

Jean Devarenne, 39, Rue Nationale, Toulon, France . . . . *Guillotine*
E. M. Shipman, 15a, Mayow Rd., Forest Hill, S.E. . . *Designing Machine*
Ernest Bullough, 391, Manchester Rd., Westhoughton, Bolton *Potato Chopper*
Ernest K. Hall, 82, Tilehurst Rd., Reading, Berks. . . . . *Roller Skate*
Eric Whiteside, 52, Northen Grove, West Didsbury, Manchester *Automatic Gong*
N. Campbell, "Aberdour," Park View, Blyth, N'umberland, *Semaphore*
Leon V. Quigley, 106, Chapin St., Holyoke, Mass., U.S.A., *Coal Hoist*
Roland Farrant, The Climb, Hitchin Rd., Luton, Beds. . . . . . . *Bridge*
Fred Goodin, 35, Glisson Rd., Cambridge.................... *Plough*
J. Pardanaud, 30, Rue Grangevieille, Le Puy (Haute-Loire), France *Mountain Transport*
A. Hirst, New Rd., Barugh Green, Nr. Barnsley. . . . . . *Coal Shaker*
Stanley Cookson, Fylde Cottage, Thornton, Lancs. . . . . *Swing Boat*
James Sutton, 26, Barnsley Rd., Wakefield. . . . . *Coronation Chair*
E. C. Large, 1, Earldom Rd., Putney, S.W., *Oscillating Steam Engine*
Jas. A. Hutcheon, 20, St. David's St., Brechin, Scotland, *Rocking Chair*
Pierre Grimont, 10, Rue de St. Quentin, Paris, France . . *Hand Cart*
Wm. Spivey, Park Rd., Norton, Malton, Yorks. .... *Easel*
Harry Oswin, 12, Causeway Head, Burnley Rd., Sowerby Bridge, York, *Doll's Carriage*
J. V. Mason, 82, Addison Way, Golder's Green, N.W., *Mixing Machine*
Ronald Green, 9, The Highlands, Keighley, Yorks. . . . . *Band Saw*
Robt. Allison, 1446, Pollokshaws Rd., Shawlands, Glasgow, *Locomotive*
Thos. Foster, 19, William St., Newfield, S.O., Newcastle-on-Tyne *Ducking Chair*
Fred Starkey, 49, Kinglake St., Edge Hill, Liverpool, *Conductor's Punch*
W. G. Conway, 9, Chesterton Rd., North Kensington, W. *Torpedo Destroyer*
F. E. Oag, 35, Capps Rd., Denmark Rd., Norwich. . . . . *Loco. Crane*
Cyril Woolley, 39, Long Row, Belper, Derbyshire . . . . . . *Swing Boat*
Marcel Tupin, 43, Rue Jean Ribault, Dieppe (Seine Inferieure), France *Aeroplane*
P. Rouillon, 75, Rue de Flandre, Paris, France . . . . . . *Invalid Chair*
Freddie Backhouse, Spark Lane, Mapplewell. . . . . . *Treadle Hammer*
A. B. Archibald, Invernettie, Private Bag, Durban, Natal, S. Africa *Maize Sheller*
R. J. M. Andrews, 16, Binswood Av., Leamington Spa *Mechanical Hammer*
D. McGregor, 4, High St., Altrincham, Cheshire. . . . . . *Aircraft Gun*
Rene Govaert, 8, St. Paul's Ter., Norton, Malton, Yorks., *Flax Cleaner*
Harry Barker, 64, Sowerby Gn., Sowerby, Nr. Sowerby Bridge, Yorks. *Crane*
R. E. Gittins, 14, Wyvis St., Poplar, E. . . . . *Overhead Crane*
D. C. Downing, 62, Greenwood Av., East Orange, N.J., U.S.A. *Automobile*
R. Reid, 725, Spring St., Elgin, Illinois, U.S.A., *Buz Saw & Wood Splitter*
J. Mosenergue, Pavillon No. 3, Route de St. Dernin, Le Creusot, Saone et Loire, France .... *Swing Saw*
Maurice Darteville, 12, Rue des Granges, Besançon (Doubs), France *Power Hammer*
Adolph Gobel, 279, Highland Boulevard, Brooklyn, New York, U.S.A. *Motor Plough*
F. Boothroyd, 65, Westgate, Almondbury, Huddersfield, *Aerial Flyer*
W. S. Morris, 217, Wilson Avenue, Montreal, Canada. . . . *Fire Escape*

25 No. 1 MECCANO OUTFITS

Mark Sturtenant, 1864 West 45th St., Cleveland, Ohio, U.S.A. *Model s.s. Mauretania*
Geo. Miller, 822, South 13th St., Quincey, Illinois, U.S.A., *Washing Machine*
E. Long, 102, Barton Ter., N. Adelaide, S. Australia. . . . *Machine Gun*
Jos. Hughes, The Craig, Bangor, Isycoed, Nr. Wrexham. . . . *Hay Tedder*

Wilfrid Whaley, 11, Witham Place, Boston, Lincs. . . *Invalid Chair*
Cedric Carr, 4, Cliff Terrace, Hartlepool............... *Swing Cot*
Geo. S. Reid, 54, Marchmont Rd., Edinburgh.......... *Bed Table*
Walter Frearson, Union St., Melbourne, Derby .... *Chair*
Sidney E. Reed, 44, Bedford Rd., Reading, Berks. . . *Coster's Barrow*
Maurice J. Allgrove, 57, Cleveleys Rd., Up. Clapton, N.E., *Ford Car*
F. Langer, 20, Fitz-Neal St., Ducane Rd., Shepherd's Bush, W. *Hand Punching Machine*
G. Everett, 97, Long St., Cerne Abbas, Dorset................ *Sifter*
J. E. Badeley, Trewyth, Northwood......................... *Ladder*
Richard L. Jones, 52, Shrewsbury St., Old Trafford, Nr. M/r. . . . . *Car*
S. H. Threadgill, 14, Belmont Rd., Clapham, S.W. . . . . *Beam Scales*
Thomas Gerrard, 31, Lord St., Leigh, Lancs. . . . . *Roman Balance*
Wm. Driver, 46, Viewland Rd., Plumstead, London. . *Roman Balance*
Albert Wroe, Four Lane Ends, Mapplewell, Barnsley, *Roman Balance*
R. K. Jeffrey, Bexley, Columbus, Ohio, U.S.A. . . . . *Rope Drive*
Nicholas Moore, 463, Willow St., Wumetka, Illinois, U.S.A. *Trench Digger*
Reggie S. Harvey, 20, Bath St., Waterloo, Nr. Liverpool, *Dinner Gong*
Roy V. Gayford, Bridge House, Hadley, Suffolk. . . . . *Bird Scarer*
Gordon Green, 8, Auckland Rd., Doncaster, Yorks., *Scissors Grinder*
Louis Elisee Guillemart (130e d'Infanterie) c/o H. Ruteau. . . . *Loom* Hospital Bénévole (Les Fontenys), Bois-le-Roi (Seine-et-Marne).
Brian Longmuir, "Ravenscrag," Wortley, Nr. Sheffield . . *Wire Cutter*

30 No. 0 MECCANO OUTFITS

George Taylor, 1, Bullfinch St., Deepdale, Preston............ *Loom*
Jas. F. Corr, Bonavista, E. Newport, Fife. . . . . . *Anti-Aircraft Gun*
M. S. Barclay, 2, Battlefield Av., Langside, Glasgow. . . . . . *Metal Saw*
A. Cureton, Darlington House, Horder Rd., Wolverhampton *Loco. Crane*
Geo. M. Belben, 39, Augustine St., Grimsby. . . . . *Sharpshooter Gun*
L. Wooldridge, "The Den," Church Lane, Highfield, Southampton *Motor Lurry*
Alan A. Whyte, 82, Castlegate, Malton, Yorks. . . . . *Mail Bag Hanger*
A. Naylor, 3, King St., Yeadon, Nr. Leeds .... *Gondola*
H. C. Ives, 19, Shandon Rd., Clapham, S.W. . . . . *Yacht*
F. E. Lyon, Navy Yard, Boston, Mass., U.S.A. . . . . *Crane*
Edwin King, 59, Queen Charlotte St., Bristol. . . . . *Jib Crane*
Tom Porter, 182, Corporation St., Birmingham. . . . . . *Horse Sleigh*
Ar. R. Jefferson, 57, Auckland Rd., Doncaster. . . . . . *Spinning Top*
Rene Pfisterer, 31, Rue de la Côte, Neuchâtel, Switzerland *Piercing Machine*
Robt. Millardet, 24, Rue Jean de Chatillon, St. Malo, France, *Hatchet*
Marcel Lerecouvreux, 10, Rue-Carrier, Belleux, Paris, France, *Anchor*
Jacques Thomas, 6, Cours Carbe, Sens, Yonne, France. . *Music Stand*
V. Aiers, Station House, Market Bosworth, Nuneaton. . *Watch Stand*
Cedric Carr, 4, Cliff Terrace, Hartlepool. . . . . *Field Roller*
J. H. Bissell, 26, Dudley Rd., Tipton, Staffs. . . . . *Scales*
Edwyn A. Birks, 565, Manchester Rd., Denton, Nr. M/r. . *Devil Wall*
H. Wilkinson, Golden Lion Inn, Hetton-le-Hole. . . . . . *Rocking Chair*
Victor Johnstone, War Signal Station, St. Alban's Head, Dorset *Morse Tapper*
Rene Prothon, Villa Blanche, Bd. Gambetta, Romans. . . . *Windmill*
Maurice Gill, 33, Newcomen St., Redcar, Yorks. . . . . *Hand Roller*
Denys Lane Walters, Fordcombe Manor, Nr. Tunbridge Wells *Fire Bellows*
Denys P. Hall, 12, Warham Rd., South Croydon. . . . *Railway Gauge*
Jack S. Thompson, 6, Lydia St., Binghamton, New York, U.S.A. *Railroad Barrier*
Monsieur Bodeau, 6, Rue des Archives, Paris. . . . . . *Operating Table*
Jean Communandat, Rue de l'Hotel de Ville, Nantua (Ain.) . . *Easel*

When you ask for Meccano, see that you get it

Nothing else is "just as good"—nothing else will do the same

LOOK FOR THE TRADE NAME "MECCANO" ON YOUR OUTFIT

MECCANO, LTD. BINNS ROAD LIVERPOOL, ENG.

Fig 4D.

Fig 5. The first of the Books of New Models.

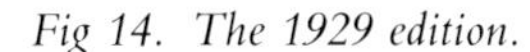
Fig 14. The 1929 edition.

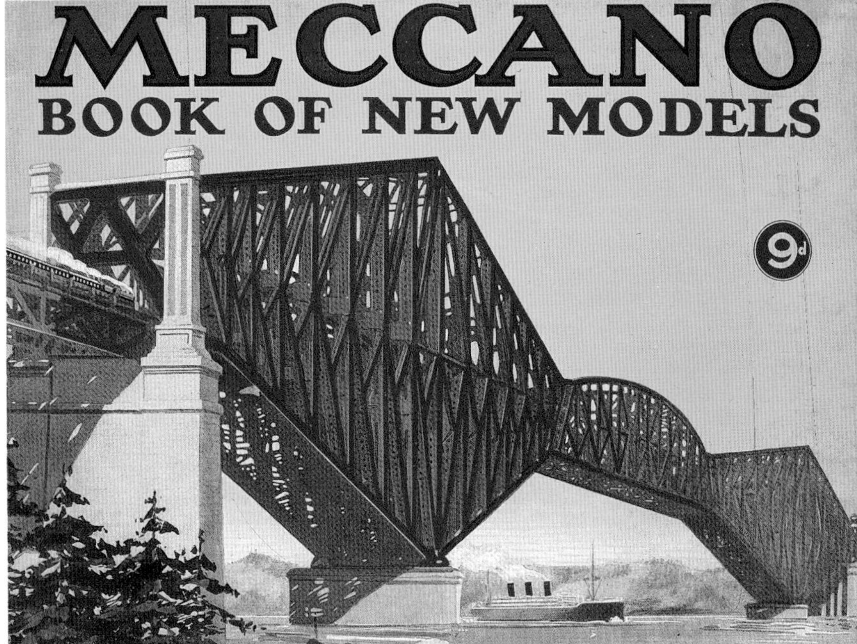

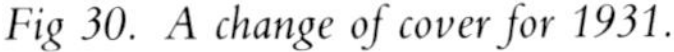
Fig 30. A change of cover for 1931.

Fig 39. The 1932 edition which reverted to the earlier cover.

At 6d it was the same price as the *Meccano Magazine* and showed 79 new models as well as nine mechanisms which had been previously featured in the 'Suggestions' columns of the *MM*. The models ranged from the very simplest (fig 7) to a very, for 1928, respectable orrery (fig 8) and a fascinating model of a Tatham Transmission Dynamometer which can be calibrated quite accurately (fig 9). The mechanisms included an Automatic Reversing Gear (fig 10) and a number of other useful devices such as an Auto Reverse Hoist (fig 11). Some of these found their way into the 1929 edition of Standard Mechanisms, for example the Two Speed Planetary Gear (see chapter 6 fig 18). Similarly many of the models were given places in the following years' manuals. To finish it off, there was a page giving details of new and recent parts (fig 12).

This first edition must have been a success because within a month a second print run was ordered. This second print was not identical, as might be thought, but had a number of small differences. The most obvious is the omission of the date on the front cover which is unlikely to have been accidental because dates were removed from a number of other pages including that showing the Tatham Transmission Dynamometer (cf with fig 9). The errors on the inside back cover relating to the pulley blocks (shown upside down) and compression spring (out of order) were also corrected. There also appear to have been some alterations to the *MM* references in mid-print.

Despite the attractiveness of this publication, it comprised in the main rather simple models and, with few exceptions, only the mechanisms were for the more advanced builder. Even so it must have been very welcome.

The 1929 edition of The Book of New Models (fig 14) was an improvement in a number of ways. Instead of concentrating on the simpler models it showed a broader and more interesting range; for example, the Electric Fan, Railway Signal Gantry and a very realistic Motor Breakdown Crane (figs 15–17). The mechanisms too were better than those of 1928. The Wobble Shaft Variable Speed Gear, The Corliss Valve Gear and the Siemens Chronometric Governor (figs 18–20) are of especial interest and also serve to show the swift progress of Meccano Modelling in a relatively short space of time.

Another departure from the 1928 format was the inclusion of four pages of prize-winning models from previous competitions and, although none would win prizes today, for their time they were generally up to standard (fig 21).

Like the 1928 edition, there were two printings – with and without the date on the front cover, although strangely both bear the same reference (see print data).

continued p. 146.

Fig 6. The Book of New Models cover as advertised but not produced.

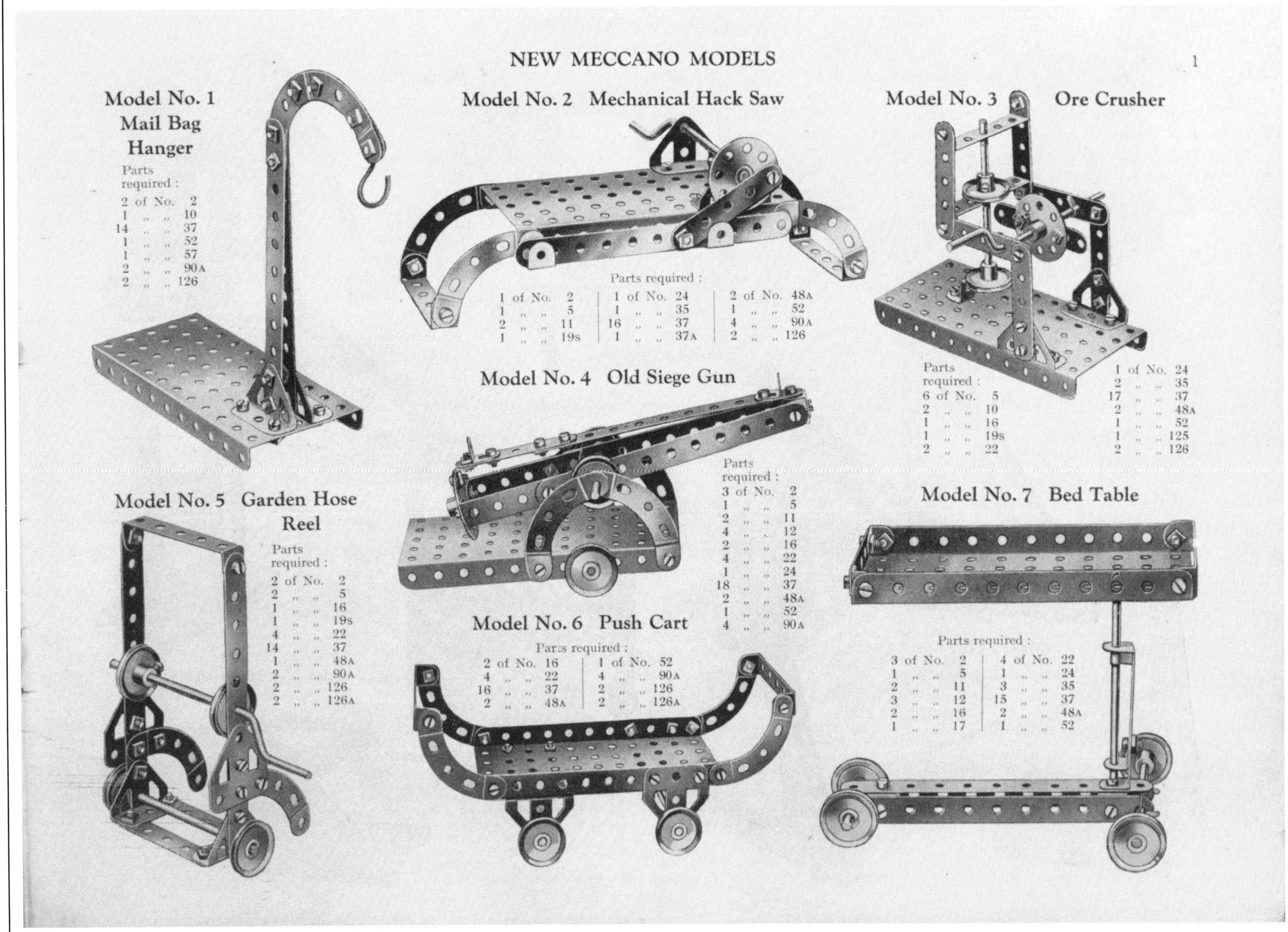

NEW MECCANO MODELS

1

Model No. 1 Mail Bag Hanger

Parts required :

Qty	No.
2 of No.	2
1	10
14	37
1	52
1	57
2	90A
2	126

Model No. 2 Mechanical Hack Saw

Parts required :

Qty	No.	Qty	No.	Qty	No.
1 of No.	2	1 of No.	24	2 of No.	48A
1	5	1	35	1	52
2	11	16	37	4	90A
1	19S	1	37A	2	126

Model No. 3 Ore Crusher

Parts required :

Qty	No.	Qty	No.
6 of No.	5	1 of No.	24
2	10	2	35
1	16	17	37
1	19S	2	48A
2	22	1	52
		1	125
		2	126

Model No. 4 Old Siege Gun

Parts required :

Qty	No.
3 of No.	2
1	5
2	11
4	12
2	16
4	22
1	24
18	37
2	48A
1	52
4	90A

Model No. 5 Garden Hose Reel

Parts required :

Qty	No.
2 of No.	2
2	5
1	16
1	19S
4	22
14	37
1	48A
2	90A
2	126
2	126A

Model No. 6 Push Cart

Parts required :

Qty	No.	Qty	No.
2 of No.	16	1 of No.	52
4	22	4	90A
16	37	2	126
2	48A	2	126A

Model No. 7 Bed Table

Parts required :

Qty	No.	Qty	No.
3 of No.	2	4 of No.	22
1	5	1	24
2	11	3	35
3	12	15	37
2	16	2	48A
1	17	1	52

Fig 7. A page of simple models for the youngest enthusiast.

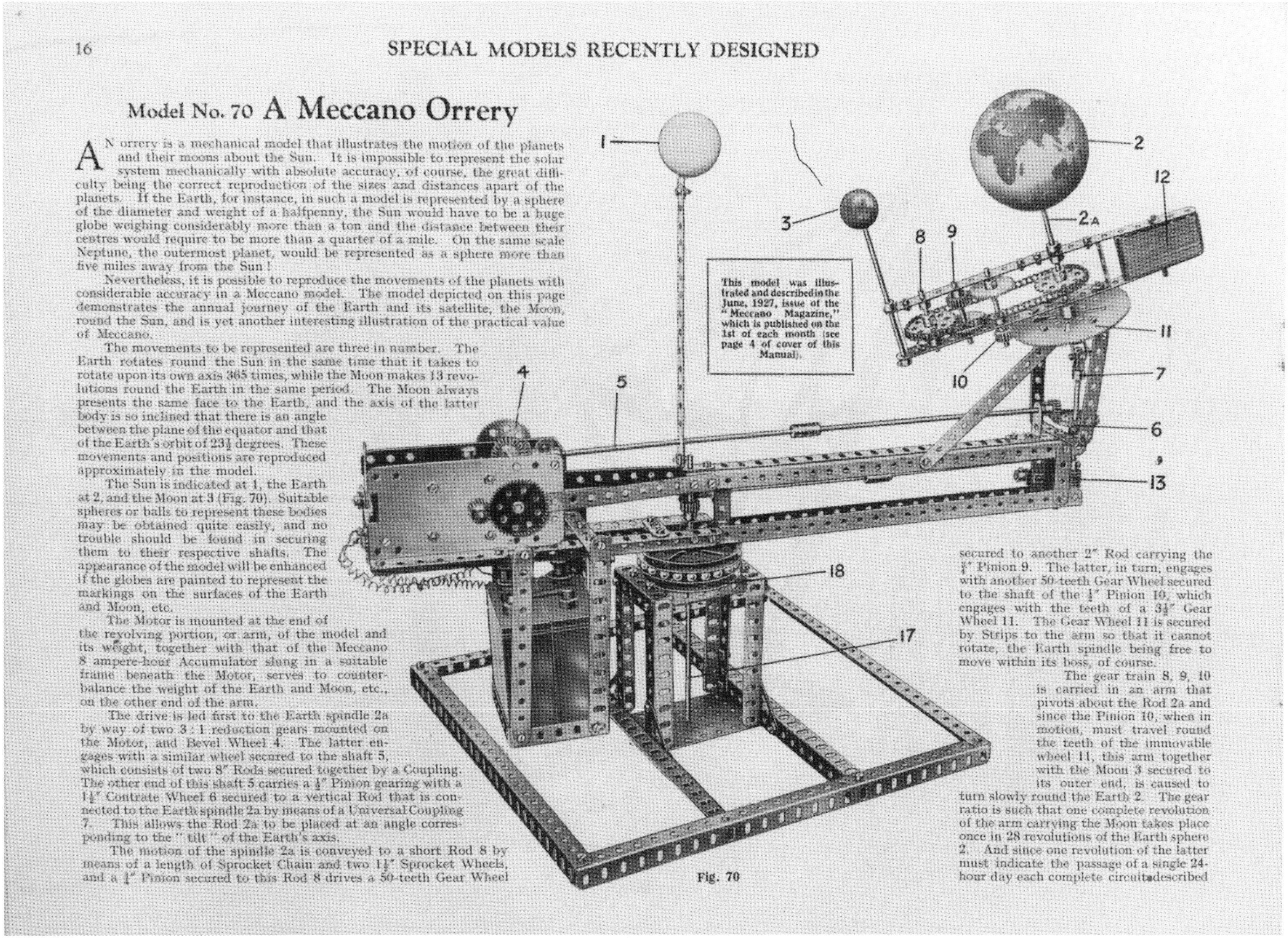

16 SPECIAL MODELS RECENTLY DESIGNED

Model No. 70 A Meccano Orrery

An orrery is a mechanical model that illustrates the motion of the planets and their moons about the Sun. It is impossible to represent the solar system mechanically with absolute accuracy, of course, the great difficulty being the correct reproduction of the sizes and distances apart of the planets. If the Earth, for instance, in such a model is represented by a sphere of the diameter and weight of a halfpenny, the Sun would have to be a huge globe weighing considerably more than a ton and the distance between their centres would require to be more than a quarter of a mile. On the same scale Neptune, the outermost planet, would be represented as a sphere more than five miles away from the Sun!

Nevertheless, it is possible to reproduce the movements of the planets with considerable accuracy in a Meccano model. The model depicted on this page demonstrates the annual journey of the Earth and its satellite, the Moon, round the Sun, and is yet another interesting illustration of the practical value of Meccano.

The movements to be represented are three in number. The Earth rotates round the Sun in the same time that it takes to rotate upon its own axis 365 times, while the Moon makes 13 revolutions round the Earth in the same period. The Moon always presents the same face to the Earth, and the axis of the latter body is so inclined that there is an angle between the plane of the equator and that of the Earth's orbit of 23½ degrees. These movements and positions are reproduced approximately in the model.

The Sun is indicated at 1, the Earth at 2, and the Moon at 3 (Fig. 70). Suitable spheres or balls to represent these bodies may be obtained quite easily, and no trouble should be found in securing them to their respective shafts. The appearance of the model will be enhanced if the globes are painted to represent the markings on the surfaces of the Earth and Moon, etc.

The Motor is mounted at the end of the revolving portion, or arm, of the model and its weight, together with that of the Meccano 8 ampere-hour Accumulator slung in a suitable frame beneath the Motor, serves to counterbalance the weight of the Earth and Moon, etc., on the other end of the arm.

The drive is led first to the Earth spindle 2a by way of two 3 : 1 reduction gears mounted on the Motor, and Bevel Wheel 4. The latter engages with a similar wheel secured to the shaft 5, which consists of two 8″ Rods secured together by a Coupling. The other end of this shaft 5 carries a ½″ Pinion gearing with a 1½″ Contrate Wheel 6 secured to a vertical Rod that is connected to the Earth spindle 2a by means of a Universal Coupling 7. This allows the Rod 2a to be placed at an angle corresponding to the "tilt" of the Earth's axis.

The motion of the spindle 2a is conveyed to a short Rod 8 by means of a length of Sprocket Chain and two 1½″ Sprocket Wheels, and a ¾″ Pinion secured to this Rod 8 drives a 50-teeth Gear Wheel secured to another 2″ Rod carrying the ¾″ Pinion 9. The latter, in turn, engages with another 50-teeth Gear Wheel secured to the shaft of the ½″ Pinion 10, which engages with the teeth of a 3½″ Gear Wheel 11. The Gear Wheel 11 is secured by Strips to the arm so that it cannot rotate, the Earth spindle being free to move within its boss, of course.

The gear train 8, 9, 10 is carried in an arm that pivots about the Rod 2a and since the Pinion 10, when in motion, must travel round the teeth of the immovable wheel 11, this arm together with the Moon 3 secured to its outer end, is caused to turn slowly round the Earth 2. The gear ratio is such that one complete revolution of the arm carrying the Moon takes place once in 28 revolutions of the Earth sphere 2. And since one revolution of the latter must indicate the passage of a single 24-hour day each complete circuit described

This model was illustrated and described in the June, 1927, issue of the "Meccano Magazine," which is published on the 1st of each month (see page 4 of cover of this Manual).

1 2 2A 3 4 5 6 7 8 9 10 11 12 13 17 18

Fig. 70

Fig 8. An interesting model for the advanced builder.

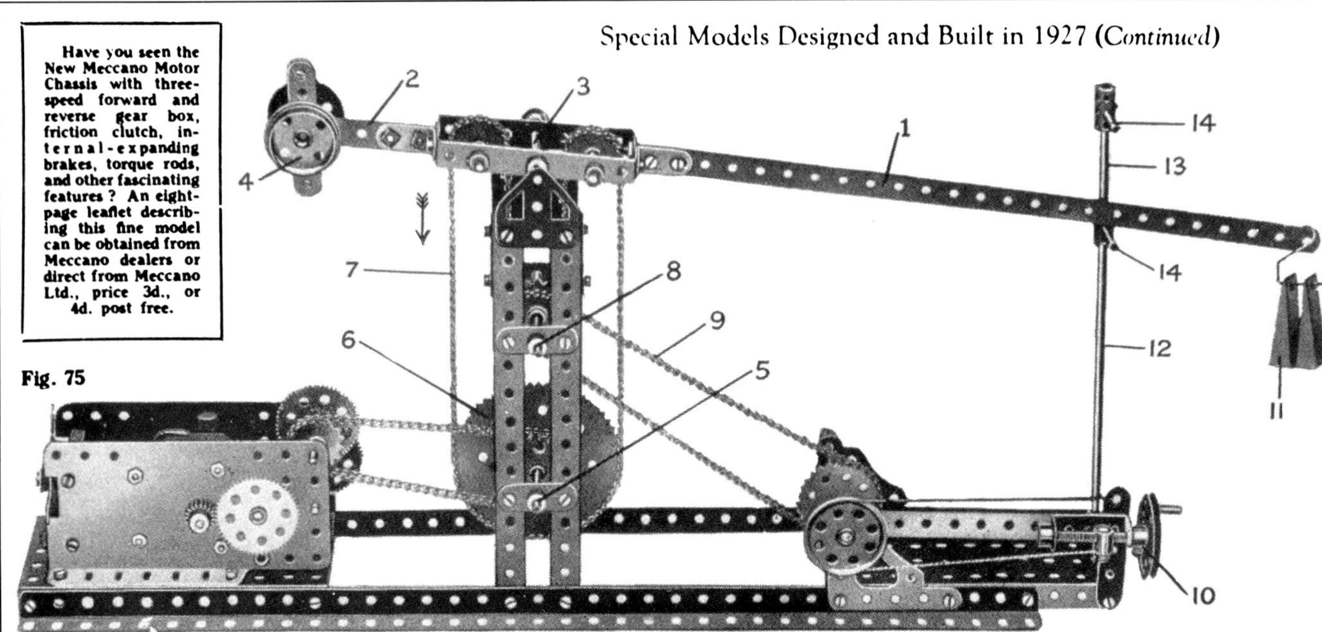

Model No. 75 Tatham Transmission Dynamometer

A transmission dynamometer is an instrument designed to measure the force of an engine while transmitting the power without other loss than that caused by friction in the apparatus.

The construction of the framework is quite simple. The upright member is built up from four 7½″ Angle Girders connected near the top by two 2½″ Strips and two Flat Trunnions. The movable arm, or steelyard 1, consists of a 12½″ Strip connected by means of two 1″ × ½″ Angle Brackets to two 3½″ × ½″ Double Angle Strips, and the other ends of the latter are connected by two further 1″ × ½″ Angle Brackets to a 2½″ Strip 2.

The arm pivots about a 3½″ Rod 3, and suitable weights should be added at 4 so that it is exactly balanced about this point.

The drive from the Motor is led on to a 2″ Sprocket Wheel secured to a 3½″ Rod 5, which carries also a 3″ Sprocket Wheel 6. A length of Sprocket Chain 7 passes round this Sprocket 6, over two 1″ Sprocket Wheels secured to 2″ Rods journalled in the arm 1, one on each side of the fulcrum 3, and round a third 1″ Sprocket Wheel secured to another 3½″ Rod 8. The drive is finally transmitted to the machinery that the Motor is required to operate by another length of Sprocket Chain 9, which passes over a second 1″ Sprocket Wheel on the Rod 8.

For testing purposes the Rod driven by the Chain 9 must have varying degrees of resistance, and the necessary adjustments are effected by a strap and screw brake 10, which is identical to Standard Mechanism No. 85. The Motor must be started in such a direction that the Chain 7 travels in the direction indicated by the arrow. The chain tends to pull down the shorter end of the arm 1 and the power of the Motor is gauged by the extent of this pull, which may be ascertained by placing the weight 11 (two Meccano 50-gramme weights attached to a Scientific Hook) in different positions on the arm. Different speed ratios should be arranged by changing the gears on the Motor, and the variation in the pull on the Chain 7 should be ascertained for each ratio.

The movement of the arm 1 is kept within certain limits by the stops 14. These consist of 1½″ Rods secured in Couplings and supported by a 6½″ Rod 12, which is gripped in the boss of a Crank
bolted to the

Fig 9. One of many scientific instruments which could be reproduced in Meccano.

No. 3 Automatic Reversing Gear

A Reversing Gear that at regular pre-arranged intervals will automatically change the direction of rotation of a driven rod is shown in Fig. 3.

The power from the Motor may be led through any convenient gearing to the driven shaft 1 via the intermediate shaft 2. This shaft 2 carries a ¾" Pinion 3, in constant engagement with a 1½" Contrate Wheel 5, and a section of a Dog Clutch 4.

A short Threaded Rod 6 is inserted in the centre of the driven shaft and is secured between Couplings mounted on the short Rods 1 and 1a. The whole driven unit 1, 6, 1a is slidable in its bearings and carries a ¾" Pinion 7 and a Dog Clutch section 8. These are so arranged that when the clutch segments 8 and 4 are in engagement the Pinion 7 is out of mesh with the Contrate Wheel 5. In this position the shafts 1 and 2 rotate as one unit and the Contrate Wheel revolves idly. In the second position of the driven shaft the clutch is disengaged and the Pinion 7 engages the Contrate Wheel 5, with the result that Rod 1 is driven in a direction opposite to that of Rod 2, the drive now being transmitted by way of the Contrate 5.

The automatic reverse motion is effected as follows: A coupling 9 is free to turn about the Pivot Bolt 10 secured to the base of the model and carries a 2" Rod that is free to slide in a Double Bracket pivotally attached to a Threaded Boss 11 mounted on the Rod 6. A Spring 12 is connected to a point 13, 2½" from the bolt 10, and its other end is attached to a ⅜" Bolt that serves to secure the Collar 14 on the 2" Rod.

The Motor must be started in a certain direction so that when the clutch segments 8 and 4 are engaged the Threaded Boss 11 advances towards the Rod 1. The clutch is held in engagement meanwhile by the Spring 12, but the Boss 11, moving slowly along the Rod 6, presently carries the Spring over the bolt 10. The Spring now tends to pull the Threaded Boss in the opposite direction and the driven unit slides over to the reverse position, wherein the Pinion 7 is engaged by the Contrate Wheel 5. The motion of the driven shaft is now reversed; hence the Boss 11 returns towards the Rod 1a until it again passes the centre point, when the driven shaft is pulled back to its original position and the cycle of operations is repeated.

The frequency at which the change-over movement occurs may be varied by (a) decreasing or increasing the speed of the shaft 2 in proportion to that of the Motor, or (b) increasing or decreasing the longitudinal sliding movement of the driven shaft and thereby varying the period required for the Threaded Boss 11 to reach the central position, where it effects the change-over.

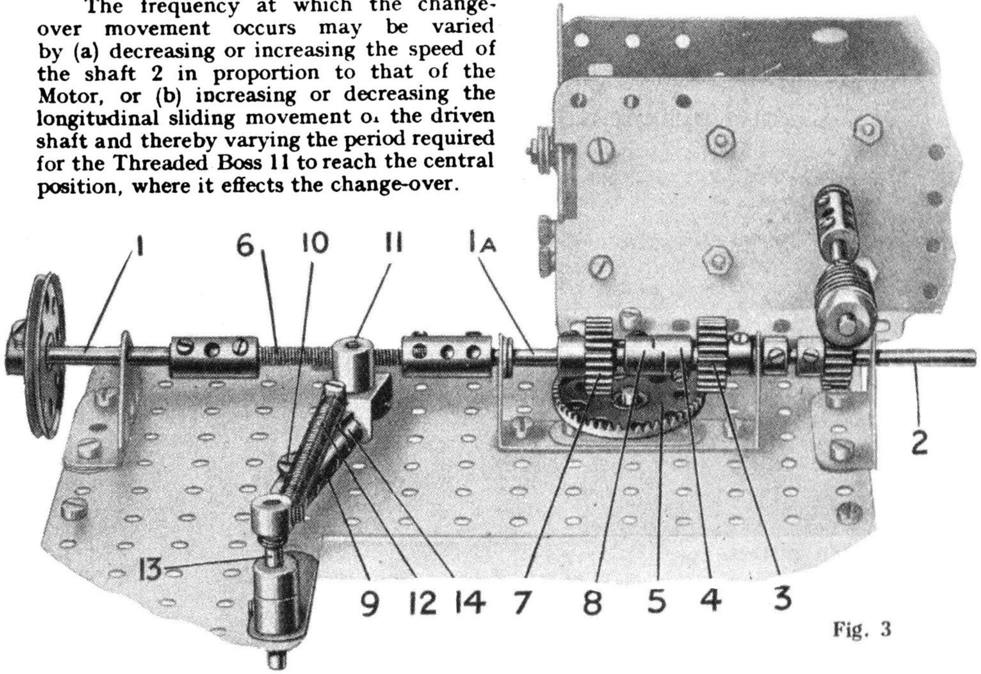

Fig. 3

No. 7 Automatic Reversing Hoist

This is a simple device by means of which a lift or similar model may be made to work for an indefinite period without attention.

The drive is taken from the Motor armature via a ½" Pinion engaging with the 57-teeth Gear Wheel 1, and a ½" Pinion on the opposite end of the rod carrying the Gear 1 meshes with another 57-teeth Gear on the 2" Rod 2. On the Rod 2 is a Worm 3 meshing with a ½" Pinion secured to a vertical 3" Rod 4, which carries at its upper extremity a second Worm meshing with a ½" Pinion on the 3½" Rod 5. This Rod 5 carries a rotating arm 6, built up from 5½" Strips secured rigidly to the Rod 5 by means of Bush Wheels. Two 1" loose Pulleys 7 are free to turn on a 2" Rod journalled in the arm 6 and two similar Pulleys 7a are mounted on a 4½" Rod attached to the Motor.

The spindle of the Pulleys 7 follows the circular path traced out by the end of the arm 6, while the spindle of the Pulleys 7a is fixed. The cord 9, which is attached to the lift, is led down and over one of the 1" loose Pulleys 7a, round one of the Pulleys 7, back to the remaining Pulley 7a and thence to the second 1" Pulley 7. After passing round the latter, it is secured to the Flat Bracket 8. As the arm 6 rotates, the cord 9 is alternately drawn in and paid out, thus working the cage up and down the shaft.

In order to counterbalance the weight of the cage, a 50-gramme weight 10 should be attached to a cord that is led over the 1" Pulleys at the lift shaft head and secured to the top of the cage. The extent of the travel of the cage may be varied considerably by altering the distance between the Rod carrying the 1" loose Pulleys 7 and the Rod 5, adding to it to increase the travel of the cage and vice versa.

The "Suggestions Section," which appears in the "Meccano Magazine" every month, is a feature that no keen Meccano boy should miss, for it will keep him informed of the very latest developments in the Meccano world. Every idea published in it will suggest several new models to him, or will help him to perfect others he may have in mind.

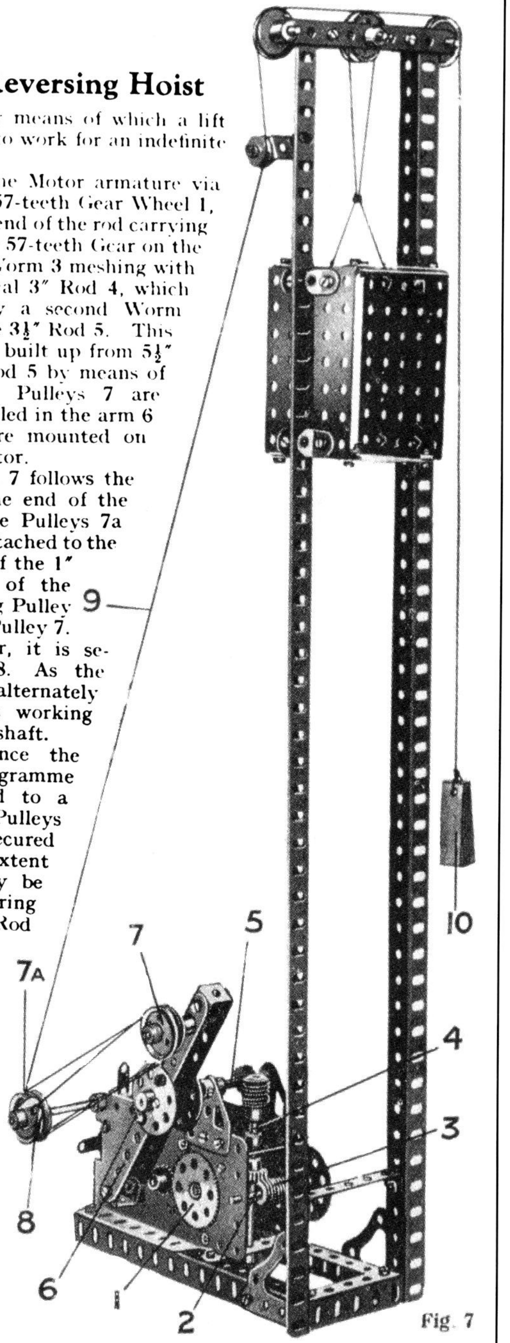

Fig. 7

Figs 10–11. Some useful devices from the 1928 Book of New Models.

NEW MECCANO ACCESSORY PARTS

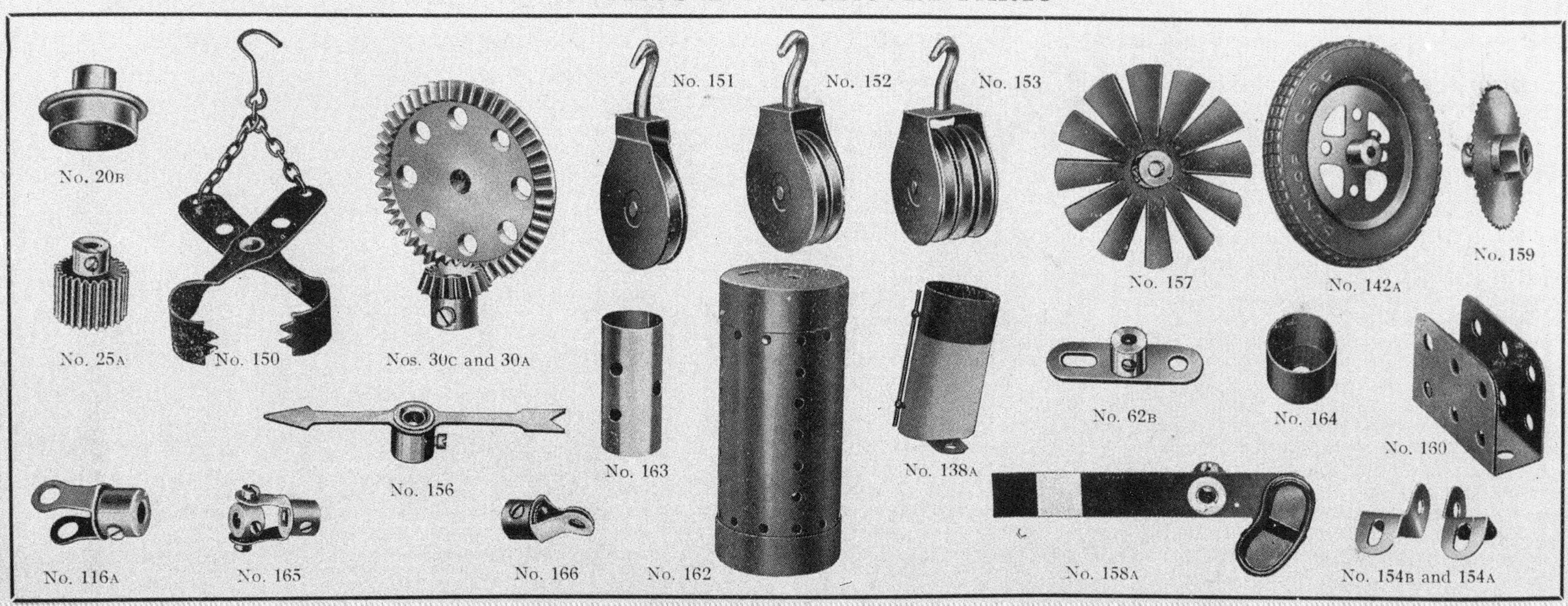

Part No. s. d.

20b. Flanged Wheels, ¾" diameter ... ... each 0 4
Designed to fit over the ends of the Sleeve Piece to form a complete cylinder unit; may also be used as travelling wheels in all models that are required to run on rails.

25a. Pinion, ¾" diam., Double-width Face each 0 9

26a. Pinion, ½" diam., Double-width Face each 0 6
These should prove extremely useful in connection with Meccano gear boxes and toothed driving mechanism, etc. They engage respectively with the 50- and 57-teeth Gear Wheels.

30a. Bevel Gear, ½" diam., 16 teeth ... each 0 6

30c. Bevel Gear, 1½" diam., 48 teeth ... each 1 3
These are designed to provide a 1 : 3 ratio right-angle drive and should only be used together. Two of 30a or two of 30c should not be mounted together to produce a 1 : 1 ratio. When such a ratio is required, two ⅞" Bevel Wheels (part No. 30) should be employed.

52. Flanged Plate, 5½"×2½" ... ... each 0 5
Improved design. Fitted with flanges on all four sides and provided with a slot to receive the blade of the Meccano Circular Saw and an elongated hole for adjusting purposes.

54. Sector Plate ... ... each 0 3
Improved design. Provided with three parallel rows of holes at centre of plate.

62b. Crank with Centre Boss ... ... each 0 3
May be used as a double-arm crank or as a reinforced bearing for shafts and as a method of securing Axle Rods to Strips, etc.

Part No. s. d.

116a. Fork Piece, small ... ... each 0 3
Designed for pivotal connections between Rods and Strips, etc. Forms an excellent bearing for ½" loose Pulleys, which may be mounted on a bolt passed through the arms of the Fork Piece.

138a. Ship's Funnel, Cunard type ... ... each 0 6
Oval in shape, raked, and fitted with a miniature steam pipe. Enamelled red with black band at top.

142a. Dunlop Tyres, 2" inside diameter ... each 0 4

142b. Dunlop Tyres, 3" inside diameter ... each 0 6
Designed to fit Meccano 2" and 3" Pulley Wheels respectively. Will add an excellent finish to Meccano model motor cars, etc.

150. Crane Grab ... ... each 0 6
For use in place of the ordinary crane hook. Miniature stone blocks, boxes, etc., may be gripped in its jaws and lifted without other aid.

151. Pulley Block, single sheave ... ... each 0 6

152. Pulley Block, two sheaves ... ... each 0 9

153. Pulley Block, three sheaves ... ... each 1 0
For use in model cranes, derricks, boat davits, etc. Very compact and of realistic appearance.

154a. Corner Angle Bracket, right-hand ...½ doz. 0 6

154b. Corner Angle Bracket, left hand ...½ doz. 0 6
For use in cases where two ½"×½" Angle Brackets bolted together would prove either too cumbersome or insufficiently rigid.

156. Pointer, with boss and set-screw ... each 0 3
For all indicating appliances, revolution counters, etc.

157. Fan, 2" diameter, with boss and set-screw each 0 3
Specially suited for use as a radiator cooling fan in Meccano motor cars, etc.

Part No. s. d.

120b. Compression Spring ... ... each 0 1
Will fit over Axle Rods and may be used for innumerable purposes.

158a. Signal Arm, " Home " type ... ... each 0 3

158b. Signal Arm, " Distant " type ... ... each 0 3
May be used in Meccano signal gantrys, etc., in conjunction with miniature railways.

159. Circular Saw ... ... each 1 0
Of specially fine steel, teeth tempered and ground. When driven at a high speed, the saw will cut thin pieces of wood, etc.

160. Channel Bearing ... ... each 0 2
Designed to form rigid bearings for Axle Rods, etc., where space is restricted.

162. Boiler, with ends ... ... each 1 0

162a. Boiler Ends ... ... each 0 3
May be incorporated in Meccano locomotives, stationary engines, and numerous other models of a similar type.

163. Sleeve Piece, 1⅜"×⅝" ... ... per pair 0 6
When fitted with a ¾" Flanged Wheel at each end, this part forms an excellent cylinder.

164. Chimney Adaptor ... ... each 0 2
Forms a suitable chimney for model locomotives, etc.

165. Swivel Bearing ... ... each 0 6
Intended for coupling two Rods together end to end, so that one may move radially about the end of the other.

166. End Bearing ... ... each 0 3
May be used as an End Bearing for connecting rods, or as a method of pivotally coupling a Rod and a Strip end to end.

Model No. 23 Oscillating Electric Fan

The fan unit is mounted on bearings consisting of fourteen Steel Balls arranged round the circumference of a Bush Wheel bolted to the interior of a Wheel Flange 1, which in turn is bolted to a Double Bent Strip 3 carried on a ¾" Bolt in the top of the 5½" vertical Girders. The unit turns on a Pivot Bolt passed through the centre hole of the 5½" × 2½" Flat Plate 4 and secured in the boss 2 of the Bush Wheel.

A Pulley 5 on the Motor armature transmits motion to a 2" Pulley 6 by means of Meccano Spring Cord, and a Worm engages with a ½" Pinion on the Rod 7 that carries a ½" Pinion 8. A 57-teeth Gear 9 is secured to a Pivot Bolt passed through the Plate 4. The bolt also carries a Crank 10, which is secured to the Wheel 9 by the ½" Bolt 11, and connected pivotally to a 3½" Strip 12 that is attached to a 2½" Strip 13 rigidly bolted to the Double Bent Strip 3.

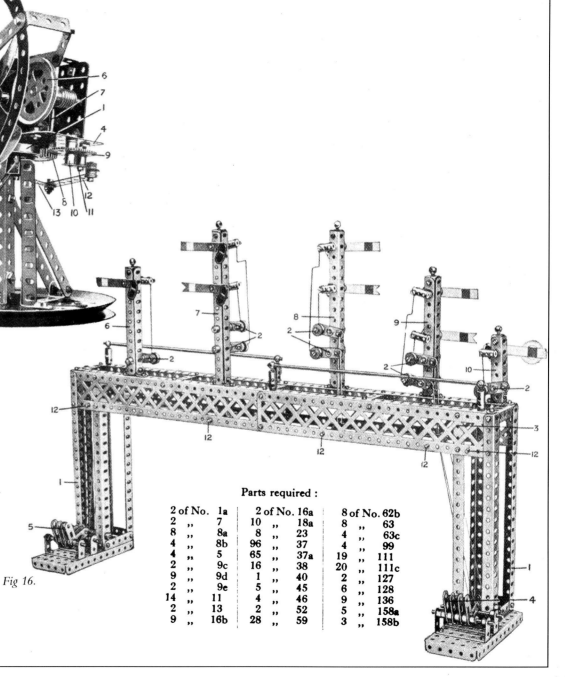

Parts required :

2 of No.	2a	1 of No.	20a	1 of No.	70
6 ,,	3	1 ,,	23a	1 ,,	77
2 ,,	5	2 ,,	24	2 ,,	111
1 ,,	6	2 ,,	26	4 ,,	111c
2 ,,	9a	1 ,,	27a	14 ,,	117
1 ,,	10	1 ,,	32	1 ,,	137
1 ,,	11	37 ,,	37	1 ,,	145
2 ,,	12	5 ,,	37a	1 ,,	147b
2 ,,	12a	4 ,,	41	1 Electric Motor (100-250 volt)	
1 ,,	16	1 ,,	45		
1 ,,	16d	4 ,,	48		
1 ,,	19c	2 ,,	59		

Fig 15. Note the use of the lethal High Voltage motor.

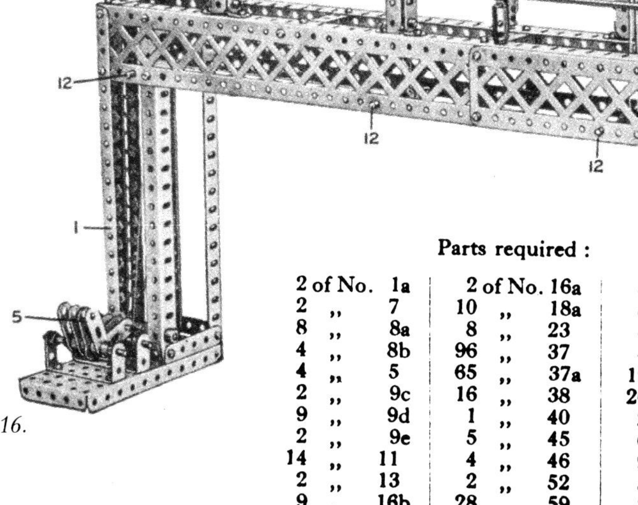

Parts required :

2 of No.	1a	2 of No.	16a	8 of No.	62b
2 ,,	7	10 ,,	18a	8 ,,	63
8 ,,	8a	8 ,,	23	4 ,,	63c
4 ,,	8b	96 ,,	37	4 ,,	99
4 ,,	5	65 ,,	37a	19 ,,	111
2 ,,	9c	16 ,,	38	20 ,,	111c
9 ,,	9d	1 ,,	40	2 ,,	127
2 ,,	9e	5 ,,	45	6 ,,	128
14 ,,	11	4 ,,	46	9 ,,	136
2 ,,	13	2 ,,	52	5 ,,	158a
9 ,,	16b	28 ,,	59	3 ,,	158b

Fig 16.

←Fig 12. A page of new parts and their uses.

Model No. 33 Motor Breakdown Crane

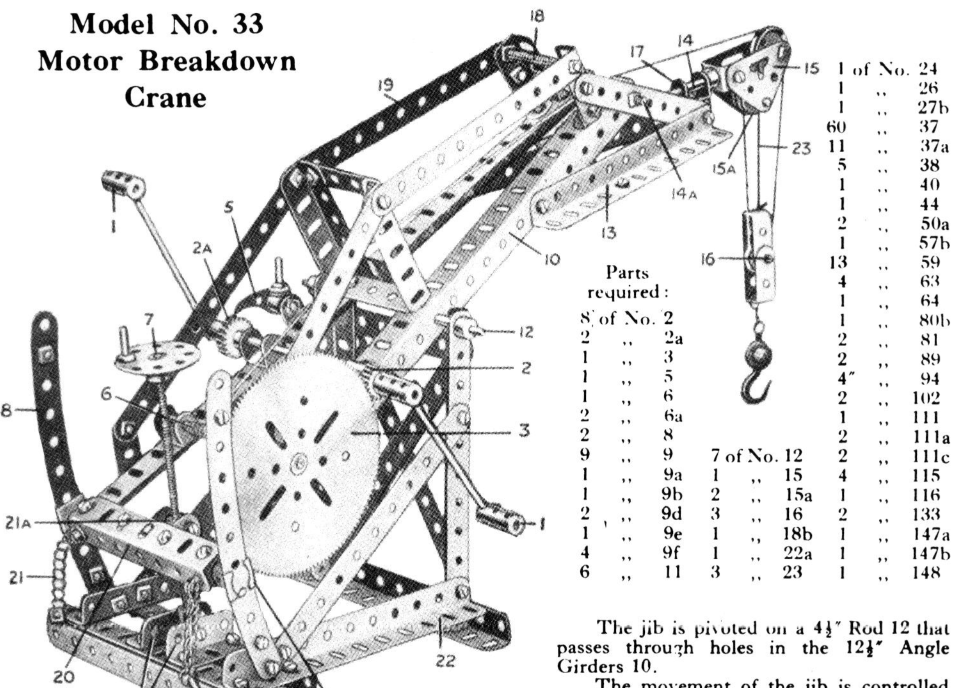

Parts required:

8	of No.	2
2	,,	2a
1	,,	3
1	,,	5
1	,,	6
2	,,	6a
2	,,	8
9	,,	9
1	,,	9a
1	,,	9b
2	,,	9d
1	,,	9e
4	,,	9f
6	,,	11
7	of No.	12
1	,,	15
2	,,	15a
3	,,	16
1	,,	18b
1	,,	22a
3	,,	23
1	of No.	24
1	,,	26
1	,,	27b
60	,,	37
11	,,	37a
5	,,	38
1	,,	40
1	,,	44
2	,,	50a
1	,,	57b
13	,,	59
4	,,	63
1	,,	64
1	,,	80b
2	,,	81
2	,,	89
4″	,,	94
2	,,	102
1	,,	111
2	,,	111a
2	,,	111c
4	,,	115
1	,,	116
2	,,	133
1	,,	147a
1	,,	147b
1	,,	148

The jib is pivoted on a 4½″ Rod 12 that passes through holes in the 12½″ Angle Girders 10.

The movement of the jib is controlled from a hand-wheel 7 secured to a 5″ Threaded Rod that passes through a Threaded Boss pivotally secured between right and left-hand Corner Angle Brackets that in turn are bolted to a 3½″ Angle Girder 20 at the rear end of the jib.

The lower end of the Threaded Rod passes through a Collar pivotally secured between 1½″ Angle Girders 4, and is held in position in the Collar by means of another Collar and two lock-nuts, the former being placed on the Rod against the upper face of the pivoted Collar while the nuts are placed against the lower face. When the hand-wheel 7 is turned the Threaded Boss is caused to rise or fall, carrying the jib with it, the jib being guided by the Eye Pieces 9 sliding on the Curved Strips 8. Short lengths of Sprocket Chain 21 secured to the rear of the jib carry Threaded Pins which may be placed in holes in the Curved Strips 8 and used to hold the jib securely in the required position.

The hoisting pulley block 15 is carried on the end of a 5½″ Rod 14 journalled in a Double Bracket 17 and in a Cranked Bent Strip, the latter being secured to a 2½″ Strip bolted to the underside of the 5½″ Angle Girders 13. The jib head Pulley is supported on a ¾″ Bolt passed through two Corner Brackets and held in position by a nut. Collars are placed on the bolt each side the jib head pulley. A ½″ Pulley 15a is journalled in a similar manner to the 1″ Pulley, but a 1″ Rod is used in place of the ¾″ Bolt. The whole pulley block is attached to the Rod 14 by a large Fork Piece.

The load is raised or lowered by turning the handles 1, which are constructed as shown and secured to a 5½″ Rod carrying a ½″ Pinion 2 and a Ratchet Wheel 2a. The Pinion 2 engages a 3½″ Gear Wheel 3 secured to a 3½″ Rod 6 that is journalled in Double Brackets secured to the Angle Girders 10. The Rod of the Pinion 2 is journalled likewise. The winding cord is attached to the Rod 6 and passes thence over a ½″ Pulley (carried on a 2″ Threaded Rod 14a) and over the 1″ jib head Pulley, then round a ½″ Pulley on the Pin 16 and back over the Pulley 15a. It is attached finally to the hoisting block, which is constructed from two Single Bent Strips.

A Pawl is pivoted in a Double Bracket bolted to one of the Girders 10 and serves to hold the load suspended by preventing the winding Rod revolving when the handles 1 are released.

Fig 17.

No. 1 Wobble Shaft Variable Speed Gear

The interesting model shown in Fig. 1 is of a new and very ingenious type of infinitely variable speed gear.

The 4½″ Rod 1, which forms the "wobble shaft," is secured to a Universal Coupling that is fixed to a Threaded Pin bolted on the end Flanged Plate. The Bush Wheel 2 is secured to the driving shaft, that carries a hand wheel by rotating which the end of the wobble shaft 1 inserted in the Bush Wheel is caused to describe a circular motion. The wobble shaft itself does not rotate of course. Two 6½″ Rods 3 are held in position in the Flanged Plates by Collars. Two Cranks are secured to each Rod, and each pair of Cranks carries a 3½″ Rod 4 in their end holes.

The 1½″ Strips 5 are free to slide on the Rods 3 and 4, and are moved simultaneously to and fro by means of the 3½″ Strip 6, each end of which is bolted to Double Brackets held between the ends of the Strips 5. The handle provided at the centre of the Strip 6 consists of a Threaded Pin, the shank of which is employed to secure another Double Bracket which slides upon a further 6½″ Rod. Each link 7 connecting the Rods 4 and the wobble shaft 1 consists of a 2″ Strip bolted to a Crank that is placed between the lower ends of the 1½″ Strips 5. These Cranks are free to slide on the Rods 4. A Crank 8, having its arm prolonged by a 2″ Strip, is secured at one end of each 6½″ Rod 3.

The Cranks on which the Pawls 9 are mounted are quite free to move about the driven shaft and are rocked to and fro by connecting links attached to the Cranks 8, and mounted loosely on the ¾″ Bolts carrying the Pawls 9. Each ¾″ Bolt is secured to its Crank by two nuts. The Pawls are held in engagement against the teeth of the Ratchet Wheel by pieces of Spring Cord.

When the 3″ Strip 6 is pushed towards the Bush Wheel end of the model—where the motion of the wobble shaft 1 is at a maximum—the maximum throw will be imparted via the links 7 to the Rod 4, and the resulting motion of the Cranks 8 imparts a maximum throw to the Pawls operating the Ratchet Wheel. Consequently the driven shaft will revolve at its highest speed. If the Strip 6 is moved in the opposite direction the throw of the links 7 decreases and the speed of the driven shaft falls.

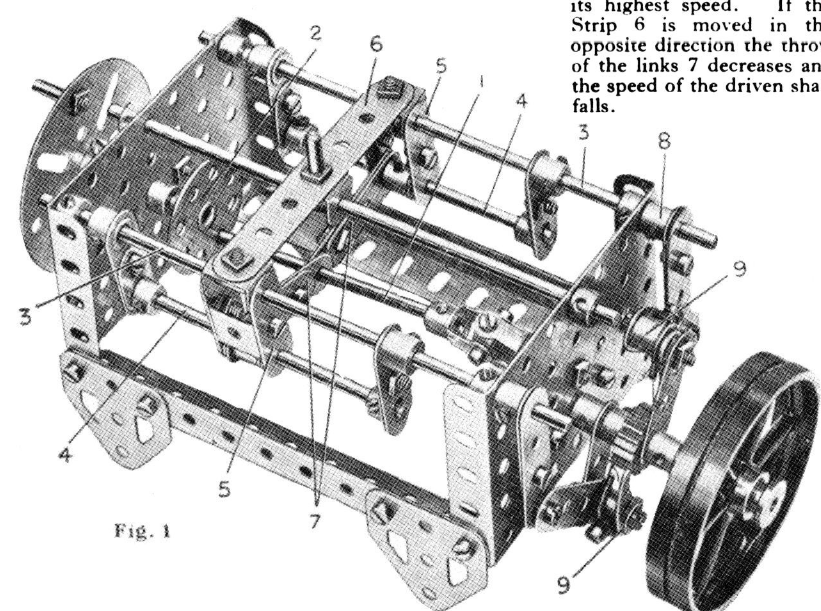

Fig 18. A novel gear mechanism.

18 INTERESTING NEW MECCANO MECHANISMS

No. 8 Demonstration Model of Corliss' Valve Gear

In the Corliss gear there is a separate exhaust and steam inlet valve for each end of the cylinder. Each valve is given an oscillatory movement and means are provided to vary automatically the cut off by a centrifugal governor as the engine speed alters.

A Bush Wheel 2 is free to turn about a Pivot Bolt secured to the $5\frac{1}{2}'' \times 3\frac{1}{2}''$ Flat Plates forming the sides of the cylinder block and links connecting the four valves 7, 7a, 11, and 11a are attached pivotally to the Bush Wheel by $\frac{3}{8}''$ Bolts. The Eccentric 1 is secured on a $4\frac{1}{2}''$ Rod and is connected to the Bush Wheel 2 by a $5\frac{1}{2}''$ Strip that is attached pivotally to the end of the Strip 14 by a Pivot Bolt.

The two exhaust valve Cranks 11 and 11a are attached pivotally to their respective links by lock-nutted bolts, the cranks being mounted on the ends of 3″ Rods that are journalled in the Flat Plates. These Rods represent the rotary Corliss valves, which, when rocked by the Bush Wheel 2, alternately open the ends of the cylinder to exhaust. The valve Cranks 7 and 7a are each operated by a trip mechanism, which trips the cranks earlier as the speed of the engine increases, so diminishing the amount of steam admitted.

The Face Plates 3 and 3a are mounted loosely on $4\frac{1}{2}''$ Rods journalled in the Flat Plates. Each trip 4 and 4a consists of two $1\frac{1}{2}''$ Strips and a Flat Bracket bolted together in the form of a triangle, the apex of which is pivoted on a Threaded Pin secured to the Face Plate 3 or 3a. In the construction of each of the trips 4 and 4a the set-screws extracted from Bush Wheels, etc., are used instead of ordinary bolts. A $\frac{1}{2}'' \times \frac{1}{2}''$ Angle Bracket is bolted to each trip as indicated in the illustration. Before placing the trips on the Threaded Pins the connecting links from the Bush Wheel 2 should be mounted on the Pins. Here it should be noted that the connecting links for the exhaust Cranks are slightly bent to form an efficient connection, as also is the connecting link to the Face Plate 3a, which has to be bent towards the Face Plate to clear the lower edge of the trip 4a.

Fig. 8

Each Bush Wheel 5, 5a (shown partly cut away) has an ordinary bolt inserted in the set-screw hole, and both must be quite free on the valve spindles. A 2″ Strip is bolted to each Bush Wheel, so that the Bolt on the boss of the Bush Wheel 5 is pointing—to use a clock face as a comparison—to 5 o'clock, while the Bolt 6 on the boss of the Bush Wheel 5a points to 10 o'clock. Two Washers are placed on each valve spindle and lastly the two Cranks 7 and 7a are secured in place. A $\frac{1}{2}'' \times \frac{1}{2}''$ Angle Bracket is bolted in the end hole of each Crank as shown. Short lengths of Spring Cord 18 are fastened to the trips 4 and 4a and to the Face Plates 3 and 3a, so that the trips normally are held against the bosses of the Bush Wheels.

The 5″ governor Rod is journalled in a $2\frac{1}{2}''$ Strip and in a hole of the $5\frac{1}{2}'' \times 2\frac{1}{2}''$ Flanged Plate forming the top of the cylinder, one Collar and three Washers on the lower end of the 5″ Rod take the downward thrust of the governor. The links 12 ($1\frac{1}{2}''$ Strips) are attached pivotally to Double Brackets bolted to the Bush Wheel 15 and at their lower extremities to the 2″ Pulley 10 that are secured rigidly together by $\frac{1}{2}''$ Bolts, a Collar and Washer on each bolt spacing the Pulleys a short distance apart. The drive for the governor is taken off the Sprocket Wheel 13 to a 1″ Sprocket on a short Rod that is journalled in a Double Bent Strip bolted to an upright Strip at the rear of the model. The short Rod carries a $1\frac{1}{2}''$ Contrate 17 that meshes with a $\frac{1}{2}''$ Pinion on the 5″ Rod.

The Simple Bell Crank 9 is bolted to a Crank secured to the 3″ Rod carrying the Bush Wheel 8 and one of its arms is extended by a 2″ Strip that has a Threaded Pin bolted to it, so that the Pin rests in the space between the Pulleys 10. Two Collars (new style) are attached in diametrically opposite holes in the Bush Wheel 8 and the $1\frac{1}{2}''$ Rod 16 is attached to the 2″ Strip by means of an End Bearing, while the 2″ Rod 15a is attached to the Strip on the Bush Wheel 5a in a similar way.

In the illustration the Crank 7a is about to be lifted by the Angle Bracket on the trip 4a engaging that on the Crank as the trip rises. As the trip moves, it rides up the Bolt 6, which thrusts it outward to the left. Presently the Crank 7a is released and flies back under the action of a piece of Spring Cord attached to a Crank secured to the valve spindle at the rear of the model. This Crank normally is held by the Spring against a stop consisting of a Threaded Pin. (The Crank 7 is controlled in a similar manner).

In the case of the left-hand valve the Crank 7 is drawn downward by the trip 4 instead of upward as in the case of the right-hand valve. When the left-hand valve is open to steam the right-hand exhaust valve is open, and vice versa.

As the governor weights fly out with increase of engine speed the Pulleys 10 rise and pull up the arm of the Bell Crank 9, so partially rotating the Bush Wheel 8. This in turn alters the position of the Bush Wheels 5 and 5a, so that the trips ride up their respective bolts and trip the Cranks 7 and 7a earlier in the stroke and cause the engine to work with a shorter cut off. The Angle Brackets on the trips and Cranks 7 and 7a must be adjusted very carefully.

The Corliss valve gear was invented by an American engineer Corliss in 1849 and is used in one of its many modifications on most of the best stationary engines. It is not, however, popular for locomotive or marine engine work.

A form of gear that is coming more and more into favour for use on locomotives is called the Walschaert gear, while for many years marine engines have been equipped with the very simple but efficient Stephenson gear. This latter was originally invented for locomotives and for a long period was very popular for this class of engine, but nowadays it has lost favour and is now used but rarely except in connection with marine engines of the reciprocating type.

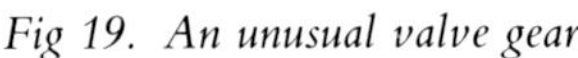

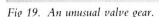

Fig 19. An unusual valve gear.

No. 11 Siemens' Chronometric Governor

In almost every type of engine, certainly in all steam engines, an efficient means of regulating the speed must be provided, and perhaps one of the most ingenious and effective methods is the Siemens' Chronometric Governor, of which a Meccano model may be constructed as shown in Fig. 11.

The ⅞" Bevel Wheel 2 is secured near the lower end of the 3½" Rod 1. The Face Plate 3 is fastened to the lower end of a 1½" Rod that is journalled as shown, and a ⅞" Bevel Wheel is secured near its upper end. The extreme ends of both the upper 3½" Rod and lower 1½" Rod are inserted in opposite ends of a Coupling, in the centre transverse hole of which is secured a 2" Rod carrying the ⅞" Bevel Gear 4. The two first-mentioned Rods are free to rotate in the ends of the Coupling and the Bevel 4 meshes with the two other Bevels.

When the handle 1 is rotated the drive is transmitted via the Bevels 2 and 4 to the third Bevel on the vertical 1½" Rod, and therefore the latter is driven in the reverse direction to that in which the handle 1 is turned. The Bevel 4 is quite free to rotate about its Rod, of course.

The pendulum 5 consists of a 5" Rod weighted with four Flanged Wheels and suspended by means of a ball-and-socket joint. The latter consists of a Swivel Bearing 6 secured to a 1½" Rod that is journalled in the 5½" × ½" Double Angle Strip 7 and also in a Double Bent Strip. As the Rod 5 must rotate freely in the collar of the Swivel Bearing 6, the set-screws inserted in the collar are provided with nuts that are locked against the sides of the collar to prevent the shanks of the screws touching the Rod 5.

Another Swivel Bearing 9 is free to turn about a Pivot Bolt, the shank of which is gripped in the boss of an Eye Piece (new style). The set-screws in this Swivel Bearing should be locked in a similar manner to those of the Bearing 6 so that their shanks do not grip the Pivot Bolt. The Eye Piece slides on a 2½" large radius Curved Strip 8, which is rigidly attached to the Face Plate 3 by means of two ½" × ½" Angle Brackets.

The Crank 10 is mounted on a spindle that in practice operates the throttle valve. It is connected to the 2" Rod 11 and the latter is attached pivotally to the Crank by means of an End Bearing, its other end being attached to the 2" Rod of the Bevel 4 by a Swivel Bearing. The movement of the Crank 10 is limited by stops in the form of two ¾" Bolts secured to each end of a 1½" Strip, and another Crank secured to its spindle carries a balance weight or counterpoise consisting of a 1" Pulley Wheel bolted to a 3" Strip.

The following is a brief summary of the action of the model. A certain amount of energy is required to maintain the pendulum 5 at a constant angle with the vertical. Since the three Bevel Wheels form an epicyclic train, either the Bevel 2 and the lower Bevel fixed to the Rod of the Face Plate 3 must turn at the same rate or Bevel 4 must run round the teeth of the lower Bevel. The latter is connected to the pendulum 5 and its rotation cannot be maintained without a constant expenditure of energy.

Therefore the tendency of the lower Bevel is to lag behind the Bevel 2 and cause the Bevel 4 to travel round its teeth. But this movement of the Bevel 4 is checked by the counterpoise.

The governor is brought into action when the velocity of the engine is sufficient to keep the counterpoise raised slightly.

Because the lower Bevel is connected to a heavy revolving mass it can only change its velocity gradually, but the counterpoise is in equilibrium. Hence the slightest increase in velocity of Bevel 2 will be sufficient to raise the counterpoise further and so vary the steam valve opening.

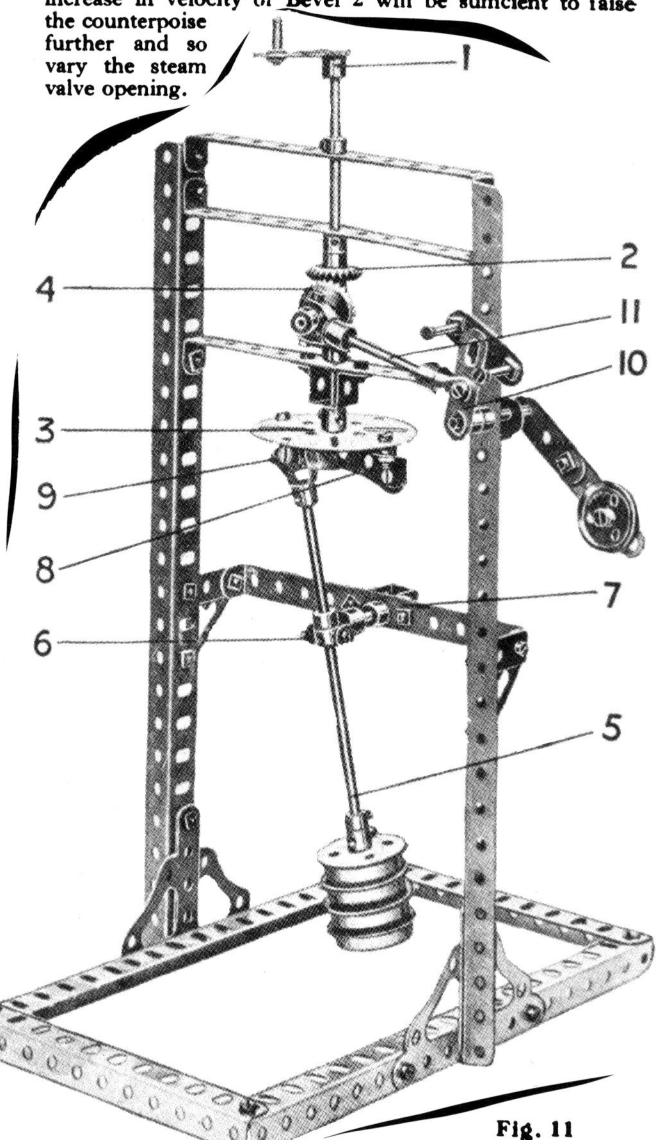

Fig. 11

*Fig 20.
An interesting demonstration model of an unusual piece of steam governing apparatus.*

20

A SELECTION OF PRIZE-WINNING MECCANO MODELS

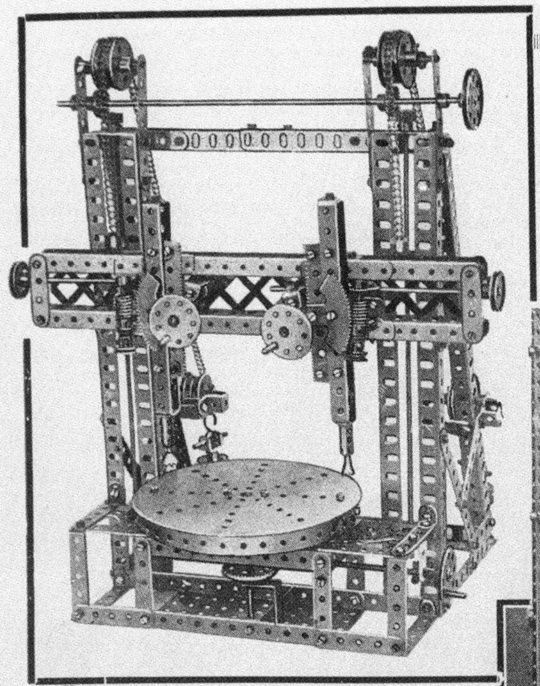

The circular planing machine (left) was built by J. Sturrock (Barrow-in-Furness). The tool holders may be adjusted to any angle and the saddles moved along the balanced cross slide by means of Threaded Rods while the elevation of the cross-slide is regulated by Threaded Rods rotated from ½″ Pinions and Contrate Wheels. Many other interesting features are included in the design of this realistic model machine tool.

The above model is a faithful reproduction of a powerful steam tractor. It was built by A. T. Locke (Shottery) and is driven by means of a Clockwork Motor. Steering is effected by chains attached to the front axle and actuated through worm and pinion mechanism. As will be seen, the model is equipped with cylinder, governor and "dynamo," the latter being driven from the engine flywheel, thus conforming to actual practice.

The cleverly-built model illustrated below is designed on the lines of Stephenson's "Rocket" locomotive. It is an excellent copy of its famous prototype. Built by N. C. Bowron (Bristol).

The above illustration shows a very fine model of Stephenson's "Locomotion No. 1." It was built by R. S. Miller (Newark) to a scale of 1-9. Note the queer position of the cylinders, with their vertical piston-rods and quaint "grasshopper" motion by which power is transmitted to the driving wheels.

On the right is a wonderful model of a sewing machine that actually works. The needle mechanism is very intricate and really excellent sewing may be done on the machine. It is undoubtedly a splendid tribute to the ingenuity and patience of its builder, Alex. Van Dam (Amsterdam).

Fig 21. Prize winners in 1928.

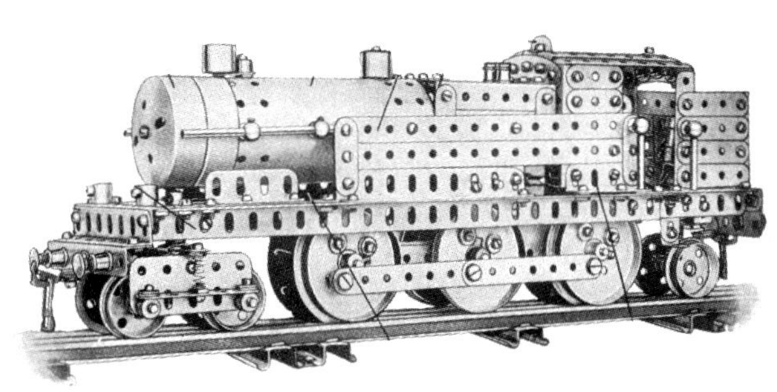

Fig 22. A Tank Engine for O gauge use.

The 1930 edition (cover as 1929 but red) unfortunately reverted to rather more simple models, although the 4–6–2 Tank Engine and the Automated Traffic Lights (figs 22–23) were worthy of attention. The locomotive especially is a good model and will run on 0 gauge track extremely well. Once again it is the mechanisms pages which provide the most interest for the advanced modeller and give further indication of the strides made in modelling technique in a very short time: the Sliding Dog Constant Mesh Gearbox (fig 24), Grisen Gearbox (fig 25) and Automatic Speed Change for Winding Gear (fig 26) are still of interest today.

As in 1929 four pages were devoted to prize-winning models, most notable of which were the Diesel Engine (fig 27), Tyne Bridge (fig 28) and 4472 modelled by one R. S. Miller (figs 29) whose locomotive models were frequent and worthy prizewinners.

1931 saw a change of cover, back to that used for the 1928 *Meccano Book of Engineering* but with a different background colour (fig 30). Contents were much as before: good models for Junior Meccano Boys and a number for the older enthusiast. The Mechanical Man (fig 31) is an excellent performer and must be one of the earliest of the genre. The four Cylinder Electric Engine (fig 32) is a particularly interesting electrical model which, when operating is most realistic in terms of the sound it makes. It is also another example of the flexibility of the system. A further good electrical model is the Telegraph Recorder (fig 33): absolutely essential for all Meccano Boys experimenting with Morse Code transmission using a length of bell wire down to the garden shed (and which Meccano Boys have not?).

The Mechanisms were again of more than passing interest. The single plate clutch (fig 34) is still a good demonstration model and the Overload Release (fig 35) foreshadowed the Hornby Circuit Breaker of some five years later. Another demonstration model, the Variable Pitch Propellor (fig 36) shows once again how quickly Meccano could cope with the latest in mechanical engineering.

Virtually since its inception, Meccano has found a place in science and the Flicker Photometer is an excellent example of a measuring instrument built at a fraction of the cost of the 'real thing' (fig 37). There were of course many others and some of these are dealt with elsewhere in this book.

As before there were several pages of prize-winning models, the best of which was the Compound Steam Engine (fig 38).

1932 saw a complete change and produced one of the finest pieces of Meccano literature of all time: in modern parlance it represented a 'quantum leap', whatever that really means. The front cover

continued p. 154.

Model No. 18. Automatic Traffic Control Signal

Three 1″ × ½″ Angle Brackets, secured to the 4½″ Angle Girders of the lamp casing, have Flat Brackets bolted in their end holes and at right angles to them, and the Lamp Holders (part No. 310) are secured to them by an insulated 6 B.A. Bolt. The sides of the lamp casing are filled in with cardboard, in which three holes are cut out and pieces of red, orange, and green transparent paper stuck over the holes. When in place the two top "glasses" on opposite sides should show red whilst the two remaining sides show green. Each of the middle glasses should be orange, and the bottom ones should be green on the sides where the top glasses are red, and red where the upper ones are green. Cardboard masks 4 also are fitted round the base of the Lamp Holders.

A wire from the Lamp 14 is connected to the terminal 5 on the base plate and a wire from the Lamp 15 connected to the terminal 6, the Lamp 16 being connected to the remaining terminal 7. These three terminals are insulated from the base plate; the terminal E, however, is in direct metallic contact with the Plate.

The Rod of the rotary switches 9, 10, 11, 12, is driven by the Electric Motor through the gearing shown. Each of the rotary switches consists of a Face Plate carrying six ½″ × ½″ Angle Brackets, which are bolted to the Face Plate and insulated therefrom by Insulating Bushes and Washers. The brushes consist of 3½″ Strips to which Double Brackets are attached by insulated Bolts. Each one is kept in proper contact by means of a short length of Spring Cord, one end of which is secured to the brush and the other end to an insulated 6 B.A. Bolt attached to the frame.

The brushes pressing on the switches 9 and 11 are connected together by a length of insulated wire 13, and a wire is taken from the latter brush to the terminal 6. The terminal 5 is connected to the brush of the switch 10 and the remaining brush to the terminal 7. One of the Motor terminals is connected to the frame whilst the other terminal of the Motor is connected to the terminal E on the Lamp standard, and also to the Accumulator. The return lead from the latter is taken to the terminal 8, which is in direct metallic contact with the Motor side plate.

The mechanism should be so arranged that when the upper Lamp is extinguished, by the brush controlling that light passing on to the first of the series of insulated Angle Brackets of the switch, the middle or orange lamp is lit immediately by the brush passing on to the uninsulated portion of the switch 9. In practice, a green light indicates "all clear," orange "caution" and red "stop."

Parts required:

Qty	No.
4 of No.	3
4 ,,	8a
4 ,,	8b
4 ,,	9a
4 ,,	9b
8 ,,	9f
3 ,,	10
4 ,,	11
33 ,,	12
4 ,	12a
1 ,,	13a
1 ,,	15
1 ,,	16a
1 ,,	26
1 ,,	27a
2 ,,	32
67 ,,	37
1 ,,	52
14″ ,,	58
10 ,,	59
4 ,,	103a
2 ,,	108
4 ,,	109
2 ,,	161
34 ,,	302
31 ,,	303
36 ,,	304
36 ,,	305
5 ,,	306
3 ,,	310
3 ,,	311
1 Electric Motor	

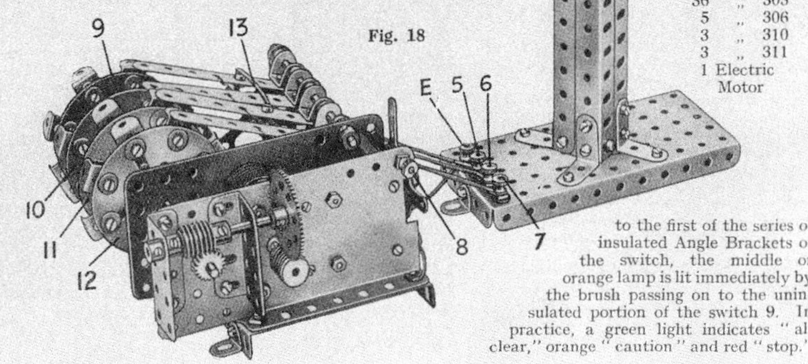

Fig. 18

*Fig 23.
An early example of an automated model.*

No. 1. Sliding Dog Constant Mesh Gear Box

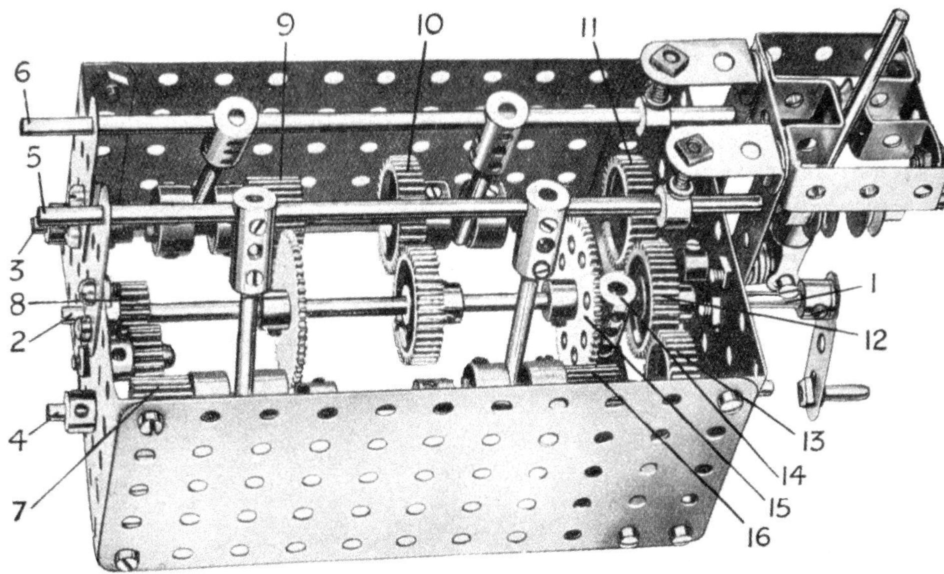

In this gear box the fact that the gears are in constant mesh reduces wear and facilitates gear-changing, while the employment of a " gate " change ensures that a particular gear cannot be engaged unless all the others are in neutral.

The shaft 1 is journalled in one of the end Plates and also half-way through the top transverse bore of the Coupling 14, which is secured to a Threaded Pin that, in turn, is secured to a 3½" × ½" Double Angle Strip bolted to the side Plates of the gear box. The Rod 1 carries a 1" Gear 12 that meshes with the Gears 11 and 13 on the Rods 3 and 4.

The Rod 3 carries two sliding clutch units 9 and 10, the former of which comprises a portion of a Dog Clutch and a ½" diam. ½" face Pinion connected together by means of a Socket Coupling. The other member of the Dog Clutch is secured on the Rod. The unit 10 is similar but a 1" Gear is used instead of the Pinion. The two clutch units on the Rod 4 are identical, each consisting of a ½" diam. ½" face Pinion and one portion of a Dog Clutch held together by a Socket Coupling. Either of these engage at will with the appropriate fixed portions of the Dog Clutches on the Rod.

The " gate " in which the gear change lever moves, prevents a false change being made, and is composed of two 1½" Strips, two Double Angle Strips and two Double Bent Strips, the entire assembly being attached to the end plate of the gear box. The gear lever is held in the boss of a Swivel Bearing and when moved sideways through the gate, engages between the pair of ½" fast Pulleys on either of the gear selector Rods 5 and 6 ; the latter may then be moved backwards or forwards to change gear. The selector Rods have short Rods secured to them by Couplings and engaging with opposite sides of the grooves of the Socket Couplings.

The device for locking each selector Rod after movement of the lever consists of a ½" Bolt mounted on a 1" × ½" Angle Bracket. The head of the bolt rests in the hole of a Collar secured to the rod to lock the gears in the neutral position. Matters must be so arranged that when both selector rods are in the neutral position, they are retained therein by the heads of the bolts of the locking devices falling into the holes of the Collars. It should then be impossible to move the gear lever across the gate, without first restoring it to the neutral position, thus preventing " jamming " and undue wear of the gear teeth.

Figs 24 and 25. Good examples of the strides made in gearbox design.

No. 4. Grisen Gear Box

The model gear box illustrated in Fig. 4 possesses several features of interest, chief amongst which may be mentioned the very novel method of changing from one gear ratio to another.

A 4½" Rod journalled in the 3½" × 2½" Flanged Plates forming the sides of the gear box, is free to slide longitudinally. It has a ¾" Pinion 1 secured to it and also a Coupling in which is held a Rod representing the gear lever. The latter has two Couplings secured to it, one carrying a 1" Gear Wheel 2 by means of a Pivot Bolt that is inserted in one of its tapped holes, and the other, which forms the top of the gear change lever, has a 1" Rod 3 sliding freely in the end transverse bore. A ¾" Pinion 5, a 1" Gear Wheel (not shown in the photograph) and a 50-teeth Gear Wheel 6 are mounted at short distances apart on the Rod 4.

The Pinion 1 and the Gear 2 are in constant mesh and the latter may be brought into engagement with the 50-teeth Gear 6 by moving the gear lever with a combined vertical and lateral movement until the plunger Rod 3 of the gear change lever is enabled to fall into the end hole of the 1½" Strip 7. This gives a reduction ratio between the driving and driven shafts. By placing the plunger rod in the end holes of the 2" Strip, as shown in the illustration, the 1" Gear 2 may be made to mesh with the other similar Gear on the driven shaft ; this gives a ratio of unity. Lastly, when the plunger rod is made to drop into the hole of the Flat Bracket 8, the 1" Gear 2 and the ¾" Pinion 5 are engaged. A step-up ratio is now obtained.

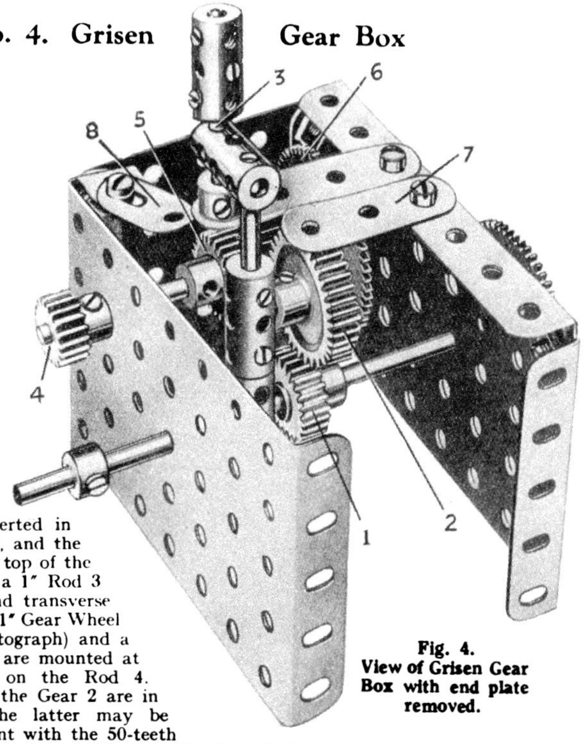

Fig. 4. View of Grisen Gear Box with end plate removed.

The distance between the 2" and 1½" Strips and the Flat Bracket should be carefully adjusted so that the Gear 2 meshes correctly with those on the shaft 4. The distance between the respective gears on the same shaft is also important ; it should be carefully adjusted so that only one Gear, and not two at a time, are engaged.

Owing to its compact nature, the gear box is particularly suitable for inclusion in a model motor chassis, and model-builders should have little difficulty in fitting their models with the device. Gear box mechanisms in their many forms are probably the most interesting of all mechanical movements. In actual engineering practice, the designing of an efficient gear box is an exceedingly difficult problem and new inventions and improvements such as are suggested in the Grisen gear box are well worthy of incorporation in suitable Meccano models.

No. 13. Automatic Speed Change for Winding Gear

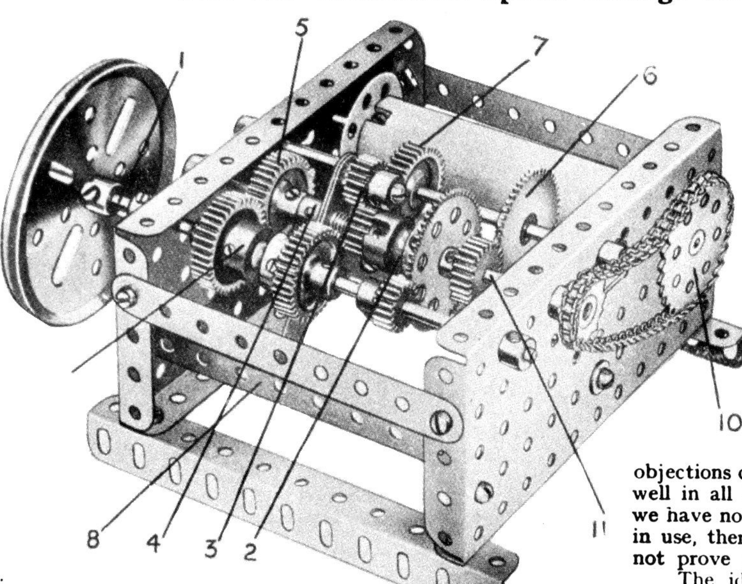

Fig. 13

Fig 26. A novel gear box for cranes.

One method of lowering the load attached to a crane hook is by throwing the hoisting barrel out of gear with the motor and allowing the load to descend under control of a brake. If this method is not practicable for reasons of safety or because of the dimensions of the load, it is necessary to lower the load by reversing the hoisting motor. This, however, causes unnecessary waste of power; also in many cases the load could safely be lowered at a greater speed than is possible when the motor is in gear with the winding mechanism.

The gear box shown in Fig. 13 provides an entirely new and very interesting method of handling the load in such a way that these objections do not apply. It should work extremely well in all kinds of Meccano cranes, and although we have no knowledge of a similar gearing actually in use, there seems to be no reason why it should not prove practicable.

The idea in brief consists in arranging the gearing so that the load is hoisted at a slower rate of speed than that at which the lowering operation is accomplished. The alteration in the speed is obtained entirely automatically on reversing the direction of rotation of the Motor.

The Rod 1 may be termed the mainshaft of the gear box, for it is the one from which the various gears derive their motion. It carries a unit 9 which consists of two 1" Gears held together by a Socket Coupling. The unit is free to revolve on the Rod, and it is prevented from moving sideways by Collars. A ½" Pinion is secured to the mainshaft in the position indicated in the illustration.

A 1" Gear Wheel 5 is fixed to a Rod 11 and next to it is a Double Arm Crank 4, freely pivoting on the Rod 11. This Crank carries a 3" Strip so that one of its arms is prolonged 2", and a ½" Pinion 3 is free to turn about a ¾" Bolt on its shorter arm. Also on the Rod 11 is the unit 2, which consists of a ½" Pinion and a 57-teeth Gear Wheel connected together by means of a Socket Coupling. The Pinion is in constant mesh with the Pinion 3 on the Double Arm Crank, and a Compression Spring is placed on the Rod between the Crank and the unit 2. The latter is of course free on the Rod 11. Finally a ¾" Pinion is secured to the Rod.

A third Rod journalled in the gear box carries a 50-teeth Gear 6 and 1" Gear 7, the latter being arranged to mesh with the ½" Pinion 3 and the former with the ¾" Pinion on the Rod 11.

With the mechanism in the position shown in the illustration, the motion of the shaft 1 is transmitted via the ½" Pinion and the 57-teeth Gear and ½" Pinion of the unit 2, to the Pinion 3, which is in mesh with the 1" Gear Wheel 7. The 50-teeth Gear 6 and the ¾" Pinion with which it is in mesh brings the drive back to the Rod 11, and the motion of the latter is conveyed by means of Sprocket Chain to the Sprocket Wheel 10 on the winding shaft. The unit 9 revolves idly. The hoisting drum now rotates slowly and the cord should be wound round it in such a manner that the crane hook is raised.

When the direction of rotation of the shaft 1 is reversed the Crank 4 will swing over and come into engagement with the Gear Wheel of the unit 9, and the drive will then be transmitted via the unit 2, which is constantly driven from the ½" Pinion on the Rod 1, and the unit 9, to the 1" Gear Wheel 5, which is secured to the Rod 11. The hoisting drum now rotates at a greater speed, lowering the load. The Compression Spring on the Rod 11 presses the boss of the Double Arm Crank lightly against that of the Gear Wheel 5 and thus aids the Crank to swing over when the direction of rotation is changed. The movement of the Crank is checked at each end of its swing by the end of the 3" Strip coming into contact with a 4½" × ½" Double Angle Strip; one of the two Double Angle Strips required may be seen at 8. This prevents the ½" Pinion 3 jamming itself between the 1" Gears that it drives. The device may be incorporated in practically any type of Meccano crane.

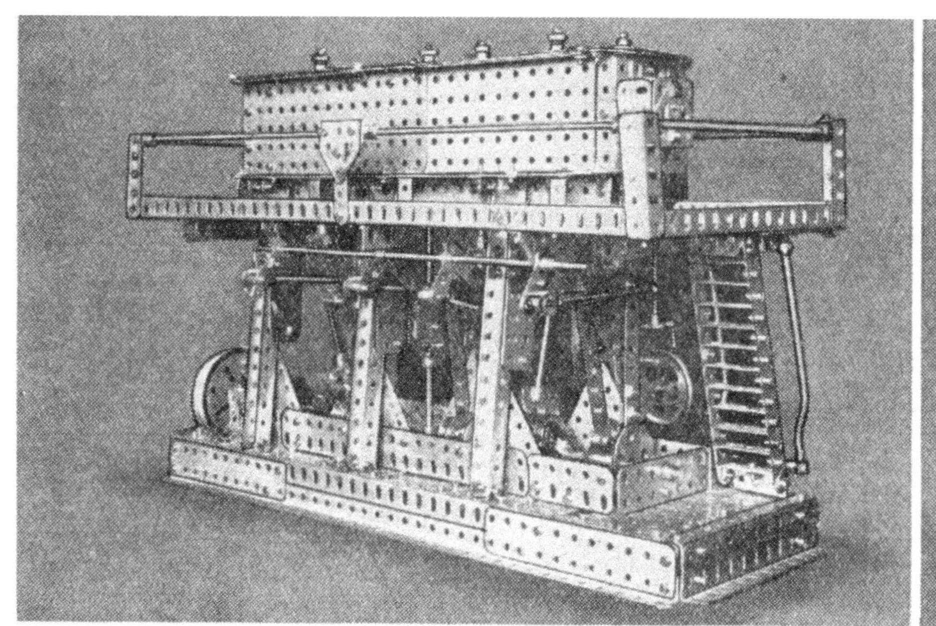

Figs 27, 28 and 29. Three notable prize-winning models from the 1930 Book of New Models.

Fig 31. An early Meccano robot.

Model No. 35. Four Cylinder Electric Engine

Parts required:

						Electrical parts:		
5	of No.	2	1	of No.	20	4	of No.	301
6	,,	6a	42	,,	37	4	,,	302
6	,,	9	18	,,	37a	2	,,	303
6	,,	9f	14	,,	38	3	,,	304
6	,,	12	9	,,	59	3	,,	305
1	,,	17	8	,,	63	2	,,	306
5	,,	17a	9	,,	82	2	,,	313
3	,,	18b	4	,,	103			
			4	,,	172			

Fig. 35

The base of the crankcase consists of a 5½" Flat Girder, to the sides of which are bolted 5½" Angle Girders; and to its ends 1½" Angle Girders are fixed. Four 1½" Angle Girders are then secured in a vertical position to the four corners of the crankcase base. Each side portion of the crankcase (one of which is shown detached in Fig. 35a) is composed of two 5½" Flat Girders and two 5½" Angle Girders, the latter being bolted together so that their flanges form a Z.

The crankshaft is of the four-throw type, each crank consisting of two Couplings secured by their centre holes to the ends of short Rods 9 that form the straight portions of the crankshaft. The crankpins each consist of a 1" Screwed Rod that is secured by lock-nuts 10 in the transverse end tapped holes of each pair of Couplings, the upper extremities of the connecting rods being carried on Set-screws inserted in Collars on the ends of the piston rods. The crankshaft is journalled in 1½" Strips 4.

Each solenoid is wound with No. 26 gauge wire, and after being covered with paper to protect its windings, is clamped in position between the Flat Girders that form the top portion of the crankcase. The Flat Girders are drawn together by means of 1" Screwed Rods.

The next item for attention is the rotary switchgear. Two similar switches are required, one on each end of the crankshaft; and each takes the form of two brushes (Pendulum Connections, part No. 172) 1, 1a, which are bent carefully to the shapes shown so that they make contact alternately with a Set-screw inserted in a Collar on the crankshaft, as the latter rotates. The brushes are attached rigidly to ½"×½" Angle Brackets that are secured by 6 B.A. Bolts to the end of the crankcase, and are insulated from it by Insulating Bushes and Washers. A similar arrangement is followed at the other end of the crankshaft, and from Fig. 35a it will be seen that the brush 6 has been removed in order to show the Set-screw 7.

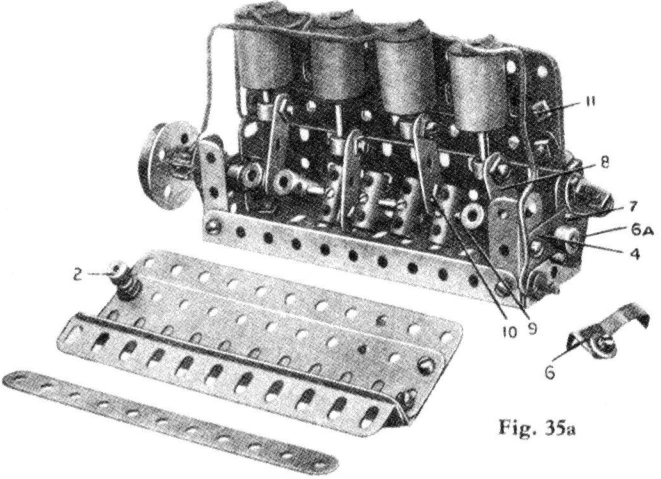

Fig. 35a

The brush 1 is connected by covered wire to the second solenoid, and the brush 1a to the third solenoid (counting from the right-hand end of the model in Fig. 35). The remaining two solenoids are connected to the brushes 6 and 6a. The other ends of the windings of the solenoids are all connected to a common "busbar" 5, which is composed of a 5½" Strip that is attached to, and insulated from, the Flat Girders by means of 6 B.A. Bolts and Insulated Bushes and Washers. A Terminal 3 is mounted on a shank of one of the 6 B.A. Bolts that serve to secure the busbar in place, and a second terminal 2 is secured in metallic contact with the frame of the model.

The path of the current is from the Accumulator to the terminal 3 on the busbar, and from there through the particular solenoid the switch of which happens to be making contact. The closing of the switch allows the current to pass through the frame of the model to the terminal 2 and to the other pole of the Accumulator, thus completing the circuit.

Fig 32. An extremely neat and well-designed electrical model.

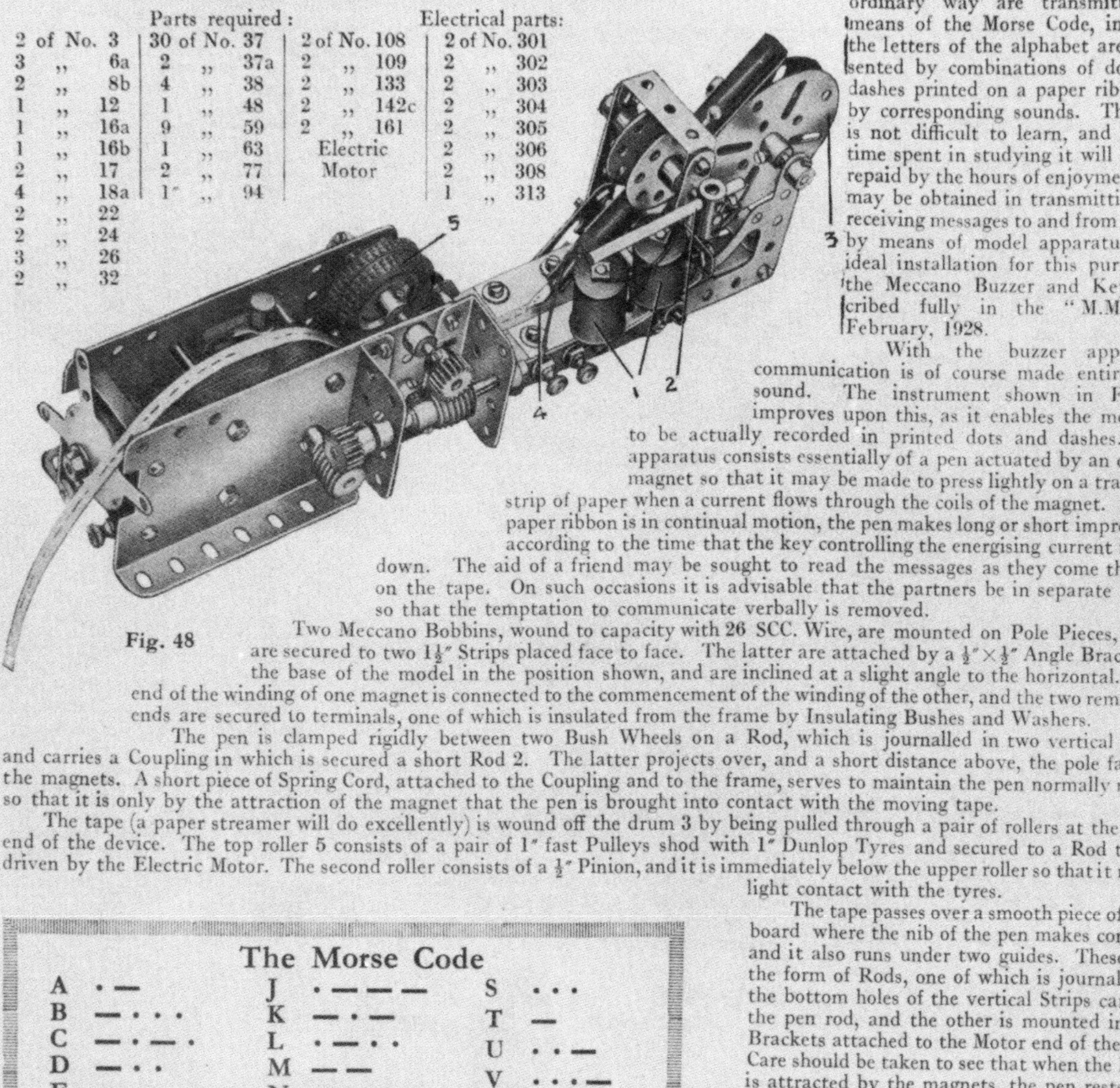

Model No. 48. A Telegraph Recorder

Parts required: Electrical parts:

2 of No. 3	30 of No. 37	2 of No. 108	2 of No. 301
3 ,, 6a	2 ,, 37a	2 ,, 109	2 ,, 302
2 ,, 8b	4 ,, 38	2 ,, 133	2 ,, 303
1 ,, 12	1 ,, 48	2 ,, 142c	2 ,, 304
1 ,, 16a	9 ,, 59	2 ,, 161	2 ,, 305
1 ,, 16b	1 ,, 63	Electric	2 ,, 306
2 ,, 17	2 ,, 77	Motor	2 ,, 308
4 ,, 18a	1" ,, 94		1 ,, 313
2 ,, 22			
2 ,, 24			
3 ,, 26			
2 ,, 32			

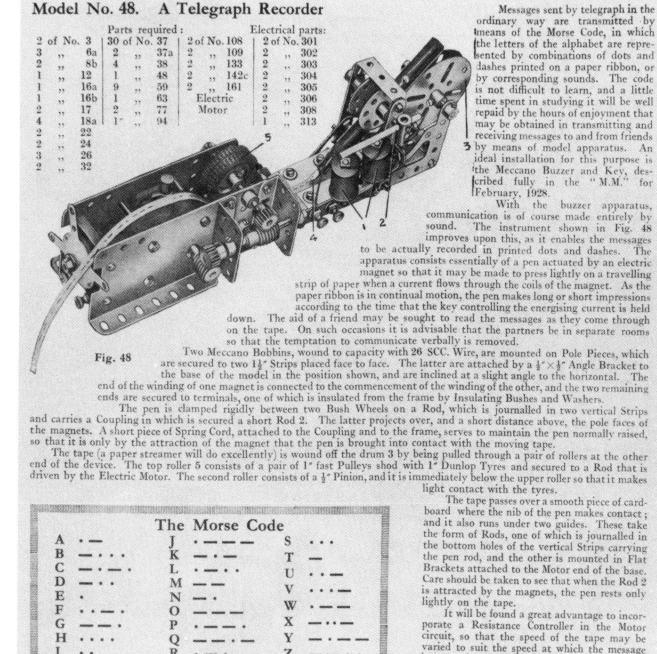

Fig. 48

Messages sent by telegraph in the ordinary way are transmitted by means of the Morse Code, in which the letters of the alphabet are represented by combinations of dots and dashes printed on a paper ribbon, or by corresponding sounds. The code is not difficult to learn, and a little time spent in studying it will be well repaid by the hours of enjoyment that may be obtained in transmitting and receiving messages to and from friends by means of model apparatus. An ideal installation for this purpose is the Meccano Buzzer and Key, described fully in the "M.M." for February, 1928.

With the buzzer apparatus, communication is of course made entirely by sound. The instrument shown in Fig. 48 improves upon this, as it enables the messages to be actually recorded in printed dots and dashes. The apparatus consists essentially of a pen actuated by an electric magnet so that it may be made to press lightly on a travelling strip of paper when a current flows through the coils of the magnet. As the paper ribbon is in continual motion, the pen makes long or short impressions according to the time that the key controlling the energising current is held down. The aid of a friend may be sought to read the messages as they come through on the tape. On such occasions it is advisable that the partners be in separate rooms so that the temptation to communicate verbally is removed.

Two Meccano Bobbins, wound to capacity with 26 SCC. Wire, are mounted on Pole Pieces, which are secured to two $1\frac{1}{2}''$ Strips placed face to face. The latter are attached by a $\frac{1}{2}'' \times \frac{1}{2}''$ Angle Bracket to the base of the model in the position shown, and are inclined at a slight angle to the horizontal. The end of the winding of one magnet is connected to the commencement of the winding of the other, and the two remaining ends are secured to terminals, one of which is insulated from the frame by Insulating Bushes and Washers.

The pen is clamped rigidly between two Bush Wheels on a Rod, which is journalled in two vertical Strips and carries a Coupling in which is secured a short Rod 2. The latter projects over, and a short distance above, the pole faces of the magnets. A short piece of Spring Cord, attached to the Coupling and to the frame, serves to maintain the pen normally raised, so that it is only by the attraction of the magnet that the pen is brought into contact with the moving tape.

The tape (a paper streamer will do excellently) is wound off the drum 3 by being pulled through a pair of rollers at the other end of the device. The top roller 5 consists of a pair of 1" fast Pulleys shod with 1" Dunlop Tyres and secured to a Rod that is driven by the Electric Motor. The second roller consists of a $\frac{1}{2}''$ Pinion, and it is immediately below the upper roller so that it makes light contact with the tyres.

The tape passes over a smooth piece of cardboard where the nib of the pen makes contact; and it also runs under two guides. These take the form of Rods, one of which is journalled in the bottom holes of the vertical Strips carrying the pen rod, and the other is mounted in Flat Brackets attached to the Motor end of the base. Care should be taken to see that when the Rod 2 is attracted by the magnets, the pen rests only lightly on the tape.

It will be found a great advantage to incorporate a Resistance Controller in the Motor circuit, so that the speed of the tape may be varied to suit the speed at which the message is transmitted, for this is liable to considerable variation with beginners.

The Morse Code

A	· —	J	· — — —	S	· · ·
B	— · · ·	K	— · —	T	—
C	— · — ·	L	· — · ·	U	· · —
D	— · ·	M	— —	V	· · · —
E	·	N	— ·	W	· — —
F	· · — ·	O	— — —	X	— · · —
G	— — ·	P	· — — ·	Y	— · — —
H	· · · ·	Q	— — · —	Z	— — · ·
I	· ·	R	· — ·		

Fig 33. A working telegraph recorder.

26 INTERESTING NEW MECCANO MECHANISMS

No. 4. Demonstration Model of a Single Plate Clutch

From a very early stage in the history of the motor car, clutches of one type or another have been standard fittings to all models. It was found at the outset by the pioneers of motoring that a gear box was necessary in order to obtain full efficiency from the engine, and also to enable the engine to do its work under varying conditions. In order to facilitate a change from one gear ratio to another, some means had to be provided for disengaging the motive power for a short time while the operation was effected. This was accomplished by means of a clutch. Like every other part of a motor car, the clutch has undergone considerable improvement during recent years and the leather-faced clutches formerly used have been replaced by more efficient devices in which metal plates are employed. Modern clutches may have one or more plates that are pressed forcibly into contact with each other in order to transmit the movement of the engine; but the present model is one of a typical single-plate clutch that is very interesting to build and operate, and is specially useful for demonstration purposes.

Fig. 4a

A suitable framework should first be built on which to mount the clutch unit. The constructional details of this should be easy to follow from Fig. 4. The clutch unit itself embodies several important parts, the main ones being the flywheel 1, the floating plate 2, and the withdrawal plate 3. These are shown, in Fig. 4a, separated from each other in order to make matters clearer. The flywheel is built up from five 6in. diam. Circular Plates, fitted with a 3″ Pulley provided with a Dunlop Tyre, which represents the "Ferodo" disc of the actual clutch. The flywheel is secured rigidly to the crankshaft, which is a Meccano Rod driven by an Electric Motor through a Sprocket Chain drive. It should be noted that the 3in. Pulley must be bolted very tightly to the flywheel in order to provide a space in which the floating plate 2 can move freely when necessary.

The floating plate consists of the geared portion of a Ball Race (part No. 168b), attached by means of $\frac{3}{8}$″ Bolts to a Bush Wheel in such a manner that it is free to slide longitudinally through a short distance. The Bush Wheel is secured to the secondary or driven shaft, the tip of which runs freely in the boss of the 3″ Pulley Wheel that is bolted to the flywheel.

The withdrawal plate 3 consists of a 6″ diam. Circular Plate, to the centre of which a Face Plate is attached by means of $1\frac{1}{2}$″ Double Angle Strips, so that both rotate freely upon the Rod as a single unit. A second 3″ Pulley Wheel, fitted with a Dunlop Tyre, is bolted on to the plate, and forms a second "Ferodo" disc.

The flywheel and the withdrawal plate revolve as one. They are connected, as shown, by 2″ Rods fixed to the flywheel by means of Cranks and passed through corresponding holes of the withdrawal plate, Compression Springs on the rods serving to keep the plate normally hard up against the driving member of the clutch. The Springs are retained in place by Collars.

Fig. 4

The withdrawal mechanism should now receive attention. An efficient clutch pedal is made from $5\frac{1}{2}$″ Angle Girders and Curved Strips, together with two $2\frac{1}{2}$″ Flat Girders, as shown in the illustration. The pedal is fixed rigidly to one end of a $11\frac{1}{2}$″ Axle Rod that is journalled in four bearings formed by several pairs of 1in. Triangular Plates. The withdrawal forks are secured very rigidly by double grub-screws to the same Rod, and each consists of a pair of Cranks fitted with a roller formed of a $\frac{1}{2}$″ loose Pulley. The Pulleys are mounted on Threaded Pins secured to the Cranks, and they are spaced centrally by Washers. When the pedal is depressed, the forks press against the edge of the Face Plate and bring the withdrawal plate out of contact with the floating plate, thus freeing the latter from the drive.

It should be noted that to limit the movement of the clutch pedal this member is extended below the $11\frac{1}{2}$″ Rod by means of a $2\frac{1}{2}$″ large radius Curved Strip, which is restricted in its movement by Threaded Pins secured to the framework. A Spring, which is attached to the lower end of the $2\frac{1}{2}$″ Curved Strip and to a $\frac{3}{4}$″ Bolt affixed to the frame-work, assists the clutch pedal to return to its normal position after operation. Owing to the fact that the withdrawal mechanism is subject to very great strain in operation, it is advisable to use two grub-screws in each of the Cranks.

Model-builders will realise, of course, that this model cannot be incorporated in a Meccano Chassis on account of its large dimensions, and it is therefore, only suitable as a demonstration model for showing the working principles of a single plate clutch.

Those who are keenly interested in constructing realistic models of motor cars should therefore endeavour to design a small compact form of this clutch, as its use in a model car will add considerably to the interest and pleasure of working the model.

It may be mentioned here that other interesting parts of a motor car transmission reproduced in Meccano, namely the gear box and the differential, are fully described and illustrated in a Special Instruction Leaflet that deals with the construction of the Meccano Motor Chassis. This Leaflet is No. 1 of a series describing the construction of Meccano Super Models, and it may be obtained from any Meccano dealer, or direct from Meccano Ltd., Old Swan, Liverpool, price 3d., plus postage.

Another interesting part of a modern motor car is the Bendix Pinion, which is designed to disconnect automatically the starting motor from the crankshaft of the engine immediately the latter starts. This remarkable mechanism was described and illustrated in the 1930 "*Book of New Models*," and model-builders will find it a splendid subject for a Meccano model.

Fig 34. A superb demonstration model of a single-plate clutch.

No. 6. Overload Release for Electric Motor

Every electrical circuit should be equipped with safety devices to protect the apparatus from damage that might arise from the passing of a heavier current than that for which the circuit is designed. In the case of electric motors it is customary to provide protection by means of a device known as an "over-load release."

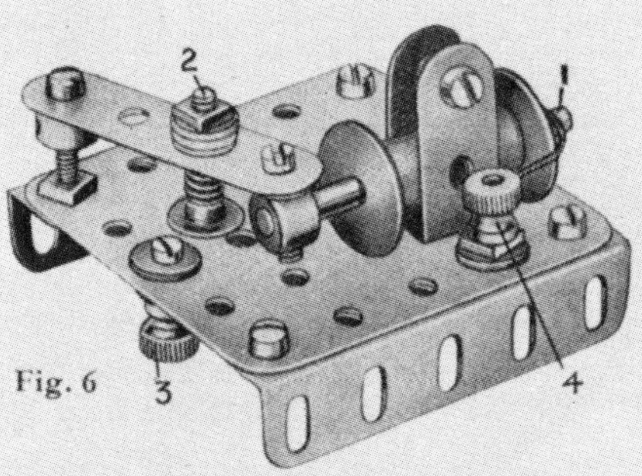

Fig. 6

Fig. 6 shows a Meccano overload release mechanism. As will be seen from the illustration, a solenoid (consisting of two layers of Meccano 26 SCC Wire wound on a Bobbin) is clamped in position on the base plate of the apparatus. The Rod 1 slides in the bore of the solenoid and is connected pivotally to a switch arm carrying the contact 2. The latter is part of a Spring Buffer (part No. 120a) and it normally makes contact with a 6 B.A. Bolt that is insulated from the Plate by insulating Bushes and Washers, and carries on its shank a terminal 3. One end of the solenoid winding is attached to the insulated terminal 4; the other end is connected to the base plate.

To connect the device in circuit with a 6-volt Motor and Accumulator, either of the two wires attached to the Accumulator should be connected to one of the terminals of the overload release, and the remaining terminal of the latter to the Motor. Hence the current is caused to flow through the turns of the solenoid and through the contacts of the overload release on its way to the Motor, and when the current rises above a certain value the plunger 1 is drawn into the interior of the solenoid, thus moving the switch arm and breaking the circuit.

Fig 35. Another useful electrical model.

No. 8. Demonstration Model of Variable-Pitch Propeller

Variable pitch propellers have recently come into use for aircraft. The amount of work demanded of an aeroplane engine varies with the height at which the machine is flying, and in order to maintain constant engine speed with an ordinary propeller the pilot can adjust the throttle according to the altitude. An alternative to this is to use an airscrew with a variable pitch.

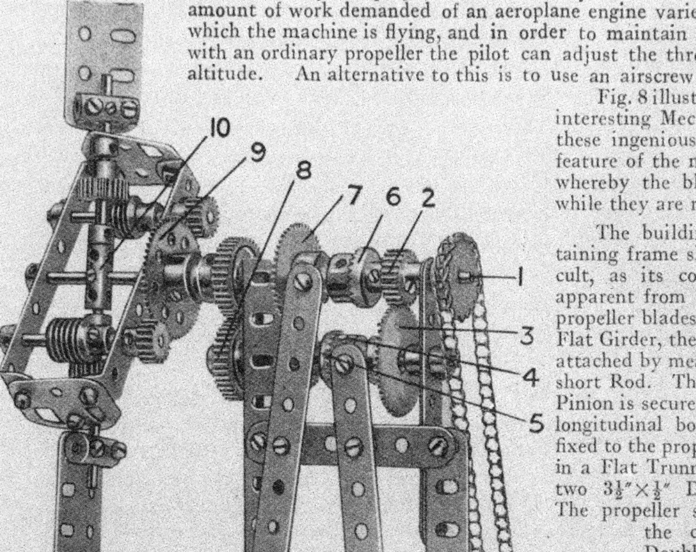

Fig. 8

Fig. 8 illustrates an exceptionally interesting Meccano model of one of these ingenious devices. The novel feature of the model is the provision whereby the blades may be angled while they are rotating.

The building of the main containing frame should not prove difficult, as its construction is clearly apparent from the illustration. The propeller blades each consist of a $5\frac{1}{2}''$ Flat Girder, the lower end of which is attached by means of a Coupling to a short Rod. This Rod, to which a $\frac{3}{4}''$ Pinion is secured, is journalled in the longitudinal bore of a Coupling 10 fixed to the propeller shaft 1, and also in a Flat Trunnion that is bolted to two $3\frac{1}{2}''\times\frac{1}{2}''$ Double Angle Strips. The propeller shaft passes through the centre holes of the Double Angle Strips, which serve also as bearings for two short Rods, on each of which is a Worm and a $\frac{1}{2}''$ Pinion. The Worms mesh with $\frac{3}{4}''$ Pinions on the Rods carrying the blades, and both the $\frac{1}{2}''$ Pinions mesh with a 57-teeth Gear 9, which is loose on the propeller shaft and is connected to a loose 1″ Gear by a Socket Coupling.

A unit comprising a 50-teeth Gear 7 and a Socket Coupling runs loosely on the propeller shaft, and a $\frac{3}{4}''$ Contrate 6 and a $\frac{3}{4}''$ Pinion 2 are fixed securely on the shaft. A movement of a lever results in the Socket Coupling coming into contact with the Contrate Wheel, which forms a clutch thus causing the unit to turn with the shaft. A similar arrangement is followed with regard to the layshaft, a 50-teeth Gear 3 of the latter unit meshing with the $\frac{3}{4}''$ Pinion, while the $\frac{3}{4}''$ Pinion on the layshaft meshes with the Gear 7. A 1″ Gear 8 fixed on the end of the layshaft meshes with that attached to the 57-teeth Gear 9.

The device works in the following manner. When the clutch on the propeller shaft is engaged by moving the appropriate handle, the Gear 7 revolves at the same speed as the shaft, thus actuating the $\frac{3}{4}''$ Pinion and the 1″ Gear of the layshaft. This angles both blades through the medium of the unit 9 and the Worm gearing contained in the boss of the propeller. When it is desired to angle the blades in the reverse direction, the clutch previously operated is withdrawn and the other then engaged.

Fig 36. The 'latest' technology demonstrated once again with Meccano.

reverted to the Blocksetter (fig 39) but was described as 'Prize-Winning Models of The Year' and consisted of 100 of them in its 40 pages printed on fine-art paper. The quality of the illustrations was quite superb and has rarely been equalled. To pick and choose from this publication is an invidious task indeed since it really deserves to be reproduced in full. That however is not possible and so the pages which follow are a personal selection of the models which in the main stemmed from the 1931 Prize Model Competition (fig 40). Most speak for themselves but text where useful has been included. Figs 41: 23, 13, 32, 25, 38, 49, 51, 61, 72/73, 92, 93/94, 95, 99. It is perhaps unfair to pick out individual models, but some points are worth a mention. The Cable Armouring Machine No. 13 is one of few by the fairer sex and No. 23 the Typewriter must be the first workable machine of this type to be produced. No. 61 the Six Wheel Lorry is very reminiscent of the No. 10 model of 1938/9 (fig 42) and another reminder of the debt Meccano owed to competition entrants. The final section on locomotives is quite exceptional: note again R. S. Miller's model, '10,000' and how like it is to the later official Meccano version published in the *Meccano Magazine* (fig 43). Good though '10,000' is, Keith Cameron's 'Fury' is even better with its superb detail and perfect proportions.

Dr. Cameron himself relates an interesting point about the picture of 'Fury':

"I had little photographic experience in those days, so I had the model photographed profession-

continued p. 167.

No. 14. An Efficient Meccano Flicker Photometer

It is practically impossible to gauge by eye the intensity of even a weak source of light, but with the aid of an instrument known as a photometer the luminosity of almost any light can be accurately measured by comparison with a given standard.

The simplest form of this instrument is that known as the Bunsen, or "grease spot," photometer, which consists essentially of a screen of moderately opaque paper having in its centre a spot of grease. The light to be measured is directed upon one side of the screen and the standard light upon the other. The distances of the lights are then adjusted until the luminosity of the grease spot is exactly the same as that of the screen. This result being achieved, the distance of each light from the screen is squared, and the relative power of the two lights thus ascertained. For example, if a small electric bulb must be four times as far away from the spot as a light of one standard candle power in order to produce the balance of light, then it will have a candle power of 16.

Another form of photometer that can be used not only for very powerful lights, but for lights of varying colours, is the flicker photometer, and Fig. 14 shows a Meccano reproduction of one of these instruments. The Meccano model is simple to build and operate, and produces remarkably accurate results.

Fig. 14

It will be seen that the apparatus consists essentially of two screens 1 and 2, that are illuminated by the lights to be compared. The screen 2 is fixed, but the screen 1 takes the form of a Maltese cross that is rotated through gears by an Electric Motor. The cross is cut out from a sheet of stout white cardboard, and is secured to a Bush Wheel or Face Plate fixed on an Axle Rod that is journalled in a $3\frac{1}{2}" \times \frac{1}{2}"$ Double Angle Strip bolted to the top of a vertical frame, consisting of Girders braced with Strips. The Double Angle Strip is arranged to make an angle of 45 degrees with the longitudinal axis of the model.

The screen 2 consists of a $3\frac{1}{2}" \times 2\frac{1}{2}"$ Flanged Plate covered with a piece of cardboard of the same texture as that employed in the Maltese cross, and is secured in such a position that its face is at right angles to the cross. The latter is driven from a countershaft 3 by means of an endless belt formed from a length of Spring Cord. The countershaft is driven in turn by a Spring Cord belt that passes over a $\frac{1}{2}"$ fast Pulley on the countershaft and over a similar Pulley 4 on the Motor.

The eye-piece 7 is composed of a short length of $\frac{1}{2}"$ diameter brass tubing, and is coated inside with lamp black. If brass tubing is not easily obtainable, a substitute may be made by wrapping a piece of gummed paper round a "former" of the right size.

The $5\frac{1}{2}"$ Angle Girder carrying the Lamp 5 is secured to a $2\frac{1}{2}" \times 2\frac{1}{2}"$ Flat Plate, which slides upon the flanges of the $24\frac{1}{2}"$ Angle Girders forming the base of the apparatus. The Plate is retained in position by a similar Plate to which it is secured by bolts, Washers being placed on the shanks of the bolts so that the flanges of the Girders slide freely between the Plates. The lamp 6 is mounted similarly.

The insulated 6 B.A. Bolt of the Lamp 5 is connected by wire to the Lamp 6, and a continuation of this wire is taken to one terminal of a 6-volt Accumulator, which is attached also to one of the Motor terminals. The other terminals of the Motor and Accumulator are connected to the framework and two terminals are attached to it for this purpose.

The two screens are each at 45 degrees to the line of sight. Hence, as the Maltese cross rotates, the eye sees alternate patches of first one screen and then the other. When the screens are illuminated differently by their respective lamps, a flickering effect is seen, but if the distance of each lamp from its screen is adjusted until the flicker is absent, then the screens are illuminated to the same degree, and the ratio of the powers of the two lamps may be determined from the squares of their respective distances from the line of sight, as in the case of the grease spot photometer mentioned earlier.

Fig 37. Another working scientific instrument for a fraction of the cost of the 'real thing'.

Tandem Compound Steam Engine

In the centre of the page is a splendid example of painstaking model-building by Mr. S. Bentley, of Bingley, Yorks. It will be seen that the model represents a tandem compound steam engine and that it is fitted with Corliss pattern valve gear, controlled by a centrifugal governor. The engine is built to a scale of one inch to the foot and all parts of the engine are correctly proportioned. Model-builders should note particularly the built-up flywheel, which is composed of Channel Segments bolted together in the usual manner. When the model was completed, it was found that the flywheel was too light to ensure satisfactory running, so Mr. Bentley filled the grooves of the Channel Segments with concrete and then enamelled the rim. The result is a very efficient wheel and a free-running engine. Considerable ingenuity has been shown in constructing the various parts of the model, and one detail in particular that savours of the master craftsman is the use of Meccano nut and bolt tins in the capacity of drip trays to catch any oil drops that may be thrown from the crankshaft journals.

The neatness of the built-up governor is a particularly noteworthy feature in the construction of which Swivel Bearings and short Rods play an important part.

Fig 38. A fine model from the prize-winners section of the 1931 Book of New Models.

MECCANO

Big Model-Building Competition

Since the last big Meccano Model-building Competition was held in 1928 many new and wonderful Meccano parts have been added to this famous constructional system, and these have made it possible for Meccano boys to build a big variety of new mechanisms and models. You should study all the Meccano separate parts before commencing to design your model. There is much help and inspiration in them and their right use may make all the difference to your chance of winning a big prize.

An Equal Chance for All

The Competition is divided into five sections in order that boys of all ages may have an equal chance. Particulars of the prizes in each section and the age limits are given below.

The closing date is the 31st March, 1932, and it is important that all entries should reach us by that date.

Sections and Prizes

Section A—For Competitors over 18 years of age on 31st March, 1932.

Section B—For Competitors over 16 years, and under 18 years of age on 31st March, 1932.

Section C—For Competitors over 12 years, and under 16 years of age on 31st March, 1932.

Section D—For Competitors over 10 years, and under 12 years of age on 31st March, 1932.

Section E—For Competitors under 10 years of age on 31st March, 1932.

Prizes will be awarded as follows :—

Section A—	Five First Prizes of £6 6 0 each	Total	£31 10 0
	Five Second Prizes of £4 4 0 each	„	£21 0 0
	Fifteen Third Prizes of £2 2 0 each	„	£31 10 0
	100 Prizes of Meccano and Hornby Train Goods.	Total Value	£60 0 0
Section B—	Five First Prizes of £5 5 0 each	Total	£26 5 0
	Five Second Prizes of £4 4 0 each	„	£21 0 0
	Fifteen Third Prizes of £1 1 0 each	„	£15 15 0
	100 Prizes of Meccano and Hornby Train Goods.	Total Value	£50 0 0
Section C—	Five First Prizes of £4 4 0 each	Total	£21 0 0
	Five Second Prizes of £3 3 0 each	„	£15 15 0
	Fifteen Third Prizes of £1 1 0 each	„	£15 15 0
	100 Prizes of Meccano and Hornby Train Goods.	Total Value	£40 0 0
Section D—	Five First Prizes of £3 3 0 each	Total	£15 15 0
	Five Second Prizes of £2 2 0 each	„	£10 10 0
	Fifteen Third Prizes of 10s. 6d. each	„	£7 17 6
	100 Prizes of Meccano and Hornby Train Goods.	Total Value	£30 0 0
Section E—	Five First Prizes of £2 2 0 each	Total	£10 10 0
	Five Second Prizes of £1 1 0 each	„	£5 5 0
	Fifteen Third Prizes of 10s. 6d. each	„	£7 17 6
	100 Prizes of Meccano and Hornby Train Goods.	Total Value	£20 0 0
Special Prizes	—In addition, there will be three special prizes of £5, £3 and £1 awarded in each section for the best models incorporating the New Meccano Aeroplane Parts.	Total Value	£45 0 0
	TOTAL VALUE OF PRIZES ...		£502 5 0

Judging the Models

In making the awards, the judges will pay special attention to the following points :—

Originality—Special marks will be given to those models showing initiative and originality and which are not simply variations of those illustrated in the Manuals.

Correct Construction—Models which in their details are constructed on correct mechanical and engineering principles will receive higher marks than those that are built incorrectly or carelessly.

General Interest—Preference will be given to those models that are likely to prove most interesting to Meccano users throughout the world.

Fig 40. Part of the competition entry form the results of which formed the basis for the 1932 Book of Prize Models.

Model No. 23. Typewriter.
(F. Pantanella, Rome).

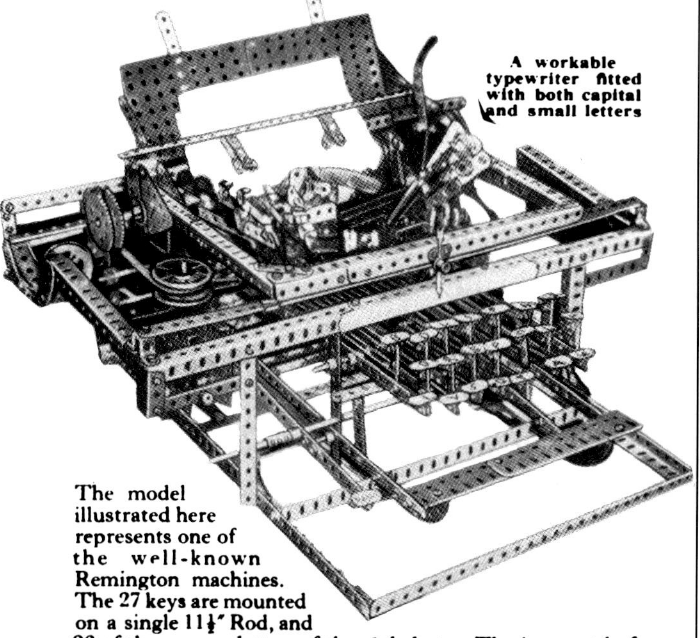

The model illustrated here represents one of the well-known Remington machines. The 27 keys are mounted on a single 11½" Rod, and 26 of them carry letters of the alphabet. The inner end of each key arm carries a short Strip that connects the arm to its respective type holder, these holders being represented by Strips of different sizes, while the letters are held in ½" × ½" Angle Brackets. The inner ends of the type holders are carried on a curved Rod so that all the types hit the paper at the same point. When a key is depressed, the corresponding type is thrown forward and passes between two Trunnions that guide it to the desired point before hitting the paper. A length of typewriter ribbon—which may be obtained from any stationer who supplies office requisites—is constantly being drawn across the space between the type guides and the paper.

The roller, together with its moving carriage, is constructed as a unit separate from the main framework of the machine. The carriage consists of a framework of Angle Girders, the underside of which is fitted with small rollers. To an Angle Girder forming the back of the frame several Rack Strips are bolted, and these engage with a ½" Pinion on the main frame of the typewriter. This Pinion is actuated by the operation of the keys and the spacing bar, and as it is rotated the moving carriage is drawn forward the space of one letter. The roller round which the paper is passed for receiving the impression is a circular wooden rod 1½" diameter. It is carried on an 11½" Rod mounted in suitable bearings, and a pawl and ratchet mechanism is fitted to one end. The ratchet enables the roller to be rotated a specified distance at the end of each line so that another line may be typed.

Fig 41: 23.

Fig 41: 32.

Model No. 32. Automatic Fortune-telling Machine. (J. Harris, Sanderstead).

When a coin is inserted in a slot at the top of the model it drops on to a pivoted lever 7 consisting of a 2½" Strip bolted to a Double Arm Crank. One end of the Strip has a piece of string tied to it and the other end carries a 1½" Strip, which points inward to prevent it fouling a trip-arm 11. This is a 5½" Strip weighted at one end with a lock-nutted 2½" Strip, and it is pivoted by means of a Crank on an Axle Rod that carries a Collar. One set-screw hole of the Collar carries a Threaded Pin, the end of which lies between two Collars mounted on a shaft, so that when the Threaded Pin is moved the Pinion 10 engages with the Contrate 9. The end hole of the trip-arm 11 carries a length of cord, the free end of which is tied to the bottom of the model.

The top of the model carries a box containing an electric light bulb that flashes intermittently and illuminates a revolving tape, which automatically stops for a short period every one and a quarter revolutions in order to attract the attention of prospective customers!

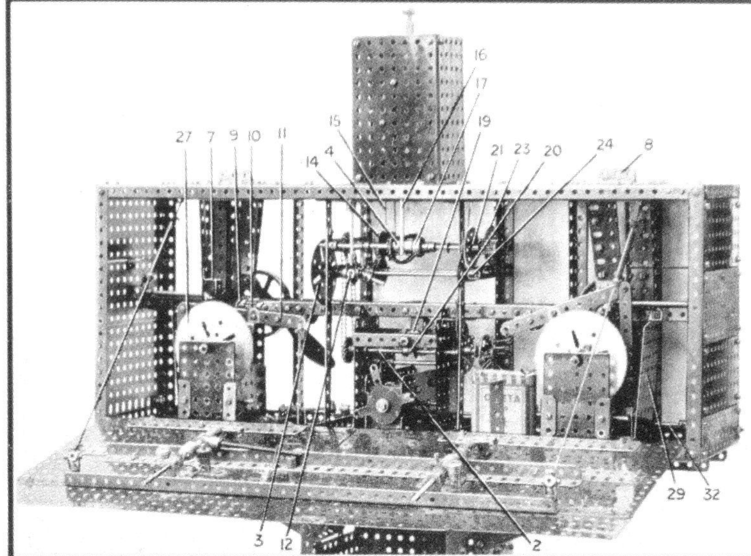

The motor drive to the tape is transmitted in the following way. A ¾" Contrate 17 secured to the Axle 21 engages with another Contrate that is carried in a Socket Coupling 4, at the other end of which is a ¾" Sprocket Wheel connected by Chain to a second similar Sprocket Wheel. This second Sprocket is held in one end of a Socket Coupling on the bottom axle of the tape roll. The Coupling carries also a 1" Pulley. The Socket Coupling units are free to turn on their respective axles, but they are held in position by a Rod 16. The automatic stop drive is operated through Gear 23 on a Rod carrying a 1" Gear Wheel 14 engaging with a second 1" Gear Wheel. The Rod of the latter Gear carries also a ½" Pinion, which meshes with a 2½" Gear Wheel 3 mounted on a 1½" Axle Rod carrying a 1" Bevel Gear. The Axle Rod 24 is secured at one end to the main frame by a Double Arm Crank, and the other end carries a Coupling forming a bearing for the 1½" Axle Rod and for the Rod 12 carrying a 1" Bevel Gear. This latter Gear meshes with the Bevel on the 1½" Axle. The opposite end of the Axle 12 carries a Coupling supporting a 1" Axle Rod. The front of the machine is filled in by means of two sheets of white cardboard on which verses respresenting the "fortunes" are written. When the propellers stop revolving the arrows on the propeller shafts indicate one of the verses.

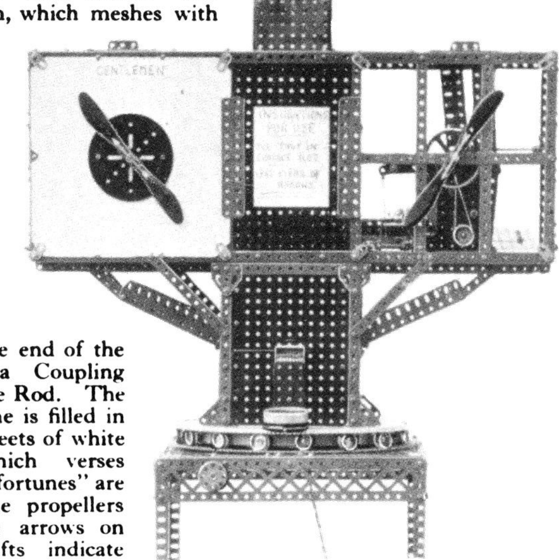

Fig 41: 13.

Model No. 13. Cable Armouring Machine.

(Miss W. Fairfield, Bowden).

This model represents a type of machine that is used for armouring electrical cables with a steel wire covering, and for stranding wire ropes. The model can be put to practical use for covering copper wire with an insulating layer of cotton strands.

It consists essentially of a revolving cage in which a number of bobbins of wire, or reels of cotton, are held on Rods. The bobbins are free to rotate on their respective Rods. The cable to be armoured is taken from a drum at one end of the machine and is passed through the interior of the cage and then through a guide, after which it is led over pulleys to a winding-in drum. The wire or cotton to be used for covering the cable is wound on the bobbins in the cage, and the free end of wire from each bobbin is passed through the boss of a Crank secured in the position shown. The cable is passed through the centre of the cage, then through the boss of the Crank, and is attached to the winding-in drum. The free ends of the wire from the bobbins are now given a few turns round the cable. When the cage is set in motion the bobbin wire is twisted around the cable. A Worm on an extension of the Crank Handle shown engages a 57-teeth Gear on the shaft of the guide pulleys and provides an effective take-up for the finished cable. The winding-in drum is driven by a belt that passes round a Pulley on the shaft of the 57-teeth Gear and another Pulley on the shaft of the winding-in drum.

The revolving cage is built up from one Hub Disc and two Circular Girders. The Circular Girders are bolted together as shown in the illustration, and are secured to the Hub Disc by means of eight 4½" Angle Girders. The complete cage revolves on and is supported by four small Flanged Wheels that are loosely carried on 1½" Rods secured to the base of the model by 1" × 1" Angle Brackets. The drive to the cage is conveyed through Sprocket Chain.

Model No. 25. Automatic Coaling Plant. (L. W. Gray, Cowes, I.O.W.).

Outstanding features of a modern dock are the huge coal handling plants that are constantly at work loading thousands of tons of coal into the bunkers of ships. Many different types of coalers are in use, and one of the best known is that constructed by Vickers-Armstrong Ltd., of which the Meccano model described here is a reproduction.

The actual coaler is 74′ in height and of this 18′ are sunk into a well in the ground that accommodates the main gear-boxes and also the coal chute when the machine is not in use. Raising and lowering of the chute and the coal truck-tipper is carried out hydraulically, and the subsidiary movements are operated by electric motors, the drive from these being transmitted through separate gear-boxes.

The frame of the model is constructed from 24½″ and 18½″ Angle Girders in two separate units, and these are braced together leaving a central space 7½″ wide. This space accommodates the cage and tip, which raises, lowers and tips the coal wagons. The cage is 7½″ wide and 9½″ long and is constructed from Angle Girders and Flat Girders of suitable lengths. The floor of the cage is hinged at the front and can be tilted by means of a ram acting on the underside. Short Angle Girders fitted to the upper side of the tip represent rails on which the wagon rests while being emptied.

The coal chute, which is 17″ long, is constructed from a number of Flat Girders and Flat Plates of various sizes, and is pivotally attached at its base to the cage carrying the wagon tip. The rate at which coal is discharged is regulated by a vertically sliding door situated about midway down the coal chute. The jib is 17″ long and the two main members are joined together by Threaded Bosses held in place by Bolts. Along the top of the jib runs a handrail carried in supports formed from Couplings and Handrail Supports. The jib is pivoted to the base of a vertical girder that is free to turn in bearings formed from a ball race at its lower end and a Pivot Bolt at its upper end. The support girder is 8″ high and is fitted with three pulley sheaves near the top. The movements of hoisting, luffing and swivelling are carried out from a gear-box at the base of the model, and the controls are situated in a small cabin at the rear. The back of the cabin is fitted with a door that gives access to a platform extending to the rear of the model, where a ladder running the entire height of the machine is held in place by ½″ × ½″ Angle Brackets.

As already mentioned, the actual machine is fitted with two hydraulic rams, one of which operates the truck cage and the other the tip. In the model link mechanism replaces the hydraulic movement and consists of Rack Strips bolted to the rams and actuated by 1″ Gear Wheels. Each ram is fitted at its lower end with a 1½″ Pulley, and a cord passed round this is attached at one end to the frame and at the other end to the cage. As a result of this arrangement the cage is raised or lowered by increasing or decreasing the length of the ram stroke. The ram piston for operating the cage is 9½″ long and that for operating the tipping movement is 7½″ long. The cord from the 9½″ piston passes from the 1½″ Pulleys to the top of the plant where it is taken over a 6″ Pulley and secured to the hoisting cage. The cords from the 7½″ ram pass from the ram pulleys to 2″ Pulleys at the head of the model, and from there are led to the ram mechanism that tips the cage.

Two separate gear-boxes are provided for operating the hydraulic rams; these are situated in the base and are operated by a Meccano 6-volt Electric Motor. When the Motor is operating the hoisting ram the greater part of the load is counterbalanced by lead weights fitted to the cage. These weights are attached to cords that pass over 1″ Pulleys at the top of the model and then down to the cage. The coal chute is luffed by means of four cords attached to winches situated in the base of the model, and the winch drums are rotated by the Clockwork Motor that works the derrick.

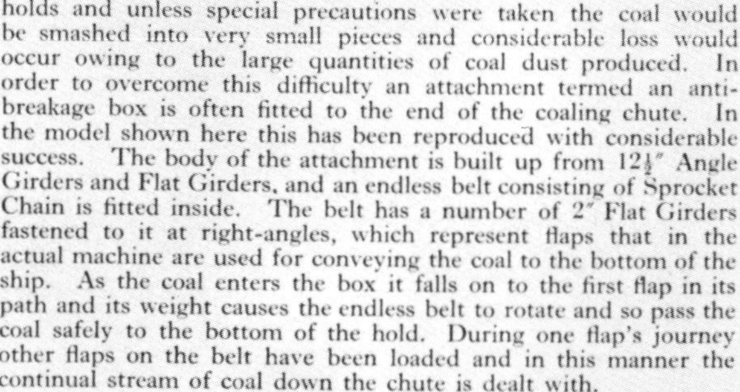

In actual practice it is frequently necessary to coal ships with very deep holds and unless special precautions were taken the coal would be smashed into very small pieces and considerable loss would occur owing to the large quantities of coal dust produced. In order to overcome this difficulty an attachment termed an anti-breakage box is often fitted to the end of the coaling chute. In the model shown here this has been reproduced with considerable success. The body of the attachment is built up from 12½″ Angle Girders and Flat Girders, and an endless belt consisting of Sprocket Chain is fitted inside. The belt has a number of 2″ Flat Girders fastened to it at right-angles, which represent flaps that in the actual machine are used for conveying the coal to the bottom of the ship. As the coal enters the box it falls on to the first flap in its path and its weight causes the endless belt to rotate and so pass the coal safely to the bottom of the hold. During one flap's journey other flaps on the belt have been loaded and in this manner the continual stream of coal down the chute is dealt with.

8

Fig 41: 25.

Model No. 38. Portable Truck Tip. (R. van Bulck, Brussels).

The Meccano model is built to a scale of 1" to 1', and is complete in every detail, including a railway wagon. The main frames are 24½" long and 1" high, and are constructed from 24½" Angle Girders and 12½" and 5½" Flat Girders. The two sides are connected together by means of a number of 5½" Angle Girders, and to the centre of the frames a 5½" × 3½" Flat Plate strengthened with 5½" Angle Girders is bolted. Each of the two swivelling bogies is constructed from two 5½" Angle Girders for the sides and four 4½" Angle Girders for the cross members, two of the 4½" Girders being used for carrying the swivel pin. The sides of the bogie are fitted with 5½" Flat Girders, and these carry the wheel springs, each of which consists of three 2½" Strips clamped together by ⅜" Bolts and secured to the bogie frame by two Threaded Bosses.

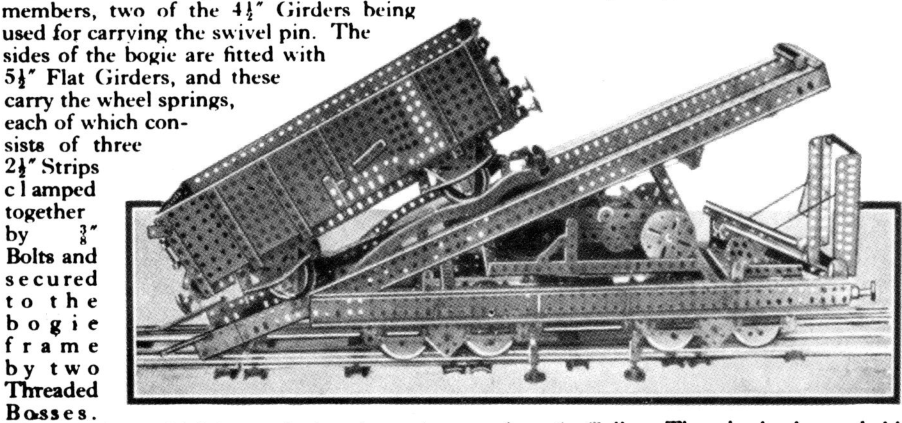

The axle-box, which is attached to the spring, consists of a Collar. The wheel axles are held in the Collars, the wheels being free to rotate.

Four screw jacks are fitted, two to each side of the main frames, and each of them consists of two Cranks bolted together with their respective bosses at opposite ends, one of the bosses being passed over and secured to a vertical pivot rod on the frames. The boss of the other Crank carries a Threaded Coupling in which a 1" Threaded Rod forming a screw jack operates. The lower end of the Threaded Rod carries a 1" fast Pulley.

The 5½" × 3½" Flat Plate bolted across the main frames carries a 4" Ball Bearing on which is mounted a framework that supports the Electric Motor used for working the model. Two Architraves, fitted one on each side of the Motor, form the pivots for the tipping girders. These are constructed in two portions from Angle Girders and Flat Girders of various sizes, and are connected together by cross members made with 5½" Angle Girders. When completed the Girders form rails on which a sliding trolley operates. The front wheels of the wagon to be tipped rest in hollows on each side of the sliding truck, and a Crane Grab is hitched to the wheel axle to prevent the wagon from breaking loose while it is being tipped. The illustration on the left is an underneath view of the model and shows the mechanism clearly.

Fig 41: 38.

This fine model Gantry Crane and Locomotive is based on the cover illustration of the "Meccano Magazine" for November, 1930.

Model No. 49. Gantry Crane and Locomotive. (E. Whalley, Blackburn).

The large girder of the crane from which the locomotive is suspended is constructed from Angle Girders, Flat Girders and Strips, as follows. First, two 24½" Angle Girders are bolted side by side to two 12½" Flat Girders. Then two 12½" and one 3½" Flat Girders are bolted together in one length, and the extended girder thus formed is bolted in turn, in the form of a bow, to each end of the 24½" Angle Girders. This bow-piece is then strengthened by a number of 2½" Flat Strips. Two of these built-up girders are placed side by side, 5½" apart, and are connected at their ends by means of Angle Girders, Plates, and Strips.

The crane gantry is fitted with two separate crabs, each of which is 9½" long and is mounted on four large Flanged Wheels, two being allotted to each end of the structure. Two separate pulley hoists are carried by each crab and each of the four blocks may be operated simultaneously or separately as desired. Each pulley system consists of two double sheave pulleys, one of which is fixed to the crab and the other to a cross beam. This cross beam couples together the two hoists fitted to each crab and is built in the form of an "H" section girder, from four 7½" Angle Girders.

The movements of the model are all controlled from one main gear-box situated at one side of the crane gantry. The power is derived from a Meccano Electric Motor, the speed of which is controlled by a rheostat. The drive from the Motor is transmitted through suitable gears to a master shaft from which it is taken to the secondary gear trains. The three traversing movements are controlled by three horizontal gear levers and the four hoists are fitted with four independent and one master lever. Thus each pulley block may be raised or lowered separately or, by moving the master lever, all four may be thrown in engagement at the same moment.

The model C.N.R. engine is of the 4-8-4 type. The boiler is made from three curved 5½" × 3½" Flat Plates, and a 5½" Flat Girder bolted to an Angle Girder forms the running board. The chimney stack is built up from four 1" loose Pulley Wheels bolted to the top of the smoke-box.

Current is conveyed to the 6-volt Electric Motor by two lengths of flexible wire, each of which is insulated from the other and also from the model.

Fig 41: 49.

Model No. 51. Electric Travelling Crane. (N. Batchelor, Westcliff-on-Sea).

This model represents an electrically operated travelling crane capable of handling loads up to 25 tons. It is fitted with a 6-volt Electric Motor and will lift 22 lb. with ease.

The travelling gantry is of very robust construction, Angle Girders being used throughout, and it is mounted on four bogies each fitted with four wheels, two of which are driven. The drive is supplied by a Motor mounted in the swivelling superstructure, and is passed through the central pivot, to be transmitted to the travelling wheels by Bevel Gears and Universal Couplings. A ladder is fitted at one corner and consists of 12½" Strips with 1" Screwed Rods secured in each hole to serve as rungs. At the upper extremity of the ladder is a miniature "gallery," as in the actual crane, to enable the operator to reach the control gear. To form the gallery 3"×1½" Flat Plates are secured to 12½" Strips and attached by ½" Reversed Angle Brackets to the gantry. A Handrail runs the entire length of the gallery, and consists of a length of heavy gauge wire held by Nuts to vertical 1" Screwed Rods.

A model of 25-ton Electric Travelling Crane. It is driven by an Electric Motor and will lift a load of 22 lbs.

The superstructure rotates on a geared Roller Bearing Unit and is constructed from 18½" and 7½" Angle Girders secured at each end to 1½" Angle Girders forming the corner members. Flat Girders are used to fill in the sides of the frame so formed, and Flat Plates cover the floor.

The jib is formed from 18½" and 12½" Angle Girders braced with Strips. Axle Rods pivotally attached to the jib head carry the Pulleys for the luffing cords, and a short Rod journalled between two 3½" Flat Girders is fitted with Pulleys from which the pulley block is suspended. This is built up in the usual manner from 2½" Triangular Plates.

The gear-box sides consist of 7½" Flat Girders bolted with the elongated holes downward, the upper holes forming the bearings for the rotating shafts. The gear-box is of the constant-mesh type, Socket Couplings fitted with clutches being used for bringing the different movements unto operation. Contrate Wheels (¾" diameter) are found more effective than Dog Clutches for this purpose as they engage quicker. They occupy more space, however, and for this reason Dog Clutches are used where space is limited. The hoisting barrel is fitted with a two-speed gear so that light loads can be dealt with quickly. A band brake, consisting of a loop of cord wound round a 1½" Pulley, is fitted on the drum and is operated by means of a handwheel and screw mechanism. The levers controlling the various movements are neatly grouped together, and the motor reversing switch is coupled up by a connecting rod and Cranks to a conveniently placed handlever.

The entire cab and gear-box is roofed in, and for this purpose four Axle Rods are mounted vertically on each side of the model to support a framework of Angle Girders. Sheet metal is cut to the required size and bolted to these, but there is no reason why standard Meccano parts should not be used instead.

Current for the Motor is supplied by a Transformer, and to prevent the wires from becoming entangled, owing to the swivelling of the superstructure, a collector ring should be fitted. This need only consist of Strips bent to form a circle and insulated from the gantry. A suitable collector attached to the rotating part should press lightly on the edge of the Strips, and should be connected to one of the Electric Motor terminals. The other terminal should be "earthed," that is, connected to the frame, and one of the Transformer terminals must also be "earthed." The other Transformer terminal should be connected to the collector ring.

Fig 41: 51.

Model No. 61. Six-wheeled Lorry. (K. W. Ingram, Chelmsford, Essex).

This model lorry is driven by an Electric Motor and will run along under its own power if an Accumulator is placed on the platform.

Each side of the main frames is 45″ long and the main girder of each consists of two 24½″ Angle Girders bolted together and overlapping each other nine holes. The shape of the finished girder is obtained with the aid of a number of shorter Angle Girders, the necessary connections being shown fairly clearly in the upper photograph. The two complete side girders are connected together by short girders so that they taper slightly towards the front. The rear cross girder is 4½″ long, and that at the front 3½″ long.

At a point 10½″ from the rear of the frames two Trunnions are fitted on each side, and these form the pivots for a Rod carrying the rear wheel compensating beams. These beams are constructed in the form of powerful leaf springs, and are pivoted at their centres by means of Double Brackets to the Rod passing through the Trunnions. The ends of the beams carry Face Plates, and in these are journalled the two rear axles. The Face Plates also form part of the brakes, which work on the internal expanding system, and are constructed in a similar manner to those incorporated in the Meccano Super Model Motor Chassis. The four brakes are coupled together by an ingenious link mechanism that ensures an even braking pressure on each wheel, and they are coupled to a hand lever by means of Boom Healds and Cranks.

The front of the frame carries two massive semi-elliptic springs, on which the steering gear is mounted. As is the case with most petrol-driven vehicles, Ackermann steering gear is fitted, but in the model slight modifications have been found necessary owing to the position of the steering column. These alterations do not impair the working of the gear, however.

A 6-volt Electric Motor that represents the engine of the actual machine is placed directly over the front axle. Ratio 3 : 1 Bevel Gearing transmits the drive to a compact single plate clutch, from which it is taken to a standard Meccano three-speed and reverse gear-box, and thence through two Universal Couplings to the differential. This latter part of the model is carried in an enlarged framework in order that an extra ratio 3 : 1 reduction gear may be incorporated.

The radiator is an almost exact replica of the original, and the typical brightly plated beading has been successfully represented by means of Spring Cord. This radiator is bolted direct to the front of the driver's cab, and the Electric Motor is placed immediately behind. The lower portion of the cab is built up from three 4½″ × 2½″ Flat Plates, and two side doors are fitted, each constructed from one 2½″ and one 3″ Flat Girder. These two Girders are bolted together edge to edge, and the unsightly extension caused by the 3″ Girder is covered by means of a 2½″ large radius Curved Strip. The complete doors are attached to the cab by means of Hinges. The back of the cab consists of two 5½″ × 2½″ Flanged Plates, and to the top of these a 5½″ × 3½″ Flat Plate is bolted. This Plate forms the roof and a 3½″ Flat Girder is fitted on each side. The sloping windscreen supports are represented by 3″ and 3½″ Strips, and the seat inside the cab is built up from four 4½″ Flat Girders.

The front mudguards each consist of a 7½″ Flat Girder attached to the underside of the cab by two 1″ × ½″ Angle Brackets.

The rear mudguards on each side of the lorry are built from 4½″ Flat Girders, and are secured to the main chassis frames by means of 1″ × ½″ and ½″ × ½″ Angle Brackets.

The petrol tank is constructed from four 7½″ Angle Girders and four 5½″ Strips, and is secured in place by 1″ × ½″ Angle Brackets at a point midway between the front and rear wheels on the left-hand side of the lorry.

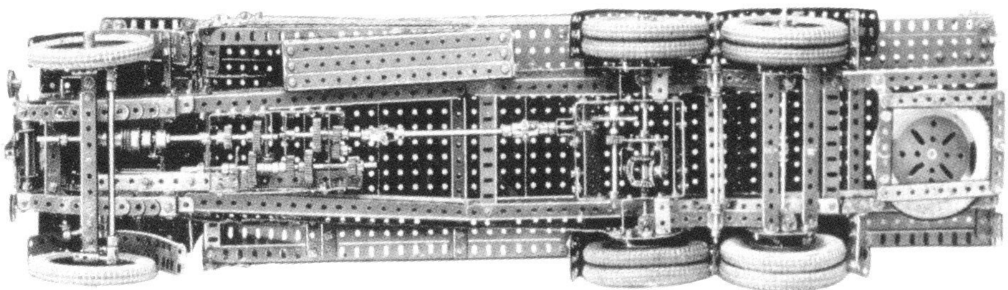

Underneath view of the Six-wheeled Lorry, showing the gear-box, clutch and differential, etc.

Fig 41: 61.

Models Nos. 72 and 73. Garner Six-wheeled Motor Chassis.

(J. K. Garner, Bickenhill, and P. M. Worfolk, Caterham Valley).

Amongst the most successful of recent commercial motor vehicles is the Garner rigid six-wheeled lorry. This incorporates many excellent features that render it useful for transport purposes over ordinary roads and the roughest ground alike.

The Garner chassis affords a splendid subject for reproduction in Meccano as will be seen from the accompanying photographs. The fine scale model shown in the upper illustration was constructed by Kenneth Garner, son of Mr. Garner, of Garner Motors Ltd., and the centre illustration shows a model by P. M. Worfolk.

The greater portion of Garner's model, namely, the frame, bogie, and articulating front axle, was developed from the original drawings of the actual chassis. The cab and bodywork are built to scale, the measurements being based on the dimensions of actual vehicles in the Garner Works.

The model is driven by a six-volt Meccano Electric Motor that is incorporated in the frame as a substitute for the orthodox engine. The gear-box gives two speeds forward, and reverse travelling is obtained by reversing the Motor. The final drive to the second and third axles is transmitted by Worm gears. Steering is by means of Ackermann type linkage, and the change-speed lever for the gear-box is placed at the driver's left-hand side. The special Garner front wheel articulation system is faithfully reproduced in the model, and it is interesting to note that, by incorporating two quarter-elliptical springs arranged in V formation and working in combination with a radius rod, a considerable difference in front wheel level is possible. The springs are centrally pivoted to the chassis and give free articulation of the front wheels within a limit of 1½".

Every part of the chassis consists of standard Meccano parts. The transmission incorporates several Universal Couplings in order to provide flexibility of the inner bogie axle for travelling over uneven ground. The six road wheels consist of 3" Pulleys fitted with 3" Meccano Dunlop Tyres, and these give to the model a very finished and realistic appearance.

In the model constructed by P. Worfolk the gear-box is of the Meccano standard type and provides three forward and reverse speeds.

A chassis of this type, in which the four rear wheels are driven, necessitates the provision of two differential gears, one for each of the twin rear axles, and for these a modified form of the standard differential that is incorporated in the Meccano Motor Chassis is used. Instead of the 1" Bevels that form a prominent feature of the standard differential, however, ½" Bevels are used in this model and function very satisfactorily.

Insufficiency of parts presumably prevented Worfolk from including a clutch in his model and therefore the Motor drives direct to the gear-box. A ½" Pinion on the Motor armature shaft meshes with a 57-teeth Gear Wheel, on the Rod of which is also a Sprocket Wheel. A length of Sprocket Chain connects the Sprocket Wheel with another Sprocket Wheel on a Rod that carries also a Worm. This is in direct engagement with a 1½" Contrate that is secured to the fixed shaft of the gear-box.

The rear axle suspension consists of two inverted semi-elliptical springs built up from Strips of various lengths on each side of the frame, and these also incorporate the bogie mounting system. An important feature of this method of suspension is that the front wheels are mounted in practically the same position fore and aft as when the usual semi-elliptical spring system is provided, thereby reducing the total length of the chassis and wheelbase without reducing the available loading space. The body is of the "well" type, and is equipped with small hooks to which a canvas covering may be attached. A hinged tail-board also is provided.

The model chassis is 24" in length overall and 8" in width, the track width being 7". The overall measurements of the body are length 15½", width 8", and height 8".

Fig 41: 72/73.

Model No. 92. C.N.R. Locomotive. (A. S. Park, Calgary, Canada).

The subject of this model is one of the latest Canadian National Railway locomotives of the K-5-a class, the numbers of which range between 5700 and 5704. These great Hudson locomotives are used for fast passenger service on two or more divisions of the Montreal and Chicago run and they are also used for hauling the *International Limited* train. They were constructed at the Montreal Locomotive Works at the end of 1930, and are amongst the most powerful locomotives designed and constructed by this firm.

They have an overall length of 92′ 6¼″ and in working order they weigh, with tender, 662,200 lbs. The boiler is of the straight top type with radially stayed fire-box and it has a diameter of 7′ 2″, with a working pressure of 275 lb. per square inch. In order to save weight this part of the engine has been constructed from high-tensile silicon steel.

The fire-box is very large and roomy, measuring 10′ 6″ in length and 7′ 1″ in width, and is constructed throughout of steel. The cylinders are 23″ in diameter with a stroke of 28″; and the driving wheels are 6′ 8″ in diameter and are fitted with steel hub liners made in a single piece. The axles on which the wheels are carried are of hammered carbon steel, quenched and drawn in oil. The driving journals are 12″ in diameter and 13″ in length.

The bogie wheels have a diameter of 2′ 10¼″ and are made from cast-iron, the tyres being of forged steel. The rear bogie, situated under the fire-box, is fitted with a booster for the purpose of increasing the nominal tractive effort of the engine from 43,300 lb. to 53,300 lb. The cylinders, valves and guide bars are lubricated by six-feed mechanical lubricators with a total capacity of 20 pints, this amount being necessary on account of the long runs made by the engines. A hydrostatic lubricator in the cab distributes oil to the various auxiliaries.

The tender is carried on 12 wheels and has a capacity of 20 tons of coal and 14,000 gallons of water, the total weight being 305,600 lb. In the actual engine the main frames, together with all cross ties, front buffer beam, rear boiler cradle, cylinders and the air reservoirs, are cast in one piece of solid steel.

The model illustrated here differs from the original in that it is fitted with Walchaerts valve gear instead of the Baker-Pillio gear fitted to the actual engine. Very close examination is necessary, however, to detect the difference between the two kinds of gear. Reversing is carried out by means of a handle in the cab of the engine, and an interesting lever mechanism is fitted that enables the movement of the reversing link to be transmitted to the reversing lever of the 6-volt Electric Motor by means of which the model is driven. In this manner the valve gear is made to appear responsible for the reversing of the locomotive. The coupled wheels are all sprung, and each separate wheel is carried on compensating levers.

The boiler of the model is 7″ in diameter over its entire length, and its fittings include safety valves, steam dome, whistle, bell and headlamp. The front of the locomotive carries an air reservoir, a neat cow-catcher, and steps that give access to a platform running the length of the boiler.

The cab is a good representation of the short vestibule type usually fitted to these engines, and the boiler fittings include water and steam gauge, power reverse lever, injector control and a brake lever. The interior is illuminated by a 6-volt. lamp situated in the roof. A battery for supplying current to this lamp, together with the head and tender lamps, is carried in the smoke-box, and separate switches are provided in the cab for each lamp. The current for the main driving Motor is supplied by a 6-volt. Transformer.

Although it is almost impossible to detect the fact from the photograph, the entire top of the boiler is hinged and may be opened to investigate the interior working of the model. The cab roof also is hinged to the cab side so that plenty of space is available for operating the controls. The two bogies of the tender are each fitted with six wheels constructed from Wheel Flanges and Face Plates, the complete units being attached to the tender frame by means of Ball Bearings. Each axle of the bogies is sprung by means of spiral springs, and realistic axle boxes are fitted to each wheel. Dummy vacuum brake cylinders and track sprinklers add to the realistic appearance of the tender. The main body, which in actual practice carries the water, is constructed from a number of 12½″ Strips, and its rear consists of a Circular Plate on which are mounted the automatic coupler, vacuum brake connections, ladder, electric lamps and buffers. The automatic coupler is built up from Flat Brackets and Couplings and its action is similar to a spring jaw trap. It is attached to the tender by means of a Double Bracket and a 1″ Axle Rod. The vacuum brake connections are represented by Springs carried on a 2″ Rod and held in place by Collars. The springs should be curved slightly in order to obtain a realistic effect. The ladder is built up from two 7½″ Strips that are secured parallel to each other by two Double Brackets, the steps being formed from 1″ Threaded Rods held in place by lock-nuts. The electric lamps, three in number, are built up from Chimney Adaptors secured to the tender by ½″ × ½″ Angle Brackets. Small bulbs fitted in these are operated by the battery in the smoke-box. The forward end of the almost circular tank is cut away in the form of a square well, which is used for carrying coal. An enclosing wall is fitted round the top of the well and a fine effect is obtained by the use of handrails. A sliding door is provided to enable the coal to be man-handled in case of emergency, but normally the furnace is fed by a mechanical stoker.

Three filling ports or manholes (Wheel Flanges) are arranged in the top of the tender and are mounted on a platform constructed from Angle Girders and Flat Plates.

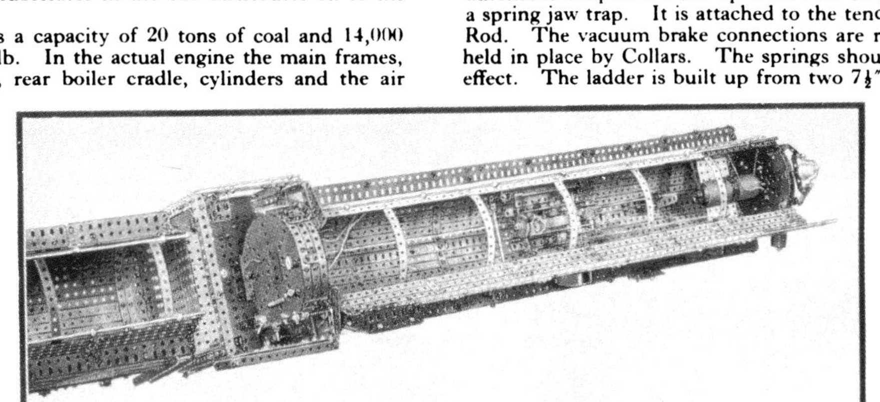

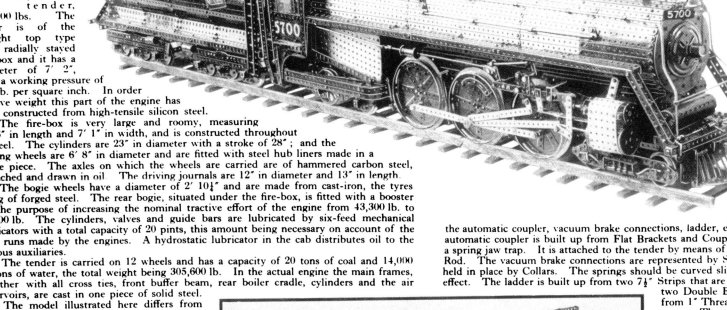

The upper photograph is a general view of the Meccano model C.N.R. locomotive, and shows the valve gear and driving-wheel arrangement. The lower illustration is a plan view of the model, showing the hinged top of the boiler open.

Fig 41: 92.

Models Nos. 93 and 94. L.N.E.R. High-Pressure Locomotive "No. 10000". (R. O. Jukes, Christchurch, N.Z., and R. S. Miller, Newark).

On this page are shown two interesting models of the wonderful L.N.E.R. high-pressure locomotive "No. 10000."

Dealing first with the model shown in the upper illustration, it will be seen that the construction of the main frame follows very closely the method adopted in the construction of actual locomotives. Although the driving wheels are not sprung as in the case of the actual engine, the appearance does not suffer greatly in consequence. The six driving wheels are each fitted with brakes operated from a handle in the driver's cab.

The front bogie is 7½" long and 3½" wide and the wheels are constructed from Face Plates and Wheel Flanges. Two 3½" Angle Girders are bolted across the centre of the bogie, and these support the sliding pivot pin. The bogie is held in a central position by means of two Springs. The axle of the front pair of wheels of the rear bogie is mounted in correctly designed axle-boxes connected to the main frames by neat leaf springs. The Bissel truck is of massive construction and is built from 3½" and 5½" Angle Girders. The rear axle is carried in two Handrail Supports attached to the truck.

A model of the L.N.E.R. Locomotive "No. 10000," by R. O. Jukes.

The boiler is cleverly constructed from 5½" × 3½" Flat Plates and 12½" Strips. By using Plates instead of Strips, a much neater appearance is obtained. The streamlined chimney is constructed from two 1" loose Pulleys and four 1½" Strips, the Strips being carefully moulded into a trailing edge in faithful imitation of the original. The handrails are represented by Rods of various sizes.

The cab is constructed from a number of 5½" × 3½" and 4½" × 2½" Flat Plates, and the curves at the roof corners are moulded with the aid of 2½" Triangular Plates and short Strips. The cab fittings include steam pressure and water gauges, vacuum gauge, brake, and valve gear levers, seats for driver and fireman, and a hinged fire-box door fitted with a draught screen. In a real engine this screen is used for the purpose of protecting the legs of the engine crew from the heat of the furnace.

The tender is a scale reproduction of an L.N.E.R. corridor-type tender and runs on eight wheels, each of which is sprung independently of the others. The corridor, which runs down one side of the tender, opens into the cab of the locomotive through a small door, and communication is also provided between the tender and the train by means of a model of an L.N.E.R. corridor connection. Small lumps of coal placed in the tender add greatly to the realism of the model.

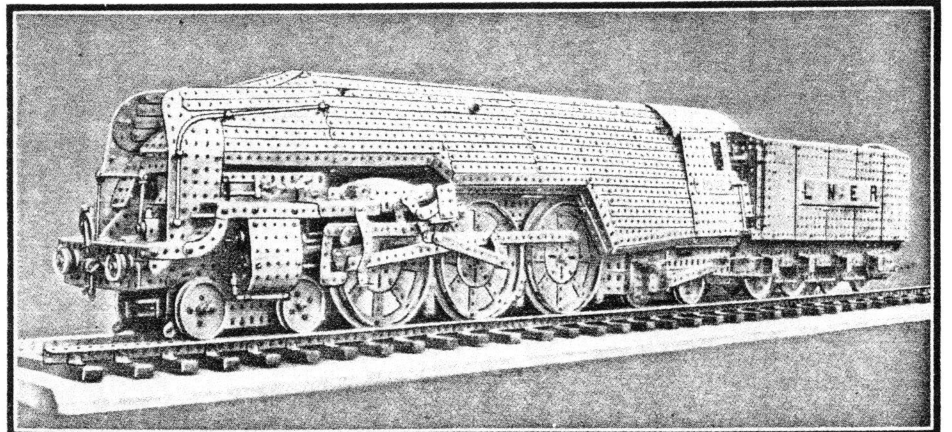

This model by R. S. Miller forms an interesting comparison with that shown above.

The model shown in the lower photograph is driven by means of a Meccano 6-volt Electric Motor. The main frames are built in a similar manner to the Meccano Super Model Baltic Tank Locomotive, and the six coupled wheels are each mounted on springs and compensating levers. The front bogie is 7½" long and 3½" wide, and is controlled by two springs that tend to keep it always in line with the main frame. What appears to be a rear bogie in the illustration is actually two separate units, one of which is mounted direct on the main frames by leaf springs and axle-boxes. The other axle unit, placed directly under the cab, is carried on a Bissel truck, constructed from Angle Girders in the form of a "T."

The end of the long arm of the Meccano Bissel truck is attached by a massive pivot to the underside of the locomotive, and the short arm carries bearings for the wheel axle.

There are four cylinders on the model, two inside and two outside, the inner pair representing the high-pressure cylinders and the outer pair the low-pressure cylinders. The outer cylinders are coupled to the centre driving wheels by 9½" Strips that represent the connecting rods, and the valves of these cylinders are operated by Gresley-Walschaerts valve motion. The inner cylinders are connected by 7½" Strips to cranks on the leading driving axle, and the valves for these are operated by links coupled to the outer sets of valve gears. These links are constructed from Double Arm Cranks and 1½" Strips, an arrangement that allows the high pressure steam to be cut off independently of the low-pressure steam. In actual practice the valves are controlled from small levers in the cab operating through telemotors, but in the Meccano model the movement of these levers is transmitted direct to the reversing links by means of rods.

The boiler, which is the most unusual part of the actual engine, presents many difficulties to the model-builder, but in the model shown here most of them have been successfully overcome. The front end is fitted with specially designed smoke deflectors and a sliding door for regulating the air supply to the furnace. The cab is equipped with all the principal fittings found in the original and a small electric light bulb is built into the cab roof.

The tender is a faithful reproduction of the original and the corridor, running down one side, is cleverly built into this section of the model. The eight wheels are all correctly sprung and fitted with brakes; the brake control being situated on the tender platform.

The rear of the tender is fitted with a vacuum pipe connection, buffers and lamp brackets, and a realistic finish is given to the model by painting appropriate letters and numbers on both sides of the locomotive cab and tender.

In the actual tender the wheels are 4¼' in diameter, and as the scale of this model happens to be slightly less than 1" to 1', it was found necessary to use 3" Pulley Wheels. Although these are a little too small the fact is not easily noticeable.

Fig 41: 93/94.

Model No. 95. L.M.S.R. High-Pressure Locomotive "Fury." (K. W. Cameron, Birkenhead).

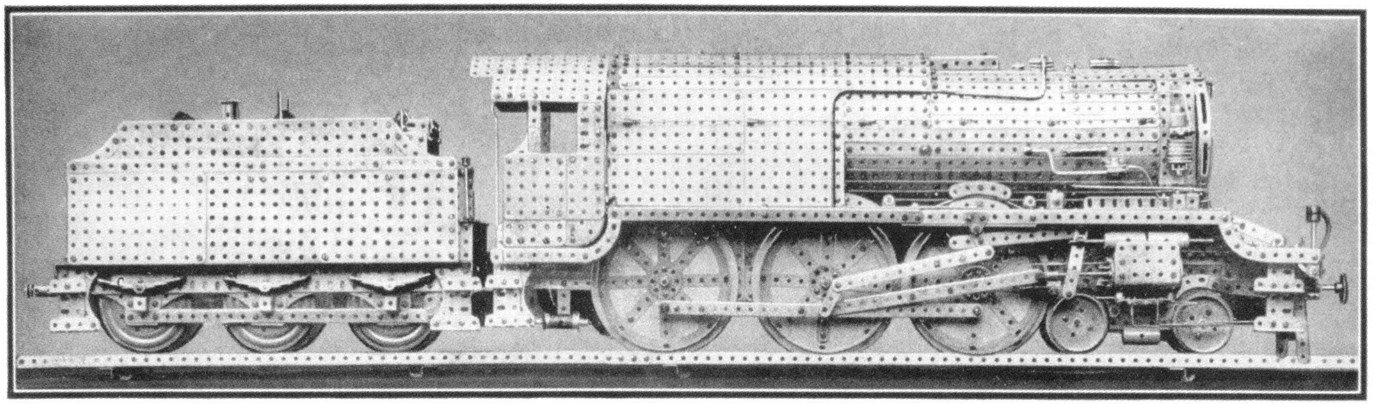

Towards the end of 1929 two experimental locomotives using high-pressure steam were produced in this country. The first of these to appear was the L. N. E. R. "No. 10000," two models of which were described on page 36. This was followed after a short interval by the L.M.S.R. "Fury," the prototype of the fine Meccano model illustrated on this page. It will greatly assist constructors in reproducing the model to know something of the special and unusual methods adopted in building the actual engine. The design follows that of the L.M.S.R. "Royal Scot" class with regard to the frames, but in this case the engine is a three-cylinder compound, the high-pressure cylinder being situated between the frames and the two low-pressure cylinders outside the frames.

The high-pressure boiler consists of three distinct systems or boilers, each carrying a different pressure. The system having the highest pressure—1,400 lb. to 1,800 lb. per sq. in., the variation in pressure depending upon the rate of firing—is in the form of a closed circuit consisting of a number of pipes that form the sides, roof, and back end of the fire-box. These pipes are connected at the bottom to a foundation ring and at the top to equalizing drums, into which they are expanded. From the equalizing drums pipes are led to evaporating elements situated in the high-pressure drum. This closed circuit is initially filled to a pre-determined level with pure water, which is the medium by means of which heat is transmitted trom the fire-box to the evaporating elements in the high-pressure drum. This drum, which furnishes steam at 980 lb. per sq. in. for the high-pressure cylinder of the locomotive, is of nickel steel, but is not in any way in contact with the fire. It is fed by water drawn as required from the low-pressure boiler by means of a pump.

The low-pressure boiler occupies the same position as the barrel of the normal locomotive boiler, and the water is evaporated by the gases passing through the boiler tubes. The barrel of this low-pressure boiler also is of nickel steel, but both tube plates are of mild steel.

The method of working the locomotive is more or less normal. The regulator handle operates both the high-pressure and the low-pressure regulator simultaneously. On opening the regulator steam is admitted into the high-pressure cylinder after passing through the high-pressure superheater situated in the lower boiler tubes. Exhausting from the high-pressure cylinder, the steam enters a mixing chamber, where it is met by low-pressure steam at 250 lb. pressure, which previously has passed through a low-pressure superheater situated in the upper boiler tubes. From the mixing chamber steam enters the two outside cylinders and goes thence to the exhaust.

The "Fury" hauls an L.M.S.R. standard tender, the carrying capacity of which is 5¼ tons of coal and 3,500 gallons of water, and a scoop is fitted for picking up water from troughs between the metals while the engine is in motion. The scoop is pivoted to the underside of the tender, and is lowered as the locomotive approaches the water trough so that it dips into the water. The speed of the engine forces the water up a pipe situated above the scoop, and at the top of the pipe it strikes a dome and is diverted so that it falls into the water tank of the tender. This system works very satisfactorily and enables about 2,000 gallons of water to be picked up in about 30 seconds when the engine is at speed.

The splendid Meccano model shown here is 5¼′ in overall length, and its particularly life-like appearance is largely due to the vast amount of detail that is incorporated.

The boiler is undoubtedly the most difficult portion of the model to construct and it will be seen that it is built in one unit. The cut-away portion of the boiler behind the smoke-box contains a very realistic reproduction of the feed pump that in actual practice feeds the high-pressure steam drum.

The valve gear of the model is similar to that fitted to the Meccano Tank Locomotive (Super Model Instruction Leaflet No. 15). The interior of the cab contains many interesting features, among which are steam gauges and water injectors for both the high and the low-pressure systems. The regulator handle, which works both the high-pressure and low-pressure regulators simultaneously, is of the standard L.M.S.R. pattern and is coupled to the starting and reversing handle of a 6-volt Electric Motor by means of a series of Cranks and Strips. This Motor is used for turning the driving wheels of the locomotive so that it is possible to "drive" the completed engine in a railway-like manner.

The tender fitted to the model is a good reproduction of the original and although no scoop is fitted all the main external features are faithfully represented. The frames are 18½″ long and are fitted with three pairs of wheels formed from Flanged Ball Races. The wheels have realistic leaf springs, and carefully shaped steps at each end give the tender a pleasing appearance. Dummy handles for the brake and for lowering and raising the water scoop are mounted on the platform.

Fig 41: 95. Note the 'lack' of left-hand driving wheels – see text.

Model No. 99. Giant Electric Shovel. (A. Bulot, Calais).

The prototype of this model has the distinction of being the largest shovel in the world. It was fully described and illustrated in the "Meccano Magazine" for December, 1930.

The main platform or base of the model is 12½″ square, each side being constructed in the shape of a massive bow girder. The four girders are secured together in the form of a hollow rectangle, and numerous members consisting of 12½″ Angle Girders are then bolted in place. These cross Girders form supports for the floor of the deck, which is built up from Flat Plates and carries the lower flange of a Roller Bearing.

The base is carried at each corner on two creeper track units, each of which is constructed in the following manner. Two side members are built up in the shape of a narrow triangle, and are secured together by means of three 1½″ × ½″ Double Angle Strips. Each corner of the double triangular frame so formed carries a Rod on which is mounted two ¾″ Contrates, and these three points support a wide canvas belt representing the creeper track. Two of these tracks are mounted on an equalising beam that facilitates travelling over uneven ground. The drive to the four sets of creepers is transmitted through Bevel Gears and Universal Couplings. The front of the base carries a short ladder built up from 5½″ Strips and 1″ Threaded Rods.

The bed of the revolving superstructure is 24½″ in length and 12½″ in width. The long sides are each constructed from two 24½″ Angle Girders joined together by Flat Girders to form a channel section girder, and the two ends are constructed in a similar manner from 12½″ Angle Girders. Flat Plates of various sizes are used for plating the bed, and the whole is bolted to the upper section of the Roller Bearing fixed to the base.

The front section of the "A" frames is built up from four 18½″ Angle Girders braced together by 7½″ Strips, and the two rear frame members are each 24½″ in length and of channel girder section. Suitable bracing members are constructed from 9½″ Angle Girders held in place by 3½″ and 2½″ Strips.

The framework of the motor and gear-box housing is constructed from 7½″, 12½″ and 18½″ Angle Girders, the 7½″ Girders serving as corner posts and the 12½″ Girders as cross members. The 18½″ Angle Girders are used as main horizontal side members and are also needed for the apex of the roof. The complete frame is covered with 5½″ × 2½″ Flat Plates and 5½″ × 3½″ Flat Plates, and two square spaces are left to represent windows and doors.

Two fine examples of Meccano Excavators. (Top) Bucket Dredger as used for excavating surface coal, by P. J. Tombeux. (Bottom) Giant Electric Shovel, by A. Bulot.

The side of the superstructure shown in the photograph carries the control platform, on which is a lever frame fitted with five levers, each controlling one of the five movements of the model. This platform and the base on which it is mounted are surrounded by a neat handrail built up from Threaded Pins, Couplings, and long Rods.

The jib is 46″ in length, and the four compound girders used in its construction are braced together by 2½″ Strips and lengths of Meccano Cord. The digger arm is built up from four 24½″ Angle Girders, and the construction of the bucket, which is a very fine replica of the original, is shown clearly in the illustration.

The racking movement for the bucket arm is driven through Universal Couplings from the main shaft of the gear-box, and is carried out by a 3½″ Rod carrying two ½″ Pinions that mesh with Rack Strips secured to the bucket arm.

Fig 41: 99.

Fig 42. The No. 10 outfit manual model of a 6-wheel lorry bearing more than a passing resemblance to the prize-winning model by K. W. Ingram (see fig 41: 61).

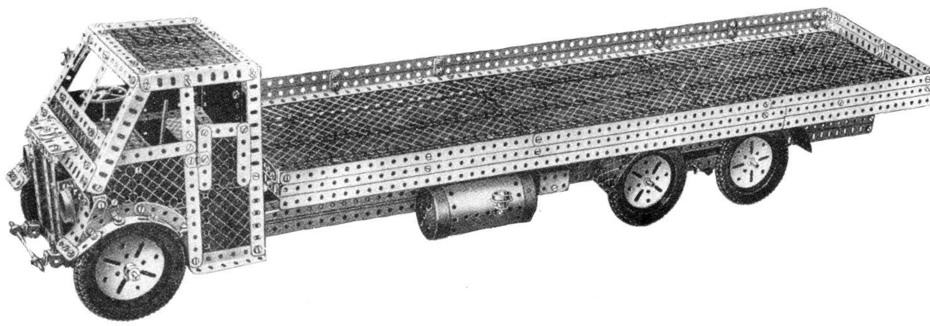

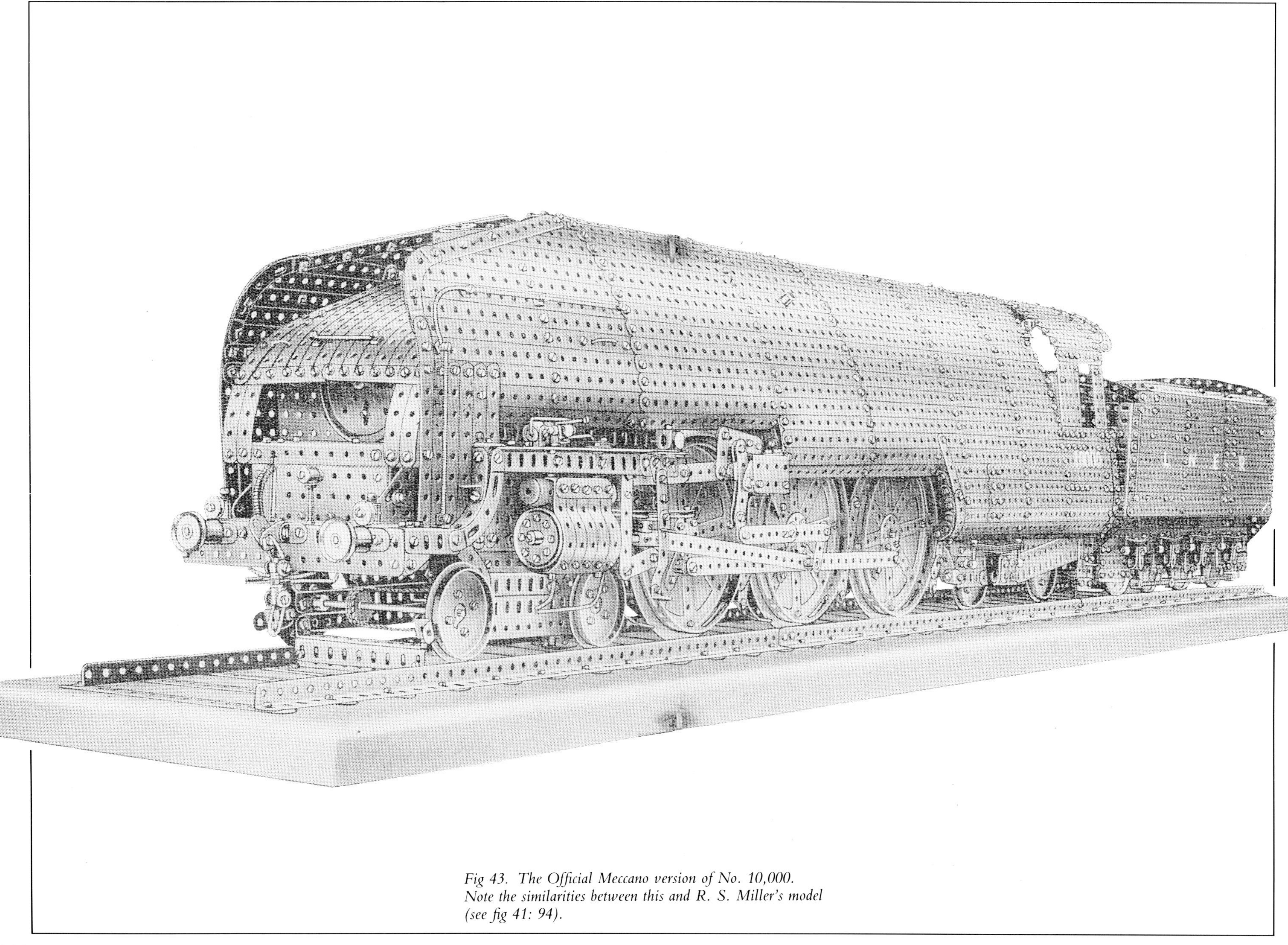

Fig 43. The Official Meccano version of No. 10,000. Note the similarities between this and R. S. Miller's model (see fig 41: 94).

ally. The photographer recommended a black background as being better for a model in nickel parts, and the original photos looked very good. But Meccano didn't like black as a background, especially for advertisements, so the touch-up artist went to work. Unfortunately in touching up the frontal view obliterated the left driving wheels!" Dr Cameron has been delighting modellers for some 60 years now and must be regarded as being the senior member of a small group of superstars whose modelling exploits are legendary.

After such a supreme effort, no 'book' was published in 1933. It was not until the following year it returned with a Book of Engineering type cover in somewhat surrealistic colours which nonetheless is most attractive (fig 44). The contents (compared with 1932) were a bit of a disappointment, reverting to the 1928–31 style with large numbers of simple models; only the Swiss Embroidery Machine (fig 45) and the Front-Wheel Drive Motor Chassis (fig 46) made it worthwhile for the more advanced builder. As before it was the mechanisms which proved to be the most interesting and a number of these such as the Hobbs Inertia Gear and the Spontan Transmission Gear found their way into Standard Mechanisms (see chapter 6). These were very advanced movements and could have been set alongside the models in the 1932 edition. It was a pity that the opportunity to build upon that standard was not taken.

At least the four pages of prize-winning models which completed the 1934 Book were to the standard of the earlier edition. Two particularly fine ones (figs 47–48) were a very nicely proportioned 4–6–4 tank engine and a locomotive coaling plant by J. Willems who was another advanced modeller of the time.

Fig 44. The somewhat surreal cover of the 1934 edition.

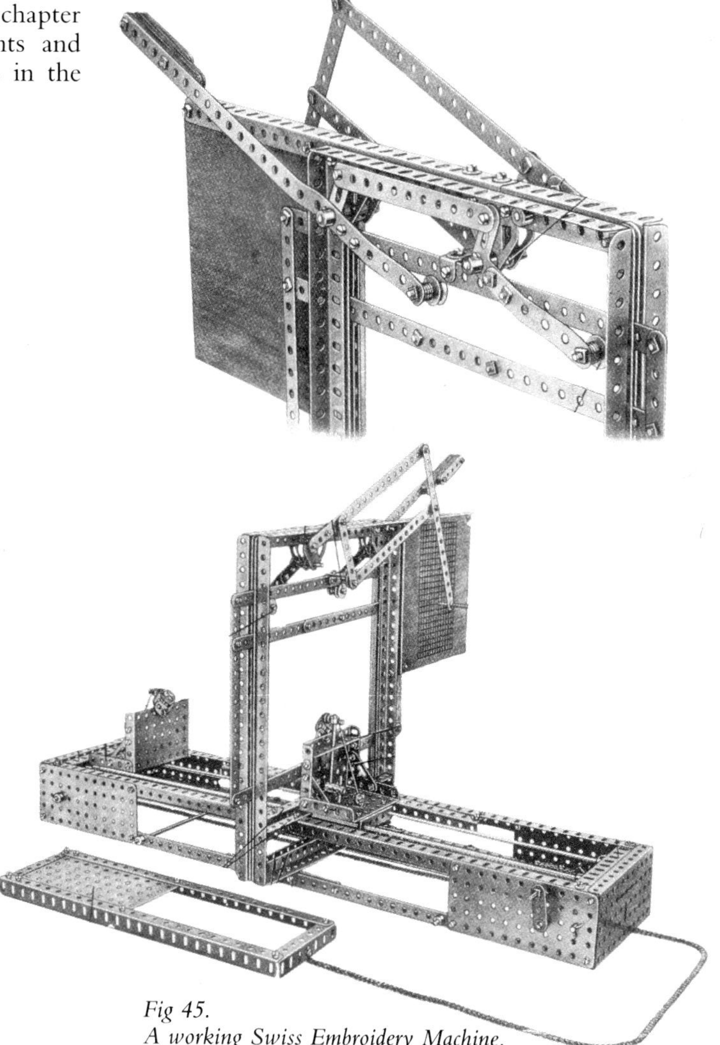

Fig 45.
A working Swiss Embroidery Machine.

Model No. 58. Front Wheel Drive Motor Chassis

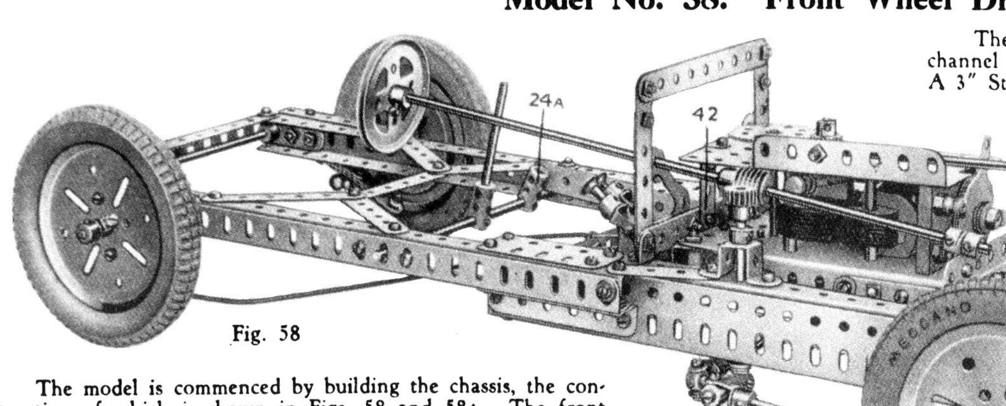

Fig. 58

The model is commenced by building the chassis, the construction of which is shown in Figs. 58 and 58A. The front springs are constructed in the following manner. There are four three-leaf springs of the quarter elliptic type on each side of the chassis, each consisting of one 2" Strip, one 1½" Strip, and one Flat Bracket bolted at one end of the chassis. The other ends of the springs terminate in Hinges attached to the frame 1, which consists of two 1½" × ½" Double Angle Strips and two 1½" Strips, the Strips being spaced away from the ends of the Double Angle Strips by Washers.

A "spider" is fixed by Set Screws to each end of a Double Arm Crank 2, the lower spider being packed out from the Crank by two Washers, while the upper one is fitted flush against the Crank. The Double Arm Crank is retained in the frame by means of a 1" Rod and a Threaded Pin inserted in the upper and lower spiders respectively, and secured in the spiders by Grub Screws. Four Washers serve to space the upper spider, and one Washer the lower spider, from the frame.

The universal-coupling drive to each of the front wheels consists of a 1" Threaded Rod 6 that forms the stub axle, to which two ½" × ½" Angle Brackets are attached by lock-nuts. The slotted portions of the Brackets must be parallel to one another, and the whole unit must be fixed very rigidly to the Rod. The arms of the Angle Brackets are bent slightly toward one another. The end of a 2" Rod 5 carries a Collar that is mounted loosely between the Angle Brackets by passing Set Screws through the slotted holes and screwing them into the tapped holes of the Collar, until the Rod 5 is nipped by them. The stub axle is inserted in the boss of the Double Arm Crank 2, and the road wheel is then secured to its end by duplicate Set Screws. It will be found that the centre of the universal coupling is practically coincident with the centre line of the pivot pin, and that the latter, if produced, would fall within ¼" of the centre of the wheel track.

A Crank 3 is fixed rigidly to the end of each 1" Rod pivot as shown in Fig. 58A, and a 5" Rod acts as a drag link by connecting the Crank to a Swivel Bearing 4 mounted on a ½" Bolt held in the end bore of a Coupling. The Coupling is secured to a Rod journalled in the chassis girders and carrying at its upper end a ½" Pinion. This Pinion will mesh eventually with a Worm on the steering column. A 1" Rod 4a is fixed in the centre transverse bore of the Coupling, and this is attached to the track rod by a Swivel Bearing.

The rear wheel suspension and the brakes are shown in detail in Fig. 58B. The spring 38 is of the cantilever type, and it consists of one 3½", one 3", one 2½" and one 2" Strip, all bolted together at one end to a 1½" Angle Girder 39 fixed to the chassis. The stub axle is held in the boss of a Crank bolted on the inside of a pivot arm 37, the two parts being separated the space of one Washer.

The pivot arm consists of two 3" Angle Girders bolted together in the form of a channel section, and mounted freely at one end on a Rod that passes through the chassis. A 3" Strip is bolted over the slotted holes of one of the Girders to provide a bearing for the pivot. The arm is connected to the spring by means of a Flat Bracket 40, which is attached pivotally by a lock-nutted Bolt to a ½"×½" Angle Bracket on the spring. The other end of the arm is inserted in the space between the Crank holding the stub axle and the pivot arm; the stub axle passes through the hole in the Flat Bracket.

The brake is of the internal expanding type, and consists of two 2" Strips mounted together at one end on a Bolt lock-nutted in the centre hole of a 1½" Strip. The end hole of the 1½" Strip is attached pivotally to the arm 37 and the other end is fitted with a Handrail Support. The 2" Strips, carrying the Collars that form the brake shoes, ride in the groove of a 1" fast Pulley 36 that is loose on the stub axle, and the strips are retained in the groove by a short length of Spring Cord fitted as shown in Fig. 58B. By moving the 1½" Strip to the left, the 2" Strips are forced apart, and consequently the Collars are pushed against the rim of a Wheel Flange forming the brake drum, which is bolted to the road wheel.

The 6-volt Motor, gear-box, clutch, differential, and front brakes, shown in Fig. 58C. all form part of a compact unit. Each of the gear-box side plates consists of a 4½" Flat Girder, that on the far side of the Motor being bolted to the flange of the Motor by its slotted holes. The plate on the near side is attached to a 4½" Angle Girder spaced away from the Motor side plates by three 2" Strips.

The Rod 8 is journalled in three bearings, a 2½" Flat Girder 33a, a 2½" × 1" Double Angle Strip 8a, and a 2½" Strip 7. The Double Angle Strip 8a is bolted to the side plates of the gear-box and it carries a Flat Trunnion in the top hole of which one end of the layshaft is journalled. The Strip 7 is one of two that are attached to the gear-box sides by means of ½" × ½" Angle Brackets. The Rod 15 runs in the second of the Strips 7, and also in another 2½"× 1" Double Angle Strip, which carries a Flat Trunnion that provides a bearing for the other end of the layshaft. Two Washers are placed under the heads of each of the Bolts retaining the Trunnion in place, so that the shanks of the Bolts do not foul the face of the 1" Gear 20. It is very important that all the bearings should be in alignment, especially those of the Rod 8, for as there are three bearings, alignment has to be carefully carried out if the Rod is to run easily.

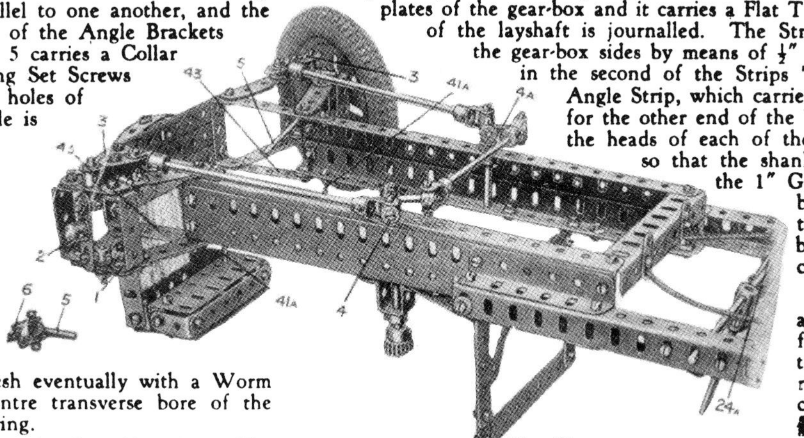

The clutch is of the single plate type and consists of a 1½" Contrate Wheel 9 free on the Rod 8, which is driven from the Motor armature spindle through a reduction gear of 3 : 1. The floating plate consists of a ½" loose Pulley fitted with a ⅜" Rubber Ring, and is pressed against the face of the Contrate Wheel by a ¾" Flanged Wheel mounted in a Socket Coupling, which represents the withdrawal plate. A Collar 10 is fixed to the Rod in such a manner that its Grub Screw is always in engagement with the slot of the Socket Coupling, thus permitting limited longitudinal movement to the unit and at the same time

Fig. 58A

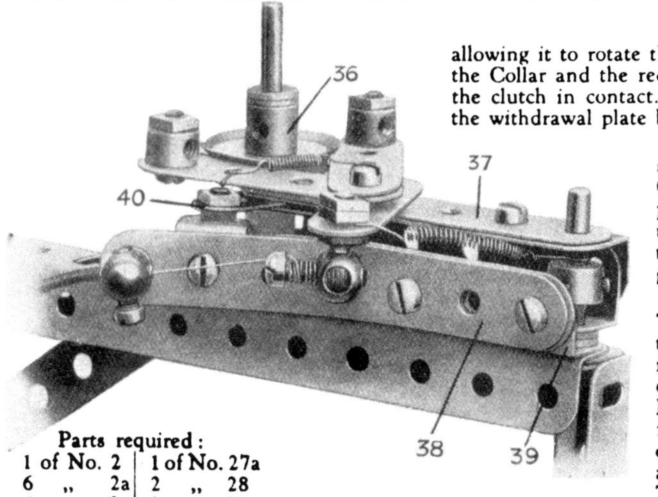

allowing it to rotate the Rod. Half of a Compression Spring is placed between the Collar and the recess in the Socket Coupling in order to keep the parts of the clutch in contact. The Contrate 9 is prevented from moving away from the withdrawal plate by a Collar secured on the Rod.

The clutch withdrawal mechanism consists of a Rod sliding in suitable bearings and carrying at one end a Coupling to which is attached a 2" Strip. This Strip pivots on the end of a Rod 33 and its upper end is joined to the clutch pedal proper 12. A Coupling 11 fixed to the Rod supports two short Rods that engage with the groove of the Socket Coupling.

Details of the differential can be seen in Fig. 58c. Two ¾" Contrate Wheels 26 are secured on the ends of two separate Rods, the outer ends of which are journalled in the ends of the gear-box side plates, and the inner ends in the longitudinal bore of a Coupling. The ¾" Pinions 27 mesh with the Contrates, and are mounted freely on Pivot Bolts inserted in the centre tapped holes of the Coupling, and screwed home sufficiently to grip a Rod in the centre transverse hole of the Coupling. This Rod carries, at each end, Collars 28 in which are inserted 1" Screwed Rods. A 1½" Contrate, free to revolve on its Rod, is locked to the Screwed Rods, and is spaced from the adjacent ¾" Contrate by two Washers.

Owing to the vertical movement of the back wheels, the brake control wire must pass through an outer flexible sheath, on the Bowden cable principle. This sheath is composed of Spring Cord, and the manner of attaching it should be clear on reference to Figs. 58A and 58B. A stop consisting of a ⅜" Bolt inserted in a Collar comes in contact with a fixed Bolt shank in order to limit the movement of the brake pedal shaft 33.

The gear change lever is carried on a cross shaft that is journalled in the chassis girders, and is prevented from free rotation by means of a Spring Clip mounted on the Rod so that its lugs press against a ½" × ½" Angle Bracket bolted to the inside of the chassis girder. The Coupling 24a on the cross shaft is connected by means of a Strip to a 2" Strip 24 pivoted on the side of the gear-box. The upper end of this Strip has a Rod attached to it by a Crank, and the Rod locates between the boss of the Gear 23 and a Collar on the layshaft, so that when the gear lever is moved the layshaft slides longitudinally in its bearings.

Parts required:

1 of No. 2	1 of No. 27a				
6 ,, 2a	2 ,, 28				
4 ,, 3	2 ,, 29				
16 ,, 4	4 ,, 31				
6 ,, 5	1 ,, 32				
23 ,, 6	1 ,, 35				
20 ,, 6a	145 ,, 37				
4 ,, 8	32 ,, 37a				
4 ,, 8a	80 ,, 38				
3 ,, 9a	1 ,, 45				
6 ,, 9c	3 ,, 46				
2 ,, 9d	6 ,, 48				
2 ,, 9f	1 ,, 58				
17 ,, 10	32 ,, 59				
3 ,, 11	8 ,, 62				
19 ,, 12	2 ,, 62b				
2 ,, 12b	7 ,, 63				
1 ,, 13	1 ,, 72				
1 ,, 13a	2 ,, 77				
1 ,, 14	4 ,, 82				
3 ,, 15	3 ,, 89a				
1 ,, 15a	2 ,, 103a				
3 ,, 16	2 ,, 103c				
3 ,, 16a	2 ,, 103e				
3 ,, 16b	1 ,, 103f				
3 ,, 17	2 ,, 108				
8 ,, 18a	1 ,, 111				
4 ,, 18b	6 ,, 111a				
4 ,, 19b	16 ,, 111c				
1 ,, 19s	8 ,, 114				
2 ,, 20	2 ,, 115				
1 ,, 20a	3 ,, 120a				
1 ,, 20b	2 ,, 126a				
2 ,, 22	7 ,, 136				
1 ,, 23	2 ,, 137				
4 ,, 23a	4 ,, 142b				
4 ,, 25	2 ,, 147b				
5 ,, 26	1 ,, 155	2 of No. 166	1 6-volt		
2 ,, 27	8 ,, 165	1 ,, 171	Motor		

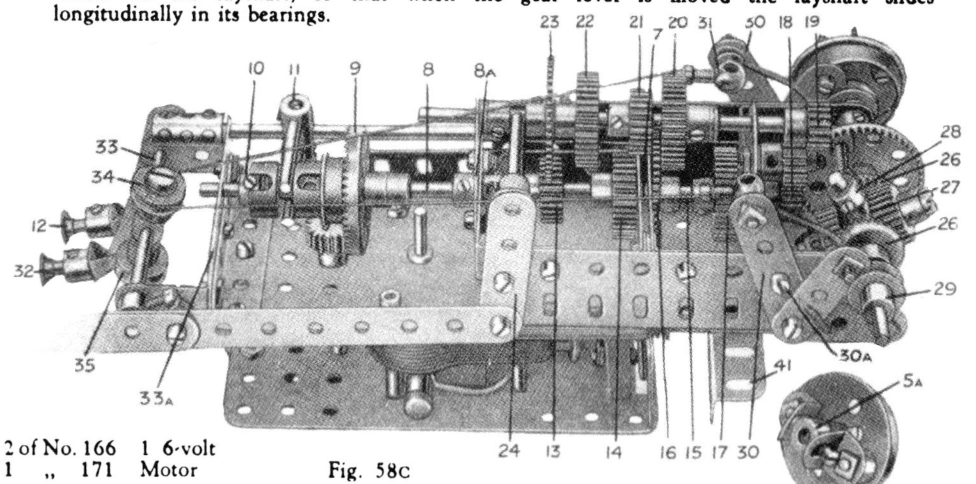

Fig. 58c

Figs 46a–b. An excellent 4-wheel drive motor chassis.

The 1934 Book of New Models was the last of that particular series. Looking at the steadily declining print runs it is easy to see why the decision was taken not to continue. Costs must have been very high and sales eventually disappointing.

Although the Books of New and Prize Models are somewhat variable there is enough in each one for them to rank as important items of Meccano literature. 1932 was exceptional and is the gem in the collection but none should be dismissed. For us they are rare and desirable pieces and no Meccano literature collection would be complete without at least one example. For the contemporary modeller they were either a useful way to get up-to-date, especially with the mechanisms, or a convenient way of collecting some of the best of the *MM*'s Meccano features in one place.

Print Data

All from the 1928–1932 series had comparatively short runs because they were soon out of date. For this reason they are all rather scarce today and strangely enough far rarer than the much earlier 1914–1915 Prize Model Book which is relatively common. U.S. versions of the earlier series did appear although not it seems of the later 1928–34 Books.

The following are the print references of editions so far discovered:

1914/15	NR
1915/16	NR
1928	228/20 (with date on front cover)
1928	328/10 (without date on cover)*
1929	229/20 (2 versions – with and without date on cover but under the same print reference.)
1930	2/230/20
1931	13/231/20
1932	7/632/15
1934	7/434/10

*See also text.

Fig 48. Two fine models which won prizes and were illustrated in the 1934 Book of New Models.

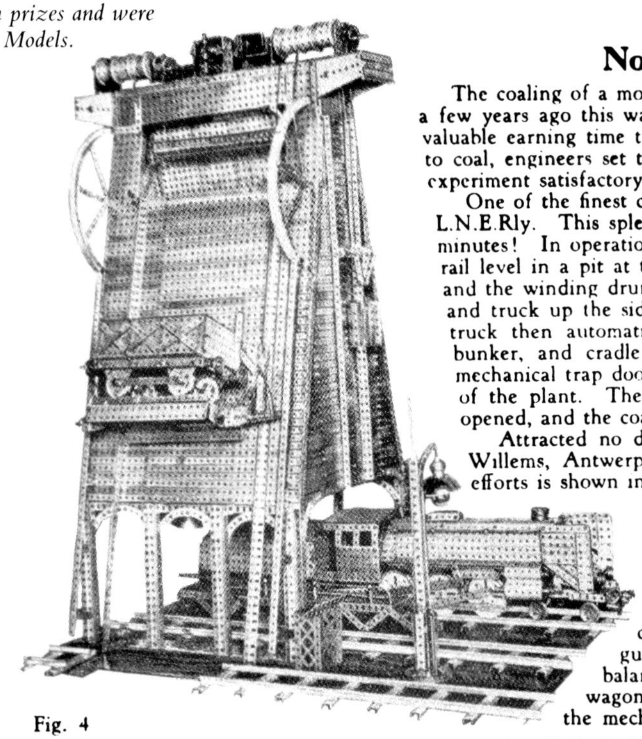

No. 4. Locomotive Coaling Plant

The coaling of a modern railway engine involves a tremendous amount of work, and until a few years ago this was nearly all done by manual labour. In order to avoid the waste of valuable earning time that occurred when engines were held up for hours waiting their turn to coal, engineers set to work to devise some mechanical means of coaling, and after much experiment satisfactory machines were produced.

One of the finest coaling plants now working in this country is that at Doncaster on the L.N.E.Rly. This splendid installation is capable of coaling the "*Flying Scotsman*" in three minutes! In operation, the loaded coal trucks are run one at a time on to a cradle lying at rail level in a pit at the bottom of an inclined elevator. The truck is secured in position, and the winding drums at the top of the tower are then set in motion and hoist the cradle and truck up the side of the tower until it reaches a hopper opening near the top. The truck then automatically cants over, its contents are tipped into a hopper or storage bunker, and cradle and truck then descend to rail level. The hopper is fitted with mechanical trap doors, controlled from a central switchboard installed in a hut at the base of the plant. The engine to be fuelled is run beneath the hopper, the trap doors are opened, and the coal falls into the engine tender.

Attracted no doubt by the mechanical perfection and massiveness of this plant, J. Willems, Antwerp, decided to build a model of it in Meccano, and the result of his efforts is shown in Fig. 4. The model is a very close copy of the original in practically every detail, but the power house, which is an imposing feature of the actual machine, has been removed to expose the winding drums.

All the operations of the actual plant are carried out faithfully in the model. The motive power for the hoisting drums is an Electric Motor mounted on the top of the tower, and the drive is transmitted to the drums through suitable reduction gearing. The wagon cradle is hoisted by cords, and is balanced by weights running on guide rails up the sides of the tower. In the actual machine the balance weights compensate for the weight of the cradle and wagon and half the load, and they form a very important part of the mechanism.

Fig. 4

No. 5. A Realistic Model 4—6—4 Tank Locomotive

Fig. 5 shows a model of a "Baltic" type tank locomotive by Mr. S. Croft-Grey, Edinburgh. A glance at the illustration will reveal several constructional details that should be helpful to model-builders interested in this kind of work.

One of the many good points of the model is to be found in the construction of the cylinders, of which there are four, one pair being mounted slightly in advance of the other. The model is driven by a 6-volt Electric Motor carried in the tender, and the drive is transmitted through a three-speed gear-box and connecting rods to a built-up crankshaft, on which the driving wheels are mounted. A gear-box is not included, of course, in the equipment of an actual steam-driven locomotive, but it is very useful in a model of this kind, as it enables considerable loads to be hauled while allowing the speed of the Motor to be kept as high as possible.

The model is fitted with Walschaerts' valve gear, which, in conjunction with the handrails, steps, buffers and vacuum pipes, makes the model look very realistic and workmanlike. The brake shoes are 1" Triangular Plates, and the brakes are applied and withdrawn by means of Rods operated from the cab.

The chassis of the model is made almost entirely of Angle Girders, braced by further Angle Girders and filled in at the front with Plates. The boiler consists of a number of Strips bolted round Hub Discs and held in place on the chassis by means of Screwed Rods. The bogies, each of which is fitted with four wheels, are fully articulated, which means that they are free to move vertically as well as horizontally. Flat Plates are used throughout in the construction of the water tanks, cab and coal bunker, and owing to the care with which they are placed together they look very neat and contribute greatly to the fine appearance of the model.

Fig. 5

A Late Splutter

Soon after the introduction of the Blue/Gold numerical series of outfits for the 1937–38 season a number of slim leaflets were issued in 1939 with the titles 'More New Models'. These were normally designated as being for certain outfits such as 0–3, 4–6 and 7–10 (fig 49). The 0–3 consisted of 3 sides, only two of which were for new models, the third being little more than a promotion of the newly introduced EO6 and EO20 electric motors (fig 50).

The 7–10 was naturally the best of them and included the most attractive Mobile Workshop (fig 51) which eventually replaced the Modern House in the 9–10 outfit manuals.

These leaflets had an understandably short life ending with the updating of the relevant manuals. Known print references are listed below:-

Outfits 0–3	13/539/170(IP)
Outfits 4–6	13/539/55
Outfits 7–10	13/739/5

At various times after the war, odd leaflets (including nine 'More New Models' leaflets of the 1960s) did appear with nominally the same aim as those of 1939. However almost without exception they are of little if any interest today.

That the 1928–1934 series of Books of New and Prize Models were an unnecessary luxury is hard to deny or disprove. Let us give thanks for such follies – our world and in particular this book would be the poorer without them.

MECCANO
MORE NEW MODELS
MECCANO is the greatest hobby in the world because it provides never-ending interest, fun and excitement. There is nothing to be compared with the joy and satisfaction of creating something new, and inventing new models in Meccano is a pastime that grows continually in fascination.
This Manual illustrates twelve splendid new models that can be built with Meccano. The building of these models will give you lots of fun, and as you build you will get ideas for models of your own invention. The possibilities of Meccano are endless !
7-10

Fig 49.
Cover of the 1939 More New Models.

Examples of Models fitted with the MECCANO Nos. EO6 and EO20 Electric Motors

CIRCULAR SAW (Outfit No. 2)

The saw is represented by a Road Wheel fastened on a 3½" Rod journalled in the 5½" × 2½" Flanged Plate. This Rod carries a 1" Pulley 1 connected by a Driving Band to the Motor pulley.

The 1" Pulley 2 is fixed to a 2½" Strip bolted to the Flanged Plate and an Angle Bracket held by Bolt 3.

Parts required

4	of No.	2
6	,, ,,	5
6	,, ,,	12
1	,, ,,	16
3	,, ,,	22
37	,, ,,	37
1	,, ,,	37a
2	,, ,,	38
2	,, ,,	48a
1	,, ,,	52
2	,, ,,	90a
3	,, ,,	111c
1	,, ,,	125
2	,, ,,	126
2	,, ,,	126a
1	,, ,,	186b
1	,, ,,	187
2	,, ,,	188
2	,, ,,	189
2	,, ,,	190
1	,, ,,	191
1	,, ,,	199
2	,, ,,	200

1 EO6 or EO20 Electric Motor

MECCANO ELECTRIC MOTORS Nos. EO6 and EO20

The Nos. EO6 and EO20 Meccano Electric Motors are realistic models of the all-enclosed type of motor used in actual engineering. The No. EO6 (6-volt) Motor can be run from A.C. mains through a Meccano T6, T6A or T6M Transformer, or from a 6-volt accumulator. The No. EO20 (20-volt) Motor is operated from A.C. mains through a Meccano T20, T20A or T20M Transformer. The Motors are non-reversing.

CABIN MONOPLANE (Outfit No. 3)

The trailing edge of each wing is formed by a 2½" × 1½" Flexible Plate, which is fastened at the rear of Flexible Plate 1, and a 5½" Strip. The Strip is secured at one end to the 2½" × 1½" Flexible Plate, and its other end is held by Bolt 2. The Motor is mounted on two Flat Brackets that are bolted to a 2½" × ½" Double Angle Strip fastened between the sides of the fuselage.

Parts required

2	of No.	1	2	of No	38	2	of No.	190
6	,, ,,	2	1	,, ,,	44	2	,, ,,	191
9	,, ,,	5	2	,, ,,	48a	2	,, ,,	192
4	,, ,,	10	4	,, ,,	90a	2	,, ,,	199
3	,, ,,	12	6	,, ,,	111c	2	,, ,,	200
1	,, ,,	15b	2	,, ,,	126	2	,, ,,	214
2	,, ,,	22	2	,, ,,	126a	3	,, ,,	215
1	,, ,,	24	2	,, ,,	187	2	,, ,,	217a
48	,, ,,	37	2	,, ,,	188	1 EO6 or EO20		
6	,, ,,	37a	2	,, ,,	189	Electric Motor		

DRAGLINE (Outfit No. 5)

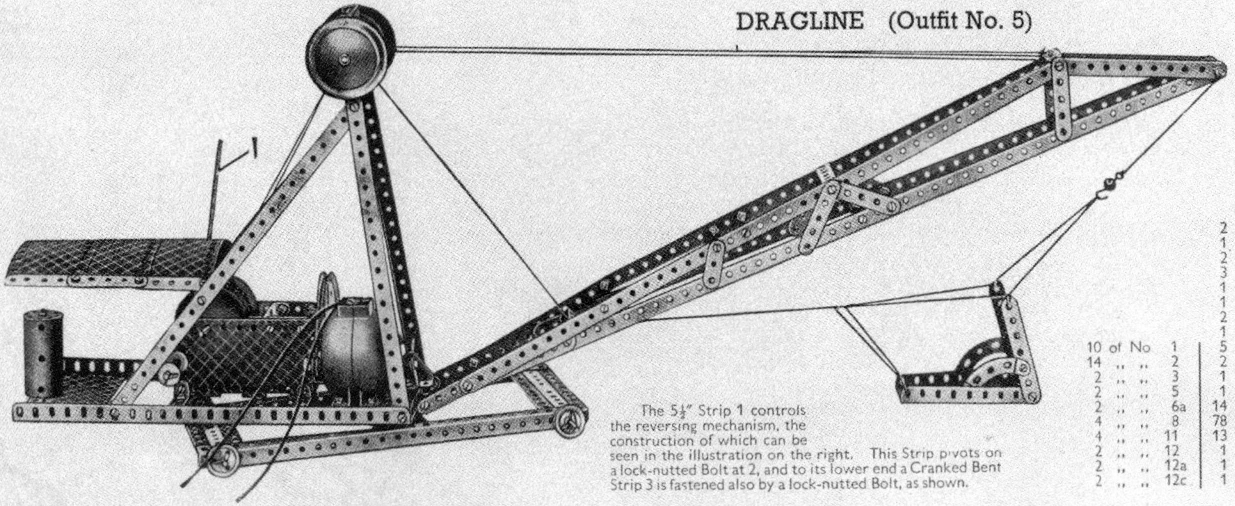

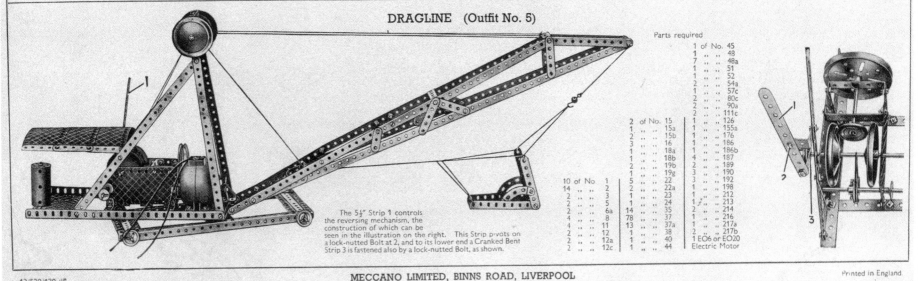

The 5½" Strip 1 controls the reversing mechanism, the construction of which can be seen in the illustration on the right. This Strip pivots on a lock-nutted Bolt at 2, and to its lower end a Cranked Bent Strip 3 is fastened also by a lock-nutted Bolt, as shown.

Parts required

						1	of No.	45
						1	,, ,,	48
						7	,, ,,	48a
						1	,, ,,	51
						1	,, ,,	52
						2	,, ,,	54a
						1	,, ,,	57c
						2	,, ,,	80c
						2	,, ,,	90a
						2	,, ,,	111c
			2	of No.	15	1	,, ,,	126
			1	,, ,,	15a	1	,, ,,	155a
			2	,, ,,	15b	1	,, ,,	176
			3	,, ,,	16	1	,, ,,	186
			1	,, ,,	18a	1	,, ,,	186b
			1	,, ,,	18b	4	,, ,,	187
			2	,, ,,	19b	2	,, ,,	189
			1	,, ,,	19g	3	,, ,,	190
10	of No	1	5	,, ,,	22	3	,, ,,	192
14	,, ,,	2	2	,, ,,	22a	1	,, ,,	198
2	,, ,,	3	1	,, ,,	23	1	,, ,,	212
2	,, ,,	5	1	,, ,,	24	1	,, ,,	213
2	,, ,,	6a	14	,, ,,	35	2	,, ,,	214
4	,, ,,	8	78	,, ,,	37	1	,, ,,	216
4	,, ,,	11	13	,, ,,	37a	1	,, ,,	217a
2	,, ,,	12	1	,, ,,	38	2	,, ,,	217b
2	,, ,,	12a	1	,, ,,	40	1 EO6 or EO20		
2	,, ,,	12c	1	,, ,,	44	Electric Motor		

13/539/170 (IF.

MECCANO LIMITED, BINNS ROAD, LIVERPOOL

Printed in England.

Fig 50. Back page of the 0–3 More New Models – little more than an advertisement for the new EO6 and EO20 motors.

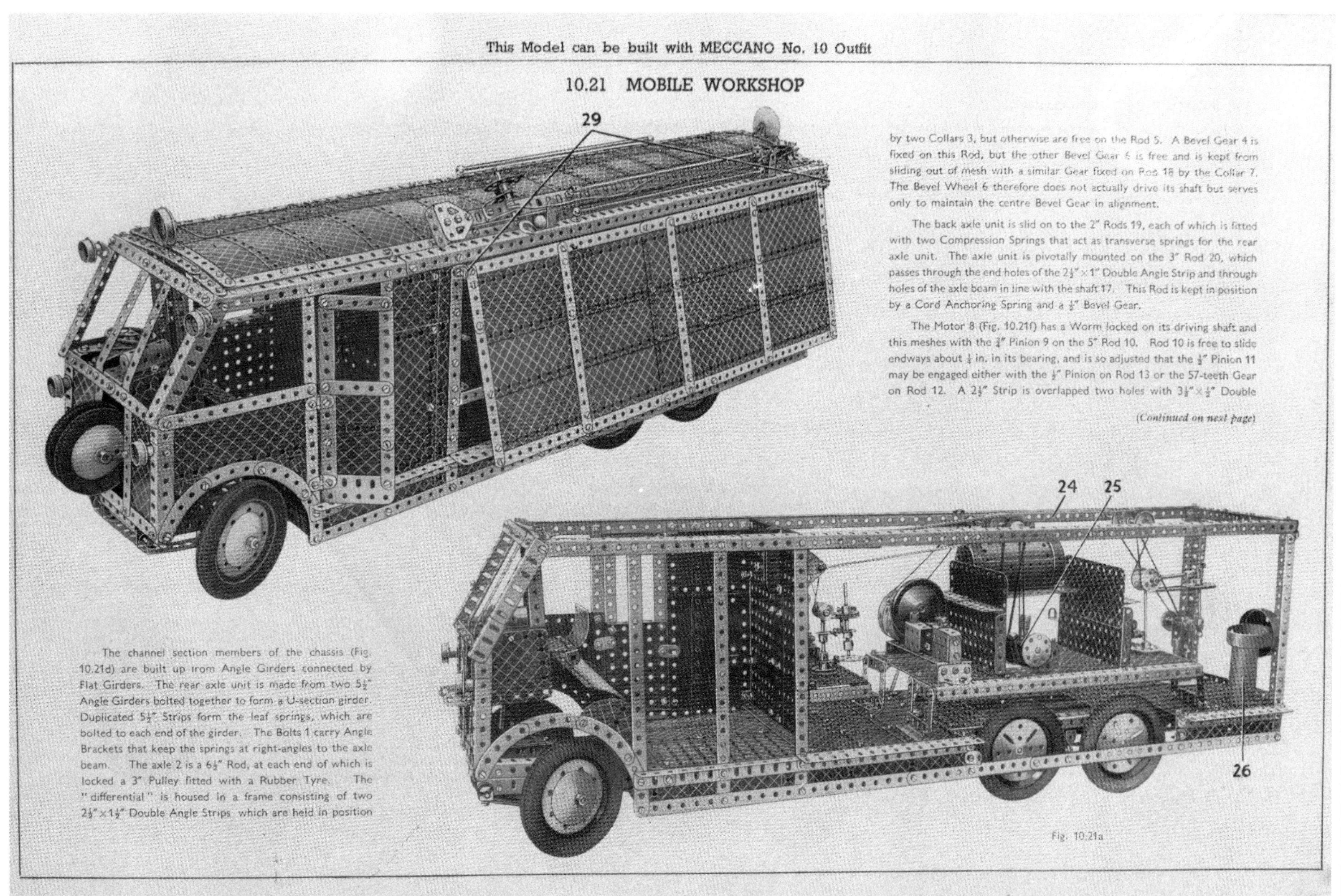

This Model can be built with MECCANO No. 10 Outfit

10.21 MOBILE WORKSHOP

The channel section members of the chassis (Fig. 10.21d) are built up from Angle Girders connected by Flat Girders. The rear axle unit is made from two 5½" Angle Girders bolted together to form a U-section girder. Duplicated 5½" Strips form the leaf springs, which are bolted to each end of the girder. The Bolts 1 carry Angle Brackets that keep the springs at right-angles to the axle beam. The axle 2 is a 6½" Rod, at each end of which is locked a 3" Pulley fitted with a Rubber Tyre. The "differential" is housed in a frame consisting of two 2½"×1½" Double Angle Strips which are held in position by two Collars 3, but otherwise are free on the Rod 5. A Bevel Gear 4 is fixed on this Rod, but the other Bevel Gear 6 is free and is kept from sliding out of mesh with a similar Gear fixed on Rod 18 by the Collar 7. The Bevel Wheel 6 therefore does not actually drive its shaft but serves only to maintain the centre Bevel Gear in alignment.

The back axle unit is slid on to the 2" Rods 19, each of which is fitted with two Compression Springs that act as transverse springs for the rear axle unit. The axle unit is pivotally mounted on the 3" Rod 20, which passes through the end holes of the 2½"×1" Double Angle Strip and through holes of the axle beam in line with the shaft 17. This Rod is kept in position by a Cord Anchoring Spring and a ½" Bevel Gear.

The Motor 8 (Fig. 10.21f) has a Worm locked on its driving shaft and this meshes with the ¾" Pinion 9 on the 5" Rod 10. Rod 10 is free to slide endways about ¼ in. in its bearing, and is so adjusted that the ½" Pinion 11 may be engaged either with the ½" Pinion on Rod 13 or the 57-teeth Gear on Rod 12. A 2½" Strip is overlapped two holes with 3½"×½" Double

(Continued on next page)

Fig. 10.21a

Fig 51. An attractive model from the 1939 More New Models for Outfits 7–10.

The Engineering Manuals

One of the things which set Meccano apart from other construction systems was the regard which Hornby and the Company had for the concept of 'Engineering for Boys'. Meccano was not just a toy, it was and is far more than that. To encourage this idea, Meccano produced a number of publications in the 1920s and 1930s including *The Meccano Book of Engineering* (reproduced in full in Volume 2), The Meccano Engineer's Pocket Book (fig 0A & 0B) and, most importantly, two special manuals which went far beyond the scope and range of the ordinary outfit manuals . . . Meccano Standard Mechanisms and How to Use Meccano Parts. Both of these have a particularly important place in the history of the system and are therefore covered in some depth.

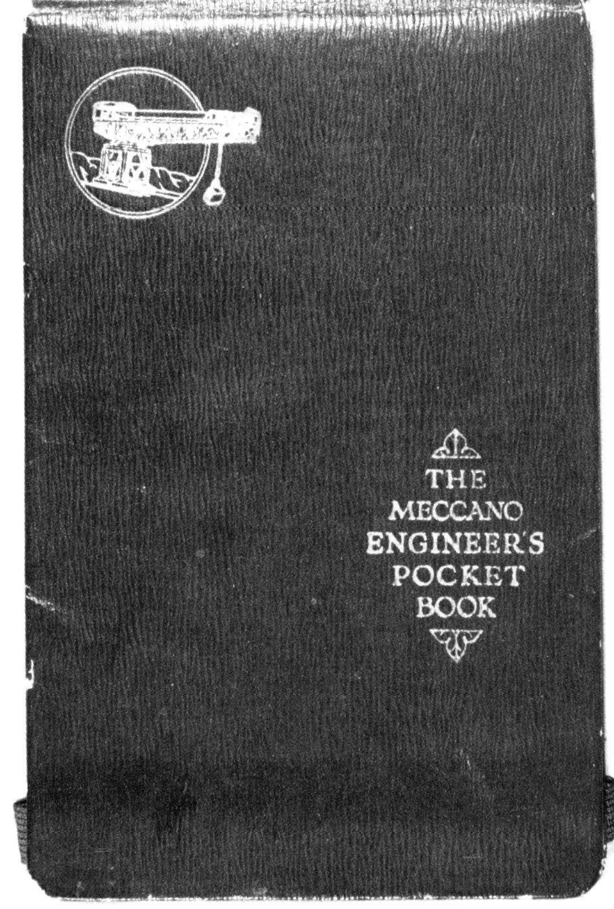

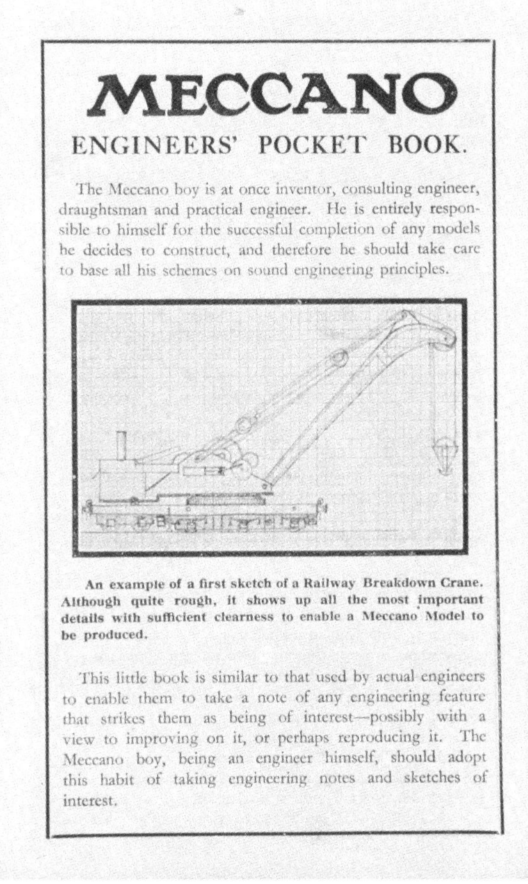

MECCANO

ENGINEERS' POCKET BOOK.

The Meccano boy is at once inventor, consulting engineer, draughtsman and practical engineer. He is entirely responsible to himself for the successful completion of any models he decides to construct, and therefore he should take care to base all his schemes on sound engineering principles.

An example of a first sketch of a Railway Breakdown Crane. Although quite rough, it shows up all the most important details with sufficient clearness to enable a Meccano Model to be produced.

This little book is similar to that used by actual engineers to enable them to take a note of any engineering feature that strikes them as being of interest—possibly with a view to improving on it, or perhaps reproducing it. The Meccano boy, being an engineer himself, should adopt this habit of taking engineering notes and sketches of interest.

Fig 0A & 0B. The Meccano Engineer's Pocket Book.

Standard Mechanisms

A cursory glance through the *Meccano Magazine* of the 1920s will demonstrate to even the most disinterested observer that Meccano models had greatly increased in both complexity and mechanical sophistication during those years. The dawn of 'Super' modelling had already broken with the coming of the series of Special Model Leaflets which comprised the Motor Chassis, Grandfather Clock, Loom and Ship Coaler. These leaflets, issued during the first half of the decade (and also featured in the *Meccano Magazine*), represented a considerable step forward and were undoubtedly a spur to modellers both amateur and professional to produce efforts of equal or greater merit. The history of the leaflets themselves is dealt with in Chapter 4 and is of course referred to in Volume 2 of The Hornby Companion Series. Suffice it to say that their appearance, which roughly coincided with the introduction and development of the No. 7 Outfit, showed the way ahead.

To help modellers build on the success of the leaflets, in 1925 Meccano embarked on what can only be described as a training programme run through the pages of the *Meccano Magazine*. For the first time basic mechanical and engineering 'building blocks' were to be properly documented with reference to their uses in Meccano. The result was to become a work of reference covering a wide variety of simple and more complex mechanical movements without which further sophistication in modelling would be impossible. The title was 'Meccano Standard Mechanisms'.

continued p. 179.

560 THE MECCANO MAGAZINE

MECCANO STANDARD MECHANISMS

GEAR RATIOS AND BELT AND ROPE MECHANISM

No Meccano boy is content to build only the models illustrated in the Meccano Manuals, for every boy who thinks is keen on inventing and likes to build models from his own ideas. With this in mind, and to assist boys to embody correct engineering practices in their new models, we have collected and classified a number of Meccano movements that have to a certain extent become standardised. That is to say, these movements may be applied to more than one model—in most cases without any alteration, but in some few cases with only slight alterations to the standard movement. A selection will be illustrated and described in the "*M.M.*" each month as "*Meccano Standard Mechanisms*," and we believe that inventive boys will find these articles of great assistance in helping to perfect their Meccano models.

S.M. 1
$\frac{3}{4}$" Pinion and 50-tooth Gear Wheel

We are also compiling a new "Standard Mechanism" manual which will comprise all these movements, divided into thirteen different Sections and indexed so that immediate reference may be made to any particular motion that it is desired to incorporate in a model. The sections dealing with "Pulleys" and "Levers" will be amplified by the description of several interesting experiments carried out with Meccano.

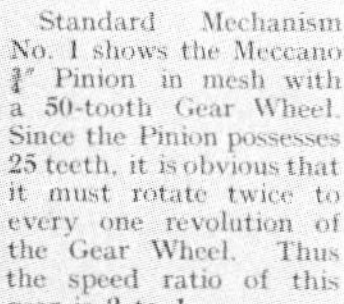

S.M. 7 Chain Gear

Other features will include Clutches, Reversing and Drive-changing Mechanism, Brakes and Retarding Appliances, Bearings, Screw Gear, Steering Gear, Traversing Mechanism, etc. The principles involved in these details will well repay the study of any boy interested in engineering.

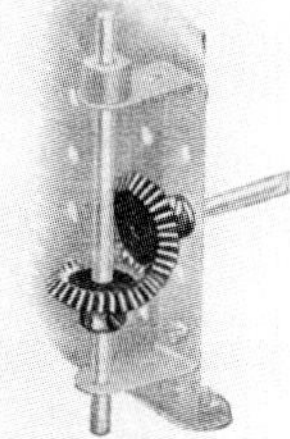

S.M. 3
Contrate Gear (for shafts at right angles)

Cutting Meccano Gears

The important part played by toothed wheels in the transmission of power, and the wonderful processes by which they are made, are described in another article in this issue (see page 554). Gear Wheels are equally indispensable in Meccano engineering, and Meccano Gear Wheels are made in much the same manner as are the gears used in actual practice.

We believe all Meccano boys would like to watch a "No. 26" or "27" as it passes through the various stages of manufacture. It is certainly very interesting to observe solid pieces of brass being transformed with amazing rapidity into beautifully finished Gear Wheels, destined, in all probability, to provide many years of hard service in hoisting loads or working hammers, drills, lathes, engines, clocks, and motor cars, at the bidding of some happy Meccano boy!

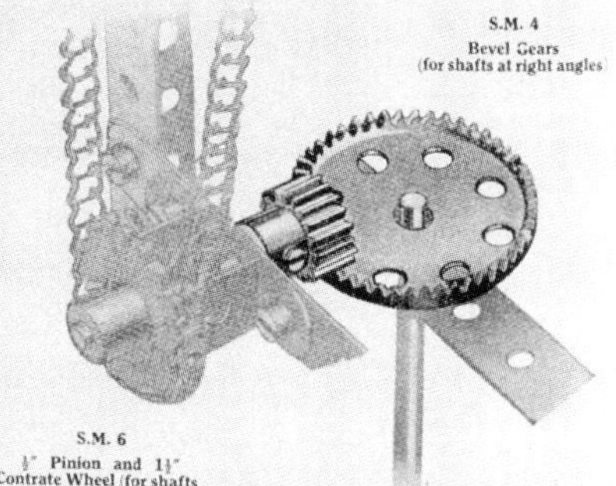

S.M. 5
Worm Gearing

The first process is the cutting and shaping of the wheel from the bars of solid brass, boring out the centres, and cutting the thread to receive the set-screws. Next a number of these blanks—still quite unfamiliar in appearance to the Meccano boy—are placed face to face and inserted on a mandril in a wonderful machine-tool. Here a circular cutting tool, revolving at a high speed, passes along the row of brass discs, and in doing so cuts out a single tooth in each wheel. When the tool has reached the end of its stroke, the blanks are rotated slightly, and the tool, returning, cuts out the next tooth. This process is repeated until all the teeth are shaped.

Section I. Gear Ratios

Standard Mechanism No. 1 shows the Meccano $\frac{3}{4}$" Pinion in mesh with a 50-tooth Gear Wheel. Since the Pinion possesses 25 teeth, it is obvious that it must rotate twice to every one revolution of the Gear Wheel. Thus the speed ratio of this gear is 2 to 1.

S.M. 2 illustrates the $\frac{1}{2}$" Pinion (19 teeth) and 57-tooth Gear Wheel, giving a ratio of 3 to 1. A larger ratio is obtained from the use of a $\frac{1}{2}$" Pinion and $3\frac{1}{2}$" Gear Wheel (133 teeth), in which the Pinion must revolve seven times as fast as the Gear Wheel.

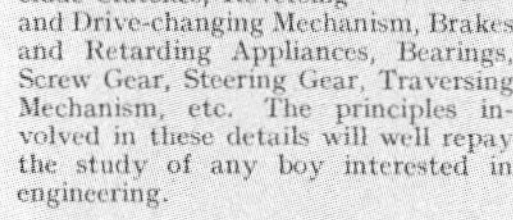

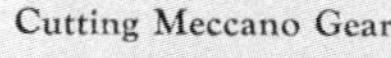

S.M. 6
$\frac{1}{2}$" Pinion and $1\frac{1}{2}$" Contrate Wheel (for shafts at right angles)

S.M. 2
$\frac{1}{2}$" Pinion and 57-tooth Gear Wheel

S.M. 4
Bevel Gears (for shafts at right angles)

Fig 2. The front cover of the first edition of Standard Mechanisms (1925).

Fig 3. The contents page of the 1925 edition.

Meccano Standard Mechanisms

CONTENTS

For easy reference purposes, the various mechanisms have been grouped under the following SECTIONS:—

Fig 1. The first Standard Mechanisms article in the MM. Nov. 1925.

Model-Building With Meccano

Real Engineering in Miniature

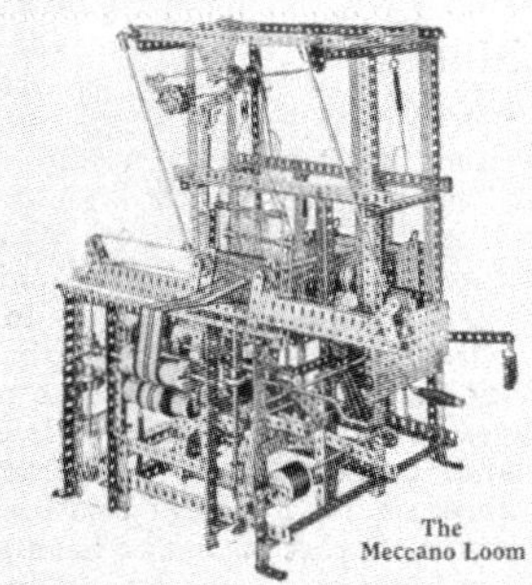

The Meccano Loom

MECCANO OUTFITS contain accurately-made and highly-finished engineering parts with which any known mechanical movement may be reproduced in model form.

Meccano owes its world-wide renown to the fact that every one of the 200 parts contained in the system is designed on correct principles. Every piece is standardised and interchangeable, so that the use of any part is not confined to one purpose only—the same part may be used in a variety of ingenious combinations.

When you build models with Meccano you use real engineering parts in miniature, for they act in a precisely similar manner to the corresponding elements in actual practice. This means that with Meccano you can accomplish more than with any other system of model construction. Other systems attempt to attain the same object by different methods, and avail themselves of constructive elements that are not based on correct engineering principles. It is important to realise this, for if you commence with badly-designed parts you can only build a very limited number of models. Even these will necessarily be constructed incorrectly and will give you faulty ideas of the laws of engineering.

For these reasons, Meccano becomes something more than a toy—it is an educational medium of very real value.

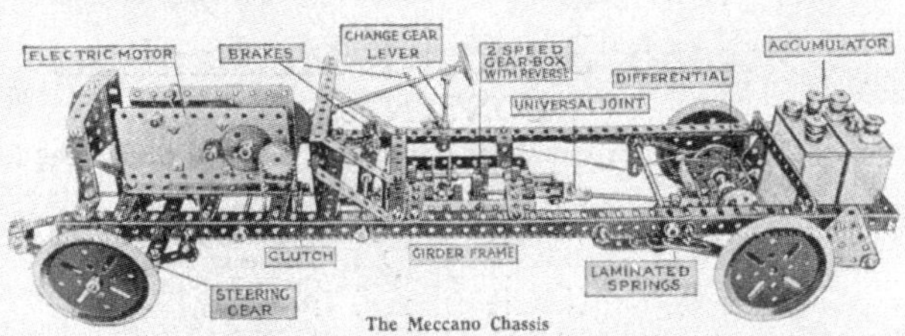

The Meccano Chassis

Professors of Engineering, bridge-building experts, draughtsmen, and others who are in a position to judge, have from time to time pronounced on the Meccano system. All have declared it to be conceived on sound lines and based on true engineering principles.

We have numerous records in our files of great engineering firms who employ Meccano every day for designing movements or engineering structures they are about to build. Famous inventors use it for experimenting and for working out ideas, while in schools and colleges it is used to demonstrate all branches of mechanics.

Clock Mechanism

Meccano Models are Real Models

There is no limit to the number of models that may be built with Meccano, and all are real working structures.

The Meccano clock is a real clock—it keeps accurate time. The Meccano Loom is a real loom, for it weaves beautiful material for hat-bands or neck-ties. The Meccano Motor Chassis, with worm-and-wheel steering, gear-box and differential, so closely resembles a real motor-car that it is used for teaching students at numerous Schools of Motoring.

It is the same with all other Meccano models—they are all accurate reproductions of the real thing and they all work because they are based on correct engineering principles.

The Meccano Standard Mechanisms

No Meccano boy is content to build only the models illustrated in the Meccano Manuals, for every boy who thinks is keen on inventing and likes to build models from his own ideas. With this in mind, and to assist boys to embody correct engineering practices in their new models, we have collected and classified a number of Meccano movements that have to a certain extent become standardised. That is to say, these movements may be applied to more than one model—in most cases without any alteration, but in some few cases with only slight alterations to the standard movement.

Those who invent with Meccano will find these movements, which we now publish as "Standard Mechanisms," of great assistance in helping to perfect their models. The various devices have been arranged so that immediate reference may be made to any particular motion that it is desired to incorporate in a model.

Moreover, we believe that certain sections of this book, such as those dealing with Pulleys and Levers, will serve as an interesting introduction to elementary Mechanics. In any event, some knowledge of the principles involved in these details will well repay the study of any boy interested in engineering.

The Meccano Clock

Fig 4. The introduction to the 1925 edition.

Section I. GEAR RATIOS.

Methods of Speed Reduction and Acceleration

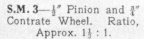

S.M. 1—$\frac{3}{4}$" Pinion and 50-teeth Gear Wheel. Ratio, 2 : 1.

S.M. 2—$\frac{1}{2}$" Pinion and 57-teeth Gear Wheel. Ratio, 3 : 1.

Further examples of Gear Ratios :

$\frac{1}{2}$" Pinion and $3\frac{1}{2}$" Gear Wheel. Ratio, 7 : 1.
Ratios of 1 : 1 may be obtained by using two 1" Gear Wheels or two $\frac{1}{2}$" Pinions.

S.M. 7—Chain Gear

$\frac{3}{4}$" and 3" diam. Sprocket Wheels. Ratio, 4 : 1.
1" and 2" diam. Sprocket Wheels. Ratio, 2 : 1.
$\frac{3}{4}$" and $1\frac{1}{2}$" diam. Sprocket Wheels. Ratio, 2 : 1. etc., etc.
Ratios of 1 : 1 may be obtained by gearing any two Sprocket Wheels of like diameter

S.M. 3—$\frac{1}{2}$" Pinion and $\frac{3}{4}$" Contrate Wheel. Ratio, Approx. $1\frac{1}{3}$: 1.

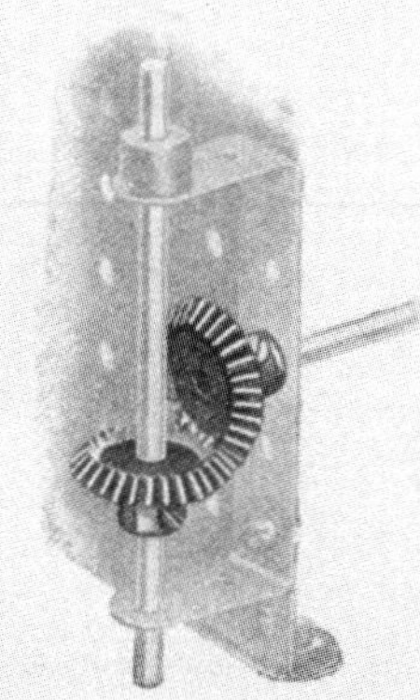

S.M. 4—Bevel Gears Ratio, 1 : 1.

S.M. 5—Worm Gearing. Worm Wheel and 57-teeth Gear Wheel. Ratio, 57 : 1.
Worm Wheel and $\frac{1}{2}$" Pinion. Ratio, 19 : 1.
The number of revolutions of any Gear Wheel to one revolution of the Worm Wheel by which it is driven may be assumed to correspond with the number of its teeth.

S.M. 6—$\frac{1}{2}$" Pinion and $1\frac{1}{2}$" Contrate Wheel. Ratio, approx. $2\frac{2}{3}$: 1.
$\frac{3}{4}$" Pinion and $1\frac{1}{2}$" Contrate Wheel. Ratio, 2 : 1.

3

Fig 5. From the simple . . .

Section XIII. Miscellaneous Appliances—(*continued*)

S.M. 254—VARIABLE SPEED: THE CONSTANTINESCO TORQUE CONVERTER

The Torque Converter—as this ingenious apparatus has become generally known—was invented recently by Mr. George Constantinesco. Briefly stated, it is an automatic infinitely-variable speed mechanism, which obviates the use of gear wheels and other forms of transmission that have been previously considered indispensable. Furthermore, it obtains the maximum efficiency from the engine to which it is fitted, since it transmits the power almost directly to the resistance which is to be overcome.

The ordinary rules of static mechanics do not apply to the Torque Converter, and it is only by the consideration of the elements "time" and "mass" that the behaviour of the converter can be explained, and for a complete understanding of its working, mathematics of a high order are required. We do not propose, therefore, to enter into detailed technical explanations, but merely to describe a Meccano model which admirably fulfils the purpose of demonstrating the remarkable principle on which the Constantinesco Converter is based.

An explanatory diagram of the model is given in Fig. 1. The crank A driven by the engine, is connected to a lever B, to the lower end of which is fixed a heavy weight C forming a pendulum. The other end of the lever B is connected to two rods D, E carrying pawls F, G which bear on a ratchet wheel J. No matter whether the rods D, E be pushed towards the ratchet or pulled away from it, a turning motion, constant in direction, is imparted by the pawls to the rod K.

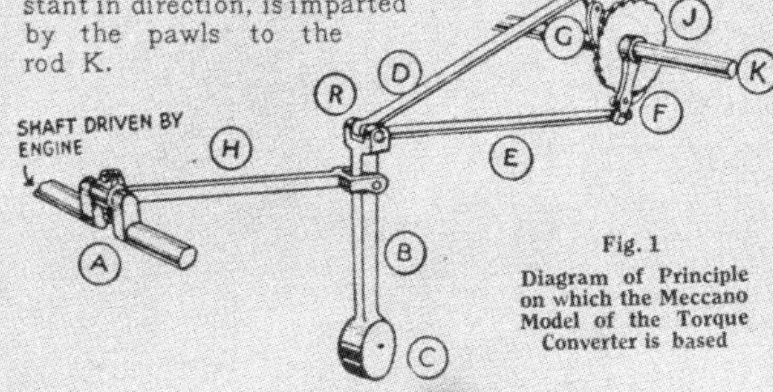

Fig. 1
Diagram of Principle on which the Meccano Model of the Torque Converter is based

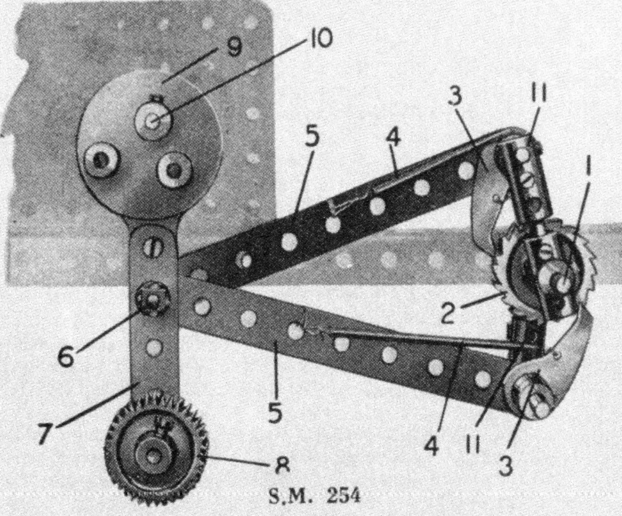

S.M. 254

HOW THE CONVERTER WORKS

When the engine is running slowly, the weighted lever B, actuated by the connecting-link H, swings to and fro, the fulcrum of oscillation being at the point of resistance (R) As the speed of the engine increases, however, the increased oscillatory movement of the lever B overcomes the resistance and the fulcrum automatically moves down to some intermediary point between R and C, resulting in a short to-and-fro motion of the levers D, E which imparts a moderate rotary motion to the rod K. If the engine is allowed to reach "top" speed a very rapid oscillatory motion is applied to the lever B; the inertia of the weight C opposes this motion and the weight becomes stationary, whilst the end R of the lever is rocked to the full extent of the throw of the crankshaft. The fulcrum is now right down in the weight C, and the levers D, E are caused to move almost as if they were driven directly from the engine.

The speed at which the engine must revolve before the inertia of the weight C completely overcomes the resistance at R, varies, of course, with the extent of the resistance on the rod K.

THE MECCANO MODEL

In the Meccano model, S.M. 254, the lever B is represented by a short Strip 7 bolted to the Eccentric 9. The latter is mounted on the driving shaft 10 and imparts the oscillatory movement to the lever 7. A 1" Gear Wheel 8 represents the weight C. Two 4½" Strips 5 are pivoted by bolt and lock-nuts 6 to the lever 7, their other ends being connected to short Rods mounted in Couplings 11 and carrying the Pawls 3. The Couplings 11 are secured by 1" Rods to further Couplings which are free to move about the Rod 1. The Pawls are opposed to one another, and engage a Ratchet Wheel 2 mounted on the driven shaft 1; portions of Spring Cord 4 exert a slight pressure on the Pawls, to ensure their proper engagement with the Ratchet Wheel. Each Pawl engages with the Ratchet Wheel intermittantly, one rotating it during the forward stroke of the levers 5, while the other is brought into operation on the reverse stroke. The combined effort of both produces a constant rotary motion in the shaft 1.

S.M. 254A is an end perspective of the Pawl and Ratchet gear.

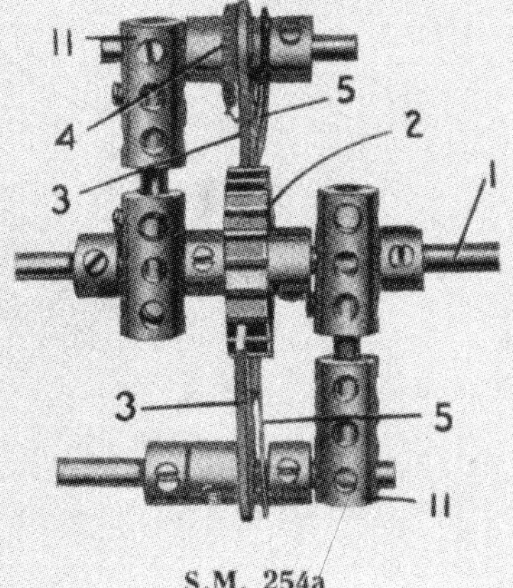

S.M. 254a

37

Fig 6. . . . to the complex.

Standard Mechanisms as it is usually known first saw the light of day in a series of articles which appeared in the *Meccano Magazine* between November 1925 and March 1927 (fig 1). Early on in the series however they were issued complete as a separate 48 page manual which conformed in size and style to the standard books of instruction. Like other manuals of the day, it had a rather dull cover (fig 2) which belied the interest of the contents, summarised on page 2 (fig 3). As can be seen from the introduction (fig 4), three of the four leaflet models are given as examples of Meccano's capabilities. It goes on to encourage invention and explain how Standard Mechanisms could be of help. That help ranged from the simple matter of gear ratios (fig 5) to the complexity of the Constantinesco Torque Convertor (fig 6). Incidentally, the large ratchet wheel shown in the illustration did not exist in that form and was simply an artist's retouching of a one inch gear wheel. Whether it was ever intended to produce such a part or whether pre-production samples were made is another matter altogether, although examination of the original drawings for this part suggest they were not.

In between these two extremes, the manual went into a great variety of mechanical devices. Some sections dealt with both the theoretical side as well as practical application. Pulleys, pulley blocks and differential pulley blocks were treated in this way (figs 7a, b & c), and first, second and third order levers were also accorded the same honour (figs 8a, b, c & d).

Meccano gear boxes were in their infancy at this time and SM 64 and SM 69 (fig 9) are typical of the period. Compare those with fig 30 from the 1934 edition and you will get a good idea of the progress which was made in what was really a very short time. SM 69 is also interesting, not for its content which is rather basic, but for the rather dim view of the 1922–23 High Voltage motor which seems to have been experimental and subsequently used for dealer's demonstration models. Aspects of its design foreshadowed the classic 1925 type as well as providing the basis for the power unit of the first Hornby electric locomotive of 1923.

continued p. 184.

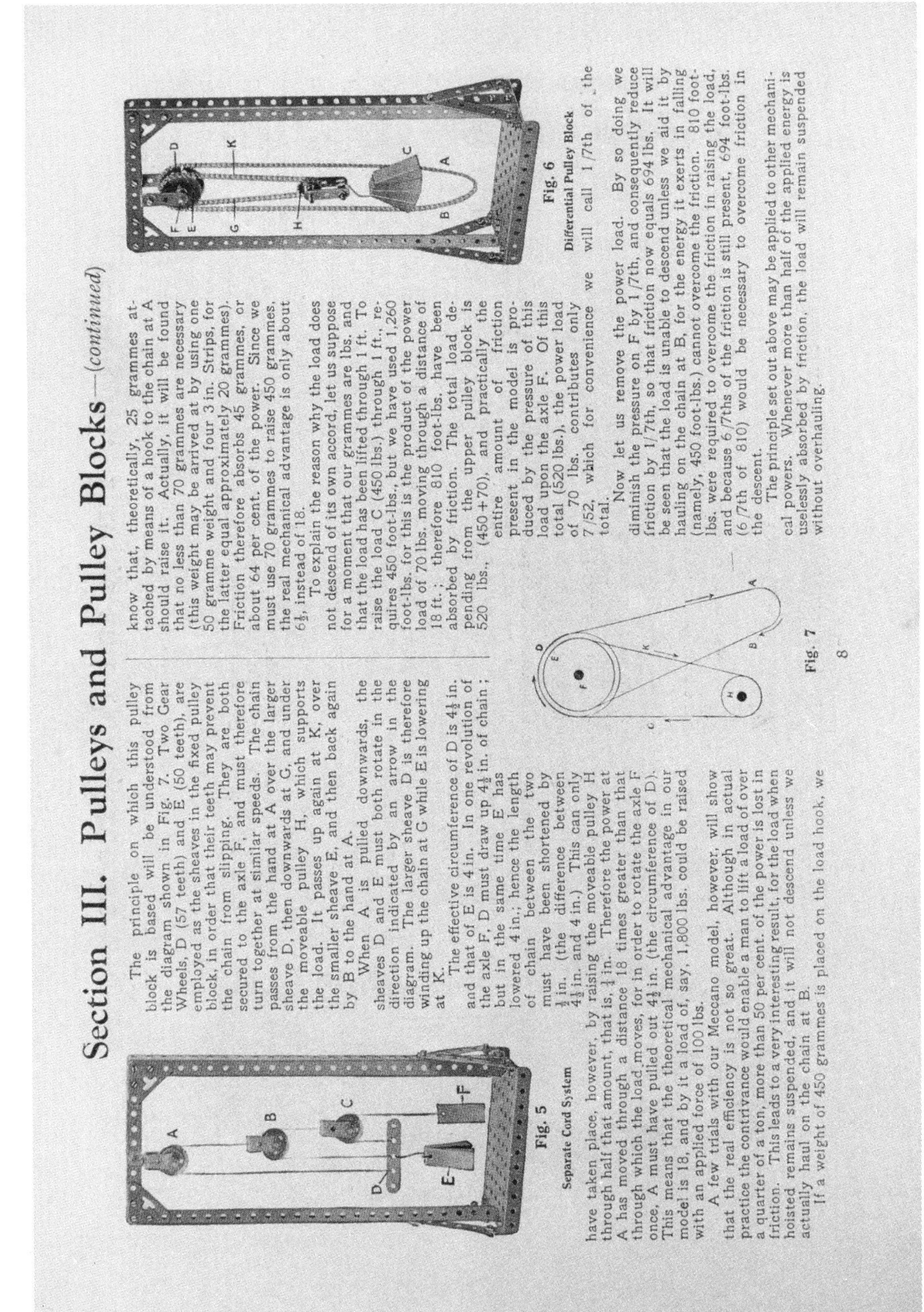

Section III. Pulleys and Pulley Blocks—*(continued)*

The principle on which this pulley block is based will be understood from the diagram shown in Fig. 7. Two Gear Wheels, D (57 teeth) and E (50 teeth), are employed as the sheaves in the fixed pulley block, in order that their teeth may prevent the chain from slipping. They are both secured to the axle F, and must therefore turn together at similar speeds. The chain passes from the hand at A over the larger sheave D, then downwards at G, and under the moveable pulley H, which supports the load. It passes up again at K, over the smaller sheave E, and then back again by B to the hand at A.

When A is pulled downwards, the sheaves D and E must both rotate in the direction indicated by an arrow in the diagram. The larger sheave D is therefore winding up the chain at G while E is lowering at K.

The effective circumference of D is $4\frac{1}{2}$ in. and that of E is 4 in. In one revolution of the axle F, D must draw up $4\frac{1}{2}$ in. of chain; but in the same time E has lowered 4 in.; hence the length of chain between the two must have been shortened by $\frac{1}{2}$ in. (the difference between $4\frac{1}{2}$ in. and 4 in.) This can only have taken place, however, by raising the moveable pulley H through half that amount, that is, $\frac{1}{4}$ in. Therefore the power at A has moved through a distance 18 times greater than that through which the load moves, for in order to rotate the axle F once, A must have pulled out $4\frac{1}{2}$ in. (the circumference of D). This means that the theoretical mechanical advantage in our model is 18, and by it a load of, say, 1,800 lbs. could be raised with an applied force of 100 lbs.

A few trials with our Meccano model, however, will show that the real efficiency is not so great. Although in actual practice the contrivance would enable a man to lift a load of over a quarter of a ton, more than 50 per cent. of the power is lost in friction. This leads to a very interesting result, for the load when hoisted remains suspended, and it will not descend unless we actually haul on the chain at B.

If a weight of 450 grammes is placed on the load hook, we know that, theoretically, 25 grammes attached by means of a hook to the chain at A should raise it. Actually, it will be found that no less than 70 grammes are necessary (this weight may be arrived at by using one 50 gramme weight and four 3 in. Strips, for the latter equal approximately 20 grammes). Friction therefore absorbs 45 grammes, or about 64 per cent. of the power. Since we must use 70 grammes to raise 450 grammes, the real mechanical advantage is only about $6\frac{3}{7}$, instead of 18.

To explain the reason why the load does not descend of its own accord, let us suppose for a moment that our grammes are lbs. and that the load has been lifted through 1 ft. To raise the load C (450 lbs.) through 1 ft., requires 450 foot-lbs., but we have used 1,260 foot-lbs. for this is the product of the power load of 70 lbs. moving through a distance of 18 ft.; therefore 810 foot-lbs. have been absorbed by friction. The total load depending from the upper pulley block is 520 lbs., (450+70), and practically the entire amount of friction present in the model is produced by the pressure of this load upon the axle F. Of this total (520 lbs.), the power load of 70 lbs. contributes only 7/52, which for convenience we will call 1/7th of the total.

Now let us remove the power load. By so doing we diminish the pressure on F by 1/7th, and consequently reduce friction by 1/7th, so that friction now equals 694 lbs. It will be seen that the load is unable to descend unless we aid it by hauling on the chain at B, for the energy it exerts in falling (namely, 450 foot-lbs.) cannot overcome the friction. 810 foot-lbs. were required to overcome the friction in raising the load, and because 6/7ths of the friction is still present, 694 foot-lbs. (6/7th of 810) would be necessary to overcome friction in the descent.

The principle set out above may be applied to other mechanical powers. Whenever more than half of the applied energy is uselessly absorbed by friction, the load will remain suspended without overhauling.

8

Fig 7A. *Simple pulleys.*

Section III. PULLEYS AND PULLEY BLOCKS

PULLEYS play such an important part in engineering that a knowledge of the principles upon which they work is essential to every engineer, whether professional or amateur.

Pulleys are a development of the lever, and when scientifically employed make possible a great saving of labour and energy. A fixed pulley cannot be described as a mechanical power, for it simply changes the direction of a force without increasing it—in fact, a small amount of energy is lost in its use owing to friction. The combination of a rope with several pulleys, however, produces a mechanical power, and with the help of a few experiments we shall endeavour to explain as simply as possible some of the interesting results so obtained.

A man carrying a sack of cement to the top of a building has to carry his own weight in addition to that of the sack. If he attaches a rope to his load and passes the rope over a pulley fixed at the top of the building, he is then able to raise the load by hauling on the other end of the rope while he remains on the ground. This is an example of the pulley used as a convenient method of changing the direction of a force, for it changes the man's downward pull to an upward force by which he is able to raise the sack of cement. It must be remembered that although the man has eliminated his own weight, he has not diminished his load. On the other hand he has increased it, for the energy he now exerts must not only equal the weight of the load but must also overcome a certain amount of friction.

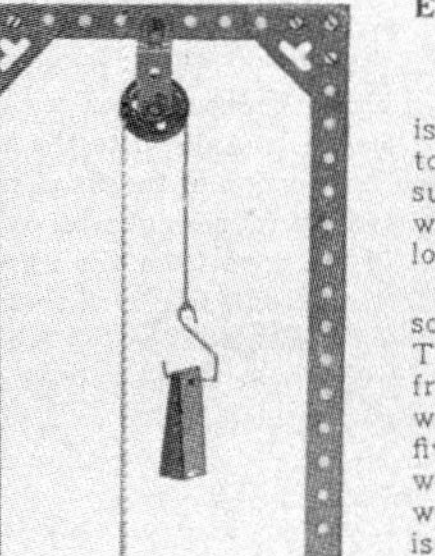

Fig. 1
Single Fixed Pulley

The Meaning of "Energy"

The amount of work, or "energy," of which a machine is capable is measured by "foot-lbs." The unit of this is based on the amount of energy necessary to raise a 1 lb. weight through a height of 1 ft. For example, suppose a weight of 2 lbs. has to be raised through a height of 1 ft.; the energy required would be exactly equal to that necessary to raise a weight of 1 lb. through a height of 2 ft.—namely, 2 foot-lbs.

If 10 lbs. be lifted 100 ft., 10 foot-lbs. are required for the first foot, the same for the second, third, and so on up to 100 ft., making a total of 1,000 foot-lbs. of energy.

Supposing a man, by hauling on a rope, lifts 1 cwt. to a height of 20 ft. The energy he expends should be sufficient to raise a load of one ton through a height of 1 ft., but it is impossible, of course, for a man to move a direct load of one ton, however short the height through which it is to be moved, although he can create sufficient energy (2,240 foot-lbs., or 1 foot-ton) when moving a load of 1 cwt. through a height of 20 ft. With the aid of a series of pulleys, however, he is able to arrange a contrivance with which he may lift one ton through 1 ft. by the same means; i.e. by moving a smaller weight, or exerting a smaller pull, through a greater height.

Friction in Pulleys

Friction plays an important part in calculating the advantages of pulleys, although in the majority of Meccano models its effect is naturally very small. In every pulley there is a slight loss of power from the necessity of bending the rope, and in actual practice, where heavy ropes are used, this loss becomes of great importance. It is for this reason that pulleys are usually made as large as possible, for the bending of a rope around the circumference of a large pulley creates less friction than when used with a smaller pulley. Small pulleys also cause damage to the rope by excessive bending.

Example 1

A simple fixed pulley is shown in Fig. 1.

If we attach a hook to the rope at the point where it is tied to the base, and suspend from this hook a weight equal to that already shown, we find that the original weight remains suspended in mid-air, in spite of the law of gravitation by which the highest weight should fall, thereby raising the lower weight.

Because this is the case, we know that there must be some force that is retaining the suspended weight in position. This force is friction, created by the bending of the cord and from the contact of the pulley on its bearings. If a 50-gramme weight is attached to each hook, we find that the addition of five Washers is required to the uppermost hook to cause the weight to fall, so raising the other hook supporting the lower weight. Thus the amount of friction present in our model is equal to the weight of five Washers.

Example 2

In Fig. 2 we have a moveable pulley B in addition to our fixed pulley A. The rope is fastened to the cross beam, passed (or "rove") through the moveable pulley B, and over the fixed pulley A.

With this arrangement it will be found that a power load of, say, 11 lbs. attached to the free or "running" end *a* of the rope will raise a weight of 20 lbs. suspended from the moveable pulley B. Here, then, the moveable pulley B is employed as a mechanical power and gives an advantage of nearly double the available force. To this mechanical advantage the fixed

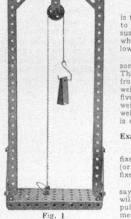

5

Fig 7B. Pulley Blocks.

Section III. Pulleys and Pulley Blocks—(*continued*)

In this case we have six lengths of cord supporting the moveable pulley block, so by a similar calculation to that made in Example 3, it will be seen that we obtain a mechanical advantage of six—that is, a force equal to one sixth of the load will be sufficient to raise it (ignoring friction).

Example 5

In Fig. 5 separate cords are substituted for the previous continuous single cord. One end of the outermost cord is attached to a Strip D and the cord then passes over the pulley A, which is bolted to the upper framework. The other end of this cord is fixed to the block B. The centre cord is also fastened to D and then passes over the pulley B to be secured to the block C. The remaining cord passes over the pulley C, and serves as the running or pulling-end of the tackle. The load E is suspended from the Strip D, and the power F is attached to the running-end of the cord C.

With this ingenious arrangement we obtain a mechanical advantage of seven; that is, it enables a load of, say, 70 lbs. to be lifted by an applied force of only 10 lbs. (ignoring friction).

The explanation is not quite so obvious, perhaps, as in our previous examples. If D is raised 1 in. the block B, suspended from the first cord that passes over A, must fall 1 in. Since the pulley B descends 1 in. that part of the second cord between B and C must be lengthened by 2 in. (We learned in Example 2 that to raise a moveable pulley 1 in., 2 in. of cord must be drawn up—therefore to drop a moveable pulley 1 in., 2 in. of cord must be let down). We must remember that D has risen 1 in. so that the second cord has been lengthened by a further inch between B and C. Therefore the pulley C has dropped 3 in. altogether. From this, again working on the theory of the moveable pulley, we find that the running end of the third cord, which passes over the pulley C, must descend through 6 in. Finally, by adding to the running end the additional length of 1 in. derived from the movement of D, we arrive at the total movement of the power load F, namely, 7 in.

Therefore if the power load is 10 lbs., it exerts 70 foot-lbs. energy for every foot the load is raised.

It should be mentioned that in the Meccano model it is first necessary to balance the weight of the pulley blocks B, C. This may be done by suspending a weight of approximately 75 grammes from the Strip at D. Then having attached a load of, say, 175 grammes, at E we find that 25 grammes on the power hook F is sufficient to balance it. By the addition of about eight Washers the load is raised; therefore the loss by friction is equal to the weight of the Washers.

This arrangement of cords and pulleys, though using a smaller number of sheaves than the continuous cord system, is seldom employed by engineers for the reason that the continuous cord is more convenient to fix and use.

Fig. 4

Example 6

Our final example deals with a very ingenious contrivance, known as Weston's differential pulley block. This apparatus consists of three parts—an upper fixed pulley block, a moveable pulley and an endless chain (Fig. 6). In our Meccano model, the load C may be raised or lowered by a slight pull on the chain at A or B.

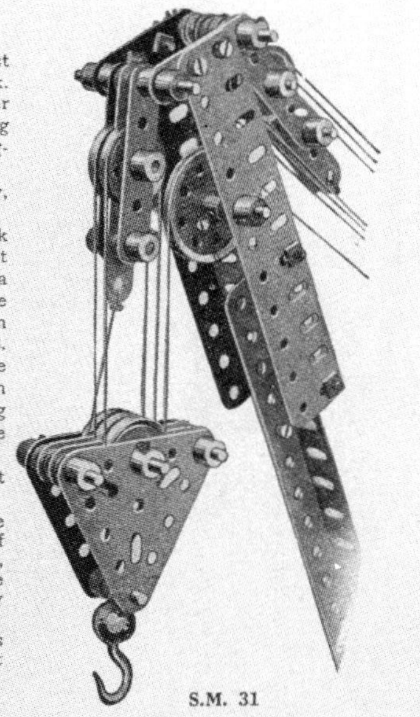

S.M. 31
Arrangement of Pulleys in Stiff-Leg Derrick
(Model No. 709)

7

Fig 7C. More complex pulley systems.

Section IV. LEVERS

Fig. 15

LEVER OF THE FIRST ORDER

THE lever is the simplest and perhaps most valuable of the various mechanical powers, for it forms a useful medium for increasing or changing the direction of a force in cases where it would be impracticable to employ pulleys. The lever is classed in three distinct groups, and is said to belong to the first, second, or third " order," according to the relative position of the fulcrum, or point at which the lever pivots, to the " power " and the " load."

A lever of the first order is illustrated in Fig. 15. The upright member of this model is constructed from two $5\frac{1}{2}''$ Angle Girders (1) secured to the base (2) by $1'' \times 1''$ Angle Brackets (3) and held together at their tops by two $\frac{1}{2}'' \times \frac{1}{2}''$ Angle Brackets. A short Rod, which supports the lever, is passed through the upright and rigidly secured in a Crank bolted to the rear $5\frac{1}{2}''$ Angle Girder.

As will be seen, the fulcrum A is situated between the load D and the power F. In order to experiment with the properties of the lever, we must first counterpoise the weight of the arm AP. This may be done by adding a weight E to the arm AC, and in the example illustrated, which shows the beam pivoted in its fifth hole, 125 grammes and two $2\frac{1}{2}''$ strips are found necessary to balance AP.

Example 1.

It will now be found that a power load of 50 grammes at B is sufficient to balance a load of 200 grammes at C; therefore this arrangement of the simple lever gives a mechanical advantage of four. The arm AB is 8 in. in length and CA only 2 in. As the radius of the point B from the fulcrum A is four times as great as that of the point C, point B must move through a distance four times greater than that through which the point C moves. This explains the mechanical advantage obtained in our model, for we have already seen (Example 2, Section III.) that a power is increased proportionally to the distance through which it moves.

Example 2.

We may further prove this rule by changing the position of the power F to the point G, which is four inches from the fulcrum A. A power of 100 grammes is now found necessary to balance the load D, for G moves through a distance only twice as great as C.

Example 3.

The rule may be expressed more generally by stating that the power is to the load as the distance of the load from the fulcrum is to the distance of the power from the fulcrum. By applying the rule, we may ascertain the power required to raise any given load, providing we know the lengths of the two arms of the lever.

Suppose for example, that it is desired to raise the load at C (200 grammes) by applying a power at the point P in the lever. The distance of the load (C) from the fulcrum (A) is 2 in., and the distance of the power P from the fulcrum (A) is 10 in. Therefore CA is only one fifth as great as AP; and since the power is to the load as CA (the distance of the load from the fulcrum) is to AP (the distance of the power from the fulcrum), then the power required is only one fifth as great as the load. Hence we find that 40 grammes at P will balance 200 grammes at C.

Further interesting experiments may be carried out with this model by altering the positions of the power and load, or by moving the fulcrum in either direction along the lever. In the latter case, it should be remembered that the weight E must be readjusted to balance the altered length of the arm AP.

11

Figs 8A–D. *Thorough treatment of levers!*

Section IV. Levers—(*continued*)

LEVER OF THE SECOND ORDER

In levers of the second order, the fulcrum is at one end, the power at the other, and the load lies between the two. This type of lever is shown in Fig. 16, in which A is the fulcrum, B the point at which the load D is applied, and C is the power.

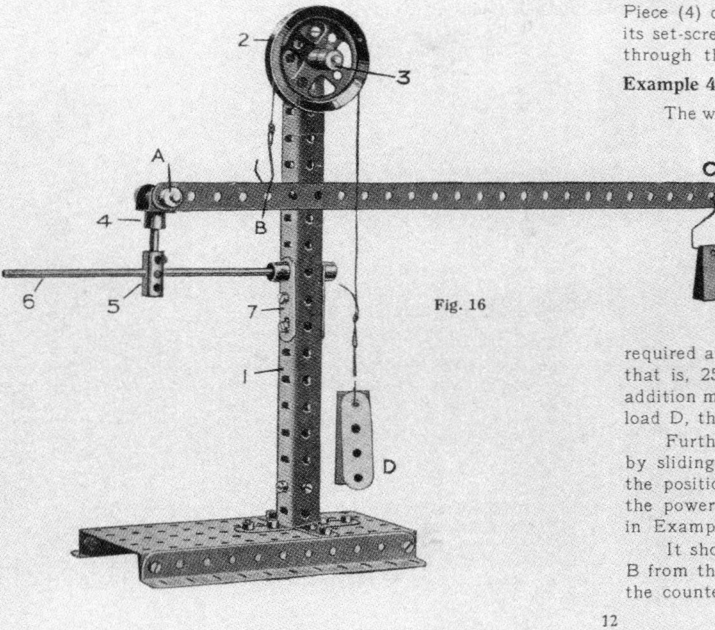

Fig. 16

The upright column (1) in this example is constructed in a similar manner to that shown in Fig. 15, but in this case the Girders are $9\frac{1}{2}''$ in length. The Pulley (2) runs freely on a short axle, and is held in place by a Collar (3). A $12\frac{1}{2}''$ Strip represents the lever, and pivots about a short axle journalled in a Fork Piece (4) carried from a Coupling (5) which may be secured by its set-screw in any position on the Rod (6). The latter passes through the upright Girders (1) and is secured in Cranks (7).

Example 4

The weight of the lever AC is balanced by placing 100 grammes and one 2″ Strip on the load-hook at D. In addition to these weights, the hook D carries a further 150 grammes to represent the load. The load-hook is suspended from a cord passing over the 2″ Pulley (2) and attached to the lever at B.

The power C is 12 in. from the fulcrum A, and the point B, at which the load D takes effect, is 2 in. distant. Therefore AC is six times as great as AB, and by applying the rule set out in Example 3 in this Section, we know that the power required at C to balance the load D is one sixth of 150 grammes, that is, 25 grammes. It will be found, however, that a slight addition must be made to the power C in order to actually raise the load D, the weight added representing the force lost by friction.

Further experiments may be carried out with this model by sliding the Coupling (5) along the Rod (6) and so altering the position of the point B, or by diminishing the distance of the power C from the fulcrum. In each case the rule set out in Example 3 will be found equally applicable.

It should be noted that whenever the distance of the point B from the fulcrum is changed, it will also be necessary to alter the counterpoise on the load-hook.

12

Fig 8B.

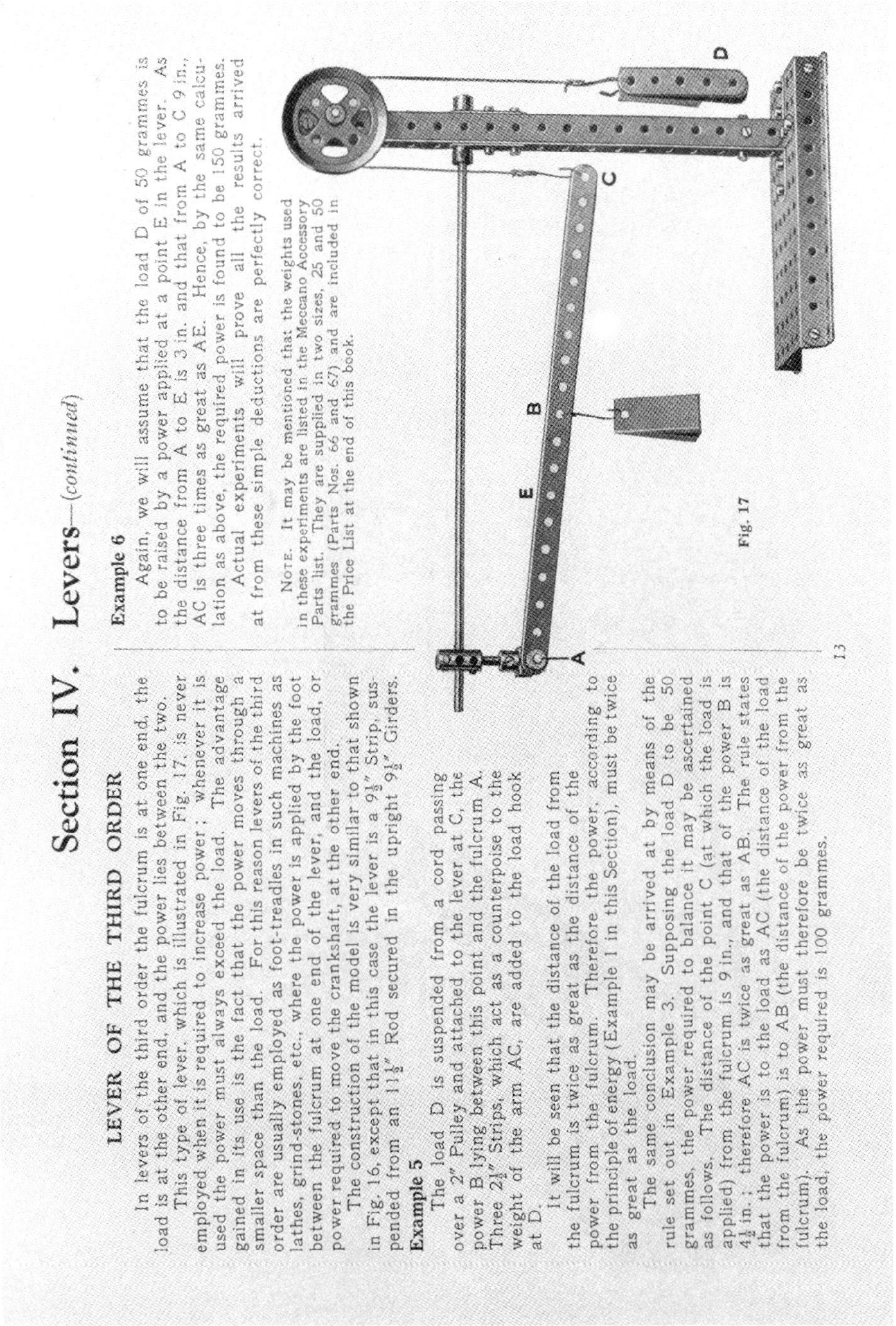

Section IV. Levers—*(continued)*

LEVER OF THE THIRD ORDER

In levers of the third order the fulcrum is at one end, the load is at the other end, and the power lies between the two.

This type of lever, which is illustrated in Fig. 17, is never employed when it is required to increase power; whenever it is used the power must always exceed the load. The advantage gained in its use is the fact that the power moves through a smaller space than the load. For this reason levers of the third order are usually employed as foot-treadles in such machines as lathes, grind-stones, etc., where the power is applied by the foot between the fulcrum at one end of the lever, and the load, or power required to move the crankshaft, at the other end.

The construction of the model is very similar to that shown in Fig. 16, except that in this case the lever is a 9½″ Strip, suspended from an 11½″ Rod secured in the upright 9½″ Girders.

Example 5

The load D is suspended from a cord passing over a 2″ Pulley and attached to the lever at C, the power B lying between this point and the fulcrum A. Three 2½″ Strips, which act as a counterpoise to the weight of the arm AC, are added to the load hook at D.

It will be seen that the distance of the load from the fulcrum is twice as great as the distance of the power from the fulcrum. Therefore the power, according to the principle of energy (Example 1 in this Section), must be twice as great as the load.

The same conclusion may be arrived at by means of the rule set out in Example 3. Supposing the load D to be 50 grammes, the power required to balance it may be ascertained as follows. The distance of the point C (at which the load is applied) from the fulcrum is 9 in., and that of the power B is 4½ in.; therefore AC is twice as great as AB. The rule states that the power is to the load as AC (the distance of the load from the fulcrum) is to AB (the distance of the power from the fulcrum). As the power must therefore be twice as great as the load, the power required is 100 grammes.

Example 6

Again, we will assume that the load D of 50 grammes is to be raised by a power applied at a point E in the lever. As the distance from A to E is 3 in. and that from A to C 9 in., AC is three times as great as AE. Hence, by the same calculation as above, the required power is found to be 150 grammes.

Actual experiments will prove all the results arrived at from these simple deductions are perfectly correct.

NOTE. It may be mentioned that the weights used in these experiments are listed in the Meccano Accessory Parts list. They are supplied in two sizes, 25 and 50 grammes (Parts Nos. 66 and 67) and are included in the Price List at the end of this book.

Fig. 17

13

Fig 8C.

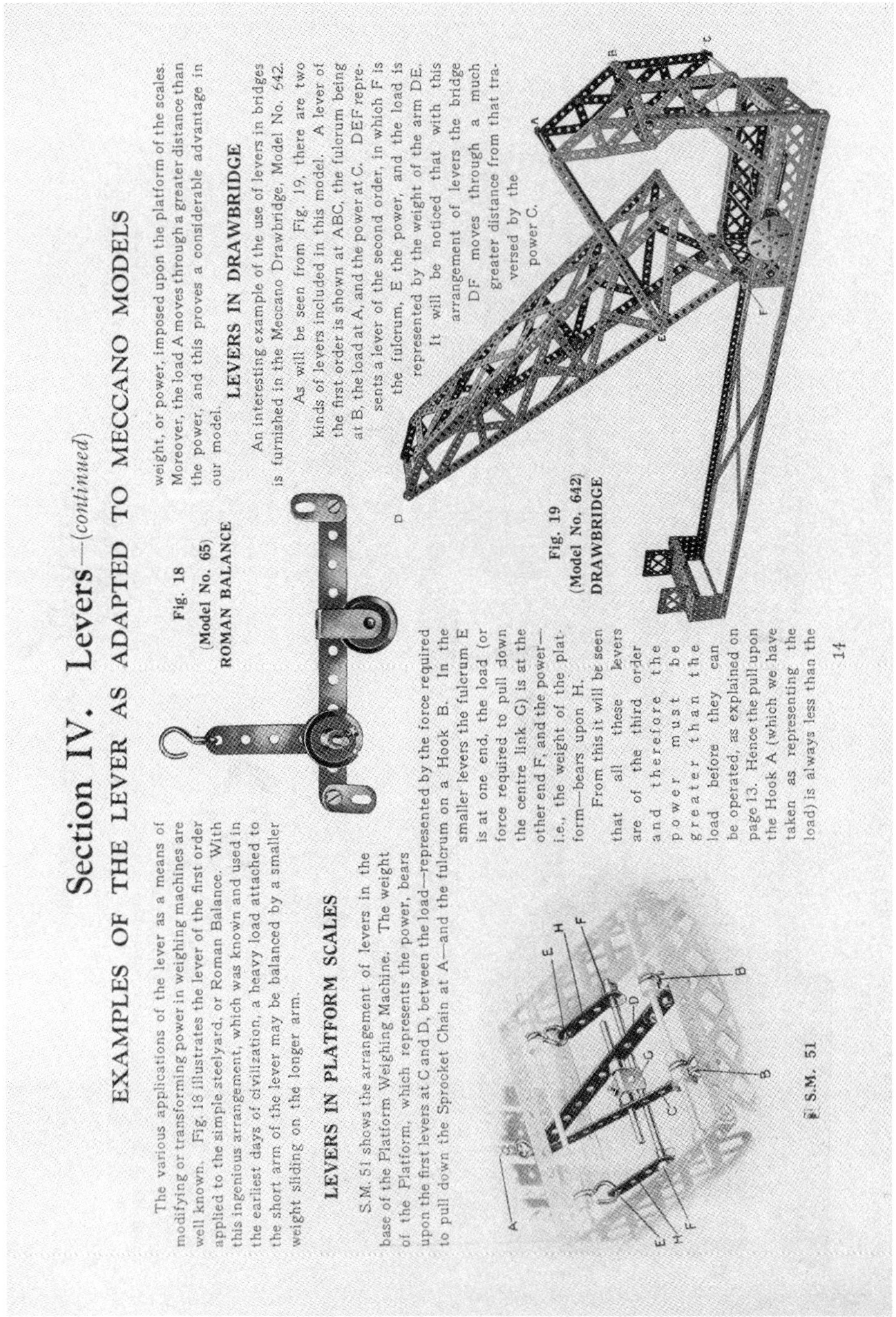

Section IV. Levers—*(continued)*

EXAMPLES OF THE LEVER AS ADAPTED TO MECCANO MODELS

The various applications of the lever as a means of modifying or transforming power in weighing machines are well known. Fig. 18 illustrates the lever of the first order applied to the simple steelyard, or Roman Balance. With this ingenious arrangement, which was known and used in the earliest days of civilization, a heavy load attached to the short arm of the lever may be balanced by a smaller weight sliding on the longer arm.

Fig. 18
(Model No. 65)
ROMAN BALANCE

LEVERS IN PLATFORM SCALES

S.M. 51 shows the arrangement of levers in the base of the Platform Weighing Machine. The weight of the Platform, which represents the power, bears upon the first levers at C and D, between the load—represented by the force required to pull down the Sprocket Chain at A—and the fulcrum on a Hook B. In the smaller levers the fulcrum E is at one end, the load (or force required to pull down the centre link G) is at the other end F, and the power—i.e., the weight of the platform—bears upon H.

From this it will be seen that all these levers are of the third order and therefore the power must be greater than the load before they can be operated, as explained on page 13. Hence the pull upon the Hook A (which we have taken as representing the load) is always less than the weight, or power, imposed upon the platform of the scales. Moreover, the load A moves through a greater distance than the power, and this proves a considerable advantage in our model.

S.M. 51

LEVERS IN DRAWBRIDGE

An interesting example of the use of levers in bridges is furnished in the Meccano Drawbridge, Model No. 642.

As will be seen from Fig. 19, there are two kinds of levers included in this model. A lever of the first order is shown at ABC, the fulcrum being at B, the load at A, and the power at C. DEF represents a lever of the second order, in which F is the fulcrum, E the power, and the load is represented by the weight of the arm DE.

It will be noticed that with this arrangement of levers the bridge DF moves through a much greater distance from that traversed by the power C.

Fig. 19
(Model No. 642)
DRAWBRIDGE

14

Fig 8D.

S.M. 69—DRIVE-CHANGING GEAR

The Rod 1 slides in its bearings and is controlled by a lever 2, which is pivoted at 3 and rests between two Collars and Set Screws 4 on the sliding Rod 1. The latter carries a Crank 5, the web of which engages between two Bevel Wheels 6 secured to a short Rod 7 driven from the Motor 8, as shown in the sectional illustration (S.M. 69A). The Crank 5 is suitably spaced with Washers 5A.

On operation of the lever 2, one of the Bevel Wheels 6 may be brought into gear with one or other of the two further Bevel Wheels 9 mounted on secondary shafts 10. This provides for two independent drives, either of which may be connected with the Motor by moving the lever 2.

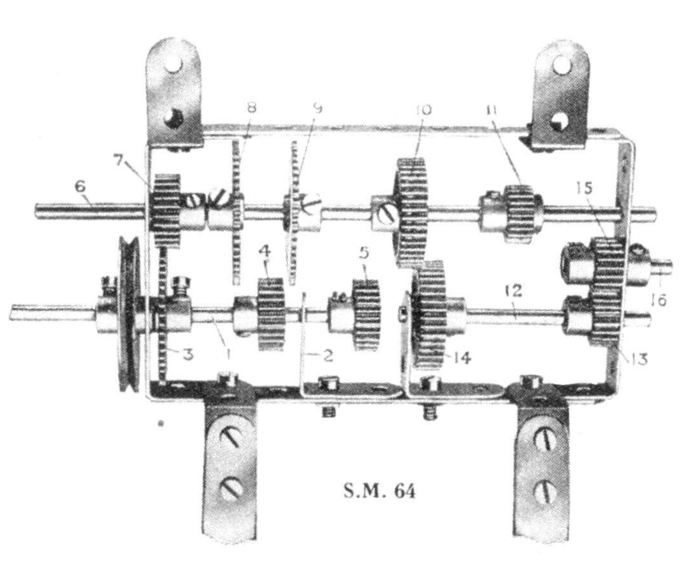

S.M. 64

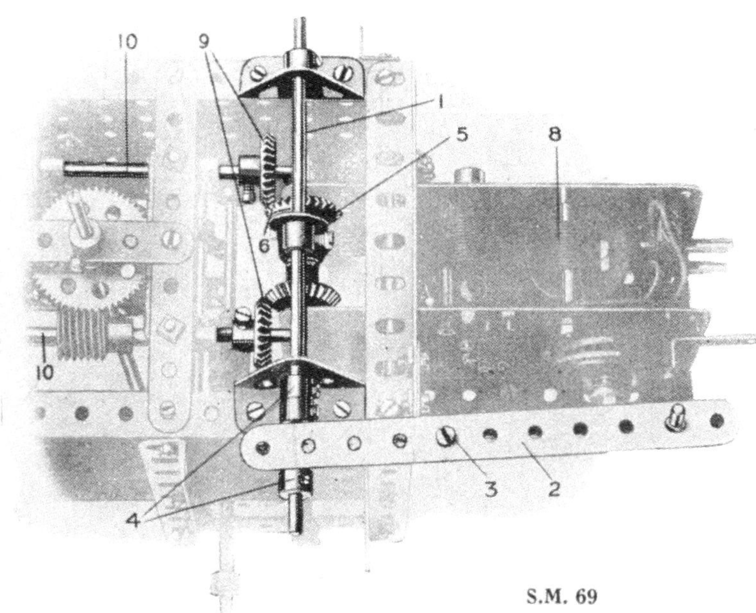

S.M. 69

S.M. 64– DRIVE-CHANGING AND REVERSING GEAR

S.M. 64 illustrates a compact example of gear box, which provides two speeds and a reverse gear. The model serves well in demonstrating the type of gear box usually fitted to automobiles.

The shaft 1 takes up the drive from the engine. This shaft, which is journalled through one end of the gear box and further supported by a 1″ × 1″ Angle Bracket 2, carries a 50-teeth Gear Wheel 3 and two ¾″ Pinions 4 and 5. A secondary shaft 6 is also inserted in the gear box and carries one ¾″ Pinion 7, two 50-teeth Gear Wheels 8 and 9, one 1″ Gear Wheel 10 and one ½″ Pinion 11. A further shaft 12 is next mounted in position, and its outer end carries the drive to the road wheels. The Rod 12 carries a ½″ Pinion 13 and a 1″ Gear Wheel 14. A ½″ Pinion 15 secured to a 1″ Rod 16 gears with the Pinion 13.

A lever should be next assembled, and serves to slide the shaft 6 in its bearings. A suitable lever for this purpose will be found in S.M. 52, and on reference to this detail it will be seen that the Rod A, connected at right angles to the lever by means of a Coupling, may readily be mounted as to lie transversely across the shaft 6, with its Collar engaging between the Gear Wheels 8 and 9. A movement of the lever will then push the Rod 6 in either direction as required.

The first position of the Rod 6 provides for a " top " speed, and in this position the Pinion 7 is in engagement with the Gear Wheel 3, Gear Wheels 10 and 14 are in engagement, while the Gears 8, 9 and 11 are all free. In this manner the Gear 3 causes the Pinion 7 on the secondary Rod 6 to revolve twice as fast as the primary Rod 1, and the propeller shaft 12 rotates at the same speed as the shaft 6, since it is driven from that shaft through the one-to-one Gear 10 and 14. The Pinion 15 revolves idly in this position.

For slow speed the shaft 6 is moved along until the Pinion 7 is out of engagement with the Gear Wheel 3 and the Gear 8 meshes with the Pinion 4, while Gear Wheels 10 and 14 are still engaged. With this arrangement the driving shaft 1 will revolve twice as fast as the driven shaft 12.

A reverse gear is obtained by sliding the Rod 6 still further, until the Gear Wheel 9 is in engagement with the Pinion 5 and the Pinions 11, 15 and 13 are all in mesh.

S.M. 69a
Detail of Drive-Changing Gear (S.M. 69)

Fig 9. Early Gearboxes. With SM 69 giving a glimpse of the 1922–3 Experimental High Voltage Motor.

Section VII. ROLLER AND BALL BEARINGS, Etc.

S.M. 101—ROLLER BEARINGS

Where a heavy mass is to be rotated about an axis, it is necessary to devise some method of relieving the tremendous strain that would be imposed upon that axis. The usual procedure is to distribute the weight of the mass over wheels or rollers arranged at a distance from and rotating round the central pivot.

Standard Mechanism No. 101 is an excellent illustration of the type of roller, or wheel, bearings frequently used for the rotation of large cranes, revolving bridges, and other heavy structures. The lower, or stationary guide rails 1 are constructed from eight Channel Segments, and form a track upon which the wheel race 2 revolves. The fixed guide is shown in detail in S.M.101A; it will be noted that the Channel Segments are bolted to the base by means of 1″ × ½″ Angle Brackets 3. The Sprocket Chain 4 shown in this

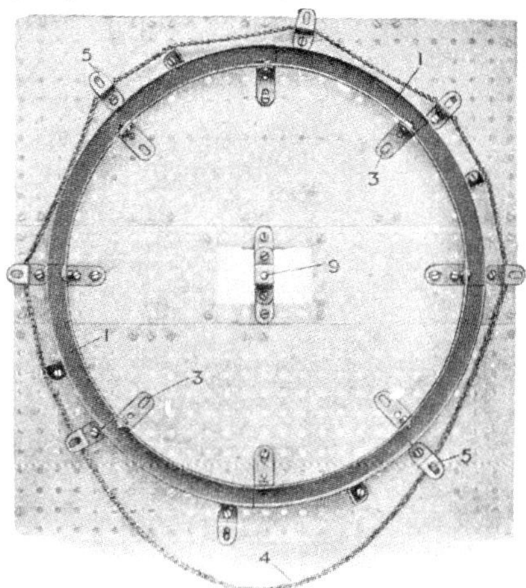

S.M. 101a

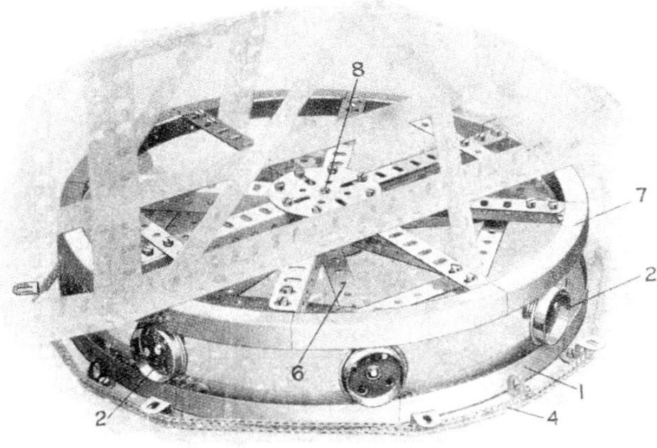

S.M. 101

figure illustrates a method of rotating the crane jib or other structure of which the track 1 forms the base; a vertical driven rod situated on the rotating structure carries a Sprocket Wheel placed *within* and engaging the chain loop 4. The latter is arranged round the series of Angle Brackets 5. On rotation of the Sprocket Wheel, the chain 4 tends to grip the brackets and becomes immovable, whereupon the Sprocket commences to travel *round the chain*, carrying the pivoted structure with it.

Eight Flanged Wheels forming the wheel race are mounted by means of 1½″ Double Angle Strips to the spider-frame 6 (S.M. 101B). The revolving guide rail 7, shown in detail in S.M.101c, is secured to the base of the upper or rotating part of the structure, and rests upon the wheels 2. A shaft 8 (S.M.101c) is journalled in the bearing 9 (S.M.101A) and forms a common axis for the spider-frame and revolving race 7, both of which rotate at different speeds. The shaft 8 should be secured in the Face Plate 10 forming the hub of the upper race 7, but the spider-frame 6 should be allowed to swivel freely upon it.

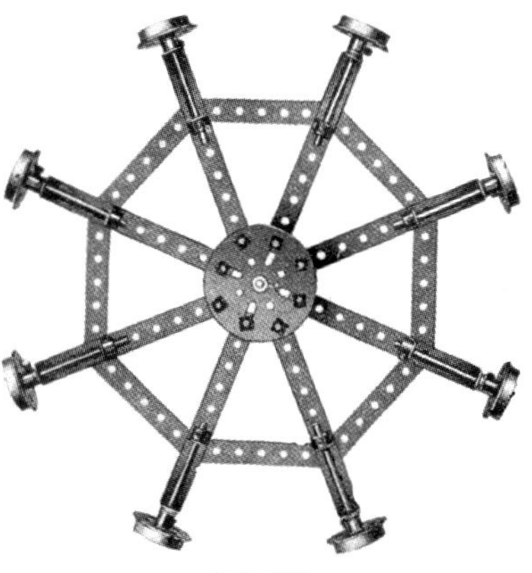
S.M. 101b

As already intimated, rollers sometimes take the place of wheels in actual practice. The rollers are of no great length but their diameters are usually made as large as possible, since an increase in size means a proportional decrease in friction. In addition, the rollers are tapered, as a rule, towards one end, in order that they shall describe a correct circle about the central pivot of the structure.

Rollers are also employed in smaller types of bearings, such as in shaft-journals, etc. Such bearings are similar in design and operation to the ordinary ball-bearings (see S.M. 104), but the advantage obtained from the employment of rollers in place of balls exists in the fact that the point of contact, or the area over which the strain is imposed, is increased considerably. Thus, in a journal-bearing, the rollers are placed longitudinally to the journal, and the latter is supported upon the entire length of each roller, whereas in ball bearings the point of contact is comparatively very small.

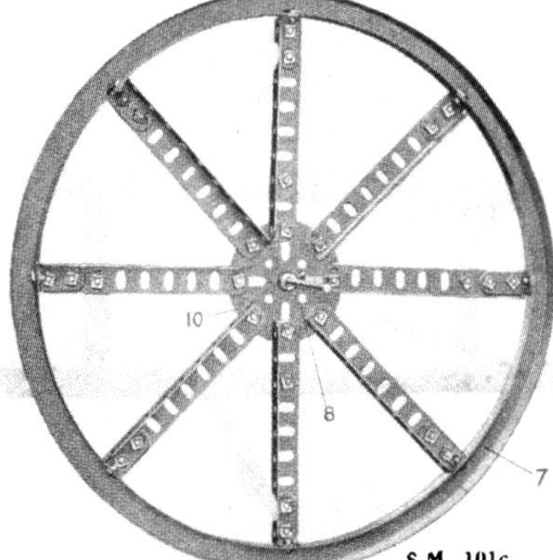

S.M. 101c

Fig 10. Before the Geared Roller Bearing.

The 1925 edition of Standard Mechanisms was published before the Geared Roller Bearing came into being and SM 106 (fig 10) presented the then current method of supporting large rotating structures. For smaller ones, SMs 104, 5, 6 (fig 11) were quite efficient. SM 106 illustrates the base from the Steam Shovel which later became Super Model Leaflet No. 19, and shows the use of part no. 145 the circular strip. This item was originally to be 6½″ in diameter and the illustration in the Leaflet (fig 12) shows this pre-production version. Standard Mechanisms was, however, updated with a different base and a new photograph showing the circular strip as was produced i.e. 7″ diameter. Since SML 19 did not appear until some three years later it is rather odd that the earlier outdated photograph was used instead of the correct one which was available. As anyone who has built this model will testify, that ½″ makes a lot of difference. The Steam Shovel is featured in the manual several times in particular for its excellent built-up digger bucket (fig 13).

Finally, having looked at locomotive valve gear (fig 14) the book was rounded off with two pages of applied mechanics (fig 15). These illustrations date from much earlier days and were perhaps another attempt by Hornby to gain educational acceptance.

All in all this first edition was an excellent work of reference and represented, for the most part, the up-to-date (in 1925) practice. Much of it was directly inspired by suggestions sent into and featured in the *Meccano Magazine* and it must have been a matter of enormous pride for a contributor to have his work enshrined in such an august publication. However the honours must eventually go to Hubert Lansley, for it was he who wrote and compiled this first pioneering edition which did so much for Meccano modelling.

The 1925 manual was reprinted at least four times in the next three years but apart from the advertising pages and a few minor alterations these later printings were similar in content and style to the first edition.

continued p. 187.

Section VII. Roller and Ball Bearings, etc. *(continued)*

S.M. 104

S.M. 104—BALL BEARINGS

This detail illustrates the standard Meccano ball-bearing. It is constructed from two 3" Pulley Wheels, one Wheel Flange, and twenty-one Steel Balls, and is applicable chiefly in models where a weight is required to impose vertically upon a pivot. The fixed ball-race is built up from the Wheel Flange and one 3" Pulley bolted together and secured to any suitable base. The balls are placed in the groove formed between the outer edges of this Pulley and the Wheel Flange, and the second Pulley, which should be bolted to the swivelling portion of the model, rests upon their upper surfaces. One of the Pulleys is secured by its set-screw to the Axle Rod shown, while the other is allowed to turn freely. When the Pulleys are placed together, it is impossible for the balls to move out of position.

S.M. 105—BALL BEARINGS APPLIED TO SWIVELLING CRANE

S.M.105 shows the jib of a small crane running on Meccano ball bearings, such as described in S.M.104. The Rod 5, about which the jib pivots, is secured in the upper Pulley 1, which is bolted to the jib. The latter is rotated from the Crank Handle 8 by means of the Worm 7 engaging with the 57-teeth Gear Wheel 6 carried on the Rod 5. The jib is secured to the base by a Collar bolted on the Rod 5 just beneath the platform.

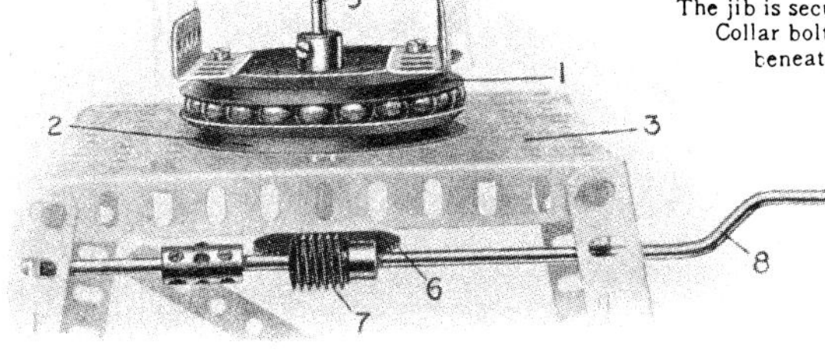

S.M. 105

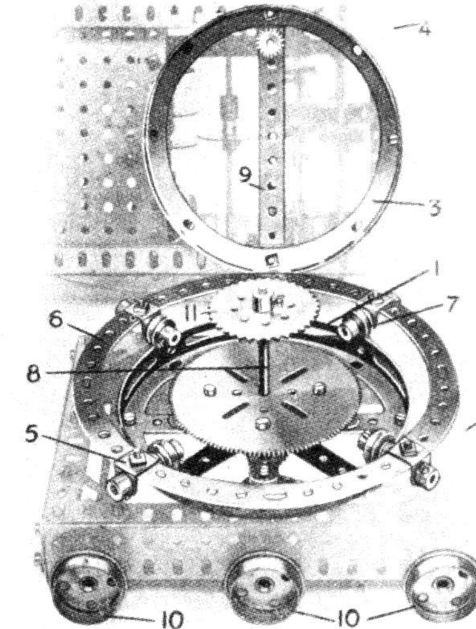

S.M. 106

S.M. 106—ROLLER BEARINGS

The swivel-bearing shown in this illustration is similar in principle to S.M.101, but is designed for lighter work. The Hub Disc 1 is bolted to the base 2 of the model and forms a guide upon which runs the wheel-race constructed from four ½" Pulleys 7, pivotly carried from a Circular Strip 6. A Circular Girder 3 bolted to the upper platform 4 of the model rests upon the Pulleys 7. The model pivots about the Rod 8, which passes through the Girder 9, but the weight of the rotating body is distributed over the Pulleys 7, so obviating the strain that would otherwise centre upon the pivot 8.

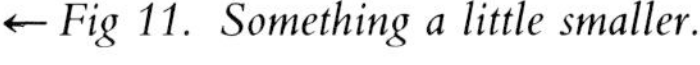

← *Fig 11. Something a little smaller.*

↓ *Fig 12. The Super Model Leaflet illustration showing the 6½" circular strip.*

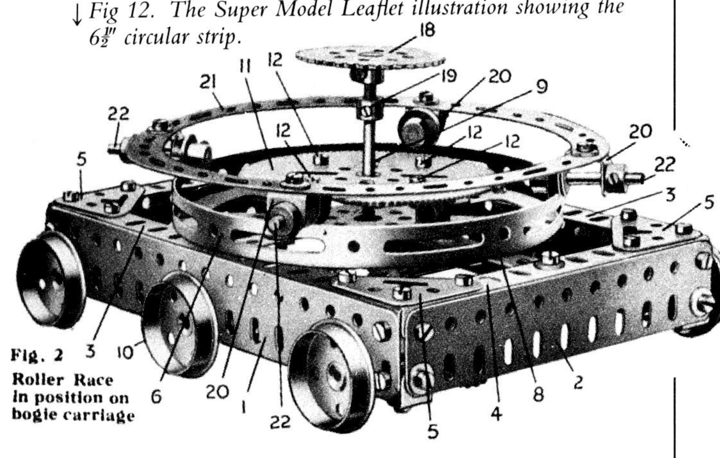

Fig. 2
Roller Race
in position on
bogie carriage

Fig 13. A made-up Digger Bucket.

S.M. 181—SHOVEL FOR GIANT EXCAVATOR

This bucket is designed for use in Steam Shovels or other excavating machines. It is bolted to the arm 1, which pivots from a point in the jib of the excavator. The bottom Plate 2 of the bucket is hinged to the Rod 3, and is closed or opened as desired by means of a sliding Rod 4, operated by a cord 5. Thus, during the cutting stroke, the Plate 2 is held in a closed position by the end of the Rod 4 engaging a Flat Bracket 6. When the loaded bucket is moved over to the point where the material is to be dumped, its contents are released by pulling the cord 5. The bucket is raised or lowered by a cord 7 engaging a Pulley 8 pivotly carried on a Rod 9. The radius of the cut is regulated by altering the length of the arm 1, which is controlled by rack and pinion mechanism in the jib.

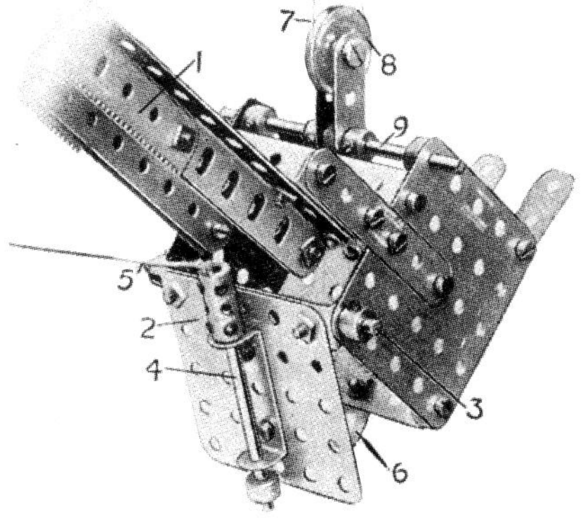

S.M. 181

S.M. 277—VALVE GEAR AND DRIVE TRANSMISSION FOR STEAM LOCOMOTIVE

S.M. 277 illustrates an interesting model of Walschaert's valve gear and also shows a typical Meccano connecting-rod gear which is applicable to most types of locomotives.

The crosshead 1 is composed of a Coupling mounted between Eye Pieces engaging slide bars 2. A Strip Coupling mounted on the end of the piston rod 3 carries the connecting rod 4 pivoted to the crank pin on the centre driving wheel 5. The coupling rod 6 is also journalled on this crank pin and on the crank pins of the leading and trailing driving wheels, thus imparting the motion of the piston over the three wheels.

The crank pins consist of short Rods passed through the driving wheels and secured in Cranks bolted to their inner sides. A Crank 7 rigidly secured to the pin of the centre driving wheel 5, pivotally carries the return crank rod 8, and the latter is pivoted to the outer end of a short Slotted Strip forming the base of the link 9, which is constructed from 2½" Curved Strips. The link rocks about a pivot 10 and pushes to and fro the radius rod 11, which is pivoted to the upper hole of the combining lever 12. This lever 12 is journalled on a short Rod secured in a Coupling 13 mounted on the end of the piston valve rod sliding in the valve chest 13A, and is connected pivotally to a guiding link 14. The latter is pivoted to a Crank 15 secured to a short Rod mounted in the Strip Coupling on the end of the piston rod.

It will now be seen that, as the wheel 5 rotates, the combining lever 12, operated by the radius rod 11 and guiding link 14, imparts a sliding movement to the valve rod 13. The radius rod 11 is pivoted at 16, by means of bolt and lock-nuts, to an Eye Piece, representing the link block, sliding on the strip 9A of the link 9. The link block is connected to a lever in the cab, so that the driver may move it to any position in the link that he may desire. By moving the block 16 towards the pivot 10, the throw of the radius rod 11 is diminished, until it reaches its minimum when the block 16 is at the centre of the link 9. Further movement of the block to any point above the pivot 10 reverses the direction of the valve rod 13, and consequently reverses the order in which the cylinder valves open, so causing the locomotive to run in an opposite direction. The alteration to the throw of the radius rod also enables the driver to vary the amount of steam which is supplied to the cylinder for each stroke of the piston, for the inlet valve is held open for a short or long period according to the extent of the " throw " of the radius rod. This variation of the steam supply is known as the "cut-off."

S.M. 277

← *Fig 14. Locomotive valve gear. The illustration is from the LMS tank which subsequently became (when expanded) the LB & SCR Baltic Tank SML 15. Note the large gauge tinplate track.*

EXPERIMENTS IN APPLIED MECHANICS

No. 1. TRIANGLE OF FORCES

This model illustrates the principle of the "Triangle of Forces." Briefly, if three forces meet at a point and balance each other, and we know one of the forces, we may determine the other two by drawing a triangle, making each side parallel to the direction of one of the forces. To demonstrate this, two large Pulleys 7 are carried on Rods in the upper 24½" Girders of the model, and cords 8, 9, are passed over these pulleys, their ends being joined to another cord 10. Weights 11, 12, and 13 are then hung on the ends of the cords 8, 9, and 10, and when the point of junction (a) of the three cords has come to rest, lines in the direction of the cords are drawn on a sheet of paper pinned to a piece of board incorporated in the model. This board is not included in Meccano Outfits on account of its size, but it may be provided at little expense. The paper is afterwards removed and a triangle drawn, as shown in the illustration, with its sides 8, 9, and 10 parallel to the directions of the three cords. This triangle is shown in dotted lines. If the sides of the triangle are measured it will be found that they are in the same proportion as the weights 11, 12 and 13. For instance, if the weight 12 were 15 units and the weight 13 were 9 units, and the weight 11 were 7 units, the lengths of the sides of the triangle would be 15, 9, and 7 units. By this experiment, therefore, we demonstrate that when three forces meet at a point, and we know their direction and the value in grammes or pounds of one of the forces, if we construct a triangle, making that side of the triangle which corresponds to the known force equal to a number of units of length, each unit representing a gramme or pound of the known force, then by scaling off the other two sides of the triangle we can determine the value of the other two forces in grammes or pounds. Several experiments with different weights should be tried and triangles drawn, and the accuracy of the apparatus for different weights tested.

As an example of the triangle of forces, when a boy pulls a bow to shoot an arrow, if we know the force he pulls with, we can find the pull along each part A and B of the string by measuring the angle which the string forms.

Little difficulty will be experienced in constructing the Meccano Demonstration Frame from this illustration. It may be well to mention, however, that the rear uprights, which consist of 18½" Angle Girders, are secured to the sides of the board shown in the illustration by ordinary wood screws. The 24½" Girder at the top is secured in the same manner, as also is the 12½" Girder at the bottom. The board is used for pinning on sheets of paper, upon which the diagrams are drawn.

43

Experiments in Applied Mechanics—*(continued)*

No. 2. INCLINED PLANE

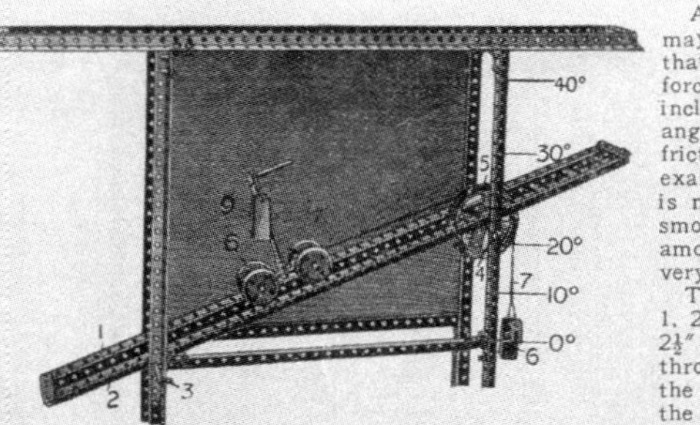

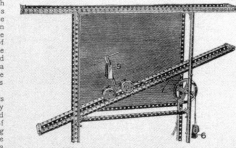

Another interesting principle which may be demonstrated on this apparatus is that known as the Inclined Plane. The force required to raise a body up an inclined plane varies according to the angle of the slope, and to the amount of friction present in the model. In the example illustrated, the load to be moved is mounted on wheels and runs upon a smooth surface, with the result that the amount of friction to be overcome is very small indeed.

The plane is made of two Angle Girders 1, 2, connected together at each end by 2½" Strips and carried on a Rod 3 passed through holes in the vertical girders of the frame and in the girders forming the plane. The other end of the plane rests on a Rod 4 which carries a 3" Pulley Wheel 5. By placing the Rod 4 through different holes in the side girders the slope or angle of the inclined plane may be varied. To obviate the need of a protractor to ascertain the slope of the plane, it may be stated that if the Rod 4 be placed in the fourth hole of the vertical girders, with the plane pivotally mounted on Rod 3 (as shown in the illustration), the surface of the plane will represent an incline of 10°. If placed in the 9th hole, 20°. If in the 15th hole 30°, and if in the 21st hole 40°. The force or weight 6 on the cord 7 is directed over the Pulley 5 in a line parallel to the plane, and the cord is connected to the carriage. The axles of the carriage wheels are journalled in Couplings bolted to either end of a 2" rod.

Before commencing the experiment, weights should be hung on the cord 7, which are just sufficient to maintain the carriage 6 in equilibrium. If a weight 9 be then hung on the carriage it should be noted what additional weight is required to be hung on the end of the cord 7 just to make the carriage slowly ascend the plane. The weight 9 should then be varied and the alteration in the weight 6 on the cord 7 to make the carriage ascend the plane noted, and these results should be tabulated.

The second example illustrated above shows the line of force acting along the cord 7 in a horizontal position instead of parallel to the inclined plane. Having exactly balanced the carriage as before, different loads should be placed on the carriage at 9 and notes made of the additional weights at 6 necessary to cause the carriage to begin to move up the plane. These results should also be tabulated.

In every case it will be found that a small force at 6 will overcome a greater one at 9. The power required to raise a given load may be ascertained by the aid of the principle of energy (see Section III., page 5), and a consideration of this principle will also explain the mechanical advantage obtained from the inclined plane. For the purpose of this experiment we will assume that a weight of 150 grammes has been attached to the carriage at 9. If the carriage is moved from the point 3 to the point 4, on reaching the latter it will have risen vertically through a space of approximately 5", but it can only have done so by travelling *longitudinally* through a distance of 15"; therefore to raise the carriage 5", the force 6 descends through three times that distance (i.e., 15"). Hence, 50 grammes attached to the power hook at 6 will be sufficient to raise 150 grammes at 9 (ignoring friction), since the number of units of energy exerted by the force is three times greater than that produced by the load.

The inclined plane is usually employed as a mechanical power in the form of a wedge or a screw (see Section IX, Screw Mechanism). The tremendous increase of power derived from the use of screw-gear forms an interesting illustration of the principle of the inclined plane, and Meccano boys may build some very instructive models, on the lines of that described above, to demonstrate the advantages so obtained.

44

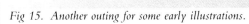

Fig 15. Another outing for some early illustrations.

A completely new edition

1929 saw a new version altogether with a brighter and more attractive cover (fig 16). There were quite a number of changes in this edition some of them significant. Gone were the lengthy sections on pulley blocks, levers and the experiments in applied mechanics. These were replaced by more useful practical mechanisms. Another casualty was the Constantinesco Torque Converter which was perhaps only to be expected in view of its limited use in such small scale modelling.

As compensation for the 'theoretical' losses, the 1929 edition placed more emphasis on gear boxes and mechanisms. For example, SMs 82 and 83 (fig 17) showed how a most useful epicyclic clutch and transmission gear could be used in Meccano; SM 84 (fig 18) pictured a simple and easy-to-understand demonstration model of a planetary gear box, and SM 86 (fig 19), showed an ingenious automated gearchange.

Electrical matters were well covered including an automatic switch, a speed governor for electric motors as well as a neat built-up resistance controller for them. SMs 113, 114 and 115 (fig 20).

The big news of 1928 had been the introduction of the Geared Roller Bearing and although the built-up version with channel segments was still shown, the obvious merits of the new part could clearly be seen (fig 21).

There were a number of other interesting features in the May 1929 edition one of which has already been noted in Volume 2 of this series. This refers to the three views of a single-motor driven version of SML 28, The Pontoon Crane (fig 22). Although single-motor operation was briefly referred to in the original leaflet (with channel segments), there was no mention of it in the 1936 Geared Roller Bearing version. In any case the gearbox shown in the 1929 Standard Mechanisms is totally different to those in the two published leaflets.

Examination of the 1929 Standard Mechanisms' gearbox reveals a rather economical use of parts which gives rise to speculation as to whether it was complete or just a mock-up for the camera. The *continued p. 191.*

Fig 16. Cover of the 1929–1933 editions.

Fig 25. The cover of the 1934–1936 'blue/gold' editions of Standard Mechanisms.

Fig 17. New Gear Mechanisms.

Section V. Clutches, Reversing and Drive-Changing Mechanism *(continued)*

S.M. 82—EPICYCLIC GEAR CLUTCH

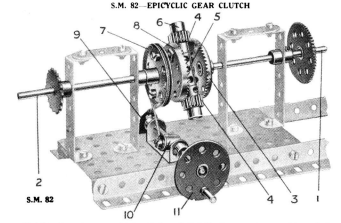

S.M. 82

Rod 1 is the primary, or driving shaft, and Rod 2 is the secondary, or driven shaft. The former carries a 1½" Contrate Wheel 3, which engages with ½" Pinions 4 mounted on 1" Rods secured in the ends of a Coupling 5. The Pinions are free to revolve, but are held in place by Collars 6. Rod 2 passes through the bosses of a Pulley 7 and the second 1½" Contrate Wheel 8, and its inner end is secured in the centre of the Coupling 5. The Pulley 7 and Contrate Wheel 8 are free to turn independently of the Rod 2, but they are secured together by two ½" Bolts, each of which is fitted with three nuts, one immediately behind Pulley 7 and one on each side of the Contrate 8.

The Wheel 7 is controlled by a friction brake consisting of a length of cord, one end of which is tied to an Angle Bracket 9 and the other end to a Threaded Boss 10 mounted on a Threaded Rod that carries a hand wheel 11.

If the brake is in the " off " position, that is with cord slack, the unit 7 and 8 is free to revolve about the Rod 2. Hence if power is applied to the Contrate Wheel 3 the Pinions 4 commence to turn upon their axles, driving the Contrate Wheel 8 in an opposite direction, and no movement is imparted to the Rod 2. If the hand wheel 11 is rotated, so gradually applying the brake, the Contrate Wheel 8 becomes increasingly difficult to turn, and the Pinions 4 commence to climb round its teeth, thereby rotating the Coupling 5 and the Rod 2.

It will be seen that by means of this clutch the power can be applied to the load very smoothly and without shock, for the Rod 2 commences to rotate immediately the resistance on the Pulley 7 becomes greater than the load (that is the resistance on Rod 2). The speed of the latter Rod increases in proportion to the increase in the resistance on Pulley 7. The gear ratio is 1 : 2 when the unit 7, 8 is immovable—that is, Rod 2 rotates once in every two revolutions of Rod 1.

S.M. 83—EPICYCLIC TRANSMISSION GEAR

This device is designed to provide a gear ratio of two to one between any two shafts. Its chief merits lie in the compactness of its construction and in the fact that the driving and driven shafts may be mounted in direct line with one another.

The handle 1 is secured to a 2" Axle Rod journalled in bearings 2. This Rod is free to rotate in the boss of a 1½" Contrate Wheel 3, but is secured in one end of the Coupling 4. A further Rod 5, which runs freely in the other end of the Coupling 4 and is journalled in further reinforced bearings 6, carries the 1½" Contrate Wheel 7 fixed in the position shown.

A 1½" Rod 8 gripped in the central transverse hole of the Coupling 4 carries a ¾" Pinion 9, which is free to rotate about the Rod but is retained in position by a Collar 10. The Pinion is engaged by the teeth of both Contrate Wheels 3 and 7.

The Double Bent Strip forming the bearing 2 for the driving Rod is bolted to the plate by two ½" Bolts, the shanks of which enter holes in the Contrate Wheel 3 and so prevent the latter from rotating.

It will be found that the secondary shaft 5 rotates twice as fast as the driving Rod carrying the handle 1. Alternatively, by using the Rod 5 as the driving shaft, a one in two reduction gear will be obtained, for the 2" Rod will revolve once only to every two revolutions of the Rod 5. By repeating the device two or three times in a straight line, a very compact transmission gear may be obtained.

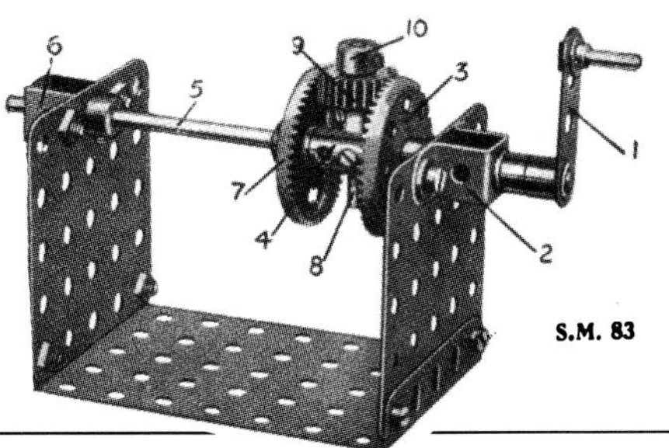

Fig 18. An early Meccano planetary gearbox.→

S.M. 84—PLANETARY GEAR BOX

A planetary gear box of the type shown in S.M. 84 is unique so far as Meccano construction is concerned. In actual practice planetary or epicyclic gears are used to a large extent, but in almost every case an internal-toothed wheel or drum is employed to actuate the planet wheels or idler pinions. The Meccano gear box provides two speeds forward, reverse, and neutral gears.

The drive is taken from the Rod 1 and the motion is transmitted through the gear box to the driven Rod 2. A ½" Pinion on the driving Rod engages with the 3½" Gear Wheel 3, which is free to rotate independently about the Rod 2. The 2½" Rod 4 is journalled in one of the holes in the face of the Gear Wheel 3 and carries a ¾" Pinion 5, 1" Gear Wheel 6 and ½" Pinion 7, all fixed to the Rod. Its other end is supported in a 2½" Strip 8 that is free to turn on the Rod 9.

The ¾" Pinion 10 is immovable, being gripped by its set-screw to a 2" Threaded Rod secured to the Gear Wheel 3 in a hole opposite to the Rod 4. Two nuts, one placed behind the 3½" Gear Wheel and the other on the Threaded Rod immediately against the boss of the Pinion 10, are screwed up very tightly to secure the Pinion and the Threaded Rod rigidly to the wheel 3. Two Washers are placed between the Pinion and the 3½" Gear Wheel.

The other end of the Threaded Rod enters a Threaded Boss 11 secured to the Strip 8 by a ⅜" Bolt. The Coupling 12 is added to assist in balancing the weight of the Rod 4 and its components. The 50-teeth Gear Wheel 13, which forms the sun wheel, is secured to the driven Rod 2, and a Compression Spring is placed between it and the wheel 3. The spring normally holds the wheel 13 in gear with the ¾" Pinion 5.

The Rod 9 is slidable in its bearings but is prevented from rotating. It carries a 1" Gear Wheel 14 and 57-teeth Gear Wheel 15, both secured in position by their set-screws. The Rod protrudes about ⅛" beyond the Gear Wheel 14. The operating lever 16, which pivots about a point 17, carries a Doubl Bracket fitted with a bolt that enters a Coupling 18 secured to the Rod 9.

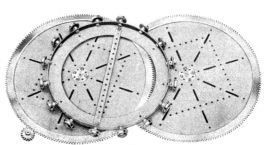

S.M. 84

The mechanism is shown in reverse gear with Gear Wheel 15 engaging Pinion 7. In this position Rod 2 rotates in the same direction as the driving Rod. "Neutral" is obtained by pushing the lever 16 forward so that the Gear Wheel 15 is disengaged from the Pinion 7; in this position the mechanism rotates bodily round the Rod 2 without turning the sun wheel 13. Additional movement of the lever brings Gear 14 into engagement with the corresponding Gear 6, thereby causing Rod 2 to turn slowly in an opposite direction to the driving Rod. This corresponds to a slow forward speed.

Further movement of the lever presses the protruding end of Rod 9 against the end of Rod 2 and throws the wheel 13 out of gear with the Pinion 5 and into engagement with the fixed Pinion 10. This locks the wheel 13 to wheel 3 and the two rotate as a single unit, thus producing, in effect, a straight-through drive. Rod 2 now rotates at maximum speed.

Fig 19. A novel automatic gear change.

S.M. 86—AUTOMATIC GEAR-CHANGE

S.M. 86 represents a gear box which, if called upon to withstand a sudden increase of load on the driven shaft, automatically changes over from high gear into low.

The driving shaft of the gear box is in two sections, 1a and 1b, and is connected to the Motor by means of Sprocket Chain or other suitable method. The countershaft 3 is connected in any convenient manner to the mechanism that is required to be set in motion. The 3" Rod 1a carries a Bush Wheel 4, which is coupled by two pieces of cord to a second Bush Wheel 5. The latter is free to ride up or down the shaft 1a.

Two 1½" Double Angle Strips secure the Bush Wheel 5 to a 57-teeth Gear 7 mounted on the end of the 3" Rod 1b. This Rod carries a 1" Gear 8 and a Compression Spring 9. The Spring tends to maintain the cords 6 outstretched as shown in the illustration, and in this position the Gear 7 is in engagement with a ½" Pinion 11 on the countershaft 3. This gives a speed ratio of 3 : 1.

The Gear 7 will continue to drive the Rod 3 considerably faster than the driving shaft so long as the load or resistance on that Rod remains light, but if the load is increased suddenly, the shaft 1a and Bush Wheel 4 commence to revolve faster than the Bush Wheel 5. But when this takes place the cords 6 are twisted slightly, with the result that the wheel 5, sliding on the Rod 1a, is drawn nearer to the wheel 4. This movement throws the Gear 7 out of engagement with the Pinion 11 and causes the Gear 8 to mesh with a similar Gear 10 on the countershaft 3, thus producing a low speed gear having a 1 : 1 ratio. To bring this about, however, the Spring 9 must be compressed; therefore the two 1" Gears will remain in engagement only while the load on the shaft 3 is greater than the pressure of the Spring.

Immediately the load drops below a certain amount, the Spring re-asserts its influence over the cords 6 and the gear is returned to its normal or "top" speed position.

S.M. 86

S.M. 137—STANDARD ROLLER BEARINGS

The standard Meccano Roller Bearings may be obtained complete (as illustrated) under part No. 167. They measure 12 ins. overall diameter and are intended to replace the built-up roller bearings shown in S.M. 131 in building large swivelling structures.

The Roller Bearings are assembled as follows: One of the Roller Races is secured to the fixed portion of the model and the 1½" Rod is fastened in the Bush Wheel bolted to its centre. The Ring Frame is then placed over the Race so that the flanges of the wheels run upon its raised rim. The second Roller Race is then placed over the Ring Frame so that its raised rim rests upon the flanges of the wheels. The 1½" Rod passes through the centre hole of the 9½" Strip that is bolted across the Ring Frame, and through the Bush Wheel in the centre of the upper Roller Race.

S.M. 137

Method of Rotation—If the driving mechanism is incorporated in the superstructure, a simple way to effect the rotation of the latter is to mount the special 16-teeth Pinion on a vertical driven Rod so that it engages with the teeth of the lower fixed Roller Race. The vertical Rod should be journalled suitably in the superstructure; then if it is set in motion, the Pinion travels round the Roller Race and carries the superstructure with it.

Alternatively, if the driving mechanism is in the fixed base of model, the Pinion should be secured to a Rod journalled in a vertical position in the base and caused to engage with the upper Roller Race.

Fig 21. The Geared Roller Bearing.

S.M. 113—SPEED GOVERNOR FOR ELECTRIC MOTOR

This is an accurate model of the governor device used in certain types of electric lift, and it can of course be used in all Meccano lifts, and in fact in all models that are driven by Electric Motors.

The governor consists essentially of two Simple Bell Cranks 4 pivoted to two horizontal 3½" Strips, which are secured rigidly by bolts inserted one in each side of a Collar secured to the governor spindle 1, two Washers on each bolt being used for spacing purposes. The 2" Pulleys 2 are connected by ½" Bolts but are spaced apart by nuts so that the Threaded Pin on the Strip 6 may easily pass between them. A Compression Spring is inserted between the Pulleys and the Collar carrying the 3½" Strips, and 1½" Strips are pivoted to the top Pulley 2 and to the Bell Cranks 4. The Strip 6 is pivoted to the Motor side plate and is provided with a contact stud (a Spring Buffer) 7.

A portion of the Rod 10 is covered with brown paper, stuck on with gum. A length of 27 B.I. Resistance Wire (part No. 312) is secured to the Collar 11 and is then laid on in a smooth spiral over the paper, and finished off a short distance from the top end of the paper. The Double-arm Crank 9 is insulated from the base and carries a terminal 12. Another terminal 13 is also insulated from the base and is connected to the Motor terminal 8, while the other Motor terminal is "earthed" by connecting it to the frame of the model. The Accumulator is connected to terminals 12 and 13.

If the speed of the Motor increases the governor weights 5 fly out and cause the Strip 6 to move up the resistance 3. If the speed increases beyond a certain limit—as may happen if the load on the Motor is suddenly withdrawn—the contact 7 moves off the resistance on to the paper, thus breaking the circuit. If the speed decreases, owing to an increase in the load, etc., the contact 7 descends and decreases the resistance, and at its lowest point touches the Collar 11, when maximum current is supplied to the Motor.

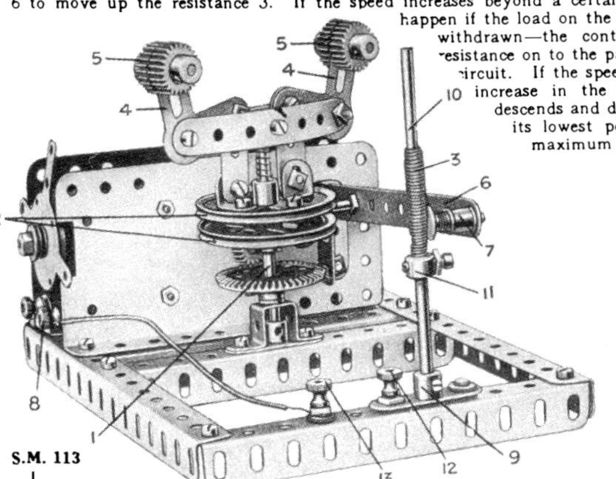

S.M. 113

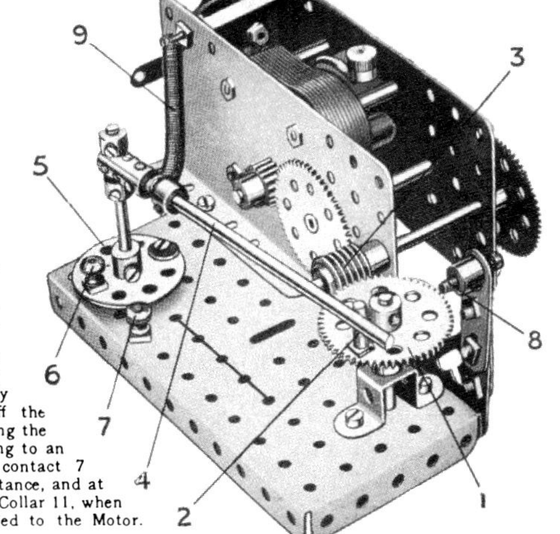

S.M. 114—AUTOMATIC SWITCH

The Motor in this device could be used to drive any Meccano model and the contact breaker used to light lamps, drive a secondary Motor, operate electro magnets, or to perform any other similar work at any pre-arranged intervals.

The 57-teeth Gear 1 meshes with a Worm 3 that is driven from the Motor. Rod 4 is mounted pivotally on a 2" Rod secured in the Bush Wheel 5, which is insulated from the base Plate by means of Insulating Bushes and Washers placed on 6 B.A. Bolts. The terminal 6 is mounted on the shank of one of these bolts.

A ¾" Bolt 8 is mounted in a Threaded Crank, which is secured to a Corner Bracket that is insulated from the base Plate by 6 B.A. Bolts and Insulating Washers and Bushes. Normally the Rod 4 is held against Bolt 8 by a Spring 9, which is anchored to the Motor by an insulated 6 B.A. Bolt. As the Gear 1 rotates, the Threaded Pin 2 presses against the Rod 4, thus allowing current to flow from the terminal 6 along Rod 4, and back through the frame of the apparatus to the uninsulated terminal 7. When the Rod 4 comes to rest against the insulated stop 8, contact between the Rod and the Pin 2 is broken until the Pin, in moving round again touches the Rod.

S.M. 115—CONTROLLER FOR ELECTRIC MOTOR

The electric controller illustrated in S.M. 115 is designed to regulate the speed of the Meccano low-voltage Electric Motor. The device may be incorporated in almost any model that is driven by the Motor.

S.M. 115 shows the complete unit connected to the Motor while S.M. 115A shows the controller dismantled. The resistances are formed from a length of Spring Cord, which must be opened out so that none of the coils are in contact. The Spring Cord is attached at equal distances to six 6 B.A. Bolts 1, which are insulated from the Bush Wheel 2 by means of Insulating Bushes and Washers. The heads of the bolts form the contact studs. The seventh stud 3 is not connected in any way and forms the "off" position of the switch. The switch arm consists of a Double Arm Crank 4 carrying a Spring Buffer 5, the head of which presses lightly on the contact studs. The switch arm pivots on the upper end of the supporting Rod 6 and is retained in place by a Collar 7.

One of the Motor terminals is earthed by connecting it to the metal frame of the model, whilst the other terminal is connected direct to one terminal of the Accumulator. The remaining terminal of the Accumulator is connected to the terminal 8 which is mounted on the shank of the first contact stud. In order to limit the movement of the switch arm, a stop 9 consisting of a portion of a Spring Buffer is bolted to the Bush Wheel 2.

When the contact 5 is pressing on the contact stud 3, no current is supplied to the Motor. If the controller handle is moved to the next contact stud, the current must pass through the whole of the resistance before reaching the Motor, with the result that the latter runs at minimum speed. Speed can now be increased gradually by moving the contact 5 further round the Bush Wheel, until it reaches the stud carrying terminal 8, when maximum current is supplied to the Motor.

22

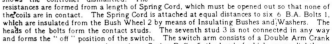

Fig 20. Motor Control.

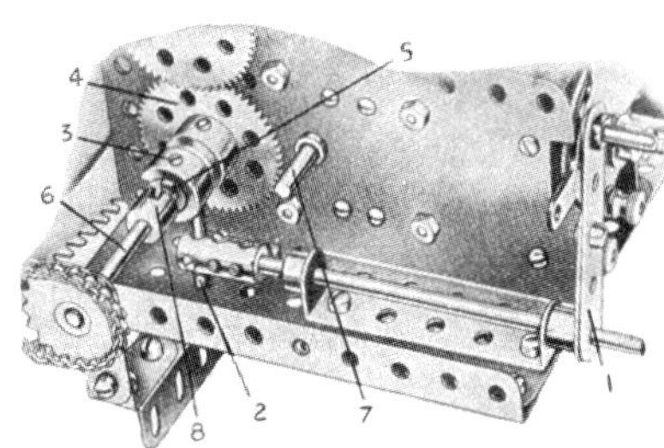

Fig 22. The three extant views of the single motor-driven pontoon crane.

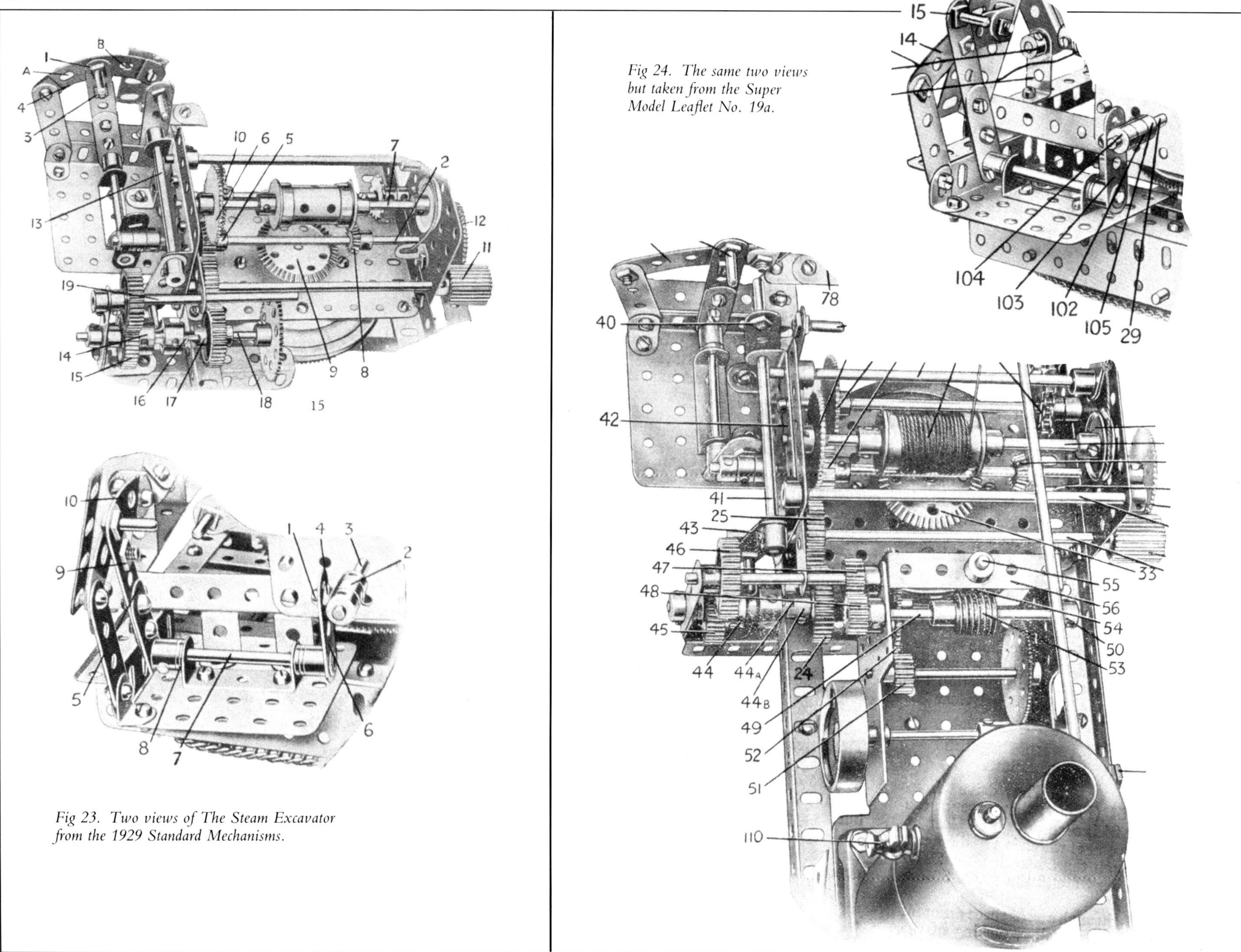

Fig 23. Two views of The Steam Excavator from the 1929 Standard Mechanisms.

Fig 24. The same two views but taken from the Super Model Leaflet No. 19a.

same can be said of the illustration extant of the non-existent SML model No. 6a which also has an economical look as well as a very 'retouched' appearance.

Equally interesting are the two views of the gearbox of SML 19a, The Steam Excavator, neither of which is the same as the illustrations in the Super Model Leaflet (figs 23 and 24). This particular model was the main one to feature the 1929 Steam Engine. The leaflet was published in December 1929 so the model must have been in existence for nearly a year before. The question is therefore, whether the SML 19a was designed or modified for the Steam Engine? A comparison between the two Standard Mechanisms illustrations and their equivalents in the SML shows that in the former the steam engine had not been fitted, but neither of course had an electric motor. No doubt the matter will be resolved one day.

The 1929 edition had a very large print run of 40,000, a much higher figure than in previous years, and, although it was used in bound versions of the Instruction Manuals, it appears to have lasted until 1933 when a virtually identical edition was produced. The only differences between the 1933 and the 1929 edition were a few very minor replacements. From the print code (2/933/3) it would appear that it was a stop-gap between the 1929 edition and the totally different version which was to be published in the following year in the 'blue/gold' style.

A new edition for the Blue/Gold era

The 1934 edition was very different from all its predecessors. It was considerably larger, conforming to the lettered series manual format (fig 25). Cross-hatching was now evident on all appropriate plates, even those of models from earlier years. The contents page shows the extended scope of the publication (fig 26), although the introduction is similar to previous editions. Not all the mechanisms in the 1934 edition were new, but a large number of the most important ones were.

The section on locomotive valve gears was much extended (fig 27), showing three demonstration models which covered the most commonly used types. Gearboxes came in for quite a lot of attention

continued p. 199.

MODEL BUILDING WITH

MECCANO

Real Engineering in Miniature

MECCANO is based on a standard system of equidistant holes spaced half an inch apart and comprises a great number of mechanical elements. These include Perforated Strips, Plates, Angle Brackets, Cranks, Couplings, Pulley Wheels, and Gear Wheels of various sizes and ratios. These elements are capable of being used in an unlimited number of ways, making possible the construction in model form of almost any movement or structure known to Mechanics or Engineering. They do this without the aid of elaborate machines and precision tools that would otherwise be necessary.

Inventing New Models

Model-building with Meccano is really fascinating. As long as one is occupied by reproducing the hundreds of models shown in the Instruction Manuals it is extremely simple and easy, and no undue brain work is necessary. No Meccano boy is content to build only the models illustrated in the Manuals, however, for every thinking boy is keen to invent and likes to build models from his own ideas.

With this in mind, and to assist boys to base their models on correct engineering practice, we have collected and classified a number of Meccano movements, that have to a certain extent become standardised. That is to say these movements may be applied to more than one model—in most cases without any alteration, but in some few instances with only slight alterations, to the standard movement.

Those who invent with Meccano will find these movements, which we now publish as "Standard Mechanisms," of great assistance in helping to perfect their models. The movements have been arrived at by careful thought and experiment, and some knowledge of the principles involved in many of them will well repay the study of any boy interested in engineering. The various devices have been arranged so that immediate reference may be made to any particular motion that it is desired to incorporate in a model. There is no finality in examples of this kind, and others will be added in subsequent editions of this book.

The Value of Meccano

While the greater proportion of boys—or even men—in every generation possess a desire to know just *why* the "wheels go round," it has never been possible, prior to the introduction of Meccano, for the unskilled to make mechanical models.

When you build models with Meccano you use real engineering parts in miniature, for they act in a manner precisely similar to the corresponding elements in actual practice. This means that with Meccano you can accomplish more than with any other system of model construction. Other systems attempt to attain the same object by different methods, and avail themselves of constructive elements that are not based on correct engineering principles. It is important to realise this, for if you commence with badly-designed parts you can only build a very limited number of models. Even these will be constructed incorrectly and will give you faulty ideas of the principles of Engineering.

For these reasons Meccano becomes something more than a toy—it is an educational medium of very real value. Professors of Engineering, bridge-building experts, draughtsmen, and others who are in a position to judge, have from time to time pronounced on the Meccano system. All have declared it to be conceived on sound lines and based on true engineering principles.

We have numerous records in our files of large engineering firms who employ Meccano for designing movements or engineering structures that they are about to build. Famous inventors use it for experimenting and for working out ideas, while in schools and colleges it is used to demonstrate all branches of mechanics.

Meccano Models are real Models

There is no limit to the number of models that can be built with Meccano, and all are real working structures. The Meccano Clock is a real clock—it keeps accurate time. The Meccano Loom is a real loom, and it weaves beautiful material for hat-bands or neckties. The Meccano Motor Chassis—with Ackermann steering gear, gear-box, clutch, and differential—so closely resembles a real motor car that it is used for teaching students at numerous schools of motoring.

It is the same with all other Meccano models—they are all accurate reproductions of the real thing, and they all work because they are based on correct engineering principles.

CONTENTS OF THIS MANUAL

For easy reference purposes, the various mechanisms have been grouped under the following SECTIONS:—

I.	Levers	VIII.	Clutches and Piston Drives	XIV.	Quick Return Mechanisms
II.	Pulley Systems	IX.	Governing Appliances	XV.	Steering Mechanisms
III.	Belt and Chain Drives	X.	Brakes	XVI.	Traversing Mechanisms
IV.	Gear Trains and Gear Boxes	XI.	Bearings and Shafting Supports	XVII.	Springs and Shock Absorbers
V.	Planetary and Epicyclic Gears	XII.	Roller and Slide Bearings	XVIII.	Special Movements
VI.	Intermittent Rotary Motions	XIII.	Applied Screw Mechanisms	XIX.	Electrically Operated Movements
VII.	Cranks, Cams and Eccentrics				

Fig 26.
The contents page of the 1934 edition.

STEPHENSON'S LINK MOTION

S.M.12. The expansion link 1 is built up from two $2\frac{1}{2}''$ large radius Curved Strips secured and spaced apart at the top and bottom by nuts placed on the shanks of $\frac{3}{8}''$ Bolts. On the centre of these Bolts, loosely mounted between the two inner spacing nuts, are the eccentric rods 13 and 14. These are bolted at their other ends to the Eccentrics 10 and 11, which are secured to the main driving axle 12 by the bosses nearest their centres, giving a throw to each Eccentric of $\frac{1}{2}''$. The Eccentrics work in opposite positions in order to rock the expansion link about its centre.

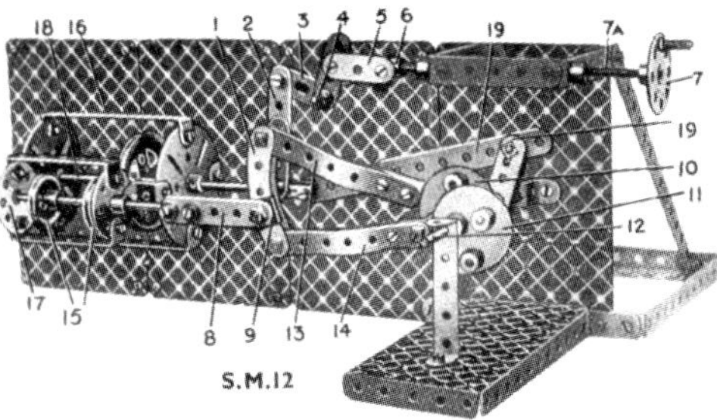

A Pivot Bolt passes through the centre hole of the rear $2\frac{1}{2}''$ Curved Strip in the expansion link, and is secured in the boss of a Crank bolted to the 2in. Strip 2 forming the suspension link, which is attached pivotally by means of bolt and locknuts to one arm of the Boss Bell Crank 3. This is secured to the shank of another Pivot Bolt 4 journalled through the outer end of a $2\frac{1}{2}'' \times \frac{1}{2}''$ Double Angle Strip, the other end of which is bolted to the rear framework. One end of a $1\frac{1}{2}''$ Strip 5 is rigidly bolted to the Threaded Boss 6, Washers being placed on the bolt to make sure that it does not touch the Threaded Rod on which the Boss moves ; and its other end is loosely connected by bolts and locknuts to the elongated hole in the upper arm of the Bell Crank. On operation of the hand-wheel 7, the Threaded Boss 6 is caused to travel to and fro along the Threaded Rod 7a, thus rocking the Bell Crank 3 about its pivot 4. In the case of a locomotive, the hand wheel is placed in a convenient handling position in the driver's cab.

The piston valves, represented by 1" Pulley Wheels 15, are connected by means of the $2\frac{1}{2}''$ Strip 8 to an Eye Piece that fulfils the functions of the die, and slides on the outer Curved Strip of the link.

The cylinder 16 and steam chest 17 are connected by $\frac{1}{2}''$ Reversed Brackets. A Rod 18 carrying a Pulley Wheel representing the piston, is attached by a Strip Coupling to the connecting rod 19, which is mounted on a $\frac{1}{2}''$ Bolt secured in the ends of two Cranks, forming part of the main axle 12.

Fig 27. A page of locomotive valve gear.

JOY'S VALVE GEAR

S.M.13. The crankshaft, or driving axle of the engine is built up from two Cranks mounted on the end of the short Rod 3 and rigidly secured together at their outer ends by a $\frac{1}{2}''$ Bolt, on the shank of which the connecting rod 5 is pivoted. A $1\frac{1}{2}''$ Pulley takes the place of the piston, and the 8" Rod to which it is secured forms the piston rod. The crosshead consists of a Strip Coupling.

The motion is derived from a point 4 in the connecting rod 5, at which point the connecting link 6 is attached pivotally by a bolt and two nuts. The lower end of the connecting link 6 is pivoted by the same means to an anchor link 7, which in turn pivots about a fixed point 8. It may be noted that the point 8 is the only fixed point in the gear. The valve lever 9 is pivoted to a point in the link 6 just below the bolt 4, and at its upper end is bolted pivotally to the valve rod 10, one end of which is connected to the valve spindle 11 by means of a Strip Coupling.

WALSCHAERTS' VALVE GEAR

S.M.14. The movement of the piston valves 1 is derived from two sources, namely, the combining lever 2, and a Crank 7 attached to the end of the crank pin in the rear driving wheel. The combining lever is connected to the crosshead by a $1\frac{1}{2}''$ Strip 4, bolted rigidly to an Angle Bracket that in turn is secured to the Strip Coupling forming the crosshead, its other end being pivoted to the Valve 5 by means of an ordinary Meccano bolt passed through the lever and inserted in a Collar. The bolt serves in place of the Grub Screw to secure this Collar to the spindle 5. The expansion link 8 consists of two $2\frac{1}{2}''$ large radius Curved Strips joined at their ends by $\frac{3}{8}''$ Bolts. Two nuts are placed on each bolt between the Strips so that the latter are spaced about $\frac{1}{4}''$ apart. The inner Curved Strip is pivoted at its centre hole by a bolt and two nuts to an Angle Bracket bolted to a Trunnion.

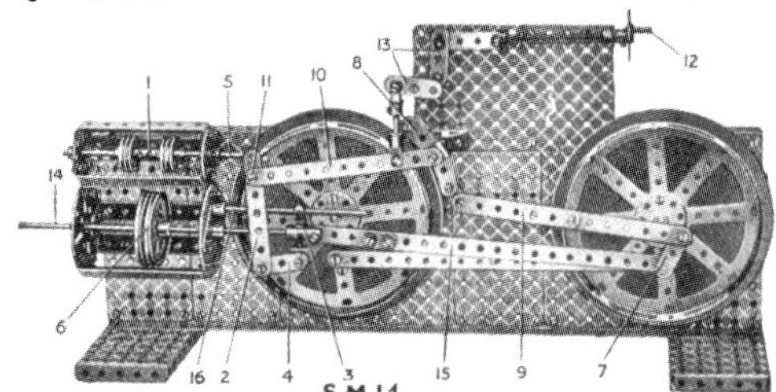

TWO-SPEED EPICYCLIC GEAR-BOX

S.M.58. This type of epicyclic gear-box has certain advantages over the more orthodox gear-box, chief of which are the smoothness with which the drive can be taken up and the fact that all gears are in constant mesh.

The gear-box illustrated is shown mounted between the side girders of a Meccano motor chassis. The driving shaft 1 carries two Face Plates, which are spaced apart about $\frac{1}{2}''$ and carry two 2" Axle Rods 3. Each Rod carries a $\frac{1}{2}''$ and a $\frac{3}{4}''$ Pinion, and a $2\frac{1}{2}''$ Strip 4 is fitted between the two Pinions, a Washer being placed between the Strip and $\frac{1}{2}''$ Pinion. Rods 3 are held in place by Collars, and it is important they rotate freely.

The driven shaft 2 is passed through the centre hole of the Strip 4 and is inserted in the boss of the Face Plate on the Rod 1 for a short distance to keep it correctly centred. A 57-teeth Gear 5, fixed on the Rod, is spaced from the Face Plate by a Washer, and from the Strip 4 by three Washers. The 50-teeth Gear 6 is held in a Socket Coupling in which also a $1\frac{1}{2}''$ Pulley is secured. The Socket Coupling unit is free on the Rod 2, and a Collar is placed between the Gear 6 and the $2\frac{1}{2}''$ Strip. A length of Cord is tied to an Angle Bracket fixed to the frame, passed round the $1\frac{1}{2}''$ Pulley, and then led round a $\frac{3}{8}''$ Bolt fixed by two nuts to the Angle Bracket and two Washers to keep the Cord in place. The Cord is finally tied to the foot pedal 8, consisting of a pivoted $1\frac{1}{2}''$ Strip to which an Angle Bracket is bolted. A Bush Wheel 7 is fixed on the driven Rod, in such a way

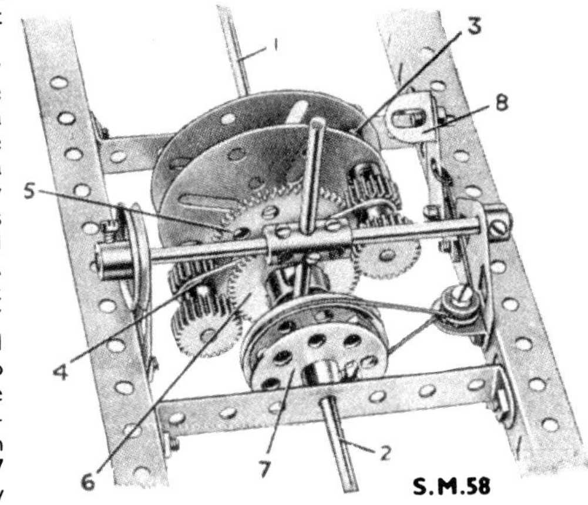

Fig 29.
A simple and easy-to-understand epicyclic gearbox.

Section IV. Gear Trains and Gear-Boxes—(continued)

engagement with one of the two $\frac{1}{2}$" Pinions on the driving Rod. If desired, a $\frac{1}{2}$" diameter $\frac{3}{4}$" face Pinion can be used in place of the two separate Pinions. Hence if the Rod 2 is used as the driven shaft and the large Contrate Wheel 5 is thrown into gear with its respective Pinion, the Rod 1 is driven nearly three times as fast as the Rod 2, the actual ratio being 2 and 12/19 : 1.

Alternatively, if the small Contrate Wheel 4 is thrown into engagement, the other Rod turns only a little faster than the driving Rod, the ratio in this case being 16/19 : 1.

COMPACT THREE-SPEED GEAR-BOX

S.M.42. This three-speed and reverse gear-box is of particular interest on account of its extreme compactness. It is in fact probably the smallest gear-box that can be built with Meccano to give three forward speeds and reverse.

The end of the Rod 1 is inserted in the bore of the $\frac{1}{2}$" Pinion 4 that is carried on a separate Rod 2 from which the final drive is taken. The latter Rod carries also a $\frac{3}{4}$" Pinion and Collar. The sliding lay-shaft is a $4\frac{1}{2}$" Rod on which are a $\frac{1}{2}$" Pinion 5, a $\frac{3}{4}$" Pinion 6, and a $\frac{1}{2}$" Pinion 7. A $\frac{1}{2}$" Pinion 8 is carried on a $\frac{3}{8}$" Bolt screwed into the transverse bore of a Threaded Boss and locked by means of a Grub Screw screwed into the opposite end of the bore. The Threaded Boss is rigidly attached to the gear-box frame by a $\frac{1}{2}$" Bolt 9, but is spaced by a Collar and two Washers.

The movement of the sliding shaft is controlled by a $\frac{3}{8}$" Bolt 10, the head of which fits between the bosses of the Pinions 6 and 7. The Bolt is fixed in a Collar on the end of a 3" Rod forming the gear change lever, and pivoted to a 1" Triangular Plate by a further Collar secured in place on the Rod by its Grub Screw, and carrying also a bolt whose shank passes through one of the holes in the Triangular Plate. The Bolt is locked in position by a nut to allow the Rod to pivot freely.

As shown in the illustration, first forward speed is in engagement, the drive passing through the $\frac{1}{2}$" Pinion on the driving shaft 1 to the $\frac{3}{4}$" Pinion 6 on the layshaft. The $\frac{1}{2}$" Pinion 7 engages the $\frac{3}{4}$" Pinion on the driven shaft, so that there are two stages of reduction gearing between driving and driven Rods. By sliding the layshaft to the right the Pinion 7 disengages, but Pinion 6 remains in engagement with its $\frac{1}{2}$" Pinion and at the same time meshes with Pinion 4. This gives a straight through drive. Further movement of the sliding Rod brings into engagement Pinions 3 and 5, and 6 and 4, in this case providing two step-up stages for top gear.

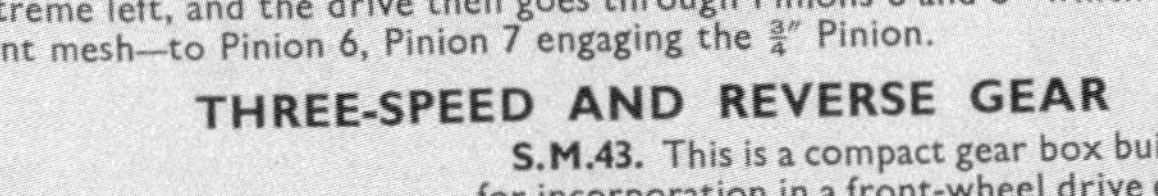

Reverse gear is obtained when the rod is slid over to the extreme left, and the drive then goes through Pinions 3 and 8—which are in constant mesh—to Pinion 6, Pinion 7 engaging the $\frac{3}{4}$" Pinion.

S.M.42

THREE-SPEED AND REVERSE GEAR

S.M.43. This is a compact gear box built specially for incorporation in a front-wheel drive chassis, but it can easily be adapted for use with a chassis of the conventional type with driven back wheels.

The sides of the gear-box consist of $3\frac{1}{2}$" Flat Girders bolted by means of $\frac{1}{2}$"×$\frac{1}{2}$" Angle Brackets to the underside of an E6 Electric Motor. These are joined together at each end by a $2\frac{1}{2}$"×$\frac{1}{2}$" Double Angle Strip fitted with Flat Trunnions, the end holes of which form bearings for the lay-shaft. The third hole from the left-hand side of the illustration, in each of the Flat Girders, carries a $\frac{1}{2}$"×$\frac{1}{2}$" Angle Bracket, and these two parts form supports for two $2\frac{1}{2}$" Strips spaced apart, as shown, by Washers.

A Rod 8 carrying a $\frac{3}{4}$" Pinion and 1" Gear, and held in place by Collars, one of which is shown at 8a, is now fitted. The inner end of this Rod is journalled in one of the $2\frac{1}{2}$" Strips already mentioned. The other $2\frac{1}{2}$" Strip supports the inner end of a second Rod that carries a 50-teeth and a 1" Gear, a $\frac{1}{2}$" Pinion 18 also being fitted outside the gear-box as illustrated. Immediately above this Pinion is mounted, on the Flat Trunnion, a second similar Pinion carried on a $\frac{3}{4}$" Bolt. This Pinion forms the connection between the two Pinions 18 and 19, when reverse gear is engaged.

The lay-shaft supports two 1" Gears 20 and 22, a $\frac{3}{4}$" Pinion 21, and a 50-teeth Gear 23. The Rod from the gear-lever is coupled up to the lay-shaft between the last-mentioned Gear and a Collar.

S.M.44

THREE-MOVEMENT GEAR-BOX

S.M.44. The outstanding feature of this gear-box is that it can be used to provide three movements each of which can be independently stopped, started or reversed. The drive is taken to the gear-box through Sprocket Chain that passes round the Sprockets 1, 2 and 3 in such a manner that the centre Sprocket 2 is driven in the reverse direction to the other two. The Sprockets are each carried on a 2" Axle Rod fitted with a Collar and $\frac{3}{4}$" Pinion. The Collars retain the Rods in place, and the Pinions on the upper and lower Rods are placed close to the outer side plate, whereas the Pinion 4 is arranged nearer the centre of its shaft. Three secondary shafts are arranged as shown, and each carries a 50-teeth Gear Wheel. These shafts are provided with a Collar on one end, and at the other end carry two Collars with a space between them to admit the head as a bolt. Three control levers are mounted in small Fork Pieces pivoted on an Axle Rod secured to the base Plates by Handrail Supports.

The method of operation is as follows. The Gear 5 is shown in engagement with the Pinion on the rod of the Sprocket 1. By moving the appropriate gear lever over to the left, this Gear is thrown out of mesh with its Pinion, so that no drive is transmitted; and by further movement of the gear lever the Gear is brought into engagement with the Pinion 4 that causes it to rotate in the opposite direction. The other two shafts each operate with a similar movement, and it will be seen that each one can be controlled independently to rotate in either direction or to remain stationary.

THREE-SPEED AND REVERSE GEAR

S.M.45. The Rod 64 forms the primary driving shaft, and is provided with a $\frac{3}{4}$" Pinion 68 and a 1" Gear Wheel 69. The countershaft consists of a $6\frac{1}{2}$" Rod 71 that is slidable in the end Double Angle Strips of the gear-box. This Rod carries the following parts—two Collars, acting as stops to limit its sliding movement; a 50-teeth Gear 72; a 1" Gear 73; two more Collars, one of which, 74, is free on the Rod; a $\frac{3}{4}$" Pinion 75; a 1" Gear 76, and a $\frac{1}{2}$" Pinion 77. The driven 3" Rod 78 carries a 50-teeth Gear 79 a 1" Gear 80, and a $\frac{1}{2}$" Pinion 81.

A Washer should be placed between the $\frac{1}{2}$" Pinion 81 and the Double Angle Strip. This Pinion is in constant engagement with another $\frac{1}{2}$" Pinion 83, which is free to turn upon a $\frac{3}{4}$" Bolt secured to the end Double Angle Strip by two nuts.

The different speeds are obtained in the following manner. Assume that the sliding Rod 71 is at the farthest limit of its travel to the left. Then the drive from the engine is led through the following gears—68, 72, 77, 83 and

S.M. 45

68 64 69 70 70A 79 78 80 81 49

71 72 73 84 74 75 76 83 77

7

Fig 28A. A selection of gearboxes from the 1934 edition.

Section IV. Gear Trains and Gear-Boxes—(continued)

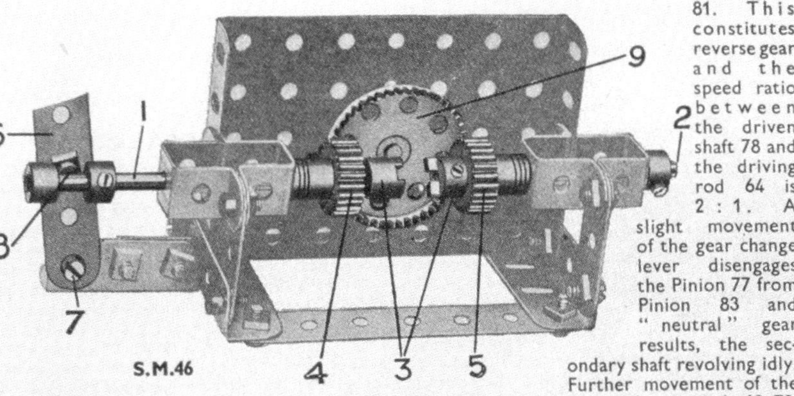

81. This constitutes reverse gear and the speed ratio between the driven shaft 78 and the driving rod 64 is 2 : 1. A slight movement of the gear change lever disengages the Pinion 77 from Pinion 83 and "neutral" gear results, the secondary shaft revolving idly. Further movement of the lever slides the Rod 71 farther to the right and causes the following gears to be engaged—68, 72, 75 and 79. This gives first speed forward, the ratio between shafts 78 and 64 being 4 : 1. Continuing the movement of the lever, the second forward speed is obtained, the drive now being directed via 69, 73, 75, and 79, and the ratio being 2 : 1. When the lever is hard over and the Rod 71 at the limit of its travel to the right, the gears in engagement are 69, 73, 76 and 80. This represents top forward speed, with a ratio of 1 : 1.

CLUTCH REVERSING GEAR

S.M.46. In this mechanism a drive transmitted through the Contrate Wheel 9 results in forward or reverse gear at the Rod 1.

The $1\frac{1}{2}''$ Contrate Gear 9 is mounted on a short Rod journalled in suitable bearings, and at one side it meshes with a $\frac{3}{4}''$ Pinion 5 mounted on the Rod 2, as shown, together with the one half of a Dog Clutch 3. The other side of the Contrate Gear is in engagement with a second $\frac{3}{4}''$ pinion 4 mounted on a sliding Rod 1. The remaining half of the Dog Clutch is also fitted on this Rod. At a suitable point along its length the Rod is fitted with two collars between which a Bolt 8 is positioned. This Bolt is carried on a lever 6 of any suitable length, the lower end of which is lock-nutted as shown at 7.

RADIAL GEAR-BOX

S.M.47. In the majority of Meccano models, especially cranes, the gear-box forms the most difficult part of the construction, especially if a centralised system of control is desired. S.M.47 shows how this can be accomplished in a remarkably simple manner, the complete mechanism being extremely compact and efficient.

The sides of the gear-box, as shown in the photograph, consist of $5\frac{1}{2}''\times3\frac{1}{2}''$ Flat Plates bolted at their bottom edges to a $5\frac{1}{2}''\times2\frac{1}{2}''$ Flanged Plate, $2\frac{1}{2}''\times\frac{1}{2}''$ Double Angle Strips being used to brace the structure at its upper edges. The driving shaft, a $4\frac{1}{2}''$ Rod carrying the 57-teeth Gear 1, carries a planetary member built up in the following manner. A Socket Coupling is fitted at one end with a $\frac{1}{2}''$ Pinion, and at the other with a Bush Wheel one of the outer holes of which is fitted with a Pivot Bolt and a $\frac{1}{2}''$ Pinion 2. This complete planetary gear is free to rotate about the Rod, and is controlled by a $\frac{1}{2}''$ Pinion meshing with the Pinion carried in one end of the Socket Coupling. This $\frac{1}{2}''$ Pinion is carried on a short Rod fitted with a Crank 3 that has a $\frac{1}{2}''$ Reversed Angle Bracket bolted to it in the position shown, a Flat Bracket being held in place by the same Bolt. A $1\frac{1}{2}''$ Rod journalled in the Flat Bracket carries at its inner end a Collar, a second Collar being fitted as shown to take the pressure of a Compression Spring fixed between the two brackets. The outer end of the Rod carries a Coupling to form a handle. It will now be seen that, on turning the handle into any of the four positions, as illustrated, the planetary member will be made to take up corresponding positions in a reverse direction.

The Pinion 2 takes the drive from the 57-teeth Gear 1, through a $\frac{1}{2}''$ Pinion secured on the shaft. Pinion 2 now meshes with any of four 50-teeth Gears arranged radially round the planetary member and mounted on Rods of suitable size to fit the gear-box, this point depending entirely on the type of model into which the mechanism has been built. If so desired 57-teeth Gears may be used in place of the 50-teeth Gear shown, the spacing of the shaft being altered accordingly. Also, if extra movements are required, these can be incorporated by offsetting their respective gears from those already fitted, but a modified selector will be necessary if this is done.

A good example of the use of this type of gear-box will be found in the Meccano Breakdown Crane, Leaflet No. 30.

1 2 3 S.M.47

FOUR MOVEMENT GEAR-BOX

S.M.48. This gear-box is specially suitable for a crane, the four separate movements that it supplies being utilised for slewing, hoisting, luffing and travelling. In the illustration it is shown fitted into the Meccano Automatic Grabbing Crane, Leaflet No. 35. The base structure is built up on a Geared Roller Bearing, not shown in this illustration, and consists of Angle Girders of various lengths, a controlling platform, formed from $5\frac{1}{2}''\times3\frac{1}{2}''$ Flat Plates, being fitted at the front. One side of the platform supports the E.6 Electric Motor forming the power unit, and the other side, in the actual model, is occupied with a resistance controller similar to S.M.110.

Each outside portion of the gear-box proper, consists of a $5\frac{1}{2}''\times2\frac{1}{2}''$ Flanged Plate, and an extra section formed from a $5\frac{1}{2}''\times2\frac{1}{2}''$ Flat Plate, is fitted for the inner bearings. A $\frac{1}{2}''$ Pinion on the Motor armature shaft meshes with a 57-teeth Gear secured on a $2\frac{1}{2}''$ Rod together with a second $\frac{1}{2}''$ Pinion. The 57-teeth Gear that is in engagement with the last-mentioned Pinion is secured on the same Rod as a 1" Gear meshing with a second similar Gear. This last Gear is locked on a Rod journalled in the gear-box, a $\frac{1}{2}''$ face, $\frac{1}{2}''$ width Pinion also being carried as shown.

Two 57-teeth Gears, on sliding Rods, mesh with this Pinion, each Rod being fitted with two Collars. The space between each pair of these Collars is occupied by a Bolt head, the Bolt being carried in the end hole of a Crank.

A long Rod, carried in suitable bearings, connects this Crank to its respective lever situated at the fore end of the control platform. When the two levers are in position they should bear against a

8

Fig 28B. Further gearboxes from the 1934 Standard Mechanisms.

Section V. Planetary and Epicyclic Gears—(continued)

that the shanks of Bolts fitted to the 1½″ Pulley can be made to engage the holes in the Bush Wheel to form a dog-clutch

The Socket Coupling unit is free to slide on its Rod, and its movement is controlled by a hand lever consisting of a 2½″ Axle Rod. The lever is held in a Coupling carrying two 2″ Rods journalled in Flat Trunnions bolted to the side girders. To engage low gear the hand lever is pulled back, thus disengaging the dog-clutch, and the foot pedal is depressed to apply the brake to the 1½″ Pulley, which is held stationary. Top gear is engaged by releasing the foot pedal and moving the hand lever forward. This engages the dog-clutch and gives a "straight through" drive, as the two Gears 5 and 6 become solid on the driven Rod 2.

S.M.59

HOBBS' INERTIA GEAR

S.M.59. The type of gear-box in which sliding gears are brought into mesh by the movements of a gear lever has never been regarded as ideal for use in motor cars in spite of the great improvements effected in its design since its introduction for this purpose. In recent years new types of gear-boxes therefore have occupied the attention of inventors, and this ingenious mechanism, developed by Mr. H. F. Hobbs, an Australian engineer, automatically provides gear ratios suitable for the load imposed on the engine of the car to which it is fitted. Its use makes the inclusion of a clutch unnecessary.

S.M.60a

9 3 7 8 5 6

The driving shaft 1 and the driven shaft 3 are arranged in line with a short intermediate shaft 2. The driving shaft corresponds to the engine crankshaft in actual practice, and is fitted with two Face Plates, bearings for the Rod being formed by the end Plate of the frame and a 3½″ × ½″ Double Angle Strip bolted between the side Plates, but spaced from them by Washers. The 2″ Rod 2 is inserted for a short distance in the boss of the end Face Plate on the Rod 1, but is free to rotate, and is supported also in a Double Angle Strip fitted between the side Plates. A 50-teeth Gear, a Collar and a Face Plate are fixed to the Rod. The driven Rod 3, which is journalled in a Double Angle Strip and the 3½″ × 2½″ Plate of the casing, carries a Ratchet Wheel, and a Pulley fitted with a band brake.

The two Face Plates on the Rod 1 carry two 1½″ Rods 4 that are free to rotate and are provided with ¾″ Pinions and Couplings. The Rods are inserted in the end transverse bores of the Couplings, and the latter each bear two Collars firmly fixed by means of ⅜″ Bolts. The Couplings are spaced from the Face Plates by a Washer on each side. The Pinions mesh with the Gear Wheel 6, and when they are correctly placed the weights 5 should be arranged in exactly opposite positions before the Grub Screws are tightened up. The correct placing of the weights in relation to each other is very important if smooth running is to be obtained, as any inaccuracy will cause excessive vibration at high speeds.

The Face Plate on the Rod 2 carries two Pawls 8, mounted on Pivot Bolts and held in constant engagement with the Ratchet Wheel 7 by means of Spring Cord. This arrangement serves as a freewheel and smooths out the drive. If the shaft 1 is rotated and the Gear 6 held stationary, the planet Pinions will rotate round the Gear, causing the weights 5 also to rotate. Centrifugal force acting on these weights imparts a series of impulses to the Gear 6, tending to turn it first in one direction and then in the other; and as the speed of the driving shaft increases a greater force is exerted on the weights 5, and the resistance offered by the Gear 6 is overcome.

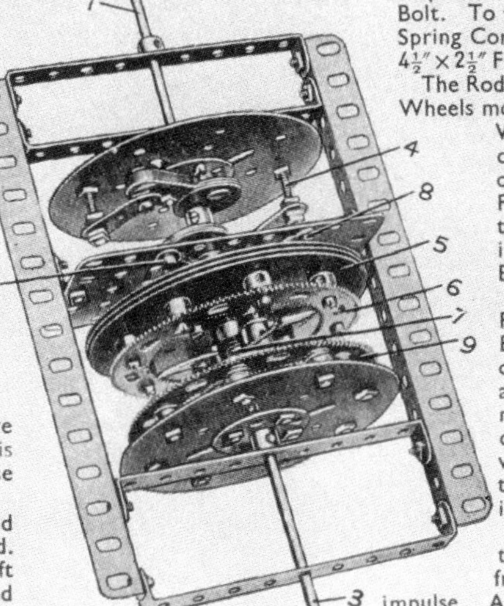

S.M.60

SPONTAN TRANSMISSION GEAR

S.M.60. The operation of this mechanism will best be understood by reference to the three photographs of the Meccano model reproduced on this page. S.M.60 shows the complete gear, and S.M.60a and S.M.60b show the components before assembly.

The working parts are housed in a frame consisting of two 7½″ Angle Girders, between which are bolted four 4½″ × ½″ Double Angle Strips and a 4½″ × 2½″ Flat Plate. These form bearings for the driving shaft 1, the intermediate shaft 2, S.M.60b, and the driven shaft 3. The Rod 1 carries a 4″ Circular Plate that is bolted to a Bush Wheel and fitted with two 1″ Screwed Rods 4, each held firmly in place by two nuts screwed tightly against the Plate. The 3½″ Rod 2 is journalled in the Flat Plate, and also in the boss of the inner Bush Wheel bolted to the Circular Plate on the Rod 3. This Bush Wheel can be seen in S.M.60a.

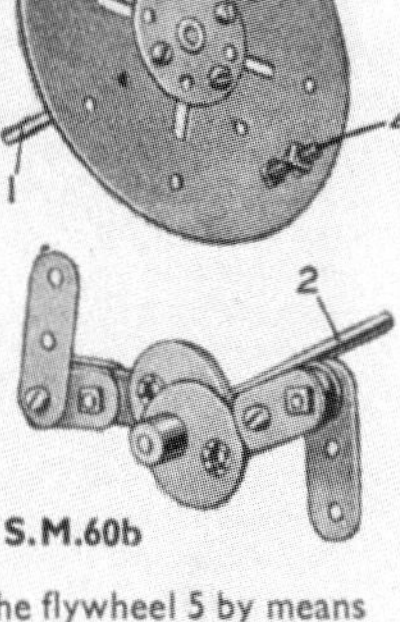

2

S.M.60b

The end of the Rod 2 carries two Single Throw Eccentrics mounted with the bosses facing outward and in directly opposite positions. The strap of each Eccentric is fitted with a weight made up of a number of Flat Brackets. The actual number used will depend upon the maximum speed of the driven shaft, and they are pivotally connected by means of 1½″ Strips to the Screwed Rods 4 on the driving Plate. The flywheel or "pendulum wheel" 5 is built up by placing the bosses of Bush Wheels through the centre holes of two 4″ Circular Plates, the two Plates then being mounted with the Bush Wheels inward on each side of a third Plate, and secured by eight ¾″ Bolts on the shanks of each of which are two Washers, one between each Plate. The same Bolts hold the Gear Ring 6, which is spaced from the Plate by a Collar and Washer on each Bolt. To the rear of the flywheel so formed lengths of Spring Cord are fitted, being attached by Bolts 8 to the 4½″ × 2½″ Flat Plate fixed to the frame.

The Rod 2 is free to rotate in the bosses of the two Bush Wheels mounted between the Plates, and carries the Bush Wheel 7, which is fitted with four Pivot Bolts carrying Pawls. The Bush Wheel is spaced from the flywheel 5 by means of Washers, and a Collar is placed between the wheel 5 and the Flat Plate. The Pawls on one side of the Bush Wheel engage the inside teeth of the Gear Ring 6, and the second pairs of Pawls engage the teeth inside the Gear Ring 9, which is bolted to a circular Plate by eight ½″ Bolts each carrying a Collar and two Washers for spacing purposes.

When the Rod 1 is rotated slowly, the connecting links attached to the Rods 4 cause the bob weights on the Eccentric straps to rotate round the Eccentrics. These unbalanced weights tend to turn the Eccentrics first in one direction and then in the other, the impulses increasing in intensity as the engine speed increases. This alternate to-and-fro motion is transmitted through the Rod 2 to the Bush Wheel 7, and backward rotation is damped out by the action of the Pawls on the flywheel 5, which is prevented from rotating by the Spring Cord. The spring-mounted wheel tends to smooth out the drive and the reaction of the springs by which it is held assists the forward motion.

The second set of Pawls on the Bush Wheel 7 rotate the Gear Ring 9, thus causing the car to travel forward, the tendency being for the car to free-wheel on the backward stroke until it receives another forward impulse. As the car picks up speed the forward impulses act on the Eccentrics for a longer period and the reverse impulses are proportionately reduced. Eventually a stage is reached when the Rod 2 rotates uniformly with the driving shaft.

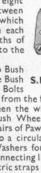

11

Fig 30. More complex gearboxes.

Section V. Planetary and Epicyclic Gears—(continued)

FOUR-SPEED and REVERSE PLANETARY GEAR-BOX

S.M.61. By means of planetary gearing it is possible to obtain a wide range of gear ratios that are not easily obtained by direct gearing. The construction of a planetary gear-box offers much scope for ingenuity, and a cleverly-designed box of this type is illustrated in S.M.61. The 6½″ Axle Rod 1 takes up the drive from the power unit, and is journalled in the centre holes of a 5½″ Angle Girder and a 5½″ × ½″ Double Angle Strip forming part of the framework for the gear-box. The driven 5″ Rod 2 is journalled in a similar manner at the other end of the frame. A cage for the planet gears is built up from two Face Plates, between which two 2″ Axle Rods are secured by means of Threaded Couplings rigidly bolted to the Plates, which are arranged with their bosses outermost. The Face Plates should be lined up carefully so that the holes through the bosses are in perfect alignment, and the complete cage is free to slide on the Rods 1 and 2. The Rod 2 carries at its inner extremity a 1″ Gear Wheel 4, in the centre hole of which the end of the Rod 1 is inserted to prevent wobble. The Rod 1 carries a fixed ¾″ Pinion 3.

The sun wheels 6 and 7, consisting of a 57 and a 50-teeth Gear Wheel, are held together by a Socket Coupling placed over their bosses, and the Rod 1 is free to rotate in their centres. The Gears are prevented from rotating by a 3½″ × ½″ Double Angle Strip attached to the 57-teeth Gear by ½″ Bolts, on the shank of each of which is a Collar for spacing purposes.

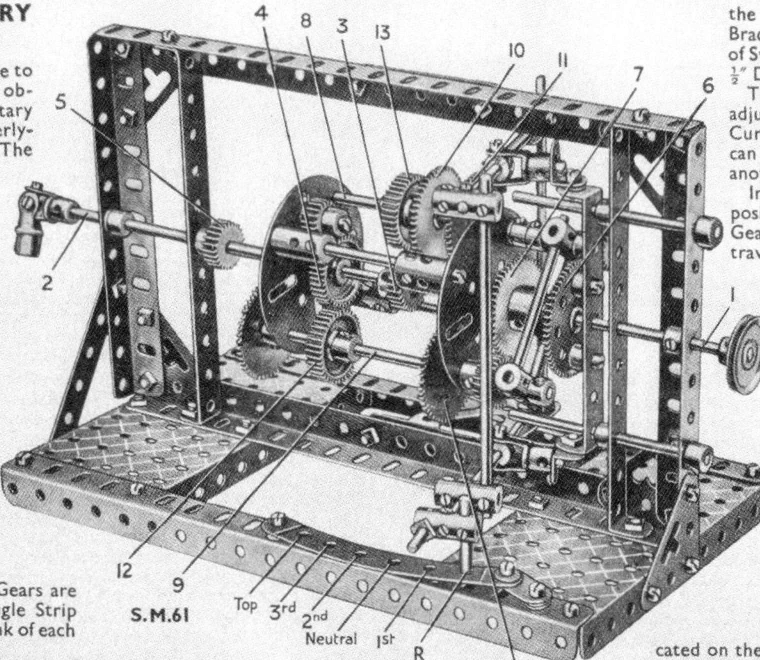

S.M.61

Two 3″ Axle Rods are placed as shown and passed through the Double Angle Strip to prevent it from rotating, at the same time allowing it to slide to and fro. The 5″ Axle Rods 8 and 9, journalled in the cage, carry the planet Pinions that rotate about the Gears 6 and 7. Rod 8 carries a ½″ Pinion engaging the Gear 6 and the Rod 9 a ¾″ Pinion that meshes with the Gear 7.

Each Rod carries a Coupling, and these Couplings are connected together by 2½″ Rods held in their end transverse bores. The two Rods engage the groove of the Socket Coupling, so that as the sun wheels are slid to and fro by means of the 3½″ × ½″ Double Angle Strip, they also cause the cage to slide with a corresponding movement, but at the same time allow it to rotate independently.

The Rod 8 carries, in addition to the planetary Pinion, two 50-teeth Gears 10 and 11, and a 1″ Gear 13. The Rod 9 carries a 50-teeth Gear 14 and a 1″ Gear 12, placed inside the cage, and another 50-teeth Gear placed outside the cage at the opposite end to the sun and planet wheels.

The 9½″ Angle Girders forming the top and bottom members of the main frame are fitted with two Flanged Brackets spaced from the Girders by three Washers on each securing Bolt. A 5″ Axle Rod is journalled in the outer holes of these Brackets, and carries two Couplings, in the upper one of which a 3½″ Axle is fitted, and in the lower one a 4½″ Axle. These Rods carry Couplings that are connected by a 4½″ Rod. A third Coupling on the lower Rod carries a Threaded Pin and a 1″ Axle Rod, the Pin forming a handle for the gear-change mechanism, while the 1″ Rod fits into the holes of a 4″ Curved Strip, fixed as shown. To allow correct placing of the Strip, one end is attached to the slotted hole of a Flat Bracket. The two horizontal Rods are connected by means of Swivel Bearings and pivoted Angle Brackets to the 3½″ × ½″ Double Angle Strip attached to the sun wheels.

The 1″ Rod at the end of the gear-change lever should be adjusted so that normally it fits into one of the holes in the Curved Strip, but by a slight upward movement of the lever can be disengaged to allow the lever to be moved in another position.

In the illustration reverse gear is in engagement. In this position the Pinion 3 on the driving shaft engages with the Gear 10, thus causing the ½″ planet Pinion on the Rod 8 to travel round the sun wheel 6. This movement causes the cage to revolve, and for reverse gear the cage is locked "solid" with the driven shaft by means of a fixed ½″ Pinion that engages the 1″ Gear 4. The Pinion is mounted on a ¾″ Bolt and spaced by two Washers from the Face Plate, the Bolt being inserted in one of the elongated holes so that the Pinion can be correctly placed for the teeth to engage the 1″ Gear.

By moving the gear lever one position to the left, the fixed Pinion is thrown out of engagement with the Gear 4, which is brought into mesh with the 1″ Gear 12 on the Rod 9. The driving Pinion 3 still remains in mesh with the Gear 10, thus causing the cage to rotate, and the ¾″ Pinion on the Rod 9 to run round the Gear 7. Thus the Gear 12 drives the Gear 4. By moving the gear lever into the next position, Pinion 3 is disengaged from the Gear 10, so that no drive is transmitted to the cage.

For second gear, the position of which is indicated on the quadrant, the Pinion 3, is brought into engagement with Gear 11, and the Gear 12 slides out of mesh with the Gear 4, which engages the Gear 13. In this case the Rod 9 rotates idly. The Gears 4 and 13 remain in mesh for third gear, but the driving Pinion is disengaged from the Gear 11 and brought into mesh with the 50-teeth Gear 14.

Further sliding movement of the cage disengages the two 1″ Gears and causes the 50-teeth Gear mounted outside the cage to engage with the Pinion 5.

Fig 30A. A complex epicyclic gear box.

Section VIII. CLUTCHES AND FRICTION DRIVES

PAWL AND RATCHET FREE WHEEL

S.M.91. A "free-wheel" movement of this type can be used in all models where it is required to transmit the drive in one direction only, as in model bicycles clock-winding mechanisms, models operated by treadles, pedal motors, etc. It is invaluable also for converting reciprocating motion into intermittent rotary motion.

The free-wheel mechanism is shown attached to a 3" Sprocket Wheel, but this may be replaced by a 3½" Gear Wheel, large Pulley, or Face Plate, etc. The Sprocket revolves freely on its axle, but is kept in position by the Ratchet Wheel secured to the axle on one side and a Collar on the other side.

Two Pawls are mounted pivotally on the face of the Sprocket by means of Pivot Bolts and lock-nuts, and are held in engagement with the Ratchet by pieces of Spring Cord attached to Set-Screws in the Pawls and also to the face of the Sprocket. It will be evident that the axle and Sprocket Wheel can each move independently in one direction only. The driving power may be imparted primarily to either the axle or the Sprocket, to suit requirements.

FRICTION FREE WHEEL

S.M.92. The usual type of free wheel makes use of pawls and ratchets as illustrated in S.M.91, but in this example an interesting substitute has been found for this noisy and often cumbersome ratchet type of mechanism.

A Coupling 3 is secured to a Rod, which also has a Flanged Wheel 1 mounted freely on it. The Flanged Wheel is spaced away from the Coupling by four Washers, and is attached to a 1" Gear by a Socket Coupling. The 1" Gear meshes with a second similar Gear secured on a Rod that carries also a 2" Sprocket Wheel.

In each of the end transverse bores of the Coupling is secured a Threaded Pin in such a manner that the square shanks are on opposite sides, and the flats of the shanks are turned at an angle to the longitudinal axis of the Coupling. Two Collars are free to "float" inside the Flanged Wheel. When the Coupling is turned in a certain direction the Collars will be found to jam between the flange of the wheel and the inclined edges of the Threaded Pin shanks, so locking the Flanged Wheel to the rotating Rod. When, on the other hand, the Coupling is turned in the reverse direction, the Collars ride idly and the Rod is free to rotate independently of the Flanged Wheel.

In practice a device of this kind has important advantages over the ordinary ratchet and pawl mechanism, in that it is quicker and smoother in action and there is less wear and tear.

These advantages render it particularly suitable for use in, say, the Meccano model of the Constantinesco Torque Converter. In the existing model a pawl and ratchet device is employed, and in certain conditions of working the pawl may fail to make proper engagement with the next tooth of the ratchet. With this apparatus, however, the slightest reverse movement of the Flanged Wheel locks the two parts of the free wheel together.

CORD OPERATED FREE WHEEL

S.M.93. Although this movement is considerably simpler than S.M.92 and almost as efficient, it is unsuitable for heavy transmission owing to excessive wear of the cord. It will be found an excellent substitute for more complicated mechanisms of a similar nature, however.

This free wheel comprises two 3" Pulleys joined together by means of two 2" Screwed Rods. Four nuts on each of the Rods serve to hold the Pulleys such a distance apart that two 1⅛" Flanged Wheels 1 can be accommodated in the space between.

The Flanged Wheels are butted together face to face and secured on a 3½" Rod that is free to turn in the bosses of the 3" Pulleys. A short length of Meccano Cord 2 is doubled and wrapped round the Wheels, and the free ends are then passed through the loop formed in the cord and secured to one of the Screwed Rods as shown in the illustration. It will be found that when the 3½" Rod is prevented from rotating it is possible to turn the 3" Pulleys easily in one direction, but in the reverse direction considerably greater effort is needed.

This apparatus could be included in the drive of a model Big Wheel or roundabout so that, when the Motor is stopped, instead of the model coming to an abrupt standstill and straining the gearing, it comes to rest gradually.

S.M.93

S.M.93a. If space is very limited and the load somewhat bigger than is thought desirable to drive through S.M.93, an Anchoring Spring for Cord will be found to act perfectly. The spring is mounted on the Rod carrying the Gear, preferably a 57-teeth Gear, that is to freewheel. A ½" × ½" Angle Bracket attached to the Gear at one of its outside holes is secured in place in such a way that its horizontally arranged hole fits over the loop of the Spring. When rotating one way the Gears tend to unwind the coil of the Spring, and it is thus prevented from gripping the Rod. When the Gear rotates in the opposite direction, however, the coiled spring tends to grip the Rod, and in this way a positive drive is imparted to the driven shaft.

The excessive friction of this mechanism when free-wheeling will prohibit it from many models, but no doubt many occasions will occure when it will be found useful.

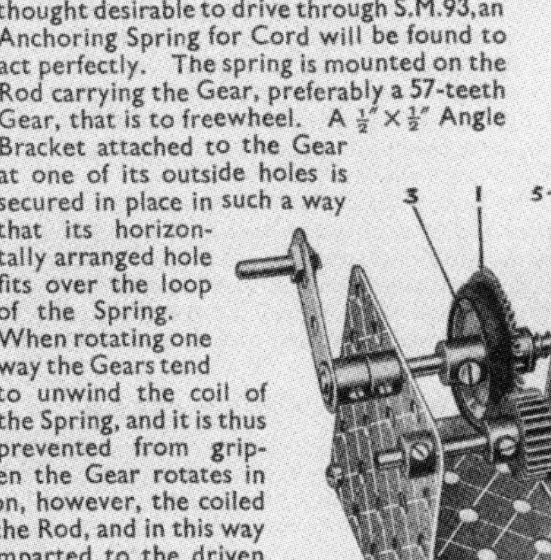

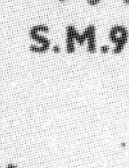

S.M.91

CLUTCH CONTROLLED GEAR-BOX

S.M.94. This example shows an extremely simple and efficient gear-box of the constant mesh type. The great advantage of this type is that the shafts do not have to be moved in order to change gear, hence the driving connections are simplified and wear and tear on gears is minimised.

The driving shaft has two 1" fast Pulleys 3 and 4 secured to it. Placed against these Pulleys, but loose on the shaft, are a 50-teeth Gear Wheel 1 and 1" Gear Wheel 2. Also on the shaft are two Compression Springs mounted between Washers and placed one on each side of a Collar 6, which is also free on the shaft.

The Collar is connected to a lever 5 that is attached pivotally to the base plate by a bolt and two locknuts. With the lever normal, or in the central position, no power is transmitted to the secondary Rod 7, but on moving the lever to one side or the other, one of the Springs is caused to press its respective Gear Wheel firmly against a rubber-shod Pulley, and consequently the Gear Wheel commences to revolve "solid" with the driving shaft, while the other Gear Wheel continues to ride idly upon it. Hence slight movements of the lever 5 will throw the Rod 7 out of engagement, cause it to be driven at the same speed as the driving shaft, or to rotate twice as fast as the driving shaft.

It should be a simple matter to construct on the lines suggested above a very efficient gearbox.

19

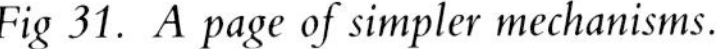

Fig 31. A page of simpler mechanisms.

Section X. Brakes—(continued).

INTERNAL EXPANDING BRAKE

S.M.117. This brake closely conforms to actual practice, and is remarkably efficient in operation on account of the comparatively large frictional surface on the brake shoes.

The brake shoes consist of 2½" Strips 1, curved to fit inside a Boiler End, and bolted at one end to a Meccano Hinge. In their centre holes they carry Threaded Pins that are free to slide in Handrail Supports 2 pivoted to the Face Plate on which the brake is mounted.

The outer ends of the shoes carry Angle Brackets between which is a Collar 3 with a Threaded Pin screwed into one of its tapped bores. The Pin is passed through the Face Plate and retained in place by a second Collar carrying the ¾" Bolt 4. This is connected to the brake operating lever.

The brake shoes fit inside a Boiler End attached to the road wheel and when the Collar 3 is turned, the shoes are expanded and the bolt heads pressed on the inside of the Boiler End, thus retarding its rotation. The shoes are normally held in the " off " position by a length of Spring Cord, the ends of which are attached to the bolts adjacent to those carrying the Hinge. In the centre the Spring Cord is fixed to the Face Plate by a nut and bolt.

S.M.117

S.M.118

"SERVO" MOTOR CAR BRAKE

S.M.118. The device illustrated demonstrates the principle of the Dewandre power braking system, used on many modern cars and omnibuses. The 1" fast Pulley 1 is secured to a Rod driven from the armature spindle of the motor through a gear train of 9:1 reduction ratio.

A crossed belt of cord 3 is passed round the Pulleys 1 and 2. The latter Pulley is mounted at the bottom end of a 2" Strip 4, which is mounted pivotally on a ⅜" Bolt and spaced from the Plate by a Washer. To the upper end of the Strip is attached pivotally a 2" Strip and a 2" slotted Strip 6 bolted together. A ⅜" Bolt is inserted in the slot of the Slotted Strip and two Washers are placed on its shank ; the bolt is then secured by locknuts, S.M.1a, and spaced so that the Strip can slide freely on its shank.

Pivoted to the link 6 is a 2½" Strip 8 to which, in turn, is pivoted the 3" Strip 5 and 1½" Strip 7, by a ½" Bolt. This Bolt is carried in the bottom hole of the 1½" Strip, a Collar and Washer on the shank of the Bolt being used for spacing purposes. The upper end of the 1½" Strip is connected pivotally to the two 1" × 1" Angle Brackets. A 2" Rod is suitably journalled and two Couplings are secured to its ends to form cranks.

To one of these Couplings a 1½" Strip 10 is attached pivotally and the centre hole of the latter is connected to the 3½" Strip as shown.

The brake cords are secured to the Strip 10 and the Coupling on the opposite end of the 3" Rod respectively, and are then passed round the 1½" Pulleys representing the brake drums. The arrangement is shown in the illustration.

The bottom of the lever 8 is connected to a point on the belt 3 by a length of cord. When the pedal 9 is depressed the link 6 is moved to the left, thus swinging the ½" Pulley to the right. As a result of this movement the belt 2 is tightened round the Pulley 1 and the cord attached to the lever 8 commences to travel towards the left and drags with it the lever 8, thus adding considerably to the pressure of the 3½" Strip representing the brake pull rod. The Motor should be running in the correct direction to ensure this result.

AUTOMATIC CLUTCH

S.M.97. Electric Motors do not develop their maximum power until the armature shaft has picked up speed, and this device ensures that the Motor has attained the necessary number of revolutions before the drive is transmitted to the model. The Rod 1 is driven from the armature shaft through a 1" Pinion and a 57-teeth Gear giving a 3:1 reduction. A 1½" Pulley 2 is fixed on the Rod which carries also a 1" loose Pulley fitted with a Dunlop Tyre and the 1½" Pulley 3.

The Pulley 3 takes the drive to the model, and is free to rotate on its Rod until it is pressed against the Dunlop Tyre, so forming a friction clutch.

A Coupling is carried on the end of the Rod 1 and has two 3" Strips attached to it by means of ¾" Bolts. Each Strip is spaced from the Coupling by two Washers, and a 3½" Strip 4 is retained in place on the Rod between the two Strips. The Couplings 5 are fastened on 1" Axle Rods and are fitted with similar Rods, each of which bears two Collars connected by Spring Cord.

When the Motor is started the Pulley 2 and the clutch operating mechanism rotate, but the Pulley 3 does not transmit the power. As the speed increases, the weights on the Couplings 5 fly outward and cause the friction clutch to engage. Suitable reduction gearing will of course have to be inserted between the Pulley 3 and the driving shaft of the model.

This novel clutch will save wear and tear of the Motor, and will ensure that it is running as fast as possible and that the maximum efficiency is being obtained. The mechanism has certain limitations, however, and precautions should be taken in models such as lifts and cranes where gravity is likely to take effect. The mechanism is of most value in demonstration models where stopping and starting have to be carried out at frequent intervals.

Fig 32.
The short-lived E20a motor in one of its few appearances.

INTERNAL EXPANDING BRAKE

S.M.120. This is similar in operation to other internal expanding brakes described in this section, but is more suitable for adapting to Bowden cable control. Two 1" Triangular Plates 1 are attached pivotally by locknutted ⅜" Bolts to a Face Plate in the positions indicated in the illustration, a Washer being placed on each Bolt for spacing purposes.

Two ⅜" Bolts secured by locknuts to the Triangular Plates serve as brake shoes,and short lengths of Spring Cord connect them together. The operating cam is a Collar 2, the tapped hole of which is screwed on to the end of a Pivot Bolt. The Collar is prevented from turning on the end of the Pivot Bolt by a Grub Screw, which is inserted in the opposite tapped hole of the Collar and screwed against the end of the Pivot Bolt.

The Pivot Bolt is journalled in a reinforecd bearing comprising a Flat Bracket spaced by a Washer from the Face Plate, and a ¾" Bolt 3 is attached by a Collar to its shank. A Loom Heald, or length of wire, connects the ¾" Bolt to the brake lever.

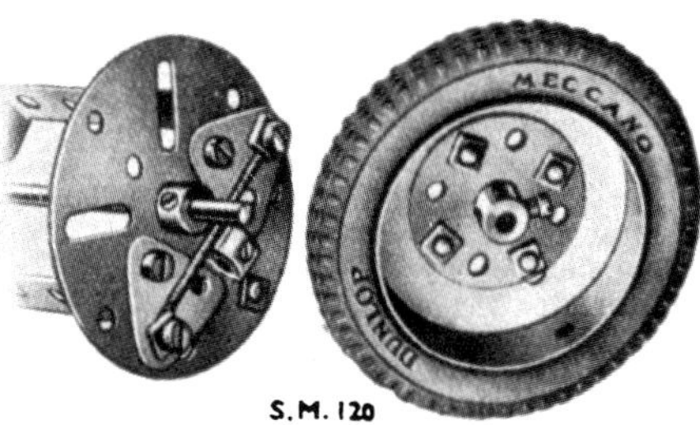

S.M. 120

Fig 33.
Various braking mechanisms showing the advances made.

(fig 28a & b), although the rather old three-speed and reverse SM 45 still survived. A new epicyclic gearbox (fig 29) and two excellent models of Hobbs Inertia Gear and Spontan Transmission Gear appeared (fig 30). The simple planetary gear in figure 29 was augmented by an interesting four-speed and reverse planetary box (fig 30a). Although perhaps not advanced by today's standards, these gearboxes are important if only to show the huge strides made between 1925 and 1934. A simple comparison is all that is needed.

Not all the mechanisms were complicated and there were a number of good simple models of which SM 94, the Clutch Controlled Gearbox (fig 31) is an example. SM 92, the Friction Free Wheel on the same page, is something of an anomaly in that it refers to the Constantinesco Torque Converter which, as a mechanism, had been deleted from the manuals in 1929.

SM 97 (fig 32) shows another clutch control mechanism which is mainly interesting because it shows the poor-selling, short-lived E20a motor. This was one of the few occasions where it is seen in a model. Nevertheless the automatic clutch is a worthwhile and sometimes useful mechanism to build.

Further evidence of the advances made by 1934 can be seen in the two internal expanding brakes and the servo braking system of SMs 117, 118 and 120 (fig 33). Similarly the models in SMs 180 and 181, the Bendix Pionion and Reversing Gear with Variable Pause (fig 34), were a long way ahead of anything produced in the middle twenties. These and others show how easily and confidently Meccano was being used for demonstrations of virtually all mechanical movements.

The 1934 edition finished with a page of electrical models which concentrated on motor control. These are amongst some of the most fascinating to watch when in action (fig 35).

The final years

There were very few alterations in the three known later editions, and only the substitution of ring frames for the withdrawn channel segments in SM

continued p. 203.

BENDIX PINION

S.M.180. This device is primarily a demonstration model of the Bendix car starting gear, but is capable of other uses.

The drive is taken from the Bevel 1 mounted on a shaft together with the Worm 2 and ½" Pinion 3. The Worm rotates a cam through the medium of a ½" Pinion, the cam being secured to the Rod by a Collar. This cam consists of a Universal Stand Clamp, Kemex Part No.K31, and a sliding Rod 4 that is in continual contact with it is connected by a Coupling to a Rod carrying the ½" Pinions 5 and 6. These Pinions engage alternately with similar Pinions mounted on the flywheel shaft and Bendix Pinion shaft respectively. The shaft carrying the Bendix Pinion consists of a 2" Threaded Rod attached to a 5" Rod by means of a Threaded Coupling.

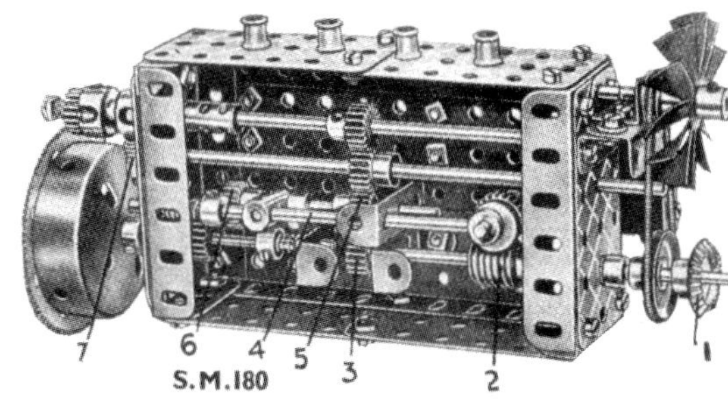

REVERSING GEAR WITH VARIABLE PAUSE

S.M.181. By means of this gear it is possible to reverse a movement and to arrange a pause of variable length at the end of each operation.

The drive is supplied to the 8" Axle Rod 1 that carries a Worm and a ½"×¾" Pinion. The Worm engages a ½" Pinion on a vertical Rod 2 that is journalled in 2" Strips secured in place by means of Angle Brackets. The Rod 2 carries a Worm that meshes with a ½" Pinion on the Rod carrying the Pinion 3, and another Rod is journalled below this and carries a 57-teeth Gear Wheel 4.

The Rod 5 is slidable in its bearings and carries two ½"×½" Pinions, one of which is in constant mesh with a ½" Pinion on the Rod 1. A loose Collar 6 on the Rod is retained in place between two fixed Collars. Two Compression Springs are fitted on the Rod on each side of the Flat Plate on the right-hand side of the frame.

The sliding movement of the Rod is controlled by a lever consisting of a 2" Strip pivoted at the base of the model and extended by means of a 2" Slotted Strip. A bolt is passed through the slot in the Strip and fitted with a nut before being screwed into the bore of the Collar 6. The nut is tightened against the Collar to prevent the shank of the bolt gripping the Axle Rod 5. At the lower end of the lever a bolt is inserted in a similar manner into the bore of the Collar 9 that is fixed to a sliding 5" Rod. The Collar 7 is loose on the Rod, and the 2" Slotted Strip 10 is pivotally attached to it. This Strip is firmly secured to a 3½" Strip that is pivoted to the Gear 4. As the Gear rotates the Collar 7 slides between the Collars 8 and 9, and as soon as it strikes either of these Collars it causes the lever to slide the Rod 5 in the corresponding direction

Owing to the arrangement of the lever the Rod 5 slides more quickly than the Collars 8 or 9 and throws one of the ½" Pinions into engagement with the ¾" Contrate Wheel on the Rod 11.

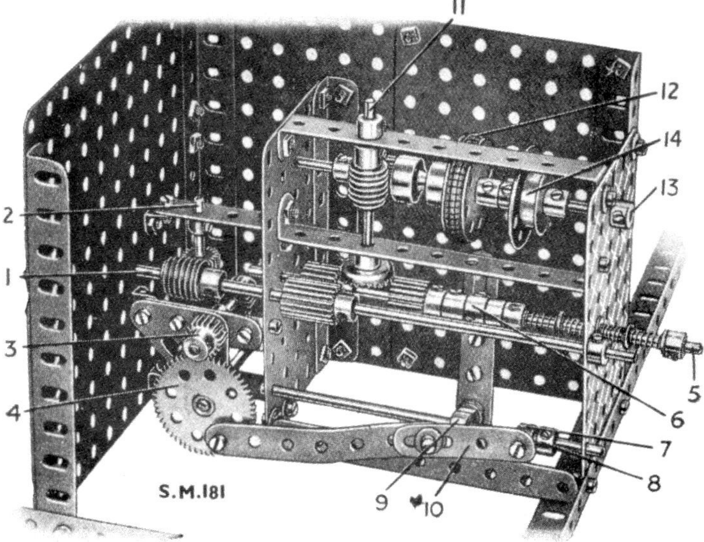

Fig 34. Two of the more advanced movements featured in the 1934 edition.

Section XIX. ELECTRICALLY OPERATED MOVEMENTS

S.M.183

OVERLOAD RELEASE FOR ELECTRIC MOTOR

S.M.183. Every electric circuit should be equipped with safety devices to protect the apparatus from damage that might arise from the passing of a heavier current than that for which the circuit is designed. In the case of electric motors it is customary to provide protection by means of a device known as an "overload release," and a mechanism of this kind is reproduced in Meccano in S.M.183.

A solenoid is wound with two layers of Meccano 26 S.C.C. Wire and clamped in position on the base plate of the apparatus. The Rod 1 slides in the bore of the solenoid and is connected pivotally to a switch arm carrying the contact 2. The latter is part of a Spring Buffer Part No. 120a. It normally makes contact with a 6 B.A. Bolt that is insulated from the Plate by insulating Bushes and Washers, and carries on its shank a terminal 3.

One end of the solenoid winding is attached to the insulated terminal 4 and the other end is connected to the base plate. In order to include the device in circuit with a 6-volt Motor and Accumulator, one of the two wires leading from the Accumulator is connected to one of the terminals of the overload release, and the remaining terminal of the latter to the Motor. The current then flows through the windings of the solenoid and through the contacts of the overload release on its way to the Motor. When it rises above a certain value the plunger 1 is drawn into the interior of the solenoid, thus moving the switch arm and breaking the circuit.

S.M.185

AUTOMATIC MOTOR BRAKE

S.M.184. One end of a Rod 3 is attached pivotally by a Swivel Bearing to the Rod 1, while its other end is connected as indicated to the end of the solenoid plunger. A small piece of Spring Cord bolted to the Strip 2 presses on the upper part of the Bush Wheel, and a second piece of Spring Cord is attached to the lower side of the Strip 2 to press similarly on the lower half of the Bush Wheel.

The solenoid is composed of a Bobbin wound with four layers of No. 23 S.C.C. wire. One of the wires is attached to a terminal that is insulated from the motor side plate by an Insulating Bush and a Washer, and the other wire is secured so that it is in metallic contact with the plate. One of the Motor terminals is treated in a similar manner, and connection is made to the Accumulator from the terminal on the Motor side plate and the remaining Motor terminal. When the Motor is running, current flows through the turns of the solenoid, which keeps the plunger down, and consequently the brake is held off. When the current is cut off, the solenoid becomes inoperative and the plunger is freed, thus allowing the Spring Cord to press the face of the Bush Wheel into contact with the Tyre on the 1" fast Pulley.

AUTOMATIC CONTRACTING BRAKE

S.M.185. A 1" fast Pulley 1 shod with a Rubber Ring is secured to a Rod driven from the armature spindle through suitable gearing. Two 1" fast Pulleys 2 are fastened rigidly to 1½" Strips that are attached pivotally by lock-nuts at their upper extremities to 2" Strips 3. At their lower ends they are mounted loosely on lock-nutted bolts attached to the side plates of the Motor. The other ends of the links 3 are attached pivotally to the 2" Slotted Strip 4, the slot in which engages with the shank of the ⅜" Bolt 4a. This Strip is also attached to a lever consisting of a 4½" Strip that is connected to the plunger of the solenoid 5. As will be seen from the illustration, this lever pivots about a lock-nutted bolt secured to the Trunnion on the Motor.

S.M.186

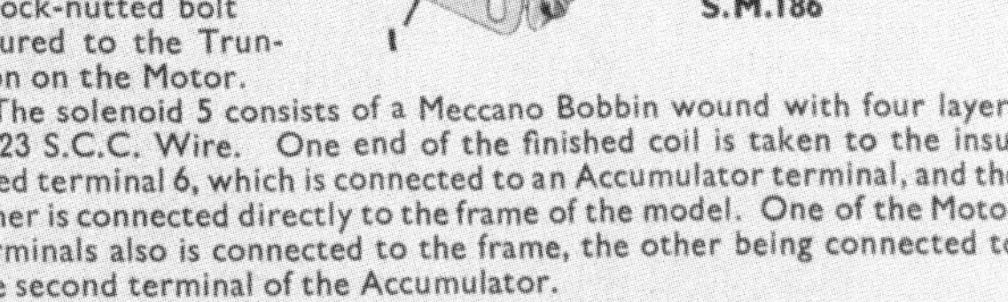

The solenoid 5 consists of a Meccano Bobbin wound with four layers of 23 S.C.C. Wire. One end of the finished coil is taken to the insulated terminal 6, which is connected to an Accumulator terminal, and the other is connected directly to the frame of the model. One of the Motor terminals also is connected to the frame, the other being connected to the second terminal of the Accumulator.

REMOTE CONTROL FOR GEAR-BOX

S.M.186. The gear control switch is shown near the Motor reversing switch for convenience, but this can be taken to any position and wired up accordingly. A 1" Triangular Plate is held on a ¾" Bolt 7 by two nuts, and two further nuts fix the Bolt in position on the motor.

Two 6 B.A. Bolts 8 and 9 mounted on the Triangular Plate are insulated from it and form studs for the contact arm, which is made from a 1½" Strip mounted on the Bolt 7 and is held against the heads of the 6 B.A. Bolts by a Compression Spring. The Bolt 8 is connected to one end of the solenoid 4, the other end of which is joined to one of the Motor terminals. The same terminal is connected to the solenoid 5, which is wired to the Bolt 9. To connect up, one of the Accumulator wires is joined to the remaining Motor terminal and the other is "earthed" by connecting it to the frame of the Motor.

With the lever as shown the solenoid 5 is in series with the Motor and causes the Crank 6 to bring the Pinion 2 into mesh with the 57-teeth Gear, at the same time throwing the Pinion 3 out of engagement with its respective Gear.

S.M.187

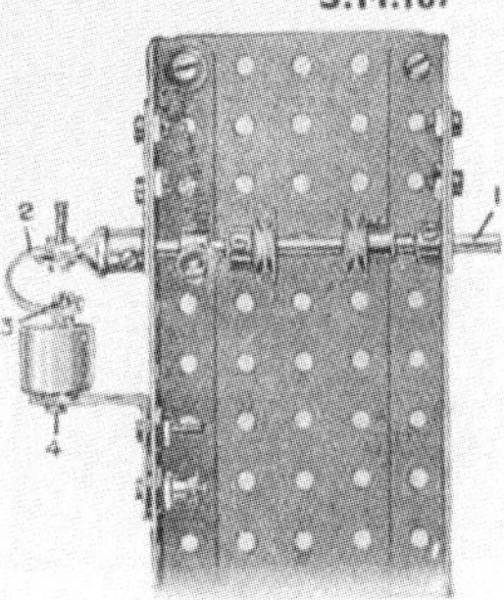

SPARK ARRESTER

S.M.187. The sliding Rod 1 carries an End Bearing fitted with a Pendulum Connection 2, which is bent as shown and carries a Silver Tipped Contact Screw 3. A Second Contact Screw 4 is passed through a hole in a 1" × 1" Angle Bracket, fitted with, but insulated from, a Chimney Adaptor. Oil is poured into the Chimney Adaptor until the top of the Contact Screw is covered.

39

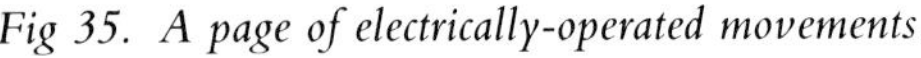

Fig 35. A page of electrically-operated movements.

LARGE BUILT-UP ROLLER BEARING

S.M.134. S.M.134 shows how an excellent roller bearing can be constructed with Ring Frames, part No. 167b. A 9½" Strip is bolted across the lower Ring Frame and has a Double Arm Crank secured to it. The Crank carries a Rod that is held in place by two Collars and passes up through the boss of a Face Plate at the centre of the frame carrying the rollers. Eight 3½" Strips are bolted radially about the Face Plate and their outer ends are connected by further 3½" Strips. The radial 3½" Strips are each fitted with a 1½" × ½" Double Angle Strip so that eight Rods radiate from the centre pivot. The Rods are 2½" in length and carry Collars on their inner ends and 1⅛" Flanged Wheels on their outer ends.

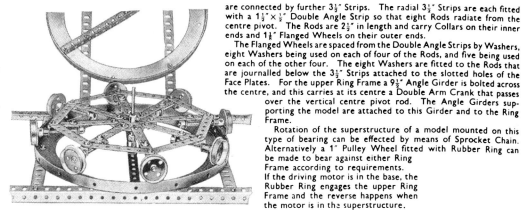

The Flanged Wheels are spaced from the Double Angle Strips by Washers, eight Washers being used on each of four of the Rods, and five being used on each of the other four. The eight Washers are fitted to the Rods that are journalled below the 3½" Strips attached to the slotted holes of the Face Plates. For the upper Ring Frame a 9½" Angle Girder is bolted across the centre, and this carries at its centre a Double Arm Crank that passes over the vertical centre pivot rod. The Angle Girders supporting the model are attached to this Girder and to the Ring Frame.

Rotation of the superstructure of a model mounted on this type of bearing can be effected by means of Sprocket Chain. Alternatively a 1" Pulley Wheel fitted with Rubber Ring can be made to bear against either Ring Frame according to requirements. If the driving motor is in the base, the Rubber Ring engages the upper Ring Frame and the reverse happens when the motor is in the superstructure.

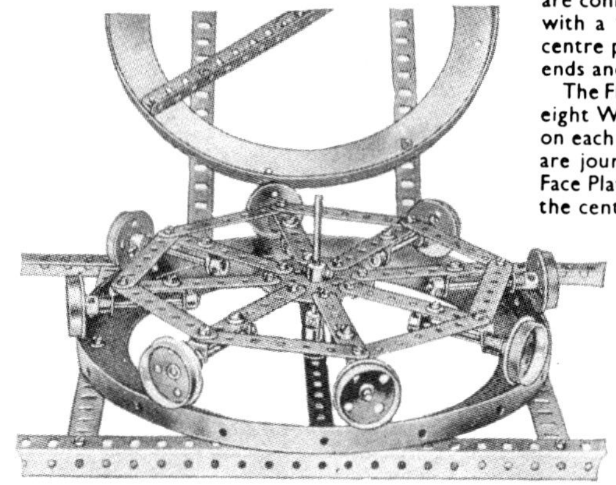

S.M.134

Fig 36.
A large built-up roller bearing after the withdrawal of part no. 119 – Channel Segment.

No. 1a MOTOR CHASSIS. This is an entirely new model, and is an accurate reproduction of a modern sports car. It embodies a four-speed gear-box and four wheel brakes.

No. 2 SHIP COALER. All the movements of a real ship coaler are reproduced in this model.

No. 5 TRAVELLING BUCKET DREDGER. In this model trucks and wagons can run underneath the chute through which falls the material raised by the dredger buckets.

No. 6 STIFF-LEG DERRICK. This model has many interesting movements, including hoisting, luffing and swivelling, which are controlled by suitable levers.

No. 7 PLATFORM SCALES. This model will weigh articles up to 4½ lbs. with remarkable accuracy.

No. 9 BAGATELLE TABLE. This is an interesting model that will give hours of fun to the players.

No. 10 LOG SAW. In this model the saw is driven rapidly to and fro while the work table travels beneath it.

No. 11a SINGLE-CYLINDER HORIZONTAL STEAM ENGINE. Fitted with balanced crankshaft, crosshead, and centrifugal governor.

No. 12 STONE SAWING MACHINE. The model is equipped with adjustable work table and overhead trolley with self-sustaining chain hoist.

No. 13 MECCANOGRAPH. This wonderful model will draw hundreds of beautiful designs.

No. 14a GRANDFATHER CLOCK. A practical example of Meccano model-building. The model keeps accurate time.

No. 18 REVOLVING CRANE. This model is fitted with screw-operated luffing gear.

No. 19 STEAM SHOVEL. This model embodies travelling, rotating, racking and digging movements, and jib hoisting and lowering gear.

No. 20 MOBILE CRANE. This model has hoisting, luffing, travelling and slewing movements. It is fitted with an automatic brake.

No. 21 TRANSPORTER BRIDGE. The carriage automatically travels to and fro for as long as the motor is driven.

No. 22 TRACTION ENGINE. A remarkably realistic model that will pull a boy of average weight. Fitted with two speeds.

No. 24 TRAVELLING GANTRY CRANE. The movements of this model comprise the traversing of the entire gantry, hoisting and lowering, and the traversing of the crane trolley.

No. 25 HYDRAULIC CRANE. The hydraulic ram is represented realistically by a powerful screw mechanism.

No. 28 PONTOON CRANE. The movements of this model include the operation of the two hoisting blocks, slewing of the entire crane and luffing.

No. 29 HAMMERHEAD CRANE. This is a very realistic and powerful model, comprising traversing, hoisting and slewing motions.

No. 30 BREAKDOWN CRANE. This model is equipped with travelling, slewing, luffing, and hoisting motions.

No. 31 WAREHOUSE WITH ELEVATORS. The two cages are driven automatically and work alternately.

No. 35 LEVEL LUFFING CRANE. The model is provided with level luffing gear, and an important feature is a grab that may be opened and closed automatically.

Fig 37.
The Super Model Leaflets remaining after the wholesale deletions of 1936.

MECCANO

STANDARD MECHANISMS

STANDARD

MECHANICAL MOVEMENTS

CONSTRUCTED AND

DEMONSTRATED WITH

MECCANO

MECCANO LIMITED · BINNS ROAD · LIVERPOOL 13

Fig 38. Norman Tudor's file copy of the post-war edition for the US market. Some examples are marked 'USA Edition'.

134 (fig 36) is of any real interest. Strangely enough the front cover was not updated at the same time and still showed the Pontoon Crane with channel segments. This illustration actually dates from some ten years earlier and originally featured the Sidelever electric motors and braced girders in the tower. The motors were later retouched to look like the 1925 type, and later still, the braced girders were erased and what appear to be strip plates were inserted. As can be clearly seen in fig 25, the three holes at the top and bottom of the tower are far too close together. This is because braced girders are two inches wide, whereas strip plates are two and a half inches. This was therefore not another version, but simply a retouched photograph.

All the Blue/Gold editions ended with a final page of advertisements for the Super Model Leaflets, but by 1936 withdrawals had reduced the list from 39 to 23 (fig 37). Within twelve months the SMLs and Standard Mechanisms would become obsolete upon the introduction of the new numbered series of outfits. These and other deletions were, in the author's opinion, representative of a change of emphasis from engineering in miniature to a flimsyness of design and construction more suited to a children's toy. It was the beginning of the end of the 'great days' which significantly coincided with the death of Frank Hornby in September 1936.

Foreign Parts

1937 wasn't quite the end of the story of Standard Mechanisms, because after the war Meccano brought out a photo-reduced version (same size as the 1925–33 editions) of the 1934–36 editions (fig 38). This was purely for the US market and does not appear to have been a good seller as up until the 1970s there were stocks at Binns Road. Oddly enough, during that edition's currency, the author's father asked Meccano's Norman Tudor (whose file copy is illustrated) if any copies of Standard Mechanisms were available and was told that there were none. However, parts of it, as well as some from the 1935 Meccano Parts and How to

CORRECTION

The caption under the left-hand illustration on page 6 should read " Fig. 3 : The Two-Sheave Pulley Block," while that under the right-hand illustration should read " Fig. 2 : The Single Moveable Pulley."

Fig 41. The correction slip in the 1925 edition.

Section III. Pulleys and Pulley Blocks—*(continued)*

pulley A does not contribute, but only changes the direction of the force, converting a downward pull on the rope at *a* to an upward force at *b*.

The explanation of the increased power, or mechanical advantage, obtained is as follows. In our model we find that to raise the load 1 in. the power must descend 2 in.—for it is clear that if B is to rise 1 in. the lengths of rope *c* and *b* must each be shortened by 1 inch—therefore *a* must be lengthened by 2 in. To raise 20 lbs. through 1 ft. requires 20 foot-lbs. But the power load of 11 lbs. descending through twice that distance—2 ft.—yields 22 foot-lbs. This is 2 foot-lbs. more than is actually necessary ; hence it may be stated that friction has absorbed 2 foot-lbs. of the energy exerted.

From this we learn that a moveable pulley enables a force to move through a greater distance than that moved by the load it lifts. We also know that the energy exerted by a force is increased proportionally to the distance through which it moves. Therefore by using a single moveable pulley we may almost halve the force that would be necessary without it, for it enables us to move the force through a distance twice as great. It should be noted here that in all the mechanical powers, the force is increased always at the expense of speed, since it must move through a greater distance than the load it lifts.

Example 3

The principle in Fig. 3 is the same as in Example 2, but two further pulleys have been added. The rope is rove through one of the pulleys, or " sheaves " as they are termed, situated in the fixed pulley block, thence under one of the sheaves in the lower moveable block, over the second fixed sheave, and down to the second moveable sheave. From here it is lead up and secured to the framework of the fixed pulley block.

The load is thus supported by four lengths of rope, and to raise the load through one inch, each of the four parts of the rope from the upper block to the lower block must be shortened one inch. Therefore, the running end of the rope must be lengthened by four inches, from which it may be calculated that, eliminating friction, one quarter of the load attached to the running end would be sufficient to raise the load, for, as we have already seen, the energy exerted by a force is increased proportionately to the distance through which it travels. In actual practice it will be found that a little more than a quarter of the load is required to raise it, the surplus being absorbed by friction.

Example 4

A popular arrangement of pulleys is well illustrated in the Meccano Model No. 709, Stiff-Leg Derrick Crane. As shown in S.M. 31 the tackle here consists of two pulley blocks, one fixed and one moveable, as in Example 3. The upper block contains two sheaves or pulley wheels, while the lower or moveable block has three sheaves. The end of the cord that passes over the large pulley in the jib of the crane is the running-end.

The model shown in Fig. 4 makes the relative arrangement of the sheaves and cords easier to understand. As will be seen, instead of all the sheaves in one block being on the same axle they are separated in this model one from another. The action of the pulleys in Fig. 4 is similar to that in the Stiff-Leg Derrick.

Fig. 3
~~The Single~~
TWO-SHEAVE ~~Moveable~~ Pulley BLOCK

Fig. 2
The ~~Two-Sheave~~ SINGLE MOVEABLE Pulley ~~Block~~

6

Fig 42. The relevant page showing the errors corrected by hand.

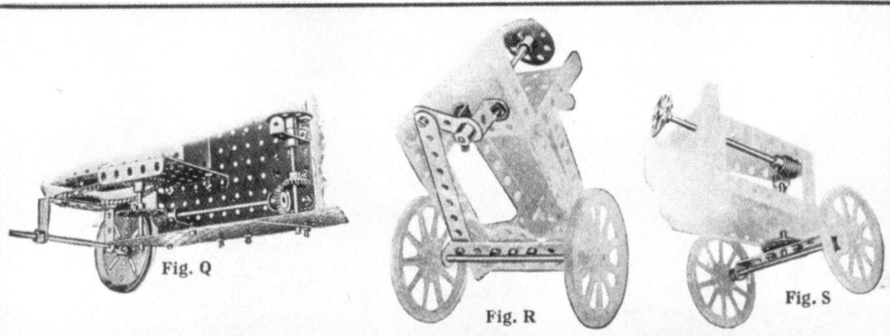

Steering Gears

The various types of steering mechanism commonly in use on vehicles of all descriptions may readily be reproduced with Meccano.

Fig. Q. This type of gear, which is particularly suitable for road tractors, etc., operates through a worm gear with chain connection, and is coupled to the hand-wheel by means of Bevel Gears.

Fig. R. In this case the road wheels are moved about their central pivot by means of a crank, which is secured to the steering shaft, and a connecting strip.

Fig. S. The road wheels in this example are secured to a central rod, which forms a pivot, and is rotated from the hand-wheel by means of a worm gear.

Three Interesting Mechanisms

Fig. T. Here is shown a method by which the table of a drill, or similar machine, may be secured quickly and rigidly in any position on the upright rod upon which it slides.

Fig. U. This illustrates the standard Meccano ball-bearing, which may be employed wherever it is required to rotate one part of a model freely upon another, with a minimum of friction.

Fig. V. A typical crankshaft built up from cranks and triangular plates (forming balance weights) etc. is shown in Fig. V. The eccentric appearing in the illustration operates the valve mechanism of the engine.

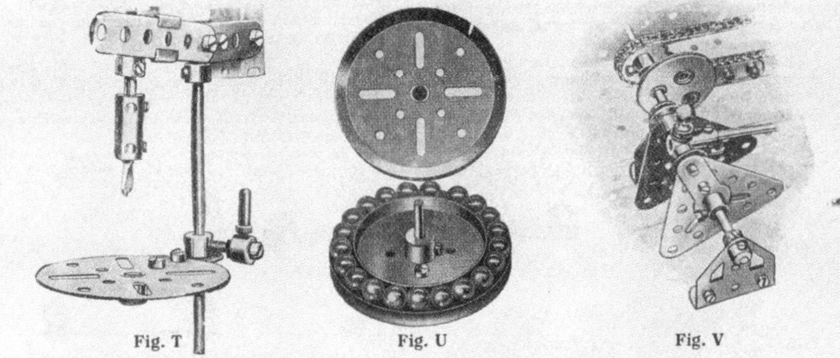

Meccano Standard Mechanisms

In December 1925 we are publishing an entirely new book, dealing with a variety of mechanisms on similar lines to those shown in this and the preceding pages. Gear Ratios, Belt and Rope Mechanisms, Levers, Clutches, Brakes, Steering Gears, Traversing Mechanisms, Grabs and many similar movements will be illustrated and described. The book, known as "Meccano Standard Mechanisms," is essential to every model builder, for the standard mechanisms are applicable to many models and may be used for a variety of purposes.

The price will be 1/- (postage 1½d. extra) and orders, accompanied by a remittance for 1/1½, may now be sent in. They will not be acknowledged but will be filed and dealt with in strict rotation, delivery being effected as soon as the book becomes available.

Fig 43. The 'Magic Carpet' reference to the publication of Standard Mechanisms.

Fig 44. The first Gears 'A' manual from 1949.

MECCANO GEARS OUTFIT "A"

HOW TO USE MECCANO SPROCKET AND CHAIN.

Sometimes it is necessary for one shaft to drive another placed in some other part of a model, and the distance between the rods makes it impracticable to use gears for the purpose. In such cases the best method of drive is the Meccano Sprocket and Chain system, an example of which is seen in Fig. E. In this illustration a ¾" diameter Sprocket is shown driving a 2" diameter Sprocket.

Fig. D

An advantage of this type of drive over ordinary pulley-and-belt drive is that the Chain drive is positive in action; that is there is no slip between the Chain and the Sprockets as may occur between a Cord belt and a pulley. This positive drive therefore makes it possible for one Sprocket to drive another at a definite rate, just as with meshing gears. The step-up or reduction ratio between any two Sprockets linked by Chain is found in exactly the same way as with the meshed gearing already explained.

Meccano Sprocket Chain is supplied in lengths of 40", and comprises six links to the inch. It can easily be separated and joined again when the requisite length has been measured off. To separate, the ends of one of the links are gently prised up with the blade of a screwdriver so that the adjacent link can be slipped out. After rejoining, the ends are bent back again carefully so that they do not grip the next link too tightly. The Chain should be passed round the wheels so that the turned-over ends of the links face outward or away from the wheel, as this will result in smoother running. The chain will also be less likely to jump the Sprocket Wheels.

Once the basic principles of gears and gear trains are understood, it is easy to assemble many interesting and useful mechanisms. In the following pages we illustrate and describe a selection of such mechanisms that will be found to meet most of the requirements of Meccano model-builders.

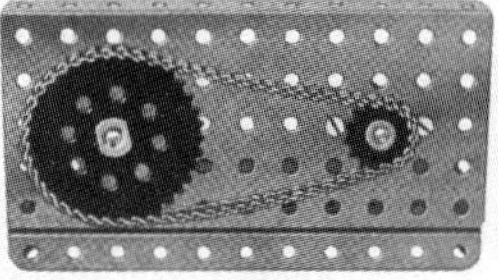

Fig. E

5

Fig 45. Some basic information from Gears 'A'.

Use Them, were supplied pasted on to Meccano notepaper.

This post-war edition differed only from its pre-war ancestors in the omission of pages and sections referring to obsolete parts, motors and Super Model Leaflets. Otherwise it was reproduced in full.

Mention of a non-UK edition brings us to the many overseas versions. There were English language editions for the USA, Australia, New Zealand, South Africa etc, together with foreign language versions such as the Dutch. Generally the content of the non-UK editions was similar to those of the British market.

Print Data

UK editions of Standard Mechanisms so far known to the author are:

1925	No reference.
1926	926/5
1927	127/10
1928	328/5
1928	728/5
1928	1128/3
1929	529/40
1933	2/933/3(IP)
1934	13/1134/15 (but see note)
1935	13/835/2.5
1936	13/636/10(UK)
1936	13/636/12.5(UK)

The 1925 edition can normally be identified by the existence of an errata slip gummed inside the front cover (fig 41). If this is missing, then reference to the illustrations on page 6 (fig 42) will settle the matter. A similar error occurred in the *Meccano Magazine* articles and was subsequently corrected. Whilst lack of a print reference makes exact dating impossible, the December 1925 edition of The Magic Carpet (fig 43) would seem to point to the latter part of that year, probably September or October. It appears to be certain that this manual was on sale for Christmas 1925, indeed it would have been very odd if it had not.

MECCANO GEARS OUTFIT 'B'

HOW TO USE MECCANO SPROCKET AND CHAIN.

Sometimes it is necessary for one shaft to drive another placed in some other part of a model. In such cases the best method of drive is the Meccano Sprocket and Chain system, an example of which is seen in Fig. F.

Fig. D

An advantage of this type of drive over ordinary pulley-and-belt drive is that the Chain drive is positive in action; that is, there is no slip between the Chain and the Sprockets, as may occur between a Cord belt and a Pulley. This positive drive therefore makes it possible for one Sprocket to drive another at a definite rate, just as with meshing gears.

Meccano Sprocket Chain is supplied in lengths of 40", and comprises six links to the inch. It can easily be separated and joined again when the requisite length has been measured off. To separate, the ends of one of the links are gently prised up with the blade of a screwdriver so that the adjacent link can be slipped out. After rejoining, the ends are bent back again carefully so that they do not grip the next link too tightly. The Chain should be passed round the wheels so that the turned-over ends of the link face outward or away from the wheel, as this will result in smoother running.

Fig. E

ROD WITH KEYWAY, AND KEY BOLT.

These parts, which are shown in Fig. E, are intended to be used in mechanisms where it is necessary to arrange a Gear or Pinion so that it turns with the Rod, but is able to slide along it. The Key Bolt 1 should be screwed into one of the threaded holes in the Gear or Pinion so that the spigot at the end of the Key Bolt enters the keyway in Rod with Keyway 2. When parts are **fixed** to the Rod with Keyway they must be arranged so that their Grub Screws or Set Screws are tightened **opposite** to the keyway.

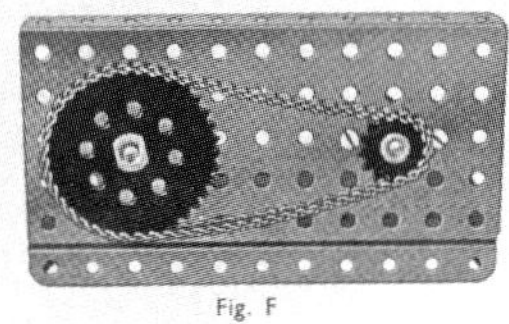

Fig. F

5

Fig 46.
The same page as in fig 45 but updated for Gears 'B' to include the new Keyway Rod.

Fig 47.
The 1959 Mechanisms Outfit manual.

MECHANICAL DEVICES BUILT WITH THE MECCANO MECHANISMS OUTFIT

PULLEY SYSTEMS FOR CRANES: *The Engineer's Power Savers*

One of the most generally useful machines in engineering is the crane, and in its many different forms it is found in shipyards, docks, engineering workshops and factories of all kinds. It is only natural, therefore, that cranes are one of the most popular subjects with Meccano model-builders.

The lifting of great weights by cranes is made possible largely by the use of pulleys, which are incorporated between the winding drum and the load. These pulley systems may be composed of two pulley blocks having any number of pulleys, but there are seldom more than six.

Pulleys, when properly used, make possible a great saving in power and energy, thus enabling great weights to be lifted with comparatively little expenditure of engine power. This increase in effective power is due to a mechanical advantage produced by passing the hoisting rope around a system of pulleys, one set of which is fixed while the other set is moveable. In a crane, the fixed set is mounted at the jib head, and the load hook is attached to the moveable set. Either set may consist of one or more pulleys. These two sets of pulleys are shown at A and B in Fig. 9, which represents the jib head of a simple model crane. Each set in this case consists of two Pulleys. Fig. 10 shows single pulley sets.

The quantity of work, or 'energy', of which any engine or machine is capable is measured by 'foot-pounds'. A 'foot-pound' is the quantity of energy that is needed to lift a 1 lb. weight through a height of 1 ft. If, for example, a weight of 2 lb. has to be raised through a height of 1 ft., the energy needed to do it would be exactly equal to that necessary to raise a weight of 1 lb. through a height of 2 ft., namely, 2 ft.-lb. If 10 lb. has to be lifted 100 ft., 10 ft.-lb. will be required for the first foot of lift, the same for the second, third, and so on up to 100 ft., making a total of 1,000 ft.-lb. of energy.

In Fig. 8 we illustrate a demonstration set-up of a pulley system using a single fixed pulley A and a single moveable pulley B. The rope is passed (or 'rove') over the fixed pulley A and around the moveable pulley B, and is then tied to the framework as shown.

A load of, say, 1 lb. attached to the 'running' end 'C' of the rope will raise a weight of approximately 2 lb. suspended from the moveable pulley B. The explanation of the increased power, or mechanical advantage as it is called, obtained, is as follows. In our model we would find that to raise a load attached to the moveable Pulley 1 in. the power load applied to the rope at C would have to descend 2 in. — for it is clear that if B is to rise 1 in. the lengths of rope 'D' and 'E' must each be shortened by 1 in. — therefore 'C' must move through a distance of 2 in.

From this is will be seen that a moveable pulley enables a force to move through a greater distance than that moved by the load it lifts. As the energy exerted by a force is increased proportionally to the distance through which it moves, by using a single moveable pulley we can almost halve the force that would be necessary without it, for it enables us to move the force through a distance twice as great. But it should be noted that the force is increased always at the expense of speed, since it must move through a greater distance than the load it lifts. In actual practice the increase in effective power is reduced slightly owing to friction.

Another and more elaborate pulley system of special interest to model-builders is shown in Fig. 7. The principle is the same here as in the system shown in Fig. 8, but two further pulleys have been added. The rope C is rove over one of the pulleys, or 'sheaves' as they are termed, situated in the fixed pulley block A, then under one of the sheaves in the lower moveable block B, over the second pulley A, and down to the second moveable pulley B. From here it is led up and secured to the framework of the fixed pulley block.

It will be seen that the load is thus supported by four lengths or 'falls' of rope, and to raise the load through a distance of 1 in. for example, each of the four 'falls' of the rope from the upper block to the lower block must be shortened 1 in. This means that the running end 'C' of the rope must be lengthened by 4 in. From this it may be calculated that, disregarding friction, a load of say 4 lb. attached to the load hook of the moveable block, could be raised by a load of 1 lb. on the running end 'C' of the rope, for as we have already seen, the energy exerted by a force is increased proportionally to the distance through which it travels. In actual practice a little more than a quarter of the load would be required to raise it, due to friction.

In Figs. 9 and 10 are shown the jib heads of two small cranes fitted with pulley systems assembled from parts in The Meccano Mechanisms Outfit. In one case two pulleys are used while in the other four pulleys are employed. Systems of these types are the most generally useful so far as the Meccano model-builder is concerned.

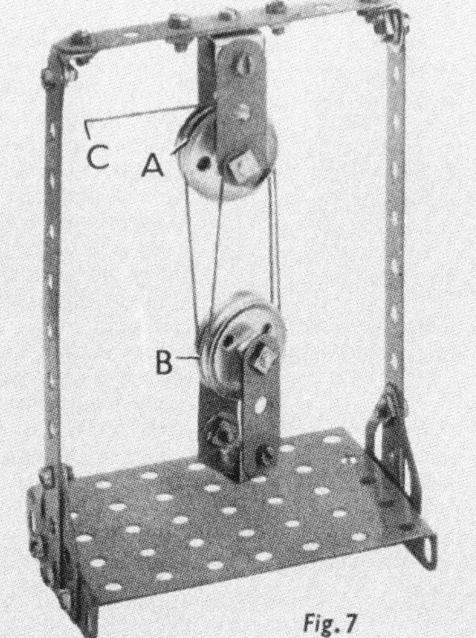

Fig. 7

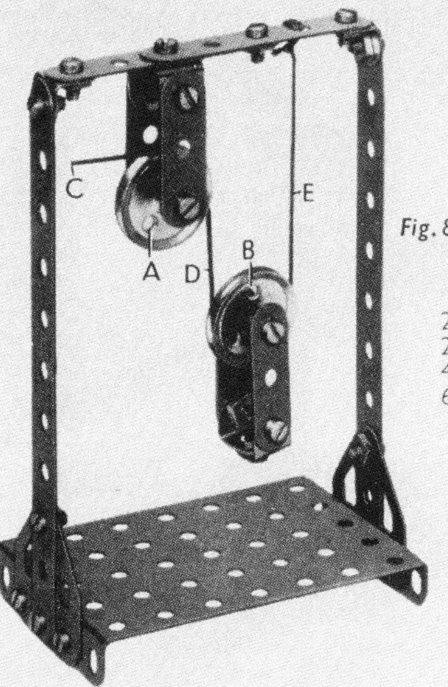

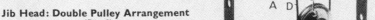

Fig. 8

Jib Head: Double Pulley Arrangement (*Fig. 9*)

4 of No.	2	4 of No.	22a	1 of No.	40
2 ” ”	6a	19 ” ”	37a	2 ” ”	59
1 ” ”	10	14 ” ”	37b	2 ” ”	111
8 ” ”	12	18 ” ”	38	2 ” ”	126a
1 ” ”	18a				

Simple Pulley Arrangement (*Fig. 8*)

2 of No.	2	19 of No.	37b
2 ” ”	5	4 ” ”	38
4 ” ”	6a	1 ” ”	40
6 ” ”	12	1 ” ”	53
2 ” ”	22a	2 ” ”	111
24 ” ”	37a	2 ” ”	126a

Fig. 9

Two-fold Pulley System (*Fig. 7*)

2 of No.	2	4 of No.	22a	1 of No.	40
2 ” ”	5	26 ” ”	37a	1 ” ”	53
4 ” ”	6a	20 ” ”	37b	2 ” ”	111
6 ” ”	12	3 ” ”	38	2 ” ”	126a

Jib Head: Single Pulley (*Fig. 10*)

2 of No.	2	5 of No.	37b
1 ” ”	10	16 ” ”	38
6 ” ”	12	1 ” ”	40
1 ” ”	18a	2 ” ”	59
2 ” ”	22a	2 ” ”	111
1 ” ”	37a	2 ” ”	126a

Fig. 10

5

Fig 48. A page from Mechanisms Book.

The 1934 edition has a different print reference in a different type face on the back cover – 13/1034/15. Which is correct is not known, though the earlier date would seem the most likely bearing in mind the proximity of Christmas and the year's peak sales. The two references for 1936 probably mean that the number to be printed was increased in mid-run from 10,000 to 12,500 and the reference changed accordingly. The two are identical.

Post-war developments. Gears 'A', 'B' and Mechanisms

Although Standard Mechanisms did not resurface in the UK after the war, some help for younger modellers did appear in 1949 when Meccano issued the Gears 'A' outfit as an adjunct to the smaller, gearless outfits. A small manual was included (fig 44) and, although it could not be compared with Standard Mechanisms, it was a useful starter for the more junior Meccano Engineers. As well as simple mechanical movements, it included a few pages on the way in which gears and sprockets could be utilised (fig 45). A number of the mechanisms were similar to pre-war examples, although new plates were used.

Gears 'B' which came out in 1956 replaced the 'A' outfit. It was very similar to Gears 'A' but it had been updated so as to include the Keyway Rod (fig 46). There were a number of minor alterations to the text and models shown in the 'B' manual.

Both Gears 'A' & 'B' only contained gears, sprockets and necessary accessories and had to be used in conjunction with standard outfits. To overcome this drawback, Meccano introduced in 1959 a new 'Mechanisms' outfit which contained a selection of standard parts as well as gears, so as to enable complete models or mechanisms to be built-up without recourse to other parts. The range of gears was more limited and so the 'Book of Mechanisms' (fig 47) issued with the outfit was less useful than those for Gears 'A' or 'B'. Fig 48 shows typical models.

The final page of the Mechanisms manual (fig 49) showed a selection of more advanced mechanisms through which, no doubt, it was hoped to lead the modeller further. Two of these are old favourites from the 1934 edition of Standard Mechanisms; the compact gear with a 243:1 reduction (though with a new plate) and the differential-type variable speed gear using the original plate from SM 96.

There are numerous printings of all three manuals but in view of their relative lack of importance, no list has yet been compiled. As with most manuals there were small changes from year to year, although none are of any significance.

A short but useful life

Standard Mechanisms manuals had a life of some twelve years only. In that relatively short time they made an important contribution to the amazing progress of model building during the golden age of Meccano which ended with the death of Frank Hornby in 1936. Although Hornby did not write the manuals, nor I suspect even contribute to them, he did create the climate which made them possible.

Of course since most modelling has for some years now been the virtual preserve of adults, many

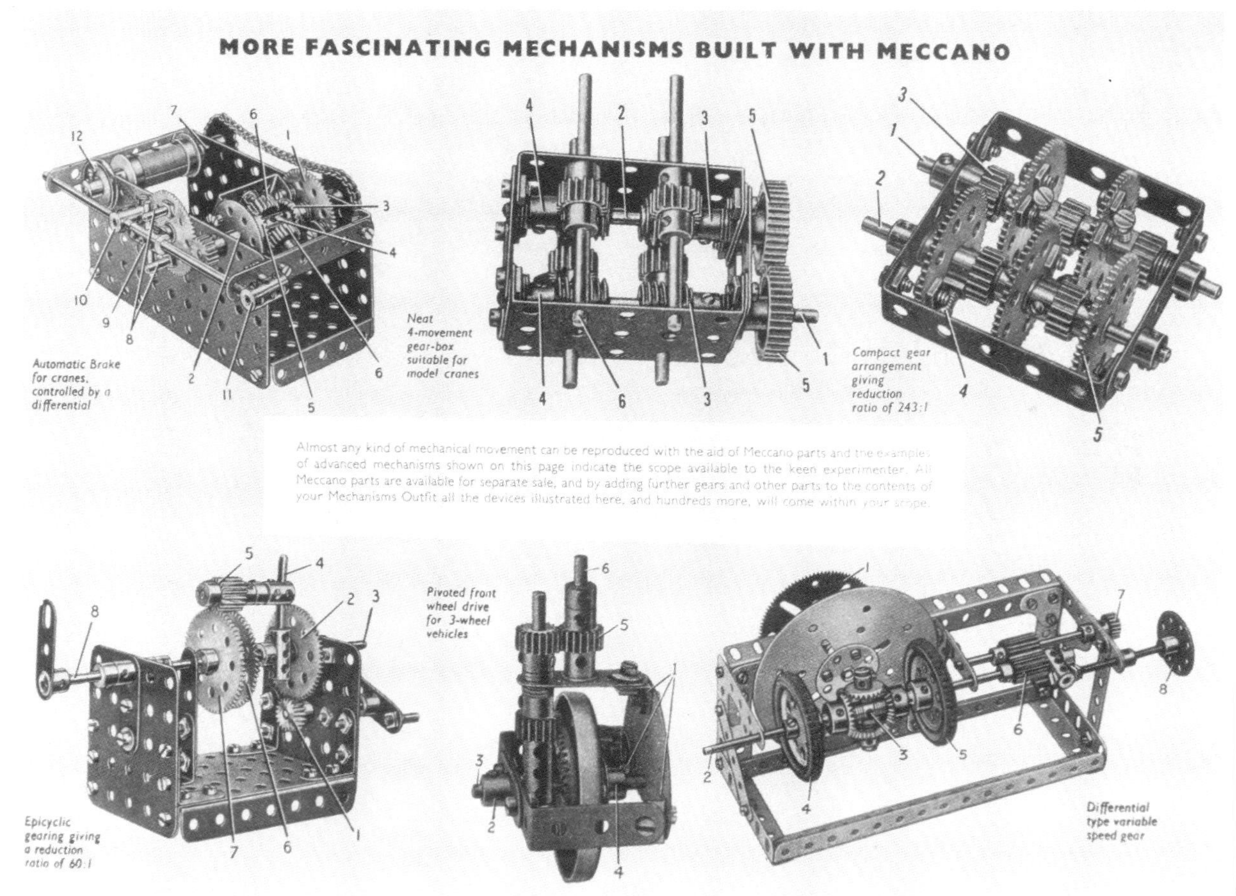

Fig 49. Something to whet the appetite.

of them highly talented men in their own fields, great strides have been made in the representation of mechanical movements and there is little which cannot now be achieved. Obviously Standard Mechanisms is no longer in the vanguard of modelling, but it can still teach the basics to newcomers. The 1934–36 editions are particularly valuable in this respect and will amply repay further study. Furthermore, they are wonderful examples of Meccano literature at its best – fascinating to look at, useful as reference material and a joy to own.

How To Use Meccano Parts

Between the years 1925, when Standard Mechanisms was first published, and 1929, the range of Meccano parts had increased quite dramatically. Some of the new ones such as the set of 26 ships' funnels, were more for appearance than for practical use. Others, such as the Digger Bucket, were for a single and obvious purpose. Many however were like the majority of Meccano parts, capable of being used for a wide variety of purposes.

As is evident in the 'Suggestions' and 'Spanner' columns in the *Meccano Magazines* of the time, the range of uses for parts was being extended all the time, both by the Model Room and *MM* readers. This, together with the frequent repetition in the column of answers to problems using standard parts, must have suggested to someone at Meccano that there was a need for a 'parts primer' which could detail the many uses of each part. It may also have been thought that such a publication might stimulate demand for some of the lesser known (and expensive) parts in the system.

Such a 'primer' first saw the light of day in the January 1929 number of the Magazine with part one of 'How to Use Meccano Parts' (fig 50). Written by Hubert Lansley (although he was not named), it was very much in the mould of Standard Mechanisms which was also a Lansley production. The series ended in April 1930 and must have been judged a success because later that year it was reprinted as a separate manual with the same title.

The First Edition

As was to be expected, How to Use Meccano Parts was a manual conforming in size to Standard Mechanisms and the normal outfit manuals (fig 51). Like Standard Mechanisms it was very comprehensive, illustrating and discussing the whole range of Meccano parts and some relevant accessories. All the parts were divided into separate sections or classifications, for ease of reference, the classification being based on a part's normal function. One can do no better than to reproduce the manual's introduction by way of explanation (fig 52).

The manual proper began with the most basic of Meccano parts, strips and girders (figs 53 & 54), giving much useful information. Indeed it would have taken a young modeller quite a deal of time

continued p. 212.

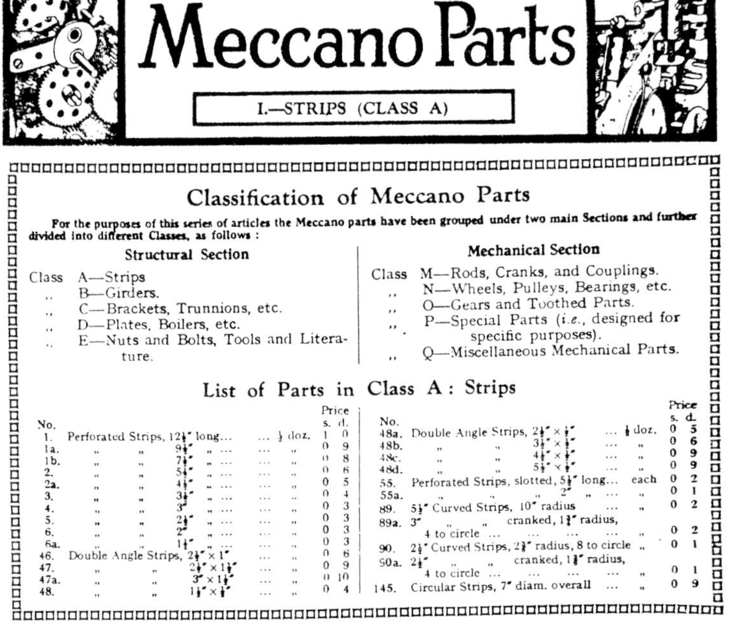

HOW TO USE

Meccano Parts

I.—STRIPS (CLASS A)

Classification of Meccano Parts

For the purposes of this series of articles the Meccano parts have been grouped under two main Sections and further divided into different Classes, as follows :

Structural Section

Class A—Strips
,, B—Girders.
,, C—Brackets, Trunnions, etc.
,, D—Plates, Boilers, etc.
,, E—Nuts and Bolts, Tools and Literature.

Mechanical Section

Class M—Rods, Cranks, and Couplings.
,, N—Wheels, Pulleys, Bearings, etc.
,, O—Gears and Toothed Parts.
,, P—Special Parts (*i.e.*, designed for specific purposes).
,, Q—Miscellaneous Mechanical Parts.

List of Parts in Class A : Strips

No.			Price s.	Price d.
1.	Perforated Strips, 12½" long...	... ½ doz.	1	0
1a.	,, ,, 9½" ,, ...	... ,,	0	9
1b.	,, ,, 7½" ,, ...	... ,,	0	8
2.	,, ,, 5½" ,, ...	... ,,	0	6
2a.	,, ,, 4½" ,, ...	... ,,	0	5
3.	,, ,, 3½" ,, ...	... ,,	0	4
4.	,, ,, 3" ,, ...	... ,,	0	3
5.	,, ,, 2½" ,, ...	... ,,	0	3
6.	,, ,, 2" ,, ...	... ,,	0	3
6a.	,, ,, 1½" ,, ...	... ,,	0	3
46.	Double Angle Strips, 2½" × 1"	... ,,	0	6
47.	,, ,, 2½" × 1½"	... ,,	0	9
47a.	,, ,, 3" × 1½"	... ,,	0	10
48.	,, ,, 1½" × ½"	... ,,	0	4
48a.	Double Angle Strips, 2½" × ½"	... ½ doz.	0	5
48b.	,, ,, 3½" × ½"	... ,,	0	6
48c.	,, ,, 4½" × ½"	... ,,	0	9
48d.	,, ,, 5½" × ½"	... ,,	0	9
55.	Perforated Strips, slotted, 5½" long...	each	0	2
55a.	,, ,, ,, 2" ,, ...	,,	0	1
89.	5½" Curved Strips, 10" radius	... ,,	0	2
89a.	3" ,, ,, cranked, 1¾" radius, 4 to circle	,,	0	2
90.	2½" Curved Strips, 2¾" radius, 8 to circle	,,	0	1
90a.	2½" ,, ,, cranked, 1⅜" radius, 4 to circle	,,	0	1
145.	Circular Strips, 7" diam. overall	... ,,	0	9

Fig 50. The first part of 'How to Use Meccano Parts' from the January 1929 Meccano Magazine.

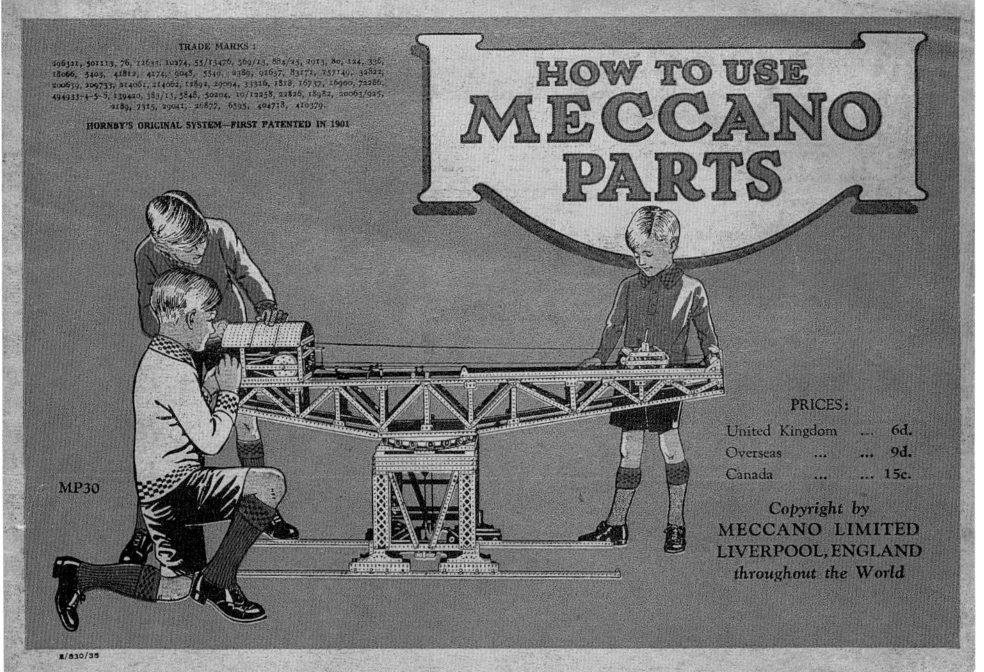

Fig 51. The first 'How to Use' manual.

How Meccano Parts are Classified

THE primary object of this booklet is to outline the principal functions of the standard parts that together constitute the Meccano system.

It would be impossible to enumerate every function of every part, but we believe that by pointing out the special purposes for which the various parts have been designed, together with a few of the other uses that have been suggested from time to time by Meccano boys themselves, we shall help Meccano enthusiasts to build more interesting models, and also construct them on scientific and practical lines.

Before any attempt could be made to describe the uses of the individual parts it was necessary to classify them in some systematic manner. For the purpose of this book we have grouped the parts first of all into two main sections, which we have termed respectively the "Structural Section" and the "Mechanical Section." Secondly, we have divided these Sections into a number of classes, each of which is dealt with separately.

The Structural Section includes all those parts that are used principally for the construction of frames, beams, bases, supports, etc., as opposed to parts intended essentially for assembly in mechanical movements (gear boxes, driving mechanisms, etc.), which are grouped under the various classes in the Mechanical Section. The grouping of the parts in the different classes will be made clear by reference to the table printed on this page.

This classification and grouping should not be taken too literally, for it is impossible to state definitely all the functions of any one Meccano part, nor can we say that certain parts are used only for frames, beams, girders, etc., and others only for gear boxes, driving mechanisms, and other mechanical movements. The Meccano Strips, for example, are used principally in the construction of frames; that is, as structural parts. They may however be used also as levers, connecting rods, and for other similar purposes; and when thus employed they would more correctly be considered, not as structural but as mechanical parts. From this it will be seen that the arranging of Meccano parts in definite groups is a difficult matter. Nevertheless we think that the method adopted will enable anyone who is not already familiar with the various components of the system to see at a glance all the parts that are most likely to fulfil any desired function.

STRUCTURAL SECTION

Class A—Strips.
„ B—Girders.
„ C—Brackets, Trunnions, etc.
„ D—Plates, Boilers, etc.
„ E—Nuts and Bolts, Tools and Literature.

MECHANICAL SECTION

Class M—Rods, Cranks, and Couplings.
„ N—Wheels, Pulleys, Bearings, etc.
„ O—Gears and Toothed Parts.
„ P—Special Accessories (i.e., designed for specific purposes).
„ Q—Miscellaneous Mechanical Parts.
„ T—Electrical Parts.
„ X—Power Units and Accessories.

The parts included in Class A, Strips, may be said to form the backbone of the Meccano system, for some of them are to be found in practically every Meccano model.

Class B deals with Girders and similar parts, which are used principally to give rigidity to various structures. Class C comprises the smaller parts that are intended to form connecting links between the larger structural parts in Classes A and B. In Class D are included all the parts intended for "filling in" the framework of models, and for building floors, gear-box frames, etc.

Class E deals with certain parts that are indispensable for all kinds of model-building, namely, Nuts and Bolts and tools. It also includes the Meccano Instruction Manuals, Super Model Leaflets, and other publications.

The contents of Classes M, N, and O are clearly indicated by their descriptive titles, and therefore need no explanation.

After the appropriate parts had been allocated to Classes M, N, and O, it was found that there still remained a large number of unclassified mechanical parts, not counting Motors and similar units. In order to deal with this remainder, the special electrical parts were grouped together into a class by themselves—Class T. Then, of the parts still left, some were found to possess characteristics quite different from the rest, and these were collected together as Special Accessories, Class P. By Special Accessories we mean those parts that are designed for specific purposes, such as Shuttles (for Looms), Signal Arms, etc. Finally, all the accessories still unclassified were placed under Class Q.

The Electric Motor, Accumulator, Transformer, Steam Engine and Clockwork Motor, are grouped under Class X, Power Units and Accessories.

Fig 52. The introduction to the 1930 'How to Use Meccano Parts' manual.

Class A: Strips

1

PERFORATED STRIPS:
No. 1, 12½″ long No. 1b, 7½″ long No. 2a, 4½″ long No. 4, 3″ long No. 6, 2″ long
No. 1a, 9½″ long No. 2, 5½″ long No. 3, 3½″ long No. 5, 2½″ long No. 6a, 1½″ long

Provided that they are placed properly, a few Strips can be converted into a perfectly rigid frame, but it is always advisable to use Angle Girders for the larger Meccano structures.

Fig. 1 shows a simple rectangle built up from 5½″ Strips and 2½″ Strips, and made perfectly rigid by the addition of a single diagonal tie composed of 5½″ and 2½″ Strips overlapped four holes.

Fig. 3 is a model of a simple roof truss. The sides 1, which have to withstand a compressive force, are constructed from Angle Girders; the side 2, which is merely in tension, consists of two 12½″ Strips overlapped and bolted together. The triangle so formed would be quite rigid for ordinary purposes, but struts and ties are usually added at 3 and 4 respectively in order to obtain still greater rigidity. Fig. 4 shows an openwork girder of the built-up truss type that is used to a large extent in the construction of bridges. The various members are arranged so that a number of triangles are formed, an arrangement that gives the girder great rigidity and strength, for the triangle is the only figure that cannot be distorted without altering the length or form of the sides. The ties are represented by 4½″ Strips and the struts by 5½″ Angle Girders.

Fig. 2 shows a braced tower such as might be used to support a crane, etc. The corner members are composed of Angle Girders, since they must withstand the compressive force exerted by the dead weight upon the structure. In order to make these girders rigid diagonal ties are added. These consist of 5½″ Strips.

DOUBLE ANGLE STRIPS:
No. 46, 2½″×1″
No. 47, 2½″×1½″
No. 47a, 3″ ×1½″
No. 48, 1½″× ½″
No. 48a, 2½″×½″
No. 48b, 3½″×½″
No. 48c, 4½″×½″
No. 48d, 5½″×½″

Similar to the ordinary Strips except that their ends are bent at right angles. They are extremely useful in the construction of frames and bearings for shafting, etc.

SLOTTED STRIPS: No. 55, 5½″ long No. 55a, 2″ long

No. 55 is provided with three ordinary holes and two slots, each 1⅛″ long, while No. 55a has two ordinary holes and a slot ⅝″ long. These slots may be used as guides for sliding mechanisms; they are also invaluable in obtaining small adjustments between parts, that would be impossible with the ½″ standard holes.

CURVED STRIPS:
No. 89, 5½″ long, 10″ radius, 12 to circle. No. 90, 2½″, 2⅜″ radius, 8 to circle.
No. 89a, 3″ cranked, 1¾″ radius, 4 to circle. No. 90a, 2½″, cranked, 1⅜″ radius, 4 to circle.

These are useful for ornamental purposes and in the construction of rotating mechanisms. Fig. 5 shows a flywheel built up from four 2½″ small radius Curved Strips. Complete circles suitable for flywheels, etc., may also be built up from eight 2½″ large radius Curved Strips or from four 3″ Curved Strips.

No. 145, CIRCULAR STRIP, 7″ diam. overall.

May be used in circular structures, as a flywheel, or in a built-up roller earing as a means of supporting the rollers (see Standard Mechanism No. 136).

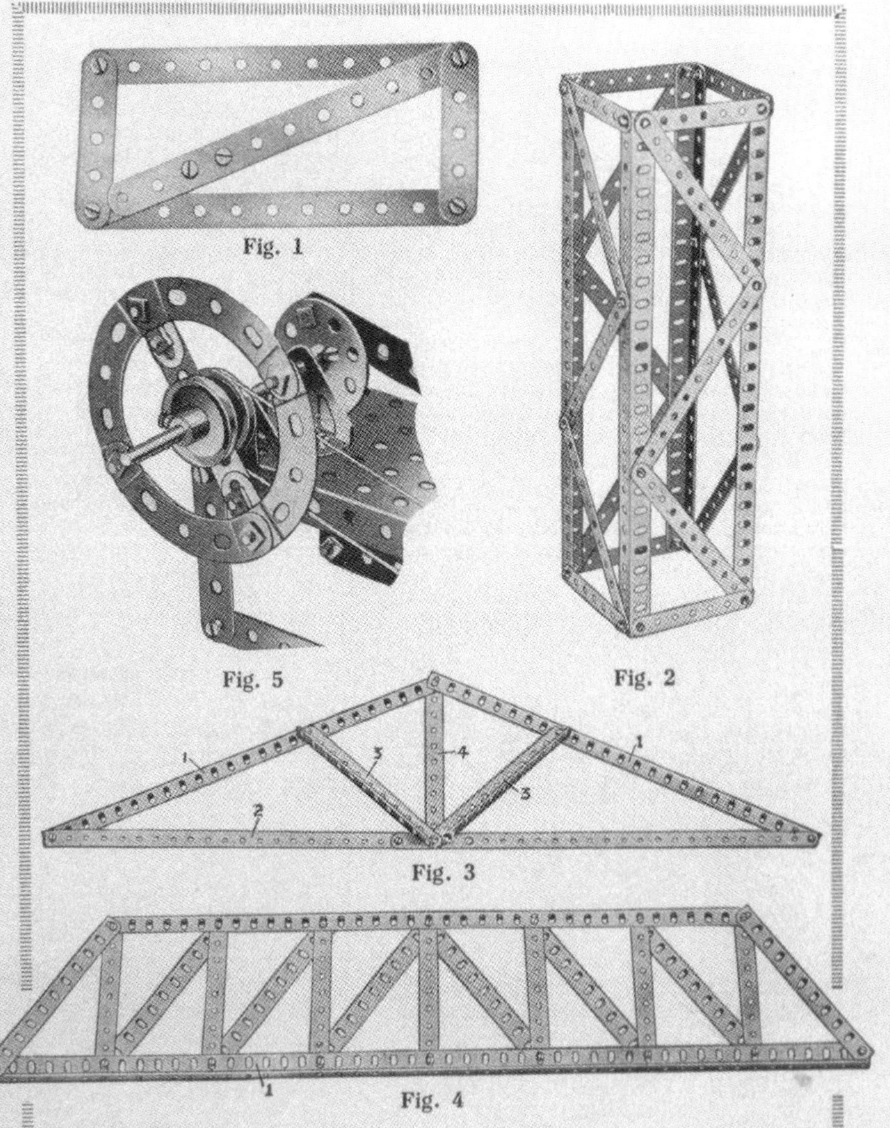

Fig 53. The manual covered even the most basic parts. Strips . . .

2

Class B: Girders

Meccano Girders play a very important part in Meccano engineering. They give great rigidity to any structure in which they are incorporated and serve admirably as bearings for shafting. A few Girders placed together with proper care and braced by one or two Strips or Rods will form a structure capable of supporting a man's weight, without the slightest disruption.

The secret of the strength of the Meccano Angle Girders is found in the right-angle formation of their flanges, which enables them to withstand bending stresses in any direction. This will become more clear from the following: If a wooden beam is mounted so that both ends only are supported and a heavy load is placed upon it, it will naturally bend. When this happens it is obvious that the upper part of the beam will be in compression and the lower part in tension. These compressive and tensional forces exert a maximum effect along the outer edges of the beam, and decrease toward the centre, in proportion with their distance from the centre, so that there is a zone between the upper and lower portions where the material of the beam is neither in compression nor in tension. It will be obvious that the more material there is above and below the neutral axis, as this zone is termed, the stronger will be the beam. Hence it will be clear that the strength of a beam is determined by its depth rather than by its width.

If a Meccano Strip is laid flat across two supports and a small load placed upon it, it will bend considerably, since the areas in compression and tension will be very small, but if the Strip is placed on edge it will withstand a very much greater load. A single Angle Girder combines the property of two ordinary Strips secured rigidly at right angles along their lengths; hence its great strength.

When a Meccano boy runs short of Girders he usually improvises by placing two Strips together lengthwise and bolting them at right angles by means of Angle Brackets.

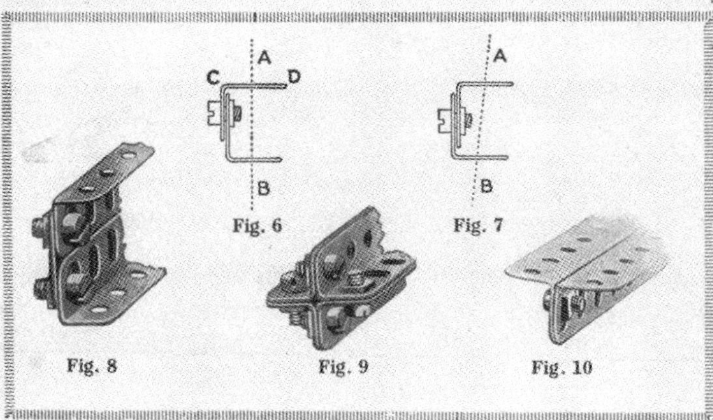

Fig. 6 Fig. 7

Fig. 8 Fig. 9 Fig. 10

ANGLE GIRDERS

No. 7 24½" long	No. 8a, 9½" long	No. 9a, 4½" long	No. 9d, 2½" long
No. 7a, 18½" long	No. 8b, 7½" long	No. 9b, 3½" long	No. 9e, 2" long
No. 8, 12½" long	No. 9, 5½" long	No. 9c, 3" long	No. 9f, 1½" long

Angle Girders differ only in their lengths. Each is perforated with round holes in one flange and elongated holes in the other. The object of the elongated holes is to provide the " play " that often is necessary when bolting a Girder to other parts. The value of this " play " is illustrated in Figs. 6 and 7, which represent sections of two Angle Girders that are bolted together to form channel-section girders, Fig. 6 showing the right method of securing the Girders and Fig. 7 the wrong method. In the former the narrow flange of one Girder is bolted to the broad flange of the other, with the result that the centres of the holes in the remaining flanges are exactly opposite—a feature that is important when it is desired to journal a Rod through the flanges of a channel girder of this type. Whenever a Rod is to be journalled through the wider flange of an Angle Girder, a short Strip should be bolted to the flange so that the Rod may pass through it as well as through the elongated hole in the Girder.

The Angle Girders lend themselves very readily to the construction of the different types of Girders used in actual practice. Fig. 12 shows a built-up I-section Girder, consisting of four Angle Girders bolted to a Flat Girder. Fig. 8 shows a built-up Channel Girder consisting of two Angle Girders connected together by Flat Girders or by Flat Brackets. Figs. 9, 10, and 13 illustrate further examples of built-up Girders that are capable of withstanding tremendous bending or compressive stresses. Figs. 11 and 14 are typical examples of complicated girder construction, the subjects being sections of the Giant Block Setting Crane (Instruction Leaflet No. 4). Fig. 11 shows a portion of the travelling gantry, viewed from underneath, while Fig. 14 is a detail view of one of the four columns that support the gantry. It will be noticed that the upper horizontal girders, which have to withstand considerable bending stresses, are of the " I " type, similar to that shown in Fig. 12 but larger. The supporting columns are in reality large rectangular girders; note the use of Braced Girders, which form two sides of the rectangle and serve to strengthen the corner Angle Girders.

BRACED GIRDERS:

No. 97, 3½" long	No. 98, 2½" long	No. 99a, 9½" long	No 100, 5½" long
No. 97a, 3" long	No. 99, 12½" long	No. 99b, 7½" long	No. 100a, 4½" long

These are not only very useful in building large structures, but are also very ornamental. They consist, in effect, of two parallel strips placed so that the opposite holes are 1½" between centres, and connected together by a series of diagonal ties and struts. Until quite recently the parallel strips were left unconnected at the ends, but all Braced Girders now being made are finished off at the ends by the addition of a narrow strip of metal at right angles to the sides. This of course is a great improvement, as each Braced Girder now forms a complete unit in itself. When connecting two Braced Girders together by overlapping, they should, wherever possible, be overlapped an odd number of holes, so that the diagonals coincide. If they overlap an even number of holes the diagonals of one Girder appear between those of the other, and the result is not so neat or realistic. The uses of Braced Girders will be obvious and a detailed description of them is not necessary therefore.

Fig 54. . . . and girders.

No. 163, SLEEVE PIECE. No. 164, CHIMNEY ADAPTOR.

The Sleeve Piece is intended primarily for use in the construction of cylinders and chimneys. To form a complete cylinder, two ¾" Flanged Wheels should be pushed over its ends as shown in Fig. 36. The Sleeve Piece may be secured in position by bolts inserted in the holes punched round its centre.

When used as a chimney the Sleeve Piece may be secured to a model by means of a ¾" Flanged Wheel clamped over one end or by a Chimney Adaptor. In building up longer chimneys, two Sleeve Pieces may be connected together by pushing them over opposite ends of a Chimney Adaptor, but a more rigid and efficient method is that adopted in the chimney shown in Fig. 32.

This consists of three Sleeve Pieces placed end to end with the centre Sleeve Piece overlapping each of the other two by ⅜". A 3½" Rod passed lengthwise through the centre of the three Sleeve Pieces carries at one end a ¾" Flanged Wheel that forms the top of the chimney. The top and bottom Sleeve Pieces are held in place by means of bolts passed through them and inserted in the holes of new style Collars carried on the 3½" Rod.

Fig. 39 shows the Chimney Adaptor used as the oil receptacle in a syphon lubricator for journal bearings.

Fig. 39

Fig 55. Some of the more unusual functions were often highlighted.

and practical model building to have gained that knowledge. All the parts were similarly treated (though with less accent on the theory), and details were given of their normal uses as well as their more interesting and unusual ones. A good example of this is the use of a chimney adaptor as a syphon wick lubricator (fig 55), although the current design with two holes in the barrel now make this impossible.

Tools, accessories and literature were, quite rightly, classed along with ordinary parts (figs 56 & 57). In fact for a time, the various manuals were themselves given part numbers (fig 58) although oddly these were not fully detailed in How to Use Meccano Parts. All the now sought-after obsolete parts were featured and page 23 (fig 59) will be enough to upset anyone who is struggling to complete a collection. The 300 series electrical parts were also included (figs 60 & 61) because, unlike the later Elektron parts, they were designed for use with standard Meccano. Following on from the electrical parts, were three pages on power units and accessories which gave much good and useful information not otherwise easily obtainable (figs 62, 63 & 64). Thus ended the first edition of How To Use Meccano Parts.

Up-Dating

There were two further editions in the same format, 1931 and 1933. They are virtually identical except for necessary up-dating. This process was not always thorough, for example, the 1933 edition does not list the $2\frac{1}{2}''$ gear wheel part no. 27c (fig 65) which was introduced in 1931. The power units' pages were better treated and showed the new motors and transformer in the 1933 edition (fig 66). The Steam Engine was omitted from this section although it was still available. Perhaps by this time its demise had already begun; certainly by this date it was not strongly featured in advertisements, although as we shall see it did make a brief reappearance in a later version of the manual.

The power units' pages also exhibit an interesting difference between the 1929–30 *Meccano Magazine* version of How to Use Meccano Parts

8

Class E: Nuts and Bolts, Tools and Literature

No. 37, NUTS AND BOLTS, 7/32".

The best method of securing nuts and bolts is with the head of the bolt on the outside of the model, for the Screwdriver forms a speedier method of tightening the nuts and bolts than the Spanner. Also, a model having all the bolt heads on the outer side will have a much neater appearance than one in which the nuts and shanks are all exposed. For ordinary model-building, sufficient rigidity can be obtained by using the Screwdriver only, merely steadying the nut with the fingers, but wherever excessive strain is expected, both Spanner and Screwdriver should be used simultaneously, the nut being held firmly by the Spanner in one hand while the bolt is turned by the Screwdriver in the other hand, or *vice versa*.

Fig. 53 shows a Meccano gear-changing lever in which a single bolt plays a novel and important part. The head of the bolt 9 presses against a $2\frac{1}{2}''$ small radius Curved Strip 10, which forms the quadrant. The head of the bolt tends to slip into the holes in the Strip 10 and thus retain the lever 5 firmly in any one of three different positions. The gearing on the shaft 3, which is controlled by the lever, should be arranged so that the different engagements are brought about in these three positions of the lever 5; then the gears will not easily ride out of engagement once the lever has been moved.

A very important use of the nut and bolt is found in the making of pivotal connections between various Meccano parts. Typical pivots so formed are described under Standard Mechanism Nos. 262 and 263. S.M. 262 is reproduced herewith (Fig. 52). In this case the bolt 1 passes through the Strip 2 and is securely held to Strip 3 by means of two nuts 4 and 5, which are screwed tight against opposite sides of the Strip. Sufficient space is left between the nut 5 and the bolt head to allow free movement of the Strip 2.

S.M. 263 is a similar arrangement except that both Strips 2 and 3 are allowed freedom of movement about the bolt instead of Strip 2 only. Both Strips are first placed on the bolt 1 and the nuts 4 and 5 are then placed together on its shank. The nuts are turned in opposite directions until they securely grip each other in position on the bolt. S.M. 262 is to be preferred wherever it is required to move only one Strip about the bolt, for this method affords a minimum amount of "play" or slackness in the joint.

Another kind of pivot formed from a bolt and nut is included in Fig. 53. Bolt 1 in this illustration passes through the end hole of a Crank 6 and enters the threaded bore of a Collar 2, without touching the Rod 3. It is secured rigidly in this position by locking a nut 4 against the Collar. Sufficient freedom is allowed for the Crank 6 to turn easily about the bolt, and the Collar 2, which is free on the shaft 3, is held in position by two further Collars. By means of this pivotal connection, easy longitudinal movement of the Rod 3 is obtained on operation of the Crank 6.

BOLTS, No. 111, $\frac{3}{4}''$. No. 111a, $\frac{1}{2}''$. No. 111c, $\frac{3}{8}''$.

There are four different sizes of Meccano bolts, i.e., $\frac{3}{4}''$, $\frac{1}{2}''$, $\frac{3}{8}''$, and 7/32" (No. 37b), but the pitch of the thread is the same in every case (32 threads to the inch). The 7/32" Bolt may be obtained separately (under part No. 37b) or complete with nut (under part No. 37). It is this size of bolt that is supplied in considerable quantities, complete with nuts, in all the Meccano Outfits. The other three kinds of bolts are for use in special cases where an extra long shank is required.

No. 69, SET SCREWS. No. 69a, GRUB SCREWS. No. 69b, 7/32" GRUB SCREWS.

No. 69 are of similar shape to the bolts but are only 3/16" in length, and are, of course, designed primarily for securing the various Meccano wheels to the Axle Rods. The Grub Screws have no head at all. They are employed for securing the smaller Meccano parts, such as Collars, Couplings, etc., to Rods. It will sometimes be found that the Set-screw of a Meccano Pulley or Gear Wheel fouls some other part of the model, in which case it may be substituted by a Grub Screw, which will fit almost flush with the boss.

No. 147b, PIVOT BOLT WITH TWO NUTS.

The Pivot Bolt is of a quite different design to the ordinary bolts. The greater portion of its shank is smooth and the part is particularly suitable for use as a small pivot or fixed pin about which a small pulley or lever may rotate. It is secured in position by clamping the two nuts on its shank to a Meccano Strip or other part, as in Fig. 52.

No. 68, WOODSCREWS, $\frac{1}{2}''$.

Woodscrews are also included in the Meccano system. These are of course, for the benefit of those boys who wish to secure their models to wooden bases. They are supplied in $\frac{1}{2}''$ lengths only. Any model that does not travel will be improved in appearance and operation if it is screwed down to a wooden base.

No. 34, SPANNER. No. 36, SCREWDRIVER.

Parts Nos. 34 and 36 (Figs. 49 and 50) are the tools that are found in every Meccano Outfit and are the only essential ones.

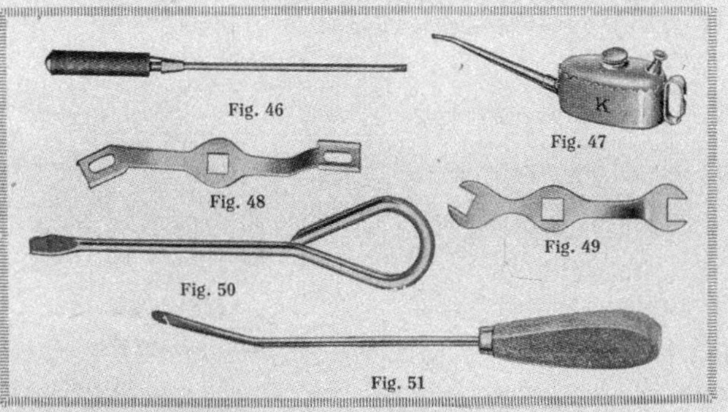

Fig 56. Tools and literature were also classed as parts of the system. See also fig 57.

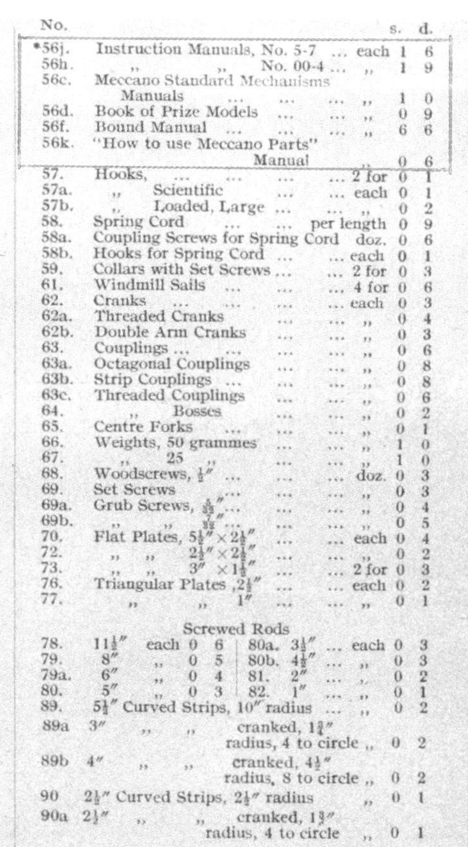

No.		s.	d.
*56j.	Instruction Manuals, No. 5-7 ... each	1	6
56h.	„ „ No. 00-4 ... „	1	9
56c.	Meccano Standard Mechanisms Manuals ... ... „	1	0
56d.	Book of Prize Models ... ... „	0	9
56f.	Bound Manual ... ... „	6	6
56k.	"How to use Meccano Parts" Manual „	0	6
57.	Hooks, ... 2 for	0	1
57a.	„ Scientific ... ... each	0	1
57b.	„ Loaded, Large ... ... „	0	2
58.	Spring Cord ... ... per length	0	9
58a.	Coupling Screws for Spring Cord doz.	0	6
58b.	Hooks for Spring Cord ... ... each	0	1
59.	Collars with Set Screws ... ... 2 for	0	3
61.	Windmill Sails ... ... 4 for	0	6
62.	Cranks ... ... each	0	3
62a.	Threaded Cranks ... ... „	0	4
62b.	Double Arm Cranks ... ... „	0	3
63.	Couplings ... ... „	0	6
63a.	Octagonal Couplings ... ... „	0	8
63b.	Strip Couplings ... ... „	0	8
63c.	Threaded Couplings ... ... „	0	6
64.	„ Bosses ... ... „	0	2
65.	Centre Forks ... ... „	0	1
66.	Weights, 50 grammes ... ... „	1	0
67.	„ 25 „ ... ... „	1	0
68.	Woodscrews, $\frac{1}{2}''$ ... ... doz.	0	3
69.	Set Screws ... ... „	0	3
69a.	Grub Screws, $\frac{5}{32}''$ ... ... „	0	4
69b.	„ „ $\frac{7}{32}''$ ... ... „	0	5
70.	Flat Plates, $5\frac{1}{2}'' \times 2\frac{1}{2}''$ ... ... each	0	4
72.	„ „ $2\frac{1}{2}'' \times 2\frac{1}{2}''$ ... ... „	0	2
73.	„ „ $3'' \times 1\frac{1}{2}''$ ... ... 2 for	0	3
76.	Triangular Plates, $2\frac{1}{2}''$ ... ... each	0	2
77.	„ „ $1''$ ... ... „	0	1
	Screwed Rods		
78.	$11\frac{1}{2}''$ each	0	6
79.	$8''$ „	0	5
79a.	$6''$ „	0	4
80.	$5''$ „	0	3
80a.	$3\frac{1}{2}''$ ... each	0	3
80b.	$4\frac{1}{2}''$ ... „	0	3
81.	$2''$ ... „	0	2
82.	$1''$ ... „	0	1
89.	$5\frac{1}{2}''$ Curved Strips, $10''$ radius ... „	0	2
89a	$3''$ „ „ cranked, $1\frac{3}{4}''$ radius, 4 to circle „	0	2
89b	$4''$ „ „ cranked, $4\frac{1}{2}''$ radius, 8 to circle „	0	2
90	$2\frac{1}{2}''$ Curved Strips, $2\frac{1}{2}''$ radius „	0	1
90a	$2\frac{1}{2}''$ „ „ cranked, $1\frac{3}{8}''$ radius, 4 to circle „	0	1

Fig 58. Part of a 1932 price list showing the numbers allocated to various manuals.

Class E: Nuts and Bolts, Tools and Literature *(continued)* 9

No. 34b, BOX SPANNER.

The Box Spanner (Fig. 48) has a kind of slot at each end into which the nut may be slipped. With the aid of this tool a nut may be placed in positions impossible to reach with the fingers.

No. 36a, EXTRA LONG SCREWDRIVER. No. 36b, SPECIAL SCREWDRIVER.

Part No. 36a is of similar pattern to part No. 36, but the blade is 5″ long instead of 3½″, and instead of the end being flattened slightly it is of the same diameter as the shaft. This enables the blade to be passed completely through the standard Meccano holes.

The Special Screwdriver (Fig. 46) is all-metal and measures 8″ in length. Like part No. 36a the blade of this tool is of such a diameter that it may be passed through standard Meccano holes.

No. 105, REED HOOK.

This is designed to facilitate the threading of the warp threads through the Meccano Loom.

OIL CANS, No. 1 (ordinary type). No. 2 ("K" type).

The latter type is reproduced herewith (Fig. 47). The oil may be ejected drop by drop by depressing the valve. The No. 2 Oil Can measures 5″ in overall length. A specially prepared lubricating oil is included in the Meccano system and may be obtained in small bottles. This oil is particularly suitable for lubricating Meccano Clockwork and Electric Motors.

MECCANO ENAMEL. Colours: Red, Grey and Green.

All Meccano parts may now be obtained enamelled in colours, and for the benefit of those boys who wish to convert nickelled parts to coloured ones, the Meccano Enamel is supplied in small tins. There are three colours available, red, grey, and green, each colour being identical in shade with the enamel used in the Meccano factory for spraying Meccano parts. The enamel should be applied with a small brush, the surface of the part having first been cleaned thoroughly with fine emery cloth. When quite dry the enamel gives a splendid finish to the Meccano parts.

MECCANO INSTRUCTION MANUALS

No. 56b, for Outfits 00-0. No. 56a, for Outfits 00-3. No. 56, for Outfits 4-7.

The greatest thrill of Meccano model-building is to be derived from building according to one's own ideas, but before a Meccano boy attempts to do this he should make a point of building all the models shown in the Meccano Instruction Manual that are within the range of his Outfit.

The Meccano Instruction Manual is obtainable in three separate portions, as listed above. The first portion, No. 56b, describes models that may be built with Outfits Nos. 00 and 0, the second shows models that may be built with Outfits Nos. 00 to 3 and the third describes models built with the larger Outfits, Nos. 4 to 7. It should be mentioned that the 00-3 Manual (No. 56a) contains all the models described in the 00-0 Manual (No. 56b) in addition to a great number of models built with Outfits Nos. 1, 2, and 3. Hence a Meccano boy who wishes to form a complete Manual need only buy the 00-3 and 4-7 Manuals.

Instructions are included wherever the illustrations are not sufficiently clear, but for the rest the Meccano boy is expected to use his own eyes and ingenuity! After a little practice it is surprising how easy it becomes to build the most elaborate model from quite a small illustration.

SPECIAL SUPER MODEL INSTRUCTION LEAFLETS.

Some of the models included in the Manuals require so many illustrations in order to show each detail clearly that they would occupy several pages. Such models therefore are dealt with in special instruction leaflets, which are beautifully printed and profusely illustrated from actual photographs. These leaflets are included in the Outfits with which the respective models can be built, and they may also be obtained separately. A complete list of the leaflets available, together with a brief description of the subject of each, appears on page 10.

STANDARD MECHANISMS MANUAL.

The Meccano Standard Mechanisms Manual is designed for the use of the more advanced model-builder. It contains details of a large number of Meccano movements that are to a large extent standardised, in that they may be applied to more than one model with very little alteration.

The various devices dealt with in the Manual have been divided into thirteen different sections, under such headings as Gear Ratios, Belt and Rope Mechanism, Clutches, Reversing and Drive-changing Mechanisms, etc., so that used in conjunction with the ordinary Instruction Manuals, the Standard Mechanisms Manual will form a very useful and instructive book.

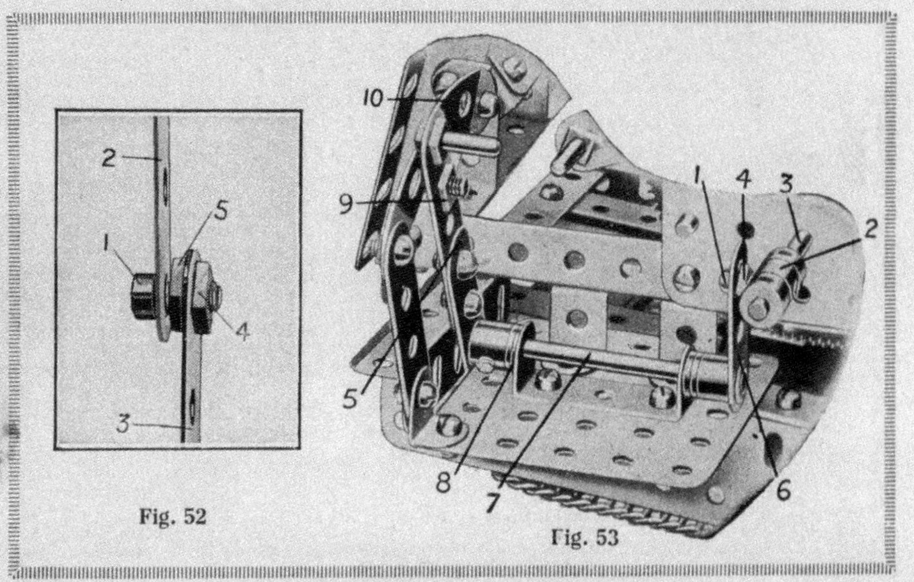

Fig. 52

Fig. 53

Fig 57. Other 'parts' in the system.

Class P: Special Accessories *(continued)* 23

Mechanisms Manual (see detail No. 134), and on reference to this it will be found that twenty-one steel Balls are placed round the circumference of a Wheel Flange that is bolted to a 3″ Pulley Wheel, while a further 3″ Pulley, which is bolted to the swivelling superstructure, rests upon the Balls. With this arrangement it is possible to rotate heavy structures easily and smoothly about a central pivot. The Steel Balls are also used in model-building for ballast purposes and for driving "gravity wheels." In the latter case the Balls are arranged to drop one at a time on to the blades of a kind of water-wheel, and the weight of the Balls causes the wheel to rotate, just as the force of the impingeing water operates the actual water-wheel.

No. 120, BUFFER. No. 120a, SPRING BUFFER.

Designed for use in models of railway vehicles. Both types are mounted on threaded shanks and fitted with standard nuts. No. 120 measures ½″ in length, excluding the shank, and is cut from the solid, while No. 120a, which measures ⅝″ in length minus shank, is provided with a separate sleeve that encloses a compression spring, and thus acts as a shock absorber.

The Spring Buffer may also be employed for other very different purposes. In Fig. 102 part No. 120a serves as a spring catch to hold a hand lever in position after the latter has been moved from one side to the other. The lever passes through the centre hole of a Coupling 19 and carries a second Coupling 20, which presses upon the Spring Buffer 21 and is provided with two 7/32″ Bolts inserted on opposite sides. These bolts act as stops to prevent the lever moving too far in either direction.

One of the most interesting adaptations of the Spring Buffer is included in Standard Mechanisms No. 115 (Meccano Electric Controller). This mechanism is reproduced at Fig. 91 and it will be seen that the Spring Buffer 5 acts as a spring-controlled contact, which ensures good contact being made with the studs of the resistance. The sleeve portion of another Spring Buffer is bolted at 9 to act as a stop.

No. 122, MINIATURE LOADED SACK.

This accessory adds a very realistic touch to Meccano models of cranes, lorries, conveyors and other types of goods-handling machinery. It may also be used with advantage in connection with Hornby goods trains. It is filled with sawdust and provided with a small loop of wire by means of which the crane hook may be attached.

The use of a number of Miniature Sacks will also add considerably to the realism and pleasure of operating the lifts in the Meccano Electric Goods Warehouse (Special Instruction Leaflet No. 31).

No. 131, DREDGER BUCKET.

Intended for use in models of excavating machinery and conveyors. Is provided with a clip which may be pushed through one of the links in a length of Sprocket Chain, the ends of the clip then being bent back as shown in Fig. 99. Great care should be exercised in bending the clips to ensure that sufficient space is left between their ends to admit the teeth of the Sprocket Wheel round which the Chain passes. The Chain 2 on which the Buckets 1 are mounted should be kept taut or it will twist when the buckets are loaded.

No. 150, CRANE GRAB.

Useful in model cranes, for picking up and depositing loads. It consists of two jaws fitted with arms that are pivoted together and connected at their upper ends by short chains to a hook, which may be attached to the main crane hook. It is illustrated in Fig. 98.

No. 169, DIGGER BUCKET.

This part is shown in Fig. 101. Designed principally for use in Meccano steam shovels, or mechanical navvies. The mouth of the Bucket measures about 1⅞″×2¼″, while the depth (over cutting teeth) is 2½″. The bottom of the Bucket is mounted on hinged levers and normally is held in place by a sliding catch that engages with a slot in the front of the bucket. A cord may be attached to the catch and on pulling this the floor falls open and so discharges the contents of the bucket. If a small quantity of gravel or grain is available a model excavator fitted with the Digger Bucket can be used to load Hornby Railway Wagons, etc.

No. 135, THEODOLITE PROTRACTOR.

The Protractor consists of a sheet of superfine ivory card on which are printed circular and semi-circular scales, marked out in degrees. These two scales are for use in the Meccano Theodolite (Model No. 6.17), the former for indicating the extent of rotation of the model in a horizontal plane and the latter for indicating the angle of the sighting arm. The scales are also very useful in a number of other models. In Fig. 95 the semi-circular scale is used to register the movement of a beam under stress, while in Fig. 94 the circular scale acts as a measure of the extent of vertical rise or fall of a lift.

No. 138, SHIP'S FUNNEL. No. 138a-z, RAKED SHIP'S FUNNEL.

Part No. 138 is placed vertically on its base while No. 138a is raked, i.e., when secured to a model, it lies at an angle to the vertical. Both are provided with two perforated lugs by means of which they may be bolted to any Meccano Strip or Plate. No. 138 is enamelled red and is designed for use in models of tramp steamers, etc. No. 138a is obtainable in twenty-six different colour-combinations to represent the principal shipping companies. It is also provided with a miniature steampipe attached to the front of the funnel.

No. 141, WIRE LINE.

For suspending the 18 lb. weight required to drive the Meccano Grandfather Clock (Instruction Leaflet No. 14). Can be used in any model where a very heavy load is to be raised, but is not suitable for small model cranes, owing to stiffness.

DUNLOP TYRES :
No. 142b, to fit 3″ diam. Pulleys. No. 142d, to fit 1½″ diam. Pulleys.
No. 142a, to fit 2″ diam. Pulleys. No. 142c, to fit 1″ diam. Pulleys.

The 3″ and 2″ sizes of the Dunlop tyres will be familiar to the majority of Meccano boys, but the 1½″ and 1″ are recent additions to the system. These solid rubber tyres are perfect miniature reproductions of the real thing and are specially made for Meccano Limited by the Dunlop Rubber Company Limited. They are suitable for use in all models of motor vehicles, etc. The dimensions given represent their inside diameters and therefore the four tyres fit the 3″, 2″, 1½″ and 1″ Pulleys respectively.

No. 142, RUBBER RINGS, 3″. No. 155, ⅝″.

No. 142 is designed to fit round the groove of a 3″ Pulley Wheel and thus represent a pneumatic tyre in models of road vehicles. Also employed to provide the frictional surface in Meccano clutch mechanisms and frictional driving apparatus. The ⅝″ Rubber Ring is incorporated in the clutch of the

Fig 59. Some of the more sought-after obsolete parts.

28

Class T: Electrical Parts

It will be noted that each part in this Class is numbered over 300, although the last number in the regular accessories is 173. The object of this is to make a more marked division between the regular and electrical components of the Meccano system.

No. 301, BOBBIN.

Designed for use in the construction of small electro-magnets and solenoids. It is about 1″ in length and its centre, which is of brass, is bored to fit round a Meccano Axle Rod. The ends are of fibre and are ¾″ in diameter. Fig. 120 shows two solenoids, formed from Meccano Bobbins, used to impart reciprocating motion to the "piston rods" 3 and 4 of a small horizontal engine. Each Bobbin is wound with several layers of No. 26 S.C.C. Wire and is covered with a strip of brown paper as extra protection. The Rods 3 and 4 are free to slide in the centre bores of the Bobbins, and matters are so arranged that current is supplied to the coils of wire alternately, thus imparting motion to the piston rods and thence to the crankshaft of the engine. Solenoids constructed in this way can be used for innumerable purposes in Meccano model-building. For example, an electric railway signal may be brought to the "off" position by supplying current to a solenoid that operates the signal arm through a "plunger" and suitable lever mechanism, as shown in Fig. 121.

No. 308, CORE OR POLE PIECE.

Consists of soft iron and may be secured in position by the nuts supplied with it. A very useful electro-magnet may easily be formed by winding a Bobbin to capacity with 26 S.C.C. Wire and inserting in its centre a Core or Pole Piece. A great advantage of the electro-magnet lies in the fact that the Pole Piece is magnetised only whilst current flows through the coils. Hence, if a magnet of this type is attached to the lifting hook of a model crane, metal objects can be picked up or dropped merely by closing or opening a switch. Other obvious adaptations for the electro-magnet—such as in bells, buzzers, relay switches and electric indicators, etc.—will immediately suggest themselves to Meccano boys. The special Pole Pieces should always be used for the magnet core, for if the ordinary Meccano steel Rods are employed they will be found to retain the magnetism after the current has ceased to flow through the coils.

Fig. 122 shows a Meccano electro-magnet incorporated in a buzzer. The magnet is seen at 1, with the end of the Pole Piece at 2 just beneath the vibrating lever or "armature" 3.

No. 307, SILVER TIPPED CONTACT SCREW.

These screws are cut with 6 B.A. Thread and are ½″ in length overall. They are shown at 4 and 5 in Fig. 122 and should always be used where a rapid make-and-break is required, for they ensure perfect contact and do not burn away or "soot-up" under the heat of the sparks like ordinary screws. The gap between the contact points may easily be adjusted by turning one of the screws.

No. 304 6 B.A SCREW   **No. 305, 6 B.A. NUT.**
No 302 INSULATING BUSH.   **No. 303, INSULATING WASHER.**

The 6 B.A. Bolts and Nuts are supplied so that Meccano parts can be bolted together and yet insulated from each other by using these bolts in conjunction with the special Insulating Bushes and Washers. These latter parts are of fibre and are similar except that the Insulating Bush has a small "shoulder" which fits inside a standard Meccano hole. Whenever it is necessary to insulate a bolt from a Meccano Strip, an Insulating Bush should be placed on one side of the Strip, with its shoulder inside a hole in the Strip, and an Insulating Washer on the other side; a 6 B.A. Bolt should then be passed through the two and secured by its nuts in the ordinary way. In this manner the bolt is prevented from making contact with the metal of the Strip. This simple means of insulation is of course, invaluable in Meccano model-building.

No. 306, TERMINAL.

The Terminal consists of a milled brass knob bored and tapped to fit the 6 B.A. Bolts. Fig. 122 shows two Terminals mounted on the shanks of bolts at 6 and 8. It will be noted that an Insulating Washer is placed under the Terminal 6; an Insulating Bush is used on the other side of the plate, so that this Terminal is insulated from the model. Terminal 8 is in metallic contact with the model.

Fig. 117 shows a Meccano two-way switch. In this the switch arm is attached pivotally to a Trunnion that is insulated from the base plate in the manner described above, and the two contact pieces 1 carrying the Terminals 2 and 3 are also insulated. Hence, by engaging one or other of the latter with the switch arm the electric circuit can be led from Terminal 5 to Terminal 3 or, alternatively, from Terminal 5 to Terminal 2.

Fig. 118 shows a 6 B.A. Bolt 5 used as the contact stud in a Meccano Morse tapping key. The bolt is insulated from the base plate, but the key 4 is in metallic contact with it. One wire is attached to the bolt 5 and another to the plate, so that the circuit is completed whenever the bolt 8 of the key touches bolt 5.

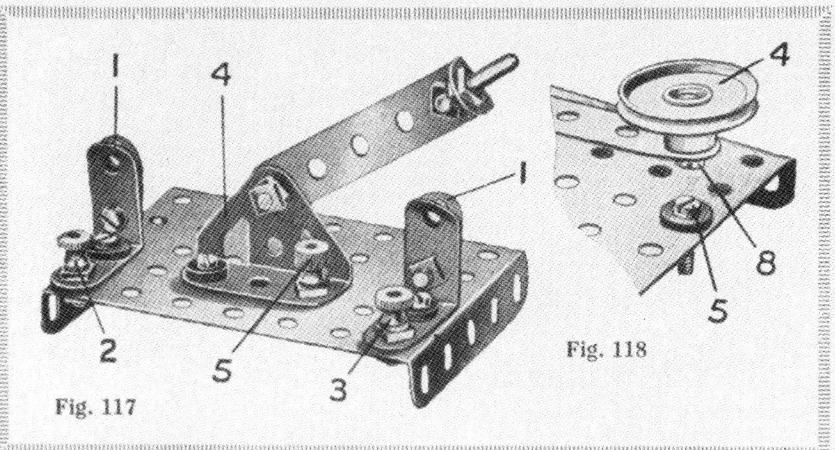

Fig. 117

Fig. 118

Fig 60. Some of the electrical parts in the system in 1930.

Class T: Electrical Parts (*continued*)

29

No. 309, COIL CHEEK.

This part is cut from ⅛" fibre sheet and measures 1¼" square. An oblong perforation is cut in its centre, so that Meccano Strips can be passed through it, and four small holes are provided to admit wire. The object of the part is, of course, to facilitate the construction of large magnetic coils.

No. 310, LAMP HOLDER. No. 311, METAL FILAMENT LAMP (6-volt).

The Lamp Holder is designed to form a screw socket for the Meccano 6-volt Lamp. Its end is of fibre and it should be secured to Meccano models as follows. A 6 B.A. Bolt is passed through the small perforation in its end, and then through a hole in a Meccano Strip, and an Insulating Bush is placed on the shank of the bolt so that its shoulder fits into the hole in the Strip. The bolt can then be secured by a nut or Terminal. When the latter is screwed up tight, the metal of the Lamp Holder will be in contact with the Strip, so that the electric current may be conducted to the lamp by attaching one wire to the 6 B.A. Bolt (the head of which presses against the contact in the end of the lamp itself), and another wire to the Meccano Strip.

Fig. 119 shows a Lamp and Holder mounted in the front of a model electric locomotive, the Holder 14 being bolted to an Angle Bracket. Current is led to the Lamp by an insulated wire slipped under the nut on the 6 B.A. Bolt by which the holder is secured, and returned to the source of supply through the Holder itself and through the frame of the model.

No. 312, 27 GAUGE, BARE IRON WIRE. No. 314, 23 GAUGE, S.C.C. COPPER WIRE. No. 313, 26 GAUGE, S.C.C. COPPER WIRE. No. 315, No. 22 GAUGE, BARE COPPER WIRE.

The 27 gauge Bare Iron Wire is intended for use when it is required to insert a resistance in an electric circuit, such as in the construction of electric speed controllers, etc. The 26 gauge Single Cotton Covered Copper Wire is usually employed in constructing electro-magnets, bobbins, etc., although it can be used for ordinary connecting purposes. The 23 gauge Copper Wire is intended for making all kinds of electrical connections in Meccano models, and the 22 gauge Bare Copper Wire is supplied for use where a conductor wire is required, such as in electric locomotives and similar models.

It is scarcely necessary to give Meccano boys detailed instructions on the subject of wiring their models, but it may be well to mention one or two important points. All connections should be made as tight as possible—that is, when connecting a wire to some part of a model it should not be merely twisted round a Strip, but secured by a nut and bolt. Insulated wire should never be allowed to rub against metal, else short circuits will quickly occur.

Another point to remember is the fact that wire exerts a certain resistance against the flow of the electric current, just as a water pipe resists the flow of water through it by the friction created between its walls and the moving liquid. In ordinary Meccano model-building, the resistance likely to be exerted by the wiring is negligible, especially if the Meccano 23 gauge wire is used, but in exceptional cases where the current is directed over considerable distances, such as in Morse Telegraph instruments, electric signals and indicators, etc., a considerable loss of current will result if thin conductor wire is used, and the Motor, bell or whatever it is required to energise, will fail to function properly. The resistance in the conductor can, however, be decreased by increasing the diameter of the wire or, if a larger wire is not obtainable, by connecting additional lengths of wire in parallel with the first.

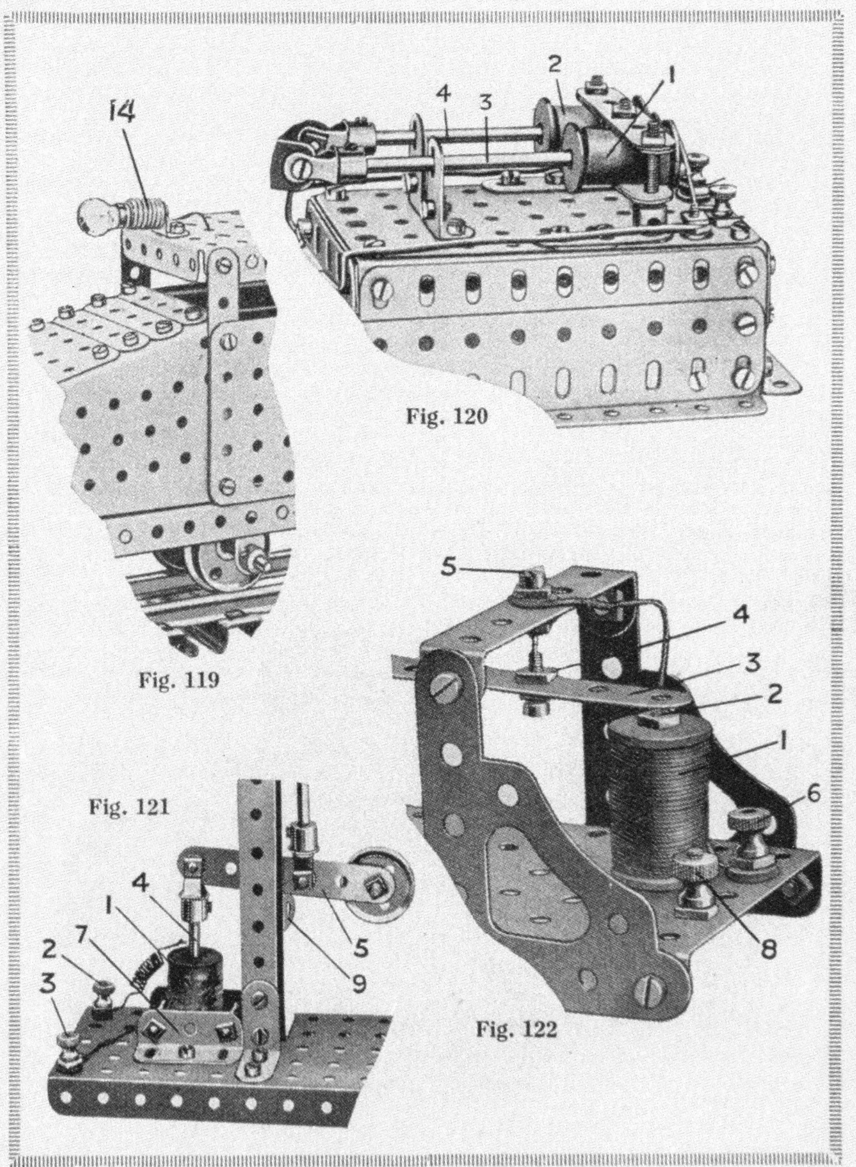

Fig 61. The remaining electrical parts.

Class X: Power Units and Accessories

For setting his model in motion, the Meccano boy has a choice of "prime movers" employing the three principal sources of power used by the model engineer—electricity, steam and clockwork. Many boys find it very difficult to decide which of these three methods to adopt. Of course, the ideal plan is to use all three methods, so that when building, say, a model electric train the Electric Motor can be employed, whilst if it is desired to represent a steam shovel or similar machine, the Steam Engine can be used, and so on, but very few boys are in a position to collect the necessary equipment!

ELECTRIC MOTOR, No. 6, 6-volt.
STEAM ENGINE, complete with Boiler, Burner, 6.5 : 1 gearing, etc.

The Meccano Electric Motor and Steam Engine are each capable of driving practically every Meccano model, provided that the intermediate gearing is designed and constructed properly.

No matter what type of model is to be driven, the Motor or Engine should always be allowed to rotate at maximum speed. This means that if it is required to operate a slow-moving model, a gear that will provide a considerable reduction in speed must be employed. The simplest means of obtaining the necessary reduction is provided by the ordinary Meccano toothed gearing (see Section 1, Standard Mechanisms Manual). If gears are not available the drive from the Motor can be transmitted through belt mechanism, and the speed can be reduced at the same time by taking the drive from a small Pulley to one of much larger diameter (see Section 2, Standard Mechanisms Manual). Sprocket Wheel and Chain gearing may, of course, be used equally well in place of belts. Meccano gearing is dealt with fully in Class O.

Fig. 123 Fig. 124 Fig. 125 Fig. 126

Whatever type of gearing is employed it is important to remember that, if the driven shaft moves more slowly than the driving shaft, a mechanical advantage is obtained and increased loads may be overcome, the apparent gain in power being roughly in proportion to the loss in speed. If the drive is led through 1 : 1 gearing (i.e., two Gears of equal size meshing together or two Pulleys of equal diameter connected by a belt), there is no gain in power to counteract the loss through friction. Such gearing should therefore be avoided as far as possible, and when it is necessary to transmit the power from one point to another, the gearing should always result in some reduction in speed in the driven shaft, unless it happens that speed is a more important consideration than power.

Another very important means by which the Engine or Motor may be used to overcome increased loads, consists of pulley blocks. By incorporating a cord and pulley system in a model, a reduction in speed is obtained, the reduction increasing in proportion to the number of pulleys or "sheaves," to give them their correct term, employed. For example, if a crane can lift a load of 10 lbs. coupled directly to the hoisting cord, then by using a single-sheave pulley block, so that the load is raised in just twice the time formerly taken, the model should be capable of lifting 20 lbs. (not allowing for loss through friction). Similarly, if a two-sheave pulley block is used so that the crane hook is raised in four times the period occupied originally, then a load of nearly 40 lb. could be raised. Therefore the mechanical advantage is "2" and "4" respectively in these examples.

Of course, the same mechanical advantage could be obtained by using extra gearing and retaining the single hoisting cord, but the use of the pulley blocks is the better method, for it is more economical and it has the very important advantage of distributing the load over several lengths of cord instead of one only, with the result that a lighter and more flexible cord can safely be used.

Fig. 129 shows the Steam Engine applied to the Meccano Stiff Leg Derrick (see Special Instruction Leaflet No. 6). In this case the gearing mounted between the side plates of the Engine gives a ratio of 58.5 : 1, that is, the crankshaft of the Engine turns 58½ times to each revolution of the winding shaft. This ratio is obtained as follows: Engine crankshaft to secondary shaft, 6.5 : 1 (the Pinion and Gear Wheel giving this ratio are supplied with the Steam Engine); secondary shaft to intermediate shaft, 3 : 1 (½" Pinion driving on to a 57-teeth Gear Wheel); intermediate shaft to winding shaft, 3 : 1 (½" Pinion and 57-teeth Gear).

Now, if we apply a load direct to the end of the hoisting cord, we shall find that the Engine can lift 9 lb. 13 oz. If we decrease still further the speed at which the load is raised by adding pulley blocks, then the amount of the load that can be raised should increase proportionately for, as already stated, power is gained in porportion to the loss in speed. In Fig. 129 a three-sheave pulley block is used, and the hoisting cord is passed between this and the jib head six times, so that the load is raised six times as slowly as it would be if attached direct to the cord. Hence it should now be possible to lift a load of nearly 59 lb. The load illustrated actually weighs 56 lb., and this the engine will raise easily, the difference between 56 and 59 representing the amount of power lost through the increased friction now existing in the various working parts of the model.

Fig 62. Power units part 1.

Class X: Power Units and Accessories *(continued)*

Meccano boys who have built the model Motor Chassis (Special Instruction Leaflet No. 1) will readily appreciate the importance of gear ratios when fitting motors to Meccano models. The chassis has three forward speeds, and the very great difference in the load that can be carried at the different speeds is obvious.

A striking illustration of the power of the Meccano 6-volt Electric Motor is afforded by the Traction Engine (Special Instruction Leaflet No. 22). This model has two forward speeds. In the first a total ratio between the Motor armature and back axle of 283.5 : 1 is obtained, but the second provides the big ratio of 567 : 1, and with this gearing truly great loads can be overcome. The Traction Engine has been made to pull over a hard, smooth surface a load of no less than 10 stone, excluding its own weight and that of the Accumulator and ballast. The latter, which was necessary to obtain sufficient adhesion on the ground, consisted of lead blocks fitted inside the boiler. Fig. 128 shows the Traction Engine hauling its driver.

The side plates of the Electric Motor measure 5″×2½″ and are perforated with the Meccano standard holes. Hence the Motors may actually form parts of the models that they are required to drive, and they can be bolted in any position. In the Traction Engine the Motor is secured on end at the rear of the boiler, in the position occupied by the fire box in the prototype, and the holes in its plates form bearings for the engine crankshaft and other parts. Fig. 127 shows an Electric Motor fitted with typical reduction gear giving a ratio of 171 : 1, the bearings for the various shafts being provided by a Channel Bearing and two 1″×1″ Angle Brackets bolted to one of the Motor side plates.

The Motor may be run from a 6-volt accumulator or from a suitable transformer connected to the main electric house supply, provided that the latter is alternating current. The Motor takes about 0.8 amperes when running free, but on load this increases up to 2.5 amps.

ACCUMULATOR, 6-volt 20 ampere-hours.
TRANSFORMER, suitable for all standard supply voltages,

Fig. 123 shows the Meccano 6-volt 20 ampere-hour Accumulator, and Fig. 125 the special Meccano Transformer designed for running the 6-volt Motor from the house supply. This transformer is available for all standard supply voltages from 100 to 250 inclusive at all standard frequencies, and is supplied complete with a length of flex and adapter for connection to an ordinary lamp socket.

The question is often asked whether the No. 6 Motor can be run from Leclanché or dry cells. For several technical reasons it is not possible to run satisfactorily any electric motor from such a source of supply, the principal reason being that these cells are not capable of delivering for any appreciable period the constant heavy current required to run even the smallest motor.

With regard to the rival merits of the two methods of running the 6-volt Motor—by accumulator or transformer—the following points should be noted. In models that are required to travel along, such as motor cars, traction engines, etc., an accumulator can be incorporated in the model or carried on a trailer behind it, and the model then becomes a self-contained power unit. The accumulator, however, will require charging at intervals. A transformer can be neatly stored in a model, but the radius of movement will always be limited by the length of the flex to the lamp socket. When using a transformer with normal loads on the Motor, the consumption of current will be something like one unit per 20 hours.

Meccano Accumulators are rated as regards their current-giving capacity in "ampere-hours." For example, the Meccano Accumulator will give a current of five amperes for four hours, or of two amperes for ten hours, and is said to have a capacity of twenty ampere-hours. It will drive the Motor continuously for 10 or 15 hours, so it will be seen that whichever method is adopted, the running of Meccano Electric Motors is not expensive.

In handling the Accumulator care should be taken to ensure that the cells are not subjected to severe knocks. Rough usage will cause particles of the chemicals of which the plates are formed to become dislodged from the lead "grids" in which they are held, and drop to the bottom of the container, where they are liable to cause short circuiting, with the result that the Accumulator will become "run down" even though not in actual use.

The Accumulator must not be used after the voltage has fallen below 1.8 volts. When this stage is reached the Accumulator should be recharged. A small voltmeter for testing the cells is very useful. These are not expensive and save a great deal of trouble and annoyance which might arise if the Accumulator is never tested, but allowed to remain at work until no further

Fig 63. Power units part 2.

32

Class X: Power Units and Accessories *(continued)*

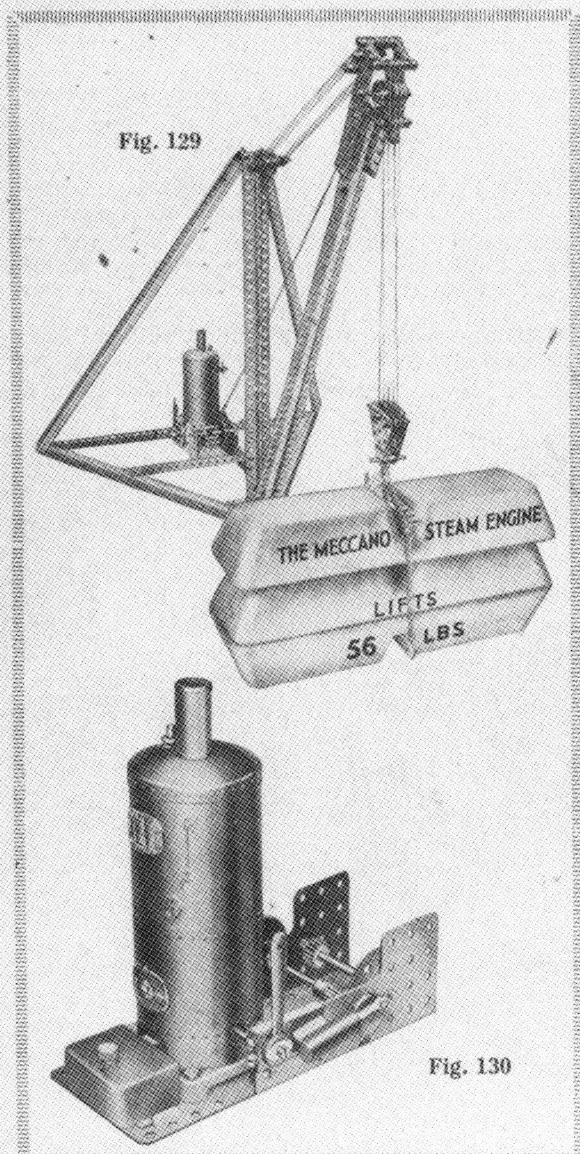

current can be obtained from it before it is recharged.

It is decidedly detrimental to the Accumulator to "spark" or "flash" the cells to see if they are charged—it should never be done. A handy method of roughly testing if the cells are charged or not is to connect an ordinary 2-volt pocket lamp bulb across the terminals of each cell in turn. If the cell is fully charged the lamp will glow very brightly, but if the cell requires charging, the lamp will be somewhat dim.

Care should be exercised to prevent the acid spilling, as it is very corrosive and will burn severely if it gets on the skin. If acid does get on the hands, however, it is a good plan to wash the skin with water in which some ordinary washing soda has been dissolved. This will prevent the skin smarting and peeling.

If an Accumulator is permitted to stand idle for a lengthy period a white deposit of lead sulphate forms on the plates. This greatly increases the resistance of the cells and might result in complete ruin of the plates. These ill effects can be prevented by always making sure that the plates are well covered with acid. If these become uncovered owing to evaporation a little distilled water should be added, but on no account should tap water be used for this purpose. If any of the acid has been spilled, the level should be brought up by adding dilute sulphuric acid of specific gravity 1.125. This may be obtained at the charging station at a small cost. Always keep the Accumulator in an upright position.

RESISTANCE CONTROLLER.

A very useful gadget for use in connection with the 6-volt Electric Motor. The Controller is shown in Fig. 124. By connecting it in series with the Motor the speed of the latter can be varied.

CLOCKWORK MOTOR.

The Clockwork Motor (Fig. 126) is the cheapest form of power, barring "gravity" and "wind" motors, which the Meccano boy sometimes fixes up for himself. It is strong, easily built into almost any model, and of course, is entirely self-contained. The remarks already given regarding the gearing to be used in connection with the Meccano Electric Motors and Steam Engine refer equally well to the Clockwork Motor, but if considerable loads are to be overcome, one must expect to have to wind the Motor frequently.

Where only a light driving power is required, the period during which the Motor will run for each winding can be increased enormously by using a suitable governing device. One of the simplest of such devices consists of a fan wheel driven by the Motor, the resistance of the atmosphere against the blades of the fan being used to prevent the Motor exceeding a certain speed. with the result that it will run for 10 minutes or more at a single winding. The fan wheel can easily be built up from Meccano parts, but the actual blades should consist of stout cardboard, or Meccano Strips covered with cardboard. Other ways to regulate the speed of the Motor are to employ some form of governing device, for example, a friction brake that is applied by the action of weights flying outward under centrifugal force (see Standard Mechanism No. 107), or a clock escapement mechanism (S.M.'s Nos. 108 and 108a). The applications of the latter are limited, however, for on referring to the S.M. Manual it will be seen that as one tooth only of the pallet wheel is released for each swing of the pendulum the movement is rather jerky. This can be overcome to a certain extent by conveying the drive through a fairly long length of loose Sprocket Chain.

The size and shape of the Clockwork Motor enable it to be incorporated in almost any model and it is often found convenient to arrange the Motor as part of the framework or the base. In small travelling models such as motor lorries and tractors, etc., it may be used to advantage as a part of the main frame or chassis.

Where a very powerful drive is required and in cases where reduction gearing cannot easily be arranged, the drive may be taken direct from the gear on the winding spindle by means of a 1″ Gear, the shaft of which may be journalled in the holes in the Motor side plates directly above the winding shaft. A tractor (Model No. 7.17 in the Instruction Manual) fitted with this gearing and a reduction of approximately 1 in 3 between the rear axle has been tested to haul a load exceeding seven stone!

Fig 64. Power units part 3.

16

Class O: Gears and Toothed Parts

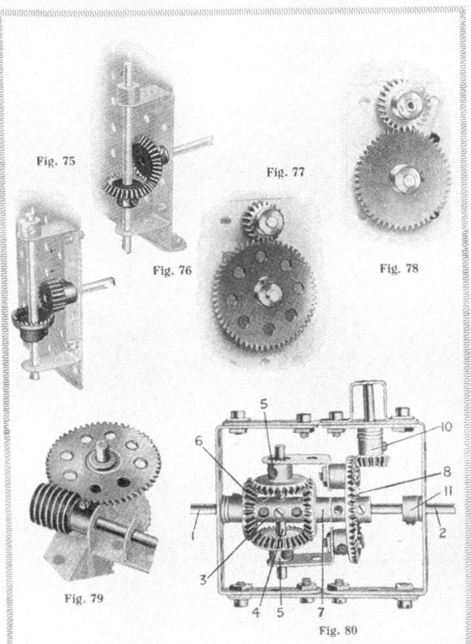

Fig. 75 Fig. 76 Fig. 77 Fig. 78 Fig. 79 Fig. 80

The Meccano range of gear wheels is very comprehensive and enables almost any speed ratio to be obtained. The gears are manufactured from solid brass, with the exception of the 3½" Gear Wheel and the Sprocket Wheels, which are of specially fine steel. The teeth are cut one at a time, not stamped out, and the precision of the finished parts is such that they are regularly used in the construction of all kinds of scientific apparatus.

The Pinions and Gear Wheels enable ordinary gear trains to be assembled, whilst the Bevel Gears and Contrate Wheels are for transmitting the drive through right angles. The Sprocket Wheels are of course designed for use in connection with chain drive transmission.

The published diameters of the various Meccano Pinions and Gear Wheels do not represent the overall measurements of the Gears, for they are measured from the " pitch line." This is an imaginary line that runs through approximately the centre of the teeth; it indicates the points on the teeth where the actual thrust is imparted from one gear to the other.

PINION WHEELS:
No. 25, ¾" diam., ¼" wide. No. 25b, ¾" diam., ¾" wide. No. 26a, ½" diam., ½" wide.
No. 25a, ¾" diam., ½" wide. No. 26, ½" diam., ¼" wide. No. 26b, ½" diam., ¾" wide.

GEAR WHEELS:
No. 27, 50-teeth, 1 5/16" diam. No. 27a, 57-teeth, 1½" diam. No. 27b, 133-teeth, 3½" diam.

In Fig. 78 a ¾" Pinion is engaged with a 50-teeth Gear Wheel. Let us assume that the Rod upon which the Pinion is fixed is rotated at a speed of 60 revolutions per minute. The ¾" Pinion has 25 teeth, and for every complete revolution that it makes it will cause the 50-teeth Gear Wheel to turn a distance occupied by 25 of its teeth, which is exactly one half of its circumference. Thus the 50-teeth Gear will turn only 30 revolutions per minute. The difference in speed obtained in this combination of Pinion and Gear is therefore as 2 to 1, and is written " ratio 2:1."

A ½" Pinion having 19 teeth is shown in Fig. 77 in mesh with a 57-teeth Gear Wheel. As the latter has three times as many teeth as the Pinion (and its pitch line diameter is three times as great), three revolutions of the Pinion are required for every complete revolution of the Gear Wheel. The ratio of this combination is therefore 3 : 1.

There are of course numerous other gear ratios obtainable, and the more usual ones are shown below, together with the alternative methods by which they may be produced. Meccano boys may find the list useful for reference.

Ratio 1 : 1—two ½" Pinions (axles ½" between centres); two 1" Gear Wheels (axles 1" between centres); two 57-teeth Gear Wheels (axles 1½" between centres); two ⅞" Bevel Gears (see Fig. 76); ¾" Pinion and ¾" Contrate Wheel. 3 : 1—½" Pinion and 57-teeth Gear Wheel (axles 1" between centres); ½" Bevel and 1½" Bevel.

7 : 1—½" Pinion and 3½" Gear Wheel (axles 2" between centres). 19 : 1—½" Pinion and Worm. 57 : 1—57-teeth Gear and Worm (see Fig. 79).

A variety of gear ratios may of course be obtained by connecting two Sprocket Wheels of varying diameter with a length of Sprocket Chain.

The ½" and ¾" diam. Pinions are each made in three widths, ¼", ½" and ¾". The ¼" width Pinion is for ordinary gearing, whilst the wider Pinions are specially designed for use in cases where the shaft on which a Pinion is secured is required to move longitudinally without disengaging the Pinion from its Gear Wheel. This movement is frequently required in Meccano gear boxes.

Fig 65. Gears page from the 1933 edition showing lack of 2½" gear introduced two years earlier.

Fig 67. Extracts from the final part of How to Use Meccano Parts as published in the April 1930 Meccano Magazine and advertising the 20-volt motor which did not appear for another two years.

Class X: Power Units and Accessories

		s.	d.
Electric Motor No. 6, 6-volt ...	... each	15	6
Electric Motor No. 20, 20-volt	... ,,	21	0
This new Meccano accessory is not yet available, but it is hoped to have supplies ready next month.			
Accumulator, 6-volt, 20 ampere-hours	,,	28	6
Transformer, for 6-volt Motor...	... ,,	30	0
Resistance Controller	... ,,	4	6
Clockwork Motor	... ,,	7	6
Steam Engine	... ,,	25	0

The 20-volt Electric Motor is an entirely new addition to the Meccano system. It is designed for running from the main supply through a transformer, and is slightly more powerful than the 6-volt Motor. We hope shortly to be able to supply a transformer for use in connection with it, and particulars and prices of this accessory will appear in an early issue of the "*M.M.*"

32

Class X: Power Units and Accessories *(continued)*

Fig. 128 Fig. 129 Fig. 130 Fig. 131 Fig. 132 Fig. 133

It is decidedly detrimental to the Accumulator to " spark " or " flash " the cells to see if they are charged—it should never be done. A handy method of roughly testing if the cells are charged or not is to connect an ordinary 2-volt pocket lamp bulb across the terminals of each cell in turn. If the cell is fully charged the lamp will glow very brightly, but if the cell requires charging, the lamp will be somewhat dim.

Care should be exercised to prevent the acid spilling, as it is very corrosive and will burn severely if it gets on the skin. If acid does get on the hands, however, it is a good plan to wash the skin with water in which some ordinary washing soda has been dissolved. This will prevent the skin smarting and peeling.

If an Accumulator is permitted to stand idle for a lengthy period a white deposit of lead sulphate forms on the plates. This greatly increases the resistance of the cells and might result in complete ruin of the plates. These ill effects can be prevented by always making sure that the plates are well covered with acid. If these become uncovered owing to evaporation a little distilled water should be added, but on no account should tap water be used for this purpose. If any of the acid has been spilled, the level should be brought up by adding dilute sulphuric acid of specific gravity 1.125. This may be obtained at the charging station at a small cost. Always keep the Accumulator in an upright position.

CLOCKWORK MOTORS.

Clockwork Motors, suitable for incorporating in Meccano Models, are now made in four different sizes. These are known as No. 1, No. 1a, No. 2, and " X " Motor. Motor No. 1 is a small non-reversing motor built specially for lightness and compactness. Motors Nos. 1a and 2 are larger than No. 1 and are fitted with a reversing lever in addition to the usual brake lever. No. 2 is fitted with a super strong spring, which gives the motor great power and length of run.

The " X " Motor is designed primarily for use with " X " series Outfits, but it is also very suitable for driving small models similar to those found in Outfits up to No. 2. It is non-reversing, but is useful in models where space is limited, such as motors, tractors and stationary engines.

The remarks already given regarding the gearing to be used in connection with the Meccano Electric Motors refer equally well to the Clockwork Motor, but if considerable loads are to be overcome, one must expect to have to wind them frequently.

Where only a light driving power is required, the period during which the Motor will run for each winding can be increased enormously by using a suitable governing device. One of the simplest of such devices consists of a fan wheel driven by the Motor, the resistance of the atmosphere against the blades of the fan being used to prevent a Motor exceeding a certain speed, with the result that it will run for 10 minutes or more at a single winding. The fan wheel can easily be built up from Meccano parts, but the actual blades should consist of stout cardboard, or Meccano Strips covered with cardboard. Other ways to regulate the speed of the Motor are to employ some form of governing device, for example, a friction brake that is applied by the action of weights flying outward under centrifugal force (see Standard Mechanism No. 107), or a clock escapement mechanism (S.M.'s Nos. 108 and 108a). The applications of the latter are limited, however, for on referring to the S.M. Manual it will be seen that as one tooth only of the pallet wheel is released for each swing of the pendulum the movement is rather jerky. This can be overcome to a certain extent by conveying the drive through a fairly long length of loose Sprocket Chain.

The size and shape of the Clockwork Motors enable them to be incorporated in almost any model and it is often found convenient to arrange them as part of the framework or the base. In small travelling models such as motor lorries and tractors, etc., they may be used to advantage as a part of the main frame or chassis.

Where a very powerful drive is required and in cases where reduction gearing cannot easily be arranged, the drive may be taken direct from the gear on the winding spindle of Motor No. 1A by means of a 1" Gear, the shaft of which may be journalled in the holes in the Motor side plates directly above the winding shaft. A tractor (Model No. 7.17 in the Instruction Manual) fitted with this gearing and a reduction of approximately 1 in 3 between the rear axle has been tested to haul a load exceeding seven stone!

Fig 66. The updated power units page from the 1933 edition.

and the 1930 manual. The Magazine announced that the No. 20 20-volt motor was in preparation was anticipated the following month (fig 67). In fact such a 20-volt motor was not generally released until 1932 and then it was designated E20b. Thus the reference to such a motor was omitted from the 1930 manual.

The 20-volt motor story of 1930 is interesting in its own right, but suffice it to say that a few do seem to have been made and most probably sold abroad together with a suitable Ferranti transformer. One of the surviving motors shows, when run, why it did not go into quantity production. The power available was little more than that of the 6-volt version and considerably less than would have been expected. Why it took another eighteen months or so to get it right must be a matter for speculation but one suspects that the ever-widening range of Meccano products issued in that time is a significant part of the answer. The development of a successful 20-volt motor would have been low on the list of priorities.

The Blue/Gold era

As with Standard Mechanisms, a 'blue/gold' edition was published although not it seems until 1935. It was given an almost identical cover to Standard Mechanisms with only the title and colour being different (fig 60). It will be noticed that the manual title had itself changed from 'How to Use Meccano Parts' to 'Meccano Parts and How to Use Them'. This was presumably to gain more impact for the word 'MECCANO'. Whatever the reason, the blue/gold edition was an improvement on the earlier ones.

The larger page size allowed for some expansion and a comparison between fig 69 and fig 53 will show how well the extra space was utilised. The section on gears was greatly increased (figs 70, 71, 72, 73), allowing a wealth of detail on gearing and design, and is perhaps the single most important part of the manual.

With the change to the electrical parts following the introduction of the Elektron Outfits, the relevant pages had already been up-dated in the

continued p. 227.

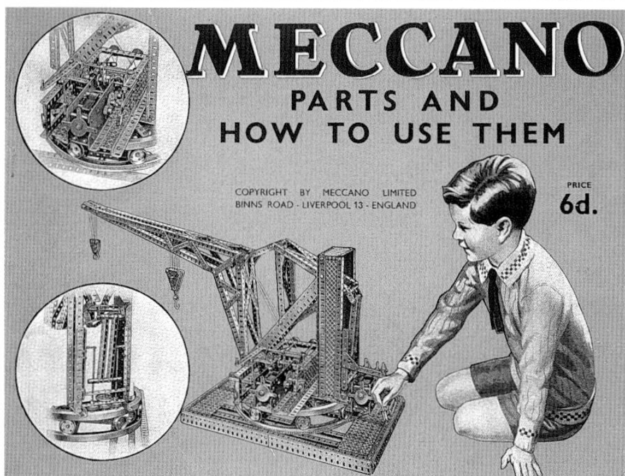

Fig 68. The 1935 'blue/gold' edition with new title.

Fig 69. Showing how the extra space was utilised.

Class A. STRIPS

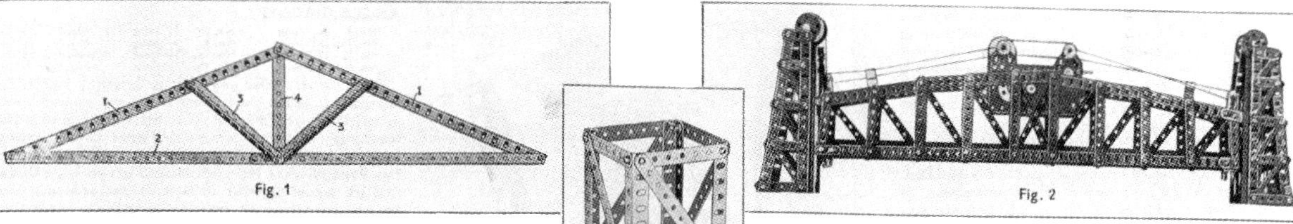

PERFORATED STRIPS.

No. 1, 12½" long. No. 1b, 7½" long. No. 2a, 4½" long. No. 4, 3" long. No. 6, 2" long.
No. 1a, 9½" long. No. 2, 5½" long. No. 3, 3½" long. No. 5, 2½" long. No. 6a, 1½" long.

There are two main uses for these parts—for bracing and for "filling-in." For the first use, a few strips, provided they are arranged correctly, will convert a normally weak framework into a rigid structure. This point is illustrated in Fig. 3. Here a vertical column, composed of four Angle Girders and eight short Strips, is made absolutely rigid by the use of twelve 5½" Strips arranged in the form of simple bracing.

An example of Strips forming compound bracing is shown in Fig. 2. The model is a small reproduction of a large vertical lift bridge the prototype of which spans the world-famous Welland Ship Canal. It will be noticed that the compression members of the main columns carrying the two slides for the lifting section of the model are represented by 12½" Angle Girders, while the corresponding tension members, which are weaker, consist only of 12½" Strips. The diagonal bracing, which is a distinctive feature of the original bridge, is reproduced in the model by means of Strips of various lengths.

Fig. 1 is a model of a simple roof truss. The sides 1, which have to withstand a compressive force, are constructed from Angle Girders ; the side 2, which is merely in tension, consists of two 12½" Strips overlapped and bolted together. The triangle so formed would be quite rigid for ordinary purposes, but struts and ties are usually added at 3 and 4 respectively in order to obtain still greater rigidity.

An excellent example of the use of Strips for filling-in is illustrated in Fig. 4. This example is the lower part of a Meccano model outboard engine, and represents the steering fin fitted to actual engines of this type. The outline of the fin is formed from Curved Strips and the space so enclosed is filled in with Strips of various lengths. As will be seen, the result is extremely neat, and gives some idea of the possibilities of this type of building in other models.

Fig. 4 shows also how a streamlined body can be constructed without distorting too many parts. This construction is shown attached to the upper face of the horizontal Boiler, and it consists of a number of vertical Strips bolted to two ellipses, each of which is constructed from two slightly bent 3½" Strips. These Strips are secured together at their ends by means of ½"×½" Angle Brackets.

Fig. 3

Fig. 4

DOUBLE ANGLE STRIPS.

No. 46, 2½"×1". No. 48, 1½"×½". No. 48c, 4½"×½".
No. 47, 2½"×1½". No. 48a, 2½"×½". No. 48d, 5½"×½".
No. 47a, 3"×1½". No. 48b, 3½"×½".

Except that their ends are bent at right-angles, these parts are exactly similar to the Strips already described. They are used in a great many ways and they are specially useful where it is necessary to join two halves of a bridge or motor-car chassis together. They can be used also in the construction of a square column or other similar unit.

Fig. 5

SLOTTED STRIPS.

No. 55, 5½" long. No. 55a, 2" long.

No. 55 is provided with three ordinary holes and two slots, each 1⅛" long ; while No. 55a has two ordinary holes and a slot ⅝" long. These slots can be used as guides for sliding mechanisms. They are invaluable also in obtaining small adjustments, between parts, that would be impossible with the standard holes spaced ½" apart.

CURVED STRIPS.

No. 89, 5½" long, 10" radius, 12 to circle. No. 90, 2½", 2⅞" radius, 8 to circle.
No. 89a, 3" cranked, 1¾" radius, 4 to circle. No. 90a, 2½", cranked, 1⅜" radius, 4 to circle
No. 89b, 4" cranked, 4½" radius, 8 to circle.

The uses for these parts are many and varied, and it will only be possible to give here a general idea of their adaptability. Their most elementary and obvious use is, of course, that of building circular figures for flywheels, roller bearings, etc. For this form of construction great care must be taken in order that a true circle may result. These circles of Curved Strips, when used in pairs and spaced apart by Washers, form excellent pulley wheels, and can be used in such models as cranes, pit-head gears, etc.

It is also possible to build correctly grooved pulleys in this way. This is accomplished by making the radius of the circle smaller than that for which the Curved Strips were designed, this causing the inner edges of the Strips to turn inward. In this manner a V shaped groove can be formed by connecting two of these circles together by means of Angle Brackets. If this construction is carried out with two Strips only, the resulting unit forms an excellent mudguard for Meccano motor cars. Bell mouths for cowls and funnels also are possible by this means.

For constructional purposes these Curved Strips are invaluable, and those used in Fig. 4 as already mentioned, form a good example of their uses in this direction. Here 4" cranked Curved Strips are used to form the framework of the steering fin of the outboard engine.

Fig. 5 is an example of the use of 2½" large radius Curved Strips. The illustration shows these parts reproducing the rear upswept end of a Meccano motor chassis. The new Meccano Motor Chassis described in Leaflet No. 1a affords other examples of Curved Strips used to reproduce the upswept ends found in an actual chassis.

These parts are also extremely useful for decorative purposes as shown in the Mantel Clock, Model L17, and also in the Single and Double Flyboats, described in Super Model Leaflet No. 33.

CIRCULAR STRIP.

No. 145. 7½" diam. overall.

Can be used in circular structures, such as a flywheel, or in a built-up roller bearing as a means of supporting the rollers (see Standard Mechanism No. 139).

Class H. GEARS & TOOTHED PARTS

The Meccano range of gear wheels is very comprehensive and enables almost any speed ratio to be obtained. The gears are manufactured from solid brass, with the exception of the $3\frac{1}{2}$" Gear Wheel and the Sprocket Wheels, which are of specially fine steel. The teeth are cut one at a time, not stamped out, and the precision of the finished parts is such that they are regularly used in the construction of all kinds of scientific apparatus.

The Pinions and Gear Wheels enable ordinary gear trains to be assembled, while the Bevel Gears and Contrate Wheels are for transmitting the drive through right angles. The Sprocket Wheels are designed for use in connection with chain drive transmission.

The published diameters of the various Meccano Pinions and Gear Wheels do not represent the overall measurements of the Gears, for they are measured from the "pitch line." This is an imaginary line that runs through approximately the centre of the teeth ; it indicates the points on the teeth where the actual thrust is imparted from one gear to the other.

PINION WHEELS.

No. 25, $\frac{3}{4}$" diam., $\frac{1}{4}$" wide. **No. 26, $\frac{1}{2}$" diam., $\frac{1}{4}$" wide.**
No. 25a, $\frac{3}{4}$" diam., $\frac{1}{2}$" wide. **No. 26a, $\frac{1}{2}$" diam., $\frac{1}{2}$" wide.**
No. 25b, $\frac{3}{4}$" diam., $\frac{3}{4}$" wide. **No. 26b, $\frac{1}{2}$" diam., $\frac{3}{4}$" wide.**

GEAR WHEELS.

No. 27, 50-teeth, 1 5/16" diam. **No. 27b, 133-teeth, $3\frac{1}{2}$" diam.**
No. 27a, 57-teeth, $1\frac{1}{2}$" diam. **No. 27c, 95-teeth, $2\frac{1}{2}$" diam.**

In Fig. 97c a $\frac{3}{4}$" Pinion is engaged with a 50-teeth Gear Wheel. Let us assume that the Rod on which the Pinion is fixed is rotated at a speed of 60 revolutions per minute. The $\frac{3}{4}$" Pinion has 25 teeth, and for every complete revolution that it makes it will cause the 50-teeth Gear Wheel to turn a distance occupied by 25 of its teeth, which is exactly one half of its circumference. Thus the 50-teeth Gear will turn only 30 revolutions per minute. The difference in speed obtained in this combination of Pinion and Gear is therefore as 2 to 1, and is written "ratio 2:1."

A $\frac{1}{2}$" Pinion having 19 teeth is shown in Fig. 97e in mesh with a 57-teeth Gear Wheel. As the latter has three times as many teeth as the Pinion and its pitch line diameter is three times as great, three revolutions of the Pinion are required for every complete revolution of the Gear Wheel The ratio of this combination is therefore 3 : 1.

In addition to these two gear ratios several others are often used. By using any two gears of a similar diameter together, 1 : 1 ratios result, these arrangements being reproduced with Meccano parts by using pairs of either $\frac{1}{2}$" Pinions, 1" Gears or 57-teeth Gears. In Fig. 97d two 1" Gears are shown used together, the distance between gear centres in this arrangement being 1". If $\frac{1}{2}$" Pinion are used, the distance is $\frac{1}{2}$", and similarly with 57-teeth Gears the distance is $1\frac{1}{2}$".

High ratios in a single stage of gearing can be obtained by employing either a $3\frac{1}{2}$" or $2\frac{1}{2}$" Gear in conjunction with a $\frac{1}{2}$" Pinion. If the larger Gear is used a 7 : 1 ratio results, this being the biggest step-up or reduction in the system that can be built up from two gears only. By meshing a $2\frac{1}{2}$" Gear with a $\frac{1}{2}$" Pinion a 5 : 1 ratio is obtained.

Two new Meccano gears are shown in Fig. 97j. These are known as $\frac{1}{2}$" and $1\frac{1}{2}$" Helical Gears, Parts Nos. 211a and 211b respectively. It is possible by using these parts to obtain a reversible right-angle drive giving a ratio of 3 : 1. They can only be used together, and are arranged similarly to a worm and worm wheel transmission unit, the latter arrangement, however, as described in this section, giving only a high ratio non-reversible drive.

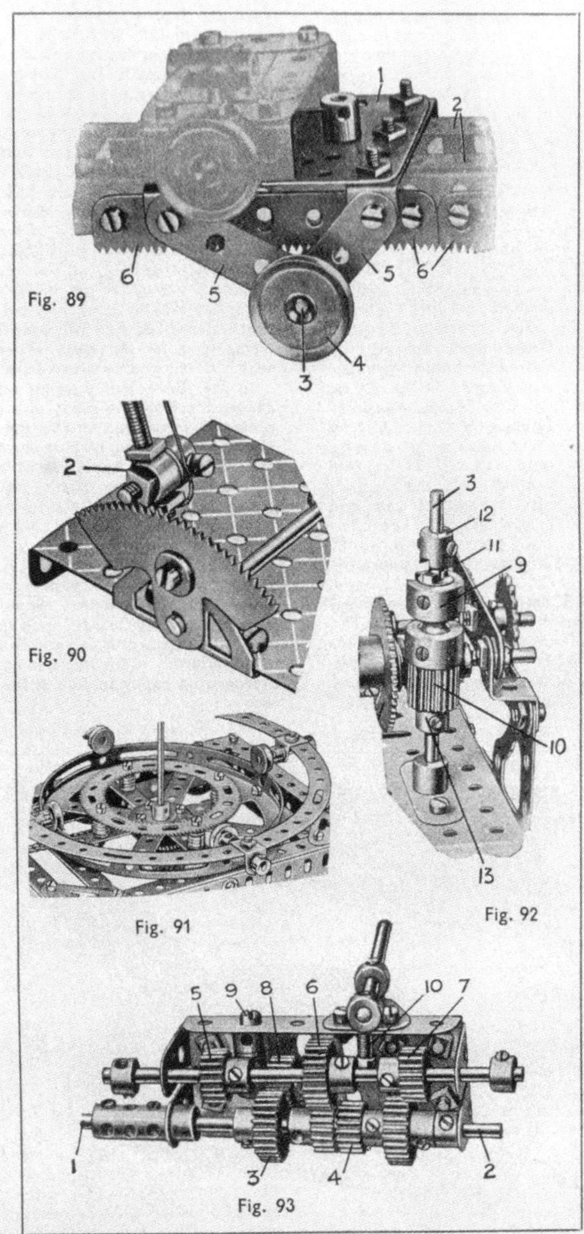

In Fig. 99 two $\frac{1}{2}$" Pinions are shown in mesh with two vertically arranged $3\frac{1}{2}$" Rack Strips. This arrangement is used on a Meccano model planing machine for raising and lowering the tool.

A variety of gear ratios can be obtained by connecting two Sprocket Wheels of varying diameter with a length of Sprocket Chain, and these are described in the chapter dealing with Sprocket Wheels.

The $\frac{1}{2}$" and $\frac{3}{4}$" diam. Pinions are each made in three widths, $\frac{1}{4}$", $\frac{1}{2}$" and $\frac{3}{4}$". The $\frac{1}{4}$" width Pinion is for ordinary gearing, while the wider Pinions are specially designed for use in cases where the shaft on which a Pinion is secured is required to move longitudinally without disengaging the Pinion from its Gear Wheel. This movement is frequently required in Meccano gear-boxes.

PINIONS IN GEAR-BOX DESIGN.

The $\frac{1}{2}$" and $\frac{3}{4}$" Pinions are seldom used together, as their centres are not a standard distance apart, and for this reason it is generally found necessary to build up a complicated framework in order to accommodate them. It is, however, occasionally possible to use them together to good effect, as shown in Fig. 93. This illustration shows a number of $\frac{1}{2}$" and $\frac{3}{4}$" Pinions, used together, in a very compact three-speed and reverse gear-box, the overall measurements of this unit being 3"×1"×1". It is probably the smallest gear-box of its type that can be built with standard Meccano parts.

The end of the Rod 1 is inserted in the bore of the $\frac{1}{2}$" Pinion 4 that is carried on a separate Rod 2 from which the final drive is taken. The latter Rod carries also a $\frac{3}{4}$" Pinion and Collar. The sliding lay-shaft is a $4\frac{1}{2}$" Rod on which are a $\frac{1}{2}$" Pinion 5, a $\frac{3}{4}$" Pinion 6, and a $\frac{1}{2}$" Pinion 7. A $\frac{1}{2}$" Pinion 8 is carried on a $\frac{3}{4}$" Bolt screwed into the transverse bore of a Threaded Boss and locked by means of a Grub Screw screwed into the opposite end of the bore. The Threaded Boss is rigidly attached to the gear-box frame by a $\frac{1}{2}$" Bolt 9, but is spaced by a Collar and two Washers.

The movement of the sliding shaft is controlled by a $\frac{3}{8}$" Bolt 10, the head of which fits between the bosses of the Pinions 6 and 7. The Bolt is fixed in a Collar on the end of a 3" Rod forming the gear change lever, and pivoted to a 1" Triangular Plate by a further Collar secured in place on the Rod by its Grub Screw, and carrying also a bolt whose shank passes through one hole in the Triangular Plate.

As shown in the illustration, first forward speed is in engagement, the drive passing through the $\frac{1}{2}$" Pinion on the driving shaft 1 to the $\frac{3}{4}$" Pinion 6 on the layshaft. The $\frac{1}{2}$" Pinion 7 engages the $\frac{3}{4}$" Pinion on the driven shaft, so that there are two stages of reduction gearing between driving and driven Rods. By sliding the layshaft to the right the Pinion 7 disengages, but Pinion 6 remains in engagement with its $\frac{1}{2}$" Pinion and at the same time meshes with Pinion 4. This gives a straight through drive. Further movement of the sliding Rod brings into engagement Pinions 3 and 5, and 6 and 4, in this case providing two step-up stages for top gear. Reverse gear is obtained when the rod is slid over to the extreme left, and the drive then goes through Pinions 3 and 8—which are in constant mesh—to Pinion 6, Pinion 7 engaging the $\frac{3}{4}$" Pinion.

14

Fig 70. Part of the greatly increased section covering gears.

Class H. Gears and Toothed Parts (Contd.)

A further example of the adaptability of the $\frac{1}{2}$" width Pinion will be found in Fig. 92. In this case a $\frac{1}{2}$" diam. $\frac{1}{2}$" width Pinion 10 is connected by a Socket Coupling 9 to the male portion of a Dog Clutch 11. The unit so formed is free on the vertical Rod 3, but on operation of a lever that carries a bolt that engages with the groove of the Socket Coupling, it can be raised so that the lower clutch section is engaged with the upper section 12 secured to the Rod 3. When out of engagement the sliding unit rests on the Collar 13. The Pinion 10 is in constant engagement with a Worm on the driving shaft ; hence the Rod 3 can be thrown in or out of engagement when desired merely by moving the control lever up or down. The $\frac{1}{2}$" width Pinion is necessary because if an ordinary $\frac{1}{4}$" width Pinion were used it would come out of engagement with the Worm as soon as the lever was raised.

GEAR RING. No. 180. $3\frac{1}{2}$" external diam. ; $2\frac{1}{2}$" internal diam.

This part resembles a Circular Strip of $2\frac{1}{2}$" inside diameter and $3\frac{1}{2}$" outside diameter, with 95 teeth cut in the inner edge and 133 teeth round the outer rim. The part is provided with 16 perforations, as will be seen in the illustration in the panel on this page, and the arrangement of these holes is such that allowance is made for adjusting and centring the part by means of slots.

The applications of this part will at once be apparent to advanced model-builders, but a few notes on its various uses will be useful to those less experienced. The chief uses will be found in the construction of epicyclic gear-boxes, and an entirely new field for experiment is opened up in this direction. A 57-teeth Gear forming the "sun wheel" can be arranged to mesh with $\frac{1}{2}$" Pinions serving as "planet wheels," and engaging the inside set of teeth of the Gear Ring. The Pinions can be mounted on $\frac{3}{4}$" Bolts each fixed by two nuts to a $3\frac{1}{2}$" Strip or 4" Circular Plate, which is free on the Rod carrying the 57-teeth Gear. If a Strip is used for this purpose, a Double Arm Crank should be bolted over the centre hole. A Socket Coupling fitted to the Boss of the Double Arm Crank or Face Plate may be provided with a Gear or Pinion for driving purposes.

The Gear Ring can be mounted on a 4" Circular Plate fitted on an independent Rod, in which case there are three rotating units, namely, the Gear Ring, the "sun wheel," and the frame carrying the "planet pinions," any one of which can be stopped while the other two are connected to driving and driven shafts. A wide variation of speed can be obtained by driving through the 57-teeth Gear and the Face Plate carrying the Pinions, and also driving the Gear Ring by means of the external set of teeth. The speed of the driven shaft will then be varied according to the variation in the speed of the Gear Ring. The part can be utilised also where a small circular strip is required.

In Fig. 91 the Gear Ring is shown used, in place of a $3\frac{1}{2}$" Gear, in the base of a travelling crane. A $\frac{1}{2}$" Pinion situated on the lower end of a vertical Rod, driven from the gear-box, engages with the inside or outside teeth of the Gear Ring.

CONTRATE WHEELS.

No. 28, $1\frac{1}{2}$" diam., 50-teeth. No. 29, $\frac{3}{4}$" diam., 25-teeth.

BEVEL GEARS.

No. 30, $\frac{7}{8}$" diam., 26-teeth. No. 30c, $1\frac{1}{2}$" diam., 48-teeth.
No. 30a, $\frac{1}{2}$" diam., 16-teeth.

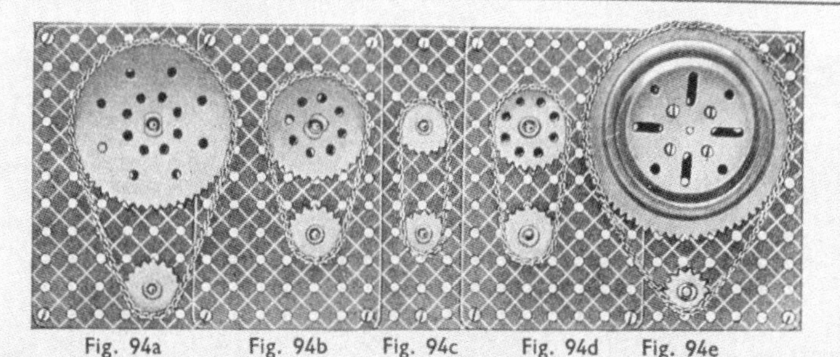

Fig. 94a Fig. 94b Fig. 94c Fig. 94d Fig. 94e

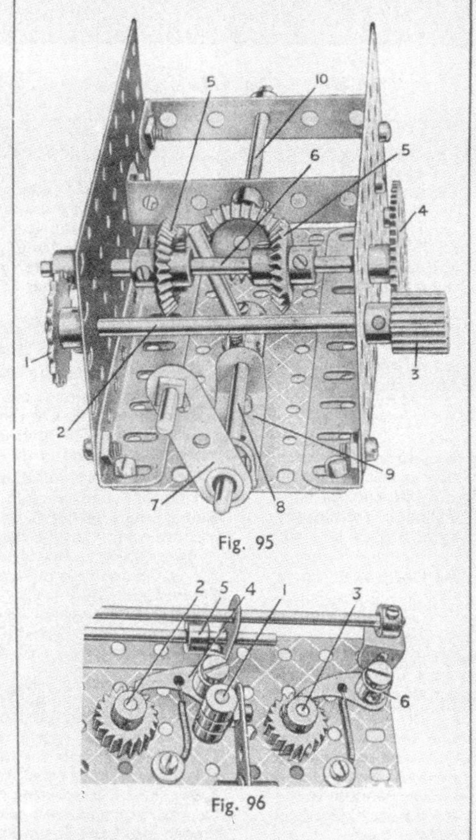

Fig. 95

Fig. 96

The primary function of the Contrate Wheels, see Fig. 97a, is similar to that of the Bevel Gears, namely, the transmission of driving power at right angles. In certain cases, however, they lend themselves to adaptations that are not possible with the Bevel Gears. For example, two Contrates of similar size mounted face to face on a common axis so that their teeth interlock will form an efficient clutch unit, and one can be thrown in or out of gear with the other.

When it is required to transmit a powerful drive at right angles it is preferable to use Bevel Gears rather than Contrate Wheels, as in the former the teeth make contact over a greater area than in the Contrate Wheels. However, Meccano boys who possess Contrate Wheels but no Bevels will find that they can employ the former in almost every case in place of Bevel Gears, with fairly good results.

It should be noted that the total space occupied by the $1\frac{1}{2}$" and $\frac{1}{2}$" Bevel Gears, when used together, is greater than that occupied by the $1\frac{1}{2}$" Contrate and $\frac{1}{2}$" Pinion. For this reason, in many models, the Contrates are used in preference to Bevels. The Meccano Motor Chassis, described in Super Model Leaflet No. 1a, illustrates this point admirably, the differential being made considerably smaller than would otherwise have been possible.

BEVEL GEARING DESIGN

In order to reduce friction to a minimum and to obtain a smooth even drive, bevel gearing is always designed so that the surfaces of the teeth of two bevels that mesh with each other lie in planes which, if extended, would all meet in a common point, and this point would coincide with the imaginary point of intersection of the axis of the shafts carrying the bevels. The Meccano Bevels are made with the teeth at such an angle that two $\frac{7}{8}$" Bevels can be meshed together, or a $\frac{1}{2}$" Bevel can be engaged with a $1\frac{1}{2}$" Bevel. Two $1\frac{1}{2}$" Bevels should not be meshed together, nor should a $\frac{7}{8}$" Bevel be engaged with a $1\frac{1}{2}$" Bevel, for although such gearing would work, the teeth would not be properly in line.

Fig. 102 should give a good idea of some of the more important adaptations of the Meccano Bevel Gears. It represents the differential gear incorporated in a Meccano motor chassis. The $\frac{1}{2}$" and $1\frac{1}{2}$" Bevel Gears are used to transmit the drive from the propeller shaft to the rear wheels, and the series of $\frac{7}{8}$" Bevels 5, 6, and 7 are arranged so that power can be applied to both road wheels under varying working conditions. Normally the Bevels 5, in rotating about the rear axle, carry the Bevels 6 and 7 bodily with them, but should one of the road wheels slow down or stop, as happens when the car turns a corner, one of the Bevels 6 or 7 slows down and the Bevels 5 tend to travel round its teeth, thus causing the opposite Bevel to turn at a greater speed.

In Fig. 95 three $\frac{7}{8}$" Bevels are employed to form a simple and compact reversing gear. The driving power is applied to the shaft 2 and is directed via the $\frac{1}{2}$" diam. $\frac{1}{2}$" width Pinion 3 to the Gear Wheel 4, which is secured to the Rod 6 carrying two Bevel Gears 5. The reverse is effected by a hand lever connected to a rocking arm that causes the Rod 6 to move longitudinally in its bearings by striking one of the Collars secured against the faces of the Bevels 5. The direction of rotation of the driven Rod 10 is changed by bringing one or other of the Bevels 5 into engagement with the third Bevel, which is rigidly fastened to the Rod 10.

15

Fig 71. Gears continued.

Class H. Gears and Toothed Parts (Contd.)

Another useful adaptation of both Bevel and Contrate Gears is found in the assembly of reduction gearing between two shafts mounted in direct line with each other. A specimen gearing of this type, in which Contrates are employed, is shown in S.M. 57. The handle 1 is secured to a 2" Axle Rod journalled in the bearings 2. This Rod is free to rotate in the boss of a 1½" Contrate Wheel 3, but is secured in one end of the Coupling 4. A further Rod 5, which runs freely in the other end of the Coupling 4, carries the 1½" Contrate Wheel 7 fixed in the position shown.

A 1½" Rod 8 gripped in the central transverse hole of the Coupling 4 carries a ¾" Pinion 9, which is free to rotate about the Rod but is retained in position by a Collar 10. The Pinion is engaged by the teeth of both Contrate Wheels 3 and 7. The Double Bent Strip forming the bearing 2 for the driving Rod is bolted to the Plate by two ½" Bolts, the shanks of which enter holes in the Contrate Wheel 3 and so prevent the latter from rotating.

It will be found that the secondary shaft 5 rotates twice as fast as the driving Rod carrying the handle 1. Alternatively, by using the Rod 5 as the driving shaft, a 1 : 2 reduction gear will be obtained, for the 2" Rod will revolve once only to every two revolutions of the Rod 5. By repeating the device two or three times in a straight line, a very compact transmission gear can be obtained.

Fig. 97h

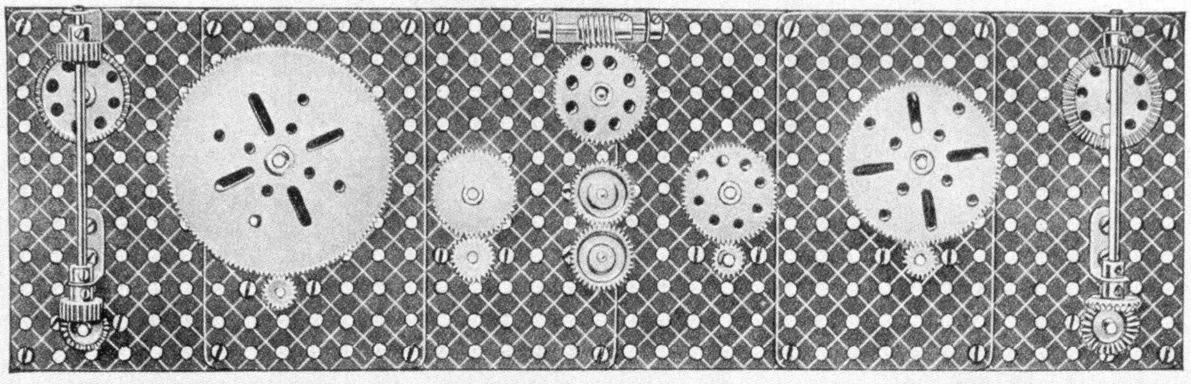

Fig. 97a Fig. 97b Fig. 97c Fig. 97d Fig. 97e Fig. 97f Fig. 97g

An idea of the value of the Meccano Worm in speed reduction mechanisms will be obtained when it is remembered that a ratio of 3249:1 can be obtained merely by duplicating the gearing shown in Fig. 97h, the second Worm being secured to the shaft of the Gear Wheel that is driven by the first Worm.

WORM. No. 32.

The Meccano Worm has a pitch of 12 threads to the inch, to enable it to mesh properly with the various Meccano Gears. It is useful for speed reducing purposes, although it should be remembered that it absorbs a good deal of power, owing to friction created by the thrust that is produced through the tendency of the Worm to move longitudinally instead of turning the Gear Wheel. A Worm drive should always be kept thoroughly lubricated.

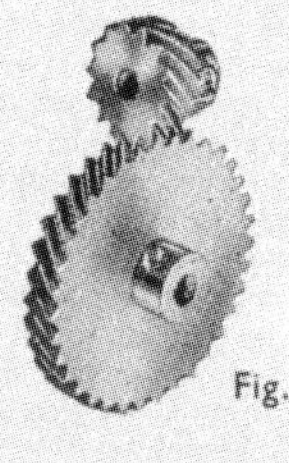

Owing to the fineness of the pitch the Meccano Worm is irreversible, that is, it cannot be rotated from a Gear Wheel but can only be used to impart motion to the Gear Wheel. This irreversibility of the Worm sometimes proves a great advantage. For example, if a Worm drive is applied to the winding drum of a hoisting gear, the load will remain suspended after the power is withdrawn, and there is no danger of the load over-running.

Each revolution of a Worm results in the Gear Wheel with which it meshes moving through a distance equal to one of its teeth. Hence the number of revolutions that must be made by a Worm in order to complete one revolution of the Gear Wheel or Pinion that it drives can be ascertained by counting the teeth on the driven wheel.

Fig. 97j

SPROCKET WHEELS.

No. 95b, 56-teeth, 3" diam.; No. 95, 36-teeth, 2" diam.; No. 95a, 28-teeth, 1½" diam.; No. 96, 18-teeth, 1" diam.; No. 96a, 14-teeth, ¾" diam.

The Meccano Sprocket Wheels and Chain provide an invaluable method for transmitting motion between two shafts where the distance is too great to enable gears to be used conveniently, and where a belt drive would not be sufficiently positive. There are five sizes of Sprocket Wheels, and the following are a few of the many different speed ratios that may be obtained with their aid. Certain of the figures shown are approximate only; the exact ratios can be ascertained by dividing the number of teeth on the smaller wheel into the number of teeth on the larger wheel.

Ratio 4 : 1—¾" and 3" diam. Sprocket Wheels. Ratio 3 : 1—1" and 3" diam. Sprocket Wheels. Ratio 2 : 1—¾" and 1½" diam. Sprocket Wheels. Ratio 1⅓ : 1—1½" and 2" diam. Sprocket Wheels.

Ratios of 1 : 1 can be obtained by using any two Sprocket Wheels of similar diameter.

The great advantage of Sprocket gearing is that power can be transmitted through almost any distance with little loss through friction. Conveyors and caterpillar track, etc., also can be built up with its aid. The method of separating and connecting lengths of Sprocket Chain is dealt with more fully in Class P, in which this part is included.

Meccano boys sometimes use their Sprocket Wheels like ordinary gear wheels, placing them so that their teeth engage. This practice is permissible in the construction of simple models where only a light driving power is transmitted through the gearing, but it should be avoided in more important models, as the teeth are not designed to engage one with the other as in ordinary spur gearing.

The Geared Ball Race, part No. 168b, which forms part of the Meccano Ball Bearing, is provided with standard sprocket teeth, and can therefore be used in chain driving mechanisms. It measures 4" in diameter and has 73 teeth. For further particulars of this part see Class N.

RACK STRIPS.

No. 110, 3½". No. 110a, 6½".

The Rack Strips, parts Nos. 110 and 110a, are designed for converting rotary motion to rectilinear motion, or vice versa. They are invaluable for obtaining the traversing movement of lathe saddles or other parts of machine tools. In model No. K.8 in the F-L Instruction Manual two 3½" Rack Strips are used to impart up and down motion to a Meccano jack, while in model No. L.36, Steam Shovel, Rack Strips are employed to

Fig. 98

16

Fig 72. Gears continued.

Class H. Gears and Toothed Parts (Contd.)

move the shovel arm toward or away from the jib. The $6\frac{1}{2}$" Rack Strip is a later addition to the Meccano system, and it has found a very large number of uses.

Two Rack Strips 6, shown in Fig. 89, are bolted to the bed 2 of a Meccano lathe, and they are in constant mesh with a $\frac{1}{2}$" Pinion. This Pinion is locked on a horizontal shaft 3 carried in bearings 5 bolted to the tool holder of the lathe. The 1" fast Pulley 4 is secured on the same Rod as the $\frac{1}{2}$" Pinion already mentioned. Thus by turning the Pulley in either direction it is possible to make the tool holder travel to and fro along the bed of the lathe.

Another use for the Rack Strip is illustrated in Fig. 99. In this example two Strips are secured by means of $\frac{1}{2}" \times \frac{1}{2}"$ Angle Brackets to the vertical Plates supporting the tool. The teeth of the Rack Strips are in engagement with $\frac{1}{2}$" Pinions 34 carried on a horizontal Rod 33, rotated by a $\frac{7}{8}$" Bevel 32. This Bevel is in mesh with a second similar part 31 that is driven from a hand wheel situated in the base of the model.

RACK SEGMENT. No. 129.

This part is intended principally for use where it is required to rotate a mechanism through part of a revolution, Fig. 101. It should be bolted to a Face Plate or other part that is capable of turning about a centre, and a 1" Gear Wheel should be engaged with its teeth. The Segment has 28 teeth and a radius of $1\frac{1}{2}$", so if four Segments are placed together to form a circle, this will measure 3" in diameter and will have 112 teeth. Great care should be taken when joining the segments together, because unless the adjoining teeth are spaced correctly they will fail to mesh properly with the Gear Wheel.

One of these parts is illustrated in Fig. 90 where it is used as a ratchet for a hand brake lever. The Rack Segment is secured to the model by means of a Trunnion, one end of a Rod being journalled in the bottom hole of this latter part. The other end of this Rod is carried in a suitable bearing bolted to the model.

The pawl 2 is represented by the nut section of a Threaded Pin, one of the corners of this section of the part being held in contact with the Rack Segment by means of a short length of Spring Cord. The pawl is held in the off position by means of a small lever situated at the upper end of the brake lever. This ratchet lever will be found useful for incorporating in a model chassis for coupling up the brakes. The connecting wires from the brakes are secured to a Coupling locked rigidly on the shaft carrying the brake lever.

DOG CLUTCH. No. 144.

Consists of one male and one female section. The object of this part is to enable two shafts to be engaged with each other or disengaged whenever desired. The shafts must be mounted end to end and one must be slidable in its bearings so that the clutch sections can be thrown in or out of engagement on operation of a suitable lever.

Alternatively, the Dog Clutch can be used, in conjunction with a Socket Coupling, to enable a Gear Wheel or Pinion, etc., to be mounted on a shaft so that it can either be carried round bodily with the shaft or allowed to remain stationary while the shaft carrying it turns in its boss. A typical example of the Dog Clutch used in this way has already been described in Fig. 92.

Fig. 108 shows the Dog Clutch employed in the construction of a reversing mechanism. In this mechanism either of the horizontal Rods can be used as a driving shaft. Each carries at its inner end one segment of a Dog Clutch 1, and one $\frac{3}{4}$" Pinion 2, and 3. The left-hand horizontal Rod is slidable in its bearings and is controlled by a suitable hand lever.

In the first position of the hand lever the $\frac{3}{4}$" Pinion 2 is caused to engage with a $1\frac{1}{2}$" Contrate Wheel, as in the illustration, while in its second position the Pinion is thrown out of engagement and the clutch members are combined. The Pinion 3 remains in constant engagement with the Contrate, and in the second position of the lever the Contrate merely revolves idly. Incidentally, this diagram indicates another important use for the $1\frac{1}{2}$" Contrate Wheel.

Fig. 101

PAWL. With Pivot Bolt and Nuts, No. 147.

PAWL. Without Pivot Bolt and Nuts, No. 147a

PAWL. Without Boss, No. 147c

RATCHET WHEEL. No. 148.

The Meccano Pawl and Ratchet Wheel may be said to be in partnership, for the one is seldom used without the other, except on those rare occasions when use can be found for the Pawl only, as in the safety device fitted to the Meccano Warehouse, Special Instruction Leaflet No. 31. Here it forms a small catch that engages with the lift guides in the event of accident to the hoisting mechanism. The Pawl may be used also in conjunction with any of the Meccano spur gears as a pawl and ratchet mechanism. Used in conjunction with each other, the Pawl and Ratchet provide a mechanism that allows the shaft on which the Ratchet Wheel is secured to rotate in one direction only.

A slight pressure should always be applied to the Pawl by means of a spring or weighted lever to ensure that it is always in proper engagement with the teeth of the Ratchet Wheel.

The Pawls can be obtained complete with a Pivot Bolt and two nuts. This Bolt forms an ideal pivot for the Pawl; it should be clamped to a Meccano part by the two nuts so that the Pawl is allowed plenty of freedom.

A section of a model self-locking gear-box is shown in Fig. 96, the locking mechanism in this example being formed from two Pawls and Ratchet Wheels. The Pawls are held in constant engagement with the Ratchet Wheels by means of short lengths of Spring Cord, and they are thrown out of engagement automatically when either of the two gear levers is operated.

By this means the hoisting shafts 2 and 3 are prevented from unwinding when they are thrown out of engagement with the main driving shaft of the gear-box.

The most recent addition to this class of parts is the Pawl without Boss. The many uses for this part will be obvious, and many unusual applications will be found for it. In Fig. 98, one of these parts is shown bolted to a Bush Wheel, a useful cam being the result.

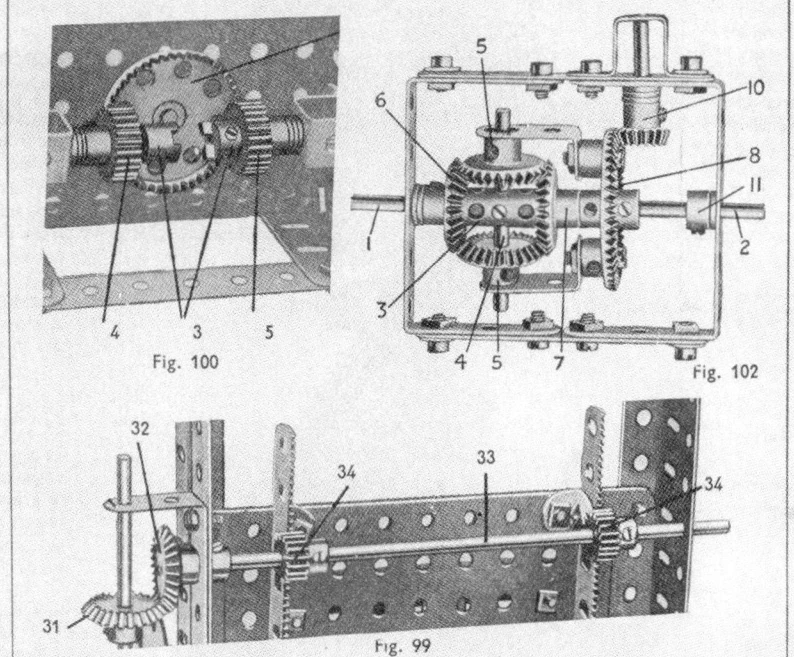

Fig. 100

Fig. 102

Fig. 99

17

Fig 73. *The final page of the expanded gears section.*

Class L. Electrical Parts (Contd.)

TERMINAL. No. 1563.

The Terminal consists of a milled brass knob bored and tapped to fit the 6 B.A. Bolts. Fig. 134 shows two Terminals mounted on the shanks of bolts at 6 and 8. It will be noted that an Insulating Washer is placed under the Terminal 6 ; an Insulating Bush is used on the other side of the plate, so that this Terminal is insulated from the model. Terminal 8 is in metallic contact with the model.

Fig. 133 shows a Meccano two-way switch. In this the switch arm is attached pivotally to a Trunnion that is insulated from the base plate in the manner described already, and the two contact pieces 1 carrying the Terminals 2 and 3 are also insulated. Hence, by engaging one or other of the latter with the switch arm the electric circuit can be led from Terminal 5 to Terminal 3, or alternatively from Terminal 5 to Terminal 2.

LAMP HOLDER. No. 183.

METAL FILAMENT LAMPS.

$2\frac{1}{2}$ volt No. 184a $3\frac{1}{2}$ volt No. 184b
6 volt No. 184c 10 volt No. 184d
20 volt No. 184e

The Lamp Holder is designed to form a screw socket for any of the Meccano Lamps. Its end is of fibre and it is secured to Meccano models as follows. A 6 B.A. Bolt is passed through the small perforation in its end, and then through a hole in a Meccano Strip, and an Insulating Bush is placed on the shank of the bolt so that its shoulder fits into the hole in the Strip. The bolt can then be secured by a nut or Terminal. When the latter is screwed up tight, the metal of the Lamp Holder will be in contact with the Strip, so that the electric current can be conducted to the lamp by attaching one wire to the 6 B.A. Bolt, the head of which presses against the contact in the end of the lamp itself, and another wire to the Meccano Strip.

Fig. 132 shows a Lamp and Holder mounted in the front of a model electric locomotive, the Holder 14 being bolted to an Angle Bracket. Current is led to the Lamp by an insulated wire slipped under the nut on the 6 B.A. Bolt by which the holder is secured, and returned to the source of supply through the Holder itself and through the frame of the model.

26 GAUGE, S.C.C. COPPER WIRE. No. 1586.

23 GAUGE, S.C.C. COPPER WIRE. No. 1587.

The 26 gauge Single Cotton Covered Copper Wire is usually employed in constructing electro-magnets, bobbins, etc., although it can be used for ordinary connecting purposes. The 23 gauge Copper Wire is intended for making all kinds of electrical connections in Meccano models.

The current consumption of a Bobbin, Part No. 181, fully wound with 26 gauge wire, is .94 amps and a Bobbin wound with 23 gauge wire takes 1.5 amps. Both of these figures are for a two-volt supply which, if increased, causes a corresponding rise in current consumption.

Fig. 135

Fig. 136

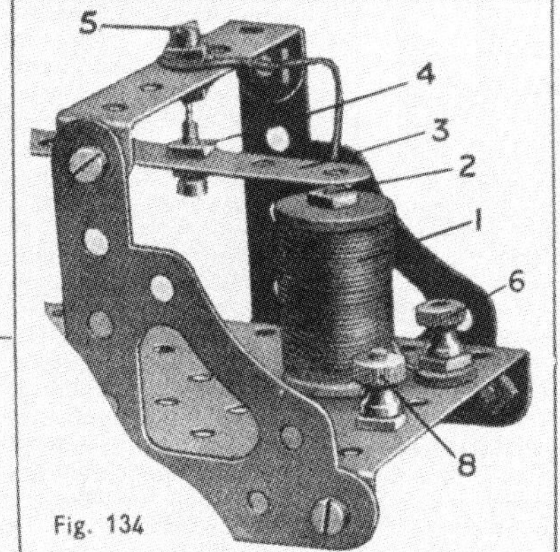

Fig. 134

It is scarcely necessary to give Meccano boys detailed instructions on the subject of wiring their models, but it may be well to mention one or two important points. All connections should be made as tight as possible—that is, when connecting a wire to some part of a model it should not be merely twisted round a Strip, but secured by a nut and bolt. Insulated wire should never be allowed to rub against metal or short circuits will quickly occur.

Another point to remember is the fact that wire exerts a certain resistance against the flow of the electric current, just as a water pipe resists the flow of water through it. In ordinary Meccano model-building the resistance likely to be exerted by the wiring is negligible, especially if the Meccano 23 gauge wire is used; but in exceptional cases where the current is directed over considerable distances, such as in Morse Telegraph instruments, electric signals and indicators, etc., a considerable loss of current will result if thin conductor wire is used, and the motor, bell or whatever it is required to energise, will fail to function properly. The resistance in the conductor can be decreased by making use of larger diameter wire or, if a larger wire is not obtainable, by connecting additional lengths of wire in parallel with the first.

PENDULUM CONNECTION. No. 172.

This part, although not included in the electrical equipment, has many uses when adapted for use with the electrical accessories. It consists of a piece of spring brass $1\frac{1}{2}''$ in length and $\frac{1}{4}''$ in width, and it can be used as a brush or as a make-and-break contact.

Two of the uses for this part are shown in Figs. 135 and 137. The first of these illustrations show a rotary trailing contact originally designed for use in a model electric roulette wheel. The wheel is secured on the spindle 7 above the roulette table, and as it spins it causes a Double Arm Crank to rotate. The Double Arm Crank carries a Pendulum Connection 5 that is held in place by a 6 B.A. nut and bolt, and the lower end of this Connection trails across the eight insulated studs of the Bush Wheel 6.

Each stud is connected to an electric lamp and the contact 5 to one terminal of an accumulator. The other terminal of the accumulator is connected to the " earth " pole of all the lamps. It will now be seen that as the contact 5 rotates, the lamps coupled up to the eight insulated studs will light alternately. When the wheel stops one lamp only will remain alight.

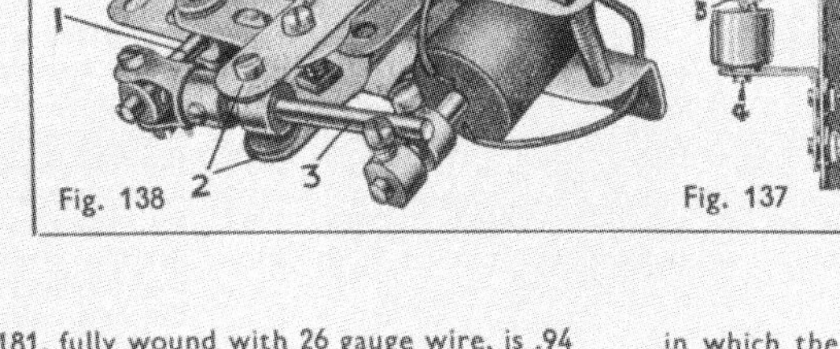

Fig. 138

Fig. 137

In Fig. 137 a Pendulum Connection is shown incorporated in an electric make-and-break fitted with a spark arrester. This unit was fitted to a Meccano Electric Mantel Clock to prevent erosion of the Contact Screws 3 and 4. The Chimney Adaptor is filled with thin oil in which the contacts work. The Pendulum Connection is bent to the shape shown and mounted on one end of the pendulum tappet rod by means of an End Bearing and 6 B.A. bolt. An extra hole must be drilled in the Pendulum Connection for this purpose.

25

Fig 74. Greater coverage of electrical parts although fig 138 is not mentioned at all!

1933 edition. The 1935 blue/gold edition, however, went further, offering an expanded text and several more examples of uses for electrical parts (fig 74). The uses for the pendulum connection are of great interest, especially the spark arrester which really was quite an advanced concept for a Meccano model at that time. The pendulum connection was a most useful part and its original use must have been much rarer than as an electrical part. The companion illustration in fig 74 (designated fig 138) is a novel automatic brake for an electric motor and is presumably meant to illustrate a further use of the bobbin although nowhere is it mentioned in the text. Both are however fully detailed in Standard Mechanisms (fig 35 page 109) which in itself is an illustration of the overlap between the two manuals. Frequently there was duplication of examples, but this was only to be expected.

The 1935 edition has a further point of interest in that it relists the 1929 Steam Engine (fig 75) in the up-dated power units pages. This is rather strange because it is not listed in product catalogues for that year. The main model to feature the Steam Engine, SML 19a The Steam Excavator, still had its leaflet listed amongst the available Super Model Leaflets, so perhaps the Steam Engine was available for a little while longer than generally supposed.

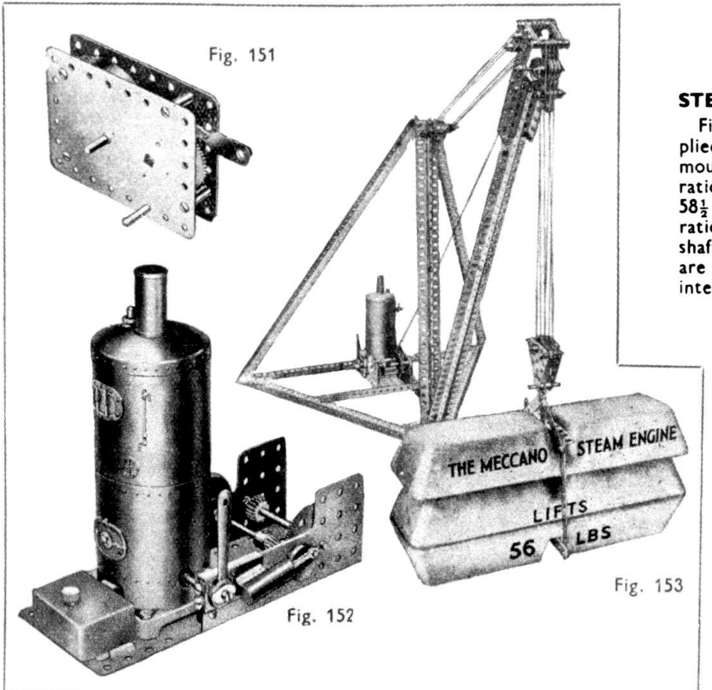

Fig 75.
The temporary return of the 1929 Steam Engine.

STEAM ENGINE.

Fig. 152 shows the Steam Engine and Fig. 153 shows it applied to a Meccano stiff leg derrick. In this case the gearing, mounted between the side plates of the Engine, gives a ration of 58.5 :1, that is, the crankshaft of the Engine turns $58\frac{1}{2}$ times to each revolution of the winding shaft. This ratio is obtained as follows—Engine crankshaft to secondary shaft, 6.5 : 1, the Pinion and Gear Wheel giving this ratio are supplied with the Steam Engine ; secondary shaft to intermediate shaft, 3 : 1, $\frac{1}{2}$" Pinion driving on to a 57-teeth Gear Wheel ; intermediate shaft to winding shaft, 3 : 1, $\frac{1}{2}$" Pinion and 57-teeth Gear.

If we apply a load direct to the end of the hoisting cord, we shall find that the Engine can lift 9 lb. 13oz. If we decrease still further the speed at which the load is raised by adding pulley blocks, then the amount of the load that can be raised should increase proportionately for, as already stated, power is gained in proportion to the loss in speed. In Fig. 153 a three-sheave pulley block is used, and the hoisting cord is passed between this and the jib head six times, so that the load is raised six times as slowly as it would be if attached direct to the cord. Hence it should now be possible to lift a load of nearly 59 lb. The load illustrated actually weighs 56 lb., and this the engine will raise easily, the difference between 56 and 59 representing the amount of power lost through the increased friction existing in the various working parts of the gear train and pulley system.

Print Data

Known UK editions of How to Use Meccano Parts & Meccano Parts and How to Use Them are:-

2/830/35	Designated MP 30
2/531/30(M)	Designated MP 31
2/1033/1	Designated MP 33
13/735/13.5(UK)	(Meccano Parts and How to Use Them)

So far only the one UK edition of Meccano Parts and How to Use Them has come to light. If that is the only one, the question arises as to why, when Standard Mechanisms was revamped for the blue/gold launch, its companion was not. It could be that sales had been rather slow since 1933 and that a new edition was not needed until 1935. Certainly there were still copies of the 1935 edition left at Binns Road long after the war so it may well be that there was only the one printing.

As with Standard Mechanisms, there were foreign language versions and in some cases separate English language editions for Australia, New Zealand, etc.

Conclusion

The How to Use Meccano Parts Manuals and their 1935 equivalent were a relatively short-lived series lasting little more than six years. That this should have been so is due in part to the changes wrought in 1936–7 following the death of Frank Hornby. However from 1933 onwards, they do not appear to have been good sellers judging by the numbers printed. Even the large runs of 1930 and 1931 may be misleading because there appear to have been few special runs for non-UK English editions. Instead the ordinary UK versions were supplied. This was possible because there were no prices listed in the manual and therefore special printings were not required.

Why these most appealing publications were not as successful as say Standard Mechanisms is a matter for conjecture although their contents were perhaps less useful to a modeller once he had learnt the 'uses'. By way of contrast, Standard Mechanisms contained much more continuously useful information.

Our interest in them today, apart from their inherent attraction, is probably due for the most part to the references to long obsolete and sought-after parts. In this respect they are like the catalogues, delightful and frustrating at the same time. On reflection it must be the finest tribute there is to Hornby and his publications department, that these catalogues and manuals, with all their shortcomings, still cast their spell.

CHAPTER 7

Promotional Material

From the earliest days, promotional material had always featured large in the scheme of things. Whilst much of it (in relation to its contents) may nowadays seem rather naive, it should not be forgotten that life, at least in the pre-war years, was much simpler. Today this material provides collectors with some of their most sought-after items. Most are visually very attractive and show just how good the advertising and artwork departments were at Binns Road.

It is difficult to produce any sort of list of promotional material, partly because it is not always easy to differentiate between what is merely informative or what is promotional; it will often be a matter of opinion. The other, more intractable problem is that we simply do not know the full extent of what was issued, new and previously unknown pieces are being unearthed all the time. However some of the most important groups of items are fairly well documented and these can be looked at in more detail. Briefly these main groups are:

The Hornby Books of Trains. 1925–1939 (See reproductions Chapter 9).
The New Meccano literature. 1926–1927
The annual folders
Adventures in Meccanoland and similar booklets
'Meccano' publicity booklets. 1920s–1930s
Products Catalogues.

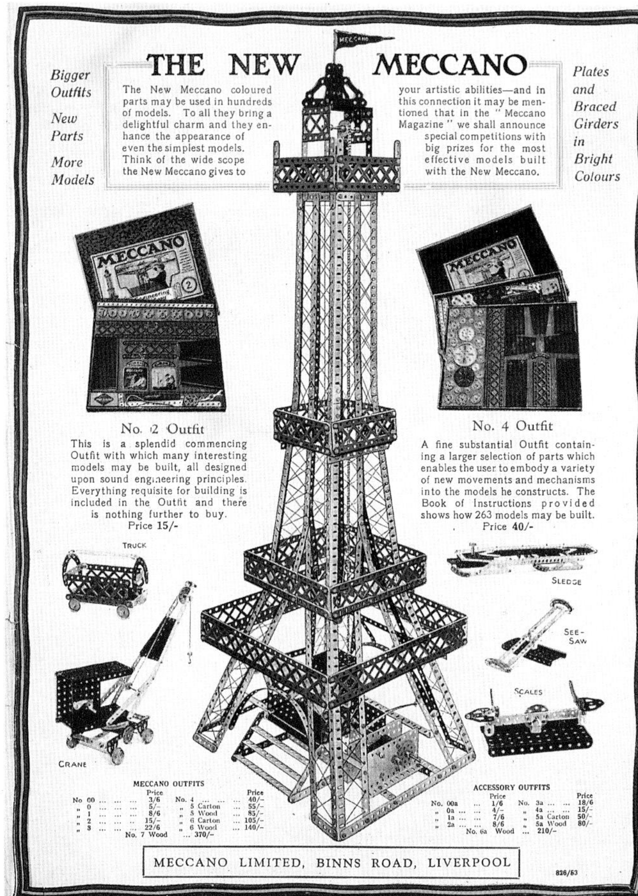

Fig 1. Special leaflet issued with the MM *advertising THE NEW MECCANO in 1926.*

Hornby Books of Trains

Perhaps of all the company's publications the various editions of the coloured Books of Trains from 1925 onwards were the most exciting. The 1935 Book of Hornby Trains and Meccano Products and The 1938–39 Hornby Book of Trains are reproduced in Volume 1 of this series. In this volume the 1925–26, 1927–28 and 1933–34 Books of Trains are reproduced giving the reader an overview of this excellent series of publications for the retail customer.

In September 1925 Meccano published the first Hornby Book of Trains to coincide with the centenary of the Stockton and Darlington Railway. Although only priced at 3d, it had a beautiful full colour cover as well as a further 20 colour pages showing the range of Hornby Trains, with the remaining 24 pages devoted to articles on real railways. This superb publication was such a success that there was a further printing (with minor corrections) issued in March of the following year.

Such was the obvious impact of the 1925 edition that it was decided to issue a new edition each year. This was continued in similar format until 1935 when a combined Book of Hornby Trains and Meccano Products was issued. The 1935 book was a magnificent publication showing all the company's products in full colour but it must have been horrendously expensive to produce. To help recoup some of its cost, the price was raised to 9d. Possibly as a result of this price increase and/or the omission of the articles on real railways in order to make room for the other products, the already reduced print run of 65,000 copies was not fully sold (assuming the print code to be correct). Remaining copies were acquired by Messrs. Halfords and were resold by them the following year at a reduced price (see Volume 5 p. 248).

After this debacle no Hornby Book of Trains was issued during the following season. 1937 saw its return, but in a slightly different style from those prior to 1935 and with many updated catalogue pictures. Obsolete printing blocks had continued to be used despite frequently bearing little resemblance to the current product.

The last Hornby Book of Trains to be published was that for 1939–1940, and although other booklets on model railway matters were to be produced

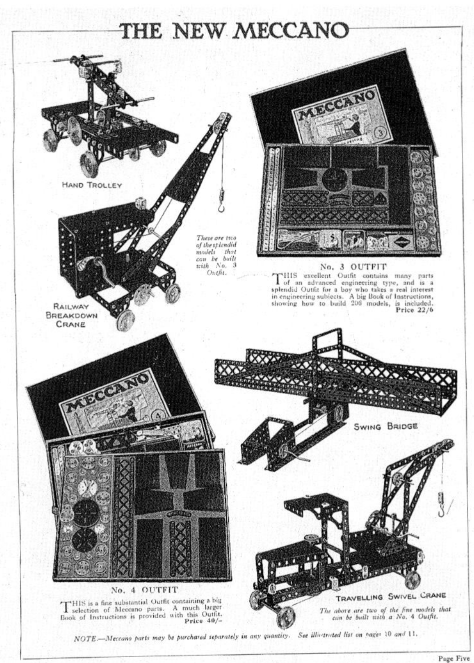

THE NEW MECCANO
HAND TROLLEY
RAILWAY BREAKDOWN CRANE
These are two of the splendid models that can be built with No. 3 Outfit.
No. 3 OUTFIT
THIS excellent Outfit contains many parts of an advanced engineering type, and is a splendid Outfit for a boy who takes a real interest in engineering subjects. A big Book of Instructions, showing how to build 206 models, is included.
Price 22/6
No. 4 OUTFIT
THIS is a fine substantial Outfit containing a big selection of Meccano parts. A much larger Book of Instructions is provided with this Outfit.
Price 40/-
SWING BRIDGE
TRAVELLING SWIVEL CRANE
The above are two of the fine models that can be built with a No. 4 Outfit.
NOTE.—Meccano parts may be purchased separately in any quantity. See illustrated list on pages 10 and 11.
Page Five

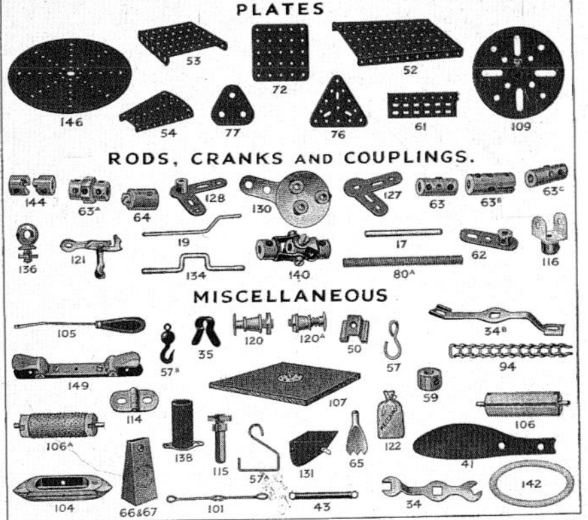

Figs 8–13.
Pages from the 1927 NEW MECCANO booklet.

PATENT.

MECHANICS MADE EASY,

AN ADAPTABLE MECHANICAL TOY.

This Invention has for its object the Training of the Young in Mechanical Construction.

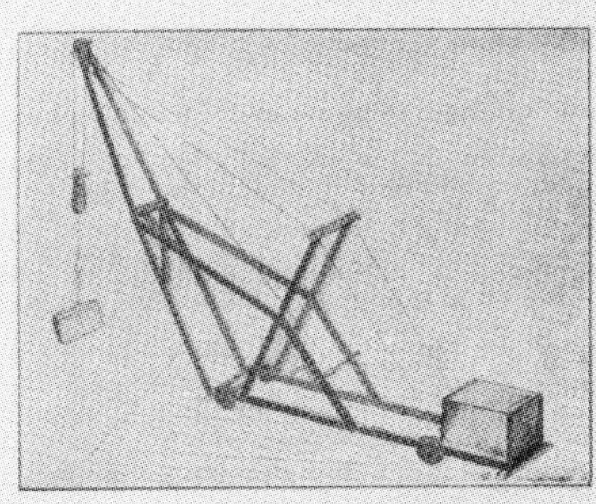

There has been a long-felt want among young people for a Mechanical Toy which will enable them to construct mechanical objects without the trouble, labour and difficulty of turning, boring, filing, &c.

It is believed this invention will fill this want, and will develop the constructive genius of the child, at the same time dispensing with expensive and intricate tools.

Everyone must have recognised how full of interest to a child's mind is "the building up of an object"; how hour after hour has been pleasantly spent in childish attempts to make models of things which have attracted its attention. If then this bent of its mind can be turned into the right groove, an educational process has been commenced which may, later on, prove of great benefit. The aimlessness of an undeveloped fancy will give way to an organised method, and from confused, hazy ideas will spring order and precision.

Upon examination it will be found this invention will help to train the child's mind on these lines; chaos will give way to order; a hazy conception to a definite idea; guess work to accuracy; whilst at the same time the various parts of this invention will give endless scope to the constructive abilities of either a child or a grown-up person.

The several parts of this invention have been so made that they easily fit into each other in a great variety of ways. This being so, it is self-evident they can be used to construct a great variety of objects. Herein lies the charm to the child's mind.

Moreover, when one object has been made, the several parts can be taken asunder, and used again and again in totally different directions.

Hence it will be found that even a young child will be able to construct Cranes, Machinery Shafting, Bridges, Wagons, Railway Lines, Inclines, Signals, &c.; and with the addition of pieces of cardboard, Railway Stations, Towers, Tunnels, &c.

Another feature of this invention is that it is practically unbreakable—notwithstanding falls, blows, and constant usage—consequently it will last much longer than the usual mechanical toy at present on the market.

CONTENTS OF BOX.

A. 12 Flat Metal Strips, 12½ inches long, ½ inch wide.
12 ,, ,, 5½ ,, ½ ,,
12 ,, ,, 2½ ,, ½ ,,
B. 18 Metal Angle Pieces.
C. 6 Brass Wheels.
D. 1 Brass Bush of Wheel.
E. 2 Pieces Grooved Steel Rod, 2 inches long.
2 ,, ,, 5 ,,
1 ,, ,, 12 ,,
F. 1 Grooved Steel Crank.
G. 1 Small Box, containing 48 Nuts and Screws and 12 Steel Keys.
H. 1 Screw Driver.

Separate parts may be obtained at the following prices:

		s.	d.
Perforated Strips, 12½ inches long	per doz.	0	9
,, ,, 5½ ,,	,,	0	6
,, ,, 2½ ,,	,,	0	4
Angle Pieces (containing 18)	,,	0	6
Large Wheels	each	0	5
Small Wheels	,,	0	2

		s.	d.
Bush	each	0	3
Grooved Rods, 2 inches long	,,	0	0½
,, ,, 5 ,,	,,	0	1
,, ,, 12 ,,	,,	0	3
Box (containing 48 Nuts and Screws, 12 Keys, 1 Hook)	,,	1	9

Figs 14–15.
Mechanics Made Easy publicity folder dating from the earliest days.

EXPLANATION OF CONTENTS.

A. Flat Strips.—The Flat Strips are pierced with holes half an inch apart. The position of these holes enables the child to arrive at the correct place where the screw is to be fixed, by simply counting the number of holes, thus dispensing with a measure.

The holes are of such a diameter as to allow the grooved steel wire to revolve freely.

B. Angle Pieces.—These pieces have an elongated hole on one side, to permit of adjustment in the construction of several of the designs.

In the construction of Railway Lines this elongated hole enables the Lines to be adjusted to the desired gauge.

C. Wheels.—Four of these wheels are made with a flat tread on the one side, and a V groove on the other, to enable them to be used as Railway Wheels or Pulleys. The other two are intended for Pulleys alone.

These wheels have a slot at the centre hole to permit of their being keyed to the rod if required.

D. Bush for Wheel.—This has four holes round the edge, to which the strips may be fastened, to form the spokes of a fly wheel. The rim of the wheel can be made by cutting out a circular piece of cardboard, and screwing it to the strips.

The bush, having a slot similar to the other wheels, may be keyed to the rods.

E. Grooved Steel Rods.—The two small pieces are intended to be used for such purposes as axles for the pulleys of cranes, &c.

The two five-inch pieces for axles of wagons, shafting, &c.

The twelve-inch piece for a shaft.

The groove in these rods permits of the wheels being fastened in any position by the special key.

F. Grooved Steel Crank.—This serves the purpose of a handle and barrel for a crane. It can be inserted in any of the holes of the strips, and is fastened in its place by the steel keys.

G. Steel Keys.—These are so shaped that the tongue can be used to fasten the wheels on to the shaft. This is done by inserting them in the slot in the wheel corresponding to the groove in the rod. When, however, the wheels are required to revolve freely, the key is reversed, and the clip grips the rod. This prevents the wheel from moving out of its place.

These keys may also be used to prevent the rod from slipping out of the holes of the strips.

Packed in handsome tin box, Price ***7/6.*** *Postage* ***6d.*** *extra.*

Letter received from PROFESSOR HELE-SHAW.

WALKER ENGINEERING LABORATORIES,

UNIVERSITY COLLEGE,
LIVERPOOL, *Nov. 5th, 1901.*

DEAR SIR,

Thank you very much for the Photographs of your clever and useful form of Toy. When it is on the market I shall certainly buy a set for my little boy, and feel sure it will afford many hours of enjoyment both to father and son. With a little ingenuity and exercise of the imagination, it should be as good as a fairy story, and what can one say more!

Yours truly,

H. S. HELE-SHAW.

To MR. F. HORNBY.

AGENTS:—

THE BIRMINGHAM MODEL ENGINEERING CO.,

MAKERS OF

LOCOMOTIVE, STATIONARY and MARINE STEAM ENGINES.

RAILS, SHIP'S FITTINGS, & ALL ACCESSORIES,

45–49, NORTHWOOD STREET, ST. PAUL'S, BIRMINGHAM.

Proprietors:—JAMES BEDINGTON & SON.

Discount 33⅓%.

Fig 15.

The Annual folders. (Figs 16–49)

Every year in time for the beginning of the season, Meccano would produce a large variety of folders and leaflets promoting one or more of their products. Some of the Meccano folders promoted just that line, but others would combine Meccano with Aeroplanes, Cars and/or other products. Hornby Trains usually had a folder to themselves which is not surprising since their range was so vast. Hornby Dublo and Dinky toys also had their own folders.

Because of the very wide variety of these annual folders, no two seem to be alike although some probably are. What is striking is the care and attention to visual presentation which marked so much of this material. One only has to study the items illustrated in this section to realise the importance with which such basically simple leaflets were treated. Right through into the 1950s the Advertising Department continued to produce eye-catching folders which must have greatly aided sales, indeed some produced in those later years are amongst the finest. Many a company has found that what might seem to be extravagant sums spent on effective advertising and promotional material, will eventually pay dividends. Naturally the product has to be right but then that was rarely a problem at Binns Road.

Figs 16–49.
A selection of annual folders and publicity leaflets from the First World War until the 1960s.

Meccano is the greatest game in the world

See the models on the next pages. They are selected from

10,000 models

sent in to us in our last big competition, all the work of young Meccano inventors. There is no limit to what you can do. You first make those in the big book of instructions, and then you do just like those 10,000 boys—commence to design your own.

See the New Meccano Girder Strip

This is the latest addition to the hobby. It gives boldness and strength to big models, such as Towers, Elevators, Bridges, etc. Beautifully made and nickelled like the regular Meccano strips.

Meccano will do all and more than any other system, and do it better. No system is complete without the Meccano patented parts. We point these facts out to you emphatically and strongly in order to guard you against the imitations and makeshift systems which are following in the wake of the great success of Meccano.

When you ask for Meccano, see that you get it. Nothing else is "just as good." Nothing else will do the same.

INSIST ON THE TRADE MARK

THESE MODELS CAN ONLY BE MADE WITH MECCANO

Each one is a prize winner. Ask your dealer for the big illustrated book of results of our last competition. 10,000 entries. Winning models illustrated. If you have any difficulty mail us your address.

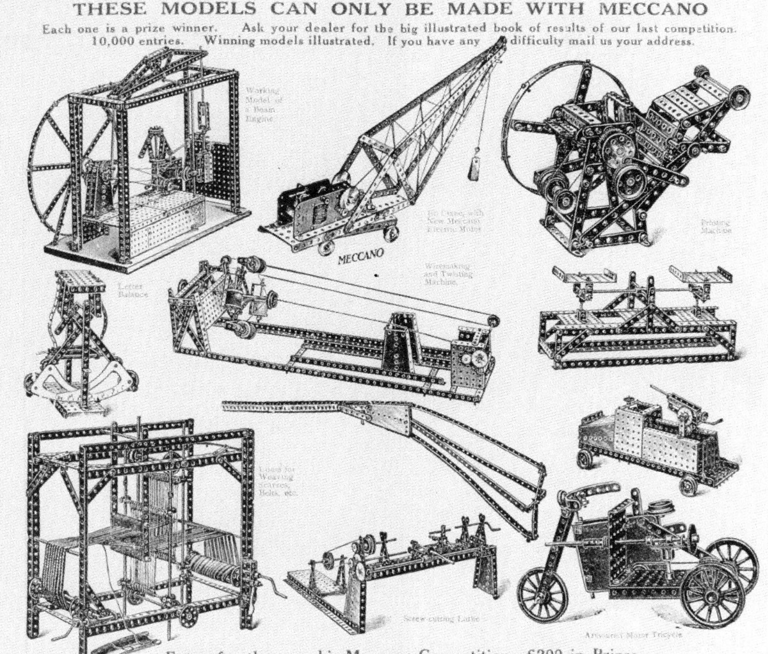

Enter for the new big Meccano Competition—£200 in Prizes.

The New Meccano Girder Strip

This model illustrates one of the many uses for the new Meccano Girder Strip. It is like the real constructional girder, with the Meccano equidistant holes along each edge. Most useful in constructing Bridges, Towers, etc. Supplied in two lengths: 12½" costing **1/6** per ½-dozen, and 5½" costing **1/-** per ½-dozen.

The Meccano Clockwork Motor

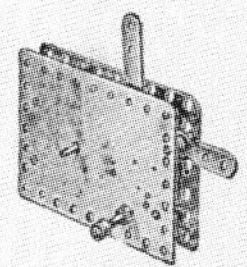

We sell very many thousands of this motor each year. It builds directly into Meccano models, to which it gives life and movement. Applied to a crane it will raise and lower a big load. It will work a merry-go-round or an elevator, or it can be made to form the chassis of a motor car to run along the ground, with stopping, starting, and reversing movements.

No. 1 5/-

Meccano Ltd., Liverpool, England

Prices of Meccano

No.			
0	Outfit with big book of instructions,		3/-
1	do.	do.	5/-
2	do.	do.	10/-
3	do.	do.	15/-
4	do.	do.	25/-
5	do.	do.	42/-
6	do.	do.	100/-

In well finished cabinet with lock and key.

Meccano outfits contain all the principal parts used in real engineering including nickel-plated girders, pulley wheels, gear wheels, brackets, plates, nuts and bolts, etc., all standardised and interchangeable. There is nothing further to buy, and the youngest boy can commence at once.

Meccano Inventor's Accessory Outfit

This is a new outfit which every Meccano user should secure. It contains the new Girder Strip, large wheels for motor cars, sprocket wheels and chain, healds for looms, new crank and coupling, and other parts hitherto contained in the higher priced outfits only. Price **5/-**

Meccano Outfits with Electric Motors

The Meccano Electric Motor is admitted to be the finest motor of its type ever produced. By means of the special gearing the maximum of power is obtained. It is specially designed to work with Meccano models, having our standard equidistant holes pierced on the sides and base. Included free in the new Meccano Outfits.

Meccano No. **1X** with non-reversing motor, **10/6**
„ **2X** „ „ **15/6**
„ **3X** with reversing motor **25/-**

These are the regular Meccano Outfits with the Electric Motor added.

The motor is also sold separately at **6/6** non-reversing type, or **10/6** reversing type, neatly boxed.

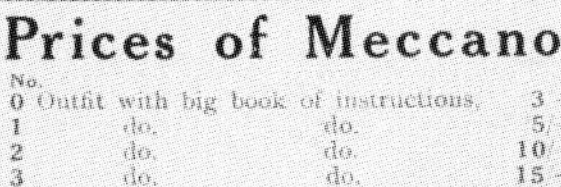

This illustration shows a combination of gearings built from Meccano parts on to the Electric Motor itself, and the lifting power obtained by such gearings.

MECCANO

The original and best constructional system. Contains more interchangeable parts than any other. The best features of Meccano are patented and cannot be imitated.

THE JOY HOBBY

Meccano Models are a long way the best, and they can only be made with Meccano.

INSIST ON THE TRADE NAME MECCANO

"Let her go, Dick!"

Watch her move out of the station like a real express. . . . See how smoothly she glides along, rapidly picking up speed. . . . Faster and faster she goes. . . Now she *is* travelling!

Playing the great game of railways with a Hornby Train is the best fun in the world. A Hornby miniature railway is exact in every detail and enables a boy to duplicate almost every operation employed in modern railway practice.

Hornby Locomotives—clockwork and electric—are splendidly built with strong and reliable mechanism, and are beautifully enamelled in correct railway colours. They are thoroughly tested before leaving the factory and are fully guaranteed.

Hornby Rolling Stock includes every type in use on the big railways, and there is also a complete range of Accessories that gives additional realism to a miniature railway. Each item built in perfect proportion and is beautifully finished in colours.

Every hour spent in playing with a Hornby railway is brimful of thrills and enjoyment! The fun and fascination are never-ending.

Prices of Hornby Trains from 5/- to 95/-

HORNBY TRAINS

BRITISH AND GUARANTEED

Ask your Dealer for a complete illustrated price list

Manufactured by
MECCANO LTD., OLD SWAN, LIVERPOOL.

1/430/280

Fig 22A.

↑
↖ *Figs 16–17.*
← *Early First World War era.*

Wonderful Mechanical Toys for Boys to make

This is part of a giant Meccano Derrick. Look at it carefully, boys! It is a typical piece of Meccano work, the real thing, just like an engineer makes it—a gem of mechanical construction. *You* can build and play with this wonderful Derrick when you buy Meccano, and you can also build hundreds of other models: a real Loom which will weave you beautiful coloured fabrics; Cranes and Bridges; Towers with elevators working up and down; in fact, every model you make is a real machine and works perfectly.

You can build this Derrick

MECCANO

Toy Engineering for Boys

Meccano Outfits contain highly finished strips, plates, girders, pulley wheels, gears, rods, nuts and bolts, &c., each representing a genuine engineering part. By fitting these parts together with the help of the big Book of Instructions, any boy can build hundreds of working mechanical models. Each outfit is a complete toy store.

If you like Cranes, you can build one—a *real* Crane which raises and lowers loads. You can then make a Bridge or an Aeroplane or an Elevator or a Motor Car or a Tank or a Submarine, hundreds of them

If you never make the same model twice, you can go on making new ones for years.

INSIST ON MECCANO

There is no other Real Engineering System

MECCANO LTD. :: Binns Road, LIVERPOOL

TOY ENGINEERING FOR BOYS

You can build models of this kind by the hundred and get loads of fun out of them.

or you can build a real Motor Car Chassis with perfect mechanism, clutch, worm steering gear, speeds, transmission, universal joint, differential, etc.;

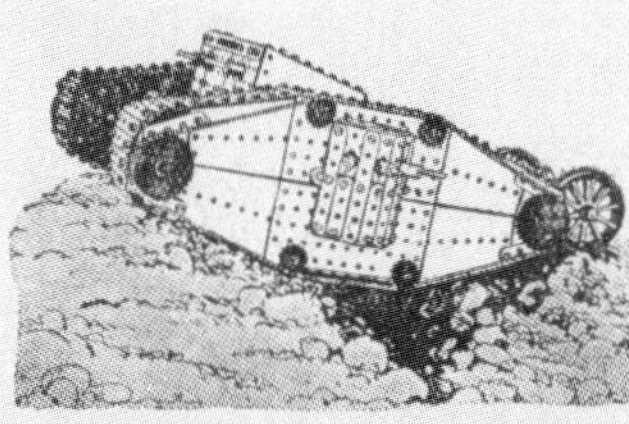

then a fine "Tank" model designed by Officers in France who fight in the real ones, a model of perfection in design;

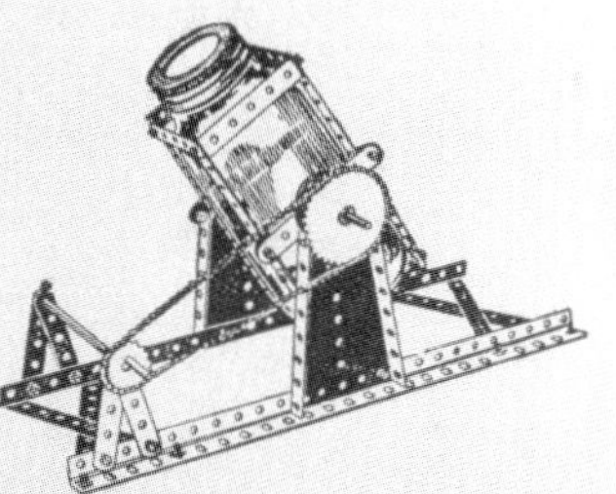

or a Butter Churn with which you can manufacture fresh butter for the family. You can set to work churning in a few minutes, the model is such an easy one to make.

Then You Can Make Your Models Run Like Real Machinery

To add to the fun of Meccano toy-building, we have introduced the most wonderful series of toy motors ever designed.

They are pierced with the regular Meccano equidistant holes, and they fit smoothly into position and become part of the model itself. They make the wheels hum round. They operate Cranes, Lifts, and the Big Wheel, Elevators, &c. They double the fun.

The Meccano Electric Motor

Especially designed to work with Meccano, having the standard equidistant holes pierced on the sides and base. Has starting, stopping, and reversing lever, interchangeable gearing, direct shaft drive. Can be run with dry batteries accumulators, or direct from the main supply with a transformer. The most powerful and reliable motor of its kind. The illustration shows a combination of gearings built from Meccano parts on to the Electric Motor itself, and the lifting power obtained by such gearings. Prices—

No. E1 Non-reversing 7/6
No. E2 With reversing gear...... 12/6

Meccano Inventor's Accessory Outfit

An accessory outfit which all users of Meccano will find useful. It contains the new Braced Girder, for building big imposing models, large wheels for wagons, motor cars, &c., sprocket wheels and chain; healds for making a loom, and other very useful parts.

Price 7/6

Figs 18–21. 1918 leaflet.

TOY ENGINEERING FOR BOYS

How to Start Meccano

The main thing is to get started, and it doesn't much matter which outfit you buy first. If you buy a No. 0 costing 5/6 you can make 78 fine models of the smaller type; and when you are ready you can get a No. 0A, costing 4/-, which makes your No. 0 into a No. 1; then you can build 105 models altogether of the better type.

If you start with a No. 3, costing 25/-, you can build 196 models of a splendid engineering type, and you can follow this by getting a No. 3A outfit, costing 18/-, which converts your No. 3 into a No. 4, giving you a range of 247 models.

The whole Meccano system is progressive, and you can work right up to No. 6 no matter where you start.

How Many Models?

425 Now—and More Coming

There is no limit to the number of models you can build with Meccano. Along with your outfit from No. 1 to No. 6 you get instructions for building 326. Then comes Book No. 2, with 100 more prize models of great beauty. This is quite a new Manual of Instructions, just published, and it costs 1/3. Before you have finished all these, there will be more models ready. Always something new.

No Study Necessary

Don't worry because you don't know anything about engineering. That doesn't matter at all.

You get with your Meccano outfit a large beautifully illustrated Book of Instructions, which makes it all delightfully simple, and you can begin to build the minute you open your outfit at home; and very soon you will know more about real engineering than all your friends put together.

PRICES

	s.	d.		s.	d.
No. 0 Meccano Outfit	5	6	No. 0a Meccano Accessory Outfit ..	4	0
,, 1 ,, ,, ...	9	0	,, 1a ,, ,, ,, ..	9	0
,, 2 ,, ,, ...	16	6	,, 2a ,, ,, ,, ..	9	6
,, 3 ,, ,, ...	25	0	,, 3a ,, ,, ,, ..	18	0
,, 4 ,, ,, ...	42	0	,, 4a ,, ,, ,, ..	14	0
,, 5 ,, ,, (Carton) ..	57	6	,, 5a (Carton) ,, ,, ..	50	0
,, 5 ,, ,, (Wood) ..	82	6	,, 5a (Wood) ,, ,, ..	77	6
,, 6 ,, ,, ...	145	0			

Each outfit contains full instructions

Fig 20.

TOY ENGINEERING FOR BOYS

This page is exactly the size of the Meccano Manual of Instructions, and this is the style of illustration which it contains.

Look at the model closely and you will see how easy it would be for you to build up this splendid Eiffel Tower.

This is no make-belief Tower. It *works*, boys, with the elevator going up and down, carrying passengers to view the wonders of Paris.

Any Boy can build this fine Tower.

The Meccano Magazine.

This is a splendid Magazine, published solely for Meccano boys. It contains announcements of new Meccano Prize Competitions, lists of awards, illustrations of new models, essays by Meccano boys, and all kinds of useful "tips" on model-building. Write to "The Editor, Meccano Magazine, Binns Road, Liverpool," who will send you a specimen copy free.

THE MECCANO EIFFEL TOWER

7/18/100

Fig 21.

You can make your Models Run like Real Machinery

To add to the fun of Meccano toy-building, we have introduced the most wonderful toy motors ever designed.

They are pierced with the regular equidistant holes, fit smoothly into position, and become part of the model itself. They operate Cranes, Lifts, and the Big Wheel, Elevators, etc. They double the fun.

Meccano Clockwork Motor

This excellent motor has been specially designed to operate Meccano models. It is powerful and reliable, and is quite free from danger. Has starting, stopping, and reversing levers.

PRICE 12/6

Meccano Electric Motor

Especially designed to work Meccano models. Has starting, stopping, and reversing levers, interchangeable gearing, direct shaft drive. Can be run with dry batteries or an accumulator. The most powerful and reliable motor of its kind.

PRICE 17/6

The Block Accumulator

This is a new and excellent type of accumulator. We have subjected it to most severe tests, and we believe it to be most suitable for use with any type of toy Electric Motor. It is non-spillable, cannot be spoiled through short circuiting, and will retain its charge for many months. Sulphating to any serious extent cannot occur, and if it is neglected or left in inexperienced hands, no serious harm can be done. Has remarkable recuperative powers, and will keep on working when nominally exhausted. A boon to any Meccano user who possesses a Meccano Electric Motor. Full instructions.

PRICE 21/-

MECCANO LTD. LIVERPOOL

Boys! Be Builders

MECCANO

Engineering for Boys

Meccano Outfits contain highly-finished strips, plates, girders, pulley wheels, gears, rods, nuts, and bolts, etc., each representing a genuine engineering part. By fitting these parts together with the help of the big Book of Instructions, any boy can build splendid working mechanical models—Cranes, Bridges, Aeroplanes, Elevators, Motor Cars—hundreds of them. Each outfit is a complete toy store.

INSIST ON MECCANO

There is no other Real Engineering System.

How to Start Meccano

No. 2 OUTFIT.

Contains 171 parts with which nearly 200 models can be built. Gives plenty of scope to the young inventor.

PRICE - - - 20/-

Meccano parts are sold in seven different sized outfits, numbered 0 to 6. All parts are of the same quality and finish, but the higher-numbered outfits contain larger quantities and a greater variety of parts.

Each outfit may be converted into the one higher by the purchase of an Accessory Outfit. Thus, a No. 2 may be converted into a No. 3 by adding to it a No. 2A. A No. 3A would then convert it into a No. 4, and so on. In this way, no matter where you start you may by degrees build up your outfit to a No. 6.

Thousands of Models

There is no limit to the number of models you can build with Meccano. Along with your outfit from No. 1 to No. 6 you get instructions for building 326. Then comes Book No. 2, with 100 more prize models of great beauty. Other Manuals are now in course of preparation, and these will contain new and striking models.

No Study Necessary

You get with your Meccano outfit a large beautifully illustrated Book of Instructions, which makes it all delightfully simple. You can begin to build the minute you open your outfit at home, and very soon you will know more about real engineering than all your friends put together.

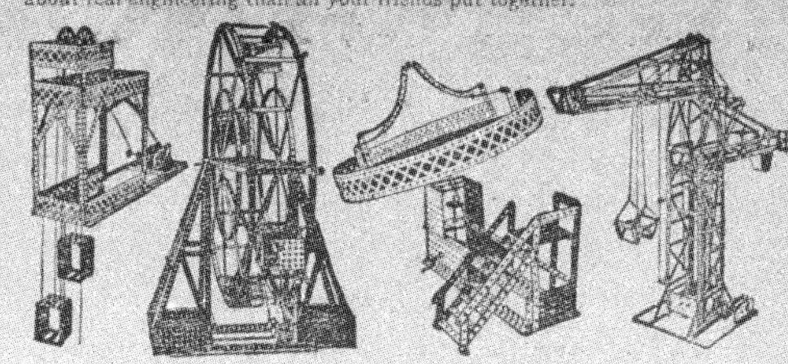

A few of the Models any Boy can Build with Meccano

Meccano Price List

No. 0 Meccano Outfit	6/-	No. 0A Accessory Outfit	5/-
No. 1 „ „	10/-	No. 1A „ „	11/-
No. 2 „ „	20/-	No. 2A „ „	12/-
No. 3 „ „	30/-	No. 3A „ „	22/-
No. 4 „ „	50/-	No. 4A „ „	17/6
No. 5 „ „ Carton..	70/-	No. 5A „ „ Carton	65/-
No. 5 „ „ Wood...	100/-	No. 5A „ „ Wood	95/-
No. 6 „ „	180/-	Clockwork Motor	12/6

Meccano Inventor's Accessory Outfits

The "A" Outfit contains 3 in. and 2 in. pulley wheels, braced girders, sprocket wheels and chain, pinion wheels, rods and washers, whilst the "B" Outfit includes bevel gears, 1 in. gear wheels, flat plates (four sizes), double-angle strips (four sizes), octagonal and strip couplings, threaded cranks, triangular plates, screwed rods, curved strips, architraves, face plates, rack strips, girder frames, hinges, buffers, and train couplings.

PRICES: "A" Inventor's Outfit 10/-
"B" „ 25/-

Meccano Electrical Accessory Outfits

The outfits contain a number of specially-designed electrical accessory parts, which, used in conjunction with any of the regular outfits, from No. 0 to No. 6, enable the user to construct models for making interesting and instructive experiments, including Electric Railway, Morse Key, Buzzer, Electric Lamps, Electric Crane, Induction Coil, Electric Iron, Motor Starter, Tapper Key, etc. The X2 Outfit includes an Electric Motor and an Accumulator.

PRICES: X1 Electrical Accessory Outfit 15/-
X2 „ „ „ 55/-

Fig 21A. Promotional leaflet from 1921 but still showing the much earlier American type motor.

Fig 22. 1924 folder.→

ANY BOY CAN BUILD THESE FINE WORKING MODELS

REAL ENGINEERING

Each Meccano Outfit contains a variety of shining steel strips, plates, and girders. These parts form the foundation of all the models, and they are pierced with equidistant holes. Then there are other parts—rods that fit into the holes; and pulleys, gear-wheels and couplings that fit on to the rods. The fact that Meccano parts are standardised and interchangeable enables you to build any model you want. Model-building with Meccano is not difficult—any boy who is able to use a screw-driver can build Meccano models.

EASY TO INVENT WITH MECCANO

No Meccano boy is content to build the models as he finds them described in the Instruction Book. It is always possible to improve them, and you set to work to do this at once. Soon new models and new designs, the creation of your brain, make their appearance.

There is no end to Meccano fun, there is always more ahead—always some new, ingenious and interesting model to build. Each one, as it is completed, "tuned up," and set to work, will bring a joy and satisfaction beyond anything that you have previously experienced.

It is a great thing to know that you are constructing a model in exactly the same manner as a real engineer builds the actual machine. This is what happens when you build models with Meccano, and because each one of the 200 Meccano parts is designed on correct engineering principles, Meccano is real engineering in miniature. No part is introduced into the Meccano system unless it is interchangeable, and each part has a variety of uses.

MECCANO MODELS WORK

When you build a Meccano model you have accomplished something. Your Meccano models will work, and work correctly. Your Motor Car is a model of the real thing, with worm-and-pinion steering, three-speed gear-box and differential. Your Crane will raise and lower loads; and your Clock ticks and keeps perfect time. Your Eiffel Tower has an elevator that moves up or down at will; and your Loom weaves real hat-bands, ties, and other fabrics in tasteful patterns.

Figs 23–25. 1930.

Fig 24.

Meccano Motors, Steam Engine, etc.

In order to obtain the fullest enjoyment from the Meccano hobby the models should be operated with a Meccano Motor or Steam Engine.

These power units are strongly made and the utmost care is taken in their manufacture to ensure that they will give satisfaction. They are specially designed to build into Meccano models.

MECCANO ELECTRIC MOTOR E.1 (6-volts)

This is a highly efficient electric motor (non-reversing) that will give excellent service. A 6-volt Accumulator will operate it, but it may also be driven from the main (alternating current only) through the Transformer described below. **Price 7/6**

MECCANO ELECTRIC MOTOR No. 6 (6-volts)

This powerful and reliable 6-volt Motor may be run from a 6-volt accumulator or, by employing the Transformer described below, from the main. It is fitted with a control mechanism that enables the motor to be started, stopped or reversed as desired. **Price 15/6**

Electric Motor No. 6

NOTE—The above Electric Motors will not run satisfactorily from dry cells.

MECCANO RESISTANCE CONTROLLER

By employing this variable resistance the speed of the Meccano 6-volt Electric Motors may be regulated as desired. The controller is connected in series with the motor and accumulator, or with the motor and transformer if a transformer is used as the source of power. It will not regulate the speed of a high-voltage motor connected to the main. **Price 4/6**

TRANSFORMER

By means of this transformer the Meccano 6-volt Electric Motors may be driven from the main supply (alternating current only). It is available for all standard supply voltages, from 100 to 250 inclusive, at all standard frequencies. The supply voltage and frequency must be specified when ordering. **Price 30/-**

MECCANO ACCUMULATOR (6-volts, 20-amps).

The Meccano Accumulator is of substantial construction and is specially recommended for running the Meccano 6-volt Electric Motors. **Price 28/6**

MECCANO CLOCKWORK MOTOR

This splendid Motor is a compact self-contained power unit. An efficient governor controls the powerful spring that is fitted on the motor and ensures a long steady run at each winding. Brake and reverse levers enable the motor to be stopped, started and reversed as required. Supplied complete with winding key and full instructions. **Price 7/6**

MECCANO STEAM ENGINE

On actual test this powerful steam unit has lifted over 56 lbs. A single cylinder of the oscillating type is employed, steam being admitted to it through a special reversing block. Operation of the reversing lever enables the crankshaft, which is fitted with a special compensating flywheel, to run in either direction.

The spirit container for the lamp is placed well outside the boiler-casing, eliminating all risk of the spirit becoming heated. There is no danger whatever of the boiler exploding. A special Manual of Instructions is supplied with each engine. **Price 25/-**

Clockwork Motor

Steam Engine

Meccano Service

The service of Meccano does not end with selling an Outfit and an Instruction Manual. When you want to know something more about engineering than is now shown in our books, or when you strike a tough problem of any kind, write to us. We receive over 200 letters from boys every day all the year round. Although all kinds of queries are put to us on all manner of subjects, the main interest is, of course, engineering. No one has such a wonderful knowledge of engineering matters as that possessed by our staff of experts. This vast store of knowledge, gained only by many years of hard-earned experience, is at your service.

MECCANO LIMITED, OLD SWAN, LIVERPOOL.

5/1030/100 (1R) U.K.

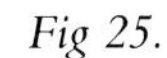

Fig 25.

Figs 26–27. 1932–3 season folder.

Figs 28–29. 1935–5 season.

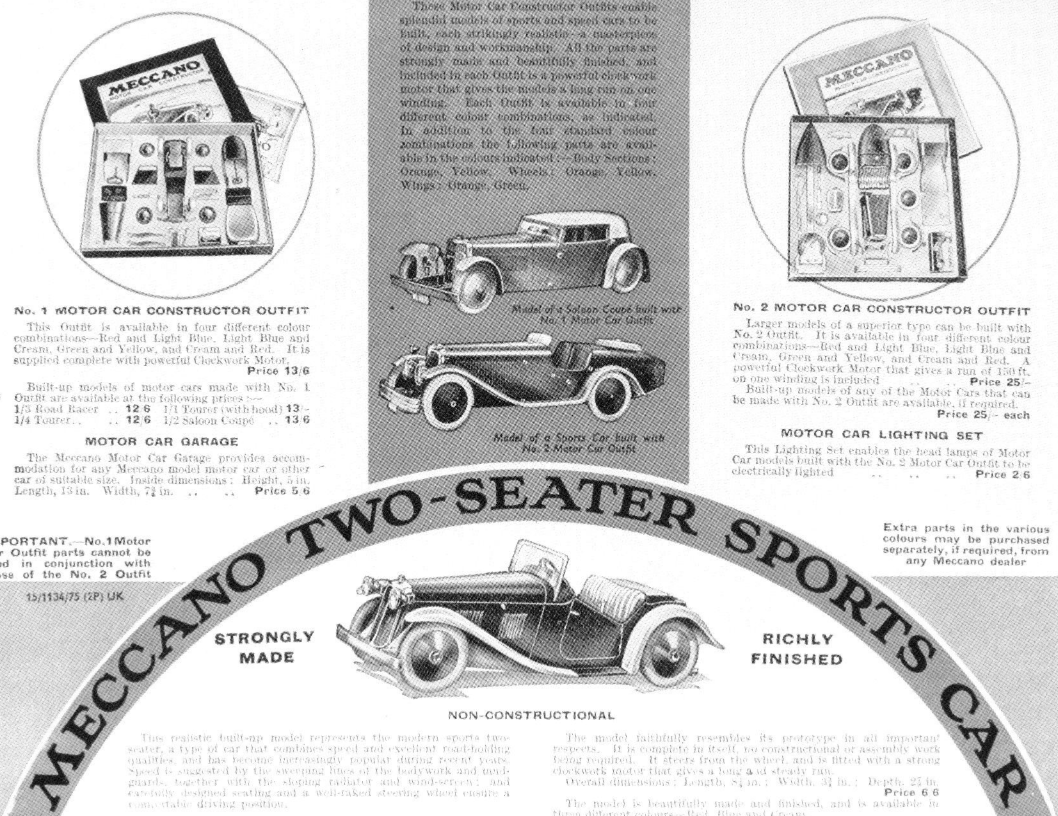

← *Fig 30. 1935–36.*
Note use of much earlier picture for cover.

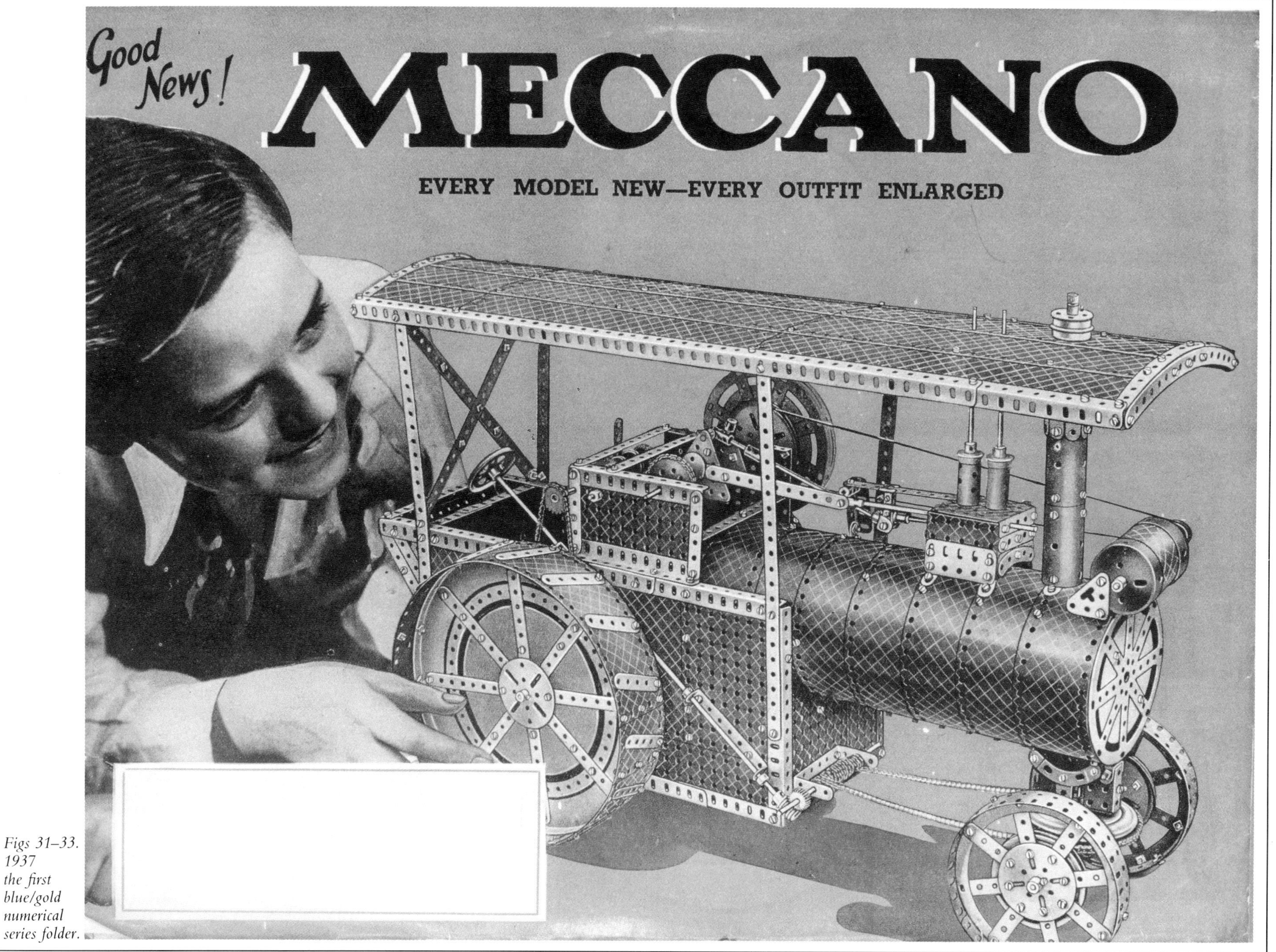
Good News!
MECCANO
EVERY MODEL NEW—EVERY OUTFIT ENLARGED

Figs 31–33. 1937 the first blue/gold numerical series folder.

1937 MECCANO—Every Model New—Ev

Boys! Here is just the toy you are looking for. A Meccano Outfit will give you lots of excitement from the very minute you get it home. You never get tired of Meccano. The more you build with it the more interesting it becomes.

You feel the thrill as soon as you begin to build. There are no complicated instructions to worry about. You open the Manual that is packed with your Outfit, choose the model you like, and set to work; the illustration shows you what to do. As you add one part after another the model grows under your fingers until it becomes a complete and perfect toy. It is the greatest fun in the world!

Nearly all Meccano models actually work. You can operate them by hand if you like, but the most wonderful thrill of all is to set them in motion by means of a Meccano Clockwork or Electric Motor. There is nothing in the world so fascinating as a Motor-driven Meccano model working away at full speed. You have built it with your own hands, and now you are the engineer-in-charge, in complete control!

Soon you will want to build another model that has caught your eye. In a few minutes you take your first model to pieces, and there are all your parts ready for you to build the new model.

So you go on, building model after model, not only those illustrated in your Manual, but others of your own design. Then you become a real inventor! There is always something new to be done. Dull evenings are a thing of the past.

Fig 32.

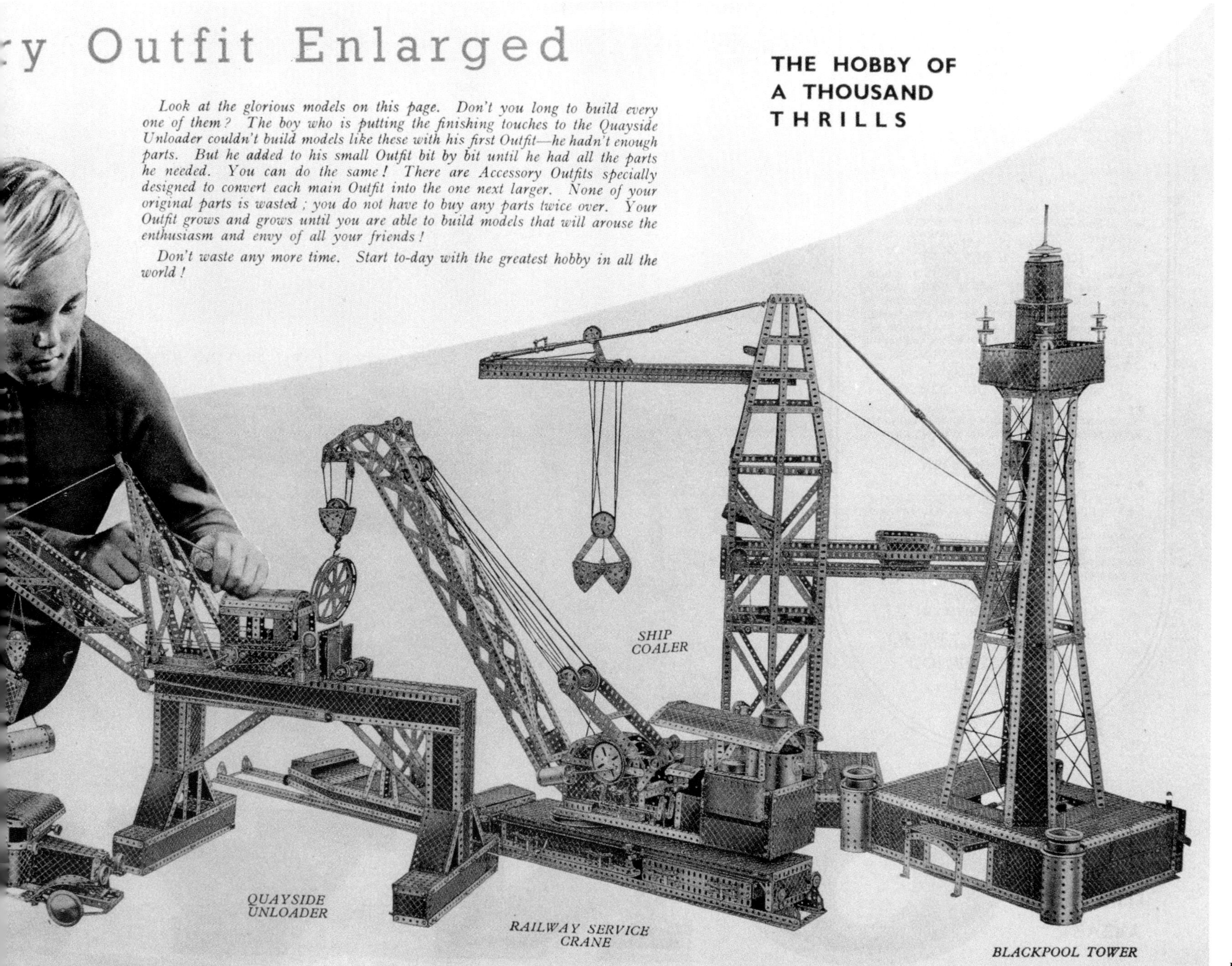

ry Outfit Enlarged
Look at the glorious models on this page. Don't you long to build every one of them? The boy who is putting the finishing touches to the Quayside Unloader couldn't build models like these with his first Outfit—he hadn't enough parts. But he added to his small Outfit bit by bit until he had all the parts he needed. You can do the same! There are Accessory Outfits specially designed to convert each main Outfit into the one next larger. None of your original parts is wasted; you do not have to buy any parts twice over. Your Outfit grows and grows until you are able to build models that will arouse the enthusiasm and envy of all your friends!
Don't waste any more time. Start to-day with the greatest hobby in all the world!
THE HOBBY OF A THOUSAND THRILLS
SHIP COALER
QUAYSIDE UNLOADER
RAILWAY SERVICE CRANE
BLACKPOOL TOWER

Fig 33.

The Secret of Meccano

The secret of the world-wide popularity of Meccano lies in the fact that it provides as much fun for the young boy with his small Outfit as for the older boy with a large collection of parts. The system is so simple that it can be understood at once from a glance at the illustrations in the Instruction Manuals packed with the Outfits. There is nothing to learn before beginning to build. The fun starts with the fitting together of the first few parts, and the excitement grows until the model is completed and set to work.

Meccano means new models day after day, week after week ; fresh interest all the time ; no more dull evenings !

A Perfect Toy

Meccano was invented by the late Mr. Frank Hornby, and was first patented in 1901. At that time the system consisted of only about 50 parts. Since then more parts have been added year by year until to-day there are more than 330 of them, together making up a perfect constructional toy. Many of the parts have been introduced as the result of suggestions from enthusiastic Meccano boys.

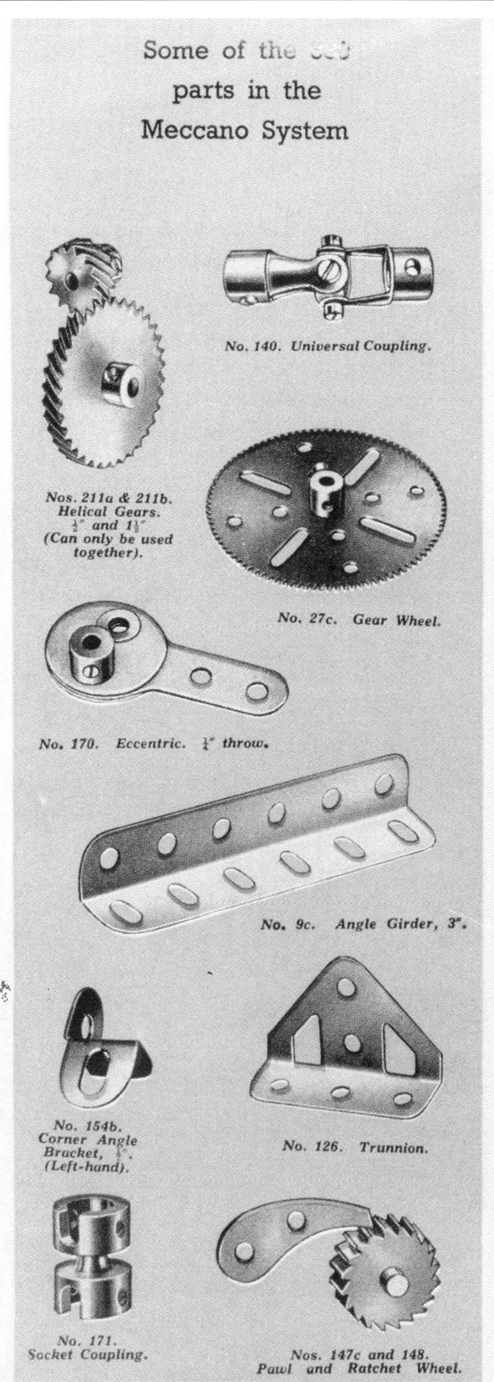

MEC

Meccano enables a boy to construct without difficulty accurate working models of almost every ty
engine, machine and mechanism. Look at the enlarged sections of the four fine models illustrated be
The first shows the steering mechanism of the Steam Lorry, simple to build but wonderfully realist
operation. Steering gears for other kinds of vehicles are just as easy to build. The second is even
interesting, showing the hoisting and traversing gears of the Gantry Crane. All the operations of the m
are carried out from the cab just as in the actual crane. It is a typical example of Meccano construc

LIVERPOOL
This realistic Steam Lorry is a typical example of the fine working models that can be built from the parts in Outfit No. 6.

Figs 34–36.
1939–1940 the last of the pre-war folders.

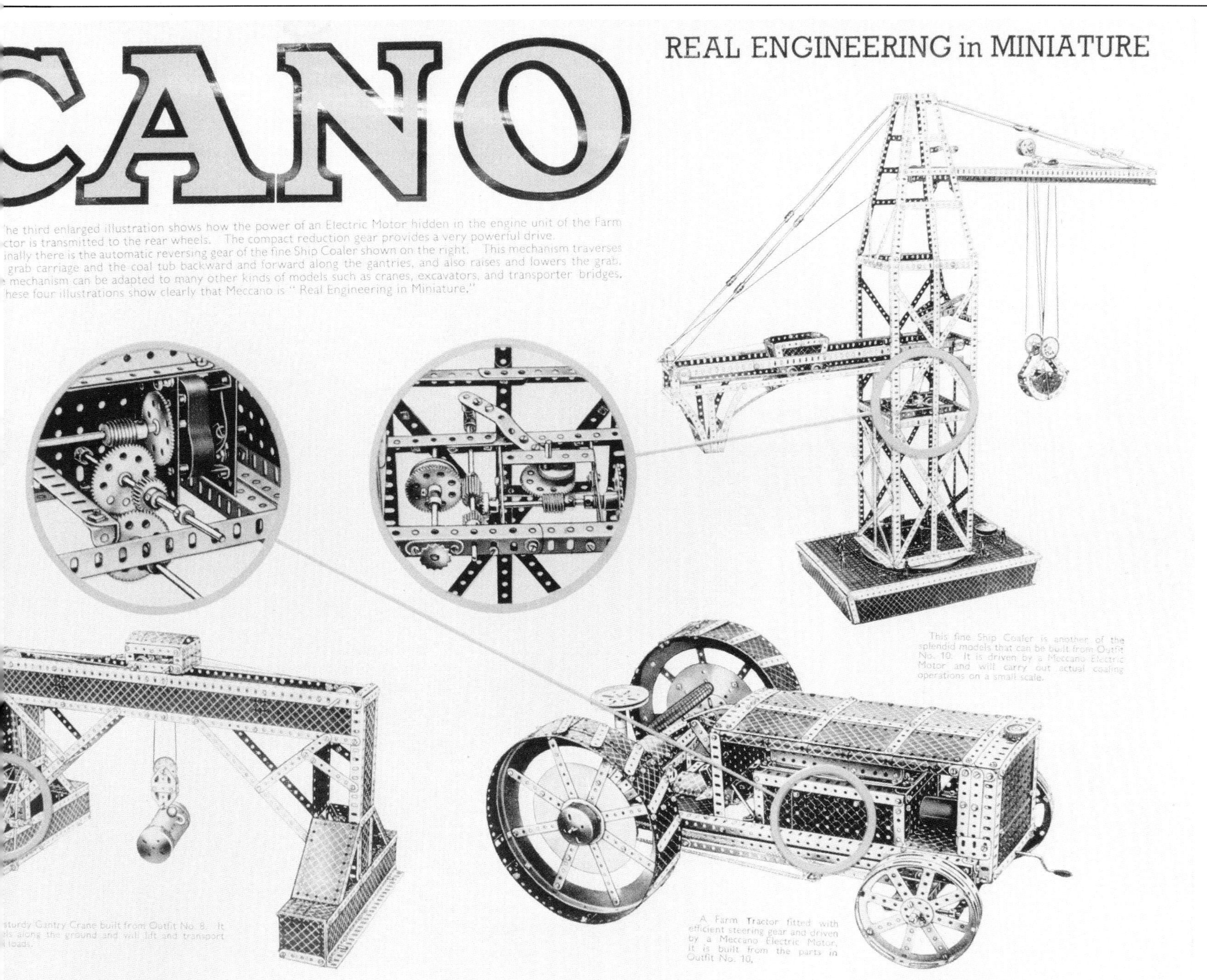
CANO
REAL ENGINEERING in MINIATURE
'he third enlarged illustration shows how the power of an Electric Motor hidden in the engine unit of the Farm
ctor is transmitted to the rear wheels. The compact reduction gear provides a very powerful drive.
inally there is the automatic reversing gear of the fine Ship Coaler shown on the right. This mechanism traverses
grab carriage and the coal tub backward and forward along the gantries, and also raises and lowers the grab.
mechanism can be adapted to many other kinds of models such as cranes, excavators, and transporter bridges.
'hese four illustrations show clearly that Meccano is " Real Engineering in Miniature."
This fine Ship Coaler is another of the splendid models that can be built from Outfit No. 10. It is driven by a Meccano Electric Motor and will carry out actual coaling operations on a small scale.
sturdy Gantry Crane built from Outfit No. 8. It
ls along the ground and will lift and transport
loads.
A Farm Tractor fitted with efficient steering gear and driven by a Meccano Electric Motor. It is built from the parts in Outfit No. 10.

Fig 35.

1939-40
MECCANO
ENGINEERING IN MINIATURE
A 50-TON
ELECTRIC CRANE
The Real Thing—in Meccano
MORE NEW MODELS!

Fig 36.

MECCANO

Meccano days are here again. The Outfits listed below, with parts beautifully enamelled in red and green, are now available; others will follow.

The Hobby of a thousand thrills

No. O OUTFIT

This Outfit contains a good selection of Meccano Parts, and is specially suitable for the younger boys. The Manual of Instructions in the Outfit gives examples of a fine selection of models that can be built—Trucks, Cranes, Mechanical Hammer, Elevator, and lots more.

Price, including Tax, **7/-**

No. I OUTFIT

This is a splendid Outfit with which to begin the Meccano hobby. The Manual of Instructions shows how a grand range of interesting models can be constructed including Ships, Cranes, Power Press, Windmill, Aeroplanes, Motor Lorry and many others.

Price, including Tax, **10/6**

No. 2 OUTFIT

No. 2 Outfit contains a wider assortment of parts and a Manual of Instructions that shows a magnificent range of models. These include a Railway Breakdown Crane, Aeroplanes, Motor Vehicles, Floating Crane and other realistic models.

Price, including Tax, **15/-**

No. 3 OUTFIT

This fine Outfit has always been a great favourite with boys. It contains a much bigger variety of Meccano parts with which an extended range of models can be built—Block Setting Crane, Battle Cruiser, Fire Engine, Marine Engine and very many others. A Manual of Instructions is included.

Price, including Tax, **21/-**

No. 4 Meccano Outfit

No. 4 OUTFIT

The owner of a No. 4 Outfit is able to build models of a more complicated and interesting type, including a Gantry Crane, Horizontal Steam Engine, Sports Car, Six-wheeled Steam Wagon, and Tank Locomotive, all designed on correct engineering principles. A Manual of Instructions is included showing these and many other fine models.

Price, including Tax, **30/6**

No. 5 OUTFIT

This superb Outfit contains a bigger and more varied range of parts, by means of which a splendid selection of realistic models can be built. These include a Military Tank, Electric Locomotive, Motor Lorry, Racing Seaplane, Tank Lorry, Railway Breakdown Crane, and many others. A fully illustrated Manual of Instructions is included.

Price, including Tax, **41/-**

No. 6 OUTFIT

Model-building possibilities are greatly increased by the large variety of parts in this fine Outfit. Excellent models of a Dockside Crane, Speed Car, Battery Locomotive, Tower Wagon and Fire Engine are among the thrilling selection featured in the Manual of Instructions supplied with the Outfit.

Price, including Tax, **53/-**

MECCANO ACCESSORY OUTFITS

Each Meccano Outfit from No. 1 upwards can be converted into the one next larger by means of an Accessory Outfit. A No. 1 Outfit can be converted into a No. 2 by adding to it a No. 1a Accessory Outfit, and a No. 2a would then convert it into a No. 3. In this way, no matter with which Outfit a boy begins, he can build it up by degrees until he has all the parts contained in the largest Outfit.

Accessory Outfit		Outfit		Outfit		Price, incl. Tax
No. **1a**	converts	No. **1**	into	No. **2**	...	5/9
No. **2a**	,,	,, **2**	,,	,, **3**	...	8/3
No. **3a**	,,	,, **3**	,,	,, **4**	...	11/-
No. **4a**	,,	,, **4**	,,	,, **5**	...	12/-
No. **5a**	,,	,, **5**	,,	,, **6**	...	12/-

MECCANO *MAGIC* **MOTOR** ... **Price,** including Tax, **5/-**

SOME USEFUL MECCANO PARTS

No.			Price, Incl. Tax s.	d.
10	Fishplate	Pkt. of 12	–	3
12	Angle Bracket ½" x ½"	,,	–	4
13	Axle Rod 11½"	Per dozen	2	6
15a	,, ,, 4½"	,,	1	6
15b	,, ,, 4"	,,	1	6
16	,, ,, 3½"	,,	1	3
20a	Pulley Wheel 2", with boss and screw	each	–	10
21	,, ,, 1½" ,, ,, ,,	,,	–	9
22	,, ,, 1" ,, ,, ,,	,,	–	6
23	,, ,, ½", without boss	,,	–	3½
25	Pinion ¾" dia. ½" face, 25 teeth	,,	1	1½
26	,, ½" ,, ¼" ,, 19 teeth	,,	–	8½
27	Gear Wheel, 1½" dia., 50 teeth	,,	–	8½
27a	Gear Wheel, 1½" dia., 57 teeth	each	–	10½
28	Contrate Wheel, 1½" dia., 50 teeth	,,	–	10½
29	,, ,, ¾" ,, 25 ,,	,,	–	6½
30	Bevel Gear, ⅞" dia., 26 teeth	,,	1	1½
32	Worm, ½" diameter	,,	–	8½
35	Spring Clips	Box of 50	2	0
37	Nuts and Bolts, 7/32"	Box of 24	1	3
38	Washers	Pkt. of 20	–	3
57c	Hook, loaded, small	each	–	2
63	Coupling	,,	1	1
94	Sprocket Chain	40" length	1	0
95	,, Wheel 2" dia., 36 teeth	each	–	11
96	,, ,, 1" ,, 18 ,,	,,	–	5

MARCH 1947

Figs 37–38. 1947 an early post-war leaflet showing the limited range available.

DINKY TOYS

The Favourite Collecting Hobby

No. 70a Avro "York" Air Liner

No. 70b Tempest II Fighter

No. 38c Lagonda Sports Coupé

No. 38f Jaguar Sports Car

No.		Price including Tax Each
16	Streamlined Train	5/6

MOTOR VEHICLES

No.		Price including Tax Each
22c	Motor Truck	1/3
23a	Small Open Racing Car	1/3
23b	Small Closed Racing Car	1/6
23c	Large Open Racing Car	1/8
23d	Large Closed Racing Car	1/8
23e	"Speed of the Wind" Record Car ...	1/8
23p	MG Record Car	1/8
23s	Streamlined Racing Car	1/9
25a	Wagon	2/3
25b	Covered Van	2/6
25d	Petrol Tank Wagon	2/3
25e	Tipping Wagon	2/9
25f	Market Gardener's Van	2/3
25h	Streamlined Fire Engine	2/–
25s	Six-Wheeled Wagon	2/9
25t	Flat Truck and Trailer	3/9
28	Delivery Van	1/5
29b	Streamlined Bus...	1/6
29c	Double Deck Bus	2/10
30b	Rolls-Royce	1/9
30c	Daimler	1/9
30d	Vauxhall	1/9
30e	Breakdown Car	2/–
30f	Ambulance	2/–
33w	Mechanical Horse and Open Wagon...	2/6
34b	Royal Mail Van	2/-
35a	Saloon Car	–/10
35b	Racer	–/9
35c	MG Sports Car	–/9
35d	Austin Seven Car	1/–
36a	Armstrong Siddeley Limousine ...	2/1
36b	Bentley 2-Seater Coupé	2/1
36c	Humber "Vogue" Saloon	2/1
36d	Rover Streamlined Saloon	2/1
36e	British Salmson 2-seater	2/1
36f	British Salmson 4-seater	2/1
36g	Taxi	2/6
38a	Frazer Nash-BMW Sports	2/3

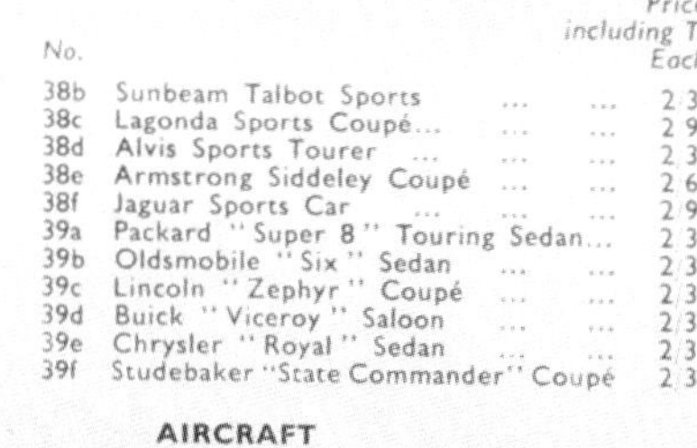

No.		Price including Tax Each
38b	Sunbeam Talbot Sports	2/3
38c	Lagonda Sports Coupé...	2/9
38d	Alvis Sports Tourer	2/3
38e	Armstrong Siddeley Coupé	2/6
38f	Jaguar Sports Car	2/9
39a	Packard "Super 8" Touring Sedan...	2/3
39b	Oldsmobile "Six" Sedan	2/3
39c	Lincoln "Zephyr" Coupé	2/3
39d	Buick "Viceroy" Saloon	2/3
39e	Chrysler "Royal" Sedan	2/3
39f	Studebaker "State Commander" Coupé	2/3

AIRCRAFT

No.		Price including Tax Each
60g	Light Racer	–/10
60k	Light Tourer	–/10
60r	Empire Flying Boat	2/3
60w	Flying Boat	2/–
62a	"Spitfire"	–/6
62b	Medium Bomber	–/9
62g	Long Range Bomber	1/7
62m	Light Transport	1/–
62p	Armstrong Whitworth Air Liner ...	2/3
62r	Four-Engined Air Liner...	1/6
62s	"Hurricane"	–/6
62y	Giant High-Speed Monoplane	1/6
63b	Seaplane	1/5
70a	Avro "York" Air Liner	3/9
70b	Tempest II Fighter	1/–
70c	"Viking" Air Liner	2/3
70d	Twin-Engined Fighter	–/10
70e	"Meteor" Twin Jet Fighter	1/3

MILITARY VEHICLES

No.		Price including Tax Each
151a	Medium Tank	3/6
151b	Transport Wagon	2/9
152a	Light Tank	3/-
152b	Reconnaissance Car	2/–
153a	Jeep	2/6
161b	Mobile Anti-Aircraft Gun	3/6
162	Field Gun Unit	4/–

No. 70c "Viking" Air Liner

No. 70e "Meteor" Twin Jet Fighter

No. 153a Jeep

No. 38e Armstrong Siddeley Coupé

HORNBY TRAINS

CLOCKWORK **GAUGE O—1¼"**

Tested and Guaranteed

Hornby M1 Goods Train Set.

A few of the famous Hornby Gauge "O" Clockwork Train Sets are now being produced and these are listed below. Each is complete with rails and attractively boxed

Hornby M1 Passenger Train Set.

MO GOODS TRAIN SET—Locomotive (non-reversing) and Tender, in either red or green, two Wagons and Rails requiring a space 2 ft. square. Price, **17/6** inc. Tax.

MO PASSENGER TRAIN SET—Locomotive (non-reversing) and Tender, in either red or green, two Pullman Coaches and Rails requiring a space 2 ft. square. Price, **18/-** inc. Tax.

MI GOODS TRAIN SET—Locomotive (reversing) and Tender, in either red or green, two Goods Wagons and Rails requiring a space 3 ft. 3 in. by 2 ft. 6 in. Price, **27/6** inc. Tax.

MI PASSENGER TRAIN SET—Locomotive (reversing) and Tender, in either red or green, two Pullman Coaches and Rails requiring a space 3 ft. 3 in. by 2 ft. 6 in. Price, **28/-** inc. Tax.

No. 201 TANK GOODS TRAIN SET—Tank Locomotive (reversing) available in L.M.S., L.N.E.R., G.W.R. and S.R. colours, one Goods Wagon, one Timber Wagon, one Oil Tank Wagon and Rails requiring a space 5 ft. 4 in. by 4 ft. 6 in. Price, **47/6** inc. Tax

16/347/50 (UK)

Made by Meccano Ltd., Binns Road, Liverpool 13

Fig 38.

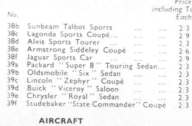

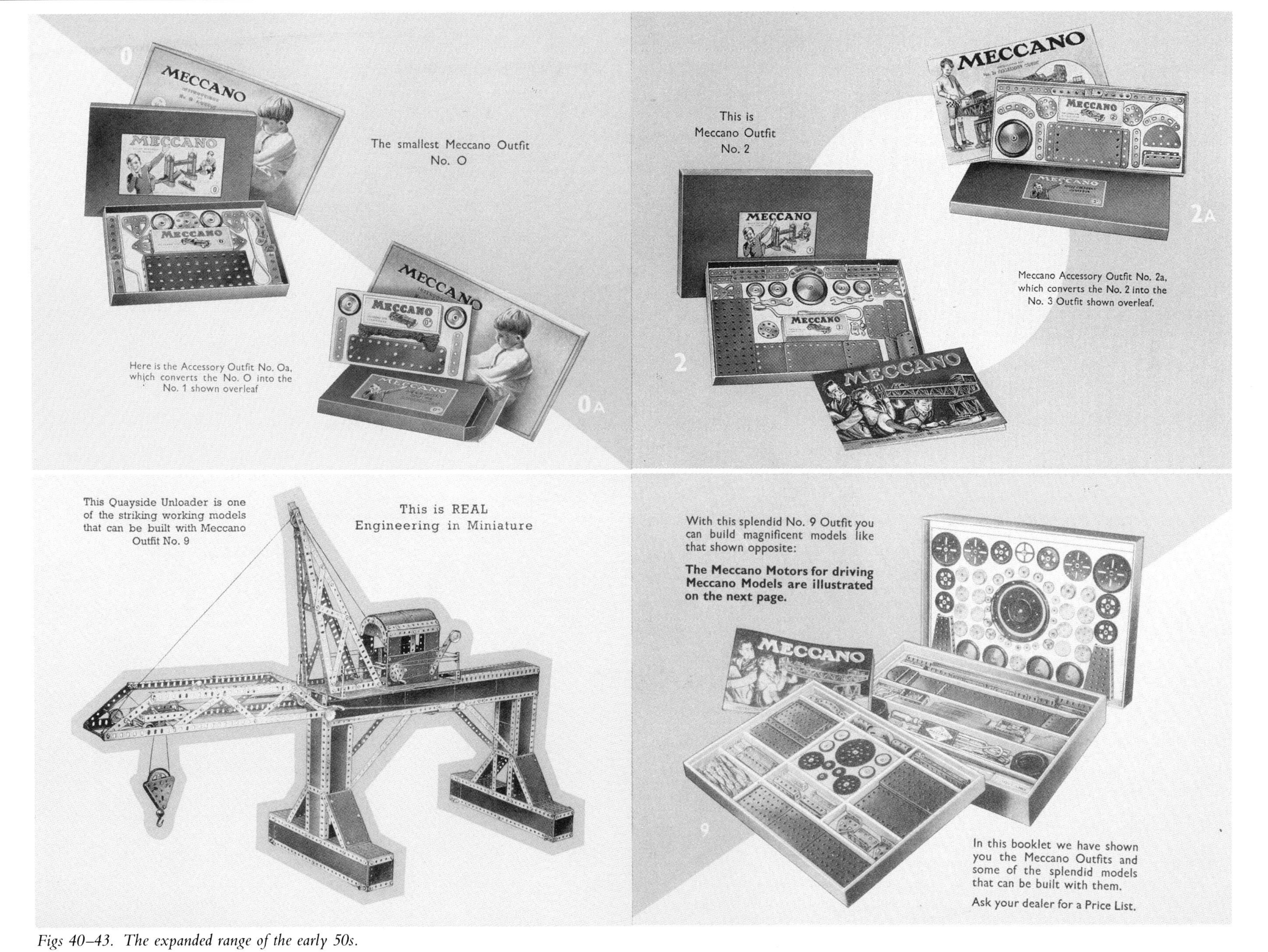

0
MECCANO
The smallest Meccano Outfit
No. O
MECCANO
Here is the Accessory Outfit No. Oa,
which converts the No. O into the
No. 1 shown overleaf
0A
This is
Meccano Outfit
No. 2
MECCANO
MECCANO
2A
Meccano Accessory Outfit No. 2a,
which converts the No. 2 into the
No. 3 Outfit shown overleaf.
2
MECCANO
This Quayside Unloader is one
of the striking working models
that can be built with Meccano
Outfit No. 9
This is REAL
Engineering in Miniature
With this splendid No. 9 Outfit you
can build magnificent models like
that shown opposite:
The Meccano Motors for driving
Meccano Models are illustrated
on the next page.
MECCANO
9
In this booklet we have shown
you the Meccano Outfits and
some of the splendid models
that can be built with them.
Ask your dealer for a Price List.

Figs 40–43. The expanded range of the early 50s.

MECCANO
A NEW TOY EVERY DAY
Clockwork Magic Motor
Clockwork Motor No. 1
E020 Electric Motor
E20R Electric Motor
MECCANO
MOTORS
After building a Meccano model there is nothing more exciting than to move a control lever and watch it working—the real thing come to life.
Four Meccano Motors are available—two clockwork and two electric. They have been designed specially to provide smooth-running power units for the operation of Meccano models.
MECCANO CLOCKWORK MOTORS
The Meccano Clockwork Motors are powerful and long-running and their precision-cut gears make them smooth and steady in operation. The Magic Motor is most suitable for driving small models built from Outfits Nos. 0 to 5. The No. 1 Motor is preferable for driving heavier models built from the larger Outfits.
Clockwork Magic Motor
This non-reversing motor is specially intended for driving small models 6/3
Clockwork Motor No. 1
A strongly-built long-running motor fitted with reversing motion 15/6
MECCANO ELECTRIC MOTORS
The special advantage of Meccano Electric Motors lies in the fact that they can be run continuously for long periods. If alternating current from the house mains is available, a Meccano 20-volt Electric Motor can be run cheaply and with perfect safety through a Meccano T20M Transformer. If alternating current is not available, an Electric Motor can be run from an accumulator.
No. E020 Electric Motor
20-volt. A sturdy non-reversing power unit of the all-enclosed type 19/3
No. E20R Electric Motor
20-volt. A powerful motor fitted with reversing motion 29/9
No. T20M Transformer
210/250 volt. A.C.; other Mains voltages to special order. For use with E020 and E20R Electric Motors 40/9
Prices include Purchase Tax
MECCANO LTD. · LIVERPOOL
16/953/220. Printed in England.

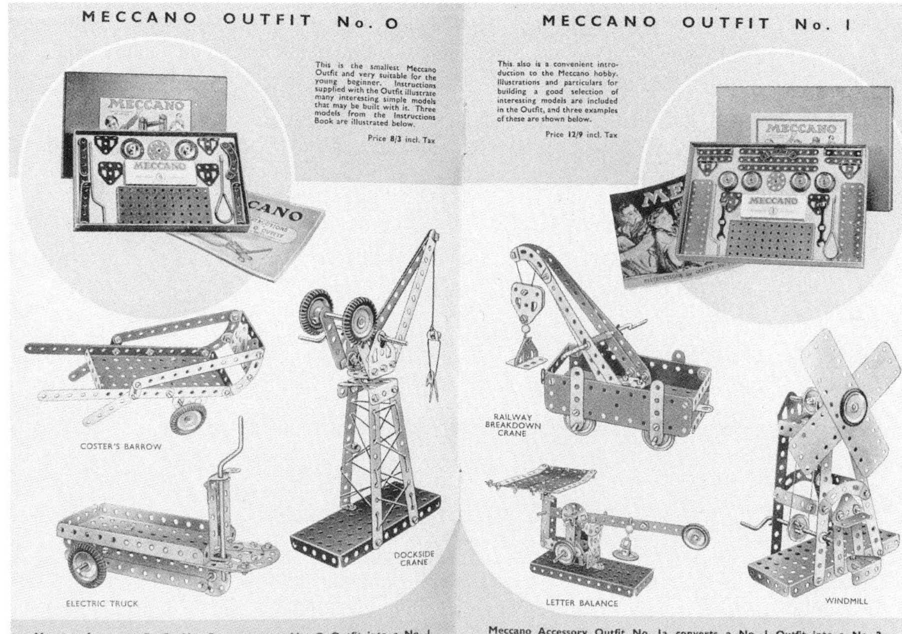

MECCANO OUTFIT No. 0
This is the smallest Meccano Outfit and very suitable for the young beginner. Instructions supplied with the Outfit illustrate many interesting simple models that may be built with it. Three models from the Instructions Book are illustrated below.
Price 8/3 incl. Tax
COSTER'S BARROW
ELECTRIC TRUCK
DOCKSIDE CRANE
Meccano Accessory Outfit No. 0a converts a No. 0 Outfit into a No. 1
MECCANO OUTFIT No. 1
This also is a convenient introduction to the Meccano hobby. Illustrations and particulars for building a good selection of interesting models are included in the Outfit, and three examples of these are shown below.
Price 12/9 incl. Tax
RAILWAY BREAKDOWN CRANE
LETTER BALANCE
WINDMILL
Meccano Accessory Outfit No. 1a converts a No. 1 Outfit into a No. 2

MECCANO OUTFIT No. 4
The owner of a No. 4 Outfit is able to build lots of more advanced models. Many examples of what can be accomplished are illustrated in the Book of Instructions. Both the fine models shown below can be built with this Outfit.
Price 35/- incl. Tax
DUMPER TRUCK
DRILLING MACHINE
Meccano Accessory Outfit No. 4a converts a No. 4 Outfit into a No. 5
MECCANO OUTFIT No. 5
Model-building possibilities are greatly increased by the large range of parts in this attractive Outfit. The Book of Instructions includes an excellent selection of models, and two of them are illustrated here.
Price 47/6 incl. Tax
PLATFORM WEIGHING MACHINE
GIANT SWING BOAT
Meccano Accessory Outfit No. 5a converts a No. 5 Outfit into a No. 6

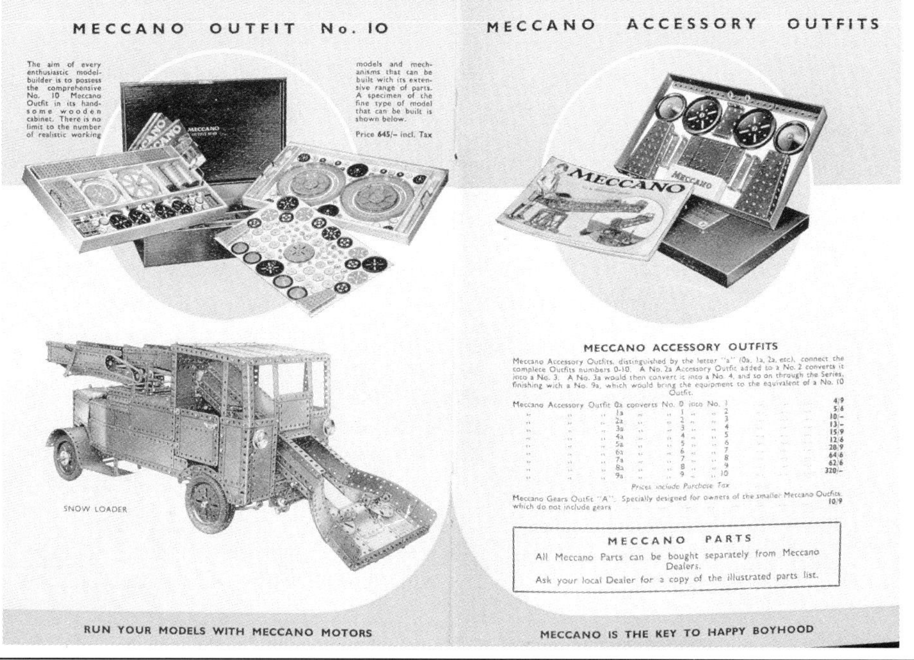

MECCANO OUTFIT No. 10
The aim of every enthusiastic model-builder is to possess the comprehensive No. 10 Meccano Outfit in its handsome wooden cabinet. There is no limit to the number of realistic working models and mechanisms that can be built with its extensive range of parts. A specimen of the fine type of model that can be built is shown below.
Price 645/- incl. Tax
SNOW LOADER
RUN YOUR MODELS WITH MECCANO MOTORS
MECCANO ACCESSORY OUTFITS
MECCANO ACCESSORY OUTFITS
Meccano Accessory Outfits, distinguished by the letter "a" (0a, 1a, 2a, etc), connect the complete Outfits numbers 0-10. A No. 2a Accessory Outfit added to a No. 2 converts it into a No. 3. A No. 3a would then convert it into a No. 4, and so on through the Series, finishing with a No. 9a, which would bring the equipment to the equivalent of a No. 10 Outfit.
Meccano Accessory Outfit 0a converts No. 0 into No. 1 4/9
" " " 1a " " 1 " " 2 5/6
" " " 2a " " 2 " " 3 10/-
" " " 3a " " 3 " " 4 13/-
" " " 4a " " 4 " " 5 15/9
" " " 5a " " 5 " " 6 12/6
" " " 6a " " 6 " " 7 28/9
" " " 7a " " 7 " " 8 64/6
" " " 8a " " 8 " " 9 62/6
" " " 9a " " 9 " " 10 320/-
Prices include Purchase Tax
Meccano Gears Outfit "A". Specially designed for owners of the smaller Meccano Outfits which do not include gears 10/9
MECCANO PARTS
All Meccano Parts can be bought separately from Meccano Dealers.
Ask your local Dealer for a copy of the illustrated parts list.
MECCANO IS THE KEY TO HAPPY BOYHOOD

Figs 44–48. 1953.

Adventures in Meccanoland and similar booklets (Figs 50–72)

From about the time of the First World War until the late 1930s, several series of booklets were produced which were aimed at the younger customer. Amongst the titles were:-

Dick's Visit to Meccanoland (figs 50–53).
Adventures in Meccanoland (figs 54–56).
Jackie Coogan Visits a Meccano Factory (figs 57–61).
The Story of Meccano by The Meccano Boy (figs 62–72).

Because of the age of the intended reader, this type of publication was somewhat juvenile in its approach, although as discussed in the opening chapter of this book, they were not quite as basic as might be supposed. Certainly some of the words contained in these booklets would cause many of today's children to rush for a dictionary.

Because these charming publications are examples of that rather patronising and paternalistic style used for young children in those days, they are mainly collected for their attractive covers and for the information contained in the advertising pages. The pages reproduced here give a good idea of the overall style.

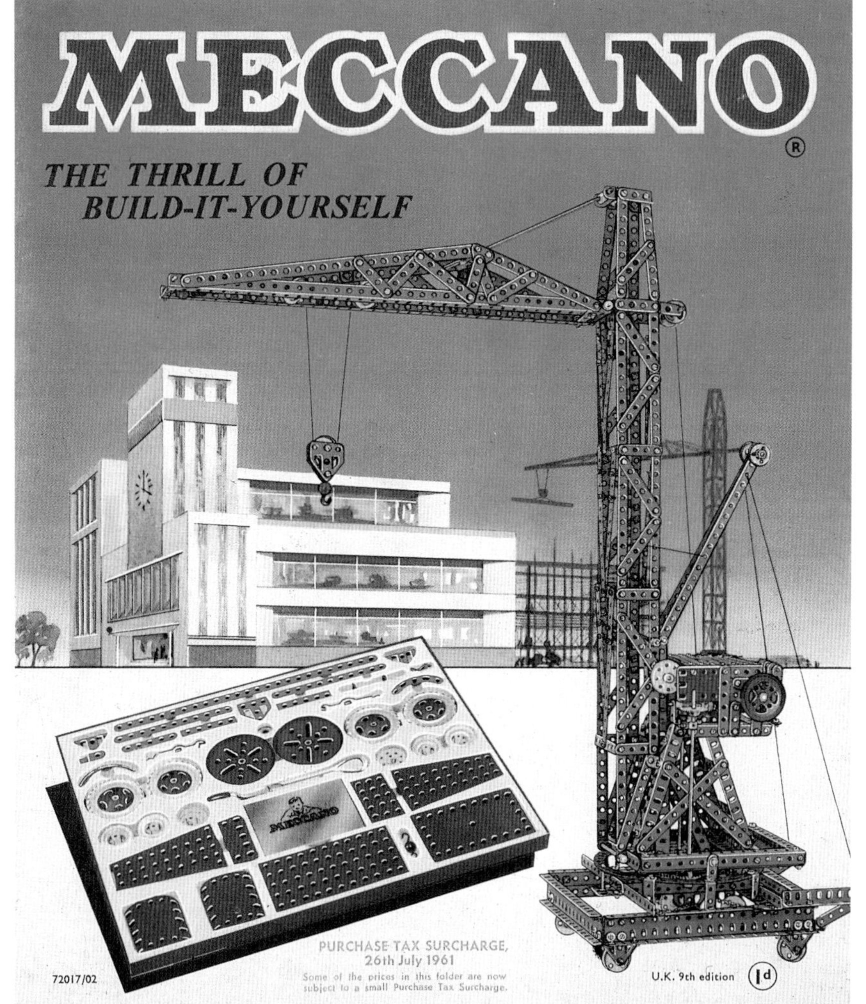

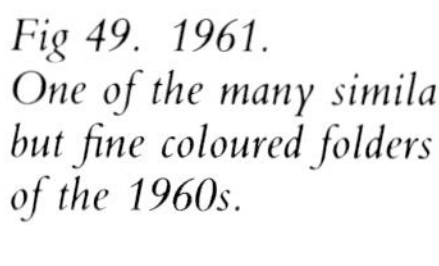

Fig 49. 1961. One of the many similar but fine coloured folders of the 1960s.

Figs 50–52. 1925 edition of Dick's Visit to Meccanoland.

THE LAND OF HAPPY BOYS

SOME BOYS have lived in Meccanoland for more than twenty years, and the longer they live there the happier they are. Every day more boys are crowding into the country, eager to learn of its wonders. The moment they arrive they feel at home, and they take their places and set to work with a will. They know that in Meccanoland they will have the time of their lives; that they will have more fun than they have ever had before. Meccano fun is healthy boys' fun—fun that makes them glad to be alive; fun that strengthens their characters, sets their brains working, and teaches them something that will make them into successful men.

The sun never sets on Meccanoland, where there is always life and joy. The gates are never closed, and the only passport you require to enter this wonderful land is a Meccano Outfit. Get your passports to-day, boys, and don't stay another minute in the cold dreary world outside.

A short time ago a bright eager boy heard about Meccano and Meccanoland, and he told his father about them. His father was so interested that he called at the Meccanoland Home Office to investigate, and what they told him there so impressed him that he set it all down. You will find it in this little book, and when you have read it through you will agree that you have never read anything so absorbing.

Dick and the Meccano Motor Chassis

2

DICK'S VISIT TO
MECCANOLAND

THE SPELL OF A WONDERFUL TOY

"MY WORD, DAD, it's great!" cried Dick, as he came running into my room with a parcel under his arm.

"What is great?" I asked, looking up from my paper.

"Why, Alan's Meccanograph. He has got . . . ."

"Alan's what did you say? What is a Meccanograph?"

"Well, I'm trying to tell you. Last Christmas, Alan got a Meccano Outfit—the engineering toy that you see advertised in all the papers. He built a most topping lot of models—a big Bridge, a Crane, a Motor Chassis, and I don't know how many more besides. Then he wanted some more parts to make bigger models. His father wouldn't hear of it at first, but said that if Alan would make a really clever model with the parts he already had, he'd buy him the parts he wanted."

"Did he do it?" I asked, becoming interested.

"Rather! Why, he made the Meccanograph, and he's lent it to me. Here it is!"

Dick placed his parcel on the table, took off the wrappings and disclosed a neat mechanical contrivance, with a little crank at one end and a wooden platform at the other.

"Lend me your fountain pen, Dad," said Dick. I did so, and he fixed it into the machine so that the point rested on a piece of paper, which he pinned on the little platform.

"Are you ready, Dad? Now watch—I'm going to show you something."

3

 Fig 51.

THE WONDERFUL MECCANOGRAPH

He turned the crank, and the pen immediately began to trace an exceedingly intricate and delicate design. It was the most magical thing I had ever seen.

" How do you work it, Dick ? " I asked. " Let me try."

" Wait a minute ! " answered Dick. " Wait till I change the design."

" What do you mean ? " I exclaimed. " Can you really make the pen draw something else besides the lovely design you have just made ? "

" Yes," replied Dick. " All you have to do is to change these little pins to other holes. I don't know how many different designs you can make altogether, but I think there must be thousands and thousands. Last night Alan and I made pictures for two hours and every one was different. There were some real beauties, and it was fearfully exciting watching the design being made, and not knowing what it was going to be. I brought the drawings with me."

He opened a thick bundle of square sheets of paper, which he handed over to me. On each was a different kind of Meccanograph design. In some the boys had used coloured inks, and had filled in parts of the design with water colours, giving a most fascinating effect. I gave up all thoughts of reading my paper, and spent the evening turning the crank and watching the pen go through its magical performance. I forgot all about going to the club, and Dick and I had the jolliest evening—the first of many such evenings we were destined to spend with Meccano.

The Meccanograph with which hundreds of beautiful designs may be made

" Where do you buy such a machine ? " I asked Dick.

" You don't buy it at all," Dick replied. " You just buy a Meccano Outfit, and make it up for yourself.

" That's a drawback, isn't it ? "

4

" Oh, no, not at all. You get full instructions for making this and hundreds of other models, and it is just as much fun building them as it is playing with them."

Three of the many beautiful designs made by the Meccanograph

I began to see what an extraordinary and instructive hobby this Meccano model-building must be, and felt very glad that Dick had run across it. I soon saw that he had a real mechanical bent that was going to be worth something to him, and that it was my duty to encourage it.

One day I asked him : " Who started Meccano ? Who's the inventor ? "

" Why, Frank Hornby, Dad," Dick quickly replied. " Every boy knows about him. He says he has a million boy friends ! "

" I shouldn't wonder if he has," I said. " Suppose we look him up some day and cross-examine him ? "

Dick's eyes glistened. " Why ! Do you think he would see us ? " he said, with doubt in his voice.

" Well, he's human like the rest of us, I suppose," I replied. " Anyhow, we will take a chance of his seeing us."

WE CALL ON MR. HORNBY

Next morning I took Dick into town with me, and, calling at the Meccano offices, asked if we could see Mr. Hornby. The attendant conducted us into the Meccano model-room, and asked us to wait there.

What a sight ! Dozens of different Meccano models were displayed on tables arranged around the room—Towers and Bridges ; Wagons and Cranes ; an electrically-operated Big Wheel, taller than Dick ; Moving Stairways ; Platform Scales ; Drilling and Punching Machines ;

5

Fig 52.

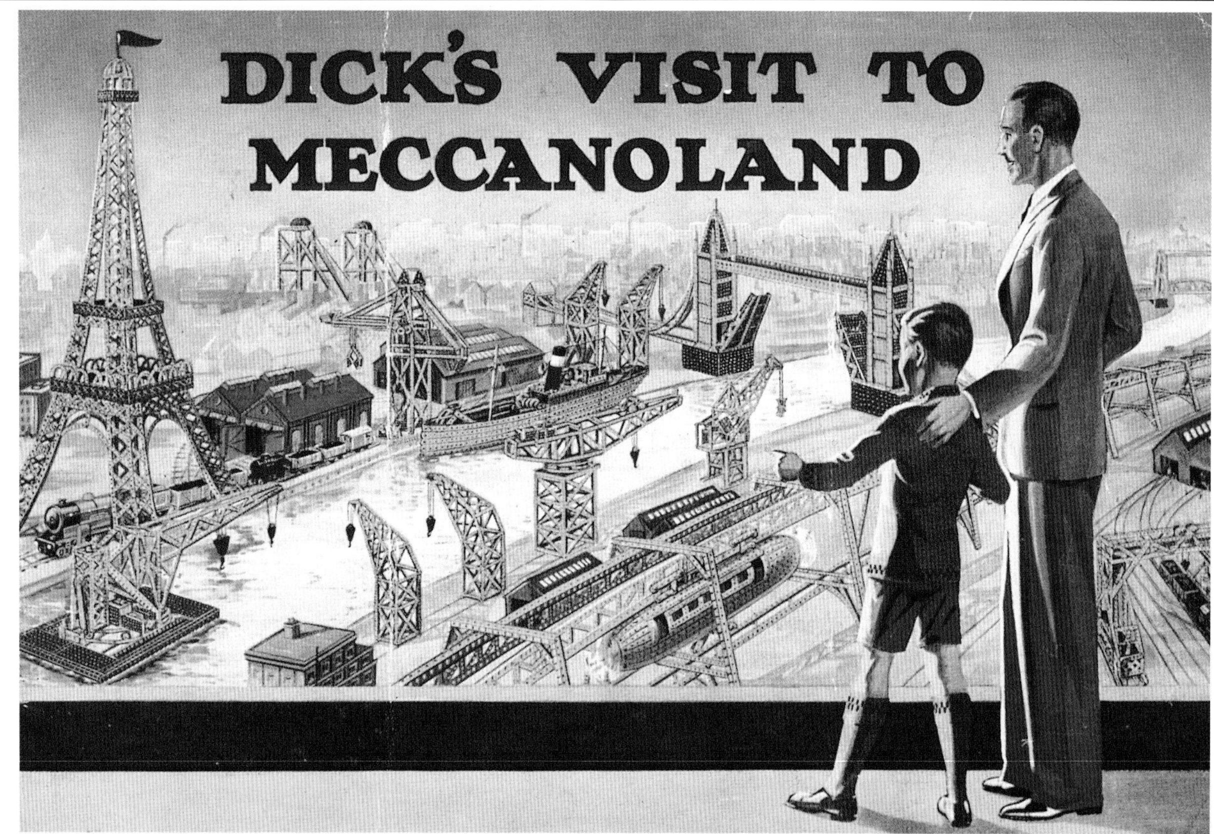

Fig 53. The 1935 edition of Dick's Visit.

Figs 53A & 53B.

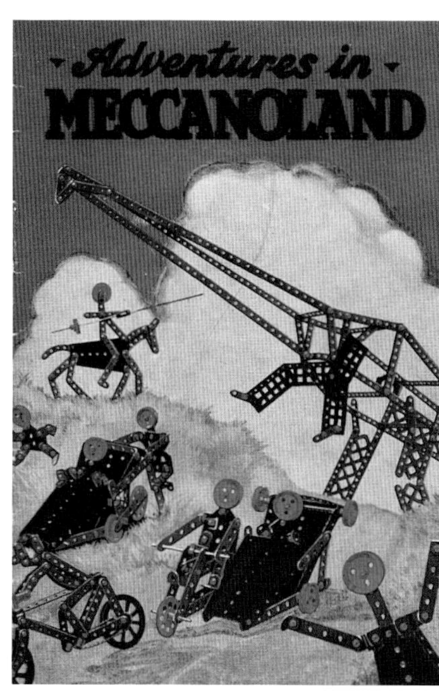

Figs 54–56. Adventures in Meccanoland (this particular copy signed by its author, Hubert Lansley).

Foreword

BEFORE you have read very far into this little story you will very likely decide that the strange adventures that befell Dick were nothing but a very extraordinary dream, brought on by a too hearty enjoyment of cakes and other delicacies provided at his birthday party. You may come rather close to the truth in taking this view of the matter, but notwithstanding this you will realise that Meccano-land is no "dream country," but a very real and glorious land where sturdy boys live a life of joy and fun.

Nearly all the inhabitants of this sunny realm are boys—millions of them—and they are all happy. The younger ones are revelling among miniature bridges, wagons, windmills, trucks and towers, that they build and set to work mechanically. The older ones are building and playing with larger structures—real engineering in miniature—and all are busily engaged in inventing new and ingenious models and movements. All these boys have their own magazine, the "*Meccano Magazine*," which deals with the topics that Meccano boys love to read about; they have their own Guild and Clubs and they spend happy hours in friendly rivalry, one striving to outdo the other in inventing and building more and better models.

Many boys have lived in Meccanoland for more than 20 years, and every day more boys are crowding into the country eager to learn of its wonders and to join the fun. Meccano fun makes boys glad to be alive; it strengthens their characters, sets their brains working and teaches them something that will make them grow up into successful men.

The sun never sets on Meccanoland—there is always life and joy. The gates are never closed and the only passport you require to enter this wonderful land is a Meccano Outfit.

Get your passports to-day, boys, and don't stay another minute in the cold dreary world outside.

Note. All the models illustrated in this book, with the exception of the Diplodocus and the Lancer, may be built with a No. 1 Meccano Outfit.

727/80

By Hubert Lansley
"Spanner" 1924–1930

ADVENTURES IN MECCANOLAND

THE STRANGE TALE OF DICK'S TRAVELS IN A WONDERFUL NEW COUNTRY

TO put it plainly, I was feeling "fed up." The previous day had been my birthday and we had had a very jolly evening, but at the time of which I write I was decidedly off colour! Of course the reason was quite clear to me for, as I explained to everyone, I had been overworked at school. I cannot imagine why my brother Jack should have chipped in just then with something about ". . . overworking yourself with birthday cakes and jam tarts you mean!" Anyway, the rest of the family were enjoying themselves in the drawing-room but I just felt that I wanted to be left alone—for a while at least!

As I wandered aimlessly about, the quietness of the house seemed most depressing after the previous night's noise and excitement. All my birthday presents still lay on the table but I couldn't take much interest in them at the time. It seemed an age since my birthday party when I took the part of Old Father Time in the charade. I had declared I could do this quite well because I already had had some experience of acting at school, and I think it really was unkind of Jack to remind everyone of the quite unnecessary fact that my début on that occasion had been in a minor part—to be candid, one of the sheep in the school pantomime "*Little Bo-Peep.*"

"I am King Meccano the Great"

As it was, things were dead against me as

Page One

Fig 55.

As I drew up with a sigh of relief by his side, the King assured me of his ability to restore me to my normal size as soon as his object was

". . . An Acrobat doing some extraordinary stunts on a see-saw"

accomplished. The boys, he explained, were ordinary Meccano boys who had been captured while asleep at their Outfits, for which crime they had been brought to the Meccanoland Court to act as the King's Body-guard. "In this capacity," said the King, "they are expected to learn the error of their ways, for in my country nobody ever sleeps! The boys seem to be enjoying themselves thoroughly, however, and, as far as I can see, they don't want ever to return to your world again."

The King then threw open a tiny door in the skirting board and beckoned me to follow him.

"We now enter the great realm of Meccanoland," he said, and as he spoke he seemed literally to glow with pride, and truly he had good cause for pride, I thought, as I stood on the frontier of the brightest and most wonderful country I had ever seen.

A vast plain lay before me, shimmering in brilliant sunshine, and prosperous-looking lands stretched away into the distance as far as I could see. Close at hand were hundreds of Meccanitians bustling about on their various occupations and presenting a scene of such activity and happiness that I could scarcely believe my eyes.

I AM INTRODUCED TO MECCANOLAND

"These wonderful lands of mine," said my royal guide, "are rich with new ideas and great possibilities, hidden from sight and kept strictly secret. There are now, however, over a million boys in all parts of your world who have sworn allegiance to me—although some do not

Page Four

know it—and the gates of my country are always open to these boys. All that they require in order to enter it is our usual passport.

"What is the passport, you ask?" His eyes twinkled and sparkled. "Why! just a Meccano Outfit, and nearly every boy has that. I welcome any and every boy, knowing that each one will do his share towards making this country even more prosperous than it is to-day, for I number among my young friends the best and brightest boys of every nation in your world.

"Those who work and seek diligently will find hidden treasure, sometimes in the most unexpected places. To let you into a secret, I may tell you that some even discover great treasures and great possibilities *hidden in themselves!* They realise the value of their finds—perhaps years later—in their life in your world, for it is there that they will reap the greatest reward for their work and devotion here."

". . . The Climber came tumbling down"

The Oldest Inhabitant

I was spellbound at the prospect unfolded by the King, and as we walked in Meccanoland my amazement increased even more. We were surrounded by hosts of little people of the same type as my companion, every one of whom seemed to be intent on cramming as much fun as possible into his or her life.

"Even the Meccanitians have their holidays as you see,"

Page Five

Fig 56.

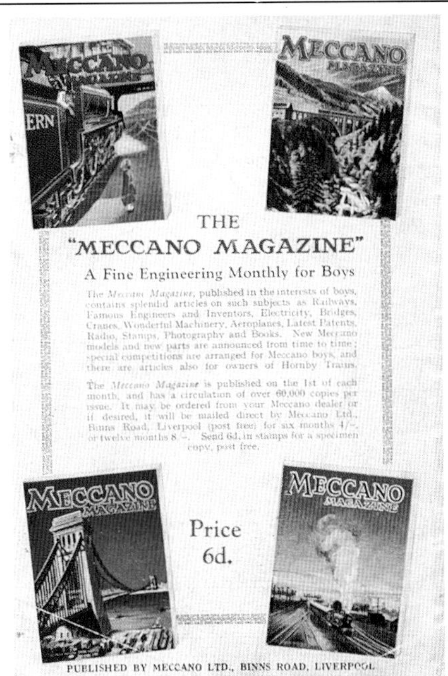

Fig 54.

adds a deposit of copper before the parts are plated with nickel, he exclaimed " Gee " at the quick change in the appearance of the parts. When he dipped them they were a dull steel colour; when he took them out they had a bright copper tint. Then he put the rack of parts in the nickel bath, rinsed them afterwards, dried them in sawdust, and with a roguish smile turned to me and said, " That's easy, isn't it ? "

The Tool Room

We next came to the Tool Room where the tools for making Meccano parts are made. All the men employed in this department are experienced and highly skilled craftsmen, on whose work depends the accuracy of the finished parts. Jackie was surprised when I told him that the machines used for making the tools work to one-thousandth part of an inch. He asked how the men were able to measure anything so finely and was more surprised still when I explained that they used an instrument known as a " Micrometer " that would measure accurately up to one-ten-thousandth part of an inch !

The Packing Department

Leaving the Tool Room we retraced our steps across the factory until we reached the entrance to the Packing Department. I had purposely

The Packing Department

Page Twelve

Jackie is shown here starting to build a new model. He is carefully following the instructions

left this Department to the last so that Jackie could see how all the finished Meccano parts were finally collected prior to being made up into bundles of the required quantities, ready to go into the various Outfits. Perforated Strips, Angle Brackets, Rods, Girders, Gear Wheels, etc., are brought to the tables, where girls wrap them up in twos, threes, sixes, tens and so on. At other tables Nuts and Bolts are counted into boxes, while at others girls are busily engaged placing the various Wheels, Pinions, etc., on cards. This work goes on all the year round, and these particular tables are busiest in the summer months preparing the stock for distribution throughout the country during the autumn and winter.

Jackie packs an Outfit

In one section of this department the complete and accessory Meccano Outfits are made up. This last operation of all greatly interested Jackie, to such an extent that he asked if he might pack up an Outfit all by himself. Of course I gave him permission at once, and I must confess that I was amazed by his cleverness

Page Thirteen

Figs 57–59. 1926 edition of Jackie Coogan visits a Meccano Factory. The packing dept appears to be Liverpool not New Jersey!

Fig 58.

Jackie and his dog spend a quiet hour with the Meccano Magazine

in successfully accomplishing an intricate job. Needless to say he was exceedingly proud of his achievement.

On the way back to my office Mr. Coogan and Jackie talked of the enjoyable time they had had and when I asked what had impressed them most of all, they both agreed that it was the extraordinary precision and accuracy with which each little part of the Meccano system is produced. Invariably when I ask visitors this question I get the same answer and it is obvious that the great care taken in the manufacture of Meccano is largely responsible for its world-wide renown as a first-class product.

An enjoyable visit

The Meccano Magazine

When we arrived at my office Jackie told me that he was a regular reader of the American edition of the "Meccano Magazine." He finds this Magazine extremely interesting and eagerly looks forward to the publishing date of each issue. I promised to send him the English Edition regularly, as this covers a much wider field, and he was delighted to think that he would have an opportunity of reading of the activities of Meccano boys in Great Britain and her colonies.

Page Fourteen

The Meccano Factories

Jackie was a little surprised to learn that we have several other factories besides the one in Elizabeth, and that the real home of Meccano is in Liverpool, where there are over 1,500 employees, and that there is another large factory in Paris. On his next trip to Europe he intends visiting both these factories. I mentioned that at Liverpool he would be able to watch the manufacture of Hornby Trains, in addition to that of Meccano. Then I told him the story of Hornby Trains and explained how they had grown in popularity until to-day they vie with Meccano for first place as the world's most popular toy.

"Say!" he exclaimed. "They must be jolly good to do that!"

As we said good-bye, he told me that, although he had met kings and princes, had been entertained as no visiting potentate is entertained, had had gifts of all kinds lavished upon him, his greatest thrill had come to him on hi: visit to the Meccano factory.

Frank Hornby

Managing Director,
Meccano Limited.

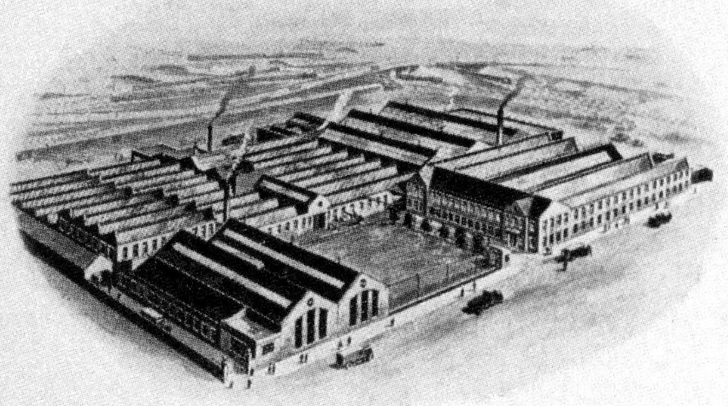

The Factories and Head Office of Meccano Limited, at Liverpool

Page Fifteen

Fig 59.

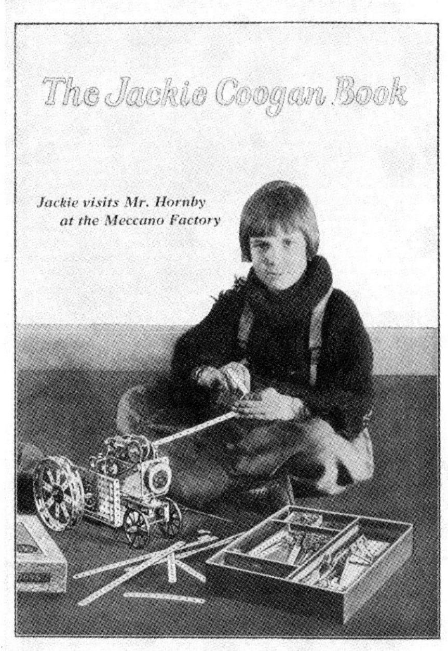

→
Figs 60–61. The American edition.

tion. He told me he had been to Paris and that when he saw the Eiffel Tower he felt sure it had been designed from Meccano. He said he had a notion that he could build an exact model of the Eiffel Tower himself every bit as big, if only he had enough parts and enough time, and then he added "Wouldn't it be fine if Meccano boys could run it and operate the elevators, and let all the other Meccano boys who came, examine the machinery and explain it all to them."

"And what would your part in the matter be, Jackie," I asked. "Oh!" he replied, "I would be an elevator boy and I would say 'Step right in; this is free day to Meccano boys; and it's all quite safe, everything's made of Meccano.'"

The Eiffel Tower in Paris

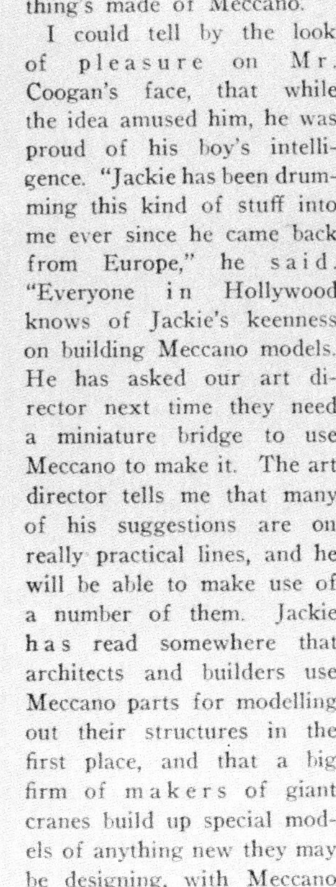

I could tell by the look of pleasure on Mr. Coogan's face, that while the idea amused him, he was proud of his boy's intelligence. "Jackie has been drumming this kind of stuff into me ever since he came back from Europe," he said. "Everyone in Hollywood knows of Jackie's keenness on building Meccano models. He has asked our art director next time they need a miniature bridge to use Meccano to make it. The art director tells me that many of his suggestions are on really practical lines, and he will be able to make use of a number of them. Jackie has read somewhere that architects and builders use Meccano parts for modelling out their structures in the first place, and that a big firm of makers of giant cranes build up special models of anything new they may be designing, with Meccano parts, and so try out the movements and mechanism first in this way; and he sees no reason why we in our business should not make similar good use of Meccano. He is especially keen on a plan for making slow motion pictures of a boy building models with Meccano in order to show other boys how easy and delightful the work is. Don't you think, Mr. Hornby, that something like that would be useful?" I, of course, agreed that the suggestion was a good one and that it might be worth planning out something of the kind. I was especially pleased to see that Jackie was so familiar with the many commercial uses to which Meccano has been applied.

All the while his father was speaking there was a grave expression on Jackie's face as he looked at us glancing from one to the other, that showed he was anxious that his ideas should be taken very seriously. The long talk that we had together gave me all the clues I needed to his strong character and showed me plainly enough why his personality and genius have impressed themselves in so marked a fashion on his audiences all over the world.

How Jackie got his start

I expressed the wish to know something of his short and wonderful career, and his father told me, with a twinkle in his eye, that his first appearance in a theatre was when he was twenty months old. Mr. Coogan himself was on the stage at the time, when he

The Eiffel Tower in Meccano

The Story of

MECCANO

by the Meccano Boy

"I built it"

MECCANO is Engineering in Miniature for Boys

I am the Meccano Boy

I am always bright, keen and happy. All the boys, big boys and little boys, young boys and "old boys" like me. Everybody knows and loves my happy smile. That's why I want *you* to know about Meccano, which is the jolliest, manliest game ever.

It's fine to be a Meccano Boy, to be able to build all sorts of splendid models. I've built a hundred models with Meccano. I've built models of great Towers and Bridges, Tremendous Cranes and Lifts. Wouldn't you like to be able to do that? I'm sure you would.

Come with me, and I will tell you in the pages of this little book all about Meccano, how you can build the models, and something of the excitements and rare times in store for every boy who gets Meccano.

1

Figs 62–68. A very early edition of The Story of Meccano by the Meccano Boy.

Meccano is so easy to understand

MECCANO is as easy as A.B.C., only you want to build the smaller and simpler models first—just to get your hand in. That's half the game, building better and bigger models every time. The other half is playing with them when they are finished.

You won't need to "swat" over instructions, because there are hardly any. You simply use your eyes and work straight from the pictures in the "Manual of Instructions" given with every set of Meccano. Thousands of boys do this and so can you.

The Manual of Instructions

You don't buy the Meccano models ready made—you build them yourself, which is far better. There are seven different outfits. Whether you start with a big outfit or a small one does not matter, although, of course, you can build more and bigger models with a big outfit.

Nut and Bolt

Steel Strip

Rectangular Plate

Double Bent Strip

The Meccano parts consist of strips of bright, plated steel with holes bored in them. The strips are of different lengths, but the holes are all the same size and the same distance apart. When building you join the strips together with bolts which pass through the holes and are held by nuts which are screwed on. Besides the steel strips, there are lengths of steel rods for axles, stays and other things; wheels and pulleys of different kinds and sizes, and beautifully made gear wheels which make the models work sweetly and smoothly. Then there are nuts and bolts galore, clips and collars and set screws, angle brackets, sector plates—in fact everything necessary for building Meccano models. Here is a box of Meccano. There is a place for every different kind of part. You can lay your hands on any one of them at once.

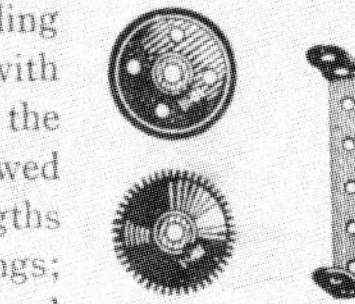

Pulley Wheel & Gear Wheel

Bent Strip

Angle Girder

Rod

Screw driver

No. 1 Outfit, 5/.

Meccano is quite easy to build

NOW I think I can give you a better idea of how to build a model if I make one myself. But whether I tell you how to build Meccano or show you how it is done won't be half the fun you will have doing it *yourself*. However, you do want to get a wrinkle from an "old hand" like me.

The part of the Crane you build first.

I like building and playing with cranes best because you can do such a lot of things with them. Here is a little beauty which I often build up and play with. You never seem to get tired of a crane. If you're playing building a house, you can carry your bricks and all your other materials around with it, or if you're playing railways you can ship the goods into the trucks and into the goods yard, and lots of things of that kind. This one is called a Travelling Jib Crane, and it's on wheels you'll notice, which makes it easy to move around.

First of all, you get your parts together. The book of Instructions always tells you just what you want although really you don't need any telling, because the pictures are so clear.

Look at figure No. 1. This is the part you make first. The large shining plate is called a rectangular plate, and that makes the base of the crane. Then you see the long strip at the end: that's $12\frac{1}{2}''$ long, so it's called a $12\frac{1}{2}''$ strip. Then there's a $5\frac{1}{2}''$ and a $2\frac{1}{2}''$ strip fastened up by nuts and bolts just as you see them. That's practically half the crane made, you see.

Then you do just the same on the other side, after which you join the two sides at the back with another strip, putting a sector plate in between the two long strips to hold the jib steady and firm and joining the two ends at the top with a nut and bolt. Look at figure No. 2. Just a little lower down you pass a small steel rod through the holes and this holds the pulley wheel in position over which the cord passes.

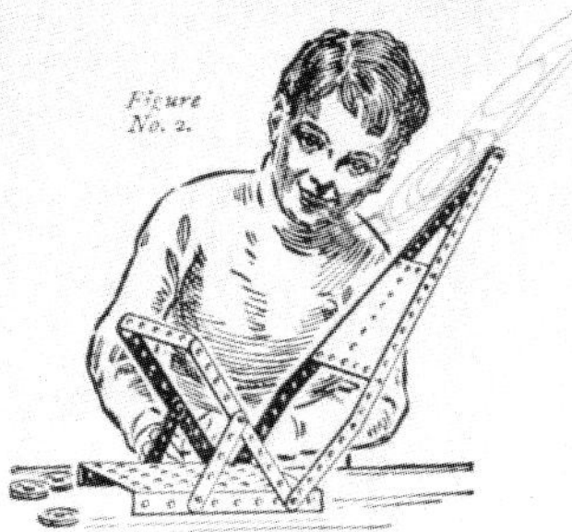

Then you do just the same on the other side.

Fig 64.

Meccano grows more and more interesting

The cord, of course, starts in the crank handle which you push through the side strips. Before pushing it through though, you fix a pulley wheel on it like you see in the picture, and this helps you to make a natty little brake. You see the strip below the wheel which is fastened at one end to the side of the crane—well, when you press that down the piece of cord which you fix over the pulley wheel holds the handle and you can stop the load which you are lowering just where you want it.

Figure No. 3.

And that's how it's done.

Now we're ready for the wheels. You push a rod through the end holes in the plate, push the wheels on and hold them in place with little clips, which you press on the rod. When you have neatly tied up the cords at the back and over to the end of the jib, you have got the whole thing complete, and I tell you it's a first-rate piece of work. Look at figure No. 3.

That's how it's done, and it isn't a bit difficult. Why, many a time I take a model like this right in pieces after I have made it, just for the fun of building it up again.

Boys, don't you feel your fingers itching to get hold of those steel strips and bolts and nuts? I fancy I hear you saying to yourself "I'm going to build that crane which the Meccano boy did, and after that I'm going to build grander models, right up to those big cranes and bridges."

Boys, that's the Meccano spirit, the same spirit that invented and improved motor cars and aeroplanes.

See how they run—for Meccano

4

Why Meccano doesn't grow stale

AFTER you have had quite a good time with the Crane it can be rapidly taken apart and a start made on a new model, using again perhaps all of the parts which were in the Crane. It may be a neat and strong little truck, a set of railway signals, a motor tipping wagon, or some other equally interesting model that you build next, but whichever it is, any one of them will give you no end of amusement. If you had bought the Crane ready-made you would simply have cast it aside when you grew tired of it. Now just think how good is Meccano.

All change here for Meccano.

There is no getting tired of it. No standing still. One thing leads on to another. You become keener and keener. Can't help it; and all the time you are learning to build like an engineer, in the very way an engineer does build, because Meccano is simply engineering in miniature. Each Meccano outfit builds a certain number of models, which are shown in the Book of Instruction. The prices are—

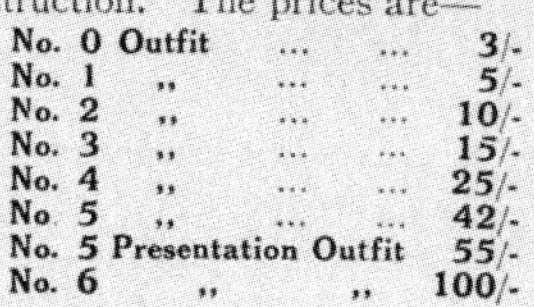

No. 0	Outfit	3/-
No. 1	,, ...	5/-
No. 2	,, ...	10/-
No. 3	,, ...	15/-
No. 4	,, ...	25/-
No. 5	,, ...	42/-
No. 5	Presentation Outfit	55/-
No. 6	,, ,,	100/-

Now, supposing you started with a No. 2 Outfit, and built all the models, you could buy an Accessory Outfit to make up the next size outfit, as explained on page 15. I think this is a jolly good arrangement for helping on a fellow who hasn't got too much pocket money.

ONE THING

LEADS ON

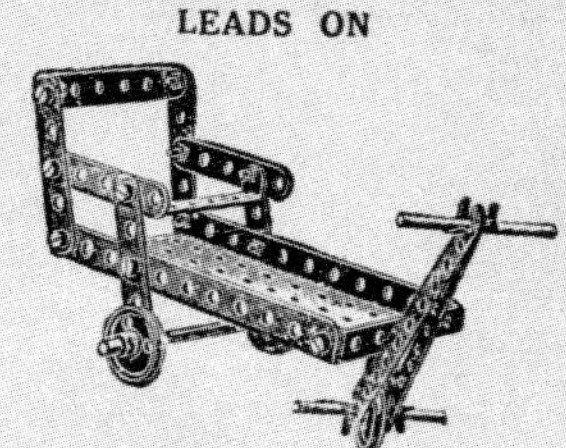

TO ANOTHER

IN MECCANO

5

Fig 65.

Inventing things with Meccano

THERE is another side to Meccano, and it's simply stunning I mean inventing models not in the "Manual" and building them with Meccano parts. When you have had good practice with Meccano, you will begin to think of things you would like to build, and you will try to build them. What you have learnt from Meccano helps wonderfully. Meccano puts you up to so many wrinkles how to do things mechanically right. Some day you might surprise father or your chums with a model of something very badly wanted, and you would feel jolly proud of being an inventor and young engineer.

Inventing a New Model from Meccano.

The Fun, the Excitement and the Triumph of Meccano

Boys, you'll agree that the building of Meccano Models is just the cutest thing ever thought out. Meccano makes dull boys bright, and bright boys brighter. Weak boys and sick boys who can't join in the sports get ever so much good from Meccano. But building is only half of Meccano, as I said before. When the models are built, whole afternoons and evenings can be spent in glorious fun. Playing with Meccano models is better than playing Red Indians and Cowboys, at which anybody can play; but only Meccano boys can turn a floor or a table into a great workshop with all the buzz and excitement of real work, drilling machines going, trucks running here and there, and travelling cranes carrying great loads; or into a dock where ships are loaded and unloaded by the big jib cranes and winches, or perhaps the vessel is being fitted with engines and boilers, then you would employ one of those giant girder cranes that are enormously powerful. A hundred other Meccano working models open up games by the score in which all your friends can join and have a right merry time.

The Meccano Boy Building a Model of a Bridge.

With this Inclined Delivery Shoot the truck runs down when loaded and returns when empty.

6

Building is only half of Meccano

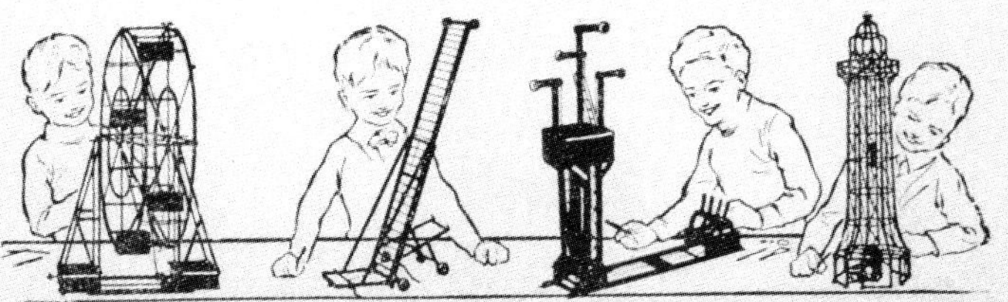

HERE I am building a model of the Big Wheel which gives huge enjoyment to the holiday folks at Blackpool. Next a Fire Escape with sliding ladder. Then a Signal Gantry with operating levers and signals all complete, just like those on the big railways. In the fourth picture you see me putting the finishing touches to a masterpiece—a copy of the famous Eiffel Tower in Paris. Any boy can build these and a hundred other models with Meccano, and be just as jolly as I am.

AGAIN you see me here busy working a Telpher Span which I have just built. This is a very interesting model, because you can fix up the pulley bracket at one end of the room and the body of the telpher at the other, and by simply lengthening the cords make the bucket travel to and fro across the room. The bucket can be loaded with anything you like. A telpher span will give you hours of enjoyment, yet it is one of the simplest of Meccano models, and can be made with a No. 1 outfit.

7

Fig 66.

Meccano Boys at Play

"Jolly Boys are we"

SOME of your chums may not have Meccano—give them a treat by letting them see you build, or better still, let them take part. It's ripping to be foreman on the job of making a big model like the London Tower Bridge or the Funicular Railway. You plan how its to be done, do a bit yourself and show the others how to do their bits. When you have built up the model and got it going full steam and all hands busy at their various duties, what more delightful than to rout out Dad or Mother and bring them to see the Show. How surprised, how amused, how delighted, they are! That is a triumph.

For Meccano's a jolly fine hobby—and so say all of us

8

What Meccano teaches

GROWN-UPS get awfully interested in Meccano, you know, because it's so clever and not a bit childish. My dad is a dab at building Meccano, and I often think he bought Meccano for himself, because he gets so keen and will sit for hours at it. But, of course, he hasn't got the hang of it like I have, so, naturally, I boss the work. But we have grand times together.

"Dad says Meccano is just miniature engineering."

DAD'S view is that Meccano is good for every boy, because it teaches him in his play a good deal about real engineering. He says Meccano is just miniature engineering. Building big things on a small scale, and building them right, so that they *work* right. "Building on correct engineering principles," dad calls it. "Other toys which attempt the same object as Meccano," he explained to me, "cannot be built on correct engineering principles, and although a boy may succeed in building playthings with them, they would be mere toys and nothing else. Worst of all, in building on wrong principles, a boy gets wrong notions which are very hard to unlearn, and when he attempts to invent or construct more elaborate models he is stopped by the faults and failings of the non-mechanical systems he has been used to." So you see, boys, Meccano is the only one for you, because it is real engineering in miniature, so make sure you get it.

9

Fig 67.

The Grown-ups come in to admire
MECCANO
A HOBBY FOR BRIGHT BOYS
I built this model of a Motor-Bus
BUILDING Meccano or playing Meccano is far finer than any fun I know, far more interesting and helpful than I can explain. You will know that when you get Meccano and with your own hands build the models, and in your own way play with them. You will feel the pride and joy of building model after model, better and bigger each time. You will become eager to excel. You will know that even when you are enjoying yourself you are learning things which will help you when you have grown to be a man. And always you will have in view the next bigger and better model, until you have mastered the whole art of Meccano and become a first-class Meccano Boy who knows how to build m ny of the things which grown-ups call "the wonders of the world." There is real satisfaction in this, isn't there?
Here I am showing the splendid model, which I have made, at work. It is an Elevated Jib Crane—a correct model of the kind you often see high up on a scaffold when a new building is being put up. My chums are having a rare time working the crane, which raises and lowers loads just like a real big crane.
10
11

Fig 68.

Figs 69–72.
A later First World War era edition.

BUILDING

It's jolly building Meccano Models

THE same Meccano parts that go to the making of a Crane are used in a Bridge, a Tower, a Ship, and scores of other models. So you see that in a Meccano Outfit there are all the materials for making very many models, all different and distinct from each other. This is wonderful enough, but perhaps it is even more wonderful to find how easy it is to build the models. Of course, you want to start building small and simple models first, just to get your hand in. It's half the fun, building better and bigger models each time.

You won't need to puzzle over instructions, because there are hardly any. You simply use your eyes and work straight from the clear pictures in the "Manual of Instructions" given with every Meccano Outfit. The only tool needed is the screwdriver supplied.

The Meccano parts include bright, plated steel strips with holes pierced in them. When building, you join the strips together with bolts, which pass through the holes and are held by nuts, which screw on just like real engineering.

2

PLAYING

—and it's rare fun making the models work

There are also steel rods for axles, stays, and other parts; brass wheels and pulleys, beautifully made gear wheels. Then there are nuts and bolts, angle brackets, sector plates—in fact, everything necessary for building models big and little.

You work like a real engineer, and piece by piece the framework of the model steadily rises. And as the steel gleams in the light like armour bright, your joy and enthusiasm mount up, for you see the model growing up, strong and rigid, bolted true and tight, under your own hands. Then comes the exciting part of fitting the mechanical parts, the gearing, spindles, cranks, and the cording. Every step is full of interest. You learn that there is a right way of doing everything, and the reasons become clear and plain without any telling. It is a proud moment, I can assure you, when you have put the finishing touches to a fine model, and you stand back to survey your handiwork. But it is an even prouder moment when you set the model to do its own particular work and note how beautifully it does it.

3

Fig 70.

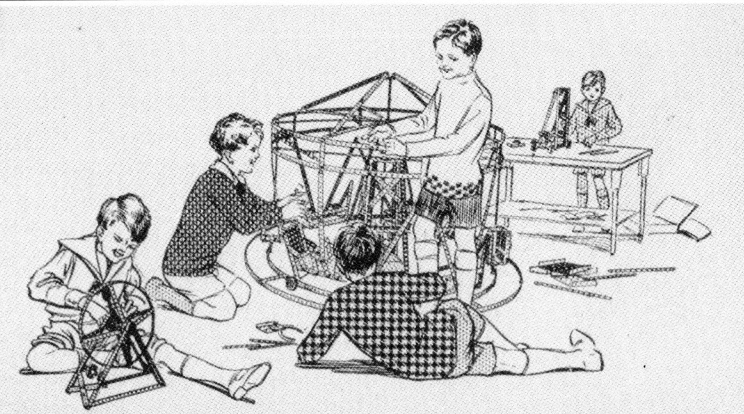

HOW TO RUN A MECCANO WORKSHOP

It's fine to be foreman on the job of making, say the Roundabout, the Funicular Railway, or the Transporter Bridge. You give each of your men a section to build whilst you superintend the work of erection. Soon there is rivalry as to who will do his best and quickest, and the fun goes fast and furious. When the model is completed everyone tumbles over himself to see it working and to get a turn at making it work. And so the happy hours spin along. Now Meccano is a great help and inspiration to boys of an inventive turn of mind. It supplies the ready means of enabling them to put their ideas into shape. Every model built with Meccano should act and work smoothly and effectively, because Meccano is based on correct engineering principles and can be applied in hundreds of ways to build models not included in the Manual — for this reason students of mechanics use Meccano for demonstration purposes.

You would be surprised to know the amount of interest grown-ups take in Meccano. Thousands of fathers like

6

Meccano is a Real Help to Parents

TO the parent who studies the welfare and future of the boy, Meccano makes an appeal so strong that it must be heard. How many thousands of pounds are spent every Christmas, and in fact every day (for every day is some child's birthday) on toys, often expensive, which are broken in a few days, and discarded! Putting the claim for Meccano on the lowest grounds, how welcome must that toy be, which will amuse and delight a boy every day in the year, and keep up his interest for many many years!

But Meccano is more than a pastime. It is a great moral force for the training of a boy. No boy who uses Meccano can be a bad boy. The hobby teaches him to think. It teaches him patience. It teaches him thoroughness because every model must be thoroughly and properly constructed and fixed up accurately and firmly before it will work properly. It teaches him order and method, because he learns to take care of the beautiful Meccano parts, and to put them away carefully and in proper order after he has used them. It teaches him to invent, because after he has made all the models shown in the book of instructions he can go on designing others for himself. There is no engineering movement which he cannot demonstrate and make use of with Meccano. He will learn to value each little Meccano part and to appreciate its accuracy and the care and skill necessary in its manufacture. Meccano is engineering; it is educational; it may be, and has been, the means of starting many a bright boy on a prosperous career in what is probably the most important field of experiment and research in modern times— engineering and mechanics.

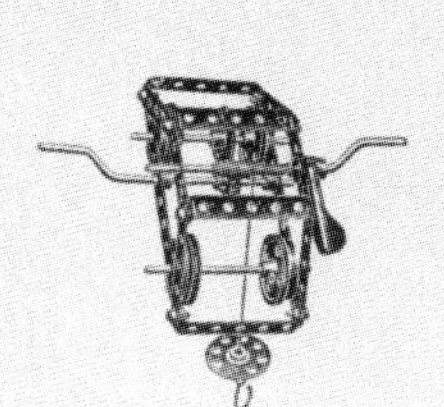

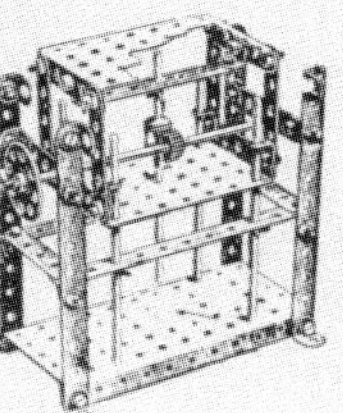

A few examples of Meccano mechanism.

11

Fig 71.

Meccano

A PAGE ABOUT THE BOOK OF INSTRUCTIONS

The Manual of Instructions

THE Meccano Book of Instructions (The Manual) is a wonderful production, consisting of 134 pages. Each model is shown in full detail, bigger and clearer than those in this book. Where printed instructions are needed, they are clearly and simply given, and many supplementary enlarged illustrations of working parts that are at all intricate are also given, so that any boy may find everything easy and straightforward.

Many new models have been added to the already large Meccano repertory. These, besides being of an exceptionally interesting character, further demonstrate the adaptability of Meccano to any design having a sound mechanical basis. The wood-turning lathe, the potter's wheel, and such like models, because of their special usefulness, are certain to have hosts of admirers.

The Manual gives also numerous designs demonstrating the main elementary fundamentals of mechanics. These convey to the growing mind the meaning and purpose of the underlying principles far more quickly and effectively than reading alone. This book of instructions accompanies all outfits from No. 1 upwards. A special edition is given with No. 0 outfit. The mere perusal of the Manual is a delight to young and old.

Here is an abbreviated list giving an idea of the variety of models shown in the Book of Instruction :—

Revolver Truck	Tower Wagon
Luggage Barrow	Pile Driver
Endless Rope Railway	Cake Walk
Drop Stamp	Pithead Gear
Automatic Dial Press	Level Crossing
Polishing Spindle	Fire Escape
Ore Crusher	Warehouse and Elevator
Stamping Mill	Cable Railway
Travelling Ladder	Coal Tip
Windmills of Various Types	Motor Bus
Railway Signal	Lighthouses
Monoplanes	Telpher Line
Turntable Gangway	Funicular Railway
Railway Footbridge with Signals	Cranes of all Types
Motor Van	Bridges of all Types
Extensible Ladder and Running Carriage	&c. &c. &c.

14

Meccano Motors *for* Meccano Models

All Meccano Models can be worked by hand or by motor, as desired.

Meccano Electric Motor—It differs from all previous types of electric motors, being totally enclosed, thus making it entirely safe to run by inexperienced users in the home. No fear of shocks. It is designed to be used in connection with models where a greater power is required than is provided by the spring motors, *e.g.*, for working the wood-turning lathe, or a number of models at one time. It is operated by a simple switch, and is readily connected to any lamp-holder. It is important when purchasing the motor to see that it corresponds to the voltage of the current it is to be connected with. Detailed specification is given in the big Book of Instructions with every Meccano outfit. Price, 45/-

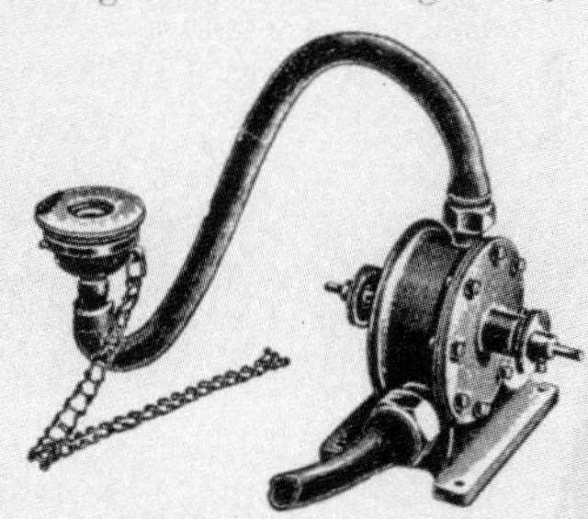

Meccano Water Motor—An admirable substitute for the Meccano Electric Motor where current is not available. It is supplied with two tubes, one with an adaptor for attachment to the water tap, and the other to carry away the waste water. It is of one-sixtieth horse-power at a pressure of 30lbs. Meccano Water Motor, complete, with tubes and fittings, price, 10/-

Meccano Spring Motor—Contains its own motive power in a simple, convenient form. It can be built into and becomes part of the model it drives. No. 1 Meccano Spring Motor may be used in connection with Outfits Nos. 1 to 3. It has a stopping and starting motion, and the movement can be reversed. Price, 5/-

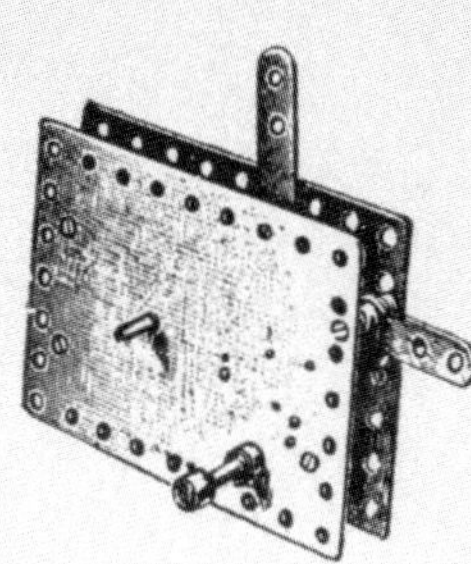

No. 2 Meccano Spring Motor is suitable for driving models made with Outfits Nos. 4 to 6. It has three driving spindles, with a clutch movement, and each can be worked independently. It has also a starting button and a reversing movement. Price, 15/-

15

Fig 72.

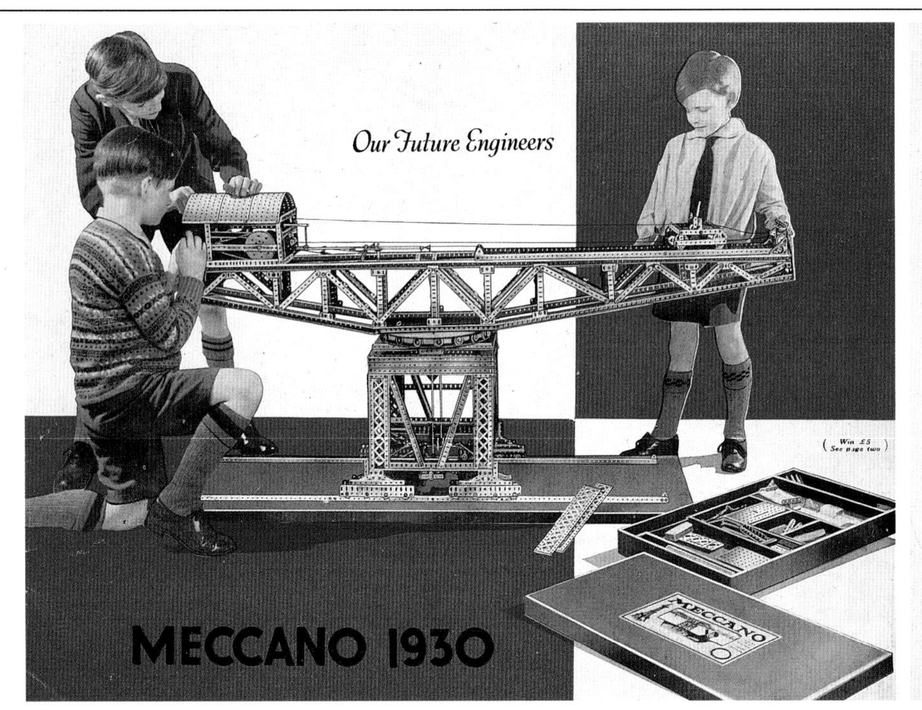

MECCANO

The Toy that made Engineering famous

Engineering for Boys

The Meccano system is composed of over two hundred different parts, mostly made of steel or brass, each one of which has a specified mechanical purpose. These parts combine to form a complete miniature engineering system with which practically any mechanical movement may be reproduced in model form. More can be accomplished with Meccano than with any other constructional toy, for no other system has such possibilities. The genius is in the parts and the youngest boy can commence to build models as soon as he gets his Outfit home.

How to Begin

Meccano is sold in nine different Outfits, numbered 00 to 7. All Meccano parts are of the same high quality and finish, but the larger Outfits contain a greater quantity and variety of parts, making possible the construction of more elaborate models. Each Outfit may be converted into the one next higher by the purchase of an Accessory Outfit (see page 14). Thus, if a No. 00 is the first Outfit bought, it may be converted into a No. 0 by adding to it a No. 00A. A No. 0A will then convert it into a No. 1 and so on up to No. 7. In this way, no matter with what Outfit a boy commences, he may build it up by degrees until he possesses a No. 7. Meccano parts may be bought separately at any time in any quantity. The border of the page shows an interesting selection of the latest additions to the Meccano System. A complete illustrated Accessory Parts list may be obtained from any Meccano dealer.

Hundreds of Models

There is no limit to the number of models that can be built with Meccano—Cranes, Clocks, Motor Cars, Ship-Coalers, Machine Tools, Locomotives—in fact everything that interests boys. The most wonderful thing about Meccano is that it is real engineering; it is fascinating and delightful and yet so simple that even an inexperienced boy may join in the fun of building models without having to study or learn anything. A beautifully illustrated Book of Instructions showing how to make hundreds of models is included with every Outfit and a screwdriver is the only tool required.

Boys, Build and Invent

The training of the eye, brain and hand in erecting Meccano is considerable, but there is also developed a faculty of immense value to every boy. No boy is content to build the models exactly as he finds them; it is always possible to improve, and he sets to work to do this almost at once. It is a boy's nature to venture into unknown fields, and the Meccano hobby opens up a new and wide world for him to explore. He very soon proceeds to invent, and new models and designs, the creation of his own brain, make their appearance.

The Meccano Service

The Meccano boy of to-day will be the famous engineer of to-morrow. When a boy wants to know something more about engineering than is now shown in our books, or when he strikes a tough problem of any kind he writes to us. We receive over 200 letters from boys every day all the year round. Some write to us because they are in difficulty, others because they want advice on their work or pleasures, or about their choice of a career. Others, again, write to us just because they like to do so—and we are glad to know that they regard us as their friends. We publish a special Magazine for them (see page16).

Although all kinds of queries are addressed to us on all manner of subjects, the main interest is, of course, Engineering. No one has such a wonderful knowledge of engineering matters as that possessed by our staff of experts, and this vast store of knowledge, gained only by many years of hard-earned experience, is at every Meccano boy's service.

Page Three

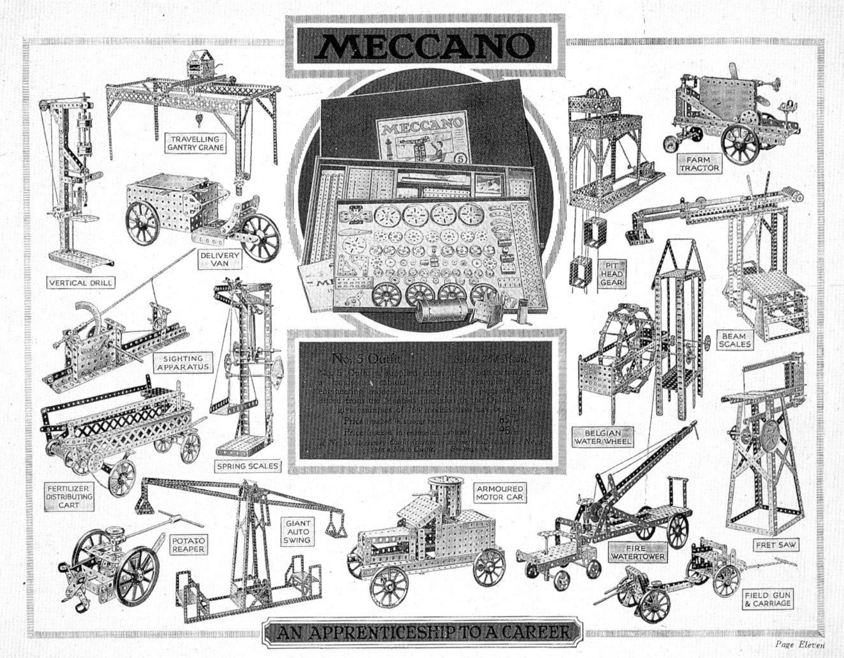

Figs 76–78. 1930 MECCANO.

 Figs 73–75. 1929 edition of MECCANO for 1930.

'Meccano' publicity booklets

From 1929 to 1933 the company issued a series of booklets entitled 'Meccano'. The first, Meccano 1930 (issued in 1929 for the 1929–30 season), was similar in contents to those editions of 'The Magic Carpet' which only contained basic details of each outfit, although in this case the parts list was excluded. Printed on art paper, its 16 Super Model leaflet sized pages were attractively set out and eye-catching. The following year a fresh edition was brought out but with only 12 pages and in reduced format. Like its predecessor, a 50,000 (assuming print codes are correct and no others come to light) print run was produced. The 1931 issue reverted to 16 pages in a slightly different and vertical format and with a reduced run of 35,000 copies. In 1932 four of the 16 pages of what was a very similar-looking edition were devoted to Aeroplane and Car Constructor outfits as well as the first speedboat. The print run was further reduced to 17,500 copies. The last of these booklets was produced for the 1933–34 season and was expanded to 24 pages. Elektron and Kemex were now included and the print run increased to 20,000.

In 1934, this series was replaced by The Meccano Book which was a much more comprehensive publication with a large number of full colour pages. This beautiful large format booklet bears a striking resemblance to the 1935 Book of Meccano Products and Hornby Trains. Its issue publicised the newly introduced Blue and Gold colour scheme, so in one sense perhaps it should be included under the New Meccano literature, but as is often the case, the distinctions are rather blurred.

Before 1929 there had been other booklets issued which could be classed as belonging to this series. For example, there were editions of 'The Magic Carpet' which dealt purely with Meccano as distinct from Hornby Trains, but on the other hand there were rather more versions which included Hornby Trains and these are perhaps more properly regarded as products catalogues. The former therefore are included here and the latter under 'Products Catalogues'.

One further publication whose contents were similar to those under discussion is *The Meccano Book of Engineering* which dates from 1928 and was not, as far as we know, reprinted although at least three slightly different front covers have been noted. The only real difference between this and the 'Meccano'/Meccano only 'Magic Carpets' was the long and detailed introduction which was in effect a review of civil engineering as at 1928. This important publication was reproduced in full in Volume 2 of this series and anyone wishing for further details should refer to that.

All of these publicity booklets were in addition to the normal products catalogues issued each year. Their function was purely promotional, the sort of thing sent out to those whose names were passed on under the '. . . if you send us the names and addresses of three of your chums we will send you . . . free of charge' system. This was a very cunning way of latching on to potential buyers and was probably the next best thing to the present practice of buying a computer file of names and addresses. As was usually the case, Meccano Ltd did not lag behind when it came to creative marketing.

MECCANO

Strong, Sturdy, Realistic Models

All Meccano models are strong and sturdy because of the quality and precision of the parts. Meccano models are real models. The Meccano Clock is a real Clock—it keeps accurate time. The Meccano Loom is a real Loom—it weaves beautiful material. The Meccano Motor Chassis—with Ackermann Steering, Gear Box and Differential—so closely resembles a real motor car that it is used for teaching students at numerous schools of motoring. It is the same with all other Meccano models—they are accurate reproductions of the real thing.

The following details of the system are of interest:—

1. STRONG METAL—STURDY MODELS. Meccano Strips and Girders are made of finest quality steel and are roll-machine surfaced. All models built with these Strips and Girders are strong and sturdy.

2. NO TURNED OVER EDGES. All Meccano Strips and Girders are flat. Only *flat* Strips and Girders can be bolted rigidly together to make perfect joints.

3. CURVED FLAT STRIPS. There are Curved Flat Strips in the Meccano System. These parts are invaluable, for they greatly add to the strength and graceful lines of those models in which they are used.

4. ALL PARTS WITH EQUIDISTANT HOLES. All Meccano parts have the equidistant holes, set ½-in. apart and spaced to 1/1000 inch, giving connections or bearings exactly where required.

The Finest Hobby in the World

5. COLOURED PARTS. All Meccano Strips and Plates are beautifully enamelled in pleasing shades that bring out the full beauty of the models.

6. CORRECTLY CUT GEAR WHEELS. Meccano Gear Wheels are cut and tested in exactly the same manner as gear wheels used for real engineering purposes. They are cut with 133, 57, 50, 38, 25 and 19 teeth that give useful ratios, no matter what combination is required.

7. MANY NEW AND SPECIAL PARTS. New Meccano parts are always being invented in order to keep Meccano model-building in line with the most modern engineering requirements.

8. INTERCHANGEABLE PARTS. Meccano parts are interchangeable and will build an endless number of models without being spoiled in the process. They may be used over and over again.

9. MECCANO IS ELECTRIFIED. Dozens of interesting and useful electrical experiments may be made with Meccano. Galvanometers, Shocking Coils, Telegraph systems, Electro Magnets, and many other interesting electrical models are all within the range of Meccano.

10. INSTRUCTIONS FOR BUILDING. Full instructions are provided with every Outfit, the Manual included containing a number of illustrations and details that make model-building delightfully simple.

Page 3

Fig 77.

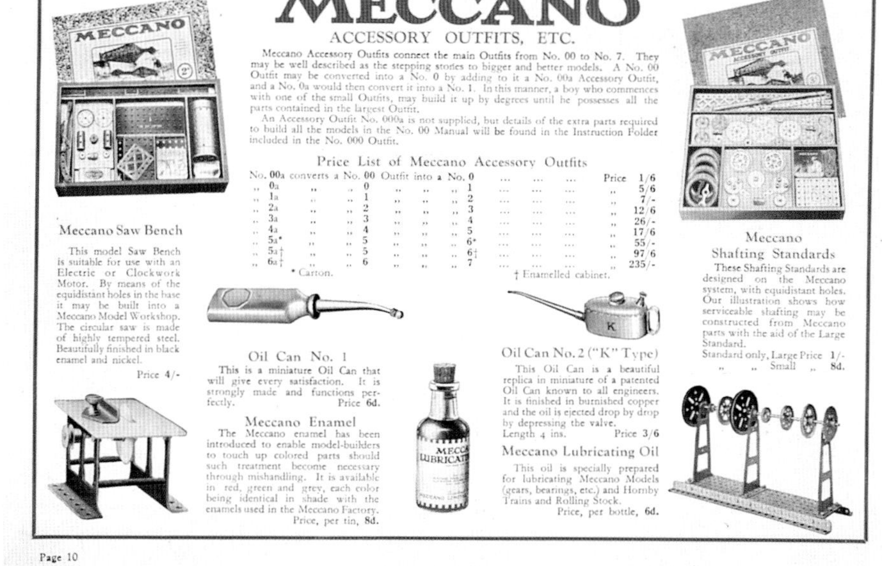

MECCANO

ACCESSORY OUTFITS, ETC.

Meccano Accessory Outfits connect the main Outfits from No. 00 to No. 7. They may be well described as the stepping stones to bigger and better models. A No. 00 Outfit may be converted into a No. 0 by adding to it a No. 00a Accessory Outfit, and a No. 0a would then convert it into a No. 1. In this manner, a boy who commences with one of the small Outfits, may build it up by degrees until he possesses all the parts contained in the largest Outfit.

An Accessory Outfit No. 000a is not supplied, but details of the extra parts required to build all the models in the No. 00 Manual will be found in the Instruction Folder included in the No. 000 Outfit.

Price List of Meccano Accessory Outfits

No. 00a	converts a No. 00	Outfit into a No. 0	... ...	Price 1/6
,, 0a	,, ,, 0	,, ,, ,, 1	... ...	,, 5/6
,, 1a	,, ,, 1	,, ,, ,, 2	... ...	,, 7/-
,, 2a	,, ,, 2	,, ,, ,, 3	... ...	,, 12/6
,, 3a	,, ,, 3	,, ,, ,, 4	... ...	,, 26/-
,, 4a	,, ,, 4	,, ,, ,, 5	... ...	,, 17/6
,, 5a*	,, ,, 5	,, ,, ,, 6*	... ...	,, 55/-
,, 5a†	,, ,, 5	,, ,, ,, 6†	... ...	,, 97/6
,, 6a†	,, ,, 6	,, ,, ,, 7	... ...	,, 235/-

* Carton. † Enamelled cabinet.

Meccano Saw Bench

This model Saw Bench is suitable for use with an Electric or Clockwork Motor. By means of the equidistant holes in the base it may be built into a Meccano Model Workshop. The circular saw is made of highly tempered steel. Beautifully finished in black enamel and nickel.

Price 4/-

Oil Can No. 1

This is a miniature Oil Can that will give every satisfaction. It is strongly made and functions perfectly. Price 6d.

Meccano Enamel

The Meccano enamel has been introduced to enable model-builders to touch up colored parts should such treatment become necessary through mishandling. It is available in red, green and grey, each color being identical in shade with the enamels used in the Meccano Factory. Price, per tin, 8d.

Oil Can No. 2 ("K" Type)

This Oil Can is a beautiful replica in miniature of a patented Oil Can known to all engineers. It is finished in burnished copper and the oil is ejected drop by drop by depressing the valve.
Length 4 ins. Price 3/6

Meccano Lubricating Oil

This oil is specially prepared for lubricating Meccano Models (gears, bearings, etc.) and Hornby Trains and Rolling Stock.
Price, per bottle, 6d.

Meccano Shafting Standards

These Shafting Standards are designed on the Meccano system, with equidistant holes. Our illustration shows how serviceable shafting may be constructed from Meccano parts with the aid of the Large Standard.
Standard only, Large Price 1/-
,, ,, Small ,, 8d.

Page 10

Fig 78.

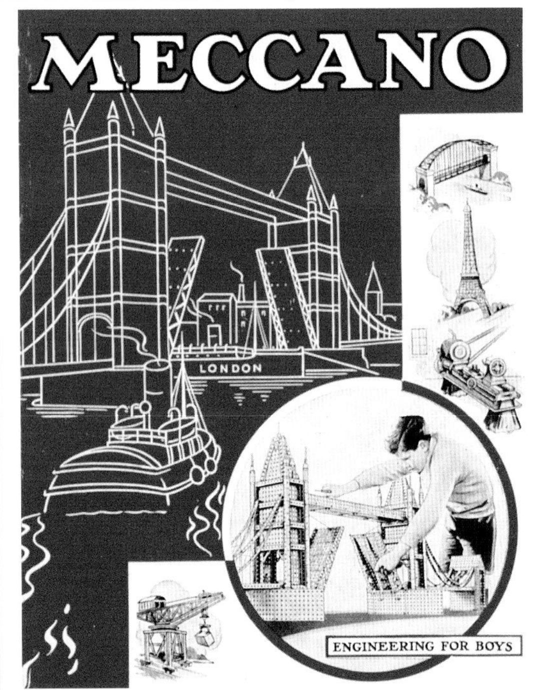

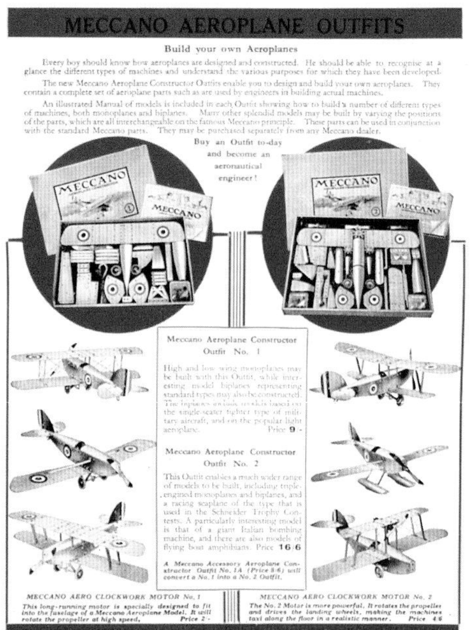

MECCANO AEROPLANE OUTFITS

Build your own Aeroplanes

Every boy should know how aeroplanes are designed and constructed. He should be able to recognise at a glance the different types of machines and understand the various purposes for which they have been developed.

The new Meccano Aeroplane Constructor Outfits enable you to design and build your own aeroplanes. They contain a complete set of aeroplane parts such as are used by engineers in building actual machines.

An illustrated Manual of models is included in each Outfit showing how to build a number of different types of machines, both monoplanes and biplanes. Many other splendid models may be built by varying the positions of the parts, which are all interchangeable on the famous Meccano principle. These parts can be used in conjunction with the standard Meccano parts. They may be purchased separately from any Meccano dealer.

Buy an Outfit to-day and become an aeronautical engineer!

Meccano Aeroplane Constructor Outfit No. 1

High and low wing monoplanes may be built with this Outfit, while interesting model biplanes representing standard types may also be constructed. The biplanes include models based on the single-seater fighter type of military aircraft, and on the popular light aeroplane. Price 9/-

Meccano Aeroplane Constructor Outfit No. 2

This Outfit enables a much wider range of models to be built, including triple-engined monoplanes and biplanes, and a racing seaplane of the type that is used in the Schneider Trophy Contests. A particularly interesting model is that of a giant Italian bombing machine, and there are also models of flying boat amphibians. Price 16/6

A Meccano Accessory Aeroplane Constructor Outfit No. 1A (Price 8/6) will convert a No. 1 into a No. 2 Outfit.

MECCANO AERO CLOCKWORK MOTOR No. 1

This long-running motor is specially designed to fit into the fuselage of a Meccano Aeroplane Model. It will rotate the propeller at high speed. Price 2/-

MECCANO AERO CLOCKWORK MOTOR No. 2

The No. 2 Motor is more powerful. It rotates the propeller and drives the landing wheels, making the machines taxi along the floor in a realistic manner. Price 4/6

Page 3

Figs 79–82.
1931 MECCANO.
Note new vertical format.

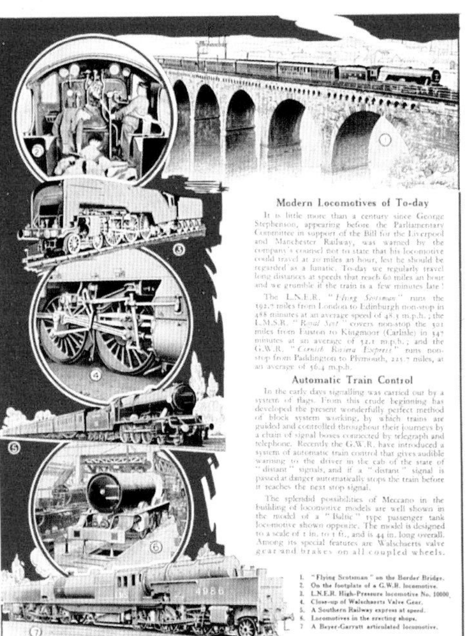

Modern Locomotives of To-day

It is little more than a century since George Stephenson, appearing before the Parliamentary Committee in support of the Bill for the Liverpool and Manchester Railway, was warned by the company's counsel not to state that his locomotive could travel at 20 miles an hour, lest he should be regarded as a lunatic. To-day we regularly travel long distances at speeds that reach 60 miles an hour and we grumble if the train is a few minutes late!

The L.N.E.R. "*Flying Scotsman*" runs the 392.7 miles from London to Edinburgh non-stop in 488 minutes at an average speed of 48.3 m.p.h.; the L.M.S.R. "*Royal Scot*" covers non-stop the 301 miles from Euston to Kingmoor (Carlisle) in 347 minutes at an average of 52.1 m.p.h.; and the G.W.R. "*Cornish Riviera Express*" runs non-stop from Paddington to Plymouth, 225.7 miles, at an average of 56.4 m.p.h.

Automatic Train Control

In the early days signalling was carried out by a system of flags. From this crude beginning has developed the present wonderfully perfect method of block system working, by which trains are guided and controlled throughout their journeys by a chain of signal boxes connected by telegraph and telephone. Recently the G.W.R. have introduced a system of automatic train control that gives audible warning to the driver in the cab of the state of "distant" signals, and if a "distant" signal is passed at danger automatically stops the train before it reaches the next stop signal.

The splendid possibilities of Meccano in the building of locomotive models are well shown in the model of a "Baltic" type passenger tank locomotive shown opposite. The model is designed to a scale of 1 in. to 1 ft., and is 44 in. long overall. Among its special features are Walschaerts valve gear and brakes on all coupled wheels.

1. "Flying Scotsman" on the Border Bridge.
2. On the footplate of a G.W.R. locomotive.
3. L.N.E.R. High-Pressure locomotive No. 10000.
4. Close-up of Walschaerts Valve Gear.
5. A Southern Railway express at speed.
6. Locomotives in the erecting shops.
7. A Beyer-Garratt articulated locomotive.

Page 8

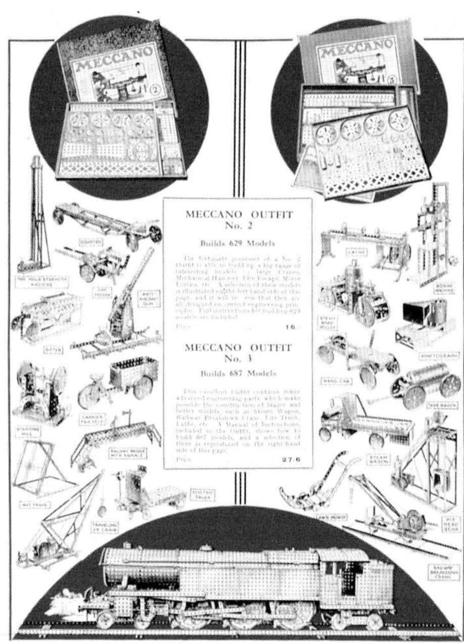

MECCANO OUTFIT No. 2

Builds 629 Models

The fortunate possessor of a No. 2 Outfit is able to build up a big range of interesting models — large Cranes, Mechanical Hammer, Fire Escape, Motor Lorries, etc. A selection of these models is illustrated on the left hand side of this page, and it will be seen that they are all designed on correct engineering principles. Full instructions for building 629 models are included.

Price 16/-

MECCANO OUTFIT No. 3

Builds 687 Models

This excellent Outfit contains many advanced engineering parts, which make possible the construction of bigger and better models, such as Steam Wagon, Railway Breakdown Crane, Fire Truck, Lathe, etc. A Manual of Instructions, included in the Outfit, shows how to build 687 models, and a selection of these is reproduced on the right hand side of this page.

Price 27/6

Meccano Model of a Baltic Tank Locomotive

Page 9

MECCANO AEROPLANE

Boys! Build realistic models of the World's Aircraft

Every boy should know how aeroplanes are designed and constructed. He should be able to recognise at a glance the different types of machines and understand the various purposes for which they have been developed.

The new Meccano Aeroplane Constructor Outfits enable you to design and build your own aeroplanes. An illustrated Manual of models is included in each Outfit showing how to build a number of different types of machines. Many other splendid models may be built by varying the positions of the parts, which are all interchangeable on the famous Meccano principle. The parts in the Nos. 1 and 2 Outfits can be used in conjunction with the standard Meccano parts.

Buy an Outfit to-day and become an aeronautical engineer!

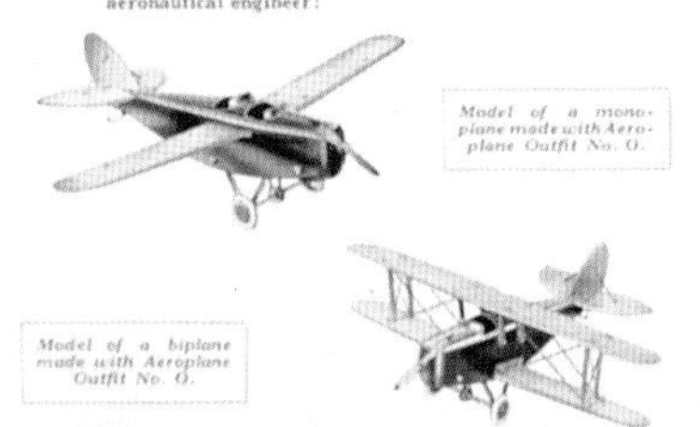

Model of a monoplane made with Aeroplane Outfit No. O.

Model of a biplane made with Aeroplane Outfit No. O.

Meccano Aeroplane Constructor Outfit No. O

The parts contained in this splendid Outfit enable an interesting range of aeroplane models to be built. The illustrated instruction folder that is included gives examples of high and low-wing monoplanes, seaplanes, standard light biplanes and an imposing light seaplane. All the parts are interchangeable. The parts in the No. O Outfit are smaller than those in Outfits Nos. 1 and 2, and are not intended for use with the larger Outfits. Price 5/-

Page 12

Fig 83. Page from the rare 1932 edition of MECCANO.

Figs 84–88.
1933 edition,
probably the most comprehensive
of the series.

MECCANO MOTOR CAR CONSTRUCTOR OUTFITS

Meccanto 538189

Every boy who is keen on model-building will ardently desire one of the fine Motor Car Constructor Outfits described on these pages.
Sports four-seaters, coupés, speed cars, and other perfect miniature reproductions of many different types of car can be built with these Outfits. All the models are driven by means of a powerful clockwork motor (included in the Outfit,) giving a long, speedy and realistic run on each winding.
The motor car parts are finished in rich enamel and nickel or chromium plate, the complete Outfits being masterpieces of miniature automobile craftsmanship. Make up your mind now to own one of these splendid Outfits!

No. 1 MOTOR CAR OUTFIT

A range of superb motor car models can be built with this Outfit. Look at the examples illustrated on this page, and think of the fun you could have building this and other types equally graceful and realistic.

No. 1 Outfit is available in four different colour combinations—red and light blue, light blue and cream, green and yellow, and cream and red. It is supplied complete with powerful Clockwork Motor... ... ... Price **14/6**

Built-up Models

Built-up models of motor cars made with No. 1 Outfit are available at the following prices:—

Road Racer ... **14/6** Sports Tourer (with hood) **15/-**
Sports Tourer ... **14/6** Saloon Coupe **15/6**

Choice Range of Colours

If extra parts in any of the colours mentioned above are required they may be purchased from any Meccano dealer. By adding separate parts in various colours you are able to construct models in a number of pleasing combinations, thus adding considerably to the interest.

In addition to the four standard colour combinations, the following No. 1 Outfit parts are available in the colours indicated:—

Body Sections: orange, yellow. Wheels: orange, yellow. Wings: orange, green.

IMPORTANT.—It should be noted that the No. 1 Motor Car Outfit parts cannot be used in conjunction with those of the No. 2 Outfit.

MOTOR CAR GARAGE

The Meccano Motor Car Garage provides accommodation for any Meccano model motor car or other car of suitable size. It is strongly built, with imitation rough-cast finish. Inside dimensions: Height, 5 in.; length, 13 in.; width, 7¾ in. Price **7/-**

Sports Tourer

Sports Tourer (with hood)

Road Racer

Page 18 Model of a Saloon Coupé built with No. 1 Motor Car Outfit

No. 2 MOTOR CAR OUTFIT

Larger models of a superior type can be built with No. 2 Motor Car Outfit. They are all perfectly designed, beautifully finished, and the most attractive examples of constructional engineering ever produced. Their handsome and realistic appearance may be judged from the illustrations on this page.

No. 2 Outfit is available in four different colour combinations—red and light blue, light blue and cream, green and yellow, and cream and red. A powerful Clockwork Motor that gives a run of 150 feet on one winding is included ... Price **25/-**

Built-up Models

Built-up models of any of the Motor Cars that can be made with No. 2 Outfit are available, if required Price **25/-** each.

Choice Range of Colours

Extra parts in any of the colours mentioned above may be purchased from any Meccano dealer.

In addition to the four standard colour combinations the following No. 2 Outfit parts are available in the colours indicated:—

Body Sections: orange, yellow. Wheels: orange, yellow. Wings: orange, green.

MOTOR CAR LIGHTING SET

This Lighting Set enables the headlamps of Motor Car models built with the 1933 No. 2 Motor Car Outfit to be electrically lighted ... ... Price **2/6**

It should be noted that the Lighting Set cannot be used with 1932 type Motor Car Outfit models unless the latest Headlamps (price **4d.** each) and Instrument Board (price **6d.**) are added.

Light Six Speed Model

Grand Prix Special

Light Sports Two Seater

Model of a Sports Car built with a No. 2 Motor Car Outfit Page 19

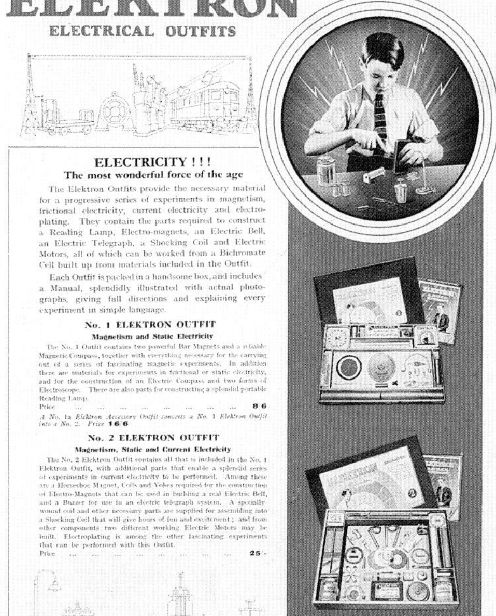

ELEKTRON

ELECTRICAL OUTFITS

ELECTRICITY!!!
The most wonderful force of the age

The Elektron Outfits provide the necessary material for a progressive series of experiments in magnetism, frictional electricity, current electricity and electro-plating. They contain the parts required to construct a Reading Lamp, Electro-magnets, an Electric Bell, an Electric Telegraph, a Shocking Coil and Electric Motors, all of which can be worked from a Bichromate Cell built up from materials included in the Outfit.

Each Outfit is packed in a handsome box, and includes a Manual, splendidly illustrated with actual photographs, giving full directions and explaining every experiment in simple language.

No. 1 ELEKTRON OUTFIT
Magnetism and Static Electricity

The No. 1 Outfit contains two powerful Bar Magnets and a reliable Magnetic Compass, together with everything necessary for the carrying out of a series of fascinating magnetic experiments. In addition there are materials for experiments in frictional or static electricity, and for the construction of an Electric Compass and two forms of Electroscope. There are also parts for constructing a splendid portable Reading Lamp.
Price **8/6**

A No. 1a Elektron Accessory Outfit converts a No. 1 Elektron Outfit into a No. 2. Price **16/6**

No. 2 ELEKTRON OUTFIT
Magnetism, Static and Current Electricity

The No. 2 Elektron Outfit contains all that is included in the No. 1 Elektron Outfit, with additional parts that enable a splendid series of experiments in current electricity to be performed. Among these are a Horseshoe Magnet, Coils and Yokes required for the construction of Electro-Magnets that can be used in building a real Electric Bell, and a Buzzer for use in an electric telegraph system. A specially wound coil and other necessary parts are supplied for assembling into a Shocking Coil that will give hours of fun and excitement; and from other components two different working Electric Motors may be built. Electroplating is among the other fascinating experiments that can be performed with this Outfit.
Price **25/-**

Page 21

HORNBY SPEED BOATS

This is the Hornby Speed Boat Club Badge. It may be purchased from your dealer, price 6d.

The 1933 Hornby Speed Boats are the finest examples of miniature speed boat construction ever seen. Their remarkable performance, perfect design, and beautiful appearance definitely establish them as the leaders in their class.

When other boats are slowing up, the Hornby Speed Boats are still good for an exciting final dash. The special design of the propeller and the unique methods employed in the construction of the hull give each model exceptional speed and length of run. Every line and every feature of the Hornby Speed Boats emphasises their excellent qualities—power, speed and reliability.

Each Hornby Speed Boat in the series is available in three different colour combinations.

	Length	Beam	Price
HORNBY SPEED BOAT No. 1. Will travel over 160 feet on one winding ...	8½in.	2⅜in.	**3/11**
HORNBY SPEED BOAT No. 2 Will travel over 300 feet on one winding ...	12½in.	3in.	**7/6**
HORNBY SPEED BOAT No. 3. Will travel over 500 feet on one winding ...	16½in.	3½in.	**12/6**
HORNBY LIMOUSINE BOAT No. 4. Will travel over 500 feet on one winding ...	16½in.	3½in.	**15/6**
HORNBY CABIN CRUISER No. 5. Will travel over 500 feet on one winding ...	16½in.	3½in.	**16/6**

Hornby Cabin Cruiser No. 5

Hornby Limousine Boat No. 4

Hornby Speed Boat No. 3

Hornby Speed Boat No. 2

Hornby Speed Boat No. 1

PENNANTS

Pennants for Hornby Speed Boats Nos. 3 and 4 may be purchased from any Meccano dealer. Price **2d.** each.

MECCANO LIMITED, BINNS ROAD, LIVERPOOL, 13

Page 24 Printed in England 20/933/20 (C.K.)

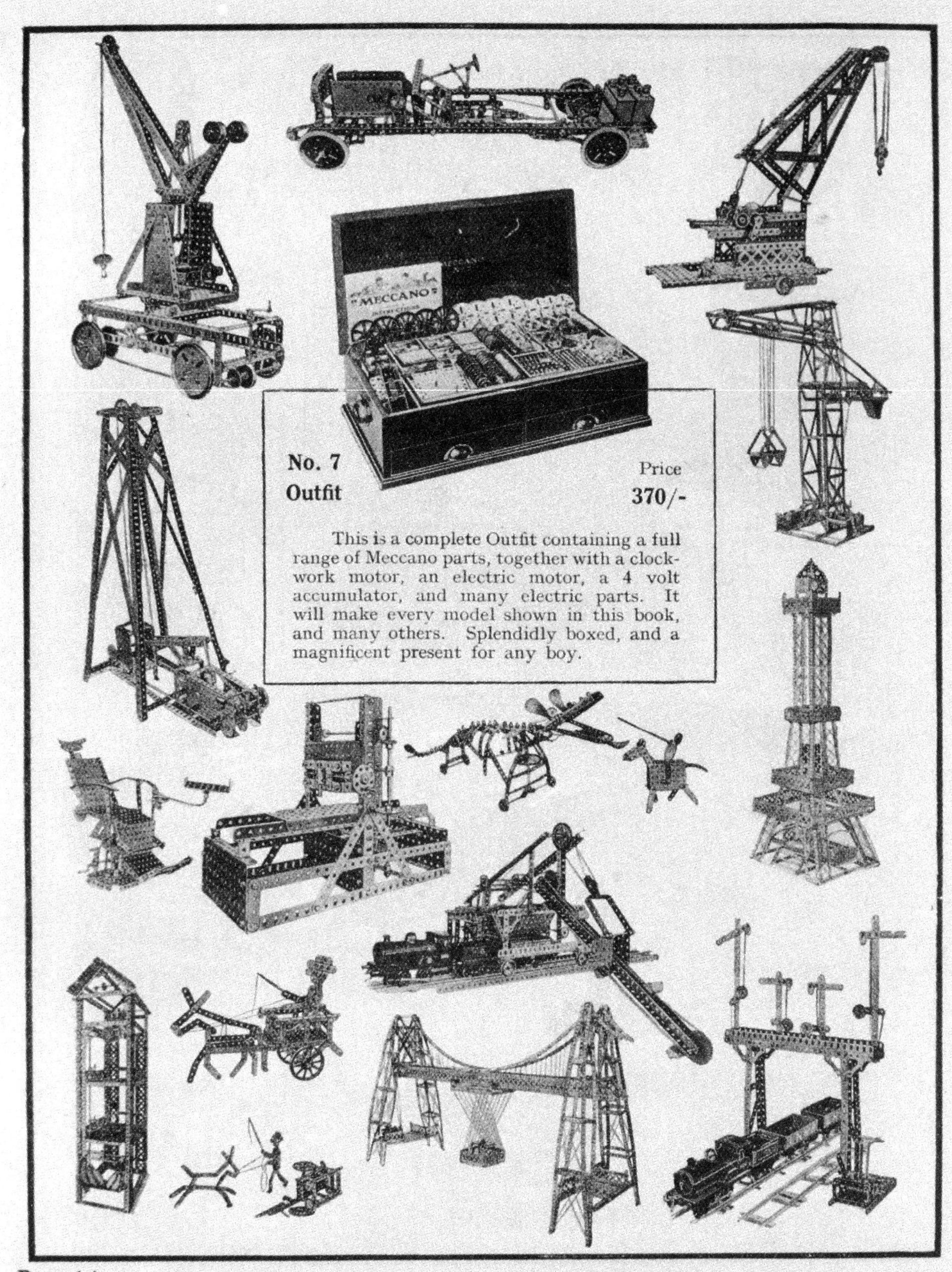

No. 7
Outfit
Price
370/-
This is a complete Outfit containing a full range of Meccano parts, together with a clockwork motor, an electric motor, a 4 volt accumulator, and many electric parts. It will make every model shown in this book, and many others. Splendidly boxed, and a magnificent present for any boy.
Page 14

Products Catalogues (Figs 96–111)

In addition to the promotional material which was produced purely to expand an existing market, Meccano issued many varied products catalogues from 1920 right through to the mid 1960s with breaks only during the war years and between the late 1950s and early 1960s. These catalogues contained full details of most or all currently available products. They should not be confused with the individual and multiple products booklets which are more correctly covered under the heading of Promotional Material. These catalogues sported some of the most colourful and attractive covers the ever produced although the earliest were rather plain as the 1920 edition demonstrates.

In the years before the war, dealers were offered catalogues with their name and address overprinted and with a variety of covers. From the evidence so far seen, it would appear that as many as six were issued at any one time, although fresh discoveries of different covers for a particular year are being made all the time. Not all of these would be new, some were available for several years running. The printing codes for catalogues seem to be the same whatever the cover, which makes it quite impossible to ascertain how many of each cover were produced. There were foreign editions of most catalogues but these generally had similar covers. Print runs were naturally very much lower.

As with much Meccano literature, there is the danger of relying on the illustrations for accurate product information. To give an example, the usual catalogue picture of the blue/gold L outfit is only a reversal of the much earlier No. 7 Outfit but with minor retouching to the plate.

← *Fig 94. Page from the 1925 edition of the Magic Carpet, the cover of which provided the picture and name for this volume.*

MECCANO PRODUCTS

MECCANO OUTFITS
ELECTRICAL OUTFITS
CLOCKWORK TRAINS
STEAM ENGINES
MOTORS, ETC.

Figs 96–99. The 1920 Products catalogue.

MECCANO

WHEN a boy takes up Meccano he begins his life afresh in a land of pleasure and brightness. A Meccano boy's life is different from the life of any other boy. He is a member of a great community of a million other boys, all friends, all with interests, pleasures and work in common. They live in a wonderful world of their own. They have their own newspaper, their clubs and meeting places. They are members of a Guild of boys who have sworn to extend the hand of friendship to each other, to play and work together, and to live clean and upright lives. They have their badges so that they may recognise and know each other wherever they may meet.

The bond which unites them in such close harmony is Meccano, the building system invented by Frank Hornby twenty years ago, and now brought to an extraordinary state of perfection. This book will tell you all about the Meccano hobby, what it is, and what it will do. If you do not actively pursue this hobby you are missing endless fun and pleasure, and sacrificing the friendship and help of a million other clever and contented boys. You are also depriving the other boys of your friendship and help. They want you and they ask you to join them in their happy pursuits.

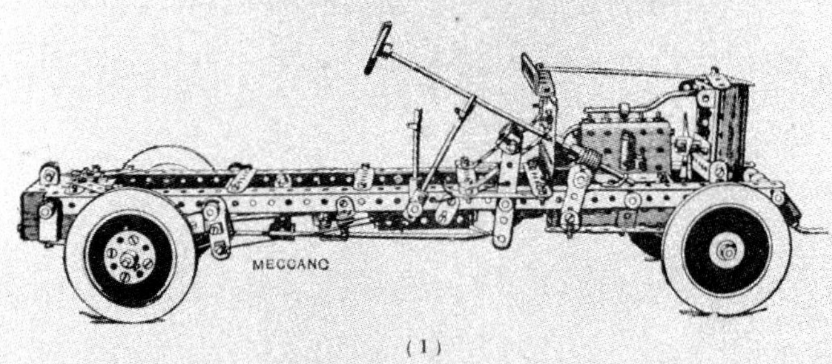

(1)

Fig 97.

MECCANO ELECTRIFIED

THE application of electricity to the Meccano system has added a further and wonderful charm. Nothing could be more fascinating and instructive than to make a loco with Meccano, fix the Meccano Electric Motor inside, attach up the Accumulator, and turn on the current from your own switchboard, making the loco start, pick up speed, slow down and come to a stop, running it through tunnels, over bridges and into sidings; or to fix up a warehouse with several floors, and an elevator worked by electricity, loading up goods and transferring them from one floor to another; or to make a real aerial Morse Signalling apparatus, for signalling messages just as a regular telegraph operator would do; or to make a mechanical Crane for raising and lowering loads by electricity; or to make your own electric Lamp, Induction Coil, and a score of other things. All these things can be done with Meccano, and the Electric side of the hobby is developing rapidly. These new Electrical Outfits contain all the electrical accessories and fittings necessary to make the full range of experiments, with a well illustrated book of instructions which makes everything simple. To the boy who already possesses a Meccano outfit, these Electrical sets are a great boon.

Meccano Electrical Accessory Outfits,

Prices:—X1 (containing electrical parts, without motor or accumulator) ... ... **15s. 0d.**

X2 (containing a Meccano Motor, 4-volt accumulator, and electrical parts) **£2 15s. 0d.**

(12)

Fig 98.

TIN PRINTED CLOCKWORK TRAINS

STRONGLY built, with reliable clockwork mechanism. One size only, Gauge 0. Each set contains Engine, Tender, and two Passenger Cars, printed in close imitation of the colours of the railway companies' rolling stock, with sets of Rails, including a circle and two straights. In London and North-Western, Midland, and Great Northern colours. The engines are fitted with reversing gear, brakes, and regulators.

Complete set, well boxed **22/6**

Engines	**14/-** each.
Tenders	**2/-** ,,
Carriages	**2/-** ,,
Rails, straight or curved	**6/-** per doz.

VERTICAL STEAM ENGINE

A FINELY finished steam engine, superior workmanship; each one carefully tested. Oxidized brass boiler; stationary cylinder, and eccentric reversing gear; whistle, spring safety valve, etc., cast base; fittings nickelled and finely finished. Dimensions of boiler, 2½in. diameter by 3½in. long.

Price ... ... **27/6** each.

(15)

Fig 99.

MECCANO

RADIO RECEIVING SETS

THE Meccano Crystal Receivers are splendid instruments, and their efficiency is guaranteed. The Crystal is a special combination of minerals, and although the effective distance of reception for Crystal Receivers is usually stated to be about 20 miles, a Meccano Receiver No. 1 is regularly receiving telephony with a standard aerial at a distance of 33 miles from the Manchester Broadcasting Station.

No. 1 CRYSTAL RECEIVER

THIS set may be used with a broadcast licence, obtainable at any post office. It is thoroughly tested on a standard aerial before leaving our works.

R.S.1	Meccano No. 1 Crystal Receiving Set, complete, tested and guaranteed	32/6
	Broadcasting Fee, according to regulations ...	7/6
	Price complete	40/-

No. 2 CRYSTAL RECEIVER

(Constructive type)

THIS set may only be used under an experimental licence, to be obtained from the Post-Master General to whom application should be made for the necessary form. Full instructions for assembling the parts are included with each Outfit.

Efficiency guaranteed.

R.S.2	Outfit containing parts to make Receiving Set, in strong carton ...	25/-
R.S.2a	,, ,, without phone	15/-

MECCANO AERIAL OUTFIT

The Meccano Aerial Outfit contains everything for the erection of a regulation aerial with the exception of the poles. The contents are as follows :—Antenna 65 ft. 18 G. Bare Copper Wire. Lead-in (soldered to Antenna) 29 ft. 16 G. Bare Copper Wire coupled to 6 ft. of Insulated 16 G. Bare Copper Wire. Earth Wire 30 ft. 18 G. Bare Copper Wire. Insulators (egg-shaped) 2, Pulleys (porcelain) 2.

Price 12/6

PRICES OF MECCANO RADIO PARTS

No.		s.	d.
403.	Insulating Triangular Plates, 2¼" (for Condenser) ... ... each	0	1
404.	Insulating Handles ... ,,	0	3
405.	Brass Washers, 1/32" ... doz.	0	4
406.	9" lengths 22G Bell Wire with Tags ... ... each	0	2
407.	Inductance Discs, hinged (Wave length approx. 500 metres) ... ... pair	4	0
407a.	Inductance Discs, hinged (not wound) ... ... each	1	0
408.	Single Telephone Receivers (2,000 Ohms) ... ,,	10	0
409.	Detector Arms, complete ,,	1	0
410.	Crystals, mounted (complete with clips No. 411) ,,	1	6
410a.	Crystals, mounted, only ,,	1	3
411.	Clips for Crystals ... ,,	0	3
412.	Mounting Boards, complete with labels ... ,,	5	0
413.	Condensers, complete ... ,,	5	6
414.	Detectors, complete, as contained in outfit of parts RS2 ... ... each	3	0
415.	Inductances, complete ,,	5	6
421.	Sliding Contacts with Rods and Brackets, complete ... ... ,,	4	6
422.	Sliding Contacts only ... ,,	1	6
423.	Pointers for Sliding Contacts ... ... ,,	0	4
424.	Rods, 5/32" Whitworth thread at ends ... ,,	0	4
425.	Brackets for Sliding Contacts Right ,,	0	3
425a.	,, ,, Left ,,	0	3
441.	Detectors, complete, as fitted to Meccano C.R.S. No. 1 ... ... ,,	4	3
442.	Detector Rods ... ... ,,	0	3
443.	Sleeves for Detector Rods ,,	0	6
444.	Cat Whiskers ... ... ,,	0	1
445.	Ball Brackets with 6 B.A. Screws ... ... ,,	0	4
446.	Plain Brackets ... ... ,,	0	2
447.	Glasses for Detectors ... each	0	4
448.	Caps for Detector Glasses, Crystal Ends ... ... ,,	0	4
449.	Caps for Detector Glasses, Detector Ends ... ,,	0	4
461.	Inductances, complete with Scales ... ... ,,	4	6
462.	Inductances, wound ... ,,	2	3
463.	,, Tube ... ,,	0	4
464.	Ends for Inductance Tubes ... ... ,,	0	6
465.	Stay Bolts for Inductance Tubes ... ... ,,	0	4
466.	Metric Scales ... ... ,,	0	6
467.	Special Insulating Washers doz.	0	6
481.	Hexagonal Nuts, tapped 5/32" Whitworth thread ,,	1	6
482.	Small Terminals, 5/32" Whitworth thread ... each	0	2
483.	Large Terminals, tapped 5/32" Whitworth thread ,,	0	2
484.	Bifurcated Rivets ... doz.	0	2
485.	Indication Labels (Phone, Earth and Aerial) ... each	0	1

8

ZULU CLOCK WORK TRAINS

Guarantee

Zulu Trains are tested and their efficiency is guaranteed. A form of Guarantee is furnished with each loco, and we undertake to repair or replace, at our option, any loco that fails to run satisfactorily from any cause other than misuse, within 60 days of date of purchase.

PASSENGER SET

Fine and durable mechanism, and strength of construction in all parts are the main characteristics of this new type of clockwork train. The Zulu Loco is well designed and efficient, and will give long and excellent service. Richly enamelled and highly finished; fitted with brake and governor; non-reversing.

Each set contains Loco, Tender, two Passenger Coaches and set of rails, consisting of two straights, and curves to form a circle of 2 ft. diameter.

Gauge 0, in black only, packed in strong cardboard box .. 25/-

ZULU GOODS SET

The Goods Set is the same as the Passenger Set but contains one Wagon in place of Passenger Coaches.

Gauge 0, in black only, packed in strong cardboard box, 18/6

Zulu Locos each 10/6 Zulu Tenders each 2/6 Zulu Passenger Coaches each 5/-

Zulu Wagons each 3/-

11

Figs 100–101. Extracts from the 1923 catalogue.

Fig 101.

MECCANO

THE TOY THAT MADE ENGINEERING FAMOUS

When a boy makes Meccano model-building his hobby he learns the secrets of real engineering in the best of all ways, for he builds with real engineering parts in miniature, all standardised and interchangeable. Meccano Strips and Plates are made of heavy steel and the big range of Meccano Gears and Pinions are all machine cut from the finest brass.

Every detail of a Meccano model follows correct engineering practice. There is scope for invention with Meccano, too, for one of its chief delights is the facility it offers for designing new mechanisms and structures, and also for trying out new ideas in model form.

This year Meccano Outfits are bigger and better than ever. They all contain a greater number and wider selection of parts than previously, enabling hundreds of new models to be built.

A selection of Meccano Super Models, showing the wonderful possibilities of the system, is illustrated on the opposite page

This splendid model of a Transporter Bridge, built entirely with Meccano, is only one of hundreds of perfect models that can be constructed by any boy.

The Meccano boy of to-day will build the Bridges of to-morrow

928/400

A Few Choice Meccano Models

Tank Locomotive

Loom

Roundabout

Steam Shovel

Ship Coaler

Giant Block-Setting Crane

Planing Machine

THE WORLD'S MOST FAMOUS TOY

1

Figs 102–103. Extracts from the 1928 catalogue.

HORNBY CONTROL SYSTEM

THE Hornby Control System enables you to manipulate Signals and Points in conjunction with the running of your trains by the operation of levers in your Signal Cabin No. 2. The installation of the system is quite a simple matter, no phase of it presenting any difficulty whatever. Large or small railway layouts may be operated with equal ease.

In order to obtain the fullest benefits from a Hornby Control Outfit the locomotive must be of a special type (fitted for Control). With certain limitations, however, the Control System may be utilised successfully with all Hornby Locomotives.

Ask your dealer for a copy of the Hornby Control System Folder, which gives full details of this splendid system.

Hornby Control Outfits

No. 1 Outfit, complete (for use with the M Series, No. O and No. 1 Locomotives). Price 35/-

No. 2 Outfit, complete (for use with No. 2, No. 3c and Metropolitan C Locomotives). Price 35/-

HORNBY TANK LOCOMOTIVES

No. 1 TANK LOCOMOTIVE. Fitted with brake mechanism and reversing gear. In L.M.S.R., G.W.R., L.N.E.R. or S.R. colours. Gauge 0 ... ... Price 12/6

***No. 1 TANK LOCOMOTIVE,** fitted for Hornby Control ... ... Price 15/-

No. 2 TANK LOCOMOTIVE. Fitted with brake mechanism and reversing gear. In L.M.S.R., G.W.R., L.N.E.R. or S.R. colours. Price 22/6

***No. 2 TANK LOCOMOTIVE,** fitted for Hornby Control ... ... Price 25/-

* *See top of page.*

STATIONS AND PLATFORMS

Hornby Series **Gauge 0**

RAILWAY STATION No. 1. Length 16¾ in., width 6 in., height 6 in. This Station is a well-made model, richly finished in bright colours. By placing one or more of these Stations at intervals along the track, and using the Railway Station No. 2 as the main terminus, a very realistic effect is given to a miniature railway layout ... ... Price 5/-

RAILWAY STATION No. 2 (Illustrated.) Excellent model, beautifully designed. Built up with three detachable sections. Length 2 ft. 9 in., breadth 6 in., height 7 in. Price 10/-

GOODS PLATFORM. Length 16¾ in., height 6¾ in., width 6 in. The crane at the end of the platform revolves on its base and is fitted with crank and ratchet mechanism for controlling the load ... ... Price 10/6

PASSENGER PLATFORM. Length 16¾ in., width 3 in. This platform may be connected to the main station or used separately. A length of white paled fencing is supplied. The device at each end enables a number of these platforms to be joined together. Price 3/6

White paled fencing may also be purchased separately ... ... Price, per length, 6d.

ISLAND PLATFORM. Length 32½ in., height 6¾ in., width 3 in. The ramps at either end are detachable, and if desired the platform may be connected to the main station. Price 7/6

The ramps may be purchased separately ... ... Price, per pair 1/6

BRITISH AND GUARANTEED

18

HORNBY ACCESSORIES

SIGNAL CABIN No. 2
Dimensions: Height 6½ in., width 3½ in., length 6½ in. Finished in colours. Roof and back open to allow Lever Frame to be fitted inside cabin if desired. Price 6/6

LATTICE GIRDER BRIDGE
Constructional type. Strong and well proportioned. Price 9/6

SIGNAL CABIN No. 1
Finished in colours. Price 2/9

TUNNEL
Realistic and finished in colours. Price 7/6

MANSELL WHEELS
These wheels are die-cast and are correctly designed. They may be fitted to Hornby Wagons, Vans, Coaches, etc., if desired. Price, per pair, 4d.

JUNCTION SIGNAL
"Home" or "Distant." Signal arms operated by levers at base. A very realistic model. Price 5/6

TELEGRAPH POLE
Price per pair 3/6

DOUBLE ARM SIGNAL No. 1
Price, per pair, 3/9
DOUBLE ARM SIGNAL No. 2 (as illustrated) Price 3/- each

SIGNAL No. 1
Price per pair 3/-
SIGNAL No. 2 (as illustrated) "Home" or "Distant" available each 2/6

PLATFORM CRANE
The Crane is fitted with a crank and ratchet mechanism. Price 4/-

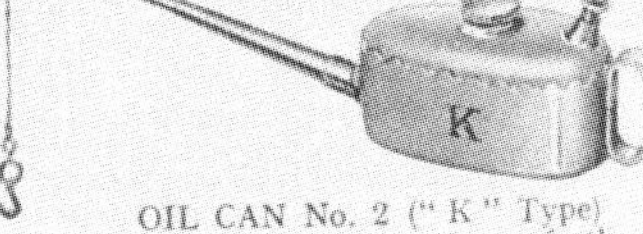

OIL CAN No. 2 ("K" Type)
This miniature Oil Can operates perfectly. The oil is ejected drop by drop by depressing the valve. Copper finish. Price 3/6

OIL CAN No. 1
This is a miniature Oil Can that will give every satisfaction. Finished in nickel. Price 6d.

(For Lubricating Oil see page 7).

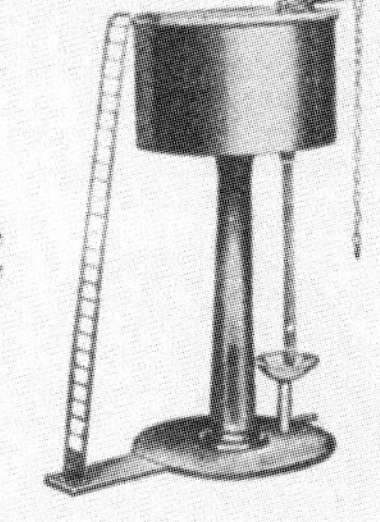

WATER TANK
Brightly coloured. Fitted with flexible tube and valve lever. Price 6/6

BRITISH AND GUARANTEED

19

HORNBY CLOCKWORK TRAINS

BRITISH AND GUARANTEED

Hornby Metropolitan Train Set C

METROPOLITAN TRAIN SET C

THIS set contains a powerful Clockwork Locomotive, two Metropolitan Coaches and set of Rails (including a Brake and Reverse Rail) to form an oval track measuring 6 ft. by 4 ft. 3 ins. The Locomotive and Coaches are modelled on the Electric Passenger Rolling stock of the famous Metropolitan Railway. Gauge 0 ... ... Price 55/-

The Locomotive and Coaches of this Set may be purchased separately, if required. The prices are as follows :—

Metropolitan Clockwork Locomotive C ... Price 22/6   Metropolitan Coach C ... Price 13/6

Hornby No. 3C Riviera " Blue " Train

THE No. 3C CLOCKWORK RIVIERA " BLUE " TRAIN SET contains Clockwork Locomotive, Riviera " Blue " Tender, Riviera " Blue " Dining Car, Riviera " Blue " Sleeping Car and Rails to form an oval track measuring 6 ft. by 4 ft. 3 ins. A Brake and Reverse Rail is included, by means of which the train may be braked and reversed from the track ... Price 62/6

The components of the Hornby Clockwork Riviera " Blue " Train Set may be purchased separately, if required. The prices are as follows :—

Hornby No. 3C Riviera " Blue " Locomotive (without Tender) ... ... Price 27/6
Hornby No. 3 Tender, Riviera " Blue " ... ... „ 5/6
Hornby Riviera " Blue " Dining Car ... ... „ 14/-
Hornby Riviera " Blue " Sleeping Car ... ... „ 14/-

Hornby No. 2 Special Pullman Set, L.N.E.R.

No. 2 SPECIAL PULLMAN SET, L.N.E.R. This set contains Locomotive, Tender, No. 2 Special Pullman Coach, No. 2 Special Pullman Coach Composite and set of Rails (including a Brake and Reverse Rail) to form an oval track measuring 5 ft. 2 ins. by 4 ft. 3 ins. The Locomotive, which is enamelled in green, is named " Yorkshire " and is a model of the famous " Shire " class ... ... Price 67/6

No. 2 SPECIAL PULLMAN SET, L.M.S.R. The contents of this set are as those of the No. 2 Special Pullman Set, L.N.E.R. The Locomotive, which is enamelled in dark red, is numbered 1185 and is a model of the L.M.S. " Standard Compound " class which are not named... ... ... Price 67/6

No. 2 SPECIAL PULLMAN SET, G.W.R. The contents of the set are as those of the No. 2 Special Pullman Set, L.N.E.R. The Locomotive, which is enamelled in Great Western green, is named " County of Bedford " and is a model of the famous " County " class ... Price 67/6

No. 2 SPECIAL PULLMAN SET, S.R. The contents of the set are similar to those of the No. 2 Special Pullman Set, L.N.E.R. The Locomotive, which is enamelled in green, is numbered A759 and is a model of the well-known new " L " class, which are not named. The Tender is also numbered A759 ... ... Price 67/6

The components of the No. 2 Special Pullman Sets may be purchased separately, if required. The prices are as follows :—

Hornby No. 2 Special Passenger Locomotive (without Tender), L.N.E.R., L.M.S.R., G.W.R. or S.R. ... ... Price 27/6
Hornby No. 2 Special Tender (L.N.E.R., L.M.S.R. and G.W.R.) ... ... „ 6/6
Hornby No. 2 Special Tender (S.R. numbered A759) ... ... „ 6/6
Hornby No. 2 Special Pullman Coach ... ... „ 15/-
Hornby No. 2 Special Pullman Coach Composite ... ... „ 16/-

For prices of Rails, Points and Crossings, see pages 30 and 31.

Page 16

HORNBY CLOCKWORK TRAINS

BRITISH AND GUARANTEED

Hornby No. 3C Train Set " Continental Express "

Hornby No. 3 Clockwork Train Sets

THE Hornby No. 3 Clockwork Train Sets are distinctive in design and beautifully enamelled in correct colours. They are available with either Clockwork or Electric Locomotives and in each case the Locomotive carries the name of a famous British Locomotive on the front wheel guards. The Clockwork sets are described below, while full details of the Electric sets are given on page 18. Gauge 0.

HORNBY No. 3C G.W. " CORNISH RIVIERA." This set contains No. 3C Locomotive, No. 2 Special Tender, No. 2 Special Pullman Coach, No. 2 Special Pullman Coach Composite and set of Rails to form an oval track measuring 6 ft. by 4 ft. 3 ins. A Brake and Reverse Rail is included, by means of which the train can be braked and reversed from the track. The train is enamelled in Great Western passenger train colours and the Locomotive is named " Caerphilly Castle " ... ... Price 67/6

HORNBY No. 3C L.M.S. " ROYAL SCOT." The contents of this set are as those of the No. 3C G.W. " Cornish Riviera " Train Set. The train is enamelled in L.M.S. passenger train colours and the Locomotive is named " Royal Scot " ... ... Price 67/6

HORNBY No. 3C L.N.E.R. " FLYING SCOTSMAN." The contents of this set are as those of the Hornby No. 3C G.W. " Cornish Riviera " Train Set. The train is enamelled in L.N.E.R. passenger train colours and the Locomotive is named " Flying Scotsman " ... Price 67/6

HORNBY No. 3C S.R. " CONTINENTAL EXPRESS." The contents of this set are similar to those of the No. 3C G.W. " Cornish Riviera " Train Set. The train is enamelled in S.R. passenger train colours and the Locomotive is named " Lord Nelson." The Tender is numbered " E850 " ... ... Price 67/6

The components of the No. 3 Clockwork Train Sets, detailed above, may be purchased separately, if required. The prices are as follows :—

Hornby No. 3 Clockwork Locomotive, L.M.S., L.N.E.R., G.W. or S.R. (without Tender) ... ... Price 27/6
Hornby No. 2 Special Tender (L.M.S.R., L.N.E.R. or G.W.R.) ... ... „ 6/6
Hornby No. 2 Special Tender (S.R. numbered E850) ... ... „ 6/6
Hornby No. 2 Special Pullman Coach ... ... „ 15/-
Hornby No. 2 Special Pullman Coach Composite ... ... „ 16/-

HORNBY CLOCKWORK TANK LOCOMOTIVES

No. 1 Tank Locomotive

No. 1 Tank Locomotive

This is a strong and durable Locomotive capable of any amount of hard work. It is richly enamelled, highly finished, and is fitted with brake mechanism and reversing gear. In colours to represent L.M.S.R., L.N.E.R., G.W.R. and S.R. Locomotives. Price 12/6

No. 1 Special Tank Locomotive

No. 2 Special Tank Locomotive

This Locomotive is fitted with a very powerful Clockwork mechanism giving great length of run and exceptional pulling power. It is a perfect model, beautifully finished in the colours of the L.M.S., L. N. E., G. W. and Southern Railways. Price 25/-

No. 2 Special Tank Locomotive

No. 1 Special Tank Locomotive

This splendid Locomotive has remarkable power and speed. It is perfect in design and finish and is available in colours of the L.M.S., L. N. E., G. W. and Southern Railways.
Gauge 0. Price 18/-

For prices of Rails, Points and Crossings, see pages 30 and 31.

Page 17

Fig 104. A typical Hornby page from the 1929 catalogue.

MECCANO AEROPLANE CONSTRUCTOR

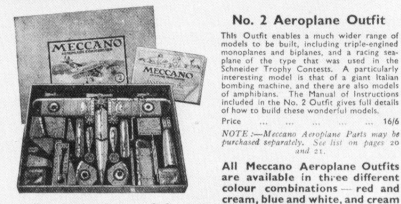

No. 2 Aeroplane Constructor Outfit

No. 2 Aeroplane Outfit

This Outfit enables a much wider range of models to be built, including triple-engined monoplanes and biplanes, and a racing seaplane of the type that was used in the Schneider Trophy Contests. A particularly interesting model is that of a giant Italian bombing machine, and there are also models of amphibians. The Manual of Instructions included in the No. 2 Outfit gives full details of how to build these wonderful models.

Price 16/6

NOTE:—Meccano Aeroplane Parts may be purchased separately. See list on pages 20 and 21.

All Meccano Aeroplane Outfits are available in three different colour combinations — red and cream, blue and white, and cream and green.

Model of a High Wing Monoplane built with No. O Aeroplane Outfit

Model of a Standard Light Biplane built with No. 1 Aeroplane Outfit

No. 1 Aero Clockwork Motor

No. I Aero Clockwork Motor

This long-running Motor is specially designed to fit into the fuselage of Meccano Aeroplane models made with No. 1, No. 2, No. 1 Special or No. 2 Special Aeroplane Outfits. It will rotate the propeller at high speed, thus greatly adding to the realism of the model.

Price 2/-

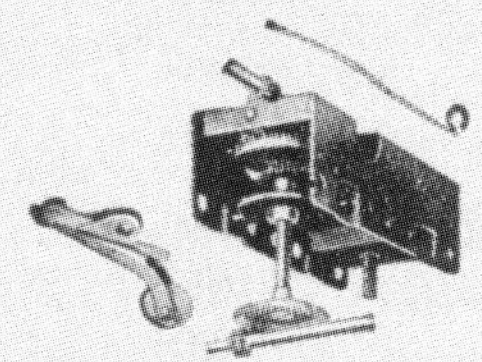
No. 2 Aero Clockwork Motor

No. 2 Aero Clockwork Motor

This is a more powerful Motor. In addition to rotating the propeller it also drives the landing wheels of No. 1 No. 2, No. 1 Special or No. 2 Special Aeroplane Outfit models, making the machines taxi along the floor in a most realistic manner. An Adjustable Tail Wheel is supplied with the Motor.

Price 4/6

RUN YOUR MODELS WITH AN AERO MOTOR

Page 18

AEROPLANE CONSTRUCTOR MECCANO

SPECIAL AEROPLANE OUTFITS

The Special Aeroplane Constructor Outfits have been designed to enable more realistic models of the latest types of aircraft to be built. They contain many new and improved parts. Each Outfit is available in three different colour combinations.

No. I Special Aeroplane Outfit

The parts in this super Aeroplane Outfit will build over 20 realistic models of different types of aircraft. The range of special parts includes main planes fitted with ailerons, tail planes with elevators, movable rudder, radial engine cowling, etc.

The Outfit is available in three different colour combinations—red and cream, blue and white, and green and cream.

Price 15/-

A No. 1a Special Aeroplane Accessory Outfit, Price 11/6, will convert a No. 1 Special Aeroplane Constructor Outfit into a No. 2 Special.

No. 1 Special Aeroplane Outfit

No. 2 Special Aeroplane Outfit

This is the finest and most attractive Aeroplane Constructor Outfit on the market. It contains a big range of aircraft parts, with which numerous models of practically any type of machine may be built—44 examples are shown in the Manual of Instructions. All the parts that are special features of the No. 1 Outfit are included, also a number of other parts of special design. As in the case of the No. 1 Special Outfit, the No. 2 is available in three different colour schemes—red and cream, blue and white, and green and cream.

Price 25/-

Run your Special Aeroplane Outfit models with a Meccano Aero Motor. Details are given on the opposite page.

No. 2 Special Aeroplane Outfit

Model of a Triple-engined Air Liner built with No. 2 Aeroplane Outfit.

Model of a Light Biplane built with No. 2 Special Aeroplane Outfit.

MECCANO TOYS OF QUALITY

Page 19

Figs 105–106. Two pages from the 1934 catalogue.

HORNBY TRAINS ELECTRIC SETS

20-VOLT TRAIN SETS (AUTOMATIC REVERSE)

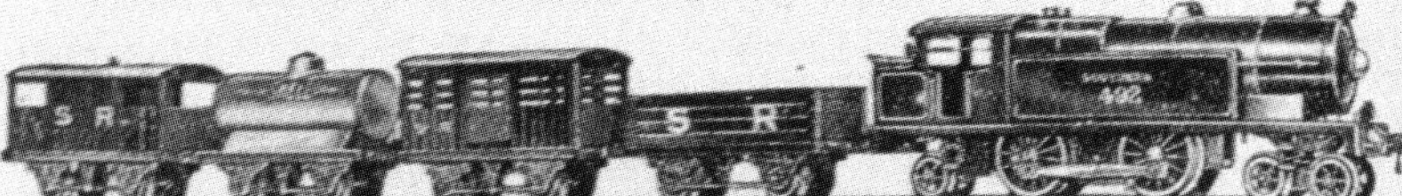

Hornby No. E220 Mixed Goods Train Set (20-volt)

This realistic Goods Set consists of a No. E220 Electric Tank Locomotive (automatic reversing) with electric headlamp, No. 1 Wagon, No. 1 Cattle Truck, Petrol Tank Wagon, Brake Van, and set of electric rails requiring a space measuring 4 ft. 6 in. square. A Terminal Connecting Plate with plug fittings is included for the connection of the power supply (20-volt Transformer) to the track. The set is supplied in L.M.S.R., L.N.E.R., G.W.R. and S.R. colours ... ... Price 47/6

The components of the above Set can be purchased separately at the following prices:

Hornby No. E220 Special Tank Locomotive (automatic reversing) ... ... Price 32/6
No. 1 Wagon ... ... Price 1/9 No. 1 Cattle Truck 2/9
Petrol Tank Wagon ... ... „ 2/- Brake Van 2/11

Hornby No. E320 Riviera "Blue" Passenger Train Set (20-volt)

The Hornby No. E320 Riviera "Blue" train is a model of the famous express that runs regularly between Calais and the Mediterranean Coast. The Set contains a No. E320 Riviera "Blue" Locomotive (automatic reversing) with electric headlamp, No. 3 Riviera "Blue" Tender, Riviera "Blue" Dining Car and Sleeping Car and a set of rails for a space measuring 4 ft. 6 in. square. A Terminal Connecting Plate with plug fittings is included for the connection of the power supply (20-volt Transformer) to the track ... Price 67/6

The components of the No. E320 Riviera "Blue" Train can be purchased separately at the following prices:

Hornby No E320 Riviera "Blue" Locomotive (automatic reversing) ... ... Price 35/-
Hornby No. 3 Riviera "Blue" Tender ... ... „ 4/6
Hornby Riviera "Blue" Dining Car ... Price 12/6 Hornby Riviera "Blue" Sleeping Car „ 12/6

Hornby No. E220 Special Pullman Sets (20-volt)

The Locomotives and Tenders in this series represent famous prototypes of the four British Railway Groups

No. E220 SPECIAL PULLMAN SET, L.N.E.R. This Set contains No. E220 Special Locomotive (automatic reversing) with electric headlamp, No. 2 Special Tender, No. 2 Special Pullman Coach, No. 2 Special Pullman Coach Composite, and set of rails requiring a space measuring 4 ft. 6 in. square. A Terminal Connecting Plate with plug fittings is included for the connection of the power supply (20-volt Transformer) to the track. The Locomotive is named "Yorkshire," and is a model of the "Shire" class. Price 75/-

No. E220 SPECIAL PULLMAN SET, L.M.S.R. The contents of this Set are similar to those of the No. E220 Special Pullman Set L.N.E.R. The Locomotive is No. 1185, and is a model of the L.M.S.R. "Standard Compound" class, which are not named ... ... Price 75/-

No. E220 SPECIAL PULLMAN SET, G.W.R. The contents of this Set are similar to those in the No. E220 Special Pullman Set L.N.E.R. The Locomotive is named "County of Bedford," and is a model of the famous "County" class ... ... Price 75/-

No. E220 SPECIAL PULLMAN SET, S.R. The contents of this Set are similar to those of the No. E220 Special Pullman Set L.N.E.R. The Locomotive is numbered "A759," and is a model of the well-known "L1" class, which are not named. The Tender also bears the number "A759" ... ... Price 75/-

The components of the No. E220 Special Pullman Sets can be purchased separately at the following prices:

Hornby No. E220 Special Loco. (L.N.E.R., L.M.S.R., G.W.R. or S.R.) automatic reversing. Price 37/6
No. 2 Special Tender (L.N.E.R., L.M.S.R., G.W.R. or S.R.) ... ... „ 6/-
No. 2 Special Pullman Coach ... Price 13/- No. 2 Special Pullman Coach Composite ... „ 14/-

READ THE "MECCANO MAGAZINE"

Page 28

ELECTRIC SETS HORNBY TRAINS

20-VOLT TRAIN SETS (AUTOMATIC REVERSE)

Hornby No. E320 Pullman Train Set (20-volt)

These Train Sets are finished in correct colours. Each of the powerful Locomotives (automatic reversing) with electric headlamp, carries the name of a famous British locomotive on the front splasher on each side.

All the doors of the coaches open. Each of the sets consists of a No. E320 Locomotive, No. 2 Special Tender, No. 2 Special Pullman Coach, No. 2 Special Pullman Coach Composite, and a set of electric rails for a space 4ft 6 in. square. A Terminal Connecting Plate is included for connecting a 20-volt Transformer to the track.

Hornby No. E320 Train Set, "The Royal Scot" (L.M.S.R.), "The Flying Scotsman" (L.N.E.R.), "Cornish Riviera" Express (G.W.R.) or "The Golden Arrow" (S.R.) ... ... Price 72/6

The components of the No. E320 Train Set are obtainable separately at the following prices:

Hornby No. E320 Locomotive (automatic reversing) "Royal Scot" (L.M.S.R.), "Flying Scotsman" (L.N.E.R.), "Caerphilly Castle" (G.W.R.), or "Lord Nelson" (S.R.) ... ... Price 35/-
Hornby No. 2 Special Tender, L.M.S.R., L.N.E.R., G.W.R. or S.R (S.R. numbered 850) ... „ 6/-
Hornby No. 2 Special Pullman Coach Price 13/- Hornby No. 2 Special Pullman Coach Composite „ 14/-

Meccano Transformers

Meccano Transformers provide a convenient means of driving 6-volt or 20-volt Electric Trains or Electric Motors from Alternating Current mains.

For all Hornby 6-volt Locomotives (except the EPM16 Special Tank) the No. T6A Transformer is the best. It has plug sockets providing three separate circuits—the first at 9 volts, controlled by a 5-stud speed regulator, for train driving; the second at 9 volts, not controlled by the speed regulator; and the third at 3½ volts, for lighting Hornby Accessories.

Other Meccano Transformers for running 6-volt Locomotives are the No. T6, which has one circuit at 9 volts controlled by a speed regulator; and the No. T6M, which is similar to the T6, but has no speed regulator.

It may be wondered why current at 9 volts should be used for 6-volt Locomotives. The reason is that motors designed to run on direct current at 6 volts from an Accumulator require an Alternating Current from a Transformer at 9 volts, on account of the impedance of the windings to Alternating Current.

For all Hornby 20-volt Locomotives the T20A Transformer is the best. It has plug sockets providing three separate circuits—one at 20 volts, controlled by a 5-stud speed regulator, for train driving; another at 20 volts, not controlled by the speed regulator; and the third at 3½ volts, for lighting Hornby Accessories.

Other Transformers for running 20-volt Locomotives are the No. T20, which has one circuit at 20 volts controlled by a speed regulator; and the No. T20M, which is similar to the T20, but has no speed regulator.

For 20-volt Locomotives fitted with Automatic Reverse, Transformers T20 or T20A should be used.

For running the Hornby 6-volt No. EPM16 Special Tank Locomotive from Alternating Current mains the Hornby Transformer-Rectifier must be used.

In ordering a Transformer or a Transformer-Rectifier the voltage and frequency of the supply must be stated. These particulars are given on the supply meter.

The prices of the full range of Meccano Transformers, Transformer-Rectifier and Accumulators are given on page 8.

No. T20 Transformer

Resistance Controller

Meccano Resistance Controllers

Where a Hornby 6-volt Train is operated from an Accumulator or from a Meccano No. T6M Transformer; or a Hornby 20-volt Train from a Meccano T20M Transformer, a variable **resistance** is required to control and regulate the speed of the train. For this purpose a Meccano Resistance Controller should be used.

Meccano Resistance Controller, 6-volt or 20-volt ... ... Price 3/9

BRITISH AND GUARANTEED

Page 29

Fig 106.

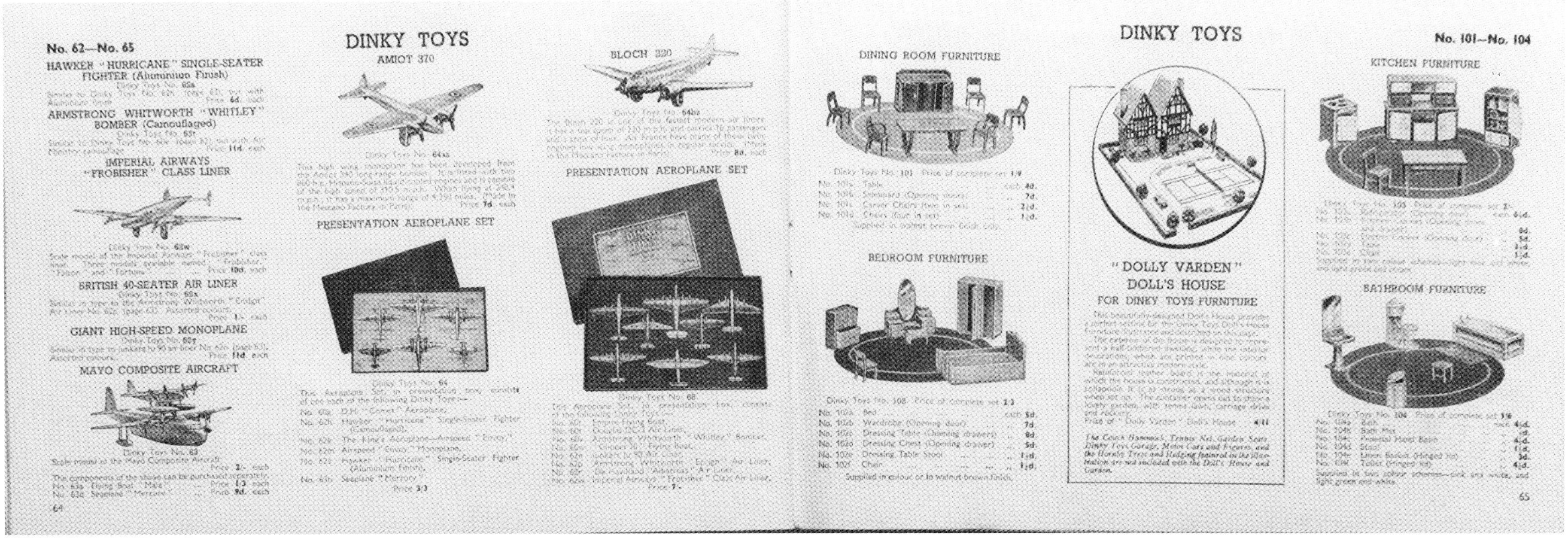

No. 62—No. 65

HAWKER "HURRICANE" SINGLE-SEATER FIGHTER (Aluminium Finish)
Dinky Toys No. 62a
Similar to Dinky Toys No. 62h (page 63), but with Aluminium finish. Price **6d.** each

ARMSTRONG WHITWORTH "WHITLEY" BOMBER (Camouflaged)
Dinky Toys No. 62t
Similar to Dinky Toys No. 60v (page 62), but with Air Ministry camouflage. Price **11d.** each

IMPERIAL AIRWAYS "FROBISHER" CLASS LINER
Dinky Toys No. 62w
Scale model of the Imperial Airways "Frobisher" class liner. Three models available named: "Frobisher," "Falcon" and "Fortuna" ... ... Price **10d.** each

BRITISH 40-SEATER AIR LINER
Dinky Toys No. 62x
Similar in type to the Armstrong Whitworth "Ensign" Air Liner No. 62p (page 63). Assorted colours. Price **1/-** each

GIANT HIGH-SPEED MONOPLANE
Dinky Toys No. 62y
Similar in type to Junkers Ju 90 air liner No. 62n (page 63). Assorted colours. Price **11d.** each

MAYO COMPOSITE AIRCRAFT
Dinky Toys No. 63
Scale model of the Mayo Composite Aircraft. Price **2/-** each
The components of the above can be purchased separately.
No. 63a Flying Boat "Maia" ... Price **1/3** each
No. 63b Seaplane "Mercury" ... Price **9d.** each

64

DINKY TOYS

AMIOT 370
Dinky Toys No. 64az
This high wing monoplane has been developed from the Amiot 340 long-range bomber. It is fitted with two 860 h.p. Hispano-Suiza liquid-cooled engines and is capable of the high speed of 310.5 m.p.h. When flying at 248.4 m.p.h., it has a maximum range of 4,350 miles. (Made in the Meccano Factory in Paris). Price **7d.** each

PRESENTATION AEROPLANE SET
Dinky Toys No. 64
This Aeroplane Set, in presentation box, consists of one each of the following Dinky Toys:—
No. 60g D.H. "Comet" Aeroplane.
No. 62h Hawker "Hurricane" Single-Seater Fighter (Camouflaged).
No. 62k The King's Aeroplane—Airspeed "Envoy."
No. 62m Airspeed "Envoy" Monoplane.
No. 62s Hawker "Hurricane" Single-Seater Fighter (Aluminium Finish).
No. 63b Seaplane "Mercury."
Price **3/3**

BLOCH 220
Dinky Toys No. 64bz
The Bloch 220 is one of the fastest modern air liners. It has a top speed of 220 m.p.h. and carries 16 passengers and a crew of four. Air France have many of these twin-engined low wing monoplanes in regular service. (Made in the Meccano Factory in Paris). Price **8d.** each

PRESENTATION AEROPLANE SET
Dinky Toys No. 68
This Aeroplane Set, in presentation box, consists of the following Dinky Toys:—
No. 60r Empire Flying Boat.
No. 60t Douglas DC-3 Air Liner.
No. 60v Armstrong Whitworth "Whitley" Bomber.
No. 60w "Clipper III" Flying Boat.
No. 62n Junkers Ju 90 Air Liner.
No. 62p Armstrong Whitworth "Ensign" Air Liner.
No. 62r De Havilland "Albatross" Air Liner.
No. 62w Imperial Airways "Frobisher" Class Air Liner.
Price **7/-**

DINING ROOM FURNITURE
Dinky Toys No. 101 Price of complete set **1/9**
No. 101a Table ... each **4d.**
No. 101b Sideboard (Opening doors) ... **7d.**
No. 101c Carver Chairs (two in set) ... **2½d.**
No. 101d Chairs (four in set) ... **1½d.**
Supplied in walnut brown finish only.

BEDROOM FURNITURE
Dinky Toys No. 102 Price of complete set **2/3**
No. 102a Bed ... each **5d.**
No. 102b Wardrobe (Opening door) ... **7d.**
No. 102c Dressing Table (Opening drawers) ... **8d.**
No. 102d Dressing Chest (Opening drawer) ... **5d.**
No. 102e Dressing Table Stool ... **1½d.**
No. 102f Chair ... **1½d.**
Supplied in colour or in walnut brown finish.

DINKY TOYS

"DOLLY VARDEN" DOLL'S HOUSE FOR DINKY TOYS FURNITURE

This beautifully-designed Doll's House provides a perfect setting for the Dinky Toys Doll's House Furniture illustrated and described on this page.
The exterior of the house is designed to represent a half-timbered dwelling, while the interior decorations, which are printed in nine colours, are in an attractive modern style.
Reinforced leather board is the material of which the house is constructed, and although it is collapsible it is as strong as a wood structure when set up. The container opens out to show a lovely garden, with tennis lawn, carriage drive and rockery.
Price of "Dolly Varden" Doll's House **4/11**

The Couch Hammock, Tennis Net, Garden Seats, Dinky Toys Garage, Motor Cars and Figures, and the Hornby Trees and Hedging featured in the illustration are not included with the Doll's House and Garden.

No. 101—No. 104

KITCHEN FURNITURE
Dinky Toys No. 103 Price of complete set **2/-**
No. 103a Refrigerator (Opening door) ... each **6½d.**
No. 103b Kitchen Cabinet (Opening doors and drawer) ... **8d.**
No. 103c Electric Cooker (Opening door) ... **5d.**
No. 103d Table ... **3½d.**
No. 103e Chair ... **1½d.**
Supplied in two colour schemes—light blue and white, and light green and cream.

BATHROOM FURNITURE
Dinky Toys No. 104 Price of complete set **1/6**
No. 104a Bath ... each **4½d.**
No. 104b Bath Mat ... **½d.**
No. 104c Pedestal Hand Basin ... **4½d.**
No. 104d Stool ... **1½d.**
No. 104e Linen Basket (Hinged lid) ... **3d.**
No. 104f Toilet (Hinged lid) ... **4½d.**
Supplied in two colour schemes—pink and white, and light green and white.

65

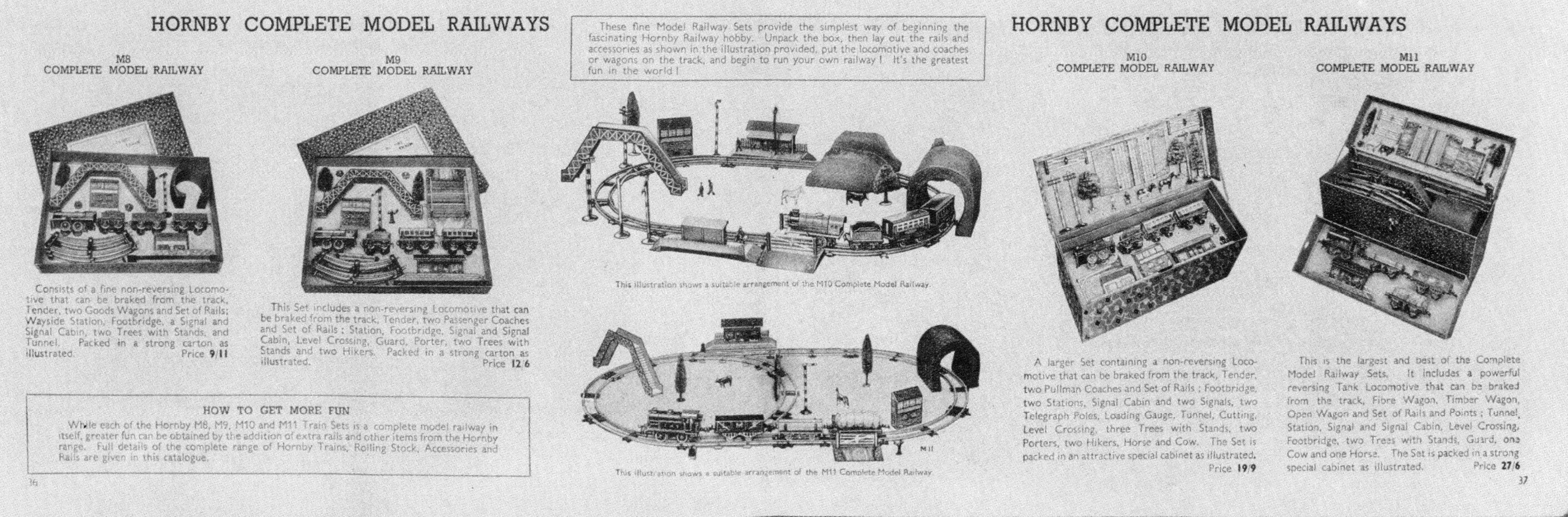

HORNBY COMPLETE MODEL RAILWAYS

These fine Model Railway Sets provide the simplest way of beginning the fascinating Hornby Railway hobby. Unpack the box, then lay out the rails and accessories as shown in the illustration provided, put the locomotive and coaches or wagons on the track, and begin to run your own railway! It's the greatest fun in the world!

M8 COMPLETE MODEL RAILWAY

Consists of a fine non-reversing Locomotive that can be braked from the track, Tender, two Goods Wagons and Set of Rails; Wayside Station, Footbridge, a Signal and Signal Cabin, two Trees with Stands, and Tunnel. Packed in a strong carton as illustrated. Price **9/11**

M9 COMPLETE MODEL RAILWAY

This Set includes a non-reversing Locomotive that can be braked from the track, Tender, two Passenger Coaches and Set of Rails; Station, Footbridge, Signal and Signal Cabin, Level Crossing, Guard, Porter, two Trees with Stands and two Hikers. Packed in a strong carton as illustrated. Price **12/6**

HOW TO GET MORE FUN

While each of the Hornby M8, M9, M10 and M11 Train Sets is a complete model railway in itself, greater fun can be obtained by the addition of extra rails and other items from the Hornby range. Full details of the complete range of Hornby Trains, Rolling Stock, Accessories and Rails are given in this catalogue.

36

This illustration shows a suitable arrangement of the M10 Complete Model Railway.

M11

This illustration shows a suitable arrangement of the M11 Complete Model Railway.

HORNBY COMPLETE MODEL RAILWAYS

M10 COMPLETE MODEL RAILWAY

A larger Set containing a non-reversing Locomotive that can be braked from the track, Tender, two Pullman Coaches and Set of Rails; Footbridge, two Stations, Signal Cabin and two Signals, two Telegraph Poles, Loading Gauge, Tunnel, Cutting, Level Crossing, three Trees with Stands, two Porters, two Hikers, Horse and Cow. The Set is packed in an attractive special cabinet as illustrated. Price **19/9**

M11 COMPLETE MODEL RAILWAY

This is the largest and best of the Complete Model Railway Sets. It includes a powerful reversing Tank Locomotive that can be braked from the track, Fibre Wagon, Timber Wagon, Open Wagon and Set of Rails and Points; Tunnel, Station, Signal and Signal Cabin, Level Crossing, Footbridge, two Trees with Stands, Guard, one Cow and one Horse. The Set is packed in a strong special cabinet as illustrated. Price **27/6**

37

Figs 107–108. Pages from the 1938 and 1939 catalogues.

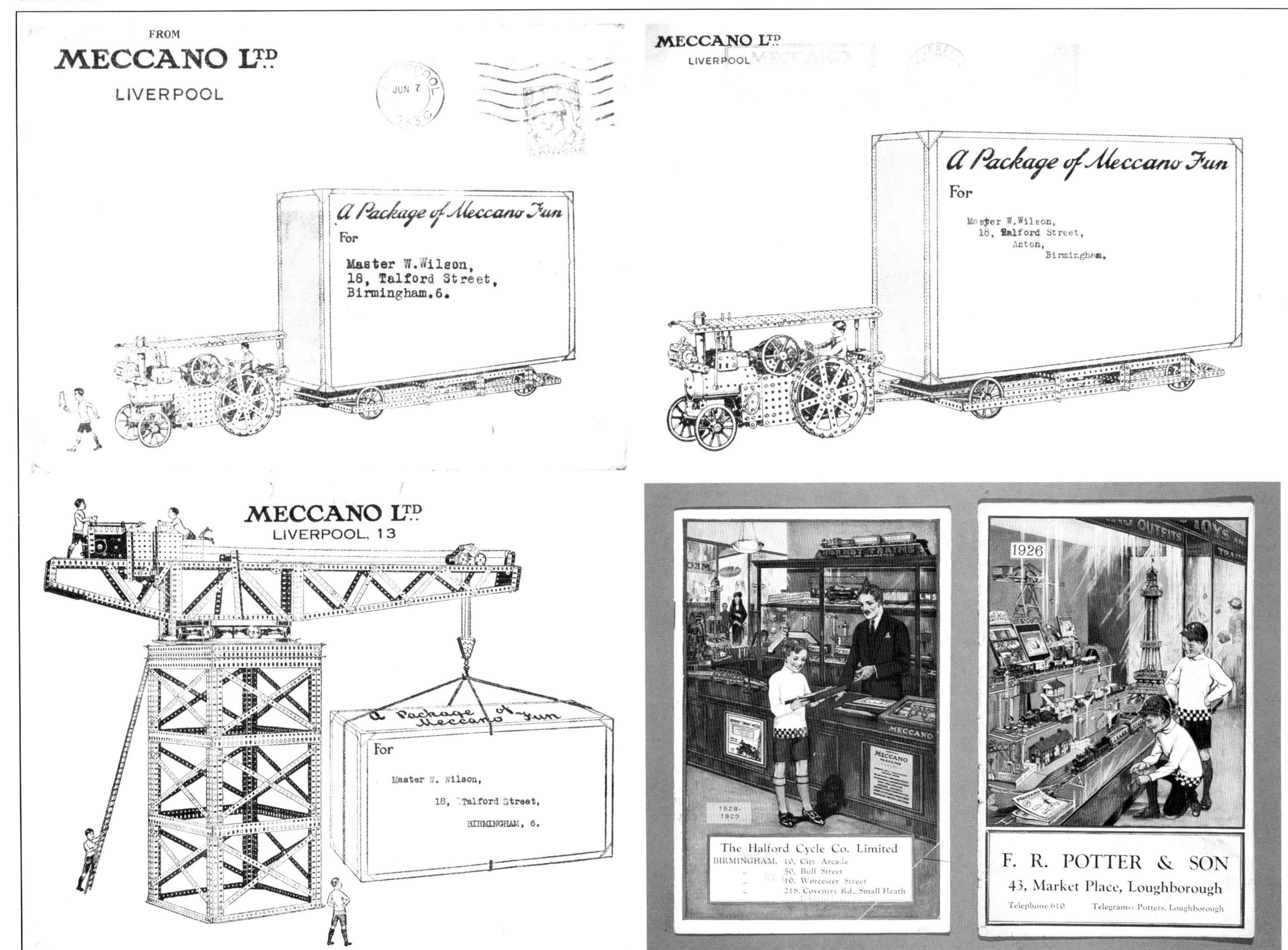
FROM
MECCANO LTD
LIVERPOOL
JUN 7
A Package of Meccano Fun
For
Master W.Wilson,
18, Talford Street,
Birmingham.6.
MECCANO LTD
LIVERPOOL
A Package of Meccano Fun
For
Master W.Wilson,
18, Talford Street,
Aston,
Birmingham,
MECCANO LTD
LIVERPOOL, 13
A Package of Meccano Fun
For
Master W. Wilson,
18, Talford Street,
BIRMINGHAM, 6.
1928-1929
The Halford Cycle Co. Limited
BIRMINGHAM. 10, City Arcade
50, Bull Street
10, Worcester Street
218, Coventry Rd., Small Heath
1926
F. R. POTTER & SON
43, Market Place, Loughborough
Telephone 610
Telegrams: Potters, Loughborough

Catalogues are in one sense unique in the history of Meccano literature in that some of the post-war editions are even better than their pre-war counterparts. The 1956 edition (similar to the 1957 edition reproduced in its entirety) is quite the finest, having a splendid cover and full colour contents with some of the richest tones one could imagine – an absolutely irresistible production. Compare the contents with some of the pages of the mid-1930s editions and it becomes obvious that the sometimes poor reproduction of illustrations is no match for the beautiful pages of the 1950s. Sadly, this state of affairs did not last and there was soon a distinct and terminal deterioration. Little from the 1960s onwards is worth more than a glance from the visual point of view and it is usually to be found in profusion on dealers disposal piles.

These then are just a few of the many different types of promotional material issued by Meccano during the great years. Although only a small fraction of the whole, they are in many ways representative. Good material may also be found in the years before and after. A selection of the best is illustrated in the pages that follow. Not all of it is rare but most is highly collectable.

There were foreign editions of many of these booklets and leaflets, but in the majority of cases they were identical except for language. An important exception was the New Meccano material issued in the US.

Frequently an overseas edition would have a different cover from the domestic one. Often it turned out that the covers used had already done service in the UK on a previous occasion or would in the future.

There is no doubt that Frank Hornby recognised the value of good promotional material, although it is unlikely that he himself ever directly (except perhaps in the early days) contributed much more than a basic overall concept to its production. For most of what is treasured today we again have to thank Ellison Hawkes and Hubert Lansley, who either directly or through inherited philosophy after they had left the company, produced or inspired the production of so much wonderful material. It is good to know that at the time of writing Hubert Lansley is still keenly interested in the future as well as the past of Meccano.

← *Figs 109–111. Three typical envelopes in which catalogues (and other material) were sent through the post.*

A selection of catalogue covers from the period 1926 to 1939. →

HORNBY TRAINS
MECCANO
Known all round the World
MECCANO LIMITED
Binns Road, Old Swan
LIVERPOOL

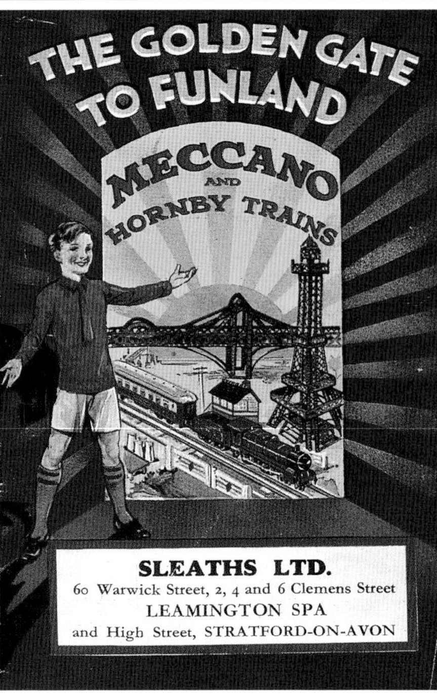
THE GOLDEN GATE TO FUNLAND
MECCANO AND HORNBY TRAINS
SLEATHS LTD.
60 Warwick Street, 2, 4 and 6 Clemens Street
LEAMINGTON SPA
and High Street, STRATFORD-ON-AVON

MECCANO
MECCANO LTD.
Binns Road, LIVERPOOL 13
1933-1934
MOTOR CAR CONSTRUCTOR
AEROPLANE CONSTRUCTOR

MECCANO AND HORNBY TRAINS
GOLDEN ELEPHANT TOYSHOPS
1a Crown Hill, CROYDON
1449 London Road, NORBURY

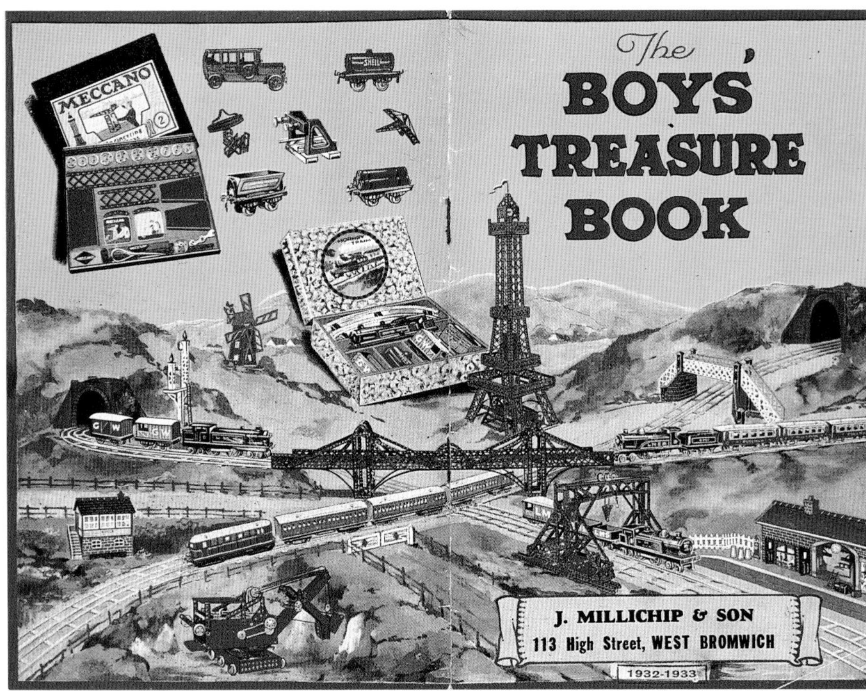
The BOYS' TREASURE BOOK
MECCANO
J. MILLICHIP & SON
113 High Street, WEST BROMWICH
1932-1933

1937
MECCANO PRODUCTS

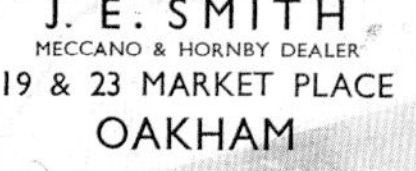
J. E. SMITH
MECCANO & HORNBY DEALER
19 & 23 MARKET PLACE
OAKHAM

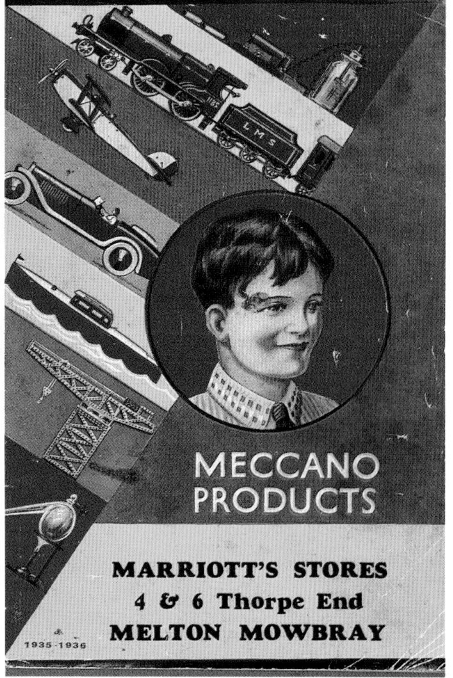
MECCANO PRODUCTS
MARRIOTT'S STORES
4 & 6 Thorpe End
MELTON MOWBRAY
1935-1936

MECCANO
QUALITY TOYS
HORNBY TRAINS
MECCANO
AEROPLANES
DINKY TOYS
MOTOR CARS
SPEEDBOATS
DINKY BUILDER
PRICE 1d
1939-1940
LUMLEY'S LTD.
Sauchiehall Street
GLASGOW, C.2
Phone : DOUGLAS 2701

MECCANO
1938
Quality Gifts for Boys
UPTON'S TOY FAIR
FINEST IN KENT
46 SANDGATE ROAD
FOLKESTONE
Phone : 2532

DINKY BUILDER
MECCANO
MECCANO
HORNBY TRAINS
1939-1940
DINKY TOYS
AEROPLANES
SPEED BOATS
MOTOR CARS
GAMIS'S STORES LTD.
High Street, YEOVIL
Telephone : 634
TOYS OF QUALITY
FROM MECCANO LAND
PRICE 1d

The Stars Send their Message
AEROPLANES
MECCANO
DINKY TOYS
HORNBY TRAINS
MOTOR CARS
1939-1940
PRICE 1d

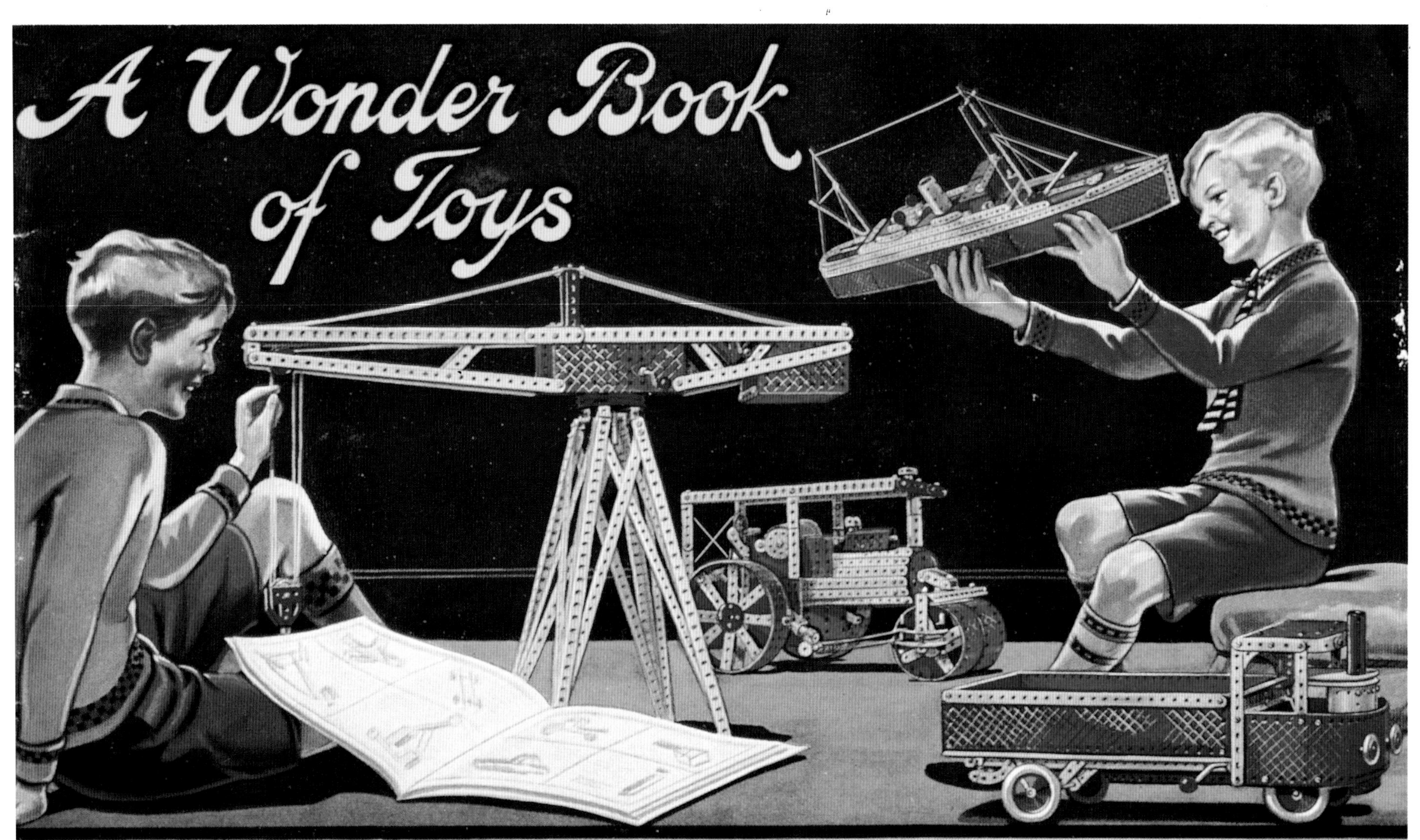
A Wonder Book of Toys
1939 - 1940
All prices in this catalogue are superseded
by a revised price list dated 1st November, 1941.
PRICE
1d

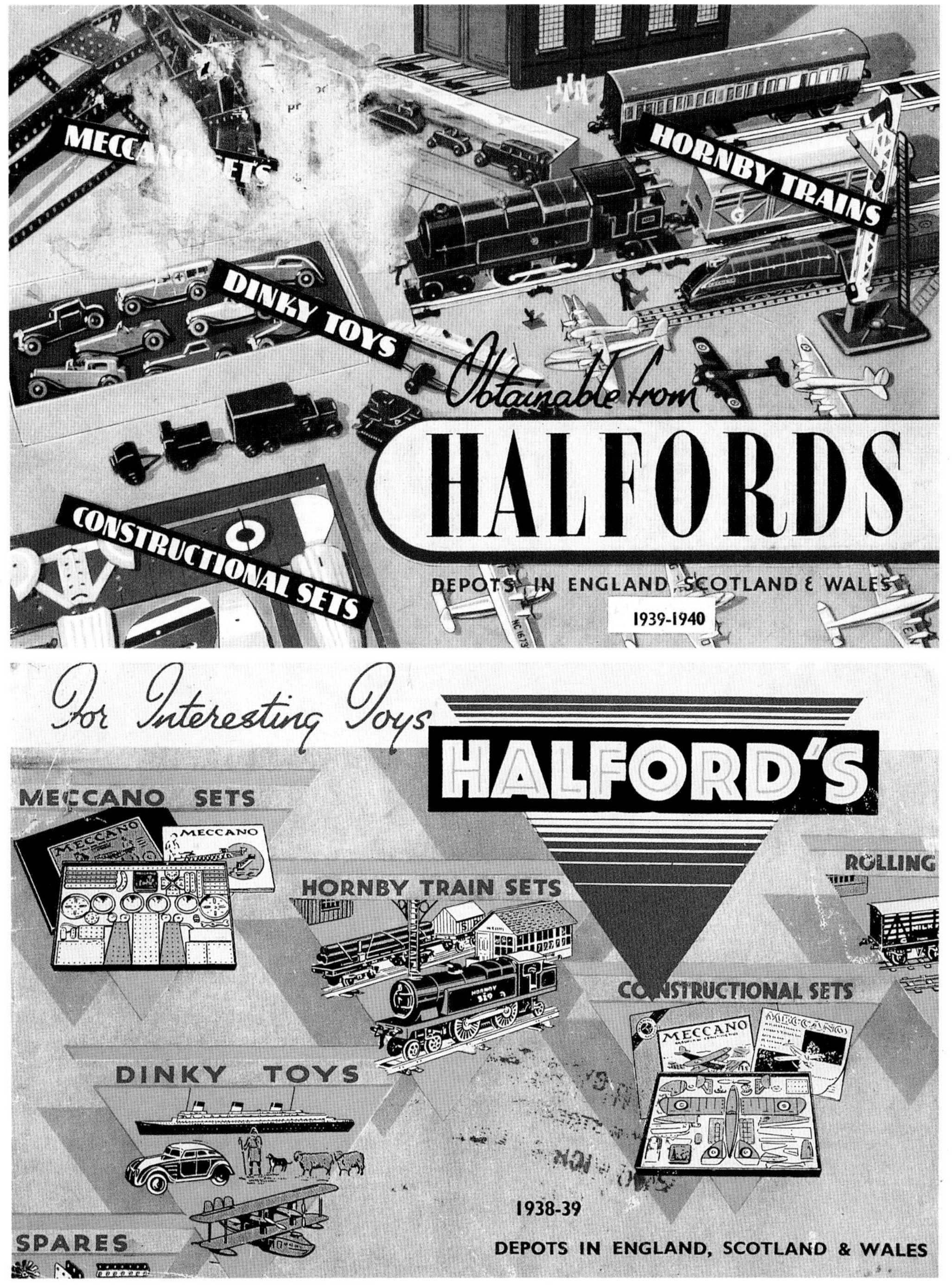
MECCANO SETS
HORNBY TRAINS
DINKY TOYS
Obtainable from
HALFORDS
CONSTRUCTIONAL SETS
DEPOTS IN ENGLAND SCOTLAND & WALES
1939-1940
For Interesting Toys
HALFORD'S
MECCANO SETS
MECCANO
HORNBY TRAIN SETS
ROLLING
CONSTRUCTIONAL SETS
MECCANO
DINKY TOYS
SPARES
1938-39
DEPOTS IN ENGLAND, SCOTLAND & WALES

CHAPTER 8

Miscellany

This is a heading which covers a multitude of sins. The range of informative material is very wide and includes price lists, announcements, competition forms, instruction leaflets and the like. It is also a class of literature which appears to have no bounds. New and previously unseen items are being discovered every day. For this reason, the choices which had to be made when considering this chapter were especially difficult, particularly since not all of it would interest the average collector (whoever he may be). What follows is of necessity a personal selection. Most items speak for themselves or need but a single line of description. Some, such as the 'How to run a Meccano Club' are worth special mention because of their social significance, and larger than usual extracts have been included. The Meccano Guild leaflets are also in this category throwing a considerable amount of light on the attitudes of the time.

Price lists can be of great use to the Meccano historian and a good range are reproduced, but these are only a tiny fraction of the total output. Indeed there are so many, that if you were to ask fifty collectors to each choose a group for inclusion you would probably end up with fifty different lots!

The other items are there simply to enjoy, which of course, is the whole purpose of this volume.

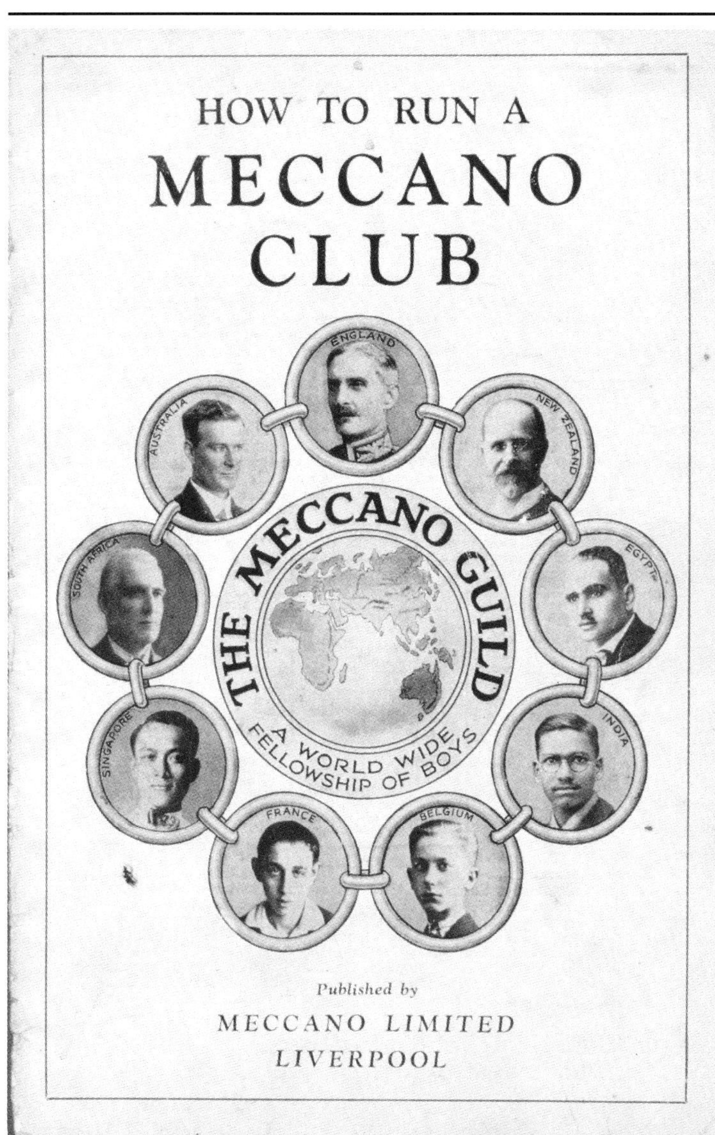

Figs 1–4.
Pages from the 1931 edition of How to Run a Meccano Club.

I. HOW THE MECCANO GUILD CAME INTO EXISTENCE

The Meccano Guild is a world-wide brotherhood of Meccano boys, and it came into existence at the earnest request of those boys.

The really happy boys throughout the world are those who have a hobby in which they take an enthusiastic interest; and the happiest of all are Meccano boys, for theirs is the greatest of all hobbies. When a boy takes up a hobby, whatever it may be, he feels a great desire to meet other boys having interests similar to his own, and to compare notes and talk things over with them. This is particularly the case with Meccano. A Meccano boy is not content for long to "play a lone hand"; he soon wants to meet other Meccano boys, to see their models and show them his own, and discuss with them plans and schemes for other and bigger models.

The Badge.

Before the days of the Guild, Meccano boys in many districts formed among themselves little clubs and societies, sometimes as branches of existing organisations and sometimes as independent units. Gradually these small clubs came to realise that their individual isolation was a serious handicap, and we began to receive repeated requests to organise some form of central organisation to which all might look for guidance. Realising the enormous amount of work that would be required to launch such a scheme, and also the great responsibility involved, action was delayed until 1919, when it was felt that we had the necessary facilities. In that year the Meccano Guild came into existence. Its success was immediate and spectacular, and since then it has made continuous progress in every civilised country in the world.

THE MECCANO GUILD

This is to Certify that

is a registered member of the Meccano Guild and is entitled to all the privileges of Membership

President

The Guild Certificate.

In thinking and speaking of the Guild, therefore, it should always be remembered that it originated in the minds and hearts of hundreds of thousands of Meccano boys. It is run quite apart from the commercial side of Meccano Ltd., and has a special staff who look after the interests of Guild members and of the clubs. The President of the Guild is Mr. Frank Hornby, who is known to hundreds of thousands of boys throughout the world as the inventor of Meccano.

I have often been asked why the name "Guild" was chosen for this great Meccano organisation. The reason is that we wished the movement to be based on the splendid ideals and traditions of the old merchant guilds—comradeship and unselfish working for mutual benefit. The old guilds have passed away, but the spirit that animated them is still alive. This spirit animates the members of the Meccano Guild, and it is because of this that the Guild has grown and prospered. Year by year it becomes an ever-wider influence for good in the world of boyhood. Its constitution has caused the Guild to be described as a "Junior League of Nations." There is no doubt that its effect on the spirit of future generations will go far toward justifying this description.

1

A happy group of members of the Thebarton High School (South Australia) M.C.

The main object of the Meccano Guild is to help every member to become a good man. It endeavours to do this by making members' lives brighter and happier; by fostering clean-mindedness, truthfulness, ambition and initiative; and by encouraging members in the pursuits of their hobbies and studies, and especially in the development of their knowledge of general mechanical and engineering principles.

The headquarters of the Guild are located at the Head Office of Meccano Ltd., Binns Road, Old Swan, Liverpool, and as Guild Secretary I am assisted by a staff of experienced workers. To us falls the pleasant task of rendering every possible assistance to Guild members, not the least part of which work is replying to a multitude of enquiries upon a wide variety of subjects, not necessarily connected with the Guild or even with Meccano. We live to help Guild members, and they show that they realise this by asking us to aid them in the many difficulties that they encounter—in their home life, at school, and later when they take their place in the world of business. They take us into their confidence and there is a constant exchange of friendly correspondence.

THE MECCANO GUILD

This is to Certify that

MECCANO CLUB

is incorporated in the Meccano Guild and is entitled to all the privileges of Membership

President

Date

The Club Certificate.

We also despatch badges and certificates to new Guild members, and special medals, such as Recruiting Medallions and Awards of Merit, to members who show particular merit or aptitude for club work. We give advice to boys who wish to form new clubs, and we co-ordinate the work of existing clubs in various parts of this country, throughout the Empire, and in foreign countries. We assist clubs in the arrangement of their programmes, furnish all available information, and generally help to make each club a success. We ensure the interchange of ideas between all Meccano Clubs, and compile the Guild pages for the *Meccano Magazine*, the official organ of the Guild. As there are now more than 300 clubs in this country and overseas, we find plenty of work to occupy our time.

2

Fig 2.

A happy party of members of the Herne Bay M.C. on a picnic.

details of each meeting and also the name of any member who carries through some special achievement. The number of members present and other details of general interest should be noted, and these "minutes" should be read over at the beginning of the next meeting and signed by the Leader.

Entries need not always be connected with Meccano. For instance, one member may win a scholarship of merit; a second may invent something of considerable importance; or a third may perform some brave deed. Such items are worthy of record and should be entered. The book should not be made "cheap," however, and every entry in it should refer to something of real importance.

It is also recommended that a Visitor's Book should be kept. When a club has thoroughly established itself, it is customary to hold Open Nights, when visitors are allowed to see members of the club at work, and as a matter of courtesy, these should always be asked to inscribe their names and addresses in a book kept for the purpose. A simple proceeding of this kind may have unexpected results. Interesting suggestions for adding to the attraction of the club's programme may be obtained in this manner, and the witty and appropriate lines that appear on page 22 of this booklet first made their appearance in the Visitor's Book of a Meccano club.

Importance of Monthly Reports to Headquarters

Reports should be sent to Headquarters each month, with a summary of the work done, and in addition the number of members on the roll should be stated, together with the average attendance at the meetings held during the month. The Record Book will be found of great assistance in compiling the monthly reports, which should contain a brief account of the club's activities and notes of any contemplated events. In large clubs it is a good plan to appoint an assistant secretary to prepare reports.

The monthly reports are of extraordinary importance. They are used as a basis for the "Club Notes" that are published monthly in the "*Meccano Magazine*," the official organ of the Meccano Guild. The members of a club are always pleased to see reports of its activities in the Guild pages of the "*M.M.*," and invariably become keener and more enthusiastic when these appear regularly. It must also be remembered that officials and members of kindred organisations judge the standing of a club very largely from these

9

reports, and therefore no effort should be spared to ensure their completeness, accuracy, and interest.

It is essential that reports should be sent in with great regularity at the end of each month. The reason for this is that the "*M.M.*" necessarily goes to press in advance of the date of publication. Reports that are sent in late therefore cannot be utilised for a considerable time and may be out of date. Secretaries should keep this point in mind, and should take special care to send immediate reports of events of importance, such as Exhibitions, Concerts, or visits and excursions of special interest.

The "*Meccano Magazine*," the Official Organ

The "*Meccano Magazine*," the official organ of the Guild, is published on the first of every month and will be found an essential feature in club life. A page of notes is published in this Magazine each month, reviewing the work and progress of the Guild in general. Suggestions are made for the improvement of club programmes with special regard to the period of the year, and attention is drawn to outstanding features in the work of particular clubs. In addition to this, each issue of the Magazine contains a page, or even more, of "Club Notes," in which the activities of the various clubs are noted. This page is of special value to Club Leaders, for by careful reading of the various events reported by the different clubs they may obtain many new ideas for the improvement of the programmes of their own clubs.

A group of Presidents of Meccano Clubs. From left to right they are: Col. The Hon. S. Peel, D.S.O. (Southall M.C.); Mr. B. McC. Barbour ("Twenty-Eight" (Edinburgh) M.C.); and Mr. F. Wiseman (Wiseman's M.C., New Zealand).

The "*Meccano Magazine*" is sold at sixpence per copy, and may be obtained from any Meccano dealer, newsagent or bookstall. It is also mailed (post free) from Headquarters for 4s. for six issues, or 8s. for twelve. Each club should keep a complete file of the Magazine for reference. A complimentary copy of the "*M.M.*" is sent each month to Club Leaders and Presidents.

Award of Special Merit Medallions

This is a convenient place to refer to the Special Merit Medallions awarded for good club work. Two of these medallions are allotted to every affiliated club at the close of each session, to be awarded to the boys who, in the opinion of the Leader, have done the best all-round work during the session. The distinction of winning this medal is keenly sought after, and every boy who is successful has good reason to feel very proud of his achievement.

The Special Merit Medallion is illustrated on pages 3 and 4 (actual size).

10

Fig 3.

A group of members of Chatellerault M.C., a prosperous French Meccano Club.

The arranging and carrying-out of competition nights will be found to be a great stimulus to the club in general. The competitions in Meccano subjects may include such events as the speedy and accurate building of specified models shown in the Meccano Manuals; improvements in the design of some particular model; clever adaptation of new Meccano parts; or accurate and intelligent description of the construction and use of a selected Meccano model, etc.

"Contractors' Nights" and the Team Spirit

Many successful Meccano Clubs have adopted an ingenious form of competition known as "contractors' nights." On certain nights the members of the club are divided into sections, each under the direction of one of the older boys, called a "contractor." The Leader then calls for "tenders" from the various contractors for constructing bridges or other structures according to given specifications. Each contractor then consults with his "gang," and finally puts forward his tender, which must describe the type of structure proposed to be erected, and give details of how it is to be completed, the amount of material (i.e., Meccano parts) it is estimated to require and the length of time it will take to complete. The club Leader then considers the merits of the various tenders and gives his decision as to which is to be accepted, when the contractor and his "gang" proceed to build the bridge. Contractors' nights are extremely popular with members of clubs in which they have been introduced. This kind of competition provides excellent training in the methods actually employed by civil engineers.

A plan that introduces the spirit of competition is to divide members into sections or groups, for then each works on behalf of his team instead of himself only. This plan has proved very popular, and there are very few clubs whose members are not divided into "Nuts," "Bolts," and "Washers," or into sections with other appropriate names, that are constantly in friendly rivalry with each other in every branch of the activities of a Meccano Club.

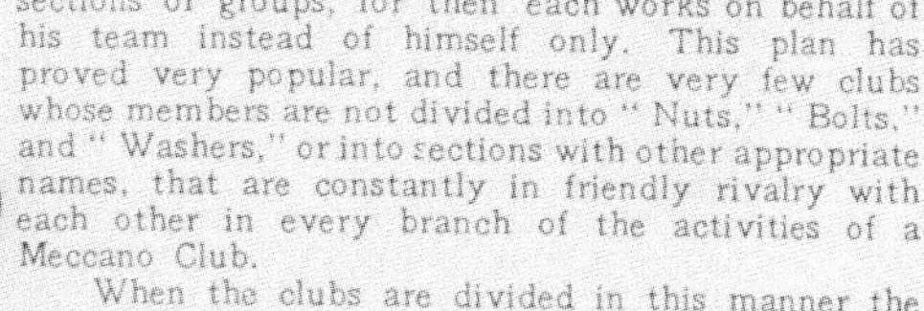

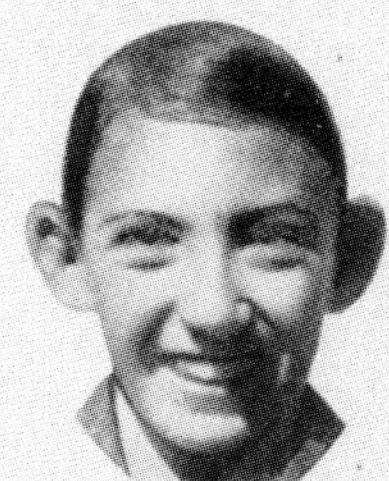

H. Jacobsen, Secretary, Clifton M.C., S.A.

When the clubs are divided in this manner the points awarded to a member for excellence in model-building, punctual attendance, or good work done on behalf of the club are placed to the credit of his section in a competition that may extend over a session or a complete year. In certain clubs a Shield or Cup is presented, and this trophy is held for a period by the

15

The Meccano Guild has penetrated into every corner of the world, as the above photograph of the members of a Chinese club shows. These Chinese Meccano boys are enthusiastic model-builders and are becoming experts.

section that earns the highest number of marks during the time allotted.

Many interesting evenings may be spent on the construction of large models by the joint efforts of members. This plan may be specially recommended for small clubs, and with modifications it may be employed successfully where members naturally fall into groups according to age, the Senior members planning and building more complicated models than the Juniors.

Special Meccano Evenings, Lectures and Talks

At certain meetings talks might be given on standard mechanisms employed in various machines that lend themselves to model-building. Of course, this should be followed by the actual building of models illustrating the particular mechanism dealt with. Suggestions for subjects may be obtained from the "*M.M.*" and other publications of Meccano Limited, while I shall always be pleased to advise Leaders who are desirous of arranging a series of meetings of this kind.

A very important feature of club activities is the arranging of a series of interesting lectures. Local gentlemen should be approached with a view to requesting them to speak to the club members on some interesting topic. Managers of the local gas, electricity, and water works, railway officials, factory managers and engineers—all these gentlemen have a wonderful story to tell if only they can be persuaded to tell it, and it is up to club Leaders and secretaries to apply the necessary persuasion. This will not require great efforts when the gentlemen approached are assured of an interested audience.

Chia Boon Hoe, Secretary, Singapore Chinese M.C.

Apart from outside lectures, the club Leader himself will be able to fill a vacant evening with a talk on some hobby or subject in which he is particularly interested. Current events at home or abroad, or some new and notable scientific

16

Fig 4.

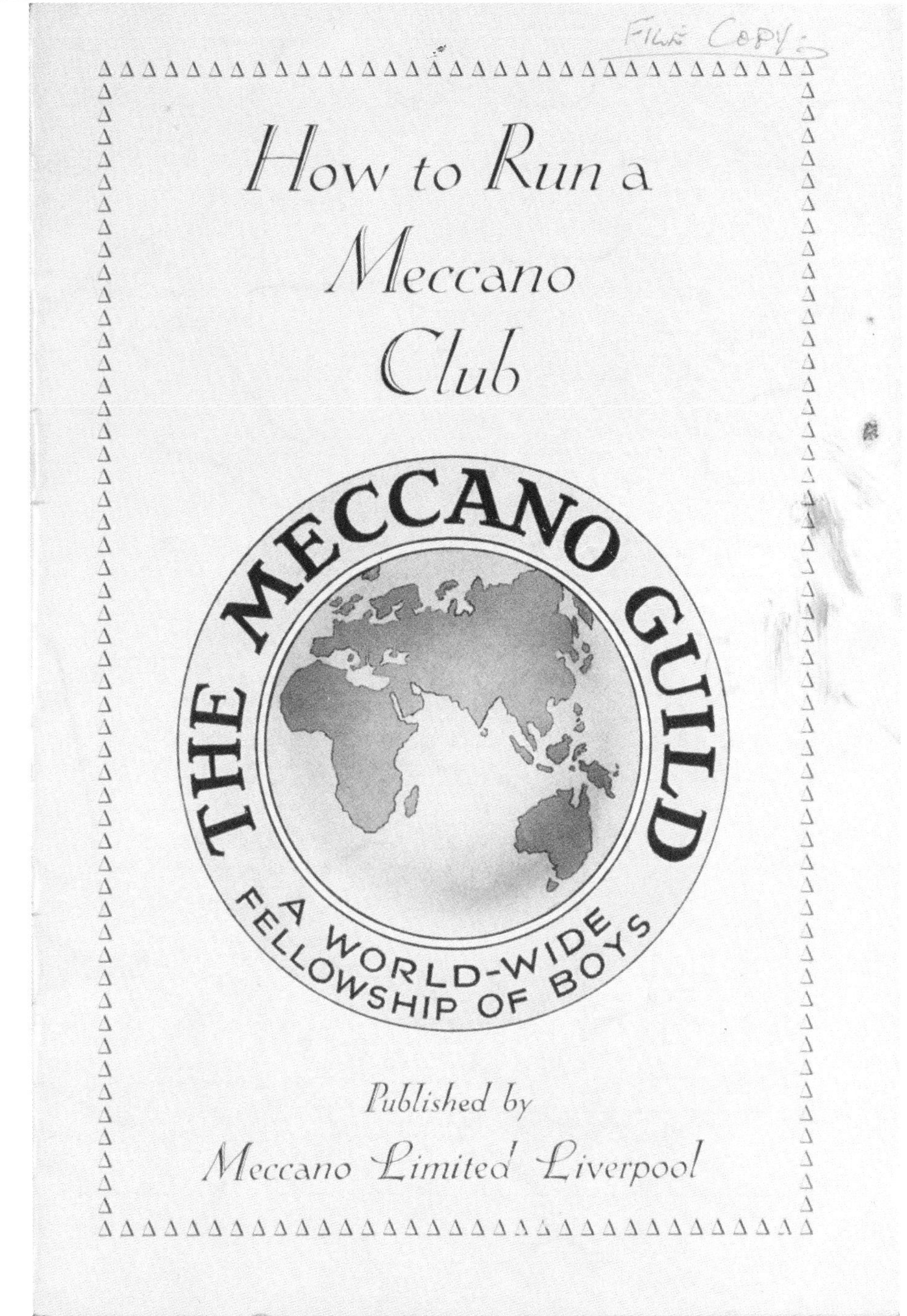

Figs 5–9.
Extracts from a later blue/gold era How to Run a Meccano Club.

After deciding on a suitable Leader, an invitation must be given to him. This may take the form of a letter, but it is better to ask for an interview, so that the position of the club can be explained and any questions on its aims and its work can be answered. In many cases I can help by writing to the prospective Leader, so I should be fully informed of members' wishes and all developments.

A good Secretary is the next official to be chosen. He keeps records of club proceedings, conducts correspondence, sends in reports to Headquarters and generally takes part in running the club. A keen and enterprising member is required for this post. Where the club is sufficiently large, a committee of say three to five members should be elected to support and assist the Leader and Secretary. The boys chosen to serve on this should be capable and enthusiastic, for they will have more to do than merely attend committee meetings and talk. It is generally fairly easy to start a club; the difficulty lies in keeping it going week after week and month after month. This throws upon the shoulders of the club officials the difficult task of giving the members a good time at every meeting by arranging a programme that will be sufficiently attractive to retain their interest, and of reviving it if their early enthusiasm shows sign of waning.

In its earliest stages a club can hold its meetings in the homes of different members in turn, but as progress is made and membership increases, search should be made for a suitable room. This should be as comfortable as possible, furnished with tables and benches, well lighted, and suitably warmed in cold weather. The choice of a room is really a matter of great importance and the success of the club will often depend upon it. If the room is cold and cheerless it will damp the ardour of even the most enthusiastic members.

If difficulty is experienced in finding a room, and if there is no boys' club in the district, application may be made for the use of a room belonging to a Church, Chapel or Institute. A schoolroom is quite suitable if one is available. It is surprising how kind people are when they know exactly what is wanted and for what purpose it is required. A polite request and a clear statement of the facts of the case will seldom fail to secure the use of a suitable room, if it is at all possible. Even if the first attempt is not successful, the effort should not be abandoned. Once it is realised for what fine objects the Meccano Guild stands, and the good it will do in the district, a room should soon be forthcoming.

Framing Rules for the Club Meetings

Some rules relating to the conduct of members at meetings are essential. It is not suggested that rigid discipline should be exercised, but members must be made to realize that disorder and rowdyism will find no place in a Meccano Club. Talk and movement are natural on model-building nights, and generally at meetings for other hobbies or games; but it should be made clear in the rules that all movement and noise should cease if the Leader or the Secretary wishes to address the members, which is often necessary during the course of a meeting. If the rule is not obeyed there can be no guarantee that important announcements are heard by everybody.

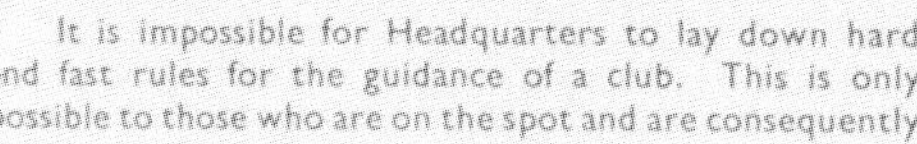

It is impossible for Headquarters to lay down hard and fast rules for the guidance of a club. This is only possible to those who are on the spot and are consequently familiar with its requirements. The officials and members of each club therefore must draw up its own rules, which should be agreed to by the members at a general meeting.

2

The Important Question of Club Funds

If possible the weekly subscriptions of members should be fixed at a figure that will enable ordinary expenditure to be met, but if necessary the income of a club can be increased by means of exhibitions, concerts and other functions, the organization of which is dealt with later in this booklet. Money raised in this way will allow the scope of club work to be extended by the purchase of material.

It is essential to the well-being of every club that its financial policy should be sound. The club Leader himself may act as Treasurer, or a member may be specially elected for the task, while in small clubs the Secretary may be able to carry out the duties. Whatever organization is adopted, strict accounts should be kept of all receipts and payments, and a balance sheet should be prepared at least half-yearly. The items in this balance sheet should be audited, and in all cases a copy signed by the Leader and the auditor should be forwarded to the Headquarters of the Guild.

The Winchmore Hill Collegiate School M.C. was affiliated in October 1925. It is now under the able Leadership of Mr. G. Watts, who is seen in the centre of this group of members.

In many cases the auditors are the Leader and a senior member, but it is a good idea to invite a friend of the club to check the accounts. For instance, if the parent or a relative of some official or member is an accountant, or is accustomed to work of the kind required, he would be pleased to give the club the benefit of his knowledge and an invitation should be given to him. Usually such an invitation leads to greater interest in the club and its proceedings on the part of the gentleman concerned, who then becomes a staunch supporter.

Every possible way of obtaining support should be explored. The aims and objects of a club have only to become known to influential people to arouse their interest, and prominent men in the district usually respond willingly to requests to become President or Vice-President when the members prove that they are thoroughly in earnest and worthy of recognition.

3

Fig 6.

A Hornby Train layout is always a great attraction at Exhibitions and Open Nights organized by Meccano Clubs. Visitors to such an Exhibition at Perse School, Cambridge, were fascinated by operations on the layout seen in this illustration.

II. How to Secure Affiliation

When a Meccano Club is thoroughly established and has an adult Leader and a club room, and when meetings are being held regularly, application may be made for affiliation with the Guild. This is done by the club Leader, who should supply the following particulars:—Number of members on the roll, a short report of meetings so far held, and a balance sheet. These particulars are placed before the President of the Guild and, subject to his approval, affiliation is granted. A certificate measuring 23 in. by 18 in., beautifully printed in colours, is then dispatched to the club. This certificate is signed by the President, and is very suitable for framing and hanging in the club room. It is illustrated on page 1 of this booklet.

Membership Cards and Club Record Books

Special membership cards are supplied free of cost by Headquarters to affiliated clubs, and on the inside of these cards space is left for the insertion of the programme for the four sessions. Subscription cards also are provided for affiliated clubs. On these are entered the weekly payments made by members in accordance with the policy adopted by the club.

Every Secretary should keep a Club Record Book, in which to enter details of each meeting, and also the names of any members who carry out some special achievement. The number of members present and other details of general interest should be noted, and these 'minutes' should be read over at the beginning of the next meeting and signed by the Leader.

Entries need not always be connected with Meccano. For instance, one member may win a scholarship of merit; a second may invent something of importance; or a third may perform some brave deed. Such items are worthy of record and should be entered.

The book should not be made 'cheap' however, and every entry in it should refer to something of real importance.

It is also recommended that a Visitors' Book should be kept. When a club has thoroughly established itself, it is customary to hold Open Nights, when visitors are

4

allowed to see members of the club at work. As a matter of courtesy these visitors should always be asked to write their names and addresses in a book kept for the purpose.

Importance of Monthly Reports to Headquarters

Reports should be sent to Headquarters each month, with a summary of the work done; and in addition, the number of members on the roll should be stated, together with the average attendance at the meetings held during the month. The Record Book will be found to be of great assistance in compiling the monthly reports, which should contain a brief account of the club's activities and notes of any contemplated events. In large clubs it is a good plan to appoint an assistant secretary to prepare reports.

A splendid subject for combined operations in a Meccano Club. This block-setting crane is seen with its builder, J. Ryall, Grimsby.

The monthly reports are of great importance. They are used as the basis for the 'Club Notes' that are published monthly in the *Meccano Magazine*, the official organ of the Meccano Guild. The members of a club are always pleased to see reports of its meetings in the Guild pages of the *M.M.*, and they become keener and more enthusiastic when these appear regularly. It must also be remembered that officials and members of other organizations judge the standing of a club very largely from these reports, and therefore no effort should be spared to make them complete, accurate and interesting.

The monthly 'Club Notes' in the *M.M.* are of special value to club Leaders, for by careful reading of the various events reported by the different clubs they may obtain new ideas for improving the programmes of their own clubs.

Award of Special Merit Medallions

This is a convenient place to refer to the Special Merit Medallions awarded for good club work. Two of these medallions are allotted to every affiliated club at the close of each session, to be awarded to the boys who, in the opinion of the Leader, have done the best all-round work during the session. The distinction of winning this Medallion is keenly sought after, and every boy who is successful has good reason to feel proud of his achievement.

Mr. F. L. Bingen, Leader of the Maastricht (Holland) M.C. since November 1933

The Special Merit Medallion is illustrated on page 2 (actual size). It is beautiful in design and finish, and on the back of each the name of the recipient is engraved. The awards are announced in the *M.M.*

Assistance in the production of their own magazines is also available for affiliated clubs. A brightly-written club magazine, clearly and neatly produced, will help to bring in new members. Some of the magazines already published are reproduced by one of various duplicating processes; others are printed. I am always pleased to lend electros of Meccano name blocks, or others that would help in the production of a journal of good appearance. These blocks are available for use in the printing of club stationery, tickets and leaflets for exhibitions, and recruiting leaflets.

5

 Fig 7.

Another type of contest that is particularly suitable for club meetings is that in which entrants are asked to construct what are called 'simplicity' models. The idea of these is to use only a small number of parts, and by skilful adaptation produce with them a model that is quickly and easily built, but gives a good idea of the form of the machine, vehicle or structure it is supposed to represent. Astonishingly realistic models can be built up with only a few parts, and model-builders enjoy such quick contests. As a variation, members can be given a certain number of parts with which to construct some simple type of model. When the parts are carefully chosen, and care is taken to include a sufficient number of bolts and nuts to allow for their proper employment, these competitions are very attractive.

A busy scene at the headquarters of the Waterlooville and Cowplain (Portsmouth) M.C., with Mr. A. A. Foster, Leader, on the left. A special feature of the work of this club is the construction of large models, including one of the 'Queen Mary', for display at exhibitions, at which large sums have been raised for charitable purposes.

'Contractors' Nights' and the Team Spirit

Many successful Meccano Clubs have adopted an ingenious form of competition known as 'Contractors' Nights'. On certain nights the members of the club are divided into sections, each under the direction of one of the older boys, called a 'contractor'. The Leader then calls for 'tenders' from the various contractors for constructing bridges or other structures according to given specifications. Each contractor then consults with his 'gang', and finally puts forward his tender, which must describe the type of structure proposed to be erected, and give details of how it is to be completed, the amount of material (that is, Meccano parts) it is estimated to require, and the length of time it will take to complete. The club Leader then considers the merits of the various tenders and gives his decision as to which is to be accepted, when the contractor and his 'gang' proceed to build the bridge. Contractors' nights are extremely popular with members of clubs in which they have been introduced. This kind of competition provides excellent training in the methods actually employed by civil engineers.

8

P. Mayo is secretary of the Barkers Butts Senior Boys' School (Coventry) M.C., a fine school club organized and led by Mr. F. Batten.

A plan that introduces the spirit of competition is to divide members into sections or groups, for then each works on behalf of his team instead of himself only. This plan has proved very popular, and there are very few clubs whose members are not divided into 'Nuts', 'Bolts' and 'Washers', or into sections with other appropriate names, that are constantly in friendly rivalry with each other in every branch of the activities of a Meccano Club

Each of these sections should have a leader, selected from the senior members of the club. Section leaders guide the activities of those under their charge, and discuss with them plans for models they are to build or for displays that they intend to arrange, so that each can be given some special part in the work required. It should be remembered that the aim is good model-building, and not merely a lot of it, for it is not in the spirit of the Guild to encourage unfinished or shoddy work. The plan drawn up therefore should be capable of completion in the time available, and the section leader should review progress from time to time in order to make sure that every part of the scheme is making headway and that everything can be properly finished off in readiness for a good display.

When the clubs are divided in this way, the points awarded to a member for excellence in model-building, punctual attendance, or good work done on behalf of the club are placed to the credit of his section in a competition that may extend over a session or a complete year. In certain clubs a Shield or Cup is presented, and this trophy is held for a period by the section that earns the highest number of marks during the time allotted.

Many interesting evenings may be spent on the construction of large models by the joint efforts of the members. This plan is specially recommended for small clubs. In larger clubs members may be divided into groups according to age, the Senior members planning and building more complicated models than the Juniors.

Special Meccano Evenings, Lectures and Talks

At certain meetings talks may be given on standard mechanisms employed in various machines that lend themselves to model-building, followed by

A successful Meccano Club has been established at the Worcester College for the Blind, members of which are seen here with their Leader, Mr. R. D. Follett.

9

Fig. 8.

Hornsea M.C. was founded by Mr. R. W. Shooter, who is seen in the centre of this group of officials and members. The club has been affiliated to the Guild since 1930.

the accident was not due to carelessness a sum may be voted towards the cost of the repairs. Should there be no accidents, and the fund be in credit at the close of the season, the balance may be transferred to the general Meccano Club fund, or perhaps expended in purchasing eatables for a final picnic!

If neither a cricket team nor a cycling club is possible, there is value in rambles to places of interest in the neighbourhood. It should be remembered that boys do not care for walks just for the sake of walking, and some special object must always be provided in order to arouse interest Thus if the Leader has any knowledge of botany, geology, bird life, etc., he will find it comparatively easy to make summer rambles lively and interesting.

Many clubs are within easy reach of the coast, and an effort should be made to arrange at least one excursion to some well-known resort, where games on the sands and similar pleasures may be enjoyed.

The Summer Session is the best time in which to arrange visits to local works and places of special interest. The officials of big engineering undertakings such as electric power stations, gasworks, etc., are almost always willing to welcome a party of Meccano boys, for they know that these boys take a genuine interest in the various things that are shown.

It is necessary to treat such visits seriously and to make application by letter at least two or three weeks beforehand. On the day of the visit the party should arrive punctually at the time agreed upon, and the number of members should be no greater than was stated in the letter of request. Finally a courteous letter of thanks should be sent the next day from the club Leader or Secretary to the officials concerned.

Visits often suggest novel subjects for model building.

This illustration is symbolic of the friendly association of two Meccano Clubs. These are Norbury M.C. and Maastricht (Holland) M.C. Mr. F. L. Bingen, founder of the latter Club, is seen with a group of members of the Norbury M.C.

14

V. How to secure Publicity

It should be the aim of every Meccano Club to become as widely known as possible in its particular district, as this is one of the surest ways of increasing membership and obtaining influential and valuable support. There are various ways of doing this, and one of the best is by means of invitation nights. Some people cannot understand the possibilities of a Meccano Club until they have attended one of the meetings, and then they become as delighted and as enthusiastic as the boys themselves. It is a good plan to arrange to open the club room to visitors one night every month, and to make a point of getting members to bring their parents and friends along to see the club 'at work'. Once parents, teachers, and others interested in boys' welfare learn of the useful work done by the club, they will give the help and support that are so necessary to its success.

The Advertising Value of an Exhibition

Model-building is the chief feature of the programme of the Kimount (Vancouver) M.C. Under the Leadership of Mr. B. I. Kershaw members have given outstanding displays at Exhibitions and Hobby Nights.

One of the best ways of making a club's activities known is to hold an exhibition, and this has the further advantage that it may be used to increase the financial resources of a club. A newly-formed club should proceed very cautiously and gain experience through one or two small functions before attempting anything more ambitious. If these are well organized, and the experience thus gained is put to good use, it will be found that the Meccano Club exhibition will become an event of local importance and one that will be looked forward to with great eagerness.

Whether an exhibition is small or large it should be well advertised, or it will be a failure. The members themselves can do excellent work in this direction by notifying their parents and friends of the forthcoming event, but personal efforts of this kind should be supplemented, if possible, by the display of attractively typed or printed notices in the windows of Meccano dealers or other shopkeepers. If funds permit, an advertisement may be inserted in a local paper. As many methods as possible of advertising the event should be adopted, but above all care must be taken to make the exhibition worthy of the efforts expended, for nothing could be more harmful than to allow visitors to go away with a feeling of disappointment.

The arrangement of the programme for an exhibition is not by any means a difficult matter, provided that members work together with the object of impressing visitors with the value of the club. A large proportion of the exhibits must, of course, be models constructed by members of the club themselves, but they may be supplemented by a display of special working models. These may be super-models constructed by older members. Naturally large models of this type attract a great deal of attention, and every

15

THE HORNBY RAILWAY COMPANY

Hundreds of thousands of boys own Hornby Trains and take pride in the possession of them, but—the lamentable fact must be recorded—most boys do not really know how to run a railway system in miniature correctly. It has always been our wish that a boy who possesses a Hornby Train should be one of the really happy kind and should get 100 per cent. fun out of his train, but the great question has always been —what can we do to make our wish come true? All our wiseacres—and we have large numbers of them in Meccanoland!—have pondered over this problem for years, and we believe that at last they have solved it. Their solution is that we should form an organisation to be known as the "Hornby Railway Company," which owners of Hornby Trains may join and which will enable them to get the best fun possible from their Hornby Trains.

The founder and chairman of the Hornby Railway Company is Mr. Frank Hornby, the inventor of Meccano and the Managing Director of Meccano Ltd.—a fact that alone is sufficient to commend the new scheme to the affections of all Hornby Train enthusiasts. Assisting Mr. Hornby is our own staff of Railway experts—trained men of long experience, full of enthusiasm for their subject, and keen to make the new venture successful. They fill the executive offices at Headquarters, and guide the affairs of the many Associated Branches of the Hornby Railway Company in local centres, which are run by boy officials.

Any owner of a Hornby Train Set, no matter what its size, may become a member. All he has to do is to fill in the official application form on the back of this folder for a share of fun and pleasure, have his signature witnessed, and send the form to Headquarters with 6d. in stamps in payment for the official badge, which he will wear in his buttonhole. This badge, here illustrated, is beautifully finished in red and green enamel, and by means of it all members are able to recognise each other when they meet. Their badges indicate at once that they have something in common—an interest in railways—and we are certain, that after a hearty handshake, conversation never flags between any "HORNBY RAILWAY COMPANY" members who may meet in this manner! Whether in your town, or at the seaside or in the country on holiday, always look out for the little badge that bears a representation of a locomotive and train, surrounded by the words "HORNBY RAILWAY COMPANY."

HORNBY RAILWAY COMPANY

This badge is worn by members of the H.R.C.

The official organ of the Hornby Railway Company is the "Meccano Magazine," a progressive Magazine which is bought each month by over 60,000 boys. Full details of the subscription rates and sources of supply may be obtained from the Editor, "Meccano Magazine," Old Swan, Liverpool. All future announcements regarding the H.R.C. will be made in the "*M.M.*"

A booklet has been prepared, which describes in detail the Hornby Railway Company, its organisation and objects. It deals with the planning, laying out and operating of a miniature railway on real railway-like principles, and shows how to obtain the utmost possible fun and excitement. This booklet will be sent from Headquarters to applicants on receipt of 2d. in stamps.

All clear for the goods special!

HORNBY

2711

G W

SHELL

Fig 10. A prospectus for the Hornby Railway Company dating from 1928.

Reprinted from "The Meccano Magazine."
A Magazine published specially for Meccano Boys. Write to the Editor, "Meccano Magazine," Binns Road, Liverpool, who will send you a Specimen Copy Free.

The Meccano Guild

A Fellowship of Meccano Boys

More than a million boys in Great Britain derive their greatest indoor pleasure from Meccano. They form local Clubs amongst themselves for the discussion of Meccano topics, and for mutual help. Thousands of them write to us and ask us to put them in correspondence with other boys, and to help them to start Meccano Clubs where they can meet their Meccano chums. We feel that the time has come for the formation of one great fraternal organisation of which all Meccano boys should become members, and we have pleasure in announcing that we have completed our plans for bringing this about in such a way that even the most lonely boy shall be able to take his part and share the happiness.

The objects of the Meccano Guild are :

(*a*) To make every boy's life brighter and happier.

(*b*) To foster clean-mindedness, truthfulness, ambition, and initiative in boys.

(*c*) To encourage boys in the pursuit of their studies and hobbies, and especially in the development of their knowledge of mechanical and engineering principles.

This is surely an ambitious programme, and we can assure our Meccano boys that we shall use every endeavour to establish an organisation of boys, for boys, and conducted as much as possible by boys, which will have a profound effect for good on the lives of all who take part in it.

The Headquarters of the Guild will be at the offices of the Meccano Works in Liverpool. At the head, guiding, controlling, and taking a personal interest in every member, will be the President, and the holder of this office will be Mr. Frank Hornby, inventor of Meccano, and Chairman and Managing Director of Meccano Limited. Associated with the Guild will be Meccano Clubs all over the country, run by Club Leaders and other officials; and finally the great army of club members—thousands upon thousands of clean, busy, happy boys, each with a definite purpose, each a member of a great happy family.

12,20/200.

Existing Meccano Clubs should at once apply for affiliation with the Meccano Guild, giving the following particulars :—

(1) Name of Club.
(2) Name and address of Club Leader.
(3) Number of Members on roll.
(4) Address where club meetings are held.
(5) The last report and balance-sheet.

The Meccano Club Certificate

Where a club can show that it is a real live organisation a Certificate of Affiliation to the Guild will be granted, and the club will be allowed to avail itself of all the privileges of membership.

Every boy who is not yet a member of a Meccano Club should apply for individual membership of the Guild, on the enclosed form.

Fig 11. 1920 Meccano Guild publicity leaflet.

The Meccano Guild

A Great Fellowship of Boys

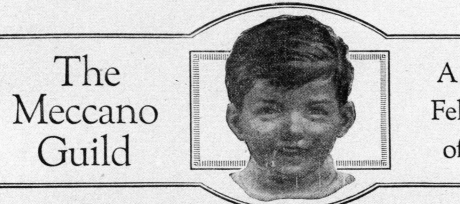

President: Mr. Frank Hornby —Inventor of Meccano

What the Guild Means The Meccano Guild is an organisation for boys, started at the request of boys, and conducted as far as possible by boys. In joining the Guild a Meccano boy becomes a member of a great brotherhood of world-wide extent, every member of which has promised to observe its three great objects; wherever he happens to be—even in strange countries—he will know he has met a friend whenever he sees the little triangular badge. The Meccano Guild is bringing together Meccano boys all over the world, and is helping them to get the very best out of life.

How it Commenced More than a million boys in Great Britain derive their greatest indoor pleasure from Meccano. Before the Guild was formed, hundreds of these Meccano boys wrote to us every week. They told us how they wished they could be put into communication with other Meccano boys and how they longed to be able to meet them. They asked if arrangements could be made so that their wishes might become an accomplished fact. We responded to their repeated and increasingly numerous appeals, and as a result the Meccano Guild came into being.

Why You Should Join Every Meccano boy should be a member of the Meccano Guild. All who have studied its objects must agree that the Guild cannot fail to have a profound effect for good on the lives of its members. It is ready to be of service to each individual member—to help or give advice whenever requested. At the head—guiding and controlling, and taking a personal interest in this great movement—is the President, Mr. Frank Hornby, Inventor of Meccano and Managing Director of Meccano Limited.

The Headquarters of the Meccano Guild are at the Head Offices of Meccano Ltd., Binns Road, Liverpool.

THE GUILD RECRUITING CAMPAIGN

Every Meccano boy should become a member of the Guild and do his utmost to help to make the objects of the Guild widely known. With this end in view, a Special Medallion is presented to each member of the Guild who obtains three new recruits. As a mark of further merit the medallion is engraved with the name of the recipient and with the words "Special Award" when six more members are recruited, making nine in all. Full particulars of the Recruiting Campaign, together with a supply of application forms, will be sent on request.

HOW TO BECOME A MEMBER

Membership of the Guild is open to every boy possessing a Meccano Outfit, or Hornby Train Set, who satisfactorily fills in the prescribed application form. The only conditions are that members promise to observe the objects of the Guild and to wear their badges on all possible occasions.

The price of the Guild membership badge is 7d. post free in the United Kingdom, but members abroad will be required to pay 5d. extra for registered postage. A remittance for the necessary amount should be sent along with the form of application. The Guild badge is beautifully enamelled in blue and white and is made for wearing in the lapel of the coat. Any boy wearing the Guild Badge is at once recognised by other Meccano boys as being a member of the Guild and one who has undertaken to live a clean, truthful and upright life.

In addition to the badge, each member receives a membership certificate, measuring 7″×9½″. This certificate is printed in orange and sepia and is a smaller edition of the large club certificate.

Write to the Secretary of the Meccano Guild, Binns Road, Liverpool, asking for an application form and full particulars. Then fill in the form and return it to Headquarters, when you will be enrolled and your badge and certificate will be sent to you. Write to-day for full particulars.

The Secretary receives hundreds of letters every week from members all over the world and he hopes that new members will also write to him as often as possible.

MECCANO CLUBS

Meccano Clubs are founded and established by enthusiastic Meccano boys under the guidance of the Guild Secretary at Headquarters. At the present time there are over 100 affiliated clubs in various towns and villages in this country and abroad, together with a much larger number not yet affiliated. Each club has its Leader, Secretary, Treasurer and other Officials, all of whom, with the exception of the Leader, are boys. If the nearest club to you is too far away for you to join, or if you are unable to join for any other reason, consider the possibility of forming a new club in your own district. A special booklet explaining "How to run a Meccano Club" is now ready, and will be sent to any reader (post free) on receipt of 2d. in stamps.

AFFILIATION WITH THE GUILD

When a Meccano Club has been successfully launched and good progress is being made, affiliation with the Guild is granted. A beautiful club certificate, suitable for framing and hanging in the club-room, is presented, and the club becomes entitled to such privileges as the loan of interesting lectures and club membership cards.

All members of the Guild are eligible for the Merit Medallion, which is awarded to those who display special ability in connection with club work, or in helping the Guild.

THE CORRESPONDENCE CLUB

Members of the Guild are able to join the Correspondence Club, by which they are placed in communication with other Guild members in some other part of the country or abroad. To those boys who are interested in foreign languages the Correspondence Club presents a splendid opportunity of obtaining a correspondent in the particular country in the language of which they are interested. They are able to write to a Meccano boy in his native language, and as he would probably reply in English, the correspondence will be of mutual benefit. Stamp collectors also find the Club of value, as they are enabled to exchange stamps with their correspondents. Full particulars and enrolment form will be sent on application.

THE MECCANO GUILD
BADGE OF MEMBERSHIP

THE THREE GREAT OBJECTS OF THE GUILD

(1) To make every boy's life brighter and happier.

(2) To foster clean-mindedness, truthfulness, ambition, and initiative in boys.

(3) To encourage boys in the pursuit of their studies and hobbies, and especially in the development of their knowledge of mechanical and engineering principles.

MECCANO LIMITED. LIVERPOOL

Fig 12. A somewhat later version of the same leaflet.

THE MECCANO GUILD

How to Join the Guild

Membership of the Guild is open to every boy possessing a Meccano Outfit or Hornby Train Set who satisfactorily fills in the application form. The only conditions are that members shall promise to observe the objects of the Guild and to wear their badges on all possible occasions.

In order to join the Guild all that is necessary is to fill up the form of application, and to forward it to the Secretary of the Meccano Guild, Binns Road, Liverpool 13, from whom an application form can be obtained if desired. A remittance to pay for the membership badge should be sent along with the completed form of application. The price of the badge is 7d. post free in the United Kingdom and 1/– post free Overseas (25 cents Canada). The applicant is then enrolled as a member of the Guild and his badge of membership is sent to him.

Boys living overseas should write to one of the Meccano agents at the following addresses: Canada: Meccano Ltd., 187-189, Church St., Toronto. Australia: Messrs. E. G. Page & Co. (P.O. Box 1832K), 52, Clarence Street, Sydney, N.S.W. New Zealand: Models Ltd. (P.O. Box 129), 9, Anzac Avenue, Auckland. South Africa: Mr. A. E. Harris (P.O. Box 1199), 142, Market Street, Johannesburg. Their badges and certificates are then forwarded without delay, while their application forms are sent to Headquarters at Liverpool, where their names are entered on the Guild roll.

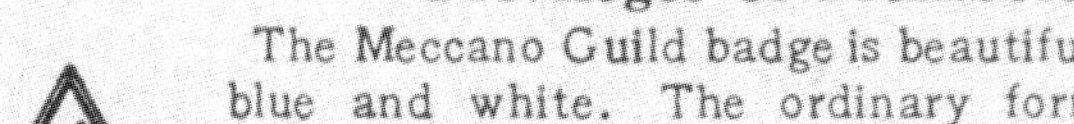

THE MECCANO GUILD

BADGE OF MEMBERSHIP

MEMBERSHIP CERTIFICATE

Privileges of Membership

The Meccano Guild badge is beautifully enamelled in blue and white. The ordinary form is made for wearing in the lapel of the coat, but brooch badges are issued to members who prefer to pin them in position, and applicants who wish to have this form of badge should indicate this when sending in their forms. In addition to the badge, each member receives a handsome Membership Certificate printed in orange and sepia. This is illustrated in the centre of the page.

A badge of membership serves as an introduction between Meccano boys. It may be seen in practically every civilised country in the world, and anyone wearing it is at once recognised by other Meccano boys as a Guild member who has undertaken to do his utmost to carry out the three great objects of the Guild.

Membership of the Guild carries with it important privileges. In addition to having the personal interest of the President, each member is entitled to the friendly advice and assistance of the Secretary in all circumstances. Every week hundreds of letters are received at Headquarters from all parts of the world. To every one of these is sent an individual reply, in which friendly advice is given, queries are answered, and suggestions are made for getting the best out of their work and play. The Secretary hopes that every member will take full advantage of this privilege by writing regularly to him.

Membership Application Form on back page

Fig 13. 1936 prospectus for the Guild.

THE MECCANO GUILD

The Correspondence Club

Members of the Guild are eligible to join the Correspondence Club, by which they are placed in communication with other Guild members in some other part of the country or abroad. To those boys who are interested in foreign languages the Correspondence Club presents a splendid opportunity of obtaining a correspondent in the particular country in the language of which they are interested. Stamp collectors also find the Club of value, as they are enabled to exchange stamps with their correspondents. Full particulars and enrolment forms will be sent post free on application to the Secretary of the Meccano Guild, Binns Road, Liverpool 13.

LEADER'S BADGE

Guild Recruiting Campaign

Every Meccano boy should become a member of the Guild and do his utmost to help to make the objects of the Guild widely known. With this end in view, the Special Medallion illustrated on this page is presented to each member of the Guild who obtains three new recruits within three months. As a mark of further merit the medallion is engraved with the name of the recipient and the words "Special Award" if three more members are recruited within a further three months, making six new members in all. Full particulars of the Recruiting Campaign together with a supply of application forms, will be sent on request.

SPECIAL MEDALLION

Meccano Clubs

Meccano Clubs are founded and established by enthusiastic Meccano boys under the guidance of the Guild Secretary at Headquarters. At the present time there are over 300 affiliated clubs in various towns and villages in this country and overseas, together with many others not yet affiliated. Each club has its Leader, Secretary, Treasurer and other Officials, all of whom, with the exception of the Leader, are boys.

Every Guild member should join a club if possible, for only in association with other Meccano boys is he able to obtain the greatest fun from his hobby. If the nearest club is too far away for him to join, or if he is unable to join it for any other reason, he should consider the possibility of forming a new club in his own district. A special booklet entitled "How to run a Meccano Club" is now ready, and will be sent post free to any reader on receipt of 2d. in stamps.

When a Meccano Club has been successfully launched and good progress is being made, affiliation with the Guild is granted. A beautiful Club Certificate, suitable for framing and hanging in the club-room, is presented, and the club becomes entitled to such privileges as the loan of interesting lectures and large models built at Headquarters.

All members of the Guild are eligible for the Merit Medallion, which is awarded to those who display special ability in connection with club work, or for good work generally on behalf of the Guild.

Membership Application Form on back page

Application for Membership of

THE

MECCANO GUILD

Headquarters:—
BINNS ROAD, LIVERPOOL.

I possess a Meccano Outfit / Hornby Train *and I hereby make application for membership of the Meccano Guild.

I approve of the objects of the Guild, and I promise on my honour

(1) To conform with the rules and regulations of the Meccano Guild.

(2) To promote its objects by my own example; to be helpful to others; to be clean in thought and habit; to be determined to learn and make progress.

(3) To wear the Meccano Guild Badge on all possible occasions.

(4) To recognise and acknowledge all other Members wearing the Guild Badge, and to render them help in case of need.

I enclose 7d. for the Guild Membership Badge.

Signature of Applicant ....

Address ....

....

Date .... Age ....

Witness ....

Address ....

....

The witness should be the Parent, Guardian, Employer, Schoolmaster or Church Minister, and should state the nature of his calling when signing.

I am a Member of the .... Meccano Club.

Signature of Club Secretary ....

If the applicant is not a member of a Meccano Club this portion should be left blank.
**Strike out words that are not applicable.*

Fig 14. A 1920s application form.

NEW SUBSCRIPTION RATES

With the December special number, the price of the "M.M." will be increased to 2d. It may be ordered from any Meccano dealer or from any bookstall or newsagent, price 2d., or post free from this office 1/6 for six months; 3/- for twelve months.

MECCANO MAGAZINE
BINNS ROAD LIVERPOOL.

CANO
AZINE PRICE 1d

CANO BOYS TO HAVE
THAN OTHER BOYS

s birthday comes along, wouldn't
which he will really appreciate?
this—

O MAGAZINE" REGULARLY.

To send him six issues will cost you 6d. or twelve issues will cost you 1/-. As each issue of this fine Magazine comes to him through the post your friend will be reminded of your thoughtfulness, and we warrant he will thoroughly enjoy reading every line of it. There are some splendid new features being added this year, and each number will be a real live one. With the first number we will write a little note to your friend telling him of your kindness and conveying your good wishes to him.

Fill in the form below and enclose the necessary stamps. You can then leave the rest to us.

ORDER FORM.

Mark with a X the kind of present you are making:—
....BIRTHDAY PRESENT.
....GIFT.
....CHRISTMAS PRESENT.
....NEW YEAR'S GIFT.
....PRESENT FOR SICK FRIEND.

To the Editor,
Meccano Magazine,
Old Swan, Liverpool.

Please post........numbers of Meccano Magazine, as issued, to—

(Name) ....

(Address) ....

....

for which I enclose..........in stamps.

Sent by (Name) ....

Address ....

Date ....

Fig 15. A selection of Meccano Magazine *inserts and the like showing the attention to detail.*

THE
"MECCANO
MAGAZINE"

The "*Meccano Magazine*" is the Meccano boy's newspaper. It appeals to all boys—whether or not they are Meccano boys—for its pages include interesting articles on such subjects as Railways, Famous Engineers and Inventors, Electricity, Bridges, Cranes, Wonderful Machinery, Latest Patents, Nature Study,
...ooks. New
...unced from
...f the com-
... There are
...nby Trains.
...each month
...o dealer or
... order to
... have each
...e
...o
...s,

Send me the names and addresses of three of your chums who are not Meccano boys, together with 3d. in stamps, and I will forward you a specimen copy of the "*M.M.*" post free. Fill in the form on the back of this leaflet.

The Editor.

OCTOBER 1926.

IMPORTANT

Commencing with the December, 1926, Number the price of the "Meccano Magazine" will be increased to 6d per copy. When ordered direct from the publishers the subscription rates will be 4/- for six issues, and 8/- for twelve issues, post free. A specimen copy will be sent you for 6d, post free.

THE EDITOR.

IMPORTANT NOTICE

The Overseas price of the "Meccano Magazine" was recently increased from 3d. to 6d. per copy. This advance was necessary on account of the heavy costs that are now entailed in the production of the Magazine and in its distribution overseas.

The increased size of the "M.M." also affects the postage on each copy and readers who obtain their Magazines direct should make a careful note of the following new subscription rates that will come into force on 1st. August 1926:-

6 months	4/-	post free
12 "	8/-	" "

Subscriptions already in hand are not affected by the change in price and will continue on the old basis until they expire.

MECCANO LTD. BINNS ROAD LIVERPOOL ENGLAND.

IMPORTANT

Commencing with the September issue, the price of the "Meccano Magazine" in Australia will be increased to 1/- per copy. The new direct subscription rates will be 7/- for six months, or 14/- for one year (post free).

Existing subscriptions will not be affected by the increase but will be completed on the present basis.

MECCANO LTD., LIVERPOOL, ENGLAND.

MECCANO
MAGAZINE
PRICE 2d
Published in the interests of Boys.

If you are already a subscriber to the Meccano Magazine, you will do a kindness by passing this copy to a friend.

SPECIAL NOTICE

The printing of a special Overseas Edition of the Meccano Magazine has been discontinued by Messrs. Meccano Ltd., and from No. 8, Vol. VIII onwards the English Edition only will be sent to subscribers.

Kindly note that English prices are now shown in the magazine, but the Australian retail prices (which of course, cover duty, freight, etc.) can be obtained from your local dealer, or :—

THE MECCANO DEPOT
379 Kent Street - Sydney
N.S.W.

IMPORTANT TO OVERSEAS READERS

Overseas readers are reminded that the prices shown throughout the "*M.M.*" both for goods manufactured by Meccano Ltd. and for goods advertised by other firms, are those relating to the home market. Current Overseas price-lists for Meccano and Hornby Trains will be mailed free on request to any of the agencies mentioned below. Application for overseas prices of other goods should be made direct to the firms mentioned and not to Meccano Agencies.

The "*M.M.*" is sold overseas at 2d. per copy, or it will be mailed (post free) direct from Meccano Ltd., Binns Road, Liverpool, or from any Meccano Agency, price 1/6 for six issues, or 3/- for twelve issues.

MECCANO AGENCIES OVERSEAS.

Australia: Messrs. E. G. Page & Co., 379, Kent Street, Sydney.
New Zealand: Messrs. Browning Ifwersen, Ltd., P.O. Box 129, Auckland.
South Africa: Mr. A. E. Harris, P.O. Box 1199, Johannesburg.
Canada: Meccano Ltd., 45, Colborne Street, Toronto.
U.S.A.: Meccano Ltd., Elizabeth, New Jersey.

Telephone
Old Swan 377
Please Address all Communications to
THE EDITOR

MECCANO MAGAZINE
To Help Meccano Boys to have More Fun than other Boys

Telegrams
Meccano, Liverpool
Editorial Office:
BINNS ROAD,
LIVERPOOL

I possess a No. .... Meccano Outfit.
Will you please send me a free copy of the "Meccano Magazine."

Name ....

Address ....

....

Fig 15.

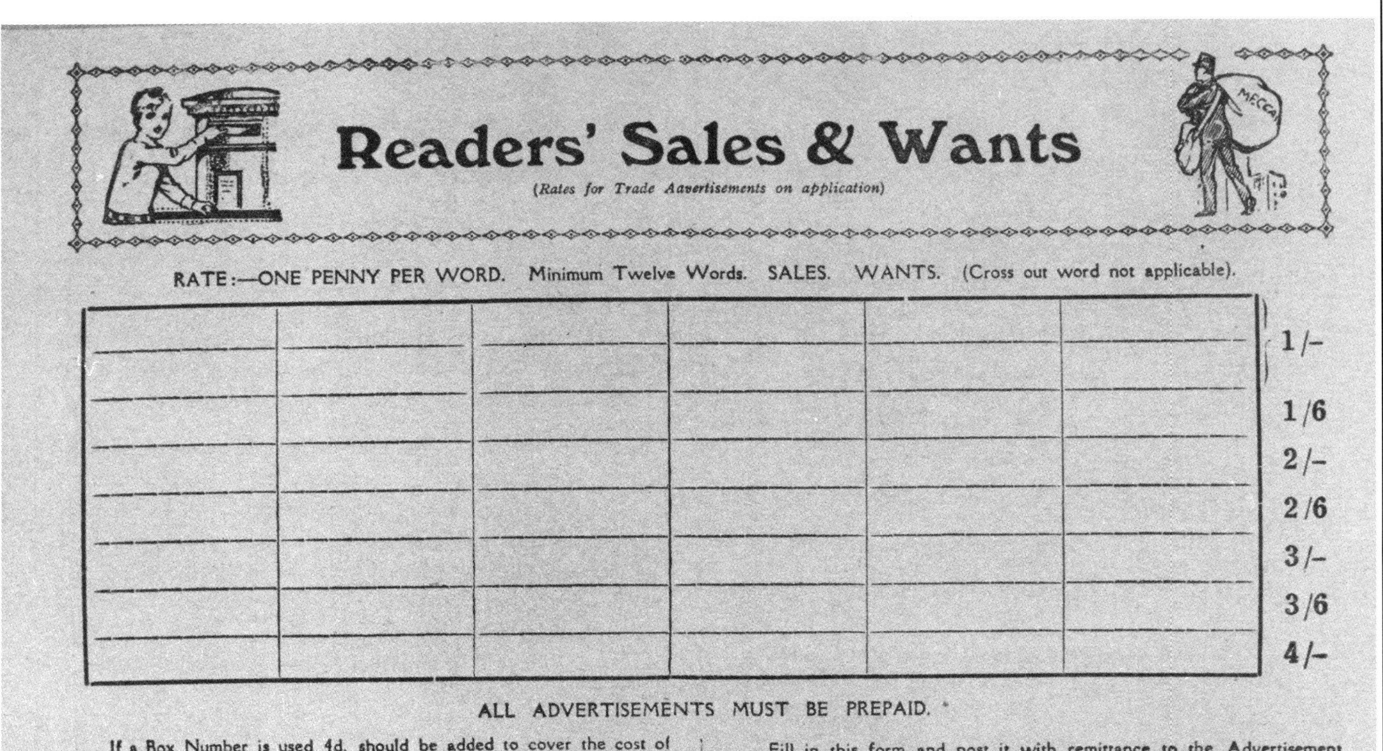

Readers' Sales & Wants

(Rates for Trade Advertisements on application)

RATE:—ONE PENNY PER WORD. Minimum Twelve Words. SALES. WANTS. (Cross out word not applicable).

						1/-
						1/6
						2/-
						2/6
						3/-
						3/6
						4/-

ALL ADVERTISEMENTS MUST BE PREPAID.

If a Box Number is used 4d. should be added to cover the cost of postage of the letters to the advertiser from this office. The letters will be posted one week after the advertisement appears and a second batch a month after the advertisement appears. They will be sent more frequently if additional postage is included with the advertisement.

Fill in this form and post it with remittance to the Advertisement Manager, *Meccano Magazine*, Binns Road, Liverpool. Advertisements must be received not later than the 10th of the month for inclusion in the following month's issue.

TESTIMONY FROM PLEASED ADVERTISERS.

LIVERPOOL.—"*Your Magazine has brought me much better results than other papers.* Through the *Meccano Magazine* I have had mail orders from South Africa, Australia and the West Indies." H.W.R.

ALFRETON.—"We are getting far more enquiries than is usually the case." N. & Co.

MANCHESTER.—"Up to the present, results have been entirely satisfactory." N.M.P.

LONDON, W.C.1.—"*I have had more satisfactory results from my advertisements in your paper than in all the other papers combined in which I advertise.* In nearly every case, each new customer has resulted in one who buys regularly from month to month." A.K.

S. WOODFORD.—"I have already obtained good customers from my last small advertisement." G.P.C.

LEYTON.—"I obtained excellent results from my advertisement in your paper." L.A.S.

UPPER NORWOOD.—"As the result of this advertisement I have received 50 enquiries, including one from Italy." A.C.M.S.

KENTISH TOWN, N.W.—"I have not repeated my advertisement, because *the number of replies was so great that I could hardly cope with them.* I have now made arrangements for dealing with a larger demand and shall be glad if you will insert the enclosed advertisement in your next issue." E.G.

MECCANO MAGAZINE FOR BOYS.

PRICE 2d

If you have anything to sell or wish to buy anything, take advantage of the service offered by a small advertisement in the *Meccano Magazine.*

The "*M.M.*" is read by approximately 100,000 people every month. It circulates in every country where the English language is spoken. If you wish to sell your duplicate stamps, to purchase a loud speaker, a steam engine, a model yacht, or any of the hundred-and-one other things in which boys delight, you will be able to do so through the columns of the "*M.M.*" Turn to page 4 of this leaflet and read what satisfied advertisers say about it.

IMPORTANT.—Advertisements dealing with any article in the current Meccano catalogue cannot be accepted.

Advertisement Manager:
Meccano Magazine, Binns Rd., LIVERPOOL.

Fig 16. An early form for readers' classified advertising using dark pink paper!

Revised Price List. March 1st, 1922.

MECCANO PRICE LIST.

MECCANO OUTFITS.

No. 0	Meccano Outfit	5/-
,, 1	,, ,,	8/6
,, 2	,, ,,	15/-
,, 3	,, ,,	22/6
,, 4	,, ,,	40/-
,, 5	,, ,, (Carton)	55/-
,, 5	,, Presentation Outfit (Wood)	85/-
,, 6	,, Presentation Outfit	140/-

ACCESSORY OUTFITS.

No. 0A	Meccano Outfit	4/-
,, 1A	,, ,,	7/6
,, 2A	,, ,,	8/6
,, 3A	,, ,,	18/6
,, 4A	,, ,,	15/-
,, 5A	,, ,, (Carton)	50/-
,, 5A	,, ,, (Wood)	80/-

INVENTOR'S ACCESSORY OUTFITS.

Inventor's Accessory Outfit "A"	8/6
,, ,, "B"	15/-

ELECTRICAL ACCESSORY OUTFITS.

X1. (Containing electrical parts, without Motor or Accumulator)	12/6
X2. (Containing Meccano Motor, 4-volt Accumulator and electrical parts)	42/-

MECCANO MOTORS.

Clockwork Motor	9/-
Electric Motor	12/6
4-volt Accumulator	17/6

Revised Price List. March 1st, 1922.

MECCANO ACCESSORY PARTS.

No.			s.	d.
1.	Perforated Strips, 12½" long	½ doz.	1	0
1A.	,, ,, 9½" ,,	,,	0	9
1B.	,, ,, 7½" ,,	,,	0	8
2.	,, ,, 5½" ,,	,,	0	6
2A.	,, ,, 4½" ,,	,,	0	5
3.	,, ,, 3½" ,,	,,	0	4
4.	,, ,, 3" ,,	,,	0	3
5.	,, ,, 2½" ,,	,,	0	3
6.	,, ,, 2" ,,	,,	0	3
6A.	,, ,, 1½" ,,	,,	0	3
7.	Angle Girders, 24½" long	each	0	8
7A	,, ,, 18½" ,,	,,	0	6
8.	,, ,, 12½" ,,	½ doz.	1	9
8A.	,, ,, 9½" ,,	,,	1	3
8B.	,, ,, 7½" ,,	,,	1	2
9.	,, ,, 5½" ,,	,,	1	0
9A.	,, ,, 4½" ,,	,,	0	10
9B.	,, ,, 3½" ,,	,,	0	8
9C.	,, ,, 3" ,,	,,	0	8
9D.	,, ,, 2½" ,,	,,	0	7
9E.	,, ,, 2" ,,	,,	0	6
9F.	,, ,, 1½" ,,	,,	0	6
10.	Flat Brackets	,,	0	2
11.	Double Brackets	each	0	1
12.	Angle Brackets	doz.	0	6
12A.	Angle Brackets, [illegible]	each	0	1
13.	Axle Rods, 11½" long	,,	0	3
13A.	,, ,, 8" ,,	,,	0	3
14.	,, ,, 6" ,,	,,	0	2
15.	,, ,, 5" ,,	,,	0	2
15A.	,, ,, 4½" ,,	,,	0	1
16.	,, ,, 3½" ,,	,,	0	1
16A.	,, ,, 2½" ,,	,,	0	1
17.	,, ,, 2" ,,	,,	0	1
18A.	,, ,, 1½" ,,	,,	0	1
19.	Crank Handles	,,	0	3
19A.	Wheels, 3" diam. with set screws	,,	0	8
20.	Flanged Wheels	,,	0	6
19B.	Pulley Wheels, 3" dia. with set screw,	each	0	8
20A.	,, 2" ,, ,, ,,	,,	0	6
21.	,, 1½" ,, ,, ,,	,,	0	6
22.	,, 1" ,, ,, ,,	,,	0	4
23A.	,, ½" ,, ,, ,,	,,	0	4
22A.	,, 1" ,, without ,,	,,	0	2
23.	,, ½" ,, ,, ,,	,,	0	2
24.	Bush Wheels	,,	0	6
25.	Pinion Wheels, ¾" diam.	,,	0	6
26.	,, ,, ½" ,,	,,	0	4
27.	Gear Wheels, 50 teeth	,,	0	9
27A.	,, ,, 57 ,,	,,	0	9
28.	Contrate Wheels, 1½" diam.	,,	0	9
29.	,, ,, ¾" ,,	,,	0	6
30.	Bevel Gears	,,	0	10
31.	Gear Wheels, 1", 38 teeth	,,	1	0
32.	Worm Wheels	,,	0	6
33.	Pawls (complete)	,,	0	4
33A.	Pivot Bolts with Nuts	,,	0	2
34.	Spanners	,,	0	2
35.	Spring Clips	per box (doz.)	0	3
36.	Screw Drivers	each	0	3
36A.	,, ,, (extra long)	,,	0	6
37.	Nuts and Bolts	per box (doz.)	0	6
37A.	Nuts	,, ,,	0	3
37B.	Bolts	,, ,,	0	3
38.	Washers	doz.	0	1
40.	Hanks of Cord	2 for	0	3
41.	Propeller Blades	per pair	0	4
43.	Springs	each	0	2
44.	Cranked Bent Strips	,,	0	1
45.	Double Bent Strips	,,	0	1
46.	Double Angle Strips, 2½" × 1"	½ doz.	0	6
50.	Eye Pieces	each	0	2
52.	Perforated Flanged Plates, 5½" × 2½"	,,	0	5
52A.	Flat Plates, 5½" × 3½"	,,	0	5
53.	Perforated Flanged Plates, 3½" × 2½"	,,	0	3
53A.	Flat Plates, 4½" × 2½"	,,	0	3
54.	Perforated Flanged Sector Plates	,,	0	3
55.	Perforated Strips, slotted, 5½" long	,,	0	2
55A.	,, ,, ,, 2" ,,	,,	0	1
56.	Instruction Manuals, No. 0	,,	0	4
	,, ,, No. 1	,,	2	6
	,, ,, No. 2	,,	1	3
	,, ,, No. 3	,,	1	3
57.	Hooks	,,	0	1
57A.	,, (scientific)	,,	0	1
57B.	,, (loaded)	,,	0	5
58.	Spring Cord	per length (1 yard)	0	9
59.	Collars with Set Screws	each	0	2

No.			s.	d.
60.	Double Angle Strips, 2½" × ½"	per ½ doz.	0	5
60A.	,, ,, ,, 1½" × ½"	,,	0	4
60B.	,, ,, ,, 3½" × ½"	,,	0	6
60C.	,, ,, ,, 5½" × ½"	,,	0	9
60D.	,, ,, ,, 4½" × ½"	,,	0	9
61.	Windmill Sails	each	0	2
62.	Cranks	,,	0	3
62A.	Threaded Cranks	,,	0	4
63.	Couplings	,,	0	6
63A.	Octagonal Couplings	,,	0	8
63B.	Strip Couplings	,,	0	8
63C.	Threaded Couplings	,,	0	6
64.	Threaded Bosses	,,	0	2
65.	Centre Forks	,,	0	2
66.	Weights, 50 gramme	,,	1	0
67.	,, 25 ,,	,,	1	0
68.	Woodscrews, ½"	doz.	0	3
69.	Set Screws	,,	0	4
69A.	Grub Screws, 5/32	,,	0	4
69B.	,, ,, 7/32	,,	0	6
70.	Flat Plates, 5½" × 2½"	each	0	3
72.	,, ,, 2½" × 2½"	,,	0	2
76.	Triangular Plates, 2½"	,,	0	2
77.	,, ,, 1"	,,	0	1
78.	Screwed Rods, 11½"	,,	0	6
79.	,, ,, 8"	,,	0	5
79A.	,, ,, 6"	,,	0	4
80.	,, ,, 5"	,,	0	3
80A.	,, ,, 3½"	,,	0	3
80B.	,, ,, 4½"	,,	0	3
81.	,, ,, 2"	,,	0	2
89.	Curved Strips, 5½"	,,	0	2
90.	,, ,, 2½"	,,	0	1
94.	Sprocket Chain	per yard	0	6
95.	Sprocket Wheels, 2" diam	each	0	5
95A.	,, ,, 1½" ,,	,,	0	4
95B.	,, ,, 3" ,,	,,	0	6
96.	,, ,, 1" ,,	,,	0	3
96A.	,, ,, ¾" ,,	,,	0	3
97.	Braced Girders, 3½" long	½ doz.	0	9
98.	,, ,, 2½" ,,	,,	0	6
99.	,, ,, 12½" ,,	,,	1	9
99A.	,, ,, 9½" ,,	,,	1	6
100.	,, ,, 5½" ,,	,,	1	0
101.	Healds, for looms	doz.	0	9
102.	Single Bent Strips	each	0	1
103.	Flat Girders, 5½" long	½ doz.	1	0
103A.	,, ,, 9½" ,,	,,	1	6
103B.	,, ,, 12½" ,,	,,	2	0
103C.	,, ,, 4½" ,,	,,	0	9
103D.	,, ,, 3½" ,,	,,	0	7
103E.	,, ,, 3" ,,	,,	0	6
103F.	,, ,, 2½" ,,	,,	0	5
103G.	,, ,, 2" ,,	,,	0	4
103H.	,, ,, 1½" ,,	,,	0	3
104.	Shuttles, for looms	each	4	0
105.	Reed Hooks, for looms	,,	0	4
106.	Cloth Rollers	,,	1	3
106A.	Sand ,,	,,	1	6
107.	Tables for Designing Machines	,,	1	0
108.	Architraves	,,	0	2
109.	Face Plates, 2½" diam.	,,	0	4
110.	Rack Strips, 3½"	,,	0	2
111.	Bolts, ¾"	,,	0	1
111A.	,, ½"	2 for	0	1
111B.	,, 3/16"	doz.	0	4
112.	Double Angle Strips, 2½" × 1½"	½ doz.	0	8
112A.	,, ,, ,, 3" × 1½"	,,	1	0
113.	Girder Frames	each	0	[illegible]
114.	Hinges	per pair	0	4
115.	Threaded Pins	each	0	2
120.	Buffers, for Locos, etc.	,,	0	2
121.	Train Couplings	,,	0	4
122.	Miniature Loaded Sacks	,,	0	2
123.	Cone Pulleys	,,	1	3
124.	Reversed Angle Brackets, 1"	½ doz.	0	10
125.	,, ,, ,, ½"	,,	0	6
126.	Trunnions	each	0	3
126A.	Flat Trunnions	,,	0	2
127.	Simple Bell Cranks	,,	0	3
128.	Boss Bell Cranks	,,	0	4
129.	Rack Segments, 3" diam.	,,	0	6
130.	Triple Throw Eccentrics	,,	1	3
131.	Dredger Buckets	,,	0	2
132.	Flywheels, 2¾" diam.	,,	2	3
133.	Corner Brackets	,,	0	3
134.	Crank Shafts, 1" stroke	,,	0	3
135.	Theodolite protractors	,,	0	3

Fig 17. 1922 Revised price list.

Revised Price List. March 1st, 192[illegible]

HORNBY CLOCK WORK TRAINS

No. 1 Hornby Train Set, Passenger	35/–
,, ,, ,, Goods	25/6
In brown leather-finished, gold-embossed box.	
No. 1 Hornby Locos ... ... each	16/–
,, ,, Tenders ... ... ,,	3/6
,, ,, Passenger Coaches, ,,	6/6
,, ,, Wagons ... ... ,,	3/9
No. 2 Hornby Train Set, Pullman	70/–
,, ,, ,, Goods	45/–
In brown leather-finished, gold-embossed box.	
No. 2 Hornby Locos ... ... each	30/–
,, ,, Tenders ... ... ,,	4/–
,, ,, Passenger Coaches, ,,	16/–
,, ,, Wagons ... ... ,,	3/9
Covered Luggage Vans ... ... ,,	4/6
Timber Wagons ... ... ,,	5/6
Lattice Girder Bridges ... ... ,,	10/6
Tin Printed Clockwork Train Set	12/6
Tin Printed Locos ... ... each	8/6
,, ,, ,, Tenders ... ... ,,	1/–
,, ,, ,, Carriages ... ... ,,	1/3

RAILS.

Gauge 0.

Rails, straight or curved (2 ft. or 4 ft. diam.) ... per doz.	5/–
Right angle Crossings ... ... each	2/6
Acute angle Crossings ... ... ,,	2/6
Points (right or left hand) for 2 ft. diameter ... ,,	3/9
,, ,, ,, ,, ,, 4 ft. ,, ... ,,	3/9

SEND FOR SPECIAL PRICE LIST OF RAILS, POINTS AND CROSSINGS.

32 / 18 / 44.

Fig 17 cont.

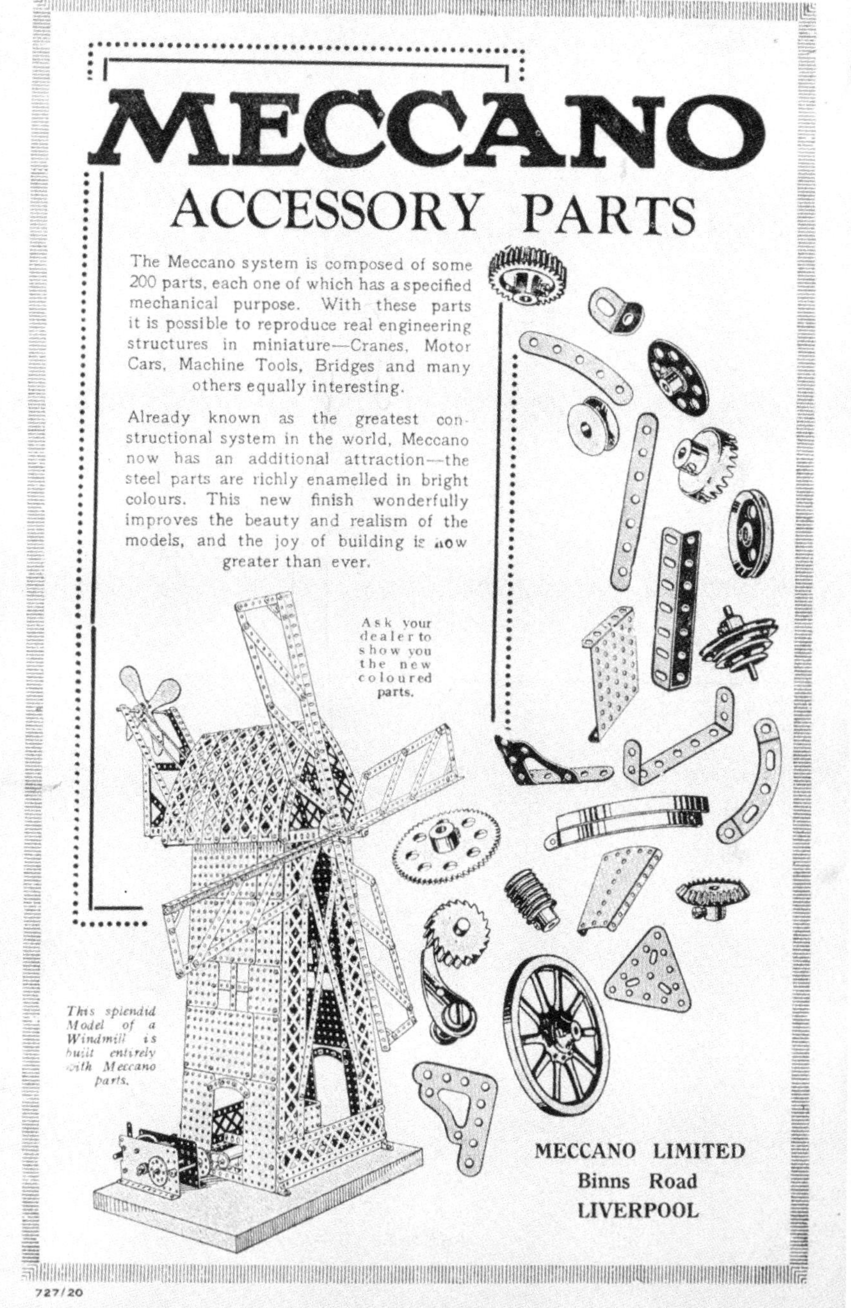

MECCANO
ACCESSORY PARTS
The Meccano system is composed of some 200 parts, each one of which has a specified mechanical purpose. With these parts it is possible to reproduce real engineering structures in miniature—Cranes, Motor Cars, Machine Tools, Bridges and many others equally interesting.
Already known as the greatest constructional system in the world, Meccano now has an additional attraction—the steel parts are richly enamelled in bright colours. This new finish wonderfully improves the beauty and realism of the models, and the joy of building is now greater than ever.
Ask your dealer to show you the new coloured parts.
This splendid Model of a Windmill is built entirely with Meccano parts.
MECCANO LIMITED
Binns Road
LIVERPOOL
727/20

Fig 18. 1927 price list.

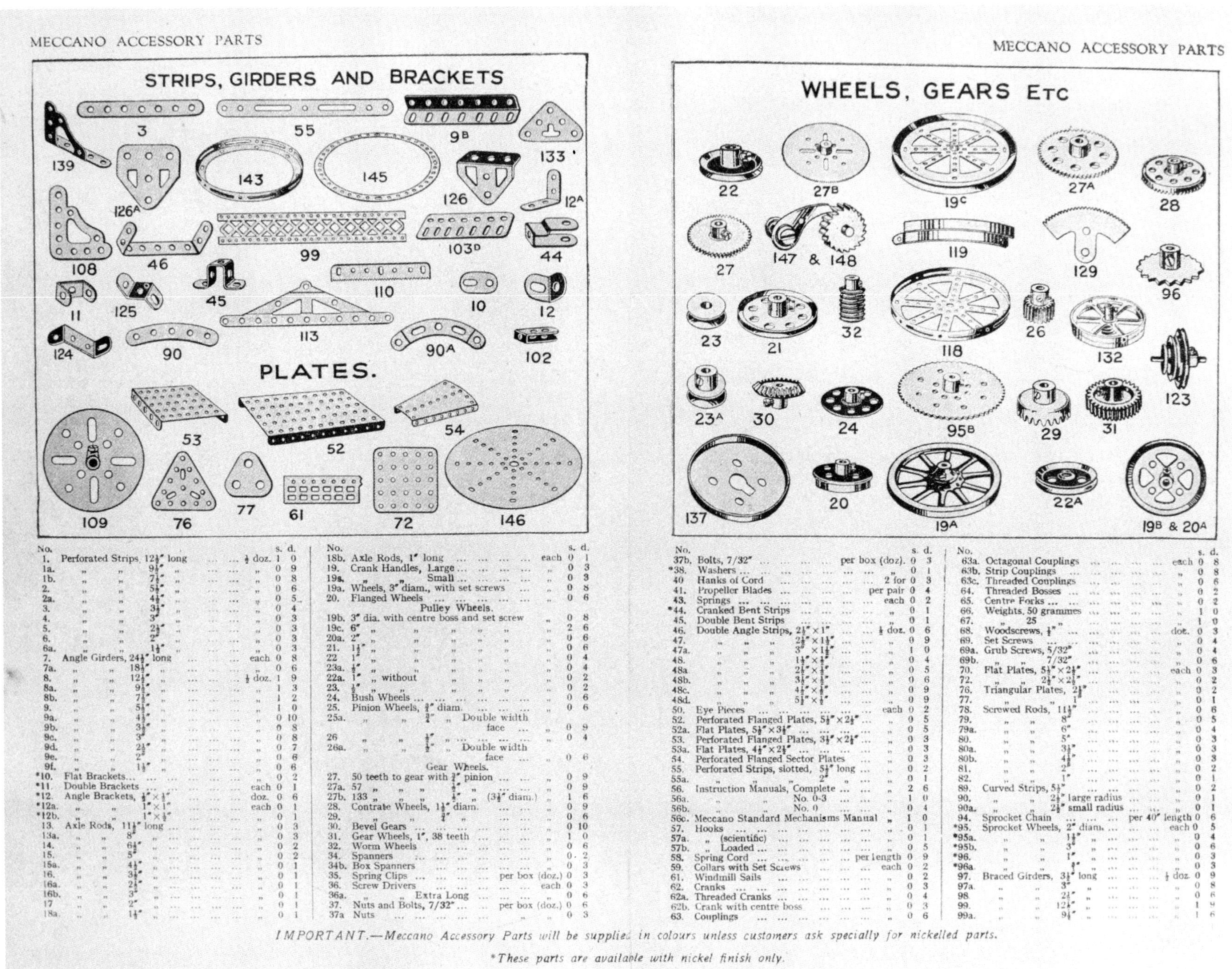

No.			s.	d.
1.	Perforated Strips, 12½" long	½ doz.	1	0
1a.	„ „ 9½" „	„	0	9
1b.	„ „ 7½" „	„	0	8
2.	„ „ 5½" „	„	0	6
2a.	„ „ 4½" „	„	0	5
3.	„ „ 3½" „	„	0	4
4.	„ „ 3" „	„	0	3
5.	„ „ 2½" „	„	0	3
6.	„ „ 2" „	„	0	3
6a.	„ „ 1½" „	„	0	3
7.	Angle Girders, 24½" long	each	0	8
7a.	„ „ 18½" „	„	0	6
8.	„ „ 12½" „	½ doz.	1	9
8a.	„ „ 9½" „	„	1	3
8b.	„ „ 7½" „	„	1	2
9.	„ „ 5½" „	„	1	0
9a.	„ „ 4½" „	„	0	10
9b.	„ „ 3½" „	„	0	8
9c.	„ „ 3" „	„	0	8
9d.	„ „ 2½" „	„	0	7
9e.	„ „ 2" „	„	0	6
9f.	„ „ 1½" „	„	0	6
*10.	Flat Brackets...	„	0	2
*11.	Double Brackets	each	0	1
*12.	Angle Brackets, ½"×½"	doz.	0	6
*12a.	„ „ 1"×1"	each	0	1
*12b.	„ „ 1"×½"	„	0	1
13.	Axle Rods, 11½" long	„	0	3
13a.	„ „ 8" „	„	0	3
14.	„ „ 6½" „	„	0	2
15.	„ „ 5" „	„	0	2
15a.	„ „ 4½" „	„	0	1
16.	„ „ 3½" „	„	0	1
16a.	„ „ 2½" „	„	0	1
16b.	„ „ 3" „	„	0	1
17	„ „ 2" „	„	0	1
18a.	„ „ 1½" „	„	0	1

No.			s.	d.
18b.	Axle Rods, 1" long	each	0	1
19.	Crank Handles, Large...	„	0	3
19s.	„ „ Small...	„	0	3
19a.	Wheels, 3" diam., with set screws	„	0	8
20.	Flanged Wheels	„	0	6
	Pulley Wheels.			
19b.	3" dia. with centre boss and set screw	„	0	8
19c.	6" „ „ „ „ „	„	2	6
20a.	2" „ „ „ „ „	„	0	6
21.	1½" „ „ „ „ „	„	0	6
22	1" „ „ „ „ „	„	0	4
23a.	½" „ „ „ „ „	„	0	4
22a.	1" „ without „ „ „	„	0	2
23.	½" „ „ „ „ „	„	0	2
24.	Bush Wheels...	„	0	6
25.	Pinion Wheels, ¾" diam.	„	0	6
25a.	„ „ ¾" „ Double width face ...	„	0	9
26	„ „ ½" „	„	0	4
26a.	„ „ ½" „ Double width face ...	„	0	6
	Gear Wheels.			
27.	50 teeth to gear with ¾" pinion	„	0	9
27a.	57 „ „ „ ½" „	„	0	9
27b.	133 „ „ „ ½" „ (3½" diam.)	„	1	6
28.	Contrate Wheels, 1½" diam.	„	0	9
29.	„ „ ¾" „	„	0	6
30.	Bevel Gears	„	0	10
31.	Gear Wheels, 1", 38 teeth	„	1	0
32.	Worm Wheels	„	0	6
34.	Spanners	„	0	2
34b.	Box Spanners	„	0	3
35.	Spring Clips ...	per box (doz.)	0	3
36.	Screw Drivers	each	0	3
36a.	„ „ Extra Long	„	0	6
37.	Nuts and Bolts, 7/32" ...	per box (doz.)	0	6
37a	Nuts	„ „	0	3

No.			s.	d.
37b.	Bolts, 7/32"	per box (doz).	0	3
*38.	Washers ...	„	0	1
40	Hanks of Cord	2 for	0	3
41.	Propeller Blades ...	per pair	0	4
43.	Springs ...	each	0	2
*44.	Cranked Bent Strips	„	0	1
45.	Double Bent Strips	„	0	1
46.	Double Angle Strips, 2½"×1"	½ doz.	0	6
47.	„ „ „ 2½"×1½"	„	0	9
47a.	„ „ „ 3" ×1½"	„	1	0
48.	„ „ „ 1½"×½"	„	0	4
48a	„ „ „ 2½"×½"	„	0	5
48b.	„ „ „ 3½"×½"	„	0	6
48c.	„ „ „ 4½"×½"	„	0	9
48d.	„ „ „ 5½"×½"	„	0	9
50.	Eye Pieces	each	0	2
52.	Perforated Flanged Plates, 5½"×2½" ...	„	0	5
52a.	Flat Plates, 5½"×3½" ...	„	0	5
53.	Perforated Flanged Plates, 3½"×2½" ...	„	0	3
53a.	Flat Plates, 4½"×2½" ...	„	0	3
54.	Perforated Flanged Sector Plates	„	0	3
55.	Perforated Strips, slotted, 5½" long ...	„	0	2
55a.	„ „ „ 2" „	„	0	1
56.	Instruction Manuals, Complete ...	„	2	6
56a.	„ „ No. 0-3	„	1	0
56b.	„ „ No. 0	„	0	4
56c.	Meccano Standard Mechanisms Manual	„	1	0
57.	Hooks	„	0	1
57a.	„ (scientific)	„	0	1
57b.	„ Loaded ...	„	0	5
58.	Spring Cord	per length	0	9
59.	Collars with Set Screws	each	0	2
61.	Windmill Sails	„	0	2
62.	Cranks	„	0	3
62a.	Threaded Cranks ...	„	0	4
62b.	Crank with centre boss	„	0	3
63.	Couplings	„	0	6

No.			s.	d.
63a.	Octagonal Couplings	each	0	8
63b.	Strip Couplings	„	0	8
63c.	Threaded Couplings	„	0	6
64.	Threaded Bosses ...	„	0	2
65.	Centre Forks ...	„	0	2
66.	Weights, 50 grammes	„	1	0
67.	„ 25 „	„	1	0
68.	Woodscrews, ½"	doz.	0	3
69.	Set Screws	„	0	4
69a.	Grub Screws, 5/32"	„	0	4
69b.	„ „ 7/32"	„	0	6
70.	Flat Plates, 5½"×2½"	each	0	3
72.	„ „ 2½"×2½"	„	0	2
76.	Triangular Plates, 2½"	„	0	2
77.	„ „ 1"	„	0	1
78.	Screwed Rods, 11½"	„	0	6
79.	„ „ 8"	„	0	5
79a.	„ „ 6"	„	0	4
80.	„ „ 5"	„	0	3
80a.	„ „ 3½"	„	0	3
80b.	„ „ 4½"	„	0	3
81.	„ „ 2"	„	0	2
82.	„ „ 1"	„	0	1
89.	Curved Strips, 5½"	„	0	2
90.	„ „ 2½" large radius	„	0	1
90a.	„ „ 2½" small radius	„	0	1
94.	Sprocket Chain	per 40" length	0	6
*95.	Sprocket Wheels, 2" diam. ...	each	0	5
*95a.	„ „ 1½" „	„	0	4
*95b.	„ „ 3" „	„	0	6
*96.	„ „ 1" „	„	0	3
*96a.	„ „ ¾" „	„	0	3
97.	Braced Girders, 3½" long	½ doz.	0	9
97a.	„ „ 3" „	„	0	8
98.	„ „ 2½" „	„	0	6
99.	„ „ 12½" „	„	1	9
99a.	„ „ 9½" „	„	1	6

IMPORTANT.—Meccano Accessory Parts will be supplied in colours unless customers ask specially for nickelled parts.

**These parts are available with nickel finish only.*

Fig 18 cont.

REVISED PRICE LIST

MECCANO

As the 1928 Meccano Outfits contain a greater number and wider selection of parts than previously, it has been found necessary to increase the prices of several of them. Actually, there is no comparison between the tremendously increased value of the Outfits and the small increase in the prices. The following is the new price list.

REVISED MECCANO PRICE LIST

Complete Outfits

No. 00 Outfit	3/6
„ 0 „	5/-
„ 1 „	10/-
„ 2 „	16/-
„ 3 „	27/6
„ 4 „	50/-
„ 5 „ (carton)	65/-
„ 5 „ (cabinet)	95/-
„ 6 „ (carton)	115/-
„ 6 „ (cabinet)	150/-
„ 7 „	380/-

Accessory Outfits

No. 00A Accessory Outfit	1/6
„ 0A „ „	5/6
„ 1A „ „	7/-
„ 2A „ „	12/6
„ 3A „ „	23/6
„ 4A „ „	15/-
„ 5A „ „ (carton)	50/-
„ 5A „ „ (cabinet)	80/-
„ 6A „ „	215/-
Special Inventor's Outfit	17/6

Many new Meccano parts have been added to the system and in some cases the prices of the existing parts have been revised. A complete new list of Meccano Accessory parts accompanies this leaflet.

HORNBY TRAINS

Alterations have been made in the contents of several Hornby Train Sets, as indicated below. In some cases new rolling stock has been added, while in others replacements of rolling stock have been effected in order to give a more realistic appearance to the sets. These additions do not increase the prices of the train sets concerned. In fact, No. 0 Passenger Set is now reduced from 22/6 to 20/-.

Revisions

No. 0 Goods Set contains two Wagons instead of one.
„ 0 Passenger Set contains one Coach and one Guard's Van instead of two Coaches.
„ 1 Goods Set contains one Brake Van in addition to one Wagon.
„ 1 Passenger Set contains one Guard's Van in addition to two Coaches.

No. 2 Goods Set contains one Brake Van in addition to two Wagons.
„ 2 Tank Passenger Set contains three No. 1 Pullman Coaches and one No. 1 Pullman Coach Composite instead of three Passenger Coaches and one Guard's Van.

It has been decided to discontinue the manufacture of CO1 Crossover (1 ft. radius) and PPR1 and PPL1 Parallel Points (1 ft. radius). We shall continue to supply the corresponding subjects in the 2 ft. radius size, as this may be used for either 1 ft. or 2 ft. radius tracks.

REVISED HORNBY TRAIN PRICE LIST

Clockwork Train Sets

No. M 1 Passenger Set	7/6
„ M 2 „	9/-
„ M 3 Goods Set	15/-
Hornby No. 0 Goods Set	17/6
„ „ 0 Passenger Set	20/-
„ „ 1 Goods Set	20/-
„ „ 1 „ „ fitted for Hornby Control	23/6
„ „ 1 Passenger Set	25/-
„ „ 1 „ „ fitted for Hornby Control	28/6
„ „ 2 Goods Set	32/6
„ „ 2 „ „ fitted for Hornby Control	37/6
„ „ 2 Pullman Set	50/-
„ „ 2 „ „ fitted for Hornby Control	55/-
Hornby No. 1 Tank Goods Set	22/6
„ „ 1 „ „ „ fitted for Hornby Control	26/-
„ „ 2 „ „ „	37/6
„ „ 2 „ „ „ fitted for Hornby Control	42/6
„ „ 2 Tank Passenger Set	40/-
„ „ 2 „ „ „ fitted for Hornby Control	45/-
„ „ 3c G.W.R. "Cornish Riviera"	60/-
„ „ 3c L.N.E.R. "Flying Scotsman"	60/-
„ „ 3c L.M.S.R. "Royal Scot"	60/-
„ „ 3c S.R. "Continental Express"	60/-
„ „ 3c Riviera "Blue" Train	62/6
„ Metropolitan Train Set C	55/-

Electric Train Sets

Hornby No. 3E G.W.R. "Cornish Riviera" (4 volt)	75/-
„ „ 3E L.N.E.R. "Flying Scotsman" (4 volt)	75/-
„ „ 3E L.M.S.R. "Royal Scot" (4 volt)	75/-
Hornby No. 3E S.R. "Continental Express" (4 volt)	75/-
„ „ 3E Riviera "Blue" Train (4 volt)	77/6
„ Metropolitan L.V. (4 volt)	95/-
Hornby Metropolitan H.V. (100-250 volt)	110/-

Rolling Stock and Accessories

The prices of the undermentioned Rolling Stock and Accessories have been revised and are now as follows —

Hornby Passenger Coach No. 0-1	2/6
Riviera "Blue" Train Coach	12/6
Seccotine Van	3/6
Guard's Van	2/6
Pullman Coach No. 2-3 (Improved Design)	11/6
Goods Platform (Improved Design)	10/6

The prices of other Hornby Rolling Stock and Accessories remain the same as previously.

1928 MECCANO LIMITED, BINNS ROAD, LIVERPOOL U.K

Fig 19. 1928 – revised price list increases are nothing new!

MECCANO

The Toy that made Engineering famous

Real Engineering in Miniature

Boys learn the secrets of real engineering in the best of all ways when they make Meccano model-building their hobby, for they build with real engineering parts in miniature, all standardised and interchangeable. The Strips and Plates are made of heavy steel and all Meccano Gears and Pinions are machine-cut from the finest brass.

One of the finest things about Meccano is that it brings the engineering wonders of the world into your own home. You can commence to build models—real engineering structures in miniature—immediately you open your Outfit. The only tool required is a screw-driver, and even this is provided.

Hundreds of Models

There is no limit to the number of models you can build—you can have a new one every day in the year if you like, and all Meccano models work.

When you build with Meccano parts you have all the thrills of a real engineer, because you build your models, piece by piece, and when they are completed you work them in exactly the same manner as an engineer would work the corresponding machines in real life.

Meccano Service

The service of Meccano does not end with selling an Outfit and an Instruction Manual. When you want to know something more about engineering than is now shown in our books, or when you strike a tough problem of any kind, write to us. We receive over 200 letters from boys every day all the year round. Some write to us because they are in difficulty, others because they want advice on their work or pleasures, or about their choice of a career. Others, again, write to us just because they like to do so, and we are glad to know that they regard us as their friends.

Although all kinds of queries are put to us on all manner of subjects, the main interest is, of course, engineering. No one has such a wonderful knowledge of engineering matters as that possessed by our staff of experts. This vast store of knowledge, gained only by many years of experience, is at your service.

The Meccano Magazine is the Meccano boys' own newspaper, and deals with all subjects of interest to boys. It is published monthly and may be had from your Meccano dealer price 6d., or direct from Meccano Ltd., Old Swan, Liverpool, price 8d., post free.

Meccano Model of a Giant Block-Setting Crane

We want the Meccano boy of to-day to be the famous engineer of to-morrow!

MECCANO LIMITED BINNS ROAD OLD SWAN LIVERPOOL ENGLAND

Fig 20. An unusual and low print run price list which appears to have become out of date within three months of issue.

MECCANO PRICE LIST

SEE REVISED PRICES MARCH 1930

COMPLETE OUTFITS

No. 00 Meccano Outfit	3/6
„ 0 „ „	5/–
„ 1 „ „	10/–
„ 2 „ „	16/–
„ 3 „ „	27/6
„ 4 „ „	50/–
„ 5* „ „ (Carton)	65/–
„ 5* „ „ (Enamelled Cabinet)	95/–
„ 6* „ „ (Carton)	115/–
„ 6* „ „ (Enamelled Cabinet)	150/–
„ 7 „ „ „ „	365/–

ACCESSORY OUTFITS

No. 00A Meccano Accessory Outfit	1/6
„ 0A „ „ „	5/6
„ 1A „ „ „	7/–
„ 2A „ „ „	12/6
„ 3A „ „ „	23/6
„ 4A „ „ „	15/–
„ 5A* „ „ „ (Carton)	50/–
„ 5A* „ „ „ (Enamelled Cabinet)	80/–
„ 6A „ „ „ „ „	200/–
Special Inventor's Outfit	17/6

* Outfits Nos. 5, 5A and 6 are supplied in neat and well-made cardboard boxes (cartons) or in superior enamelled cabinets, with lock and key.

MECCANO MOTORS, Etc.

Meccano Clockwork Motor	7/6
„ Electric Motor No. 1 (6-Volt)	15/6
Transformer	30/–
Meccano Accumulator (6-Volt, 20 Amps.)	28/6
Resistance Controller (for low voltage motors)	3/6
No. 1 Meccano Storage Box	10/6
„ 2 „ „ „	21/–
„ 3 „ „ „	30/–
Meccano Steam Engine	21/–

SEE REVISED PRICES MARCH 1930

HORNBY TRAIN PRICE LIST

M0 Passenger Set	6/–
M1 „ „	7/6
M2 „ „	9/–
M Goods Set	8/6
Hornby No. 0 Goods Set	15/–
„ „ 0 Passenger Set	15/–
„ „ 1 Goods Set	20/–
„ „ 1 Passenger Set	25/–
„ „ 1 Tank Goods Set	22/6
„ „ 1 Special Goods Set	30/–
„ „ 1 „ Passenger Set	32/6
„ „ 2 „ Goods Set	35/–
„ „ 2 „ Pullman Set	55/–
Hornby No. 2 Mixed Goods Set	37/6
Metropolitan Train Set, L.V. (6-Volt Electric)	95/–
„ „ „ C (Clockwork)	55/–
Riviera "Blue" Train Set No. 3E (6-Volt Electric)	77/6
„ „ „ „ 3C (Clockwork)	62/6
Hornby No. 3C "Cornish Riviera" (Clockwork)	60/–
„ „ 3E „ „ (6-Volt Electric)	75/–
„ „ 3C "Flying Scotsman" (Clockwork)	60/–
„ „ 3E „ „ (6-Volt Electric)	75/–
„ „ 3C "Royal Scot" (Clockwork)	60/–
„ „ 3E „ „ (6-Volt Electric)	75/–
„ „ 3C "Continental Express" (Clockwork)	60/–
„ „ 3E „ „ (6-Volt Electric)	75/–

2/1229/1

1st March 1930

REVISED PRICES

The prices of a number of Meccano Outfits, Hornby Train Sets, Hornby Rolling Stock and Accessories have been revised as indicated below.

MECCANO

COMPLETE OUTFITS.

Item	s.	d.
No. 4 Outfit	52	6
„ 5 „ (Carton) ..	70	0
„ 5 „ (Wood Cabinet)	100	0
„ 6 „ (Carton) ...	125	0
„ 6 „ (Wood Cabinet)	155	0
„ 7 „ (Wood Cabinet)	450	0

ACCESSORY OUTFITS, ETC.

Item	s.	d.
No. 3a	26	0
„ 4a	17	6
„ 5a (Carton)	55	0
„ 5a (In a No. 6 Wood Cabinet)	97	6
„ 6a (Wood Cabinet)	235	0
Resistance Controller....	4	6
Meccano Steam Engine ...	25	0

NOTE:— The Special Inventor's Outfit has been withdrawn.

MECCANO ACCESSORY PARTS.

Item	s.	d.
No. 37 Nuts & Bolts 7/32" ... per box (doz).	0	4
„ 37a Nuts „ „ ... „ „	0	2
„ 37b Bolts 7/32" ... „ „	0	2

HORNBY TRAINS

TRAIN SETS (CLOCKWORK).

Item	s.	d.
No. 1 Special Goods	32	6
No. 1 Special Passenger	35	0
No. 2 Special Pullman	67	6
No. 2 Mixed Goods	40	0
No. 3c Pullman	67	6

TRAIN SETS (ELECTRIC).

Item	s.	d.
No. 3E Pullman, L.M.S., L.N.E.R., G.W. or S.R.	85	0
No. 3E Riviera "Blue"	80	0

LOCOMOTIVES.

Item	s.	d.
No. 1 Special	18	0
No. 2 Special	27	6
No. 1 Tank Special	18	0
No. 2 „ „	25	0
No. 3E, L.M.S., L.N.E.R., G.W. or S.R.	40	0
No. 3E Riviera "Blue"	40	0

TENDERS.

Item	s.	d.
Riviera "Blue"	5	6
No. 1 Special	3	6
No. 2 Special	6	6

COACHES.

Item	s.	d.
No. 1 Pullman....	3	6
No. 1 Pullman Composite	4	0
No. 2/3 Pullman	15	0
No. 2/3 Pullman Composite	16	0
Riviera "Blue"	14	0

ROLLING STOCK.

Item	s.	d.
Guard's Van	3	0
Milk Tank Wagon	6	0
Wine Wagon, Single Barrel	4	0
„ „ Double „	5	0
Bitumen Tank Wagon "Colas"	5	3
Covered Wagon	3	0
Cattle Truck No. 1	3	3
Gunpowder Van	3	6
Hopper Wagon	3	6
Trolley Wagon	4	6

ACCESSORIES.

Item	s.	d.
Buffer Stops No. 2	5	6
Engine Shed No. 1	15	0
„ „ No. 2	22	6
Footbridge No. 1	4	0
Footbridge No. 2	7	6
Footbridge No. 3 (Lattice Girder)....	12	6
Junction Signal	6	0
Lamp Standard No. 1	3	6
„ „ No. 2	4	6
Level Crossing No. 2	5	6
Loading Gauge	2	3
Platform Crane	4	9
Platform, Goods	12	6
Ramps, pairs	2	6
Shunter's Pole	0	3
Signals No. 1, pairs	3	3
„ Double Arm, No. 1, pairs	4	3
Signals for Footbridge No. 2 pairs	3	9
Station No. 1	6	0
„ No. 2	12	6
Tarpaulin Sheet	0	3
Telegraph Poles, pairs	4	0
Turntable No. 1	2	9
„ No. 2	4	6
Viaduct Centre	4	9
Electric Viaduct Centre	5	3
Water Tank	8	6
Signal Cabin No. 2	5	6

RAILS, ETC.

Item	s.	d.
DS1 Straight rails, double track, ½-doz.	6	6
DC 2 Curved rails, double track, (2 ft. radius) ½-doz.	7	6
Crossings, CA1 and CR1 each	2	0
„ CA2 and CR2 „	1	9
Points on solid base, (2 ft. radius) pairs	8	6

NOTE:— The No. 2 Special Goods Set has been withdrawn.

MECCANO LIMITED, Old Swan, LIVERPOOL

1/330/10(2) U.K.

Fig 21. The full list of price revisions of March 1930.

Fig 22. Front and rear sides of another unusual price list of 1932.→

MECCANO

A THOUSAND TOYS IN ONE

If you want to have the happiest possible boyhood, be a Meccano model-builder. There is no other hobby in the world half so wonderful or half so fascinating.

A Meccano boy is able to build hundreds of splendid working models with the greatest of ease. One day a crane, the next day a bridge, the day after a motor car. Day in and day out there is always something different to build, some new thrill to enjoy.

Meccano models are real engineering models, because they are built with real engineering parts in miniature that can be used over and over again to make hundreds of different models.

Meccano is the finest hobby in the world for boys!

MECCANO OUTFITS

MECCANO X SERIES OUTFITS

MECCANO AEROPLANE CONSTRUCTOR OUTFITS

MECCANO MOTOR CAR CONSTRUCTOR OUTFIT

MECCANO MOTORS AND STEAM ENGINE

MECCANO PARTS AND ACCESSORIES

PRICE LIST

COMPLETE OUTFITS

Item		s.	d.
X Series Outfit No. 1	Price	1	3
X Series Outfit No. 2	„	2	0
No. 000 Outfit	„	2	6
No. 00 „	„	3	6
No. 0 „	„	5	0
No. 1 „	„	10	0
No. 2 „	„	16	0
No. 3 „	„	27	6
No. 4 „	„	52	6
No. 5 „ ... ... (carton)	„	70	0
No. 5 „ ... ... (cabinet)	„	100	0
No. 6 „ ... ... (carton)	„	125	0
No. 6 „ ... ... (cabinet)	„	155	0
No. 7 „ ... ... (cabinet)	„	450	0

ACCESSORY OUTFITS

Item		s.	d.
X Series Accessory Outfit No. 1a	Price	1	0
No. 00a Accessory Outfit	„	1	6
No. 0a „ „	„	5	6
No. 1a „ „	„	7	0
No. 2a „ „	„	12	6
No. 3a „ „	„	26	0
No. 4a „ „	„	17	6
No. 5a „ „	„	55	0
No. 5a „ „ (with No. 6 Outfit cabinet)	„	97	6
No. 6a „ „ (cabinet)	„	235	0

MECCANO MOTORS AND STEAM ENGINE

Item		s.	d.
Meccano X Series Clockwork Motor (non-reversing)	Price	2	6
Meccano Clockwork Motor No. 1 (non-reversing)	„	5	0
Meccano Clockwork Motor No. 1a (reversing)	„	7	6
Meccano Clockwork Motor No. 2 (reversing)	„	10	0
Meccano No. E1 Electric Motor (6-volt non-reversing)	Price	7	6
Meccano No. E6 Electric Motor ... (6-volt, reversing)	„	15	6
Meccano No. E20A Electric Motor (20-volt, non-reversing)	„	16	6
Meccano No. E20B Electric Motor (20-volt, reversing)	„	18	6
Meccano Steam Engine	„	25	0

MECCANO AEROPLANE CONSTRUCTOR OUTFITS

Item		s.	d.
Aeroplane Outfit No. 0	„	5	0
„ „ No. 1	„	9	0
Aeroplane Outfit No. 2	„	16	6
„ Accessory Outfit No. 1a	„	8	6

MECCANO AERO MOTORS

Item		s.	d.
Aero Clockwork Motor No. 1 ...	„	2	0
Aero Clockwork Motor No. 2 ...	„	4	6

These motors will not drive models built with Aeroplane Outfit No. 0

MECCANO MOTOR CAR CONSTRUCTOR OUTFIT 25/-

A. STOCKWIN & C
16, WORCESTER ST.
BIRMINGHAM

MECCANO
AEROPLANE CONSTRUCTOR PARTS

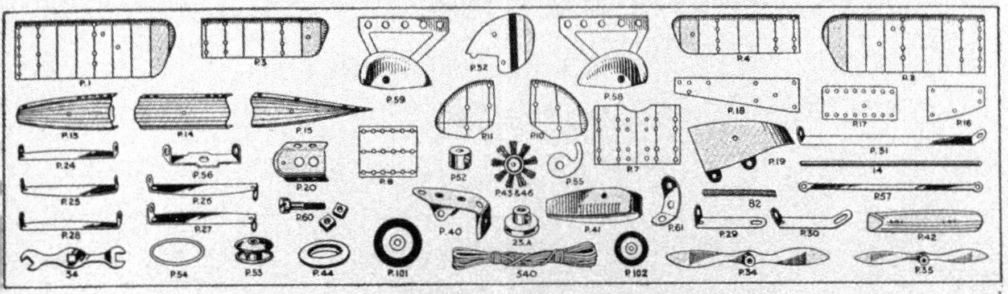

No.			s.	d.
P1	Main Plane—Large—R.H.	each	0	6
P2	„ „ — „ —L.H.	„	0	6
P3	„ „ —Small—R.H.	„	0	3
P4	„ „ — „ —L.H.	„	0	3
P7	Centre Section Plane	„	0	5
P8	Extension Plane	„	0	3
P10	Tail Plane—R.H.	„	0	2
P11	„ „ —L.H.	„	0	2
P13	Fuselage Top—Front	„	0	3
P14	„ „ —Middle	„	0	4
P15	„ „ —Rear	„	0	4
P16	„ Side—Front	„	0	2
P17	„ „ —Middle	„	0	2
P18	„ „ —Rear	„	0	2
P19	„ Underside...	„	0	2
P20	„ Front	„	0	1
P24	Interplane Strut—Staggered—R.H.	„	0	1
P25	„ „ — „ —L.H.	„	0	1
P26	„ „ —Angled—R.H	„	0	1
P27	„ „ — „ —L.H....	„	0	1
P28	„ „ —Straight	„	0	1
P29	Centre Section Strut—Straight	„	0	1
P30	Float and Centre Section Strut—Angled ...	„	0	1
P31	Wing Stay	„	0	1
P32	Rudder	„	0	4
P34	Propeller—Large	„	0	4
P35	„ —Small	„	0	4
P40	Base for Engine Casing	„	0	3

No.			s.	d.
P41	Top for Engine Casing	each	0	3
P42	Float, complete	„	0	9
P43	Radial Engine, small	„	0	7
P44	Tyre for Aeroplane Landing Wheel	pair	0	3
P46	Radial Engine, large	each	0	9
P52	Collar	2 for	0	3
P53	Aeroplane Landing Wheel	each	0	3
P54	Rubber Driving Band	„	0	1
P55	Tail Skid	„	0	1
P56	Rear Bracket for Propeller	„	0	1
P57	Tie Rod for floats	„	0	1
P58	Undercarriage piece and wheel shield—R.H. ...	„	0	5
P59	„ „ „ „ —L.H. ...	„	0	5
P60	Pivot Bolt with two nuts	„	0	2
P61	Engine Bracket	„	0	1
P62	Axle Rod. 3½" long	2 for	0	1
P63	Screwdriver	each	0	3
*P101	Identification Markings, Large } Packet of 4	(2 Large	0	6
*P102	„ „ , Small }	2 Small)		
12	Angle Bracket, ½"×½"	doz.	0	3
14	Axle Rod —6½" long	each	0	1
16A	„ „ —2½" „	2 for	0	1
23A	Fast Pulley—½" dia.	each	0	3
34	Spanner	„	0	2
82	Screwed Rod 1"	„	0	1
537A	Nuts	doz.	0	2
537B	Bolts 7/32" long	„	0	2
540	Hank of Cord	2 for	0	3
611C	Bolts ⅜" long	doz.	0	3

**The Aero Identification Markings included in the series represent the national markings of 16 different countries*
IMPORTANT.—These Aeroplane parts can only be used in conjunction with the parts contained in Meccano Aeroplane Outfits Nos. 1 and 2

MECCANO X SERIES PARTS

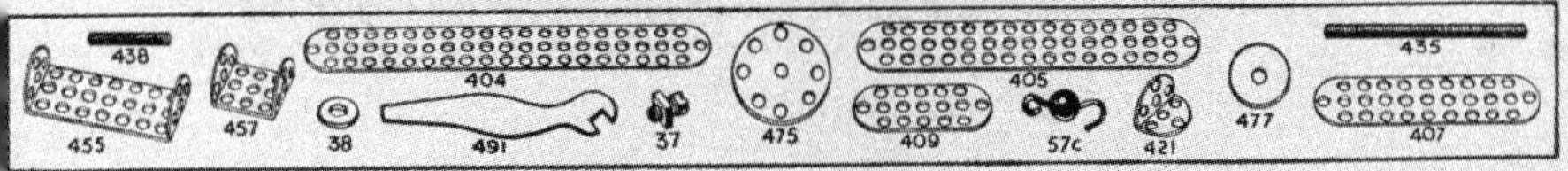

No.			s.	d.
X404	Strips, 5½"	per doz	1	2
X405	„ 4½"	„	1	0
X407	„ 2½"	„	0	7
X409	„ 1½"	„	0	6
X421	Angle Brackets	„	0	3
X435	Screwed Rods, 2½"	„	0	5
X438	Screwed Rods, 1"	„	0	3
X455	Double Angle Strips, 1½"×½" ...	„	0	9
X457	„ „ „ ½"×½" ...	„	0	7

No.			s.	d.
X475	Discs, 1½"	per doz.	0	6
X477	„ ½"	„	0	3
X491	Combined Spanner and Screwdriver	each	0	1
37	Nuts and Bolts, 7/32" ...	per box (doz.)	0	3
37a	Nuts	„ „ „	0	2
37b	Bolts 7/32"	„ „ „	0	2
38	Washers	„ „ „	0	1
57c	Loaded Hooks, small	each	0	1

MECCANO LTD.
OLD SWAN · LIVERPOOL · ENGLAND

/1032/10 (2P) U.K

Fig 22 cont.

MECCANO
PRICE LIST

COMPLETE OUTFITS

	s.	d.
No. 0 Outfit ...	2	6
No. 1 „ ...	3	6
No. 2 „ ...	5	0
No. 3 „ ...	7	6
No. 4 „ ...	10	0
No. 5 „ ...	15	0
No. 6 Outfit ...	20	0
No. 7 „ ...	30	0
No. 8 „ ...	55	0
No. 9c „ ...	80	0
No. 9w „ ...	105	0
No. 10 „ ...	231	0

MECCANO MOTORS

ELECTRIC

	s.	d.
No. E1 (6-volt non-reversing) Motor ...	7	6
No. E120 (20-volt non-reversing) Motor ...	7	6
No. E6 (6-volt reversing) Motor ...	12	9
No. E20b (20-volt reversing) Motor ...	13	6

CLOCKWORK

	s.	d.
Magic Motor (non-reversing) ...	2	0
No. 1 „ „ „ ...	4	6
No. 1a „ (reversing) ...	6	6
No. 2 „ „ ...	9	0

ACCESSORY OUTFITS

	s.	d.
No. 1a Accessory Outfit converts either a No. 1 Outfit or an Outfit O (Old Style) into a No. 2 Outfit ...	1	6
No. 2a „ „ „ No. 2 „ „ „ A „ „ No. 3 „ ...	2	9
No. 3a „ „ „ No. 3 „ „ „ B „ „ No. 4 „ ...	3	9
No. 4a „ „ „ No. 4 „ „ „ C „ „ No. 5 „ ...	6	6
No. 5a „ „ „ No. 5 „ „ „ D „ „ No. 6 „ ...	6	6
No. 6a „ „ „ No. 6 „ „ „ E „ „ No. 7 „ ...	12	0
No. 7a „ „ „ No. 7 „ „ „ F „ „ No. 8 „ ...	28	6
No. 8a Accessory Outfit converts a No. 8 Outfit into a No. 9 Outfit...	25	0
No. 9a „ „ „ No. 9 „ „ No. 10 „ ...	110	0

The necessary parts to connect G, H and K Outfits of the alphabetical series to Nos. 8, 9 and 10 Outfits, respectively, of the numerical series, are specially boxed and are available at the following prices:—
G—8 Connecting Outfit **10/6** H—9 Connecting Outfit **23/6** K—10 Connecting Outfit **82/6**

If a No. 10 Outfit Cabinet is required for the purpose of storing the parts contained in K—10 Connecting Outfit, it can be obtained separately at the price of 47/6

MECCANO PARTS

Perforated Strips.

No.			s.	d.	No.			s.	d.
1.	12½"	½ doz.	1	0	3.	3½"	½ doz.	0	4
1a.	9½"	„	0	9	4.	3"	„	0	3
1b	7½"	„	0	8	5.	2½"	„	0	3
2.	5½"	„	0	6	6.	2"	„	0	3
2a.	4½"	„	0	5	6a.	1½"	„	0	3

Angle Girders.

No.			s.	d.	No.			s.	d.
7.	24½"	each	0	7	9a.	4½"	½ doz.	0	8
7a.	18½"	„	0	6	9b.	3½"	„	0	7
8.	12½"	„	0	3	9c.	3"	„	0	6
8a.	9½"	„	0	2½	9d.	2½"	„	0	5
8b.	7½"	„	0	2	9e.	2"	„	0	5
9.	5½"	„	0	1½	9f.	1½"	„	0	4

No.			s.	d.
10.	Flat Brackets ...	doz.	0	1
11.	Double Brackets ...	„	0	3
12.	Angle Brackets, ½"×½" ...	„	0	2
12a.	„ „ 1"×1" ...	„	0	6
12b.	„ „ 1"×½" ...	„	0	4
12c.	Obtuse Angle Brackets, ½"×½"	„	0	2

Axle Rods.

No.			s.	d.	No.			s.	d.
13.	11½"	each	0	1	16.	3½"	... 3 for	0	1
13a.	8"	„	0	1	16a.	2½"	... 4 for	0	1
14.	6½"	„	0	½	16b.	3"	... „	0	1
15.	5"	„	0	½	17.	2"	... 5 for	0	1
15a.	4½"	„	0	½	18a.	1½"	... „	0	1
15b.	4"	3 for	0	1	18b.	1"	... 6 for	0	1

No.			s.	d.
19g.	Crank Handles 3½", with Erinoid grip...	each	0	2
19h.	Crank Handles 5", with Erinoid grip...	„	0	2
19s	Crank Handles 3½"	„	0	1
19a.	Wheels, 3" diam., with set-screws,	each	0	6
20.	Flanged Wheels, 1½" diam. ...	„	0	3
20b.	„ „ ¾" „ ...	„	0	2

Pulley Wheels.

No.		s.	d.
19b.	3" dia., with centre boss & set-screw each	0	4
19c.	6" „ „ „ „ „ „	1	9
20a.	2" „ „ „ „ „ „	0	3
21.	1½" „ „ „ „ „ „	0	2½
22.	1" „ „ „ „ „ „	0	1½
23a.	½" „ „ „ and grub-screw	0	2
22a.	1" „ without „ „ each	0	1
23.	½" „ „ „ „ „	0	1

No.		s.	d.
24.	Bush Wheels ... ... each	0	2
25.	Pinion Wheels, ¾" diam., ½" face „	0	4
25a.	„ „ ¾" „ ¾" „ „	0	6
25b.	„ „ ¾" „ 1" „ „	0	8
26.	„ „ ½" „ ¼" „ „	0	3
26a.	„ „ ½" „ ½" „ „	0	4
26b.	„ „ ½" „ ¾" „ „	0	5

Gear Wheels.

No.		s.	d.
27.	50 teeth to gear with ¾" Pinion... each	0	4
27a.	57 „ „ „ ½" „ „	0	5
27b.	133 „ „ „ ½" „ (3½" diam.)	1	3
27c.	95 „ „ „ ½" „ (2½" diam.)	0	9

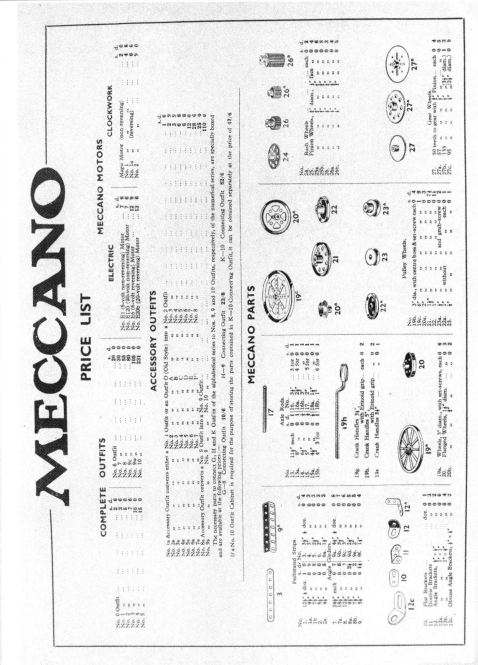

Fig 23. First 1937 price list covering the numerical series and special connecting outfits enabling conversion from lettered series.

REVISED PRICES OF MECCANO PRODUCTS

KEEP THIS FOR REFERENCE

It contains the latest prices of Meccano Products

1st JANUARY, 1938

Continuous increases in the costs of raw materials and labour, have compelled us to make a number of increases in prices and the following new prices came into force on the 1st January, 1938. Where increases are shown, they have been made as small as possible, and Meccano users may always rely upon our keeping the prices as low as is consistent with maintaining high quality.

A separate list is available showing the revised prices of Hornby Trains, Rolling Stock and Accessories.

Meccano Outfits

COMPLETE OUTFITS	s.	d.		s.	d.		s.	d.
No. 0 Outfit	3	0	No. 4 Outfit	12	6	No. 8 Outfit	66	0
No. 1 ,,	4	6	No. 5 ,,	18	0	No. 9c ,,	95	0
No. 2 ,,	6	0	No. 6 ,,	24	0	No. 9w ,,	125	0
No. 3 ,,	9	0	No. 7 ,,	35	0	No. 10 ,,	255	0

ACCESSORY OUTFITS	s.	d.		s.	d.		s.	d.
No. 1a Accessory Outfit	1	9	No. 5a Accessory Outfit	7	0	No. 9a Accessory Outfit	120	0
No. 2a ,, ,,	3	3	No. 6a ,, ,,	12	6	G—8 Connecting Outfit	12	6
No. 3a ,, ,,	4	3	No. 7a ,, ,,	33	6	H—9 Connecting Outfit	27	6
No. 4a ,, ,,	6	6	No. 8a ,, ,,	29	0	K—10 Connecting Outfit	95	0

If a No. 10 Outfit Cabinet is required for the purpose of storing the parts contained in K—10 Connecting Outfit, it can be obtained separately at the price of **55/-**.

Meccano Parts

Perforated Strips.

No.		s.	d.	No.		s.	d.
1.	12½" ½ doz.	1	3	3.	3½" ½ doz.	0	5
1a.	9½" ,,	1	0	4.	3" ,,	0	4½
1b	7½" ,,	0	10½	5.	2½" ,,	0	4
2.	5½" ,,	0	7½	6.	2" ,,	0	4
2a.	4½" ,,	0	6	6a.	1½" ,,	0	3

Angle Girders.

No.		s.	d.	No.		s.	d.
7.	24½" each	0	8½	9a.	4½" ½ doz.	0	10½
7a.	18½" ,,	0	6	9b.	3½" ,,	0	9
8.	12½" ,,	0	3½	9c.	3" ,,	0	7½
8a.	9½" ,,	0	3	9d.	2½" ,,	0	6
8b.	7½" ,,	0	2½	9e.	2" ,,	0	6
9.	5½" ,,	0	2	9f.	1½" ,,	0	4½

No.		s.	d.
10.	Flat Brackets ... doz.	0	1
11.	Double Brackets ... ,,	0	3
12.	Angle Brackets, ½"×½" ... ,,	0	2
12a.	,, ,, 1"×1" ... ,,	0	8
12b.	,, ,, 1"×½" ... ,,	0	5
12c.	Obtuse Angle Brackets, ½"×½" ,,	0	2

Axle Rods.

No.		s.	d.	No.		s.	d.
13.	11½" each	0	1	16.	3½" doz.	0	4½
13a.	8" doz.	0	9	16a.	2½" ,,	0	3½
14.	6½" ,,	0	8	16b	3" ,,	0	4
15.	5" ,,	0	7	17.	2" ,,	0	3
15a.	4½" ,,	0	6	18a.	1½" ,,	0	2½
15b.	4" ,,	0	5	18b.	1" ,,	0	2

No.		s.	d.
19g.	Crank Handles 3½", with Erinoid grip each	0	2½
19h.	Crank Handles 5", with Erinoid grip ,,	0	2½
19s.	Crank Handles 3½" ... ,,	0	1
19a.	Wheels, 3" diam., with set-screws ,,	0	6
20.	Flanged Wheels, 1½" diam. ... ,,	0	3½
20b.	,, ,, ¾" ,, ... ,,	0	2½
	Pulley Wheels.		
19b.	3" dia., with centre boss & set-screw each	0	4
19c.	6" ,, ,, ,, ,, ,,	1	9
20a.	2" ,, ,, ,, ,, ,,	0	3½
21.	1½" ,, ,, ,, ,, ,,	0	3
22.	1" ,, ,, ,, ,, ,,	0	2
23a.	½" ,, ,, and grub-screw ,,	0	2
22a.	1" ,, without ,, ,, ,,	0	1
23.	½" ,, ,, ,, ,, ,,	0	1½
24.	Bush Wheels ... ,,	0	2½
25.	Pinion Wheels, ¾" diam., ½" face ,,	0	4½
25a.	,, ,, ¾" ,, ¾" ,, ,,	0	6
25b.	,, ,, ¾" ,, 1" ,, ,,	0	8
26.	,, ,, ½" ,, ¼" ,, ,,	0	3½
26a.	,, ,, ½" ,, ½" ,, ,,	0	4½
26b.	,, ,, ½" ,, ¾" ,, ,,	0	6
	Gear Wheels.		
27.	50 teeth to gear with ¾" Pinion ,,	0	4
27a.	57 ,, ,, ,, ½" ,, ,,	0	5
27b.	133 ,, ,, ,, ½" ,, (3½" diam.)	1	3
27c.	95 ,, ,, ,, ½" ,, (2½" diam.)	0	9
28.	Contrate Wheels, 1½" diam. ... each	0	6
29.	,, ,, ¾" ,, ... ,,	0	4
30.	Bevel Gears, ⅞", 26 teeth ... ,,	0	6
30a.	,, ,, ⅝", 16 ,, *Can only be*	0	4
30c.	,, ,, 1½", 48 ,, *used together*	1	6
31.	Gear Wheels, 1", 38 teeth ... each	0	9
32.	Worms ... ,,	0	3½
34.	Spanners ... ,,	0	1
34b.	Box Spanners ... ,,	0	2
35.	Spring Clips ... box of 20	0	2
35s.	,, ,, ... box of 60	0	6
36.	Screwdrivers ... each	0	2½
36a.	,, Extra Long ... ,,	0	3½
36b.	,, Special ... ,,	1	0
37.	Nuts and Bolts, 7/32" ... box doz.	0	2
37af.	Nuts ... box of 50	0	4

No.		s.	d.
37bf.	Bolts, 7/32" ... box of 50	0	5
37f.	Nuts and Bolts, 7/32" ... ,, ,,	0	8
37g.	,, ,, ,, ... box of 144	1	9
38.	Washers ... packet of 20	0	1
38g.	,, ... box of 60	0	3
40.	Hanks of Cord ... each	0	1½
41.	Propeller Blades ... ,,	0	3
43.	Springs ... ,,	0	2
44.	Cranked Bent Strips ... ,,	0	1
45.	Double Bent Strips ... ,,	0	1
46.	Double Angle Strips, 2½"×1" ½ doz.	0	8
47.	,, ,, ,, 2½"×1½" ,,	0	10½
47a.	,, ,, ,, 3"×1½" ,,	1	0
48.	,, ,, ,, 1½"×½" ,,	0	5
48a.	,, ,, ,, 2½"×½" ,,	0	6
48b.	,, ,, ,, 3½"×½" ,,	0	8
48c.	,, ,, ,, 4½"×½" ,,	0	10½
48d.	,, ,, ,, 5½"×½" ,,	1	0
50a.	Eye Pieces, with boss ... each	0	3½
51.	Perforated Flanged Plates, 2½"×1½" ea.	0	2½
52.	,, ,, ,, 5½"×2½" ,,	0	4½
52a.	,, Flat Plates, 5½"×3½" ,,	0	4
53.	,, Flanged Plates, 3½"×2½" ,,	0	3
53a.	,, Flat Plates, 4½"×2½" ,,	0	2½
54a.	Perforated Flanged Sector Plates, 4½" long each	0	3½
55.	,, Strips, slotted, 5½" long doz	1	3
55a.	,, Strips, ,, 2" ,, ,,	0	9
57.	Hooks ... each	0	0½
57a.	,, Scientific ... ,,	0	1
57b.	,, Loaded, large ... ,,	0	2
57c.	,, Loaded, small ... ,,	0	1
58.	Spring Cord ... 40" length	0	10
58a.	Coupling Screws for Spring Cord each	0	0½
58b.	Hooks for Spring Cord ... doz.	0	4
59.	Collars with Grub Screws ... ,,	1	3
61.	Windmill Sails ... Set of 4	0	9
62.	Cranks ... each	0	2½
62a.	Threaded Cranks ... ,,	0	2½
62b.	Double Arm Cranks... ,,	0	2½
63.	Couplings ... ,,	0	5
63a.	Octagonal Couplings ... ,,	0	8
63b.	Strip Couplings ... ,,	0	6
63c.	Threaded Couplings ... ,,	0	6
64.	,, Bosses ... doz.	1	3
65.	Centre Forks ... each	0	1
66.	Weights, 50 grammes ... ,,	0	9
67.	,, 25 ,, ... ,,	0	6
68.	Woodscrews, ½" ... doz.	0	3
69.	Set Screws ... ,,	0	2
69a.	Grub Screws, 5/32"... ,,	0	2½
69b.	,, ,, 7/32"... ,,	0	3
69c.	,, ,, 5/64"... ,,	0	2
70.	Perforated Flat Plates, 5½"×2½" each	0	3
72.	,, ,, ,, 2½"×2½" ,,	0	2
73.	,, ,, ,, 3"×1½" ,,	0	2
76.	Perforated Triangular Plates, 2½" ,,	0	2
77.	,, ,, ,, 1" ,,	0	1

Screwed Rods.

No.		s.	d.	No.		s.	d.
78.	11½" each	0	8	80a.	3½" ... each	0	3
79.	8" ,,	0	6	80b.	4½" ... doz.	3	9
79a.	6" ,,	0	4½	80c.	3" ... ,,	0	9
80.	5" ,,	0	4	81.	2" ... ,,	0	6
				82.	1" ... 3 for	0	1

No.		s.	d.
89.	5½" Curved Strips, 10" radius each	0	2
89a.	3 ,, ,, cranked, 1¾" radius, 4 to circle ,,	0	2
89b.	4" Curved Strips, cranked, 4½" radius, 8 to circle ,,	0	2
90.	2½" Curved Strips, 2¾" radius ,,	0	1
90a.	2½" ,, ,, cranked, 1⅜" radius, 4 to circle ,,	0	1
94.	Sprocket Chain ... 40" length	0	6

No.		s.	d
95.	Sprocket Wheels, 36 teeth, 2" diam. each	0	5½
95a.	,, ,, 28 ,, 1½" ,, ,,	0	4
95b.	,, ,, 56 ,, 3" ,, ,,	0	7
96.	,, ,, 18 ,, 1" ,, ,,	0	3
96a.	,, ,, 14 ,, ¾" ,, ,,	0	2½
97.	Braced Girders, 3½"... ½ doz.	1	1½
97a.	,, ,, 3" ... ,,	1	0
98.	,, ,, 2½" ... ,,	0	10½
99.	,, ,, 12½" ... ,,	3	0
99a.	,, ,, 9½" ... ,,	2	6
99b.	,, ,, 7½" ... ,,	2	3
100.	,, ,, 5½" ... ,,	1	3
100a.	,, ,, 4½" ... ,,	1	1½
101.	Healds, for looms ... doz.	0	3
102.	Single Bent Strips ... each	0	1
103.	Flat Girders, 5½" ... ½ doz.	1	0
103a.	,, ,, 9½" ... ,,	1	6
103b.	,, ,, 12½" ... ,,	1	9
103c.	,, ,, 4½" ... ,,	0	10½
103d.	,, ,, 3½" ... ,,	0	9
103e.	,, ,, 3" ... ,,	0	7½
103f.	,, ,, 2½" ... ,,	0	6
103g.	,, ,, 2" ... ,,	0	6
103h.	,, ,, 1½" ... ,,	0	4½
103k.	,, ,, 7½" ... ,,	1	3
104.	Shuttles for looms ... each	0	6
105.	Reed Hooks, for looms ... ,,	0	4
106.	Wood Rollers ... ,,	1	0
106a.	Sand Rollers ... ,,	1	3
107.	Tables for designing machines ,,	1	6
108.	Architraves ... doz.	1	9
109.	Face Plates, 2½" diam. ... each	0	3½
110.	Rack Strips, 3½" long ... ,,	0	2
110a.	,, ,, 6½" ,, ... ,,	0	3
111.	Bolts, ¾" ... doz.	0	3
111a.	,, ½" ... ,,	0	2
111c.	,, ⅜" ... ,,	0	1½
113.	Girder Frames ... each	0	3
114.	Hinges ... ,,	0	3
115.	Threaded Pins ... ,,	0	2
116.	Fork Pieces, large ... ,,	0	2½
116a.	,, ,, small ... ,,	0	2
117.	Steel Balls, ⅜" diam. ... doz.	0	9
118.	Hub Discs, 5½" diam. ... each	1	0
120.	Buffers ... ,,	0	2
120a.	Spring Buffers ... ,,	0	3
120b.	Compression Springs ... ,,	0	1
121.	Train Couplings ... ,,	0	1
122.	Miniature Loaded Sacks ... ,,	0	1½
123.	Cone Pulleys ... ,,	1	0
124.	Reversed Angle Brackets, 1" ½ doz.	0	4½
125.	,, ,, ,, ½" ,,	0	3
126.	Trunnions ... each	0	1½
126a.	Flat Trunnions ... ,,	0	1
127.	Simple Bell Cranks ... ,,	0	3
128.	Boss Bell Cranks ... ,,	0	5
129.	Rack Segments, 3" diam. ,,	1	0
130.	Eccentrics, Triple Throw ... ,,	0	2½
131.	Dredger Buckets ... ,,	2	0
132.	Flywheels, 2¾" diam. ... ,,	0	1
133.	Corner Brackets, 1½" ... ,,	0	1
133a.	,, ,, 1" ... ,,	0	1
134.	Crank Shafts, 1" stroke ... ,,	0	1
135.	Theodolite Protractors ... ,,	0	2
136.	Handrail Supports ... ,,	0	3
136a.	,, Couplings ... ,,	0	5½
137.	Wheel Flanges ... ,,	0	2½
138.	Ships' Funnels ... ,,	0	4
138a-z.	,, ,, Raked ... ,,	0	9
139.	Flanged Brackets (right) ... ,,	0	2
139a.	,, ,, (left) ... ,,	0	2
140.	Universal Couplings ... ,,	0	9

Fig 24. One of the many revised price lists for 1938.

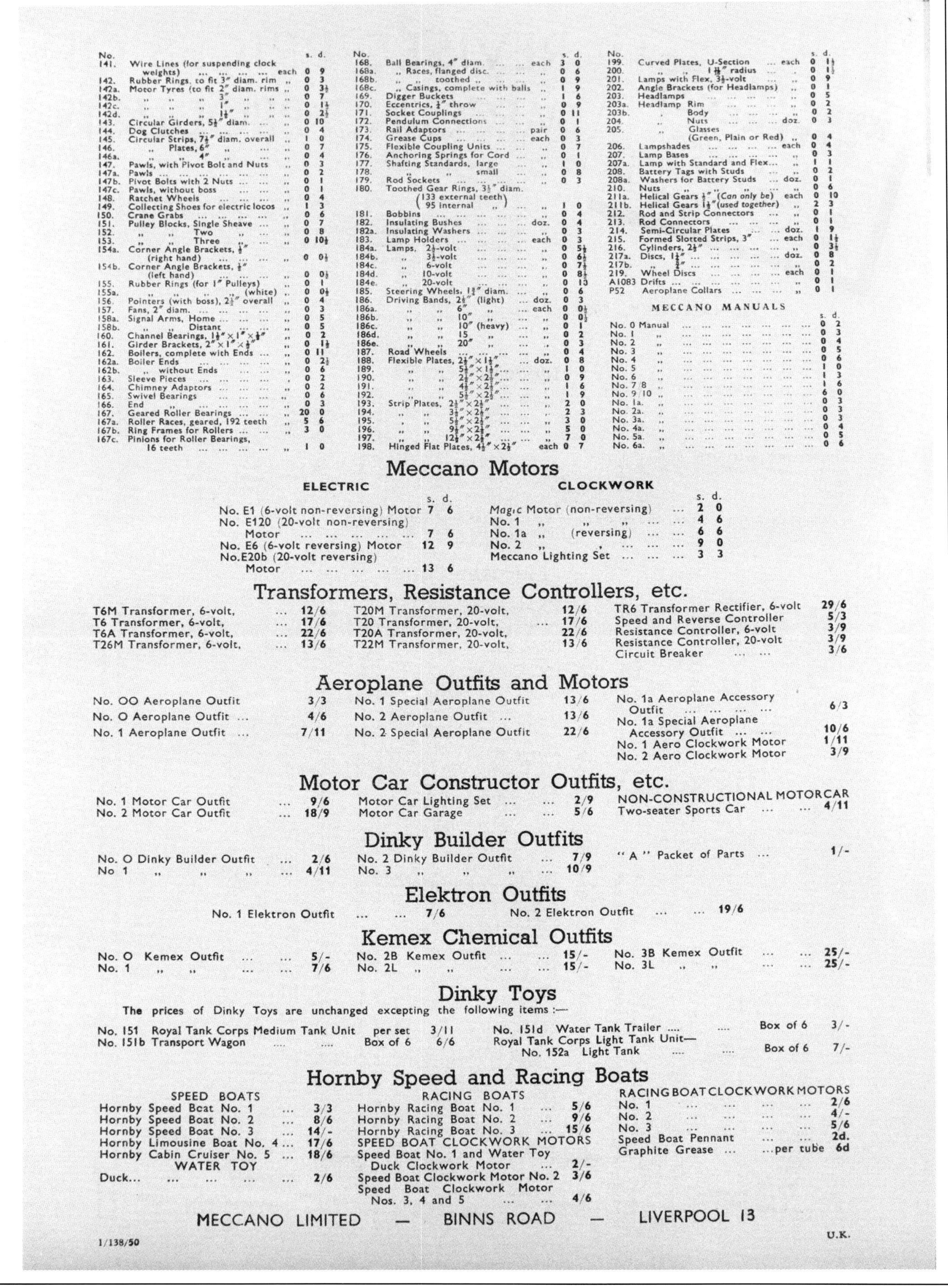

No.			s.	d.
141.	Wire Lines (for suspending clock weights)	each	0	9
142.	Rubber Rings, to fit 3" diam. rim	,,	0	3
142a.	Motor Tyres (to fit 2" diam. rims	,,	0	3½
142b.	,, ,, ,, 3" ,, ,,	,,	0	7
142c.	,, ,, ,, 1" ,, ,,	,,	0	1½
142d.	,, ,, ,, 1½" ,, ,,	,,	0	2½
143.	Circular Girders, 5½" diam. ...	,,	0	10
144.	Dog Clutches	,,	0	4
145.	Circular Strips, 7½" diam. overall	,,	1	0
146.	,, Plates, 6" ,, ...	,,	0	7
146a.	,, ,, 4" ,, ...	,,	0	4
147.	Pawls, with Pivot Bolt and Nuts	,,	0	3
147a.	Pawls	,,	0	2
147b.	Pivot Bolts with 2 Nuts	,,	0	1
147c.	Pawls, without boss	,,	0	1
148.	Ratchet Wheels	,,	0	4
149.	Collecting Shoes for electric locos	,,	1	3
150.	Crane Grabs	,,	0	6
151.	Pulley Blocks, Single Sheave ...	,,	0	7
152.	,, ,, Two ,, ...	,,	0	8
153.	,, ,, Three ,, ...	,,	0	10½
154a.	Corner Angle Brackets, ½" (right hand)	,,	0	0½
154b.	Corner Angle Brackets, ½" (left hand)	,,	0	0½
155.	Rubber Rings (for 1" Pulleys)	,,	0	1
155a.	,, ,, ,, ,, (white)	,,	0	0½
156.	Pointers (with boss), 2½" overall	,,	0	4
157.	Fans, 2" diam.	,,	0	3
158a.	Signal Arms, Home	,,	0	5
158b.	,, ,, Distant	,,	0	5
160.	Channel Bearings, 1½"×1"×½"	,,	0	2
161.	Girder Brackets, 2"×1"×½"	,,	0	1½
162.	Boilers, complete with Ends ...	,,	0	11
162a.	Boiler Ends	,,	0	2½
162b.	,, without Ends	,,	0	6
163.	Sleeve Pieces	,,	0	2
164.	Chimney Adaptors	,,	0	2
165.	Swivel Bearings	,,	0	6
166.	End ,, ...	,,	0	3
167.	Geared Roller Bearings	,,	20	0
167a.	Roller Races, geared, 192 teeth	,,	5	6
167b.	Ring Frames for Rollers	,,	3	0
167c.	Pinions for Roller Bearings, 16 teeth	,,	1	0

No.			s.	d.
168.	Ball Bearings, 4" diam.	each	3	0
168a.	,, Races, flanged disc.	,,	0	6
168b.	,, ,, toothed ,, ...	,,	0	9
168c.	,, Casings, complete with balls	,,	1	9
169.	Digger Buckets	,,	1	6
170.	Eccentrics, ½" throw	,,	0	9
171.	Socket Couplings	,,	0	11
172.	Pendulum Connections	,,	0	1
173.	Rail Adaptors	pair	0	6
174.	Grease Cups	each	0	3
175.	Flexible Coupling Units	,,	0	7
176.	Anchoring Springs for Cord ...	,,	0	1
177.	Shafting Standards, large ...	,,	1	0
178.	,, ,, small ...	,,	0	8
179.	Rod Sockets	,,	0	3
180.	Toothed Gear Rings, 3½" diam. (133 external teeth / 95 internal ,,) ...	,,	1	0
181.	Bobbins	,,	0	4
182.	Insulating Bushes	doz.	0	4
182a.	Insulating Washers	,,	0	3
183.	Lamp Holders	each	0	3
184a.	Lamps, 2½-volt	,,	0	5½
184b.	,, 3½-volt	,,	0	6½
184c.	,, 6-volt	,,	0	7½
184d.	,, 10-volt	,,	0	8½
184e.	,, 20-volt	,,	0	10
185.	Steering Wheels, 1½" diam. ...	,,	0	6
186.	Driving Bands, 2½" (light) ...	doz.	0	3
186a.	,, ,, 6" ,, ...	each	0	0½
186b.	,, ,, 10" ,, ...	,,	0	0½
186c.	,, ,, 10" (heavy) ...	,,	0	1
186d.	,, ,, 15 ,, ...	,,	0	2
186e.	,, ,, 20" ,, ...	,,	0	3
187.	Road Wheels	,,	0	4
188.	Flexible Plates, 2½"×1½" ...	doz.	0	8
189.	,, ,, 5½"×1½"	,,	1	0
190.	,, ,, 2½"×2½"	,,	0	9
191.	,, ,, 4½"×2½"	,,	1	6
192.	,, ,, 5½"×2½"	,,	1	9
193.	Strip Plates, 2½"×2½"	,,	2	0
194.	,, ,, 3½"×2½"	,,	2	3
195.	,, ,, 5½"×2½"	,,	3	0
196.	,, ,, 9½"×2½"	,,	5	0
197.	,, ,, 12½"×2½"	,,	7	0
198.	Hinged Flat Plates, 4½"×2½"	each	0	7

No.			s.	d.
199.	Curved Plates, U-Section ...	each	0	1½
200.	,, ,, 1 11/16" radius ...	,,	0	1½
201.	Lamps with Flex, 3½-volt ...	,,	0	9
202.	Angle Brackets (for Headlamps)	,,	0	1
203.	Headlamps	,,	0	5
203a.	Headlamp Rim	,,	0	2
203b.	,, Body	,,	0	2
204.	,, Nuts	doz.	0	3
205.	,, Glasses (Green, Plain or Red)	,,	0	4
206.	Lampshades	each	0	4
207.	Lamp Bases	,,	0	3
207a.	Lamp with Standard and Flex...	,,	1	1
208.	Battery Tags with Studs ...	,,	0	2
208a.	Washers for Battery Studs ...	doz.	0	1
210.	Nuts ,, ,, ,, ...	,,	0	6
211a.	Helical Gears ½" (Can only be)	each	0	10
211b.	Helical Gears 1½" (used together)	,,	2	3
212.	Rod and Strip Connectors ...	,,	0	1
213.	Rod Connectors	,,	0	1
214.	Semi-Circular Plates	doz.	1	9
215.	Formed Slotted Strips, 3" ...	each	0	1½
216.	Cylinders, 2½"	,,	0	3½
217a.	Discs, 1½"	doz.	0	8
217b.	,, ¾"	,,	0	2
219.	Wheel Discs	each	0	1
A1083	Drifts	,,	0	1
P52	Aeroplane Collars	,,	0	1

MECCANO MANUALS

	s.	d.
No. 0 Manual	0	2
No. 1 ,, ...	0	3
No. 2 ,, ...	0	4
No. 3 ,, ...	0	5
No. 4 ,, ...	0	6
No. 5 ,, ...	1	0
No. 6 ,, ...	1	3
No. 7/8 ,, ...	1	6
No. 9/10 ,, ...	6	0
No. 1a. ,, ...	0	3
No. 2a. ,, ...	0	3
No. 3a. ,, ...	0	3
No. 4a. ,, ...	0	4
No. 5a. ,, ...	0	5
No. 6a. ,, ...	0	6

Meccano Motors

ELECTRIC

	s.	d.
No. E1 (6-volt non-reversing) Motor	7	6
No. E120 (20-volt non-reversing) Motor	7	6
No. E6 (6-volt reversing) Motor	12	9
No.E20b (20-volt reversing) Motor	13	6

CLOCKWORK

	s.	d.
Magic Motor (non-reversing) ...	2	0
No. 1 ,, ,, ...	4	6
No. 1a ,, (reversing)	6	6
No. 2 ,, ,, ...	9	0
Meccano Lighting Set	3	3

Transformers, Resistance Controllers, etc.

T6M Transformer, 6-volt, ...	12/6
T6 Transformer, 6-volt, ...	17/6
T6A Transformer, 6-volt, ...	22/6
T26M Transformer, 6-volt, ...	13/6
T20M Transformer, 20-volt,	12/6
T20 Transformer, 20-volt, ...	17/6
T20A Transformer, 20-volt,	22/6
T22M Transformer, 20-volt,	13/6
TR6 Transformer Rectifier, 6-volt	29/6
Speed and Reverse Controller	5/3
Resistance Controller, 6-volt	3/9
Resistance Controller, 20-volt	3/9
Circuit Breaker	3/6

Aeroplane Outfits and Motors

No. OO Aeroplane Outfit	3/3
No. O Aeroplane Outfit ...	4/6
No. 1 Aeroplane Outfit ...	7/11
No. 1 Special Aeroplane Outfit	13/6
No. 2 Aeroplane Outfit ...	13/6
No. 2 Special Aeroplane Outfit	22/6
No. 1a Aeroplane Accessory Outfit	6/3
No. 1a Special Aeroplane Accessory Outfit	10/6
No. 1 Aero Clockwork Motor	1/11
No. 2 Aero Clockwork Motor	3/9

Motor Car Constructor Outfits, etc.

No. 1 Motor Car Outfit ...	9/6
No. 2 Motor Car Outfit ...	18/9
Motor Car Lighting Set	2/9
Motor Car Garage	5/6
NON-CONSTRUCTIONAL MOTORCAR	
Two-seater Sports Car	4/11

Dinky Builder Outfits

No. O Dinky Builder Outfit ...	2/6
No 1 ,, ,, ,, ...	4/11
No. 2 Dinky Builder Outfit ...	7/9
No. 3 ,, ,, ,, ...	10/9
"A" Packet of Parts ...	1/-

Elektron Outfits

No. 1 Elektron Outfit	7/6
No. 2 Elektron Outfit	19/6

Kemex Chemical Outfits

No. O Kemex Outfit	5/-
No. 1 ,, ,, ...	7/6
No. 2B Kemex Outfit	15/-
No. 2L ,, ,, ...	15/-
No. 3B Kemex Outfit	25/-
No. 3L ,, ,, ...	25/-

Dinky Toys

The prices of Dinky Toys are unchanged excepting the following items:—

No. 151 Royal Tank Corps Medium Tank Unit	per set	3/11
No. 151b Transport Wagon	Box of 6	6/6
No. 151d Water Tank Trailer	Box of 6	3/-
Royal Tank Corps Light Tank Unit— No. 152a Light Tank	Box of 6	7/-

Hornby Speed and Racing Boats

SPEED BOATS

Hornby Speed Boat No. 1 ...	3/3
Hornby Speed Boat No. 2 ...	8/6
Hornby Speed Boat No. 3 ...	14/-
Hornby Limousine Boat No. 4 ...	17/6
Hornby Cabin Cruiser No. 5 ...	18/6

WATER TOY

Duck...	2/6

RACING BOATS

Hornby Racing Boat No. 1 ...	5/6
Hornby Racing Boat No. 2 ...	9/6
Hornby Racing Boat No. 3 ...	15/6

SPEED BOAT CLOCKWORK MOTORS

Speed Boat No. 1 and Water Toy Duck Clockwork Motor ...	2/-
Speed Boat Clockwork Motor No. 2	3/6
Speed Boat Clockwork Motor Nos. 3, 4 and 5	4/6

RACING BOAT CLOCKWORK MOTORS

No. 1	2/6
No. 2	4/-
No. 3	5/6
Speed Boat Pennant	2d.
Graphite Grease ... ...per tube	6d

MECCANO LIMITED — BINNS ROAD — LIVERPOOL 13

1/138/50

U.K.

MECCANO PRODUCTS

January 1941 and until further notice.

Prices "With Tax" relate to goods delivered to addresses in Great Britain, Northern Ireland and the Isle of Man. In countries where English selling-prices apply, but English Purchase Tax is not levied, the "List" prices are appropriate.

SPECIAL NOTE.—Items marked with an asterisk (*) are not at present available; items marked with a dagger (†) are available in limited quantities.

MECCANO

COMPLETE OUTFITS

	Retail Prices List	Retail Prices With tax
0 Outfit	5/-	6/-
1 ,,	7/6	9/-
2 ,,	9/6	11/6
3 ,,	14/6	17/6
4 ,,	21/-	25/6
5 ,,	30/9	37/6
6 ,,	39/-	47/6
7 ,,	55/-	67/6
8 ,,	105/-	127/6
9c ,, (carton)	158/6	192/6
9w ,, (cabinet)	201/6	245/-
10 ,, ,,	402/6	490/-

ACCESSORY OUTFITS

	Retail Prices List	Retail Prices With tax
1a Outfit	2/9	3/3
2a ,,	5/9	7/-
3a ,,	7/6	9/-
4a ,,	9/6	11/6
5a ,,	8/9	10/9
6a ,,	17/3	21/-
7a ,,	49/6	60/-
8a ,,	47/3	57/6
9a ,,	195/6	237/6
Meccano Lighting Set	4/6	5/6
Mechanised Army Outfit	17/3	21/-

MECCANO MOTORS

	Retail Prices List	Retail Prices With tax
*"Magic" Clockwork Motor	3/9	4/6
†No. 1 Clockwork Motor	8/3	10/-
†No. 2 Clockwork Motor	16/6	20/-
†No. 1A Clockwork Motor	12/-	14/6
No. EO6 Electric Motor (6-volt)	9/6	11/6
†No. EO20 Electric Motor (20-volt)	9/6	11/6
*No. E1 Electric Motor (6-volt)	13/-	16/-
No. E120 Electric Motor (20-volt, non-reversing)	13/-	16/-
†No. E6 Electric Motor (6-volt, reversing)	21/9	26/6
*No. E20B Electric Motor (20-volt, reversing)	22/6	27/6
Klaxon High-volt Elec. Motor	50/-	63/-

TRANSFORMERS, RESISTANCE CONTROLLERS AND CIRCUIT BREAKERS

	List	With tax
T6M Transformers, 6-volt	18/9	23/6
T20M ,, 20-volt	18/9	23/6
T6 ,, 6-volt	25/-	31/-
T20 ,, 20-volt	25/-	31/-
T6A ,, 6-volt	30/-	37/6
T20A Transformer, 20-volt	30/-	37/6
T26M ,, 6-volt	20/-	25/-
T22M ,, 20-volt	20/-	25/-
Transformer Rectifier No. TR6, 6-volt	29/6	36/6
*Resistance Controller, 6-volt	6/-	7/6
*Resistance Controller, 20-volt	6/-	7/6
Circuit Breaker, 6-volt	6/-	7/6
†Circuit Breaker, 20-volt	6/-	7/6

MECCANO PARTS AND ACCESSORIES

No.						
1	Perforated Strips, 12½"	doz.	5/-	ea.	-/6
1a	,, ,, 9½"	,,	3/3	,,	-/4
1b	,, ,, 7½"	,,	2/9	,,	-/3½
2	,, ,, 5½"	,,	2/6	,,	-/3
2a	,, ,, 4½"	,,	2/-	,,	-/2½
3	,, ,, 3½"	,,	1/9	,,	-/2
4	,, ,, 3"	,,	1/3	,,	-/1½
5	,, ,, 2½"	,,	1/3	,,	-/1½
6	,, ,, 2"	,,	-/10	,,	-/1
6a	,, ,, 1½"	,,	-/10	,,	-/1
7	Angle Girders, 24½"	,,	14/9	,,	1/6
7a	,, ,, 18½"	,,	9/9	,,	1/-
8	,, ,, 12½"	,,	6/3	,,	-/7½
8a	,, ,, 9½"	,,	5/-	,,	-/6
8b	,, ,, 7½"	,,	4/-	,,	-/5
9	,, ,, 5½"	,,	3/3	,,	-/4
9a	,, ,, 4½"	,,	2/9	,,	-/3½
9b	,, ,, 3½"	,,	2/6	,,	-/3
9c	,, ,, 3"	,,	2/-	,,	-/2½
9d	,, ,, 2½"	,,	1/9	,,	-/2
9e	,, ,, 2"	,,	1/3	,,	-/1½
9f	,, ,, 1½"	,,	1/3	,,	-/1½
10	Flat Brackets	,,	-/1½	doz.	-/2
11	Double Brackets	,,	-/5	,,	-/6
12	Angle Brackets, ½" × ½"	,,	-/3	,,	-/3½
12a	,, ,, 1" × 1"	,,	1/3	,,	1/6
12b	,, ,, 1" × ½"	,,	-/10	,,	1/-
12c	Obtuse Angle Brackets ½" × ½"	,,	-/3	,,	-/3½
†13	Axle Rods 11½"	,,	1/9	,,	2/3
†13a	,, ,, 8"	,,	1/3	,,	1/6
†14	,, ,, 6½"	,,	1/-	,,	1/3
†15	,, ,, 5"	,,	-/10½	,,	1/1
†15a	,, ,, 4½"	,,	-/10	,,	1/-
†15b	,, ,, 4"	,,	-/9	,,	-/11
†16	,, ,, 3½"	,,	-/8	,,	-/10
†16a	,, ,, 2½"	,,	-/6½	,,	-/8
†16b	,, ,, 3"	,,	-/7	,,	-/9
†17	,, ,, 2"	,,	-/6	,,	-/7
†18a	,, ,, 1½"	,,	-/5	,,	-/6
†18b	,, ,, 1"	,,	-/4	,,	-/5
*19g	Crank Handles (with Erinoid Grip), 3½"	,,	4/-	ea.	-/5
*19h	Crank Handles (with Erinoid Grip), 5"	,,	4/6	,,	-/5½
†19s	Crank Handles (without Erinoid grip), 3½"	,,	1/9	,,	-/2
19a	Wheels, 3", with set screws	,,	12/3	,,	1/3
20	Flanged Wheels, 1½"	doz.	5/9	ea.	-/7
20b	,, ,, ¾"	,,	5/-	,,	-/6
	Pulley Wheels				
*19b	3" with boss & set screw	,,	8/3	,,	-/10
19c	6" ,, ,, ,, ,,	,,	34/6	,,	3/6
*20a	2" ,, ,, ,, ,,	,,	5/9	,,	-/7
21	1½" ,, ,, ,, ,,	,,	5/-	,,	-/6
*22	1" ,, ,, ,, ,,	,,	3/3	,,	-/4
†23a	½" with boss & grub screw	,,	4/-	,,	-/5
22a	1" without boss & grub screw	,,	1/9	,,	-/2
*23	½" without boss & grub screw	,,	2/6	,,	-/3
24	Bush Wheels	,,	4/-	,,	-/5
*25	Pinion Wheels ¾", ¼" face	,,	7/9	,,	-/9½
*25a	,, ,, ¾", ½" ,,	,,	11/6	,,	1/2
25b	,, ,, ¾", ¾" ,,	,,	14/9	,,	1/6
†26	,, ,, ½", ¼" ,,	,,	5/9	,,	-/7
*26a	,, ,, ½", ½" ,,	,,	7/3	,,	-/9
†26b	,, ,, ½", ¾" ,,	,,	9/9	,,	1/-
	Gear Wheels				
*27	50 teeth, gears with ¾" Pinion	,,	6/6	,,	-/8
27a	57 ,, ,, ½" ,,	,,	8/3	,,	-/10
27b	133 ,, ,, ½" ,,	,,	24/6	,,	2/6
27c	95 ,, ,, ½" ,,	,,	12/3	,,	1/3
28	Contrate Wheels, 1½", 50 t'th	,,	9/9	,,	1/-
29	,, ,, ¾", 25 t'th	,,	5/-	,,	-/6
*30	Bevel Gears ⅞", 26 teeth	,,	9/9	,,	1/-
*30a	,, ,, ½", 16 ,,	,,	6/6	,,	-/8
*30c	,, ,, 1½", 48 ,,	,,	29/6	,,	3/-
	(30a & 30c can only be used together)				
*31	Gear Wheels, 1", 38 teeth	,,	17/3	,,	1/9
†32	Worms	,,	5/9	,,	-/7
34	Spanners	,,	1/9	,,	-/2
34b	Box Spanners	,,	3/3	,,	-/4
35	Spring Clips box of 20	,,	3/3	,,	-/4
35s	,, ,, box of 60	,,	9/9	,,	1/-
36	Screwdrivers	,,	3/3	,,	-/4
*36a	,, Extra Long	,,	5/9	,,	-/7
*36b	,, Special	,,	19/9	,,	2/-
†37	Nuts & Bolts, 7/32" box of 12	,,	3/3	,,	-/4
†37af	Nuts box of 50	,,	5/9	,,	-/7
†37bf	Bolts, 7/32" box of 50	,,	7/3	,,	-/9
†37f	Nuts & Bolts, 7/32" box of 50	,,	12/3	,,	1/3
†37g	,, ,, ,, box of 144	,,	32/-	,,	3/3
38	Washers pkt. of 20	,,	1/9	,,	-/2
38s	,, box of 60	,,	5/-	,,	-/6
40	Hanks of Cord	,,	2/6	,,	-/3
41	Propeller Blades	,,	4/-	,,	-/5
†43	Springs	doz.	3/3	ea.	-/4
44	Cranked Bent Strips	,,	1/3	,,	-/1½
45	Double Bent Strips	,,	2/-	,,	-/2½
46	Dble Angle Strips, 2½" × 1"	,,	2/6	,,	-/3
47	,, ,, ,, 2½" × 1½"	,,	2/9	,,	-/3½
47a	,, ,, ,, 3" × 1½"	,,	3/3	,,	-/4
48	,, ,, ,, 1½" × ½"	,,	1/3	,,	-/1½
48a	,, ,, ,, 2½" × ½"	,,	1/9	,,	-/2
48b	,, ,, ,, 3½" × ½"	,,	2/-	,,	-/2½
48c	,, ,, ,, 4½" × ½"	,,	2/9	,,	-/3½
48d	,, ,, ,, 5½" × ½"	,,	3/3	,,	-/4
50a	Eye Pieces, with boss	,,	5/-	,,	-/6
51	Perf. Flanged Plates 2½" × 1½"	,,	3/3	,,	-/4
52	,, ,, ,, 5½" × 2½"	,,	7/3	,,	-/9
52a	Perf. Flat Plates, 5½" × 3½"	,,	7/-	,,	-/8½
53	Perf. Flanged Plates 3½" × 2½"	,,	5/-	,,	-/6
53a	Perf. Flat Plates 4½" × 2½"	,,	4/6	,,	-/5½
†54a	Perf. Flanged Sector Plates, 4½" long	,,	5/9	,,	-/7
55	Perf. Strips, slot'd, 5½" long	,,	2/-	,,	-/2½
55a	Perf. Strips, slot'd, 2" long	,,	1/9	,,	-/2
57	Hooks	,,	-/10	,,	-/1
57a	,, Scientific	,,	1/3	,,	-/1½
57b	,, Loaded, Large	,,	3/3	,,	-/4
57c	,, Loaded, Small	,,	1/9	,,	-/2
58	Spring Cord, 40" length	,,	14/9	,,	1/6
58a	Coupling Screws for Spring Cord, box of 12	,,	8/3	,,	-/10
58b	Hooks for Spring C'd, box of 12	,,	6/6	,,	-/8
*59	Collars, with grub screws	,,	2/-	,,	-/2½
61	Windmill Sails	,,	3/9	,,	-/4½
*62	Cranks	,,	3/3	,,	-/4
*62a	Threaded Cranks	,,	3/9	,,	-/4½
*62b	Double Arm Cranks	,,	3/3	,,	-/4
*63	Couplings	,,	8/3	,,	-/10
*63a	Octagonal Couplings	,,	12/3	,,	1/3
†63b	Strip Couplings	,,	9/9	,,	1/-
*63c	Threaded Couplings	,,	9/-	,,	-/11
64	Threaded Bosses	,,	2/6	,,	-/3
65	Centre Forks	,,	1/9	,,	-/2
66	Weights, 50 grammes	,,	14/9	,,	1/6
67	,, 25 ,,	,,	9/9	,,	1/-
68	Woodscrews, ½" box of 12	,,	5/-	,,	-/6
*69	Set Screws ,,	,,	2/6	,,	-/3
*69a	Grub Screws, 5/32" ,,	,,	4/-	,,	-/5
*69b	,, ,, 7/32" ,,	,,	5/-	,,	-/6
*69c	,, ,, 5/64" ,,	,,	3/3	,,	-/4

* Not available. † Limited supplies.

HORNBY TRAINS GAUGE O

TINPLATE RAILS, POINTS AND CROSSINGS, ELECTRIC, GAUGE O, 1¼"

		Retail Prices List	Retail Prices With tax
CURVED RAILS.			
EA1 Curved Rails	doz.	10/-	12/-
EA1½ Curved Half Rails	,,	9/-	11/-
EA1¼ Curved Quarter Rails	,,	8/3	10/-
EA2 Curved Rails	,,	10/-	12/-
EA2½ Curved Half Rails	,,	9/-	11/-
EA2¼ Curved Quarter Rails	,,	8/3	10/-
EDC2 Curved Rails, dble track	½-doz.	17/3	21/-
STRAIGHT RAILS.			
EB1 Straight Rails	doz.	10/-	12/-
EB½ Straight Half Rails	,,	9/-	11/-
EB¼ Straight Quarter Rails	,,	8/3	10/-
EDS1 Straight Rails, dble track	½-doz.	14/9	18/-
PARALLEL POINTS.			
EPPR2 Parallel Points, right; EPPL2 Parallel Points, left	Pair	12/3	15/-
POINTS.			
EPR1 Right-hand Points; EPL1 Left-hand Points	pair	12/-	14/6
EPR2 Right-hand Points; EPL2 Left-hand Points	pair	13/3	16/-
CROSSOVER POINTS.			
ECOR2 Crossover points, Right-hand; ECOL2 Crossover Points, Left-hand	pair	41/-	50/-
CROSSINGS.			
ECA Acute-Angle Crossings	ea.	4/-	5/-
ECR Right-angle Crossings	,,	4/-	5/-
DOUBLE SYMMETRICAL POINTS.			
EDSR1 Double Symmetrical Points, Right-hand; EDSL1 Double Symmetrical Points, Left-hand	Pair	12/3	
EDSR2 Double Symmetrical Points, Right-hand; EDSL2 Double Symmetrical Points, Left-hand	Pair	12/3	
CONNECTING PLATES, ELECTRIC			
*TCP6 Terminal Connecting Plates (6-volt)	ea.	1/3	
†TCP20 Terminal Connecting Plates (20-volt)	,,	1/3	

SOLID STEEL RAILS AND POINTS, ELECTRIC, GAUGE O 1¼" 3 FT. RADIUS.

		List	With tax
CURVED RAILS.			
EA3 Curved Rails	ea.	3/-	3/8
EA3½ Curved Half Rails	,,	1/9	2/1½
AP Adapting Pieces	box of 6	1/-	1/3
STRAIGHT RAILS.			
EB3 Straight Rails	ea.	3/-	3/8
EB3½ Straight Half Rails	,,	1/9	2/1½
EB3¼ Straight Quarter Rails	,,	1/3	1/6½
FP Fishplates	doz.	-/7	-/8½
POINTS.			
EPR3 Right-hand Points	ea.	10/-	
EPL3 Left-hand Points	,,	10/-	
TSR Terminal	box of 12	2/6	

SUNDRIES

		List	With tax
*Cable Drum	ea.	-/5	-/6
Combined Rail Gauge, Screwdriver and Spanner	,,	-/3	-/4
Goods Container	,,	-/10	1/-
†Hedging, 10½" lengths on base	doz.	5/-	6/-
†Imitation Bricks	box	1/3	1/6
Imitation Coal	,,	-/10	1/-
Lighting Access, Buffer Stops	ea.	-/10	1/-
Bonding Clips	,,	-/5	-/6
†Mansell Wheels	pr.	-/5	-/6
Detachable Lamps for Locos	ea.	-/1½	-/2
Milk Cans	ea.	-/1½	-/2
Oil, Lubricating	bottle	-/10	1/-
Oilcan No. 1	ea.	-/10	1/-
†Oilcan No. 2 ("K" type)	,,	5/9	7/-
Poster Boards (3 large, 3 small)	set	-/6	-/8
Posters in Miniature, No. 1	,,	-/10	1/-
Posters in Miniature, No. 2	,,	-/10	1/-
*Shunter's Pole	ea.	-/3	-/4
*Spoked Wheels, die-cast	pr.	-/5	-/6
*Plugs	ea.	-/5	-/6
*Sockets	,,	-/5	-/6
Tarpaulin Sheets (assorted)	ea.	-/3	
Train Name Boards, set of 4 of a kind		-/6	
Roof Clips No. 2	doz.	1/8	
Roof Clips No. 2S	,,	1/8	
Trees with Stands	box of 12	3/3	
Trees, Oak, with stands	doz.	3/3	
Trees, Poplar, with stands	,,	3/3	
Stands for Trees	,,	-/10	
Fuse Wire, 24G	card	-/5	
Fuse Wire, 32G	,,	-/5	
Fuse Wire, 41G	,,	-/3	
*Connecting Wire	coil	-/7	

DINKY TOYS

No.				
1	Station Staff	set	2/8	3/3
2	Farmyard Animals	,,	2/10½	3/6
3	Passengers	,,	3/3½	4/-
4	Engineering Staff	,,	2/8	3/3
5	Train and Hotel Staff	,,	2/8	3/3
6	Shepherd Set	,,	1/10	2/3
12	Postal Set	,,	3/11	4/9
12a	Pillar Box, G.P.O.	ea.	-/5½	-/7
12b	Pillar Box, Air Mail	,,	-/5½	-/7
12c	Telephone Call Box	,,	-/7½	-/9
12d	Telegraph Messenger	,,	-/5½	-/7
12e	Postman	,,	-/5½	-/7
13	Hall's Distemper Advertisement	set	1/3	1/6
15	Signals	set	2/5½	3/-
15a	Signal, single arm	ea.	-/3	-/4
15b	Signal, double arm	,,	-/5	-/6
15c	Signal, junction	,,	-/6½	-/8
18	Goods Train Set	,,	3/11	4/9
19	Mixed Tank Goods Train Set	,,	4/4	5/3
22c	Motor Truck	,,	-/10	1/-
22e	Tractor	,,	1/3	1/6
22g	Streamlined Tourer	,,	-/8	-/10
22h	Streamlined Saloon	,,	-/8	-/10
22s	Searchlight Lorry (Small)	,,	1/5½	1/9
23	Racing Cars	set	3/3½	4/-
23a	Racing Car	ea.	-/7½	-/9
23b	Hotchkiss Racing Car	,,	-/8	-/10
23c	Mercedes-Benz Racing Car	,,	1/1	1/4
23d	Auto-Union Racing Car	,,	1/1	1/4
23e	"Speed of the Wind" Racing Car	,,	1/1	1/4
23m	"Thunderbolt" Speed Car	,,	1/5½	1/9
23p	Gardner's M.G. Record Car	,,	1/5½	1/9
23s	Streamlined Racing Car	,,	1/3½	1/7
24a	Ambulance	ea.	1/-½	1/3
24c	Town Sedan	,,	1/-½	1/3
24g	Sports Tourer (4-seater)	,,	1/-½	1/3
24h	Sport Tourer (2-seater)	,,	1/-½	1/3
25	Commercial Motor Vehicles	set	7/-	8/6
25a	Wagon	ea.	1/3	1/6
25b	Covered Van	,,	1/3	1/6
25c	Flat Truck	,,	1/3	1/6
25d	Petrol Tank Wagon	,,	1/3	1/6
25e	Tipping Wagon	,,	1/3	1/6
25f	Market Gardener's Van	,,	1/3	1/6
25g	Trailer	,,	-/10	1/-
25h	Streamlined Fire Engine	,,	1/3	1/6
25s	Six-Wheeled Wagon	,,	1/7½	2/-
28/1	Delivery Vans	set	5/6	6/9
28/2	,, ,,	,,	5/6	6/9
28/3	,, ,,	,,	5/6	6/9
29b	Streamlined Motor Bus	ea.	-/10	1/-
29c	Double Decker Motor Bus	,,	2/1½	2/7
30	Motor Vehicles	set	7/5	9/-
30a	Chrysler "Airflow" Saloon	ea.	1/-½	1/3
30b	Rolls-Royce	,,	1/5½	1/9
30c	Daimler	,,	1/5½	1/9
30d	Vauxhall	,,	1/5½	1/9
30e	Breakdown Car	,,	1/3	1/6
30f	Ambulance	,,	1/-½	1/3
30g	Caravan Trailer	,,	-/10	1/-
33	Mechanical Horse and four Assorted Trailers	set	4/4	5/3
33a	Mechanical Horse	ea.	-/8	-/10
33b	Flat Truck	,,	-/10	1/-
33c	Open Wagon	,,	-/10	1/-
33d	Box Van	,,	1/-½	1/3
33e	Dust Wagon	,,	1/-½	1/3
33f	Petrol Tank	,,	1/-½	1/3
33R	Railway Mechanical Horse and Trailer Van	set	2/3	2/9
33Ra	Rly Mechanical Horse	ea.	1/-½	1/3
33Rd	Trailer Van	,,	1/3	1/6
34a	Royal Air Mail Service Car	ea.	-/10	
34b	Royal Mail Van	,,	1/5½	
*35	Small Cars	set	1/7½	
35a	Saloon Car	ea.	-/6½	
35b	Racer	,,	-/6½	
35c	"M.G." Sport Car	,,	-/6½	
35d	Austin Seven Car	,,	-/6½	
36	Motor Cars	set	8/8	
36a	Armstrong Siddeley	ea.	1/5½	
36b	Bentley	,,	1/5½	
36c	Humber	,,	1/5½	
36d	Rover	,,	1/5½	
36e	British Salmson (2-seater)	,,	1/5½	
36f	British Salmson (4-seater)	,,	1/5½	
36g	Taxi, with Driver	,,	1/5½	
37a	Motor Cyclist (civilian)	,,	-/10	
37b	Motor Cyclist (police)	,,	-/10	
37c	Royal Corps of Signals Dispatch Rider	,,	-/10	
38a	Frazer-Nash B.W.N. Sports Car	,,	1/10	
38b	Sunbeam-Talbot Sports Car	,,	1/10	
38d	Alvis Sports Tourer	,,	1/10	
39	U.S.A. Saloon Cars	set	11/-	
39a	Packard "Super 8" Tourer	ea.	1/10	
39b	Oldsmobile Sedan	,,	1/10	
39c	Lincoln "Zephyr" Coupe	,,	1/10	
39d	Buick "Victory" Saloon	,,	1/10	
39e	Chrysler "Royal" Sedan	,,	1/10	
39f	Studebaker "State Commander" Coupe	,,	1/10	
42	Police Box, Motor Cycle Patrol and Policeman	set	3/2½	
42a	Police Box	ea.	-/10	
42b	Motor Cycle Patrol	,,	1/5½	
42c	Point Duty Policeman (in white coat)	,,	-/5½	
42d	Point Duty Policeman	,,	-/6½	

* Not available. † Limited supplies.

Fig 25. A wartime price list.

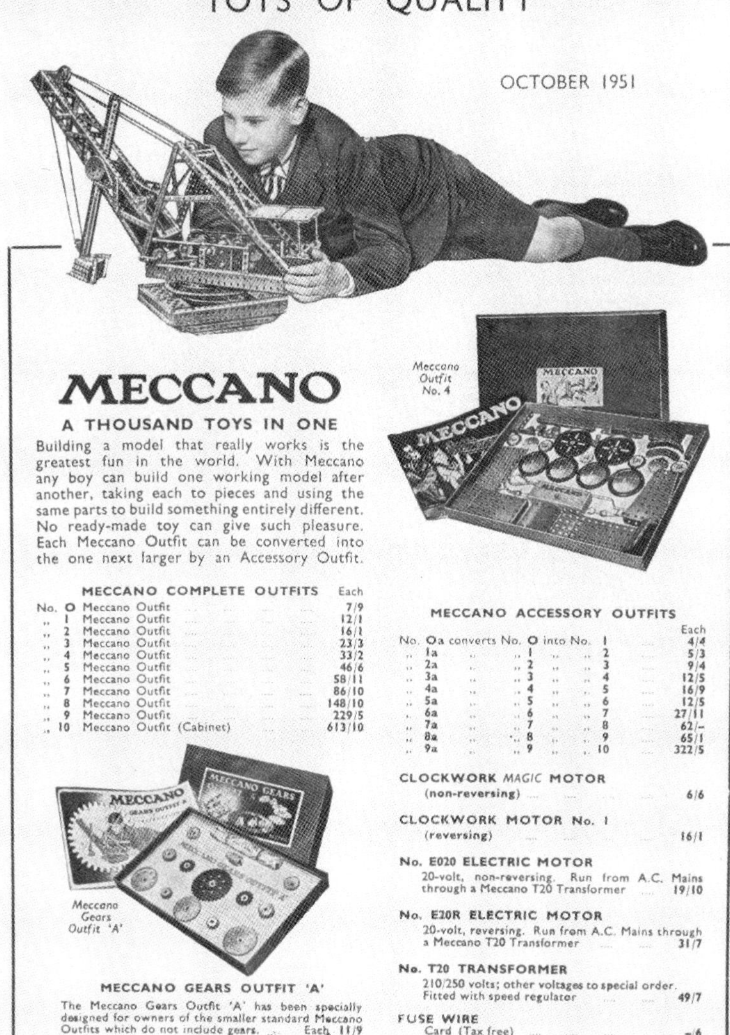

TOYS OF QUALITY

OCTOBER 1951

MECCANO

A THOUSAND TOYS IN ONE

Building a model that really works is the greatest fun in the world. With Meccano any boy can build one working model after another, taking each to pieces and using the same parts to build something entirely different. No ready-made toy can give such pleasure. Each Meccano Outfit can be converted into the one next larger by an Accessory Outfit.

MECCANO COMPLETE OUTFITS

		Each
No. O	Meccano Outfit	7/9
,, 1	Meccano Outfit	12/1
,, 2	Meccano Outfit	16/1
,, 3	Meccano Outfit	23/3
,, 4	Meccano Outfit	33/2
,, 5	Meccano Outfit	46/6
,, 6	Meccano Outfit	58/11
,, 7	Meccano Outfit	86/10
,, 8	Meccano Outfit	148/10
,, 9	Meccano Outfit	229/5
,, 10	Meccano Outfit (Cabinet)	613/10

MECCANO GEARS OUTFIT 'A'

The Meccano Gears Outfit 'A' has been specially designed for owners of the smaller standard Meccano Outfits which do not include gears. Each 11/9

MECCANO ACCESSORY OUTFITS

			Each
No. Oa	converts No. O	into No. 1	4/4
,, 1a	,, ,, 1	,, ,, 2	5/3
,, 2a	,, ,, 2	,, ,, 3	9/4
,, 3a	,, ,, 3	,, ,, 4	12/5
,, 4a	,, ,, 4	,, ,, 5	16/9
,, 5a	,, ,, 5	,, ,, 6	12/5
,, 6a	,, ,, 6	,, ,, 7	27/11
,, 7a	,, ,, 7	,, ,, 8	62/–
,, 8a	,, ,, 8	,, ,, 9	65/1
,, 9a	,, ,, 9	,, ,, 10	322/5

CLOCKWORK *MAGIC* MOTOR
(non-reversing) 6/6

CLOCKWORK MOTOR No. 1
(reversing) 16/1

No. E020 ELECTRIC MOTOR
20-volt, non-reversing. Run from A.C. Mains through a Meccano T20 Transformer 19/10

No. E20R ELECTRIC MOTOR
20-volt, reversing. Run from A.C. Mains through a Meccano T20 Transformer 31/7

No. T20 TRANSFORMER
210/250 volts; other voltages to special order. Fitted with speed regulator 49/7

FUSE WIRE
Card (Tax free) –/6

PRICES INCLUDE PURCHASE TAX U.K.

Fig 26. 1951 price list. *Fig 27. Prospectus for 1919–1920 Inventors Competition designed to increase sales of various new parts!*

MECCANO INVENTORS' COMPETITION

1919—20.

ONE of the most excellent features of Meccano is the constant freshness and variety imparted to the hobby by the introduction of new engineering elements, and this is a line of progress which we shall always develop strongly. We have recently added a number of new parts to the system, and each one of them adds to the pleasure and interest of Meccano model building, and to the beauty and efficiency of the models themselves. Every Meccano boy should add them to his outfit because they will give him a lot of help. We are preparing a new Manual of Instructions containing models which will illustrate the usefulness of these new parts, but before this is issued we wish to encourage Meccano boys to think things out for themselves, and we are therefore offering valuable prizes for suggestions for the improvement of the models in the Meccano Manuals of Instructions, by the use of any of the following new parts.

No. 109. Face Plate.	No. 62a. Threaded Crank.	No. 52a. Flat Plates $5\frac{1}{2} \times 3\frac{1}{2}$ in.
,, 110. Rack Strip.	,, 108. Architrave.	,, 53a. ,, ,, $4\frac{1}{2} \times 2\frac{1}{2}$,,
,, 63a. Octagonal Coupling	,, 20a. Pulley Wheel, 2 in.	,, 70. ,, ,, $5\frac{1}{2} \times 2\frac{1}{2}$,,
,, 63b. Strip Coupling.	,, 19b. Pulley Wheel, 3 in.	,, 72. ,, ,, $2\frac{1}{2} \times 2\frac{1}{2}$,,
,, 64. Threaded Boss.	,, 80 & 81. Screwed Rod.	,, 7. Angle Girders, $24\frac{1}{2}$ in. long
	,, 90. Curved Strip.	,, 7a. ,, ,, $18\frac{1}{2}$ in. ,,

HOW TO COMPETE. Look carefully over the models in the No. 1 and No. 2 Manuals of Instructions, and decide how any of these could be improved by the use of any of the above new parts, then send to us a sketch or photograph of the alterations which you suggest, together with a short description.

First Prize—a No. 6	**Meccano Outfit**	....	**value**	**£9 0 0**
Second ,, ,, 5	**,,**	**,,**	**,,**	**£5 0 0**
Third ,, ,, 5	**,,**	**,, (carton)**	**,,**	**£3 10 0**

Additional Prizes will be awarded to competitors whose entries shew special merit.

All entries for this competition should be addressed—

INVENTORS' COMPETITION,
MECCANO LIMITED,
BINNS ROAD,
LIVERPOOL.

<u>Closing date, March 1st, 1920.</u>

The judges will be Meccano Ltd., and the sole copyright of the photos, sketches or models which win prizes will be vested in the Company. Photographs or sketches will not be returned.

No special Form of Entry is required in this competition.

MECCANO LIMITED. **LIVERPOOL.**

919/35

MECCANO
Model Building Contest
For the best original Models made with Meccano

Every year thousands of new Meccano models are invented and built by Meccano boys. We want to encourage these inventive boys, and have accordingly arranged a grand Model-building Contest, with valuable Prizes.

All you have to do is to build an original Meccano model and send us a photograph or a neat sketch of it, together with an explanation of the original points in its mechanism and design. These details should be written carefully on one side of the paper only (they should be as brief as possible) and, together with your entry form, should be securely attached to the photograph or sketch of your model.

Neither photographs nor drawings need be your own work, but **the model itself must be the result of your own unaided efforts.**

Don't forget that your model will stand a better chance of winning a prize if it is constructed on correct mechanical and engineering principles.

The contest is divided into two groups—United Kingdom & Overseas—and particulars of the awards in each group are given below. The closing date for the United Kingdom is 31st January, 1929, but in order to give Overseas entrants time in which to build their models we have extended the closing date for the Overseas group to 30th April, 1929.

PRIZES

UNITED KINGDOM GROUP

Section A: For Competitors over 16 years of age on 31st January, 1929. First Prize, £12; Second Prize, £8; Third Prize, £5.

Section B: For Competitors over 12 and under 16 years of age on 31st January, 1929. First Prize, £8; Second Prize, £5; Third Prize, £3.

Section C: For Competitors under 12 years of age on 31st January, 1929. First Prize, £5; Second Prize, £3; Third Prize, £2.

OVERSEAS GROUP

Section D: For Competitors over 16 years of age on 30th April, 1929. First Prize, £5; Second Prize, £3; Third Prize, £2.

Section E: For Competitors under 16 years of age on 30th April, 1929. First Prize, £3; Second Prize, £2; Third Prize, £1.

For models showing special merit there will also be 100 special prizes, consisting of Meccano Outfits, Hornby Train Sets, Electric Motors, Clockwork Motors, Inventor's Outfits, Meccano Radio Sets, and Earphones, etc., and 100 copies of the "Meccano Standard Mechanisms" Manual as consolation prizes, bringing the total value of the prizes up to ONE HUNDRED POUNDS.

Meccano Electric Motor

(4-VOLT)

This Electric Motor may be employed for any purpose for which a 4-volt motor is suitable, but it is specially designed for running Meccano models.

The motor may be run from a 4-volt accumulator or from a suitable transformer connected to the mains (alternating current only).

The two terminals of the accumulator or transformer should be connected to the terminals of the motor. It is of no consequence which motor terminal is connected to the positive and which to the negative terminal of an accumulator. For making these connections insulated copper bell wire is advised, and this may be obtained from any electrical stores.

Running, free, the motor takes about 1 ampere, but on full load this is increased to 2.5 amperes.

In disconnecting the motor from an accumulator, always release the wire from the accumulator terminal first in order to avoid the risk of a short circuit, which would damage the accumulator.

The bearings of the motor should be oiled occasionally, care being taken to prevent the oil from coming into contact with the windings, commutator or brushes, each of which should be kept clean.

If the motor does not run satisfactorily, examine it to ensure that (a) the leads to the terminals of the motor do not touch the plates of the latter, (b) the carbon brushes make good contact with the commutator, (c) the brush springs are exercising sufficient pressure on the brushes.

Should the examination fail to reveal any faults of this description, do not take the motor to pieces, but send it to us for complete overhaul.

The parcel containing it should be addressed to Service Department, Meccano Ltd., Old Swan, Liverpool.

Printed in England.

Moteur Electrique Meccano

(4-VOLTS)

Ce moteur électrique Meccano peut servir partout où convient un moteur de 4 volts, mais il s'adapte particulièrement au fonctionnement des modèles Meccano.

Il peut être actionné par un accumulateur de 4 volts, ou par un transformateur convenable branché sur le courant de la ville (courant alternatif seulement).

Fonctionnement par Accu.—La borne positive ou la négative peuvent être indistinctement raccordées aux bornes du moteur. Pour établir ces connexions, il convient de se servir de fil isolé de cuivre pour sonnerie que l'on peut trouver chez tous les électriciens.

Afin d'éviter des courts-circuits quand on sépare l'accumulateur du moteur, il est recommandé de démonter en premier lieu une des bornes de l'accumulateur.

Consommation.—Le moteur Meccano tournant à vide prend environ, 1 ampère; à pleine charge il peut prendre 2.5 ampères, sans crainte de détérioration du moteur.

Les parties tournantes du moteur doivent être huilées légèrement, mais on doit s'abstenir de toucher aux parties électriques, comme induits, balais ou collecteur.

Si le moteur ne fonctionne pas d'une manière satisfaisante, examinez-le afin de vous assurer: (a) que les fils reliés aux bornes du moteur ne touchent pas aux flasques; (b) que les balais entrent bien en contact avec le collecteur; (c) que les ressorts des balais exercent suffisamment de pression sur ces derniers.

Si cet examen ne fait pas connaître de défauts de cette nature, ne démontez pas le moteur mais envoyez-le nous pour être révisé.

Le colis devrait être adressé au Département Service, Meccano Ltd., Old Swan, Liverpool, Angleterre.

Imprimé en Angleterre.

Motor Eléctrico Meccano

(4-VOLTIOS)

Este Motor Eléctrico **Meccano**, puede emplearse en cuantos casos convenga usar un motor de 4 voltios, pero particularmente es apropiado para hacer funcionar los modelos del **Meccano.**

El motor se pone en funcionamiento mediante un acumulador de 4 voltios o mediante un transformador conveniente conexionado con la linea principal (corriente alternativa solamente).

Los dos bornes del acumulador o transformador han de estar conveniente conexionados con los dos bornes del motor. Cualquier borne del motor puede conexionarse con el borne positivo ó negativo del acumulador. Las conexiones se establecen mediante alambre corriente de la clase que se usa para instalaciones de timbres y se puede adquirir en todos los almacénes de material eléctrico.

El motor sin carga consume 1 amperio y á plena carga consume 2.5 amperios.

Para desmontar la instalación, téngase la precaución de desprender primeramente el alambre del borne del acumulador con el fin de evitar el riesgo de que se forme un circuito corto que puede ocasionar la descarga rápida del mismo.

Es conveniente lubrificar regularmente los cojinetes evitando que el aceite ensucie los contactos de las escobillas del motor ya que dichas partes deben conservarse limpias.

Caso de no funcionar á satisfaccion, examine el motor para cerciorarse

(a) que los alambres colocados en los bornes del motor no estén en contacto con las placas laterales del mismo.

(b) que las escobillas de carbón tengan buen contacto con el conmutador,

(c) que los muelles ejerzan bastante presión sobre las escobillas.

Caso de no descubrir defectos de la índole indicada, no desmonte el motor, sino que puede enviarnoslo con una carta de aviso.

Dirijase el paquete á la Sección de Servicio, Meccano **Ltd., Old Swan, Liverpool, Inglaterra.**

Impreso en Inglaterra.

Der Meccano Elektromotor

(4-VOLT)

Dieser Elektromotor kann für jeden für einen 4-Volt Motor geeigneten Zweck Verwendung finden, er ist aber im besonderen für den Antrieb der Meccano-Modelle entworfen worden.

Der Motor wird durch einen 4-Volt Akkumulator betrieben, oder durch einen geeigneten Transformator der mit der Stadtleitung (nur Wechselstrom) verbunden wird.

Die beiden Polenden des Akkumulators oder des Transformators müssen mit den Polen des Motors verbunden werden. Es spielt hierbei keine Rolle, welches Polende des Motors mit dem positiven oder negativen Polende des Akkumulators verbunden wird. Als Verbindungen benütze man gewöhnlichen für elektrische Glocke geeigneten Isolierdraht, der in jedem Elektrizitäts-Geschäft erhältlich ist.

Läuft der Motor frei, dann verbraucht er 1 Ampère, jedoch wird der Verbrauch bei voller Belastung auf 2, 5 Ampères, erhöht.

Bei der Entkuppelung des Motors vom Akkumulator muss der Draht stets zuerst von dem Polende des Akkumulators entfernt werden, um Kurzschluss, welcher den Akkumulator ruinieren würde, zu vermeiden.

Das Lager des Motors muss hin und wieder geölt werden, wobei darauf geachtet werden muss, dass das Oel nicht mit den Spulen, dem Kollektor und den Bürsten, die alle sauber gehalten werden müssen, in Berührung kommt.

Wenn der Motor nicht zur Zufriedenheit läuft, so untersuche man ihn, um sich zu versichern, dass (a) die Leitungen nach den Polenden des Motors nicht die Platten des letzteren berühren, (b) die Kohlenbürsten guten Kontakt mit dem Kollektor geben und (c) die Bürstenfedern einen genügenden Druck auf die Bürste ausüben.

Sollte die Untersuchung keinen der in dieser Beschreibung genannten Fehler ergeben, so nehme man den Motor nicht auseinander sondern sende ihn zur gründlichen Durchsicht an uns.

Das den Motor enthaltende Paket muss an die Dienstabteilung, Meccano Ltd., Old Swan, Liverpool, gerichtet werden.

In England gedruckt.

6/632/2 **Meccano Ltd., Liverpool, England**

Fig 28. Application form for the 1928 competition.

Fig 29. 1932 instructions for the US-style Meccano motors some of which were repatriated after the demise of the New Jersey operation.

Meccano Electric Motor (20 Volt)

No. E20b Reversing

INSTRUCTIONS

The E20b Electric Motor may be employed for any purpose for which a 20-volt motor is suitable, but it is specially designed for running Meccano models.

The Motor can be run from the mains by means of a transformer that will give an output of 20 volts. We manufacture transformers specially for use with our Electric Motors and Train Sets. Meccano Transformers types T20A, T20 and T20M are suitable for use with this Motor. It should be specially noted that transformers must be used with alternating current only. If the mains supply is direct current, a rotary converter that will give an output of 20 volts should be used.

The two terminals of the transformer or rotary converter must be connected to the terminals of the Motor. For making these connections, insulated wire of 18 or 20 gauge is suggested.

Running free, the Motor takes approx. 0.5 ampere. The current increases under load up to a maximum of 1 ampere.

The Motor is provided with a reversing switch A, as shown in the illustration. When the switch is in the central position, the Motor is stopped; it should be set in this position before making the connections described above. To reverse the direction of the drive, the switch is moved over from one extreme position to the other.

When connecting or disconnecting the Motor it is important that the transformer or rotary converter should be switched off from the mains supply.

The bearings of the Motor should be oiled occasionally, care being taken to prevent the oil from coming into contact with the windings, commutator or brushes, each of which should be kept clean.

If, after a period of use, the Motor loses power, examine it to ensure that (a) the leads to the terminals of the Motor do not touch the plates of the latter—metal to metal, (b) the carbon brushes make good contact with the commutator, (c) the brush springs are exercising sufficient pressure on the brushes, and (d) the commutator and brushes are clean and free from oil. When the brushes have become worn, it may be found necessary to increase the tension of the brush springs by extending the coils a little.

Should the examination fail to reveal any fault of this description, send the Motor for complete overhaul to Service Department, Meccano Ltd. Binns Road, Liverpool 13.

Printed in England

Moteur Electrique Meccano (20 Volt)

Avec renversement de marche E20b

INSTRUCTIONS

Le Moteur Electrique peut être employé dans tous les cas où convient un Moteur de 20 volts, mais il est tout spécialement destiné à actionner les modèles Meccano

Le Moteur peut fonctionner sous le courant de la ville (courant alternatif exclusivement) au moyen d'un transformateur Meccano T20A, T20 ou T20M donnant 22 volts au plus.

Les deux bornes du transformateur doivent être connectées à celles du Moteur. Chaque borne du Moteur peut être connectée indifféremment à la borne positive ou négative. Nous conseillons d'effectuer ces connexions au moyen de fil isolé, de diamètre 0.914 ou 1.22 mm.

En tournant à vide, le Moteur consomme 0.5 ampère. Le courant augmente suivant la résistance imposée au moteur et ce courant arrive à consommer jusqu'à un maximum de 1 ampères

Le Moteur est muni d'un levier de renversement de marche A, comme indiqué sur la gravure. Quand l'interrupteur est dans sa position centrale, le Moteur est arrêté; il faut le ramener à cette position avant d'établir les connexions décrites ci-dessus. Pour renverser la marche du Moteur, on pousse le levier à la position opposée.

Il est important que la communication entre le courant de la ville et le transformateur soit interrompue lorsqu'on branche ou enlève le Moteur.

Les paliers du Moteur doivent être graissés de temps en temps mais on prendra soin d'empêcher l'huile de venir en contact avec l'enroulement, le commutateur et les balais qui doivent rester secs.

Si le Moteur perde de puissance examinez-le pour vous assurer: (a) que les fils venant des bornes du Moteur ne touchent pas aux parois de ce dernier, (b) que les balais en charbon sont en bon contact avec le commutateur, et (c) que les ressorts des balais exercent une pression suffisante sur ces derniers, (d) que le commutateur et les balais sont nets et libres d'huile. Il se peut qu'après un certain temps de service, quand les balais seront usés, on doive augmenter la tension de leurs ressorts en les étirant légèrement.

Au cas où cet examen ne révèle aucune de ces défectuosités, veuillez écrire au Service Réparations, Meccano Limited, Binns Road, Liverpool 13, Angleterre.

Imprimé en Angleterre

Meccano Elektromotor (20 Volt)

Type E20b Umsteuerbar

GEBRAUCHSANWEISUNG

Der Meccano Elektromotor kann für alle Zwecke bei denen ein 20 Volt Motor anwendbar ist, benutzt werden. Er ist jedoch nach besonderen Entwürfen konstruiert worden, um hauptsächlich Meccano Modelle zu betreiben.

Dieser Motor kann von der Hausleitung (nur Wechelstrom) durch Meccano Transformator T20A, T20, oder T20M, (die eine Leistung von nicht mehr als 22Volt liefern) angetrieben werden. Die beiden Pole des Transformators werden an die Polklemmen des Motors angeschlossen. Bei der Herstellung dieser Verbindungen benutzt man Isolierdraht von 1.22 oder 0.914mm. Diam. Der Motor läuft frei mit 0.5 Ampère, kann jedoch bis zu höchstens 1 Amp. gesteigert werden.

Die Umschaltung des Motors ist durch den Buchstaben A der Abbildung gekennzeichnet. Befindet sich der Schalter in Mittelstellung, so ist der Motor abgestellt. Es ist darauf zu achten, dass bei Herstellung der Verbindung mit dem Transformator der Motor stets *abgestellt* ist. Um den Gang umzukehren muss der Schalter von seiner äussersten Stellung bis zur entgegengesetzten gedreht werden.

Bei jedem Ver -und Abkuppeln des Motors ist es wichtig, dass *vorher* die Verbindung zwischen Hausleitung und Transformator *unterbrochen* wird.

Die Wellen-Lager des Motors müssen ab und zu geölt werden. Das Oelen muss sehr vorsichtig geschehen damit das Oel nicht mit den Wickelungen, dem Kommutator und den Bürsten in Berührung kommt. Diese müssen stets sehr sauber gehalten werden.

Wenn der Motor nach Dauerlauf Kraft verliert, vergewissere man sich :—

a) dass die Leitung zu dem Motore nicht die Platten des Motors berührt,
b) dass die Kohlenbürsten in gutem Kontakt mit dem Kommutator stehen,
c) dass die Bürstenfedern genügenden Druck auf die Bürsten ausüben. Bei Abnutzung der Bürsten empfiehlt es sich, die Spannung der Bürstenfedern dadurch etwas zu erhöhen, dass man die Spiralen etwas auseinander zieht,
d) dass der Kommutator sowie die Bürsten sauber und ölfrei sind.

Ist trotz dieser Massnahmen die Fehlerquelle nicht zu entdecken, so schreibe man an Meccano Limited, Binns Road, Liverpool 13, England.

Meccano Electromotor (20 Volt)

E20b Omkeerbaar

GEBRUIKSAANWIJZING

De Electromotor kan worden gebruikt voor alle doeleinden waarvoor een 20-Volt Motor geschikt is, doch is in het bijzonder bestemd voor het aandrijven van Meccano-modellen.

De Motor kan worden aangedreven door stroom uit de lichtleiding door middel van een transformator, die een secundaire spanning geeft van niet meer dan 22 Volt. De Meccano Transformatoren T20A, T20 of T20M zijn ontworpen om deze Motor te drijven. In verband hiermede moge in het bijzonder vermeld worden, dat transformatoren slechts met wisselstroom gebruikt kunnen worden.

De beide klemmen van den transformator moeten met de klemmen van den motor verbonden worden. Voor het maken van deze verbindingen wordt het gebruik van geisoleerd draad of snoer van minstens 0.914 mM. of 1.22 mM. diam. aanbevolen.

Bij het onbelast loopen gebruikt de Motor 0.5 ampère. De stroom loopt, al naarmateb elasting plaats vindt, op tot een maximum van 1 ampère.

De Motor is voorzien van een omschakelaar A, zooals in de illustratie afgebeeld is. Wanneer de schakelaar in het midden staat, is de Motor gestopt; deze schakelaar moet in dien stand gezet worden, alvorens de hierboven omschreven verbindingen gemaakt worden. Om de richting van de aandrijving om te keeren, wordt de schakelaar van den eenen uitersten stand in den anderen gebracht.

Bij het aansluiten of afkoppelen van den Motor is het van belang de verbinding van den transformator met de lichtleiding te verbreken.

De lagers van den Motor dienen van tijd tot tijd gesmeerd te worden, waarbij men er voor zorge, dat de olie niet op de windingen, collector of borstels komt; elk van deze onderdeelen moet goed schoon gehouden worden.

Indien de Motor kracht verliezt, onderzoekt men hem om zekerheid te verkrijgen, dat (a) de leiding naar de klemmen van den Motor niet de platen van dezen laatsten raakt, (b) dat de kool-borstels een goed contact met den collector maken, (c) dat de borstelveeren een voldoenden druk op de borstels uitoefenen, en (d) dat de collector en borstels schoon en olievrij zijn. Wanneer de borstels afgesleten zijn, kan het noodzakelijk blijken de spanning van de borstelveeren te vergrooten, door de spiraalveeren een weinig uit te rekken.

Mochten bij het onderzoek geenerlei fouten van bovengenoemden aard aan het licht komen schrijf aan Meccano Ltd., Binns Road, Liverpool 13, Engeland.

1/139/1.5 **MECCANO LTD. — LIVERPOOL 13 — ENGLAND**

Fig 30. 1939 instructions for E20b electric motor.

INSTRUCTIONS

Meccano Transformer Type T20A

Output: 35 VA at 20/3.5 Volts

This Transformer provides an economical and perfectly safe means of running a Meccano 20-volt Motor or a Hornby 20-volt Electric Train. It transforms the high voltage of the electric light supply to the requisite low voltage. The Transformer can be used in connection with any apparatus requiring an Alternating Current supply up to 1 ampere at 20 volts. It will run for 28 hours on one unit.

Transformers work only on Alternating Current (A.C.) **A Transformer must not be connected to direct or continuous current (D.C.)**

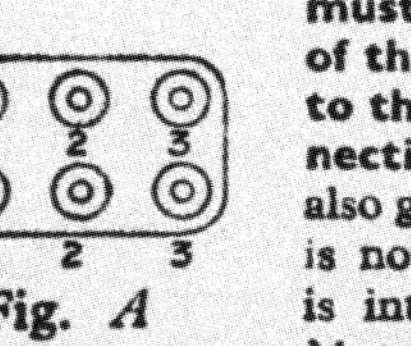

Fig. *A*

The three-core flex provided with this Transformer is intended to be used with a three-pin plug and socket. If your plug is of this type, connect the two free ends of the flex to the terminals of the two smaller pins, which are the supply terminals; and the end tied back and labelled "Earth" to the terminal of the remaining larger pin, which is the earthing terminal. **On no account must the earth lead be connected to either of the supply terminals**

If you have a two-pin plug, connect the free ends of the flex to the terminals of these pins, leaving the earth lead disconnected. As an extra safety precaution the earth lead may be connected to earth. This should certainly be done where the Transformer is to be used on a stone or concrete floor. If in doubt, consult your electrical supplier.

Fig. A is a diagram of three pairs of plug sockets on one side of the Transformer The first pair, numbered 1, gives current at 20 volts under control of the 5-stud speed regulator fitted to the Transformer as shown in Fig.B. The current from this pair is intended for driving a 20-volt Hornby Train.

RUNNING A TRAIN

To start a train, move the regulator handle over to the stud at the extreme right, without pausing on the intermediate studs. Then, by moving the handle toward the left, the speed is gradually increased until the maximum is reached when the handle is in contact with the stud next to the "off" stud which is at the extreme left. Fig C shows the Transformer connected to the track or driving a 20-volt Hornby Train. The connection between the Transformer and the rails is made by means of the flexible leads supplied with the Transformer. The plug ends of the leads are inserted in the upper and lower sockets of the pair marked 1, the socket fittings of these leads being connected to the plug fitting on the Terminal Connecting Plate. **The lead connected to the lower socket must always be connected to the outer rails of the track, that is to the plug connected to the locking lever on the Terminal Connecting Plate.** The second pair of sockets 2, also gives current at 20 volts, but this current is not controlled by the speed regulator. It is intended for driving a Meccano 20-volt Motor, as shown in Fig. B. **The first and second pair of sockets must not be used at the same time.** That is to say, either a train or a motor can be run, but not both together.

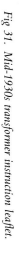

CURRENT CONSUMPTION

The maximum permissible current that can be taken from the sockets marked 1 and 2 is 1 amp., and from the socket marked 3 is 4.5 amps. These values should not be exceeded, as continuous overloading causes damage to the windings. Overload is indicated by heating or by a loud buzzing noise, but it may occur though these symptoms are absent. As a guide to determining the load on the Transformer the following current consumptions are given:- 20-volt Locomotive, .75 ampere; 20-volt Headlamp on Locomotive .15 ampere; 3½-volt Flashlamp, as used in the Hornby Accessories fitted for lighting, ·3 ampere; 20-volt Meccano Motor 1 ampere.

PROTECTING THE TRANSFORMER

The 20-volt train circuit is protected by the fuse in the Terminal Connecting Plate attached to the rails. The correct Fuse Wire to use with the Terminal Connecting Plate to suit this Transformer is No. 32 S.W.G. Lead. In the event of a short circuit the wire melts and disconnects the power supply to the track. When this happens the current must be switched off, the fault cleared and the fuse wire then renewed.

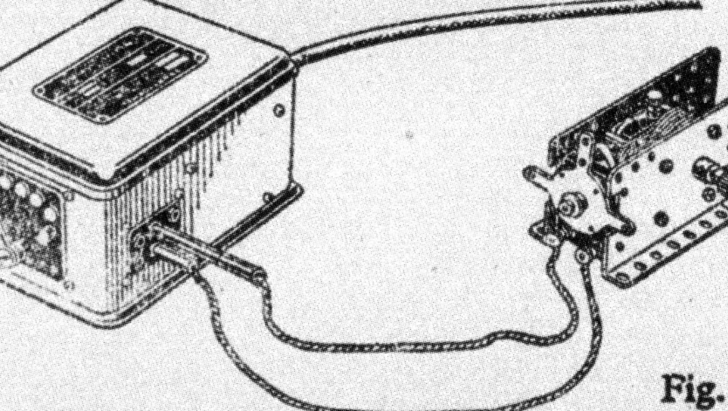
Fig. *B*

Fig 31. Mid-1930s transformer instruction leaflet.

INSTRUCTIONS

Lighting Set for use with Meccano Models

The Lanterns. The accompanying illustration shows how a lantern (1) is fixed in position on a model by means of one of the special angle brackets (2) supplied with the set. The lantern carries a nut (3) with which it is secured to the bracket, and the latter is attached to the model by means of an ordinary Meccano nut and bolt

The pea lamp is carried by a short tube (4) in a slot (5) in the side of the lantern, the flex (6) being connected to the battery clips (7) by means of the terminals (8). The clips are pushed on to the brass strips of an ordinary 4½-volt flashlamp battery (not included in the set).

The small illustration inset shows a front view of a lantern with pea lamp in position.

The Reading Lamp. The reading lamp is assembled by passing the flex down through the centre hole in the base and leading it out through the hole in the side. The shade is held in position by the cork mounting. The flex is connected to the battery in the manner described above for the lantern.

Printed in England

INSTRUCTIONS

Système d'Eclairage pour Modèles Meccano

Les lanternes (1) sont fixées au modèle au moyen d'attaches spéciales (2) comprises dans le Système. Les lanternes sont munies d'écrous (3) à l'aide desquels elles sont fixées aux attaches. Des écrous et des boulons Meccano servent à fixer les attaches aux modèles dans la position voulue.

Au besoin, les lanternes peuvent être fixées à un modèle sans l'aide d'attaches spéciales.

Les ampoules (4) sont introduites dans les fentes (5) aménagées sur les côtés des lanternes, le fil flexible (6) étant relié aux bornes (7) des broches (8), celles-ci sont glissées sur les lames en laiton d'une pile de poche (4.5 volts).

On procède au montage de la Lampe de Chevet en faisant passer le fil flexible dans le trou central de la base et en l'introduisant ensuite dans le trou latéral. L'abat-jour est fixé au modèle à l'aide d'un bouchon-monture. La connexion à la pile est effectuée comme indiqué ci-dessus.

Imprimé en Angleterre

ISTRUZIONI

Impianto d'illuminazione per l'uso nelle costruzioni di Modelli Meccano

Le lampade (1) si applicano ai modelli Meccano mediante le squadrette speciali (2) fornite coll'impianto. Queste lampade sono munite di dadi (3) che servono per fissarle alle squadrette o supporti. Per il fissaggio dei supporti in qualunque punto di un modello Meccano, si usano le comuni viti con dado Meccano.

Volendo, si possono applicare le lampade ai modelli anche senza le squadrette speciali.

Le lampadine (4) vanno infilate nei ricettacoli ai lati delle lampade, attaccando il filo conduttore (6) ai ferma pila (7) per mezzo dei terminali (8). I ferma pila sono quindi adattati ai contatti di metallo di una comune pila a secco, per lampadine tascabili.

Per montare la lampada da lettura, passare il filo nel foro centrale alla base e condurlo fuori del foro laterale. Il riflettore è tenuto a posto dalla guarnizione di sughero. Si fa quindi l'attacco alla pila come sopra indicato.

Stampato in Inghilterra

GEBRUIKSAANWIJZING

Verlichtings-Garnituur voor gebruik bij Meccano-Modellen

De lantaarns (1) worden in den juisten stand op het model vastgezet door middel van de speciale hoeksteunen (2), die bij het garnituur geleverd worden. De lantaarns worden geleverd met moeren (3), waarmede ze aan de steunen worden bevestigd. Meccano moeren en bouten worden gebruikt om de steunen in elken gewenschten stand aan een model aan te brengen.

Desgewenscht kunnen de lantaarns aan een model worden gemonteerd zonder de speciale steunen.

De gloeilampen (4) worden geplaatst in de gleuven (5) aan de zijkanten van de lantaarns, het snoer (6) wordt verbonden met de batterijklemmen (7) door middel van de aansluitklemmen (8). De klemmen worden op de koperen strooken van een gewone zaklantaarnbatterij gedrukt

Om de leeslamp samen te stellen, steke men het snoer naar beneden door de middenopening in het voetstuk en voert het naar buiten door de opening in den zijkant. Het scherm wordt op zijn plaats gehouden door het kurkmontuur. Aansluiting met de batterij wordt verkregen op de reeds omschreven wijze.

1/1134/2 **MECCANO LIMITED - LIVERPOOL 13 - ENGLAND**

Fig 32. Lighting Outfit instructions.

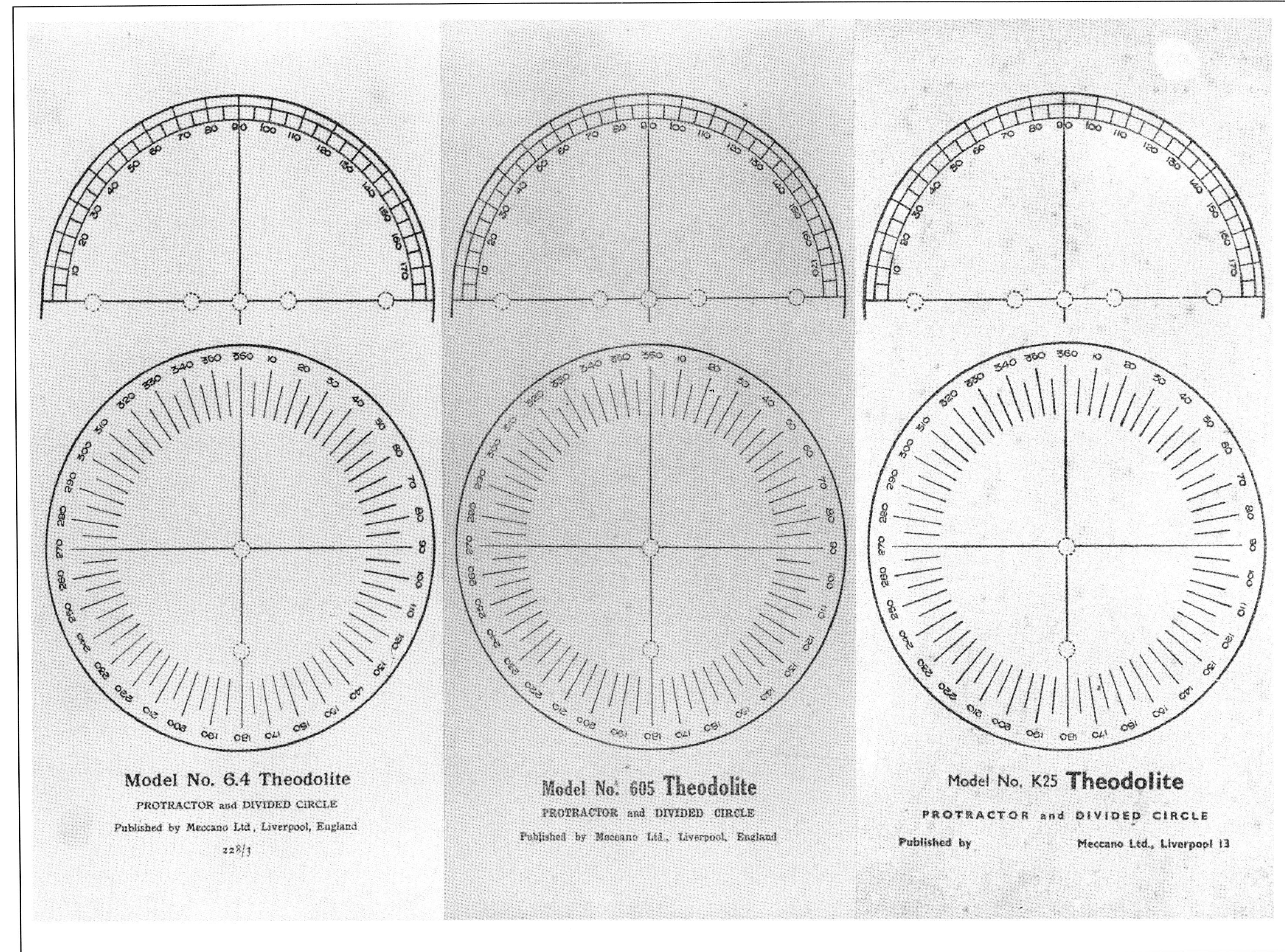
Model No. 6.4 Theodolite
PROTRACTOR and DIVIDED CIRCLE
Published by Meccano Ltd, Liverpool, England
228/3
Model No. 605 Theodolite
PROTRACTOR and DIVIDED CIRCLE
Published by Meccano Ltd., Liverpool, England
Model No. K25 Theodolite
PROTRACTOR and DIVIDED CIRCLE
Published by Meccano Ltd., Liverpool 13

ENGLISH.

Instructions for the First Charge of Accumulator Battery Type 4/5 M 1.

The cells should be filled with Sulphuric Acid, of a specific gravity of 1.200 (to be obtained from any chemist) until the liquid is ¼-in. above the top of the plates. Allow the accumulator to stand for one hour before being placed on charge for 30/40 hours at the rate of ½ ampere. On completion of charge the accumulator is ready for service. Do not spill the acid as it is a corrosive and quickly burns through clothing, &c.

FRENCH.

Instructions pour la charge initiale à l'accumulateur, Batterie Type 4/5 M 1.

Les accumulateurs doivent être remplis d'acide sulfurique d'un poids spécifique de 1,200 jusqu'à ce que le liquide se trouve à 6mm. au-dessus du haut des plaques. L'acide peut être obtenu dans n'importe quelle pharmacie. L'accumulateur, après avoir été laissé rester pendant une heure, doit être mis en charge sous un régime de ½ d'ampère au maximum, et cela pendant 30 à 40 heures. Une fois la charge terminée, l'accumulateur peut être mis en service. Prendre garde de ne pas renverser l'acide, lequel, étant corrosif, pourrait endommager les vêtements.

MECCANO LTD., Binns Road, LIVERPOOL.

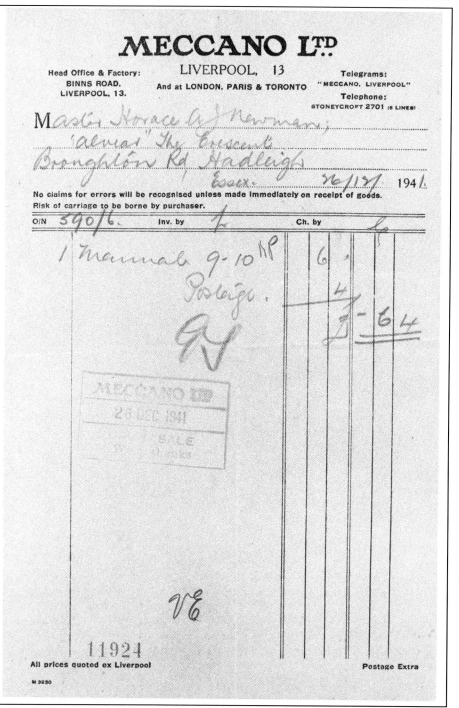

Fig 34. Printed luggage-type ticket giving instructions for the first charge of the 4-volt Meccano accumulator (circa 1925).

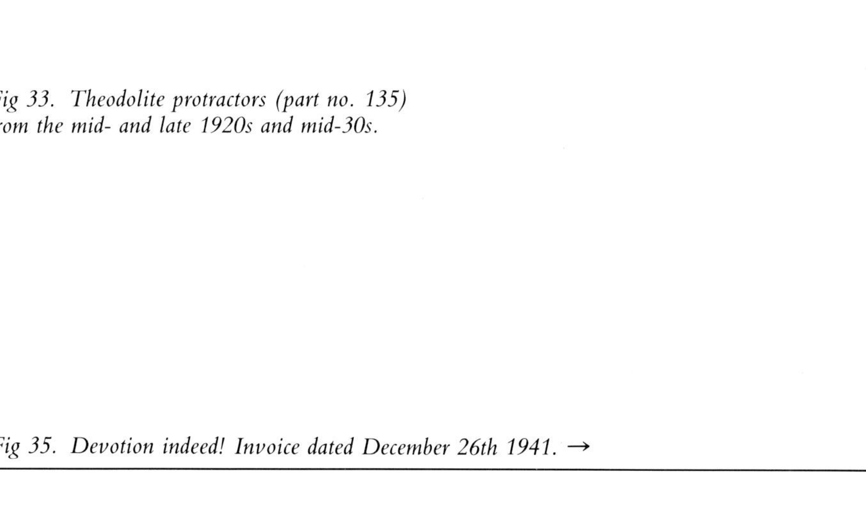

← *Fig 33. Theodolite protractors (part no. 135) from the mid- and late 1920s and mid-30s.*

MECCANO LTD.

Head Office & Factory:
BINNS ROAD.
LIVERPOOL, 13.

LIVERPOOL, 13
And at LONDON, PARIS & TORONTO

Telegrams:
"MECCANO, LIVERPOOL"
Telephone:
STONEYCROFT 2701 (6 LINES)

M aster Horace A J Newman,
"alvias" The Crescent
Broughton Rd Hadleigh
Essex. 26/12/ 1941

No claims for errors will be recognised unless made immediately on receipt of goods.
Risk of carriage to be borne by purchaser.

O/N 590/6. Inv. by Ch. by

1 Manual 9-10 HP 6 .
Postage. 4
7 - 6 4

MECCANO LTD
26 DEC. 1941
SALE
thanks

VE

11924

All prices quoted ex Liverpool

Postage Extra

M 3930

Fig 35. Devotion indeed! Invoice dated December 26th 1941. →

CHAPTER 9

Retail and Trade Literature, Showcards and Catalogues

Meccano Ltd had as we have seen, a very paternalistic and benevolent regard for its customers, however young. This attitude was not dissimilar to that exhibited towards the dealers who sold their products – they too were taken care of in a way which today's dealers would find hard to imagine. Not only did Meccano ensure that there were never too many dealerships for an area to support (and this in itself made a Meccano dealership a valuable property), but it also provided a complete selling service. One only has to look at a pre-war edition of the trade booklet 'Our Selling Service' to realise just how much the company was prepared to do in order to help its retailers.

For the shop, display models and Hornby Train layouts were available, some of which were allied to the special Meccano and Hornby Train weeks. These were well-advertised events for which dealers were supplied special invitation cards for customers. Designs for window displays were shown which must have been a great help to the dealers who lacked the necessary skills in window presentation. Other in-shop aids were showcards, window bills, floor mats, signs, parts cabinets, price tickets and a host of additional items to help the dealer. Meccano even supplied special printing blocks so that the shopkeeper could make use of local press advertising. These blocks were supplied either as complete stereos or as individual pictures for insertion in the dealer's own layout. The range of available blocks was extensive and continually enlarged. This was one service which did continue after the war albeit in a somewhat reduced form. Further assistance with advertising came in the form of lantern slides which were for use in local cinemas. These were hand coloured $3\frac{1}{4}''$ glass transparencies and were, like the printing blocks, for loan only. These slides degraded easily and are consequently extremely rare with very few existing today. Indeed the author is only aware of another 10 or so apart from those in his own collection and it is these which are reproduced for the first time in this volume. They are some of the most beautiful examples of the Artwork department's handiwork and it is sad to think that only a handful have survived. Should any more come to light, the author would dearly like to have details.

Apart from the 'Our Selling Service' booklets, there were regular bulletins advising details of new parts and products as well as further assistance for dealers. Even these were laid-out most attractively in pre-war days and are a joy to the eye. As with most pre-war trade literature (and sales aids) these bulletins are extremely scarce which in view of the small print runs (four to five thousand was not untypical) is not surprising.

For the historian, trade literature is an invaluable source of information because it gives details of the introduction, deletion or alteration of parts and other items thus removing the need for inspired guesswork or difficult research. One can only hope that caches of trade literature are still to be discovered in old shops which once sold Meccano.

The examples illustrated here do not of course tell the whole story of Meccano but they are representative of the care lavished upon dealers – care which paid commercial dividends.

Meccano News No. 1. (Fig. 1)

An exceedingly rare publication, and it seems certain that this is the only issue. It contains much of interest and is written in a far more factual and less propagandist style than might have been expected. It was, as stated on the front cover, designed for both dealers and staff alike – an early exercise in 'in house' communication. The Works Notes are especially interesting. I wonder what happened to Nurse Birchell and did they get more Gramophone records? (Capital G for Gramophone since it is a proprietory name as Alfred Clark pointed out to Sir Compton Mackenzie) And 'Verily we are a thrifty community'. How true!

Our Selling Service. (Figs 2 & 3)

Several of these fascinating publications are illustrated but it is almost impossible to highlight particular features because each page contains so much of interest. Some of the items shown in the booklets, such as glass slides, printing blocks, showcards and 'odds and ends' are illustrated.

Meccano Electrotypes. (Fig 4)

An early 20s leaflet detailing the printing blocks available to dealers. See illustrations of impressions of actual blocks. (Fig 11)

Which Trade Do You Get? (Fig 5)

An extremely rare US leaflet dating from the mid-1920s, it used the pulling power of the child film star Jackie Coogan. (See also the chapter on promotional material).

Trade Bulletins. (Figs 6–9)

Extracts from those of 1928 and 1929 plus a page from the 1940 issue and the display model pages from a 1953 leaflet. Note how visually unattractive the post-war layout is compared with the pre-war equivalent in the 'Our Selling Service' booklets.

'Coles of Sheffield'. (Fig 10)

An example of a dealer initiative which must have assisted the Christmas trade in Sheffield for 1936.

Trade Material

A selection of items supplied to the trade and described in the various trade publications already illustrated.

MECCANO NEWS

Published as a means of cultivating good-will and friendliness between Head Office, Works, Associated Companies, Customers, and Friends of Meccano Limited.

No. 1 Nov. 1920

MECCANO LTD.
LIVERPOOL

MECCANO NEWS

Published as a means of cultivating good-will and friendliness between Head Office, Works, Associated Companies, Customers, and Friends of Meccano Limited.

No. 1. NOVEMBER. 1920.

OUR FUTURE.

I welcome the advent of the *Meccano News*, and the opportunities which it will provide for cultivating and improving the spirit of friendliness and esteem which already exists between the Head Office, Works, Associated Meccano Companies, and friends of Meccano Limited. I also welcome the opportunities which it will give me of from time to time saying something of the progress which we are making, and of our plans and hopes for the future.

Just now is a critical time for industry in this and in all countries. Trade in the home market, as we all know, is fraught with all kinds of troubles with labour, raw materials, and the reduced purchasing power of money, whilst trade with foreign countries is hampered by constant and disconcerting changes in rates of exchange, tariffs, freight charges, delays, and, in some instances, the prohibition of imports except under certain difficult conditions. The only right course, as I see it, is to produce goods of the best possible type, to endeavour to give a square and equitable deal to our employees, to the trade, and to the public, and to bend our energies towards so consolidating our business that when the nation sails into calmer waters, as it inevitably will, Meccano Limited will take the high place in British industry which, I am convinced, is its natural destiny.

Fig 1. Meccano News No. 1.

During the war Meccano fully held its own, and since the Armistice, when we again devoted our full energies to it, its progress in the affections of boys of all nations, has been continuous. In every country, in every home where there are boys, Meccano has become a household word, and it is gratifying to me, and gratifying, I am sure, to all who read the *Meccano News*, to know that there are few businesses which are responsible for the dissemination of so much pleasure as our own. There is every indication that the popularity of Meccano will further increase in the years to come.

The manufacture of clockwork trains, lines, crossings, signals, stations, vertical steam boilers, &c., which we have now commenced, marks a very important step in the history of our Company. Before the war this class of toy was almost entirely imported from the Continent, and it was apparently accepted as a fact that it was impossible to manufacture goods of this type satisfactorily in this country. The war has created new conditions, which have brought with them new opportunities, and I believe that it is now possible to produce clockwork trains and other metal toys equal to anything previously imported, and at prices which will make them commercially profitable. The types which we have so far produced, and which are already selling well have been designed and perfected in our own factory. The Hornby clockwork train is quite a departure from the recognised type, and I am convinced that it has a wonderful future.

Only those who are actually engaged in the production of these new lines can appreciate the enormous amount of organisation they call for, and the labour, space and plant which are necessary. Our new wing, which is now almost complete, and which will have a floor space of 30,510 sq. ft. will be devoted entirely to this new work. This will give us a total floor space of 154,000 sq. ft. Even this is not the end of it, however, and you will be interested to know that the Company has purchased the vacant plot of land between the present factory and Rathbone Road, and the entire block of houses on the west side of Garnet Street, in order that the future development of our business may not be hampered from lack of space.

If we succeed in this new work, as I firmly believe we shall, we shall have added an asset to the nation's wealth in the shape of a new industry, which will provide employment for very large numbers of British workpeople. The benefit to the nation will not stop at that point even; our purchases of metal, cartons, printed matter, and a thousand other commodities will increase enormously, and will form a substantial contribution to the prosperity of the country. There have been, and there will be, difficulties, disappointments and delays all along the line, but none, I believe, which we cannot overcome, and I am fully convinced that we shall in due time arrive at the goal for which we are striving.

It has been a matter of considerable regret to me that we have not yet been able to get our new canteen going. The building was finished some time ago, and everything ready, when we were faced with the difficulty of lack of space for the production of our new goods. The choice lay between clockwork trains, and meals in greater comfort, and clockwork trains won the day. I believe this was a right decision, as any delay in pushing along with our new lines would have meant loss of very valuable time, and would have been a highly dangerous proceeding in my opinion, and when the progress which we have made is taken into consideration, together with the additional employment which we have provided for so many girls, I do not think any of us has cause to regret the course adopted.

I am looking forward to the time when the whole of this work will be transferred to the new building, and I can assure you that it will be a real pleasure to see the canteen in full swing. It is a splendid building, with 16,200 sq. ft. floor space. We have had the floor specially laid in order to make it suitable for dancing, and at one end we propose erecting a stage so that concerts and other entertainments may be held. There is no doubt that the canteen will add a very great deal to the enjoyment and comfort of our employees. I hope that it will be ready for occupation early next year.

At the present time we have well over 1,200 employees in the works, and I have every hope that this number will greatly increase in the future. As we all know, there is considerable unrest in the labour world at the present time, due to a variety of causes over which no-one appears to have control. I am happy to think that these troubles have so far touched us but lightly, and I believe that this is due mainly to the fact that our workers recognise and understand the spirit of fair-mindedness and sincerity with which we have dealt with those questions which concern their welfare. If this understanding continues in the future, and if it is applied to both sides, as I feel sure it will be, there is every reason to believe that whatever misunderstandings or differences of opinion may arise in the future, will be dealt with in a friendly and satisfactory way.

F. Hornby

Fig 1 cont.

MECCANO WORKS COMMITTEE ACTIVITIES.

MEMBERS OF THE COMMITTEE.

Mr. J. A. Welsh, President.
Miss C. Caldwell, Vice-President.
Mr. G. Rotherham, Secretary.
Mr. W. Atherton, Assist. Secretary.
Mr. H. Dyson, Treasurer.
Mrs. A. Hughes, Sick Visitor.
Miss K. Canning.
Miss E. Quinn.
Mr. S. Hardman.
Mr. L. Armes.
Miss N. King.
Miss E. Lockwood.
Miss S. Flynn.
Miss E. Hannigan.
Miss I. Yeo.
Mr. A. Ashworth.
Mr. D. Cuthbertson.
Mr. S. Doodson.
Miss J. Griffiths.

The functions of this Committee are briefly as follows :—

(a) This Committee is for the purpose of promoting the general welfare of the workers employed by Messrs. Meccano Limited.

(b) The Committee will act as medium between the management and the workers, and will consider complaints and grievances as they arise, whether from the management or the workers.

(c) The Committee will discuss and submit to the management suggestions for improvement and betterment of working conditions when necessary.

(d) The Committee will co-operate with the management with a view to facilitating and preserving harmonious relations between the management and general body of workers, thereby endeavouring to attain that desirable condition of contentment and satisfaction necessary to our mutual benefit.

During the past 12 months much useful work has been done by the Works Committee. Many helpful suggestions have been made and put into practice, and the happy relationships which exist between the Company and its employees are due in no small measure to the spirit in which the Committee has co-operated with the management.

BENEVOLENT FUND.

A Benevolent Fund was established in the Works in October, 1919, by the Works Committee, and during the first twelve months 40 cases have been dealt with, and grants made varying from 15s. to £5.

The total contributions by employees were £118. 2s. 11d., and the total grants made amounted to £46. 3s. 5d., leaving a balance in hand of £71. 19s. 6d.

The contribution of each employee is 1d. per week, and the fund is applied to the immediate relief of any employee needing help, or who meets with an accident, and to bridge over the period of 14 days before anything is paid by the Insurance Company. The collection and distribution is in the hands of the Works Committee, who are to be congratulated upon the success with which the Benevolent Fund has been administered during its first twelve months.

HOSPITAL COLLECTION.

Twelve months ago a weekly collection was established by the Works Committee amongst our employees for the benefit of hospitals and convalescent homes, and the contributions were fixed as follows :—

For those in receipt of a weekly wage of £2 and over, 1d. per week.

For those in receipt of a weekly wage less than £2, ½d. per week.

Our Managing Director, Mr. Frank Hornby, made a contribution of £50 to the fund for the first year, and up to September 23rd the amount collected totalled £114. 11s. 9d. This sum has been distributed amongst the local hospitals as follows :—

	£	s.	d.
Royal Infirmary	55	0	0
Myrtle Street Eye Hospital ..	27	10	0
St. Paul's Eye & Ear Hospital	27	10	0
Carried forward	4	11	9
	£114	11	9

The collections will be continued throughout the coming year.

WORKS NOTES.

There is a lot of football talent amongst us in the works aching to show its prowess, and we are badly in need of a suitable recreation ground. This is being searched for, and when secured, the Meccano Football Club will at once come into being.

———

The new works' gramophone has been a big success and there is much jazzing and song each day after dinner. Some of our records are suffering from putting in too much overtime, and the new ones each week are welcome.

———

Nurse Birchall, who has been with us since September, 1917, left us on October 23rd, and on November 8th she will sail on the "Metagama" to Ontario, her new home. Before her departure the workpeople presented her with a splendid travelling rug, and the staff gave her a warm and serviceable pair of fur gloves. Nurse Birchall will follow the nursing profession in her new home, and she carries with her the best wishes of all in the works. She is succeeded by Nurse Cartwright, who commenced her duties on October 24th.

———

About fifty of the Office Staff spent a most enjoyable afternoon at Chester on September 11th.

Preparatory to taking the train, lunch was provided in the staff dining-room by the directors.

The party arrived at Chester at 3 p.m., and some of the most interesting features of this old cathedral city were visited.

An excellent tea was provided at the City Café, after which the party repaired to the "Roodee" where a varied programme of sports was thoroughly enjoyed both by spectators and participants.

Before leaving, many members of the party had a pleasant row up the river, returning in time to catch the 8-55 p.m. train to Liverpool.

It was a most enjoyable event, and hopes were expressed that there might be many others to come.

It has been felt in the works for some time that if the working hours on Saturday could be fixed from 8 to 12, the extra half hour gained by the earlier closing down would be a great convenience to many, and a few weeks ago the Works Committee brought the suggestion and the benefits which would follow before the Management. They also suggested that wages be paid on Friday night instead of Saturday in order that all might get away promptly at 12 o'clock. The Management received the suggestions sympathetically, and finally it was arranged that the working hours on Friday should be from 8 to 12-30, and from 1-30 to 6, with wages to be calculated up to Wednesday, and paid on Friday, and that the hours on Saturday should be from 8 to 12. The Works Committee undertook, on behalf of the employees, that there should be no greater loss of time on Saturdays than there had previously been under the old arrangement.

———

The Superintendents and Foremen to the number of about thirty travelled by char-a-banc to Llangollen on Saturday, September 11th, and they had a most enjoyable outing.

Leaving Woodside Ferry at 1-30 p.m., the party reached their destination at about 4-30 p.m. A substantial tea was enjoyed at the "Ponsonby Arms," after which many of the well-known places of interest were visited.

The local bowling green proved a great attraction, and many members of the party displayed their prowess. So far as we have heard, no records were broken, and the actual results were only spoken of in whispers, but the enjoyment was great.

After a most exhilarating ride, Birkenhead was reached at 9-30 p.m.

The best thanks are due to Mr. C. W. Rush for the excellent arrangements which contributed so much to the day's enjoyment.

———

As we go to press we learn that the contributions to the Employees' Savings Club amount to £475 on November 1st. Verily we are a thrifty community.

Fig 1.

EDITORIAL.

Meccano Popularity.

Meccano may now be said to be the most popular indoor recreation for boys in every civilised country, and every new announcement made by our Company is eagerly read in hundreds of thousands of homes. Apart from its great intrinsic merits as an enjoyable and educational hobby it appeals to both boys and parents by its excellent manufacture and presentation. The efficiency of our plant, the quality of our tools, the care exercised in our Inspection Departments, and the efficiency of our workpeople and our factory methods have contributed to the high reputation which Meccano now holds.

Future Plans.

Our plans for the future include the further development of Meccano by the introduction of valuable new parts and new models. The interest of boys in this and other countries will be stimulated by our advertising, by the *Meccano Magazine* which already has an enormous circulation, and by the activities of the Meccano Guild, a movement founded a year ago for the purpose of showing boys how to have good times in their play hours and encouraging them to lead their lives upon wholesome, active, and ambitious lines.

The successes of both the *Meccano Magazine* and Meccano Guild have been remarkable, and future generations will bear testimony to the benefits which Meccano and its producers have conferred upon the youth of this and other countries.

Electrical Side of Meccano.

Much progress has been made in the development of the electrical side of Meccano, and soon a good deal of our factory space will be required to produce the parts necessary to enable boys to make electrical experiments with their Meccano parts. The uses and possibilities of electricity are becoming more and more recognised and understood in this country, and the electrical side of Meccano will undoubtedly develop rapidly.

Our Clockwork Trains.

The Hornby clockwork trains, Tin Printed clockwork trains, vertical steam boilers, &c., have evoked a lively and gratifying response from British toy dealers, many of whom have hitherto held the opinion that home manufacturers could not produce quality goods of this type. If we can continue to supply these lines and follow them with others of the same quality and excellence, and in sufficient quantities—and we have no doubts whatever on these points—we are well on the way towards creating a new and valuable industry in this country.

In France.

Our work in France this year has been of a most difficult nature. Our business has grown rapidly in that country and there are still greater possibilities before us. In April this year the French Government announced that until further notice no toys of any description would be allowed into the country. If we were not to lose our French trade entirely it was necessary for us to buy or build a factory in France, and manufacture the goods on the spot. Our Managing Director and Works Manager proceeded to Paris at once, and found it possible to purchase land and commence building operations which, if properly carried through, would give us production in time for the Christmas season. Fortunately, however, in July the French Government raised the embargo on toys, and it was unnecessary to proceed further with our plans.

It would have been regrettable in our opinion if we had been compelled to withdraw the manufacture of Meccano for the French market from our own factories, and we are glad to know that this business will remain with us in Binns Road. We trust that it may not be necessary at any time for us to establish further factories in other countries and so decrease the size and importance of our works in Binns Road.

In Australasia.

In August we received a visit from Mr. H. Hooper, representing the Overseas Sales Agency of Sydney, who are the Agents for Meccano Limited in Australia. Mr. Hooper reported continued interest in Meccano products throughout the whole of the Colony, and now that the country is settling down after the war, he anticipates great success for the big Meccano campaign which is now being launched. During Mr. Hooper's visit we were able to arrange for the Overseas Sales Agency to take charge of the Meccano business in New Zealand. They have stock houses and representatives in the important centres in North and South Islands, and we have every confidence that they will do full justice to our goods.

In South Africa.

We have also had a visit from Mr. Arthur E. Harris, who represents our Company in South Africa, with depots in Johannesburg, Cape Town and Durban. This was Mr. Harris' first visit to our factory, and he returns much impressed with the care and thought devoted to the manufacture of Meccano and our other lines. He anticipates a healthy and increasing trade throughout his colony.

Other Countries.

We are now well represented in Spain, the Argentine, Brazil, Turkey, Palestine, etc., and in most cases we correspond with our Agents and the merchants who sell our goods in the language of the country. The advantage of this is, of course, very great, our progress being in consequence more rapid, and our relationships with our correspondents being on a much more cordial footing.

Fig 1 cont.

In Italy.

Early this year our Managing Director paid a visit to Italy in order to study the prospects of the Meccano business in that country. Italy has suffered severely from the effects of the war, and some time must elapse before there can be a return to normal trading conditions. There is a serious shortage of coal, the country being dependent almost entirely upon England for that commodity. There is no coal whatever for domestic purposes, factories can only run on short time, and the train service has been cut down most drastically. For some time an order has been in force which prohibits the importation of toys into Italy except through parcels post, and our own business there is much handicapped in consequence. Meccano, however, is much sought after by Italian boys, and when the embargo is removed we are confident that excellent business will follow. Our agent, Sr. Alfredo Parodi, of Genoa, is putting in much good work under difficult circumstances, and he entertains no doubt that Meccano will prosper in Italy as it has prospered in all other countries. Our photograph was taken at S. Margherita on the Italian Riviera. It shows (from left to right) Mr. Frank Hornby, Mrs. G. Jones, Senor Alfredo Parodi, and Mrs. Frank Hornby.

EMPLOYEES' SAVINGS CLUB.

COMMITTEE OF MANAGEMENT.

Mr. J. E. Jones ..	Shipping Dept.
Miss E. Lockwood	Meccano Inspection.
Miss E. Graham ..	Packing Dept.
Mr. F. L. Murray	Tool Dept.
Miss F. Meadows	Barrel Dept.
,, H. Dignum ..	Plating Dept.
,, L. Hannigan	Train Inspection.
,, H. Davies ..	Trains and Clockwork Motors.
,, N. E. Tompkins	H.O. Staff.
,, N. McKelvie	Works Staff.
,, H. Burton ..	Works Mess.
,, Rees	Enamelling Dept.
,, E. Williams	Woodworking Dept.
Mr. A. Dutton ..	Hon. Secretary.

A man or woman who has saved money is a contented and satisfied individual; a man or a woman who has saved nothing whatever is a discontented and unhappy individual. There are no arguments against those statements, and as a firm we like to have as many happy and contented employees around us as possible. The success of the Meccano Employees' Savings Club since its inception at the end of August this year is gratifying. There are now 460 members and the contributions up to October 6th amounted to £338. 6s. 3d.

Amongst the benefits of the Savings Club are interest at the rate of 6 per cent., or 6½ per cent. when the total deposit amounts to £10, and 7½ per cent. on deposits which have been left in the Club after the end of any financial year.

Full information will be given to any employee intending to join the Club by the Secretary, Mr. A. Dutton.

MECCANO ADVERTISING.

It is not necessary nowadays to bring forward arguments to prove the value of advertising in the marketing of merchandise; there can hardly be a manufacturer of any consequence in the country who does not accept advertising in some form as an essential department in his business. At all events, it plays a very important part in the selling of Meccano, and it accounts in no small measure for the rapid progress which we have made.

Our own Advertising Department is one of the busiest sections of the business. It controls the announcements which are placed in the big dailies, weeklies, and monthlies, which have a national circulation; the preparation of showcards for the use of dealers in their shop windows; price lists, catalogues, competition literature, &c.; the preparation and distribution of the *Meccano Magazine*, which has already attained great popularity amongst Meccano boys; and towards the end of the year it deals with the many thousands of enquiries from boys in response to our advertisements, and sees that all these boys are provided with attractive literature, which describes and makes clear to them the joys of the Meccano hobby.

Since the close of the war the work in this Department has increased enormously. This year, in addition to the British advertising, we have taken space in the most important publications in France, Belgium, Spain, Holland, Sweden, Denmark, Norway, the Argentine, Brazil, and in the South African, Australian, and New Zealand colonies. The whole of the translations have been made in our own offices, set up in type in London, and the matrices despatched to the various publications for use during the Christmas buying season.

In addition to this, our Advertising Department distributes Meccano literature in nine different languages:—

French,
German,
Spanish,
Portuguese,
Danish,
Swedish,
Italian,
Dutch,
Chinese.

More will be added to this number as we spread further afield.

Meccano advertising has always been very successful, and has attracted a great deal of attention. The preparation of our advertisements has always received our most serious thought, each sentence being weighed carefully in order that it may give to the reader a clear impression of Meccano and a full understanding of what it will do.

We are, of course, selling what is largely a boys' hobby, and in order to make our advertisements more appealing to boys, we have always made a strong feature of introducing into them attractive drawings of boys who are obviously enjoying the pleasure of building or playing with Meccano models.

THE MECCANO BOY.

Many years ago we created the Meccano boy, a sturdy, happy-faced young man, with joy and fun oozing from every feature and limb. He is always dressed in the same way in the characteristic Meccano jersey, and is always enjoying himself. Our advertisements would now seem incomplete without him, and we are quite sure that his sturdy form adds distinction and attractiveness to all our announcements.

Fig 1.

He is now on his way to all the foreign countries which we have already mentioned to spread the Meccano gospel amongst the boys in those countries.

From the beginning of September, when our big advertising commences, up to the end of the year, is a very busy time indeed in our Advertising Department. Each day hundreds of enquiries have to be replied to, and at a low estimate the number of communications addressed to this Department during the season from boys who want full particulars of Meccano, and others who communicate with the Editor of the *Meccano Magazine*, the Secretary of the Meccano Guild, &c., is not less than 80,000 to 100,000.

The Department also issue about 40,000 of each number of the *Meccano Magazine* to boys, and in addition to distributing showcards, literature, advertising blocks, competition forms, &c., to dealers, they periodically send out to the entire toy trade particulars of our new lines, notifications of changes in prices, &c.

Printers' strike, shortage of paper, the slowness of production, and irritating delays of all kinds, have recently made the work of this Department very trying, and the fact that they have dealt with all matters promptly, and that no one has been kept waiting for advertising supplies or information regarding Meccano, is a tribute to the efficiency of the Department.

Edward Jones and Walter Moore.

Two of our oldest employees who, through long and faithful service, have well merited the high regard of both management and fellow employees.

OUR BELGIAN BUSINESS.

M. Fr. Fremineur.

No country is recovering so quickly from the effects of the war as Belgium, and we are glad to say that the affairs of our Company there are in capable hands, and are in a flourishing condition. M. Fr. Fremineur was living in Brussels during the whole of the time Belgium was in the hands of Germany and can tell moving tales of the events during that dreadful time. We were able to set enquiries going during the war which resulted in our finding that he and his family, though in difficulties, were quite well. Within a few weeks of the Armistice he came over to spend a week with us, and we then made arrangements for him to represent our Company in Belgium, Holland, Norway, Sweden, Denmark, and Switzerland, with headquarters and stockhouse in Brussels. It was a great relief to Mr. Fremineur when freedom of action was restored to him after a dead period of five years, and he has since made up for lost time by active and vigorous work in all the countries in his charge. The good results which he has achieved so far have demonstrated that our business is in safe hands. Last summer Mr. Fremineur's son, Paul, spent several months in our Head Office, studying our methods of business, and perfecting his knowledge of English, and he is now back again in Brussels actively assisting his father.

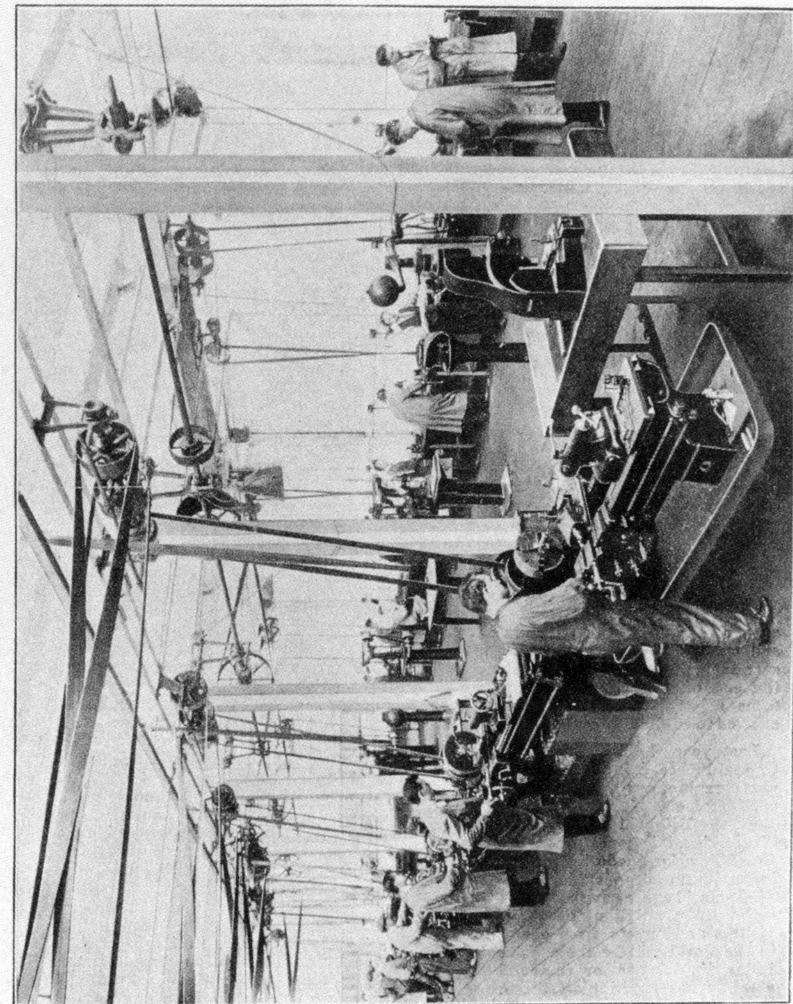

A Section of Our Toolmaking Department.

Fig 1.

OUR LONDON OFFICE AND STOCK ROOMS.

The position in regard to office and warehouse accommodation is probably worse in London than in any other city, and we recently found ourselves in the unhappy position of being liable to be turned out of our London premises at short notice. We have solved the problem by buying the entire building in which our offices and warehouse are located, and we are thus able to ensure a continuance of our excellent service to London dealers, and the rapid distribution of Meccano products to all towns within range of London.

The Meccano building is very centrally situated in Marshall Street, just behind Regent Street and Oxford Street, and in a very short time it is our intention to occupy the whole of the building as offices, stock rooms and show rooms. Our London business is in the capable hands of Mr. E. R. Robinson who joined up with the Company at the close of the war.

The busiest period at our London Office is between October 1st and the end of the year. Most of our London business is fed from there, and this in itself is no small undertaking. In addition, the principal towns in the Southern Counties and within a radius of 50 miles north of London draw largely from our London Stock Rooms.

About the end of November, most of the big stores in London hold special Meccano demonstrations, devoting considerable space to the sale of the outfits and the display of working models. These displays are the centre of attraction in most of the stores, and are the rendezvous of crowds of delighted and fascinated boys. Our representatives in London visit these displays daily for the purpose of seeing that they are in good shape, and that all the models are working correctly. They also see that there are sufficient stocks of outfits on hand of all kinds to provide for each day's requirements.

This year there will be additional demonstrations of Hornby Clockwork Trains, and we have every confidence that these will prove as attractive to boys as the big Meccano demonstrations.

MECCANO IN AMERICA

MR. J. P. PORTEUS.

The manager of our American business is Mr. J. P. Porteus, who went out to New York for us in 1917.

The last three years have been very busy ones indeed for him, but he has had the satisfaction of seeing our American business make good progress. The difficulties in that country have been greatly increased through the extent and nature of the competition which we have had to encounter. A protracted and costly law case has recently been decided in our favour, and it has finally been established that no other firm can be permitted to manufacture and sell a flagrant imitation of Meccano. The way has thus been made clear for Meccano to pursue its business undisturbed by this form of unfair competition, and our future in America is full of decided promise.

Our Managing Director has just returned from a visit to New York, and it is his belief that whilst the difficulties of doing business, due to labour troubles, high costs, and transport delays, are very great indeed, there is an abundance of money in the country, and trade generally during the winter will be good. Our business has already gone well ahead this year; American boys are keenly interested in Meccano doings, the Meccano Magazine, our big £250 Competition, and all the novelties which we introduce from time to time to add to the pleasure of Meccano model building, and the vogue of the hobby is rapidly spreading all over the country. Mr. Porteus, assisted by Mr. H. H. Dobson, who hails from Wallasey, will be fully occupied this winter in coping with the increased demand for Meccano products.

A SECTION IN OUR NEW YORK OFFICE.

Fig 1.

MARCH 1928 TO THE TRADE

OUR SELLING SERVICE

MECCANO

HORNBY TRAINS AND ACCESSORIES

MECCANO LIMITED, BINNS ROAD, LIVERPOOL

Fig 2. Our Selling Service 1928.

Meccano and Hornby Train Selling Service
1928

Meccano for 1928 has been entirely transformed. Every set is new, new in presentation, new in contents with new parts, and new manuals.

Our 1928 advertising campaign will be planned on new and bolder lines and will be unusually effective. A greater number of national publications will be used, and bigger spaces will be taken.

A Meccano Week

A Meccano Week will be organised, and fuller details will be furnished to you later. During the Meccano Week we shall commence a Grand New Meccano Model Building Competition with cash prizes for both competitors and dealers. Full particulars will be found on page 5.

An Additional Advertising Campaign for Meccano

Our dealers are familiar with the special leaflets that we publish, containing instructions for building such special models as the new Motor Car Chassis, Clock, Loom, etc., and will have noticed the rapidly increasing demand for them. This year the range of these special models will be extended and the instructions revised and much amplified. During the summer and autumn months we shall run a special advertising campaign featuring these models, as we believe large numbers of Meccano enthusiasts who have not already heard of these, will be glad to know of, and build them. We are confident that this additional special advertising will result in extra sales of Outfits and parts.

The Meccano Book of Engineering

We believe this new and beautiful book will prove to be the finest piece of Meccano propaganda we have ever issued. It will be widely distributed throughout the country to enquirers through our advertisements. The price will be 3d. per copy and the publication date will be 16th November, 1928. Those dealers who desire to have reserved for them a number of these books for distribution amongst their special customers, should let us know their requirements as soon as possible and not later than 1st October, so that extra copies may be printed. A reprint of this book before Christmas will not be possible. The price to dealers will be 3d. nett per copy.

Page One

HORNBY TRAINS

The great demand for Hornby Trains during the 1927-28 season has proved that these splendid trains, British and Guaranteed, are more popular than ever. Their strength and durability, combined with their beautiful finish and superior appearance, have firmly established their name and reputation amongst all miniature railway enthusiasts.

Success of The Hornby No. 3 Trains

The new Hornby No. 3 Trains have met with a remarkably good reception. The locomotives in these sets bear the names of famous British Locomotives—"Flying Scotsman," "Caerphilly Castle" and "Royal Scot," and their attractive appearance and great efficiency have made a strong appeal to all boys. It is certain that the success these trains have gained will be maintained next season.

Hornby No. 3C Train "Flying Scotsman"

New Rolling Stock and Accessories

Several new items have been added to the Hornby Series this year, details of which have already been given to dealers. These goods will be featured in all our advertising literature and good stocks should be carried to meet the demand thus created.

Introduction of Southern Railway Rolling Stock

Arrangements have now been made to supply Hornby Trains and Rolling Stock in the colours of the Southern Railway. For some time past there has been a demand for trains representing those in the services of this Company, and we believe their introduction will be welcomed both by boys and by our dealers. The Southern Railway Trains and Rolling Stock will be illustrated and described in our advertising literature during the coming season.

1928 Hornby Book of Trains

Over 100,000 copies of the 1927 edition of the Hornby Book of Trains were distributed last year.

The 1928 edition will be entirely re-written and will be an even better production than its predecessors. It will penetrate into thousands of homes and will make business wherever it goes.

The 1928 Hornby Book of Trains will be supplied at 3d. net per copy as usual, and the publishing date will be the 16th November, 1928. To ensure supplies dealers should place their orders early, and not later than 1st October.

Page Two

Fig 2.

Hornby Train Week

Many of our dealers have suggested that it would be beneficial to organise a Meccano Week this year and to reduce the usual period for the Hornby Train event from a fortnight to a week. We also are of the opinion that this would be a good plan, and are therefore making arrangements to carry it into effect.

Next season Hornby Train Week will commence on the 7th December and terminate on the 14th December. It will follow immediately after the Meccano Week, which begins on the 30th November and ends on the 7th December.

During Hornby Train Week our press advertising in national publications will be intensified. Special layouts and copy will be used, and mention will be made of the fact that big displays are on view at all dealers' stores.

No. 2 Display Board

Hornby Train Display Boards

Hundreds of these boards are now in use throughout the country, and all our dealers are agreed that they have proved an excellent means of displaying Hornby Trains and Accessories, making sales easier and more numerous.

Prices

No. 1 DISPLAY BOARD.
Dimensions: 4ft. 4in. square. Fitted with rails. Price £3. 10. 0. net.

No. 2 DISPLAY BOARD.
Dimensions: 8ft. long by 4ft. 6in. wide. Fitted with rails, points and crossings, buffer stops, level crossing, viaduct and turntable. Price £7. 3. 4. net.

No. 3 DISPLAY BOARD. HORNBY CONTROL.
Dimensions: 8ft. long by 4ft. 6in. wide. Fitted with the Hornby Control System, rails, points, level crossing, viaduct, turntable and buffer stops. Price £7. 10. 0. net.

If a dealer has not sufficient space to accommodate any of the boards mentioned, we are prepared to quote a price for special boards made to the dealer's own dimensions. On these we shall lay out suitable rail formations.

Invitation Cards

100,000 personal invitations were sent out by our dealers prior to Hornby Train Fortnight last year. A suitable quantity, printed with his own name and address, will be furnished to each dealer again this year, free of cost. It is intended thay they shall be posted by the dealer to his special customers a few days before the Hornby Train Week, inviting them to come to a special demonstration of Hornby Trains in the dealer's store.

Page Four

Meccano Week

A Meccano Week will be a feature of our Meccano selling scheme this year. It will take place during the week preceding the Hornby Train Week, from 30th November to 7th December.

A most effective Meccano display can be made if one or more demonstration models are employed, and there is no greater stimulus to trade. In this connection we would draw special attention to the models illustrated and described on pages 6 to 9, which we are prepared to supply at cost, making no charge for labour.

The Meccano Week will be well advertised in the national press and emphasis will be laid on the fact that Meccano is being demonstrated in all the shops.

Grand Model-Building Competition

In order to strengthen the Meccano Week scheme we are arranging for a Grand £100 Meccano Model-Building Competition to commence during the same week. This Competition will be open during the succeeding winter months and will close on 20th April, 1929.

In addition to the awards to prize-winners in all the classes, we are also giving special cash prizes to the dealers who supply the prize winners with their Outfits and Accessory Parts. Good supplies of entry forms will be available, free of charge, and these will be distributed only through our dealers.

Local Advertising

Advertisements in the local press always prove an excellent means of stimulating sales, and every dealer is urged to identify himself and his store with our big advertising campaign during the Meccano and Hornby Train Weeks.

We have a number of blocks that are specially suitable for the purpose, and any of these will be loaned, free of charge, on request (see pages 14 to 21). If desired our Advertising Department will draw up special layout and copy, and in this connection we would mention the necessity of supplying full particulars as to space advertisement will occupy, and whether it is intended for newspaper or catalogue.

Reproductions of special coloured lantern slides, which will be issued for Hornby Train and Meccano Weeks, appear on page 11.

Page Five

Fig 2.

Meccano Demonstration Models

The dealer who devotes a generous portion of his window space to a Meccano display may rest assured that increased sales will result. In the following pages we reproduce a selection of special models that we are prepared to make up for any of our dealers who desire to give an effective window display. These are models that have been selected as being very attractive in appearance and suitable in size for the average window. They are supplied at the cost of parts required to make them, no charge being made for labour. When ordering Model No. 2, 6, 8, 9, 10, 12, 13, 14, 15 or 16, please state whether it is required with or without a base-board. Orders for Demonstration Models should be placed early. We are unable to guarantee delivery of models ordered later than October.

Model No. 2

Motor Chassis

The new Meccano Motor Chassis model is a triumph of model building. It includes all the important details of real automobile practice—Differential Gear, Ackermann Steering, Gear Box (3-speed and reverse) and Internal-expanding Rear Wheel Brakes.

Length 26½in. Breadth 7in.

Price, complete with 4-volt motor and accumulator, £5 : 3 : 9 subject

Extra for Sprayed Board, £0 : 9 : 9

Model No. 1

Horizontal Steam Engine

This Model is specially adapted to window display. It is supplied without a motor, as illustrated, or with a 4-volt electric motor.

Price, with 4-volt motor .. .. £2 : 14 : 0 subject

Price, without motor .. .. £1 : 15 : 6 subject

Page Six

Meccano Demonstration Models

(continued)

Model No. 6

Big Wheel

The Big Wheel stands 32in. high. It is fitted with eight special passenger compartments.

Price (with Electric Motor No. 2) £4 : 18 : 6 subject

Extra for sprayed board, 13/6 nett

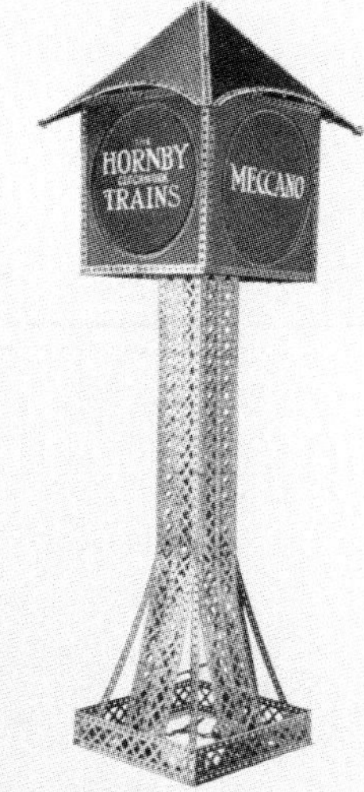

Model No. 3

Meccano Lamp

This standard lamp stands 43in. high and the lamp portion is fitted with coloured transparencies.

Price (complete with electrical fittings) £1 : 9 : 6 subject

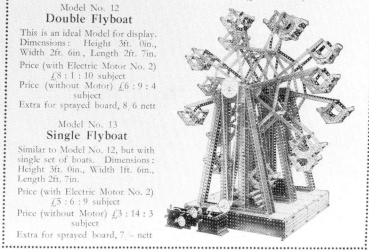

Model No. 12

Double Flyboat

This is an ideal Model for display. Dimensions: Height 3ft. 0in., Width 2ft. 6in., Length 2ft. 7in.

Price (with Electric Motor No. 2) £8 : 1 : 10 subject

Price (without Motor) £6 : 9 : 4 subject

Extra for sprayed board, 8/6 nett

Model No. 13

Single Flyboat

Similar to Model No. 12, but with single set of boats. Dimensions: Height 3ft. 0in., Width 1ft. 6in., Length 2ft. 7in.

Price (with Electric Motor No. 2) £5 : 6 : 9 subject

Price (without Motor) £3 : 14 : 3 subject

Extra for sprayed board, 7/- nett

Page Seven

Fig 2.

Meccano Demonstration Models

(continued)

Model No. 8. **Windmill**

The sails in the front and fan at the rear are rotated by means of a Meccano Electric Motor No. 2 (100–250-volt). Dimensions: Height (to top of sail) 29in., Width 19in., Length (across sails) 25½in.
Price (with motor) £4 : 4 : 2 subject
Extra for sprayed board, 6/– nett

Model No. 14. **Small Warehouse**

The Small Warehouse is a splendid display model, and is particularly suitable in cases where window space is limited.
Height 3ft. 10½in., Width 1ft. 2½in., Length 1ft. 2½in.
Price (with Electric Motor No. 2) £6 : 18 : 0
,, (without motor) £5 : 5 : 6 subject
Extra for sprayed board, £0 : 6 : 6 nett

Model No. 15. **Large Warehouse**

The elevators of this model work up and down automatically.
Height 5ft. 9½in., Width 1ft. 8in., Length 1ft. 9in.
Price (with Electric Motor No. 2) £10 : 18 : 0
,, (without motor) £9 : 5 : 6 subject
Extra for sprayed board, £0 : 7 : 0 nett

Model No. 16.
Baltic Tank Loco

This fine Meccano model of a tank locomotive is certain to attract a great deal of attention when used for display.

Length 36in., Depth 12¼in., Width 9½in.

Price (with Electric Motor No. 2) £8 : 16 : 3 subject
Price (without motor) £7 : 3 : 9 subject

Extra for sprayed board £0 : 13 : 0 nett

Meccano Demonstration Models

(continued)

Model No. 10
Double Beam Engine

Massive in construction and realistic in design, this model clearly shows the possibilities of Meccano and is sure to arouse interest.
The over-all dimensions of the model are: Height 21in., Width 15½in., Length 45in.
A Meccano Electric Motor No. 2 (100-250 volt) provides the motive force.
Price (with motor and necessary gearing) £8 : 16 : 4 subject
Price (without motor) - - - - - £6 : 19 : 3 subject
Extra for sprayed board - - - £0 : 9 : 0 nett

Model No. 9
Laxey Wheel

This is a new Meccano demonstration model, distinctive in appearance and eminently suitable for display. A Meccano Electric Motor No. 2 drives the wheel and pump.
The over-all dimensions of the model are: Height 28in., Width 15in., Length 42in.
Price (with motor and necessary gearing) £6 : 3 : 0 subject
Price (without motor) - - - - - £4 : 6 : 0 subject
Extra for sprayed board - - - £0 : 6 : 6 nett

Fig 2.

Display Cabinets for Meccano Parts

Special Display Cabinet

The trade in Meccano Accessory Parts, which has always been very big, has increased considerably now that so many parts in colours are available. In order to take full advantage of this important side of the business, the parts must be well displayed and carefully stocked. Our Special Display Cabinet enables the dealer to do this, and we loan it free of charge when an order for the contents is placed with us. The Display Cabinet includes a full range of the best-selling parts, and the cost to the dealer is £11 : 3 : 6, less the usual discount. The case is made of polished mahogany, with a plate-glass top, through which a sample of each part may be seen mounted on a velvet pad.

Display Cabinet Extension

For those dealers who find the accommodation of the above Display Cabinet too small for their stock of Accessory Parts, we provide an Extension containing a selection of the latest Meccano Accessory Parts. It is mahogany finished, and measures: Length 25 ins., breadth 27 ins., height 5 ins. The Display Cabinet fits on the top of the Extension, and the two drawers are conveniently partitioned to accommodate the parts. The contents, together with those of the Display Cabinet, cover the full range of Meccano parts.

We supply the extension on loan to those dealers who already have the Display Cabinet, and who order from us its contents value £11 : 1 : 9, less the usual discount.

We also provide smaller assortments of Meccano parts in strong partitioned boxes in two sizes. Assortment "A" is suitable for the small dealer and comprises a good range of the quickest selling parts to the value of £2 : 17 : 8, subject. Assortment "B" consists of a wider range of the best sellers and costs £5 : 4 : 1, subject. Both boxes are made of strong leather board and will do good service for years. No charge is made for the boxes when the contents are ordered. Each assortment is accompanied by an illustrated list of all Meccano parts, with prices.

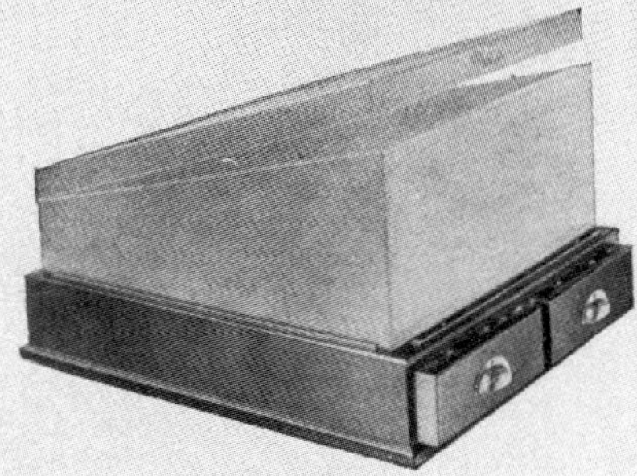

Showing Display Cabinet Extension in position

Coloured Lantern Slides

Slide No. 1

Slide No. 2

Slide No. 3

Slide No. 4

Slide No. 5

These slides are suitable for showing on the screen in theatre or cinema and form an attractive and economical means of local advertising. They are beautifully coloured in tints that are appropriate to the subjects employed. In the Meccano slides the colouring is particularly effective as it shows to advantage the attractiveness of the enamelled parts.

There are five Meccano and five Hornby Train slides and they are supplied free on loan, on application. When ordering please state the exact wording you wish inscribing in the address panel, and in this connection it is important to note that the panel will only accommodate three lines of matter. The slides should be ordered by number only.

As the preparation of the slides requires a week or two it is advisable to requisition early.

Special Slides for Meccano Week and Hornby Train Week

Slides Nos. 5 and 10 have been specially designed for use in connection with the 1928 Meccano Week and Hornby Train Week. They draw attention to the special displays, and every dealer who participates in either or both of the events should make use of them, if possible. The same remarks regarding the ordering of these slides apply as to the ordinary slides described above.

Slide No. 6

Slide No. 7

Slide No. 8

Slide No. 9

Slide No. 10

Fig 2.

Showcards and Window Bills

The range of Showcards and Window Bills that we have available for the use of dealers is illustrated on this and the opposite pages. Brightly coloured advertising material adds much to the effectiveness of a window display, and we strongly recommend our dealers to take full advantage of the facilities that we place at their disposal in this connection.
We are prepared to supply, free of charge, any of the material illustrated. Please order by number only.

No. 14. Cut-out Showcard. Beautifully coloured. Size 10¾in. × 9¼in. Fitted with supporting ring at back.

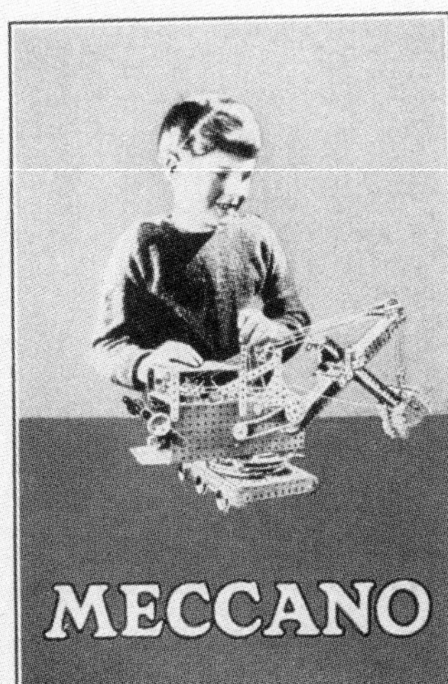

No. 18. Poster. Size double-crown (30in. × 20in.). This splendid poster is certain to increase sales at all stores where it is prominently displayed. It is artistically designed and beautifully coloured.

THE HORNBY CLOCKWORK TRAINS

No. 13. Hornby Train Window Transparency. Size 9in. in diameter. Yellow on blue. This transparency makes an attractive advertisement by day or night.

HORNBY TRAIN PRICE LIST

No. 15. Hornby Train Price List. Mounted on cardboard and fitted with cord hanger. Size 9in. × 10¾in.

MECCANO PRICE LIST

No. 10. Meccano Price List. Mounted on cardboard and fitted with cord hanger. Size 7in. × 10½in.

HORNBY TRAIN WEEK

No. 11. Special Window Bill for use in connection with Hornby Train Week. Lettered black on red ground. Size 5¾in. × 39in.

THESE ARE MECCANO DAYS

No. 17. Window Bill. Black lettering on bright yellow ground. Size 8in. × 30in.

HORNBY CLOCK WORK TRAINS
STANDARDISED PARTS · BEAUTIFUL FINISH · PERFECT MECHANISM

No. 16. Showcard. Green outline lettering on bright yellow ground. Size 5¾in. × 20in. Fitted with two supporting rings at back.

No. 12. Cut-out Showcard. Attractively coloured. Size 5¾in. × 19¾in. Fitted with two struts at back.

Page Twelve

Showcards and Window Bills

(continued)

MECCANO
ENGINEERING FOR BOYS

No. 4. Cut-out Showcard. Richly coloured in maroon with white lettering. Size 4½in. × 18¾in. Fitted with two supporting rings at back.

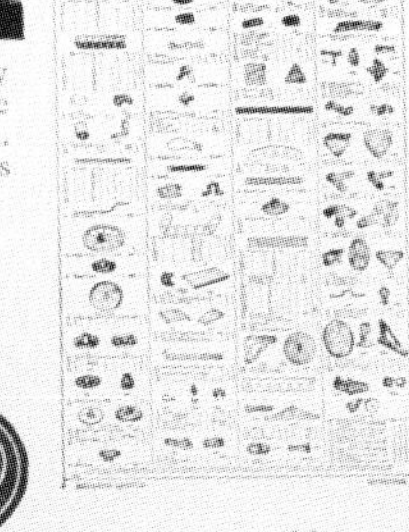

No. 20. Meccano Accessory Parts Price List. Mounted on cardboard. Size 14in. × 10in. May be used either for display or for reference purposes.

MECCANO
ENGINEERING FOR BOYS

No. 2. Cut-out Showcard. Bright red and green with white letters. Size 6in. × 18¾in. Fitted with two supporting rings at back.

No. 3. Similar to No. 2 but smaller. Size 4in. × 12½in. Fitted with two struts at back.

MECCANO

No. 6. Meccano Window Transparency. Black and white on orange. Size 7¾in. × 15in. Attractive by day or night.

MECCANO ACCESSORIES

No. 5. Window Bill. Red lettering on buff ground. Size 8in × 14½in.

HORNBY CLOCKWORK TRAINS

No. 21. Window Bill. Blue lettering on bright yellow ground. Size 6in. × 36in.

MECCANO

No. 1. Window Bill. Red lettering on buff ground. Size 11in. × 39in.
No. 19. Window Bill. Similar to above but lettered dark blue on light blue ground. Size 7in. × 36in.

No. 7. Showcard. Blue and red lettering on pink ground. Size 15in. × 10in. Fitted with cord hanger.

No. 8. Special Showcard for display during Hornby Train Week. Orange lettering, purple ground, green border. Size 14½in. × 24in. Fitted with cord hanger.

Price Tickets

The price tickets for Meccano Outfits, Motors, Hornby Trains, Rolling Stock and Accessories that we issued last year proved very popular with dealers and were used to great advantage. Our illustrations show the style of price tickets supplied.
An appropriate selection of these tickets will be sent to each dealer at the commencement of the season.

HORNBY TRAINS
No. 2 GOODS SET
32/6
L.M.S., L.N.E.R., G.W. or S.R.

Price Ticket for Hornby No. 2 Goods Set.

Hornby Series
3/6

Price Ticket for a 6/6 article in the Hornby Series.

Price Ticket for Meccano Outfit No. 1.

Page Thirteen

Fig 2.

Complete Stereos—Meccano

For the convenience of dealers we have prepared four Meccano advertisements which are reproduced below. Complete stereos are available and when passing these to the printer he should be instructed to pierce as necessary and insert details of name and address in type. The layouts and dimensions of the advertisements are particularly suitable for newspaper advertising, but they may also be used for circulars, throwaways, and the backs of invoice forms, etc. Please order by number only.

MECCANO

ENGINEERING IN MINIATURE

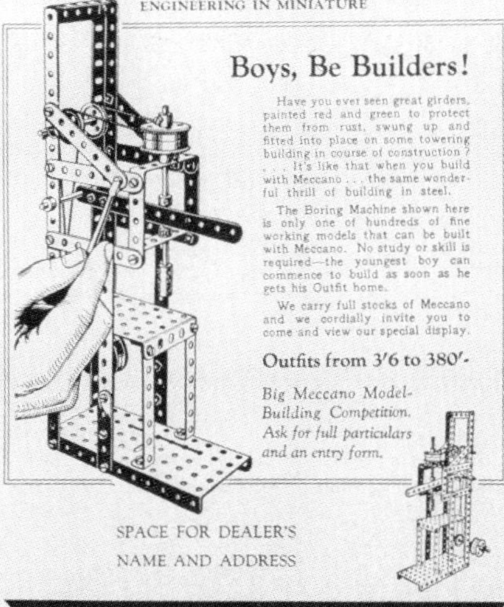

Boys, Be Builders!

Have you ever seen great girders, painted red and green to protect them from rust, swung up and fitted into place on some towering building in course of construction? . . . It's like that when you build with Meccano . . . the same wonderful thrill of building in steel.

The Boring Machine shown here is only one of hundreds of fine working models that can be built with Meccano. No study or skill is required—the youngest boy can commence to build as soon as he gets his Outfit home.

We carry full stocks of Meccano and we cordially invite you to come and view our special display.

Outfits from 3/6 to 380/-

Big Meccano Model-Building Competition. Ask for full particulars and an entry form.

SPACE FOR DEALER'S NAME AND ADDRESS

No. 1 M.—6 in. Double Column advertisement. This is a very attractive advertisement that will create sales for the dealer who uses it freely in connection with his own local advertising. It is also of a suitable size for circulars and backs of invoice forms.

ALL COLOURED

You can build a thousand different working models with Meccano—and Dad can join in the fun if he likes. All Meccano models are correct engineering models that work in exactly the same way as their big brothers in real life. No skill or study is required—the youngest boy can commence to build as soon as he gets his Outfit home. Ask Dad to buy you an Outfit for Christmas.

Outfits from 3/6 to 380/-

Big Meccano Model-Building Competition. Ask for full particulars and an entry form.

MECCANO

SPACE FOR DEALER'S NAME AND ADDRESS

No. 2 M.—6 in. Single Column advertisement. The outstanding merits of Meccano are clearly explained in the few short sentences that comprise the copy of this advertisement.

BOYS! THIS IS

MECCANO WEEK

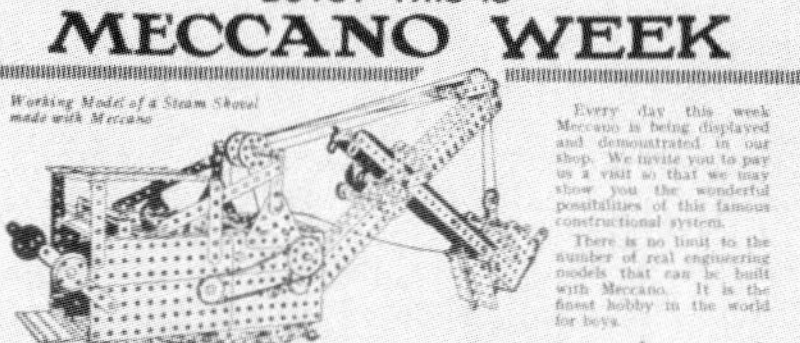

Working Model of a Steam Shovel made with Meccano

Every day this week Meccano is being displayed and demonstrated in our shop. We invite you to pay us a visit so that we may show you the wonderful possibilities of this famous constructional system.

There is no limit to the number of real engineering models that can be built with Meccano. It is the finest hobby in the world for boys.

Outfits from 3/6 to 380/-

SPACE FOR DEALER'S NAME AND ADDRESS

No. 3 M.—3 in. Double Column advertisement. This is a special Meccano Week advertisement. Dealers using it during Meccano Week will link up their stores with our own intensive advertising during that period.

MECCANO

ENGINEERING FOR BOYS

The finest thing about Meccano is that it brings the engineering wonders of the world into your own home. You can commence to build beautiful models—real engineering structures in miniature—immediately you open your Outfit. There is no limit to the number of models you can build with Meccano.

OUTFITS FROM 3/6 TO 380/-

SPACE FOR DEALER'S NAME AND ADDRESS

No. 4 M.—3 in. Single Column advertisement. This advertisement emphasises the fact that Meccano parts are real engineering units in miniature.

Complete Stereos—Hornby Trains

The four advertisements shown below are similar, as regards size, to the Meccano advertisements illustrated on the opposite page. Here again complete stereos are available and when passing these to the printer he should be instructed to pierce as necessary and insert details of name and address in type. Dealers are advised to use these advertisements freely during the period our own publicity campaign is in progress.

"That's her signal . . . and here she comes, dead on time as usual!"

Whether on passenger service, goods traffic or carrying out shunting operations, Hornby locos may be depended upon to give the utmost satisfaction. They are British-made throughout, fully guaranteed and beautifully enamelled in correct railway colours.

We have a special display of Hornby Trains and cordially invite you to favour us with a visit so that we can show you the sterling qualities of these famous trains.

Prices of Hornby Trains from 7/6 to 110/-

HORNBY TRAINS

BRITISH AND GUARANTEED

SPACE FOR DEALER'S NAME AND ADDRESS

No. 1 H.T.—6 in. Single Column advertisement. A striking advertisement that may be used either for general advertising or during Hornby Train Week.

BRITISH AND GUARANTEED
Shunting with a Hornby Train is fine fun

Watch a real locomotive shunting at the station. Then, when you get home, carry out similar operations with your Hornby railway. It's fine fun and just like the real thing.

A miniature railway is exact in every detail when it is constructed with Hornby Rolling Stock and Accessories. Every part is beautifully made in perfect proportion and all trains and rolling stock are finished in correct railway colours and appropriately lettered.

We invite you to see our special display of Hornby Trains.

PRICES OF HORNBY TRAINS FROM 7/6 TO 110/-

HORNBY TRAINS

SPACE FOR DEALER'S NAME AND ADDRESS

No. 2 H.T.—6 in. Double Column advertisement. This layout is based on one of the advertisements that we used with great success last year. Every boy who reads this announcement will ardently desire a Hornby Train.

HORNBY TRAINS

BRITISH AND GUARANTEED

Only when you've got a real train like the Hornby can you enjoy the fun of running your own railway system. It's the finest fun in the whole world. Bring Dad to see our special display of Hornby Trains and Accessories. Tell him you must have a Hornby Train for Christmas.

Prices from 7/6 to 110/-

SPACE FOR DEALER'S NAME AND ADDRESS

No. 3 H.T.—3 in. Single Column advertisement. This advertisement is strongly recommended as a "follow-up" after the 6 in. Double Column advertisement—No. 2 H.T.

This is Hornby Train Week

This week we have a special display of the famous Hornby Trains. Make a point of seeing these trains. Examine every detail of their excellent construction and beautiful finish. You will then understand the reason why they are so popular with boys all over the world.

Hornby Trains are "British and Guaranteed" and they may be depended upon to give the utmost satisfaction. Give your boy a Hornby Train for Christmas.

Prices from 7/6 to 110/-

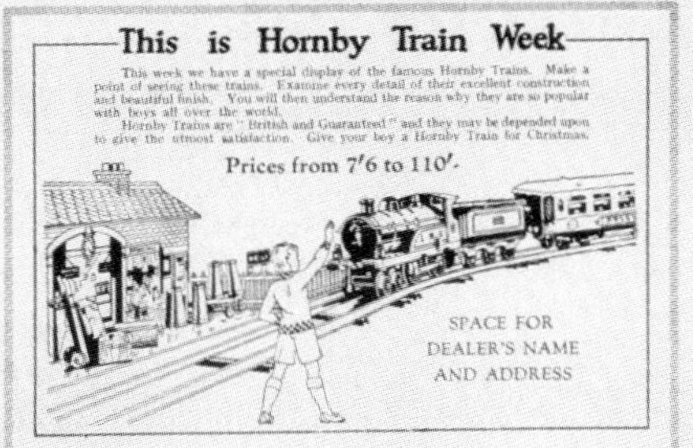

SPACE FOR DEALER'S NAME AND ADDRESS

No. 4 H.T.—3 in. Double Column advertisement. This is a special Hornby Train Week advertisement. The copy employed will stimulate interest in the event, and the majority of people who read it will undoubtedly make a point of seeing the special displays of trains in the shops.

Fig 2.

MARCH 1929 TO THE TRADE

OUR SELLING SERVICE

MECCANO

HORNBY TRAINS
AND
ACCESSORIES

MECCANO LIMITED, OLD SWAN, LIVERPOOL

Meccano and Hornby Train
Selling Service
1929

MECCANO

The Big Sales of 1928 will be exceeded in 1929

The 1929 Meccano Outfits will remain substantially the same as the 1928 Outfits as regards contents, but they will have a better presentation. All the Meccano Manuals have again been considerably improved and a large number of new and attractive models have been added. For instance, the 1929 00-3 Manual shows how to build 663 models, as compared with 447 models illustrated in the corresponding 1928 Manual. Never before have we shown so many models in a Meccano Manual of Instructions.

Meccano Week

The 1928 Meccano Week proved so successful that we have decided to repeat the event next season. It is clear from reports received from dealers that the first week in December is the most suitable period for the Meccano Week and we are making arrangements accordingly. Full details of the event are given on page 4.

HORNBY TRAINS

More Popular than Ever

The name " Hornby " is a household word in every home where there are boys—it stands for everything that is best in model railways. Hornby Trains have many features that place them in a category of their own. They will be even more popular this year as a result of the big improvements that are being made, particulars of which are given in pages 2 and 3 of this book.

Hornby Train Week

The Hornby Train Week scheme is a never-failing method of creating interest, and its advertising value has been well proved during the years that it has figured in our advertising campaign. Next season Hornby Train Week will be held during the second week in December and we look to all our dealers to give it their support. Full details of the event are given on page 5.

Christmas Clubs

Many of our dealers have suggested that a Meccano and Hornby Train Christmas Club scheme would be popular. We feel that this trading method has possibilities and we have decided to co-operate with those dealers who desire our help. Our traveller will give full particulars of the service we are prepared to give in this connection.

Page One

Fig 3. Our Selling Service 1929.

HORNBY TRAINS

"True-to-Type" Locomotives and Tenders

Hornby No. 2 Special Pullman Sets

Hornby No. 2 Special Pullman Set

We have produced a range of "true-to-type" locomotives and tenders, representing famous types in the services of the leading railway companies in this country. The engines have been carefully designed and are fitted with an entirely new mechanism giving great length of run and exceptional pulling power. These special models will supersede the existing No. 2 type and will be known as No. 2 Special. They will be well advertised and will be certain to meet with a good reception from the public. Retail prices—Locomotives 22/6. Tenders 5/6. The retail price of the Hornby No. 2 Special Pullman Set is 55/- (L.M.S., L.N.E.R., G.W. or S.R.).

Hornby No. 2 Special Goods Set

Hornby No. 2 Goods Set will be replaced by Hornby No. 2 Special Goods Set. The contents will include two wagons and a brake van, as hitherto, but a newly designed tank locomotive will replace the No. 2 Locomotive and Tender.
The retail price of the Hornby No. 2 Special Goods Set is 35/- (L.M.S., L.N.E.R., G.W. or S.R.).

Hornby No. 1 Special Train Sets

Hornby No. 1 Special Goods Set

An entirely new Hornby No. 1 Locomotive and Tender has been designed and will be known as the No. 1 Special. This will not supersede the existing No. 1 type, which is being retained and this year is fitted with longer running mechanism. The new Locomotive and Tender will be included in both goods and passenger sets. Retail prices—Hornby No. 1 Special Passenger Set, 32/6 (L.M.S., L.N.E.R., G.W. or S.R.). Hornby No. 1 Special Goods Set, 30/- (L.M.S., L.N.E.R., G.W. or S.R.).
The No. 1 Special Locomotive and Tender will also be available for separate sale. Retail Price—Locomotive 16/6. Tender 3/-.

New M. Series Trains

M.O. Passenger Set

In response to the big demand for a low-priced train set, we are placing on the market a Train Set to be known as the M.O. Passenger Set. This set will contain M. Locomotive and Tender, one Pullman Coach and set of rails, including a brake rail, to make a circle 2 ft. in diameter. Retail price, 6/-.
The M.3 Goods Set is no longer listed but is replaced by a Goods Set that will be known as the M. Goods Set. This new set will contain one M. Locomotive and Tender (as in the M. Passenger Set), two of the new tin-printed Wagons, and set of rails. Retail price 8/6.

Page Two

HORNBY TRAINS

New Tank Locomotives

Hornby No. 1 Electric Tank Locomotive (6-Volt)

Hornby No. 1 Electric Tank Locomotive, 6-Volt

This new electric locomotive is perfect in design and workmanship. It is of the permanent magnet type and may be run from a 6-volt Accumulator. It will be supplied with a terminal connecting plate, speed and reverse control switch and 3 ft. of flex, and will be available in the colours of the L.M.S., L.N.E., G.W. and Southern locomotives. Retail price, 32/6.

Hornby No. 1 Special Tank Locomotive

Hornby No. 1 Special Tank Locomotive

This new locomotive is fitted with an exceptionally powerful clockwork mechanism giving great length of run and pulling power. In every respect it is a very fine model and is beautifully finished in the colours of the L.M.S., L.N.E., G.W. and Southern Railways. **It is only available as a separate unit and is not included in any Hornby Train Set.** Retail price, 16/6.

Alterations to Existing Hornby Train Sets

6-Volt Electric Locomotives

The Hornby Electric Locomotives included in the No. 3E and Metropolitan Train Sets will in future be fitted with 6-volt motors, not 4-volt. The prices of the complete Electric Train Sets, or the Locomotives supplied for separate sale, will not be altered. A new 6-volt Accumulator is being introduced.

Hornby No. 2 Tank Sets

The new Hornby No. 2 Special Tank Locomotive will be included in the No. 2 Tank Goods Set in future and the set will be known as Hornby No. 2 Mixed Goods Set. The Hornby No. 2 Tank Passenger Set will not appear in future lists.

Hornby No. 0 Train Sets

Hornby No. 0 Passenger Set

The popular Hornby No. 0 Sets have been revised and are much superior in every respect to the No. 0 Sets supplied previously.

The 1929 Hornby Book of Trains

Over 100,000 copies of the 1928 edition of the Hornby Book of Trains were distributed last year. The 1929 edition will be entirely re-written and will be an even better production than its predecessors. It will be supplied at 3d. net per copy as usual, and the publishing date will be the 16th November, 1929. To ensure supplies dealers should place their orders early, and not later than 1st October.

Page Three

Fig 3.

Meccano Week

29th November to 6th December, 1929

It is certain that the Meccano Week of 1928 was largely responsible for the big increase in Meccano sales. Dealers everywhere gave their whole-hearted support to the scheme. They made attractive window displays and advertised in the local press, thus linking up with our national advertising campaign.

A Meccano Week will again be included in our Meccano selling scheme this year. It will take place during the week preceding Hornby Train Week, from 29th November to 6th December, and will be well advertised in the national press.

A good Meccano window display is the most effective method of stimulating interest. In this connection we would draw special attention to the demonstration models illustrated and described on pages 8, 9, 10 and 11, any of which we are prepared to supply at cost, making no charge for labour. A number of suggestions for attractive window displays are contained in a special folder described on page 7. We shall be pleased to send a copy of this folder on request.

Invitation Cards

We shall supply special invitation cards for Meccano Week to any dealer who requires them. These cards are beautifully printed and carry the dealer's name and address. They invite the recipient to visit the dealer's store in order to see the special Meccano display and, because of the personal element that is associated with them, we believe them to be very effective.

Local Advertising

Advertisements in the local press always prove an excellent means of stimulating sales, and every dealer is urged to identify himself and his store with our big advertising campaign during the Meccano and Hornby Train Weeks.

We have a number of blocks that are specially suitable for the purpose, and any of these will be loaned, free of charge, on request (see pages 17 to 24). If desired our Advertising Department will draw up special layout and copy, and in this connection we would mention the necessity of supplying full particulars as to space advertisement will occupy, and whether it is intended for newspaper or catalogue.

Reproductions of special coloured lantern slides, which will be issued for Meccano and Hornby Train Weeks, appear on page 16.

Page Four

Hornby Train Week

6th to 13th December, 1929

A special Hornby Train Week will again be an outstanding feature of our advertising campaign next season. The event will commence on the 6th December and terminate on the 13th December. It will follow after the Meccano Week, which begins on the 29th November and ends on the 6th December.

During Hornby Train Week our press advertising in national publications will be intensified. Special layouts and copy will be used, and mention will be made of the fact that big displays are on view at all dealers' stores.

We urge all our dealers to identify their stores with this big advertising campaign by making special displays of Hornby Trains in their windows and also, if space permits, inside their shops.

No. 2 Display Board

Hornby Train Display Boards

Hundreds of these boards are now in use throughout the country, and all our dealers are agreed that they have proved an excellent means of displaying Hornby Trains and Accessories, making sales easier and more numerous.

Prices

No. 1 DISPLAY BOARD.
Dimensions: 4 ft. 4 in. square. Fitted with rails. Price £3 10s. 0d. net.

No. 2 DISPLAY BOARD.
Dimensions: 8 ft. long by 4 ft. 6 in. wide. Fitted with rails, points and crossings, buffer stops, level crossing, viaduct and turntable. Price £7 3s. 4d. net.

No. 3 DISPLAY BOARD. HORNBY CONTROL.
Dimensions: 8 ft. long by 4 ft. 6 in. wide. Fitted with the Hornby Control System, rails, points, level crossing, viaduct, turntable and buffer stops. Price £7 10s. 0d. net.

If a dealer has not sufficient space to accommodate any of the boards mentioned, we are prepared to quote a price for special boards made to the dealer's own dimensions. On these we shall lay out suitable rail formations.

Invitation Cards

Over 100,000 invitations were sent out by our dealers prior to Hornby Train Week last year. A suitable quantity, printed with his own name and address, will be furnished to each dealer again this year, free of cost. It is intended that they shall be posted by the dealer to his special customers a few days before the Hornby Train Week, inviting them to come to a special demonstration of Hornby Trains and Accessories.

Page Five

Fig 3.

THE

"MECCANO MAGAZINE"

The "*Meccano Magazine*" has made extraordinary progress during the past few years. All readers are keen model-builders and miniature railway enthusiasts and most of them obtain their Meccano Outfits and Hornby Trains at the shops from which they regularly purchase their Magazines. You will undoubtedly increase your sales if you display the Magazine prominently in your store and thus bring it to the notice of all your customers. It is published on the first day of each month and sells at 6d. per copy.

The net sales of the "Meccano Magazine" during the past six months have averaged over 65,000 copies per issue. The Magazine is supplied on trade terms (i.e., 33⅓ per cent. discount) carriage paid, "firm sale," and an attractive double crown poster is supplied with each issue to dealers placing regular orders. If you do not already stock the "Meccano Magazine," we shall be pleased to send a trial half dozen copies on the above-mentioned terms.

The above are reproductions of 12 striking "Meccano Magazine" Covers

Page Six

Meccano and Hornby Train Window Displays

Window Display No. 14

Meccano and Hornby Trains are commodities that lend themselves admirably to effective window displays. They draw public attention like a magnet, and big business is assured to the dealer who gives his careful and personal attention to the arranging of his window and counter displays.

Suggestions for Window Displays

For the benefit of our dealers we have had fourteen Meccano and Hornby Train window displays specially laid out by experts. These displays are all reproduced in a special folder, beautifully printed on art paper, a copy of which will gladly be sent to any dealer on request. The above illustration is included in the range of suggestions and from this it will be seen how interesting and attractive a combined Meccano and Hornby Train display can be made. This particular display is specially suitable for use in cases where space is limited.

Material for Window Displays

With the exception of the Meccano Outfits and Models, Hornby Train goods, crepe paper and empty cartons, the requisite amount of advertising material for any of the displays will be provided to dealers free of charge, on application. The crepe paper used in connection with our layouts is made by the Dennison Manufacturing Co. Ltd., 52, Kingsway, London, W.C.2, and is specially recommended for making distinctive and tasteful backgrounds and floor coverings.

Page Seven

Fig 3.

Meccano Demonstration Models

The dealer who devotes a generous portion of his window space to a Meccano display may rest assured that increased sales will result. In the following pages we reproduce a selection of special models that we are prepared to make up for any of our dealers who desire to give an effective window display. These are models that have been selected as being very attractive in appearance and suitable in size for the average window. They are supplied at the cost of parts required to make them, no charge being made for labour. When ordering Model No. 1, 3, 4, 5, 6, or 7, please state whether it is required with or without a base-board. Orders for Demonstration Models should be placed early. We are unable to guarantee delivery of models ordered later than October.

Model No. 1

Motor Chassis

The Meccano Motor Chassis model is a triumph of model building. It includes all the important details of real automobile practice—Differential Gear, Ackermann Steering, Gear Box (3-speed and reverse) and Internal-expanding Rear Wheel Brakes.

Length, 26½ in. Breadth, 7 in.

Price, including Meccano 6-volt Motor, £2 12s. 0d. nett.

Extra for Sprayed Board, 4/9 nett nett.

Model No. 2

Cantilever Bridge

Although not a working model this well-constructed cantilever bridge is exceedingly attractive in appearance and is an ideal model for display. It has the advantage of being suitable for a combined Meccano and Hornby Train exhibit, since one or two engines with rolling stock can be placed on the rails that are fastened in position on the roadway of the bridge.

The outside dimensions of the model are: Height, 14 in.; Width, 5 in.; Length, 50 in.

Price, complete with rails, 15/2 nett.

Page Eight

Meccano Demonstration Models

(continued)

Model No. 3

Revolving Aeroplanes

This is a new Meccano demonstration model, distinctive in appearance and eminently suitable for display. It stands 27 ins. high and when travelling at top speed the aeroplanes describe a circle 42 ins. in diameter.

Price, complete with Meccano Electric Motor No. 2 (100-250 volt), £2 6s. 4d. nett.

Extra for Sprayed Board, 2/3 nett nett.

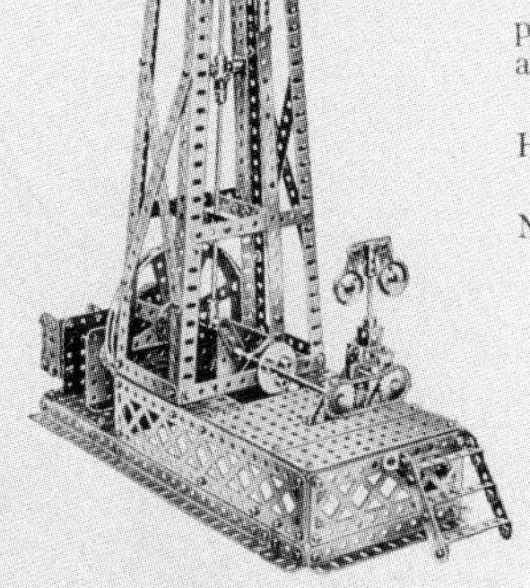

Model No. 4

Vertical Steam Engine

This well-constructed model clearly shows the possibilities of the Meccano system and it always attracts a considerable amount of attention.

The outside dimensions of the model are: Height, 20 in.; Width, 7½ in.; Length, 18 in.

Price, complete with Meccano Electric Motor No. 2 (100-250 volt), £2 7s. 4d. nett.

Extra for Sprayed Board, 4/6 nett nett.

Model No. 5

Windmill Pump

This new display model has been specially designed for the use of dealers who have limited window accommodation. When it is working the sails rotate, whilst the pivoted superstructure oscillates from one side to the other in a very realistic manner.

Height, 26 in.; Width, 9 in.; Length, 12 in.

Price, complete with Meccano Electric Motor No. 2 (100-250 volt), £1 15s. 4d. nett.

Extra for Sprayed Board, 2/3 nett nett.

Page Nine

Fig 3.

Meccano Demonstration Models

(continued)

Model No. 6

Meccano Workshop

This fine Meccano Model Workshop is certain to attract a great deal of attention when used for display. All the machines in the workshop are driven simultaneously by means of a Meccano Electric Motor, which is connected to the shafting.

The overall dimensions of the model are: Height, 14 in.; Length, 27 in.; Width, 14 in.

Price, complete with Meccano Electric Motor No. 2 (100-250 volts), £2 11s. 0d. nett.

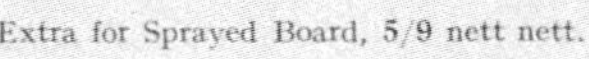

Extra for Sprayed Board, 5/9 nett nett.

Model No. 7

Dredger

This new Dredger is a very attractive model. The buckets are secured to an endless chain which is driven from a Meccano Electric Motor No. 2.

The overall dimensions of this model are: Height, 19½ in.; Length, 37½ in.; Width, 9 in.

Price, complete with Meccano Electric Motor No. 2 (100-250 volt), £3 17s. 4d. nett.

Extra for Sprayed Board, 9/- nett nett.

Page Ten

Meccano Demonstration Models

(continued)

Model No. 8

Hanging Lantern

This attractive lantern may be hung in the window, doorway, or inside the shop. It is supplied with lamp-holder, adapter and length of flex. **Please specify length of flex required when ordering and also state whether a "Flasher" is to be fitted.**

Price 10/6 nett, plus flex 1d. per foot nett.
Extra for "Flasher," 5/- nett nett.

Model No. 9

Meccano Standard Lamp

This standard lamp stands 43 in. high and the lamp portion is fitted with coloured transparencies. **Please specify length of flex required when ordering and also state whether a "Flasher" is to be fitted.**

Price £1 2s. 0d. nett, plus flex 1d. per foot nett. Extra for "Flasher," 5/- nett nett.

Model No. 10

Electric Sign (Small)

This handsome electric sign may be used in the same manner as the Meccano Hanging Lantern. It is supplied with lamp-holder, adapter and length of flex. **Please specify length of flex required when ordering and also state whether a "Flasher" is to be fitted.**

Price 5/- nett, plus flex 1d. per foot nett.
Extra for "Flasher," 5/- nett nett.

Model No. 11

Electric Sign (Large)

This is a larger electric sign. It is supplied with lamp-holder, adapter and length of flex. **Please specify length of flex required when ordering and also state whether a "Flasher" is to be fitted.**

Price 7/6 nett, plus flex 1d. per foot nett.
Extra for "Flasher," 5/- nett nett.

Page Eleven

Fig 3.

Display Cabinets for Meccano Parts

Display Cabinet No. 1 (Front and Side View)

In all Meccano advertising literature we emphasise the fact that bigger and better models may be built by Meccano boys who add extra parts to their equipment. As a result of this the trade in Meccano Accessory Parts is very considerable. In order to take full advantage of this important side of the business, the parts must be well displayed and carefully stocked. Our Display Cabinet No. 1 enables the dealer to do this, and we loan it free of charge when an order for the contents is placed with us. This cabinet contains a good quantity of every Meccano part, with the exception of Nos. 104, 105 and 167. All these parts are accommodated in the six spacious drawers that are fitted in the back (see illustration below). The cost of the parts contained in the cabinet to the dealer is £29/10/0, less the usual discount. The cabinet is made of polished mahogany, with a plate-glass front, through which a sample of each part may be seen mounted on a velvet pad. The overall dimensions are :—Length 22½ in., depth 26¼ in., width 20½ in.

Assortments "A" and "B"

We also provide smaller assortments of Meccano parts in strong partitioned boxes, in two sizes. Assortment "A" is suitable for the small dealer and comprises a good range of the quickest selling parts to the value of £2/13/3, subject. Assortment "B" consists of a wider range of the best sellers and costs £4/19/3, subject. Both boxes are made of strong leather board and will do good service for years. No charge is made for the boxes when the contents are ordered. Each assortment is accompanied by an illustrated list of all Meccano parts, with prices.

Display Cabinet No. 1 (Rear View)

Page Twelve

Display Cabinets for Meccano Parts

Display Cabinet No. 2 (Front and Side View)

We have been asked by many of our dealers for a display cabinet that will be capable of accommodating more Meccano Accessory Parts than the cabinets now supplied. We have therefore designed a bigger cabinet which, we are sure, will fill the requirements of these dealers.

The attractive design of the new cabinet and its beauty as a piece of counter furniture will be seen from the accompanying illustrations. The ten partitioned drawers fitted at the back accommodate a much larger quantity of accessory parts than any other Meccano display cabinet. A special note should be made of the fact that we do not supply parts with this new cabinet, other than the range mounted on the velvet-covered display panels.

The new cabinet will be known as Display Cabinet No. 2 and it will be sold at a net manufacturing cost price of £10/15/–, carriage extra. It will not be possible for us to supply the cabinet on loan. It will be supplied unglazed to avoid the risk of breakage in transit. The expense of glazing will be borne by the purchaser.

The dimensions of the cabinet are as follows :—Length 40″, depth 28½″, and width 19½″.

Display Cabinet No. 2 (Rear View)

Page Thirteen

Fig 3.

Showcards and Window Bills

The range of Showcards and Window Bills that we have available for the use of dealers is illustrated on this and the opposite pages. Brightly coloured advertising material adds much to the effectiveness of a window display, and we strongly recommend our dealers to take full advantage of the facilities that we place at their disposal in this connection.

We are prepared to supply, free of charge, any of the material illustrated. Please order by number only.

No. 14. Cut-out Showcard. Beautifully coloured. Size 11¾ in. × 8⅞ in. Fitted with supporting ring at back.

No. 18. Poster. Size double-crown (30 in. × 20 in.). This splendid poster is certain to increase sales at all stores where it is displayed. It is artistically designed and beautifully coloured.

THE HORNBY CLOCKWORK TRAINS

No. 13. Hornby Train Window Transparency. Size 9 in. in diameter. Yellow on blue. This transparency makes an attractive advertisement by day or night.

HORNBY TRAIN PRICE LIST

HORNBY TRAINS ARE BRITISH AND GUARANTEED

No. 15. Hornby Train Price List. Mounted on cardboard and fitted with cord hanger. Size 9½ in. × 10⅞ in.

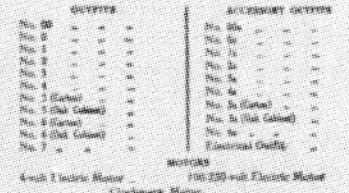

No. 10. Meccano Price List. Mounted on cardboard and fitted with cord hanger. Size 7 in. × 10½ in.

HORNBY CLOCK WORK TRAINS

STANDARDISED PARTS · BEAUTIFUL FINISH · PERFECT MECHANISM

No. 16. Showcard. Green outline lettering on bright yellow ground. Size 5¼ in. × 20⅞ in. Fitted with two supporting rings at back.

HORNBY TRAINS

BRITISH AND GUARANTEED

No. 12. Cut-out Showcard. Attractively coloured. Size 5⅝ in. × 19¾ in. Fitted with two struts at back.

HORNBY TRAIN WEEK

No. 11. Special Window Bill for use in connection with Hornby Train Week. Lettered black on red ground. Size 5¾ in. × 39 in.

HORNBY TRAINS

No. 21. Window Bill. Blue lettering on orange ground. Size 6 in. × 36 in.

No. 1. Window Bill. Red lettering on buff ground. Size 11 in. × 38 in.

No. 19. Window Bill. Lettered dark blue on light blue ground. Size 7 in. × 36 in.

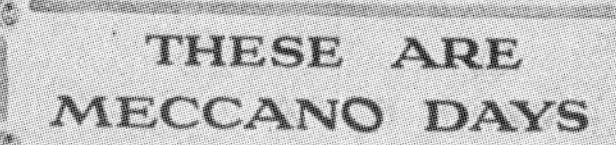

No. 17. Window Bill. Black lettering on bright yellow ground. Size 8 in. × 30 in.

Page Fourteen

Showcards and Window Bills

(continued)

MECCANO ENGINEERING FOR BOYS

No. 4. Cut-out Showcard. Richly coloured in maroon with white lettering. Size 4½ in. × 18¼ in. Fitted with two rings at back.

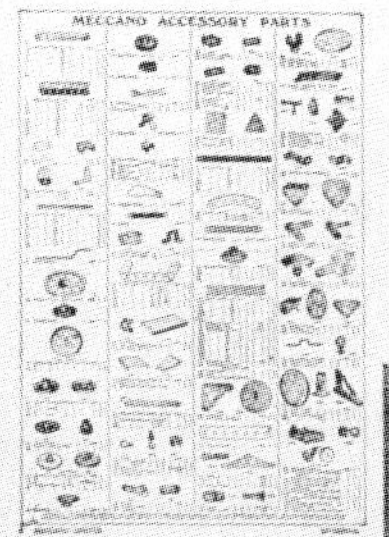

No. 20. Meccano Accessory Parts Price List. Mounted on cardboard. Size 17¼ in. × 10¼ in.

MECCANO ENGINEERING FOR BOYS

No. 2. Cut-out Showcard. Bright red and green with white letters. Size 6 in. × 18¼ in. Fitted with two rings at back.

No. 3. Similar to No. 2 but smaller. Size 4 in. × 12¼ in. Fitted with two struts at back.

No. 6. Meccano Window Transparency. Black and white on orange. Size 7¼ in. × 15 in. Attractive by day or night.

MECCANO ACCESSORIES

No. 5. Window Bill. Red lettering on buff ground. Size 8 in. × 14¼ in.

No. 22. Showcard. Size 14¼ in. × 24 in. Fitted with cord hanger.

No. 8. Showcard. Size 14¼ in. × 24 in. Fitted with cord hanger.

The Best Age to Start Meccano is Anywhere Between 5 and 70

No. 7. Showcard. Dark red lettering on green ground. Size 15 in. × 10 in. Fitted with cord hanger.

Price Tickets

The price tickets for Meccano Outfits, Motors, Hornby Trains, Rolling Stock and Accessories that we issue are used to great advantage by our dealers. Their colours blend very attractively with the general colour scheme of the goods and containers.

An appropriate selection of these tickets will be sent to each dealer with his stock order. If a selection is required separately we shall be glad to send it, on request.

No. 23. Special Window Bill for use in connection with Meccano Week. Lettered in purple on orange ground. The cube border is purple on white ground. Size 11 in. × 44 in.

Page Fifteen

Fig 3.

Coloured Lantern Slides

Slide No. 1

Slide No. 2

Slide No. 3

These slides are suitable for showing on the screen in theatre or cinema and form an attractive and economical means of local advertising. They are beautifully coloured in tints that are appropriate to the subjects employed. In the Meccano slides the colouring is particularly effective as it shows to advantage the attractiveness of the enamelled parts.

There are five Meccano and five Hornby Train slides and they are supplied free on loan, on application. When ordering please state the exact wording you wish inscribing in the address panel, and in this connection it is important to note that the panel will only accommodate three lines of matter. The slides should be ordered by number only.

As the preparation of the slides requires a week or two it is advisable to requisition early.

Slide No. 4

Slide No. 5

Special Slides for Meccano Week and Hornby Train Week

Slides Nos. 5 and 10 have been specially designed for use in connection with the 1929 Meccano Week and Hornby Train Week. They draw attention to the special displays, and every dealer who participates in either or both of the events should make use of them, if possible. The same remarks regarding the ordering of these slides apply as to the ordinary slides described above.

Slide No. 6

Slide No. 7

Slide No. 8

Slide No. 9

Slide No. 10

Page Sixteen

Complete Stereos—Meccano

For the convenience of dealers we have prepared four Meccano advertisements which are reproduced below. Complete stereos are available and when passing these to the printer he should be instructed to pierce as necessary and insert details of name and address in type. The layouts and dimensions of the advertisements are particularly suitable for newspaper advertising, but they may also be used for circulars, throwaways, and the backs of invoice forms, etc. Please order by number only.

MECCANO

The Toy that made Engineering famous

When a boy makes Meccano model-building his hobby he learns the secret of real engineering in the best of all ways, for he builds with real engineering parts in miniature, all standardised and interchangeable. Meccano Strips and Plates are made of heavy steel thickly coated with enamel, and the big range of Meccano Gears and Pinions are all machine-cut from the finest brass. Every detail of a Meccano model follows correct engineering practice.

There is scope for invention with Meccano, too, for one of its chief delights is the facility it offers for designing new mechanisms, and also for trying out new ideas.

There is no other hobby in the world to compare with Meccano model-building.

Prices of Outfits from 3/6 to 365/-

We carry full stocks of Meccano and we cordially invite you to come and view our special display

SPACE FOR DEALER'S NAME AND ADDRESS

No. 1 M.—6 in. Double Column advertisement. This is a very attractive advertisement that will create sales for the dealer who uses it freely in connection with his own local advertising. It is also of a suitable size for circulars and backs of invoice forms.

Here's a splendid working model

This model of a Traction Engine is only one of hundreds that any boy can build with Meccano. All the thrills of the real engineer are experienced by the keen Meccano boy, who constructs his models piece by piece, and when they are completed works them in exactly the same manner as the corresponding machines are worked in real life.

The above model is capable of pulling its driver along the ground with ease. This is evidence of the sturdy and accurate construction of Meccano models.

Outfits from 3/6 to 365/-

MECCANO

The Toy that made Engineering famous amongst boys

SPACE FOR DEALER'S NAME AND ADDRESS

No. 2 M.—6 in. Single Column advertisement. The new Meccano model of a Traction Engine is prominently featured in this advertisement.

BOYS! THIS IS

MECCANO WEEK

This is the greatest week in the year for boys interested in engineering. Everywhere there is talk of Gears and Girders, Cranks and Couplings, Pinions and Pulleys, and every boy should see our special demonstration of Meccano.

There is no hobby in the world to equal Meccano Model-building, and there is no other hobby that will satisfy the boy who prides himself on knowing something about machinery, because Meccano is the only constructional system that is based on correct engineering principles.

This year Meccano Outfits are bigger and better than ever.

Prices of Outfits from 3/6 to 365/-

SPACE FOR DEALER'S NAME AND ADDRESS

No. 3 M.—3 in. Double Column advertisement. This is a special Meccano Week advertisement. Dealers using it during Meccano Week will link up their stores with our own intensive advertising arranged for that period.

MECCANO

Meccano gives boys practical engineering experience, for the system is composed of real engineering parts in miniature that fit together and work perfectly. There is no limit to the number of splendid working models that can be built with Meccano.

Prices of Outfits from 3/6 to 365/-
Obtainable from

SPACE FOR DEALER'S NAME AND ADDRESS

No. 4 M.—3 in. Single Column advertisement. This advertisement emphasises the fact that Meccano parts are real engineering units in miniature.

Page Seventeen

Fig 3.

Complete Stereos—Hornby Trains

The four advertisements shown below are similar, as regards size, to the Meccano advertisements illustrated on the previous page. Here again complete stereos are available and when passing these to the printer he should be instructed to pierce as necessary and insert details of name and address in type. Dealers are advised to use these advertisements freely during the period when our own publicity campaign is in progress.

All Clear for the Express Goods!

Prices from 6/- to 110/-

HORNBY TRAINS

BRITISH AND GUARANTEED

SPACE FOR DEALER'S NAME AND ADDRESS

No. 1 H.T.—6 in. Single Column advertisement. A striking advertisement that will attract attention and create a demand for Hornby Trains and Accessories.

HERE THEY ARE, DAD!
Hornby Trains are British and Guaranteed

There are Hornby Trains from 6/- to 110/-

HORNBY TRAINS

SPACE FOR DEALER'S NAME AND ADDRESS

No. 2 H.T.—6 in. Double Column advertisement. This layout is based on one of the advertisements that we used with great success last year. Every boy who reads this announcement will ardently desire a Hornby Train.

HORNBY TRAINS

BRITISH AND GUARANTEED

Prices from 6/- to 110/-

SPACE FOR DEALER'S NAME AND ADDRESS

No. 3 H.T.—3 in. Single Column advertisement. This advertisement is strongly recommended as a "follow-up" after the 6 in. Double Column advertisement—No. 2 H.T.

This is Hornby Train Week

Prices of Hornby Trains from 6/- to 110/-

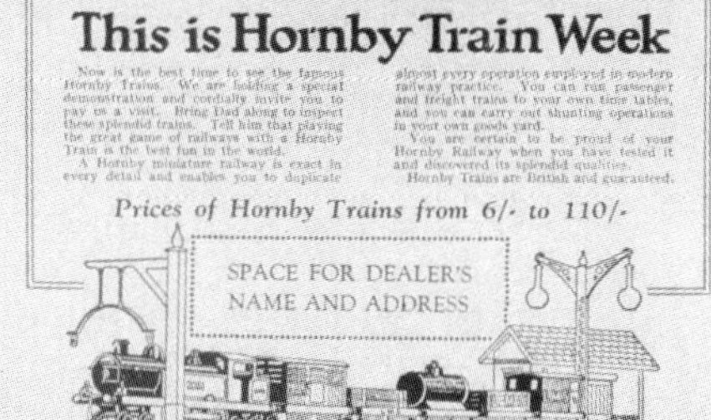

No. 4 H.T.—3 in. Double Column advertisement. This is a special Hornby Train Week advertisement. The copy employed will stimulate interest in the event, and the majority of boys who read it will want to see the special displays of Hornby Trains and Accessories in the shops.

Page Eighteen

Meccano Advertising Blocks

During the winter months Meccano and Hornby Trains are extensively advertised in all the best national publications, and the resulting demand is very great.

Over 75,000,000 Copies

of daily, weekly and monthly publications containing attractive Meccano and Hornby Train advertisements will be circulated this year. It is to your interest to let the public know that *you* keep full stocks of our products. In the following pages are shown illustrations of blocks that will assist you in your local advertising. They will be loaned to you free on the understanding that after use they are returned to us, and that they are not used in connection with goods other than those manufactured by us. When requisitioning blocks, it is important to quote the reference numbers and to state whether half-tone or line subjects are required.

We shall be pleased to help you in the preparation of layouts and copy for your advertisements and catalogues, and the experience of our advertising staff is entirely at your disposal in this connection.

*G.2715 1¾" wide
G.2773 1⅛" „

G.133 1½" wide
G.614 2" „
G.4519 2½" „

*G.2666 1¾" wide
G.2771 1⅛" „

*G.434 1½" wide
*G.824 1½" „
G.1700 1¼" „
G.730 2" „

*G.4184 2¾" wide
G.2014 2¼" „
G.1392 3¼" „
G.2011 4¼" „

*G.26 1¼" wide
*G.227 1½" „
G.1689 1½" „
G.1876 2½" „

*G.4056 4½" wide
G.4057 4½" „
*G.4061 4¾" „
G.4062 6¼" „

*G.238 1½" deep
G.1626 1¼" „

**These are half-tone blocks. All subjects not marked with an asterisk are line blocks*

Page Nineteen

Fig 3.

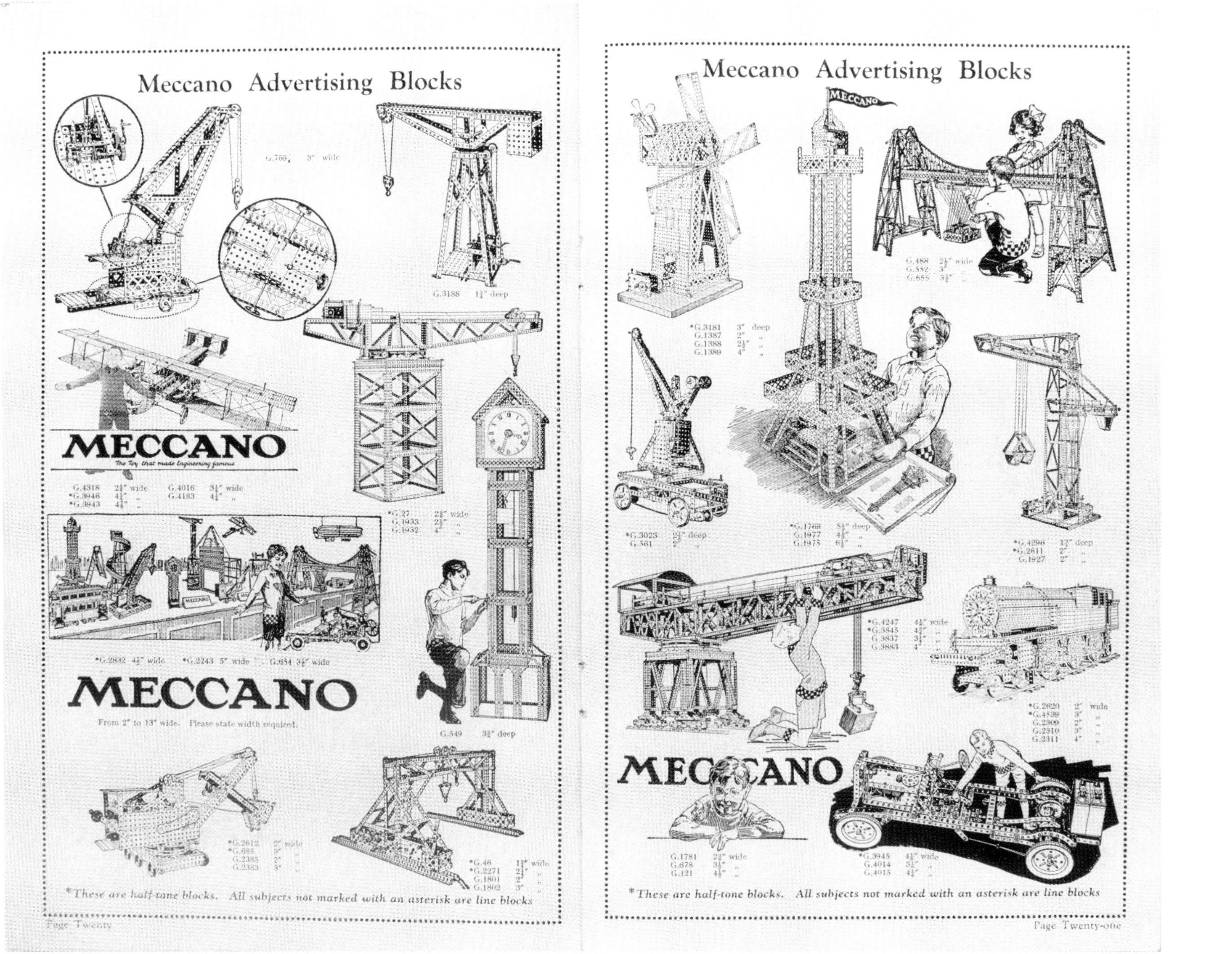

Meccano Advertising Blocks

G.769½ 3" wide

G.3188 1¾" deep

MECCANO

The Toy that made Engineering famous

G.4318 2⅞" wide
*G.3946 4¼" "
*G.3943 4⅞" "

G.4016 3¼" wide
G.4183 4¼" "

*G.27 2⅞" wide
G.1933 2½" "
G.1932 4" "

*G.2832 4½" wide *G.2243 5" wide G.654 3¼" wide

MECCANO

From 2" to 13" wide. Please state width required.

G.549 3⅜" deep

*G.2612 2" wide
*G.685 3" "
G.2385 2" "
G.2383 3" "

*G.46 1¾" wide
*G.2271 2¼" "
G.1801 2" "
G.1802 3" "

*These are half-tone blocks. All subjects not marked with an asterisk are line blocks

Page Twenty

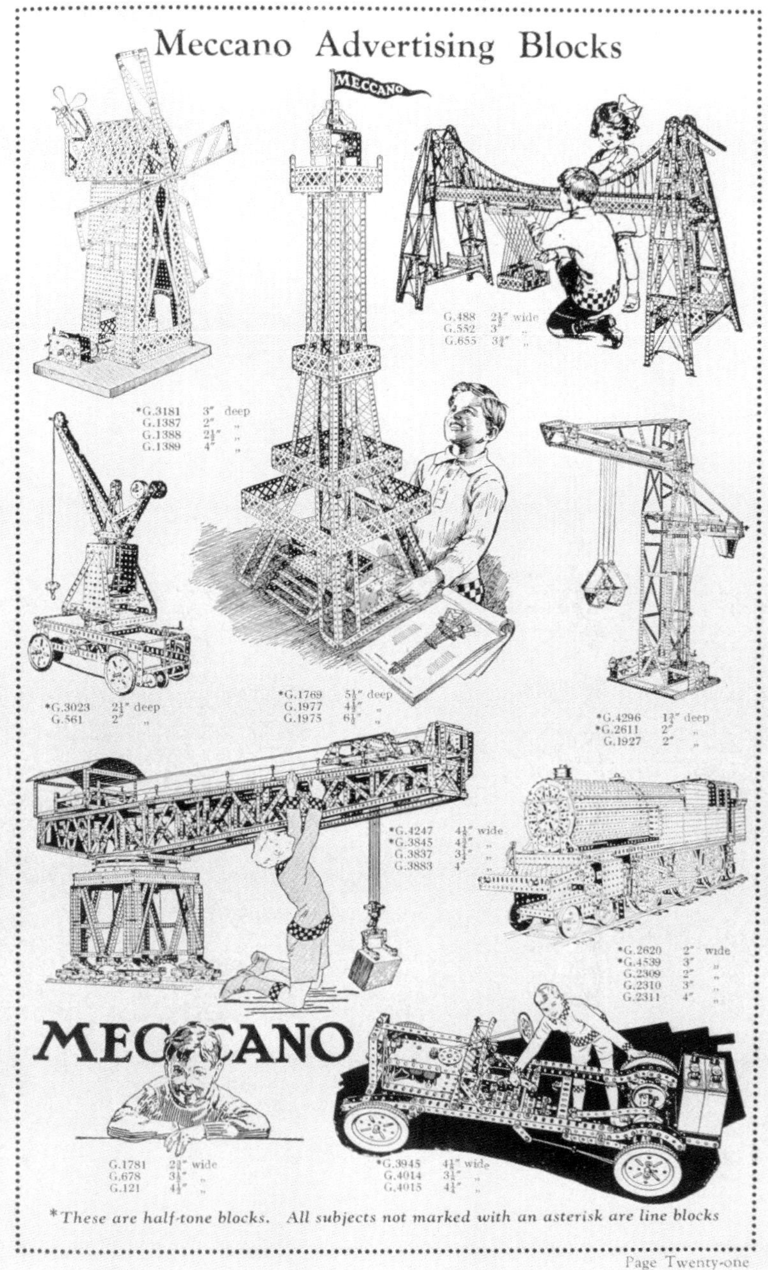

Meccano Advertising Blocks

G.488 2¼" wide
G.552 3" "
G.655 3¾" "

*G.3181 3" deep
G.1387 2" "
G.1388 2½" "
G.1389 4" "

*G.3023 2½" deep
G.561 2" "

*G.1769 5¼" deep
G.1977 4⅜" "
G.1975 6¼" "

*G.4296 1¾" deep
*G.2611 2" "
G.1927 2" "

*G.4247 4¼" wide
*G.3845 4⅜" "
G.3837 3¼" "
G.3883 4" "

*G.2620 2" wide
*G.4539 3" "
G.2309 2" "
G.2310 3" "
G.2311 4" "

MECCANO

G.1781 2¾" wide
G.678 3¼" "
G.121 4½" "

*G.3945 4¼" wide
G.4014 3¼" "
G.4015 4¼" "

*These are half-tone blocks. All subjects not marked with an asterisk are line blocks

Page Twenty-one

Fig 3.

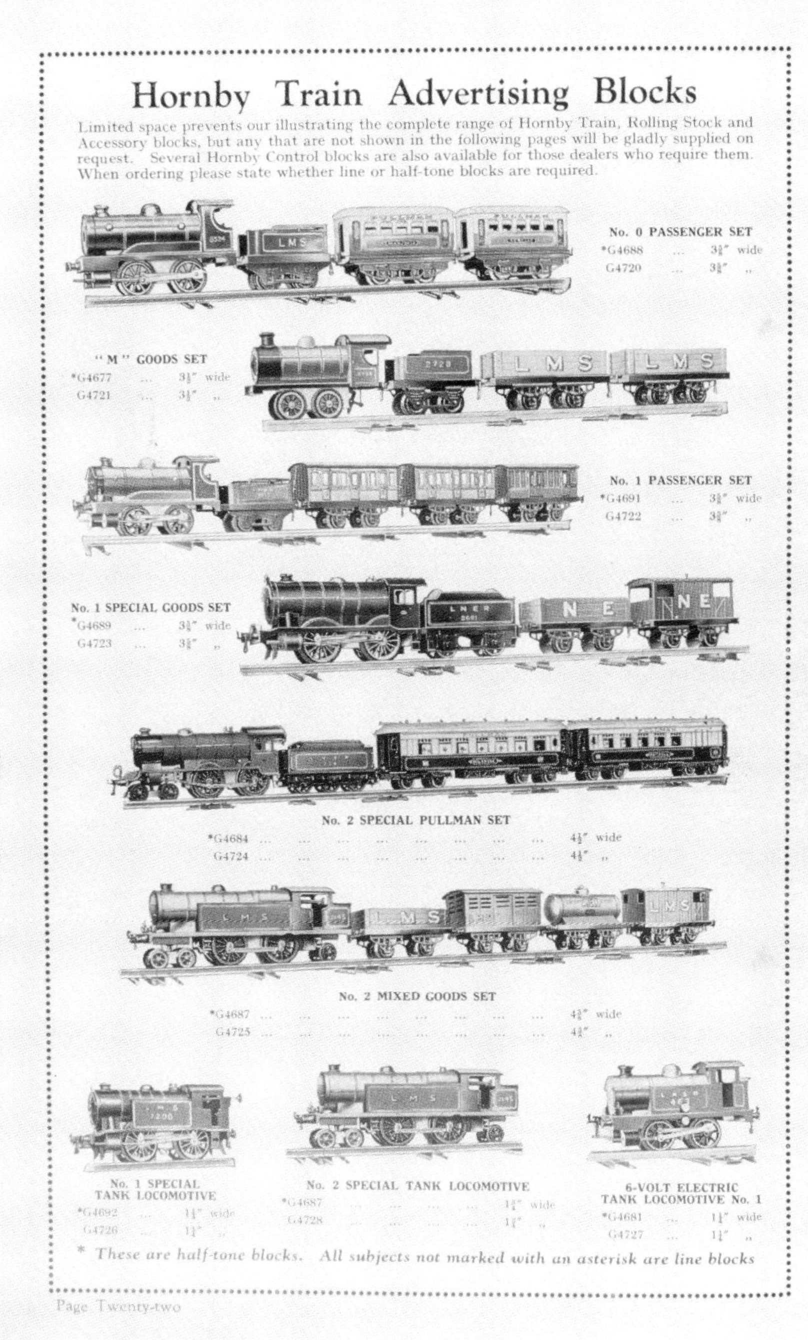
Hornby Train Advertising Blocks
Limited space prevents our illustrating the complete range of Hornby Train, Rolling Stock and Accessory blocks, but any that are not shown in the following pages will be gladly supplied on request. Several Hornby Control blocks are also available for those dealers who require them. When ordering please state whether line or half-tone blocks are required.
No. 0 PASSENGER SET
*G4688 ... 3⅜" wide
G4720 ... 3⅜" „
"M" GOODS SET
*G4677 ... 3½" wide
G4721 ... 3½" „
No. 1 PASSENGER SET
*G4691 ... 3⅜" wide
G4722 ... 3⅜" „
No. 1 SPECIAL GOODS SET
*G4689 ... 3⅜" wide
G4723 ... 3⅜" „
No. 2 SPECIAL PULLMAN SET
*G4684 ... 4½" wide
G4724 ... 4⅜" „
No. 2 MIXED GOODS SET
*G4687 ... 4⅜" wide
G4725 ... 4⅜" „
No. 1 SPECIAL TANK LOCOMOTIVE
*G4692 ... 1¼" wide
G4726 ... 1¼" „
No. 2 SPECIAL TANK LOCOMOTIVE
*G4687 ... 1¼" wide
G4728 ... 1¼" „
6-VOLT ELECTRIC TANK LOCOMOTIVE No. 1
*G4681 ... 1¼" wide
G4727 ... 1¼" „
* These are half-tone blocks. All subjects not marked with an asterisk are line blocks
Page Twenty-two

Rolling Stock Advertising Blocks
*G.3265 1¼" wide
G.3273 1¼" „
*G.35 2" wide
G.1475 1⅞" „
*G.3294 1¼" wide
G.3304 1⅛" „
CEMENT
SECCOTINE STICKS EVERYTHING
LMS
NORD
*G.457 ⅞" wide
G.521 1¼" „
*G.465 1" wide
G.472 1" „
*G.58 1" wide
G.482 1¼" „
*G.464 1" wide
G.478 1¼" „
*G.2259 1" wide
G.2529 1½" „
LNER
SR
*G.572 1½" wide
G.599 1¾" „
*G.3290 1" wide
G.733 1¼" „
*G.579 1" wide
G.559 1⅜" „
*G.571 1½" wide
G.138 1¾" „
LMS
*G.3267 1" wide
G.3422 1¼" „
*G.575 1" wide
G.483 1⅜" „
*G.462 ⅞" wide
G.137 1¼" „
*G.466 1" wide
G.1554 ⅞" „
*G.3157 1" wide
G.3127 1¼" „
*G.36 1⅜" wide
G.1476 1⅜" „
*G.451 1¼" wide
G.485 1¼" „
*G.3293 2" wide
SR
*G.3627 1¼" wide
*G.63 1" wide
G.372 1¼" „
*G.463 1" wide
G.1650 ¾" „
*G.55 ⅞" wide
G.484 1¼" „
*G.3289 1" wide
G.1649 ⅞" „
*G.347 2" wide
G.595 2" „
*G.59 1" wide
G.479 1¼" „
*G.510 2" wide
G.596 1¾" „
CRAWFORD'S BISCUITS
MOTOR SPIRIT
LMS
LMS
*G.574 1" wide
G.476 1¼" „
*G.1980 1" wide
G.1837 1¼" „
*G.373 1" wide
G.475 1¼" „
*G.50 1" wide
G.486 1¼" „
*G.578 1" wide
G.471 1¼" „
NORD
*G.3287 2¼" wide
G.3275 2" „
*G.2260 1" wide
G.2530 1⅛" „
*G.3288 2¼" wide
G.3274 2" „
* These are half-tone blocks. All subjects not marked with an asterisk are line blocks
Page Twenty-three

Fig 3.

Code Numbers for Meccano and Hornby Train Goods

Second List—Previous List Cancelled

The following code numbers, covering every article we manufacture, will facilitate the ordering of Meccano and Hornby Train goods. It should be noted that the code system is for the use of the trade only and must only be used **when ordering goods by telegram.** We shall continue to list all goods in our catalogues under the titles and identification numbers hitherto employed.

Meccano Outfits, Accessory Outfits, Accessory Parts, Motors, Model Instruction Leaflets, Miscellaneous Literature, etc.

MECCANO OUTFITS

	CODE NUMBER		CODE NUMBER		CODE NUMBER		CODE NUMBER
No. 00 Outfit ...	**00**	No. 1a Outfit ...	**1a**	No. 4 Outfit ...	**4**	No. 5aw Outfit ...	**5aw**
No. 00a " ...	**00a**	No. 2 " ...	**2**	No. 4a " ...	**4a**	No. 6c " ...	**6c**
No. 0 " ...	**0**	No. 2a " ...	**2a**	No. 5c " ...	**5c**	No. 6w " ...	**6w**
No. 0a " ...	**0a**	No. 3 " ...	**3**	No. 5w " ...	**5w**	No. 6aw " ...	**6aw**
No. 1 " ...	**1**	No. 3a " ...	**3a**	No. 5ac " ...	**5ac**	No. 7 " ...	**7**

Special Inventor's Outfit ... **S1**

MECCANO ACCESSORY PARTS

No. 1	**01**	No. 4	**04**	No. 7a	**07a**	No. 9a	**09a**
No. 1a	**01a**	No. 5	**05**	No. 8	**08**	No. 9b	**09b**
No. 1b	**01b**	No. 6	**06**	No. 8a	**08a**	No. 9c	**09c**
No. 2	**02**	No. 6a	**06a**	No. 8b	**08b**	No. 9d	**09d**
No. 2a	**02a**	No. 7	**07**	No. 9	**09**	No. 9e	**09e**
No. 3½	**03**					No. 9f	**09f**

Remainder of Meccano Accessory Parts will retain the numbers by which they have always been identified.

MECCANO MOTORS, OILCANS, ENAMEL, ETC.

Meccano Clockwork Motor ...	**201**	Shafting Standard, Large ...	**2082**
Meccano Electric Motor No. 1 (6-volt) ...	**202**	Saw Bench ...	**209**
Meccano Electric Motor No. 2 (100-250 or 200-250 volt) ...	**203**	Lamp Board ...	**210**
Accumulator, 6-volt, 20 amps. ...	**204**	Lubricating Oil, in bottles ...	**211**
Resistance Controller ...	**205**	Oilcan No. 1 (Ordinary Type) ...	**212**
Rheostat ...	**206**	Oilcan No. 2 ("K" Type)...	**213**
Transformer ...	**207**	Enamel, in Tins (Red) ...	**2141**
Shafting Standard, Small ...	**2081**	Enamel, in Tins (Green) ...	**2142**
		Enamel, in Tins (Grey) ...	**2143**

MECCANO ELECTRICAL PARTS

301 Bobbin ...	**301**	309 Coil Check ...	**309**
302 Insulating Bush (Dozen) ...	**302**	310 Lamp Holder ...	**310**
303 Insulating Washer (Dozen) ...	**303**	311 Best Metal Filament Lamp (3½ volts) ...	**311**
304 6 B.A. Screws (Dozen) ...	**304**	312 Bare Iron Wire (27 Gauge) 30 in. ...	**312**
305 6 B.A. Nuts (Dozen) ...	**305**	313 SCC Insulated Copper Wire (26 Gauge) 50 yds.	**313**
306 Terminal... ...	**306**	314 SCC Insulated Copper Wire (23 Gauge) 25 yds.	**314**
307 Silver-tipped Contact Screw ...	**307**	315 Bare Copper Wire (22 Gauge) 4 yds.... ...	**315**
308 Core or Pole Piece ...	**308**	316 Meccano Electrical Manual ...	**316**

Instruction Leaflets for Super Meccano Models

Leaflet	No. 1	Motor Chassis, Model No. 7.1 ...	**L1**
"	No. 2	High-speed Ship-coaler, Model No. 7.30 ...	**L2**
"	No. 3	Motorcycle and Sidecar, Model No. 7.33 ...	**L3**
"	No. 4	Block-setting Crane, Special Model ...	**L4**
"	No. 5	Dredger, Model No. 7.35 ...	**L5**
"	No. 6	Stiff Leg Derrick, Model No. 7.10 ...	**L6**
"	No. 7	Platform Scales, Model No. 6.20 ...	**L7**
"	No. 8	Roundabout, Special Model ...	**L8**
"	No. 9	Bagatelle Table, Model No. 6.15 ...	**L9**
"	No. 10	Log Saw, Model No. 6.21 ...	**L10**
"	No. 11	Horizontal Steam Engine, Model No. 6.28 ...	**L11**
"	No. 12	Stone Sawing Machine, Model No. 6.42 ...	**L12**
"	No. 13	Meccanograph, Model No. 7.9 ...	**L13**
"	No. 14	Grandfather Clock, Model No. 7.21 ...	**L14**
"	No. 15	Baltic Tank Locomotive, Special Model ...	**L15**
"	No. 16	Loom, Model No. 7.23 ...	**L16**
"	No. 17	Planing Machine, Model No. 7.5 ...	**L17**
"	No. 18	Revolving Crane, Model No. 7.7 ...	**L18**
"	No. 19	Steam Shovel, Model No. 7.8 ...	**L19**
"	No. 20	Mobile Crane, Model No. 7.15 ...	**L20**
"	No. 21	Transporter Bridge, Model No. 7.14 ...	**L21**
"	No. 22	Traction Engine, Special Model ...	**L22**
"	No. 23	Vertical Log Saw, Model No. 7.6 ...	**L23**
"	No. 24	Travelling Gantry Crane, Model No. 7.25 ...	**L24**
"	No. 25	Hydraulic Crane, Model No. 7.4 ...	**L25**
"	No. 26	Twin Elliptic Harmonograph, Model No. 7.31 ...	**L26**
"	No. 27	Dragline, Special Model ...	**L27**
"	No. 28	Pontoon Crane, Special Model ...	**L28**
"	No. 29	Hammerhead Crane, Special Model ...	**L29**
"	No. 30	Railway Breakdown Crane, Special Model ...	**L30**
"	No. 31	Warehouse, Model No 7.12 ...	**L31**
"	No. 32	Two Cylinder Horizontal Steam Engine, Special Model ...	**L32**
"	No. 33	Single and Double Flyboats, Special Models ...	**L33**
"	No. 34	Aeroplane, Special Model ...	**L34**

Page Twenty-five

Fig 3.

Meccano Outfits, Accessory Outfits, Accessory Parts, Motors, Model Instruction Leaflets, Miscellaneous Literature, etc.

(continued)

Meccano Storage Boxes and Display Cabinets

	CODE NUMBER		CODE NUMBER
Storage Box No. 1	SB1	Display Cabinet No. 1 Extension	DC2
Storage Box No. 2	SB2	Display Cabinet No. 2	DC3
Storage Box No. 3	SB3	Box of Accessory Parts, Assortment " A " ...	DC4
Display Cabinet No. 1	DC1	Box of Accessory Parts, Assortment " B " ...	DC5

Miscellaneous Literature, Binders, etc.

Magazine Binder, Spring Back (to hold 6 copies)	B1	The Hornby Book of Trains	B7
Magazine Binder, Spring Back (to hold 12 copies)	B2	The Hornby Railway Company Booklet	B8
Magazine Binding Case (to hold 6 copies)	B3	" How to Get more Fun out of Hornby Trains "	B9
Magazine Binding Case (to hold 12 copies) ...	B4	" Famous Trains " Book, by C. J. Allen	B10
" Adventures in Meccanoland " Booklet	B5	Meccano Writing Pad (Small)	B111
" Dick's Visit to Meccanoland " Booklet	B6	Meccano Writing Pad (Large)	B112

Meccano Engineers' Pocket Book B12

Hornby Train Sets, Rolling Stock and Accessories

HORNBY TRAIN SETS

M.0. Passenger	4010	Hornby No. 1 Tank Goods, S.R.	4154
M.1. Passenger	4011	„ No. 2 Special Pullman, L.N.E.	4211
M.2. Passenger	4012	„ No. 2 Special Pullman, L.M.S.	4212
M. Goods, L.N.E.	4021	„ No. 2 Special Pullman, G.W.	4213
M. Goods, G.W.	4022	„ No. 2 Special Pullman, S.R.	4214
M. Goods, S.R.	4023	„ No. 2 Special Goods, L.N.E.	4251
Hornby No. 0 Goods, L.N.E.	4051	„ No. 2 Special Goods, L.M.S.	4252
„ No. 0 Goods, L.M.S.	4052	„ No. 2 Special Goods, G.W.	4253
„ No. 0 Goods, G.W.	4053	„ No. 2 Special Goods, S.R.	4254
„ No. 0 Goods, S.R.	4054	„ No. 2 Mixed Goods, L.N.E.	4261
„ No. 0 Passenger, L.N.E.	4061	„ No. 2 Mixed Goods, L.M.S.	4262
„ No. 0 Passenger, L.M.S.	4062	„ No. 2 Mixed Goods, G.W.	4263
„ No. 0 Passenger, G.W.	4063	„ No. 2 Mixed Goods, S.R.	4264
„ No. 0 Passenger, S.R.	4064	„ No. 3E G.W. " Cornish Riviera " (6 volt)	4311
„ No. 1 Goods, L.N.E.	4111	„ No. 3C G.W. "Cornish Riviera" (Clockwork)	4312
„ No. 1 Goods, L.M.S.	4112	„ No. 3E L.M.S. " Royal Scot " (6 volt) ...	4321
„ No. 1 Goods, G.W.	4113	„ No. 3C L.M.S. " Royal Scot " (Clockwork)	4322
„ No. 1 Goods, S.R.	4114	„ No. 3E L.N.E.R. " Flying Scotsman " (6 volt)	4331
„ No. 1 Passenger, L.N.E.	4121	„ No. 3C L.N.E.R. " Flying Scotsman " (Clockwork)	4332
„ No. 1 Passenger, L.M.S.	4122	„ No. 3E S.R. " Continental Express " (6 volt)	4341
„ No. 1 Passenger, G.W.	4123	„ No. 3C S.R. " Continental Express " (Clockwork)	4342
„ No. 1 Passenger, S.R.	4124	„ No. 3E Riviera " Blue Train " (6 volt)...	4351
„ No. 1 Special Goods, L.N.E.	4131	„ No. 3C Riviera " Blue Train " (Clockwork)	4352
„ No. 1 Special Goods, L.M.S.	4132	Metropolitan H.V. (100-250 volt)	4411
„ No. 1 Special Goods, G.W.	4133	Metropolitan L.V. (6 volt)	4412
„ No. 1 Special Goods, S.R.	4134	Metropolitan C. (Clockwork)	4413
„ No. 1 Special Passenger, L.N.E.... ...	4141		
„ No. 1 Special Passenger, L.M.S.	4142		
„ No. 1 Special Passenger, G.W.	4143		
„ No. 1 Special Passenger, S.R.	4144		
„ No. 1 Tank Goods, L.N.E.	4151		
„ No. 1 Tank Goods, L.M.S.	4152		
„ No. 1 Tank Goods, G.W.	4153		

LOCOMOTIVES

M. Locomotive (Green)	5011	Hornby No. 1 Special Tank, S.R. (Green) ...	5166
Hornby No. 0 L.N.E. (Black)	5051	„ No. 1 Special Tank, G.W. (Green) ...	5167
„ No. 0 L.N.E. (Green)	5052	„ No. 1 6 v. Electric Tank, L.N.E. (Black)	5171
„ No. 0 L.M.S. (Black)	5053	„ No. 1 6 v. Electric Tank, L.N.E. (Green)	5172
„ No. 0 L.M.S. (Red)	5054	„ No. 1 6 v. Electric Tank, L.M.S. (Black)	5173
„ No. 0 S.R. (Black)	5055	„ No. 1 6 v. Electric Tank, L.M.S. (Red)...	5174
„ No. 0 S.R. (Green)	5056	„ No. 1 6 v. Electric Tank, S.R. (Black)...	5175
„ No. 0 G.W. (Green)	5057	„ No. 1 6 v. Electric Tank, S.R. (Green)...	5176
„ No. 1 L.N.E. (Black)	5111	„ No. 1 6 v. Electric Tank, G.W. (Green)...	5177
„ No. 1 L.N.E. (Green)	5112	„ No. 2 Special, L.N.E. (Green)	5211
„ No. 1 L.M.S. (Black)	5113	„ No. 2 Special, L.M.S. (Red)	5212
„ No. 1 L.M.S. (Red)	5114	„ No. 2 Special, S.R. (Green)	5213
„ No. 1 S.R. (Black)	5115	„ No. 2 Special, G.W. (Green)	5214
„ No. 1 S.R. (Green)	5116	„ No. 2 Special Tank, L.N.E. (Black) ...	5261
„ No. 1 G.W. (Green)	5117	„ No. 2 Special Tank, L.N.E. (Green) ...	5262
„ No. 1 Special, L.N.E. (Black)	5121	„ No. 2 Special Tank, L.M.S. (Black) ...	5263
„ No. 1 Special, L.N.E. (Green)	5122	„ No. 2 Special Tank, L.M.S. (Red) ...	5264
„ No. 1 Special, L.M.S. (Black)	5123	„ No. 2 Special Tank, S.R. (Black) ...	5265
„ No. 1 Special, L.M.S. (Red)	5124	„ No. 2 Special Tank, S.R. (Green) ...	5266
„ No. 1 Special, S.R. (Black)	5125	„ No. 2 Special Tank, G.W. (Green) ...	5267
„ No. 1 Special, S.R. (Green)	5126	„ No. 3E G.W. (6 volt Electric)	5311
„ No. 1 Special, G.W. (Green)	5127	„ No. 3C G.W. (Clockwork)	5312
„ No. 1 Tank, L.N.E. (Black)	5151	„ No. 3E L.M.S. (6 volt Electric)	5321
„ No. 1 Tank, L.N.E. (Green)	5152	„ No. 3C L.M.S. (Clockwork)	5322
„ No. 1 Tank, L.M.S. (Black)	5153	„ No. 3E L.N.E. (6 volt Electric)	5331
„ No. 1 Tank, L.M.S. (Red)	5154	„ No. 3C L.N.E. (Clockwork)	5332
„ No. 1 Tank, S.R. (Black)...	5155	„ No. 3E S.R. (6 volt Electric)	5341
„ No. 1 Tank, S.R. (Green)	5156	„ No. 3C S.R. (Clockwork)	5342
„ No. 1 Tank, G.W. (Green)	5157	„ No. 3E Riviera " Blue Train " (6 volt Electric)	5351
„ No. 1 Special Tank, L.N.E. (Black) ...	5161	„ No. 3C Riviera " Blue Train " (Clockwork)	5352
„ No. 1 Special Tank, L.N.E. (Green) ...	5162	Metropolitan H.V. (100-250 volt)	5411
„ No. 1 Special Tank, L.M.S. (Black) ...	5163	Metropolitan L.V. (6 volt)	5412
„ No. 1 Special Tank, L.M.S. (Red) ...	5164	Metropolitan C. (Clockwork)	5413
„ No. 1 Special Tank, S.R. (Black) ...	5165		

Hornby Train Sets, Rolling Stock and Accessories

(continued)

TENDERS

	CODE NUMBER		CODE NUMBER
M. Tender (Green)	6011	Hornby No. 1 Special, S.R. (Black)	6065
Hornby No. 0 & 1 L.N.E. (Black)	6051	„ No. 1 Special, S.R. (Green)	6066
„ No. 0 & 1 L.N.E. (Green)	6052	„ No. 1 Special, G.W. (Green)	6067
„ No. 0 & 1 L.M.S. (Black)	6053	„ No. 2 Special, L.N.E. (Green)	6111
„ No. 0 & 1 L.M.S. (Red)	6054	„ No. 2 Special, L.M.S. (Red)	6112
„ No. 0 & 1 S.R. (Black)	6055	„ No. 2 Special, S.R. (Green)	6113
„ No. 0 & 1 S.R. (Green)	6056	„ No. 2 Special, G.W. (Green)	6114
„ No. 0 & 1 G.W. (Green)	6057	„ No. 3 G.W.	6151
„ No. 1 Special, L.N.E. (Black)	6061	„ No. 3 L.M.S.	6152
„ No. 1 Special, L.N.E. (Green)	6062	„ No. 3 L.N.E.	6153
„ No. 1 Special, L.M.S. (Black)	6063	„ No. 3 S.R.	6154
„ No. 1 Special, L.M.S. (Red)	6064	„ No. 3 Riviera " Blue Train "	6155

COACHES

M. Series & No. 0 Pullman Coach " Marjorie " ...	6251	Hornby No. 1 Pullman Coach " Niobe "	6273
M. Series & No. 0 Pullman Coach " Aurelia " ...	6252	„ No. 1 Pullman (Composite) " Ansonia "	6281
M. Series & No. 0 Pullman Coach " Viking " ...	6253	„ Nos. 2 & 3 Pullman Coach " Iolanthe "	6291
Hornby No. 1, L.N.E.	6261	„ Nos. 2 & 3 Pullman (Composite) "Arcadia"	6301
„ No. 1, L.M.S.	6262	„ No. 3 Riviera " Blue Train " (Dining) ...	6311
„ No. 1, S.R.	6263	„ No. 3 Riviera " Blue Train " (Sleeping)	6312
„ No. 1, G.W.	6264	Metropolitan H.V.	6321
„ No. 1 Pullman Coach " Corsair " ...	6271	Metropolitan L.V.	6322
„ No. 1 Pullman Coach " Cynthia " ...	6272	Metropolitan C.	6323

WAGONS

M. Series, L.N.E.	6351	Hornby No. 0, G.W.	6414
M. Series, L.M.S.	6352	„ No. 1, L.N.E.	6421
M. Series, S.R.	6353	„ No. 1, L.M.S.	6422
M. Series, G.W.	6354	„ No. 1, S.R.	6423
Hornby No. 0, L.N.E.	6411	„ No. 1, G.W.	6424
„ No. 0, L.M.S.	6412	French Type Wagon, Nord	6451
„ No. 0, S.R.	6413	Covered Wagon, French Type, Nord	6461

MISCELLANEOUS ROLLING STOCK

Carr's Biscuit Van	6511	Luggage Van No. 1, S.R.	6634
Crawford's Biscuit Van	6512	Luggage Van No. 2, L.N.E.	6641
Jacob's Biscuit Van	6513	Luggage Van No. 2, L.M.S.	6642
Brake Van, L.N.E.	6521	Luggage Van No. 2, G.W.	6643
Brake Van, L.M.S.	6522	Luggage Van No. 2, S.R.	6644
Brake Van, G.W.	6523	Lumber Wagon No. 1, L.N.E.	6651
Brake Van, S.R.	6524	Lumber Wagon No. 1, L.M.S.	6652
Brake Van, French Type, Nord	6531	Lumber Wagon No. 1, G.W.	6653
Breakdown Van & Crane, L.N.E....	6541	Lumber Wagon No. 1, S.R.	6654
Breakdown Van & Crane, L.M.S.	6542	Lumber Wagon No. 2, L.N.E.	6661
Breakdown Van & Crane, G.W.	6543	Lumber Wagon No. 2, L.M.S.	6662
Breakdown Van & Crane, S.R.	6544	Lumber Wagon No. 2, G.W.	6663
Cattle Truck No. 1, L.N.E....	6551	Lumber Wagon No. 2, S.R.	6664
Cattle Truck No. 1, L.M.S.	6552	Milk Traffic Van, L.N.E.	6671
Cattle Truck No. 1, G.W.	6553	Milk Traffic Van, L.M.S.	6672
Cattle Truck No. 1, S.R.	6554	Milk Traffic Van, G.W.	6673
Cattle Truck No. 2, L.N.E....	6561	Milk Traffic Van, S.R.	6674
Cattle Truck No. 2, L.M.S.	6562	Petrol Tank Wagon, " Shell "	6681
Cattle Truck No. 2, G.W.	6563	Petrol Tank Wagon, " Pratts "	6682
Cattle Truck No. 2, S.R.	6564	Motor Spirit Tank Wagon, " B.P."	6683
Cement Wagon, L.N.E.	6571	Petrol Tank Wagon, " Redline "	6684
Cement Wagon, L.M.S.	6572	Refrigerator Van, L.N.E.	6691
Cement Wagon, G.W.	6573	Refrigerator Van, L.M.S.	6692
Cement Wagon, S.R.	6574	Refrigerator Van, G.W.	6693
Crane Truck, L.N.E.	6581	Refrigerator Van, S.R.	6694
Crane Truck, L.M.S.	6582	Snow Plough, L.N.E.	6701
Crane Truck, G.W.	6583	Snow Plough, L.M.S.	6702
Crane Truck, S.R.	6584	Snow Plough, G.W.	6703
Gas Cylinder Wagon, L.N.E.	6591	Snow Plough, S.R.	6704
Gas Cylinder Wagon, L.M.S.	6592	Timber Wagon No. 1, L.N.E.	6711
Gas Cylinder Wagon, G.W....	6593	Timber Wagon No. 1, L.M.S	6712
Gas Cylinder Wagon, S.R.	6594	Timber Wagon No. 1, G.W.	6713
Guard's Van, L.N.E.	6601	Timber Wagon No. 1, S.R.	6714
Guard's Van, L.M.S.	6602	Timber Wagon No. 2, L.N.E.	6721
Guard's Van, G.W.	6603	Timber Wagon No. 2, L.M.S.	6722
Guard's Van, S.R.	6604	Timber Wagon No. 2, G.W.	6723
Gunpowder Van, L.N.E.	6611	Timber Wagon No. 2, S.R.	6724
Gunpowder Van, L.M.S.	6612	Side Tipping Wagon	6731
Gunpowder Van, G.W.	6613	Rotary Tipping Wagon	6741
Gunpowder Van, S.R.	6614	Trolley Wagon, L.N.E.	6751
Hopper Wagon, L.N.E.	6621	Trolley Wagon, L.M.S.	6752
Hopper Wagon, L.M.S.	6622	Trolley Wagon, G.W.	6753
Hopper Wagon, G.W.	6623	Trolley Wagon, S.R.	6754
Hopper Wagon, S.R.	6624	Seccotine Van	6761
Luggage Van No. 1, L.N.E.	6631	Single Wine Wagon	6771
Luggage Van No. 1, L.M.S.	6632	Double Wine Wagon	6772
Luggage Van No. 1, G.W.	6633	Milk Tank Wagon, "United Dairies Ltd." ...	6781
		Mansell Wheels	6901

ACCESSORIES

Footbridge No. 1	7011	Station No. 1...	7061
Footbridge No. 2	7012	Station No. 2...	7062
Signals for Footbridge (Pair)	7013	Station Approach (Right)	7063
Footbridge Signal (Short)	7014	Station Approach (Left)	7064
Footbridge Signal (Long)	7015	Signal No. 1 (Home and Distant) One Pair ...	7071
Buffer Stops No. 1 (Spring)	7021	Signal No. 2 (Home)	7081
Buffer Stops No. 2 (Hydraulic)	7022	Signal No. 2 (Distant)	7082
Lamp Standard No. 1 (Single)	7041	Junction Signal (Home)	7091
Lamp Standard No. 2 (Double)	7042	Junction Signal (Distant)	7092
Loading Gauge	7051	Signal Cabin No. 1	7101

Fig 3.

Hornby Train Sets, Rolling Stock and Accessories
(continued)

ACCESSORIES (Contd.)	CODE NUMBER
Signal Cabin No. 2	7102
Tunnel	7111
Telegraph Poles (One Pair)	7121
Water Tank	7131
Level Crossing No. 1	7141
Level Crossing No. 2	7142
RailwayAccessories No. 1 (Miniature Luggage)	7151
Railway Accessories No. 2 (Milk Cans and Truck)	7152
Railway Accessories No. 3 (Platform Machines, etc.)	7153
Railway Accessories No. 4 (All pieces contained in Nos. 1, 2 and 3 sets)	7154
Railway Accessories No. 5 (Gradient Posts and Mile Posts)	7155
Railway Accessories No. 7 (Watchman's Hut, Brazier, Shovel and Poker)	7156
Railway Accessories No. 8 (Notice Boards)	7157
Railway Accessories No. 9 (Station-name Boards)	7158
Milk Cans	7159
Viaduct	7161
Viaduct, Centre Portion only	7162
Viaduct Approach (Right)	7163
Viaduct Approach (Left)	7164
Viaduct, Electrical	7171

ACCESSORIES (Contd.)	CODE NUMBER
Viaduct, Centre Portion only (Electrical)	7172
Viaduct Approach (Electrical) Right	7173
Viaduct Approach (Electrical) Left	7174
Island Platform	7181
Passenger Platform	7191
Goods Platform	7201
White Paled Fencing (One Length)	7211
Ramps (Pair)	7221
Turntable No. 1	7231
Turntable No. 2	7232
Platform Crane	7241
Double Arm Signal No. 1 (One Pair)	7251
Double Arm Signal No. 2 (One only)	7252
Engine Shed No. 1	7261
Engine Shed No. 2	7262
Shunter's Pole	7271
Lattice Girder Bridge	7281
Signal Gantry	7291
Tarpaulin Sheets, L.N.E. (Dozen)	7301
Tarpaulin Sheets, L.M.S. (Dozen)	7302
Tarpaulin Sheets, S.R. (Dozen)	7303
Tarpaulin Sheets, G.W. (Dozen)	7304
Speed and Reverse Control Switch (for use with the 6-volt Electric Tank Locomotive No. 1)	7311

HORNBY CONTROL SYSTEM—OUTFITS AND COMPONENTS

Item	Code
Outfit No. 1	8011
Outfit No. 2	8012
Lever Frame	8021
Control Points (One Pair R.H. and L.H., 1 ft. radius)	8031
Control Points (One Pair R.H. and L.H., 2 ft. radius)	8032
Single Control Signal (Home)	8041
Single Control Signal (Distant)	8042
Junction Control Signal (Home)	8051
Junction Control Signal (Distant)	8052
Control Rail No. 1	8061
Control Rail No. 2	8062
Rodding Compensator	8071
Control Couplings	8081
Wire, 24 ft. Coil	8091
Guide Brackets (One Dozen)	8101
Wire Cutters (One Pair)	8111
Nuts and Bolts (Box of 36)	8121
Crossover, right / Crossover, left } per pair	8131
Electric Control Points (One Pair R.H. and L.H., 2 ft. radius)	8211

HORNBY TRAINS FITTED FOR CONTROL

Item	Code
No. 1 Goods Set, L.N.E.	8311
No. 1 Goods Set, L.M.S.	8312
No. 1 Goods Set, G.W.	8313
No. 1 Goods Set, S.R.	8314
No. 1 Passenger Set, L.N.E.	8321
No. 1 Passenger Set, L.M.S.	8322
No. 1 Passenger Set, G.W.	8323
No. 1 Passenger Set, S.R.	8324
No. 1 Tank Goods Set, L.N.E.	8331
No. 1 Tank Goods Set, L.M.S.	8332
No. 1 Tank Goods Set, G.W.	8333
No. 1 Tank Goods Set, S.R.	8334

HORNBY LOCOMOTIVES FITTED FOR CONTROL

Item	Code
Hornby No. 1 L.N.E. (Black)	8711
„ No. 1 L.N.E. (Green)	8712
„ No. 1 L.M.S. (Black)	8713
„ No. 1 L.M.S. (Red)	8714
„ No. 1 S.R. (Black)	8715
„ No. 1 S.R. (Green)	8716
„ No. 1 G.W. (Green)	8717
Hornby No. 1 Tank, L.N.E. (Black)	8811
„ No. 1 Tank, L.N.E. (Green)	8812
„ No. 1 Tank, L.M.S. (Black)	8813
„ No. 1 Tank, L.M.S. (Red)	8814
„ No. 1 Tank, S.R. (Black)	8815
„ No. 1 Tank, S.R. (Green)	8816
„ No. 1 Tank, G.W. (Green)	8817

RAILS FOR CLOCKWORK AND STEAM TRAINS

Item	Code
A1 Curved Rails (1 ft. radius), doz.	9011
A1½ Curved Half Rails (1 ft. radius), doz.	9012
A1¼ Curved Quarter Rails (1 ft. radius), doz.	9013
AB1 Curved Brake Rails (1 ft. radius), one	9021
A2 Curved Rails (2 ft. radius), doz.	9031
A2½ Curved Half Rails (2 ft. radius), doz.	9032
A2¼ Curved Quarter Rails (2 ft. radius), doz.	9033
AB2 Curved Brake Rails (2 ft. radius), one	9041
B1 Straight Rails, doz.	9051
B½ Straight Half Rails, doz.	9052
B¼ Straight Quarter Rails, doz.	9053
BB1 Straight Brake Rails, one	9061
BBR1 Straight Brake and Reverse Rail, one	9062
DS1 Straight Rails, Double Track, ½ doz.	9071
DC2 Curved Rails, Double Track (2 ft. radius), ½ doz.	9081
CA1 Acute Angle Crossings (for 1 ft. radius tracks), one	9211
CA2 Acute Angle Crossings (for 2 ft. radius tracks), one	9212
CR1 Right Angle Crossings (for 1 ft. radius tracks), one	9221
CR2 Right Angle Crossings (for 2 ft. radius tracks), one	9222
COR2 Crossover, right hand / COL2 Crossover, left hand } per pair	9253
PR1 & PL1 Points, 1 pair, Right-hand and Left-hand (1 ft. radius)	9311
PR2 & PL2 Points, 1 pair, Right-hand and Left-hand (2 ft. radius)	9312
PSR2 & PSL2 Points on Solid Base, 1 pair, Right-hand and Left-hand (2 ft. radius)	9322
DSR1 & DSL1 Points, 1 pair Double Symmetrical, Right-hand and Left-hand (1 ft. radius)	9351
DSR2 & DSL2 Points, 1 pair Double Symmetrical, Right-hand and Left-hand (2 ft. radius)	9352
PPR2 & PPL2 Points, 1 pair Parallel, Right-hand and Left-hand	9412
RCP Rail Connecting Plates, ½ doz.	9511

RAILS FOR ELECTRIC TRAINS

Item	Code
EA1 Curved Rails (1 ft. radius), doz.	9611
EA1½ Curved Half Rails (1 ft. radius), doz.	9612
EA1¼ Curved Quarter Rails (1 ft. radius), doz.	9613
EA2 Curved Rails (2 ft. radius), doz.	9621
EA2½ Curved Half Rails (2 ft. radius), doz.	9622
EA2¼ Curved Quarter Rails (2 ft. radius), doz.	9623
EB1 Straight Rails, doz.	9631
EB½ Straight Half Rails, doz.	9632
EB¼ Straight Quarter Rails, doz.	9633
ECA Acute Angle Crossings, one	9651
ECR Right Angle Crossings, one	9661
EPR2 & EPL2 Points, 1 pair, Right-hand and Left-hand (2 ft. radius)	9711
EDSR2 & EDSL2 Points, 1 pair Double Symmetrical, Right-hand and Left-hand (2 ft. radius)	9751
EPPR2 & EPPL2 Points, 1 pair Parallel, Right-hand and Left-hand (2 ft. radius)	9811
TCPH Terminal Connecting Plates (High Voltage) one	9851
TCPL Terminal Connecting Plates (Low Voltage) one	9852

Page Twenty-eight

Fig 3.

A selection of pages from the 1930 edition → of 'Our Selling Service'. Note the wider range of demonstration models and suggestions for window displays.
The print reference on the inside front cover (15/439/4.5) should read 15/430/4.5.

The Products of Meccano Ltd. are sold to the Trade subject to the following terms and conditions of sale:

CONDITIONS OF SALE

All goods are supplied on the understanding that they are to be resold by retail only, and at the prices in our current price lists, without deduction.

Goods of our manufacture are not to be offered for sale at a dealer's branch establishment unless a separate account for the branch has been opened.

Acceptance of goods will be treated as an acknowledgment of these conditions.

TERMS

Trade Discounts

All goods 33⅓% (except accumulators and transformers, 25%; storage cabinets, 15%).

Settlement Terms

Settlement discount 2½% on all items appearing in the subject column of our statements when payment is made by the 15th of the month following the date of our invoice. Accounts are due nett at the end of the same month.

References

Two trade references (not bankers') should accompany a dealer's first order.

Carriage

Carriage paid by goods train on orders of net value of £2 and over, to any part of Great Britain and Northern Ireland. During the period immediately preceding Christmas (Scotland, New Year also) goods are sent by passenger train at our discretion, the additional cost being debited to the dealer.

Packing

Packing cases extra; credited in full if returned carriage paid, within fourteen days. Half price is not allowed for cases retained.

EXECUTION OF ORDERS

Each order received is immediately passed to our Despatch Department for attention. It is rarely practicable to include with an original consignment any further small items that may be ordered later.

MECCANO LIMITED
BINNS ROAD
OLD SWAN
LIVERPOOL

15/439/4.5

OUR SELLING SERVICE

HOW WE HELP YOU TO INCREASE YOUR SALES AND PROFITS.

We spend many thousands of pounds annually in a nation-wide advertising campaign, which stimulates interest and creates a big demand for our products. We advertise in the leading national newspapers and periodicals; we send interesting literature to thousands of boys throughout the country; we organise Meccano and Hornby Train Weeks to give the boys something to talk about, and we have many other forms of propaganda designed for the express purpose of bringing our goods to the notice of the public. Although this publicity inevitably creates a big demand for Meccano and Hornby Trains which benefits all our dealers equally, the dealer who organises and conducts a local advertising campaign on his own account gets a double advantage.

We hope that every dealer will make the fullest use of our Selling Service, by utilising the "helps" shown in this booklet, and especially by requisitioning the aid of our Advertising Department in the preparation of layouts and copy for local advertisements. Dealers should call on us for suggestions or help at any time when they encounter difficulties in connection with their advertising.

Page One

Fig 3a.

Suggestions for Window Displays

(Continued.)

Material required for Display No. 3.

Ruby, White, and Black Crepe Papers.

SHOWCARDS, ETC.

2 Meccano Cutouts No. 2.
1 Meccano Cutout No. 4.
1 Showcard No. 7 " Best Age."
1 Showcard No. 22, " These are Meccano Days."
1 Window Bill No. 23, " This is Meccano Week."
Price Tickets.

MECCANO GOODS.

2 No. 00a Outfit Cartons (Empty).
2 No. 0a Outfit Cartons (Empty).
2 No. 1a Outfit Cartons (Empty).
2 No. 2a Outfit Cartons (Empty).
2 No. 00 Outfit Cartons (Empty).
2 No. 0 Outfit Cartons (Empty).
2 No. 1 Outfit Cartons (Empty).
2 No. 2 Outfit Cartons (Empty).
2 No. 0 Outfits.
1 No. 2 Outfit.
1 Steam Engine.
1 Oilcan No. 1.
1 Oilcan No. 2 (" K " type).
1 Bottle of Lubricating Oil.
1 Clockwork Motor.
1 Electric Motor No. 6 (6-volt).
1 Transformer.

MODELS.

1 Manual Mo'el No. 2.48 Aeroplane.
Price 6/- net.
1 Marine Engine Display Model.
Price £3 6s. 8d. net, with gearing and H.V. Motor.
2 Meccano Pedesta's, 7".
Price 2/2 each net.

Window Display No. 3.

Material required for Display No. 9.

Ruby and Orange Crepe Paper

SHOWCARDS.

1 Showcard No. 22, " These are Meccano Days."
2 Showcards No. 7, " Best Age."
1 Meccano Screen.
2 Boy Cutouts No. 14.
1 Meccano Cutout No. 3.

MECCANO GOODS.

1 No. 0a Meccano Carton (Empty).
1 No. 1a Meccano Carton (Empty).
2 No. 0 Outfits.
2 No. 1 Outfits.
1 No. 2 Outfit.
1 Clockwork Motor.
1 Electric Motor No. 6 (6-volt).
1 Oilcan No. 2 (" K " type).
1 Oilcan No. 1.
1 Bottle of Lubricating Oil.
1 Steam Engine.
1 Transformer.
1 Meccano Magazine.

MODELS, Etc.

1 Meccano No. 6 Model Tug.
Price 15/4 net.
1 Manual Model No. 1.69 Elevated Crane.
Price 5/6 net.
1 Oval Velvet-covered Card of Parts.
2 Meccano Pedestals, 5". Price 2/3 each net.

Window Display No. 9.

Page Six

Suggestions for Window Displays

(Continued.)

Material required for Display No. 5.

Yellow, Light Orange, and Blue Crepe Paper.

SHOWCARDS.

1 Showcard No. 8, " This is Hornby Train Time."
2 Hornby Train Showcards No. 16.
1 Hornby Train Screen.
2 Hornby Train Talking Cards.
Price Tickets.

HORNBY GOODS.

1 Footbridge No. 3 (Lattice Girder).
1 Platform Crane.
1 Lamp Standard No. 1.
1 Lamp Standard No. 2.
1 Buffer Stop No. 2.
1 Buffer Stop No. 1.
1 Gunpowder Van.
1 Cement Wagon.
1 " B.P." Petrol Tank Wagon.
1 Crane Truck.
1 No. 0 Locomotive and Tender.
1 No. 1 Special Locomotive and Tender.
1 No. 2 Special Locomotive and Tender.

HORNBY GOODS (*continued*).

1 Junction Signal.
1 Signal No. 2.
1 Double Arm Signal No. 2.
1 Station No. 1.
1 Signal Cabin No. 2.
1 Water Tank.
1 Telegraph Pole.
1 Set Railway Accessories No. 2.
1 Set Railway Accessories No. 3.
1 Milk Tank Wagon.
1 Side Tipping Wagon.
1 Covered Wagon NORD
1 Refrigerator Van.
1 Gas Cylinder Wagon.
1 Breakdown Van and Crane.
1 M2 Passenger Set.
1 No. 1 Special Passenger Set.
1 No. 2 Mixed Goods Set.
1 No. 2 Special Pullman Set.
1 No. 3 Pullman Set.
1 Wagon with lookout, NORD.
Suitable quantity of Rails.

---

1 Set of 6 Meccano Pedestals.
Price 15/2 net.

Window Display No. 5.

Material required for Display No. 4.

Orange Crepe Paper.

SHOWCARDS, ETC.

Price Tickets.
2 Showcards No. 7, " Best Age."
1 Meccano Cutout No. 2.
1 Meccano Cutout No. 4.
2 Boy Cutouts No. 14.
1 Meccano Screen.

MODELS.

1 Special Model Dredger.
Price £3 13s. 9d. net, with gearing and H.V. Motor.
1 Hanging Lantern No. 8.
Price 10/6 net, plus flex 1d. per foot, net.
Extra for " Flasher," 5/- net net.

MECCANO GOODS.

2 No. 00 Outfit Cartons (Empty).
2 No. 0 Outfit Cartons (Empty).
2 No. 1 Outfit Cartons (Empty).
1 No. 0a Outfit Carton (Empty).
1 No. 1a Outfit Carton (Empty).
1 No. 1 Outfit.
1 No. 2 Outfit.
1 Clockwork Motor.
1 Electric Motor No. 6 (6-volt).
1 Resistance Controller.
1 Steam Engine.
1 Oilcan No. 1.
1 Oilcan No. 2 (" K " type).
1 Bottle of Lubricating Oil.

---

1 Oval Velvet-covered Card of Parts.

By Selling the " Meccano Magazine " you will increase your sales of Meccano and Hornby Trains.

Window Display No. 4.

Page Seven

C

 Fig 3.

Meccano Demonstration Models

On this and the following three pages we reproduce a selection of special Demonstration Models that we are prepared to make up for any of our dealers who desire to give an effective window display. These models have been selected because of their attractive appearance and also because they are suitable in size for the average window. If desired, they may be used in conjunction with any of the suggested Meccano Window Displays illustrated on pages 4 to 8, instead of the models that are shown in these displays.

Meccano Demonstration Models are supplied at the cost of the parts required to make them, no charge being made for the labour of assembling. When ordering any of the models (excepting No. 7) please state whether they are required with or without base boards. Orders for demonstration models should be placed early; we are unable to guarantee delivery of models ordered later than October.

When the models are no longer required for display they may be dismantled and the parts taken into stock. Alternatively, the models may be returned to us for credit at half invoice value against an order for new models of at least the equivalent value. Credit for returned models and our debit for new models ordered will appear in the same month's account.

Model No. 3 Drop Hammer

Model No. 4

Large Windmill

(As illustrated)

This new Meccano demonstration model is distinctive in appearance and is an exceptionally good display model.

Dimensions: Height, 4'; Length, 1' 9"; Breadth, 1' 8". Sails span 3' 2".

Price, complete with special Meccano H.V. Motor (100-250 Volt), £3/5/4 net.

Extra for Sprayed Base Board, 5/9 net net.

Model No. 2

Drop Hammer

This well-constructed model has been specially designed for the use of dealers who have limited accommodation. Its action when in operation is very realistic and it may be depended upon always to create considerable interest.

Dimensions: Height, 1' 8½"; Length, 1' 4½"; Breadth, 5½"

Price, complete with special Meccano H.V. Motor (100-250 Volt), £1/15/8 net.

Extra for Sprayed Base Board, 2/9 net net.

Model No. 3. **DROP HAMMER.** A 6-volt Meccano Electric Motor is fitted into this model instead of a high voltage motor. Otherwise the model is exactly the same as model No. 2, described above.

Price, complete with Meccano 6-volt motor, £1/4/8 net.

Extra for Sprayed Base Board, 2/9 net net.

Model No. 5

Small Windmill

The Small Windmill is similar in design, and works in the same manner, as the large Windmill described above. The difference in size will be seen on comparing the respective dimensions.

Dimensions: Height, 2' 6"; Length, 11"; Breadth, 11"; Sails span, 2' 1½".

Price, complete with special Meccano H.V. Motor (100-250 Volt), £2/1/0 net.

Extra for Sprayed Base Board, 3/– net net.

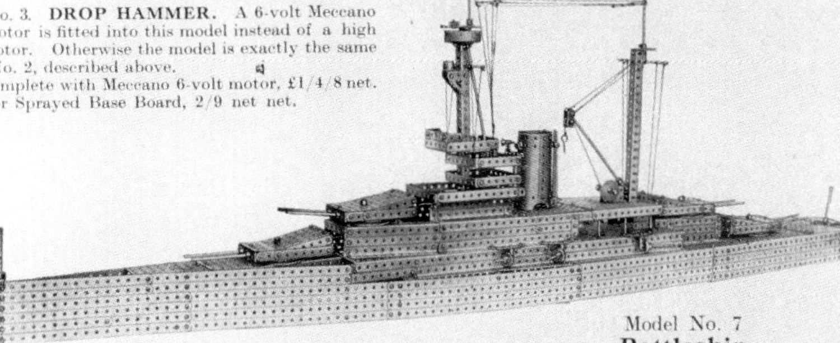

Model No. 7

Battleship

Although it does not work, this well-constructed and exceedingly realistic model of a Battleship (Revenge class) is an ideal subject for window display.

Dimensions: Height, 1' 7"; Length, 4' 10"; Breadth, 9½".

Price £2/4/6 net.

Page Ten

Meccano Demonstration Models

(*Continued*)

Model No. 14

Baltic Tank Locomotive

This fine Meccano model of a Tank Locomotive is designed on the most modern type of Tank Locomotive, and is fitted with many of the latest appliances, including Walschaerts' Valve Gear. It may be used for display independently, but we strongly recommend that it should be shown with Model No. 15 in order to demonstrate the wonderful progress that has been made in locomotive construction during the past century. When the models are ordered together we provide a suitably worded card to be shown with them.

Dimensions: Height, 12¾"; Length, 36"; Breadth, 9½".

Price, complete with special Meccano H.V. Motor (100-250 Volt), £4/19/8 net.

Price without H.V. Motor, £3/15/0 net. Extra for Sprayed Base Board, 7/– net net.

Model No. 15

Stephenson's "Locomotion No. 1"

This splendid model of Stephenson's Locomotive may be used independently but, for the reason explained above, much more attention will be attracted if it is used in conjunction with the Baltic Tank Locomotive.

Dimensions: Height, 1' 1½"; Length, 1' 7½"; Breadth, 7".

Price £1/4/0 net.

Extra for Sprayed Base Board, 3/3 net net.

Model No. 16

Stephenson's "Rocket" Locomotive

This is a model of Stephenson's famous Locomotive that was used on the original Liverpool-Manchester railroad in 1830. In common with all other replicas of the "Rocket" it has a great fascination for boys. It is an admirable model for display purposes.

Dimensions: Height, 1' 8¾"; Length, 2' 3½"; Breadth, 10".

Price, complete with special Meccano H.V. Motor (100-250 Volt) £3/10/0 net.

Price without H.V. Motor, £2/8/4 net.

Extra for Sprayed Base Board, 6/3 net net.

Page Eleven

Fig 3.

Meccano Demonstration Models

(Continued)

Model No. 6

Workshop

This splendid Meccano model clearly shows the possibilities of the Meccano system. All the machines are driven simultaneously by means of a Meccano H.V. Electric Motor, which is connected to the shafting.

Dimensions: Height, 14″; Length, 27″; Breadth, 14″.

Price, complete with special Meccano H.V. Motor (100-200 Volt), £2/9/6 net.

Extra for Sprayed Base Board, 5/9 net net.

Model No. 12

Marine Engine

The new Marine Engine is a very attractive model and is particularly suitable for window display. It is designed on the triple-expansion type of steam engine, and includes a four-bearing balanced crank-shaft, crossheads with guide bars, balanced flywheel, etc.

Dimensions:
Height, 1′ 8½″;
Length, 1′ 8¼″;
Breadth, 10″.

Price, complete with special Meccano H.V. Motor (100-250 Volt), £3/6/8 net.

Extra for Sprayed Base Board, 5/– net net.

Model No. 1

Motor Chassis

The Meccano Motor Chassis is a triumph of model building. It includes all the important details of real automobile practice—Differential Gear, Ackermann Steering, Gear Box (3-speed and reverse), and Internal expanding rear wheel brakes.

Dimensions: Height, 9″; Length, 26½″; Breadth, 7″.

Price, complete with Meccano 6-volt Electric Motor, £2/10/0 net.

Extra for Sprayed Base Board, 4/9 net net.

Page Twelve

Complete Stereos—Meccano

The four Meccano advertisements reproduced below have been specially prepared for the use of our dealers. Complete stereos of these advertisements will be supplied, free of charge, on request. When passing these to the printer or newspaper publisher he should be instructed to insert details of the name and address in type in the panel provided. The layouts and dimensions of the advertisements are particularly suitable for newspaper advertising, but they may also be used for circulars, throwaways and the backs of invoice forms, etc. Please order by number only.

BUILD HUNDREDS OF WORKING MODELS

When a Meccano boy wants a new toy he builds it himself—a different one every day if he feels so inclined. Not only does he build toys, he also builds real working models of Motor Cars, Aeroplanes, Cranes, Bridges, and hundreds of other engineering structures. He builds them with Meccano parts, because they are real engineering parts in miniature. All the parts are standardised and the same units can be used in hundreds of different models.

Meccano, the most thrilling hobby in the world, becomes more fascinating every day.

Prices of Meccano Outfits from 2/- to 450/-

MECCANO

SPACE FOR DEALER'S NAME AND ADDRESS

No. 1 M.—6 in. Double Column advertisement.

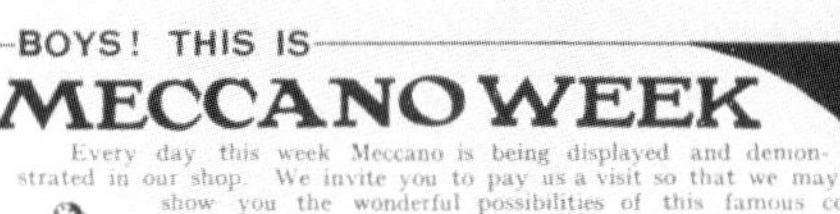

BOYS! THIS IS MECCANO WEEK

Every day this week Meccano is being displayed and demonstrated in our shop. We invite you to pay us a visit so that we may show you the wonderful possibilities of this famous constructional system.

There is no limit to the number of real engineering models that can be built with Meccano. Cranes, Bridges, Motor Cars, Locomotives, Clocks—in fact everything that interests boys. No skill or study is required—the youngest boy can commence to build as soon as he gets his Outfit home.

PRICES OF MECCANO OUTFITS from 2/- to 450/-

Meccano Model of Steam Shovel.

SPACE FOR DEALER'S NAME

No. 3 M.—3 in. Double Column advertisement.

Boys, Be Builders!

There is no limit to the number of splendid models that you may build with Meccano—Cranes, Bridges, Machine Tools, Motor Cars and hundreds of others.

Meccano is the finest hobby in the world for boys. We cordially invite you to come and see our range of 1930 Meccano Outfits.

MECCANO

Outfits from 2/- to 450/-

SPACE FOR DEALER'S NAME

No. 4 M.—3 in. Single Column advertisement.

BOYS, BUILD LIKE REAL ENGINEERS!

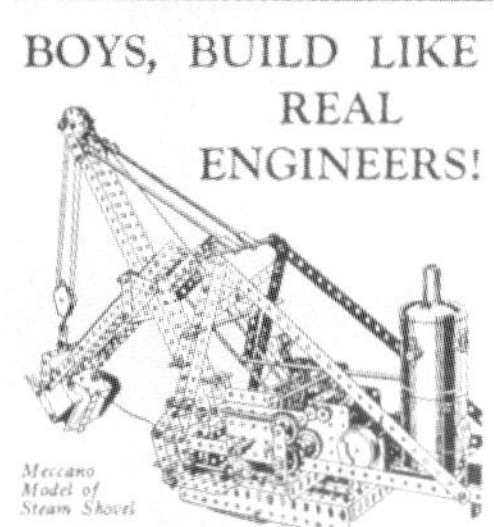

Meccano Model of Steam Shovel

Meccano is the finest hobby in the world for boys. All the parts in the Meccano system are miniatures of the corresponding parts in real engineering practice. They are all standardised and interchangeable and can be used to make hundreds of different models.

Meccano becomes more fascinating every day. This year the scope of the Outfits is greater than ever, and hundreds of new and better Models are shown in the Manuals of Instructions. Come and see the 1930 Meccano Outfits.

We carry a full stock of Meccano Accessory Parts

Prices of complete Outfits from 2/- to 450/-

MECCANO

SPACE FOR DEALER'S NAME

No. 2 M.—6 in. Single Column advertisement.

Page Nineteen

Fig 3.

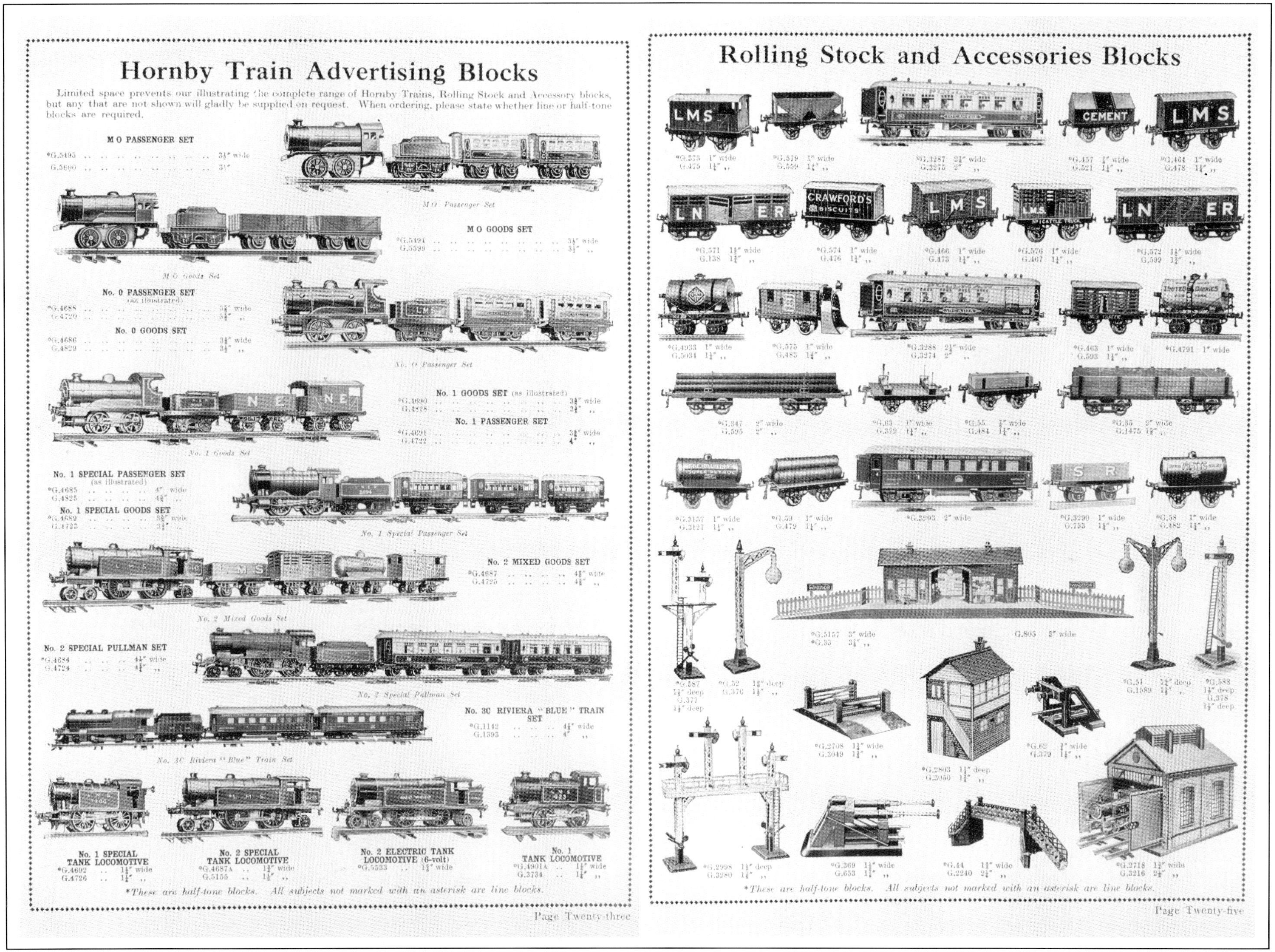

Hornby Train Advertising Blocks

Limited space prevents our illustrating the complete range of Hornby Trains, Rolling Stock and Accessory blocks, but any that are not shown will gladly be supplied on request. When ordering, please state whether line or half-tone blocks are required.

M O PASSENGER SET

*G.5495 .. .. 3¼" wide
G.5600 .. .. 3½"

M O Passenger Set

M O Goods Set

M O GOODS SET

*G.5491 .. .. 3¼" wide
G.5599 .. .. 3½" ,,

No. 0 PASSENGER SET
(as illustrated)

*G.4688 .. .. 3⅝" wide
G.4720 .. .. 3⅜" ,,

No. 0 GOODS SET

*G.4686 .. .. 3⅝" wide
G.4829 .. .. 3½" ,,

No. 0 Passenger Set

No. 1 Goods Set

No. 1 GOODS SET (as illustrated)

*G.4690 .. .. 3⅝" wide
G.4828 .. .. 3⅜" ,,

No. 1 PASSENGER SET

*G.4691 .. .. 3⅝" wide
G.4722 .. .. 4" ,,

No. 1 SPECIAL PASSENGER SET
(as illustrated)

*G.4685 .. .. 4" wide
G.4825 .. .. 4⅛" ,,

No. 1 SPECIAL GOODS SET

*G.4689 .. .. 3⅝" wide
G.4723 .. .. 3⅝" ,,

No. 1 Special Passenger Set

No. 2 MIXED GOODS SET

*G.4687 .. .. 4⅜" wide
G.4725 .. .. 4⅜" ,,

No. 2 Mixed Goods Set

No. 2 SPECIAL PULLMAN SET

*G.4684 .. .. 4¼" wide
G.4724 .. .. 4¾" ,,

No. 2 Special Pullman Set

No. 3C RIVIERA "BLUE" TRAIN SET

*G.1142 .. .. 4¼" wide
G.1393 .. .. 4" ,,

No. 3C Riviera "Blue" Train Set

No. 1 SPECIAL TANK LOCOMOTIVE
*G.4692 .. 1¼" wide
G.4726 .. 1¼" ,,

No. 2 SPECIAL TANK LOCOMOTIVE
*G.4687A .. 1⅝" wide
G.5155 .. 1½" ,,

No. 2 ELECTRIC TANK LOCOMOTIVE (6-volt)
*G.5533 .. 1⅝" wide

No. 1 TANK LOCOMOTIVE
*G.4901A .. 1½" wide
G.3734 .. 1¼" ,,

**These are half-tone blocks. All subjects not marked with an asterisk are line blocks.*

Rolling Stock and Accessories Blocks

*G.373 1" wide
G.475 1¼" ,,

*G.579 1" wide
G.559 1⅛" ,,

*G.3287 2¼" wide
G.3275 2" ,,

*G.457 ⅞" wide
G.521 1¼" ,,

*G.464 1" wide
G.478 1¼" ,,

*G.571 1⅝" wide
G.138 1¾" ,,

*G.574 1" wide
G.476 1¼" ,,

*G.466 1" wide
G.473 1¼" ,,

*G.576 1" wide
G.467 1¼" ,,

*G.572 1½" wide
G.599 1¾" ,,

*G.4933 1" wide
G.5034 1¼" ,,

*G.575 1" wide
G.483 1⅜" ,,

*G.3288 2¼" wide
G.3274 2" ,,

*G.463 1" wide
G.593 1¼" ,,

*G.4791 1" wide

*G.347 2" wide
G.595 2" ,,

*G.63 1" wide
G.372 1¼" ,,

*G.55 ⅞" wide
G.484 1¼" ,,

*G.35 2" wide
G.1475 1⅞" ,,

*G.3157 1" wide
G.3127 1¼" ,,

*G.59 1" wide
G.479 1¼" ,,

*G.3293 2" wide

*G.3290 1" wide
G.733 1¼" ,,

*G.58 1" wide
G.482 1¼" ,,

*G.5157 3" wide
*G.33 3¾" ,,

G.805 3" wide

*G.587
1¾" deep
G.377
1¼" deep

*G.52 1⅝" deep
G.376 1½" ,,

*G.51 1⅝" deep
G.1589 1½" ,,

*G.588
1½" deep
G.378
1½" deep

*G.2708 1¼" wide
G.3049 1¾" ,,

*G.2803 1¼" deep
G.3050 1¾" ,,

*G.62 ¾" wide
G.379 1⅛" ,,

*G.2998 1½" deep
G.3280 1⅝" ,,

*G.369 1½" wide
G.653 1⅞" ,,

*G.44 1⅝" wide
G.2240 2¼" ,,

*G.2718 1½" wide
G.3216 2¼" ,,

**These are half-tone blocks. All subjects not marked with an asterisk are line blocks.*

Fig 3.

MECCANO
ELECTROTYPES

3 Sizes.
No. 22. 3¾ × 3 ins.
No. 22a. 3 × 2½ ins.
No. 22b. 2¼ × 2 ins.

DURING the winter months Meccano is advertised on a big scale in all the best national publications, and the demand created is very great.

OVER 20,000,000 COPIES

of daily, weekly, and monthly publications containing attractive Meccano advertisements will be sold to the public this year, and will reach every home in the country.

It is to your interest to let the public know that you keep full stocks of Meccano and can supply all requirements. Advertise in your local papers, and give Meccano prominence in your price lists.

On this sheet are shown the illustrations which we shall use in our national advertising, and electros of any of them will be loaned to you free on request. If it will help you, we will also prepare the copy for your own advertisements and catalogues, and send it to you along with the electros. When ordering it is sufficient to quote the reference numbers of the electrotypes required. After use they are to be returned to us, and they are loaned on the understanding that they are not to be used in connection with goods other than those manufactured by us.

MECCANO, LIMITED,
LIVERPOOL.

Meccano Electrotypes.

2 Sizes.
No. C.M. 1. 2¼ × 1⅞ ins.
No. C.M. 1a. 1½ × 1⅛ ins.

No. 114.

2 Sizes.
No. 736. 3 × 1½ ins.
No. 736a. 2 × ⅞ ins.

No. 01.

No. 0. 7a.

No. 0. 7b.

No. 02.

2 Sizes.
No. E.M. 1. 2 × 2 ins.
No. E.M. 1a. 1½ × 1$\frac{5}{16}$ ins.

No. 04.

No. 0. X2.

No. 06.

Fig 4. Meccano Electrotypes. Blocks available in the early 1920s.

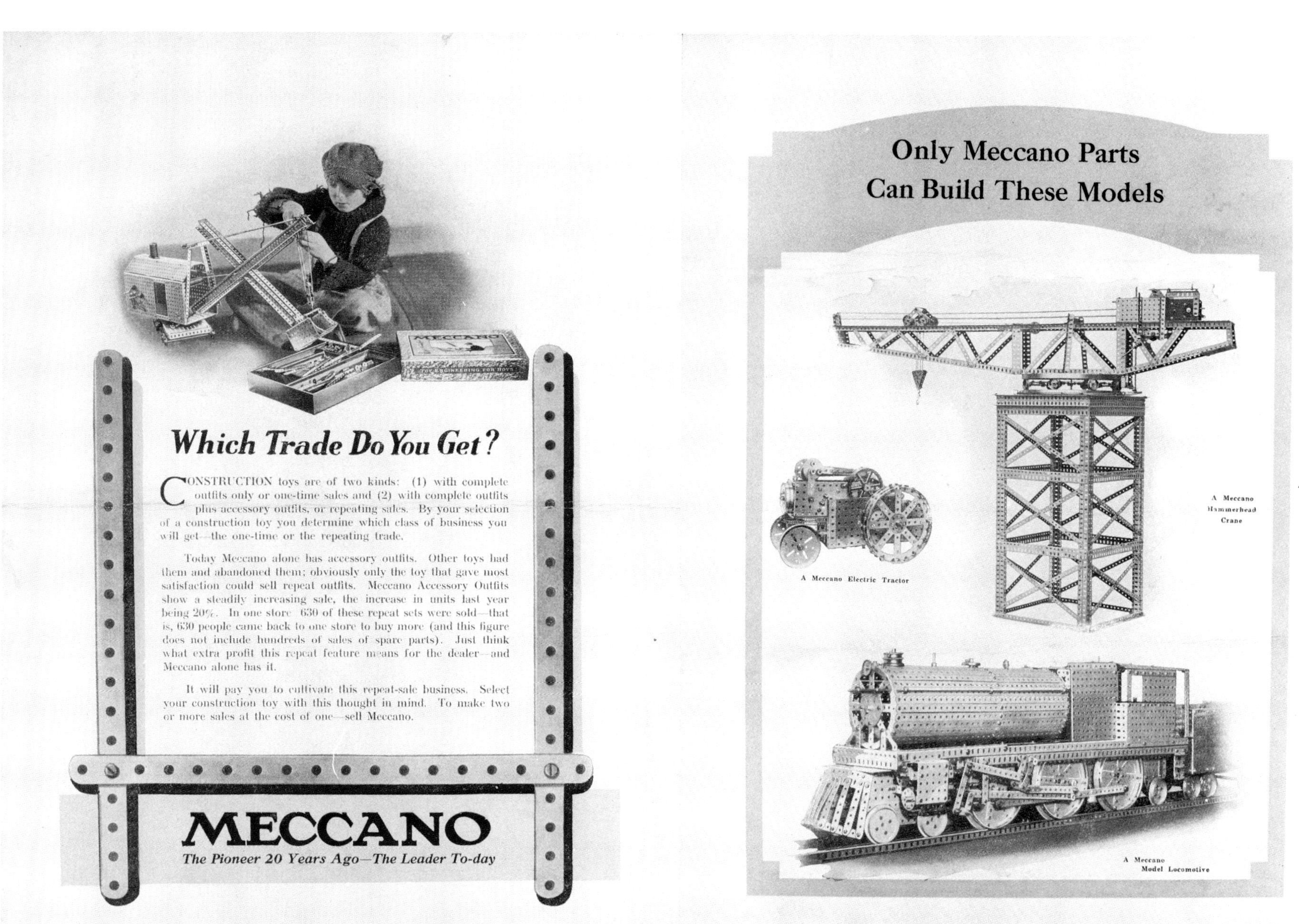

Fig 5. An American promotion booklet aimed at dealers.

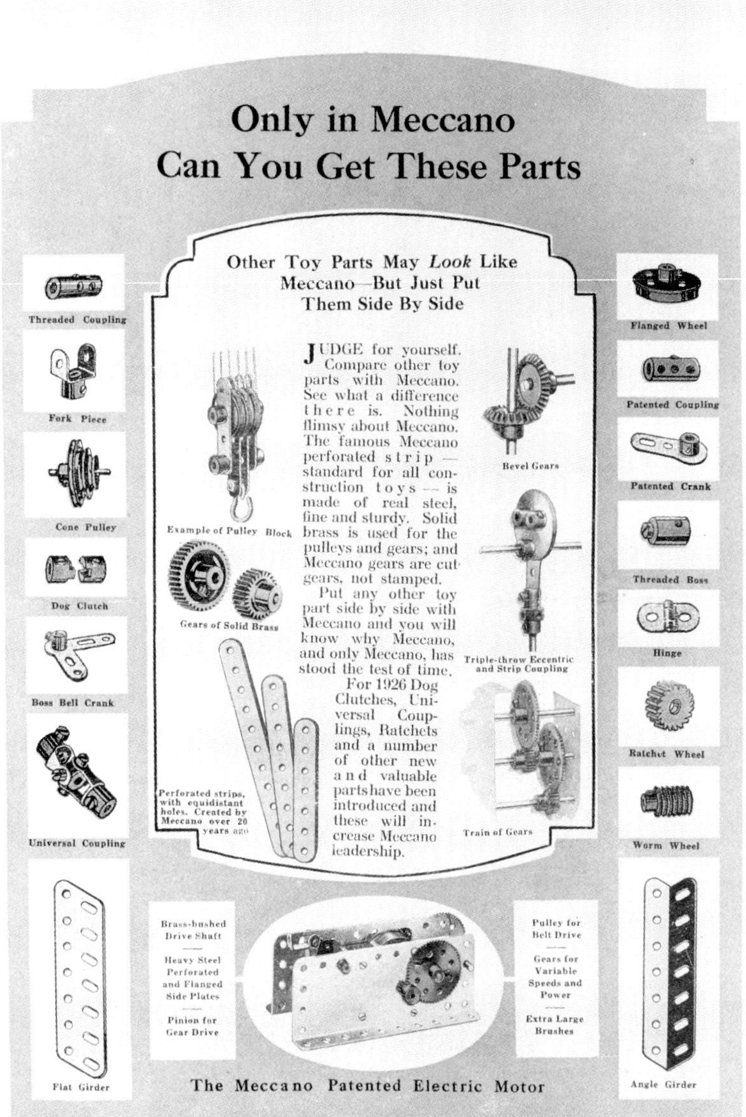

Only in Meccano
Can You Get These Parts
Other Toy Parts May *Look* Like
Meccano—But Just Put
Them Side By Side
JUDGE for yourself. Compare other toy parts with Meccano. See what a difference there is. Nothing flimsy about Meccano. The famous Meccano perforated strip — standard for all construction toys — is made of real steel, fine and sturdy. Solid brass is used for the pulleys and gears; and Meccano gears are cut gears, not stamped.
Put any other toy part side by side with Meccano and you will know why Meccano, and only Meccano, has stood the test of time.
For 1926 Dog Clutches, Universal Couplings, Ratchets and a number of other new and valuable parts have been introduced and these will increase Meccano leadership.
Example of Pulley Block
Gears of Solid Brass
Perforated strips, with equidistant holes. Created by Meccano over 20 years ago
Bevel Gears
Triple-throw Eccentric and Strip Coupling
Train of Gears
Threaded Coupling
Fork Piece
Cone Pulley
Dog Clutch
Boss Bell Crank
Universal Coupling
Flat Girder
Flanged Wheel
Patented Coupling
Patented Crank
Threaded Boss
Hinge
Ratchet Wheel
Worm Wheel
Angle Girder
Brass-bushed Drive Shaft
Heavy Steel Perforated and Flanged Side Plates
Pinion for Gear Drive
Pulley for Belt Drive
Gears for Variable Speeds and Power
Extra Large Brushes
The Meccano Patented Electric Motor

Meccano Price List

Meccano parts are packed in a series of progressive outfits numbered 00 to 6. There is no difference in the quality or finish of the parts in any of them. Each outfit contains all necessary tools and a well illustrated book of models. An unlimited number of models can be made with each set, and the manual shows only a selection of models of the most appealing kinds—such things as the alphabet and numerals are not shown.

No. 1 Meccano Outfit.............$3.00

Meccano Outfits

No. 00	Meccano Outfit		Price	$1.00
" 0	"	"	"	2.00
" 1	"	"	"	3.00
" 1X*	"	"	"	5.00
" 2	"	"	"	6.00
" 2X*	"	"	"	8.50
" 3	"	"	"	9.00
" 3X*	"	"	"	11.50
" 4 *	"	"	"	15.00
" 5 *	"	"	"	25.00
" 6 *	"	"	"	45.00

* Has electric motor.

No. 2X Meccano Outfit.........$8.50

Meccano Accessory Outfits

Meccano Accessory Outfits are the big repeat-sale feature described on the first page. Only Meccano has this feature and it is a source of constant and profitable repeat business—two or more sales at the cost of one.

No. 0A *makes a No. 0 into a No. 1*..Price $1.25
No. 1 A *makes a No. 1 into a No. 2*..Price 3.00
No. 2 A *makes a No. 2 into a No. 3*..Price 3.00
No. 3A *makes a No. 3 into a No. 4, except motor*.......Price $6.00
No. 4A *makes a No. 4 into a No. 5, except transformer*. Price 7.50
No. 5A *makes a No. 5 into a No. 6*..............Price 20.00

Accessory Outfits do not contain motors or transformers

Meccano Motors and Transformer

MECCANO ELECTRIC MOTORS

The famous Meccano Electric Motor—see illustration on second page—has been specially designed for operating Meccano models. Its heavy flanged side-plates are perforated with the Meccano equidistant holes for attaching gearing. The side-plates are not a makeshift attachment, but are an integral part of the motor—an exclusive patented Meccano feature. The driving shaft is brass-bushed, just like a big motor. Operates on 6-8 volts. The motor is furnished either with or without reversing switch and gears:

E1 Motor—One-way, with pulley and pinion ....Price $3.50
E2 Motor—Reversing, with extra gears ....Price 4.50

The Meccano Clockwork Motor

MECCANO CLOCKWORK MOTOR

A simple and sturdy motor which can be built into the models and form a rigid part of them. Equipped with start, stop and reverse levers.

Price..........$3.00

MECCANO TRANSFORMER

For operating Meccano Electric Motors direct from the house current. Simple, safe and convenient. For 110 volts, 60 cycles, alternating current only.

Price..........$2.50

A complete price list of spare parts sent on request

MECCANO COMPANY
INCORPORATED

New York Showroom—Fifth Ave. Building   Office and Factory—Elizabeth, N. J.

Fig 5.

MECCANO

The Toy that made Engineering Famous

1928—A Big Meccano Year

This will be a record Meccano year! It could not be otherwise, considering the wonderful improvements that have been made. Every Outfit is new—new presentation, new contents, new parts and new Manuals. Meccano already has the distinction of being the most famous boys' hobby in the world—this year we are confident that it will be more popular than ever.

During the coming season we are embarking on a bigger advertising campaign than any we have yet undertaken. Larger sums will be expended on advertising Meccano in the national press, supported by a new scheme for a Meccano Week and by a big Model-building Competition.

Revised Meccano Outfits

As the 1928 Meccano Outfits contain a greater number and wider selection of parts than previously, it has been found necessary to increase the prices of several of them; as already advised. Actually, there is no comparison between the tremendously increased value of the Outfits and the small increases in the prices. This will be more clearly understood when it is explained that the new No. 1 Outfit builds over 348 models whereas the old style built only 106.

The new prices come into force on the 1st September and the first announcement to the public concerning them will appear in the September number of the "*Meccano Magazine.*"

Meccano Retail Price List, 1928

Complete Outfits				Accessory Outfits			
No. 00	3/6	No. 5 (carton)	65/-	No. 00A	1/6	No. 4A	15/-
,, 0	5/-	,, 5 (cabinet)	95/-	,, 0A	5/6	,, 5A (carton)	50/-
,, 1	10/-	,, 6 (carton)	115/-	,, 1A	7/-	,, 5A (cabinet)	80/-
,, 2	16/-	,, 6 (cabinet)	150/-	,, 2A	12/6	,, 6A (cabinet)	215/-
,, 3	27/6	,, 7 (cabinet)	380/-	,, 3A	23/6	Special Inventor's Outfit	17/6
,, 4	50/-						

Meccano Super Models

This year we are giving considerable prominence to a range of Meccano super models, in connection with which we are publishing special Instruction Leaflets. The object of this special propaganda is to make known the wonderful possibilities of the Meccano system and we are certain that our efforts will result in extra sales of Outfits and Parts. We hope that dealers will co-operate with us by ordering a supply of each leaflet published and by bringing the leaflets to the notice of all their best customers.

"One of the New Super Models"

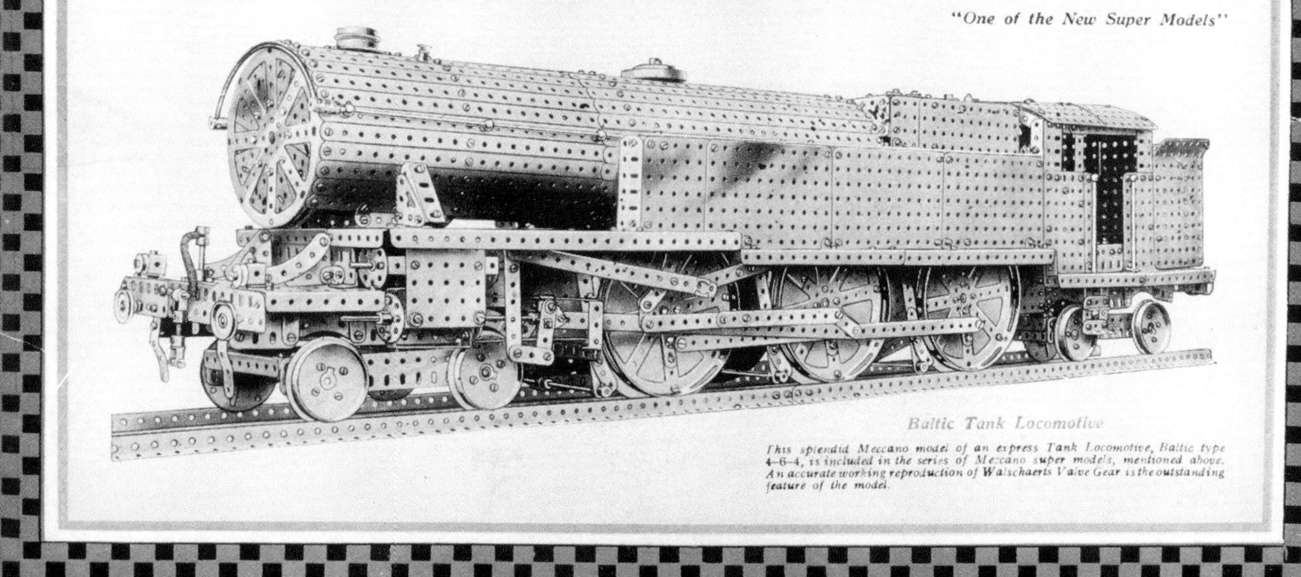

Baltic Tank Locomotive

This splendid Meccano model of an express Tank Locomotive, Baltic type 4-6-4, is included in the series of Meccano super models, mentioned above. An accurate working reproduction of Walschaerts Valve Gear is the outstanding feature of the model.

Fig 6. 1928 Trade Bulletin.

"*Meccano Magazine*" Coupon Scheme

The majority of our dealers appreciate the value of the "*Meccano Magazine*" as a sales promoter, and take every opportunity of bringing this popular monthly to the notice of their customers. We have devised a scheme that we feel sure will have a beneficial influence on Magazine sales. We are including a coupon in all Meccano Outfits from No. 1 upwards, all Hornby Train Sets from No. 1 upwards and all Hornby Locomotives from No. 1 upwards. This coupon will enable the purchaser to obtain a copy of the "*Meccano Magazine*" at half price over a period of six months. Naturally, almost every boy who buys one of the Meccano Outfits or Hornby Train Sets containing a coupon will take advantage of this generous offer. *The fact that he does so will result in his visiting your shop regularly each month for six months.* This will give you an opportunity of bringing to his notice the latest lines in Meccano and Hornby Trains.

After filling in his name and address on the back of the coupon, as directed, the boy will present it to his dealer, at the same time paying the sum of 1/6, and he will then be entitled to a copy of each of the six ensuing numbers of the Magazine. In effect he pays 3d. per copy instead of the usual 6d. The boy keeps the coupon in his possession and brings it with him each time he calls for his Magazine when the dealer will cancel the month from the list on the coupon.

When the period covered by the subscription has expired the coupon is sent in to us by the dealer, whose account is credited with 1/6, this being the difference between the amount he received from the boy and the full retail value of the six Magazines. When the coupons are sent in they should be stamped with the dealer's name and address in order to obviate mistakes.

The Magazine is an important factor in creating and maintaining interest in Meccano products. It is a silent salesman of inestimable worth and the business it brings is incalculable. Already over 50,000 copies of every issue are sold and we hope that the new scheme will rapidly increase these figures.

"*Meccano Magazine*"

Will dealers please note that, commencing with the July Number, we shall discontinue the practice of allowing 2½% settlement discount on payments against Magazine invoices. This arrangement applies to "*Meccano Magazine*" orders only.

Meccano Storage Boxes

For some time there has been a growing demand from boys for boxes suitable for storing Meccano parts. We have now introduced three different sized Storage Boxes that enable extra parts purchased by Meccano boys to be stored neatly and in such an orderly manner that they are always easily accessible. These boxes will be featured in our new Manuals and in our lists. Details are as follows:—

No. 1 Storage Box.
Stained and varnished in rich oak finish, and fitted with partitions. The lid is hinged and is secured by means of lock and key. Dimensions: Length 15¼ in. Width 8¾ in. Depth 2¾ in.
Retail price 10/6

No. 2 Storage Box.
Finished as No. 1 Box and provided with lock and key. The tray with which it is fitted enables a much larger quantity of parts to be accommodated. Dimensions: Length 14½ in. Width 11 in. Depth 3¾ in.
Retail price 21/-

No. 3 Storage Box.
Finished similarly to the No. 1 and No. 2 boxes. In addition to accommodation in the bottom section of the box there are two partitioned trays which fit neatly in position one above the other.
Dimensions: Length 20 in. Width 14 in. Depth 5¼ in.
Retail price 30/-

The Trade Discount on Meccano Storage Boxes is 15% only

New Meccano Parts

Will dealers please note that part No. 131, Dredger Bucket, will be superseded by an improved type of Bucket. The retail price of the new type Bucket is 1/- per half-dozen.

The No. 00-3, 4-7 and Standard Mechanisms Manuals are now available, attractively bound in full cloth cover, lettered in gold. This bound Manual will be packed in Outfits Nos. 6 and 7 and it will also be available for separate sales. The identification number of the Manual in the parts list is 56f. Retail price 7/6. Trade price 6/2 net.

A new screwdriver, B & S type, with long blade, will be available. The identification number of this new line is 36b. Retail price 1/-.

We are also introducing a further new part—No. 161 Girder Bracket. Size 2″ × 1″ × ½″. This part has innumerable uses in the construction of gear boxes and frames, etc. Retail price ~~2d. per pair~~.

Meccano Model-Building Competition

A Meccano Week will be a feature of our Meccano Selling scheme this year. It will take place from 30th November to 7th December—the week preceding Hornby Train Week. Our travellers will explain the project to all dealers as they make their calls and we shall publish a special notice concerning the scheme later in the year.

In order to strengthen the Meccano Week event, we are arranging for a grand £100 Meccano Model-building Competition to commence during the same week. In addition to the awards to prize winners in all classes, we are giving special cash prizes to the dealers who supply the prize-winners with their Outfits and Accessory Parts. Good supplies of entry forms will be available, free of charge, and these will be distributed only through our dealers.

New Demonstration Model

We illustrate a new model that has been added to our range of Demonstration Models. The Hanging Lantern is an attractive model, specially introduced at the request of a number of dealers, and we are sure that it will create much interest.

The price is 10/6 net, plus flex 1d. per foot net

Fig 6.

The Hornby Railway Company

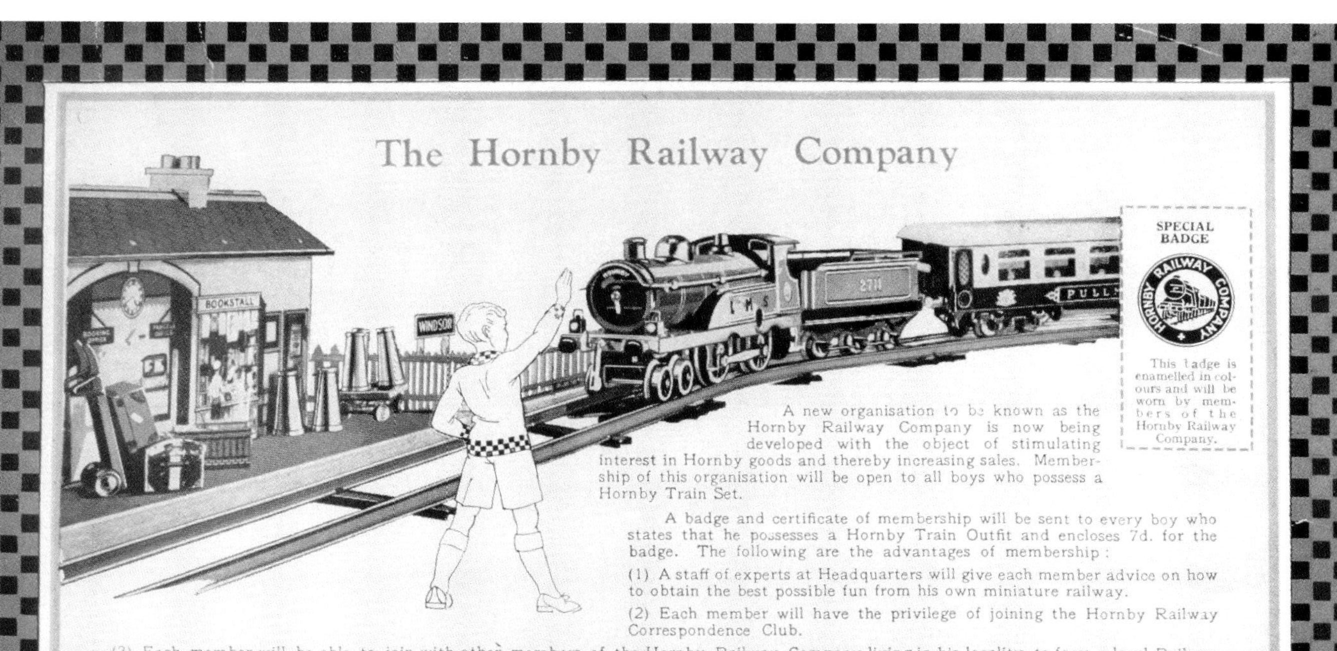

This badge is enamelled in colours and will be worn by members of the Hornby Railway Company.

A new organisation to be known as the Hornby Railway Company is now being developed with the object of stimulating interest in Hornby goods and thereby increasing sales. Membership of this organisation will be open to all boys who possess a Hornby Train Set.

A badge and certificate of membership will be sent to every boy who states that he possesses a Hornby Train Outfit and encloses 7d. for the badge. The following are the advantages of membership:

(1) A staff of experts at Headquarters will give each member advice on how to obtain the best possible fun from his own miniature railway.

(2) Each member will have the privilege of joining the Hornby Railway Correspondence Club.

(3) Each member will be able to join with other members of the Hornby Railway Company living in his locality, to form a local Railway Company of their own. Each local company will have a special name and officials and will ultimately be affiliated with the Parent Company.

As soon as we are in a position to do so, we shall give the fullest information to our dealers. We believe that the Hornby Railway Company will have the effect of greatly increasing the interest and enthusiasm of every boy who possesses a Hornby Train.

Talking Cards

A number of talking cards, artistically printed, have now been added to our range of advertising material. These cards are intended for use in connection with dealers window displays and they will be found very effective in drawing attention to the goods exhibited. A selection will be included with all stock orders and in cases where additional cards are required we shall be pleased to supply them, on request.

Three of the cards in the series are illustrated below. They measure 2½ ins. × 5 ins.

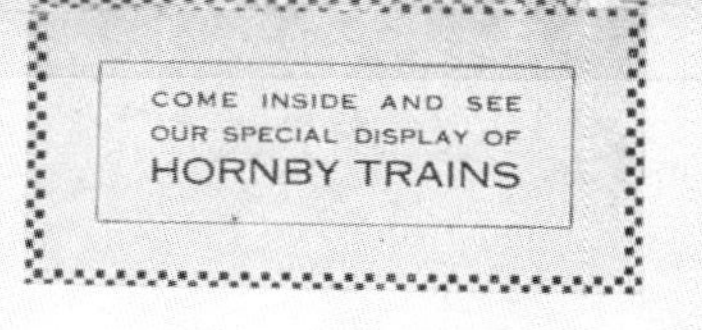

COME INSIDE AND SEE
OUR SPECIAL DISPLAY OF
HORNBY TRAINS

BUY YOUR BOY A HORNBY TRAIN FOR CHRISTMAS

Daylight Signs

Daylight signs are now popular and we believe they will become a permanent method of publicity. There is no doubt that this form of advertising is very effective and compels a great deal of attention.

For the benefit of our dealers we have been making numerous enquiries with a view to ascertaining the best source from which to obtain these signs, and we shall be pleased to give dealers all the information we have obtained, on request.

The usual type of daylight sign enables new stencils to be inserted, as required. We are able to loan (free of charge) special stencils with the wording "Meccano and Hornby Trains" for use in connection with these signs. We shall be glad if dealers who desire to take advantage of this service will communicate with us, giving the overall dimensions of the stencils required.

Control Demonstration Board No. 4

A board for demonstrating the working principle of the Hornby Control System is now available. On the board, which measures 14 ins. by 30 ins., is mounted a lever frame, point, and brake rail, as illustrated. The board is attractively finished and enables a counter demonstration of the Hornby Control System to be given without inconvenience. Price 18/- net. 31/- × 14"

Code Numbers of New Lines

A system of code numbers, covering every article we manufacture, has been introduced to facilitate the ordering of Meccano and Hornby Train goods **by telegram.** All the numbers are given in the 1928 Selling Service booklet, but since this was published in March last further new lines have been introduced and new code numbers have been allotted. These code numbers are given in the enclosed slip, which should be pasted on page 3 of the cover of the dealers' Selling Service booklet.

MECCANO LIMITED - Binns Road - LIVERPOOL

London Office and Warehouse: Walnut Tree Walk, Kennington Road, S.E.11

Fig 6.

To Meccano Dealers

November, 1929

MECCANO
The Toy that made Engineering Famous

Boys will flock to see *your* display of Meccano and Hornby Trains

The display shown here is most attractive, and it has the additional advantage of being compact. It includes both Meccano and Hornby Trains. The requisite amount of advertising material for this display (with the exception of the Meccano Outfits, the Meccano model, Hornby Train goods and crepe paper) will be sent free of charge on application.

SUGGESTIONS FOR MECCANO AND HORNBY TRAIN WINDOW DISPLAYS

This is the title of a special folder that we have prepared for the use of our dealers. It contains illustrations in half-tone of fourteen particularly attractive window displays with many useful suggestions for showing Meccano and Hornby Trains to the best advantage.

We shall be happy to send a copy to you on request.

Brighter Displays—Increased Sales

The object of this circular is to remind you that Meccano Week and Hornby Train Week will soon be here. The importance of these two events, from the retailer's point of view, cannot be too strongly emphasised. If you link up your store with our special advertising campaign you will increase your sales, and have correspondingly bigger profits.

In case you have not already made provision for a special window or counter display during Meccano Week or Hornby Train Week, please let us know. We will then send you a selection of advertising material for the purpose.

Extract from a Letter received from an enthusiastic Meccano Dealer:

"You may be pleased to hear we are doing remarkable business with Hornby Trains and Accessories. We have every reason to believe that we will enjoy a phenomenal demand for your products. We are convinced that our displays are the secret, as we have the bottom of two windows set out like a miniature railway. We run the trains round at constant intervals and this collects quite a crowd of parents and children, a large percentage of whom become 'Hornby' enthusiasts."

Fig 7. 1929 Trade Bulletin.

MECCANO WEEK

29th November to 6th December

For one week commencing 29th November we are running a special advertising campaign in the national press announcing Meccano Week. Every boy in your district will want to know all about the 1929 Meccano and will look for your display. We hope you will prepare for big business.

A proof is enclosed showing the attractiveness of the special advertisements that are being employed. Dealers' window displays are mentioned particularly in the copy, and the illustration shows an imaginary shop window with a crowd of typical Meccano boys keenly interested in the model displayed.

In conjunction with this press advertising our dealers are distributing over 100,000 special cards, inviting parents and boys to visit their establishments. This big propaganda will be supported by screen advertising and by the use of special showcards, window streamers and other display matter. The "*Meccano Magazine*," with 250,000 readers, will also add its weight and influence to make the scheme a success.

The Meccano Week proved its worth last season, when it was a huge success. We confidently invite your co-operation again this year in order to make the 1929 event even more successful.

The New Meccano Steam Engine

It is already evident that the new Meccano Steam Engine will be a popular line, and a big seller. This Steam Engine is specially designed for building into and driving Meccano models. When suitably geared it is capable of developing remarkable power, sufficient to drive any of the models shown in the Meccano Manuals.

The Meccano Steam Engine is being featured very prominently in all our advertising literature and every Meccano boy should have its many unique advantages explained to him.

Retail Price 21/–

We are sending you a copy of the new window streamer that has been prepared advertising this engine. Will you please give this a place in your display.

The New Meccano Steam Engine

Meccano Dunlop Tyres

Meccano Dunlop Tyres are very popular with all Meccano model-builders. They are now obtainable in four different sizes as follows:—

Part No.		Price each
142a,	2″ Dunlop Tyre, to fit 2″ Pulleys	4½d.
142b,	3″ ,, ,, ,, 3″ ,, ...	6d.
142c,	1″ ,, ,, ,, 1″ ,, ...	3d.
142d,	1½″ ,, ,, ,, 1½″ ,, ...	4d.

The tyres are specially made for Meccano Limited by the Dunlop Rubber Co. Ltd., and they are perfect miniature reproductions of the famous Dunlop Cord Tyres. They will be advertised specially in forthcoming issues of the "*Meccano Magazine*" and we advise you to stock an assortment in order to meet the steady demand that will be created.

Meccano Dunlop Tyres

Alterations to Meccano Parts

The price of Part No. 104, Shuttles for Looms, has been reduced from 7/6 to 5/–.

It has been necessary to increase the price of Part No. 142a, Dunlop Tyre to fit 2″ rim, from 4d. to 4½d.

Meccano Retail Price List for 1929

COMPLETE OUTFITS

No. 00 Outfit	**3/6**	No. 5 Outfit (carton)	**65/–**
,, 0 ,, ...	**5/–**	,, 5 ,, (enamelled cabinet)	**95/–**
,, 1 ,, ...	**10/–**	,, 6 ,, (carton)	**115/–**
,, 2 ,, ...	**16/–**	,, 6 ,, (enamelled cabinet)	**150/–**
,, 3 ,, ...	**27/6**	,, 7 ,, ,, ,,	**365/–**
,, 4 ,, ...	**50/–**		

ACCESSORY OUTFITS

No. 00a Accessory Outfit...	**1/6**	No. 4a Accessory Outfit	**15/–**
,, 0a ,, ,, ...	**5/6**	,, 5a ,, ,, (carton)	**50/–**
,, 1a ,, ,, ...	**7/–**	,, 5a ,, ,, (enamelled cabinet)	**80/–**
,, 2a ,, ,, ...	**12/6**	,, 6a ,, ,, ,,	**200/–**
,, 3a ,, ,, ...	**23/6**	Special Inventor's Outfit ...	**17/6**

MECCANO MOTORS, etc.

Meccano Clockwork Motor	**7/6**	Meccano Steam Engine...	**21/–**	Meccano Accumulator (6-volt, 20 amps) ...	**28/6**
Meccano No. 1 Electric Motor (6-volt) ...	**15/6**	Resistance Controller	**3/6**	Transformer	**30/–**

Fig 7.

HORNBY TRAINS

British and Guaranteed

HORNBY TRAIN WEEK

From
6th December
to
13th December

Meccano Week will be followed by a special Hornby Train Week, which will begin on the 6th December and end on the 13th December.

During Hornby Train Week our press advertising in National publications will be intensified, large spaces having been booked to appear in all the leading daily newspapers and weekly periodicals. The style of layout we are using in this important campaign is exceptionally effective, as you will see on looking at the enclosed proof. The first part of the copy is similar to that used for the Meccano Week advertisement, considerable emphasis being laid on the fact that big displays are on view at all dealers' shops. We urge you to identify your shop with this big advertising campaign by making a special display of Hornby Trains in your window and also inside your shop.

The leading toy dealers in the United Kingdom are taking part in this great campaign. They are backing up our efforts by local advertising, by using the lantern slides we loan in cinemas and theatres, by distributing Hornby Train literature, and by making good use of the showcards, window streamers and other display matter that we supply. In addition, they are inviting thousands of boys to visit their establishments in order to see the special displays of Hornby Trains and Accessories.

The result of this advertising will be a greatly increased demand for Hornby Trains and Accessories during the Christmas shopping season. We hope you will again help us to make the event an outstanding success.

Boys!
HORNBY TRAIN WEEK
will soon be here
DURING THE PERIOD 6TH–13TH DEC
WE ARE ARRANGING A SPECIAL
DISPLAY OF HORNBY TRAINS.
YOU ARE CORDIALLY INVITED TO
THIS EXHIBIT. MAKE A NOTE OF
THE DATE.
Prices of Hornby Trains
from 6/- to 95/-

A Special Lantern Slide

The lantern slide reproduced here is intended to create interest in Hornby Train Week before the event takes place. Boys who see the slide reproduced on the screen will look forward to this special week and will tell all their chums about it. In this manner, we believe, excellent publicity will be obtained.

If you can make use of one of these special slides (supplied free, on loan) kindly let us know **by return o' post** so that we can effect delivery in good time. The preparation of the slides requires a few days.

Retail Price List of Hornby Trains for 1929

CLOCKWORK

MO Passenger Set	6/-	Hornby No. 1 Goods Set	20/-	Hornby No. 2 Special Pullman Set	55/-
M1 „ „	7/6	„ „ 1 Passenger Set	25/-	„ „ No. 2 Mixed Goods Set	37/6
M2 „ „	9/-	„ „ 1 Special Goods Set	30/-	„ „ 3 C Train Set (L.M.S., L.N.E.R., G.W., or S.R.)	60/-
M Goods Set	8/6	„ „ 1 Special Passenger Set	32/6	Hornby No. 3C Train Set (Riviera "Blue")	62/6
Hornby No. O Goods Set	15/-	„ „ 1 Tank Goods Set	22/6	Metropolitan Train Set C	55/-
„ „ O Passenger Set	15/-	„ „ 2 Special Goods Set	35/-		

ELECTRIC (6-volt)

Hornby No. 3E Train Set (L.M.S., L.N.E.R., G.W., S.R.), **75/-** | Hornby No. 3E Train Set (Riviera "Blue"), **77/6** | Metropolitan Train Set L.V., **95/-**

 Fig 7.

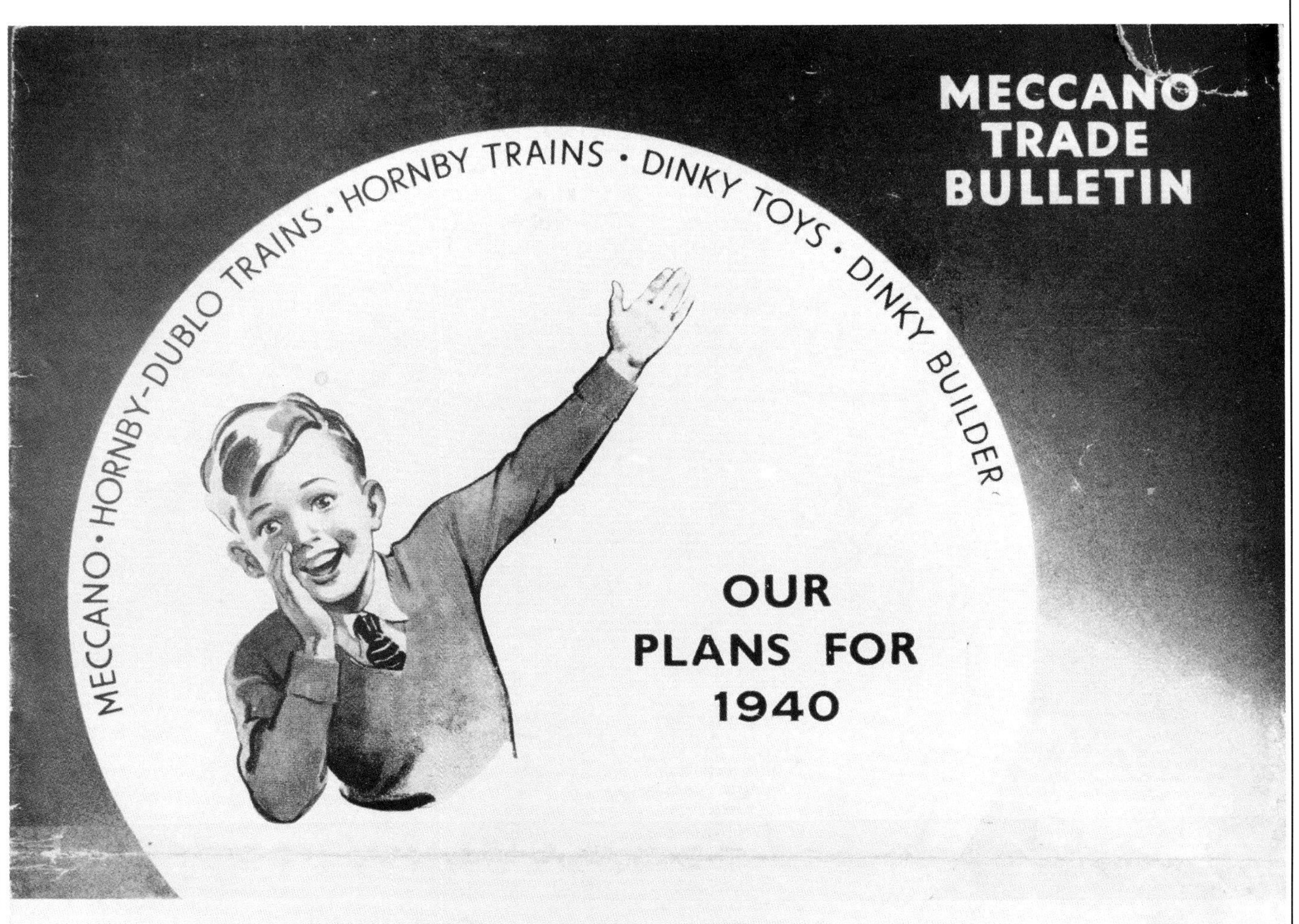

MECCANO
TRADE
BULLETIN
MECCANO · HORNBY-DUBLO TRAINS · HORNBY TRAINS · DINKY TOYS · DINKY BUILDER
OUR
PLANS FOR
1940

TO MECCANO DEALERS

One of the most difficult problems in the Toy Trade at present is that of forecasting what is going to happen next season. There is little definite knowledge to work upon, but there are one or two factors that seem fairly sure. Our Government have announced that they are preparing for a war of at least three years' duration; and they warn us not to indulge in easy optimism, but to brace ourselves for the grim struggle ahead. It seems pretty certain that the war will last at least until 1941.

Our own view of the position as it will be at the end of the year is that unemployment will be almost non-existent, and that in spite of heavy taxation, trade will be reasonably good. The supplies of imported toys available will be so small as to be negligible, and there will be a shortage of home products due to the scarcity of available labour and raw materials. We feel so strongly that this view of the situation is correct that before and since Christmas we have pushed forward the manufacture of all our best lines at highest pressure, and we shall continue to do so as long as possible.

We are faced with certain difficulties. One is that all our plant that is suitable for the purpose is on Government work, and cannot be used on our own products. A second difficulty is that metals are strictly rationed. We cannot count on supplies for more than a few weeks ahead, and as time goes on rationing is becoming more strict. Still another trouble is that supplies of cardboard for making boxes - a very important commodity indeed - are also becoming scarcer, and the quality is deteriorating. We shall just go on manufacturing as long as possible; but it is unlikely that we shall be able to complete sufficient stocks to take care of the season's trade.

We increased our prices on 1st January, and we are glad to say there is no immediate prospect of a further increase. Nevertheless, rising costs of raw material and increased rates of pay to employees may compel us to revise our prices again at a later stage.

Most of the big Stores and other large retailers are buying well ahead, and this appears to be the wise course. If we could buy our own raw materials ahead for twelve months we should certainly do so. From the retailers' point of view the things to be feared are scarcity of goods, deterioration in quality, rising prices and slow and uncertain transport. Where finances permit, the purchase of suitable goods at the present moment is a sound investment.

In a short time we shall be in a position to commence deliveries of stock orders. Our representatives, who will call on as many of our dealers as travelling conditions permit, are instructed to accept season's orders for delivery as soon as the goods are ready, on current monthly account; and these orders will be executed in full, as long as we are in a position to supply. We believe the best advice we can give to Meccano dealers is that they should safeguard their businesses in this way, as far as their financial situation allows. All goods will be charged at the prices ruling at the time of despatch.

Meccano Ltd.

Fig 8. 1940 Trade Bulletin.

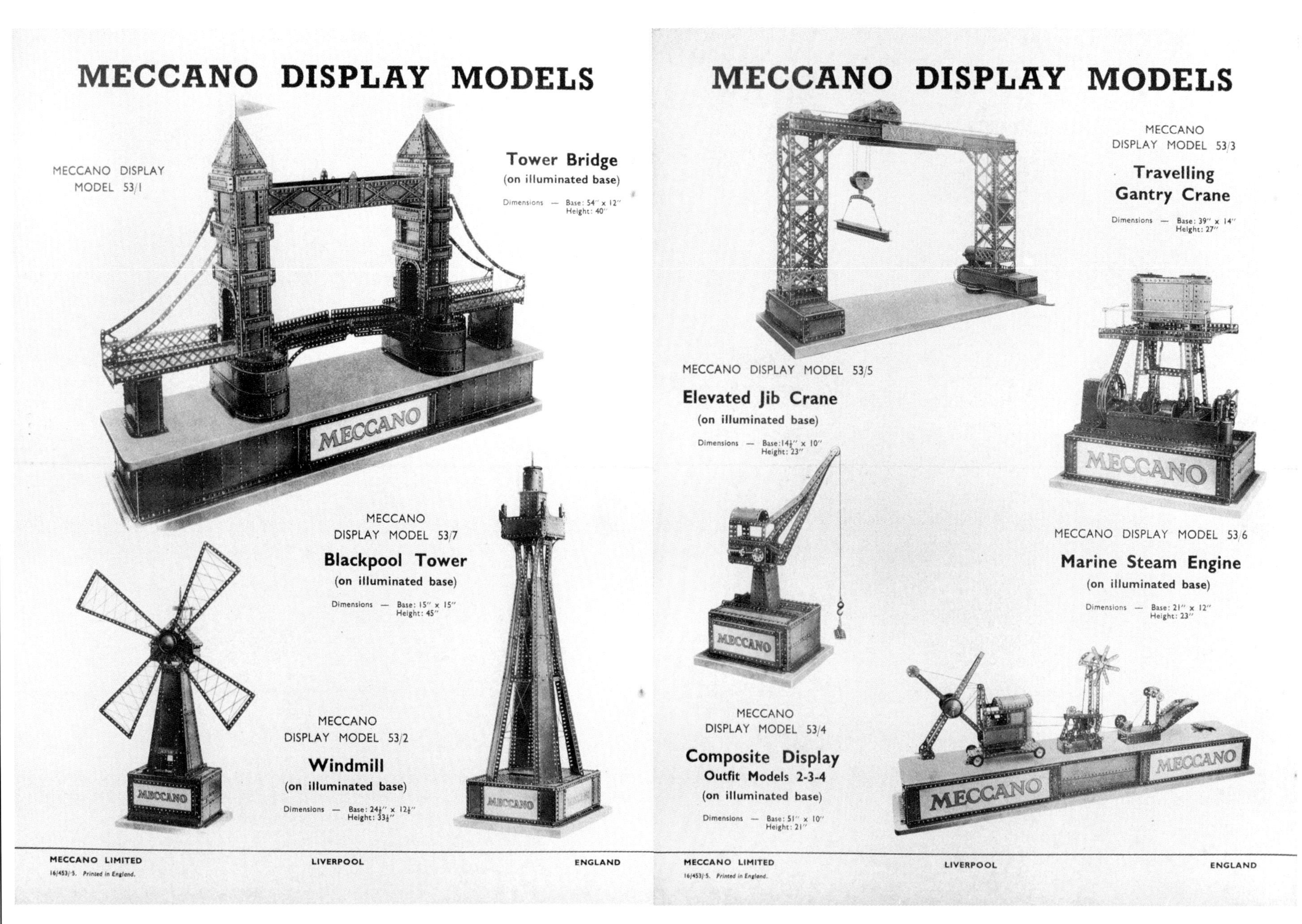

MECCANO DISPLAY MODELS
MECCANO DISPLAY MODEL 53/1
Tower Bridge
(on illuminated base)
Dimensions — Base: 54" x 12" Height: 40"
MECCANO
MECCANO DISPLAY MODEL 53/7
Blackpool Tower
(on illuminated base)
Dimensions — Base: 15" x 15" Height: 45"
MECCANO DISPLAY MODEL 53/2
Windmill
(on illuminated base)
Dimensions — Base: 24½" x 12½" Height: 33½"
MECCANO
MECCANO
MECCANO LIMITED
LIVERPOOL
ENGLAND
16/453/5. Printed in England.
MECCANO DISPLAY MODELS
MECCANO DISPLAY MODEL 53/3
Travelling Gantry Crane
Dimensions — Base: 39" x 14" Height: 27"
MECCANO DISPLAY MODEL 53/5
Elevated Jib Crane
(on illuminated base)
Dimensions — Base: 14½" x 10" Height: 23"
MECCANO
MECCANO
MECCANO DISPLAY MODEL 53/6
Marine Steam Engine
(on illuminated base)
Dimensions — Base: 21" x 12" Height: 23"
MECCANO DISPLAY MODEL 53/4
Composite Display
Outfit Models 2-3-4
(on illuminated base)
Dimensions — Base: 51" x 10" Height: 21"
MECCANO
MECCANO
MECCANO LIMITED
LIVERPOOL
ENGLAND
16/453/5. Printed in England.

Fig 9. 1953 display models.

Coles of Sheffield

"MECCANO" MODEL COMPETITION:

For Boys and Girls

CLASSES

A Models built with a No. D Outfit (costing 15/-) or with only the parts to be found in that outfit.

B Models built with a No. F Outfit (costing 30/-) or with only the parts to be found in that Outfit.

C Models built with any Outfit or with any number of parts. This is the "No Limit Class"!

PRIZES:

CLASS A.—1st Prize—Voucher for goods value 10/-
2nd Prize—Voucher for 5/-
CLASS B.—1st Prize—Voucher for goods value 10/-
2nd Prize—Voucher for 5/-
CLASS C.—1st Prize—Voucher for goods value £1.
2nd Prize—Voucher for 10/-

Closing Date - - - October 31st, 1936
Presentation of Prizes - November 7th, 1936

Tie to Model here:

ENTRY FORM:

Class.......... Title of Model..........

Any special features claimed..........

....

Age of Entrant on Nov. 7th.......... Years.......... Months

★ *I declare that this model is my own unaided work. I accept the conditions governing the competition, and the decision of the judge as final.*

Signature..........

Address..........

The CHILDREN'S THIRD FLOOR at "Coles of Sheffield"

TELEPHONE 21071

TELEGRAMS "COLE SHEFFIELD"

12th. October 1936.

Dear Jumbo Member,

I expect you have often seen a train running, or a Meccano model, working in the Toy Department on the Children's Third Floor. Well, this Christmas we have such a lot of fine things to show you, that we have had to move upstairs to the Fourth Floor, where the whole of our "Exhibition Room" is already full of Meccano and model trains.

When you come you will find several fine Meccano models, and two large railways. One of them is our special test track, and on it I shall be very pleased to try out your present engine (free, of course!). You will discover too that there are more fine trains than ever, including an American Streamliner-which whistles!- the new 00 gauge trains (with engines no higher than a matchbox), all the Hornby and Lionel trains, and a fine display of Milbro' Sheffield made models. These last are just like the real thing, and include a new type of steel track on wooden sleepers which is so strong that you can stand on it, and which has been made specially for Lionel and Hornby rolling stock.

And last, but by no means least, there is our Meccano competition. All details are on the leaflet enclosed, and I'm expecting to receive a model from you.

Come and see us as soon as you can, and get your copy of the new catalogue.

Yours sincerely,

LAWRENCE ROGERS.

Model Engineering Dept.
Fourth floor.

Cole Brothers Ltd. (One of the Selfridge Stores) Church Street & Fargate, Sheffield.

Fig 10. A dealer's initiative from 1936.

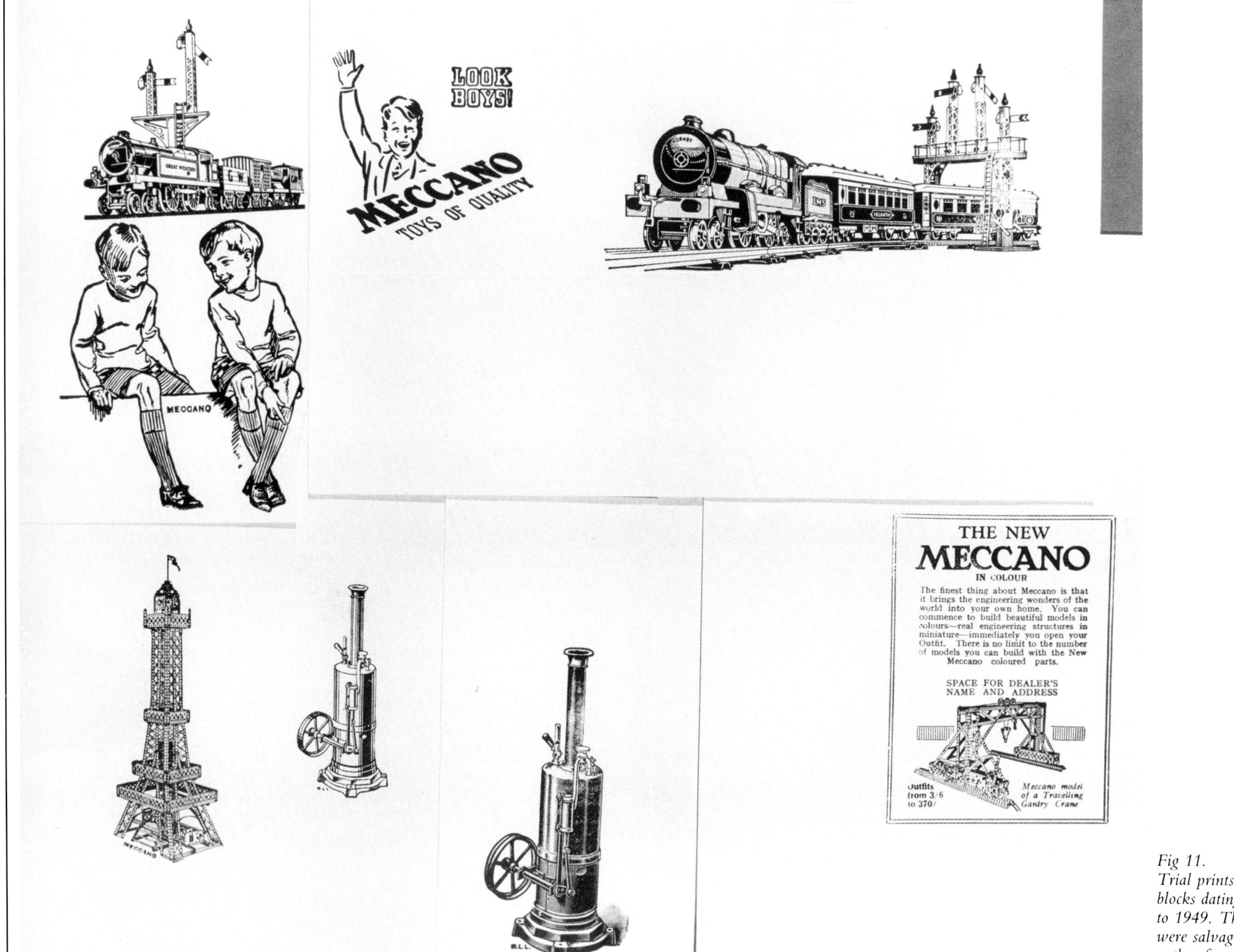

Fig 11.
Trial prints from printing blocks dating from 1918 to 1949. These blocks were salvaged by the author from a shop which was giving up business.

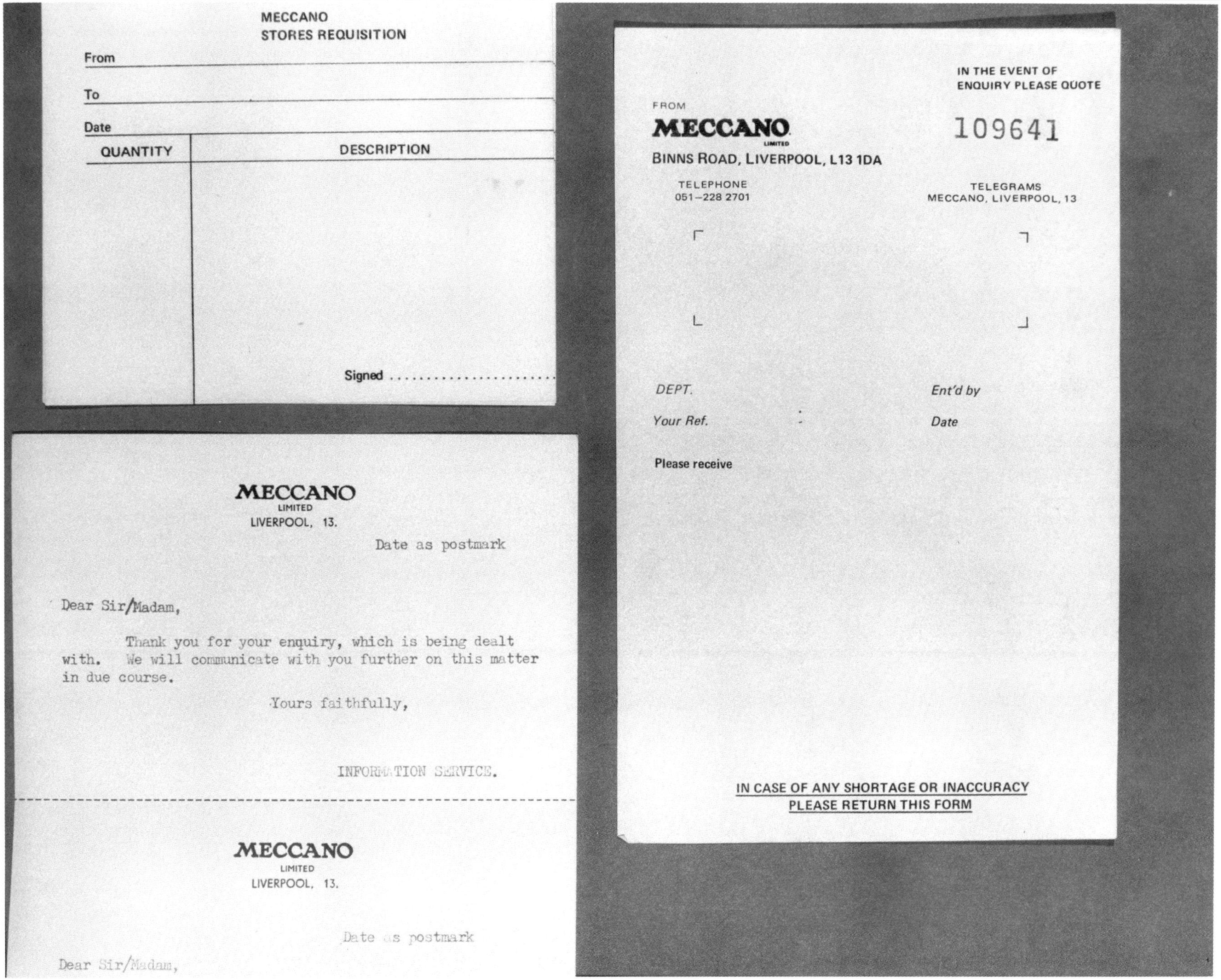

MECCANO
STORES REQUISITION

From

To

Date

QUANTITY	DESCRIPTION

Signed ....

MECCANO
LIMITED
LIVERPOOL, 13.

Date as postmark

Dear Sir/Madam,

Thank you for your enquiry, which is being dealt with. We will communicate with you further on this matter in due course.

Yours faithfully,

INFORMATION SERVICE.

MECCANO
LIMITED
LIVERPOOL, 13.

Date as postmark

Dear Sir/Madam,

IN THE EVENT OF
ENQUIRY PLEASE QUOTE

109641

FROM
MECCANO
LIMITED
BINNS ROAD, LIVERPOOL, L13 1DA

TELEPHONE
051–228 2701

TELEGRAMS
MECCANO, LIVERPOOL, 13

DEPT.

Ent'd by

Your Ref.

Date

Please receive

IN CASE OF ANY SHORTAGE OR INACCURACY
PLEASE RETURN THIS FORM

Fig 12. Various factory items from the 1950s.

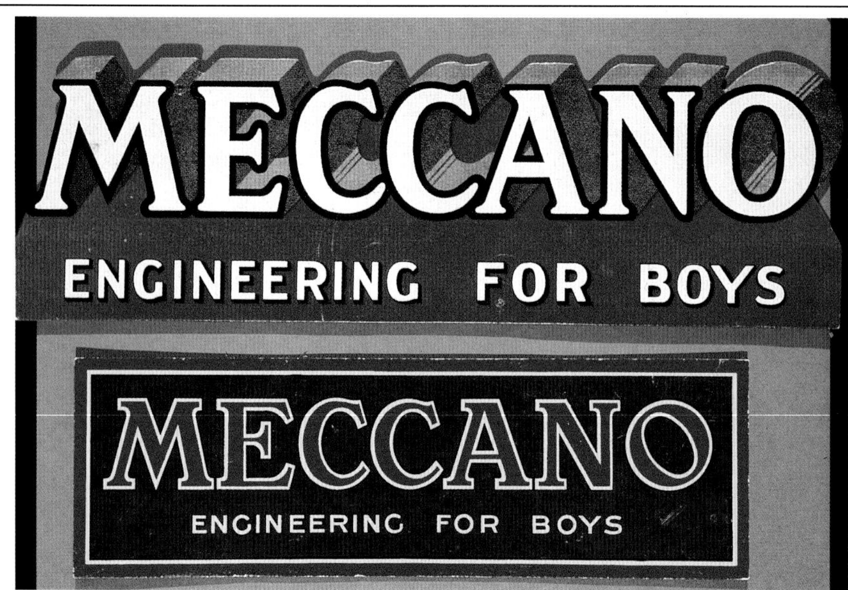

Fig 13. *Two showcards as advertised in Our Selling Service.*

MECCANO
THE NEW MECCANO
ALL COLOURED NEW PARTS
BETTER MODELS
70/-
HORNBY
11/6
4/-
MECCANO
17/6 MECCANO
MECCANO
OUTFIT No. 0
5/-
MECCANO
MECCANO
ELECTRIC MOTOR No. 2
(100-250-Volt A. or D.C.)
32/6
MECCANO
MECCANO
EASIEST MODEL-BUILDING METHOD
"You Just Count the Holes"
Nuts, Bolts
Clips, Etc.
8/6 HORNBY
MECCANO
ELECTRIC MOTOR No. 1
(4-Volt)
15/6

Fig 15. *Various trade and other related ephemera.*

MECCANO

PRICE LIST

MECCANO COMPLETE OUTFITS		MECCANO ACCESSORY OUTFITS	
X Series Outfit No. 1 ...	1/3	X Series Accessory Outfit No. 1a	1/-
X ,, ,, No. 2 ...	2/-	No. 00a Accessory Outfit	1/6
No. 000 ,, ...	2/6	,, 0a ,, ,, ...	5/6
,, 00 ,, ...	3/6	,, 1a ,, ,, ...	7/-
,, 0 ,, ...	5/-	,, 2a ,, ,, ...	12/6
,, 1 ,, ...	10/-	,, 3a ,, ,, ...	26/-
,, 2 ,, ...	16/-	,, 4a ,, ,, ...	17/6
,, 3 ,, ...	27/6	,, 5a ,, ,, (carton)	55/-
,, 4 ,, ...	52/6	,, 6a ,, ,, (cabinet)	225/-
,, 5 ,, ... (carton)	70/-		
,, 5 ,, ... (cabinet)	100/-		
,, 6 ,, ... (carton)	125/-		
,, 6 ,, ... (cabinet)	155/-		
,, 7 ,, ... (cabinet)	415/-		

MECCANO MOTORS

X Clockwork Motor (non-reversing)	2/6	E1/20 Electric Motor (20-Volt, non-reversing)	10/-
No. 1 Clockwork Motor ,,	5/-	E6 Electric Motor (6-Volt, reversing)	15/6
,, 1a Clockwork Motor (reversing)	7/6	E20a Electric Motor (20-Volt, non-reversing)	16/6
,, 2 Clockwork Motor ,,	10/-	E20b Electric Motor (20-Volt, reversing)	18/6
E1 Electric Motor (6 Volt, non-reversing)	9/-	Steam Engine	25/-

MECCANO AEROPLANE CONSTRUCTOR OUTFITS

No. 0 Aeroplane Outfit ...	5/-	No. 1 Special Aeroplane Outfit	15/-
,, 1 Aeroplane Outfit ...	9/-	,, 1a Special Aeroplane Accessory Outfit	11/6
,, 1a Aeroplane Accessory Outfit	8/6	,, 2 Special Aeroplane Outfit	25/-
,, 2 Aeroplane Outfit ...	16/6		

MECCANO AERO MOTORS

No. 1 Aero Clockwork Motor	2/-	No. 2 Aero Clockwork Motor	4/6

MECCANO MOTOR CAR CONSTRUCTOR OUTFITS

No. 1 Motor Car Outfit ...	14/6	No. 2 Motor Car Outfit ...	25/-

ELEKTRON ELECTRICAL OUTFITS

No. 1 Elektron Outfit ...	8/6	No. 1a Elektron Accessory Outfit	16/6
No. 2 Elektron Outfit ...	25/-		

KEMEX CHEMICAL OUTFITS

No. 1 Kemex Outfit	7/6	No. 2 Kemex Outfit	15/-	No. 3 Kemex Outfit	25/-

6/633/7 MECCANO LIMITED — BINNS ROAD — LIVERPOOL 13 U.K.

Fig 14. *A card price list of 1933.*

Fig 16.
A magnificent showcard advertising the car constructor outfits.

Hurrah! right away
Working Model of a Girder Crane
MECCANO
Engineering for Boys,
Give your Boy a Meccano to-day
Complete Outfits 5/- to 370/-

ENGINEERING FOR BOYS
BEAUTIFUL MODELS IN COLOURS
MECCANO
COMPLETE OUTFITS FROM 3/6 TO 365/-
WE CARRY FULL STOCKS
CRASKE & SMITH
191 Cleethorpe Road
GRIMSBY

MECCANO
REAL ENGINEERING IN MINIATURE
THE FINEST HOBBY IN THE WORLD FOR BOYS
PRICES OF COMPLETE OUTFITS FROM 2/6 TO 450/-
H. STANLEY
75 Fleetgate
BARTON-ON-HUMBER

YOU CAN BUILD ANY MODEL YOU LIKE WITH
MECCANO
ENGINEERING FOR BOYS
COMPLETE OUTFITS FROM 3/6 to 365/-
WE CARRY FULL STOCKS
MODEL TANK LOCO MADE OF MECCANO PARTS
CRASKE & SMITH
191 Cleethorpe Road
GRIMSBY

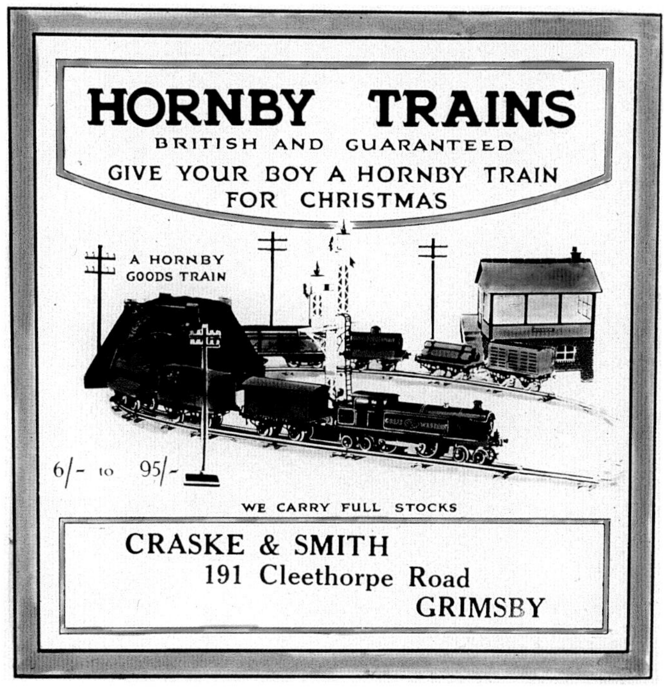

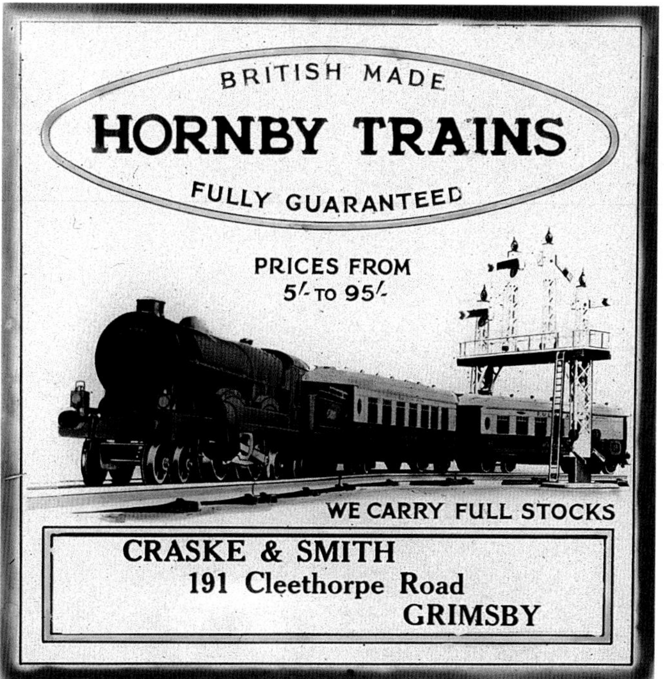

Fig 17. A group of seven glass lantern slides used for cinema advertising. These are amongst the most beautiful of all Meccano items.

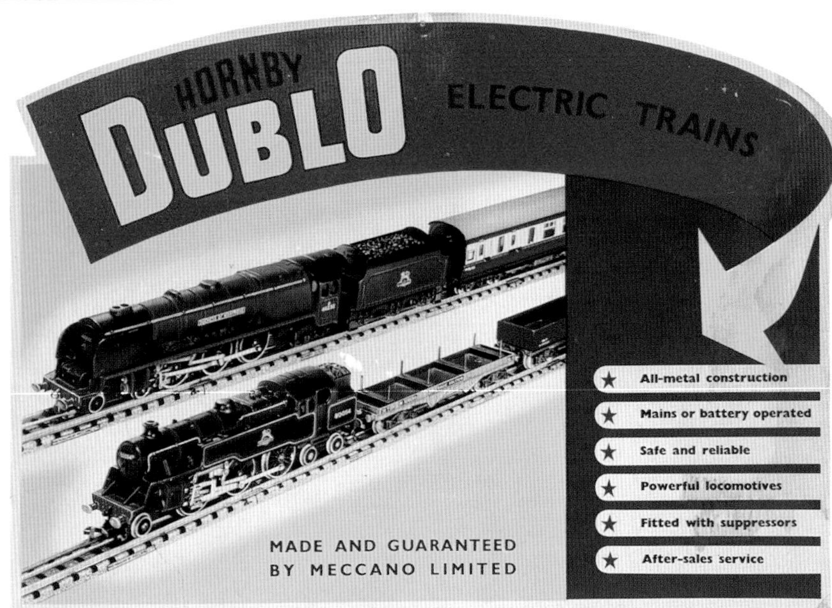

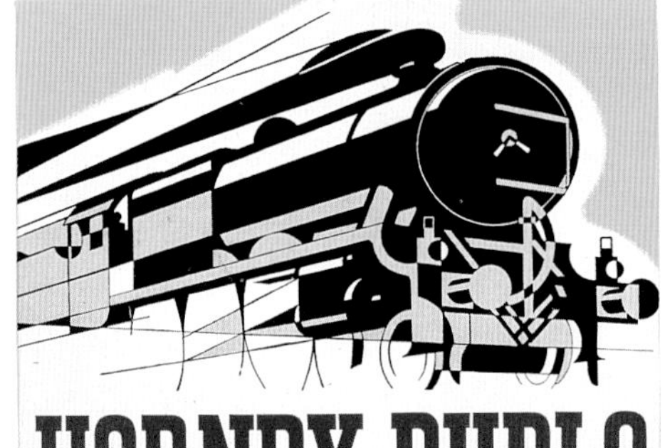

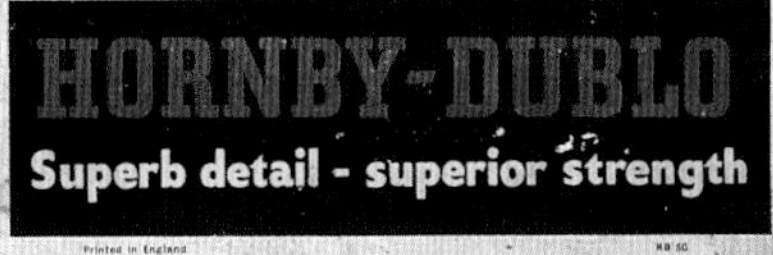

A selection of Hornby Dublo showcards.

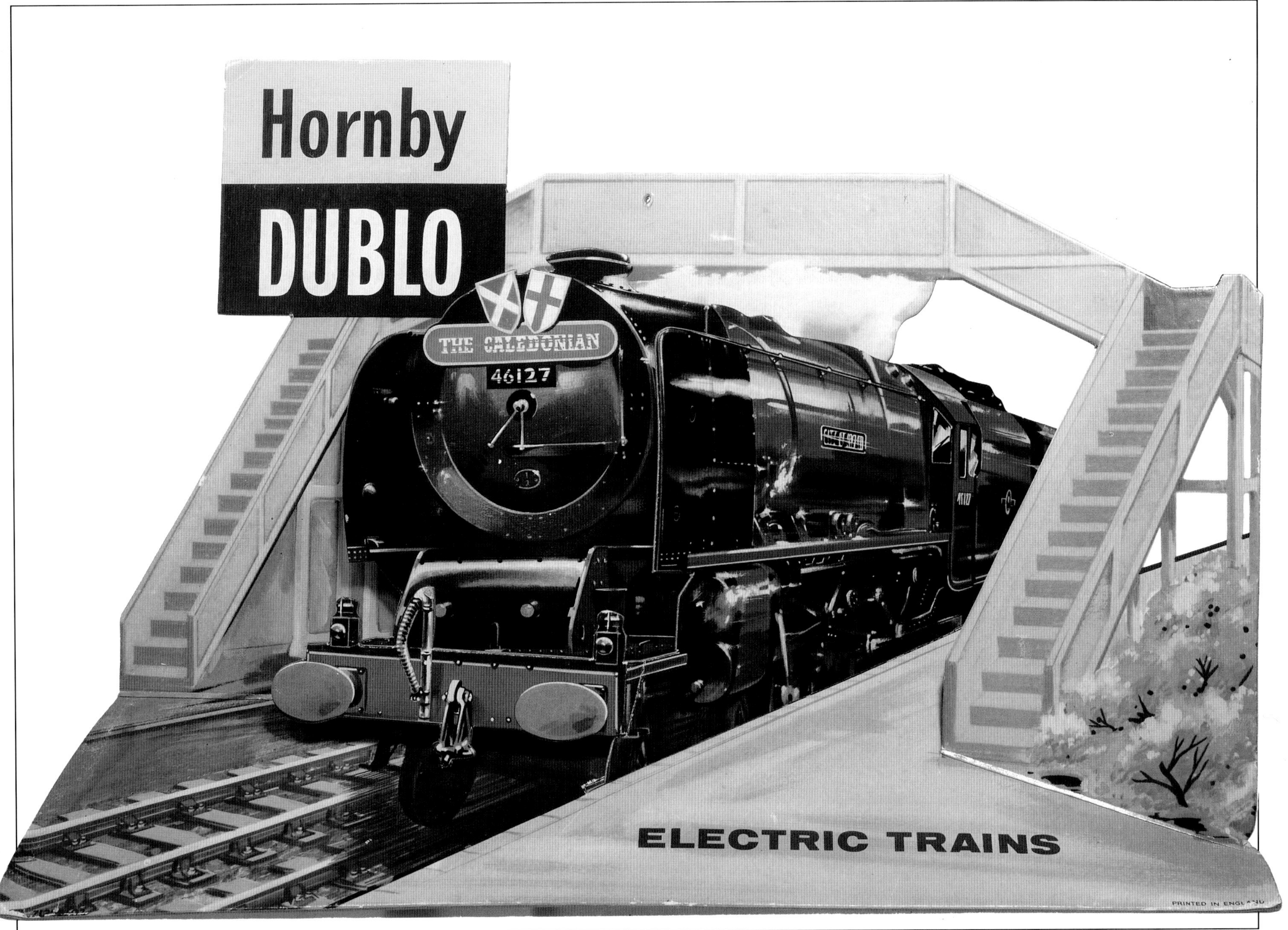
Hornby
DUBLO
THE CALEDONIAN
46127
ELECTRIC TRAINS
PRINTED IN ENGLAND

MECCANO
The Magic Carpet

The Magic Carpet

EVERY boy who has read the "Arabian Nights" knows the story of Prince Houssain's carpet and how everyone who stood on it had only to express the wish, and he was instantly whisked off to any part of the world he wanted to see. Most boys have thought what a wonderful time they would have if only they owned such a carpet. Well! even fairy tales come true sometimes and this one has surely been realized.

Any carpet with Meccano and a boy on it becomes a Magic Carpet. The boy can wish himself into a workshop filled with fascinating and ingenious machinery; into a factory where he can weave his own gorgeously coloured silks and into hundreds of other places equally entrancing. He can wish for Automobiles, great Bridges, Looms, Cranes that raise and lower real loads and which he can operate himself. *And all his wishes come true!*

Prince Houssain's Carpet was not half so wonderful as the Meccano Magic Carpet. His was only imaginary, but the Meccano Carpet is *real*. It is ready now to take you into lands of brightness, joy, and fun. Step on to it, boys, and commence wishing!

WHEN a boy takes up Meccano he begins his life afresh in a land of pleasure and brightness. A Meccano boy's life is different from the life of any other boy. He is a member of a great community of a million other boys, all friends, all with interests, pleasures and work in common. They live in a wonderful world of their own. They have their own newspaper, their clubs and meeting places. They are members of a Guild of boys who have sworn to extend the hand of friendship to each other, to play and work together and to live clean and upright lives. They have their badges so that they may recognize and know each other wherever they may meet.

The bond which unites them in such close harmony is Meccano, the building system invented by Frank Hornby twenty years ago and now brought to an extraordinary state of perfection. This book will tell you all about the Meccano hobby, what it is, and what it will do. If you do not actively pursue this hobby you are missing endless fun and pleasure and sacrificing the friendship and help of a million other clever and contented boys. You are also depriving the other boys of your friendship and help. They want you, and they ask you to join them in their happy pursuits.

MECCANO

Engineering for Boys

The Meccano system is composed of some two hundred different parts, mostly made of steel or brass, and each one has a specified mechanical purpose. The parts combine to form a complete miniature engineering system with which practically any movement known in mechanics may be duplicated.

The finest machines are used in the manufacture of Meccano parts, which are all standardized and interchangeable. The steel parts are heavily coated with nickel and the brass parts are finely finished and lacquered.

By employing these parts any boy may build all the hundreds of working models shown in the Meccano literature—and this without previous knowledge or study. He may build Cranes, Wagons, Bridges, Towers, etc., using the same parts over and over again. A fully-illustrated Book of Instructions is included in each Outfit, and he is in no difficulty at any time.

The training of the eye, brain, and hand in erecting Meccano models is considerable, and there is also developed a faculty of immense value to every boy. No Meccano boy is content to build the models just as he finds them ; it is always possible to improve, and he sets to work to do this almost at once. It is a boy's nature to venture into unknown fields, and the Meccano hobby opens up a new and wide world for him to explore. He very soon proceeds to invent, and new models and designs, the creation of his own brain, make their appearance.

How to Begin

For convenience Meccano parts are sold in nine Outfits of varying size, numbered 00 to 7. The quality and finish of the parts are of the same high standard throughout the series, but as the Outfits increase in size they contain larger quantities and greater varieties of parts. Each Outfit may be converted into the one next higher by the purchase of an Accessory Outfit (see page 6). Thus, if a No. 2 is the first Outfit bought, it may be converted into a No. 3 by adding to it a No. 2A. A No. 3A would then convert it into a No. 4 and so on up to No. 7. In this way, no matter with what Outfit the boy commences, he may build it up by degrees to a No. 7 and so be able to make all of the many hundreds of models shown in the Books of Instructions.

The separate Meccano parts may be bought at any time in any quantity (see pages 19 and 20).

MECCANO OUTFITS

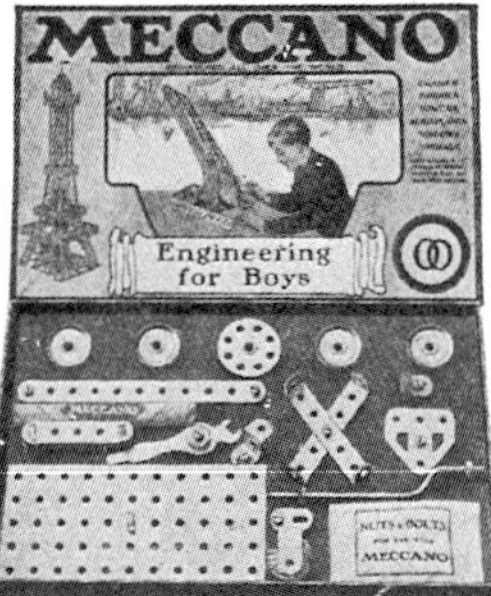

No. 00 OUTFIT

THE No. 00 Outfit is specially adapted to the requirements of very young boys. With it 43 simple models may be constructed, each of which is illustrated in the Instruction Sheet included in the Outfit. A No. 00A Accessory Outfit, costing 1/6 will convert the No. 00 into a No. 0 Outfit.

Price 3/6

No. 0 OUTFIT

THE No. 0 Outfit contains a good assortment of Meccano Strips, Rods, Wheels, Plates, Nuts, Bolts, etc., and a special Book of Instructions for building 70 fine working models, including Trucks of all types, Wheel-barrows, Potter's Wheel, Signals, Drilling, Sawing and Stamping Machines, Cranes, etc., each a perfect toy, capable of providing hours of fun. Everything necessary for commencing to build immediately is included.

Price 5/-

No. 1 OUTFIT

THIS Outfit is very popular. It contains a greater number and variety of Meccano parts with which larger models may be built, including fine Cranes, Trucks, Roundabout, Windmill, Fire Alarm, Snow Plough, etc. A big fully-illustrated Book of Instructions is included, which makes everything clear and shows how 106 models may be made with the Outfit.

Price 8/6

No 2 OUTFIT

THE fortunate possessor of a No. 2 Outfit is able to build up models of a more complicated and interesting type. Large Cranes, Gangways, Motor-Wagons, Roundabouts, well-constructed Monoplane, Turntable, Joy Wheel, Mechanical Hammer, etc., all designed on sound engineering principles, with hours of pleasure stored up in each. This is a splendid commencing Outfit. As in all Meccano Outfits, full instructions for building are provided, everything requisite is included in the Outfit, and there is nothing further to buy. No study is necessary, and the youngest boy can commence to build as soon as he gets his Outfit home.

Price 15/-

No. 3 OUTFIT

THIS excellent Outfit contains many parts of an advanced engineering type. They include correctly-cut Gear-Wheels, Worm-Wheels, Pinion-Wheels, Collars with set screws, Cranks and Strips in greater variety. It is a splendid Outfit for a boy who takes a real interest in engineering subjects. The Cranes and Bridges that it builds are of a better type, and in addition such excellent models as Bob Sleigh, Tower Wagon, Flax Cleaner, Oscillating Steam Engine, Wire Rope Maker, Pit Head Gear, and Lawn Swing, etc., may be constructed. It is packed in a stout box with wooden sides and includes a big Book of Instructions showing how to build 206 models.

Price 22/6

No. 4 OUTFIT

THIS is a fine substantial Outfit containing a large selection of Meccano parts. Engineering parts such as Contrate-Wheels (that enable the user to construct reversing gears, etc.) greatly improve the working of the models, and make possible a variety of new movements and mechanisms. Amongst the No. 4 models illustrated in the Manual are Travelling and Girder Cranes, Swivelling and Luffing Jib Cranes, Cable Railway, Swing Bridge, Sextant and Theodolite, Anti-Aircraft Gun, etc. A much larger Book of Instructions is provided with this Outfit, showing how to construct 263 working models.

Price 40/-

No. 5 OUTFIT

THE No. 5 Outfit is supplied either in a stout carton or in a handsome oak cabinet with lock and key. The contents are the same in each case. The building possibilities are very greatly increased and with it fine engineering models may be constructed. These include a Farm Tractor, Field Gun and Carriage, Motor Plough, Vertical Drill, Giant Auto Swing, an improved Pit Head Gear, Beam Scales, etc. A big Book of Instructions is included, showing how to build 309 models. The Carton Outfit is strong and serviceable, the carton itself being stoutly made with partitions for the various parts, and it will last for years. The Cabinet Outfit is very handsome, the cabinet being made of oak, French-polished. This Outfit makes a splendid present.

Price (packed in strong carton) 55/-
Price („ „ superior oak cabinet, fitted with lock and key) .. 85/-

No. 6 OUTFIT

THE No. 6 Meccano Outfit is supplied either in a stout carton or in a handsome oak cabinet with lock and key. With it may be constructed all the models of the earlier Outfits, and many more, including a Big Wheel, Beam Engine, Stone-Sawing Machine, Jack Knife Bridge, Punching and Profiling Machines, Radial Travelling Crane, Tower Bridge, etc.—359 models in all. Some of the models stand several feet high and they represent the genius of generations of engineering and mechanical experts. No greater benefit could be conferred upon any boy than to make him a present of such an Outfit as this. It will enable him to acquire a sound knowledge of the great engineering feats of the world, and will cause him to take a deeper interest in one of the most attractive sides of life. If he intends to pursue an engineering career, it is an indispensable part of his education and will make his initiation into an intricate subject easy and pleasant.

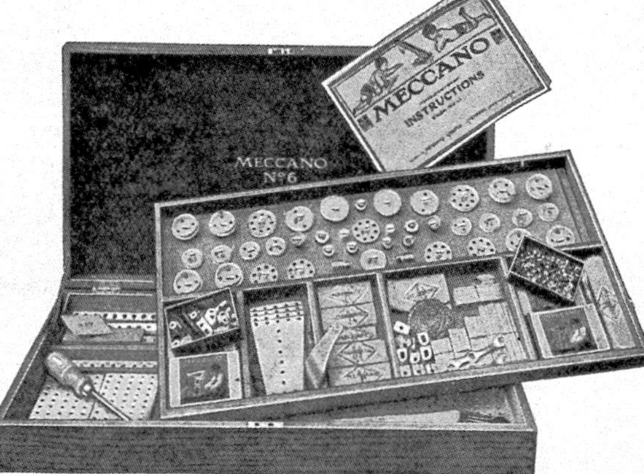

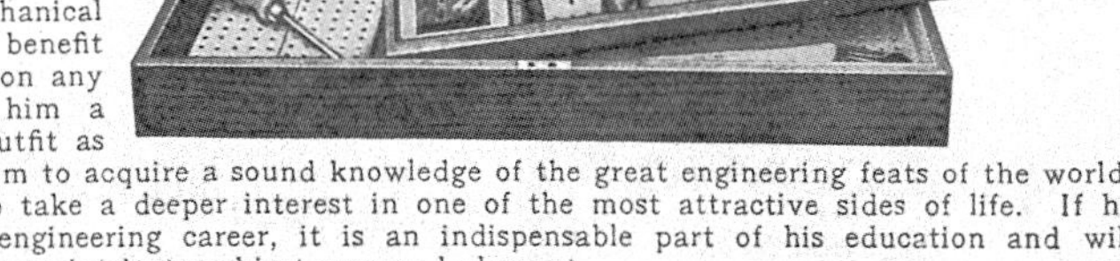

Price (packed in stout carton) 105/-
Price („ „ superior oak cabinet, fitted with lock and key) .. 140/-

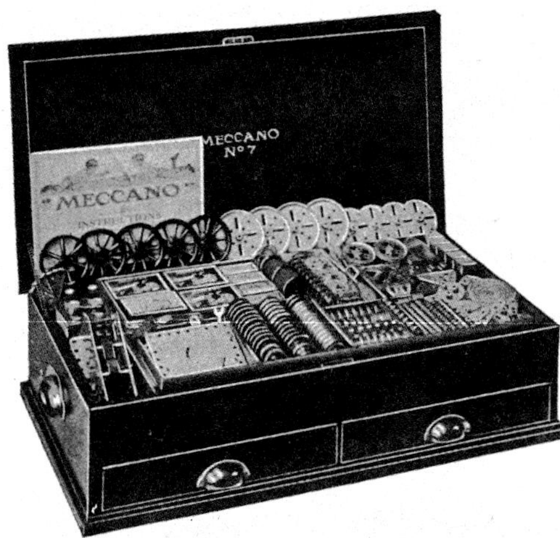

No. 7 OUTFIT

THIS is a complete and comprehensive Outfit, containing all Meccano parts necessary to build each of the models in the new big Manual of Instructions, including Stiff Leg Derrick, Meccanograph, Eiffel Tower, Transporter Bridge, Forth Bridge, Hydraulic Crane, Dredger, etc., as well as such special models as the High Speed Ship Coaler, the Loom (for real weaving) and the Motor Chassis.

The No. 7 Outfit also contains Clockwork Motor, 4-volt Electric Motor and Accumulator, a selection of all the new Meccano electrical accessory parts, with full instructions for building electrical models.

An ideal present for a boy interested in mechanics or electricity.

Price (packed in beautifully-finished oak cabinet fitted with lock and key) . . 370/–

ACCESSORY OUTFITS

OUR illustration shows one of the Meccano Accessory Outfits. As has already been explained, these Outfits connect the main Outfits from No. 00 to No. 7, making it possible for a boy who commences with one of the earlier Outfits to build up his equipment by easy stages, until he is the possessor of parts that cover the entire system.

Meccano Accessory Outfits.

No. 00a	converting No.	00	into No.	0	..	1/6
„ 0a	„	„ 0	„ „	1	..	4/–
„ 1a	„	„ 1	„ „	2	..	7/6
„ 2a	„	„ 2	„ „	3	..	8/6
„ 3a	„	„ 3	„ „	4	..	18/6
„ 4a	„	„ 4	„ „	5	..	15/–
„ 5a*	„	„ 5	„ „	6	..	50/–
„ 5a†	„	„ 5	„ „	6	..	80/–
„ 6a†	„	„ 6	„ „	7	..	210/–

*Carton. †Wood.

MANUALS OF INSTRUCTIONS

THE complete Meccano Manual of Instructions is beautifully illustrated and contains all directions necessary for the construction of 400 splendid models. It includes a large number of entirely new models — Transporter Bridge, Rotating and Hydraulic Cranes, Theodolite, Travelling Gantry, Dredger, Lathe, Coal Cutting Machine and many others of special interest. Every Meccano boy should possess a copy of this fine Manual. Price 2/6 (postage 4d. extra).

The Meccano 0-3 Manual comprises a section of the above Complete Manual illustrating the models that may be built with Nos. 00, 0, 1, 2 and 3 Outfits. It gives full instructions for building 206 fine models, including Fire Escape, Wire-Rope Maker, Roundabout, Railway and Travelling Cranes, Scales, Oscillating Steam Engine, Pile Driver and many other interesting and instructive models that will provide hours of fun. Beautiful illustrations in half-tone throughout. Price 1/– each (postage 2½d. extra).

ELECTRICAL OUTFIT

THE application of Electricity to the Meccano system adds a further and wonderful charm. The joys of model-building are now increased by the fascinating pastime of carrying out delightful electrical experiments.

THE MECCANO ELECTRICAL OUTFIT contains a number of specially designed electrical accessory parts, and, used in conjunction with any of the regular Outfits, enables the user to construct models for making interesting and instructive experiments. These include the Electric Railway, Morse Key, Tapper Key, Buzzer, Electric Lamps, Electric Crane, Induction Coil, Electric Iron, Motor-Starter, etc.

Price 42/–

ELECTRIC MOTORS

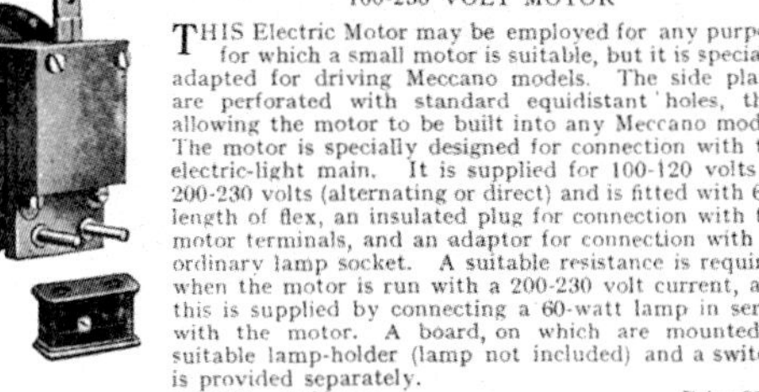

100-230 *Volt Motor*

4 *Volt Motor*

100-230 VOLT MOTOR

THIS Electric Motor may be employed for any purpose for which a small motor is suitable, but it is specially adapted for driving Meccano models. The side plates are perforated with standard equidistant holes, thus allowing the motor to be built into any Meccano model. The motor is specially designed for connection with the electric-light main. It is supplied for 100-120 volts or 200-230 volts (alternating or direct) and is fitted with 6ft. length of flex, an insulated plug for connection with the motor terminals, and an adaptor for connection with an ordinary lamp socket. A suitable resistance is required when the motor is run with a 200-230 volt current, and this is supplied by connecting a 60-watt lamp in series with the motor. A board, on which are mounted a suitable lamp-holder (lamp not included) and a switch, is provided separately.

100-230-volt Motor ... ... Price 32/6
Lamp Board (with Lamp-holder and switch) „ 4/6

4-VOLT MOTOR

The 4-volt motor is also specially designed to build into Meccano models. It is a most reliable and powerful model and when properly geared will lift over 30lbs. dead weight. It may be run by a 4-volt accumulator or, by employing a suitable transformer, direct from the main. Fitted with reversing motion, provided with stopping and starting controls, and the gearing is interchangeable.

Price... ... ... 12/6

4-VOLT ACCUMULATOR

THIS new and excellent type of accumulator has been adapted to drive the Meccano 4-volt Electric Motor. It has remarkable recuperative powers, and will continue to supply current when nominally exhausted. Price 17/6

CLOCKWORK MOTOR

Clockwork Motor

This is a splendid piece of mechanism, simple, powerful, reliable and free from all danger. It is fitted with starting, stopping and reversing levers, and all its movements are fully explained in the instructions that accompany it. Price 7/6

SHAFTING STANDARDS

THESE Shafting Standards are designed on the Meccano system, with equidistant holes. Our illustration shows how strong and serviceable shafting may be constructed from Meccano parts with the aid of the Large Standard.

PRICES.

Standard only, Large ... ... Price 1/–
„ „ Small ... ... „ 8d.

SAW BENCHES

THIS model Saw Bench is suitable for use with an Electric or Clockwork Motor. By means of the equidistant holes in the base it may be built into a Meccano Model Workshop. Beautifully finished in black enamel and nickel.

Price 4/–

Revised Prices

Revisions in the prices and designs of several items in this catalogue have recently taken place as indicated below.

ELECTRIC MOTORS

4-Volt Motor

Page 7. 4-Volt Electric Motor

This motor has been greatly improved in design as will be seen from the accompanying illustration. The price is increased to 15/6.

Page 7. 100-230-Volt Electric Motor

Similarly this high-powered electric motor has been altered in design, and its efficiency is now considerably increased. The price remains unchanged.

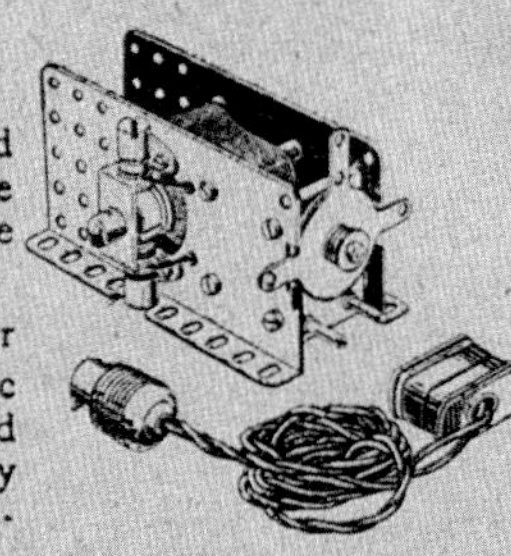

100-230-Volt Motor

TRAIN SETS

	Price		Price
Page 10 Hornby No. 1 Passenger Set	27/6	Page 12 Hornby No. 0 Passenger Set	24/-
,, 10 Hornby No. 1 Goods Set	21/-	,, 13 No. 00 Clockwork Train Set	10/6

ROLLING STOCK AND ACCESSORIES

	Price		Price
Page 10 Hornby No. 1 Loco ..	13/6	Page 13 No. 00 Carriage	1/-
,, 10 Hornby Passenger Coach	3/6	,, 13 No. 00 Tender	9d.
,, 12 Hornby Passenger Coach No. 0	3/6	,, 16 Guard's Van	3/6
,, 13 No. 00 Loco	6/6	,, 16 Turntable	5/-

RAILS, POINTS AND CROSSINGS

	Price		Price
Page 18 ECA Acute Angle Crossing	4/6	Page 18 ECR Right Angle Crossing	4/6

NOTE.—Zulu Clockwork Trains are now replaced by Hornby No. 0 Clockwork Trains. George V. Clockwork Trains will in future be known as No. 00 Clockwork Trains. Electrical Points, various types, are now supplied for 2 ft. radius curves only.

New items have been added to the range of Meccano Products as follows:—

HORNBY TRAIN SETS

Electric Train	Price 110/-	No. 2 Tank Goods Set ..	Price 45/-
No. 1 Tank Goods Set ..	,, 25/-	No. 2 Tank Passenger Set ..	,, 45/-

ROLLING STOCK AND ACCESSORIES

Pratts Petrol Wagon ..	Price 3/-	Centre Section for Viaduct	Price 4/6
Viaduct	,, 7/6	Electrical Viaduct	,, 8/-

Centre Section for Electrical Viaduct 5/-

RAILS, POINTS AND CROSSINGS

CO1 Crossovers, 1 ft. Radius	Price 6/6	CO2 Crossovers, 2 ft. Radius	Price 7/6

MECCANO ACCESSORY PARTS

No. 121 Couplings ..	Each 2d.	No. 148 Ratchet Wheel ..	Each 9d.
,, 147 Pawls, with Bolts and Nuts	,, 3d.	,, 149 Collecting Shoes for Electric Locos ..	,, 1/6
,, 147a Pawls	,, 2d.		
,, 147b Pivot Bolt and Two Nuts	,, 2d.		

NOTE.—Part No. 121, Coupling, is replaced by a new one designed on different lines. In the same way parts Nos. 33 and 33a are replaced by parts No. 147, 147a, and 147b.

A FEW CHOICE MECCANO MODELS

Dragline

Big Wheel

Hydraulic Crane

Revolving Crane

Punching Press

Mechanical Dredger

Platform Crane

Forth Bridge

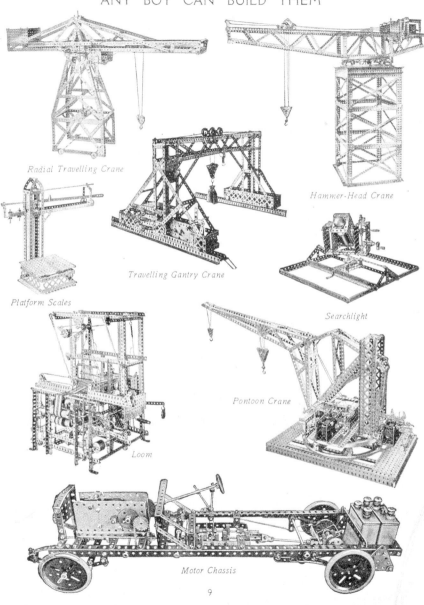

ANY BOY CAN BUILD THEM

Radial Travelling Crane

Hammer-Head Crane

Travelling Gantry Crane

Platform Scales

Searchlight

Pontoon Crane

Loom

Motor Chassis

Guarantee
Hornby Trains are tested and their efficiency is guaranteed. A form of guarantee is furnished with each loco and we undertake to repair or replace, at our option, any loco that fails to run satisfactorily from any cause other than misuse, within 60 days of date of purchase.

HORNBY CLOCK WORK TRAINS

No. 1 PASSENGER SET

A most valuable feature of the Hornby Loco is that all the parts are standardised and any lost or damaged part may be replaced with a new one.

The Clockwork is a splendid piece of mechanism with accurately-cut gears, ensuring smooth running, and the workmanship and finish are of the highest quality. The Loco is fitted with reversing gear, brake and governor. Loco, Tender and Coaches are superb in appearance and finish, enamelled in colour and stoved at a high temperature to ensure durability. The doors of the Coaches open.

Gauge 0 in colours to represent the L.M.S or L.N.E.R. Companies' rolling-stock. Each set contains Loco, Tender, two passenger coaches and set of rails consisting of two straights and curves to form a circle of 2ft. diameter.

Hornby No. 1 Passenger Set complete, well boxed .. Price 30/-

No. 1 GOODS SET

Gauge 0 in colours to represent the L.M.S. or L.N.E.R. Companies' rolling-stock. Each Loco is fitted with reversing gear, brake and governor. Each set comprises Loco, Tender, one Wagon and set of rails as in the No. 1 Passenger Set. Superb finish to all parts of train.

Hornby No. 1 Goods Set complete, well-boxed .. .. Price 22/6

No. 1 Hornby Loco .. .. Price 15/-
„ „ Tender .. .. „ 2/6
Hornby Passenger Coach .. .. Price 5/-
No. 1 Hornby Wagon .. .. „ 2/6

HORNBY CLOCK WORK TRAINS

Guarantee
Hornby Trains are tested and their efficiency is guaranteed. A form of guarantee is furnished with each loco and we undertake to repair or replace, at our option, any loco that fails to run satisfactorily from any cause other than misuse, within 60 days of date of purchase.

No. 2 PULLMAN SET

The Loco in this set is built of standardized parts, and any lost or damaged part may be replaced at once by the user. The Loco with Tender measures 17in. in length. The Loco is fitted with superior mechanism and the accurately-cut gears ensure smooth running. Loco, Tender and Coaches are superb in appearance and finish, enamelled in colours and stoved at a high temperature to ensure durability.

Gauge 0 in colours to represent the L.M.S. or L.N.E.R. Companies' rolling-stock. Each set contains Loco, Tender and two Coaches, with set of rails to form a circle of 4ft. diameter. The Loco is fitted with reversing gear, brake and governor.

Hornby No. 2 Pullman Set complete, well-boxed .. .. Price 60/-

No. 2 GOODS SET

Gauge 0 in colours to represent the L.M.S. or L.N.E.R. Companies' rolling-stock. This set contains Loco, Tender and Rails as in the No. 2 Pullman Set, and two Wagons. Superb enamel finish to all parts of train. The Loco is fitted with reversing gear, brake and governor.

Hornby No. 2 Goods Set complete, well-boxed .. .. Price 37/6

No. 2 Hornby Loco .. .. Price 22/6
„ „ Tender .. .. „ 3/6
Hornby Pullman or Dining Car Price 15/-
No. 2 Hornby Wagon .. .. „ 2/6

Guarantee

Zulu Trains are tested and their efficiency is guaranteed. A form of guarantee is furnished with each loco and we undertake to repair or replace, at our option, any loco that fails to run satisfactorily from any cause other than misuse, within 60 days of date of purchase.

ZULU CLOCK WORK TRAINS

ZULU PASSENGER SET

Fine and durable mechanism, and strength of construction in all parts are the main characteristics of this new type of clockwork train. The Zulu Loco is well designed and efficient, and will give long and excellent service. Richly enamelled and highly finished; fitted with brake and governor; non-reversing.

Each set contains Loco, Tender, two Passenger Coaches and set of rails, consisting of two straights and curves to form a circle of 2ft. diameter.

Gauge 0, in colours to represent the L.M.S. or L.N.E.R. Companies' rolling-stock.

Packed in strong cardboard box .. .. .. Price 22/6

ZULU GOODS SET

The Goods Set is the same as the Passenger Set but contains one Wagon in place of Passenger Coaches.

Gauge 0, in colours to represent the L.M.S. or L.N.E.R. Companies' rolling-stock.

Packed in strong cardboard box .. .. .. Price 17/6

Zulu Loco, Price 10/6. Zulu Tender, Price 2/-. Zulu Passenger Coach, Price 4/-. Zulu Wagon, Price 2/6

HORNBY No. 1 TANK LOCO

The Hornby No. 1 Tank Loco is strong and durable and is capable of any amount of hard work. Richly enamelled and highly finished; fitted with reversing gear, brake and governor.

Gauge 0, in colours to represent the L.M.S. or L.N.E.R. Companies' locos.

Price 12/6

HORNBY No. 2 TANK LOCO

The Hornby No. 2 Tank Loco is a powerful model embodying all the characteristics of the Hornby Train. It is 11½in. in length and is fitted at both ends with a four-wheeled bogie.

Beautifully finished in colours to represent the L.M.S. or L.N.E.R. Companies' locos. Fitted with reversing gear, brake and governor.

Price 30/-

GEORGE V. CLOCKWORK TRAINS

Strongly built, with reliable clockwork mechanism. One size only, Gauge 0. Each set contains Loco, Tender and two Passenger Coaches printed in imitation of the colours of the principal British Railway Companies' rolling-stock, with set of rails including a circle and two straights. The Loco is fitted with brake and regulator; non-reversing.

Complete set, well-boxed .. .. Price 12/6

Loco .. .. .. Price 8/6 Carriage .. .. Price 1/3

Tender .. Price 1/-

ROLLING STOCK AND ACCESSORIES FOR TRAINS

HORNBY SERIES GAUGE 0

RAILWAY STATION
Excellent model, beautifully designed and finished. Dimensions: Length, 2ft. 9ins.; Breadth, 6ins.; Height, 7ins. ... ... Price 12/6

L.M.S. BRAKE VAN
Finished in colours. Opening doors
Price 4/-

*REFRIGERATOR VAN
Enamelled in white. Opening doors ... ... Price 4/-

*GUNPOWDER VAN
Finished in Red. Opening doors
Price 4/-

L.N.E.R. BRAKE VAN
Finished in colours. Opening doors ... ... Price 4/-

*MILK TRAFFIC VAN
Fitted with sliding door, and complete with milk cans ... Price 4/6

*No. 2 CATTLE TRUCK
Splendid model, fitted with double doors. Suitable for 2ft. radius rails only ... Price 6/6

*No. 1 CATTLE TRUCK
Fitted with sliding door. Very realistic design ... Price 4/

CARR'S BISCUIT VAN
Finished in dark blue. Opening doors ... ... Price 4/-

JACOB'S BISCUIT VAN
Finished in crimson lake. Lettered in gold and black. Opening doors ... ... Price 4/-

CRAWFORD'S BISCUIT VAN
Finished in red. Opening doors
Price 4/-

*No. 1 LUGGAGE VAN
Representative colours.
Opening doors, Price 4/-

*No. 2 LUGGAGE VAN
Finished in colour. Fitted with double doors. Suitable for 2ft. radius rails only ... Price 6/6

SECCOTINE VAN
Finished in blue. Opening doors
Price 4/-

** Lettered L.M.S. or L.N.E.R.*

ROLLING STOCK AND ACCESSORIES FOR TRAINS *(contd.)*

HORNBY SERIES GAUGE 0

"SHELL"
PETROL TANK WAGON
Finished in colour .. Price 3/-

SIDE TIPPING WAGON
Excellent design and finish
Price 3/6

ROTARY TIPPING WAGON
Finished in colour ... Price 4/-

"NATIONAL BENZOLE"
PETROL TANK WAGON
Finished in colour .. Price 3/-

LOADING GAUGE
Price ... 1/9

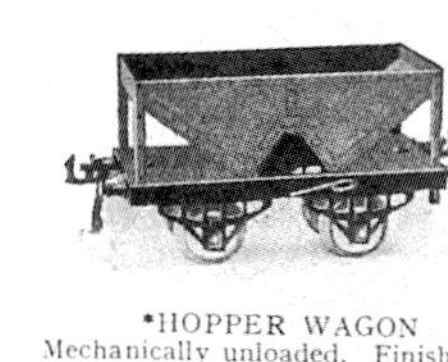

*HOPPER WAGON
Mechanically unloaded. Finished in colour ... ... Price 4/-

*SNOW PLOUGH
With revolving plough driven from front axle
Price 5/6

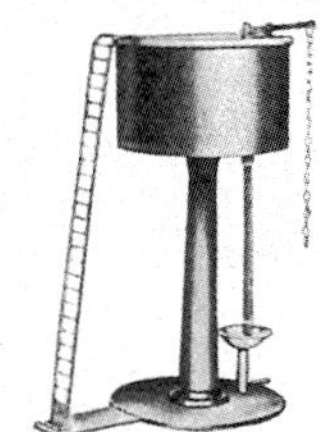

WATER TANK
Brightly coloured, stands 8½in. high, fitted with flexible tube and valve lever ... Price 6/6

VIADUCT ... ... Price 7/6

*CRANE TRUCK
Finished in grey and black
Price 4/6

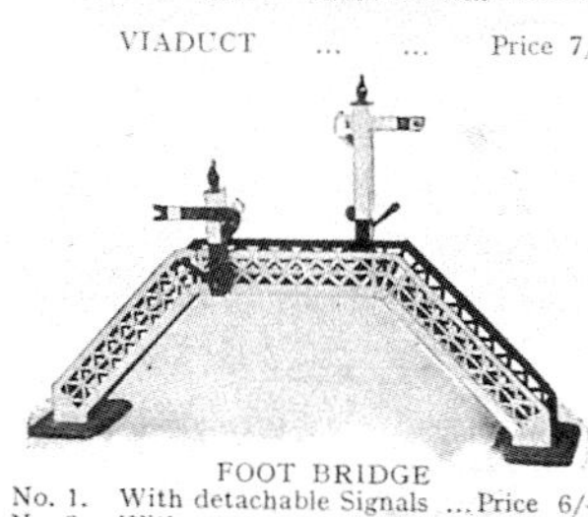

FOOT BRIDGE
No. 1. With detachable Signals ... Price 6/-
No. 2. Without " " ... " 3/6
Signals only ... ... per pair " 2/9

LATTICE GIRDER BRIDGE
This bridge is of the constructional type, strong and well proportioned.
Price 10/6

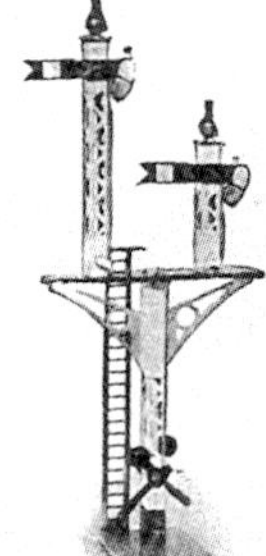

JUNCTION SIGNAL
Signal arms operated by levers at base. Very realistic model standing 14in. in height.
Price ... 5/6

SINGLE LAMP STANDARD
A 4-volt bulb may be fitted into the globe ... Price 3/-

TELEGRAPH POLE
Price 2/6

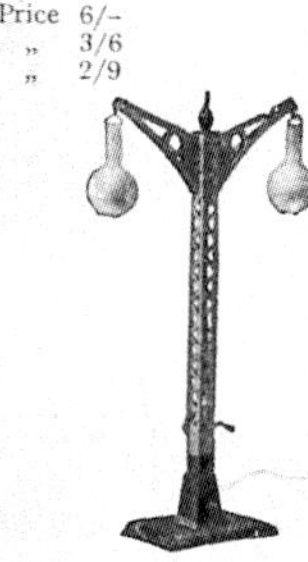

DOUBLE LAMP STANDARD
Four-volt bulbs may be fitted into the globes ... Price 4/-

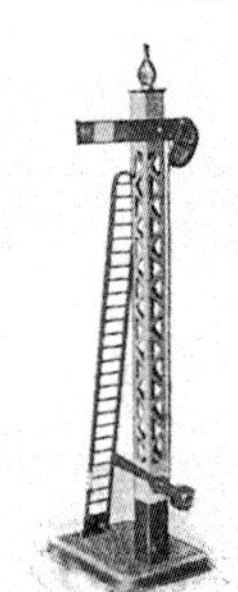

SIGNAL
Price ... 2/6

** Lettered L.M.S. or L.N.E.R.*

ROLLING STOCK AND ACCESSORIES FOR TRAINS *(contd.)*

HORNBY SERIES — GAUGE 0

No. 1

No. 2

LUMBER WAGONS

Provided with bolsters and stanchions for log transport. (NOTE.—The No. 2 Wagons are suitable for 2ft. radius rails only).

*No. 1 Lumber Wagon ... Price 2/-

*No. 2 „ „ ... „ 5/-

SIGNAL CABIN

Dimensions: Height, 6½in.; Width, 3¼in.; Length, 6½in. Finished in colour and lettered "Windsor." Roof and back open to allow signal levers to be fitted inside cabin if desired. Price ... 6/6

No. 1

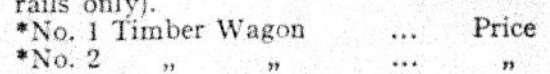

No. 2

TIMBER WAGONS

Beautifully enamelled in colour and stoved. Complete with loads of timber. (NOTE.—The No. 2 Wagons are suitable for 2ft. radius rails only).

*No. 1 Timber Wagon ... Price 2/-

*No. 2 „ „ ... „ 4/6

*BREAKDOWN VAN AND CRANE

Beautifully coloured. Opening doors. Suitable for 2ft. radius rails only ... ... Price 7/-

TURNTABLE

Price ... 4/6

LEVEL CROSSING

Beautifully designed in colour. Measures 11¼in. × 7¼in. with Gauge 0 rails in position.

Price 6/6

*GUARD'S VAN

Finished in crimson lake. Each side fitted with single and double opening doors. Price 5/-

*TROLLEY WAGON

Finished in colour. Suitable for 2ft. radius rails only ... ... Price 6/-

TUNNEL

Realistic and finished in colours ... Price 7/6

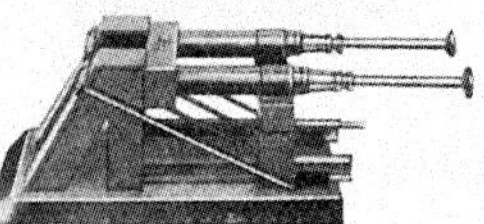

HYDRAULIC BUFFER STOP

Price 5/-

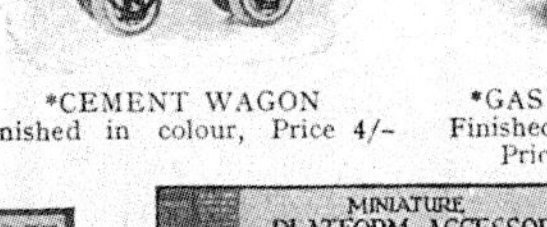

*CEMENT WAGON

Finished in colour, Price 4/-

*GAS CYLINDER WAGON

Finished in red, lettered gold

Price 3/-

SPRING BUFFER STOP

Price ... 1/6

PLATFORM ACCESSORIES

No. 1. Miniature Luggage

Price ... ... per set 2/-

PLATFORM ACCESSORIES

No. 3. Platform Machines, etc.

Price ... ... per set 2/-

PLATFORM ACCESSORIES

No. 2. Milk Cans and Truck

Price ... ... per set 2/-

* *Lettered L.M.S. or L.N.E.R.*

RAILS, POINTS AND CROSSINGS

Gauge 0, 1⅜". **(Hornby Series)** **Alternate Pegs**

HORNBY Rails, Points and Crossings are built for hard wear and for smooth running. They are made of the finest materials and hold together rigidly and strongly, for real workmanship is put into them. Note the great superiority, both in quality and appearance, of the Hornby rails, and note also the extra sleepers, giving added strength and steadiness to the track. Each sleeper on rails, points and crossings is stamped with the name, and you should look for this name in order to ensure getting the genuine article.

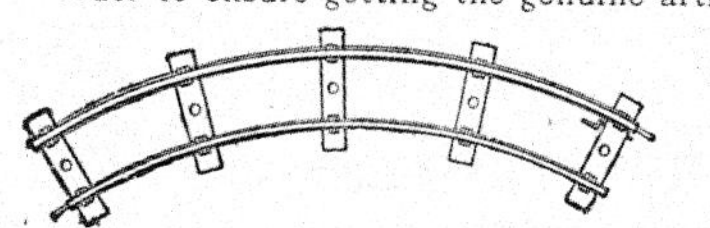

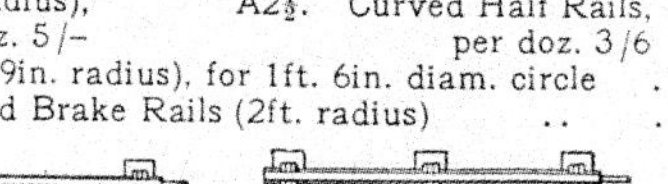

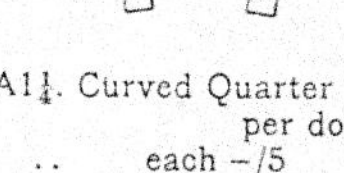

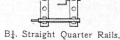

FOR 2ft. DIAMETER CIRCLE

A1. Curved Rails (1ft. radius), per doz. 4/-

A1½. Curved Half Rails, per doz. 3/-

A1¼. Curved Quarter Rails, per doz. 2/6

AB1. Curved Brake Rails (1ft. radius) .. .. each -/5

FOR 4ft. DIAMETER CIRCLE

A2. Curved Rails (2ft. radius), per doz. 5/-

A2½. Curved Half Rails, per doz. 3/6

A2¼. Curved Quarter Rails, per doz. 3/-

A9. Curved Rails (9in. radius), for 1ft. 6in. diam. circle .. .. per doz. 3/-

AB2. Curved Brake Rails (2ft. radius) .. .. .. each -/6

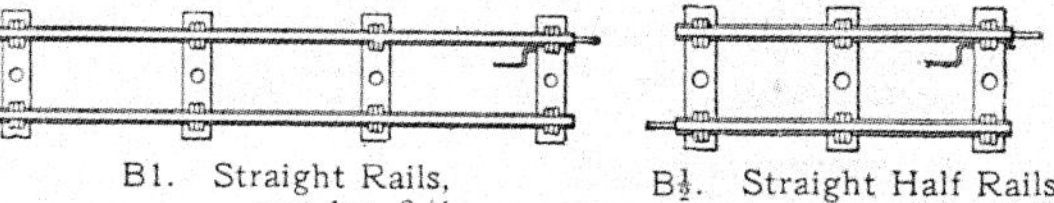

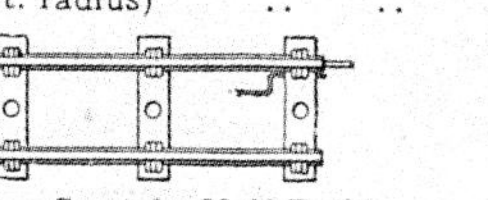

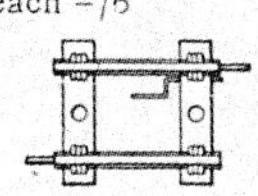

B1. Straight Rails, per doz. 3/6

B½. Straight Half Rails, per doz. 2/6

B¼. Straight Quarter Rails, per doz. 2/-

BB1. Straight Brake Rails .. .. each -/4½

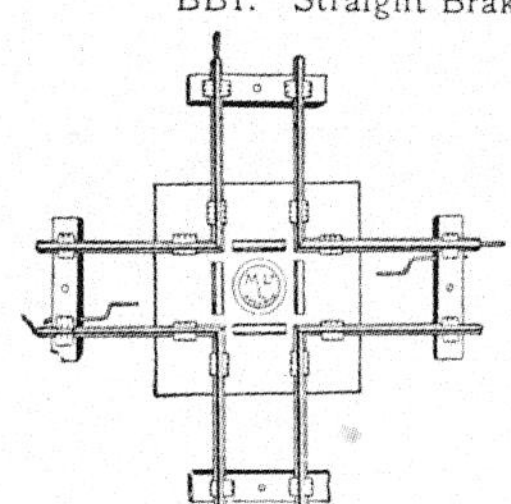

CROSSINGS

CA. Acute-angle Crossing, Price 1/9

CR. Right-angle Crossing, Price 1/9

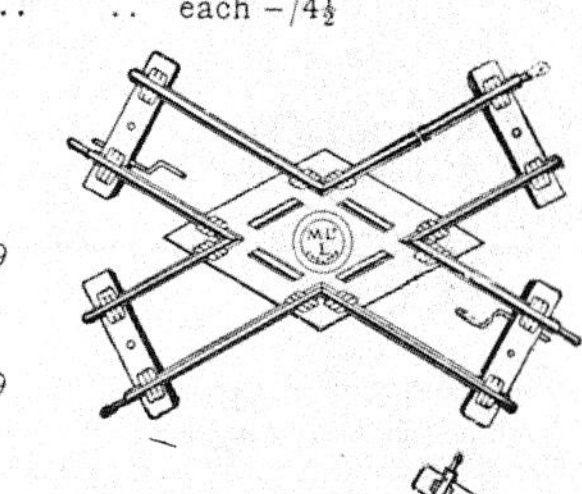

POINTS

For 9in. Radius Curves.

PR9. Right-hand Points .. .. .. Price 2/3

PL9. Left-hand Points .. .. .. „ 2/3

For 1ft. Radius Curves.

PR1. Right-hand Points .. .. .. Price 2/3

PL1. Left-hand Points .. .. .. „ 2/3

For 2ft. Radius Curves.

PR2. Right-hand Points .. .. .. Price 2/3

PL2. Left-hand Points .. .. .. „ 2/3

Left-hand Points (1-ft. radius)

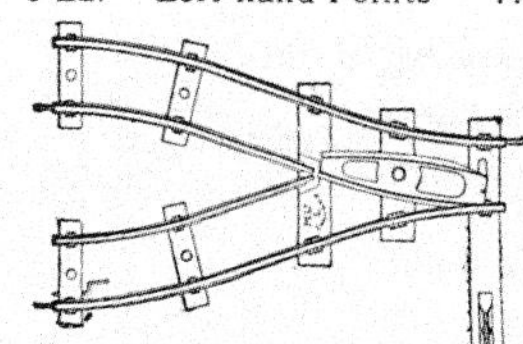

Parallel Points, right

PARALLEL POINTS

For 1ft. Radius Curves

PPR1. Parallel Points, right, Price 2/6

PPL1. Parallel Points, left .. .. Price 2/6

For 2ft. Radius Curves

PPR2. Parallel Points, right .. .. Price 2/6

PPL2. Parallel Points, left .. .. „ 2/6

RAILS, POINTS AND CROSSINGS—*continued*

D.S. Points, right
(1ft. radius)

DOUBLE SYMMETRICAL POINTS

For 1ft. Radius Curves

DSR1.	Double Symmetrical Points, right ..	Price 2/6
DSL1.	,, ,, ,, left ..	,, 2/6

For 2ft. Radius Curves

DSR2.	Double Symmetrical Points, right ..	Price 2/6
DSL2.	,, ,, ,, left ..	,, 2/6

RAILS FOR ELECTRIC TRAINS

GAUGE 0, 1¼in.

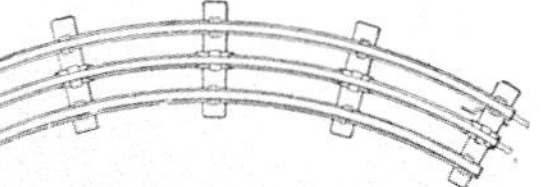

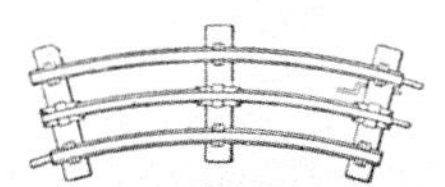

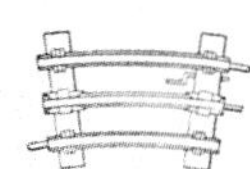

EA1. Curved Rails (1ft. radius), per doz. 8/-

FOR 2ft. DIAMETER CIRCLE

EA1½. Curved Half Rails, per doz. 5/-

EA1¼. Curved Quarter Rails, per doz. 4/6

EA2. Curved Rails (2ft. radius), per doz 8/-

FOR 4ft. DIAMETER CIRCLE

EA2½. Curved Half Rails, per doz. 5/-

EA2¼. Curved Quarter Rails, per doz. 4/6

EAT1.	Curved Rail with Terminals (1ft. radius)	Price 1/2
EAT2.	,, ,, ,, ,, (2ft. radius)	,, 1/3

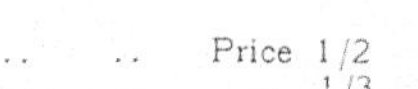

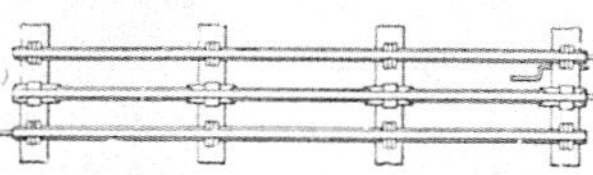

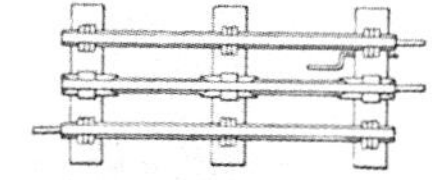

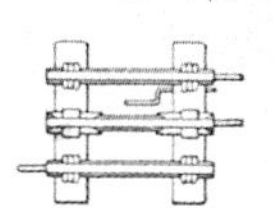

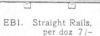

EB1. Straight Rails, per doz 7/-

EB½. Straight Half Rails, per doz. 4/6

EB¼. Straight Quarter Rails, per doz. 4/-

POINTS

For 1ft. Radius Curves

EPR1. Right-hand Points, Price 5/-

EPL1. Left-hand Points, Price 5/-

For 2ft. Radius Curves

EPR2. Right-hand Points, Price 5/-

EPL2. Left-hand Points, Price 5/-

CROSSINGS

ECA.	Acute-angle Crossing	Price 2/6
ECR.	Right-angle ,, ...	,, 2/6

DOUBLE SYMMETRICAL POINTS

For 1ft. Radius Curves

EDSR1.	Double Symmetrical Points, right ..	Price 6/-
EDSL1.	,, ,, ,, left ..	,, 6/-

For 2ft. Radius Curves

EDSR2.	Double Symmetrical Points, right ..	Price 6/-
EDSL2.	,, ,, ,, left ..	,, 6/-

MECCANO ACCESSORY PARTS

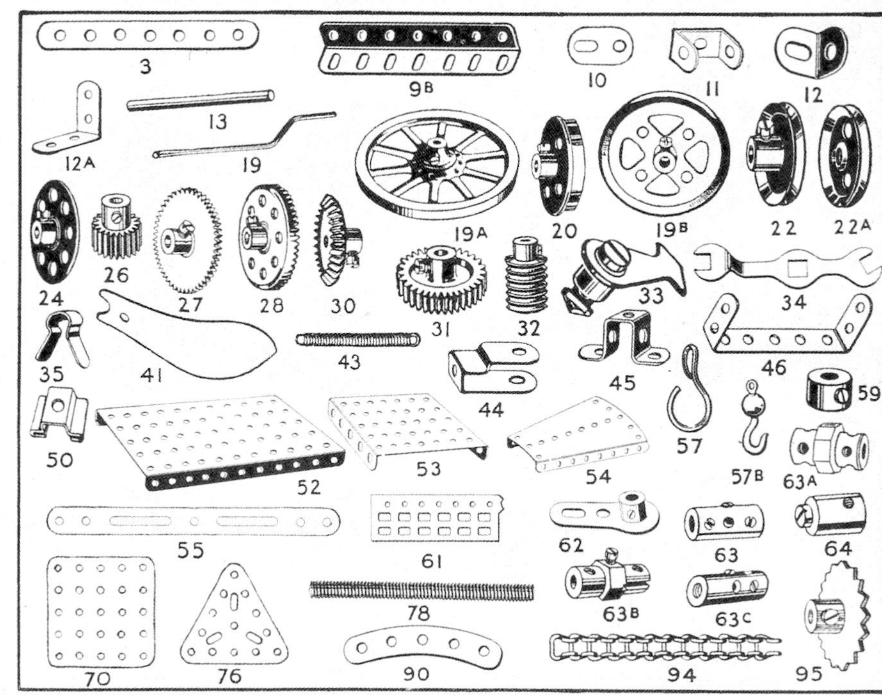

No.		s.	d.
1.	Perforated Strips, 12½" long ½ doz.	1	0
1a.	,, ,, 9½" ,, ,,	0	9
1b.	,, ,, 7½" ,, ,,	0	8
2.	,, ,, 5½" ,, ,,	0	6
2a.	,, ,, 4½" ,, ,,	0	5
3.	,, ,, 3½" ,, ,,	0	4
4.	,, ,, 3" ,, ,,	0	3
5.	,, ,, 2½" ,, ,,	0	3
6.	,, ,, 2" ,, ,,	0	3
6a.	,, ,, 1½" ,, ,,	0	3
7.	Angle Girders, 24½" long ... each	0	8
7a.	,, ,, 18½" ,, ... ,,	0	6
8.	,, ,, 12½" ,, ... ½ doz.	1	9
8a.	,, ,, 9½" ,, ... ,,	1	3
8b.	,, ,, 7½" ,, ... ,,	1	2
9.	,, ,, 5½" ,, ... ,,	1	0
9a.	,, ,, 4½" ,, ... ,,	0	10
9b.	,, ,, 3½" ,, ... ,,	0	8
9c.	,, ,, 3" ,, ... ,,	0	8
9d.	,, ,, 2½" ,, ... ,,	0	7
9e.	,, ,, 2" ,, ... ,,	0	6
9f.	,, ,, 1½" ,, ... ,,	0	6
10.	Flat Brackets ... ... ,,	0	2
11.	Double Brackets ... ... each	0	1
12.	Angle Brackets, ½" × ½" ... doz.	0	6
12a.	,, ,, 1" × 1" ... each	0	1
12b.	,, ,, 1" × ½" ... ,,	0	1
13.	Axle Rods, 11½" long ... ,,	0	3
13a.	,, ,, 8" ,, ... ,,	0	3
14.	,, ,, 6½" ,, ... ,,	0	2
15.	,, ,, 5" ,, ... ,,	0	2
15a.	,, ,, 4½" ,, ... ,,	0	1
16.	,, ,, 3½" ,, ... ,,	0	1
16a.	,, ,, 2½" ,, ... ,,	0	1
16b.	,, ,, 3" ,, ... ,,	0	1

No.		s.	d.
17.	Axle Rods, 2" long ... each	0	1
18a.	,, ,, 1½" ,, ... ,,	0	1
18b.	,, ,, 1" ,, ... ,,	0	1
19.	Crank Handles ... ... ,,	0	3
19a.	Wheels, 3" diam., with set screws ... ... ,,	0	8
20.	Flanged Wheels ... ... ,,	0	6
	Pulley Wheels		
19b.	3" diam., with centre boss and set screw ,,	0	8
19c.	6" ,, ,, ,, ,, ,, ,,	2	6
20a.	2" ,, ,, ,, ,, ,, ,,	0	6
21.	1½" ,, ,, ,, ,, ,, ,,	0	6
22.	1" ,, ,, ,, ,, ,, ,,	0	4
22a.	1" ,, without ,, ,, ,, ,,	0	2
23.	½" ,, ,, ,, ,, ,, ,,	0	2
23a.	½" ,, with ,, ,, ,, ,,	0	4
24.	Bush Wheels ... ... ,,	0	6
25.	Pinion Wheels, ¾" diam. ... ,,	0	6
26.	,, ,, ½" ,, ... ,,	0	4
	Gear Wheels		
27.	50 teeth, to gear with ¾" pinion ,,	0	9
27a.	57 ,, ,, ,, ½" ,, ,,	0	9
27b.	133 ,, ,, ,, ½" ,, (3½" diam.) ,,	1	6
28.	Contrate Wheels, 1½" diam. ,,	0	9
29.	,, ,, ¾" ,, ,,	0	6
30.	Bevel Gears ... ... ,,	0	10
31.	Gear Wheels, 1", 38 teeth ,,	1	0
32.	Worm Wheels ... ... ,,	0	6
33.	Pawls (complete) ... ... ,,	0	4
33a.	Pivot Bolts with Nuts ... ,,	0	2
34.	Spanners ... ... ,,	0	2
34b.	Box Spanners ... ... ,,	0	3
35.	Spring Clips ... per box (doz.)	0	3

No.		s.	d.
36	Screw Drivers ... ... each	0	3
36a.	,, ,, (extra long) ,,	0	6
37.	Nuts and Bolts ... per box (doz.)	0	6
37a.	Nuts ... ... ,, ,,	0	3
37b	Bolts ... ... ,, ,,	0	3
38.	Washers ... ... doz.	0	1
40.	Hanks of Cord ... ... 2 for	0	3
41.	Propeller Blades ... ...per pair	0	4
43.	Springs ... ... each	0	2
44.	Cranked Bent Strips... ... ,,	0	1
45.	Double Bent Strips ... ... ,,	0	1
46.	Double Angle Strips, 2½" × 1" ½ doz.	0	6
47.	,, ,, ,, 2½" × 1½" ,,	0	9
47a.	,, ,, ,, 3" × 1½" ,,	1	0
48.	,, ,, ,, 1½" × ½" ,,	0	4
48a.	,, ,, ,, 2½" × ½" ,,	0	5
48b.	,, ,, ,, 3½" × ½" ,,	0	6
48c.	,, ,, ,, 4½" × ½" ,,	0	9
48d.	,, ,, ,, 5½" × ½" ,,	0	9
50.	Eye Pieces ... ... each	0	2
52.	Perforated Flanged Plates, 5½" × 2½" ... ... ,,	0	5
52a.	Flat Plates, 5½" × 3½" ... ,,	0	5
53.	Perforated Flanged Plates, 3½" × 2½" ... ... ,,	0	3
53a.	Flat Plates, 4½" × 2½" ... ,,	0	3
54.	Perforated Flanged Sector Plates ... ... ,,	0	3
55.	Perforated Strips, slotted, 5½" long ... ... ,,	0	2
55a.	2" ,, ... ,,	0	1
56.	Instruction Manuals complete	2	6
56a.	,, ,, No. 0-3 ,,	1	0
56b.	,, ,, No. 0 ,,	0	4
57.	Hooks ... ... ,,	0	1

MECCANO ACCESSORY PARTS—*(continued)*

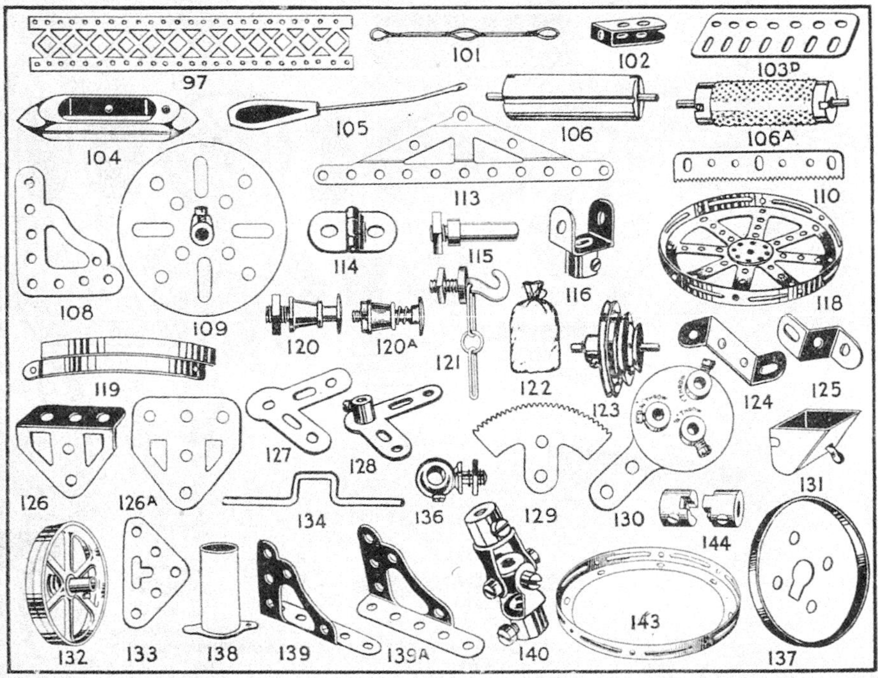

No.			s.	d.
57a.	Hooks (scientific)	each	0	1
57b.	„ (loaded)	„	0	5
58.	Spring Cord	per length	0	9
59.	Collars with Set Screws ...	each	0	2
61.	Windmill Sails	„	0	2
62.	Cranks...	„	0	3
62a.	Threaded Cranks	„	0	4
63.	Couplings	„	0	6
63a.	Octagonal Couplings ...	„	0	8
63b.	Strip Couplings	„	0	8
63c.	Threaded Couplings	„	0	6
64.	Threaded Bosses	„	0	2
65.	Centre Forks	„	0	2
66.	Weights, 50 gramme ...	„	1	0
67.	„ 25 „ ...	„	1	0
68.	Woodscrews, ½″	doz.	0	3
69.	Set Screws	„	0	4
69a.	Grub Screws, 5/32″	„	0	4
69b.	„ „ 7/32″	„	0	6
70.	Flat Plates, 5½″×2½″ ...	each	0	3
72.	„ „ 2½″×2½″ ...	„	0	2
76.	Triangular Plates, 2½″ ...	„	0	2
77.	„ „ 1″ ...	„	0	1
78.	Screwed Rods, 11½″ ...	„	0	6
79.	„ „ 8″	„	0	5
79a.	„ „ 6″	„	0	4
80.	„ „ 5″	„	0	3
80a.	„ „ 3½″ ...	„	0	3
80b.	„ „ 4½″ ...	„	0	3
81.	„ „ 2″	„	0	2
82.	„ „ 1″	„	0	1
89.	Curved Strips, 5½″	„	0	2
90.	„ „ 2½″	„	0	1
94.	Sprocket Chain	per length	0	6
95.	Sprocket Wheels, 2″ diam.	each	0	5
95a.	Sprocket Wheels, 1½″ diam.	each	0	4
95b.	„ „ 3″ „	„	0	6
96.	„ „ 1″ „	„	0	3
96a.	„ „ ¾″ „	„	0	3
97.	Braced Girders, 3½″ long	½ doz.	0	9
98.	„ „ 2½″ „	„	0	6
99.	„ „ 12½″ „	„	1	9
99a.	„ „ 9½″ „	„	1	6
100.	„ „ 5½″ „	„	1	0
101.	Healds, for looms	doz.	0	9
102.	Single Bent Strips	each	0	1
103.	Flat Girders, 5½″ long ...	½ doz.	1	0
103a.	„ „ 9½″ „ ...	„	1	6
103b.	„ „ 12½″ „ ...	„	2	0
103c.	„ „ 4½″ „ ...	„	0	9
103d.	„ „ 3½″ „ ...	„	0	7
103e.	„ „ 3″ „ ...	„	0	6
103f.	„ „ 2½″ „ ...	„	0	5
103g.	„ „ 2″ „ ...	„	0	4
103h.	„ „ 1½″ „ ...	„	0	3
103k.	„ „ 7½″ „ ...	„	1	3
104.	Shuttles, for looms	each	4	0
105.	Reed Hooks, for looms ...	„	0	4
106.	Wood Rollers	„	1	3
106a.	Sand „	„	1	6
107.	Tables for Designing Machines	„	1	0
108.	Architraves	„	0	2
109.	Face Plates, 2½″ diam. ...	„	0	4
110.	Rack Strips, 3½″	„	0	2
111.	Bolts, ¾″	„	0	1
111a.	„ ½″	2 for	0	1
111b.	„ 7/32″	doz.	0	4
113.	Girder Frames	each	0	2
114.	Hinges	per pair	0	4
115.	Threaded Pins	each	0	2
116.	Fork Pieces	each	0	3
117.	Steel Balls, ⅜″ diam. ...	doz.	0	6
118.	Hub Discs, 5½″ diam. ...	each	1	3
119.	Channel Segments (8 to circle, 11½″ diam.) ...	„	0	4
120.	Buffers, for Locos, etc. ...	„	0	2
120a.	Spring Buffers ...	per pair	0	8
121.	Train Couplings	each	0	4
122.	Miniature Loaded Sacks	„	0	2
123.	Cone Pulleys	„	1	3
124.	Reversed Angle Brackets, 1″	½ doz.	0	10
125.	„ „ „ ½″	„	0	6
126.	Trunnions	each	0	3
126a.	Flat Trunnions	„	0	2
127.	Simple Bell Cranks	„	0	3
128.	Boss Bell Cranks	„	0	4
129.	Rack Segments, 3″ diam.	„	0	6
130.	Triple Throw Eccentrics...	„	1	3
131.	Dredger Buckets	„	0	2
132.	Flywheels, 2¾″ diam. ...	„	2	3
133.	Corner Brackets	„	0	3
134.	Crank Shafts, 1″ stroke ...	„	0	3
135.	Theodolite Protractors ...	„	0	3
136.	Handrail Supports	„	0	3
137.	Wheel Flanges	„	0	4
138.	Ships' Funnels	„	0	4
139.	Flanged Brackets (right)	„	0	2
139a.	„ „ (left) ...	„	0	2
140.	Universal Couplings ...	„	0	9
141.	Wire Lines	„	0	9
142.	Rubber Rings	„	0	4
143.	Circular Girders, 5½″ diam.	„	1	0
144.	Dog Clutches	„	0	6
145.	Circular Strips, 7″ diam. over all	„	1	0
146.	Circular Plates, 6″ diam.	„	1	3

The Meccano Magazine

THE *Meccano Magazine*, published in the interests of boys, contains splendid articles on such subjects as Famous Engineers and Inventors, Electricity, Bridges, Cranes, Wonderful Machinery, Latest Patents, Radio, Stamps, Nature-Study and Books. Special competitions are announced from time to time.

The *Meccano Magazine* is published on the 1st of each month and may be ordered from your Meccano dealer or from any newsagent or bookstall. If desired it will be mailed direct from Meccano Limited, Binns Road, Liverpool (post free), for six months 2/–, or twelve months 4/–. Write to the Editor, *Meccano Magazine*, Liverpool, for a free copy.

The Meccano Guild

The Meccano Guild Badge

THIS is the little enamelled badge showing that the wearer has joined up with thousands of other Meccano boys for more fun, more friends, good fellowship and mutual help. Each member obtains one of these badges when he joins the Meccano Guild, and he at once becomes the acknowledged friend of every other Meccano boy throughout the world.

Any boy possessing a Meccano Outfit may join the Meccano Guild. Send for full particulars and a form of application to the Secretary, Meccano Guild, Binns Road, Liverpool.

MECCANO CLUBS.—There are now Meccano Clubs in most towns, run by enthusiastic Meccano boys and guided by adult Club Leaders. They hold regular meetings, arrange exhibitions and concerts and generally enjoy themselves in the ways in which boys find delight. They are all affiliated to the Meccano Guild, whose officials tell the boys how to form and run the Clubs so as to make them successful.

The Meccano Guild Secretary will let you know if there is a Meccano Club in your town, and if you write to him he will give you interesting information about this great world-wide boys' movement.

THE HORNBY ELECTRIC TRAIN

The Hornby Electric Train

The Metropolitan Railway

THE famous Metropolitan Railway, on which the Hornby Electric Train system is modelled, was incorporated in 1853 as the North Metropolitan Railway, and re-incorporated in the following year as a mixed gauge line. It was worked for six months—in 1863—by the Great Western Railway with broad gauge rolling stock, but in consequence of a disagreement between the two Companies, the Metropolitan Railway had to provide rolling stock and work the line on the narrow gauge at seven days' notice in August 1863.

Electrical working was commenced in 1905, and to-day the entire route is operated by both steam and electric trains. Automatic signalling (all-electric) is installed on several sections of the line, and a similar system of signalling, but with "upper-quadrant" semaphores in the open, is also used.

The system covers a considerable area to the North of London, and serves Wembley, Harrow, Uxbridge, Rickmansworth, Chesham, Aylesbury, etc., and exercises running powers over short sections of other London Railways. Every year the Metropolitan Railway carries over a hundred million passengers!

The Latest Hornby Thrill

THE Hornby Electric Train is modelled on the lines of the well-known Metropolitan Railway, and is most realistic in appearance. Both Loco and Coaches are fitted with electric lights, which may be switched on and off at will. The finish and workmanship are of the highest quality.

The motor is the most efficient ever fitted into a model loco. It is adapted to be used on the ordinary town current of 100 to 240 volts, either alternating or direct. Neither accumulators nor dry batteries are needed. A regulator is provided to control the speed.

Any boy can fit up the track and operate the train. Full instructions accompany each set, and there are no difficulties. All the regular Hornby Series rolling stock and practically all the accessories, may be used with the Hornby Electric Train.

Loco, Coaches and rails are fully covered by our usual guarantee.

Electric Train, London Metropolitan Railway

HORNBY EL

BRITISH AN

The Hornby Electric Loco measures 9¾″ in length, from buffer to buffer, and weighs, complete, 1 lb. 14 ozs. The Passenger Coaches are each 13″ long, and Loco and Coaches are beautifully enamelled in realistic colours. The Loco mechanism is well built and carefully tested.

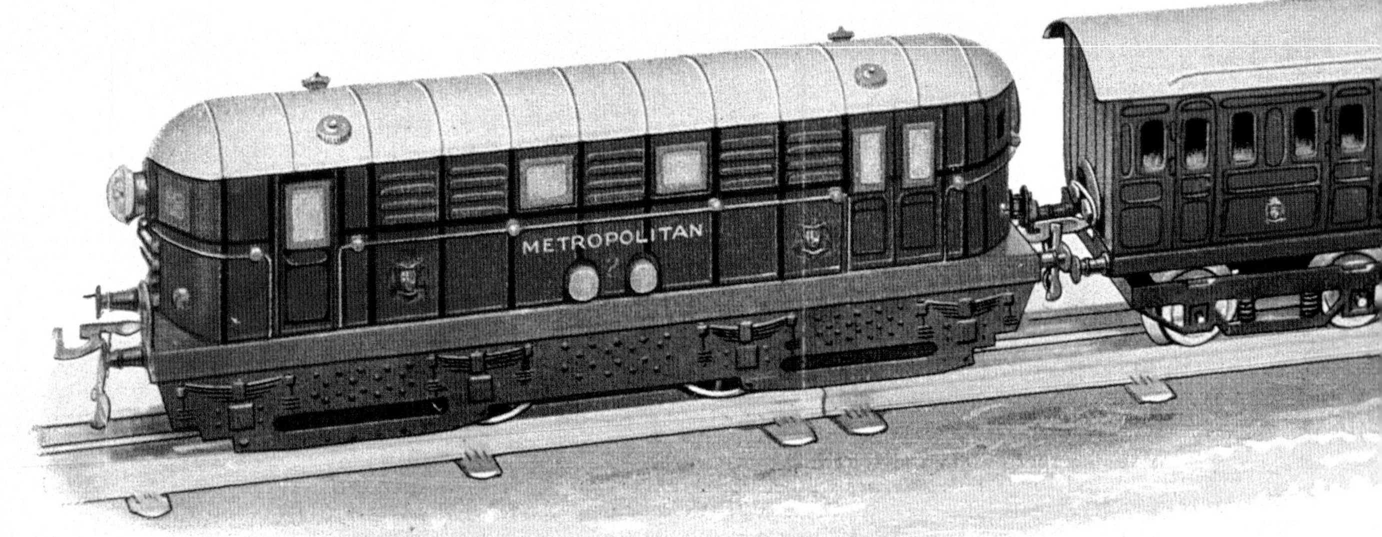

THE Hornby Electric Train is designed for hard and continual wear ; its massive construction is indicated to some extent in the illustration. Nuts and bolts are used wherever possible in holding the various sections together, with the result that all its components may be removed with ease in order to repair or replace.

The Loco is an exceptionally powerful model, and will start on, and climb, a steep gradient. The field winding is 150 yards in length and consists of Double Silk Covered wire which eliminates any possibility of insulation breakdown.

G

Hornby Trains are teste
A form of guarantee is furnish
repair or replace, at our opt
factorily from any cause other
of

TRIC TRAIN

UARANTEED

Hornby Electric Train Set

Each Set contains Electric Loco, two Metropolitan Passenger Coaches, and Electrical Rails to form a circle 4 ft. in diameter, together with a rheostat, complete with regulating handle by which the speed of the train may be controlled, and rail terminal plate. The Loco is fitted with reversing gear.

Complete Set, well boxed	Price 110/-
Hornby Electric Loco	52/6
Hornby Coach, Metropolitan	18/-

ee

heir efficiency is guaranteed. each loco, and we undertake to loco that fails to run satis- isuse, within 60 days of date se.

As soon as you have obtained your set, all that you require is a 60-watt electric lamp of the same voltage as your house supply. Everything else is included in the Set. Place the lamp in the socket of the regulator switch panel, fix the adapter in a lamp socket of the house supply, and your train is ready to start at a touch on the control handle.

The Loco and Coaches are fitted with electric lamps and may be illuminated as desired, on operation of the switches provided at either end of the vehicles.

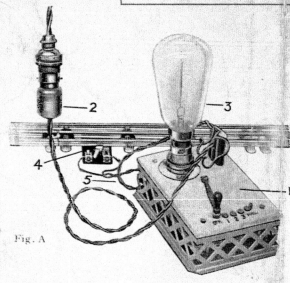

IMPORTANT FEATURES OF THE HORNBY ELECTRIC TRAIN

CURRENT

The Hornby Electric Train is adapted to be used on alternating or direct current of 100 to 240 volts. Included in the set is a regulator (1, Figure A) for controlling the speed of the train. This should be connected to the house lighting system by means of an adapter (2), and a 60-watt lamp (3), of the same voltage as the supply, placed in the socket on the regulator. (This lamp is not supplied in the set).

A fully illustrated sheet of instructions is included in every Hornby Electric Train Set.

Fig. A

Fig. B

CONNECTIONS

The regulator (1) is connected to the rail terminal plate (4) which is included in the set) by a twin flexible wire (5). Whilst connections are made, it is important to see that the regulator handle is at the OFF position.

When the loco is on the rails it is absorbing practically the whole of the current, so that if the centre or "live" rail be inadvertently touched there is no danger of an unpleasant shock.

If the connections have been properly made, the train will start running immediately the regulator handle is placed on the first stud, and the speed may be gradually increased by moving the handle to the second, third, and "full" positions.

CARE OF THE LOCOMOTIVE

Care should be given both to the motor and cars, in order to ensure satisfactory running. The collecting shoes (1, Figure B), wheel flanges (2), and rails should be kept clean and free from oil, in order to make good contact. The axles (3), gear bearings (4), and both ends of the armature shaft (5), should be lubricated with a little light oil, but not used too freely. One end of the armature shaft may be oiled from the bottom of the loco at (5), but to obtain access to the other end it will be necessary to remove the roof by unscrewing the four screws, when a pointed match stick should be used in order to prevent the oil spreading to the commutator and brushes. The commutator and brushes should not be oiled. The regulator (1, Figure A) should always be used to stop the train and care should be taken to see that it is in the OFF position before making any adjustments to the system.

Fig. C

THE HEAD-LIGHT

There are two switches at each end of the loco for the purpose of lighting the train (Figure C). The head-light (1) may be lighted separately by moving the switch handle (2) off the stud (3).

LIGHTING THE COACHES

To light the coaches, the switch handle (4, Figure D) at the rear of the loco must be moved off the stud (5) and the two-pin plug (6) of the first coach inserted in the sockets (9) and (5) on the loco. The second coach is connected in a similar manner, the only difference being that the sockets (7) on the coaches are in a horizontal instead of a vertical position.

It is not necessary to insert a lamp in the rear socket of the loco, but the switch handle (2) should be in a vertical position.

REVERSING THE LOCO

To reverse the direction of the loco the lever (10, Figure C) should be pushed in or drawn out as far as it will go.

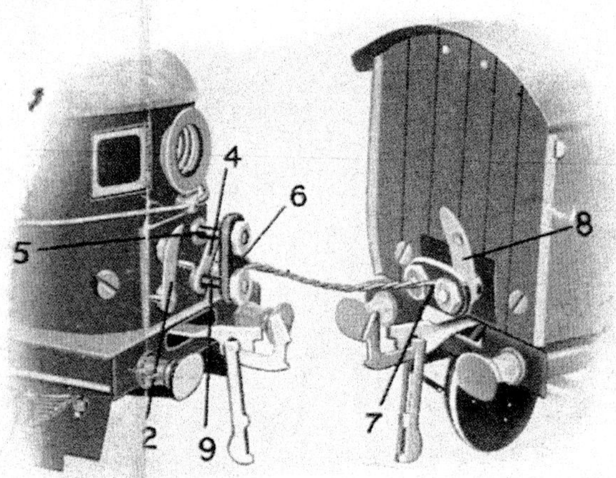

Fig. D

MECCANO LTD., BINNS ROAD, LIVERPOOL

The HORNBY BOOK of TRAINS

PRICE THREEPENCE

THE HORNBY BOOK OF TRAINS

Richard Trevithick

"I believe you will live to see the day when railways will supersede almost all other methods of conveyance in this country—when mail coaches will go by railway, and railroads will become the great highway for the King and all his subjects. The time is coming when it will be cheaper for a working man to travel upon a railway than to walk on foot."—*From a speech by George Stephenson shortly before the opening of the Stockton and Darlington Railway.*

George Stephenson

FOREWORD

ALTHOUGH the Stockton and Darlington Railway was the first public railway to carry passengers under Parliamentary sanction, it was not the first railway to be constructed under Parliamentary powers. This honour belongs to the Surrey Iron Railway, opened in 1804. The Surrey Railway was only intended for goods traffic, however, whereas the Stockton and Darlington Railway was not only organised for public goods traffic of all kinds, but also had definite rights with regard to conveying passengers.

The opening of the Stockton and Darlington Railway on 27th September 1825 is regarded rightly as one of the great events of history. Some of the onlookers treated the ceremony with ridicule, but a considerable number must have realised that there was a great future before the locomotive. Yet it is unlikely that the most imaginative spectator present could have foreseen the stupendous changes that the railway was destined to effect in the conduct of the world's affairs.

London to Edinburgh: 1825, ten days; 1925, eight hours

At the dawn of the nineteenth century man moved about very much in the same manner as he had been doing for generations past. Unless he was able to afford a horse he could only get from one place to another by walking, although, if blessed with sufficient means, he would sometimes use a Sedan chair for short distances, making longer journeys by coach. People who lived in Edinburgh and wished to travel to London had the opportunity of making the journey by stage coach only once every month. The journey required ten days in summer, but in winter twelve days or even more were required, because then floods and impassable roads were often encountered.

In addition to the discomfort of a journey by coach there was always the possibility of an encounter with highwaymen, and it is no matter for surprise that travelling in those days was regarded as a highly adventurous undertaking. There is little wonder that to most people the country outside a radius of some twenty miles of their homes was remote as a foreign land.

A Hundred Years Hence?

All this has been altered by the railway and to-day every town in the Kingdom is linked to a vast network of over twenty-four thousand miles of railroad. We travel in comfort, eat and sleep on board the train, and the ten days' coach journey from Edinburgh to London is accomplished in eight hours. The "iron horse," as the early locomotive was at first quaintly termed, has overcome every obstacle, mechanical and geographical. It travels across valleys; crosses gaping chasms; tunnels through the great mountain ranges; penetrates jungles; and safely traverses dangerous swamps and bogs—even wide rivers fail to check its progress.

Whatever steps may be taken in the future to modify or develop means of transport, it seems very unlikely that the railway can be superseded by any more satisfactory system. In these days of turbine-locomotives, far-seeing inventors, and keen business men, however, it is unwise to prophesy that the method of locomotion will always remain the same. The day may not be far distant when the Age of Steam must give way to the Age of Electricity, with consequent changes that we can foresee as little as the spectators of 1825 foresaw the *"Flying Scotsman"* or the giant locos of America.

One Hundred Years of Railways.

The Development of Iron Rails

THE iron rail may be said to have developed to meet the requirements of the English coal industry, particularly in the northern counties. When the coal is brought to the surface it is immediately necessary to transport it to a place of shipment. At first this was done by carrying it on horseback in sacks or otherwise, but later, two-wheeled carts came into use, thus enabling larger quantities to be transported. The next step was to improve the running of these carts by providing a "tram-way" of flagstones, which again led to the carts being enlarged and mounted on four wheels, such vehicles being known as wagons.

Considerable attention was next paid to making easier the haulage of the wagons, and it was not long before a form of wooden rail was introduced. These rails consisted of pieces of planking either laid parallel upon wooden sleepers or embedded in the ordinary track. The resulting decrease in friction enabled a single horse to draw a large wagon fully loaded.

It was found that the wooden rails quickly wore away and so thin iron plates were nailed to them to protect them. Later, cast iron rails were introduced to avoid trouble through the rotting of the wooden rails. A cast iron road of this kind was called a "plate-way" on account of the plate-like form in which the rails were cast. The men who laid down the track were known as "platelayers"—a name that continues to be used to-day.

Jessop's Iron Rail

Section of Flanged Wagonway

In 1789 William Jessop built a railway at Loughborough, using a cast iron edge rail and wheels with an inner flange. Jessop's rails were cast with a kind of foot, through which they were spiked down to cross-sleepers. This foot was abandoned later and the rails were placed on "chairs," the lines being braced with cross-sleepers.

The introduction of the locomotive made it necessary that rails of greater strength should be constructed and consequently the cast iron rail was followed by the wrought iron rail, which gave place, in turn, to the present steel rail, now universally used.

Modern track is made of steel rails over 44 ft. in length and weighing $97\frac{1}{2}$ lbs. per yard. These are held in position by cast iron chairs, into which they are wedged by blocks of compressed wood, called "keys." The chairs are bolted firmly to "sleepers," which consist of cross-pieces of timber, treated with creosote or other preservative to make them weatherproof, and laid about 30 in. apart upon a bed of "ballast" about a foot in depth. The ballast consists of some good draining material such as slag or gravel, and lateral movement of the sleepers is prevented by tightly packing the ballast under and round them. Adjoining rails are connected by what are known as "fish-plates," the joints overhanging and not resting upon the sleepers. At curves the outer rail is raised a little above the level of the inner rail in order to counteract the centrifugal force of trains passing round the curve at high speed.

Flanged Wagon, 1765.

Early Steam Locomotives

THE considerable benefits derived from the use of the railway in the transport of coal, suggested its employment for the conveyance of other commodities. Those with vivid imaginations even dared to suggest that it would be useful for the conveyance of passengers! Experiments were tried in various parts of the country and at the time of the opening of the Stockton and Darlington Railway, in 1825, there were already twenty different railways in operation, but they were all worked by horses and conveyed merchandise only. Of course, with either of these limitations the railway could never have become more than a localised system of transport, and it was not until after the introduction of the locomotive that its most important development began.

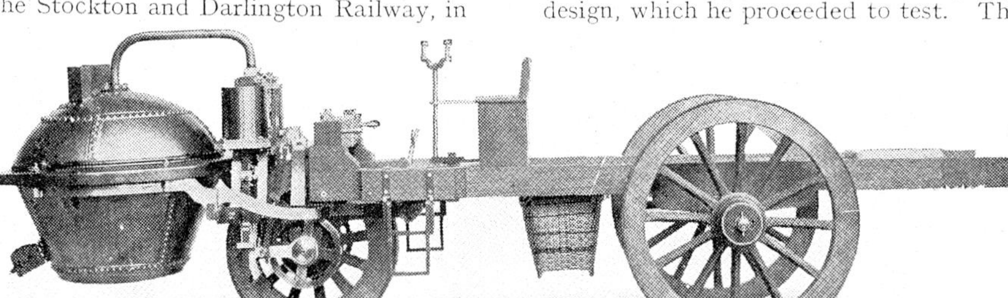

Cugnot's Steam Engine (1770)

A large share of the credit for the introduction of the locomotive is due to George Stephenson. It was through his ingenuity in demonstrating the practicability of the locomotive that the Act, covering the working of railways by mechanical power, was at last passed by Parliament. Stephenson cannot be regarded as the inventor of the locomotive, however, for it originated in the collective work of a number of earlier workers. Had it not been for such men as James Watt, Newcomen, and his partner Cally; Matthew Murray of Leeds, and other pioneers, the locomotive could never have been brought to perfection by Stephenson.

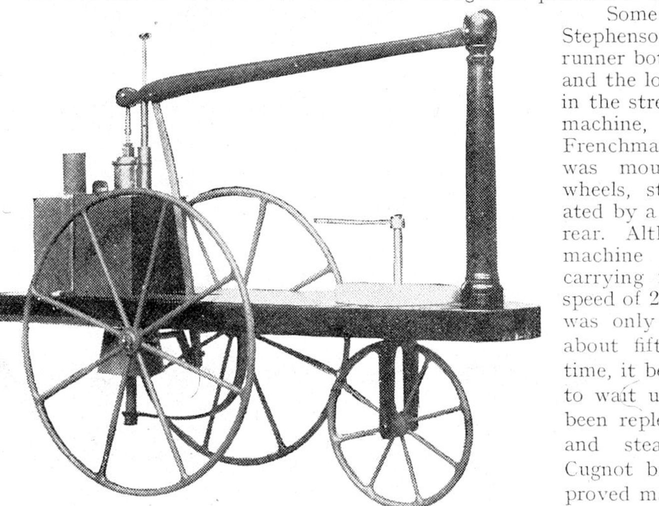

Murdock's Steam Carriage (1786)

Some 50 years before Stephenson's time, the forerunner both of the motor car and the locomotive appeared in the streets of Paris. This machine, invented by a Frenchman named Cugnot, was mounted upon three wheels, steam being generated by a small boiler at the rear. Although this peculiar machine was capable of carrying four persons at a speed of 2¼ miles per hour, it was only able to work for about fifteen minutes at a time, it being then necessary to wait until the boiler had been replenished with water and steam raised again. Cugnot brought out an improved machine in 1770, but when it was tried in the streets of Paris it was deemed to be a public danger and was locked up in the Arsenal!

In 1784 a somewhat similar machine was constructed by William Murdock, inventor of coal gas lighting. Murdock was employed by the famous firm Boulton & Watt, whose engines he considerably improved. Then he built an engine of his own design, which he proceeded to test. The extreme difficulty with which trials of this machine were carried out affords a striking example of the conditions prevalent in those days. It was within Murdock's memory that people had been burned at the stake for witchcraft, and probably this consideration decided him to make his tests with as much secrecy as possible. One Sunday night, however, whilst he was giving his machine a trial run down a narrow country lane, it ran on ahead of him and encountered some people on their way home from Church. We can imagine the consternation caused in the minds of these simple country folk at the sight of the snorting machine, rushing on them out of the darkness! No wonder that they scattered in all directions, convinced that the "Evil One" was really upon them at last!

If any one man can claim the invention of the steam locomotive that man is Richard Trevithick, a Cornishman, for his was certainly the first engine to run on rails and to haul wagons on a railway. On a wagon-way at Merthyr Tydvil, his locomotive proved itself capable of drawing five wagons laden with 10 tons of iron and 70 passengers, a distance of 9 miles, at a rate of nearly five miles an hour. This historic experiment was made in 1804 at Trevithick's own expense, for he was convinced that his machine would work with sufficient success to recommend it for general use. The wagon-way was unable to stand the unusual strain, however, and since the owners would not incur the necessary expense of keeping the track in good condition, Trevithick could not develop his invention. After designing a locomotive to the order of Christopher Blackett, the owner of Wylam Colliery, Trevithick appears to have turned his attention to other branches of engineering. He endeavoured to tunnel the Thames, worked at the idea of the double-expansion and triple-expansion engine, made the first steam threshing machine and was the first to design a propeller for steamships. This very remarkable man has been described as being "one of the greatest geniuses who ever lived," and he is commemorated by a window in Westminster Abbey.

Trevithick's First Locomotive (1804)

Matthew Murray and William Hedley

In 1811, Matthew Murray devised an engine to the order of John Blenkinsop, of Middleton Colliery, near Leeds. This engine exerted a tractive power five times as great as Trevithick's, although it was itself no heavier. A toothed driving wheel was made to engage in projecting lugs fixed at the side of the rail to eliminate any possible wheel-slip. Stephenson visited Leeds in 1812 to inspect this railway, the fame of which had spread far and wide.

Another successful attempt to employ steam as a motive power on railways was carried out in 1813 by William Hedley, on the Wylam wagon-way, which now forms part of the London and North Eastern Railway. Hedley constructed several engines embodying important improvements on the designs of both Trevithick and Blenkinsop. These quaint old locomotives became known as "Puffing Dillies"—the former horse-wagons having been termed "Dillies"—but the title later became corrupted to "Puffing Billies." In Hedley's engines the drive from the cylinders was distributed over four pairs of wheels, connected by spur-gears, the improved grip on the rails thus obtained enabling Blenkinsop's rack and pinion to be eliminated. It appears that Hedley had not complete faith in adhesive working, however, for he also provided wheels with teeth to grip the ground between the rails.

All these locomotives were built and were actually running before Stephenson came on the scene to perfect the locomotive that was the foundation of the railway system as we now know it.

A quaint colliery engine at work at Leeds in 1812. Built by Matthew Murray to the design of John Blenkinsop, the loco was propelled by a toothed-wheel engaging in a rack alongside the rails

From Lowly Cow-Herd to Famous Engineer

The story of George Stephenson's life is one that must appeal to all boys, for it is a story of perseverance and industry that fires the imagination. He was born on 9th June 1781, at Wylam-on-Tyne, and the family lived in one of the lower rooms of a small two-storeyed house near the colliery. His father, the fireman of the old pumping engine at Wylam Colliery, received a wage of only 12/ a week, and not only lived on his wage, but also managed to maintain his wife and six children! It was in these modest circumstances that the great engineer spent his childhood, little dreaming of the wonderful career that lay before him. He did not go to school—indeed, after rent and food had been paid for, there was but little left from his father's scanty wage to pay for anything but clothing.

In his early days Stephenson was fully employed helping to nurse his younger brothers and sisters, but later he obtained his first situation. His duties were to keep the cows off the tram-road that ran from the colliery to the wharf, and to close the gates at night after the last wagon had passed, for which work he received a wage of 2d. per day.

Matthew Murray of Leeds (1765-1826)

Stephenson Appointed Engineman

As he grew older, Stephenson was set to harder work, ploughing the fields and hoeing turnips for 4d. a day, but he was not particularly interested in this work, his great ambition being to work at the colliery. At last he went there as a "picker," to separate stones from the coal sent up from the mine below. At 14 years of age, he was appointed to assist his father in firing the engines, at what seemed the princely wage of 1/- per day.

Stephenson was very fond of trying feats of strength with his friends and had frequent trials of lifting heavy weights, throwing the hammer and putting the stone. Although he could not acquire the requisite knack in the last-named, he was unbeaten in throwing the hammer. He was successful, too, at weight-lifting, and on one occasion lifted as much as 60 stones.

Taking the Colliery Engine to Pieces

When he was fifteen years of age his wages were raised to 12/– per week, and it is related that on coming out of the foreman's office on the Saturday night on which he received the advance, he announced the fact to a fellow-workman, adding triumphantly: "I am now a made man for life."

A new pit being opened at Newburn, Stephenson was appointed engineman, his work being to watch the engine and to see that the pumps were efficient in drawing water. If his engine stopped through some defect that he could not remedy, it was his duty to call in the chief engineer of the colliery to set it right. He endeavoured to learn as much as he could regarding the working of his engine and in this task we may imagine that he was in his element. He studied his engine from morning to night until he knew exactly how it was constructed, and he was never tired of inspecting and watching it. When the colliery was closed at week-ends or at holiday time he would take the engine to pieces so as to be better able to understand how it worked. He must have felt very confident in himself to do this, for it would have proved disastrous had he not been able to reconstruct the engine so as to have it working when the colliery re-opened.

The Second Locomotive constructed by Stephenson at Killingworth

Stephenson Constructs his First Loco

"High Street House," Wylam-on-Tyne, the humble cottage in which George Stephenson was born

While the locomotive experiments on the Wylam wagon-way were proceeding, Stephenson was giving anxious attention to the problem of hauling coal from the Killingworth mines to the river with greater speed and economy. The idea was gradually forming itself in his brain that the haulage of the future would be carried out by steam. He frequently went to inspect the Wylam locomotives and also visited Leeds, where he saw the Blenkinsop-Murray locomotive at work—drawing 16 wagons and laden to 70 tons—at a speed of three miles an hour.

Smooth Wheels and Forced Draught

It was not long before Stephenson determined to set about building a locomotive himself and with this idea in view, he approached Lord Ravensthorpe, the principal partner in the Killingworth colliery, urging him to give the new motive power a trial. Lord Ravensthorpe considered the matter carefully and ultimately authorised Stephenson to proceed with the construction of a locomotive, advancing money for the purpose. Stephenson pressed forward with the greatest eagerness. His first locomotive, completed after about ten months' work, had a wrought-iron boiler and two vertical cylinders of 8 in. diameter and 2 ft. stroke, the motion of the crank being transferred to the wheels by spur-gearing. This loco was tried on the Killingworth railway on 25th July 1814 and succeeded in hauling eight loaded wagons of 30 tons weight, at a speed of about four miles an hour on a rising gradient of 1 in 450.

Although this loco, popularly known as "*Blucher*," was a considerable improvement upon the Wylam locos, it was very cumbersome, noisy and inefficient. One noteworthy feature was that it had smooth wheels, for Stephenson had satisfied himself by experiment that the adhesion between the wheels of the loco and the rails was sufficient for the purpose of traction. Stephenson afterwards more than doubled the power of this loco by turning the waste steam into the funnel, considerably increasing combustion by means of the draught thus set up. The actual invention of the steam-blast, as this arrangement is called, has been claimed for various inventors. In the following year Stephenson constructed a second loco known as "No. 2," which combined the good points of all previous locos. Its pistons were connected direct to the wheels by cross-bars and connecting-rods and it has strong claims to be regarded as the ancestor of the railroad giants of to-day. Stephenson later attached the connecting rod to a pin direct to the driving wheels—an arrangement that continues in use to this day. Many other improvements followed and Stephenson soon attained some degree of fame throughout the north of England.

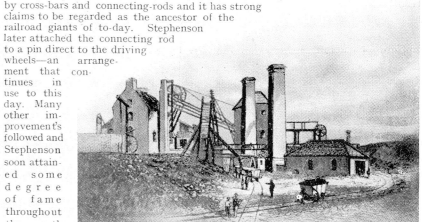

Westmoor Colliery, Killingworth, Northumberland, where Stephenson was at one time employed as brakesman

The Stockton and Darlington Railway

In the early part of the nineteenth century it was realised that a considerable amount of traffic might be done in the export of coal from the Durham coal-fields to London and elsewhere, if some means of communication, other than the road, could be provided to deal with this traffic to the coast.

As early as 1810 a committee had considered a proposal to provide communication between Stockton and Darlington, the two towns principally affected, by means of a railway or canal. During the deliberations, which extended over several years, each method of transit alternatively gained favour at different times. A meeting held in 1813 decided upon a canal, but in 1816 the decision was amended to the undertaking being a joint project of a canal and railway. In 1820 a further and final decision was made in favour of a railway only.

The promoters of the scheme founded the Stockton and Darlington Railway Company, the ultimate success of which was largely due to Edward Pease, a Quaker resident of Darlington. Pease is described as having been a "thoughtful and sagacious man who could see a hundred years ahead," and it is evident that he fully earned the title of "the Father of Railways" by which he afterwards became known.

The Opening of the Stockton and Darlington Railway, 27th September, 1825

Stephenson Visits Darlington

At the outset, the directors of the railway found themselves confronted with numerous difficulties, the most formidable of which was the strong opposition they encountered when the first application was made to Parliament for the necessary power to construct a tram-road. As a consequence of this opposition, organised by the Duke of Cleveland, who owned some fox-covers through which the railway was to pass, the Bill was rejected.

A new survey was made, however, and a second application to Parliament in 1819 was successful. The Bill provided for the making and maintaining of tramroads for the passage of "wagons and other carriages" with "men and horses or otherwise." Between certain hours of the day the public would, on payment of the usual fees, be allowed to use the tramroads formed by the company "with horses, cattle and carriages." Thus we see that the employment of locomotives did not enter into the original scheme.

About this time George Stephenson and Nicholas Wood, the viewer of Killingworth Colliery, visited Edward Pease at Darlington. Stephenson explained that he had heard of the proposals regarding the new railway, and the reason of his visit was to urge the use of locomotives instead of horses. Mr. Pease was so much impressed by Stephenson's open manner and apparent ability, that he consented to visit Killingworth to inspect his locomotives.

Appointed Engineer

The outcome of this was that at the next meeting of the directors of the Stockton and Darlington Company it was decided to request Stephenson to make a new survey of the line with a view to using it as a mechanically-operated railway. Stephenson undertook the task and submitted his report at the end of six weeks. The result was that he was appointed the company's engineer at a salary of £300 per annum, and the reconstruction of the line commenced shortly afterwards. The amended Stockton and Darlington Act, with a clause inserted giving power to work the railway by means of locomotive engines, was sanctioned in 1823.

It was decided to give Stephenson's engines a fair trial in the haulage of coal and merchandise, but it was arranged that at first the passenger traffic should be worked by horses. It is curious to note, by the way, that very little provision had been made for the conveyance of passengers and in estimating the yearly revenue, the probable receipts from this source were reckoned as negligible.

Three locomotives were ordered from Stephenson & Co., of Newcastle, a firm established by George Stephenson to specialise in the construction of locomotives. The first of the three to be delivered was "*Locomotion No. 1*" and this engine embodied all the improvements that Stephenson had introduced up to that time. It weighed about 8 tons, and had one large flue through the boiler, by which the heated air passed direct from the furnace at one end, lined with firebrick, to the chimney at the other end. Combustion in the furnace was quickened by the adoption of the steam-blast in the chimney, and indeed the heat raised was sometimes so great that the chimney became almost red hot. "*Locomotion No. 1*" was capable of speeds of from 12 to 16 miles an hour, but was particularly adapted for hauling trains of coal wagons at low speeds.

On the 27th of September 1825, the day appointed for the opening of the Stockton and Darlington line, a great concourse of people assembled to witness the event. Those who had interests in coaches and posting houses, or those whose land had been cut through during the progress of the line, were hoping to see the complete failure of the "travelling-engine." Farmers, too, were very much opposed to the introduction of the locomotive, for they had been told that it would cause panic amongst their cattle, and that the smoke and ashes issuing from the chimney would ruin their crops and fruit trees. Many other fallacies were circulated and special handbills were printed, to make known to all and sundry the terrible effects that would follow the introduction of the locomotive.

The First Passenger Train

Those who hoped to see the engine fail were disappointed, however, for the opening was successful in every way. The "*Locomotion,*" driven by Stephenson himself, hauled a train of thirty-eight vehicles made up as follows :—six wagons, loaded with coal and flour ; a special passenger coach, carrying the directors and their friends ; twenty-one wagons, fitted with temporary seats for passengers ; and, lastly, six more wagon-loads of coal.

The train was drawn up Brusselton Incline by means of ropes hauled by a fixed engine, the locomotive waiting to receive it on the other side. The event was thus described: "A signal being given, the engine started off with its immense train of carriages; and such was its velocity that in some parts its speed was frequently twelve miles an hour." The train reached Stockton on time, with about 600 passengers, either in or hanging on to the wagons, all anxious to be able to lay claim to having ridden in the first train.

The Historic "Locomotion No. 1" built by the Stephensons in 1825

Unexpected Sources of Revenue

The Stockton and Darlington Railway enabled an enormous amount of coal to be shipped from Stockton and Middlesbrough. At that time Middlesbrough as a town was unknown, there being then only a few cottages, and it may be truly said that the prosperity of Middlesbrough and surrounding district is the direct outcome of the success of Stephenson's "*Locomotion No. 1.*"

Even the railway company were surprised at the amount of traffic that came to them, principally the haulage of coal to the coast for export to London and elsewhere. In comparison with this export traffic, the amount of coal carried for sale at the stations along the line was very small, although this was expected to be the main source of the company's revenue.

Another famous engine, "Puffing Billy," built (in 1813) twelve years before "Locomotion No. 1," by William Hedley, of Newcastle-on-Tyne

When the Bill for the establishment of the railway was before Parliament, the Earl of Durham had succeeded in having a clause inserted limiting the railway company's charge for carrying coal to Stockton to one halfpenny per ton per mile. The object of this was to protect the Earl's own trade in the export of coal. The directors of the railway believed that the very low rate thus imposed would make it impossible for the company to carry coal to the ports at a profit. In this they were wrong, however, for the shipment of coal to the ports became enormous and this work soon formed the main traffic of the railway. The trains caused many new businesses to come into existence in the district served by the railway, and this again reacted beneficially on the traffic in the haulage of coal from the mines.

In a similar manner, the passenger traffic, which had not been thought of seriously in the original estimates, became considerable. The single passenger coach that took part in the opening procession was built by Stephenson and was named "*The Experiment.*" This vehicle was little more than a caravan. It had a row of seats along each side and a long table fixed down the centre, and the door was at the rear end as in the case of an omnibus.

The Liverpool and Manchester Railway

THE success of the Stockton and Darlington Railway suggested the possibility of a railway from Liverpool to Manchester, to deal with the ever-increasing traffic between the two towns. The promoters consulted Stephenson on the matter, and he eventually moved to Liverpool to take charge of the work. The difficulties encountered in the construction of the Stockton and Darlington line seemed of little account in comparison with those that now confronted him. Not only were there treacherous bogs to be crossed and great masses of rock to be tunnelled, but there were also political and financial difficulties of a nature sufficient to have disheartened any man other than Stephenson.

As in the case of the Stockton and Darlington promotion, there was considerable opposition to the Bill. This came not only from stage-coach owners and others, who all believed that the development of the railway would mean a serious financial loss, but also from land-owners through whose estates it was proposed to lay the line. More than once, Stephenson appeared in person before the Parliamentary Committee, to throw the whole of his weight into the argument in favour of the Bill. His wonderful enthusiasm for the locomotive and the future of the railway contributed greatly to the ultimate success of the Bill.

The Locomotive Contest at Rainhill (1830)

Before one of the sittings commenced, he informed the leading counsel for the railway company that he was confident he could make his locomotive travel at twenty miles an hour. This thoroughly alarmed the lawyer, who warned Stephenson that unless he moderated his views and brought his estimated speed within "reasonable limits" he would not only wreck the Bill but would be regarded as a maniac fitted only for the lunatic asylum.

Awkward "For the Coo"

An amusing incident occurred when the Committee were inquiring as to the dangers of travelling in a train going at such high speed as nine miles an hour. One of the members of the Committee, addressing Stephenson, said :—

"Suppose, now, one of your engines to be going along a railroad at the rate of nine or ten miles an hour, and that a cow were to stray upon the line and get in the way of the engine. Would not that, think you, be a very awkward circumstance ?"

"Yes," replied Stephenson with a twinkle in his eye, "very awkward—for the coo !"

On the first occasion that the Liverpool and Manchester Bill came before Parliament it was rejected and a new survey of the line had to be made. The second time the Bill was brought up the promoters were more fortunate, however, and in spite of opposition it was passed, and work on the line was commenced.

Stephenson Attempts "An Impossible Task"

Stephenson decided to begin by laying the portion of the line that was to cross Chat Moss, a great peat bog between Manchester and Liverpool. The bog, twelve miles square, was composed of a mass of rotten vegetation, the growth and decay of ages—in fact local tradition said that the bog had originated at the time of the Flood ! In wet weather it absorbed the rain as easily as a huge sponge, and its centre stood several feet higher than its edges. In the summer, when the water evaporated, the bog was left saucer-shaped and it was impossible at any time for a man to walk across the bog, or even stand on it. Mr. Dixon, the resident engineer, was inspecting the bog one day, when he slipped off the plank on which he was walking and sank to his knees. His struggles only sent him deeper, and he would have disappeared altogether but for the fact that workmen hastened to his assistance. After this experience it was not unnatural that Mr. Dixon should wonder if his chief was wise in endeavouring to construct a road for heavy locomotives, hauling trains of passengers and goods, across a bog that was found incapable of supporting the weight of a man !

Previously when the Bill was before Parliament some very scathing remarks had been made in regard to Stephenson's suggestion to cross Chat Moss. "The making of an embankment out of this pulpy and wet moss" declared counsel, "is no easy task. Who but Stephenson would have thought of entering into it ? It is ignorance almost inconceivable. It is perfect madness to propose such a plan." An eminent engineer, called as expert witness by the opposition, said : "In my opinion, unless a solid embankment can be built up from its bed, no railway can be carried across the Moss without going to the bottom." The cost of this embankment, the witness estimated, would be £270,000. Another leading engineer—one of the most distinguished of his day—declared that the laying of the line across Chat Moss was "an impossible task that no man in his senses would undertake."

The Conquest of Chat Moss

Stephenson was not to be put off by such assertions as these, however, and argued that as snow-shoes distribute a man's weight over an area much greater than that occupied by his feet, so, too, would a platform bear a railway track well above the bog. He did not propose to build an embankment such as had been recommended, it being his intention to construct a track of cross-sleepers, supported by a matting of heather and branches, so that the track would really be a floating road or elongated raft. He commenced by forming a workman's foot-path of heather across the bog, next strengthening this footpath so that it would carry a narrow-gauge railway for the transport of the materials necessary for constructing the permanent-way.

Great difficulty was experienced in carrying the work to a successful conclusion, especially at the Manchester end of the line. Here the situation became alarming, for thousands of loads of heather, grass, tree-branches and turf were spread on each side of the narrow pathway. No sooner had they attained the height of a few feet than they sank out of sight in the bog. After several weeks' toil there was so little trace of the workings that, had it not been for the ever-increasing total of the wages bill, it could almost have been supposed that the task had never been commenced.

Describing this anxious time, Stephenson wrote: "After working for weeks and weeks in filling in materials to form the road, there did not yet appear to be the least sign of our being able to raise the solid embankment one single inch; in other words, we went on filling in without the slightest apparent effect. Even my assistants began to feel uneasy and to doubt the success of the scheme. The directors spoke of it as a hopeless task and at length they became seriously alarmed—so much, indeed, that a board meeting was held on Chat Moss to decide whether we should proceed any farther. There was no help for it, however, but to go on, as an enormous outlay had been incurred and great loss would have been occasioned had the scheme been abandoned and the line taken by another route. So the directors were compelled to go on with my plans—of the ultimate success of which I myself never for one moment doubted."

Olive Mount Cutting in 1831, showing early type of carriages with guard and luggage on the roof

Opening of the Liverpool-Manchester Railway, 15th September, 1830. The scene at Edge Hill

Stephenson's great confidence in himself was surprising. He never lost heart but true to his motto "Persevere" he went steadily on with the work. At length the time came when his optimism was rewarded. The material had been slowly sinking through the bog and resting on the solid bottom of the Moss until gradually a bank rose above the surface. Before long this bank was joined to the floating road already laid across the Moss from the Liverpool side, and on New Year's Day 1830 the first train passed across. Chat Moss was vanquished, and at a cost of only £28,000—a great difference from the £270,000 estimated by the eminent engineer already mentioned. As a matter of fact, instead of being the most expensive part of the line, the line across the Moss was almost the cheapest!

Great Feats of Engineering

Another obstacle, of a different nature but no less formidable, was a great ridge of red sandstone at Olive Mount, outside Liverpool. Even to-day the excavation of Olive Mount Cutting—which, by the way is only a few minutes' walk from the factory where Hornby Trains are made—would be considered a formidable task, for nearly 500,000 cubic yards of rock were removed. In Stephenson's time, when skilled workmen and modern labour-saving devices were unknown, the achievement was all the more remarkable. The Cutting extends for over two miles through the solid rock and in places the walls rise to a height of over 100 ft. Standing on one of the bridges that cross the Cutting one cannot help paying tribute to the imagination of the man who conceived this great work, only by the completion of which was it possible to bring the line into Liverpool.

The conquest of Olive Mount was not the end of Stephenson's troubles, however, for between this point and Liverpool is another mass of rock through which it was necessary to cut a tunnel a mile and a half in length. This also proved to be a matter of great difficulty, but in blasting and hewing the rock Stephenson's colliery experience was of great service. On several occasions water penetrated into the workings, and when wet sand was encountered it became necessary to prop and under-pin the roof. More than once the workmen ceased work, refusing to continue with so dangerous a task. Stephenson was always ready to share danger with his men, however, and on at least one occasion he took off his coat and, picking up a spade, made his way into the workings. His good example immediately reflected itself upon his men and they followed him into the tunnel to continue the work.

Engineers Disagree

The directors did not at first contemplate that many passengers would be forthcoming to swell the company's revenue, The question of how the trains would be hauled was therefore not of such importance as it would have been had the railway been catering for passenger traffic alone.

Several board-meetings were held to discuss the form of power that was to be used. At some it was suggested that the trains should be hauled by ropes, actuated by a number of stationary steam engines placed at regular distances along the line. At others the opinion was in favour of employing horses to draw the wagons, as had been done in the early railways at the collieries in the north of England. Celebrated engineers, when asked to report on the matter, stated that they had no confidence in the future of the locomotive and they did not even take the trouble to examine the details of the locomotives that were running so successfully on the Stockton and Darlington Railway. They were probably actuated by jealousy arising from the fact that Stephenson, the one-time colliery fireman, had appeared before Parliament in the role of a leading engineer in support of a Railway Bill. As it was, nothing but contradictory opinions could be obtained from the experts, and this did not help the directors in coming to a decision.

This excellent model of Messrs. Braithwaite & Ericsson's "Novelty" locomotive is to be seen in the Kensington Science Museum

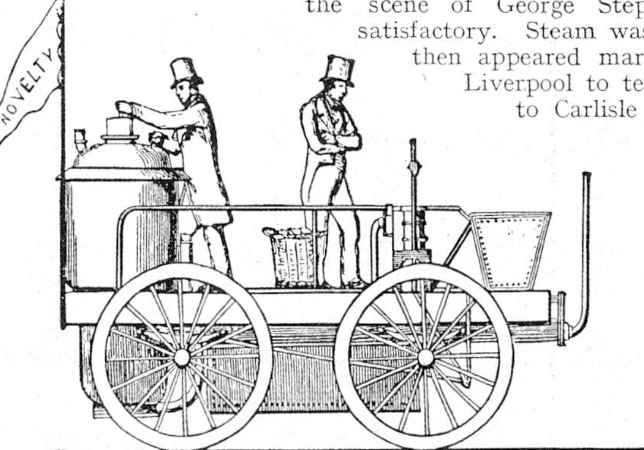

The "Novelty" (1830) was an unsuccessful competitor at the Rainhill Trials

£500 for a Locomotive

Of course, Stephenson himself had not the slightest doubt on the question and he persevered in advocating that locomotives should be employed on the new railway. Although he had scarcely any supporters, both the engineering profession and public opinion being against him, his persistent earnestness and his arguments at last had their effect. The directors determined to stimulate enterprise by offering a reward of £500 for a locomotive that would satisfactorily perform certain tests, one of which included the maintenance of a speed of ten miles an hour.

Stephenson's son, Robert, had recently returned from South America, and both father and son determined to build a locomotive for the competition. Together they produced the "*Rocket*," in which was embodied many improvements upon Stephenson's earlier engines, including a cylindrical boiler 6 ft. in length with 25 copper tubes passing through the water. These tubes were 3 in. in diameter and the heated air passed through them on its way to the chimney. The fire-box, immediately behind the boiler, was surrounded by water, the cylinders being placed obliquely on each side of the boiler, with the piston rods connected directly to the cranks on the front wheels. The tender carried a water cask as well as a supply of fuel, and engine and tender, with full load of water, weighed 4½ tons.

When the "*Rocket*" was completed it was tried on the Killingworth colliery railway, the scene of George Stephenson's early exploits. The results were thoroughly satisfactory. Steam was raised rapidly and continuously and in quantities that then appeared marvellous, and Robert Stephenson wrote to his father at Liverpool to tell him all was well. Shortly afterwards the loco was sent to Carlisle to be shipped to the Mersey.

The official trials were held at Rainhill, a village a few miles east of Liverpool, and here, on the day appointed, the ground was thronged with thousands of spectators from all parts of the country. The following engines were entered in the competition:—"*Novelty*" (constructed by Braithwaite and Ericsson); "*Sanspareil*" (Hackworth); "*Rocket*" (Stephenson); "*Perseverance*" (Burstall); and "*Cycloped*" (Brandreth). Several other engines had been under construction in different parts of the country, but as they were not ready in time they could not appear. Before the competition began the "*Cycloped*" was disqualified, for it was found that instead of the loco being driven by a steam engine it depended for its motive power on a horse in a frame—a kind of "squirrel-wheel" or tread-mill!

By the conditions of the contest each engine was to make 20 journeys over two miles of railroad at a speed of ten miles an hour, and the four engines made preparations to get up steam. With characteristic thoroughness the Stephensons had their engine ready first, and it was ordered out for an experimental trip, which it performed satisfactorily. The other competitors were less fortunate, however, for the "*Novelty*" had to retire, the bellows for forcing the air through the furnace having collapsed, while the "*Sanspareil*" was equally unlucky, developing a defect in her boiler. In the meantime the "*Rocket*" was again brought out and with 30 passengers in the wagons attached to it, it travelled along the line at a speed of 30 miles an hour, to the amazement of the spectators.

The Triumph of the "Rocket"

On the third day of the trials the "*Rocket*" was tried again, steam being raised from cold to a pressure of 50 lb. to the square inch in just under an hour.

The loco started on its journey, dragging after it about thirteen tons weight in wagons, and made the first ten trips backward and forward along the two miles of road, running the thirty-five miles, including stoppages, in an hour and forty-eight minutes. The second ten trips were performed in two hours and three minutes, and the maximum velocity attained during the trial was twenty-nine miles an hour.

In the meantime the "*Novelty*" had been patched up and was tried again, but soon after commencing to run she burst a pipe from the forcing pump. The "*Sanspareil*" had also been repaired, but now it was discovered that she was 4 cwt. over the weight limit. The judges allowed her to run, however, but before she had completed eight journeys her water pump went wrong and she came to a standstill.

While all this was taking place the engineers in charge of the "*Perseverance*" had been using strenuous efforts to get their engine into working order, but as they had been unsuccessful in making her move at more than five miles an hour they withdrew from the contest. On the following day, when the result was to be announced, Braithwaite and Ericsson pleaded hard for another trial for the "*Novelty*," and although this was granted, they had no better luck for the engine broke down again. There was now only the "*Rocket*" left in the competition, and as it had more than conformed with all the stipulated conditions the Stephensons were awarded the prize of £500.

The hostility displayed by many of the railway directors against Stephenson's plans now miraculously disappeared, for the competition had firmly established the efficiency of the locomotive and showed conclusively that a new power had arrived. Stephenson's bitterest enemies now became loudest in their praise of the "great skill and unwearied energy" that had resulted in the success of the "*Rocket*." Needless to say, nothing more was heard of the 21 fixed engines, engine houses, ropes, etc., with which it had been proposed to work the route!

Timothy Hackworth's "Sanspareil," now standing in the Science Museum, South Kensington

Opening of the Railway

The directors of the Liverpool and Manchester Railway enthusiastically pushed ahead with the completion of the line. The tunnel at Liverpool was finished about the middle of 1829 and gas-lighting having been installed, it was thrown open to the public one day a week. Thousands of people came to view the great engineering achievement, and a charge of one shilling each was made for admission, the money thus raised being devoted to the support of the families of labourers who had been injured upon the line and to the Manchester and Liverpool Infirmaries.

The first trial run between Manchester and Liverpool was made on 14th June 1830, the train being drawn by a new locomotive, the "*Arrow*," with Stephenson in charge. On the return journey to Liverpool the "*Arrow*" crossed Chat Moss at a speed of nearly 27 miles an hour.

Stephenson then commenced the necessary preliminary arrangements for handling traffic and in particular for the rapid conveyance of passengers, and for nearly three months prior to the formal opening trial trips were made every week.

The public opening of the line took place on the following 15th September and attracted vast numbers of spectators from all over the country. Eight locomotives took part in the opening and the carriages of the eight trains accommodated about six hundred people. The "*Northumbrian*," driven by Stephenson himself, headed the procession. It was followed by the "*Phœnix*" driven by Robert Stephenson and the "*North Star*" driven by Robert Stephenson senior (brother to George). The procession was cheered enthusiastically by thousands of spectators throughout the whole route.

In conclusion, it is interesting to note that whereas the projectors had based their estimated revenue almost entirely upon the conveyance of merchandise, the receipts derived from passenger traffic were considerably greater, and the carrying of goods was for some time a subsidiary branch of the traffic. Shortly after its opening the railway was carrying an average of some 1,200 passengers daily, and five years later it was carrying nearly half-a-million people per year.

The "Sanspareil" as it appeared in the historic Rainhill Trials in 1830

The First Railway Companies

ALTHOUGH writers on early railways generally close the subject after describing the two railways already mentioned, we must remember that there were several other lines opened only a little later that deserve mention. For instance, while work on the Liverpool and Manchester Railway was proceeding, Stephenson was asked to undertake the construction of a short line of about 16 miles to open up communication between Leicester and the colliery districts in the western part of the county. He felt that he must decline to undertake any additional work, however, but recommended his son Robert for the post. Towards the end of 1830 Robert Stephenson commenced the construction of the line, which became known as the Leicester and Swannington Railway, and it was opened in 1832. At the Swannington end the line terminated in a long incline of one in seventeen, which was worked by ropes and a stationary engine. This engine was put down by Stephenson in 1833 and we believe it is still used occasionally.

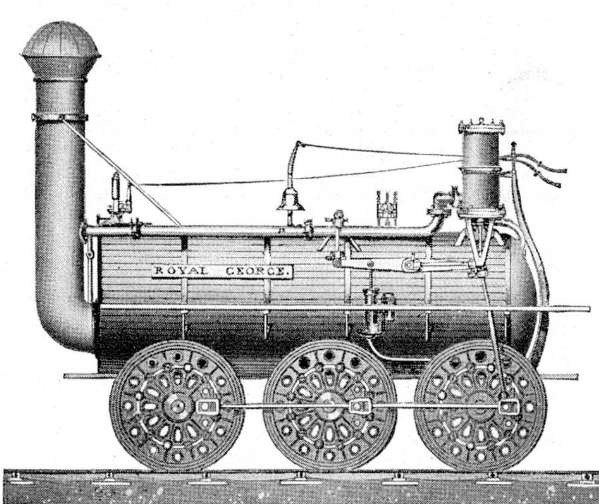

The "Royal George," the first loco with six coupled wheels

The London-Birmingham Railway

The construction of a railway between London and Birmingham was next taken in hand, and Stephenson, having been consulted as to the route, was appointed engineer of the line in conjunction with his son. In spite of the usual strong opposition from landowners, canal proprietors and others, the Bill was passed in 1833, and by the beginning of 1840 work was making satisfactory progress, Robert Stephenson, with the consent of his father having been appointed sole engineer.

The length of the line to be constructed was about 112 miles and the engineering difficulties proved to be very great. In order to construct a level road from valley to valley considerable excavations had to be made. These included Tring Cutting, 2½ miles in length and 75 ft. in depth, and the Blisworth cutting, 1½ miles in length and 65 ft. in depth. Eight tunnels, with a total length of 7,336 yards, were necessary, the most difficult problem of all being the construction of the tunnel under Kilsby Ridge. Here the inrush of water was such that it was necessary to pump continuously for eight months before the workings were cleared. The London and Birmingham Railway was finally completed in September 1838.

Another important railway constructed at this period was the Grand Junction Railway, from Birmingham to Manchester and Liverpool by way of Crewe and Warrington. George Stephenson and Joseph Locke were the engineers, and the line was opened in 1837.

The great importance of the London and Birmingham and Grand Junction Railways lay in the fact that they opened up direct railway communication between London and the great provincial towns of Birmingham, Manchester, and Liverpool.

Origin of Present-day Railway Grouping

By this time England was fully awake to the value of railways. Companies for the promotion of railway schemes sprang up like mushrooms all over the country and an enormous amount of public capital was raised for the purpose. Some lines were well planned and quickly proved successful, but many others were planned so badly that their financial failure was inevitable. It soon became evident that the numerous railways could not be worked separately with economy, and gradually the larger and better-managed companies began to absorb their smaller neighbours. It was in this manner that the great railway companies of pre-war days came into existence and reached a wonderful pitch of efficiency.

Although the ancestry of the North Eastern Railway may be traced back to the Stockton and Darlington Railway, the line grew up more directly from a series

A "Single-Driver" Express Passenger Loco, built at Doncaster in 1870

The most recent design in Railway Carriages—Articulated Sleeping Car, King's Cross to Aberdeen

of amalgamations of railways covering the area between York, Newcastle, and Berwick. Before the War, the North Eastern had a larger tonnage of mineral and coal traffic than any other railway in the Kingdom, and it was also the largest dock-owning railway company.

The Midland Railway was formed in 1844 by an amalgamation of the Midland Counties Railway, which met the London and Birmingham line at Rugby; the North Midland, from Derby to Sheffield and Leeds; and the Birmingham and Derby Railway. In pre-war days the Midland Railway had more capital invested in it than any other and once on its feet it grew rapidly, expanding in all directions. Its greatest constructional undertaking was the Settle to Carlisle line running through Kirkby Stephen and Penrith. The Midland was the first company in England to run Pullman cars and the first to abolish second-class carriages.

The London and North Western Railway grew out of the first big line leading out of London—Robert Stephenson's London and Birmingham Railway. Its rise took place in 1846 from the amalgamation of the Manchester and Liverpool, the Grand Junction, and the London and Birmingham lines. Afterwards it acquired the Lancaster and Carlisle Railway and subsequently the Chester and Holyhead line. Later it penetrated into Yorkshire and on 31st December 1921 amalgamated with the Lancashire and Yorkshire railway.

The Lancashire and Yorkshire Railway assumed the title in 1847, and possessed a wonderful network of lines traversing the most densely populated areas of industrial England. The company was composed of a large number of smaller railways including the Manchester and Bolton, Manchester and Leeds, Huddersfield and Sheffield, Wakefield, Pontefract and Goole, East Lancashire, West Lancashire and other companies.

The Great Western Railway was planned and built by I. K. Brunel, the famous engineer. Once the main line from London to Bristol was in active operation the railway proceeded to develop by a steady process of extension and amalgamation. It received a set-back through having to change its gauge, but having surmounted that trouble it made rapid progress. In 1906 the Fishguard–Rosslare route was opened, providing the shortest sea passage between England and Ireland. The Great Western has always been famous for fast running, and in 1906 the company commenced the "*Cornish Riviera*" express service from Paddington to Plymouth, a distance of 226 miles—the longest non-stop run in the world.

The Great Northern Railway from its earliest days was a fighting line, persistently striving for greater speed. It originally consisted of a main line between London and York, but later obtained a strong grip on Lincolnshire and finally obtained running powers to Manchester and Liverpool. The Great Northern was the first British company to introduce restaurant cars, this innovation taking place in 1879 between King's Cross and Leeds.

The Great Eastern Railway grew out of a combination of the Eastern Counties line and the Northern and Eastern line, which originally were of 5 ft. gauge. Afterwards one small line after another was absorbed, and the resulting company took the name of Great Eastern in 1862. At one time the Great Eastern had the reputation of being nearly the worst railway in the country, and the story of its growth to one of the best in the country is a romance worth reading.

The London and South Western Railway began its career with a line from London to Southampton. In 1830 the shippers and merchants of Southampton, who had watched with keen interest the progress of the Liverpool and Manchester Railway, realised the tremendous effect that the railway was likely to have upon the shipping of Liverpool. Consequently they decided that Southampton must follow Liverpool's example and in 1834 an Act was obtained for a line to connect the port with the Metropolis. The line was opened in the same year as the London and Birmingham Railway and

An "Old-Timer": Early Coach of Eastern Counties Railway, which Company was incorporated in 1836 and its title changed to Great Eastern in 1862

it was originally called the London and Southampton Railway. Later, Portsmouth wanted a railway but refused to be served by a branch of a line in which the name of the rival port appeared. After some discussion tact prevailed and the line was re-named the London and South Western.

This railway connected the three great naval stations of Portsmouth, Portland, and Plymouth with the great military camps at Salisbury and Aldershot, and possessed more military stations than any other line. It was also the first line to give a trial to automatic signalling, the tests taking place in April 1902.

The London Brighton and South Coast Railway consisted of a network of lines covering a large portion of south London, almost the whole of Sussex and extending into Surrey, Kent and Hampshire. The construction of this line was first suggested in 1825 but nothing happened for some ten years. The London and Brighton Company was incorporated in 1837 and the first portion of it from Brighton to Shoreham was opened in 1840.

Ancient and Modern : "Locomotion No. 1" (1825), the forerunner of the world's railways compared with L.N.E.R. Pacific Loco, "City of York" (1925)

Part of the main line to Brighton passes along what was formerly the bed of a canal belonging to the London and Croydon Railway. This latter line is noteworthy as having been one of the lines on which the atmospheric system was tried, but the scheme failed here, as elsewhere, owing to the extreme difficulty of keeping the pipes airtight. In 1899 the company introduced trains consisting entirely of Pullman cars, and was the first to adopt electricity for train lighting.

The South Eastern and Chatham Railway resulted from an arrangement for united working made in 1899 between the South Eastern and the London, Chatham and Dover Companies. The South Eastern Railway included two of the oldest railways in the south of England—the London and Greenwich, opened in 1837, and the Canterbury and Whitstable, opened in 1830.

The story of the London, Chatham and Dover Railway is closely connected with Thomas R. Crampton, born at Broadstairs in 1816. In his early days Crampton was an assistant to Sir Marc Brunel and afterwards served on the Great Western Railway under Daniel Gooch. Later he commenced designing locomotives, in which he was extremely successful. It was Crampton who, in 1851, came forward with £15,000 and thus made possible the laying of the cable between Dover and Calais, the first successful submarine cable in the world.

The Great Central Railway appeared at a later date than the other great trunk lines of the country. It began in 1837 as the Sheffield, Ashton-under-Lyne and Manchester Railway, which afterwards became the Manchester, Sheffield and Lincolnshire railway. This consisted mainly of cross-country lines from Manchester to Sheffield, Lincoln, Grimsby and Cleethorpes, with branches to Barnsley, Wakefield and elsewhere. The line ultimately succeeded in getting to London at Marylebone and then changed its name to the Great Central. One great undertaking carried through by the Great Central was the development of the huge dock at Immingham.

In Scotland, the North British Railway dates back to 1844 when the original company was incorporated for a line from Edinburgh to Berwick with a branch to Haddington. Subsequently the Edinburgh, Perth and Dundee, the West of Fife, the Edinburgh and Glasgow and the Monkland and other railways were added. Two of the great engineering works of this line were the bridges over the Forth and the Tay. The first Tay bridge, which was opened for traffic in 1878, was partially destroyed during a storm in December 1879. A second bridge was constructed alongside the original and opened in 1887.

The Caledonian Railway practically originated with the Glasgow and Garnkirk line opened in 1831. The company grew steadily by amalgamation, particularly in the years 1865–1867. This railway owned many docks and possessed a fine fleet of steamers on the various lochs and rivers.

The Glasgow and South Western Railway originated in 1840 as the Glasgow, Paisley, Kilmarnock and Ayr Railway, and took this title on amalgamation with the Glasgow, Dumfries and Carlisle Railway. It included the line between Kilmarnock and Troon, the first railway opened in Scotland, dating from 1811 and worked by horse-haulage. A great feature of the Glasgow and South Western Railway was its splendid fleet of Clyde steamers.

The Highland Railway originated with the Inverness and Nairn line, 15 miles in length, which opened in November 1855, and followed the usual course of growth by extension and absorption. One of the features of this line is its extensive use of the snow plough.

The great North of Scotland Railway Company was incorporated in 1846 for a line between Aberdeen and Inverness, with various branches. This line made far more extensive use of the electric telegraph than the other Scottish railways, and it never had any second-class carriages.

The Present Four Groups

The foregoing railway companies maintained their independent existence until 1921, when an Act of Parliament was passed requiring them to arrange themselves in four groups to commence operation in 1923. The main object of this grouping was economy in working, with a view to a corresponding reduction in charges to the public.

The four groups are now as follows :—London, Midland and Scottish (7,525 miles), consisting of the London and North Western ; Midland ; Caledonian ; Glasgow and South Western ; Highland and other smaller lines. London and North Eastern (6,714 miles), comprising the North Eastern ; Great Northern ; Great Central ; Great Eastern ; North British ; Great North of Scotland, and some smaller lines. Great Western (3,795 miles), consisting of the old Great Western line with the addition of the whole of the Welsh Railways. Finally, the Southern Railway (2,199 miles), consisting of the South Eastern and Chatham, London, Brighton and South Coast, and London and South Western Railways with smaller lines.

Development of the Passenger Carriage

The first railway coach that ran on the Stockton and Darlington Railway at its opening—George Stephenson's *"Experiment"*—was little more than a box on four wheels, but it served the purpose of showing that passengers could be carried successfully by rail. By the time the Liverpool and Manchester line was opened the passenger vehicles had improved a good deal. They were then in fact stage coaches on railway wheels, and from early illustrations it may be seen how close was the resemblance. Many people indeed travelled on the railway in their own private carriages that were run on to flat trucks.

"The Experiment"—First Passenger Coach (1825)

In these early stage coach vehicles there were usually three compartments, one first-class in the centre and a second-class at each end. Luggage was placed on the roof and the guard also was given a seat at the end of one of the carriage-tops. Third-class passengers received very little consideration. At first they travelled in open trucks, and even when these trucks gave place to carriages of sorts no attempt was made to make the vehicles comfortable. Windows were only fitted in the doors, and the seats were of plain hard wood. The cartoonists and humorous writers of those days found much material in the unfortunate third-class passenger and his rough and ready treatment!

Passenger traffic grew with surprising rapidity on all the important lines and gradually longer carriages with more comfortable fittings were introduced. After a while it was found that the length could not be increased further if the coaches were to negotiate curves with safety, and this resulted in the introduction from America of bogie trucks by means of which coaches of great length could ride easily round curves.

"Queen Adelaide" coach used in London—Birmingham Railway (1842)

Dining cars were adopted by the Gt. Northern Railway in 1879 but the trains were not then fitted with corridors and vestibules. Incidentally the meals were cooked before the train began its journey and were kept as hot as possible until the meal hour! The credit for the first corridor express with dining cars attached must be given to the old L.N.W.R. which ran a well-fitted express daily from Euston to Scotland.

Pullman cars were introduced from America by the Midland Railway in 1875, and that company also took the drastic step of abolishing second-class carriages and making every train available for third-class passengers. The first Pullmans were very successful. It was found that these smooth-riding cars were the safest portion of the train and this fact led directly to the adoption of much heavier coaches on most of our main lines. Many of the long-distance expresses to-day have Pullman cars attached, and for a small additional charge both first-class and third-class passengers may travel in these luxuriously-fitted vehicles. Pullman carriages are the property of the Pullman Car Company, and run on the various railways by agreement.

Old Chaldron Wagon—the only surviving wagon used in the first S. & D. train (1825)

Sleeping cars were first used in America and consisted of large vehicles the seating arrangements in which could be easily adapted for night use. In this country they were first used between England and Scotland on the West Coast route in 1873. These vehicles have been improved and enlarged until at the present day they are as comfortable as it is possible to imagine and even the noise of the train is practically eliminated by means of their thick rubber floors.

In the old days very little consideration was given to the lighting of railway coaches. As the number of passengers increased, however, it became necessary to have some regular system of lighting, and oil lamps were introduced. From the accounts of passengers in those days these lamps were evil-smelling affairs giving a miserably poor light. The next step was the introduction of oil gas with flat flame burners. This improved matters considerably, but a really efficient light was not obtained until the introduction of the incandescent burner which is still largely used.

A "Dandy Coach"—a horse-drawn carriage used on the N.B.R.

Incandescent lighting has certain disadvantages, however, the chief of which is danger from fire, and on account of this danger the present-day tendency is to abolish gas entirely and to light trains throughout by electricity. On electrified railways the current for lighting purposes exists already, but on steam-driven trains a small dynamo is fitted beneath each coach and driven from one of the bogie axles. In order to maintain the light when the train is at a standstill, or running too slowly for the dynamo to generate sufficient current, an accumulator battery is provided and this is charged by the dynamo during the periods in which the train is travelling at 25 miles per hour or more.

Two Famous British Locomotives

"Caerphilly Castle" (4-6-0), No. 4073, G.W.R. and "Great Northern" (4-6-2) No. 4470, L.N.E.R.

The Classification of Locos

IN the modern method of classifying locos, based on the number and arrangement of the wheels, the normal arrangement of wheels in every loco is assumed to be :—first, leading wheels ; second, coupled driving wheels ; and third, trailing wheels. The wheels of tenders are left out of consideration. For example, a loco having four leading wheels, four coupled driving wheels, and two trailing wheels would be described as being of 4–4–2 type, the figures indicating quite clearly the wheel arrangement. If a loco has either no leading wheels or no trailing wheels, a cipher, "0," is used instead of a figure, to indicate the absence of either or both of these sets of wheels. Stephenson's famous "*Rocket*," the winner of the Rainhill contest, was a 0–2–2 loco, being without leading wheels and having only two driving wheels and two trailing wheels.

It is interesting to note that in France, and certain other Continental countries, the number of axles is counted instead of the number of wheels, so that the figures are halved. Thus a loco that we should describe as being of 4–4–2 type would be described in France as 2–2–1.

Some Famous Early Types

Many of the different types of locos have been given distinctive names. Among the early types were the handsome "single-wheelers" or "single drivers," so called because they had no coupled wheels, the single pair of driving wheels being larger than the other wheels and not connected with them. For fast running with comparatively light loads the "single-wheelers" were excellent, but they were not capable of dealing efficiently with the heavy trains of modern times. The principle that as many wheels as possible must be coupled together in order to achieve the best results is now established, and thus the "single-wheeler" has gradually disappeared. The effect of coupling wheels together is to distribute the driving force among the wheels, giving greater adhesion to the rails and greater stability.

ARRANGEMENT	NAME	FORMULA
	ATLANTIC	4-4-2
	PACIFIC	4-6-2
	BALTIC	4-6-4
	MOGUL	2-6-0
	PRAIRIE	2-6-2
	CONSOLIDATION	2-8-0
	MIKADO	2-8-2
	MASTODON	4-8-0
	MOUNTAIN	4-8-2
	DECAPOD	0-10-0
	CENTIPEDE	0-12-0

Table showing classification of locos by wheel arrangement

The simplest type of "single-wheeler" was the 2–2–2, and among the last of these to be scrapped were the celebrated L.N.W.R. "*Problems*." The only other form of single-wheeler to be used extensively was the 4–2–2, and of this type a few ex-Midland, Great Central, and North Eastern locos are the sole survivors. Probably the most celebrated and graceful singles were the "8-footers" of Mr. Patrick Stirling's design on the old G.N.R., one of which we are illustrating on page 13.

The earlier types of coupled locos were the 0–4–0, 0–4–2, and 2–4–0. Except for shunting and industrial locos the first type is obsolete, and the others are represented by an ever-decreasing family, most members of which bear honoured records. Thus a few 0–4–2 locos survive in the famous old Brighton "*Gladstones*," and also on the L. & S.W.R. section in some mixed traffic locos. The 2–4–0's are more common, and no better representatives could be found than the favourite "*Precedents*" of the L.N.W.R. With the introduction of a leading bogie, a type regarded as the standard British passenger loco was evolved, although abroad this is known as the "American" type as its first example was built in the United States. This class is too numerous and well known to require further comment.

"Atlantics" and "Pacifics"

The next development of the four coupled loco was in 1897 when the G.N.R. introduced the first 4–4–2 "*Atlantics*," the advantage of which was in the wider firebox that could be fitted. Modern train loads are often beyond even the powers of an "Atlantic," however, and these locos are now giving pride of place to the 4–6–2 "*Pacifics*."

Coming now to the six-coupled types, all these owe their origin to that "maid-of-all-work," the 0–6–0, which will never be excelled for all-round usefulness. (The L.M.S. company are to build no fewer than 180 Class Four 0–6–0's during the present year). The type is termed "*Goods*" in a general way, although its activities are by no means confined to this kind of work. The addition of a leading pony truck made possible a longer boiler and heavy outside cylinder fittings, and so developed the 2–6–0 or "Mogul" type, originated in America and imported into England in the "eighties" of last century when there was a shortage of locos on the Great Northern, Great Eastern and Midland Railways. More recently this type was revived on the G.W.R. and is now becoming increasingly popular for mixed traffic working. An additional trailing pony truck is a feature of Continental and American locos, the resulting 2–6–2 being known as the "*Prairie*" type.

The latest and most powerful Garratt Articulated Loco (2-8-0 : 0-8-2), No. 2395, L.N.E.R.

Origin of the "Castles"

For express or fast goods work the 4–6–0 class is in common use, and locos having this wheel arrangement are commonly referred to as "ten-wheelers." Among them are the famous Great Western "*Castles*," and the type dates back in this country to the first 4–6–0 goods engines built for the Highland Railway in 1898. Nowadays many designers are forsaking the 4–6–0 in order to take advantage of the much larger firebox that can be fitted to a "*Pacific*," or 4–6–2 type. Recent developments in the railway world have made this type well known and the huge boilers of its members on the L.N.E.R. have captured public imagination.

Some interesting tests were recently carried out between a G.W. "*Castle*," Loco No. 4029 "*Pendennis Castle*," which worked between King's Cross and Grantham, and the L.N.E.R. "*Pacific*," Loco No. 4474 on the G.W. line, hauling the "*Cornish Riviera*" express between Paddington and Plymouth.

There are, as yet, no British tender locos of the 4–6–4 or "*Baltic*" type, although several were built for the Nord Railway of France.

"Mineral" and "Mikado"

Locos with eight wheels coupled, 0–8–0, are generally referred to as the "*Mineral*" type, their original purpose being the haulage of slow but heavy coal and mineral trains. With a leading pair of small wheels the type becomes 2–8–0 or "*Consolidation*," another name derived from American practice. Large numbers of locos built by the Government to the Great Central 2–8–0 design were used in France during the war. Many were not completed before the Armistice and most of these are now absorbed into the loco stock of the L.N.E.R., L.M.S., and G.W.R. The last-mentioned railway also has a fine type of 2–8–0 of its own design with coupled wheels large enough to attain a high speed with passenger trains. The 2–8–2 or "*Mikado*" type, so called because its first representatives were built for Japan, was introduced recently into this country by a single narrow-gauge loco, one-third scale size, for the well-known 15 in. gauge Eskdale Railway in Cumberland. An entirely new design of "*Mikado*" type is now making its appearance on the L.N.E.R. and handling with great success the heavy coal trains between Peterborough and London. Powerful locos of the 4–8–0 or "*Mastodon*" type, and the 4–8–2 or "*Mountain*" type, are used for heavy work on the *Etat* Railway of France, but these types are not represented in the United Kingdom.

Ten-coupled wheels are suitable only for special work on heavy gradients and for short runs. The Great Eastern tried a loco "*Decapod*" of this type many years ago for suburban work, the experiment showing that it was capable of more rapid acceleration than had been thought possible. The "*Decapod*" was too heavy for the track, however, and was converted into a 0–8–0 mineral loco, only to be scrapped soon afterwards. At present the L.M.S. have one "*Decapod*" at Bromsgrove for pushing trains up the Lickey Incline, which for two miles has a gradient of 1 in 37. The Austrian State Railways built some 0–12–0 banking engines before the war, but there is little likelihood of any addition to these "*Centipede*" designs.

In the present system of classification, tank locos are distinguished from locos having tenders by placing the letter "T" below or following the classification figures, as for example 4–4–0T or 2–4–2T. Type names are not used, except in the case of the "*Baltic*" (4–6–4) and "*Prairie*" (2–6–2) types, so that a 4–4–2 Tank is not called an "*Atlantic*," but is described simply as 4–4–2T.

In the case of "articulated" locos of the "Garratt" and other types, which really consist of two locos having a single boiler, the separate engine units are regarded as having separate sets of coupled wheels. Thus, from a description such as 2–8–0 : 0–8–2, the wheel arrangement is readily understood.

Famous Trains

L.N.E.R. "Flying Scotsman"

The most famous of all British trains is undoubtedly the "*Flying Scotsman*," the fame of which is world-wide. The train has been running regularly since 1850 and its comfort and punctuality quickly brought it into such favour that its name soon became a household word. For twelve years the express left London at 9.30 a.m. but in June 1862, in order to meet public wishes, the time was altered to 10 a.m., and for 63 years the train has left King's Cross daily at that hour without a break.

The corresponding train in the other direction leaves Edinburgh also at 10.0 a.m., the distance of 395 miles in each case being covered in the schedule time of 8 hours. As in the case of all other up-to-date expresses, this East Coast express is steam-heated and electrically-lighted throughout. It has always been the last word in advanced railway practice and its coaches are now constructed on the articulated principle.

G.W. "Cornish Riviera"

Very little behind the "*Flying Scotsman*" in reputation, and nothing behind it in popularity, is the Great Western Railway's "*Cornish Riviera*" Express, also known as the "10.30 *Limited*." This train daily covers the 225·7 miles, Paddington to Plymouth, without a stop in 247 minutes, this being the longest regular non-stop run in the world. The final destination of this famous train is Penzance, between which and Plymouth there are some extraordinarily difficult gradients and several stretches of single line. To accomplish this run of 305 miles in 6½ hours from start to finish necessitates the very best locomotive work. The train is composed of 10 or 12 of the latest 70ft. carriages, the seats in which are all numbered and may be booked in advance.

Few trains can surpass the "10.30 *Limited*" for smooth and easy running. It is hauled by one of the latest and most powerful express locos, and there is no difficulty in maintaining the speed schedule. Indeed, the "10.30 *Limited*" frequently runs into North Road Station, Plymouth, several minutes in advance of booked time.

The "Southern Belle" and "Harrogate Pullman"

A train for long regarded as one of the most luxurious in the world, is the "*Southern Belle*," a Pullman Train, running on the Southern Railway between London and Brighton. This train, inaugurated on 1st November, 1908 originally accommodated first-class passengers only and ran only on Sundays, but later third-class cars were added and the train ran every day. Ordinarily this luxurious train consists of nine Pullman cars, vestibuled throughout, with accommodation for 368 passengers.

The fame of the "*Southern Belle*" has been somewhat over-shadowed by the inauguration (in July, 1923) of the "*Harrogate Pullman*." This fine train was originally intended to run between London and Harrogate only, but the L.N.E.R. subsequently decided to extend the service to Newcastle, and this summer to Edinburgh. The timing of the run is so smart that the train reaches Tyneside only a few minutes later than would be the case if it were booked to run direct via Selby and York.

The "*Harrogate Pullman*" was intended in the first instance to be a summer luxury, but it proved so popular that it was retained in the winter time-table, and is likely to remain a permanent feature.

The train starts from King's Cross and the first stop is Leeds, a distance of 185¾ miles, which is covered in three hours 25 minutes. Harrogate, 203¾ miles, is reached in four hours, and the whole journey of 395¼ miles between London and Edinburgh, including stops, is accomplished in 8 hours.

The "Flying Scotsman"

The "Wild Irishman" and other famous Trains

Among other popular long-distance expresses is the "*Sunny South Special*," composed of up-to-date L.M.S. stock and starting daily, in separate sections, from the northern termini at Liverpool and Manchester. The sections are united at Crewe, and travel thence to Willesden Junction with an intermediate stop at Rugby. From Willesden a Southern Railway loco hauls the "*Sunny South*" to Brighton, Eastbourne and the Kentish coast resorts. The inception of this train was due to the unpopularity of the Southern watering places with north-country folk, owing to the trouble of transferring themselves and their luggage across London to Victoria or Charing Cross.

The "*Wild Irishman*" or "*Irish Mail*" is one of the fastest out of Euston, which it leaves every night in connection with the Holyhead-Greenore steamers. The section from Chester to Holyhead, including the difficult approaches to the Britannia Tubular Bridge crossing the Menai Straits, is covered at an average speed of over 52 m.p.h.

No list of famous British express trains would be complete without mentioning two Scottish services. The "*Tinto*" express, which for many years has left Glasgow Central at 1 p.m. for the residential districts of Lanarkshire, is a most comfortably equipped train. Special twelve-wheeled corridor carriages were built for this run, and prior to the new grouping arrangements, the "*Tinto*" and "*Grampian*" expresses were the pride of the Caledonian Railway. "*Tinto*," incidentally, is the name of a great conical hill, which overlooks Lanarkshire and Central South Scotland, where, in the neighbouring hills the Clyde has its source. The "*Grampian*" Express goes north to Aberdeen via the Caledonian main line, and on account of the severe gradients to be surmounted it needs the best efforts of the Scottish locos to keep to time.

"The Southern Belle"

Both the "*Tinto*" and the "*Grampian*" expresses are unique in having their respective names permanently emblazoned in gold letters on the carriage sides, the special rolling stock being reserved for these particular trains.

Famous Continental Trains

On the Continent there are many trains whose names are familiar to everyone interested in the world's railways. The most familiar one is probably the "*Orient Express*," which links up London with Constantinople. Before the war this famous train reached Vienna via Strasbourg, Stuttgart and Munich, but a more southerly route is now followed, via the Simplon Tunnel, Milan, Trieste and Belgrade. This alternative route saves 263½ miles between Paris and Constantinople.

Leaving Paris three times weekly, the eastbound "*Orient*" runs over the P.L.M. Railway via Dijon and Lausanne to Brigue, 408¾ miles, and near the latter station it plunges into the Simplon, the longest tunnel under the Alps (12½ miles). The express is now in Italy, and the next important point is Milan, where another section of the train from Amsterdam, Ostend, and Brussels—via Strasbourg and Basle, and through the Alps by the first Swiss tunnel, the St. Gothard—joins the Paris portion. The train now continues through Venice and Trieste to Vinkovci, 1,141¼ miles from Paris, and at this junction the Bukarest portion turns northward via Orsova. The Constantinople section continues eastward through Belgrade, drops at Nisch the carriages destined for Athens, and after halts at Sofia and Adrianople pulls up for the last time, on the shores of the Bosphorus, having covered in all 1,905¾ miles. The full time taken is 84 hours, including halts, and making allowance for the time spent at stations, frontiers, passport points, etc., the average speed works out at 27 miles an hour.

Luxurious Pullmans

Another famous train linking the capitals of Spain, Portugal, and France is the "*Sud Express.*" Its run is 1,187 miles from Paris to Lisbon, and 909½ miles to Madrid. The first section of the journey, Paris-Biarritz, 497½ miles, is run with eight stops at the good average speed of 50.5 m.p.h. (excluding halts). On the final sections to Lisbon and Madrid—the express being divided at Medina del Campo, 772 miles south of Paris—the average speed is only about 35 m.p.h.

A splendid express known as the "*Cote d'Azur Limited*" serves the Pyrenees and Basque Coast and, as its name indicates, provides only restricted passenger accommodation. The most recently inaugurated express, and certainly the most palatial one, is the "*Calais-Mediterranean Express*," more familiarly called the "*Riviera Limited*" or the "*Blue Express.*" This train has been put on to meet the requirements of wealthy passengers from London, and America via London, to the fashionable French watering places, and in the matter of luxurious sleeping-car accommodation it is unequalled. The vehicles are the property of the International Sleeping Car Company and are built of steel, wood being used for internal decoration only. The exteriors are elaborately finished in royal blue panelling with gold-leaf lining, hence the title of the train.

"The Cornish Riviera"

In conjunction with the "*Blue Express*," the Southern Railway has introduced a "*Pullman Limited*" upon the 77 miles between London and Dover, and the luxurious train awaits the boat at Calais. By this train it is possible to travel from London to Cannes or Nice in about 24 hours in the utmost comfort.

Famous Trains of Canada

As might be expected, Canada, with its vast distances, provides some interesting examples of expresses, and to-day the Canadian National Railways, comprising 22,660 miles of line, have nothing to fear in comparison with other railways throughout the world. One of the most famous of Canadian trains is the "*Continental Limited*," which leaves Montreal and Vancouver every day. The route is through the Rocky Mountains by way of the Albreda and Yellowhead Passes and across wide stretches of prairie. Each train consists of eight coaches, including first-class and colonist or third-class cars; sleepers; dining car and observation car, the last-named providing unrestricted views of the magnificent scenery through which the railway passes.

Two other famous trains are the "*National*," running between Toronto and Vancouver, and the "*Maritime Express*," the latter covering the 842 miles between Halifax and Montreal in one day, 11 hours, 35 minutes.

The trans-continental trains of the Canadian National Railways are hauled by fast locos of what is known as the "*Medium Pacific*" type. These locos have cylinders 23½ in. by 28 in., driving wheels 69 in. in diameter, boiler 70⅝ in. in diameter, supplying steam at a pressure of 200 lb. The eight-wheeled tender carries 6,500 gallons of water and 22,400 lb. of coal. The complete loco in working order weighs 416,600 lb. and the total wheel-base of loco and tender is 66 ft. 4¾ in.

The C.N.R. were the first railway system in the world to adopt wireless as a part of their regular service. To-day all the C.N.R. trans-continental trains are equipped with receiving sets—headphones and loud speakers—which keep passengers in touch with the events of the day and provide entertainment during the journey of 2,937 miles, occupying four days, 9 hours, 10 minutes.

The enormous weight of the Canadian trans-continental trains has led to the development of specially heavy and powerful locos. These include the famous "6,000" type which were built at the Kingston, Ontario, works for the C.N.R., and which are the largest passenger locos operated in Canada. An even more powerful loco, No. 4100, has been built for hauling heavy freight trains. This loco, which is of the Santa Fé type, is 92 ft. in length overall and weighs 325 tons. Its height is 15 ft. 3 in. and the smoke-box alone has a diameter of 97 in.

This monster is capable of developing 3,200 h.p.

The Largest Passenger Loco in the Empire: New 6,000" Type Loco, Canadian National Railways

Australian Expresses

Railway development in Australia has been hampered to some extent by the differences of gauge in use in the different States. None the less, the Australian railway service to-day has reached a very high standard and all the State capitals are linked up by efficient services. Starting from Central Station, Sydney, for instance, the "*Melbourne Limited*" completes its journey of 401 miles in exactly 12 hours, and taking into consideration the gradients to be encountered and the many stops to take in water, this is an excellent performance. Again in South Australia the "*Broken Hill*" express accomplishes a journey of 334 miles from Adelaide in 15 hours, and another train running to Oodnadatta in the interior covers 689 miles in 34 hours' actual running time. The Australian "*Transcontinental Limited*" is undoubtedly one of the finest trains in the world. It consists of drawing room—complete with piano—smoking, observation, dining and sleeping cars, each of which is fitted up in luxurious style. The express is electrically lighted throughout. The average speed for the whole distance of 1,051 miles between Port Augusta and Kalgoorlie is a little over 27 miles per hour, but this speed will almost certainly be increased later. The whole distance is covered in 38¾ hours. An interesting and rather unusual feature of this train is a special car accommodating eight travellers, which can be engaged by a party desiring to travel in private.

In pre-war days one of the most remarkable railways in the world was the trans-Siberian Railway. This remarkable line, 5,425 miles in length, brought London within 15 or 16 days' travel of Japan. Leaving London on a Monday morning and travelling via Ostend, it was possible to be in Moscow on Wednesday night and ten days later to steam into Vladivostok station. The trans-Siberian trains had everything possible in the way of comfort, and no matter what might be a traveller's nationality he was certain to find attendants able to speak his language. A noteworthy feature of these trains was the provision of a Church car in which services were held en route.

Famous Trains in the United States

Railway travelling in the United States is highly developed and the long-distance expresses are very fine as regards both speed and comfort. The first through service linking the East and West coasts was inaugurated in 1869, and in the following year a luxurious Pullman train known as the "*Hotel Train of* 1870" was in service. This train ran once a week and it carried two complete crews who took duty in turn.

To-day five magnificent "*Limited*" expresses are run between San Francisco, Los Angeles and Chicago. These five are known as the "*Overland*," "*Pacific*," "*Los Angeles*," "*San Francisco*" *and* "*California Mail*" respectively, and each is really a travelling hotel with every possible comfort and convenience for passengers. Another interesting train is that known as the "*Katy Flyer*." This train runs between St. Louis and Galveston, a distance of 1,134 miles, in about 36½ hours. The curious name of this express has resulted from the combination of the initials of two of the States forming the title of the company—The Missouri-Kansas-Texas Railway.

Another magnificent express on this line is the "*Texas Special*," the "*Pacific*" locos hauling which are oil fired. The "*Panama Limited*," running between Chicago and New Orleans, is a specially luxurious train that carries only one class of passengers. The distance of 922 miles is accomplished in an actual running time of 22¾ hours and the train has a splendid reputation for punctuality. One other United States train may be mentioned, that known as the "*Merchants' Limited*," running between New York and Boston. This train runs daily, except Sundays, and from its inauguration in 1903 it has been extremely popular with business men. Its scheduled time for the 229 miles is 5 hours 10 minutes. The appointments of this train have been specially devised to meet the requirements of business men and it resembles to a great extent a palatial travelling office. Normally the train consists of four 36-seat parlour cars; two 32-seat drawing room parlour cars; two 42-seat dining cars; a composite baggage and smoking car and a 40-seat observation car. Each dining car cost about £5,300 and each parlour car about £4,000.

The No. 2 Pullman Train is superb in appearance and finish, beautifully enamelled and stoved at a high temperature to ensure durability. The Loco with Tender measures 17 ins. in length, and each of the two Pullman coaches are 13 ins. from buffer to buffer. The Loco mechanism is well-built and carefully tested, and the accurately-cut gears result in a smooth-running that is a pleasure to see. It is the most attractive and satisfactory clockwork train yet produced.

UNTIL quite recent years, all that was considered necessary in a model train was something on wheels—preferably with a chimney and boiler—to run round in a circle. Boys soon became tired of such toys, however, and a demand grew for miniature trains, rails, and signals that resembled the real thing, and with which they could construct and operate a model railway, just as real railways are operated.

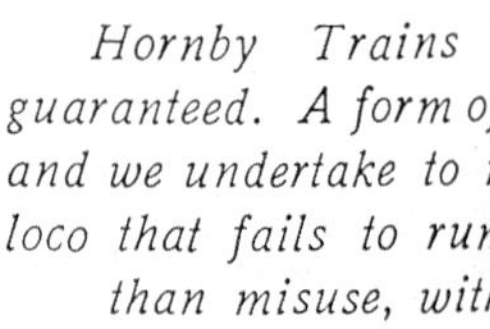

Hornby Trains
guaranteed. A form o
and we undertake to
loco that fails to ru
than misuse, wit

Hornby No. 2 Pullman Set

Each set contains Loco, Tender, and two Pullman Coaches, as illustrated, with a set of rails to form a circle 4-ft. in diameter, including one brake rail. The Loco is fitted with reversing-gear, brake and governor.

Complete Set, well boxed ... Price **60**/-

The No. 2 Pullman Train, L.N.E.R., is illustrated on page **28**.

ınd their efficiency is
furnished with each loco,
ace, at our option, any
· from any cause other
f date of purchase.

To the boy who takes an intelligent interest in railway engineering—and there must be very few boys nowadays who do not—Hornby Trains exert an irresistible appeal. He finds in them those qualities for which he has waited so long, and he knows that no pains have been spared in their construction to make them as realistic and accurate as possible. Moreover, they are made from the finest materials only, and they are stoutly built and thoroughly tested before leaving the factory. Should he break or lose any part, it may be replaced immediately, for every piece is standardised.

HORNBY CLOCK WORK TRAINS
BRITISH AND GUARANTEED

HORNBY No. 0 PASSENGER SET, L.M.S.

Each set contains Loco, Tender, and two Coaches, as illustrated, with Curved Rails to form a circle 2 ft. in diameter and two Straight Rails. One of the Curved Rails carries a brake, by means of which the train may be stopped from the track. The Loco is fitted with brake and governor; non-reversing.

Hornby No. 0 Passenger Set, complete, packed in strong cardboard box, Price 24/–

HORNBY No. 0 GOODS SET, L.M.S.

The set comprises Loco, Tender and one Wagon, with Curved Rails to form a circle 2-ft. in diameter and two Straight Rails. One of the Curved Rails is fitted with a brake, by means of which the train may be stopped from the track. The Loco is equipped with brake and governor; non-reversing.

Hornby No. 0 Goods Set, complete, packed in strong cardboard box, Price 17/6

Hornby No. 0 Loco	**Price 10/6**	**Hornby Passenger Coach**	**Price 3/6**
Hornby Tender	**,, 2/6**	**Hornby Wagon**	**,, 2/6**

HORNBY No. 0 GOODS SET, L.N.E.R.

This set contains Loco, Tender, one Wagon, and Rails as in the No. 0 Goods L.M.S., and is identical to that set with the exception of the lettering. The Hornby No. 0 is a strong and useful Goods Train, richly enamelled in realistic colours and highly finished.

Hornby No. 0 Goods Set complete, packed in strong cardboard box, Price 17/6

HORNBY No. 0 PASSENGER SET, L.N.E.R.

The contents of this set are similar to those of the No. 0 Passenger L.M.S., namely Loco, Tender, two Coaches, and Rails to form a circle of 2-ft. diameter (including one Brake Rail) and two Straight Rails. The Loco is fitted with brake and governor; non-reversible.

Hornby No. 0 Passenger Set complete, packed in strong cardboard box, Price 24/-

Hornby No. 0 Loco	**Price 10/6**	**Hornby Passenger Coach**	**Price 3/6**
Hornby Tender	**„ 2/6**	**Hornby Wagon**	**„ 2/6**

HORNBY CLOCK WORK TRAINS
BRITISH AND GUARANTEED

HORNBY No. 1 PASSENGER SET, L.N.E.R.

The set comprises Loco, Tender, two Passenger Coaches and Rails to form a circle 2-ft. in diameter (including one Brake Rail, by means of which the train may be stopped from the track) and two Straight Rails. The Loco is fitted with reversing-gear, brake and governor ; the doors of the coaches open.

Hornby No. 1 Passenger Set, complete, well boxed, Price 27/6

HORNBY No. 1 GOODS SET, L.N.E.R.

Each set contains Loco, Tender and one Wagon, with Rails to form a circle 2-ft. in diameter and two Straight Rails. One of the Curved Rails is fitted with a brake by means of which the train may be stopped from the track. The Loco is equipped with reversing-gear, brake and governor.

Hornby No. 1 Goods Set complete, well boxed, Price 21/–

Hornby No. 1 Loco	**Price 13/6**	**Hornby Passenger Coach**	**Price 3/6**
Hornby Tender	**„ 2/6**	**Hornby Wagon**	**„ 2/6**

HORNBY No. 1 PASSENGER SET, L.M.S.

This set comprises Loco, Tender, two Coaches and Rails as in the No. 1 Passenger L.N.E.R., and is identical to that set except that the colouring represents the L.M.S. Railway Company's rolling-stock instead of that of the L.N.E.R. In the No. 1 Hornby Loco the brake and reversing-gear are controlled by levers situated in the engine cab.

Hornby No. 1 Passenger Set complete, well boxed, Price 27/6

HORNBY No. 1 GOODS SET, L.M.S.

The contents of this set are similar to those of the No. 1 Goods L.N.E.R., namely, Loco, Tender, one Wagon and Rails to form a circle 2-ft. in diameter (including one Brake Rail) and two Straight Rails. The Loco is fitted with reversing-gear, brake and governor.

Hornby No. 1 Goods Set, complete, well boxed, Price 21/–

Hornby No. 1 Loco	**Price 13/6**	**Hornby Passenger Coach**	**Price 3/6**
Hornby Tender	**,, 2/6**	**Hornby Wagon**	**,, 2/6**

HORNBY No. 2 PULLMAN SET, L.N.E.R.

This set is identical in every way to the No. 2 Pullman L.M.S. illustrated and described on pages ~~21-22,~~ 22-23 except that in this case the lettering and colouring are modelled from London and North Eastern rolling-stock. The No. 2 Hornby Loco may be braked and reversed from the track.

Hornby No. 2 Pullman Set, complete, well boxed, Price 60/-

Hornby No. 2 Loco ... ... Price 22/6 **Hornby No. 2 Tender ... ... Price 3/6**

Hornby Pullman Car ... ... Price 15/-

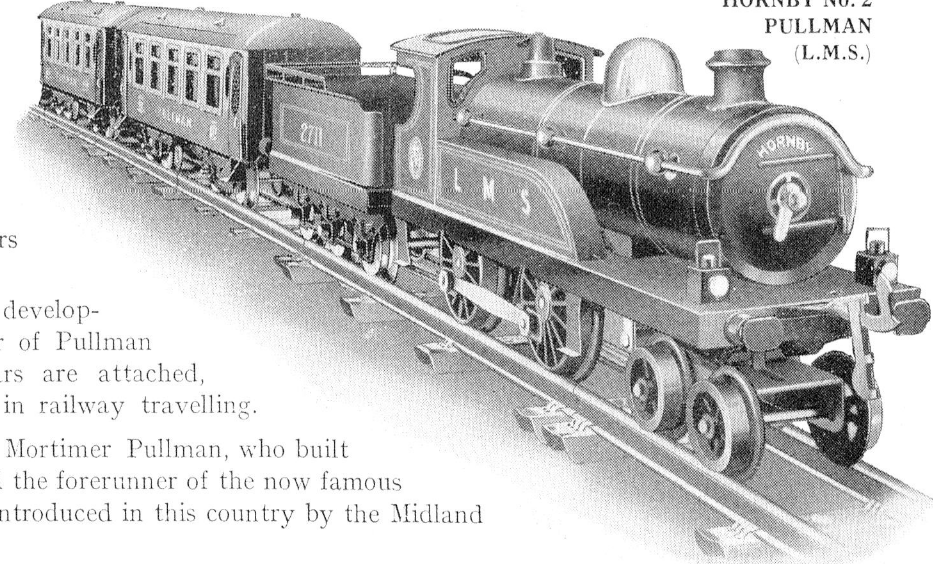

HORNBY No. 2 PULLMAN (L.M.S.)

THE FIRST PULLMAN IN ENGLAND

IN George Stephenson's time railway carriages were built on somewhat similar lines to road coaches. Stephenson's first carriage, which he appropriately named the "*Experiment*," was more like a bathing machine than a railway carriage! It is difficult for travellers of the present day to realise the immense improvements that have taken place since the time when outside passengers were carried, and the tops of the coaches were heaped with luggage.

In this connection one of the most interesting of recent railway developments in Great Britain is the considerable increase in the number of Pullman cars. There are now more than 185 trains to which Pullman cars are attached, and some of these trains undoubtedly represent the height of luxury in railway travelling.

Pullman cars were originated by an American inventor, George Mortimer Pullman, who built the first sleeping car at Chicago in 1859. Four years later he produced the forerunner of the now famous type of railway coach which bears his name. Pullman cars were first introduced in this country by the Midland Railway in 1874.

HORNBY CLOCK WORK TRAINS
BRITISH AND GUARANTEED

HORNBY No. 2 GOODS SET, L.N.E.R.

The Loco, Tender, and Rails in this set are similar to those in the Pullman Set, but two Wagons take the place of the Coaches. As in all other No. 2 Hornby Trains, the Loco may be both braked and reversed from the track.

Hornby No. 2 Goods Set, complete, well boxed, Price 37/6

HORNBY No. 2 GOODS SET, L.M.S.

This set is identical with the No. 2 Goods Train illustrated above, except that the lettering and colouring represent L.M.S. rolling-stock instead of L.N.E.R.

Hornby No. 2 Goods Set, complete, well boxed, Price 37/6

Hornby No. 2 Loco ... ... **Price 22/6** **Hornby No. 2 Tender** ... ... **Price 3/6**

Hornby Wagon ... ... **Price 2/6**

HORNBY No. 1 TANK GOODS SET, L.N.E.R.

This set contains a Hornby No. 1 Tank Loco, Hornby Wagon, Petrol Tank Wagon, Brake Van and set of Rails to form a circle 2-ft. in diameter (including one Brake Rail) and two Straight Rails. The Loco is fitted with brake, which may be operated by a lever in the cab or from the track, reversing gear and governor.

Hornby No. 1 Tank Goods Set, complete, well boxed, Price 25/–

HORNBY No. 1 TANK GOODS SET, L.M.S.

This set is similar to that described above with the exception of colouring and lettering. The No. 1 Hornby Tank Goods Sets are strong and realistic, and form a valuable addition to any model railway. The Locos and component wagons of the sets may also be obtained separately. Prices are given elsewhere in these pages.

Hornby No. 1 Tank Goods Set, complete, well boxed, Price 25/–

HORNBY No. 2 TANK GOODS SET, L.M.S.

The rolling-stock of this realistic goods train consists of a No. 2 Tank Loco, Hornby Wagon, Petrol Tank Wagon, No. 1 Cattle Truck, and Brake Van. The Loco may be braked and reversed from the track, which forms a circle 4-ft. in diameter.

Hornby No. 2 Tank Goods Set, complete, well boxed, Price 45/-

HORNBY No. 2 TANK GOODS SET, L.N.E.R.

This set is identical to that described above, except that in colouring and lettering it is modelled from L. & N.E. rolling-stock instead of L.M.S. The No. 2 Hornby Tank Loco is $11\frac{1}{2}''$ in length and is fitted with leading and trailing four-wheeled bogies. The Locos and component wagons of the Hornby Tank Goods Sets may also be obtained separately. Prices are given elsewhere in these pages.

Hornby No. 2 Tank Goods Set, complete, well boxed, Price 45/-

HORNBY CLOCK WORK TRAINS
BRITISH AND GUARANTEED

HORNBY No. 2 TANK PASSENGER SET, L.M.S.

This set comprises the famous No. 2 Hornby Tank Loco, three Passenger Coaches, Guard's Van and set of Rails to form a circle 4-ft. in diameter. One of the Rails is fitted with levers by means of which the Loco may be both braked and reversed from the track.

Hornby No. 2 Tank Passenger Set, complete, well boxed, Price 45/–

HORNBY No. 2 TANK PASSENGER SET, L.N.E.R.

This set comprises a Hornby No. 2 Tank Loco, three Passenger Coaches, Guard's Van and Rails as in the No. 2 Tank Passenger Set described above. The trains are realistically modelled from representative rolling-stock of the two great Railway Companies.

Hornby No. 2 Tank Passenger Set, complete, well boxed, Price 45/–

No. 2 Hornby Tank Loco ... ... Price 30/– **Hornby Passenger Coach ... ... Price 3/6**
Guard's Van ... ... Price 3/6

No. 00 CLOCKWORK TRAINS

(GAUGE 0)

No. 00 TRAIN SET, G.N.R.

Strongly built with reliable clockwork mechanism. Each set contains Loco, Tender and two Passenger Coaches, with set of Rails including a circle and two Straight Rails. The Loco is fitted with brake and regulator, non-reversing.

Complete Set, well boxed, Price 10/6

Loco ... ... Price 6/6 **Coach ... ... Price 1/–**
Tender ... ... Price 9d.

No. 00 TRAIN SET, MIDLAND

Strongly built with reliable clockwork mechanism. Each set contains Loco, Tender and two Passenger Coaches, with set of Rails including a circle and two Straight Rails. The Loco is fitted with brake and regulator, non-reversing.

Complete Set, well boxed, Price 10/6

Loco ... ... Price 6/6 **Coach ... ... Price 1/–**
Tender ... ... Price 9d.

No. 00 CLOCKWORK TRAINS

(GAUGE 0)

No. 00 TRAIN SET, L.N.W.R.

Strongly built, with reliable clockwork mechanism. Each set contains Loco, Tender and two Passenger Coaches, with set of Rails including a circle and two straight rails. The Loco is fitted with brake and regulator, non-reversing.

Complete Set, well boxed, Price 10/6

Loco ... ... Price 6/6 **Coach ... ... Price 1/-**

Tender ... ... Price 9d.

HORNBY RAIL FORMATIONS

There is practically no limit to the number of interesting combinations to which Hornby Rails, Points and Crossings lend themselves, and a carefully-planned track adds realism and greatly enhances the fun to be obtained from your model railway. An eight-page folder illustrating 62 suggested rail layouts for both large and small radius Hornby Rails, is included with every Hornby Train Set. Additional copies of the folder may be obtained by writing direct to Meccano Ltd., Liverpool, price 3d. each or 4d. post free.

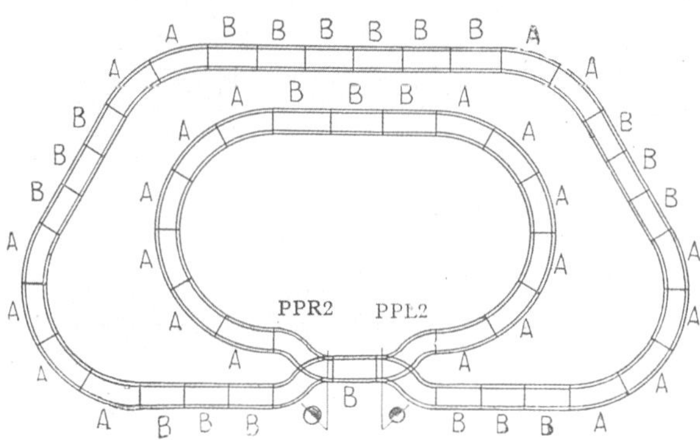

A specimen layout for Hornby Rails, reproduced from the Rail Formations folder. The letters and figures indicate the type of rails employed.

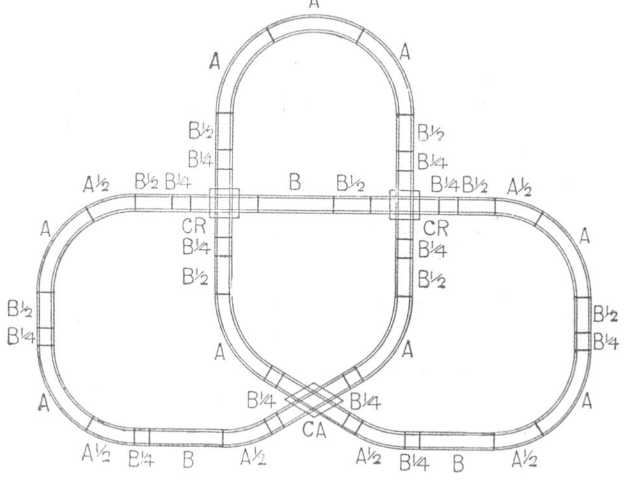

Another typical design for Hornby Track.

As every boy knows, in actual practice tank locos are chiefly employed on comparatively short runs, where smaller quantities of water and coal are necessary for each trip. One of their chief advantages is that they may be run as readily backwards as forwards. This fact enables them to be used independently of turntables, thus effecting economy in both time and money. The development of tank locos has increased rapidly during recent years, and they now form an important addition to every railway in the world.

HORNBY No. 1 TANK LOCO, L.M.S. GOODS

The Hornby No. 1 Tank Loco is strong and durable and is capable of any amount of hard work. It is richly enamelled and highly finished in three different colours, representing L.M.S. goods and passenger locos and L.N.E.R. locos. The reversing gear and brake are operated from levers in the cab, and the brake may also be applied from the track. The clockwork mechanism is fitted with a governor, which maintains a steady and constant speed. Every loco is thoroughly tested before leaving the factory, and is sold only under the Hornby guarantee.

Price 12/6

HORNBY No. 1 TANK LOCO, L.N.E.R.

HORNBY No. 1 TANK LOCO, L.M.S.

THE Hornby No. 2 Tank Loco is a powerful model embodying all the characteristics of the Hornby Train. It represents a type of loco that is being developed rapidly by our Railway Companies for main line goods and passenger traffic. It is richly enamelled and beautifully finished in colours to represent L.M.S. goods and passenger locos and L.N.E.R. locos. It is $11\frac{1}{2}''$ in length and is fitted with four coupled wheels and a leading and trailing four-wheeled bogie.

The brake and reversing gear may be operated from levers in the cab or from the track. Special rails with levers for this purpose are supplied in all No. 2 Hornby Sets, or may be obtained separately.

Each loco is carefully tested before leaving the factory, and is sold under the Hornby guarantee.

Price 30/-

HORNBY No. 2 TANK LOCO, L.M.S. GOODS

HORNBY No. 2 TANK LOCO, L.M.S.

HORNBY No. 2 TANK LOCO, L.N.E.R.

HORNBY CLOCK WORK TRAINS
BRITISH AND GUARANTEED

No. 1 LUGGAGE VAN

Realistic and highly finished. The doors are mounted on hinges and may be opened. Lettered L.M.S. or L.N.E.R.

Price 4/-

No. 2 LUGGAGE VAN

Mounted on two four-wheeled bogies, and fitted with double opening doors. Suitable for 2-ft. radius rails only. Lettered L.M.S. or L.N.E.R.

Price 6/6

No. 1 TIMBER WAGON

Beautifully enamelled in green, complete with load of timber.

Price 2/-

No. 2 TIMBER WAGON

Highly finished and stoved. Complete with load of timber. Suitable for 2-ft. radius rails only. Lettered L.M.S. or L.N.E.R.

Price 4/6

THE Hornby system includes a complete range of Rolling-Stock, Train Accessories, and Rails, Points and Crossings, with which the most elaborate model railway can be fully equipped. Every item in the Hornby Series is well thought out and carefully modelled from actual practice.

Any boy may gradually build up a complete miniature railway by making use from time to time of the items included in the series.

TROLLEY WAGON

Trolley Wagons are designed to carry exceptionally heavy loads, and their low-built construction necessitates only a minimum lift when loading. Fitted with four-wheeled bogies and stanchions. Suitable for 2-ft. radius rails only. Lettered L.M.S. or L.N.E.R.

Price 6/-

BREAKDOWN VAN AND CRANE

Beautifully coloured in grey and black with opening doors. The crane is provided with a handle by means of which the hoisting cord may be operated, and swivels about a pivot. Suitable for 2-ft. radius rails only. Lettered L.M.S. or L.N.E.R.

Price 7/-

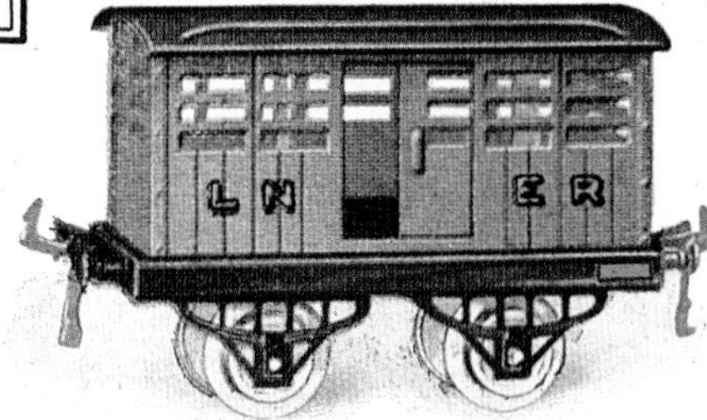

No. 1 CATTLE TRUCK

Fitted with sliding door. Very realistic design. Lettered L.M.S. or L.N.E.R.

Price 4/-

No. 2 CATTLE TRUCK

Splendid model, fitted with double doors and two four-wheel bogies. Suitable for 2-ft. radius rails only. Lettered L.M.S. or L.N.E.R.

Price 6/6

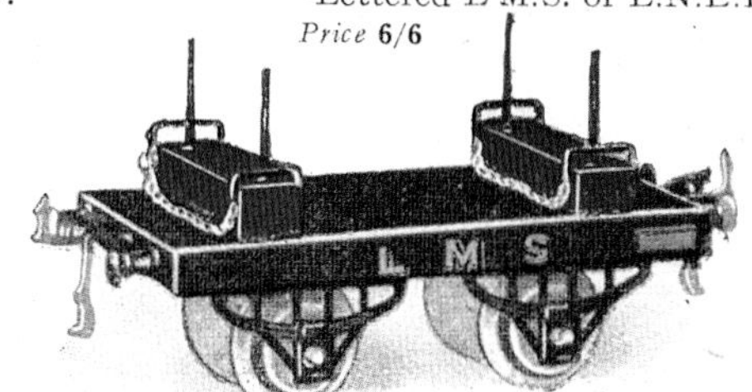

No. 1 LUMBER WAGON

Fitted with bolsters and stanchions for log transport. Lettered L.M.S. or L.N.E.R.

Price 2/-

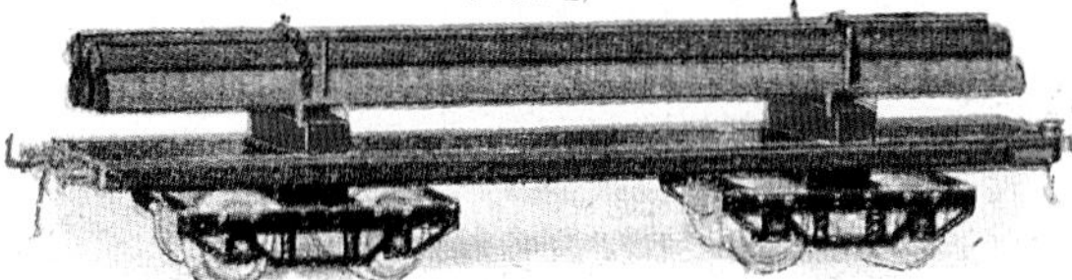

No. 2 LUMBER WAGON

Fitted with bolsters and stanchions and complete with logs. Suitable for 2-ft. radius rails only. Lettered L.M.S. or L.N.E.R.

Price 5/-

HORNBY CLOCK WORK TRAINS
BRITISH AND GUARANTEED

BRAKE VAN L.N.E.R.

Finished in colours with opening doors; a very realistic model.

Price 4/-

CRAWFORD'S BISCUIT VAN

Finished in red with opening doors.

Price 4/-

CARR'S BISCUIT VAN

Finished in dark blue with opening doors.

Price 4/-

BRAKE VAN L.M.S.

Finished in grey with opening doors.

Price 4/-

PETROL TANK WAGON, "SHELL"

Finished in red and strongly built.

Price 3/-

"SECCOTINE" WAGON

Beautifully finished in blue with opening doors.

Price 4/-

JACOB'S BISCUIT VAN

Finished in crimson lake with opening doors.

Price 4/-

PETROL TANK WAGON, "PRATT'S"

Stoutly built.

Price 3/-

REFRIGERATOR VAN

Enamelled in white, with opening doors. Lettered L.M.S. or L.N.E.R.

Price 4/-

PETROL TANK WAGON, "NATIONAL BENZOLE"

Realistic and well made.

Price 3/-

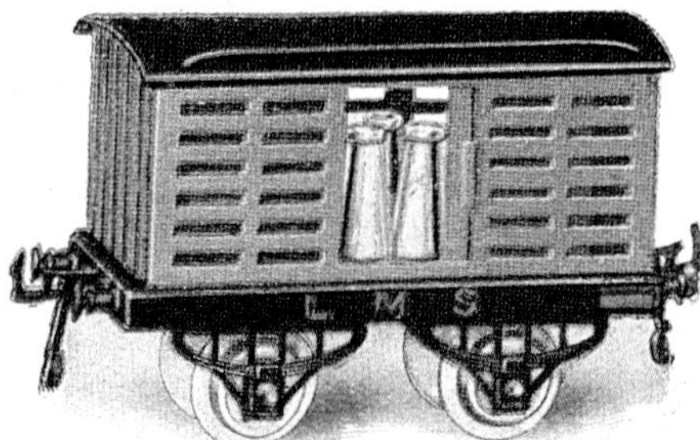

MILK TRAFFIC VAN

Fitted with sliding door, and complete with three milk cans. Lettered L.M.S. or L.N.E.R.

Price 4/6

GUNPOWDER VAN

Beautifully finished with opening doors. Lettered L.M.S. or L.N.E.R.

Price 4/-

HORNBY CLOCK WORK TRAINS

BRITISH AND GUARANTEED

GUARD'S VAN

Realistic design. Fitted each side with double and single opening doors. Lettered L.M.S. or L.N.E.R.

Price 3/6

CRANE TRUCK

The crane swivels about a pivot, and is operated by a crank fitted in its base. Lettered L.M.S. or L.N.E.R.

Price 4/6

CEMENT WAGON

Lettered L.M.S. or L.N.E.R. Hinged portion of the cover may be opened.

Price 4/-

SNOW PLOUGH

Runs on specially constructed heavy wheels, and the plough is driven from the front axle. Lettered L.M.S. or L.N.E.R.

Price 5/6

GAS CYLINDER WAGON

Lettered L.M.S. or L.N.E.R.

Price 3/-

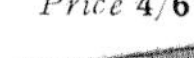

SIDE TIPPING WAGON

Arranged to tip to either side of the track.

Price 3/6

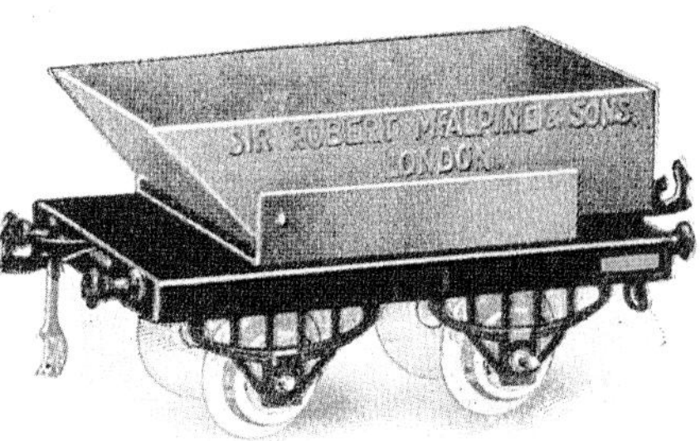

ROTARY TIPPING WAGON

The body rotates and will tip in all directions.

Price 4/-

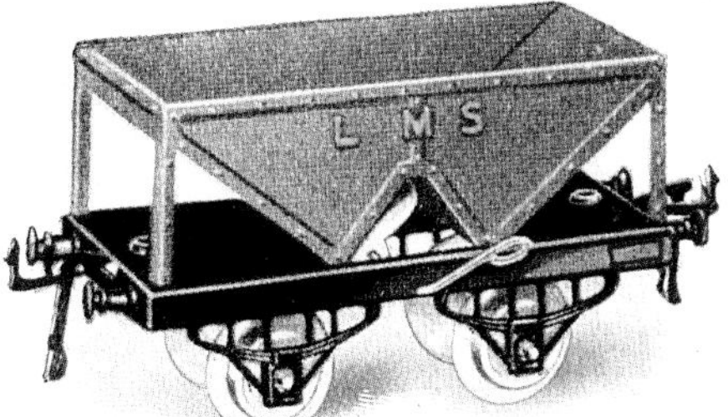

HOPPER WAGON

May be automatically unloaded on operation of the lever shown. Lettered L.M.S. or L.N.E.R.

Price 4/-

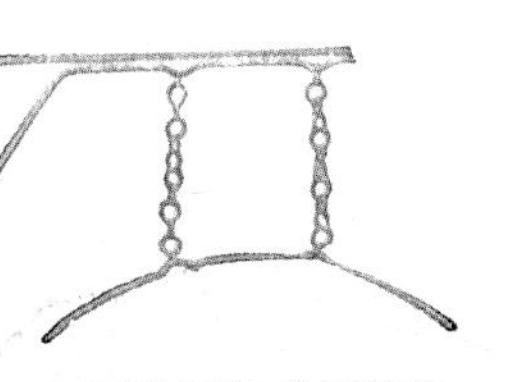

LOADING GAUGE

$7\frac{3}{4}''$ in height.

Price 1/9

TELEGRAPH POLE

11″ in height.

Price 2/6

PLATFORM ACCESSORIES No. 2

Milk Cans and Truck.

Price 2/-

PLATFORM ACCESSORIES No. 1

Miniature Luggage.

Price 2/-

The three sets of Platform Accessories shown form an interesting and very realistic addition to the Hornby Station. In addition to figuring on the platform the miniature luggage shown may of course be carried in the Guard's Van, and the Milk Cans in the Milk Traffic Van, etc.

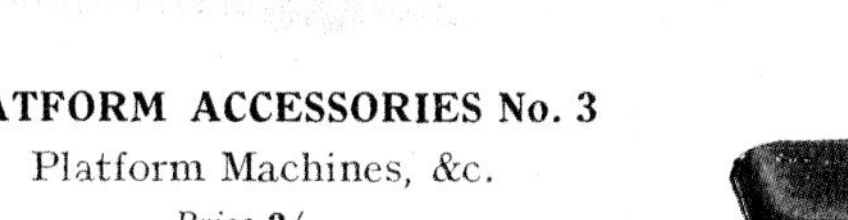

PLATFORM ACCESSORIES No. 3

Platform Machines, &c.

Price 2/-

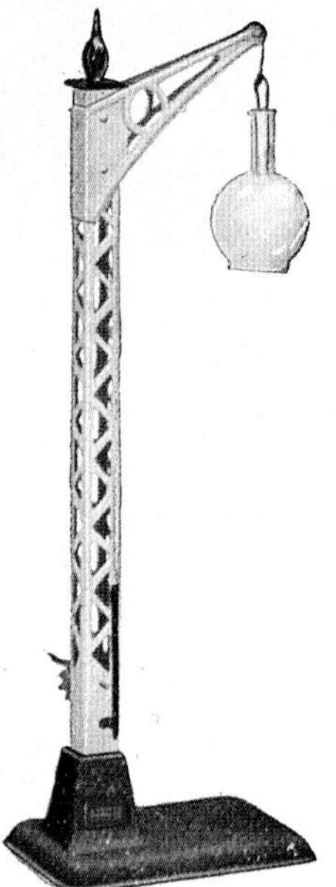

SINGLE LAMP STANDARD

The Lamp, into which a 4-volt bulb may be fitted, is hoisted or lowered from a crank-handle at the base and controlled by a ratchet.

Price 3/-

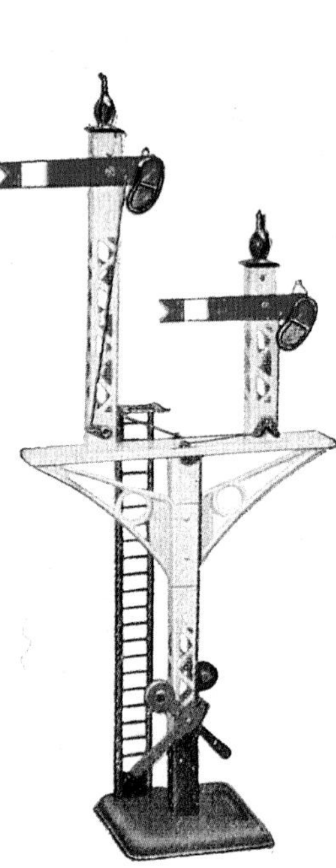

JUNCTION SIGNAL

Signal arms operated by weighted levers at base. Complete with imitation lamps, ladder, etc. Very realistic model standing 14″ in height.

Price 5/6

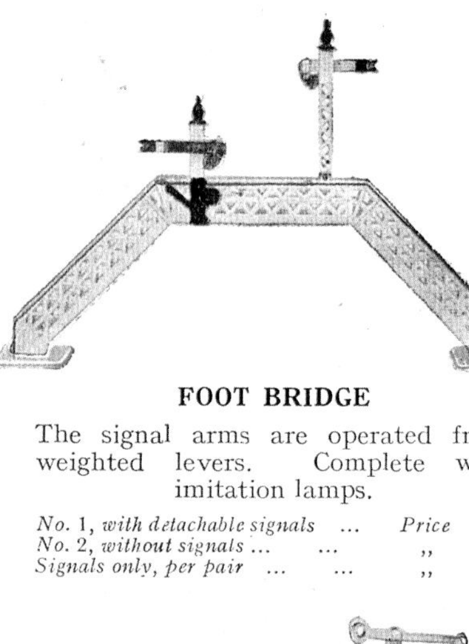

FOOT BRIDGE

The signal arms are operated from weighted levers. Complete with imitation lamps.

No. 1, with detachable signals ...	*Price*	6/-
No. 2, without signals	,,	3/6
Signals only, per pair	,,	2/9

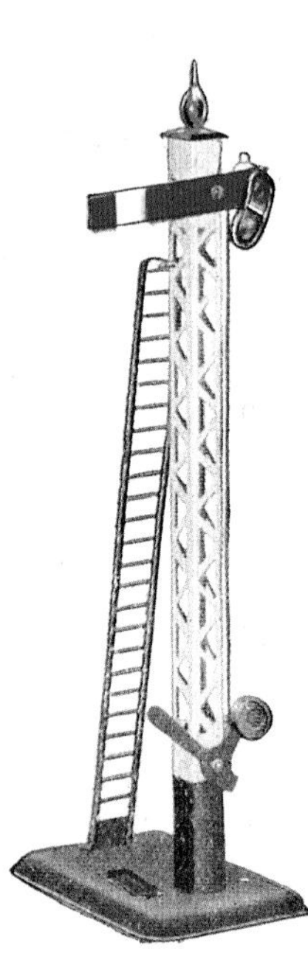

SIGNAL

Operated by weighted levers at base and complete with ladder and imitation lamp.

Price 2/6

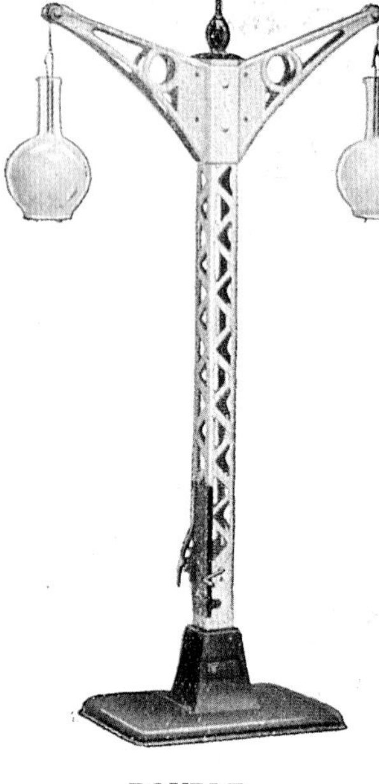

DOUBLE LAMP STANDARD

4-volt bulbs may be fitted in the globes, which are hoisted and lowered from crank handles in the base and controlled by ratchets.

Price 4/-

SPRING BUFFER STOP

May be attached to all Hornby Rails.

Price 1/6

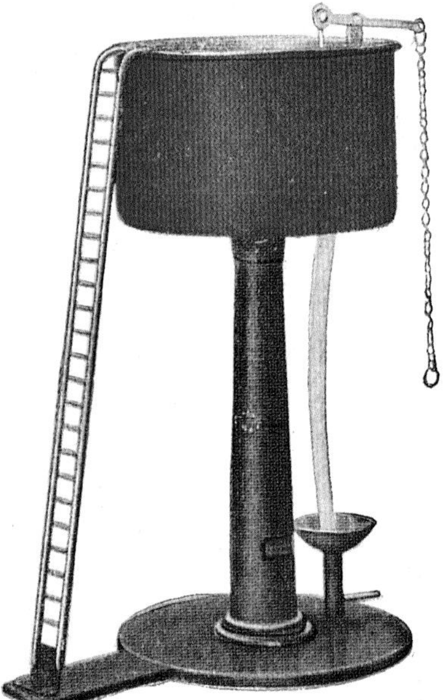

WATER TANK

Stands $8\frac{1}{2}''$ in height, fitted with rubber tube and spring controlled valve, operated from a chain and lever.

Price 6/6

HYDRAULIC BUFFER STOP

Realistic and very stoutly built. May be fitted to all Hornby rails.

Price 5/-

HORNBY CLOCK WORK TRAINS

BRITISH AND GUARANTEED

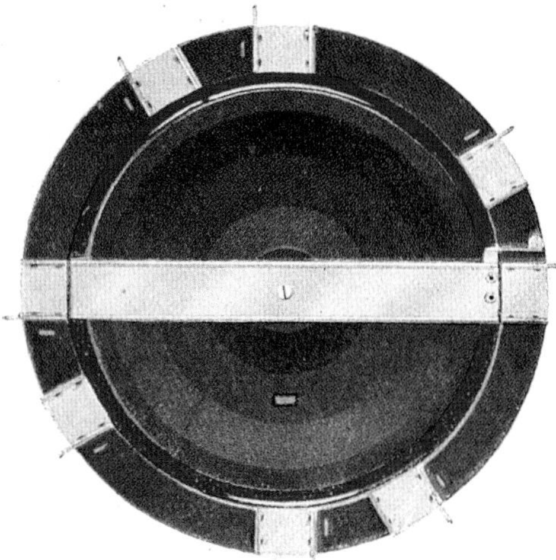

TURNTABLE

Fitted with catch to lock the revolving portion in certain positions as required.

Price 5/-

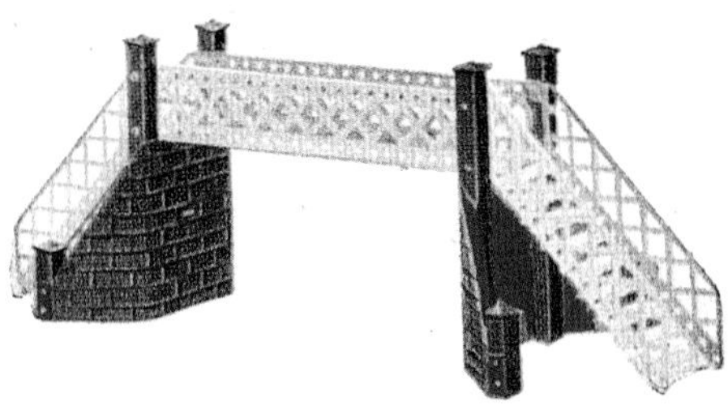

LATTICE GIRDER BRIDGE

Constructional type, strong and well proportioned. Meccano strips for signals, etc., may be secured to its sides.

Price 10/6

SIGNAL CABIN

Dimensions: Height $6\frac{1}{2}''$, Width $3\frac{1}{2}''$, Length $6\frac{1}{2}''$. Beautifully finished and lettered "Windsor." Roof and back open to allow signal levers to be fitted inside cabin if desired.

Price 6/6

RAILWAY STATION

Excellent model, beautifully designed and finished. Constructed in three sections, which may be easily detached.

Dimensions: Length, 2-ft. 9-in. Width 6-in. Height 7-in.

Price 12/6

LEVEL CROSSING

Beautifully designed and finished, with double track of gauge "0" rails in position. Measures $11\frac{1}{2}''$ by $7\frac{1}{4}''$.

Price 6/6

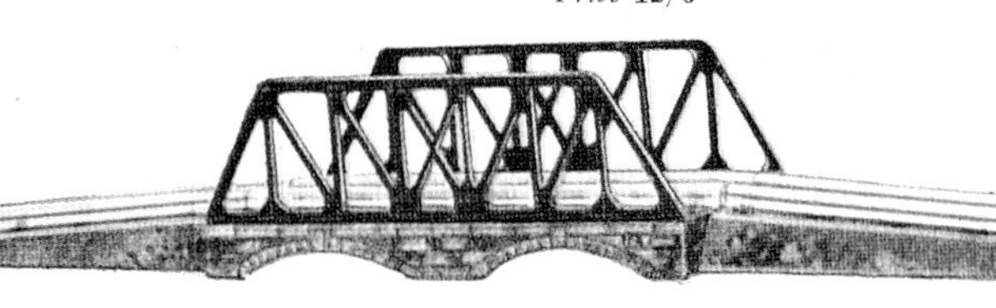

VIADUCT

Constructed in three sections which may be easily detached.

Price 7/6

Centre section only, *Price* 4/6

Viaduct for Electric Trains with "live" rails in position, *Price* 8/-

Do. do. do. centre section only, *Price* 5/-

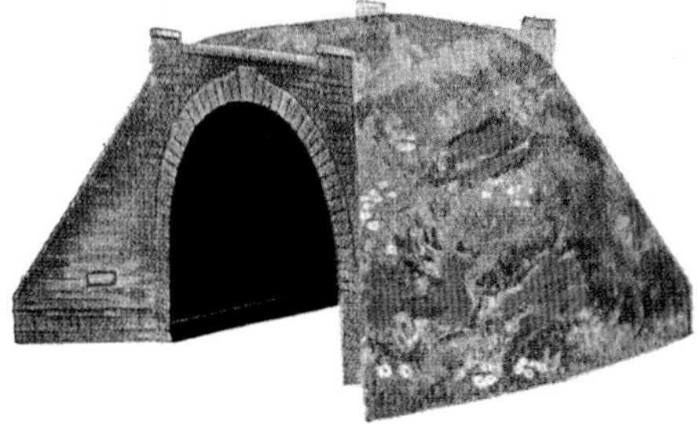

TUNNEL

Beautifully designed and finished in realistic colours.

Price 7/6

Gauge 0, 1¼″

Rails, Points and Crossings

Alternate Pegs

Hornby Series

HORNBY Rails, Points and Crossings are designed to meet the most exacting requirements of model railway enthusiasts. They are made of the finest materials and hold together rigidly and strongly, for real workmanship is put into them. The variety of Points, left-hand and right-hand turnout, together with the Crossings, make possible an almost endless number of realistic and railway-like layouts. The adaptability of the rails is well shown in the specimen layouts in the " Rail Formations " folder, which is included in every Hornbv Train Set.

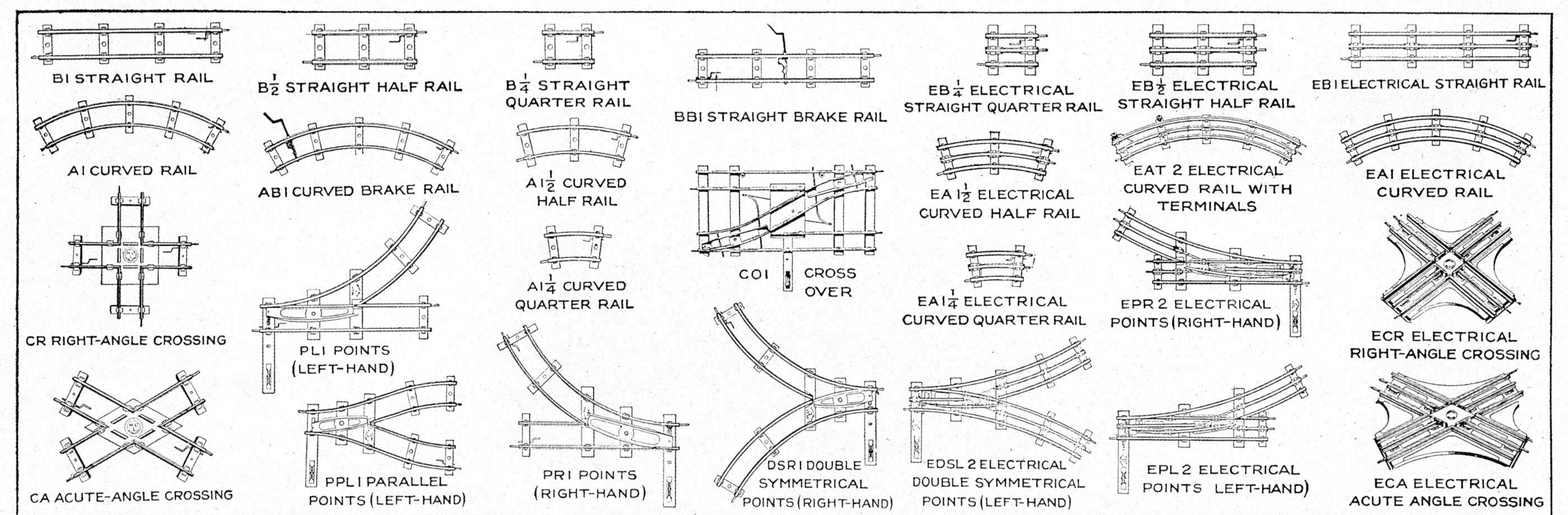

Rails for Clockwork and Steam Trains

	CURVED RAILS.		
	For 1-ft. 6-ins. diameter circle.		
A9	Curved rails (9-in. radius) ...	per doz.	3/–
	For 2-ft. diameter circle.		
A1	Curved rails (1-ft. radius) ...	per doz.	4/–
A1½	Curved half rails	„	3/–
A1¼	Curved quarter rails ...	„	2/6
AB1	Curved brake rails (1-ft. radius)	each	**5d.**
	For 4-ft. diameter circle.		
A2	Curved rails (2-ft. radius) ...	per doz.	5/–
A2½	Curved half rails	„	3/6
A2¼	Curved quarter rails ...	„	3/–
AB2	Curved brake rails (2-ft. radius)	each	**6d.**
	STRAIGHT RAILS.		
B1	Straight rails	per doz.	3/6
B½	Straight half rails	„	2/6
B¼	Straight quarter rails ...	„	2/–
BB1	Straight brake rails	each	**4½d.**
	CROSSINGS.		
CA	Acute-angle crossings ...	each	1/9
CR	Right-angle crossings ...	„	1/9
	CROSSOVERS.		
CO1	Crossover (1-ft. radius) ...	each	6/6
CO2	Crossover (2-ft. radius) ...	„	7/6

	POINTS.		
	For 9-ins. radius curves.		
PR9	Right-hand points	each	2/3
PL9	Left-hand points	„	2/3
	For 1-ft. radius curves.		
PR1	Right-hand points	each	2/3
PL1	Left-hand points	„	2/3
	For 2-ft. radius curves.		
PR2	Right-hand points	each	2/3
PL2	Left-hand points	„	2/3
	DOUBLE SYMMETRICAL POINTS.		
	For 1-ft. radius curves.		
DSR1	Double symmetrical points, right	each	2/6
DSL1	Double symmetrical points, left	„	2/6
	For 2-ft. radius curves.		
DSR2	Double symmetrical points, right	each	2/6
DSL2	Double symmetrical points, left	„	2/6
	PARALLEL POINTS.		
	For 1-ft. radius curves.		
PPR1	Parallel points, right ...	each	2/6
PPL1	Parallel points, left	„	2/6
	For 2-ft. radius curves.		
PPR2	Parallel points, right ...	each	2/6
PPL2	Parallel points, left	„	2/6

Rails for Electric Trains

	CURVED RAILS.		
	For 2-ft. diameter circle.		
EA1	Curved rails (1-ft. radius) ...	per doz.	8/–
EA1½	Curved half rails	„	5/–
EA1¼	Curved quarter rails ...	„	4/6
EAT1	Curved rail with terminals (1-ft. radius)	each	1/2
	For 4-ft. diameter circle.		
EA2	Curved rails (2-ft. radius) ...	per doz.	8/–
EA2½	Curved half rails	„	5/–
EA2¼	Curved quarter rails ...	„	4/6
EAT2	Curved rail, with terminals (2-ft. radius)	each	1/3
	STRAIGHT RAILS.		
EB1	Straight rails	per doz.	7/–
EB½	Straight half rails	„	4/6
EB¼	Straight quarter rails ...	„	4/–
	CROSSINGS.		
ECA	Acute-angle crossings ...	each	4/6
ECR	Right-angle crossings ...	„	4/6

	POINTS.		
	For 2-ft. radius curves.		
EPR2	Right-hand points... ...	each	5/–
EPL2	Left-hand points	„	5/–
	DOUBLE SYMMETRICAL POINTS.		
	For 2-ft. radius curves.		
EDSR2	Double symmetrical points, right	each	6/–
EDSL2	Double symmetrical points, left	„	6/–
	PARALLEL POINTS.		
	For 2-ft. radius curves.		
EPPR2	Parallel points, right ...	each	6/–
EPPL2	Parallel points, lef ...	„	6/–

Electrical Points, Double Symmetrical Points and Parallel Points for 1-ft. radius curves are not supplied.

NOTE.—The addition of straight and curved brake rails supplied for Clockwork Trains, makes possible a great deal more fun. By the use of the straight brake rail, trains may be brought to a standstill at the station platform. With these rails the No. 1 Hornby Trains may be braked from the track, while the No. 2 Hornby Trains may be both braked and reversed from the track, thus greatly facilitating shunting operations.

Covers of seven recent issues of the

"Meccano Magazine"

Articles dealing with new Railway activities, latest progress, inventions, and improvements culled from all over the world form interesting features every month in the *Meccano Magazine*. It also contains articles on such subjects as Famous Engineers and Inventors, Electricity, Bridges, Cranes, Wonderful Machinery, Latest Patents, Radio, Stamps, Photography, Nature-Study and Books. Special competitions are announced from time to time.

The *Meccano Magazine* is published (on the 1st of each month) in the interests of boys. It may be ordered from any Meccano dealer or from any newsagent or bookstall, price threepence. If desired it will be mailed direct from Meccano Limited, Binns Road, Liverpool (post free), for six months 2/–, or twelve months 4/–. Write to the Editor, *Meccano Magazine*, Liverpool, for a free specimen copy.

A Fine Engineering Monthly for Boys

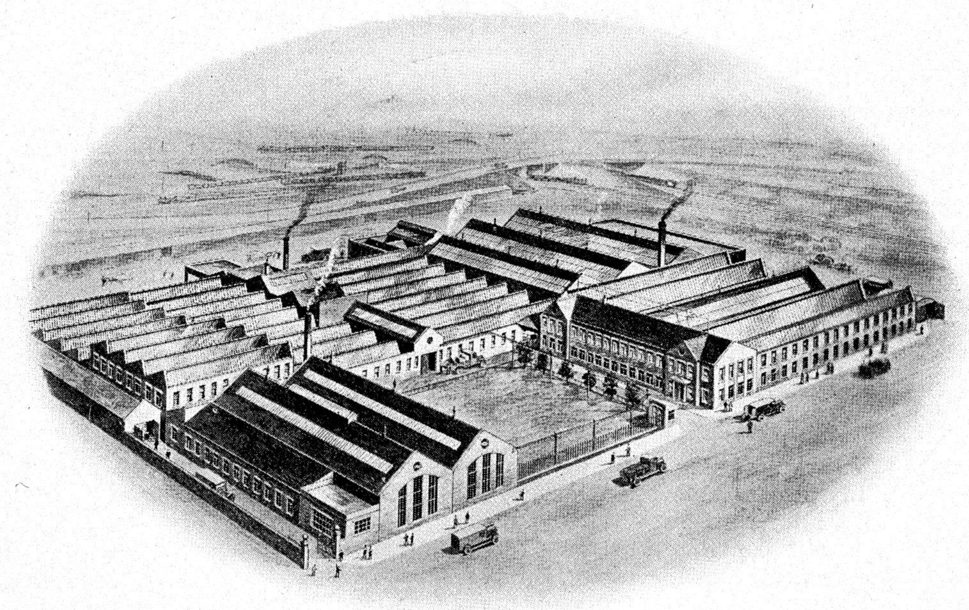

Head Office and Factory, Liverpool.

Published by

MECCANO LTD., BINNS ROAD, LIVERPOOL

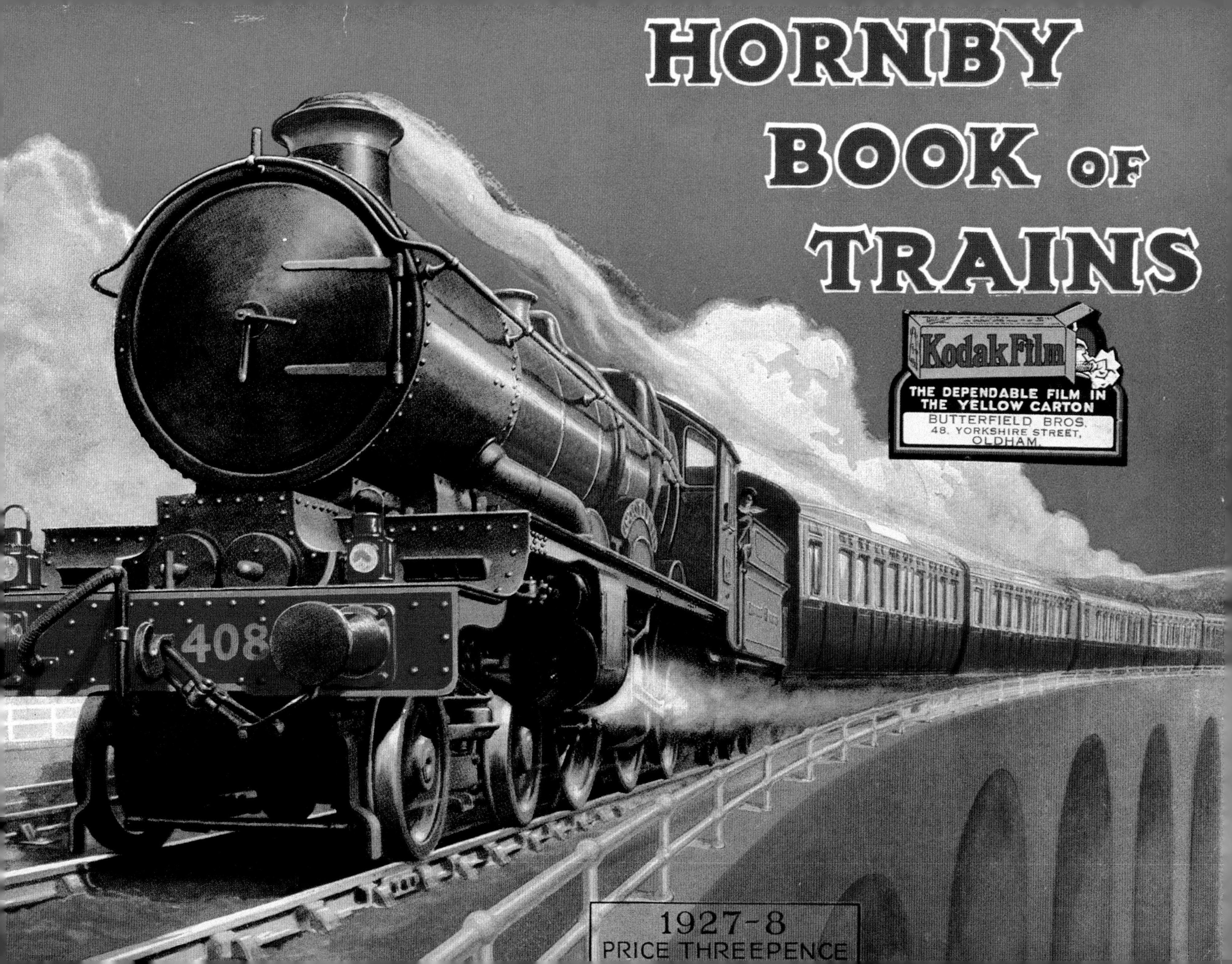
HORNBY
BOOK OF
TRAINS
Kodak Film
THE DEPENDABLE FILM IN
THE YELLOW CARTON
BUTTERFIELD BROS.
48, YORKSHIRE STREET,
OLDHAM.
408
1927-8
PRICE THREEPENCE

THE HORNBY BOOK OF TRAINS
1927-8

Foreword

IN the 1925 Hornby Book of Trains we described the gradual development of the locomotive and of railways in general, and in the 1926 edition the operation of the more important railway mechanisms was explained. This year we deal with the life-history of a typical locomotive.

Commencing with a survey of the different types of locomotives and of the special purposes for which each is intended, we pass on to the designing of a locomotive for express passenger traffic. From the preparation of the plans in the drawing office we trace the gradual growth of the engine through foundry, fitting and machine shops and boiler and erecting shops, up to its trial and testing and its painting and finishing ready for the road.

Finally we follow our locomotive on to the road and through its various replacements and repairs up to the time when it is no longer efficient for its work and, withdrawn in favour of some new locomotive of more modern design and greater power, is condemned and finally relegated to the scrap heap.

Specially interesting features of the book are the descriptions of the equipment and operation of a dynamometer car and of the work of the breakdown train and its crew.

On this page and on the cover we illustrate the famous Great Western "*Cornish Riviera*" express. The train is seen approaching Westbury, which is 95½ miles from Paddington. At Westbury the railway curves abruptly into the station, necessitating severe application of the brakes and a reduction of speed from the "70's" down to some 30 miles per hour.

The locomotive is No. 4082, "*Windsor Castle*," a well-known member of the famous "Castle" class of 4–6–0 locomotives. The "Castles" have won for themselves a great reputation for hauling heavy loads at high speeds on a remarkably low consumption of fuel and water. The success of these fine locomotives is largely due to their high working pressure of 225 lb. per sq. in.

In the preparation of this book we have received a good deal of valuable assistance and we wish to express our indebtedness particularly to the Great Western Railway for the series of photographs of various sections of the Swindon Railway Works; to the Great Southern Railways (Ireland) for the drawing of a 4–6–0 express passenger locomotive; to the London North Eastern Railway for the illustrations of a dynamometer car and of a breakdown train; and to the Southern Railway for photographs of "Baltic" and "Pacific" tank locomotives.

Some Members of the Locomotive Family

In the early days of the steam locomotive, as in the early days of all inventions, there was no specialisation. Cugnot and Murdock with their road locomotives and Trevithick with his first railway locomotive were concerned almost entirely with the problem of constructing an engine that would "go." In this they succeeded, but many years elapsed before engineers began to design special types of locomotives for different purposes.

The gradual development of the railway locomotive from its original crude and inefficient state was described in the 1925 Hornby Book of Trains and need not be repeated. We are now concerned with the modern engine and its life history, and propose to follow the course of its construction and period of service down to the time when it qualifies for the scrap heap.

Southern Railway "Baltic" type Tank Engine "*Remembrance*"
employed on the heaviest trains between London and Brighton, including the "Southern Belle" Pullman. This engine was named in memory of the employees of the Brighton section who fell in the Great War

Railway engines may be divided broadly into two classes—tender engines, which have coupled to them a separate vehicle to carry the necessary fuel and water, and tank engines, which have not a separate vehicle attached, but carry their own supplies. It is obvious that the fuel and water capacity of the engine with separate tender must be greater than that of the tank engine, and until recent years the tender engine was employed for long-distance traffic and the tank engine almost exclusively for short journeys. The distinction still holds good to a considerable extent, but recent developments in tank engines have brought the two classes nearer together.

The tender engine is clearly ideal for very long runs. The capacity of the tender of a main line engine may be anything between 3,000 and 5,000 gallons of water and five to eight tons of coal, and thus journeys of 350 miles or more become possible on one filling up. Tenders of such size, when full, are very heavy, and this weight has to be hauled by the engine in addition to the weight of the train behind. The hauling of this weight is justified in the case of long-distance expresses but it is utterly uneconomical when short distances only are to be run, and here the tank engine scores heavily.

In addition to carrying no more fuel and water than is necessary for its work, the tank engine possesses the important feature of being able to run equally well backward as forward, thus being independent of the turntable. A tender engine is capable of running backward, but when doing so it has to push its tender before it, which makes fast running undesirable if not altogether unsafe. The tank engine has no such disability, and in addition its driver has as clear a view when running backward as forward, which is not the case when there is a tender in the way. Thus a tank engine has greater flexibility and this, in conjunction with its economical running, makes it the best type for suburban and other short-distance work and for shunting and similar purposes.

Many other considerations must be taken into account in settling the type of engine required for any particular work.

In dealing with the design of engines for different purposes the number, size, and arrangement of the wheels carrying the engine are of vital importance. The early types of engines for passenger work were mostly what are known as "single wheelers," that is engines with one pair of driving wheels. Between the years 1840 and 1850 some extraordinary locomotives of this type were designed, characterised by enormous driving wheels, some of them even up to 10 ft. in diameter. The idea was that a large driving wheel was necessary to secure high speeds. Gradually it was found that satisfactory speeds could be obtained quite easily with wheels of more reasonable size, and by about 1850 the day of freak engines was past. From then onward the development of engines was along proved and standard lines.

Conspicuous among the "single wheelers" of the following years were the famous 4–2–2 Stirling "eight-footers," so called from the size of their driving wheels. These were designed by Mr. Patrick Stirling, the locomotive engineer of the Great Northern Railway. Their efficiency was undoubted and their handsome appearance attracted wide-spread attention. Trains were lighter then than they are now and the "eight-footers" put up some striking performances on long journeys. This was particularly the case in the closing years of last century, when the Stirling "eight-footer" achieved great distinction in the railway race from London to the North between the trains of the East and West Coast companies. The first of these engines, by the way, ran well over a million miles, and is still preserved at the King's Cross locomotive sheds. The heaviest of the type weighed 90 tons with its tender, while its successor, the "*Flying Scotsman*" weighs no less than 150 tons.

Increasing loads—"Flying Scotsman's" 400-ton train

In the following years there was a great increase in the loads that engines were called upon to draw. In the case of passenger traffic the increase in the weight of trains was accounted for by the more massive construction of the coaches. This has led to an immense improvement in the accommodation for passengers, including the provision of such luxuries as corridor coaches, dining cars and sleeping cars. The latest type of coach used for the famous "*Flying Scotsman*" weighs over 34 tons, so that a 12-coach train weighs well over 400 tons. As an illustration of the increase of engine power it may be noted that only 25 years ago a 200-ton express was regarded as heavy, and two locomotives were thought necessary to draw a 300-ton train.

It was soon found that excessive load caused wheel-slip in single-wheelers. The driving power of a locomotive depends entirely on the grip of its driving wheels on the rails, and while the adhesion between the smooth surfaces of the rail and the wheel may be increased by the use of sand, the only satisfactory method in practice is to increase the weight bearing down on the driving wheel.

This increase, however, has its limits. For safety's sake the maximum axle weight allowable to-day is 20 tons, or 10 tons to each wheel. This figure was much less, of course, in the early days of the locomotive, so that another method of procuring greater adhesion was adopted. This was the use of a second pair of driving wheels of exactly the same size as the first pair, and coupled to it as in the well known 4–4–2 "Atlantics," a type that derives its name from the fact that it was first used on the Atlantic City express from New York. From this it was a natural development to couple more wheels together so as to obtain the maximum of adhesion and also greater stability, and thus the 2–6–0, 4–6–2, and similar types came into use.

The function of the remaining wheels is to assist in carrying weight, and their number and position is settled for any engine by the design of boiler and firebox adopted and the total weight of the engine. The "idle" wheels, as they are called, are either leading or trailing wheels, the names referring to their position with regard to the driving wheels. The provision of leading wheels is absolutely essential for any engine designed for express work, as they fulfil an important duty in "feeling" for the track, so rendering high speeds safe.

Southern Railway "Pacific" type Tank Engine, having "Stephenson" link motion. Employed on fast business trains between London and Brighton. The two S.R. engines of this class were the first 4-6-2 standard gauge Tank Engines in this country

Modern Passenger Express Locomotives

The actual arrangement of the wheels of an engine depends on its proposed use, as does also the size of the coupled wheels. An engine to be used for fast passenger traffic only will almost certainly be planned nowadays with six coupled wheels to enable it to cope with the weight of modern express trains. As it will make long runs, a considerable weight of fuel will be necessary, so that an engine with a tender is required. Further, the weight of the boiler and fire-box usual for this type of work suggests six "idle" wheels, the best arrangement for which will be a four-wheeled bogie in front with two trailing wheels. This is, of course, the arrangement of the well-known 4–6–2 "Pacific" engines, the famous "*Flying Scotsman*" being an example of this type.

It is of interest to note that the first engines of this type were built in the United States to the design of the locomotive engineers of the New Zealand Government Railways, while a similar engine was built independently for the West Australian Railways. The name "Pacific" indicates the origin of the type and also its association with the 4–4–2 type.

Practically all fast passenger express engines now constructed have six coupled wheels, as the modern express train loads are beyond the powers of the 4–4–2 "Atlantics," which for years were the standard engines for work of this kind. Another type of engine with six coupled wheels in common use for express work is the 4–6–0, and engines having this wheel arrangement are commonly referred to as "ten-wheelers." Among them are the famous Great Western "Castles." The "*Caerphilly Castle,*" the most famous example of this class, is one of the most graceful engines ever built, and it is probable that no engine has ever had a wider circle of enthusiastic admirers. A splendid photograph of this remarkable engine appeared in the 1926 Hornby Book of Trains, the cover of which showed another engine of this class drawing the "*Cornish Riviera*" express. The 4–6–0 type is losing favour with many designers, however, as a much larger firebox can be fitted to "Pacific" engines. This is a matter of some importance in view of the greater steam pressures necessitated by the increased loads that engines are now called upon to bear. If engines using pressures of 230 lbs. to the sq. in. are to be of any use a generous steaming capacity is essential.

Giants that Haul Goods Trains

Similar considerations have influenced the development of engines for goods traffic. The general tendency has been towards heavier loads, which has involved heavier and more powerful engines. It is not difficult to realise the type of engine required for hauling heavy goods trains when high speed is unnecessary. As the main thing is to get along with a huge load, the number of coupled wheels may be increased with advantage to eight or even more. In fact all the wheels may be coupled together, so that the whole of the weight of the engine is available for adhesion. The diameter of the wheels may be reduced from 6 ft. 9 in., the usual size for passenger express engines, to 4 ft. 6 in. or 5 ft., since small wheels have the advantage of giving more hauling power in covering any given distance, at the expense of speed which is not essential for this traffic.

Engines with eight wheels coupled, 0–8–0, are generally referred to as the "Mineral" type, their original purpose being the haulage of slow but heavy coal and mineral trains. With a leading pair of small wheels the type becomes 2–8–0 or "Consolidation," another name derived from American practice. The first engine of this type was christened "Consolidation" to commemorate the fusion of two American Railways. It was introduced to haul coal traffic over a heavy section of road on the Lehigh Valley Railroad and proved so conspicuously successful that it was eventually adopted, and the name with it, as the type best fitted for similar work, all over the world. A remarkable feature was the number of engines of this type built during the War, both in Great Britain and in America. The number required was so large that the plant of the famous Baldwin Locomotive Company in Philadelphia was organised for an output of 300 a month!

A further development from this type is the 2–8–2 or "Mikado" type, now handling with great success the heavy coal trains between Peterborough and London on the London & North Eastern Railway. This locomotive owes its origin to the inferior quality of the coal formerly available for the Japanese railways. This necessitated a larger grate area and a bigger firebox than was possible on the "Consolidation" type, and these requirements were met by setting a wide firebox behind the driving wheels and providing a trailing truck to give the necessary extra support.

Other special requirements, either greatly increased loads or formidable inclines, have produced many types of engines with more wheels. Thus the 4–8–0 "Mastodon" was altered to suit the conditions met with on the Natal railways by adding trailing wheels, the new type being known as the "Mountain." As in the case of the "Mikado," the object was improved steaming capacity. The 4–8–2 type is now commonly used for express passenger work in America.

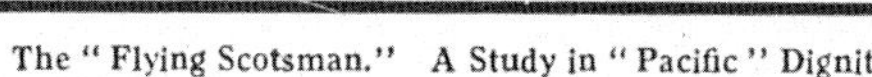

The "Flying Scotsman." A Study in "Pacific" Dignity

The 0–10–0 "Decapod" was introduced as long ago as 1882, when the rails of a long gradient over the mountains on the Southern Pacific Railway were increased in weight from 50 lb. per yard to 62 lb. The President of the company remarked that he would like to see an engine representing as great an advance in size and power over those existing as the new rails did over the old ones. The result was a tremendously heavy and powerful 4–10–0 locomotive known as "*The Guv'nor*," that unfortunately suffered a similar fate to the steamship "*Great Eastern*," and for similar reasons. The main difficulty was to keep steam up, two firemen sometimes being necessary.

"*The Guv'nor*" was undoubtedly premature, and even to-day it may be said that "Decapods" are only suitable for special work on heavy gradients and for short runs. The Great Eastern Railway tried a locomotive of this type many years ago for suburban work, the experiment showing that it was capable of more rapid acceleration than had been thought possible. The "Decapod" was too heavy for the bridges, however, and eventually was scrapped.

The grip on the rails given by the coupled wheels of a "Decapod" makes it very suitable for banking, and an engine of this type is used for this purpose on the

Lickey Incline, near Birmingham. On American railways, where restrictions on the size of engines are less harassing, more use is made of engines of this type, and there 2–10–2 goods engines are more common.

The magnificent engine illustrated on this page, for instance, is used to haul incredibly long and heavy freight trains through mountainous sections on the Pennsylvania Railroad. On these sections wonderful curves and loops have been constructed in the search for easier running, but there still remain gradients to be surmounted. This is done successfully both by ten-coupled engines of the type illustrated and by the standard 4–8–2 passenger express engines of that railroad.

To distribute the increased weight of engines and to enable curves to be negotiated easily, an articulated type was introduced such as the "Fairlie," the "Mallet" and the "Garratt." These engines have usually been required either for heavy banking or for work on railways in mountainous country, as the articulation principle allows for the provision of a large number of driving wheels. Thus we find "Garratts" with 16 driving wheels, arranged in two sets of eight. Four pairs of cylinders are fitted and supplied with steam from a common boiler. Engines of this class are in use in many parts of the world, such as South Africa and Queensland, where severe gradients exist, that have to be surmounted with long and heavy trains. On other American railways the tendency is to use engines of these types, most of which are now fitted with such refinements as feed water heaters and boosters.

Pennsylvania Railroad "Decapod" 2–10–0

The Mallet "Triplex": The World's Largest Locomotive

The world's biggest locomotive, the famous "Triplex" of the Erie Railroad, U.S.A., is of the "Mallet" type. It has three sets of eight coupled wheels, so that its wheel arrangement is 2–8–8–8–2. Engines of this size and power make light of trains a mile in length carrying 10,000 tons of coal!

In addition to these specialised locomotives, it is also necessary on most railways to provide engines for all-round work and mixed traffic. An engine that has proved of great value for this purpose is the 0–6–0 type, which will never be excelled for all-round usefulness. The type is termed "Goods" in a general way, although its activities are by no means confined to this kind of work. The addition of a leading pony truck made possible a longer boiler and heavy outside cylinder fittings, and so developed the 2–6–0 or "Mogul" type, originated in America and imported into England in the "eighties" of last century, when there was a shortage of engines on the Great Northern, Great Eastern and Midland Railways. More recently this type was revived on the G.W.R. and is now becoming increasingly popular for mixed traffic working. Good speeds are often attained although big wheels are rare. In the United States and Canada "Moguls" are fast disappearing, enormous locomotives of the type already described displacing them.

Tank engines have followed a similar course of development to that of tender engines. So long as this type of engine was confined almost exclusively to short-distance work the first essential was power rather than speed, for with the kind of passenger train worked by these engines good starting is essential. Accordingly the earlier tank engines had small wheels.

The design of tank engines lends itself to quaint-looking variations. Usually the water is carried in tanks situated on the frames at the sides of the boiler, but in the case of small engines "saddle" tanks, fitted on top of the boiler, are often employed. This type is used particularly on engines running on narrow gauge lines in engineering works or on small local railways, and the fussy appearance of these small locomotives is familiar to most people. By way of contrast we have at the other end of the scale enormously powerful tank engines, often of the articulated type, with eight or more coupled wheels, that are used for banking, for working the "humps" in marshalling yards, or for running short-distance coal and mineral trains.

The most striking recent development has been the construction of large tank engines for express passenger work. On the Southern Railway, for instance, 4–6–2 and 4–6–4, or "Baltic" tank engines have been put into operation on the journeys of 50 or 60 miles from London to the towns on the south coast. These are genuine express engines capable of running at very high speeds.

Drawing Office and Pattern Shop

FROM general considerations regarding the design of a locomotive we will turn now to the actual process of producing one.

The official of a railway company responsible for the design of new locomotives is the Chief Mechanical Engineer, who is instructed by the Board of Directors speaking through the General Manager. Much correspondence and discussion takes place between the officers of the company before the Board is in a position to issue an order for the construction of a new engine.

Possibly the Operating Superintendent finds that the long-distance express passenger traffic on one section of the system is increasing in such a manner that the existing engines cannot cope adequately with it. On the other hand, some of the bridges on that section are not strong enough to take heavier engines. The chief officers of the company then confer to decide upon the policy to be recommended to the Board, who review the whole of the circumstances before making a decision.

Generally speaking, if the traffic is sufficiently important and likely to yield a fair return on the expenditure, the necessary bridge-strengthening will be put in hand while the Mechanical Engineer is going ahead with his design for the new engine. This is a process that has been necessary on the Southern Railway, as the bridges on the lines between London and Dover were unable to carry the weight of the " King Arthur " locomotives. Rebuilding and strengthening have been carried out so as to make no less than three routes available.

We will suppose that after a thorough investigation it is decided to adopt a locomotive of the 4–6–0 type with a tractive effort greater than that of any passenger engine so far owned by the company. The permissible axle load is fixed by the Chief Civil Engineer, account being taken of all sections where the engine is likely to run. In getting out designs for new engines an attempt is made to keep them within such limits of weight and size that they can work over any part of the system. This is especially important in this country since the big amalgamations were effected but, of course, a balance has to be struck between the general availability of the engine and the restrictions imposed by various parts of the line. Curves and gradients are extremely important in making decisions of the type of locomotive to be constructed, while another point to be considered is that larger turntables may be required to accommodate the new engine.

Portion of Drawing Office : G.W.R. Swindon Works

A 4–6–0 design having been decided upon, the Drawing Office receives its instructions from the Chief Mechanical Engineer and makes a start on the work. The Drawing Office is responsible for the issuing of all drawings and instructions required by the shops for the building of the engines. Certain leading features of the design probably will be standard practice with this particular line—for instance, two cylinders outside and either one or two inside ; Walschaerts' valve gear ; possibly a tapered boiler ; the Belpaire firebox or the wide Wootten type so much used on the L.N.E.R., and so on. This to a large extent governs the design, for wherever possible standard parts are used as this is a source of economy. The Stores Department thereby has a smaller variety of articles to keep in stock, which helps to reduce the value of the stores held. The importance of economy in this respect will be realised when it is stated that the value of the stores may run into many millions of pounds, the interest on which is a large drain on the company's resources every year.

It will be necessary also to settle the coal and water capacity of the tender, which depends upon the location of these supplies on the line. Nowadays tenders are largely standardised, especially in regard to wheel arrangements.

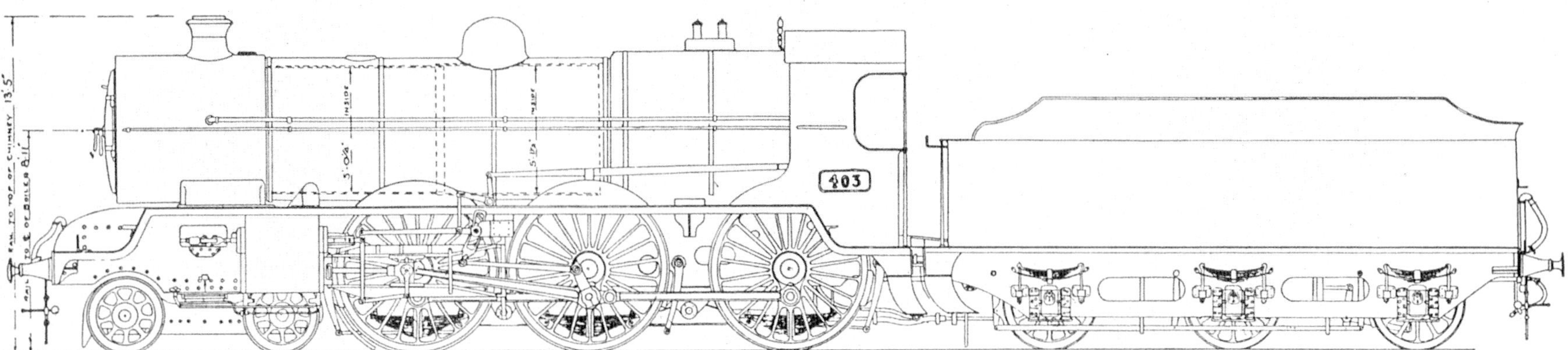

Example of Drawing Office Work. General elevation of a 4-6-0 four-cylinder, superheated express passenger engine

A general outline and end-view drawing of the proposed locomotive is gradually evolved and then a great deal of tedious work has to be done in order to find where the centre of gravity of the engine will come, so that the loads on the axles when the engine is in working order may be settled. Several modifications and sets of calculations may be required before a suitable weight distribution, giving no axle weight in excess of that permitted by the Civil Engineer, is arrived at. The labour is not so great when there are in existence many drawings of engines that in some respects resemble the new one, as the weights already have been taken out in detail.

An essential feature of all well-conducted drawing offices is a well thought out filing system whereby any particular drawing or data may be quickly turned up for reference. New drawings are usually roughed out in pencil on drawing paper and from them tracings are made on transparent tracing cloth, from which in turn any number of photo-copies can be made. The tracings are kept in the Drawing Office and only prints are sent out to the various officials concerned.

District Engineers' Reports

Several prints of the general drawing are sent to the Chief Civil Engineer, who distributes them to his district engineers for their comments in regard to any restrictions on the running of the engine. Where small alterations will give the necessary clearances these are carried out. Larger works have to be specially sanctioned and possibly modifications in the design of the engine may be called for. The expense of removing restrictions on certain sections of the line may not be justified, in which event all concerned are notified in due course, through the Appendix to the Working Timetable, that the new engines referred to as Class so-and-so may not run on these sections.

General approval of the outline design having been obtained, the detailed drawings are put in hand and may amount to several hundred sheets for an engine such as we are considering. Many of the fittings, such as injectors and lubricators, are specialities manufactured by outside firms and for these nothing but an outline giving the overall size is required. But for the boiler, motion, firebox and tender every detail has to be drawn out. The drawings are arranged with a view to giving each part of the workshops just those particulars they require for their work, so that they have not to waste time in picking out their information from the general mass of material provided by the complete set of drawings.

One very important set of drawings is that which deals with the castings required. The steel castings for such parts as wheel centres, pistons and motion plates, are probably ordered from outside firms; whereas iron castings such as the cylinders are made in the company's foundry. For the latter wooden patterns will be made in the Pattern Shop, to which we will now pay a visit.

The Pattern Maker's Art

Pattern making is a highly specialised trade quite distinct from ordinary carpentry and demanding a very high degree of skill from those who practise it. Where large numbers of castings are required from one pattern, that pattern can be made with advantage of metal to resist wear, but even this metal pattern would originally be made from a wooden one.

When the pattern maker gets the drawing of the part that is to be cast, he has to decide first of all how the cast is to be made. Iron and brass are cast in what is called "moulding sand." Impressions in this are made by the pattern which, when removed, leaves cavities to be filled by the molten metal. The whole art of pattern making lies in scheming things out so that it is possible to withdraw the pattern without disturbing the sand.

Another important point for the pattern maker is that the molten metal shrinks as it solidifies, and therefore if the pattern were made the exact size of the finished casting as given on the drawing, the casting produced would be too small. All patterns therefore are made larger than the required casting by an amount known as the "shrinkage." This varies for different materials, but is about $\frac{1}{8}$th in. in 15 in. for cast iron and $\frac{1}{8}$th to $\frac{1}{4}$ in. in 12 in. for brass.

All but the very simplest patterns have to be jointed otherwise they could never be withdrawn from the moulding boxes without disturbing the sand. "Coring" is another very important consideration to bear in mind where hollow castings such as cylinders have to be made. Large patterns also have to be made with what is called "taper" or "draught," so that they can be lifted out without breaking down the sand. A machining allowance is also made where required as, for instance, for the bedding of the cylinder covers, but this will be indicated on the drawings.

Foundry, Fitting and Machine Shops

FROM the pattern shop the next step is obviously to the foundry, always one of the most spectacular parts of the works, at any rate when casting is going on. Casting does not take place at all hours of the day, but usually only in the afternoons, the morning being taken up in moulding.

The first objects that claim our attention here are the cupolas, in which the molten iron is produced. The brass foundry, where brass, copper and phosphor bronze castings are made, is a separate building, containing tilting and crucible furnaces, but the work of casting, except for the difference in the furnaces, is much as will be described for the iron foundry. The brass foundry at Swindon Works, which is one of the best arranged in the country, has an output of some 1,700 tons per annum.

The cupolas consist of vertical cylinders built of steel plates. They are lined with firebrick and have a loading platform built near the top. Before charging up, the tapping hole in the front of the cupola near the bottom is plugged with fireclay and the delivery channel smoothed off with fireclay plaster. A small fire having been lit in the cupola this is now charged with alternate layers of coke, limestone and a mixture of pig and scrap iron. When it is nearly full, the air blast is turned on and enters the cupola by several pipes or tuyeres near the bottom. It forces its way up through the mass, which very soon attains a very high temperature, and the iron begins to melt. By looking through a peep-hole of dark glass one can see the drops of iron falling to the bottom. The limestone unites with the impurities to form a slag, which luckily floats on the molten iron. At all costs slag must be kept out of the castings, as any inclusions of this kind seriously impair their strength.

The furnaceman removes the fireclay plug when the men with the fireclay-lined ladles are ready and the ladles are charged and taken to the mould boxes. The flow of molten iron from the furnace is readily stopped at any time by a fireclay plug pushed home by an iron rod. As molten iron is tapped from the cupola, fresh charges of coke, limestone and pig iron are added from the charging platform. The whole process is thus continuous throughout the period during which casting is in progress so that there is no risk of shortage of metal. The greatest care must be taken at the same time to see that the metal used is homogeneous.

A Railway Iron Foundry showing the preparation of the moulding boxes used for large castings

Meanwhile, the various moulding boxes have been got ready by using the appropriate patterns. Moulding is a skilled art, which does not generally receive the recognition due to it. The moulding is done in special moulding sand, which must be damp enough to make it workable, but not so wet that the hot metal will produce dangerous amounts of steam. A great deal of skill and experience is required to enable the moulder to know where the pouring holes should be placed so as to ensure a good sound casting free from blow holes and porosity.

Most of the large and complicated moulding is done by hand, but a lot of the smaller work is done by machine moulders, which are capable of turning out a lot of work in a short time and are of great value in a modern iron foundry.

Some locomotive castings are of very large size. We are told that in order to cast the combined saddle and cylinder for one of the Great Western Railway "Castle" type locomotives, it is found necessary to use moulding boxes made in four separate parts. These moulding boxes are rectangular iron frames, with lifting handles, arranged so that they can be piled up on the top of one another and secured together by bolts. One is apt to forget that the boxes may sometimes contain many hundredweights of molten metal, and therefore must be very strong. To get the necessary holes in this casting, twenty cores have to be used in the moulding. These are of clay, usually baked to hardness in an oven. When the four moulds are fastened together they are taken to a casting pit, from 6 ft. to 8 ft. in depth, and finished off with the runner boxes to guide the molten iron into the mould.

From the foundry we naturally pass to the fitting and machine shops, the exact arrangement of which varies with the size of the establishment concerned. As there is no hard and fast dividing line between the two sets of shops we may quite well consider them together.

Boring and Facing Cylinders

Following up the cylinders from the foundry and the "fettling" shop, where the rough edges and spare bits of metal are knocked off, we can see in the fitting shops how the cylinders are bored and faced—operations requiring a high degree of accuracy. The sides of the castings have to be planed so as to fit tightly against the main frames of the engine, and numerous bolt and stud holes require to be drilled. All important shops are now supplied with large multiple drills which are set by means of "jigs," and may then be used to drill many holes in a casting simultaneously. Some wonderful machinery is to be seen at Crewe, where, among a host of appliances, is a circular saw, 7 ft. in diameter, the edge of which travels at the rate of 13,000 ft. per minute, and can cut through a 9-inch steel axle in 25 seconds!

Part of a Machine Shop with lathe and twist drill grinder in foreground

The frame plates are a feature of particular interest. There are two of these to each engine, and they run the full length of the engine. There are generally two lighter outer frames also, which support the footplating, splashers, etc., and in some designs they have to carry the wheel bearings. Although of practically uniform thickness, the frame plates have a very elaborate contour, to accommodate the outlines of the buffer plate, cylinders, bogie centre pin casting, axle box guides, boiler expansion brackets, footplate, and trailing buffer plate. As received from the steelworks, the plates are about 4 ft. in width, and $1\frac{1}{4}$ in. thick, and of suitable length to avoid a joint. After marking off they are roughly punched out to the required shape, afterwards being slotted and otherwise machined to the exact dimensions, then levelled by hammering or rolling, and finally drilled. To save time, 8 or 10 plates are piled on top of one another and all are slotted together, the top one having been carefully marked off and forming a template for the others. On the conclusion of drilling, the frames are sent to the erecting shop where they are set up on timber trestles and accurately spaced and levelled as described in the course of the next chapter.

Piston valves are an essential feature of all modern superheated locomotives and at Swindon works there is very complete plant for dealing with these. For good working there should be no leakage of steam past the piston valves, so it will be appreciated that very accurate machining is called for. The piston valve consists of two pistons, or heads, on a stem, which reciprocate in a valve chamber. This has to be bored with great exactitude and the valve heads have to be turned to equally fine limits. The finished surface is obtained by hand scraping.

The valve gear and motion require a good deal of attention in the machine and fitting shops, especially if the much favoured Walschaerts' gear is used, as they enter the shops as rough castings and forgings. The piston heads are turned, bored and screwed in the lathe, and then screwed on to the piston rods, which have been turned and screwed ready to receive them. The finishing touches are given by means of a grinding lathe, and we may notice that grinding now plays a very important part in machine shop operations, especially since very hard alloy steels have come into favour. The brake gear is similarly dealt with. Milling machines are an essential part of the equipment of up-to-date machine shops, and we shall probably find them engaged on the milling of valve rods, connecting and coupling rods. The latter are milled out to an "I" section, which gives the maximum of rigidity with a minimum of weight.

Wheel centres, crank axles, axle boxes, and a multitude of small brass fittings also have to be dealt with in this part of the locomotive works.

Boiler and Erecting Shops

THE largest individual item in the make-up of the locomotive is the boiler, and we will now pay a visit to the boiler shop, easily distinguishable by the deafening noise it creates.

The boiler is built up of steel plates of acid open hearth steel, which are first passed through rollers to straighten them, after which one plate is carefully marked off to serve as a template for the others. Where necessary, the edges are planed and trimmed, and a certain amount of drilling is then done. The next process is to curve the plates to the required cylindrical form, which is done by passing them many times through sets of bending rollers. The three rings forming the boiler are then assembled vertically, the circumferential joints being covered by a joint ring, or belt, previously heated to a red heat before it is put on. The longitudinal seams are covered by butt strips. The plates are all "tacked" together by means of drift pins to keep them in position while the final riveting is done. Special multiple drilling machines are used to drill the large number of holes required, the usual size of rivet being $\frac{7}{8}$ in. Hydraulic riveters are much used for riveting up the boiler shell, after all the joints have been carefully cleaned with sal ammoniac. At one time all locomotives had boilers with a round topped firebox, which were a little easier to construct than the more popular modern "Belpaire" type, in which the outer firebox top is flat, so as to be parallel with the top of the inner firebox.

Erecting shop showing engines in various stages

Some locomotive boilers are made with the ring nearest the firebox, conical in shape. This gives greater steam space over the firebox.

The firebox outer casing or wrapper plate, also the throat and back plates, are more complicated, requiring flanging work done on them. The foundation ring, which unites the inner and outer fireboxes, has to be drilled and machined where necessary, for which special machinery is usually employed. The wrapper plate is secured to the barrel temporarily while the back and throat plates are fitted, and then dismantled again while the firebox end of the boiler is riveted up.

The inner firebox is of copper and the necessary flanging is done by hand, whereas for the steel plates it is done in a hydraulic press. After the necessary drilling has been done, the foundation ring is attached to the inner firebox, which is then placed inside the outer shell. After this the back plate is riveted in, then the tapping and screwing for the stays follows, the stays then being put in by hand from the outside. Every stay is carefully tested when in position. Special expansion stays are used for part of the firebox roof. The ends of the copper stays are hammered over by pneumatic riveters, and an extra powerful machine is used for riveting the foundation ring and the firehole.

When the boiler is completely assembled, the various mountings are put on it, and the ordinary and superheater fire tubes are fitted in. Next comes the hydraulic test, during which the boiler is stressed to a pressure 50 per cent. above that at which it will have to work. This is followed by a steam test at 10 lb. above the working pressure, with another steam test after the superheater header and elements have been added. The object of having the hydraulic test before the steam test is that if anything gives way, or if any of the seams leak, no great damage is done. By reason of water being practically incompressible, it only escapes in small quantities, in the event of a mishap, and the pressure is immediately reduced.

The smith's shop, in which we include the stamping shop and the coppersmith's shop, now claim our attention, and the stamping shop comes a good second to the boiler shop for noise. In it are produced by what is called "drop forging," a great variety of the small parts required on the locomotive and for which castings would not be good enough. The drop stamp is simply a large hammer, steam driven, the face of the hammer containing half the mould or die required to produce the forging. The other half of the die is in the anvil, so that a piece of metal placed under the hammer takes the shape of the two dies together. By this means sound forgings of clean outline are rapidly obtained, and the method has made great progress within recent times. Under the larger hammers such articles as connecting rods and valve rods, are forged. In the smith's shop proper are many small hearths and a few steam hammers, by the aid of which a great variety of the smaller smithing jobs required on a locomotive are carried out.

In the copper and tin smiths' shops a great deal of interesting work goes on, largely in connection with the pipe details of the locomotive, but lamps and other sheet iron articles are also made.

Looking now for a few moments into the wheel shop, we notice the large wheel lathes of special construction into which a pair of wheels on their axle can be rolled for the tyres to be turned. In this shop the axles are hydraulically pressed into the bosses of the cast steel wheel centres, and the heated tyres are shrunk on to the previously turned rims. The balancing of the wheels of a locomotive, especially the driving wheels, is very important, as unbalanced wheels cause bad running and severe wear on the permanent way, so that all up to date wheel shops have a machine for testing the balance. A good deal of the work of a wheel shop consists of the trueing-up of tyres that have become worn in service, and hence the liberal provision of wheel lathes.

All the work done in the shops so far described has been a necessary preliminary to the assembly or erection of the locomotive, a process we will now proceed to study in the erecting shop. To most visitors this will undoubtedly be the most interesting part of the works, because here they see all the five thousand or so parts of the engine put together to form the finished article.

First of all the frames of the locomotive, as received from the machine shop, are laid on trestles and the various centre lines marked out. They are then placed upright in forked supports and adjusted so as to be square with one another and truly vertical and level. The levelling is carefully done by straightedge and spirit level. The footplate brackets, cross stays, etc., are then riveted in after being bolted up temporarily. The bogie pivot casting and motion plate are fixed in at this stage. Then the cylinders are lowered into position, the weight being taken on jacks until the exact final settling is reached. The cylinders must be fixed with great accuracy, as on this depends the smooth working of the machine.

A typical Boiler Shop, showing drilling machines

(*Continued on page 35*)

HORNBY TRAINS

BRITISH AND GUARANTEED

No. 2 Pullman Train, L.M.S.

No. 2 Goods Train, L.M.S.

Perfect Miniature Railways

Every boy is fascinated by railways and longs for a railway of his own. But it must be a real railway, correctly laid out with main line, branch lines and sidings, stations, tunnels and bridges, and fully equipped with points, signals, etc. A railway of this kind is easily built from the component parts of the Hornby Train System.

The splendid fun of running a Hornby railway is real and lasting because of the exceptional strength and reliable mechanism of the Hornby Locomotives, the realistic Hornby Rolling Stock, and the wide range of Hornby Accessories—all built in perfect proportion and all beautifully finished.

Gas Cylinder Wagon

Level Crossing

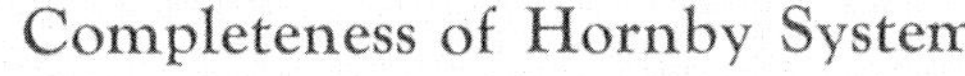

Completeness of Hornby System

From the day of their introduction Hornby Trains have always represented the latest model railway practice. Designs are continually being improved and new items added so that the system is complete in every detail. There is a comprehensive range of Locomotives, driven by clockwork or electric motors; Rolling Stock of all kinds—Passenger Coaches, Pullman Cars, Trucks, Wagons and Vans; and Accessories—Stations, Tunnels, Bridges, Signals and Level Crossings.

Finally, there is the new Hornby Control System that enables every model railway enthusiast to control his trains, signals, and points by operating levers in the Signal Cabin, just as a signalman does on a real railway.

The Hornby system has many unique features that place it in a category quite by itself. The motors in the locomotives are of the highest possible quality, being perfect pieces of mechanism with accurately cut gears that ensure smooth and steady running. The trains throughout are beautifully finished in every respect and are enamelled in standard railway colours.

In the following pages the Hornby Trains, Rolling Stock, and Accessories are fully described, and are beautifully illustrated in their *actual colours.*

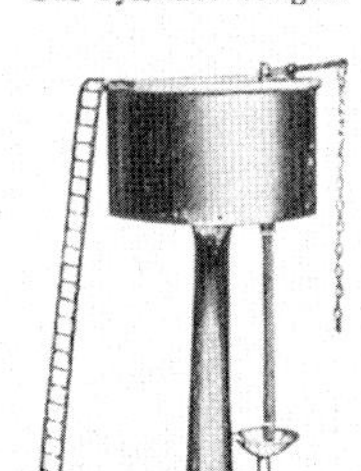

Water Tank

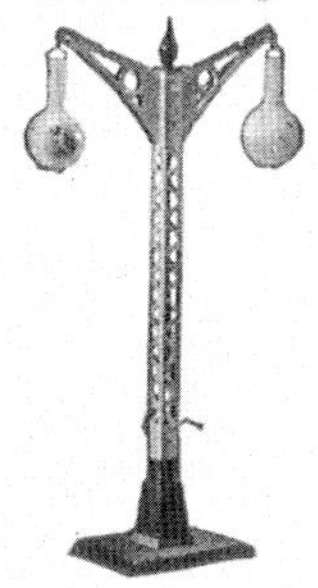

Double Lamp Standard

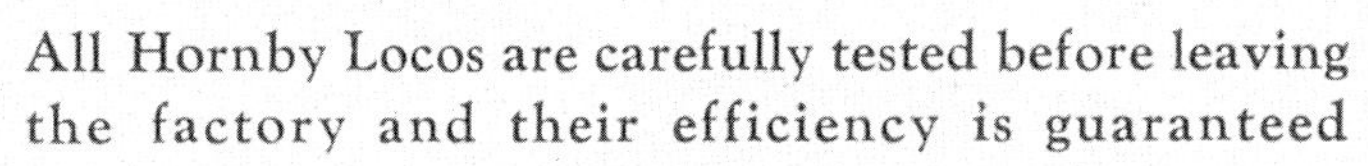

All Hornby Locos are carefully tested before leaving the factory and their efficiency is guaranteed

No. 1 Lumber Wagon

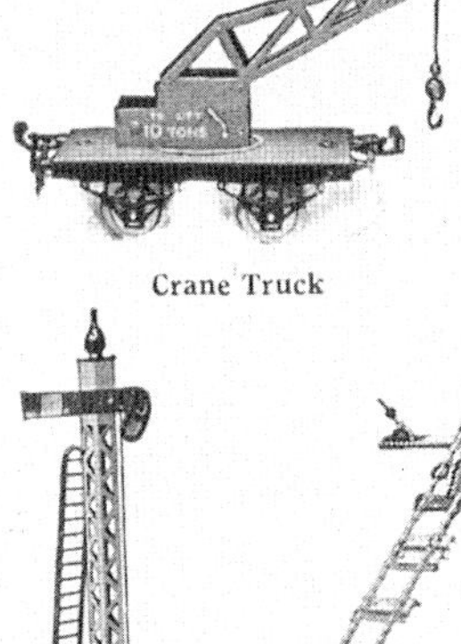

Crane Truck

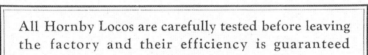

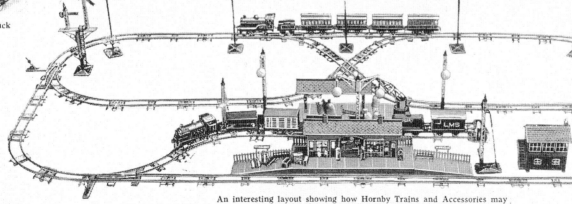

Signal

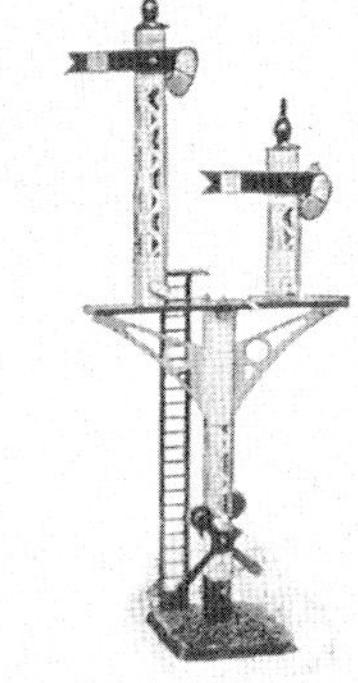

Junction Signal

An interesting layout showing how Hornby Trains and Accessories may be used for the construction of a miniature railway

HORNBY TRAINS

BRITISH AND GUARANTEED

No. M1 PASSENGER SET

This set contains a fine Loco, Tender, two Pullman Coaches and set of Rails. One of the rails is fitted with a braking device by means of which the train may be braked from the track. Each Loco is fitted with brake mechanism. The set is richly coloured and well finished. Non-reversible type. Gauge 0.

No. M1 Passenger Set, complete, packed in strong cardboard box, Price 7/6

No. M2 PASSENGER SET

Similar in every way to the above excepting that it has three Pullman Coaches instead of two, and additional Rails.

No. M2 Passenger Set, complete, packed in strong cardboard box, Price 9/-

No. M1 or M2 Loco ... ... Price 3/- No. M1 or M2 Tender ... ... Price 9d.

No. M1 or M2 Pullman Coach ... ... Price 1/-

No. M3 GOODS SET

Strongly built with reliable clockwork mechanism. This set comprises Loco, Tender, two Goods Wagons and set of Rails. A rail fitted with a special device is included by means of which the train may be braked from the track. The locos and tenders are supplied in three colours—red, black and Great Western green. Wagons lettered L.M.S. are supplied with the red and black locos and tenders. Wagons lettered G.W. are supplied with the Great Western green locos and tenders. Each Loco is fitted with brake mechanism, and is of the non-reversible type. Gauge 0.

No. M3 Goods Set, complete, packed in strong cardboard box, Price 15/-

No. M3 Loco ... ... Price 8/6 No. M3 Tender ... ... Price 9d.

No. M3 Wagon ... ... Price 1/6

HORNBY TRAINS

BRITISH AND GUARANTEED

HORNBY No. 0 PASSENGER SET, L.M.S.

Each set contains Loco, Tender, and two Coaches, as illustrated, with Curved Rails to form a circle 2-ft. in diameter, and two Straight Rails. One of the rails is fitted with a braking device by means of which the train may be stopped from the track. The Loco is fitted with brake mechanism. Non-reversible type. Gauge 0.

Hornby No. 0 Passenger Set, L.M.S., complete, packed in strong cardboard box, Price 22/6

HORNBY No. 0 GOODS SET, L.M.S.

This set comprises Loco, Tender and one Wagon, with Curved Rails to form a circle 2-ft. in diameter, and two Straight Rails. One of the rails is fitted with a braking device by means of which the train may be stopped from the track. The set is supplied with either red or black loco and tender and the colour required should be stated when ordering. The Loco is equipped with brake mechanism. Non-reversible type. Gauge 0.

Hornby No. 0 Goods Set, L.M.S., complete, packed in strong cardboard box, Price 17/6

The Locos, Tenders, Coaches and Wagons of the above train sets may also be purchased separately. Prices are as follows:—

Hornby No. 0 Loco	Price 10/6	Hornby Passenger Coach	Price 3/6
Hornby Tender	„ 2/6	Hornby Wagon	„ 2/6

HORNBY TRAINS

BRITISH AND GUARANTEED

HORNBY No. 0 GOODS SET, L.N.E.R.

This set contains Loco, Tender, one Wagon, and Rails as in the No. 0 Goods L.M.S., and is identical with that set except for the lettering. It is supplied with either green or black loco and tender and the colour required should be stated when ordering. Richly enamelled in realistic colours and highly finished. Gauge 0.

Hornby No. 0 Goods Set, L.N.E.R., complete, packed in strong cardboard box, Price 17/6

HORNBY No. 0 PASSENGER SET, L.N.E.R.

The contents of this set are similar to those of the No. 0 Passenger L.M.S., namely, Loco, Tender, two Coaches, and Rails to form a circle of 2-ft. diameter and two Straight Rails (including one brake rail). The Loco is fitted with brake mechanism. Non-reversible type. Gauge 0.

Hornby No. 0 Passenger Set, L.N.E.R., complete, packed in strong cardboard box, Price 22/6

HORNBY No. 0 GOODS AND PASSENGER SETS, G.W.

The No. 0 Goods and Passenger Sets are also lettered to represent G.W. rolling stock. In each case the locos and tenders are coloured Great Western green only. The contents of each set are similar to those in the L.M.S. and L.N.E.R. sets.

Hornby No. 0 Goods Set, G.W., complete, packed in strong cardboard box, Price 17/6 **Hornby No. 0 Passenger Set, G.W., complete, packed in strong cardboard box, Price 22/6**

The Locos, Tenders, Coaches and Wagons of the above train sets may also be purchased separately. Prices are as follows :—

Hornby No. 0 Loco	**Price 10/6**	**Hornby Passenger Coach**	**Price 3/6**
Hornby Tender	**„ 2/6**	**Hornby Wagon**	**„ 2/6**

HORNBY TRAINS
BRITISH AND GUARANTEED

HORNBY No. 1 PASSENGER SET, L.M.S.

This set comprises Loco, Tender, two Passenger Coaches, Rails to form a circle 2-ft. in diameter and two Straight Rails. One of the rails has a braking device by means of which the train may be stopped from the track. The Loco is fitted with reversing-gear and brake mechanism, and the doors of the coaches open. Gauge 0.

Hornby No. 1 Passenger Set, L.M.S., complete, well boxed, Price 25/-

HORNBY No. 1 GOODS SET, L.M.S.

Each set contains Loco, Tender and one Wagon, with Rails to form a circle 2-ft. in diameter and two Straight Rails. One of the rails is fitted with a braking device by means of which the train may be stopped from the track. The set is supplied with either red or black loco and tender and the colour required should be stated when ordering. The Loco is equipped with reversing-gear and brake mechanism. Gauge 0.

Hornby No. 1 Goods Set, L.M.S., complete, well boxed, Price 20/-

***Hornby No. 1 Goods Set, L.M.S., complete, well boxed, fitted for Hornby Control, Price 23/6**

The Locos, Tenders, Coaches and Wagons of the above train sets may also be purchased separately. Prices are as follows :—

Hornby No. 1 Loco	**Price 12/6**	**Hornby Passenger Coach**	**Price 3/6**
Hornby Tender	**„ 2/6**	**Hornby Wagon**	**„ 2/6**

***Hornby No. 1 Loco, fitted for Hornby Control, Price 15/-**

** For particulars of the Hornby Control System, see page 26.*

HORNBY TRAINS
BRITISH AND GUARANTEED

HORNBY No. 1 PASSENGER SET, L.N.E.R.

This set comprises Loco, Tender, two Coaches and Rails as in the No. 1 Passenger Set L.M.S., described on the previous page, and is identical with that set except that the colouring is representative of the L.N.E.R. Company's locos and rolling-stock. Gauge 0.

Hornby No. 1 Passenger Set, L.M.S., complete, well boxed, Price 25/-

HORNBY No. 1 GOODS SET, L.N.E.R.

The contents of this set are similar to those of the No. 1 Goods L.M.S., namely, Loco, Tender, one Wagon, Rails to form a circle 2-ft. in diameter and two Straight Rails (including one brake rail). The set is supplied with either green or black loco and tender and the colour required should be stated when ordering. The Loco is fitted with reversing-gear and brake mechanism. Gauge 0.

Hornby No. 1 Goods Set, L.N.E.R., complete, well boxed, Price 20/-

***Hornby No. 1 Goods Set, L.N.E.R., complete, well boxed, fitted for Hornby Control, Price 23/6**

HORNBY No. 1 GOODS AND PASSENGER SETS, G.W.

The No. 1 Goods and Passenger Sets are also lettered to represent G.W. rolling stock. In each case the locos and tenders are coloured Great Western green only. The contents of each set are similar to those in the L.M.S. and L.N.E.R. sets.

Hornby No. 1 Goods Set, G.W., complete, well boxed ... ... **Price 20/-** **Hornby No. 1 Passenger Set, G.W., complete, well boxed** ... ... **Price 25/-**

***Hornby No. 1 Goods Set, G.W., complete, well boxed, fitted for Hornby Control, Price 23/6**

The Locos, Tenders, Coaches and Wagons of the above train sets may also be purchased separately if required. Prices are as follows :—

Hornby No. 1 Loco	**Price 12/6**	**Hornby Passenger Coach**	**Price 3/6**
Hornby Tender	**,, 2/6**	**Hornby Wagon**	**,, 2/6**

***Hornby No. 1 Loco, fitted for Hornby Control, Price 15/-**

* *For particulars of the Hornby Control System,* *see page* 26.

HORNBY TRAINS
BRITISH AND GUARANTEED

HORNBY No. 1 TANK GOODS SET, L.N.E.R.

This set contains a Hornby No. 1 Tank Loco, Hornby Wagon, Petrol Tank Wagon, Brake Van and set of Rails to form a circle 2-ft. in diameter and two Straight Rails (including one brake rail). It is supplied with either green or black loco and the colour required should be stated when ordering. The Loco is fitted with brake mechanism and reversing gear. Gauge 0.

Hornby No. 1 Tank Goods Set, L.N.E.R., complete, well boxed, Price 22/6
***Hornby No. 1 Tank Goods Set, L.N.E.R., complete, well boxed, fitted for Hornby Control, Price 26/-**

HORNBY No. 1 TANK GOODS SET, L.M.S.

This set is similar to the L.N.E.R. set, described above, with the exception of colouring and lettering. It is supplied with either red or black loco and the colour required should be stated when ordering. Gauge 0.

Hornby No. 1 Tank Goods Set, L.M.S., complete, well boxed, Price 22/6
***Hornby No. 1 Tank Goods Set, L.M.S., complete, well boxed, fitted for Hornby Control, Price 26/-**

HORNBY No. 1 TANK GOODS SET, G.W.

No. 1 Tank Goods Set is also available with G.W. lettering. In this set the loco is coloured Great Western green only. The contents are the same as those of the L.M.S. and L.N.E.R. sets. Gauge 0.

Hornby No. 1 Tank Goods Set, G.W., complete, well boxed, Price 22/6
***Hornby No. 1 Tank Goods Set, G.W., complete, well boxed, fitted for Hornby Control, Price 26/-**

The components of the above train sets may also be purchased separately if required. Prices are as follows :—

Hornby No. 1 Tank Loco	**Price 12/6**	**Petrol Tank Wagon ... ...**	**Price 2/6**
Hornby Wagon	**„ 2/6**	**Brake Van ... ...**	**„ 3/6**

***Hornby No. 1 Tank Loco fitted for Hornby Control, Price 15/-**

* *For particulars of the Hornby Control System, see page 26.*

HORNBY No. 2 TANK PASSENGER SET, L.M.S.

This set contains the famous No. 2 Hornby Tank Loco, three Passenger Coaches, Guard's Van and set of Rails. One of the rails is fitted with a device by means of which the Loco may be both braked and reversed from the track. Gauge 0.

Hornby No. 2 Tank Passenger Set, L.M.S., complete, well boxed, Price 40/-

***Hornby No. 2 Tank Passenger Set, L.M.S., complete, well boxed, fitted for Hornby Control, Price 45/-**

HORNBY No. 2 TANK GOODS SET, L.M.S.

This realistic goods train consists of a No. 2 Hornby Tank Loco, Hornby Wagon, Petrol Tank Wagon, No. 1 Cattle Truck, Brake Van, and set of Rails, including a brake rail. It is supplied with either red or black loco and the colour required should be stated when ordering. Gauge 0.

Hornby No. 2 Tank Goods Set, L.M.S., complete, well boxed, Price 37/6

***Hornby No. 2 Tank Goods Set, L.M.S., complete, well boxed, fitted for Hornby Control, Price 42/6**

The components of the above train sets may also be purchased separately if required. Prices are as follows :—

Hornby No. 2 Tank Loco	**Price 22/6**	**Petrol Tank Wagon**	**Price 2/6**
Hornby Passenger Coach	**„ 3/6**	**Brake Van**	**„ 3/6**
Hornby Wagon	**„ 2/6**	**No. 1 Cattle Truck**	**„ 3/6**

***Hornby No. 2 Tank Loco, fitted for Hornby Control, Price 25/-**

* *For particulars of the Hornby Control System, see page 26*

HORNBY TRAINS

BRITISH AND GUARANTEED

HORNBY No. 2 TANK PASSENGER SET, L.N.E.R.

This set contains a Hornby No. 2 Tank Loco, three Passenger Coaches, Guard's Van and Rails as in the No. 2 Tank Passenger Set L.M.S., described on the opposite page but the lettering and colouring are representative of L.N.E.R. Locos and rolling stock. Gauge 0.

Hornby No. 2 Tank Passenger Set, L.N.E.R., complete, well boxed, Price 40/-

***Hornby No. 2 Tank Passenger Set, L.N.E.R., complete, well boxed, fitted for Hornby Control, Price 45/-**

HORNBY No. 2 TANK PASSENGER SET, G.W.

The contents of this set are identical with those of the L.M.S. and L.N.E.R. sets, except that they are coloured and lettered to represent G.W. rolling stock.

Hornby No. 2 Tank Passenger Set, G.W., complete, well boxed, Price 40/-

***Hornby No. 2 Tank Passenger Set, G.W., complete, well boxed, fitted for Hornby Control, Price 45/-**

HORNBY No. 2 TANK GOODS SET, L.N.E.R.

No. 2 Tank Goods Set L.N.E.R. consists of a No. 2 Tank Loco, Hornby Wagon, Petrol Tank Wagon, No. 1 Cattle Truck, Brake Van and set of Rails including one brake rail. It is supplied with either green or black loco and the colour required should be stated when ordering. Gauge 0.

Hornby No. 2 Tank Goods Set, L.N.E.R., complete, well boxed, Price 37/6

***Hornby No. 2 Tank Goods Set, L.N.E.R., complete, well boxed, fitted for Hornby Control, Price 42/6**

HORNBY No. 2 TANK GOODS SET, G.W.

No. 2 Tank Goods Set is also available with G.W. lettering and colouring. The loco in this set is only supplied in Great Western green. The contents of the set are exactly the same as those of the L.M.S. and L.N.E.R. sets.

Hornby No. 2 Tank Goods Set, G.W., complete, well boxed, Price 37/6

***Hornby No. 2 Tank Goods Set, G.W., complete, well boxed, fitted for Hornby Control, Price 42/6**

The components of the above train sets may also be purchased separately if required. Prices are as follows :—

Hornby No. 2 Tank Loco	**Price 22/6**	**Petrol Tank Wagon**	**Price 2/6**
Hornby Passenger Coach	**,, 3/6**	**Brake Van**	**,, 3/6**
Hornby Wagon	**,, 2/6**	**No. 1 Cattle Truck**	**,, 3/6**

***Hornby No. 2 Tank Loco, fitted for Hornby Control, Price 25/-**

* *For particulars of the Hornby Control System, see page 26*

HORNBY TRAINS
BRITISH AND GUARANTEED

HORNBY No. 2 PULLMAN SET, G.W.

Each set contains Loco, Tender and two Pullman Coaches, as illustrated, with set of Rails The rails include one brake rail by means of which the Loco may be both braked and reversed from the track. Gauge 0.

Hornby No. 2 Pullman Set, G.W., complete, well boxed, Price 50/-
***Hornby No. 2 Pullman Set, G.W., complete, well boxed, fitted for Hornby Control, Price 55/-**

HORNBY No. 2 PULLMAN SET, L.M.S.

This set is the same as the No. 2 Pullman Set, G.W., excepting that the components are coloured and lettered to represent L.M.S. Locos and rolling stock.

Hornby No. 2 Pullman Set, L.M.S., complete, well boxed, Price 50/-
***Hornby No. 2 Pullman Set, L.M.S., complete, well boxed, fitted for Hornby Control, Price 55/-**

HORNBY No. 2 GOODS SET, L.M.S.

The Loco, Tender, and Rails in this set are similar to those in the No. 2 Pullman Sets, but two Wagons take the place of the Pullman Coaches. The set is supplied with either red or black loco and tender and the colour required should be stated when ordering. Gauge 0.

Hornby No. 2 Goods Set, complete, well boxed, Price 32/6
***Hornby No. 2 Goods Set, complete, well boxed, fitted for Hornby Control, Price 37/6**

The Locos, Tenders, Pullman Coaches and Wagons of the above train sets may also be purchased separately if required. Prices are as follows :—

Hornby No. 2 Loco ... ... Price 20/-
Hornby Pullman Car ... ... „ 12/6
Hornby Wagon ... ... Price 2/6
Hornby No. 2 Tender ... ... „ 3/6
***Hornby No. 2 Loco, fitted for Hornby Control, Price 22/6**

** For particulars of the Hornby Control System,* *see page 26*

HORNBY TRAINS
BRITISH AND GUARANTEED

HORNBY No. 2 PULLMAN SET, L.N.E.R.

This set is identical in every way with the No. 2 Pullman Sets described on the opposite page, except that in this case the lettering and colouring are representative of the London and North Eastern Locos and rolling stock. Gauge 0.

Hornby No. 2 Pullman Set, L.N.E.R., complete, well boxed, Price 50/-
***Hornby No. 2 Pullman Set, L.N.E.R., complete, well boxed, fitted for Hornby Control, Price 55/-**

HORNBY No. 2 GOODS SET, L.N.E.R.

The Loco, Tender, and Rails in this set are similar to those in the No. 2 Pullman Sets, but two Wagons take the place of the Pullman Coaches. The set is supplied with either green or black loco and tender and the colour required should be stated when ordering. Gauge 0.

Hornby No. 2 Goods Set, L.N.E.R., complete, well boxed, Price 32/6
***Hornby No. 2 Goods Set, L.N.E.R., complete, well boxed, fitted for Hornby Control, Price 37/6**

No. 2 Goods Set is also supplied with G.W. lettering. In this set the loco is coloured G.W. green only. The contents are the same as those of the L.M.S. and L.N.E.R. No. 2 Goods Sets. Gauge 0.

Hornby No. 2 Goods Set, G.W., complete, well boxed, Price 32/6
***Hornby No. 2 Goods Set, G.W., complete, well boxed, fitted for Hornby Control, Price 37/6**

The Locos, Tenders, Pullman Coaches and Wagons of the above train sets may also be purchased separately if required. Prices are as follows :—

Hornby No. 2 Loco	**Price 20/-**	**Hornby Wagon**	**Price 2/6**
Hornby Pullman Car	**„ 12/6**	**Hornby No. 2 Tender**	**„ 3/6**

***Hornby No. 2 Loco, fitted for Hornby Control, Price 22/6**

* *For particulars of the Hornby Control System, see page 26.*

HORNBY METROPOLITAN TRAIN SET

The Locos and Coaches in these train sets are modelled on the electric passenger rolling stock of the Metropolitan Railway. Three different sets are available and particulars of the motive power and contents of each are given below. The components of each set may be purchased separately, if required.

HORNBY METROPOLITAN TRAIN SET No. 1 contains Electric Loco, two Coaches and Electrical Rails for a 4-ft. diameter circle. The motor in the Loco is designed to run from the main supply, either alternating or direct, of 100-250 volts, connection being made by an adaptor that will fit in a lamp socket of the house supply. A suitable rheostat is included for speed regulating. The train is electrically lighted. Gauge 0.

Hornby Metropolitan Electric Train, Set No. 1, complete, well boxed, Price 110/-

Metropolitan Electric Loco No. 1 ... Price 52/6 Metropolitan Coach No. 1 ... Price 18/- Rheostat ... Price 18/6

HORNBY METROPOLITAN TRAIN SET No. 2 contains Electric Loco, two Coaches, Resistance Controller, and Electrical Rails. The Loco is fitted with an electric motor which is operated from a 4-volt Accumulator or from a suitable transformer connected to the main (alternating current only). Gauge 0.

Hornby Metropolitan Electric Train Set No. 2, complete, well boxed, Price 95/-

Hornby Metropolitan Electric Loco No. 2 ... Price 47/6 Hornby Metropolitan Coach No. 2 ... Price 18/- Resistance Controller ... Price 3/6

***HORNBY METROPOLITAN TRAIN SET No. 3** contains a powerful Clockwork Loco, two Coaches, and set of Rails including a Control Rail. The Loco is fitted for Control.

Hornby Metropolitan Train Set No. 3, complete, well boxed, Price 55/-

Hornby Metropolitan Clockwork Loco No. 3 ... Price 22/6 Hornby Metropolitan Coach No. 3 ... Price 13/6

THE RIVIERA "BLUE" TRAIN SET

This splendid train set is a model of the famous express that runs regularly between Calais and the Mediterranean Coast. It is beautifully finished and is available with either Clockwork or Electric Loco. Gauge 0.

RIVIERA "BLUE" TRAIN SET No. 1 contains Electric Loco, Tender, two Coaches, Resistance Controller and Electrical Rails. The Loco is fitted with an electric motor which is operated from a 4-volt Accumulator or from a suitable transformer connected to the main (alternating current only). Gauge 0.

Riviera "Blue" Train Set No. 1, complete, well boxed, Price 85/-

***RIVIERA "BLUE" TRAIN SET No. 2** contains a powerful Clockwork Loco, Tender, two Coaches and set of Rails including a Control Rail. The Loco is fitted for Control.

Riviera "Blue" Train Set No. 2, complete, well boxed, Price 70/-

The components of the Riviera "Blue" Train Sets may also be purchased separately if required. Prices are as follows:

Riviera "Blue" Train Loco No. 1 ... Price 37/6 Riviera "Blue" Train Tender ... Price 4/6
Riviera "Blue" Train Coach ... ... „ 16/6 Riviera "Blue" Train Loco No. 2 ... „ 27/6
Resistance Controller ... ... Price 3/6

* *For particulars of the Hornby Control System, see page 26*

HORNBY TRAINS
BRITISH AND GUARANTEED

Hornby No. 1 Tank Loco, L.M.S. Passenger

Hornby No. 1 Tank Loco, L.N.E.R. Passenger

Hornby No. 1 Tank Loco L.N.E.R. Goods, coloured black, is also supplied.

The Hornby No. 1 Tank Loco is strong and durable and is capable of any amount of hard work. It is richly enamelled and highly finished in four different colours, representing L.M.S., L.N.E.R. and G.W. goods and passenger locos. The Loco is fitted with brake and reversing-gear.

Hornby No. 1 Tank Loco, Price 12/6 ***Hornby No. 1 Tank Loco, fitted for Hornby Control, Price 15/-**

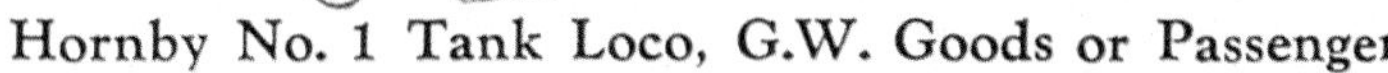

Hornby No. 1 Tank Loco, G.W. Goods or Passenger

Hornby No. 1 Tank Loco, L.M.S. Goods

* *For particulars of the Hornby Control System, see page 26*

HORNBY TRAINS

BRITISH AND GUARANTEED

Hornby No. 2 Tank Loco, L.M.S. Passenger

Hornby No. 2 Tank Loco, L.N.E.R. Passenger

Hornby No. 2 Tank Loco, L.N.E.R. Goods, coloured black, is also supplied.

The Hornby No. 2 Tank Loco is a powerful model, beautifully designed and finished. It represents a type of loco that is being developed rapidly by our Railway Companies for main line goods and passenger traffic. It is richly enamelled in colours to represent L.M.S., L.N.E.R. and G.W. goods and passenger locos, and is fitted with four coupled wheels and leading and trailing four-wheeled bogies. Length 10½". The brake and reversing-gear may be operated from levers in the cab or from the track. Each loco is carefully tested before leaving the factory.

Hornby No. 2 Tank Loco, Price 22/6 ***Hornby No. 2 Tank Loco, fitted for Hornby Control, Price 25/–**

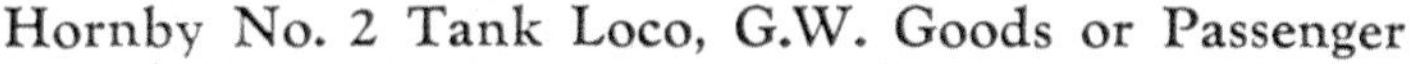

Hornby No. 2 Tank Loco, G.W. Goods or Passenger

Hornby No. 2 Tank Loco, L.M.S. Goods

** For particulars of the Hornby Control System, see opposite page.*

THE HORNBY CONTROL SYSTEM

Trains, Signals and Points operated from the Signal Cabin

Control Signal

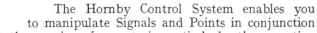

The Hornby Control System enables you to manipulate Signals and Points in conjunction with the running of your trains entirely by the operation of levers in your Signal Cabin. The installation of the System is quite a simple matter, no phase of it presenting any difficulty whatever. Large or small railway layouts may be operated with equal ease.

In order to obtain the fullest benefits from a Hornby Control Outfit, the loco used must be of the Special type (fitted for Control). With certain limitations, however, the Control System may be utilised successfully with all Hornby locos.

Both the No. 1 and No. 2 Control Outfits operate Signals and Points in exactly the same manner. The only difference between the Outfits is that No. 1 contains 1 ft. radius Control Points and a No. 1 Control Rail (15″) whereas No. 2 contains 2 ft. radius Control Points and a No. 2 Control Rail (20″).

By means of the No. 1 Control Rail included in the No. 1 Outfit the M Series and No. 0 Locos may be stopped from the Signal Cabin, while No. 1 Locos (latest type) may be stopped or reversed. After stopping, however, these locos cannot be re-started automatically. The No. 1 Control Rail will either stop, re-start or reverse the Special No. 1 Locos (fitted for Control).

The No. 2 Control Rail contained in the No. 2 Outfit is designed for operating the Special No. 2 (fitted for Control), Metropolitan Clockwork, " Blue " Train Clockwork and other Locos of this type, enabling them to be stopped, re-started or reversed from the Signal Cabin. The ordinary No. 2 Locos may be similarly stopped or reversed but must be re-started by the cab lever.

The most important component in the system is the Lever Frame, which is provided with six levers and is specially designed to fit the Hornby Signal Cabin. This Lever Frame is the central point controlling the whole system and its position depends upon the nature of the layout. The best fun is to be obtained, of course, by placing the frame alongside the Station as in real railway practice. It is then a simple matter to carry out a variety of operations in the most fascinating manner. For instance, by manipulating the various levers you can control the signals giving the right of entry to or exit from the station. Also you are able to operate two sets of Points and thus transfer any train from the main line, or vice versa, just whenever you choose. These operations are controlled entirely from the Signal Cabin without touching the Signals or Points at all.

After a great deal of experiment a frame of six levers has been adopted as the most generally suitable. By placing one or more additional Lever Frames at different points of the layout the number of points and signals that can be controlled may be extended almost indefinitely.

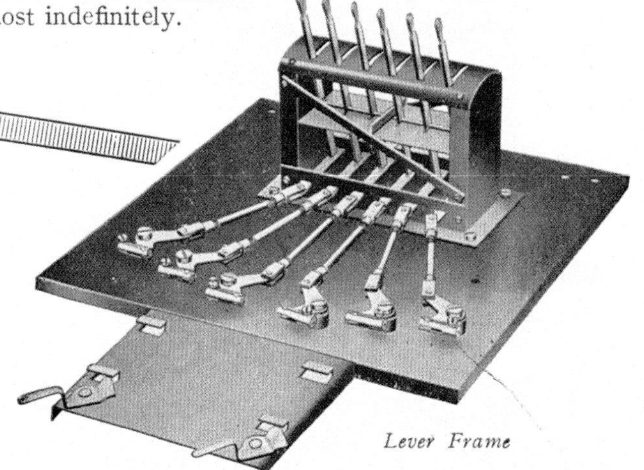

Lever Frame

Price List of Control Outfits and Components

No. 1 Outfit complete ... ... each 35/– **No. 2 Outfit complete ... ... each 35/–**

Item		Price	Item		Price
Lever Frame, complete	each	12/6	No. 2 Control Rail (20 in.) as in No. 2 Outfit	each	2/3
Control Points, L.H., 1 ft. or 2 ft.	pair	6/–	Rodding Compensator	„	1/6
Control Points, R.H., 1 ft. or 2 ft.	„	6/–	Control Couplings	„	3d.
Control Signals, Single	each	3/6	Wire, 24 ft. coil	„	9d.
Control Signals, Junction	„	7/6	Wire Cutters	pair	1/6
Signal Cabin	„	6/6	Guide Brackets	doz.	1/–
No. 1 Control Rail (15 in.) as in No. 1 Outfit	„	2/–	Meccano Nuts and Bolts	box of 36	1/6

*Hornby Train Sets fitted for Hornby Control

No. 1 Goods Set	23/6	No. 2 Tank Goods Set	42/6
No. 1 Tank Goods Set	26/–	No. 2 Tank Passenger Set	45/–
No. 2 Pullman Set	55/–	No. 2 Riviera " Blue " Train Set	70/–
No. 2 Goods Set	37/6	No. 3 Metropolitan Train Set	55/–

*A Hornby Control Rail of the correct size is included in each of these sets.

HORNBY TRAINS

BRITISH AND GUARANTEED

THE Hornby system consists of a complete range of Rolling-Stock, Train Accessories, and Rails, Points and Crossings, with which the most elaborate model railway may be constructed. Every component in the Hornby Series is well designed and carefully modelled on its prototype in real life.

Any boy may gradually build up a complete miniature railway by employing the various elements that comprise the Hornby Series of Rolling Stock, Accessories, and Rails, Points and Crossings.

No. 1 LUGGAGE VAN

Realistic and highly finished. The doors are mounted on hinges and may be opened. Lettered L.M.S., L.N.E.R. or G.W.

Price 3/6

No. 2 LUGGAGE VAN

Mounted on two four-wheeled bogies, and fitted with double opening doors. Suitable for 2-ft. radius rails only. Lettered L.M.S., L.N.E.R. or G.W.

Price 5/9

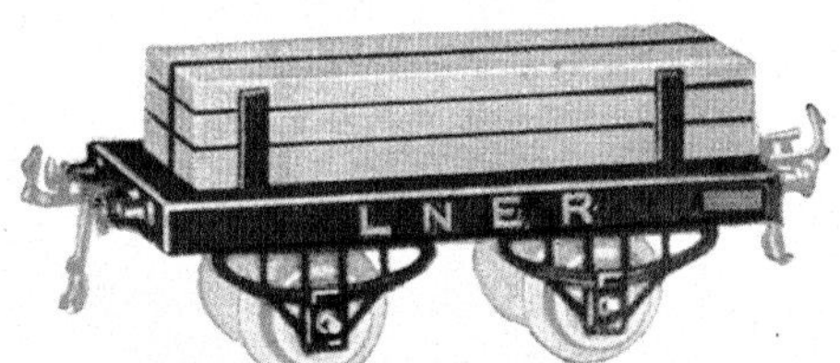

No. 1 TIMBER WAGON

Beautifully enamelled in green, complete with load of timber. Lettered L.M.S., L.N.E.R. or G.W.

Price 1/9

No. 2 TIMBER WAGON

Highly finished and stoved. Complete with load of timber. Suitable for 2-ft. radius rails only. Lettered L.M.S., L.N.E.R. or G.W.

Price 3/6

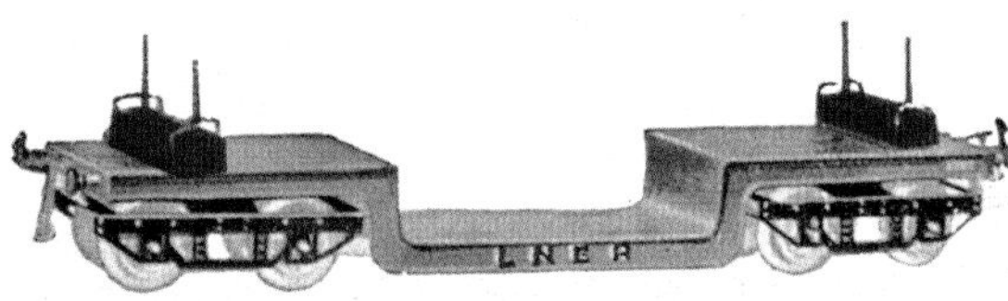

TROLLEY WAGON

Trolley Wagons are designed to carry exceptionally heavy loads, and their low-built construction necessitates only a minimum lift when loading. Fitted with four-wheeled bogies and stanchions. Suitable for 2-ft. radius rails only. Lettered L.M.S., L.N.E.R. or G.W.

Price 5/6

BREAKDOWN VAN AND CRANE

Beautifully coloured in brown and blue, with opening doors. The crane is provided with a handle, by means of which the hoisting cord may be operated, and swivels about a pivot. Suitable for 2-ft. radius rails only. Lettered L.M.S., N.E. or G.W.

Price 6/3

No. 1 CATTLE TRUCK

Fitted with sliding door. Very realistic design. Lettered L.M.S., L.N.E.R. or G.W.

Price 3/6

No. 2 CATTLE TRUCK

Splendid model, fitted with double doors and two four-wheel bogies. Suitable for 2-ft. radius rails only. Lettered L.M.S., L.N.E.R. or G.W.

Price 5/9

No. 1 LUMBER WAGON

Fitted with bolsters and stanchions for log transport. Lettered L.M.S., L.N.E.R. or G.W.

Price 2/-

No. 2 LUMBER WAGON

Fitted with bolsters and stanchions and complete with logs. Suitable for 2-ft. radius rails only. Lettered L.M.S., L.N.E.R. or G.W.

Price 4/-

HORNBY TRAINS

BRITISH AND GUARANTEED

WAGON, FRENCH TYPE

Lettered Nord. Modelled on type of Goods Wagon used in France. Highly finished in colours.

Price 3/3

BRAKE VAN L.N.E.R.

Finished in colours with opening doors; a very realistic model.

Price 3/6

BRAKE VAN G.W.

Enamelled in grey and black with white roof. Opening doors.

Price 3/6

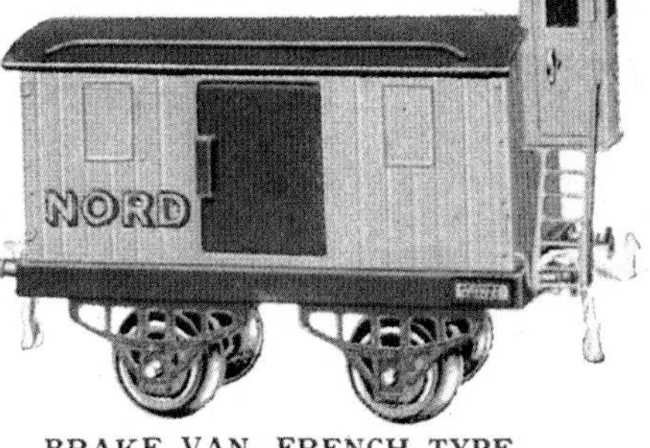

BRAKE VAN, FRENCH TYPE

Lettered Nord. Modelled on type of Brake Van used in France. Beautifully finished in colours. Opening doors.

Price 4/-

The Brake Van is also available with L.M.S. lettering.

"SECCOTINE" WAGON

Finished in blue. The doors open.

Price 4/-

JACOB'S BISCUIT VAN

Finished in crimson lake. The doors open.

Price 3/6

CRAWFORD'S BISCUIT VAN

Finished in red. The doors open.

Price 3/6

CARR'S BISCUIT VAN

Finished in dark blue. The doors open.

Price 3/6

MOTOR SPIRIT TANK WAGON "B.P."

Realistic in design and appropriately coloured.

Price 2/6

PETROL TANK WAGON, "SHELL"

Realistic in design and appropriately coloured.

Price 2/6

PETROL TANK WAGON, "PRATTS"

Realistic in design and appropriately coloured.

Price 2/6

MOTOR SPIRIT TANK WAGON, "NATIONAL BENZOLE"

Realistic in design and appropriately coloured.

Price 2/6

HORNBY TRAINS
BRITISH AND GUARANTEED

GUARD'S VAN

Realistic design. Fitted each side with double and single opening doors. Lettered L.M.S., L.N.E.R. or G.W.

Price 3/6

GUNPOWDER VAN

Enamelled in red. The doors open. Lettered L.M.S., L.N.E.R. or G.W.

Price 3/9

REFRIGERATOR VAN

Enamelled in white, with opening doors. Lettered L.M.S., L.N.E.R. or G.W.

Price 3/9

SNOW PLOUGH

Runs on specially constructed heavy wheels, and the plough is driven from the front axle. Lettered L.M.S., L.N.E.R. or G.W.

Price 5/6

GAS CYLINDER WAGON

Lettered L.M.S., L.N.E.R. or G.W.

Price 2/6

SIDE TIPPING WAGON

Arranged to tip to either side of the track.

Price 2/6

ROTARY TIPPING WAGON

The body rotates and will tip in all directions.

Price 3/-

HOPPER WAGON

May be automatically unloaded on operation of the lever shown. Lettered L.M.S., L.N.E.R. or G.W.

Price 4/-

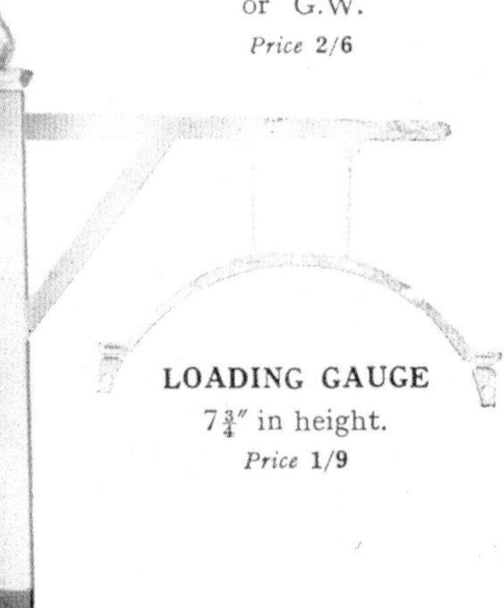

LOADING GAUGE

$7\frac{3}{4}''$ in height.

Price 1/9

CRANE TRUCK

The crane swivels about a pivot, and is operated by a crank fitted in its base. Lettered L.M.S., L.N.E.R. or G.W.

Price 3/6

CEMENT WAGON

Lettered L.M.S., L.N.E.R. or G.W. Hinged portion of the cover may be opened.

Price 3/-

MILK TRAFFIC VAN

Fitted with sliding door, and complete with three milk cans. Lettered L.M.S., L.N.E.R. or G.W.

Price 3/6

HORNBY TRAINS
BRITISH AND GUARANTEED

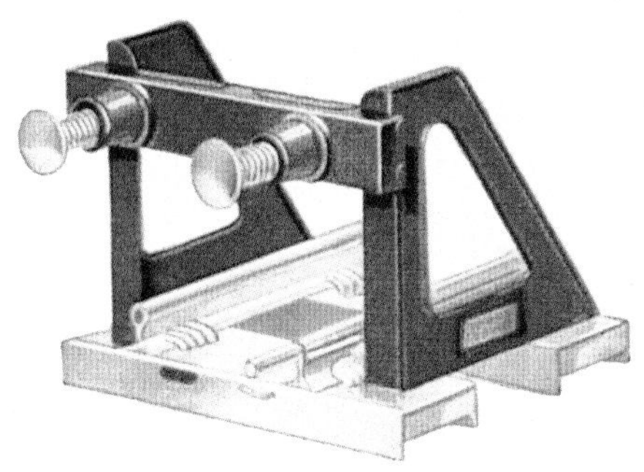

SPRING BUFFER STOPS

May be connected to all Hornby Rails.

Price 1/-

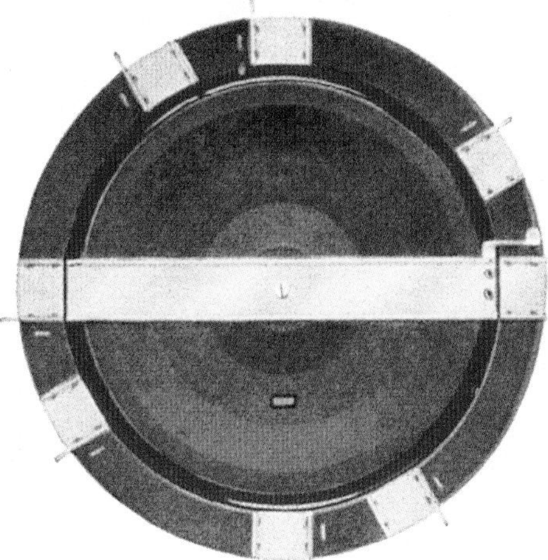

TURNTABLES

The revolving portion of these Turntables may be locked in certain positions, as required.

Large Turntable, Price 4/-
Small ,, ,, 2/6

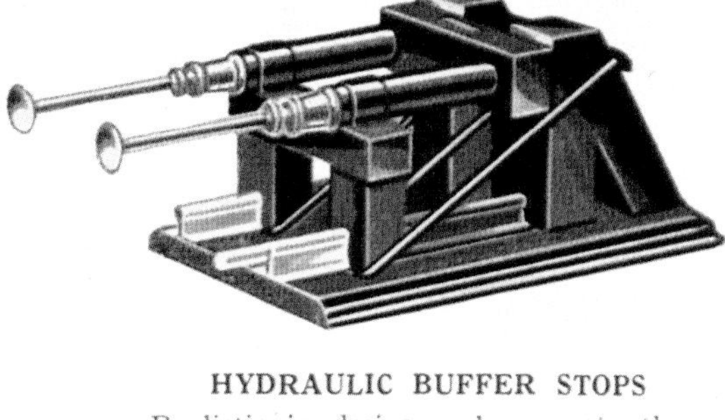

HYDRAULIC BUFFER STOPS

Realistic in design and very stoutly built. May be connected to all Hornby rails.

Price 5/-

DOUBLE LAMP STANDARD

4-volt bulbs may be fitted in the globes, which are hoisted and lowered by means of crank handles in the base, and controlled by ratchets.

Price 4/-

JUNCTION SIGNAL

Signal arms operated by weighted levers at base. Complete with imitation lamps, ladder, etc. Very realistic model standing 14″ in height.

Price 5/6

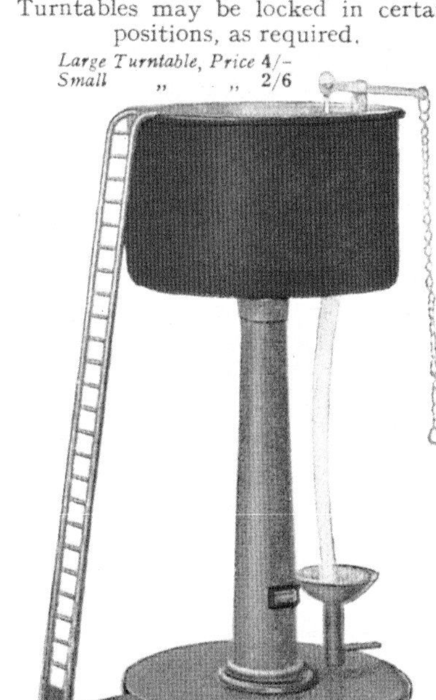

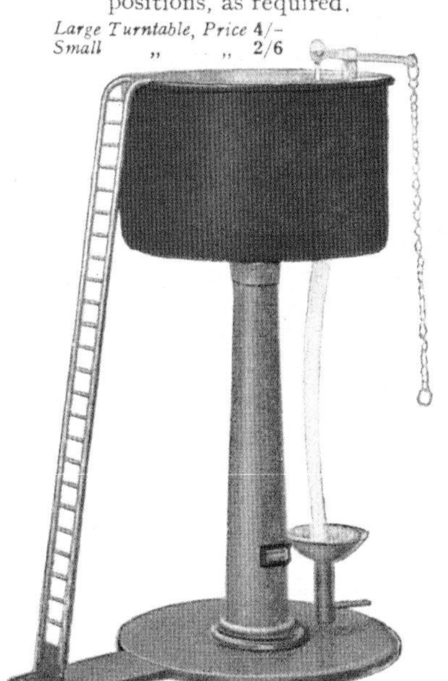

WATER TANK

Stands 8½″ in height. Fitted with rubber tube and spring controlled valve, operated by a chain and lever.

Price 6/6

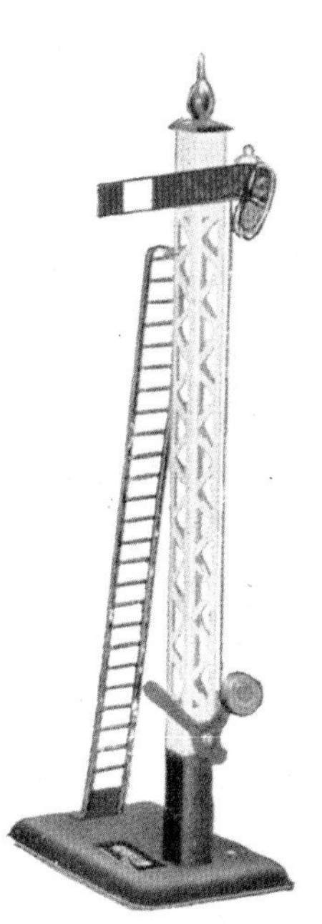

SIGNAL

Operated by weighted levers at base and complete with ladder and imitation lamp. " Home " or " Distant."

Price 2/6

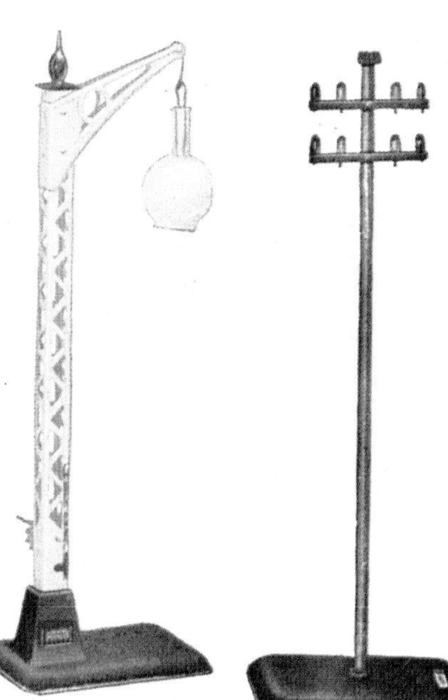

SINGLE LAMP STANDARD

The Lamp, into which a 4-volt bulb may be fitted, is hoisted or lowered by means of a crank-handle at the base, and controlled by a ratchet.

Price 3/-

TELEGRAPH POLES

11″ in height.

Price, per pair, 3/6

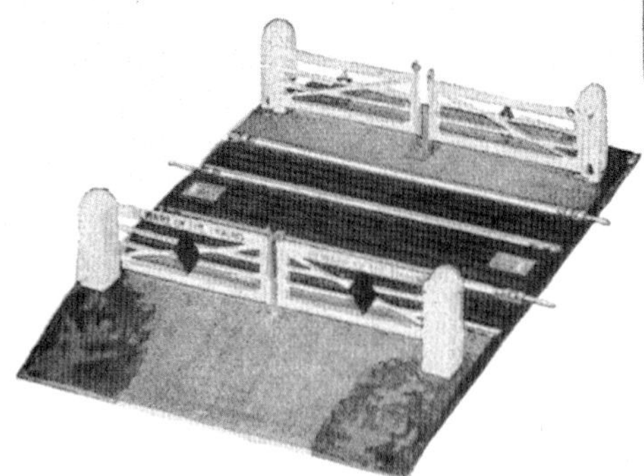

LEVEL CROSSING

Beautifully designed and finished, with double track of gauge "0" rails in position. Measures 11½" by 7¼".

Price 5/-

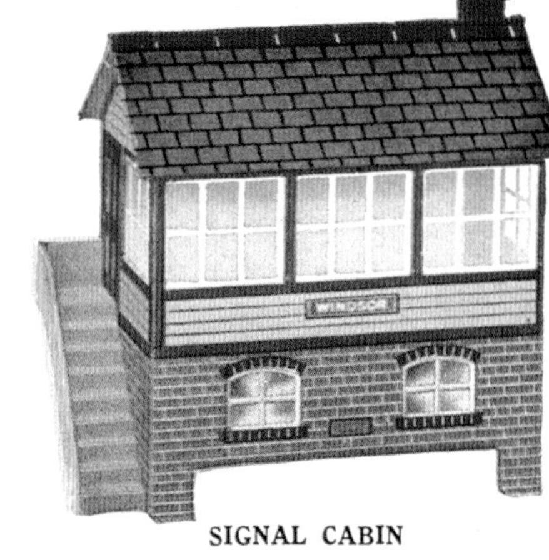

SIGNAL CABIN

Dimensions: Height 6½", Width 3½", Length 6½". Beautifully finished and lettered "Windsor." Roof and back open to allow a signal lever frame to be fitted inside cabin, if desired.

Price 6/6

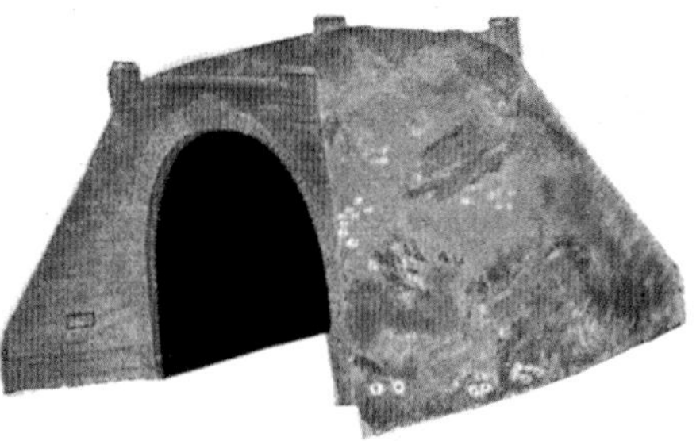

TUNNEL

Beautifully designed and finished in colours.

Price 7/6

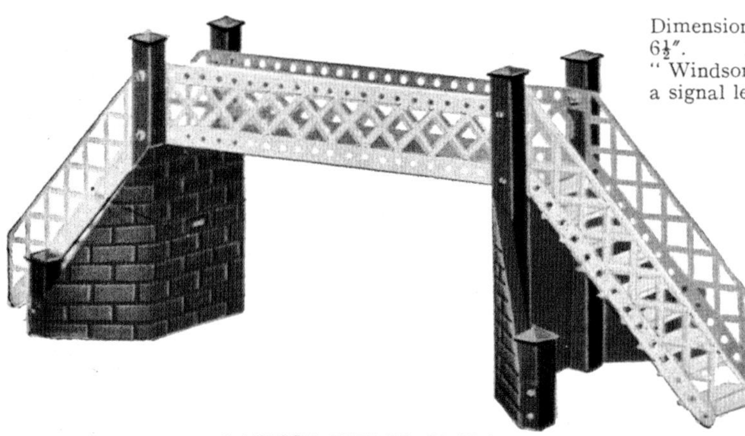

LATTICE GIRDER BRIDGE

Constructional type, strong and well proportioned. Meccano strips for signals, etc., may be secured to its sides.

Price 9/6

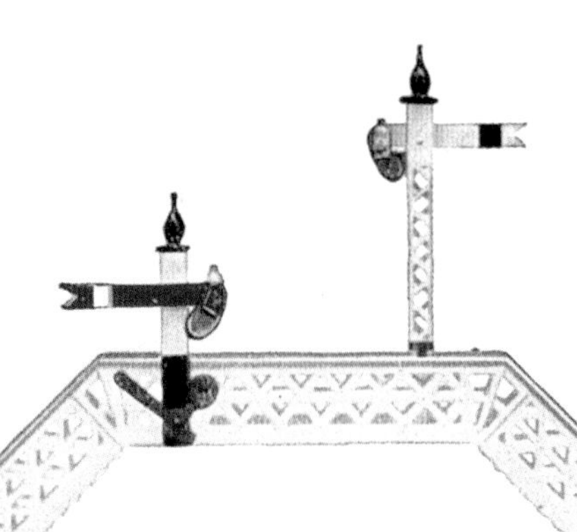

FOOT BRIDGE

The signal arms are operated from weighted levers. Complete with imitation lamps.

No. 1, with detachable signals ...	*Price*	6/-
No. 2, without signals ...	"	3/6
Signals only, per pair ...	"	2/9

VIADUCT

Constructed in three sections which may be easily disassembled.

Price 7/-

Centre section only,

Price 4/6

The Viaduct is also made with "live" centre rails in position for Electric Trains.

Price 8/-

Centre section only.

Price 5/-

HORNBY TRAINS

BRITISH AND GUARANTEED

RAILWAY STATION

Excellent model, beautifully designed and finished. Constructed in three sections which may be easily detached.

Dimensions: Length, 2-ft. 9-in. Width 6-in. Height 7-in.

Price 10/-

WAYSIDE STATION

This Wayside Station is a well-made model, richly finished in bright colours. By placing one or more of these Stations at intervals along the track, and using the Windsor Railway Station (illustrated above) as the main terminus, a very realistic effect is given to a miniature railway layout.

Dimensions of Wayside Station.

Length 16¾-in., Width 6-in., Height 6-in.

Price 5/-

PLATFORM ACCESSORIES

The three sets of Platform Accessories shown below form an interesting and very realistic addition to the Hornby Station. In addition to figuring on the platform the miniature luggage shown may of course be carried in the Guard's Van, and the Milk Cans in the Milk Traffic Van, etc.

PLATFORM ACCESSORIES No. 1

Miniature Luggage.

Price 1/6

PLATFORM ACCESSORIES No. 2

Milk Cans and Truck.

Price 1/6

PLATFORM ACCESSORIES No. 3

Platform Machines, &c.

Price 1/6

MODEL RAILWAY STATIONS

The Island, Goods and Passenger Platforms, illustrated on this page, may be used separately or in conjunction with the Windsor Railway Station to which they may be connected. It is possible to build up very realistic railway terminus stations with these Platforms, interesting examples of which are illustrated in a special booklet entitled "How to get more fun out of Hornby Trains," price 3d., post free. Application for a copy of this booklet should be made to your dealer or a remittance in stamps should be sent to Meccano Ltd., Binns Road, Liverpool.

PASSENGER PLATFORM

Length, 16¾-in. Width, 3-in. This platform may be connected to the main station or used separately. The interlocking device at each end enables a number of these platforms to be joined together.

Price 3/6

Paled fencing, as supplied with the Passenger Platform, may be purchased separately.

Price per length 6d.

ISLAND PLATFORM

Length, 32½-in. Height, 6¾-in. Width, 3-in. The ramps at either end are detachable, and if desired the platform may be connected to the main station.

Price 7/6

Ramps similar to those fitted to the Island Platform may be purchased separately.

Price, per pair, 1/6

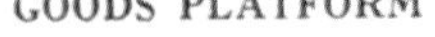

GOODS PLATFORM

Length, 16¾-in. Height, 6¾-in. Width, 6-in. The crane at the end of the platform revolves on its base. It is enamelled in bright red and is fitted with a crank and ratchet mechanism for controlling the load.

Price 10/-

Gauge 0, 1¼″

Rails, Points and Crossings

Alternate Pegs

Hornby Series

HORNBY Rails, Points and Crossings are designed to meet the most exacting requirements of model railway enthusiasts. They are made of the finest materials and hold together rigidly and strongly, for real workmanship is put into them. The variety of Points, left-hand and right-hand turnout, together with the Crossings, make possible an almost endless number of realistic and railway-like layouts. The adaptability of the Rails is well shown in the booklet "How to get more fun out of Hornby Trains," which is obtainable from your dealer or from Meccano Limited, Binns Road, Liverpool, price 3d. post free.

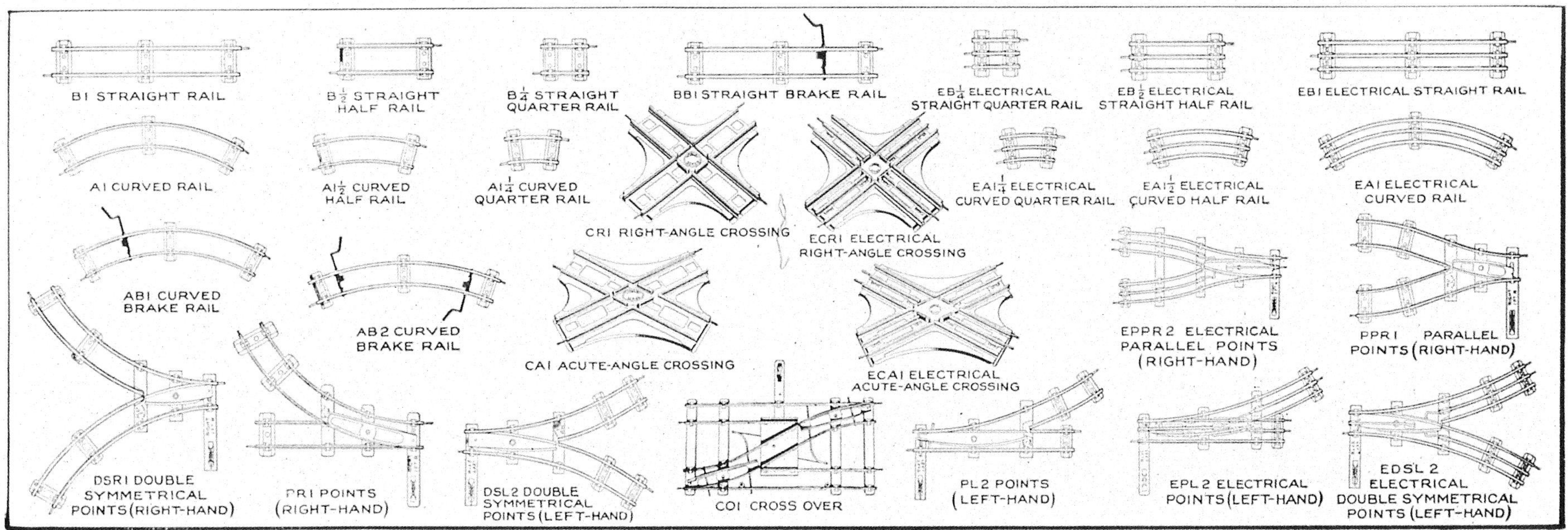

Rails for Clockwork and Steam Trains

CURVED RAILS.

For 2-ft. diameter circle.

A1	Curved rails (1-ft. radius) ...	per doz.	4/6
A1½	Curved half rails	,,	3/6
A1¼	Curved quarter rails ...	,,	3/-
AB1	Curved brake rails (1-ft. radius)	each	6d.

For 4-ft. diameter circle.

A2	Curved rails (2-ft. radius) ...	per doz.	4/6
A2½	Curved half rails	,,	3/6
A2¼	Curved quarter rails ...	,,	3/-
AB2	Curved brake rails (2-ft. radius)	each	6d.

STRAIGHT RAILS.

B1	Straight rails	per doz.	4/-
B½	Straight half rails	,,	3/-
B¼	Straight quarter rails ...	,,	2/6
BB1	Straight brake rails	each	5d.
BBR1	Straight brake and reverse rails	,,	1/6

CROSSINGS.

CA1	Acute angle crossings (for 1-ft. radius tracks)	each	1/6
CA2	Acute angle crossings (for 2-ft. radius tracks)	,,	1/6
CR1	Right-angle crossings (for 1-ft. radius tracks)	,,	1/6
CR2	Right-angle crossings (for 2-ft. radius tracks)	,,	1/6

CROSSOVERS.

CO1	Crossover (1-ft. radius) ...	each	6/6
CO2	Crossover (2-ft. radius) ...	,,	7/6

POINTS.

For 1-ft. radius curves.

PR1	Right-hand points ...	per pair	4/-
PL1	Left-hand points ...		

For 2-ft. radius curves.

PR2	Right-hand points ...	per pair	4/-
PL2	Left-hand points ...		

DOUBLE SYMMETRICAL POINTS.

For 1-ft. radius curves.

DSR1	Double symmetrical points, right	per pair	5/-
DSL1	Double symmetrical points, left		

For 2-ft. radius curves.

DSR2	Double symmetrical points, right	per pair	5/-
DSL2	Double symmetrical points, left		

PARALLEL POINTS.

For 1-ft. radius curves.

PPR1	Parallel points, right	per pair	5/-
PPL1	Parallel points, left		

For 2-ft. radius curves.

PPR2	Parallel points, right	per pair	5/-
PPL2	Parallel points, left		

CP Rail Connecting Plates, ½ doz. 4d.

Rails for Electric Trains

CURVED RAILS.

For 2-ft. diameter circle.

EA1	Curved rails (1-ft. radius) ...	per doz.	8/-
EA1½	Curved half rails	,,	5/-
EA1¼	Curved quarter rails ...	,,	4/6

For 4-ft. diameter circle.

EA2	Curved rails (2-ft. radius) ...	per doz.	8/-
EA2½	Curved half rails	,,	5/-
EA2¼	Curved quarter rails ...	,,	4/6

STRAIGHT RAILS.

EB1	Straight rails	per doz.	7/-
EB½	Straight half rails	,,	4/6
EB¼	Straight quarter rails ...	,,	4/-

CROSSINGS.

ECA	Acute-angle crossings ...	each	4/-
ECR	Right-angle crossings ...	,,	4/-

POINTS.

For 2-ft. radius curves.

EPR2	Right-hand points ...	per pair	10/-
EPL2	Left-hand points ...		

DOUBLE SYMMETRICAL POINTS.

For 2-ft. radius curves.

EDSR2	Double symmetrical points, right	per pair	12/-
EDSL2	Double symmetrical points, left		

PARALLEL POINTS.

For 2-ft. radius curves.

EPPR2	Parallel points, right	per pair	12/-
EPPL2	Parallel points, left		

Electrical Points, Double Symmetrical Points and Parallel Points for 1-ft. radius curves are not ***supplied.***

TCPH	Terminal Connecting Plates (High voltage)	each	1/6
TCPL	Terminal Connecting Plates (Low voltage)	each	1/6

NOTE.—The addition of straight and curved brake rails, supplied for Clockwork Trains, makes possible a great deal more fun. By the use of the straight brake rail, trains may be brought to a standstill at the station platform in a very realistic manner.

(*Boiler and Erecting Shop—continued from page 11*)

Once the cylinders are fixed the slide bars may be put in position and fixed. As there are top and bottom bars they have to be set truly parallel, and special gauges are made to ensure that this result is achieved. A "dummy" slide block is used to check the work and must be a free sliding fit between the bars. At this stage it is possible to check over the reciprocating parts of the engine and ensure that everything is true.

The boiler, having been tested under steam, has been sent to the erecting shop, and can now be lowered on to the frames and secured. The boiler is possibly 5/16 in. longer when hot than it is when cold, and therefore allowance has to be made for this. The front end is fixed but the back end is carried on expansion brackets that rest on top of the frames. Having fixed on the boiler, the next step is to bolt the front tube plate to the cylinder casting, at the same time attaching the expansion bracket guides to the frames at the firebox end.

Locomotives in embryo. Overhead crane lifting 2-8-0 tank

The material we see when we look at a locomotive boiler in a railway station is, of course, only the outer covering or cleading, of thin sheet metal, protected from the heat of the boiler by asbestos lagging, which also serves to retain the heat in the boiler. We have now reached the stage in the erection at which this lagging and cleading may be put on. On completion of this operation the smokebox, cab, splashers, etc., are fitted.

While one gang is thus employed, another is fitting up the axle boxes in the horn guides. These are made by hand scraping to be a tight sliding fit in the guides, as they soon wear slack in service. After this the axle boxes are carefully fitted on to their respective journals.

Our locomotive has now decidedly taken shape, but it is still without wheels, a defect the erectors will now proceed to remedy. The engine is lifted up by an overhead crane, the wheels are rolled underneath on the track provided in the shop floor, and the axle boxes are guided into the horn blocks. Packings are put in until the springs are fitted.

The motion is now put in, and that highly specialised and skilled job known as valve setting is taken in hand. Upon its accuracy depends the hauling capacity of the locomotive, and it demands an intimate knowledge of the steam distribution of the valve gear. With this fixed, the springs can be put in and adjusted and the buffer beam attached, followed by such details as brake gear, feed pipes, cylinder drain cocks and operating rods. The engine is then put on a siding, the boiler filled with water, and coupled to the tender, with its supply of coal and water. The erection of the tender has been proceeding simultaneously with that of the engine, the method followed being similar, except that the work is simpler, on account of the absence of moving parts.

The completed locomotive now goes to the weighing machine, which is so designed that each axle can be weighed separately. Any slight irregularities in the weights on the various wheels are smoothed out by adjustments to the springs. It is very important to ensure that each axle is carrying its correct proportion of the total weight. An engine of the type we have followed through the works would probably have on its driving axles the maximum load allowed by the permanent way engineer, and therefore it is very essential to make sure that this weight is not exceeded. Elaborate calculations have of course been made in the drawing office with this object in view, but many of the weights used in those calculations are only estimated, so there is room for small discrepancies. The adjustment possible by altering the springs is very slight.

The Swindon Works, where the locomotives and rolling stock of the Great Western Railway are built and maintained, are among the most extensive in the world, and occupy an area of 310 acres, of which 65 are roofed. The railway line through Swindon was opened on 16th December 1840, and the erection of shops for the construction and repair of locomotives was commenced in 1841. Although the machinery was started in November of the following year, the shops were not put into general working until 1st January 1843. It is of interest to note that Brunel was mainly responsible for the planning of the Works.

The number of men employed at Swindon has increased from 4,500 in 1876 to over 13,500. The extensive equipment of the erecting shop is such that from 60 to 70 new locomotives can be turned out per annum, while the number of locomotives repaired amounts to about 600 yearly.

Trial Run, Testing and Painting

OUR locomotive has now arrived at the stage at which it is capable of running under its own power and hauling a load after it. In appearance it still looks very unfinished, however, because it has not received any final painting. Before it proceeds to the paint shop it has to go on a trial trip. Nowadays a preliminary trial is not likely to reveal any serious defects, but is a necessary part of the life of the engine.

Nothing in the way of high speed is attempted on the trial run as the engine will have to run many hundred miles before the moving parts work easily and sweetly. Just as a new motor car never runs as well as a slightly used one, because the bearings have not been "run in," so the locomotive at first does not give the best work of which it is capable. Trained observers ride upon it during the trials, which usually are carried out on some quiet stretch of line as near the works as possible. Probably no elaborate measurements are taken until the engine has seen a moderate amount of service, and then if a complete test is to be made, this is carried out by means of a dynamometer car. The construction and operation of such a car is described fully in the next section.

For the present we will assume that our engine has passed successfully her preliminary trial. She now returns to the sheds to receive her numerous coats of paint and the finishing necessary before she goes into active service.

The final stages in engine construction

Engine given its First Coat of Grey

While the locomotive is going through the final stages in the erecting shop, a coat of lead-coloured paint is given to it to protect the metal from oxidisation, which would make the subsequent painting unsatisfactory. It is in this grey livery that the engine runs its trial trip. Before this first or "priming" coat of paint is applied all dirt and grease must be removed from the metal with turpentine and sand paper, otherwise the paint would not adhere properly.

When the locomotive comes back to the paint shop from its trial trip, the priming coat is scraped in places to see if it adheres firmly. If it does, it is left on; if not, it shows that the metal surface was not sufficiently clean and all the priming must come off.

First of all the whole surface is covered with a stopping consisting of white lead and ochre, mixed with gold size, and this is well worked into the surface. After being allowed to harden, it is rubbed down with flat pieces of pumice stone and "worked" with water until a perfectly smooth surface is obtained, with all the small hollows filled up. After this the first coat of lead colour is applied, and when this is dry the first coat of the final colour is put on. The lettering, figures, lines and stripes are now added after the final coat has been applied, "transfers" being used for this purpose. An elaborate system of "lining out" the locomotive adds greatly to the cost of painting, although improving the appearance of the finished job.

When all is dry, a first coat of varnish is applied, which, after drying, is rubbed down with powdered pumice stone applied on a horsehair pad, giving a smooth surface to which a second and possibly a third coat is applied. For varnishing a copal varnish is used, which sets hard and lasts well. Only the very best material is used, because the changes in temperature and the exposure to all sorts of weather are a very severe test.

Finishing Touches

If the engine is urgently required for work on the line the time it spends in the paint shop will be cut down to the absolute minimum, usually by trying to speed up the time of drying of the various coats of paint and varnish. If possible, however, the engine should be allowed to stand a week in the paint shop after the last coat of varnish is applied, the shop being meanwhile kept at a uniform temperature. Dirt in paint shops is also to be avoided as far as can possibly be managed. If the painting and varnishing work is scamped, or the subsequent shed cleaning badly done, the engine soon loses its smart appearance.

The engine smokebox gets a good deal hotter than any of the other painted surfaces, so that one of the specially prepared "smokebox blacks" is usually adopted for it. Such parts as the brake gear, springs and under portions of the tender, which are more or less out of sight, may be coated with the same material. The object of painting is of course primarily to resist corrosion and secondly for appearance. For the benefit of the engine men, the inside of the cab is usually painted some light colour, say buff, although this is by no means universal. The inside of the frames and the motion are also painted a light shade, so that when the driver is going round the lubricating points with an oil lamp at night he has a better chance to see whether or not everything is all right.

The painting of the engine wheels after the engine is assembled is an awkward job, as owing to the splashers covering a large part of the driving wheels, the engine has to be moved along to enable all parts to be reached. In some shops, therefore, it is the practice to paint and line the wheels before they are put under the engine.

Engine on turntable ready for trial run

The cost of painting a locomotive, particularly other than black, is a considerable item. Mr. Webb, one of the most outstanding locomotive engineers this country has produced, was once asked why he painted the London and North Western engines black, and is credited with the reply that he would paint them with gold leaf when the shareholders dividend warranted it!

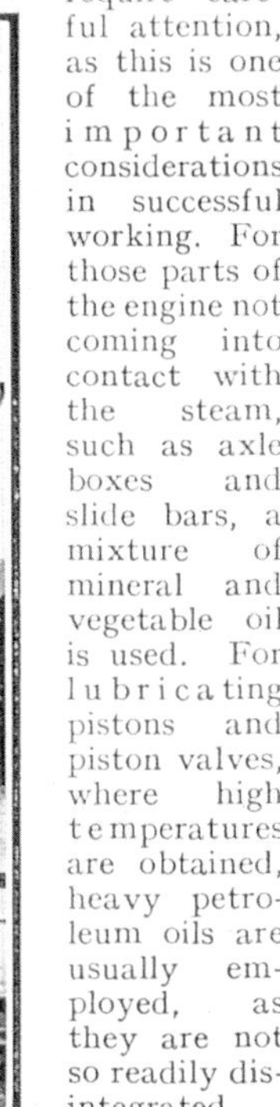

Before our locomotive is fit to do much running in service, the lubrication will require careful attention, as this is one of the most important considerations in successful working. For those parts of the engine not coming into contact with the steam, such as axle boxes and slide bars, a mixture of mineral and vegetable oil is used. For lubricating pistons and piston valves, where high temperatures are obtained, heavy petroleum oils are usually employed, as they are not so readily disintegrated.

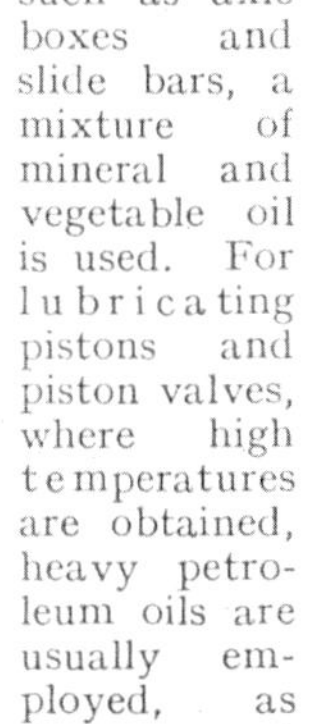

Various methods are adopted to convey the oil to the places where it is required, depending on the location of the part and the importance of its lubrication. Oil cups with worsted trimmings are used on slide bars and bearings, but for the pistons and valves the oil is fed in from a lubricator, usually fitted in the cab and working on the displacement principle, whereby the condensation of steam causes oil to be discharged down a supply pipe. A mechanical lubricator, placed on the running plate, and acting as a pump, is now coming into favour, owing to its great reliability.

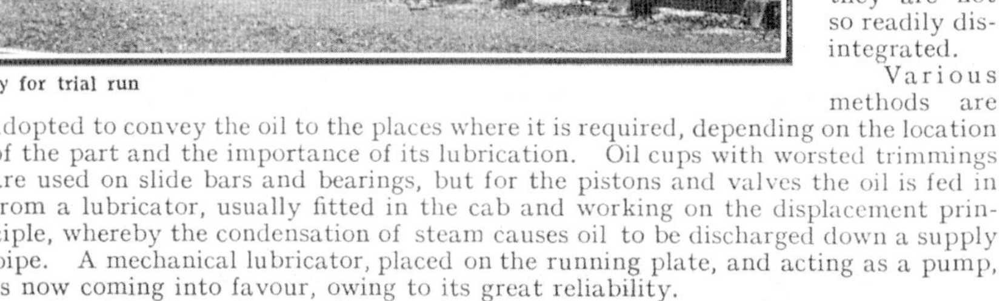

Provision is made on all locomotives for the carrying of a supply of sand, and arrangements for dropping it on the rails immediately in front of the driving wheels, if it should be required to help the engine to start on slippery rails with a heavy load. Care has to be taken to keep the sand dry, and most running sheds have a sand furnace for this purpose. One authority states that a locomotive will use about five tons of sand in the course of a year.

Mysteries of the Dynamometer Car

WE have traced now the engine through its embryo stages in the designing and drawing offices, through the constructional sheds and through its preliminary tests, until now it is ready for the road. Its working days are about to commence, and, like every boy who aspires to rank high in his chosen profession, the engine must first serve an apprenticeship or probationary period during which it is subjected to a series of very exhaustive tests, designed to reveal its working habits, its strength and weaknesses.

The medium through which these searching tests are made is the "Dynamometer Car." Most of our readers who were fortunate enough to visit the British Empire Exhibition at Wembley in 1924 will recall the mysteriously fitted-up car, very like an ordinary saloon coach, that was exhibited on the Great Western Railway's stand at that exhibition. That was a typical Dynamometer Car.

"Sir Lamorak," Southern Railway, fitted with Indicating Shelter

Make-Up of Car

The body of the car is mounted on two 4-wheeled bogies and is divided into three compartments, the largest over 25 ft. in length. This compartment is fitted with plate-glass windows so built that the best look-out possible can be obtained from the interior. Behind the main compartment are cupboards for stores, two lockers, and a battery of accumulators for the electrically-operated instruments. The third compartment is equipped with a table and benches for the crew, which consists of five engineers. The dynamometer car is usually placed at the head of the train immediately behind the tender of the locomotive to be tested, that is, between the engine and the leading van.

The most important recording device of the car is a long spiral spring of the finest possible workmanship, which is fitted beneath the floor and connected to the coupling of the locomotive ahead. This huge spring works on roller bearings and is so delicately adjusted that it registers accurately the exact pulling power of the engine at every state of the run, or as the engineers say, records the "drawbar pull."

A technical description of the apparatus would make rather tedious reading and it is sufficient to note that the attachments to the spring are coupled to a bar running longitudinally with the car and across the instrument table. The pull on the drawbar is recorded by an instrument known as the "integrator," and the gearing of the whole apparatus is so arranged that one complete revolution of the roller represents 330,000 ft. lb. of work. An electric counter tots up the revolutions, which are recorded by an electro magnetic pen. Also beneath the floor of the car is a heavy additional wheel that can be raised clear or lowered so that it runs along the rail, as required. This wheel is constructed to such a diameter that it makes 440 revolutions for every mile that it runs, and also it provides the motive power for the operation of several of the recording instruments.

Wonderful Mechanical Fingers

Connected with the wheel and the spring is the central recording instrument, an uncanny-looking device, which consists principally of a number of moving metal fingers each holding a stylographic pen.

At the commencement of each test, a thick roll of paper, 12 in. in width, is threaded through this central recorder beneath the pens, and as the train leaves the station the wheel commences to move, the spring begins to register and the pens, guided by their metal fingers, write the story of the journey in the wandering lines of a graph on the paper roll, which is made to move across the recording machine. Each of these lines has a particular meaning. There is, for example, a line of speed recorded by a clock, electrically connected with the speed pen. As the paper that moves across the recorder is driven by the special wheel, referred to above, it passes the pen point at a rate proportionate to the speed of the train. Wheel and clock thus combine to give automatically what may be called a "speed trail," which can be read off in miles per hour by means of a scale measurement.

The wheel also records the distance travelled, and the spring beneath the floor gives the power exerted by the engine from second to second, a separate metal finger and pen recording the deflections of the drawbar in a sinuous line.

On the footplate of the engine ahead of the car an inspector travels and supplements the information automatically recorded by means of a portable telephone, which is connected by a cable over the coals in the tender to a loud speaker fitted inside the roof of the car. Such particulars as steam pressure, cut off, opening of regulator and height of water in gauge glasses are continually passed through this telephone to the car engineers, who note them down on the moving chart.

Indicating Shelter

Among the most important of the engine's efficiency tests are those classed as "indicating." Readers probably have often heard the expression "fitted with indicating shelter" used in connection with locomotive reports, and particularly relating to new engines. The explanation is that observation is being made of the locomotive's behavour from the front of the engine. The work here is the hardest of all. In the narrow space afforded by the hut-like shelter erected on the buffer beams, the draughts coming through the chinks in the shield nearly freeze the occupant's back, while the front part of his body is almost roasted by the heat given off by the smoke box!

Instruments known as "U" type manometers are used for recording vacuum and pressure in the smoke box, and an apparatus known as a 6-station pyrometer gives the temperatures of the superheater and smoke box. The operation of this latter apparatus depends on the fact that when two dissimilar metals are brought into contact, and the ends in contact are hotter than the other ends, a small electro-motive force is generated, and by attaching wires to the cold ends and leading them to a meter, the difference in temperature between the hot and the cold ends can then be read off.

Dynamometer Car ready for the run

A separate telephone line is led direct to the dynamometer car and through this the engineers in the shelter transmit all special readings regarding the temperature of the steam in the superheater, the vacuum and pressure in the smoke box, the effects of the draught through the boiler tubes, and the number of revolutions per minute made by the driving wheels. The readings are marked on the dynamometer car chart at the exact point in the run at which they are taken.

Recording the Behaviour of Steam

One of the most important of the indicating tests is the recording of the behaviour of the steam in the cylinders. The pen of the indicator is directly connected with the interior of the cylinders and rises and falls as the steam enters and expands inside them. This up-and-down motion is recorded on a piece of paper that moves backward and forward on the indicating cylinder chart in a precisely similar manner to the forward and backward motion of the piston in the engine cylinder. The drawing produced represents roughly the shape of a boot, and so long as the engine continues to use the steam steadily and evenly the same drawing is produced with each successive cycle of the cylinder's motions.

Interior of Dynamometer Car showing central Recorder and metal fingers

The importance of the indicating tests will be understood when it is stated that from the charts produced it is possible to calculate definitely the exact horse-power exerted by the engine at any point on the run.

Inside the dynamometer car itself, three engineers watch and control the ever-moving strip of paper beneath the mechanical fingers of the central recorder, note down messages from their colleagues ahead, and separately record by other instruments the direction of the wind, the wind pressure, the temperature of water in the tender (by means of ordinary mercury thermometers) and other facts about the journey for subsequent comparison with the corresponding results obtained from similar tests made on other trains.

At the end of the run the coal, water and oil consumption is carefully ascertained, and so exhaustive are the tests that samples of the ashes are taken from the ash pan for subsequent analysis in the laboratory.

Determining Fuel and Water Consumption

Only the coal actually used in the run is determined, for the fire is made up with unmeasured coal before starting and as nearly as can be gauged a similar quantity is placed in the fire box at the end. The tender with its tank full of water, which was weighed before the start, is weighed again at the end of the run, the tank having been refilled to the previous level, and the difference between the first and second weights represents the weight of coal consumed.

The water consumption is checked by a special indicator fitted to the tender and worked from the ordinary indicator float. This indicator is carefully marked up by measuring the water as it passes into the tank through a specially tested water meter. A certain quantity of water is used in watering the coal and this must, of course, be deducted from the total water consumption before the quantity used in the engine boiler is known. The quantity involved is checked by determining the amount passed by the coal-watering cock in a given time. A record of the total length of time that the cock is open is kept on the foot-plate and this gives the required figure.

The oil consumption is easily ascertained. A known quantity is issued to the driver before the trip and the surplus is returned at the end. All oil cups and lubricators are filled with unmeasured oil before the trials and again at the end of the run, the difference between the quantity remaining and that issued to the driver thus representing the actual consumption.

When all the data possible have been obtained, the engineers have an elaborate system of calculations to work out in order that a complete report of each journey may be made.

Value of the Tests

Innumerable conclusions are drawn from the calculations, any weakness in the performance of the locomotive engine and the train en route being quickly located. In addition, the driving of one driver and that of another can be compared. The necessary quantities of fuel and lubricants for efficient working become known and a definite check on the actual conditions to be met with on every yard of the way is obtained. Each dynamometer car record is therefore of great value and is carefully preserved for comparison purposes.

As previously mentioned, a portion of the dynamometer car is equipped with a table and benches for, when engaged on long distance tests, there is little time for the engineers to obtain food. Equipment is also provided on the car so that the staff may spend the night aboard if necessary. Sometimes when making tests with freight trains that journey from colliery sidings to the shipping bunkers at the docks, or when special tests are made with an experimental locomotive on a quiet stretch of the line in some country district miles from anywhere, the staff are indeed glad to avail themselves of the facilities for food and rest.

Dynamometer Car, interior view taken en route

The apparatus of the car is very valuable and delicate, and an attendant is always aboard night and day, except when the strange carriage is safely stowed away and locked up in its place in the carriage sheds.

The nature of the work of the dynamometer car and the close application necessary for the proper production of accurate results make it one of the greatest honours of the service to be appointed to serve as one of its crew.

A locomotive travelling at high speed receives many jolts and jars owing to irregularities of the track, and the length of its career is, therefore, largely dependent on the condition of the track. An ingenious instrument has been invented by a French railway engineer that acts as an inspector of the permanent way.

The track register is placed on the floor of a railway carriage immediately above the wheels and records oscillations in three directions (1) movements parallel to the track, (2) transverse movements and (3) vertical movements. A record is also made of the quarter mile posts and the stations passed, which record is controlled by an operator who presses a pneumatic bulb when one or the other is sighted, and thus the irregularities of the track are quickly located.

The movements are recorded by three needles, working through sheets of carbon, which mark a thin strip of paper mounted on a drum rotated by a geared clockwork mechanism. The result is a chart something similar to that of a barometer composed of lines of varying amplitude. Each portion of the record can be interpreted at a glance by the engineers, and any portion of the track requiring attention is easily picked out at the end of the journey. This instrument, which is known as the Hallade track register, often reveals defects that are not visible to the eye.

On the Road—Repairs and Renewals

OUR locomotive is now ready for handing over to the operating department for regular duty on the line, but it does not go straight away into main line high speed service. It may start work on pick-up goods trains or possibly make several trips on local passenger trains, to enable the lubrication to be properly adjusted, and to allow the rubbing surfaces of axles, eccentrics, coupling rod pins and so on to acquire a glassy smoothness and hardness. Until this is done the engine cannot be considered to be in perfect working order, fit to run for four or five hours at express speed without a stop and without anything "heating up," an essential condition in modern railway working.

Eating up the Miles. "Flying Scotsman" express passing Hatfield

Provided the boiler is regularly washed out and no mud is allowed to collect in the water spaces, the engine should require very little in the way of repairs for the first few months after leaving the shops. Boiler washing is done at intervals which may vary from every third trip for long-distance passenger engines to once a week for shunting engines. It is done at the shed at which the engine is stationed, with the idea of removing scale, which is a bad conductor of heat and injurious to the boiler. At the same time the fire brick arch should be cleaned and the fire tubes swept out, although the latter operation may very well be carried out after each trip. Jets of steam or compressed air from a portable apparatus are used for this purpose in some sheds.

After the engine has been hard at work for two or three months, however, it begins to show signs of decreasing efficiency, due to wear having taken place in the valves, more particularly when piston valves are concerned, on the piston and the slide blocks. The steam tightness of the pistons and piston valves depends on the split rings, which probably have lost their spring. If the engine has ordinary flat valves, these probably have worn unevenly, which necessitates facing up in the planing machine. The slide block may be so worn as to require liners inserting.

By this time, especially if the water used is not of first-class boiler quality, two or three dozen fire tubes will require taking out on account of leaking, caused by an accumulation of scale and the consequent burning of the ends of the tubes. An especially heavy deposit of scale is to be expected on the top of the firebox, where the ebullition is most violent, and this has to be removed, otherwise apart from loss of evaporative efficiency, there is danger of the plates being burnt. Small cracks that develop through the stay holes may be dealt with in the running shed by drilling out, tapping, screwing in a rivet and riveting the end over. When the boiler feed water is of particularly bad character, tubes may have to be removed for the purpose of cleaning the boiler about every four months, and the fusible plugs may be changed every three months.

The Long, Long Trail

One authority on locomotive running states that each locomotive should have one recognised shed day each week, on which occasion the boiler should be thoroughly washed out, the firebox, bars and smokebox cleaned, and trimmings and bearings attended to, in addition to a general "look round."

Driver's Examination and Report

All the foregoing work is carried on in what are called the running sheds, to one of which all locomotives are attached. When a driver brings his engine into the locomotive yard after the completion of its run, it is his duty to thoroughly inspect all parts of it, so as to make sure everything is in order, or, if not, to enable him to report the defects. A book is kept in the shed for the purpose of receiving reports from drivers as to repairs required.

One of the jobs frequently undertaken in the running shed is the refitting of the brasses in the axle boxes of the driving wheels, which under certain conditions, tend to heat up and cause the white metal linings to run out, after which the brasses become badly scored. Many up-to-date sheds have a device known as a "wheel drop pit," by means of which a pair of wheels on their axle can be dropped right down beneath the engine, brought to one side, and lifted up to floor level again. Otherwise, some appliance, such as a "sheer legs," must be used to lift up one end of the engine while the wheels are pulled out.

Besides the examination by the driver after his daily trip, all locomotives are periodically examined in the shed by an examiner, who pays special attention to looking for such defects as cracks in axles, which are quite difficult to find, and defective springs, often due to a broken leaf. The liability of flaws occurring in such parts as crank shafts, connecting and coupling rods has nowadays been greatly reduced by highly scientific design and the use of special alloy steels. This, of course, does not do away with the necessity of great vigilance in the inspection of these parts, as the breakage of one of them with the engine in motion would probably cause a serious accident.

Treatment of Various Defects

Piston rings in a modern locomotive have a fairly strenuous time and require frequent renewal. They wear thin and are liable to break up, in which event some of the pieces may get into the valve chest, doing great damage, and finally being blown up the chimney by the exhaust steam. The difficulty or otherwise of renewing piston rings depends on the accessibility of the cylinder covers, which, of course, have to be removed before the pistons can be drawn out. After the cylinder cover has been removed, the connecting rod is disconnected from the sliding cross head, allowing the piston to be drawn out of the cylinder so that the rings are released.

We have already seen how, by weighing each pair of wheels separately on a special weighing machine, it can be ascertained whether or not each axle is carrying its correct share of the total weight of the locomotive. When a locomotive comes into the sheds for the renewal of a broken spring, it is important to adjust the weights after the renewal has taken place, because the new spring will be much stiffer than those that have been in use for some time.

Other jobs carried out in the running sheds are the making of cylinder and valve cover joints, that is, the provision of new packing to render the covers steam tight, also the remaking of safety valve and dome cover joints. Water accumulating in the cylinder due to condensation of the steam is a fruitful cause of leaky cylinder covers, although the general adoption of superheating has done much to reduce the liability to this. The remaking of the front covers of the cylinders is fairly straightforward, but the back covers are more troublesome owing to the dismantling of the motion they necessitate.

Mr. C. J. Bowen Cooke, lately chief mechanical engineer of the London and North Western Railway, says in one of his books, that if no special defect occurs, a locomotive may run from 80,000 to 100,000 miles between visits to the works for heavy repairs, but it is advisable to send the engine to the shops after 70,000 miles or so, because by this time the tyres will have worn hollow and the flanges consequently become deeper. The axle boxes will require attention also, and some fire tubes will be in need of replacement. Fairly heavy repairs can be done in some running sheds, which may have a wheel lathe, but heavy boiler repairs are always done in the main locomotive shops. It would not pay to keep the expensive plant and skilled operators for this work at so many different places.

The Essential Breakdown Crane

Average Life of a Locomotive

Some figures dealing with the life of the locomotive and the most important parts of it may be of some interest here. It may be remembered that arising out of the Railways Act, by which the British railways were amalgamated into four large groups, a Rates Tribunal was set up which, among other things, held an enquiry into the working costs of the four new systems. This involved the production of figures giving the life of the chief items of equipment, and the figure taken as an average for the locomotive was 33 years. During this time, of course, very heavy replacements will have been made, possibly quite changing the appearance of the engine.

For instance, the life of the boiler will be about eight to ten years, during which time the locomotive may have run 300,000 to 350,000 miles. A locomotive is said to be rebuilt when it receives a new boiler. Definite mileages are laid down to mark the times for testing boilers, which may be 200,000 to 250,000 miles, representing five to six years' life, and further tests at closer intervals should follow this.

Copper fireboxes last from five to nine years, but the nature of the water and fuel is the deciding factor. Steel fire tubes will last about four years if they have been renewed previous to this at their firebox ends, and a good deal of "spot" replacement, that is renewal of the worst tubes, will have been done in this time.

The tyres of driving wheels will survive a mileage of 50,000 before requiring to be returned, but leading bogie wheels will require "shopping" at half this mileage. Their job of "finding the road" puts a lot of work on them. Trailing wheels and the tender wheels will have a tyre life of 30,000 to 40,000 miles.

The brick arch, that is the structure inside the firebox that prevents cold air from the fire door getting direct access to the tubes, has a very short life, lasting only 10 to 14 weeks. Fortunately its renewal is neither a very expensive nor difficult job, and can be carried out in the running shed. All the figures quoted are, of course, averages, but careful inspection of all new materials used tends to uniformity in rate of wear.

Regular shed inspections and regular visits to the works will keep our express passenger engine fit for duty for many years. As time goes on its efficiency will grow less, however, and new and improved designs will come to the front. Presently we shall find that it is taken off the heaviest duties and put to lighter tasks. This is the beginning of the end. The next visit to the shops reveals that very extensive repairs are required. A consultation is held, a sort of consultation of physicians over a death-stricken patient, and the verdict is announced—scrapping!

Somewhere round at the back of the works a gang of specialists get busy and after removing all re-usable fittings and parts, rapidly reduce the remainder to pieces of convenient size and the one-time pride of the road becomes just a heap of iron and brass, some of which may quite possibly find its way into new castings and a useful life in a locomotive of a later type.

Breakdown Trains and Their Work

THE locomotive whose career we have described in the preceding sections may run its life calmly and peacefully, or it may be less fortunate and on some occasion come to grief. Probably the mishap is nothing more than a derailment, but however trifling the accident the engine for the time being is out of action and the aid of the ever-ready breakdown train has to be requisitioned to restore normal working conditions.

Typical Breakdown Train

In this country railway mishaps are rare, thanks to the highly efficient systems of the railway companies and the skill and care of their staffs. When an accident does occur, however, one of the earliest steps taken is to report it by telegraph, or the quickest means available, to various specified points, including the nearest Locomotive Depot where a complete breakdown train is always kept in readiness to serve the whole of the district at the shortest notice.

Call for the Breakdown Crew

On receipt of a call for the breakdown train steps are immediately taken to collect the crew, which consists of men specially selected and assigned to the train and including some well-versed in ambulance work. If the call is received during the day these men, who probably are assistant fitters, fitter labourers, etc., are withdrawn at once from their jobs. If the message comes at night the running shed foreman despatches men on cycles to round-up the train foreman and his gang. At busy traffic centres the members of the crew are required to live near the depot in order that they may be available quickly at any time. The number of men in a breakdown gang varies, but at large depots is about 16.

By the time the gang turn up at the shed the running shed foreman has procured an engine, engine-men and a guard, and the steam crane is well fired. During ordinary working hours a breakdown train is got away in less than 20 minutes and even at night the period required is less than an hour. The train's mission is sufficient to secure a clear line and special orders at the scene of the mishap allow it to proceed on the wrong road if necessary. As regards signalling a breakdown train is treated as an ordinary express passenger train.

The breakdown train consists of the engine and tender followed by the travelling crane, the chain van containing chains and wire ropes of every variety, the riding van in which the men travel and the tool van containing the miscellaneous appliances required. The number of articles in the tool van runs into several hundreds and all are neatly and systematically stored on shelves and racks. It would take a page of this book to enumerate them all, but mention must be made of the hydraulic jacks, capable of lifting as much as 30 tons; the screw jacks; various tools for relaying torn tracks; hammers, wrenches, files and a vice. There are also oil flares and acetylene lamps, engine parts, ambulance equipment, and a supply of cups, coffee, condensed milk and biscuits for the gang.

Arrival at Scene of Accident

On arrival of the breakdown train at the scene of the accident no time is lost in getting to work. Every mishap has its own peculiarities of circumstance, and personal judgment on the part of the foreman of the train plays a large part in organising systematic clearance operations. The earliest steps in the task of restoring normal conditions are directed to assisting those engaged in the rescue of sufferers, should there be any.

The wreckage after an accident of any magnitude presents a wild scene. Everywhere lie fragments of timbers from coaches either torn to matchwood or telescoped one into another. The locomotive, completely off the road, may be lying upon its side with wheels wrenched off, frames twisted in amazing fashion, and other parts torn and distorted — a mangled mass enveloped in escaping steam.

The clearing away of the heaps of debris and the restoration of the permanent way, which often suffers severely in a smash-up, involves a variety of operations by the break-down gang. In these the all-important crane is well to the fore, although its use often has to be preceded by much patient hacking and sawing to separate the shattered vehicles. This is especially the case when the impact of a collision has been unusually severe and coaches have been telescoped.

Considering the weight of modern locomotives and rolling stock it is not surprising that many modern breakdown cranes are capable of lifting loads of from 35 tons to 60 tons. They are specially constructed to enable them to travel with ordinary rolling stock. Although run where required by attaching a locomotive, they are also equipped with self-propelling gear. When not in use, the jib or arm of the crane is always lowered to prevent it from fouling overhead and wayside structures, and it then rests upon a trestle erected on the " guard " or " match " truck always attached to the crane. In this portion the crane is spoken of as being in running order or " running trim," and it will pass under the railway standard loading gauge of 13 ft. During hoisting operations, however, the highest point of the jib may be more than 25 ft. above the level of the rails.

The crane is provided with special equipment to enable it to lift heavy loads without damaging the permanent way, for an enormous weight is concentrated upon the rails when the crane is engaged in hoisting. There is a set of rail clips by which a firm grip on the rails is secured for the crane, prior to performing heavy work, and adjustable blocks also are provided to take the load off the springs.

A very important feature of the special equipment is the blocking girders, sometimes called " draw-out " bars or " outriggers." These short lengths of girder are an integral part of the crane and are housed in a special casing underneath the frame, between the wheels. There are two girders to each side, and when required each is drawn outward and jacked up at the outer end so as to form an extended base to the crane and thus ensure the stability and rigidity of the whole structure. It is due to the use of these blocking girders that the crane is enabled to lift such heavy loads.

A derailed engine frequently may be lifted back on to the rails by jacks, or drawn up on to them by means of rerailing ramps.

Two 36-ton Steam Cranes lifting "Castle" Class Engine

"MECCANO MAGAZINE"

ALL boys who are interested in Locomotives, Railways, and in developments connected with them, will find the *"Meccano Magazine"* a valuable source of information. It contains articles dealing with the latest railway activities throughout the world, and owners of Hornby Trains are specially catered for so that they may get all the enjoyment possible out of their hobby.

In addition, the *"M.M."* contains interesting articles on such subjects as Famous Engineers and Inventors, Electricity, Aeroplanes, Bridges, Cranes, Wonderful Machinery, Latest Patents, Nature Study, Radio, Stamps, Photography and Books—in fact the Magazine deals with those subjects in which all healthy boys are interested. It has a larger circulation than any similar boys' magazine, and is read in every civilised country in the world.

The *"M.M."* is published on the 1st of each month (price 6d.) and it may be obtained from your Meccano dealer or newsagent, with one of whom you should place a regular order to prevent disappointment. If you prefer to have each issue sent direct the Editor will be pleased to arrange this on receipt of a Postal Order for 4/- to cover six issues or 8/- to cover twelve issues, post free.

Send 6d. in stamps for a specimen copy of the *"M.M.,"* which will be forwarded post free

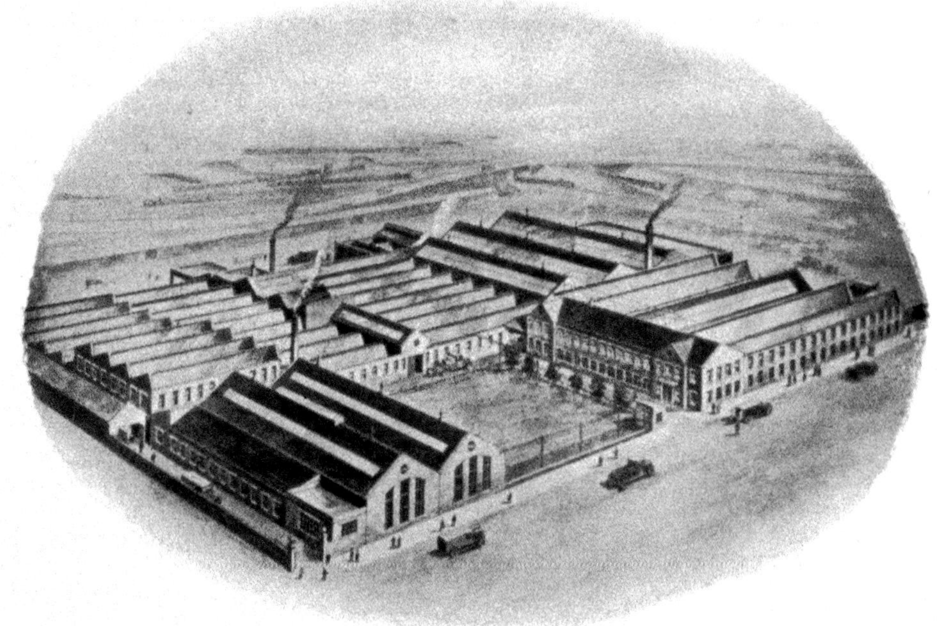

Head Office and Factory, Liverpool

Published by:

MECCANO LTD., BINNS ROAD, LIVERPOOL

1127/15

HORNBY BOOK OF TRAINS

1933-1934

THE HORNBY BOOK OF TRAINS

1933-34

The present year has been notable for the successful opening of the first British main line electrification, that of the Southern Railway route to Brighton. This development has aroused new interest in electric traction generally, and in our first article we give a brief survey of the electric railways of the British Isles. The pioneer part played by many of these lines is of considerable interest and importance. For instance, the Giant's Causeway Electric Railway in Northern Ireland was the first hydro-electric railway in the world ; the City and South London line was the first tube railway ; and the Liverpool Overhead Railway was the first elevated electric line.

It is difficult to appreciate fully the remarkable efficiency of the railways of to-day without some knowledge of the various developments that have preceded it. In our second article we pass in review the principal landmarks in the history of British railways, and trace the steps leading up to the great expresses that are now world famous.

In the course of our railway journeys we must all have noticed the variations that exist in the nature of the line in different parts of the country. Our third article shows how the railway engineer adapts his methods of construction to the type of country across which the line runs, and explains why a railway that passes through fenland necessarily differs so greatly from one in a hilly region.

Finally we deal with the railways as the main carriers of the nation's goods, and describe some of the interesting and remarkable vehicles that have been designed to transport different forms of traffic in the most effective manner. In this article reference is made to the curious and often puzzling code names that are given by the railway companies to goods vehicles of unusual type to save long descriptions.

Our cover shows the L.M.S.R. "*Royal Scot*" express hauled by the locomotive of the same name ; and above we illustrate the L.M.S.R. "Pacific" express locomotive "*The Princess Royal,*" the first of this type to be built by the company. This giant is the longest and heaviest express locomotive in the British Isles. It has an overall length of more than 74 ft., and with its tender holding nine tons of coal and 4,000 gallons of water, the total weight is 158 tons 12 cwt.

For assistance in the preparation of this book we wish to express our indebtedness to the London, Midland and Scottish Railway ; the London and North Eastern Railway ; the Great Western Railway, and the Southern Railway. We have also to thank the London Passenger Transport Board, the Westinghouse Brake and Saxby Signal Company, the Anglo-American Oil Co., Ltd., the British Thomson-Houston Co., Ltd., and Railway Photographs (Liverpool) for the use of illustrations.

The Electric Railways of the British Isles

THE electrification of our railways has made considerable progress this year by the conversion of the Southern Railway Company's line between Purley and Brighton, with the branch to Worthing. This ranks as the first main line electrification in these islands, and its successful working has made the subject of railway electrification a very live one. This is therefore a good time at which to take stock of the present position, and to see what has already been done in this way by the railways of this country.

Taking the biggest installation first, the Southern Railway have now 359 miles of route electrified, but actually the length of track so equipped is 978 miles. This is the largest suburban electrification in the world, and is all on the 600-volt direct current third-rail system, the current rail being outside the running rails. The company have only one power-house of their own, which was built near Wimbledon by the L.S.W.R. A large part of their current is obtained from the London Power Company, and for the Brighton line, south of Purley, power is taken from the national electric "grid." The electrical arrangements for this part of the line are controlled from a control room at Three Bridges.

The standard electric train on the Brighton line consists of five corridor coaches and one composite first and third class Pullman car, and at times of heaviest traffic two such six-coach trains are coupled together. The trains are designed for a maximum service speed of 75 m.p.h. During slack hours on the suburban electrified sections of the Southern, the ordinary trains consist of three coaches, eight-coach trains being used at busy times. The electric "*Southern Belle*" is composed of Pullman coaches only, and takes the place of the famous steam-operated train of the same name that first ran in 1908.

Next in mileage electrified comes the group of lines operated by the London Passenger Transport Board, consisting of the systems forming the late "Underground" group and the Metropolitan Railway, and including therefore all the Tube railways except the Waterloo and City, which belongs to the Southern. These are all on the 600-volt direct current third-rail system, taking most of their power from the Lots Road and Neasden power stations. These lines are notable for the very dense services of trains they carry, which are made possible by automatic and power signalling. For efficiency of operation they set a standard that is not exceeded in any other country in the world.

A special design of all-steel rolling stock has been evolved for the Tube lines, as it has to run in tunnels of 11 ft. 8¼ in. diameter. Particular attention has been paid to lighting, ventilation, and rapid loading and unloading, with the use of air-worked doors. The stock on what were the District and Metropolitan Railways conforms more to main line dimensions.

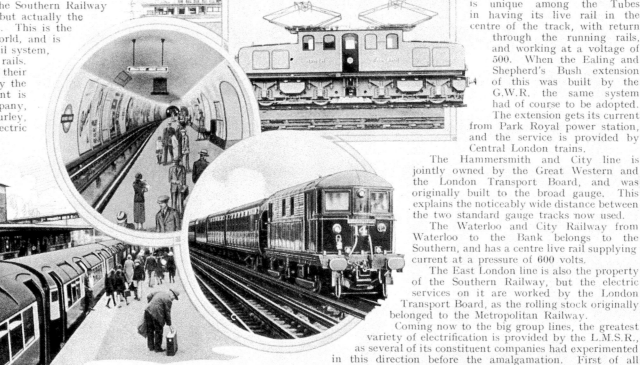

(Top, right.) L.N.E.R. electric goods locomotive. (Top, left.) A typical "Underground" station. (Bottom, right.) Metropolitan locomotive and train. (Bottom, left.) A "Tube" train at a surface station.

The Central London Railway is unique among the Tubes in having its live rail in the centre of the track, with return through the running rails, and working at a voltage of 500. When the Ealing and Shepherd's Bush extension of this was built by the G.W.R. the same system had of course to be adopted. The extension gets its current from Park Royal power station, and the service is provided by Central London trains.

The Hammersmith and City line is jointly owned by the Great Western and the London Transport Board, and was originally built to the broad gauge. This explains the noticeably wide distance between the two standard gauge tracks now used.

The Waterloo and City Railway from Waterloo to the Bank belongs to the Southern, and has a centre live rail supplying current at a pressure of 600 volts.

The East London line is also the property of the Southern Railway, but the electric services on it are worked by the London Transport Board, as the rolling stock originally belonged to the Metropolitan Railway.

Coming now to the big group lines, the greatest variety of electrification is provided by the L.M.S.R., as several of its constituent companies had experimented in this direction before the amalgamation. First of all there are the numerous lines in the London area, including the old Tilbury section, from Bow Road to Barking, recently extended to Upminster. This is worked by the trains of the late District Railway, but the track, stations, signals, etc., belong to the L.M.S.R. Current is supplied by the Lots Road power station. The electrified lines from Broad Street and Euston to Richmond and Watford are worked by L.M.S.R. rolling stock of main line type, with a high standard of comfort. The recent addition of automatic colour-light signals on the Watford line has enabled a better service to be given, with probably less delays in fog. Over this section run also certain trains of Tube stock, which emerge from what was the Bakerloo Tube at Queen's Park, and join the lines from Euston. These trains are jointly owned by the L.M.S.R. and the London

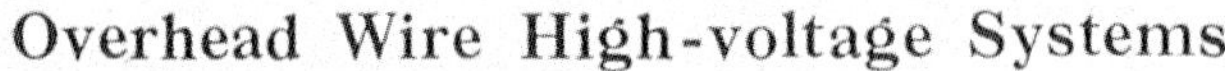

Extensive Developments on the L.M.S.R. Overhead Wire High-voltage Systems

Passenger Transport Board. Electric power for these L.M.S.R. lines is supplied by the company's power station at Stonebridge Park, near Wembley. The third rail carrying current at 600 volts is the system used, being fixed by the necessity of running in conjunction with the Tubes from Queen's Park to Watford and the District Railway at Earl's Court.

The late Lancashire and Yorkshire Railway, now part of the L.M.S.R., was very early in the field with electrification, and the first conversion was on the Liverpool to Southport line. This has been a very successful venture, and it caters well for the growing residential district through which it passes, and which it has done a great deal to create. Power is supplied by the Formby power station, owned by the company, and owing its apparently isolated position to the presence of a good supply of cooling water from the River Alt. A third rail, fixed outside the track, feeds current to the trains at 600 volts, the return being through the rails. Electrification was also introduced some years ago on the line through Aintree to Maghull and Ormskirk.

The L. & Y. R. electrified their Manchester to Bury line before amalgamation. This was notable for the use of exceptionally wide rolling stock, built entirely of steel, and a third rail working at 1,200 volts, direct current, and therefore having to be protected on top by boarding to prevent accidental contact by workmen. Power was originally supplied by a specially-built power station at Clifton Junction, but is now taken from the "grid."

Another pioneering effort in electrification was that of the Midland Railway, which equipped the line from Lancaster to Morecambe and Heysham with an overhead wire carrying single-phase current at a voltage of 6,600, supplied by a power station at Heysham Harbour. Wooden poles are used for the support of the overhead wire. A frequent service is maintained, the traffic being chiefly residential, together with workmen travelling between Lancaster and Heysham.

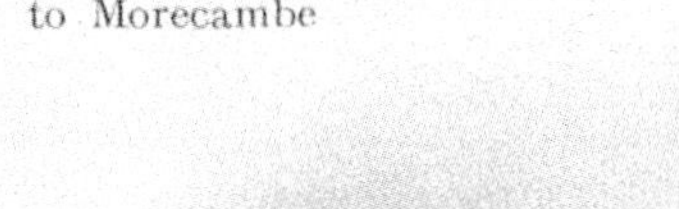

Some years ago the Government appointed a Committee to prepare a schedule of requirements for future railway electrification in this country, and the first line to conform to this schedule was the Manchester, South Junction and Altrincham, owned by the L.M.S.R. and the L.N.E.R. This is about nine miles long, and serves a residential area to the south-west of Manchester. It is equipped with an overhead wire carrying direct current at 1,500 volts. The rolling stock employed is of the compartment type, and ordinarily the trains consist of three coaches, but during the rush periods two such trains are coupled together. It is understood that the results so far obtained by electric working have been satisfactory, and it is likely that further electrifications in populous areas will be undertaken on this system of working.

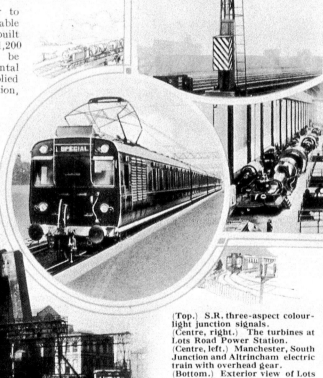

The L.N.E.R. have only a small electrified mileage, and it is all on the former North Eastern system. In the Newcastle district there are suburban lines equipped with a third rail carrying direct current at 600 volts. The Newport and Shildon line, which deals principally with coal traffic, has an overhead wire carrying direct current at 1,500 volts, and the coal trains are worked by electric locomotives. It is interesting to note that the North Eastern, before amalgamation, built the first electric locomotive for main line passenger service in this country, as an experiment in connection with the proposal to electrify the main line from York to Darlington. This scheme was put forward after the War but has not developed further.

(Top.) S.R. three-aspect colour-light junction signals.
(Centre, right.) The turbines at Lots Road Power Station.
(Centre, left.) Manchester, South Junction and Altrincham electric train with overhead gear.
(Bottom.) Exterior view of Lots Road Power Station.

The Multiple-Unit System of Control

The Liverpool Overhead Railway, the first overhead electric railway in the world, is 40 years old, and the original rolling stock is still running. There is a positive rail outside the running rails, working at 500 volts, direct current, and a centre negative rail. The line is equipped with automatic colour-light signals, and serves almost the full length of the docks.

The Mersey Railway, which was opened originally as a steam line, connects Liverpool and Birkenhead by a tunnel under the Mersey. It has its own terminus under the Cheshire Lines Central Station in Liverpool, and in Birkenhead has two branches, one connecting with the Wirral section of the L.M.S.R. at Park Station, the other joining the G.W.R. and L.M.S.R. joint line from Birkenhead to Chester at Rock Ferry. It has been re-signalled with colour-light signals, and was the first railway in the world to adopt a system of automatic working of points, which enables the Liverpool terminus to be worked without a signalman during the slack hours of the day.

The Manx Electric Railway is built to the 3 ft. and 3 ft. 6 in. gauges, and has a route mileage of 22½, of which 18 are of the 3 ft. gauge, with 31 motor-cars and 25 trailers. There are also 28 goods vehicles.

This year the Giant's Causeway Electric Railway, in Northern Ireland, celebrates its fiftieth anniversary. It was the first hydro-electric railway in the world. Some would call it a tramway, but for part of its eight-mile length it has its own right-of-way. It is on the 3 ft. gauge, and has gradients as steep as 1 in 24. It was at first arranged with a conductor rail, but for many years the overhead wire system has been employed.

Electrifications of railways in this country have been practically all on what is known as the multiple-unit system, which is the opposite to the system in which a locomotive is used to haul a train. It is only practicable to use the multiple-unit system for passenger trains, however, and even then, although the Brighton main line is worked on this principle, it does not follow that other main lines would be so worked. In this system the electric motors are carried on the bogies of the vehicles, and are situated at various parts of the train; but they all work together, and are controlled from one end or other of the train as desired. Thus a great number of wheels become driving wheels, which enables rapid acceleration to be achieved; and also it becomes an easy matter to alter the size of the trains to suit the traffic. There is also the great advantage that terminal working is much simplified, as there is no engine to be run round the train. The driver and guard simply change places, which results in a great saving of time.

(Top.) A moving stairway or escalator.
(Left.) Former L.B.S.C. "overhead wire" train.
(Centre.) Driver's compartment on an "Underground" train, showing the "dead man's handle."
(Bottom.) A station on a "Tube" surface extension.

Automatic Devices to Ensure Safety

To secure the full benefits from electrification, which, with its rapid acceleration and braking, increases the capacity of the line, it is usually found necessary to remodel the signalling of the railway concerned. Hence, in electrifying to Brighton, the Southern have completely changed the signalling south of Purley, and, adopting colour-light signals controlled by track circuit, have done away with a number of signal-boxes, and yet increased the capacity for traffic of that part of their line.

When a steam locomotive is hauling a train there are never less than two men on it, so that if one suddenly becomes ill, or is injured in some way so as to become unfit for work, the other can bring the train safely to a standstill. On electric trains, as there is no need for a fireman, it is usual to have only one man in the driving compartment, and unless precautions were taken his sudden incapacity might be very dangerous. It has therefore become the usual practice to adopt the so-called "dead man's handle." The controller handle, which corresponds to the steam regulator, is similar to a tram controller, but in the top of it there is a small knob that the driver holds down with the palm of his hand. If he lets go of this for any reason, the current is cut off and the brakes are applied, no matter in what position the handle happens to be. In addition it is usual for electric trains to be fitted with what are known as "trip-cocks." These are mounted on the motor bogie, and work in conjunction with trips at the side of the line. Each trip is connected to a signal and is horizontal when the line is clear, but rises vertically when the signal is at danger. It is thus in a position to actuate the trip-cock on the motor bogie, and this causes the current to be cut off and the brakes to be applied, in the event of a train overrunning a signal that is at danger.

A Short History of British Railways

IT is interesting to look back from time to time over the history of our British railways. Indeed, only by doing this can we form any real idea of the tremendous development that has taken place since the days of Trevithick, George Stephenson and other famous pioneers of steam locomotion.

Wooden rail ways were used more than 300 years ago, but the first iron railway was laid at the Nunnery Colliery near Sheffield in 1776. In 1801 Parliament agreed to the building of the Surrey Iron Railway, and this railway has the distinction of being the first to receive Parliamentary sanction. Richard Trevithick, whose centenary has been celebrated this year, built in 1804 a locomotive that hauled a train on the Merthyr Tydvil tram road. Seven years later the first railway in Scotland, the Kilmarnock and Troon, was opened, but was not worked by a steam locomotive until 1817. "*Puffing Billy*" appeared at Wylam in 1813, and Stephenson's first locomotive, "*Blucher*," at Killingworth in the following year. In 1825 the Stockton and Darlington Railway was opened, and the success of the "*Rocket*" at the Rainhill trials held four years later definitely gave the railway locomotive the foremost place as an agent of transport.

The opening of the Liverpool and Manchester Railway in 1830 marked the beginning of a period of great activity in railway building. The Canterbury and Whitstable Railway was opened in the same year, and was followed in 1831 by two or three short lines in Scotland. Important developments took place in 1837, which year saw the opening of a portion of the London and Birmingham Railway and the Grand Junction Railway. These ultimately formed part of the London and North Western Railway and now of course are included in the L.M.S.R. system. About a year later the whole of the London and Birmingham Railway was opened, and also the first section of the broad gauge Great Western line, from Paddington to Maidenhead Bridge.

In that year also were opened the Manchester and Bolton line, the first section of the Lancashire and Yorkshire Railway, and the first portion of the London and Southampton Railway from Nine Elms to Woking. Two important events in 1839 were the installation on the G.W.R. between Paddington and West Drayton of Cook and Wheatstone's electric telegraph, and the first publication of Bradshaw's Railway Timetable. In the same year came into being the London and South Western Railway, and the first part of the London and Croydon Railway, and of the Eastern Counties Railway on the 5 ft. gauge.

(Top.) A replica Liverpool and Manchester inaugural train. (Centre, right.) Famous broad gauge locomotive "North Star." (Centre, left.) The first Stockton and Darlington locomotive. (Bottom.) "Locomotion" at work in 1825 on the opening train.

The L.S.W.R. was opened to Southampton in 1840, and by the following year the G.W.R. had reached Bristol, and the London to Brighton line was complete. In the same year was held the first conference of railway managers, the forerunner of regular meetings to decide questions of common interest, such as rules and regulations; and in the next year the Railway Clearing House began work. Howe's link motion for locomotives was introduced. The Midland Railway was constituted in 1844, the Yarmouth and Norwich line was opened and worked on the telegraph block system, and the Bristol and Exeter line opened.

By this time the existence of different gauges had begun to prove troublesome. In 1845 the Eastern Counties Railway was converted from 5 ft. gauge to the 4 ft. 8½ in. that had been adopted from the first by George Stephenson, and a Royal Commission was appointed to consider the whole question. That Commission ultimately reported in favour of 4 ft. 8½ in., and in 1848 Parliament decided upon this gauge as standard, but the broad gauge lingered on until 1892. In 1846 began the period that is known as the "Railway Mania," which was

Lines Constructed during the "Railway Mania"

marked by a wild rush of legislation and construction. During that year there were passed by Parliament no less than 272 Acts for new lines. The London and North Western Railway and the London, Brighton and South Coast Railway were constituted, and the first sections of the North British Railway and the Furness Railway were opened. In the following year the Lancashire and Yorkshire, the North Staffordshire, and the Manchester, Sheffield and Lincolnshire Railway—the last-named being the forerunner of the Great Central Railway—were constituted, and the first section of the Caledonian Railway was opened. In 1850 the Great Northern Railway was opened for its full length, the Glasgow and South Western was completed to Carlisle, and the Royal Border Bridge at Berwick and the High Level Bridge at Newcastle were opened. The G.W.R. was completed on the broad gauge to Birmingham in the following year, and King's Cross Station was opened.

(Top.) Brunel's Saltash Bridge.
(Centre, left.) Mail exchange apparatus.
(Centre, right.) Picking up water at speed.
(Bottom.) Royal Border Bridge, Berwick.

The train staff system for working single lines was introduced by the L.N.W.R. in 1853, and three years later Saxby took out a patent for the interlocking of points and signals. It was on this railway, in 1860, that the water pick-up apparatus now used on most of our main lines was first employed, by Ramsbottom between Llanfairfechan and Aber.

The North Eastern Railway was constituted in 1854, and five years later there was first applied to the locomotive the injector which, in an improved form, still holds the field. During 1862 the Eastern Counties line changed its name to Great Eastern Railway, and the famous *"Flying Dutchman"* train began to run on the G.W.R. Gas lighting was first used on trains in 1863, the North London being the line concerned. Other events in this year were the opening of the Isle of Wight Central Railway and the Highland line from Perth to Inverness via Forres. In the following year Charing Cross Station of the South Eastern was brought into use, and the Cambrian Railway was constituted. In 1868 the G.W.R. commenced

Period of Rapid Development

the big task of converting their broad gauge to standard, and St. Pancras Station, the London terminus of the Midland Railway, was opened.

The Midland and Great Eastern Railways began to carry third-class passengers by all trains in 1872, and a year later sleeping carriages were introduced on the West Coast route to Scotland. In 1875 the Midland Railway abolished second class and introduced a number of Pullman cars that they imported from America. Dining cars were first run on the Great Northern Railway between King's Cross and Leeds in 1879, which was the year of the collapse of the first Tay Bridge. In 1885 the L.N.W.R. ran the first train exclusively for mails. The Mersey Tunnel was opened for steam traffic in 1886, and the new Tay Bridge came into use in 1887, the Severn Tunnel in 1888, and the Forth Bridge in 1891. In the following year the G.W.R. introduced corridor trains and finished their gauge conversion of the whole line, and the L.S.W.R. took over Southampton Docks. Steam heating of trains was introduced on the G.W.R. in 1893, which year was notable also for the opening of the first part of the Liverpool Overhead Railway, the first overhead electric railway in the world. The West Highland line was completed in 1894, and the Snowdon Railway in 1895. In the latter year took place the famous race to Aberdeen, one result of which was the fixing for several years of the timing of the fast trains to Scotland.

The Great Central Railway first got its name in 1897, and two years later was extended to London. Chain communication in railway carriages was adopted by the G.W.R. in 1901, and automatic signalling was introduced on the L.S.W.R. in 1902. This latter year is noteworthy as a speed year. The N.E.R. began to run a train that took 43 minutes for the 44¼ miles between Darlington and York, which was the fastest booked run in the British Empire; and the L.Y.R. introduced the 40-minute expresses between Liverpool and Manchester.

Electric traction commenced on the Liverpool to Southport line in 1903, and in the Newcastle area of the N.E.R. in 1904, in which year also was set up a world's record locomotive speed that still holds. This was set up on the G.W.R. by the running of the *"City of Truro"* at a speed of 102·3 m.p.h. in the descent of Wellington Bank. The Great Western Railway

Railway Steamer Services Commenced

Formation of the Four Great Groups

(Top.) "Queen of Scots" Pullman Express at speed. (Centre, left.) G.W.R. broad gauge conversion in progress. (Centre, right.) Latest pattern of L.M.S.R. mail stowage van. (Bottom.) Typical three-aspect colour-light signals, with route indicators above and shunting signals below.

also inaugurated in this year the "*Cornish Riviera Express*," running non-stop from Paddington to Plymouth via Bath and Bristol.

The development of railway steamship services should here be noted. The Manchester, Sheffield and Lincolnshire Railway, the forerunner of the Great Central, commenced a steamer service in 1865 between Grimsby and Hamburg, and the Larne and Stranraer steamers began to sail in 1872. The Harwich to Hook of Holland service began in 1893. A joint steamer service by the G.W.R. and the L.S.W.R. was started in 1899 between Weymouth, Southampton and the Channel Islands, and in 1904 the Midland Railway introduced a service between Heysham and Belfast. In 1906 the L.Y.R. and the N.E.R. opened the Hull-Zeebrugge route, and the Rosslare-Fishguard service was commenced.

The first section of the City and South London Railway was opened in 1890, and the Central London Railway in 1900. The Mersey Railway was electrified in 1903. Other important line openings were those of the Great Northern and City in 1904, the Baker Street and Waterloo Tube and the Piccadilly Tube in 1906, and the Hampstead Tube in 1907.

Automatic signalling was introduced on the District Railway in 1906, in which year also all-electric signalling was put into operation at Crewe. In 1908 a system of electro-pneumatic signalling was introduced at Glasgow Central, and automatic signals came into use over a part of the Metropolitan Railway. The American Boat Specials of the L.N.W.R. began to run between Riverside Station, Liverpool, and Euston in 1907. In the following year the Midland Railway electrified the Lancaster to Morecambe and Heysham lines; the famous L.B.S.C.R. train, the "*Southern Belle*," began to run between London and Brighton in one hour for the 51½ miles; and the Cowlairs Incline out of Glasgow, Queen Street, ceased to be worked by cable haulage. The Brighton company introduced electric trains on the overhead high-tension system on the South London line in 1909, and a year later the L.N.W.R. began to run what were known as the "City to City" expresses between Birmingham and Broad Street, London. In this year the Birmingham two-hour expresses were commenced by the G.W.R. over their shortened route, and this line also abolished second class.

The Metropolitan Railway commenced in 1911 a system of automatic signalling, in which upper-quadrant arms were used for the signals. The upper-quadrant arm has now been standardised on all main lines. In 1911 also the L.S.W.R. introduced two-hour expresses to Bournemouth, and tea cars became a feature of certain L.N.W.R. expresses. The first escalator came into use at Earl's Court. Electric traction commenced on the East London line in 1913, and the G.W.R. began the "Safety First" movement in regard to railways.

An interesting event was the disappearance in 1914 of the last survivor of the old horse-worked vehicle on a railway, except for shunting, as the result of the introduction of steam working on the Port Carlisle branch of the North British Railway in place of the "horse dandy." The declaration of War in August of that year was followed by the taking over of the railways by the Government, and the working of them by the Railway Executive Committee. In 1919 the Ministry of Transport was established and took the place of the Board of Trade in regard to the safety of railway working.

The railways were decontrolled in 1921, and the Railways Act was passed, as a result of which the four great groups were formed. On 1st January, 1923, the Southern, Great Western, London Midland and Scottish, and London and North Eastern Railways, as constituted by this Act, commenced to operate 123 railway undertakings that previously had been independent concerns. In that year a successful experiment was made in which a wireless programme was received by passengers on an L.M.S.R. express train at full speed, and an installation of colour-light signals was brought into use by the L.N.E.R. between Marylebone and Wembley.

The group undertakings gradually began to develop fresh principles in their operations and services, combining with the experience of the formerly independent companies the developments suggested by modern progress. In 1924 the G.W.R. adopted the arrangement whereby the departure times of trains from Paddington were standardised according to their destinations. This had been introduced on the old L.S.W.R. in 1919, when the timetables and services were reconstructed after the decelerations of the War

Competition for Traffic to the North

Modern Developments and Experiments

period. The train ferry service between Harwich and Zeebrugge also began in 1924, thus enabling Continental traffic to be dealt with without transhipment. In 1925 the centenary of the Stockton and Darlington Railway occurred, and all groups sent examples of their locomotives, both ancient and modern, to take part in the celebrations at Darlington. Towards the end of the year the Metropolitan Railway opened a branch to Watford, and the Southern extended their system of electrified lines to Epsom, Leatherhead, Dorking and Guildford.

The year 1927 was notable for the long-distance running competition between the L.M.S.R. and the L.N.E.R. The latter company commenced to run the 9·50 a.m. from King's Cross—the "*Junior Scotsman*" relief of the famous 10 a.m. "*Flying Scotsman*"—without a stop to Newcastle, 268½ miles. The L.M.S.R., on the other hand, in bestowing the name "*The Royal Scot*" on their 10 a.m. service, made Carnforth, 236 miles from Euston, the first halting place. These runs applied to the summer services. At the commencement of the winter services the non-stop run of "*The Royal Scot*" was extended to Carlisle, a distance of over 300 miles to the point where the halt was made for engine-changing purposes. In the following year the L.N.E.R. instituted the 392¾-mile run of "*The Flying Scotsman*" to and from Edinburgh. This was anticipated by a sporting effort of their rivals in running the two portions of "*The Royal Scot*" to Glasgow and Edinburgh respectively without a halt. The L.M.S.R. feat was not repeated, however, whereas the L.N.E.R. non-stop run took its place in the regular summer timetables.

An important event of 1928, as showing the democratic tendency in railway travel, was the introduction of sleeping cars for third-class passengers on all groups except the Southern. In 1929 the G.W.R. "*Cheltenham Flyer*," which had been withdrawn in the previous year, was reinstated, and from its former average of 61·8 m.p.h. over the 77¼-mile course from Swindon to Paddington it was accelerated to 66·2 m.p.h. The first appearance of the famous L.N.E.R. engine "No. 10000," with its water-tube boiler carrying a pressure of 450 lb. per sq. in., was made towards the end of the year. This was a sign of the times, as also was the appointment in 1930 by the L.M.S.R. of a Director of Technical Research.

The completion of several important works was witnessed in 1931. The widening of the L.M.S.R. main line in the neighbourhood of Barnt Green on the Birmingham and Bristol section included the opening out of Cofton Tunnel. The Exchange and Victoria stations in Manchester were joined by an exceptionally long platform, and at the same time the whole area was provided with colour-light signals of the four-aspect variety. Electric services began on the Manchester, South Junction, and Altrincham Railway, this being the first example in this country of the use of the 1,500-volt direct current overhead system recommended by the Ministry of Transport. The experimental Ro-Railer of the L.M.S.R.—a vehicle able to run on either road or rail—was put into service between Stratford-on-Avon and the company's Welcombe Hotel.

Further widenings and signalling developments have to be chronicled for 1932. The L.M.S.R. works at Mirfield were completed, together with the pioneer installation of "Speed" colour-light signalling. The G.W.R. introduced colour-light signals between Paddington and Southall, and the Barking to Upminster widening on the Tilbury section of the L.M.S.R. was opened to traffic. Numerous accelerations of train services came into force, and in September the "*Cheltenham Flyer*" was speeded up to an average of 71·3 m.p.h., making it the fastest steam train in the world.

A feature of the present year has been the first appearance of the "Pacific" type of express passenger locomotive on the L.M.S.R., and the number of experiments made with heavy oil engines as applied to railway working, both in separate locomotives and rail cars.

The experience of the century of development that we have thus recorded so briefly, together with the most modern technical improvements, are embodied in the best-known train services of to-day. Of the many famous expresses run by the "*Big Four*," as our chief companies are sometimes known, there is little doubt that the most celebrated quartette is made up of "*The Royal Scot*" of the L.M.S.R.; "*The Flying Scotsman*" of the L.N.E.R.; the "*Cornish Riviera Express*" of the G.W.R.; and "*The Golden Arrow*" of the Southern Railway.

(Top.) L.M.S.R. 1st class sleeping saloon running on two six-wheeled bogies. (Centre, right.) S.R. steamer "Brighton." (Centre, left.) Southern electric motor coach as used on the Brighton service. (Bottom.) Harwich-Zeebrugge Train Ferry loaded with railway wagons.

Luxurious Anglo-Scottish Travel

Each of these famous trains is renowned for its luxurious comfort, and each of them has practically all the amenities of a first-class hotel. A journey in "*The Royal Scot*" convinces one that the "comfort, smooth riding and dustless tracks" claimed by the L.M.S.R. are not empty boasts. The engine in charge takes out of Euston some "four hundred tons (or more) of wheeled comfort," and has to cover in summer just over 300 miles to the Border City before the first stop is made. Even this stop is for changing engines only, at Kingmoor sheds, Carlisle, not for traffic purposes, so that those joining the train at Euston are assured of an uninterrupted journey throughout. At Symington a halt is made to separate the Glasgow and Edinburgh portions, which then proceed to their respective destinations.

In the early days "*The Flying Scotsman*" made its name for speed and punctuality. It is now one of the world's luxury trains, with its hairdressing saloon, Louis XVI restaurant, and Vita glass windows to allow passengers to obtain the full benefit of the healthful rays of the sun. The train as a whole is indeed as perfect as the skill of the engineer, the imagination of the hotelier, or craftsmanship of the decorative expert, can make it.

"*The Flying Scotsman*" whisks us to Edinburgh non-stop in the summer in 7½ hours at the average rate of 52·4 m.p.h. In this age we take such things for granted, but the earliest through coaches to run between King's Cross and Edinburgh, which were first-class only, took 11 to 12 hours to reach their destination.

Originality and boldness form the keynote of Great Western enterprise, and these features certainly characterise the "*Cornish Riviera Express*," the most famous G.W.R. train, in spite of the claims of the record-breaking "*Cheltenham Flyer*." From the tip of the handsome locomotive to the tail of the luxurious train there are embodied features that do not apply collectively to any service of any other company. The elegantly-finished "King" locomotive with its green paint, bright steel, copper and brass work, and its tapered domeless boiler, has a smarter appearance than most engines in these days. The train, too, is remarkable in that except during the summer it carries no less than three slip portions. These are detached at Westbury, Taunton, and Exeter, for Weymouth, Minehead and Ilfracombe, and Torquay respectively. In the summer season the Westbury slip only is made, as complete trains for the other destinations are necessary to cope with the traffic.

West Country and Continental Services

For 20 years on end this train made the longest non-stop run in the world—225¾ miles from Paddington to Plymouth. From 1906 the time of 4 hours 7 min. held good, except for the War period, until 1927, when the advent of the famous "Kings" enabled a reduction to the even four hours to be made. This last summer, however, a further acceleration of three minutes was made on the previous year's summer timing. Thus Plymouth for the first time was reached in less than four hours from Paddington, at an average speed of 57·1 m.p.h.

(Top, left.) The S.S. "Duke of Lancaster," L.M.S.R. (Top, right.) S.S. "Isle of Guernsey," engaged on the Southern Railway Channel Islands service. (Centre, left.) Widening operations on the L.N.E.R. (Centre, right.) L.M.S.R. Upminster Station. (Bottom.) The S.S. "St. Helier," G.W.R.

The splendid all-Pullman "*Golden Arrow*" train has developed from the introduction in 1910, more or less experimentally, of first-class Pullman cars in certain of the Continental boat trains. It provides a fast journey to Dover, which, followed by a swift Channel crossing and a luxurious run on the "Nord," enables Paris to be reached from London in 6 hours 35 min. Overcrowding is avoided, as the number of passengers travelling is limited to the accommodation of the trains.

"*The Golden Arrow*" has been styled the most fashionable train in Europe. It is extremely popular, and this is not surprising when the excellence of Pullman service is borne in mind. The unusual character of this train—which recalls the exclusive "Limiteds" of earlier years in view of its restriction to "first-class only"—is reflected in the title appearing on its roof boards—"*The Golden Arrow—London and Paris.*" This is considerably more striking than the prosaic "*Continental Boat Express*" formerly used. Many a train may claim to be "Continental Boat Express," but there is only one "*Golden Arrow*."

HORNBY TRAINS

Guarantee

Every Hornby Locomotive is thoroughly tested and is guaranteed to be in good running order when it leaves our factory. Hornby Trains are manufactured by Meccano Limited, Liverpool, and are made from the finest materials obtainable.

Key to the Hornby Railway Layout illustrated below.

1. Lattice Girder Bridge.
2. The Signal Cabin protecting the station.
3. Telegraph Pole for lineside use.
4. A realistic Water Tank.
5. A useful Double Arm Signal
6. No. 1 Lumber Wagon for short logs.
7. Lamp Standards for goods yard.
8. A realistic Station.
9. Fine bogie Lumber Wagon No. 2.
10. Platform Crane loading up a wagon.
11. Brake Van for use at end of goods train.
12. Trolley Wagon carries bulky loads.
13. No. 2 Special Pullman Coach.
14. One of the Hornby L.M.S.R. Standard Compound Locomotives.

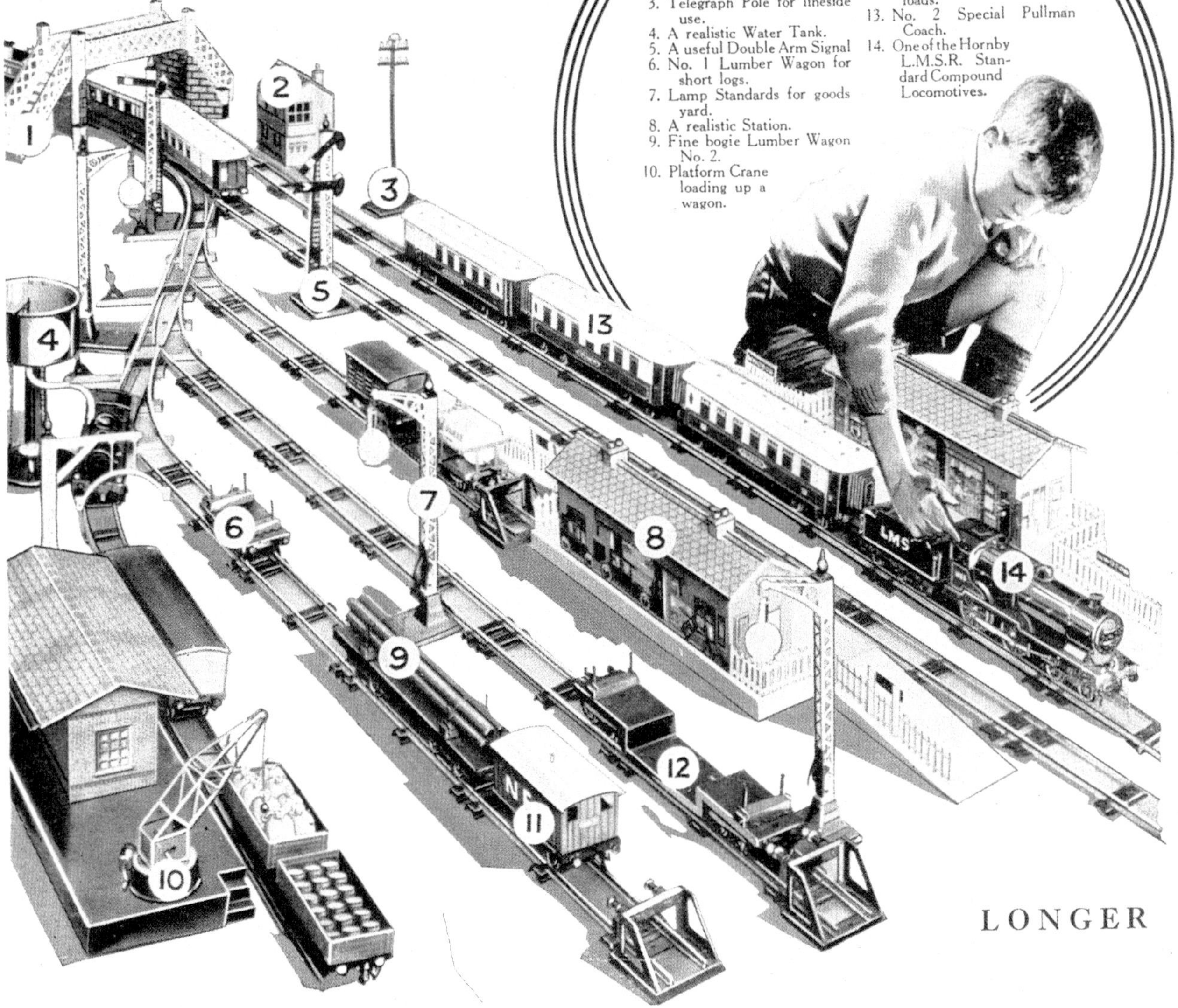

A Perfect Miniature Railway

The splendid fun of running a Hornby Railway is real and lasting because of the exceptional strength and reliable mechanism of the Hornby Locomotives, the realism of the Hornby Rolling Stock, and the wide range of Hornby Accessories —all designed and built in perfect proportion and all beautifully finished.

Hornby Clockwork Locomotives are the longest-running locomotives in the world. The motors that are fitted are of the highest possible quality, being perfect pieces of mechanism with accurately cut gears that ensure smooth and steady running. Hornby Electric Locomotives are fitted with powerful motors giving very high speeds, but always under perfect control.

The trains throughout are beautifully finished in every respect and in almost every case are available in the colours of the L.M.S., L.N.E., G.W. and Southern Railways.

Completeness of The Hornby System

From the day of their introduction Hornby Trains have always represented the latest model railway practice. Designs are continually being improved and new items added so that the system is complete in almost every detail. There is a comprehensive range of Locomotives, driven by clockwork or electric motors: and Rolling Stock of all kinds—Passenger Coaches, Pullman Cars, Trucks, Wagons and Vans. The Accessories are now better than ever. In addition to Stations, Bridges, Signals and Level Crossings, there are Countryside Sections to provide a splendid scenic setting for any layout; Cuttings and Tunnels to add realism to the track; miniature Railway Staff and Passengers to give "life" to station platforms; and Animals for lineside fields. The Rails, Points and Crossings enable an endless variety of layouts to be constructed.

In the following pages the components of the Hornby Series—Locomotives, Rolling Stock and Accessories—are fully described. Many of them are illustrated in actual colours, so that their beautiful finish can be judged.

LONGER RUNS—HIGHER SPEEDS

HORNBY TRAINS

Gauge 0, 1¼ in.

CLOCKWORK TRAIN SETS

The MO Sets are the smallest members of the Hornby Train Series. They are strongly built and well finished, and the Locomotives are fitted with a very efficient clockwork mechanism that gives a long run. They may be obtained with the Locomotive and Tender coloured in either red or green.

MO Goods Train Set consists of a Locomotive and Tender (available in either red or green), two Goods Wagons and Rails requiring a space measuring 2 feet square. One of the rails is a Brake Rail, by means of which the train may be braked from the track. Non-reversible .. .. Price 5/-

The prices of the components of the above Train Set are indicated at the foot of this page.

MO Passenger Train Set. This set consists of a Locomotive and Tender (available in red or green), two MO Pullman Coaches and set of Rails requiring a space measuring 2 feet square. One of the rails is a Brake Rail, by means of which the train may be braked from the track. Non-reversible .. .. Price 5/9

The components of the MO Train Sets may be purchased separately at the following prices :—

MO Locomotive (without Tender) .. Price 2/9 MO Tender .. Price 6d. MO Wagon .. Price 7d. MO Pullman Coach .. Price 10d.

RAILS FOR MO TRAIN SETS

BM Straight Rails .. .. Price, per doz. 2/9

MR9 and ML9 Points (9 in. radius), Right-hand and Left-hand .. Price, per pair 3/-

M9 Curved Rails (9 in. radius) .. .. .. Price, per doz. 3/-

MB9 Curved Brake Rails (9 in. radius) .. .. Price, each 3½d.

HORNBY TRAINS

CLOCKWORK TRAIN SETS

Gauge 0, 1¼ in.

M1 Passenger Train Set. (Illustrated above.) This set contains M1/2 Locomotive (reversing), M1/2 Tender, two M1 Pullman Coaches and set of Rails requiring a space measuring 3 ft. 3 in. by 2 ft. 6 in. One of the rails is a Brake Rail, by means of which the train may be braked from the track. The set is richly coloured and well finished. The Locomotive and Tender are available in two colours—green and red .. .. **Price 9/3**

M2 Passenger Train Set. This set is similar to the M1/2 Passenger Set, but it has three M1/2 Pullman Coaches instead of two, and the set of Rails requires a space measuring 4 ft. 3 in. by 2 ft. 6 in. .. .. **Price 10/9**

The components of the M1 and M2 Passenger Sets may be purchased separately at the following prices :—

M1 Locomotive (without Tender) .. **Price 4/6** **M1 Tender** .. .. **Price 9d.** **M1 Pullman Coach** .. .. **Price 1/-**

M1 Goods Train Set. This strongly-built train set contains M1/2 Locomotive (reversing), M1/2 Tender, two M1 Wagons (lettered L.M.S., N.E., G.W. or S.R.) and set of Rails requiring a space measuring **3 ft. 3 in.** by **2 ft. 6 in.** One of the rails is a Brake Rail, by means of which the train may be braked from the track. The Locomotive and Tender are available in red (with wagons lettered L.M.S.) and green (with wagons lettered N.E., G.W. or S.R.) .. .. **Price 10/-**

The components of the M1 Goods Set may be purchased separately at the following prices :—

M1 Locomotive (without Tender) .. **Price 4/6** **M1 Tender** .. .. **Price 9d.** **M1 Wagon** .. .. **Price 1/-**

The prices of Hornby Rails, Points and Crossings are specified on page 41.

Gauge 0, 1¼ in.

CLOCKWORK TRAIN SETS

M3 Tank Goods Train Set. This fine goods train is composed of a tank Locomotive (reversing) fitted with a clockwork motor of exceptional power, Goods Wagon (lettered L.M.S., N.E., G.W. or S.R.), Petrol Tank Wagon, Timber Wagon and set of Rails requiring a space measuring 3 ft. 3 in. by 2 ft. 6 in. One of the rails is a Brake Rail, by means of which the train may be braked from the track. The Locomotive is available in either red (with L.M.S.R. lettering) or green (with L.N.E.R., G.W.R. or S.R. lettering) **Price 15/-**

The M3 Tank Locomotive may be purchased separately.

M3 Tank Locomotive (Reversing) .. .. Price 7/6

Complete Model Railway M10

This interesting addition to the Hornby M range is a complete railway outfit, consisting of a non-reversing Locomotive, with a reliable mechanism that can be braked from the track, Tender, 2 Pullman Coaches, set of Rails, Footbridge, 2 Stations, Signal Cabin, 2 Telegraph Poles, 2 Signals, Loading Gauge, Tunnel, Cutting, Level Crossing, 3 Trees and 6 Die-cast Figures.

The Outfit is attractively packed in a special box, as illustrated .. .. .. **Price 21/-**

A suitable arrangement of the M10 Complete Railway is shown in the above illustration. This may be varied, as required.

The separate prices of Hornby Rails, Points and Crossings are specified on page 41.

CLOCKWORK TRAIN SETS

Gauge 0, 1¼ in.

Hornby No. O Passenger Train Set. This handsome train set is composed of a reversing No. O Locomotive, No. O/1 Tender, two No. O Pullman Coaches and set of Rails requiring a space measuring 3 ft. 3 in. by 2 ft. 6 in. One of the rails is a Brake Rail, by means of which the train may be braked from the track. The set is available with the Locomotive and Tender finished in L.M.S.R., L.N.E.R., G.W.R., or S.R. passenger traffic colours .. .. Price 17/6

The components of the Hornby No. O Passenger Train Set may be purchased separately at the following prices :—

Hornby No. O Locomotive, reversing (without Tender) .. Price 11/6 Hornby No. O/1 Tender .. Price 2/- No. O Pullman Coach .. Price 1/3

Hornby No. O Goods Train Set. This realistic goods set contains a long-running No. O Locomotive (reversing), No. O/1 Tender, No. O Wagon, No. 1 Timber Wagon, and set of Rails requiring a space measuring 3 ft. 3 in. by 2 ft. 6 in. One of the rails is a Brake Rail, by means of which the train may be braked from the track.

The Locomotive and Tender are supplied in the regulation goods traffic colours—black for L.N.E.R., L.M.S.R., and S.R., and dark green for G.W.R. If required, the set may be obtained with Locomotive and Tender in passenger traffic colours—green for L.N.E.R., red for L.M.S.R., and dark green for G.W.R. and S.R. .. .. .. Price 18/6

The components of the Hornby No. O Goods Train Set may be purchased separately at the following prices :—

Hornby No. O Locomotive, reversing (without Tender) .. Price 11/6 Hornby No. O/1 Tender .. .. Price 2/-
No. O Wagon .. .. „ 1/6 No. 1 Timber Wagon .. .. „ 1/6

The separate prices of Hornby Rails, Points and Crossings are specified on page 41.

Gauge 0, 1¼ in.

CLOCKWORK TRAIN SETS

Hornby No. 1 Tank Goods Train Set. A Hornby No. 1 Tank Locomotive, fitted with a powerful reversing clockwork motor that gives great length of run, is supplied with the popular Hornby No. 1 Tank Goods Train Set. The set consists of No. 1 Tank Locomotive, No. 1 Wagon, Petrol Tank Wagon, Brake Van and set of Rails requiring a space measuring 4 ft. 6 in. square. An AB2 Brake Rail is included, by means of which the train may be either braked or reversed from the track. The Locomotive is supplied in the regulation goods traffic colours—black for L.N.E.R., L.M.S.R., and S.R., and dark green for G.W.R. If required, the set may be obtained with Locomotive in passenger traffic colours—green for L.N.E.R., red for L.M.S.R., and dark green for G.W.R. and S.R. .. .. Price 25/-

The components of the Hornby No. 1 Tank Goods Set may be purchased separately at the following prices :—

Hornby No. 1 Tank Locomotive (reversing)	Price 13/6	Petrol Tank Wagon	Price 2/6
No. 1 Wagon	„ 1/9	Brake Van	„ 3/6

THE HORNBY CONTROL SYSTEM

MORE FUN—MORE THRILLS!

There is a certain amount of fascination about even the cheapest and simplest Miniature Railway. For a time we can take a keen interest in a single train running round a plain oval track, but presently we realise that we need something more. Then we add points and crossings and so make possible layouts with branch lines and sidings. Still later, perhaps, we add further interest by introducing a more or less complete system of signals.

By this time our railway has become a source of keen enjoyment to us and to our friends, and for a while we feel that nothing more is needed. Sooner or later, however, our thoughts turn to the Signal Cabin on a real railway and we wish that, like the signalman, we could control the operation of our railway by means of levers enabling us to manipulate signals and points.

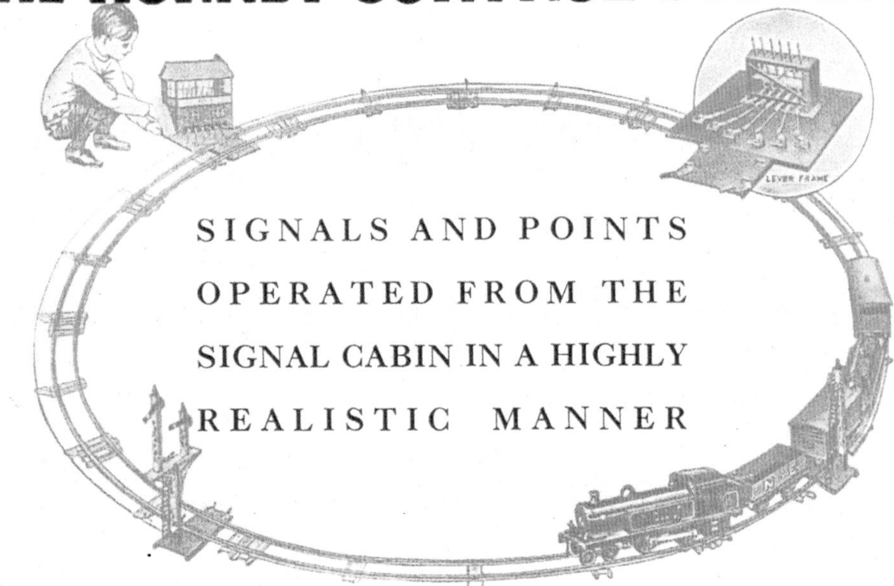

LEVER FRAME
SIGNALS AND POINTS OPERATED FROM THE SIGNAL CABIN IN A HIGHLY REALISTIC MANNER

The Hornby Control System has been specially devised to enable this desire to be fulfilled.

The Control System is easy to install on our Hornby Railway and once it is in operation we are in the position of the signalman whom we have previously envied. Instead of being obliged to manipulate individually the points and signals situated at various positions along the track, we are able to control them from one central point, namely, the Signal Cabin.

Our railway thus makes a tremendous advance in realism and the possibilities of fun are now unlimited.

Ask your dealer for the free illustrated price list that tells all about the Hornby Control System.

CLOCKWORK TRAIN SETS

Gauge 0, 1¼ in.

Hornby No. 1 Passenger Train Set. This very attractive train set consists of No. 1 Locomotive (reversing), No. O/1 Tender, two No. 1 Passenger Coaches, Guard's Van, and set of Rails requiring a space measuring 4 ft. 6 in. square. An AB2 Brake Rail is included, by means of which the train may be either braked or reversed from the track. The set is supplied in L.M.S.R., L.N.E.R., G.W.R. or S.R. passenger traffic colours. The doors of the Coaches open .. .. **Price 28/6**

The components of the Hornby No. 1 Passenger Train Set may be purchased separately at the following prices :—

Hornby No. 1 Locomotive, reversing (without Tender) ..	**Price 14/-**	**Hornby No. O/1 Tender**	**Price 2/-**
No. 1 Passenger Coach	„ **2/6**	**Guard's Van**	„ **2/9**

Hornby No. 1 Goods Train Set. This splendid goods set contains a powerful, long-running No. 1 Locomotive (reversing), No. O/1 Tender, No. 1 Wagon, Brake Van, and set of Rails requiring a space measuring 4 ft. 6 in. square. An AB2 Brake Rail is included by means of which the train may be either braked or reversed from the track. The Locomotive and Tender are supplied in the regulation goods traffic colours—black for L.N.E.R., L.M.S.R., and S.R., and dark green for G.W.R. If required, the set may be obtained with Locomotive and Tender in passenger traffic colours—green for L.N.E.R., red for L.M.S.R., and dark green for G.W.R. and S.R. .. .. **Price 25/-**

The components of the Hornby No. 1 Goods Set may be purchased separately at the following prices :—

Hornby No. 1 Locomotive, reversing (without Tender) ..	**Price 14/-**	**Hornby No. O/1 Tender**	**Price 2/-**
No. 1 Wagon	„ **1/9**	**Brake Van**	„ **3/6**

The prices of Hornby Rails, Points and Crossings are specified on page 41.

HORNBY TRAINS

Gauge 0, 1¼ in.

CLOCKWORK TRAIN SETS

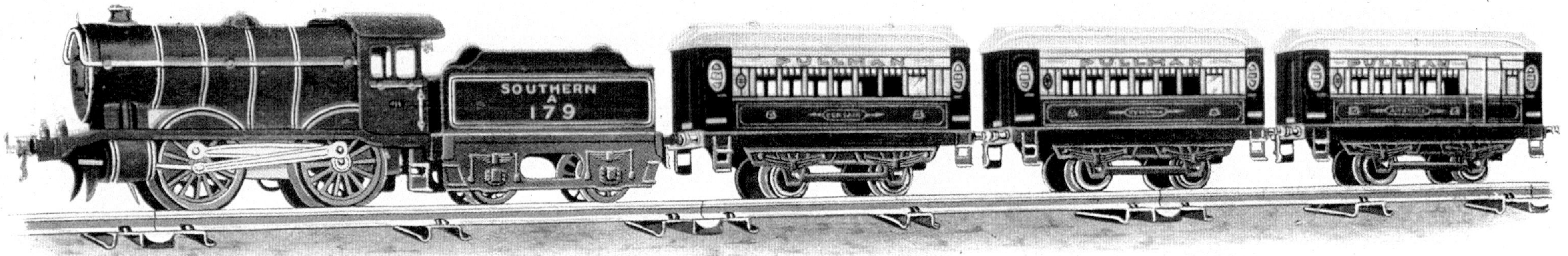

Hornby No. 1 Special Passenger Train Set. This excellent train set consists of a No. 1 Special Locomotive (fitted with reversing gear and brake mechanism), No. 1 Special Tender, two No. 1 Pullman Coaches, one No. 1 Pullman Coach Composite, and set of Rails requiring a space measuring 5 ft. 4 in. by 4 ft. 6 in. One of the rails is a Brake and Reverse Rail, by means of which the train may be braked or reversed from the track. The doors of the Coaches open. The Locomotive and Tender are supplied in the correct passenger traffic colours—green for L.N.E.R., red for L.M.S.R., and dark green for G.W.R. and S.R. .. .. **Price 35/-**

The components of the No. 1 Special Passenger Train Set may be purchased separately at the following prices :—

Hornby No. 1 Special Locomotive, reversing (without Tender) .. **Price 18/-**
Hornby No. 1 Special Tender .. .. „ **3/6**
Hornby No. 1 Pullman Coach .. .. **Price 3/-**
Hornby No. 1 Pullman Coach Composite .. .. „ **3/3**

Hornby No. 1 Special Goods Train Set. This realistic and highly efficient train set contains No. 1 Special Locomotive (reversing), No. 1 Special Tender, No. 1 Wagon, Brake Van and Rails requiring a space measuring 5 ft. 4 in. by 4 ft. 6 in. One of the rails is a Brake and Reverse Rail, which enables the train to be braked or reversed from the track. The Locomotive and Tender are supplied in the regulation goods traffic colours—black for L.N.E.R., L.M.S.R., and S.R., and dark green for G.W.R. If required, the set may be obtained with Locomotive and Tender in passenger traffic colours—green for L.N.E.R., red for L.M.S.R., and dark green for G.W.R. and S.R. **Price 32/6**

The components of the Hornby No. 1 Special Goods Train Set may be purchased separately at the following prices :—

Hornby No. 1 Special Locomotive, reversing (without Tender) .. **Price 18/-**
Hornby No. 1 Special Tender .. .. „ **3/6**
Hornby Brake Van .. .. **Price 3/6**
Hornby No. 1 Wagon .. .. „ **1/9**

The prices of Hornby Rails, Points and Crossings are specified on page 41.

HORNBY TRAINS

CLOCKWORK TRAIN SETS

Gauge 0, 1¼ in.

Hornby No. 2 Mixed Goods Train Set. This handsome Goods Train Set consists of No. 2 Special Tank Locomotive (reversing), Hornby No. 1 Wagon, Cattle Truck No. 1, Petrol Tank Wagon, Brake Van, and set of Rails requiring a space measuring 5 ft. 4 in. by 4 ft. 6 in. One of the rails is a Brake and Reverse Rail by means of which the train may be braked or reversed from the track. The Locomotive is supplied in the regulation goods traffic colours—black for L.N.E.R., L.M.S.R., and S.R., and dark green for G.W.R. If required, the set may be obtained with Locomotive in passenger traffic colours—green for L.N.E.R., red for L.M.S.R., and dark green for G.W.R. and S.R. **Price 40/-**

The components of the Hornby No. 2 Mixed Goods Set may be purchased separately at the following prices :—

Hornby No. 2 Special Tank Locomotive (reversing) .. .. **Price 25/-**

Hornby Wagon No. 1 .. .. **Price 1/9** **Brake Van** .. .. „ 3/6

Petrol Tank Wagon .. .. „ 2/6 **Cattle Truck No. 1** .. .. „ 3/-

Hornby Metropolitan Train Sets

The Locomotive and Coaches of the Hornby Metropolitan Train Set are modelled on the electric passenger rolling stock of the London Metropolitan Railway. The set is available with either clockwork or 6-volt electric locomotive. Details of the former are given below ; the latter is described on page 22.

Hornby Metropolitan Train Set C. This popular set contains a powerful Clockwork Locomotive (reversing), two Metropolitan C Coaches and set of Rails requiring a space measuring 6 ft. 3 in. by 4 ft. 6 in. A Brake and Reverse Rail is included, by means of which the train may be braked or reversed from the track. The train is well designed and is richly finished in correct colours .. .. **Price 45/-**

The components of the set may be purchased separately at the following prices :—

Metropolitan Clockwork Locomotive C (reversing) .. **Price 22/6** **Metropolitan Coach C** .. .. **Price 8/6**

The prices of Hornby Rails, Points and Crossings are specified on page 41.

HORNBY TRAINS

Gauge 0, 1¼ in.

CLOCKWORK TRAIN SETS

Hornby No. 3C Riviera "Blue" Passenger Train Set. The Hornby No. 3C Riviera "Blue" Train is a model of the famous express that runs regularly between Calais and the Mediterranean Coast. It is available with either Clockwork or 6-volt Electric Locomotive. Details of the Electric Train Set are given on page 22.

The No. 3C Clockwork Riviera "Blue" Train Set contains Clockwork Locomotive (reversing), Riviera "Blue" Tender, Riviera "Blue" Dining Car, Riviera "Blue" Sleeping Car, and set of Rails requiring a space measuring 6 ft. 3 in. by 4 ft. 6 in. A Brake and Reverse Rail is included, by means of which the train may be either braked or reversed from the track. The Locomotive, Tender and Coaches are enamelled in the correct colours of the Riviera "Blue" Train .. .. **Price 62/6**

The components of the Hornby Clockwork Riviera "Blue" Train Set may be purchased separately at the following prices :—

Hornby No. 3C Riviera "Blue" Locomotive (reversing) .. **Price 27/6**
Hornby No. 3 Riviera "Blue" Tender .. .. .. ,, **4/6**
Hornby Riviera "Blue" Dining Car .. .. **Price 14/-**
Hornby Riviera "Blue" Sleeping Car .. .. ,, **14/-**

Hornby No. 2 Special Pullman Sets

The Locomotives and Tenders in this splendid series of Hornby Train Sets are "true-to-type." They are models of famous types in the services of the leading railway companies, as described below. Each Locomotive is fitted with a powerful clockwork mechanism that gives great length of run and enables big loads to be drawn with ease.

Hornby No. 2 Special Pullman Set, L.N.E.R. (as illustrated above). This set contains No. 2 Special Locomotive (reversing), No. 2 Special Tender, No. 2 Special Pullman Coach, No. 2 Special Pullman Coach Composite, and set of Rails requiring a space measuring 5 ft. 4 in. by 4 ft. 6 in. One of the rails is a Brake and Reverse Rail by means of which the train may be braked or reversed from the track. The Locomotive, which is enamelled in green, is named "Yorkshire," and is a model of the famous "Shire" class. **Price 67/6**

Hornby No. 2 Special Pullman Set, L.M.S.R. The contents of this set are as those of the No. 2 Special Pullman Set, L.N.E.R. The Locomotive is enamelled in dark red and numbered "1185." It is a model of the L.M.S.R. "Standard Compound" class locomotives, which are not named .. .. **Price 67/6**

Hornby No. 2 Special Pullman Set, G.W.R. The contents of this set are as those of the No. 2 Special Pullman Set, L.N.E.R. The Locomotive, which is enamelled in Great Western green, is named "County of Bedford." It is a model of the well-known "County" class .. .. **Price 67/6**

Hornby No. 2 Special Pullman Set, S.R. The contents of this set are similar to those of the No. 2 Special Pullman Set, L.N.E.R. The Locomotive is enamelled in green and numbered "A 759." It is a model of the "L1" class locomotives, which are not named. The Tender is also numbered "A 759" .. .. **Price 67/6**

The components of the No. 2 Special Pullman Sets may be purchased separately at the following prices :—

Hornby No. 2 Special Locomotive, reversing (without Tender), L.N.E.R., L.M.S.R., G.W.R., or S.R. .. .. **Price 27/6**
Hornby No. 2 Special Tender .. **Price 6/6** **Hornby No. 2 Special Pullman Coach Composite** .. **Price 16/-** **Hornby No. 2 Special Pullman Coach** .. **Price 15/-**

The prices of Hornby Rails, Points and Crossings are specified on page 41.

HORNBY TRAINS

CLOCKWORK TRAIN SETS

Gauge 0, 1¼ in.

Hornby No. 3C Train Sets

These Train Sets are distinctive in design and are beautifully enamelled in correct colours. Each Locomotive carries the name of a famous British locomotive on the front wheel guard at each side. All the doors of the Coaches open. The trains in this Series are "Cornish Riviera" (G.W.R.), "Flying Scotsman" (L.N.E.R.), "Royal Scot" (L.M.S.R.), and "Golden Arrow" (S.R.). In each case the Train Set is available with either Clockwork or 6-volt Electric Locomotive. Particulars of the 6-volt Electric Sets are given on page 22.

Hornby No. 3C Train Sets (Clockwork) contain a No. 3C Clockwork Locomotive (reversing), No. 2 Special Tender, No. 2 Special Pullman Coach, No. 2 Special Pullman Coach Composite, and set of Rails requiring a space measuring 6 ft. 3 in. by 4 ft. 6 in. A Brake and Reverse Rail is included, by means of which the train may be braked or reversed from the track.

Hornby No. 3C Train Set (Clockwork), "Cornish Riviera" (G.W.R.), "Flying Scotsman" (L.N.E.R.), "Royal Scot" (L.M.S.R.) or "Golden Arrow" (S.R.) .. .. Price 67/6

The components of the No. 3C Train Sets may be purchased separately at the following prices :—

Hornby No. 3C Locomotive, "Caerphilly Castle" (G.W.R.), "Flying Scotsman" (L.N.E.R.), "Royal Scot" (L.M.S.R.) or "Lord Nelson," (S.R.) (without Tender) .. .. Price 27/6

Hornby No. 2 Special Tender, L.M.S.R., G.W.R. or L.N.E.R. .. .. Price 6/6

Hornby No. 2 Special Tender, S.R. No. E850 .. .. Price 6/6

Hornby No. 2 Special Pullman Coach .. .. Price 15/-

Hornby No. 2 Special Pullman Coach Composite .. .. Price 16/-

HORNBY CLOCKWORK LOCOMOTIVES

On this and the two following pages are illustrated all the Clockwork Locomotives in the Hornby System. These include types suitable for every kind of model railway traffic. The M Series are splendid for all-round work on small layouts. Light traffic is well catered for by No. O and No. 1 Locomotives, and for heavier duties there are the No. 1 Specials. For express services the No. 2 Special and No. 3C Locomotives are ideal. The various Tank Locomotives are useful for all short-distance traffic.

MO LOCOMOTIVE

Non-reversing. Available in either red or green.

Price 2/9

M3 TANK LOCOMOTIVE

L.M.S.R. illustrated

Reversing. Available in red with L.M.S.R. lettering, or green with L.N.E.R., G.W.R. or S.R. lettering.

Price 7/6

M1/2 LOCOMOTIVE

Reversing. Available in either red or green.

Price 4/6

The prices of Hornby Rails, Points and Crossings are specified on page 41.

Gauge 0, 1¼ in.

CLOCKWORK LOCOMOTIVES

HORNBY No. O LOCOMOTIVE

L.M.S.R. Passenger illustrated

Reversing. Available in the goods or passenger traffic colours of the L.M.S.R., L.N.E.R., G.W.R. and S.R.

Price 11/6

HORNBY No. 1 LOCOMOTIVE

G.W.R. illustrated

Reversing. Available in the goods or passenger traffic colours of the L.M.S.R., L.N.E.R., G.W.R. and S.R

Price 14/-

HORNBY No. 1 TANK LOCOMOTIVE

L.M.S.R. Goods illustrated

Reversing. Available in the goods or passenger traffic colours of the L.M.S.R., L.N.E.R., G.W.R. and S.R.

Price 13/6

HORNBY No. 1 SPECIAL TANK LOCOMOTIVE

S.R. Passenger illustrated

Reversing. Available in the goods or passenger traffic colours of the L.M.S.R., L.N.E.R., G.W.R. and S.R.

Price 18/-

HORNBY No. LEC 1 LOCOMOTIVE

Reversing. This locomotive is modelled on the type in use on the Swiss Federal Railways.

Price 15/-

HORNBY No. 1 SPECIAL LOCOMOTIVE

L.M.S.R. Goods illustrated

Reversing. Available in the goods or passenger traffic colours of the L.M.S.R., L.N.E.R., G.W.R., and S.R.

Price 18/-

The prices of Hornby Rails, Points and Crossings are specified on page 41.

CLOCKWORK LOCOMOTIVES

Gauge 0, 1¼ in.

HORNBY No. 3C LOCOMOTIVE

S.R. " Lord Nelson " illustrated

Reversing. The Locomotives in this series are modelled on the following famous British locomotives :—" Caerphilly Castle" (G.W.R.), " Flying Scotsman " (L.N.E.R.), " Royal Scot " (L.M.S.R.), " Lord Nelson " (S.R.). They are all beautifully finished in the correct colours of their prototypes.

Price 27/6

HORNBY No. 2 SPECIAL LOCOMOTIVE

G.W.R. " County of Bedford " illustrated

Reversing. The No. 2 Special Locomotives are " true to type." They are models of the following locomotives in the services of the leading railway companies: L.M.S.R. Numbered " 1185 " (" Standard Compound " class), G.W.R. " County of Bedford " (" County" class), L.N.E.R. "Yorkshire " (" Shire " class), S.R. Numbered " A759 " (" L1 " class).

Price 27/6

HORNBY No. 3C RIVIERA " BLUE " LOCOMOTIVE

Reversing. This is modelled on the Locomotive that hauls the famous Riviera " Blue " Train that runs regularly between Calais and the Mediterranean Coast

Price 27/6

HORNBY METROPOLITAN LOCOMOTIVE C

Reversing. This Locomotive is modelled on the type employed on the London Metropolitan Railway. It is a very handsome model .. .. .. **Price 22/6**

HORNBY No. 2 SPECIAL TANK LOCOMOTIVE *G.W.R. illustrated*

Reversing. Available in the goods or passenger traffic colours of the L.M.S.R., L.N.E.R., G.W.R. and S.R. .. .. **Price 25/-**

The separate prices of Hornby Rails, Points and Crossings are specified on page 41.

HORNBY TRAINS

Gauge 0, 1¼ in.

6-volt ELECTRIC TRAIN SETS

The Hornby Electric Train Sets and Locomotives are perfect in design, workmanship and efficiency. They have withstood the severest tests, and each one carries the Hornby guarantee. They are simple and perfectly safe to use, and are remarkably realistic in operation.

The 6-volt Electric Locomotives and Trains, with the exception of the No. 1 Electric Tank, may be operated either from a 6-volt Accumulator or through a Transformer direct from the mains, provided that the supply is alternating current. The No. 1 Electric Tank has a permanent magnet motor and can only be run from a 6-volt Accumulator.

Hornby No. E3/6 Train Sets (6-volt) contain an Electric Locomotive (6-volt), No. 2 Special Tender, No. 2 Special Pullman Coach, No. 2 Special Pullman Coach Composite, Resistance Controller and set of Electrical Rails requiring a space measuring 4 ft. 6 in. square. In the case of the Riviera "Blue" Train Set a Dining Car, a Sleeping Car, and a No. 3 Riviera Tender are included in place of the No. 2 Special Pullman Coach, No. 2 Special Pullman Coach Composite, and No. 2 Special Tender.

Hornby No. E3/6 Train Set (6-volt Electric), "Cornish Riviera" (G.W.R.), "Flying Scotsman" (L.N.E.R.), "Royal Scot" (L.M.S.R., as illustrated) or "Golden Arrow" (S.R.) .. .. .. **Price 85/-**

Hornby No. E3/6 Riviera "Blue" Train Set (6-volt Electric) .. .. .. **„ 80/-**

The components of the above Train Sets may be purchased separately at the following prices :—

Hornby No. E3/6 Locomotive (without Tender), "Caerphilly Castle," "Flying Scotsman," "Royal Scot," or "Lord Nelson" .. .. **Price 40/-**

Hornby No. E3/6 Locomotive, Riviera "Blue" (without Tender) .. .. **„ 40/-**

Hornby No. 2 Special Tender, L.M.S.R., G.W.R., or L.N.E.R. .. .. **„ 6/6**

Hornby No. 2 Special Tender, S.R. No. E850 .. .. **Price 6/6**

Hornby No. 3 Tender, Riviera "Blue" .. .. **„ 4/6**

Hornby No. 2 Special Pullman Coach .. .. **„ 15/-**

Resistance Controller .. .. **„ 3/9**

Hornby No. 2 Special Pullman Coach Composite .. .. **„ 16/-**

Hornby Riviera "Blue" Dining Car .. .. **„ 14/-**

Hornby Riviera "Blue" Sleeping Car .. .. **„ 14/-**

For prices of Accumulators and Transformers, see page 25

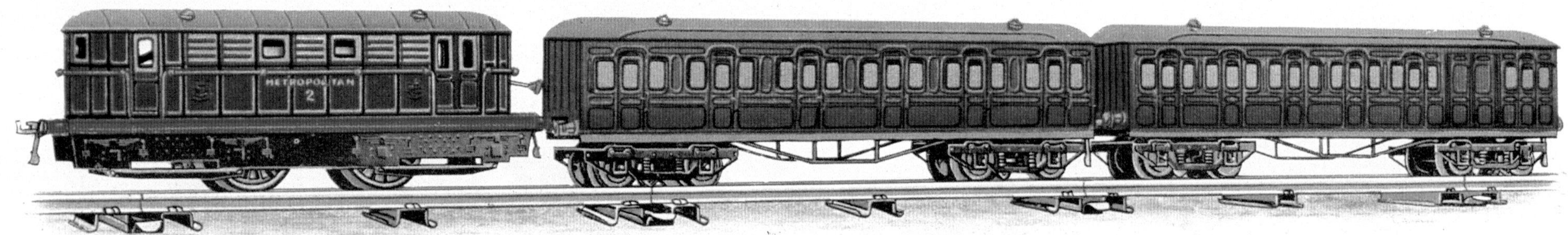

Hornby Metropolitan Train Set (6-volt)

The contents of the Hornby Metropolitan Train Set are Metropolitan Locomotive, two Metropolitan Coaches, Resistance Controller, and set of electrical rails requiring a space measuring 4 ft. 6 in. square. The 6-volt Electric Motor in the Locomotive may be operated from a 6-volt Accumulator or direct from the mains (alternating current only) through a Transformer capable of supplying 2·5 amps. at 9 volts .. .. .. **Price 85/-**

The Locomotive, Coaches and Resistance Controller contained in this Set may be purchased separately at the following prices :—

Metropolitan Electric Locomotive .. **Price 47/6** Metropolitan Coach .. **Price 13/-** Resistance Controller .. **Price 3/9**

The separate prices of Hornby Rails, Points and Crossings are specified on page 41.

HORNBY TRAINS

20-volt ELECTRIC TRAIN SETS

Gauge 0, 1¼ in.

The 20-volt Train Sets illustrated and described below are the latest additions to the Hornby range of electric trains. These trains are most conveniently operated through a 20-volt Transformer from the mains supply (alternating current only). The Transformer, as regards voltage and frequency, must correspond to the supply with which it is connected.

Hornby LST 1/20 Tank Goods Train Set (20-volt Electric). This attractive Electric Goods Set consists of a 20-volt Electric Tank Locomotive with Headlamp, No. 1 Wagon, Petrol Tank Wagon, Brake Van, Terminal Connecting Plate, and set of electric rails requiring a space measuring 4 ft. 6 in. square. The Locomotive is supplied in the regulation goods traffic colours—black for L.N.E.R., L.M.S.R. and S.R., and dark green for G.W.R. If required, the set may be obtained with Locomotive in passenger traffic colours—green for L.N.E.R., red for L.M.S.R., and dark green for G.W.R. and S.R. .. .. **Price 40/-**

The components of the LST 1/20 Tank Goods Train Set may be purchased separately at the following prices :

Hornby No. LST 1/20 Tank Locomotive (20-volt Electric) .. Price 25/- No. 1 Wagon .. Price 1/9 Petrol Tank Wagon .. Price 2/6 Brake Van .. Price 3/6

Hornby LST 2/20 Mixed Goods Train Set (20-volt Electric). This realistic Electric Goods Set consists of a 20-volt Electric Tank Locomotive with Headlamp, No. 1 Wagon, No. 1 Cattle Truck, Petrol Tank Wagon, Brake Van, Terminal Connecting Plate, and set of electric Rails requiring a space measuring 4 ft. 6 in. square. The Locomotive is supplied in the regulation goods traffic colours—black for L.N.E.R., L.M.S.R., and S.R., and dark green for G.W.R. If required, the set may be obtained with Locomotive in passenger traffic colours—green for L.N.E.R., red for L.M.S.R., and dark green for G.W.R. and S.R. .. .. **Price 55/-**

The components of the LST 2/20 Mixed Goods Train Set (20-volt electric) may be purchased separately at the following prices :

Hornby LST 2/20 Special Tank Locomotive (20-volt Electric) .. .. Price 37/6
No. 1 Wagon .. .. Price 1/9 Brake Van .. .. .. „ 3/6
Petrol Tank Wagon .. .. .. „ 2/6 No. 1 Cattle Truck .. .. .. „ 3/-

For prices of Hornby Rails, Points and Crossings, see page 41.

HORNBY TRAINS

Gauge 0, 1¼ in.

6-VOLT ELECTRIC LOCOMOTIVES

The 6-volt Locomotives, with the exception of the No. 1 Tank Locomotive (6-volt P.M. type), may be operated either from a 6-volt Accumulator or through a Transformer (capable of supplying 2·5 amps. at 9 volts) direct from the mains, provided that the supply is alternating current.

HORNBY No. E3/6 ELECTRIC LOCOMOTIVE (6-volt)

A well-designed and popular Locomotive, modelled on the locomotives of the following famous classes :—" Caerphilly Castle " (G.W.R.), " Flying Scotsman " (L.N.E.R.), " Royal Scot " (L.M.S.R., as illustrated), " Lord Nelson " (S.R.), and the Continental Riviera " Blue Train " Locomotive .. .. **Price 40/-**

HORNBY No. 2 ELECTRIC TANK LOCOMOTIVE (6-volt)

This fine electric Locomotive is powerfully built and is perfect in design. In every respect it is a very fine model, and it is available finished in the goods or passenger traffic colours of the L.M.S.R., L.N.E.R., G.W.R., or S.R. The realistic appearance and beautiful lines may be judged from the above illustration of the G.W.R. locomotive. **Price 37/6**

HORNBY No. 1 TANK LOCOMOTIVE (6-volt P.M. Type). This strongly built Locomotive is of the Permanent Magnet type and must be operated from a 6-volt accumulator. The unique feature is that it can be stopped, restarted, reversed and the speed varied by the operation of levers at the side of the track. Available in the passenger or goods traffic colours of the L.M.S.R. (passenger illustrated), L.N.E.R., G.W.R., or S.R. It is supplied with a Terminal Connecting Plate, Speed and Reverse Control Switch and 3 ft. of flex .. .. **Price 32/6**

Separate prices of No. 1 Tank Locomotive (6-volt. P.M. Type) Components :—

Locomotive .. 25/- **Speed and Reverse Control Switch** .. 7/6
Terminal Connecting Plate 1/6

Combined Rail Gauge, Screwdriver and Spanner for Hornby Locomotives Price 3d.

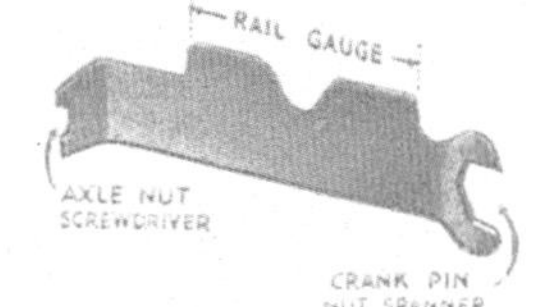

HORNBY METROPOLITAN LOCOMOTIVE (6-volt)

This is a model of one of the famous Metropolitan Railway Locomotives. It is richly finished in correct colours, and is an exceptionally attractive model Locomotive. **Price 47/6**

HORNBY TRAINS

20-VOLT ELECTRIC LOCOMOTIVES

Gauge 0, $1\frac{1}{4}$ in.

Hornby 20-volt Locomotives are designed to run from the mains supply, alternating current only, through a 20-volt Transformer capable of supplying 1 amp. at 20 volts. In ordering Transformers, the voltage and frequency of the mains supply must be stated in every case.

HORNBY LST M3/20 TANK LOCOMOTIVE (20-volt). This strongly built electric Locomotive is obtainable in red, lettered L.M.S., or green, lettered L.N.E.R., Great Western or Southern .. .. .. **Price 22/6**

HORNBY LE 1/20 LOCOMOTIVE (20-volt) is modelled on the type in use on the Swiss Federal Railways. It is a very handsome Locomotive .. .. **Price 26/6**

HORNBY LST 1/20 TANK LOCOMOTIVE (20-volt) is a perfectly finished model. It is obtainable in the goods or passenger traffic colours of the L.M.S.R., L.N.E.R., G.W.R. or S.R. .. .. **Price 25/-**

HORNBY LST 2/20 ELECTRIC TANK LOCOMOTIVE (20-volt). This Locomotive is exactly the same as the No. 2 Electric Tank Locomotive (6-volt) (illustrated at the top of the opposite page) except that it is wound for 20 volts instead of 6. It is available finished in the goods and passenger traffic colours of the L.M.S.R., L.N.E.R., G.W.R., or S.R. **Price 37/6**

HORNBY LE 2/20 LOCOMOTIVE (20-volt) is an exceptionally fine model. It is built to stand hard wear, and is attractively finished in a combination of pleasing colours. Two pantagraphs are fitted on the roof similar to those shown on the roof of Hornby LE 1/20 Locomotive, illustrated above .. .. **Price 33/-**

TRANSFORMERS AND ACCUMULATORS

A Meccano Transformer provides a convenient means of driving a Hornby Electric Train. There are six Transformers in the series, all of which are available for the following A.C. supplies :—100/110 volts, 50 cycles ; 200/225 volts, 50 cycles ; 225/250 volts, 50 cycles. Any of these Transformers can be specially wound for supplies other than the above.

T20 Transformer.

Resistance Controller.

No. T6 Transformer (Output 25 VA at 9 volts) for 6-volt Electric Locomotives. Fitted with a 5-stud speed regulator. **Price 21/-**

No. T6M Transformer (Output 25 VA at 9 volts) for 6-volt Electric Locomotives. This is similar to No. T6, but is not fitted with a speed regulator .. .. **Price 16/6**

No. T6A Transformer (Output 40 VA at 9/$3\frac{1}{2}$ volts) for 6-volt Electric Locomotives. Similar to No. T6, but fitted with three pairs of plug sockets. The first pair is the train-driving circuit and has a 5-stud speed regulator incorporated. The second pair gives an output at 9 volts and is not subject to control by the speed regulator. The third pair gives an output at $3\frac{1}{2}$ volts for lighting Hornby Accessories .. .. **Price 26/6**

No. T20 Transformer (Output 20 VA at 20 volts) for 20-volt Electric Locomotives. Fitted with 5-stud speed regulator. **Price 21/-**

No. T20M Transformer (Output 25 VA at 20 volts) for 20-volt Electric Locomotives. This is similar to No. T20, but is not fitted with speed regulator .. .. **Price 16/6**

No. T20A Transformer (Output 35 VA at 20 volts) for 20-volt Electric Locomotives. Fitted with three pairs of plug sockets. The first pair is the train-driving circuit and has a 5-stud speed regulator incorporated. The second pair gives an output at 20 volts, and is not subject to control by the speed regulator. The third pair is for connecting Hornby Accessories fitted for electric lighting .. .. **Price 26/6**

When ordering a Transformer the voltage and frequency of the supply must always be stated.

MECCANO ACCUMULATORS

6-volt 20 amps. Meccano Accumulator. This is specially suitable for running Hornby 6-volt Trains .. .. **Price 28/6**

2-volt 20 amps. Meccano Accumulator is supplied for converting 4-volt Accumulators to 6 volts .. .. **Price 10/6**

RESISTANCE CONTROLLER

This variable resistance enables the speed of Hornby 6-volt Trains to be regulated .. .. **Price 3/9**

6-volt 20 amps. Meccano Accumulator.

HORNBY TRAINS

Guage 0, $1\frac{1}{4}$ in.

ROLLING STOCK

THE Hornby System consists of a complete range of Rolling Stock, Railway Accessories and Rails, Points and Crossings with which the most elaborate model railway may be constructed. Every component in the Hornby Series is well designed and carefully modelled on its prototype.

BRAKE VAN, S.R. & N.E.

Enamelled in brown with white roof. Opening doors. Lettered S.R. or N.E. .. **Price 3/6**

GUARD'S VAN

Realistic design. Fitted each side with double and single opening doors. Obtainable in the colours of the L.M.S.R., L.N.E.R., G.W.R., or S.R. **Price 2/9**

BREAKDOWN VAN AND CRANE

Beautifully coloured and fitted with opening doors. The crane, which swivels about a pivot, is provided with a handle for hoisting loads. Suitable for 2 ft. radius rails only. Lettered L.M.S., N.E., G.W. or S.R. **Price 6/3**

CABOOSE, AMERICAN TYPE

This is a realistic model of the brake van used on the American railroads. Beautifully finished and appropriately coloured .. .. **Price 2/6**

TANK CAR, AMERICAN TYPE

Modelled on the type of oil tank wagon used in America. Well proportioned and beautifully finished .. .. **Price 1/9**

BOX CAR, AMERICAN TYPE

A realistic model of the type of vehicle used in American for the conveyance of luggage and perishables .. .. **Price 2/6**

BRAKE VAN, L.M.S. & G.W.

Enamelled in grey with white roof. Opening doors. Lettered L.M.S. or G.W. **Price 3/6**

BRAKE VAN, FRENCH TYPE

Lettered NORD only. Modelled on the type of brake van used in France. Beautifully finished. Opening doors .. **Price 4/-**

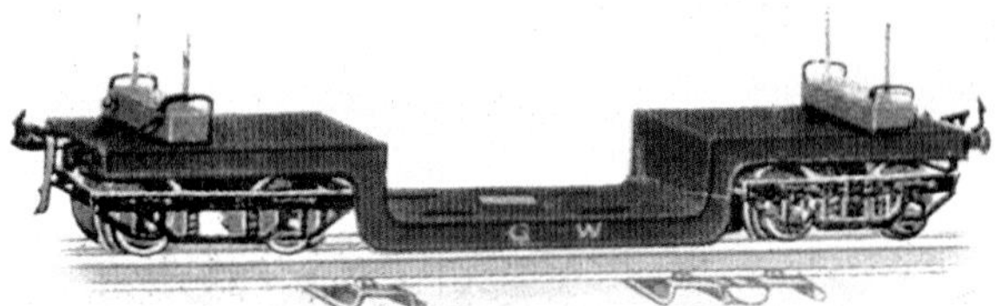

TROLLEY WAGON

Trolley Wagons are designed to carry exceptionally heavy loads, as their low-built construction necessitates only a minimum lift when loading. Fitted with four-wheel bogies, bolsters and stanchions. Suitable for 2 ft. radius rails only .. .. **Price 4/6**

HORNBY TRAINS

ROLLING STOCK

Gauge 0, 1¼ in.

No. 1 PULLMAN COACH

Distinctive in design and beautifully finished. Named " Cynthia," " Corsair " or " Niobe "
Price 3/-

No. 1 PULLMAN COACH COMPOSITE

One part of this coach is designed for passenger accommodation and the other for conveyance of luggage. Named " Ansonia " .. Price 3/3

No. 2 SPECIAL PULLMAN COACH

As supplied with No. 2 Special Pullman and No. 3 Pullman Train Sets. This splendid Coach is perfect in detail and finish. Lettered " Iolanthe," " Zenobia " and " Grosvenor." Suitable for 2-ft. radius rails only
Price 15/-

No. 2 SALOON COACH

A well-proportioned model, realistically finished in the colours of the L.N.E.R. (as illustrated) or L.M.S.R. Companies. Suitable for 2-ft. radius rails only
Price 11/6

RIVIERA " BLUE " TRAIN COACH

" Dining Car " or " Sleeping Car "

This is a beautiful model, substantially built and well finished. Suitable for 2-ft. radius rails only Price 14/-

CONTINENTAL " MITROPA" COACH No. 3

Similar in design to above. Beautifully finished in red, with white roof and lettered "Mitropa" in gold Price 14/-

No. 1 PASSENGER COACH

Realistic in design and fitted with opening doors. Lettered L.M.S., L.N.E.R., G.W.R. or S.R. Price 2/6

M1 PULLMAN COACH

Named " Marjorie," " Aurelia " or " Viking." As supplied with the M1 and M2 Passenger Train Sets .. Price 1/-

PULLMAN CAR

Imported from U.S.A. Product of Meccano Factories

American type. Green or yellow. Lettered " Washington " or " Madison " .. Price 1/6

Continental type " Mitropa " Coach No. O. Red with white roof. Lettered " Mitropa "
Price 1/6

No. 2 SPECIAL PULLMAN COACH COMPOSITE

As supplied with No. 2 Special Pullman and No. 3 Pullman Train Sets. One part is designed for passenger accommodation and the other for the conveyance of luggage. Lettered "Arcadia," "Alberta " and " Montana." Suitable for 2-ft. radius rails only .. .. Price 16/-

No. 2 PULLMAN COACH

This model is substantially built and distinctive in design. Suitable for 2-ft. radius rails only .. .. Price 11/6

HORNBY TRAINS

Gauge 0, 1¼ in.

ROLLING STOCK

CARR'S BISCUIT VAN

Finished in dark blue. The doors open
Price 3/-

JACOB'S BISCUIT VAN

Finished in brown. The doors open
Price 3/-

CRAWFORD'S BISCUIT VAN

Finished in red. The doors open
Price 3/-

"SECCOTINE" VAN

Finished in blue. The doors open
Price 3/-

No. 2 CATTLE TRUCK

Splendid twin bogie model, fitted with double doors. Suitable for 2-ft. radius rails only. Lettered L.M.S., N.E., G.W., or S.R. .. .. .. **Price 5/9**

No. 1 CATTLE TRUCK

Fitted with sliding doors. Realistically designed. Lettered L.M.S., N.E., G.W., or S.R. .. .. .. **Price 3/-**

No. 2 LUGGAGE VAN

Mounted on twin bogies, and fitted with opening doors. Suitable for 2-ft. radius rails only. Lettered L.M.S., N.E., G.W., or S.R. .. .. .. **Price 5/9**

No. 1 LUGGAGE VAN

Realistic and highly finished. Opening doors. Lettered L.M.S., N.E., G.W., or S.R. .. .. **Price 3/-**

GUNPOWDER VAN

Enamelled in red. The doors open. Lettered L.M.S., N.E., G.W., or S.R.
Price 3/-

REFRIGERATOR VAN

This is a very realistic model, fitted with opening doors. Lettered L.M.S., N.E., G.W., or S.R. .. .. **Price 3/-**

MILK TRAFFIC VAN No. 1

Fitted with sliding doors, and complete with four milk cans .. **Price 3/-**
Separate Milk Cans .. **Price 2d.** each

HORNBY TRAINS

ROLLING STOCK

Gauge 0, 1¼ in.

BANANA VAN

An attractive model. Fitted with opening doors .. .. .. **Price 3/-**

HOPPER WAGON

This wagon is unloaded by operating the handle shown. Lettered L.M.S., N.E., G.W., or S.R. .. .. **Price 3/6**

FIBRE WAGON

This is an interesting model of a type of wagon used in France and other European countries .. .. .. **Price 1/9**

SNOW PLOUGH

Runs on specially designed heavy wheels. The plough is driven from the front axle .. .. .. **Price 5/6**

FISH VAN

This is an excellent model, distinctive in design and finish. Lettered N.E. only .. .. .. **Price 2/6**

MEAT VAN

This is a very realistic model, sturdily built and well-finished. Lettered L.M.S. only .. .. **Price 2/6**

MILK TRAFFIC VAN No. O

This is a well-designed and attractively finished model. Lettered G.W. only **Price 2/6**

CADBURY'S CHOCOLATE VAN

Finished in blue, with white roof. The doors open .. .. **Price 3/-**

CRANE TRUCK

The crane swivels about a pivot, and is operated by a crank handle .. **Price 3/6**

BARREL WAGON

An interesting model of a type of wagon used on European railways .. **Price 2/9**

COAL WAGON

This is similar to Hornby Wagon No. 1. It is fitted with an embossed representation of coal .. .. **Price 2/3**

OPEN WAGON "B"

Similar to Hornby Wagon No. 1, but fitted with centre tarpaulin-supporting rail. Lettered L.M.S., N.E., G.W., or S.R. **Price 2/-**

Gauge 0, 1¼ in.

ROLLING STOCK

MILK TANK WAGON
"UNITED DAIRIES"

A very realistic model .. **Price 6/-**

PETROL TANK WAGON
"PRATTS"

Realistic in design and appropriately coloured .. .. .. **Price 2/6**

PETROL TANK WAGON
"SHELL"

Realistic in design and appropriately coloured .. .. .. **Price 2/6**

PETROL TANK WAGON
"B.P."

Realistic in design and appropriately coloured .. .. .. **Price 2/6**

PETROL TANK WAGON
"REDLINE-GLICO"

Realistic in design and appropriately coloured .. .. .. **Price 2/6**

OIL TANK WAGON "CASTROL"

An attractive model, beautifully coloured **Price 2/6**

OIL TANK WAGON
"MOBILOIL"

An attractive and realistic model **Price 2/6**

BITUMEN TANK WAGON
"COLAS"

This model represents the type of wagon employed by Colas Products, Ltd. **Price 5/3**

CEMENT WAGON

Fitted with opening door in roof **Price 2/9**

ROTARY TIPPING WAGON

The body of the wagon rotates and will tip in all directions .. **Price 2/6**

SIDE TIPPING WAGON
ROBERT HUDSON, LTD.

Arranged to tip to either side of the track **Price 2/-**

GAS CYLINDER WAGON

Realistic in design and appropriately coloured .. .. .. **Price 2/6**

ROLLING STOCK

TIMBER WAGON No. 1

Beautifully enamelled. Complete with load of timber .. .. **Price 1/6**

LUMBER WAGON No. 1

Fitted with bolsters and stanchions for log transport .. .. **Price 1/9**

COVERED WAGON (FRENCH TYPE)

This attractive-looking Wagon is fitted with a special frame and is supplied complete with sheet. French type, lettered "NORD."

Price 3/-

WAGON, FRENCH TYPE

Lettered "NORD" only. Modelled on type of goods wagon used in France

Price 3/3

HORNBY WAGON No. 1

As supplied with No. 1 Goods and No. 2 Mixed Goods Sets. Obtainable finished in grey and black, lettered L.M.S., N.E., or G.W. Also in brown and black, lettered S.R.

Price 1/9

TARPAULIN SHEETS

Strongly made. Lettered L.M.S., N.E., G.W., or S.R.

Price 3d.

WINE WAGON

DOUBLE WINE WAGON

Modelled on the double-barrelled type of wine wagon used in France .. .. **Price 5/-**

HORNBY WAGON No. 0

As supplied with Hornby No. 0 Goods Set. Available lettered L.M.S., N.E., G.W., or S.R. **Price 1/6**

LUMBER WAGON No. 2

Fitted with bolsters and stanchions, and complete with logs. Suitable for 2-ft. radius rails only .. **Price 3/6**

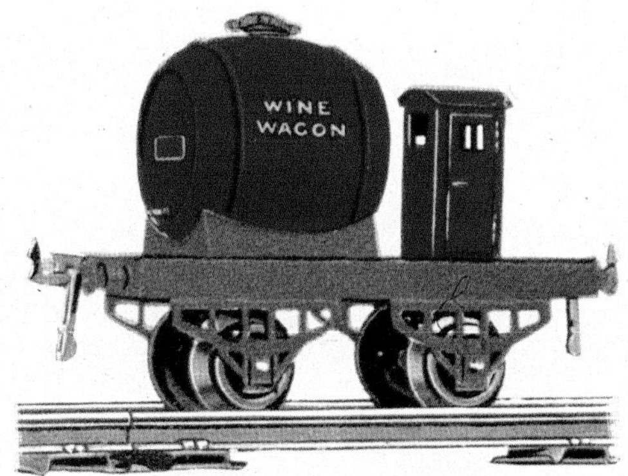

SINGLE WINE WAGON

This interesting model represents the single-barrel type of wine wagon used in France

Price 3/6

TIMBER WAGON No. 2

Highly finished. Complete with load of timber. Suitable for 2-ft. radius rails only .. .. .. **Price 3/-**

HORNBY TRAINS

Gauge 0, $1\frac{1}{4}$ in.

ACCESSORIES

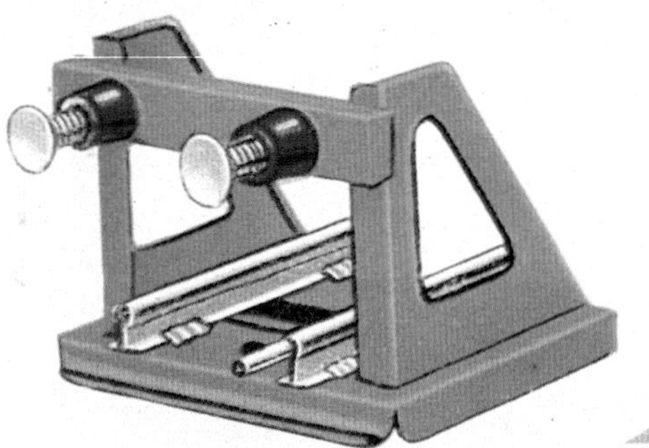

BUFFER STOPS No. 1
(Spring Type)
May be connected to all Hornby Rails .. .. **Price 1/-**

BUFFER STOPS No. 1E
Similar to above, but wired and fitted for electric lighting .. **Price 2/-**

RAILWAY STATION No. 1
This Station is a well-made model, richly finished in colours. By placing one or more of these stations at intervals along the track, and using Station No. 2 (illustrated below) as the main terminus, a very realistic effect is obtained.
Length $16\frac{3}{4}$ in. Width 6 in. Height 6 in. .. .. **Price 6/-**

BUFFER STOPS No. 2
(Hydraulic Type)
Realistic in design and very stoutly built .. .. .. **Price 5/6**

BUFFER STOPS No. 2E
Similar to above, but wired and fitted for electric lighting **Price 7/-**

VIADUCT

Constructed in three sections, which may be easily disassembled	**Price 7/-**
Centre section only	„ 4/9
The Viaduct is also made with electrical rails in position for electric tracks	„ 8/-
Centre section only (with electrical rails)	„ 5/3

TUNNEL (Metal)
Beautifully designed and finished in colours .. .. .. **Price 5/9**

TURNTABLE No. 1	Price 2/9
TURNTABLE No. 2 (as illustrated)	„ 4/6
TURNTABLE No. 2E (Electrical)	„ 8/6

WINDSOR

WINDSOR

RAILWAY STATION No. 2
This excellent model is constructed in three sections, which are detachable. Length 2 ft. 9 in. Width 6 in. Height 7 in. **Price 10/-**

RAILWAY STATION No. 2E
Similar to Railway Station No. 2, but wired and fitted for electric lighting. **Price 12/6**

HORNBY TRAINS

ACCESSORIES

Gauge 0, $1\frac{1}{4}$ in.

Engine Shed No. 2.

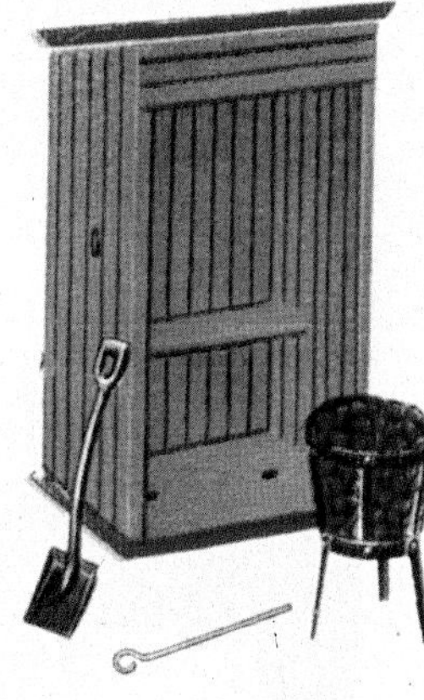

ENGINE SHED No. 1
Will accommodate Locomotives and Tenders of the M Series, and No. 1 Tank and No. 1 Special Tank Locomotives
Price 15/-

ENGINE SHED No. E1E
Similar to above, but wired and fitted for electric lighting .. .. **Price 18/6**

ENGINE SHED No. 2
Will accommodate any Locomotive and Tender in the Hornby Series **Price 22/6**

ENGINE SHED No. E2E
Similar to above, but wired and fitted for electric lighting .. .. **Price 26/-**

SIGNAL CABIN No. 1
Price 2/9

SIGNAL CABIN No. 2
(as illustrated) **Price 4/6**
Roof and back of Signal Cabin No. 2 open to allow a Hornby Control Lever Frame to be fitted inside.

SIGNAL CABIN No.2E
Wired and fitted for electric lighting.
Price 5/6

RAILWAY ACCESSORIES No. 7
Watchman's Hut, Brazier, Shovel, and Poker.
Price 1/6

M LEVEL CROSSING
Suitable for single track, with rails in position
Price 1/6

LEVEL CROSSING No. 1
(*Illustrated above*) Suitable for single track, with rails in position .. .. .. **Price 3/6**

LEVEL CROSSING No. E1 (Electrical)
Price 4/-

LEVEL CROSSING No. E1E
Wired and fitted for electric lighting .. **Price 7/-**

LEVEL CROSSING No. 2
(*Illustrated below*) Suitable for a double track, with rails in position .. .. .. **Price 5/6**

LEVEL CROSSING No. E2 (Electrical)
Price 7/6

LEVEL CROSSING No. E2E
Wired and fitted for electric lighting .. **Price 11/-**

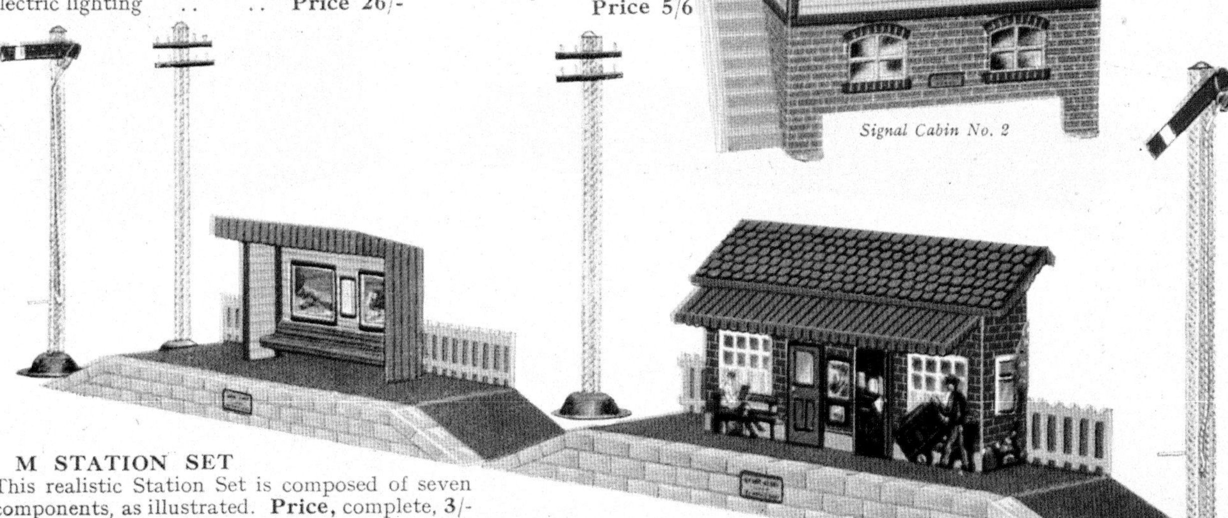

Signal Cabin No. 2

Level Crossing No. 2.

M STATION SET
This realistic Station Set is composed of seven components, as illustrated. **Price,** complete, **3/-**

The components may be purchased separately at the following prices:—

M Wayside Station .. **Price 10d.**
M Signal Box .. .. „ **4d.**
M Signal .. .. .. „ **4d.**
M Station .. .. .. **Price 1/-**
M Telegraph Pole No. 1 „ **3d.**

SHUNTER'S POLE
Price 3d.

HORNBY TRAINS

Gauge 0, 1¼ in.

ACCESSORIES

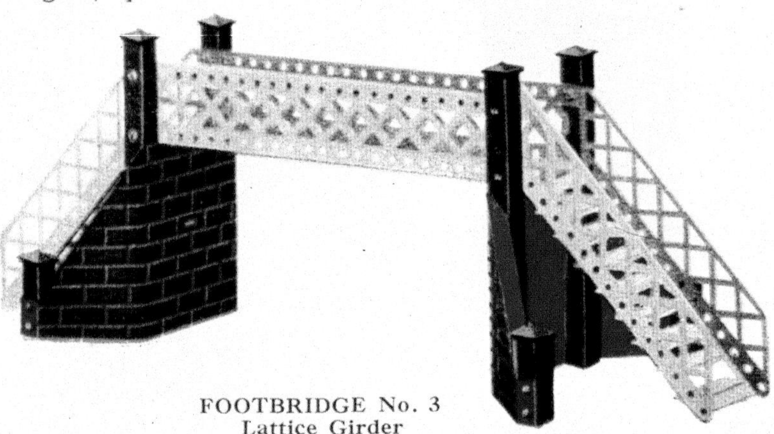

FOOTBRIDGE No. 3
Lattice Girder

Constructional type, strong and well proportioned. Meccano strips for signals, etc., may be secured to the sides of the bridge.
Price 10/6

GOODS PLATFORM

Length 16¾ in. Height 6¾ in. Width 6 in. The crane at the end of the Platform revolves on its base. It is fitted with a crank and ratchet mechanism for controlling the load .. .. **Price 12/6**

GOODS PLATFORM E

Similar to the above, but wired and fitted for electric lighting. **Price 15/-**

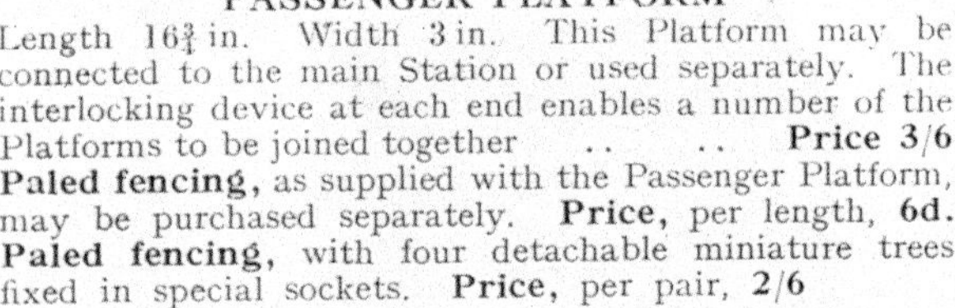

PASSENGER PLATFORM

Length 16¾ in. Width 3 in. This Platform may be connected to the main Station or used separately. The interlocking device at each end enables a number of the Platforms to be joined together .. .. **Price 3/6**

Paled fencing, as supplied with the Passenger Platform, may be purchased separately. **Price,** per length, **6d.**

Paled fencing, with four detachable miniature trees fixed in special sockets. **Price,** per pair, **2/6**

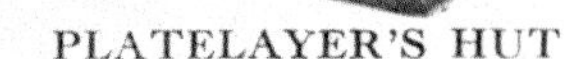

PLATELAYER'S HUT

This is an extremely attractive accessory, beautifully designed and finished .. **Price 2/-**

ISLAND PLATFORM

Length 32¼ in. Height 6¾ in. Width 3 in. The Ramps at either end are detachable, and if desired the Platform may be connected to the main Station .. .. **Price 7/6**

Ramps similar to those fitted to the Island Platform may be purchased separately. **Price,** per pair, **2/6**

ISLAND PLATFORM E. Similar to the above, but wired and fitted for electric lighting .. .. .. **Price 9/-**

HORNBY TRAINS

ACCESSORIES

Gauge 0, $1\frac{1}{4}$ in.

RAILWAY ACCESSORIES No. 1
Miniature Luggage and Truck.
Price 1/6

OIL CAN No. 2 ("K" Type)
Polished Copper
This Miniature Oil Can operates perfectly. The oil is ejected drop by drop by depressing the valve.
Price 3/6

OIL CAN No. 1
This strongly made Miniature Oil Can functions perfectly. **Price 6d.**

LUBRICATING OIL
Specially prepared for Hornby Trains, Rolling Stock and Accessories. **Price,** per bottle, **6d.**

GRAPHITE GREASE
An ideal lubricant for the springs of Hornby Locomotives and Hornby Speed Boats, Meccano and Aero Clockwork Motors, and Meccano Motor Cars. **Price,** per tube, **6d.**

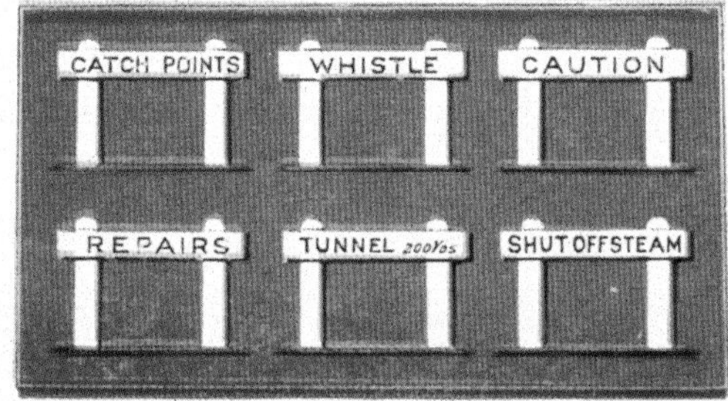

RAILWAY ACCESSORIES No. 8
Notice Boards. **Price 2/3**

RAILWAY ACCESSORIES No. 2
Milk Cans and Truck. **Price 1/6**

RAILWAY ACCESSORIES No. 4
Railway Accessories No. 4 is a composite set consisting of all the pieces contained in Railway Accessories Nos. 1, 2 and 3. **Price 3/9**

STATION or FIELD HOARDING
This is a realistic accessory, suitable for placing on the station platform or in the fields adjacent to the track.
Price 8d.

POSTER BOARDS
To carry Hornby Miniature Posters. Provided with lugs for attachment to Paled Fencing, etc. Packet of 6 (3 large, 3 small), **Price 6d.**

POSTERS IN MINIATURE
These posters are reproductions of familiar national advertisements. They are intended to be pasted on the Station Hoardings or the Poster Boards described above, and are beautifully printed in full colours. Packet of 51, **Price 6d.**

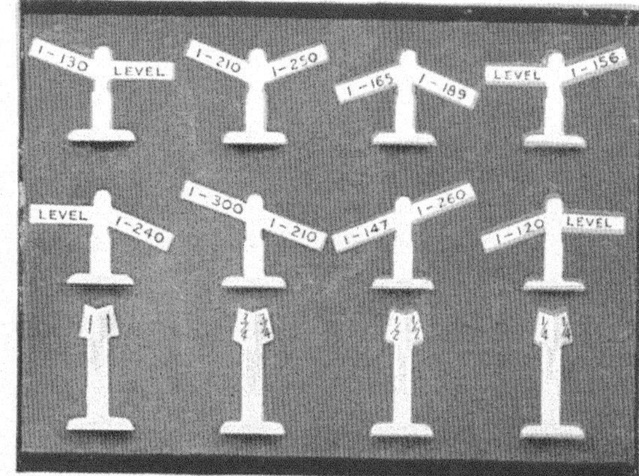

RAILWAY ACCESSORIES No. 5
Gradient Posts and Mile Posts. **Price 2/-**

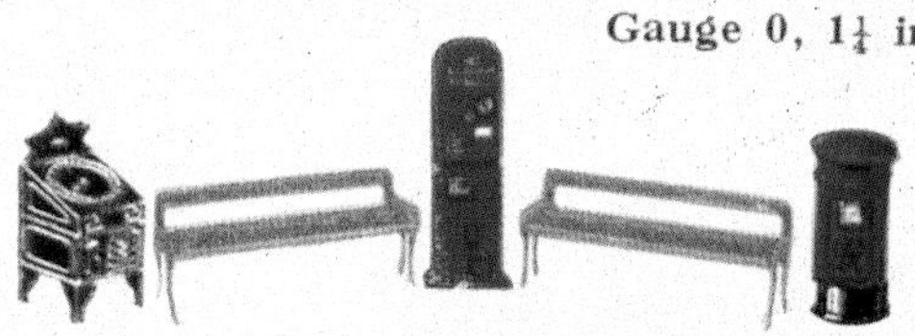

RAILWAY ACCESSORIES No. 3
Platform Machines, etc. **Price 1/6**

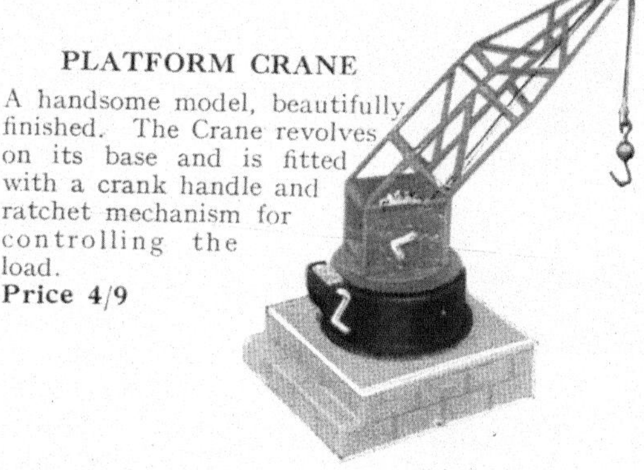

PLATFORM CRANE
A handsome model, beautifully finished. The Crane revolves on its base and is fitted with a crank handle and ratchet mechanism for controlling the load.
Price 4/9

MANSELL WHEELS
These wheels are die-cast and are correctly designed. They may be fitted to Hornby Vans, Coaches, etc.
Price, per pair, **4d.**
Die-cast Spoked Wheels for fitting to Hornby Wagons, Tenders, etc. **Price,** per pair, **3d.**

RAILWAY ACCESSORIES No. 9
Station Name Boards. **Price 2/6**

Gauge 0, 1¼ in.

COUNTRYSIDE SECTIONS

Copyright. Provisional Patent No. 4655/32

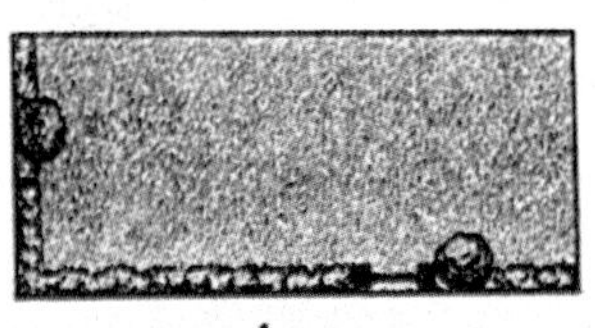

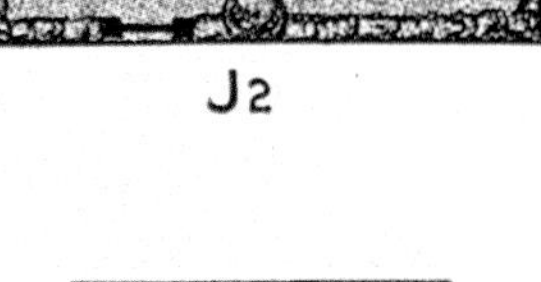

The Hornby Countryside Sections provide model railway owners for the first time with scenery in a ready-made form that is suitable for any kind of 2 ft. radius layout. The accompanying illustrations show the shapes of the various components and give a good idea of the wide range of effects that can be produced by means of them.

The space enclosed by a plain circular track is filled by the F Sections, and the G1 and G2 Sections. In an oval, Sections J1 and J2 are laid opposite the full straight rails, but if a half-rail is used, the narrow Section J3 is required. The No. 1 Level Crossing necessitates the use of road Section H. This imitates the surface of the average road in a realistic manner, and it fits under the approach to the Crossing. Packing piece R preserves the level on the opposite side. Triangular Sections K1 and K2 fit between the arms of the right-angle Crossing. Sections L1 and L2, M1 and M2, are available for the curved outer edges of the track.

The natural appearance of the Sections is their greatest charm. The fields represent rich meadowland with hedges of appropriately darker green, and some of the Sections have five-barred gates leading from field to field. These gates, which are made to open, are painted white, and look very attractive against the green of the fields and hedges. Trees to represent oaks are included with all the Sections except J3 and R, and are arranged to be mounted in special sockets provided in the fields and roads. In addition, these trees, and also poplars, are available separately mounted in neat bases, and the poplars can be obtained in sets of four with a section of Paled Fencing (see page 40).

Splendid effects may be obtained by inserting the Hornby miniature animals (Modelled Miniatures No. 2, see page 41) as shown in the accompanying illustration.

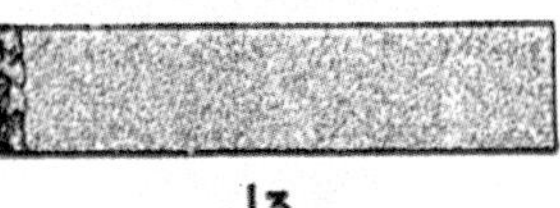

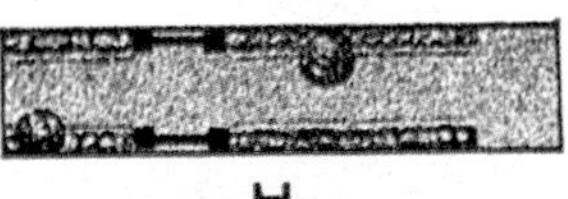

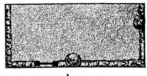

PRICE LIST OF COUNTRYSIDE SECTIONS

Fields F	Box of four	10/-
Fields G1 and G2	Box of eight (four G1 and four G2) ..	11/-
Roads H and Supports R	Box of two H with R Supports	5/6
Fields J1 and J2	Box of four (two J1 and two J2)	11/-
Fields J3	Box of two	2/-
Fields K1 and K2	Box of four (two K1 and two K2)	8/-
Fields L1 and L2	Box of four (two L1 and two L2)	7/-
Fields M1 and M2	Box of four (two M1 and two M2)	5/-

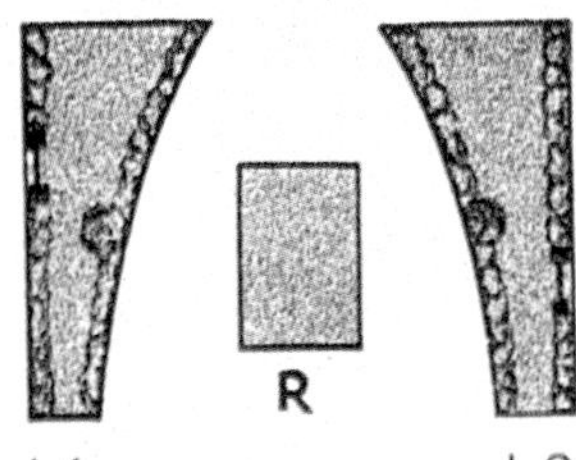
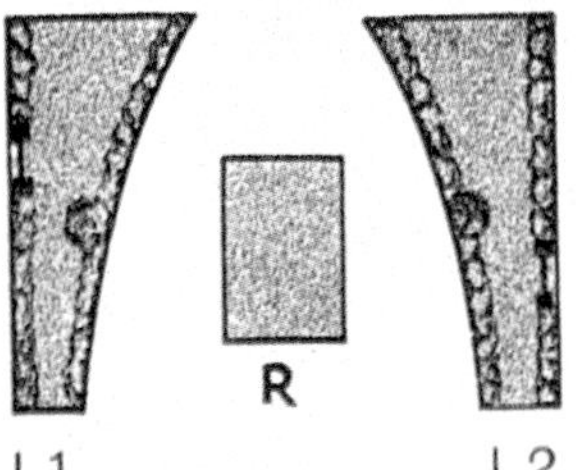

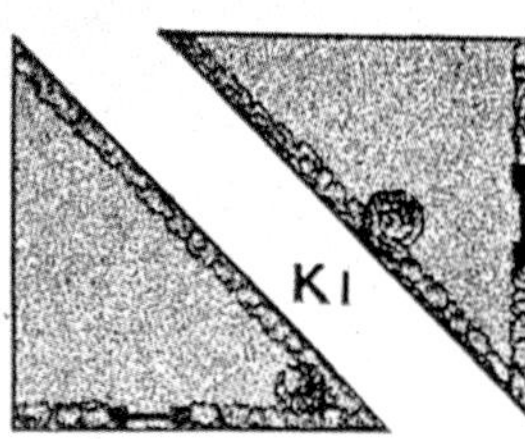

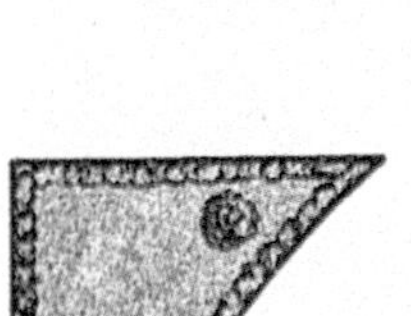

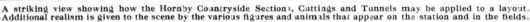

A striking view showing how the Hornby Countryside Sections, Cuttings and Tunnels may be applied to a layout. Additional realism is given to the scene by the various figures and animals that appear on the station and in the fields.

ACCESSORIES

Gauge 0, 1¼ in.

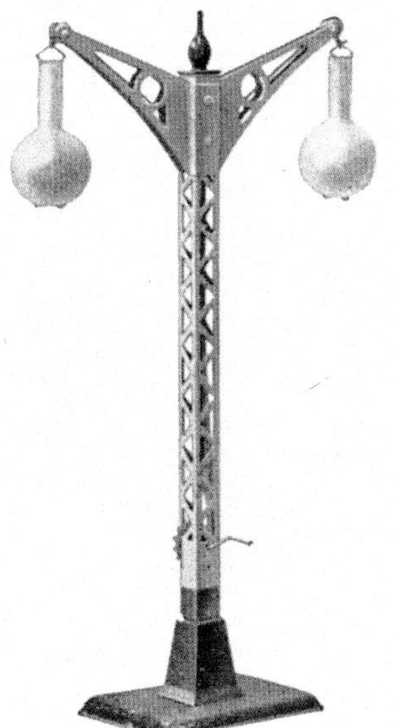

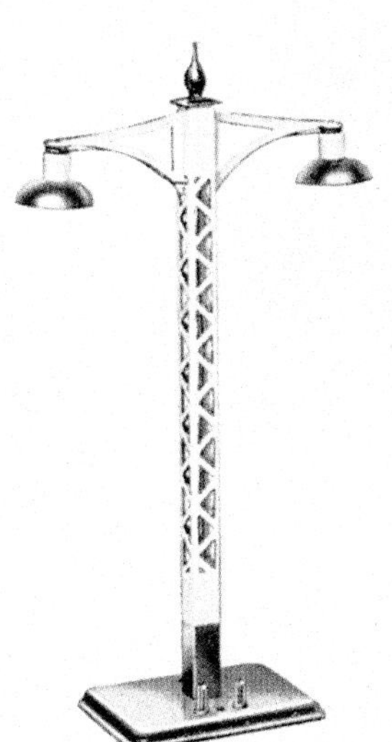

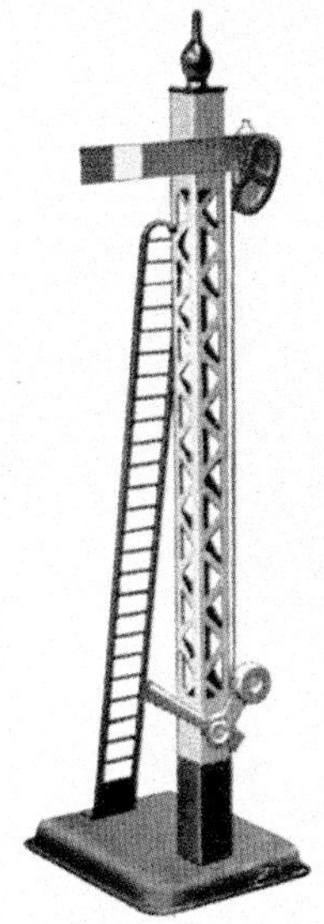

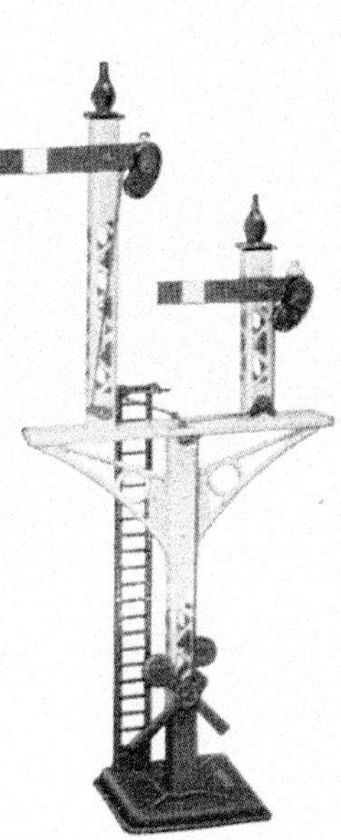

LAMP STANDARD No. 1 (**Single**) Price 3/6

LAMP STANDARD No. 2 (**Double**) (As illustrated) Electric flashlamp bulbs may be fitted in the globes, which can be hoisted or lowered as required. **Price 4/6**

LAMP STANDARD No. 1E, ELECTRICAL (Single) **Price 3/6**

LAMP STANDARD No. 2E, ELECTRICAL (Double) (as illustrated) **Price 4/3**

The above Lamp Standards are wired and fitted for electric lighting.

DOUBLE ARM SIGNAL No. 1
Price, per pair, **4/3**

DOUBLE ARM SIGNAL No. 2
(as illustrated) **Price, 3/-**

DOUBLE ARM SIGNAL No. 2E
Wired and fitted for electric lighting.
Price 6/6

SIGNAL No. 1
Price, per pair, **3/-**
(One "Home," one "Distant")

SIGNAL No. 2
(as illustrated)
"Home" or "Distant."
Price, per pair, **4/6**

SIGNAL No. 2E
Wired and fitted for electric lighting.
Price 4/6

JUNCTION SIGNAL
"Home" or "Distant"
Price 6/-

JUNCTION SIGNAL E
Similar to the above, but wired and fitted for electric lighting
Price 10/-.

Each Hornby Accessory illustrated on this page is tastefully finished in attractive colours.

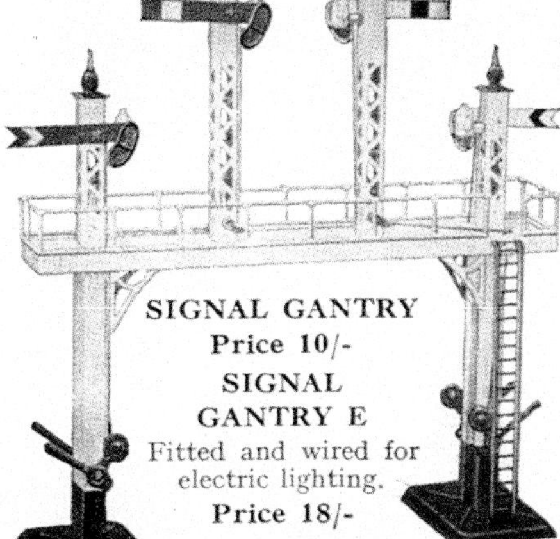

SIGNAL GANTRY
Price 10/-

SIGNAL GANTRY E
Fitted and wired for electric lighting.
Price 18/-

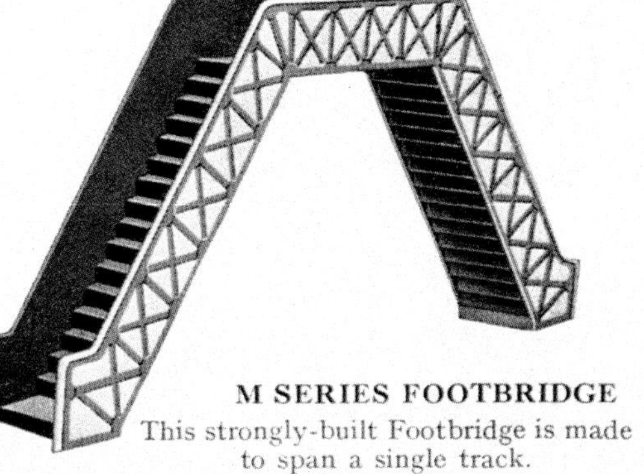

M SERIES FOOTBRIDGE
This strongly-built Footbridge is made to span a single track.
Price 1/3

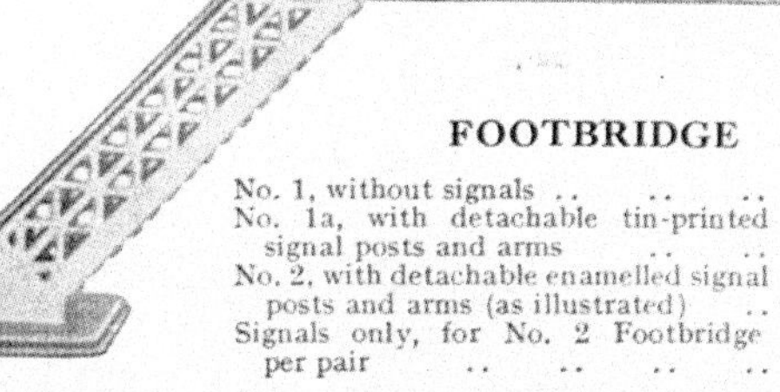

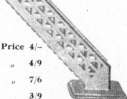

FOOTBRIDGE

No. 1, without signals	Price 4/-
No. 1a, with detachable tin-printed signal posts and arms	„ 4/9
No. 2, with detachable enamelled signal posts and arms (as illustrated) ..	„ 7/6
Signals only, for No. 2 Footbridge per pair	3/9

Gauge 0, 1¼ in.

ACCESSORIES

Two No. 1 and one No. 2 Cuttings are illustrated here.

TUNNEL No. O (Straight)

Length 6 in., width 6¼ in. **Price 1/6**

TUNNEL No. 1 (Straight)

Length 7¾ in., width 6¼ in. (as illustrated) **Price 2/-**

TUNNEL No. 2 (Straight)

Length 15⅝ in., width 9⅝ in. **Price 4/-**

CUTTING No. 1 (end section)
(illustrated)

Base measurement: Length 7¾ in., width 6 in. **Price,** per pair, **3/-**

CUTTING No. 2 (centre section, straight)
(illustrated)

The addition of these Centre Sections enables a Hornby Railway Cutting to be extended to any length. They are intended to be used in conjunction with the End Sections (Cutting No. 1), between which they are fitted. Base measurement: Length 10¼ in., width 6 in. **Price 2/-**

CUTTING No. 3 (centre section, curved)

This is used for curved tracks in the same manner as the straight Centre Section, described above, is used for straight tracks. It is suitable for both 1-ft. and 2-ft. radius tracks. **Price 2/-**

TUNNEL No. 3 (Curved)

Base measurement: Length 13 in., width 9⅝ in. For 2-ft. radius tracks only. **Price 4/6**

Each Hornby Accessory illustrated on this page is tastefully finished in attractive colours.

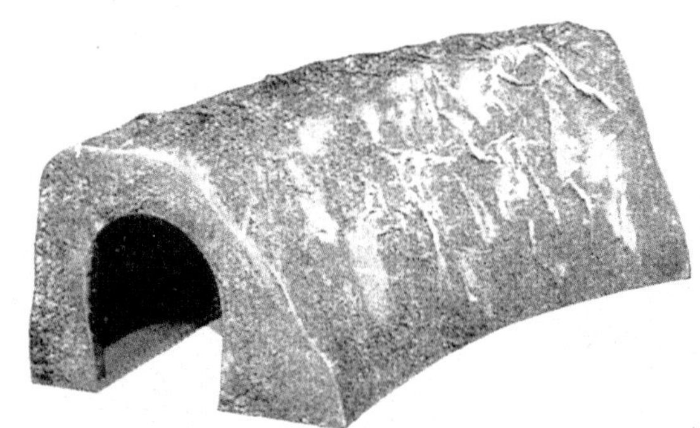

TUNNEL No. 4 (Curved)

Base measurement: Length 20 in., width 9⅝ in. For 2-ft. radius tracks only. **Price 5/6**

CUTTING No. O (Straight)

This is a double cutting, mounted on a base over which the railway track is laid. Base measurement: 8 in. × 8 in. **Price 2/6**

CUTTING No. 4

This double cutting (illustrated) is similar in design to Cutting No. O. The base measurements are: Length 15⅝ in. width 15 in. **Price 6/-**

TUNNEL No. 5 (left-hand, curved) (illustrated)

This Tunnel is in the form of a small hill, through which the track runs obliquely. For 2-ft. radius tracks only. Base measurement: 16 in. × 14¾ in. Length of track 17¼ in. **Price 7/6**

TUNNEL No. 6 (right-hand, curved)

Similar to No. 5 Tunnel, but with track in the reverse position. For 2-ft. radius tracks only. Base measurement 16 in. × 14¾ in. Length of track 17¼ in. **Price 7/6**

ACCESSORIES

Gauge 0, 1¼ in.

MODELLED MINIATURES No. 1 STATION STAFF

These splendid models, which are beautifully enamelled in colours, add the final touch of realism to Hornby Station Platforms. **Price,** per set, **1/6**

The figures in the above set may be purchased separately.

MODELLED MINIATURES No. 4 ENGINEERING STAFF

This set comprises six figures representing Electrician, two Fitters, Storekeeper, Greaser and Engine Room Attendant. **Price,** per set, **1/6**

The figures in the above set may be purchased separately.

MODELLED MINIATURES No. 22 MOTOR VEHICLES

This very attractive die-cast set consists of two Motor Cars, two commercial Vehicles, one Tractor and one Army Tank. **Price,** per set, **4/-**

The items in the above set may be purchased separately.

MODELLED MINIATURES No. 13 HALL'S DISTEMPER ADVERTISEMENT

This miniature of a well-known line-side advertisement is intended to be placed in the fields adjoining the railway track. **Price 9d.**

TRAIN NAME BOARDS

These Name Boards are for Pullman and Saloon Coaches and add greatly to the realistic appearance of the coaches. Details are as follows :—

No. 2 The Scarborough Flier.
No. 3 The Royal Scot.
No. 4 The Merseyside Express.
No. 5 Golden Arrow.
No. 6 Bournemouth Belle.
No. 7 Cornish Riviera Express.
No. 8 Torbay Limited Express.
No. 9 King's. Cross, York and Edinburgh.
No. 10 King's Cross, Edinburgh and Aberdeen.
No. 11 London (Euston) and Liverpool (Lime Street).
No. 12 London (Euston) and Glasgow (Central).
No. 13 Victoria and Dover.
No. 14 Waterloo, Salisbury and Exeter.
No. 15 Paddington, Exeter and Plymouth.
No. 16 Paddington and Bristol.
No. 1 The Flying Scotsman.

Price, per packet of four of a kind, **4d.**

Each Hornby Accessory illustrated on this page is tastefully finished in attractive colours.

CLIPS FOR TRAIN NAME BOARDS

These Clips are for use with coaches that are not fitted with brackets to take the Name Boards. There are two types : No. 2S, for No. 2 Special Pullman and No. 2 Special Pullman Composite Coaches ; and No. 2 for No. 2 Pullman and No. 2 Saloon Coaches. .. Price, per packet of 12, **1/-** (either kind).

MODELLED MINIATURES No. 21 TRAIN SET

This new Miniature Train Set is a very attractive model. It includes die-cast Locomotive, Wagon, Crane Truck, Lumber Wagon and "Shell" Petrol Tank Wagon. **Price 2/6**

The components of the above train set may be purchased separately.

MODELLED MINIATURES No. 3 PASSENGERS

This set contains figures as illustrated representing various types of railway passengers. **Price,** per set, **1/6**

The figures in the above set may be purchased separately.

MODELLED MINIATURES No. 5 TRAIN AND HOTEL STAFF

Five figures are included in this set, including Pullman Car Conductor, two Pullman Car Waiters and two Hotel Porters. **Price,** per set, **1/3**

The figures in the above set may be purchased separately.

MODELLED MINIATURES No. 2 FARMYARD ANIMALS

Comprises six animals : Sheep, Pig, two Cows, and two Horses. **Price,** per set, **1/6**

The animals in the above set may be purchased separately.

HORNBY TRAINS

Gauge 0, 1¼ in.

ACCESSORIES

POPLAR TREE
Price, per doz. **2/-**
Die-cast stands for above.
Price, per doz. **1/-**

OAK TREE
Price, per doz. **2/6**
Die-cast stands for above.
Price, per doz. **1/-**

ASSORTED TREES
Six Oak and six Poplar, complete with die-cast stands.
Price, per doz. **3/-**

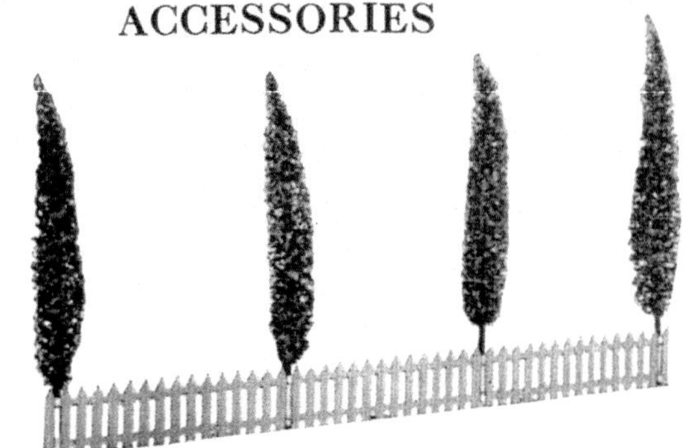

FENCING, with four trees
Length 16½ in. **Price,** per pair, **2/6**

HEDGING
Length 10¼ in. **Price,** per doz. lengths, **3/-**

M TELEGRAPH POLE No. 2
Price, each, **4d.**

TELEGRAPH POLE
Price, per pair, **4/-**

Each Hornby Accesory illustrated on this page is tastefully finished in attractive colours.

WATER TANK
Stands 8½ in. in height. Fitted with rubber tube and spring-controlled valve, operated by a chain and lever.
Price 8/6

WATER TANK E
Wired and fitted for electric lighting.
Price 10/-

HORNBY ACCESSORIES FITTED FOR ELECTRIC LIGHTING

The following Hornby Accessories are available suitably wired and fitted for electric lighting. These items are additional to the ordinary range.

	Price		Price
Engine Shed No. E1E	**18/6**	Signal Gantry E	**18/-**
Engine Shed No. E2E	**26/-**	Level Crossing No. E1E ..	**7/-**
Station No. 2E	**12/6**	Level Crossing No. E2E ..	**11/-**
Island Platform E	**9/-**	Buffer Stops No. 1E	**2/-**
Goods Platform E	**15/-**	Buffer Stops No. 2E	**7/-**
Signal Cabin No. 2E	**5/6**	Water Tank E	**10/-**
Signal No. 2E	**4/6**	Lamp Standard No. 1E ..	**3/6**
Double Arm Signal No. 2E ..	**6/6**	Lamp Standard No. 2E ..	**4/3**
Junction Signal E	**10/-**		

In order to facilitate the electrical connection of the above range of accessories, we supply a series of flexible leads, fitted with plugs at one end and sockets that fit the accessories at the other. These leads are available in three lengths: 9 in., 18 in., and 36 in., prices **1/4**, **1/5**, and **1/6** respectively.

DISTRIBUTION BOX

This special Distribution Box enables two or more accessories to be lighted simultaneously. This appliance is fitted with a pair of plugs, for connection to the transformer or accumulator, and also with five pairs of sockets to accommodate the flexible leads described above. Price of Distribution Box **2/6**.

LOADING GAUGE
(illustrated)
Height 7¾ in. **Price 2/3**

M LOADING GAUGE
Height 7¾ in. **Price 1/-**

Every owner of a Hornby Railway should have one or two of these Loading Gauges in his goods yard.

RAILS POINTS & CROSSINGS
HORNBY SERIES

Gauge 0, 1¼ in.

HORNBY Rails, Points and Crossings are designed to meet the most exacting requirements of model railway enthusiasts. They are made of the finest materials and hold together rigidly and strongly, for real workmanship is put into them. The adaptability of the rails is well shown in the booklet "How to Plan your Hornby Railway," which is obtainable from your dealer, price 3d., or direct from Meccano Limited, Binns Road, Liverpool, 13, price 4d. post free.

Rails for Clockwork and Steam Trains

CURVED RAILS

9-in. radius (for MO Trains)

M9	Curved rails	per doz.	3/-
MB9	Curved brake rails	each	3½d.

1-ft. radius

A1	Curved rails	per doz.	4/6
A1½	Curved half rails	„	3/6
A1¼	Curved quarter rails	„	3/-
AB1	Curved brake rails	each	6d.

2-ft. radius

A2	Curved rails	per doz.	4/6
A2½	Curved half rails	„	3/6
A2¼	Curved quarter rails	„	3/-
AB2	Curved brake rails	each	6d.
DC2	Curved rails, double track	½ doz.	7/6

STRAIGHT RAILS

BM	Straight rails (for MO trains)	per doz.	2/9
B1	Straight rails	„	4/-
B½	Straight half rails	„	3/-
B¼	Straight quarter rails	„	2/6
BB1	Straight brake rails	each	5d.
BBR1	Straight brake and reverse rails	„	1/6
DS1	Straight rails, double track	½ doz.	6/6

DOUBLE SYMMETRICAL POINTS

For 1-ft. radius curves

DSR1	Double symmetrical points, right hand	per pair	5/-
DSL1	Double symmetrical points, left-hand		

For 2-ft. radius curves

DSR2	Double symmetrical points, right-hand	per pair	5/-
DSL2	Double symmetrical points, left-hand		

PARALLEL POINTS

PPR2	Parallel points, right-hand	per pair	5/-
PPL2	Parallel points, left-hand		

CROSSINGS

CA1	Acute-angle crossings (for 1-ft. radius tracks)	each	2/-
CA2	Acute-angle crossings (for 2-ft. radius tracks)	„	1/9
CR1	Right-angle crossings (for 1-ft. radius tracks)	„	2/-
CR2	Right-angle crossings (for 2-ft. radius tracks)	„	1/9

CROSSOVER POINTS

COR2	Crossover points, right-hand	per pair	12/-
COL2	Crossover points, left-hand		

POINTS

9-in. radius (for MO Trains)

MR9	Right-hand points	per pair	3/-
ML9	Left-hand points		

1-ft. radius

PR1	Right-hand points	per pair	4/-
PL1	Left-hand points		

2-ft. radius

PR2	Right-hand points	per pair	4/-
PL2	Left-hand points		
PSR2	Points on solid base, right-hand	per pair	8/6
PSL2	Points on solid base, left-hand		
RCP	Rail connecting plates	½ doz.	2d.

Rails for Electric Trains

CURVED RAILS

1-ft. radius

EA1	Curved rails	per doz.	6/6
EA1½	Curved half rails	„	4/6
EA1¼	Curved quarter rails	„	4/-

2-ft. radius

EA2	Curved rails	per doz.	6/6
EA2½	Curved half rails	„	4/6
EA2¼	Curved quarter rails	„	4/-
EDC2	Curved rails, double track	½ doz.	9/-

STRAIGHT RAILS

EB1	Straight rails	per doz.	6/-
EB½	Straight half rails	„	4/6
EB¼	Straight quarter rails	„	4/-
EDS1	Straight rails, double track	½ doz.	8/6

CROSSINGS

ECA	Acute-angle crossings	each	4/-
ECR	Right-angle crossings	„	4/-

POINTS

For 2-ft. radius curves

EPR2	Right-hand points	per pair	7/6
EPL2	Left-hand points		

DOUBLE SYMMETRICAL POINTS

For 2-ft. radius curves

EDSR2	Double symmetrical points, right-hand	per pair	8/6
EDSL2	Double symmetrical points, left-hand		

PARALLEL POINTS

EPPR2	Parallel points, right-hand	per pair	8/6
EPPL2	Parallel points, left-hand		

CROSSOVER POINTS

ECOR2	Crossover points, right-hand	per pair	24/-
ECOL2	Crossover points, left-hand		
TCP6	Terminal connecting plates (6-volt)	each	1/6
TCP20	Terminal connecting plates (20-volt)	„	1/6

Electrical Points for 1-ft. radius curves are not supplied

Centre Rails for Converting Ordinary Track to Electrical

CURVED CENTRE RAILS

1-ft. radius

AC1	Curved centre rails	per doz.	1/-
AC1½	Curved centre half rails	„	9d.
AC1¼	Curved centre quarter rails	„	6d.

2-ft. radius

AC2	Curved centre rails	„	1/-
AC2½	Curved centre half rails	„	9d.
AC2¼	Curved centre quarter rails	„	6d.

STRAIGHT CENTRE RAILS

BC1	Straight centre rails	per doz.	1/-
BC½	Straight centre half rails	„	9d.
BC¼	Straight centre quarter rails	„	6d.
ICR	Insulators for insulating centre rails	per doz.	3d.
CCR	Clips for fixing centre rails	„	6d.

A1½ CURVED HALF RAIL

PPR2 PARALLEL POINTS (RIGHT-HAND)

B1 STRAIGHT RAIL

DC2 CURVED RAILS DOUBLE TRACK

AB1 CURVED BRAKE RAIL

PR1 POINTS (RIGHT-HAND)

CR2 RIGHT-ANGLE CROSSING

COL2 CROSSOVER POINTS

EB½ ELECTRICAL STRAIGHT HALF RAIL

DSL2 DOUBLE SYMMETRICAL POINTS (LEFT-HAND)

EA1 ELECTRICAL CURVED RAIL

EPPR2 ELECTRICAL PARALLEL POINTS (RIGHT-HAND)

BB1 STRAIGHT BRAKE RAIL

PSR2 POINTS ON SOLID BASE

PL2 POINTS (LEFT-HAND)

ECA ELECTRICAL ACUTE-ANGLE CROSSING

Railway Scenery and the Causes to which it is Due

ON account of the necessity of constructing railways with gradients as flat as possible, and with curves of as great a radius as can be secured, it very seldom happens that a railway lies exactly at the level of the ground on either side of it. This difference in level may be produced in various ways, and it causes a change in the surface features of the land lying between the railway fences. It is to this altered landscape that we refer when we speak of railway scenery, and not to the wider country to be seen at a distance. Let us examine briefly some of the reasons for certain common types of railway scenery.

In the British Isles it is only in such districts as the Fens, peat bogs such as Chat Moss, and boglands of Central Ireland, that a railway can be built with practically no disturbance of surface level. In order to ensure good drainage of the track, however, it is usual to keep the rail level a few feet above that of the surrounding ground, and thus the line appears to run on a very low embankment. This embankment has been formed by dumping large quantities of earth into the soft marshy ground on top of a mat of branches and brushwood first put down. Sometimes, in order to assist in keeping the foundation dry, a line of trees, such as willows, may be planted on each side of the line, which then appears to run through an avenue. Generally speaking, railways in areas of this kind have few curves because, on account of the level nature of the ground, there is nothing to prevent them from being straight.

Next to these areas, for ease in railway building, come such districts as the Cheshire Plain, and large parts of Yorkshire and Lincolnshire. Here the ground is much firmer and not quite so flat, so that low embankments and shallow cuttings may occasionally be necessary, and curves of large radius will appear. The width of land required by, and fenced off for, the railway will increase at the cuttings and embankments to allow for the slopes. In these areas, as compared with the boglands and fenlands, there will be a much greater population, with more villages and small towns, and busier roads. For this reason, instead of level and occupation crossings, we shall find bridges, probably of brick if the district is a clay area, or of stone if this is easily obtainable from quarries in the neighbourhood.

Gradients, which were practically non-existent in the flat country, will make their appearance and tend to become steeper. Curves will be more frequent, and will be required not only for the purpose of following the lie of the ground, but also for giving better crossings of rivers and roads, and bringing the line nearer villages. Possibly some curves will be made in order to avoid certain property. Stations will tend to be more frequent and of greater importance, and whereas, on account of difficult foundations, timber buildings may be usual in fenland, brick and stone will be more often used on this firmer ground, or, as in modern practice, reinforced concrete.

As the country passed through becomes more undulating, the railway will necessarily make increasing use of cuttings and embankments, and curves will tend to become more frequent and sharper. The observant railway traveller will soon notice that the slopes of the cuttings and embankments in different parts of the country vary very considerably. This variation is caused by the fact that different materials have different "angles of repose," this angle being the steepest slope at which the material will stand unsupported. As a matter of fact, in order to avoid risk of slipping, the slope of a cutting or embankment must be rather less than the theoretical angle of repose. Clays have a very flat angle of repose, and near London there are to be seen many clay cuttings that demonstrate this in a striking manner.

In parts of the country where land is very valuable and the cuttings are to be deep, it may be cheaper to build retaining walls with vertical or nearly vertical faces for the bottom parts of the sides of the cutting. In this way the width of land taken between tops of slopes is reduced, as compared with the amount required by an ordinary cutting. The task of the engineer is to work out the relative costs of tunnel, ordinary cutting

(Top.) Straight track through level country.
(Left.) Running between the sea wall and cliffs at Teignmouth.
(Centre.) Totley Tunnel, L.M.S.R., 3 miles 950 yards long.
(Right.) A cutting through clay with surface drains.

Cuttings in Clay, Chalk and Limestone

and cutting with retaining walls, to reduce excavation and width of land required. Thus near large towns we find walled cuttings are very frequent, and often the full depth of the cutting is between walls. In a similar manner embankments may be reduced in width by forming the bottom portion between two walls, but this is not a usual form of construction.

Clay is a treacherous material with which to form slopes, as it is very liable to slip if water gets behind the slope. In the sides of cuttings there are often to be noticed patterns formed by stonework on the surface, or simply by a series of stone strips running down the slopes. These are "surface drains," the object of which is to collect the water off the slope and lead it to the drains at the bottom along the line out of harm's way. The surface drains are not just laid on the surface, but often are cut down many feet into the slope.

All the railways running north and south from London have to cut through the chalk ridges that are known as the Chiltern Hills on the north side, and the Downs on the south. Thus we get chalk cuttings, such as Tring on the L.M.S.R., and as the angle of repose of chalk is very steep, the sides of these cuttings are almost vertical and seem to be very close to the carriage windows.

When the depth of cutting would be excessive, say over about 75 ft., tunnelling becomes cheaper, and thus we have Elstree, Watford, Potter's Bar, Merstham, Polhill, and other tunnels through the chalk. In the same way, when an embankment would be very high, and therefore costly both for land and for construction, a viaduct may be cheaper. So we get such structures as the Ouse Viaduct on the Brighton line, and Welwyn Viaduct on the L.N.E.R. main line from London to the North.

Limestone resembles chalk in having a very steep angle of repose, and so on the old Midland line in Derbyshire we get cuttings with almost vertical sides. But whereas the chalk generally occurs in large rounded masses like the Downs, the limestone is usually broken up into irregular crags and tors, giving rise to a much more varied railway scenery than is possible in the chalk, which is monotonously regular in the cuttings as most travellers will know.

Line Construction in Mountainous Country

Olive Mount Cutting, near Liverpool, on the Liverpool and Manchester line built by Stephenson, is one of the deepest in the country and, as it is cut in good sandstone, it has vertical sides. It must have been nearly as costly as a tunnel, but it is said that much of the stone from it was used for bridges on the line, and thus Stephenson may have used it as a sort of quarry.

The east and west lines across England, through the Pennines, provided some of the most mountainous country, and therefore most difficult construction, for our railways. Thus we find many long tunnels, such as Cowburn, Totley, Woodhead and Standedge, deep cuttings, sharp curves, and steep gradients. The old Lancashire and Yorkshire route is specially notable for the number of towns served in a short distance, and thus it has a particularly devious route and expensive construction, with many bridges over roads, rivers and canals, and viaducts in the towns. This route is characterized also by its great number of junctions, and many of the diverging lines are practically as important as the main line itself.

(Top.) Cowburn Tunnel, L.M.S.R., 2 miles 182 yards long.
(Centre, left.) Cutting and tunnel through limestone.
(Centre, right.) Stephenson's Menai Tubular Bridge.
(Bottom.) Viaduct crossing a valley at Penkridge.

Lines passing through mountainous country provide another form of railway scenery, not strictly either cutting or embankment, but a combination, more or less, of these two features; and this is found where the line follows a river valley, or a pass through the hills. It is then often cut into the side of the mountain as a kind of ledge, so that one side of it appears to be in a cutting and the other side on an embankment. Parts of the Callander and Oban and West Highland lines in Scotland have many miles built like this, and some of the Welsh coastal lines have the same feature. Heavy curvature is of course almost unavoidable with this type of construction, and some remarkable examples are to be observed.

Every type of railway scenery has its own special reason, and the interest of journeys by rail is greatly increased by observing the railway scenery passed through, and trying to think out the conditions to which it is due.

The Vehicles that Carry our Goods Traffic

IN this article, for the sake of simplicity, we have used the term "goods" in regard to wagons as being the opposite of "passenger." Actually there are on our railways hundreds of vehicles, fitted with vacuum or Westinghouse brakes, that generally run in passenger trains but are not used for carrying passengers, among them being postal vans, parcel vans, pigeon vans, etc. For our purpose we shall consider such vehicles as being used for goods traffic.

The variety of goods handled by our railways is enormous, and to deal with it a great many different kinds of vans and wagons are necessary. Strenuous efforts have been made in recent years to reduce the number of types, but there is still a great variety in use. In studying these types two leading features of the operation of our railways should be noticed, for in some respects these add greatly to the difficulty of working. The first is the fact that Great Britain, with Ireland, is the only important railway country to retain the use of the loose link coupling for goods trains. This is a convenience in shunting, but it makes long trains more difficult to handle, and is apt to lead to breakages of drawgear, through sudden snatching. The other feature is the very high proportion of privately-owned wagons on our railways, a state of affairs found nowhere else. These wagons are generally built by contract firms and maintained by these firms, who have repair depots at all important junctions. As the wagons can be used only for the traffic of the owner, it follows that there is great waste in hauling them about empty to where they can be loaded, and in shunting and marshalling them into the places to which they belong. On the other hand, this practice enables the railways to work the traffic with the investment of less capital than would be required if they had to supply all the wagons. As the bulk of these privately-owned wagons are for coal traffic they would generally travel empty in one direction in any event.

(Top, left.) A 10,000-gallon bogie tank wagon for petrol.
(Top, right.) L.M.S.R. hopper-bottom ballast wagon.
(Bottom, left.) A modern 25-ton goods brake van.
(Bottom, right.) Locomotive trolley with detachable ends.

At the present time there are roughly 700,000 railway-owned wagons on our railways, of which about 215,000 are open wagons for coal and mineral traffic. Of the remainder some 390,000 are open trucks, and the other 95,000 are covered wagons. There are some 640,000 privately-owned wagons, of which about 620,000 are open trucks for coal, coke, and mineral traffic, which shows the large proportion of such wagons.

Years ago, all goods vehicles had axle-boxes that were kept filled with thick yellow grease for lubrication purposes. This was not altogether satisfactory, as its action depended too much on the weather, being apt to be too free in summer and too hard in winter. At the best it did not give such good results as oil. For some years now all the railways have been changing over from grease-boxes to oil-boxes, in which a pad of soft material is kept full of oil, and produces much less friction in the axle-box than grease would do.

Let us look at the wagon list of the late Midland Railway, and take first of all the vehicles classed as passenger stock, but which do not take passengers. Among these are the covered carriage truck, fish and poultry trucks, horse box, hound van, milk and fruit van, motor van, open carriage truck (16 ft. and 20 ft.), parcel van, and prize-cattle van. Among the goods vehicles proper we have banana and fruit vans, ventilated van, ventilated meat van, locomotive coal wagon, manure wagon, armour-plate truck, bogie-rail wagon, bogie tram car truck, boiler truck, circular plate wagon, deep case wagon, flat case wagon, girder wagon, glass wagon, gun truck (60 and 100 tons), gunpowder vans and implement wagons. From a G.W.R. list we notice ventilated and refrigerator vans, 30-ton covered goods van, 20-ton coal wagon, sleeper wagon, portable engine wagon, bolster truck, double bolster timber truck, roll wagon, and wheel and propeller wagon. There are also oil tanks of 10, 11, 12 and 20 tons.

In describing some of these wagons in more detail we shall make use of certain terms, the meaning of which may not be well known, and may therefore be defined here. The "tare" weight of a wagon is its empty weight. The

Advantages of High-capacity Wagons

"wheelbase" is the length along the rail from the point at which one end wheel touches it to the point at which the wheel at the other end touches it. The "solebar" is the main frame member at each side of the truck, running lengthways, the "headstock" being the end member of the frame. When a wagon is described as of so many tons, say 10, this refers to the load that it is designed to carry, not to its own empty weight.

The commodity of which the largest quantities are conveyed on our railways is coal, and we may now turn our attention to the vehicles for carrying it. By far the commonest is the 10-ton wooden wagon, with side doors, which has been in use for a great many years by both private owners and by the railways. The Railway Clearing House has a design for a standard 12-ton wagon, both for coal and for general merchandise, and large numbers of these have been built. They have four wheels and side lever hand brakes, and a tare weight of 6½ tons.

The North-Eastern area of the L.N.E.R. is unique in that about 90 per cent. of the coal traffic originating in it is carried in railway-owned wagons. Most of these are of 20 tons capacity, of the steel hopper type, unloading through the bottom. A great deal of coal from this area is of course unloaded direct into ships at the various ports.

The advantages of using large wagons instead of small ones are fairly easy to see when material like coal is considered, which is dealt with in full loads. Neither the length nor the weight of the truck increases as fast as its capacity, so that the greater the size of the wagon for the conveyance of any particular commodity the smaller becomes its own weight in proportion to that of the load. Unfortunately, a great many of our colliery sidings are unfit for anything bigger than a 12-ton wagon, and the coal screens will not permit anything larger to pass under, so that progress in this matter is necessarily rather slow.

A few years ago the G.W.R. management felt so strongly about the advantages of large wagons that they put into operation a system by which a reduced rate was given for coal conveyed in 20-ton wagons supplied by them. They also altered

Special Wagons for Rapid Discharge

the coal tips at most of their docks to take these wagons. The wagons are 21 ft. 6 in. over headstocks and 8 ft. 6 in. in overall width, have a wheelbase of 12 ft., and measure 24 ft. over buffers. The wheels are 3 ft. 2 in. in diameter—a very usual wagon wheel size—and the tare weight is 9 tons 12 cwt. The total cost of these wagons is about £280 each. They were designed to take Welsh coal, which averages 40·6 cu. ft. to the ton. For the same weight of coal, 20 tons, from North Country or Midland mines, the sides would have to be made higher, as this coal is lighter. These wagons are often called steel wagons, but actually the body is made of iron, because the sulphur in the coal attacks iron less readily, so that it lasts about one-third longer than steel. The response to this scheme was slow but steady. More recently the G.W.R. have introduced another scheme by which the company build the wagons and rent them to the collieries, the wagons becoming the property of the renting colliery at the end of an agreed period. All the railways are themselves of course users of great quantities of coal, and for this they have special wagons, generally marked very plainly "Loco Coal Only," "Loco Coal" or in many cases just "Loco."

There are many types, chiefly steel or iron. The L.M.S.R. introduced about three years ago a special set of 40-ton wagons for hauling coal to their Stonebridge Park power station near London. These are of the hopper type, with side-discharging doors for quick unloading, and are fully engaged running between the colliery and the power station. Many of the big electricity concerns also have their own coal wagons, usually of a hopper type. The G.W.R. have a number of 40-ton bogie wagons for locomotive coal.

(Top, left.) **L.N.E.R. covered van for banana traffic.**
(Top, right.) **A container mounted on a motor lorry.**
(Bottom, left.) **A special transformer wagon with a transformer loaded on the main girders.**
(Bottom, right.) **A container on a railway wagon.**

Closely akin to coal is coke, and most of the railways possess or run special coke wagons. This material is comparatively light, so that a 12-ton coke wagon is much deeper for the same length than a coal wagon of that capacity. The extra depth is often provided by an openwork, light timber fence round the top of the wagon. In 1930 the L.M.S.R. built 100 steel wagons for coke, with eight bottom doors, each of which can be worked independently. There are side lever

Interesting L.N.E.R. Vehicles for Chemicals

brakes and the wheels are of 3 ft. 2 in. diameter, the wheelbase, with four wheels, being 12 ft. Over headstocks is 25 ft. and over the buffers 28 ft., the greatest height being 11 ft. The tare weight, or simply tare as it is usually called, is 11 tons 5 cwt.

The district just south of Peterborough on the old Great Northern main line is well known as a brick-making centre, and the tall chimneys of the kilns can be seen for miles over the flat countryside. So great was the demand for bricks in London in the years following the War that the Great Northern built in 1920 a number of wagons carried on bogies and capable of holding 50 tons of bricks; and these made regular trips between Peterborough and London. They could be used also for other traffic, of course, although it was difficult to secure full loads, hence the general use of four-wheeled wagons.

Near Stockton-on-Tees, in the North-Eastern area of the L.N.E.R., is a very large chemical works, one of whose principal products is sulphate of ammonia, used for fertilising the ground. The L.N.E.R. have built 80 wagons each capable of holding 50 tons of the chemical in 2 cwt. bags, the tare weight being $20\frac{3}{4}$ tons. The wagons are all steel except the two doors in each side, and are labelled "Sulphate" in 12 in. letters. They have lever-operated, either side hand brakes, and are mounted on bogies identical with those of the brick wagons. They measure 39 ft. over headstocks, are 9 ft. wide, and 5 ft. deep inside. The chemical has a corrosive action if it gets damp, and hence the wagons are painted with a special protective bituminous paint.

Several designs of ore wagon are in use, many of them of the bottom-door type; and there are many private owner's wagons for this traffic. The L.N.E.R. have some 20-ton wagons used for hauling pig iron, the raw material for the manufacture of steel.

As already mentioned, the two standard wagons for ordinary merchandise are the 12-ton open and 12-ton covered wagon, each on four wheels, with steel underframes and timber bodies. In 1931, however, the G.W.R. built 100 high-capacity wagons to hold 20 tons. These measure 30 ft. long over headstocks, and are 7 ft. 7 in. high inside. They have a wheelbase of 19 ft. 6 in. and weigh nearly 11 tons, and are fitted with the automatic vacuum brake, and a quick-action coupling called the "Instanter." They are capable of going round a two-chain curve, which is sharper than most curves, even in sidings. The G.W.R. have some 25-ton open goods wagons and some 30-ton covered vans, both being mounted on bogies and measuring 36 ft. over headstocks. The L.N.E.R. also have some 25-ton covered wagons, built in the early years of this century.

(Top.) Special steel vehicle for bulk grain traffic.
(Centre, left.) A high-capacity covered goods van.
(Centre, right.) Special truck for road-rail milk tanks.
(Bottom.) A road-rail milk tank loaded on its truck.

Curious Code Names for Special Wagons

All the railway companies have code names for their special wagons, which reduce the labour of ordering them from place to place, especially by telegraph. The G.W.R. code name "*Bloater*" immediately gives a clue to the purpose of the van to which it applies; as also does "*Fruits*," a general term for fruit vans, the particular variety being denoted by a letter following the code name. The purpose of "*Siphons*" and "*Micas*" is not so clear, but actually these names refer to milk and meat vans respectively. The uses of a "*Mex*" and a "*Paco*" are apparently more mysterious, but quite ordinary vehicles—cattle trucks and horse-boxes—are meant. "*Macaw*" and "*Crocodile*" have no relation to the tropical jungles, but are the names for rail wagons and well wagons respectively. "*Damo*" and "*Asmo*" indicate different types of vans for motor-car traffic. Every G.W.R. goods train is provided with a "*Toad*," this being the goods brake van. "*Toad A*," fitted with vacuum brake apparatus, is a superior vehicle to a plain "*Toad*," which is provided with hand brakes only.

The L.N.E.R. code includes some curious terms, but the names on the whole suggest the actual names or purpose of the wagons concerned. Thus "*Traction*" means a traction engine wagon, "*Powder*" a gunpowder van, and "*Boiler*" a flat wagon for the conveyance of boilers. "*Miser*" does not sound pleasant, but is actually a special wagon for carrying the economisers used in many commercial power plants. "*Rect*" refers to a special bogie wagon for carrying military tanks and adapted for end loading, while "*Twin Imps*" are nothing more dangerous than twin machine wagons.

Others can be determined without much difficulty. "*Flatrol*" means a flat trolley wagon; a "*Weltrol*" a trolley wagon with a well; "*Protrol*" a special vehicle for ships' propellers; "*Boplate*" a bogie wagon for steel plates; and "*Arm*," an armour-plate wagon. "*Quads*" and "*Quints*" are a little puzzling, but are the code names for four-bolster and five-bolster bogie plate wagons. The 25-ton vans mentioned previously are known as "*Covfits*," implying brake-fitted covered vans.

The L.M.S.R. have a number of 12-ton ventilated goods vans fitted with automatic vacuum brake as well as with either side hand brakes and screw couplings, so that they are able to run in fast passenger trains or express goods trains. They have oil axle-boxes

New types of General-purpose Vans

timber sides, and corrugated steel ends. The roofs are of ⅞ in. tongued and grooved boards, covered with Ruberoid.

Recently the L.M.S.R. have put into service a new type of vehicle designed to carry a wide range of traffic, such as ordinary luggage, parcels, pigeons, fruit, theatrical scenery and motor-cars. The vans are straight-sided and built with a lofty elliptical roof. At each end are double folding doors with loading plates to facilitate the loading of motor-cars, and adjustable wheel bars and racks are fitted to allow for differences in the lengths of various cars. Two pairs of double doors on each side are provided for loading from the platform. Along each side of the interior are arranged two rows of folding shelves for pigeon crates, fruit baskets, and similar articles. The sides and roofs are steel panelled, and the floor is composed of fireproof material, drain holes being arranged at frequent intervals for cleaning-down purposes. The underframe is constructed of steel sections, and is carried on two four-wheeled bogies. The vans have a length over buffers of 45 ft. 8 in., and an overall width of 8 ft. 6 in. The tare weight is 25 tons and the load 8 tons.

The Southern Railway built a number of rather ingenious general-purpose wagons, on four wheels, with a wheelbase of 21 ft. They have both end and side doors, and by means of a special series of movable fittings they can be adapted to take passengers' luggage, milk cans, motor-cars, road vehicles, fruit baskets, theatrical scenery, aeroplane parts, and many other things.

For a long time the railways have been handling large quantities of milk, which until recently was always sent in churns. These churns were generally transported in special milk wagons, which were covered, but had sides made of open boarding so as to keep a current of air circulating among the cans and prevent over-heating. Some of the big milk distributors have now adopted a system by which the milk is railed in large tanks, carried on four- or six-wheeled trucks. These tanks are glass-lined for cleanliness, and are thoroughly washed out with hot water after each trip. Speed of transit is essential with these vehicles, which often run in express passenger trains; and they are therefore fitted with the vacuum brake, and are provided with pipes for steam-heating connection to passenger coaches. They have, in addition, either side hand brakes and screw couplings. The tanks are specially anchored on the steel underframes.

All the companies use these special milk vehicles, but we may here notice

Road-Rail Milk Tanks and Containers

one type, as used on the G.W.R. It is carried on a six-wheeled frame, and holds 3,000 gallons. The tank is 18 ft. 0½ in. long, and 6 ft. 1 in. in diameter, and at 3,000 gallons the load is 13 tons 6 cwt., the tare weight being 14 tons 9 cwt. The wheelbase is 13 ft. The tank is fitted with an outlet cock at each end, a manhole for access, an air cock, and safety and inlet valves at the top; and there are fixed ladders at each side for reaching the manhole and valves. It is important that the milk should not be exposed to extremes of temperature, and the tank is therefore coated with 2 in. of cork, covered with thin metal sheets welded together. There is also a sheet-metal canopy over the top half of the tank, with an air space of 1⅜ in.

Some of the tanks are of the "road-rail" variety running on a road-type chassis, and loaded for their railway journeys upon special flat wagons. Milk is thus transported from dairy farms in the heart of the country to town distributing depots in the minimum of time.

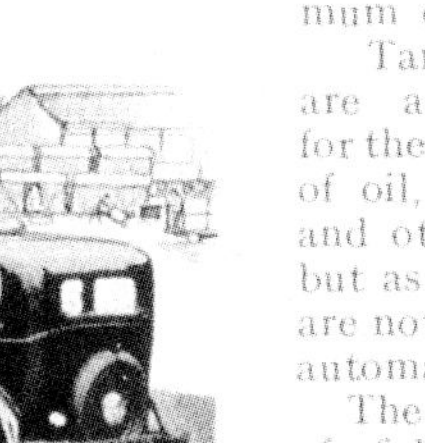

Tank wagons are also in use for the conveyance of oil, petrol, tar and other liquids, but as a rule they are not fitted with automatic brakes.

The conveyance of fish has long been a regular feature of railway goods working, and in general there are four types of vehicle in use—the closed van, the ventilated van, the insulated van, and the open truck. The closed vans usually have louvres to provide ventilation, and the ventilated vans have the sides made of boards fixed ¾ in. to 1 in. apart. Refrigerated vans are usually only provided for frozen fish and cold-stored cured fish. The open truck is really only suitable for carrying fish for short distances, and is not greatly used. It is interesting to note that for calculating wagon capacity, fish, ice and boxes altogether are taken at 46 cu. ft. to the ton.

Containers, which are really only a form of box, are now much used on the railways. They have been designated the "Suitcases of Commerce," and in view of their useful and handy character they well merit the name. As they can be carried equally well on a road lorry and on a railway wagon, they can be quickly and easily packed at a factory, taken by lorry to the goods yard, and loaded on to flat trucks. Another road journey brings them to the merchant's premises, where they can be unpacked, thus affording door-to-door service. There are different sizes of

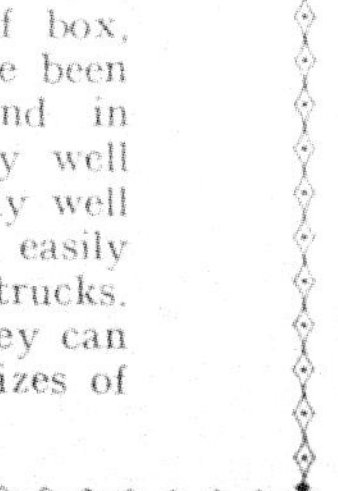

(Top.) Side-discharging hopper wagon for coal traffic. (Centre, left.) An L.N.E.R. all-metal gunpowder van. (Centre, right.) End-loading motor cars in S.R. vans. (Bottom.) All-metal 20-ton wagon for South Wales coal.

The Largest British Goods Vehicle

open and closed containers, which are more or less similar to open and covered wagon bodies; and special insulated containers for perishable traffic have now become familiar objects. The earlier containers were built of wood, but steel construction is now becoming general. The S.R. built 100 steel containers each to hold four tons of bricks. The L.M.S.R. have made a special feature of furniture removal by container, and built 100 of their "K" type containers for this traffic in 1932. They measure 15 ft. by 6 ft. 9 in. by 7 ft. high, and have a system of vertical and horizontal movable partitions inside. They are lifted on and off the flat trucks by the mobile cranes that have recently been provided in most goods yards.

Among specially large goods wagons may be mentioned the 20-ton and 40-ton flat wagons for steel tubes, timber, and similar traffic, owned by the L.N.E.R. This company also have 20-ton, 25-ton and 30-ton wagons for the carriage of iron and steel flats, which are long, narrow plates; and a 30-ton wagon with a well to take a plate 40 ft. long and 13 ft. 6 in. wide. This wagon is 60 ft. long and weighs 25¾ tons. The G.W.R. have some tinplate bar wagons for use in South Wales, similar in design to the ordinary open goods wagon. They have wood bodies on steel underframes, carried on four wheels, and they can carry 20 tons. The tare is 7 tons 15 cwt.

The largest goods vehicle in the country is really a set of wagons, and belongs to the L.N.E.R. It can carry 150 tons, it rests on 56 wheels, and is 221 ft. long. The centre portion, called the "*Weltrol*," is on 24 wheels, and can itself carry 110 tons. By making up the set with two 60-ton flat wagons each on 12 wheels, and two 20-ton trolley wagons each on four wheels, and using the cantilever beam principle to spread the load, a total of 150 tons can be carried without difficulty.

The introduction of the "grid" system that covers Great Britain with a network of high-tension electric cables has involved the provision of a great number of transformers, and the transport of these has set the railways some awkward problems. Most of the companies have built special wagons for the purpose, among which may be mentioned the L.N.E.R. 70-ton set. This consists of two armour-plate wagons connected by two strong beams, which can be moved sideways. The transformer hangs down between the beams, the whole conveyance resting on 16 wheels and weighing

(Top, left.) A special G.W.R. motor-car van.
(Top, right.) L.M.S.R. all-steel coke wagon.
(Bottom, left.) A typical large cattle wagon.
(Bottom, right.) Standard 12-ton open wagon of wooden construction.

Trolleys for Transformers and Locomotives

42½ tons. The G.W.R. have a transformer set, consisting of trolleys and detachable side girders, capable of carrying 120 tons and itself weighing 76 tons.

The conveyance of locomotives for abroad, where the gauge may be different from ours, has often to be arranged. In 1932 the L.M.S.R. built two 65-ton trolley wagons, the first of their type in the world, capable of carrying a locomotive of any gauge from 3 ft. 6 in. to 5 ft. 6 in. Each is carried on two six-wheeled bogies and weighs 49½ tons. Briefly the idea is that by detaching one end, or both, the middle portion may be opened out and the engine be run into it, and then picked up on the main beams to which rails are fixed. These rails are adjustable to various gauges. By the use of hydraulic jacks the wagon can then be assembled again.

For carrying omnibuses, mobile cranes, and agricultural machinery, the L.N.E.R. have some 20-ton flat trolley wagons, measuring 55 ft. over buffers, carried on two four-wheeled bogies, and weighing 24½ tons. They have a specially low deck for easy loading.

The railways require a good number of vehicles for handling their own requirements, in addition to the locomotive coal and goods already mentioned. Trucks are required also for rails, sleepers and ballast, and a good example of modern practice for the latter is the L.M.S.R. 25-ton steel hopper wagon, of which 108 have been built. They weigh 16 tons each, and are V-shaped in section. The sides of the V's open at the bottom to discharge the ballast, and are controlled by a screw shaft and hand-wheel. The idea of the wagons is to deposit the ballast in a long heap between the rails. The guard's van used with them has a steel blade like a plough set underneath it, and as the whole train is drawn along the plough levels down the ballast to within an inch or two of rail level, so that trains can safely run over the line immediately. Rapid unloading and distribution of the ballast is thus a feature and the efficiency of this method has frequently been proved. On one of the first occasions when a ballast train of this kind was used, three men unloaded 12 wagons in 15 minutes. A special loading test of this type of train with Penmaenmawr granite showed that, once the wagons were in positon, three men could load 12 wagons in 40 minutes. The S.R. also have some hopper ballast wagons, of 40 tons capacity and running on bogies.

THE HORNBY RAILWAY COMPANY

A World-wide Organisation for Owners of Hornby Trains

The Hornby Railway Company is a world-wide organisation formed for the sole purpose of enabling all Hornby Railway owners to obtain one hundred per cent. fun from their hobby.

Membership of the Hornby Railway Company entitles a boy to the great privilege of expert advice, entirely free, on all the problems that arise in connection with his own railway. By following out the advice given to him from Headquarters, he has the great satisfaction of knowing that he is not only obtaining the best possible results, but also the maximum amount of fun from the operation of his railway.

This is the badge worn by Hornby Railway Company members.

The founder and chairman of the Hornby Railway Company is Mr. Frank Hornby, the inventor of Meccano and the Managing Director of Meccano Ltd. Assisting him is our own staff of railway experts—trained men of long experience and full of enthusiasm for their subject. They fill the executive offices at Headquarters, and guide the affairs of the many Associated Branches of the Hornby Railway Company in local centres which are run by boy officials.

The Headquarters of the Hornby Railway Company are at Binns Road, Liverpool 13, where a complete railway system has been installed for experimental and test purposes.

Any owner of a Hornby Train Set, no matter what its size, may become a member. All he has to do is to fill in the official application form, have his signature witnessed, and send the form to the Headquarters of the Hornby Railway Company with 6d. in stamps in payment for the official badge, which he will wear in his button-hole. This badge, illustrated above, is beautifully finished in blue and green enamel, and by means of it all members are able to recognise each other wherever they may meet. Their badges indicate at once that they have something in common—an interest in railways—and we are certain that, after a hearty handshake, conversation will never flag for a moment between any "HORNBY RAILWAY COMPANY" members who may happen to meet in this manner.

The official organ of the Hornby Railway Company is the "Meccano Magazine," a progressive Magazine that is bought each month by over 70,000 boys. Full details of the subscription rates and sources of supply are given on the back page of this book.

The Hornby Railway Company is divided into two sections—Senior, for members aged 12 and upwards, and Junior, for members under 12. A special booklet dealing in an attractive manner with the details of model railway working has been prepared for each of these sections, and the appropriate booklet will be sent post free to every member of the H.R.C. at the time of his enrolment.

The booklets contain excellent advice on the running of model railways, large or small, and will be found equally helpful by the boy whose Hornby equipment can be accommodated on the dining-room table and by the boy with an extensive range of components requiring a large amount of space.

The two Hornby Railway Company booklets together form a complete guide to the equipment and operation of a model railway. They may also be obtained by non-members for 2d. each, post free from Meccano Limited, Binns Road, Liverpool 13.

If you are not already a member, join the H.R.C. to-day!

"Get ready to Switch her, Dad!"

This is No. 2 Special Pullman Train, one of the famous trains in the Hornby System.

"MECCANO MAGAZINE"

PRICE 6d.
MONTHLY

PRICE 6d.
MONTHLY

The World's Best Magazine for Boys

All boys who are interested in Railways and in developments connected with them will find the *Meccano Magazine* a valuable source of information. It contains articles dealing with the latest railway activities throughout the world, and owners of Hornby Trains are specially catered for in articles on the working of Model Railways. In addition, the "M.M." deals with Engineering in all its branches—Aviation, Ships, Motor Cars, Hydro-Electric Schemes, Bridges, Cranes, etc. Specially attractive articles are devoted to Model Aeroplanes, Model Speed Boats, and Home Experiments in Electricity and Chemistry. Other sections deal with Books of interest to boys, Stamps, New Inventions, etc.

The *Meccano Magazine* has a larger circulation than any similar boys' magazine. It is published on the 1st of each month, and has a net sale of over 70,000 copies each month. It may be ordered from your Meccano dealer or newsagent, price 6d. If desired, it will be mailed direct by Meccano Ltd., Liverpool, six months for 4/–, or 12 months for 8/–, post free. Send 6d. for a specimen copy.

Price
6D.
Monthly

MECCANO LIMITED
Binns Road
LIVERPOOL 13

16/833/100.

Published by Meccano Limited, Binns Road, Liverpool 13.

Printed in England.

Cambrian Road
NEWPORT

4 St. John Square
CARDIFF

4d.

U.K./57

MECCANO

Trade Mark Reg.

THE TOY THAT GROWS WITH THE BOY

All boys like to know how things are made and work — nothing gives them greater pleasure than finding out what makes the wheels go round: Meccano is just the toy for them.

Meccano enables boys to build fascinating models of motor cars, bridges, cranes, looms, clocks, and many other of the wonderful machines and mechanisms they see around them today. Meccano caters for that urge to construct and experiment that exists in every boy.

The hobby can be started with any main Outfit; Accessory Outfits soon convert small Outfits into big ones. The appeal and scope of Meccano grow steadily over the years as Accessory Outfits and spare parts are added, enabling bigger and better models to be built.

Read the Meccano Magazine every month for the latest news of Meccano model-building, Hornby and Hornby-Dublo train running and Dinky Toys. Each issue contains attractive articles, for readers of all ages, on engineering, railways, aircraft, stamps, etc. You can obtain the Meccano Magazine from your Meccano dealer or newsagent, 1/3 monthly.

For those who prefer to have each issue sent direct by post, the subscription rate in the U.K. is 18/- for twelve months or 9/- for six months.

It works . . . it's realistic . . . it's Meccano !

MECCANO OUTFIT No. OO

This Outfit makes an ideal introduction to the Meccano hobby for very young boys. It contains a selection of standard interchangeable Meccano parts—with instructions for building many simple and interesting toys like the three illustrated.

High Flyers
(*Outfit No. OO*)

Pointer
(*Outfit No. OO*)

Scales
(*Outfit No. OO*)

MECCANO OUTFIT No. O

Another small Meccano Outfit which is very suitable for the beginner. Instructions are included for building a number of simple models. Three of them are illustrated here.

Ship-building Crane
(*Outfit No. O*)

Windmill Pump
(*Outfit No. O*)

Electric Truck
(*Outfit No. O*)

MECCANO OUTFIT No. 1

This Outfit, too, is a convenient introduction to the Meccano hobby. A good selection of interesting models is illustrated in the Book of Instructions; three examples are shown here.

Windmill
(*Outfit No. 1*)

Steam Wagon
(*Outfit No. 1*)

Lifting Bridge
(*Outfit No. 1*)

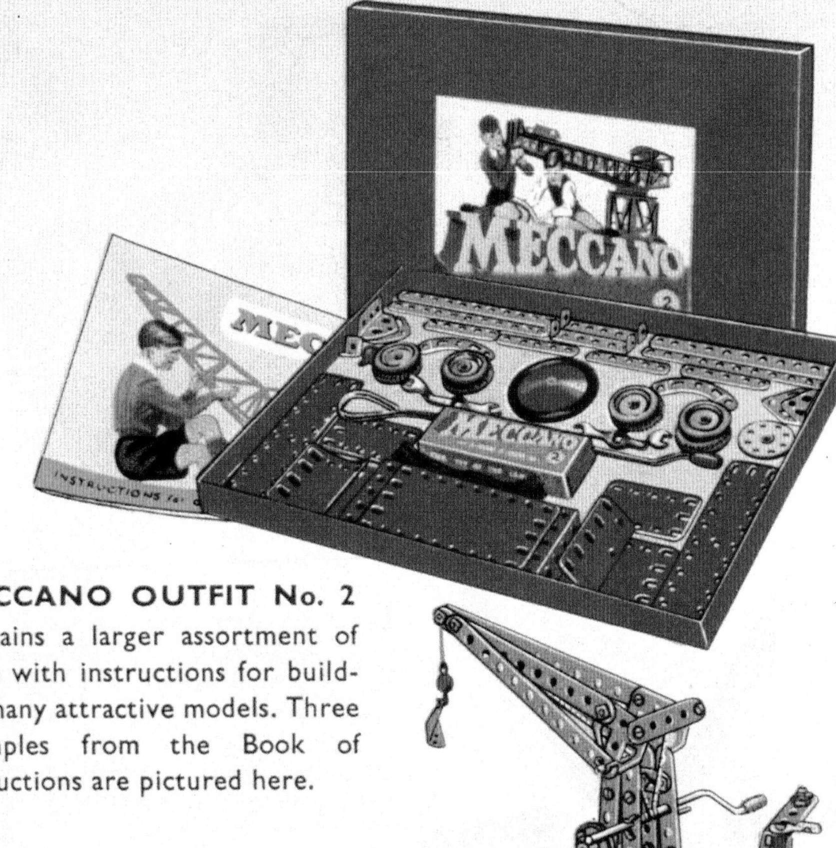

MECCANO OUTFIT No. 2

Contains a larger assortment of parts with instructions for building many attractive models. Three examples from the Book of Instructions are pictured here.

Crane Truck
(*Outfit No. 2*)

Beam Engine
(*Outfit No. 2*)

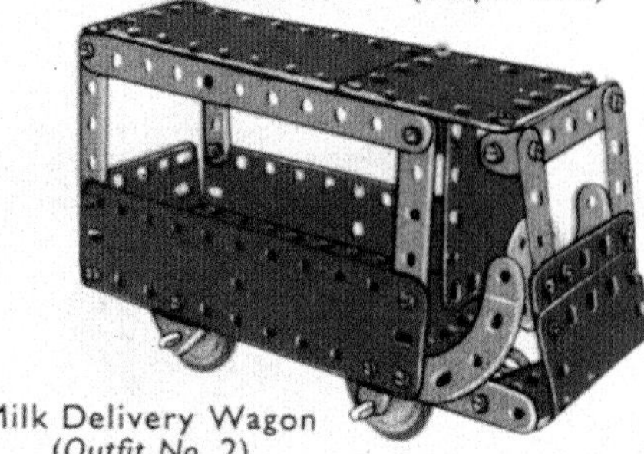

Milk Delivery Wagon
(*Outfit No. 2*)

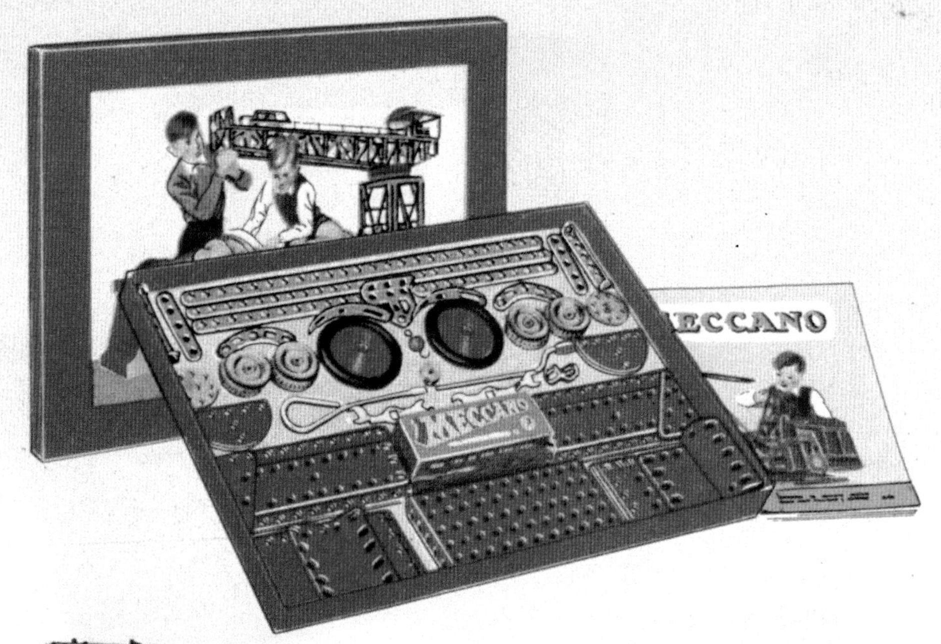

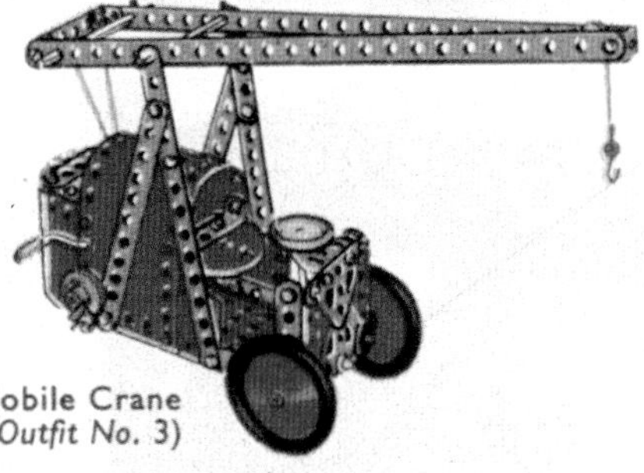
Mobile Crane
(Outfit No. 3)

MECCANO OUTFIT No. 3

Always a great favourite. This Outfit contains parts in greater number and variety, with instructions for building a range of superior models, three of which are shown here.

Electric Crane Truck
(*Outfit No.* 3)

Dumper Truck
(*Outfit No.* 3)

MECCANO OUTFIT No. 4

The owner of a No. 4 Outfit is able to build lots of more advanced models with the greater number and variety of parts at his disposal.

Two examples from the Book of Instructions are illustrated here.

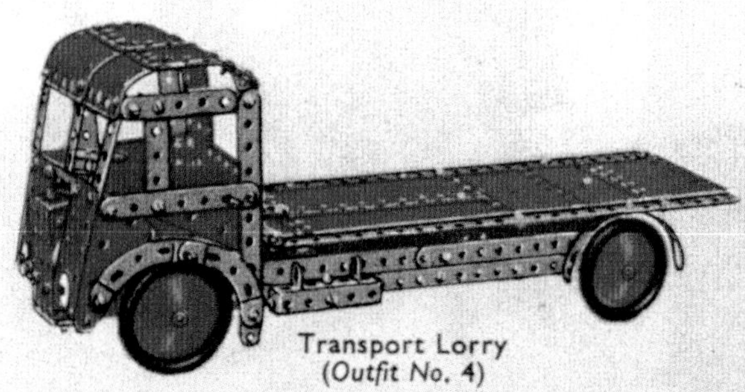
Transport Lorry
(*Outfit No.* 4)

Drilling Machine
(*Outfit No.* 4)

MECCANO OUTFIT No. 5

Model-building possibilities are greatly increased by the large range of parts —including gears—in this attractive Outfit. Two examples from the Book of Instructions are illustrated below.

Pithead Gear
(*Outfit No 5*)

Giant Swing-Boat
(*Outfit No. 5*)

MECCANO OUTFIT No. 6

The inclusion of a greater variety of parts in this Outfit makes possible the construction of even bigger and better models. Among the many attractive models described in the Instructions Book are the two pictured here.

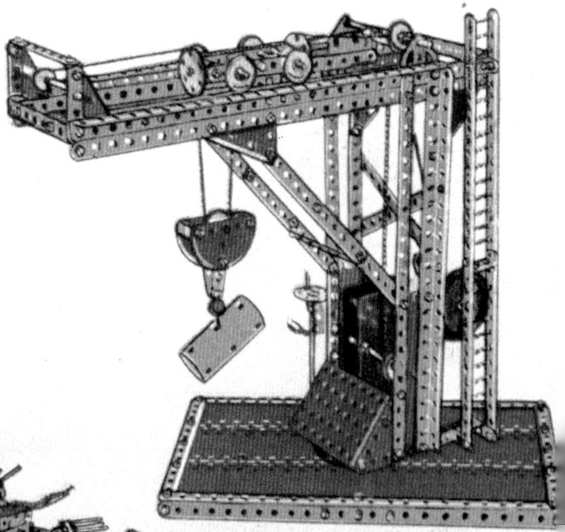

Forge Crane
(*Outfit No. 6*)

Naval Frigate
(*Outfit No. 6*)

MECCANO OUTFIT No. 7

This excellent Outfit is particularly suitable for a boy with an inventive turn of mind, for the wide range of parts encourages originality in the construction of mechanisms and large models like those shown below.

MECCANO OUTFIT No. 8

Continuing the progressive principle of Meccano, many fascinating working models come within the scope of this Outfit. Two are illustrated here.

Coaling Tower
(Outfit No. 7)

Engineers' Lathe
(Outfit No. 7)

Road Sweeper
(Outfit No. 8)

'Jumbo' Mobile Crane
(Outfit No. 8)

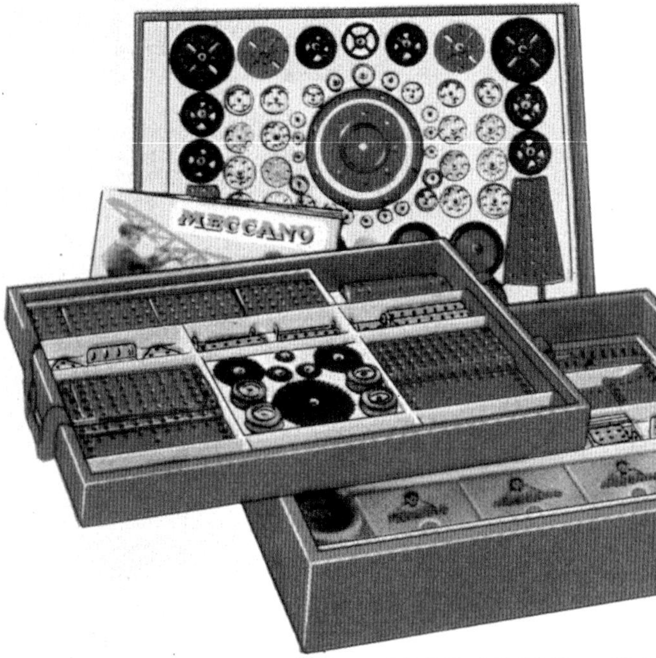

MECCANO OUTFIT No. 9

The proud owner of a No. 9 Outfit has the equipment to build an indefinite number of attractive working models and mechanical movements. An excellent variety is illustrated in the Book of Instructions, and the Floating Crane shown below is a typical example.

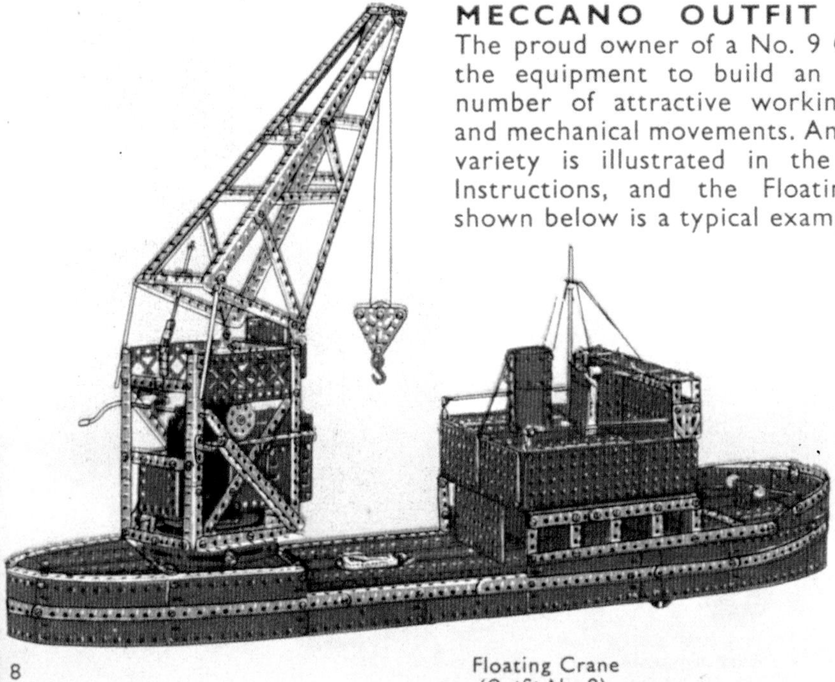

Floating Crane
(*Outfit No. 9*)

MECCANO OUTFIT No. 10

There is no known limit to the number of realistic working models and mechanisms that can be built with this excellent Outfit. A set of Instructions Books is supplied, and also 12 Special Leaflets, each describing in detail the construction of a fascinating working model. In handsome wooden cabinet.

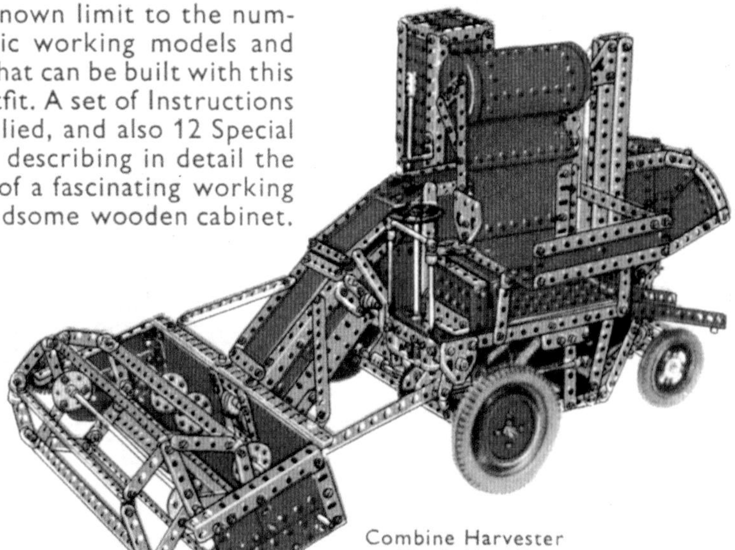

Combine Harvester
(*Outfit No. 10*)

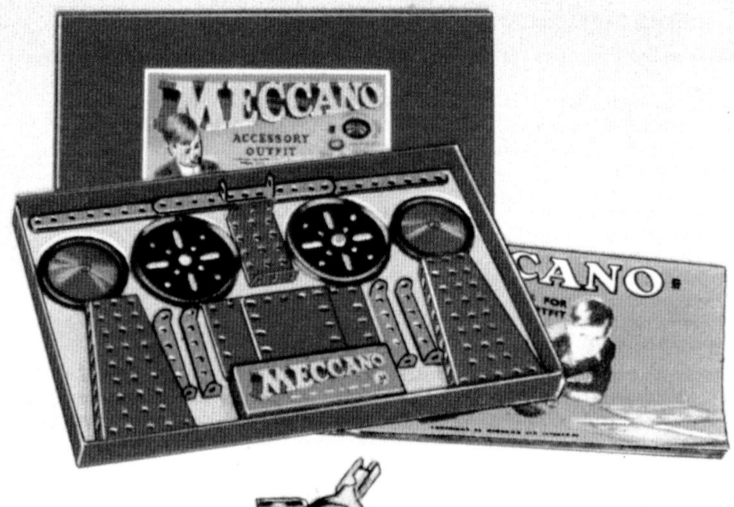

No. 213b

No. 133a

No. 22

No. 128

No. 200

MECCANO ACCESSORY OUTFITS

Each Meccano complete or main Outfit can be converted into the one next larger by the addition of the appropriate Accessory Outfit. No matter with which main Outfit a boy begins, he can build it up by degrees until he has all the parts contained in the largest Outfit.

Accessory Outfit No. OOa converts No. OO to No. O
Accessory Outfit No. Oa converts No. O to No. 1
Accessory Outfit No. 1a converts No. 1 to No. 2
Accessory Outfit No. 2a converts No. 2 to No. 3
Accessory Outfit No. 3a converts No. 3 to No. 4
Accessory Outfit No. 4a converts No. 4 to No. 5
Accessory Outfit No. 5a converts No. 5 to No. 6
Accessory Outfit No. 6a converts No. 6 to No. 7
Accessory Outfit No. 7a converts No. 7 to No. 8
Accessory Outfit No. 8a converts No. 8 to No. 9
Accessory Outfit No. 9a converts No. 9 to No. 10

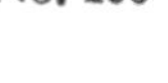

No. 21

No. 133a

No. 51

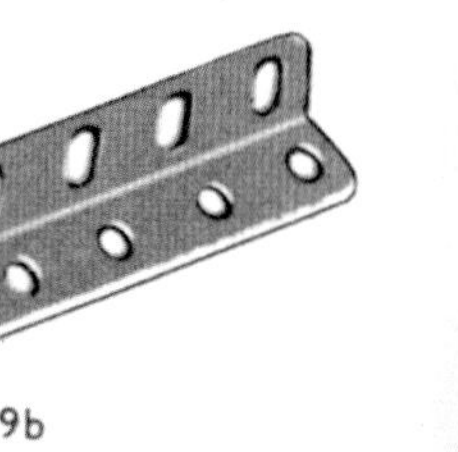

No. 9b

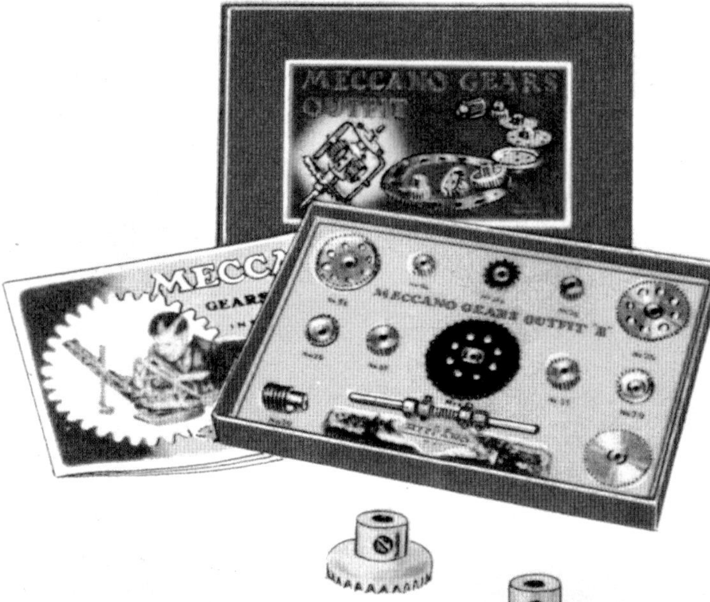

MECCANO GEARS OUTFIT 'B'

This Gears Outfit, used in conjunction with a main Meccano Outfit, makes possible the building of a wide range of interesting mechanisms driven through gears, as in real engineering. The machine-cut brass gears, steel sprockets and Rod with Keyway in the Outfit have been selected as having the widest possible uses.

The various mechanisms, steering and reversing gears, etc., described and illustrated in the Instructions Book are quite simple to assemble and to fit into models.

Two examples from the Instructions Book are reproduced below.

No. 29

No. 96a

No. 25

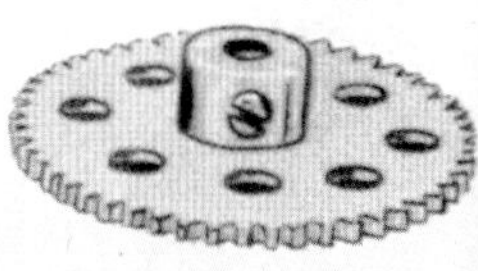

No. 27a

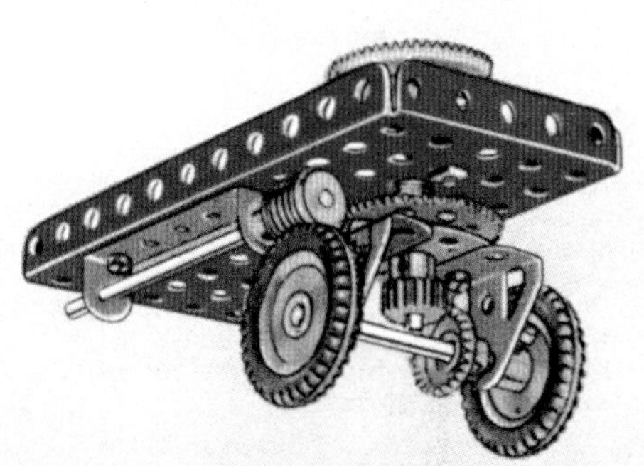

Castor Steering

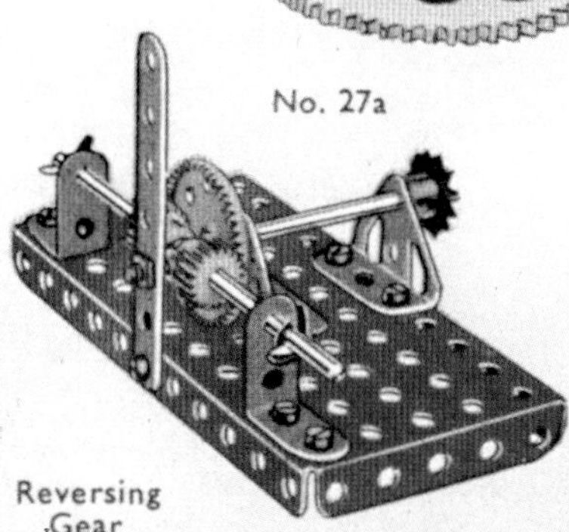

Reversing Gear

Clockwork *Magic* Motor

No. 1 Clockwork Motor

EO20(S) Electric Motor

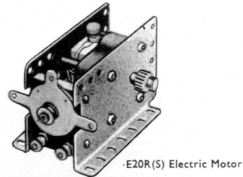

E20R(S) Electric Motor

MECCANO MOTORS

Meccano models can be operated by hand, but the greatest thrill is to set them in motion by means of a Meccano Clockwork or Electric Motor.

MECCANO CLOCKWORK MOTORS

The Meccano Clockwork Motors fit easily into Meccano models, and their precision-cut gears make them smooth and steady in operation.

Meccano Magic Motor. Non-reversible. Specially suitable for driving small models.

Meccano No. 1 Clockwork Motor. Suitable for driving many of the larger models. It is fitted with reversing mechanism.

MECCANO ELECTRIC MOTORS

The great advantage of Electric Motors is that they can be run continuously for long periods. If alternating current is available from the house mains a Meccano 20-volt Electric Motor can be run cheaply, and with perfect safety, through a suitable Transformer. If A.C. current is not available, the E20R(S) Electric Motor will be found to give adequate power when run from a 12-volt car battery.

Meccano No. EO20(S) Electric Motor. A sturdy 20-volt non-reversing motor of the enclosed type. Fitted with radio and T.V. interference suppressors.

Meccano No. E20R(S) Electric Motor. A powerful 20-volt motor with reversing mechanism. Fitted with radio and T.V. interference suppressors.

43903 'S' Key for *Magic* Motor   43901 'B' Key for No. 1 Clockwork Motor

MECCANO BOOKS OF INSTRUCTIONS

Books of Instructions for Meccano Outfits can be purchased separately from Meccano Dealers.

No. OO Book of Instructions
No. O Book of Instructions
No. 1 Book of Instructions
No. 2 Book of Instructions
No. 3 Book of Instructions
No. 4 Book of Instructions
No. 5 Book of Instructions
No. 6 Book of Instructions
No. 7/8 Book of Instructions
No. 9 Book of Instructions
No. 10 Outfit Wallet (containing 12 Special Model Leaflets)
No. Oa Book of Instructions
No. 1a Book of Instructions
No. 2a Book of Instructions
No. 3a Book of Instructions
No. 4a Book of Instructions
No. 5a Book of Instructions
No. 6a Book of Instructions
Gears Outfit 'B' Book of Instructions

Twenty Meccano Special Model Leaflets for Outfit No. 10 are available for the delight of enthusiastic model-builders. Each leaflet contains full instructions for building an attractive, realistic model, with many excellent sectional photographs and particulars of the parts required.

No.	
1	Railway Service Crane
2	Sports Motor Car
3	Coal Tippler
4	Cargo Ship
5	Double Deck Bus
6	Lifting Shovel
7	Block-setting Crane
8	Beam Bridge
9	Dumper Truck
10	Automatic Gantry Crane
11	Automatic Snow Loader
12	4-4-0 Passenger Locomotive and Tender
13	Combine Harvester
14	Eiffel Tower
15	Showman's Traction Engine
16	Twin-cylinder Motor Cycle Engine
17	Trench Digger
18	Bottom Dump Truck
19	Road Surfacing Machine
20	Mechanical Loading Shovel

Instructions for Meccano Outfit No. 10, comprising leaflets 1 to 12, are available in an attractive wallet.

MECCANO PARTS

Meccano model-building becomes more and more fascinating as spare parts are added to build bigger and better models. The full range of Meccano parts is listed on this and the two following pages. Most Meccano dealers can supply Meccano parts from stock.

No. 151

No. 142a

PERFORATED STRIPS

No.		No.	
1	12½in.	3	3½in.
1a	9½in.	4	3in.
1b	7½in.	5	2½in.
2	5½in.	6	2in.
2a	4½in.	6a	1½in.

ANGLE GIRDERS

7	24½in.	9a	4½in.
7a	18½in.	9b	3½in.
8	12½in.	9c	3in.
8a	9½in.	9d	2½in.
8b	7½in.	9e	2in.
9	5½in.	9f	1½in.

10 Fishplate
11 Double Bracket

ANGLE BRACKETS

12	½in. × ½in.	12b	1in. × ½in.
12a	1in. × 1in.	12c	Obtuse, ½in. × ½in.

AXLE RODS

No.		No.	
13	11½in.	16	3½in.
13a	8in.	16a	2½in.
14	6½in.	16b	3in.
15	5in.	17	2in.
15a	4½in.	18a	1½in.
15b	4in.	18b	1in.

CRANK HANDLES

No.	
19g	3½in. shaft, with grip
19h	5in. shaft, with grip
19s	3½in. shaft, without grip

19a Spoked Wheel, 3in. diam.
20 Flanged Wheel, 1⅛in. diam.
20b Flanged Wheel, ¾in. diam.

PULLEYS

19b	3in. diam., with boss and screw
19c	6in. diam., with boss and screw
20a	2in. diam., with boss and screw
21	1½in. diam., with boss and screw
22	1in. diam., with boss and screw
22a	1in. diam., without boss
23	½in. diam. without boss
23a	½in. diam., with boss and screw

No.	
24	Bush Wheel, 1⅜in. diam., 8 holes
24a	Wheel Disc, 1⅜in. diam., 8 holes, without boss
24b	Bush Wheel, 1⅜in. diam., 6 holes
24c	Wheel Disc, 1⅜in. diam., 6 holes, without boss

PINIONS

25	¾in. diam., ¼in. face, 25 teeth
25a	¾in. diam., ½in. face, 25 teeth
25b	¾in. diam., ¾in. face, 25 teeth
26	½in. diam., ¼in. face, 19 teeth
26a	½in. diam., ½in. face, 19 teeth
26b	½in. diam., ¾in. face, 19 teeth
26c	7/16in. diam., ¼in. face, 15 teeth

GEAR WHEELS

27	1¼in. diam., 50 teeth
27a	1½in. diam., 57 teeth
27b	3½in. diam., 133 teeth
27c	2½in. diam., 95 teeth
27d	1⅝in. diam., 60 teeth

CONTRATE WHEELS

28	1½in. diam., 50 teeth
29	¾in. diam., 25 teeth

No. 97

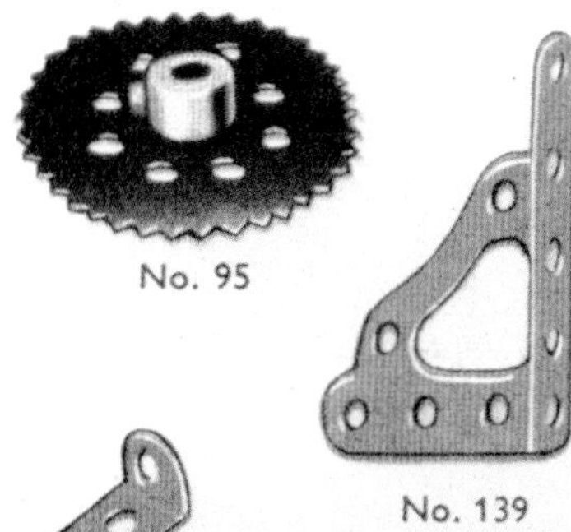

No. 95

No. 139

No. 12b

No. 140

No. 76

No. 20b

No. 187

No. 113

No. 24c

No. 62

No. 213a

No. 160

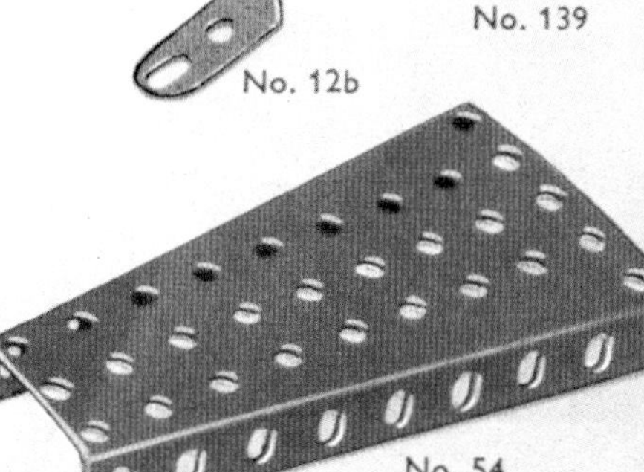

No. 54

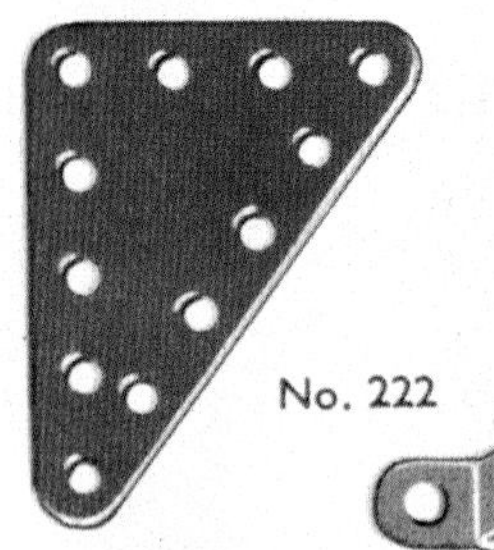
No. 222

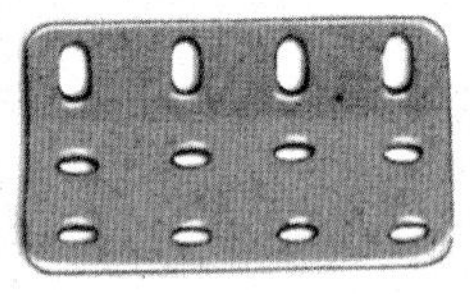
No. 161

No. 130

No. 31

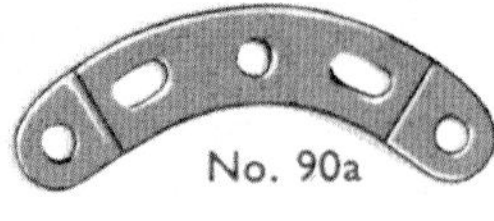
No. 90a

No. 110

No. 63

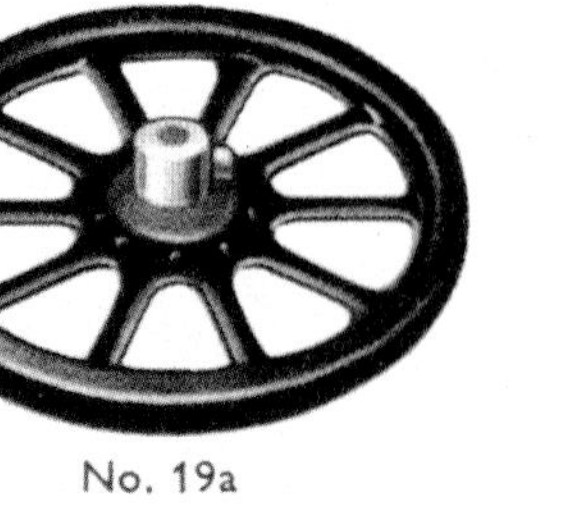
No. 19a

No. 221

No. 154a

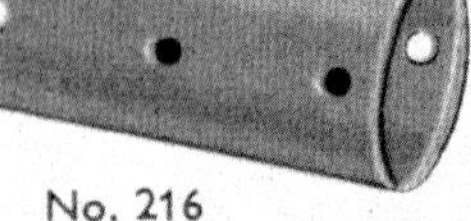
No. 216

No. 147

No. 57b

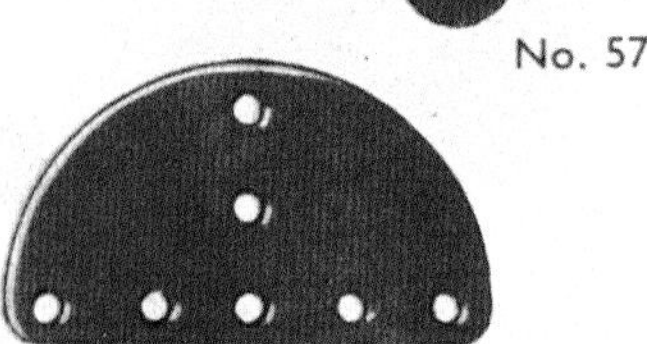
No. 214

No. 23

No. 136a

No. 20a

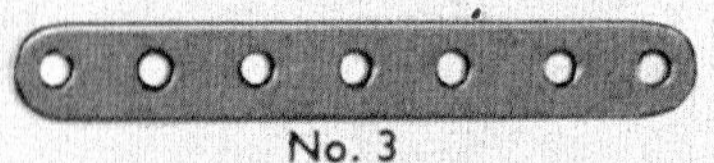
No. 3

No.	
30	Bevel Gear, $\frac{7}{8}$in. diam., 26 teeth (for use in pairs)
30a	Bevel Gear, $\frac{1}{2}$in. diam., 16 teeth
30c	Bevel Gear, $1\frac{1}{2}$in. diam., 48 teeth (30a & 30c can only be used together)
31	Gear Wheel, 1in. diam., $\frac{1}{4}$in. face, 38 teeth
32	Worm, $\frac{1}{2}$in. diam.
34	Spanner
34b	Box Spanner
35	Spring Clip
36	Screwdriver
36a	Screwdriver (longer)
36c	Drift (for levering bolt holes into line)
37	Nut and Bolt, 7/32in.
37a	Nut
37b	Bolt, 7/32in.
38	Washer
38d	Washer, $\frac{3}{4}$in.
40	Hank of Cord
41	Propeller Blade
43	Tension Spring, 2in. long
44	Bent Strip, stepped
45	Double Bent Strip

DOUBLE ANGLE STRIPS

46	$2\frac{1}{2}$in. $\times$ 1in.	48a	$2\frac{1}{2}$in. $\times$ $\frac{1}{2}$in.
47	$2\frac{1}{2}$in. $\times$ $1\frac{1}{2}$in.	48b	$3\frac{1}{2}$in. $\times$ $\frac{1}{2}$in.
47a	3in. $\times$ $1\frac{1}{2}$in.	48c	$4\frac{1}{2}$in. $\times$ $\frac{1}{2}$in.
48	$1\frac{1}{2}$in. $\times$ $\frac{1}{2}$in.	48d	$5\frac{1}{2}$in. $\times$ $\frac{1}{2}$in.

50 Slide Piece

PLATES

51	Flanged Plate, $2\frac{1}{2}$in. $\times$ $1\frac{1}{2}$in.
52	Flanged Plate, $5\frac{1}{2}$in. $\times$ $2\frac{1}{2}$in.
52a	Flat Plate, $5\frac{1}{2}$in. $\times$ $3\frac{1}{2}$in.
53	Flanged Plate, $3\frac{1}{2}$in. $\times$ $2\frac{1}{2}$in.
53a	Flat Plate, $4\frac{1}{2}$in. $\times$ $2\frac{1}{2}$in.
54	Flanged Sector Plate, $4\frac{1}{2}$in. long

No.	
55	Perforated Strip, slotted, $5\frac{1}{2}$in. long
55a	Perforated Strip, slotted, 2in. long
57b	Hook, Loaded, large
57c	Hook, Loaded, small
58	Spring Cord, 40in. length
58a	Coupling Screw for Spring Cord
58b	Hook for Spring Cord
59	Collar, with screw
61	Windmill Sail
62	Crank
62a	Threaded Crank
62b	Double Arm Crank
63	Coupling
63b	Strip Coupling
63c	Threaded Coupling
63d	Short Coupling
64	Threaded Boss
65	Centre Fork
69	Set Screw, 5/32in.
69a	Grub Screw, 5/32in.
69b	Grub Screw, 7/32in.
69c	Grub Screw, 7/64in.

PLATES

70	Flat Plate, $5\frac{1}{2}$in. $\times$ $2\frac{1}{2}$in.
72	Flat Plate, $2\frac{1}{2}$in. $\times$ $2\frac{1}{2}$in.
73	Flat Plate, 3in. $\times$ $1\frac{1}{2}$in.
76	Triangular Plate, $2\frac{1}{2}$in.
77	Triangular Plate, 1in.

SCREWED RODS

78	$11\frac{1}{2}$in.	80b	$4\frac{1}{2}$in.
79	8in.	80c	3in.
79a	6in.	81	2in.
80	5in.	82	1in.
80a	$3\frac{1}{2}$in.		

CURVED STRIPS

89	$5\frac{1}{2}$in. (10in. radius)
89a	Stepped, 3in. ($1\frac{3}{4}$in. radius)
89b	Stepped, 4in. ($4\frac{1}{2}$in. radius)

No.	Curved Strips (Cond.)
90	$2\frac{1}{2}$in. ($2\frac{3}{8}$in. radius)
90a	Stepped, $2\frac{1}{2}$in. ($1\frac{3}{8}$in. radius)

94 Sprocket Chain, 40in. length

SPROCKET WHEELS

95	2in. diam., 36 teeth
95a	$1\frac{1}{2}$in. diam., 28 teeth
95b	3in. diam., 56 teeth
96	1in. diam., 18 teeth
96a	$\frac{3}{4}$in. diam., 14 teeth

BRACED GIRDERS

97	$3\frac{1}{2}$in. long	99a	$9\frac{1}{2}$in. long
97a	3in. long	99b	$7\frac{1}{2}$in. long
98	$2\frac{1}{2}$in. long	100	$5\frac{1}{2}$in. long
99	$12\frac{1}{2}$in. long	100a	$4\frac{1}{2}$in. long

101	Heald for Loom
102	Single Bent Strip

FLAT GIRDERS

103	$5\frac{1}{2}$in. long	103e	3in. long
103a	$9\frac{1}{2}$in. long	103f	$2\frac{1}{2}$in. long
103b	$12\frac{1}{2}$in. long	103g	2in. long
103c	$4\frac{1}{2}$in. long	103h	$1\frac{1}{2}$in. long
103d	$3\frac{1}{2}$in. long	103k	$7\frac{1}{2}$in. long

106	Wood Roller (complete with Rod and two Collars)
108	Corner Gusset
109	Face Plate, $2\frac{1}{2}$in. diam.
110	Rack Strip, $3\frac{1}{2}$in. long
110a	Rack Strip, $6\frac{1}{2}$in. long

BOLTS

111	$\frac{3}{4}$in.	111c	$\frac{3}{8}$in.
111a	$\frac{1}{2}$in.	111d	$1\frac{1}{8}$in.

113	Girder Frame
114	Hinge

No.
115 Threaded Pin
116 Fork Piece, large
116a Fork Piece, small
118 Hub Disc, $5\frac{1}{2}$in. diam.
120b Compression Spring, $\frac{9}{16}$in. long
122 Loaded Sack
123 Cone Pulley, $1\frac{1}{4}$in., 1in. and $\frac{3}{4}$in. diam.
124 Reversed Angle Bracket, 1in.
125 Reversed Angle Bracket, $\frac{1}{2}$in.
126 Trunnion
126a Flat Trunnion
128 Bell Crank, with boss
130 Eccentric, Triple Throw, $\frac{1}{4}$in., $\frac{3}{8}$in. and $\frac{1}{2}$in.
130a Eccentric, Single Throw, $\frac{1}{4}$in.
133 Corner Bracket, $1\frac{1}{2}$in.
133a Corner Bracket, 1in.
134 Crank Shaft, 1in. stroke
136 Handrail Support
136a Handrail Coupling
137 Wheel Flange
138 Ship's Funnel, Raked
139 Flanged Bracket (right)
139a Flanged Bracket (left)
140 Universal Coupling

MOTOR TYRES

142a To fit 2in. diam. rim
142b To fit 3in. diam. rim
142c To fit 1in. diam. rim
142d To fit $1\frac{1}{2}$in. diam. rim

143 Circular Girder, $5\frac{1}{2}$in. diam.
144 Dog Clutch
145 Circular Strip, $7\frac{1}{2}$in. diam. overall
146 Circular Plate, 6in. diam. overall
146a Circular Plate, 4in. diam. overall
147 Pawl, with Pivot Bolt and Nuts
147a Pawl
147b Pivot Bolt, with two Nuts
147c Pawl, without boss
148 Ratchet Wheel
151 Single Pulley Block
153 Triple Pulley Block
154a Corner Angle Bracket, $\frac{1}{2}$in. (right-hand)
154b Corner Angle Bracket, $\frac{1}{2}$in. (left-hand)

No.
155 Rubber Ring (for 1in. Pulley)
157 Fan, 2in. diam.
160 Channel Bearing, $1\frac{1}{2}$in. × 1in. × $\frac{1}{2}$in.
161 Girder Bracket, 2in. × 1in. × $\frac{1}{2}$in.
162 Boiler, complete, 5in. long × $2\frac{1}{16}$in. diam.
162a Boiler End, $2\frac{1}{16}$in. diam. × $\frac{3}{4}$in.
163 Sleeve Piece, $1\frac{1}{2}$in. long × $\frac{11}{16}$in. diam.
164 Chimney Adaptor, $\frac{5}{8}$in. diam. × $\frac{1}{2}$in. high
165 Swivel Bearing
166 End Bearing
167b Flanged Ring, $9\frac{7}{8}$in. diam.
168 Ball Thrust Bearing, 4in. diam.
168a Ball Thrust Race, flanged disc, $3\frac{3}{4}$in. diam.
168b Ball Thrust Race, toothed disc, 4in. diam.
168c Ball Cage, $3\frac{5}{8}$in. diam., complete with balls
168d Ball, $\frac{3}{8}$in. diam.
171 Socket Coupling
173a Adaptor for Screwed Rod
175 Flexible Coupling Unit
176 Anchoring Spring for Cord
179 Rod Socket
180 Gear Ring, $3\frac{1}{2}$in. diam. (133 ext. teeth, 95 int.)
185 Steering Wheel, $1\frac{3}{4}$in. diam.

DRIVING BANDS

186	$2\frac{1}{2}$in. (light)	186c	10in. (heavy)
186a	6in. (light)	186d	15in. (heavy)
186b	10in. (light)	186e	20in. (heavy)

187 Road Wheel, $2\frac{1}{2}$in. diam.
187a Conical Disc, $1\frac{7}{8}$in. diam.

FLEXIBLE PLATES

188	$2\frac{1}{2}$in. × $1\frac{1}{2}$in.	190a	$3\frac{1}{2}$in. × $2\frac{1}{2}$in.
189	$5\frac{1}{2}$in. × $1\frac{1}{2}$in.	191	$4\frac{1}{2}$in. × $2\frac{1}{2}$in.
190	$2\frac{1}{2}$in. × $2\frac{1}{2}$in.	192	$5\frac{1}{2}$in. × $2\frac{1}{2}$in.

STRIP PLATES

196 $9\frac{1}{2}$in. × $2\frac{1}{2}$in.
197 $12\frac{1}{2}$in. × $2\frac{1}{2}$in.

198 Hinged Flat Plate, $4\frac{1}{2}$in. × $2\frac{1}{2}$in.
199 Curved Plate, U-section, $2\frac{1}{2}$in. × $2\frac{1}{2}$in. × 9/32in. radius
200 Curved Plate, $2\frac{1}{2}$in. × $2\frac{1}{2}$in. × $1\frac{11}{16}$in. rad.

No.
211a Helical Gear, $\frac{1}{2}$in. } Can only be
211b Helical Gear, $1\frac{1}{2}$in. } used together
212 Rod and Strip Connector
212a Rod and Strip Connector, right angle
213 Rod Connector
213a 3-way Rod Connector
213b 3-way Rod Connector, with boss
214 Semi-Circular Plate, $2\frac{1}{2}$in.
215 Formed Slotted Strip, 3in.
216 Cylinder, $2\frac{1}{2}$in. long, $1\frac{1}{4}$in. diam.

TRIANGULAR FLEXIBLE PLATES

221	$2\frac{1}{2}$in. × $1\frac{1}{2}$in.	224	$3\frac{1}{2}$in. × $1\frac{1}{2}$in.
222	$2\frac{1}{2}$in. × 2in.	225	$3\frac{1}{2}$in. × 2in.
223	$2\frac{1}{2}$in. × $2\frac{1}{2}$in.	226	$3\frac{1}{2}$in. × $2\frac{1}{2}$in.

230 4in. Rod with Keyway
231 Key Bolt (doz.)

Tower Wagon
(Outfit No. 6)

Any Meccano dealer will be pleased to supply—free of charge—a copy of the folder illustrating the entire range of parts in the Meccano System.

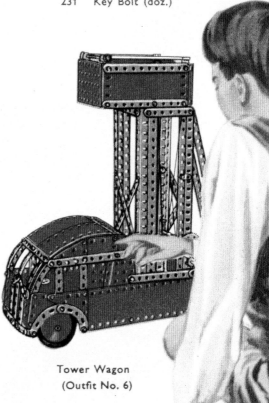

HORNBY DUBLO
ELECTRIC TRAINS

SAFE AND RELIABLE

POWERFUL LOCOMOTIVES

FITTED WITH SUPPRESSORS

AUTOMATIC COUPLINGS

MAINS OR BATTERY OPERATED

GAUGE OO $\frac{5}{8}$in. (16·5 mm.)

When you start a model railway it is obviously something you intend to enjoy for many years. Start off right—with Hornby-Dublo, precision engineered for lasting service. The Hornby-Dublo System, with remote control, can reproduce all the working of a real railway—on a table!

MASTERPIECES IN MINIATURE. Hornby-Dublo trains are accurate reproductions of real trains, made of the finest materials and with engineering precision. The locomotive housings and other components are die-cast under pressure, a process that gives a product of great strength and durability, with perfect surface detail. Locomotives and rolling stock are handsomely finished in British Railways colours, with names and numbers correctly reproduced.

EASY TO RUN. The Hornby-Dublo system operates on D.C. at 12 volts, and is therefore safe for the youngest owners. Current may be obtained in any one of three different ways, as follows:

1. From A.C. mains through a suitable self-contained power unit.
2. From three 4·5-volt dry bell batteries (Ever-Ready 126 or Drydex H30), using a Hornby-Dublo Battery Control Unit.
3. From a 12-volt accumulator, of 10 or 20 amp-hr. capacity, using the Hornby-Dublo C3 Controller.

SIMPLE TO CONTROL. Trains can be started either forward or backward and stopped by just moving the single handle of the Controller, which also varies their speeds. Thus trains on a Hornby-Dublo layout can be operated realistically from a central control position.

TRACK COMPONENTS. The Straight and Curved Rails, Points and Crossings which are available allow for a wide variety of layouts, and there are special Large Radius Curves that, with the Standard Curved Rails, provide double track, like that of a real railway.

AUTOMATIC COUPLING AND UNCOUPLING. Hornby-Dublo Locomotives, Coaches and Wagons couple immediately on impact, and the Uncoupling Rail is used to disengage automatically the couplings of vehicles passing over it. Thus trains can be made up, or broken up, by remote control, without handling them at all.
Two forms of Uncoupling Rail are available. One is hand-operated; the other is electrically-operated, brought into action by means of a push-button switch.

ELECTRICALLY-OPERATED ACCESSORIES. Other electrically-operated components of the Hornby-Dublo System include Points and Signals, with neat and efficient Switches specially designed for operating them. The Switches can be grouped alongside the Controller, so that there is complete remote control over all train movements, including shunting. With the T.P.O. Mail Van Set, trains can be run that pick up mail and set it down without stopping—just as on real railways. In addition to the components and accessories already noted, the system includes hand-operated Signals, a Water Crane, a Loading Gauge, a Signal Cabin, Girder Bridge, Turntable and Buffer Stops. Two handsome Stations are available, each with buildings and ramps. These and other components of the System are illustrated in the following pages of this booklet.

Guarantee

All Hornby-Dublo components are thoroughly tested before despatch from the Meccano Works, and their efficiency is guaranteed.

HORNBY-DUBLO TRAIN SETS

EDP10 Hornby-Dublo 0-6-2 Tank Passenger Train Set B.R.

EDP14 Hornby-Dublo 2-6-4 Tank Passenger Train Set B.R.

EDP15 Hornby-Dublo 'Silver King' Passenger Train Set B.R.

EDP10 HORNBY-DUBLO 0-6-2 TANK PASSENGER TRAIN SET B.R.

This set contains Hornby-Dublo EDL17 Tank Locomotive 0-6-2 B.R., D14 Suburban Coach 1st/2nd D14 Suburban Coach Brake/2nd, and rails forming an oval track requiring a space of 3ft. 6in. by 3ft.

EDP14 HORNBY-DUBLO 2-6-4 TANK PASSENGER TRAIN SET B.R.

This set contains Hornby-Dublo EDL18 Tank Locomotive 2-6-4 B.R., D14 Suburban Coach 1st/2nd, two D14 Suburban Coaches Brake/2nd, and rails forming an oval track requiring a space of 4ft. by 3ft.

EDP15 HORNBY-DUBLO 'SILVER KING' PASSENGER TRAIN SET B.R.

This set contains Hornby-Dublo Streamlined Locomotive EDL11 'Silver King', D11 Tender, D12 Coach 1st/2nd, D12 Coach Brake/2nd and rails forming an oval track requiring a space of 4ft. by 3ft.

With the exception of EDP10, each of the above Hornby-Dublo Train Sets is supplied with the following rails—1 EDB1 Straight Rail, 1 EDB 1½ Straight Half Rail, 1 EDBX½ Straight Half Rail with Roadway, 7 EDA1 Curved Rails, 1 EDAT1 Curved Terminal Rail.

Power supply and control units are not included in the sets.

HORNBY-DUBLO TRAIN SETS

EDG16 Hornby-Dublo 0-6-2 Tank Goods Train Set B.R.

EDG17 Hornby-Dublo 0-6-2 Tank Goods Train Set B.R.

EDG19 Hornby-Dublo 2-6-4 Tank Goods Train Set B.R.

12-volt

EDG16 HORNBY-DUBLO 0-6-2 TANK GOODS TRAIN SET, B.R.
This set contains Hornby-Dublo 0-6-2 Tank Locomotive EDL17, two D1 Open Wagons, D1 Goods Brake Van and rails forming an oval track requiring a space of 3ft. 6in. by 3ft.

EDG17 HORNBY-DUBLO 0-6-2 TANK GOODS TRAIN SET, B.R.
This set contains Hornby-Dublo 0-6-2 Tank Locomotive EDL17, D1 Meat Van, D1 Open Wagon, D1 Tank Wagon 'Mobil', D1 Goods Brake Van and rails forming an oval track requiring a space of 3ft. 6in. by 3ft.

EDG19 HORNBY-DUBLO 2-6-4 TANK GOODS TRAIN SET, B.R.
This set contains Hornby-Dublo 2-6-4 Tank Locomotive EDL18, D1 Ventilated Van, D1 Tank Wagon 'Mobil', D2 Double Bolster Wagon, D1 20-ton Tube Wagon, D1 Goods Brake Van and rails forming an oval track requiring a space of 4ft. by 3ft.

EDG18 HORNBY-DUBLO 2-6-4 TANK GOODS SET, B.R.
(not illustrated)

With the exception of EDG18 and EDG19, each of the above Hornby-Dublo train sets is supplied with the following rails—1 EDB1½ Straight Half Rail, 1 EDBX½ Straight Half Rail with Roadway, 7 EDA1 Curved Rails, 1 EDAT1 Curved Terminal Rail. 1 EDB1 Straight Rail is also included in Hornby-Dublo Train Sets EDG18 and EDG19 and the space required for these Sets is 4ft. by 3ft.

Suppressors are fitted to all Hornby-Dublo Locomotives and effectively counter interference with radio and television reception.

HORNBY-DUBLO TRAIN SETS

12-volt

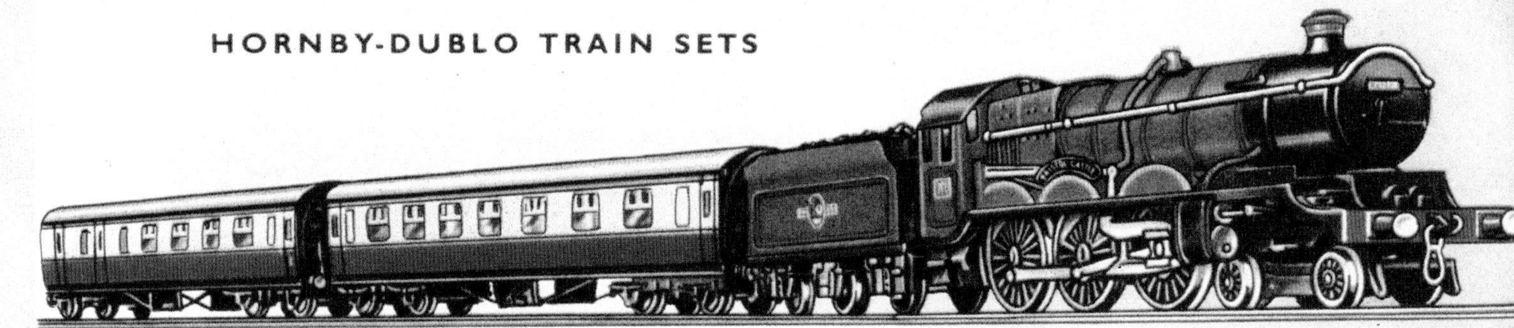

EDP20 Hornby-Dublo 'Bristolian' Passenger Train Set B.R.

EDP20 HORNBY-DUBLO 'BRISTOLIAN' PASSENGER TRAIN SET, B.R. (W.R.)

This Set contains Locomotive and Tender EDLT20 'Bristol Castle', D21 Coach 1st/2nd, D21 Coach Brake/2nd and rails forming an oval track requiring a space of 4ft. by 3ft. *(available later)*

EDP22 Hornby-Dublo 'Royal Scot' Passenger Train Set B.R.

EDP22 HORNBY-DUBLO 'ROYAL SCOT' PASSENGER TRAIN SET, B.R. (L.M.R.)

This Set contains Locomotive EDL12 'Duchess of Montrose' D12 Tender, D22 Coach 1st/2nd, D22 Coach Brake/2nd and rails forming an oval track requiring a space of 4ft. by 3ft.

EDP12 HORNBY-DUBLO 'DUCHESS OF MONTROSE' PASSENGER SET, B.R.
(not illustrated)

HORNBY-DUBLO CONTROL UNITS

Hornby-Dublo Battery Control Unit

32,849 HORNBY-DUBLO BATTERY CONTROL UNIT

A Hornby-Dublo Locomotive can be worked efficiently from dry batteries using the Hornby-Dublo Battery Control Unit. Current at 12 volts is required and this can be obtained from three 4½-v. dry bell batteries (Ever-Ready No. 126 or Drydex H.30).

32,304 HORNBY-DUBLO C3 CONTROLLER

For use with any convenient 12–15 volt A.C. supply for controlling a Locomotive. It can also be used with a 12 volt Accumulator, or any other 12 volt D.C. supply.

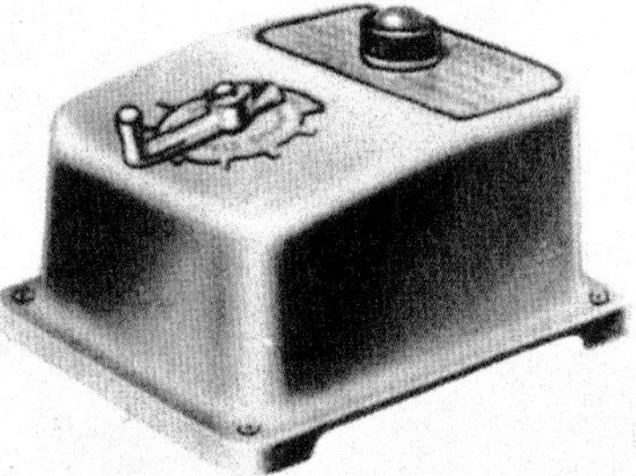

Hornby-Dublo C3 Controller

Your local dealer will be pleased to advise the most suitable power control unit.

HORNBY-DUBLO LOCOMOTIVES AND TENDERS

Hornby-Dublo Locomotives are scale-proportioned models finely-detailed, with accurate reproduction of valve gear. Suppressors are fitted which effectively counter interference with radio and television reception.

EDLT20 Locomotive and Tender 'Bristol Castle' B.R. (W.R.). Sold only as a unit.

EDL12 Locomotive 'Duchess of Montrose' and D12 Tender B.R. (L.M.R.)

EDL11 Locomotive 'Silver King' and D11 Tender B.R. (E.R.)

EDL17 Tank Locomotive 0-6-2, B.R.

EDL18 Tank Locomotive 2-6-4, B.R.

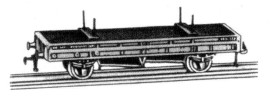

32,052 D2 Double Bolster Wagon (long wheelbase) Length 5in.

32,076 D1 20-ton Tube Wagon (long wheelbase) Length $5\frac{5}{16}$in.

32,058 D1 Ventilated Van (long wheelbase) Length $5\frac{5}{16}$in.

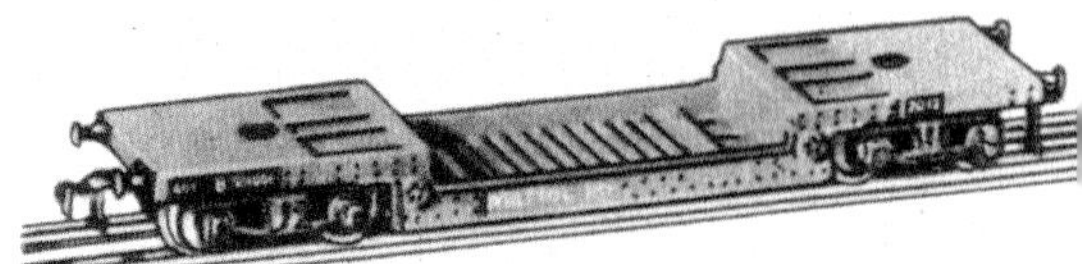

32,053 D1 40-ton Bogie Well Wagon Length $6\frac{3}{4}$in.

HORNBY-DUBLO ROLLING STOCK WITH AUTOMATIC COUPLINGS

32,051
D1 Bogie Bolster Wagon
Length $6\frac{3}{8}$in.

32,050
D1 High Capacity Wagon
Length $6\frac{3}{8}$in.

32,022
D22 Corridor Coach, 1st/2nd, B.R. Maroon Livery
(with corridor partitions and transparent windows)
Length $9\frac{1}{16}$in.

32,018
D12 Corridor Coach, Brake/2nd B.R.
(with corridor partitions and transparent windows)
Length $9\frac{1}{16}$in.

32,017
D12 Corridor Coach, 1st/2nd B.R.
(with corridor partitions and transparent windows)
Length $9\frac{1}{16}$in.

32,023
D22 Corridor Coach, Brake/2nd, B.R. Maroon Livery
(with corridor partitions and transparent windows)
Length $9\frac{1}{16}$in.

32,095
D21 Corridor Coach, Brake/2nd B.R. (W.R.)
(with corridor partitions and transparent windows)
Length $9\frac{1}{16}$in.

32,094
D21 Corridor Coach, 1st/2nd B.R. (W.R.)
(with corridor partitions and transparent windows)
Length $9\frac{1}{16}$in.

32,092
D14 Suburban Coach, 1st/2nd B.R.
(with transparent windows)
Length $7\frac{15}{16}$in.

32,097
D20 Composite Restaurant Car B.R.
(with transparent windows and internal fittings)
Length $9\frac{1}{16}$in. (*available later*).

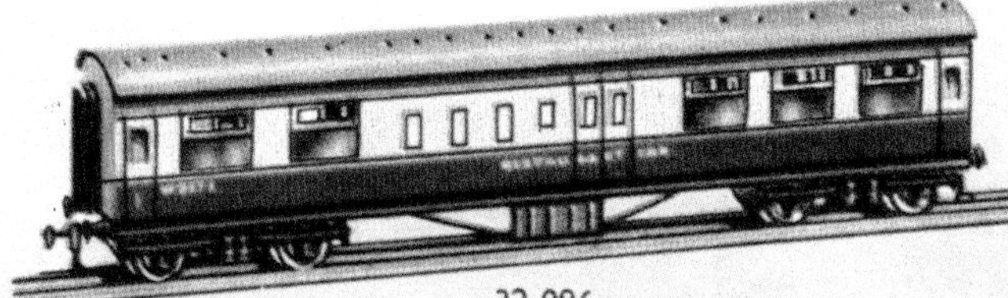

32,096
D20 Composite Restaurant Car B.R. (W.R.)
(with transparent windows and internal fittings)
Length $9\frac{1}{16}$in. (*available later*)

32,093
D14 Suburban Coach, Brake/2nd B.R.
(with transparent windows)
Length $7\frac{15}{16}$in.

The overall dimensions given above are measured over the Couplings

HORNBY-DUBLO ROLLING STOCK WITH AUTOMATIC COUPLINGS

32,085
D1 Low-Sided Wagon
Length $3\frac{7}{8}$in.

32,056
D2 Mineral Wagon
Length $3\frac{1}{2}$in.

32,075
D1 Open Wagon
Length $3\frac{1}{2}$in.

32,065
D1 Meat Van
Length $3\frac{1}{2}$in.

32,020
D1 Cattle Truck
Length $3\frac{1}{2}$in.

32,086
D1 Low-Sided Wagon with Cable Drums. Length $3\frac{7}{8}$in.

32,084
D1 Tank Wagon 'MOBIL'
Length $3\frac{1}{2}$in.

32,083
DI Tank Wagon 'VACUUM'
Length $3\frac{1}{2}$in. *(not illustrated)*

32,025
D1 Coal Wagon
Length $3\frac{1}{2}$in.

32,060
D1 Horse Box
Length $3\frac{1}{2}$in.

32,046
Goods Brake Van B.R. (E.R.)
Length $4\frac{5}{16}$in.

32,088
D1 Low-Sided Wagon
with Insulated Meat Container
Length $3\frac{7}{8}$in.

32,081
D1 Tank Wagon 'ESSO'
Length $3\frac{1}{2}$in.

32,055
D2 High-Sided Wagon
Length $3\frac{1}{2}$in.

32,035
D1 Fish Van
Length $3\frac{1}{2}$in.

32,045
D1 Goods Brake Van
B.R. (L.M.R.)
Length $4\frac{5}{16}$in.

32,087
D1 Low-Sided Wagon
with Furniture Container
Length $3\frac{7}{8}$in.

32,082
D1 Tank Wagon
'SHELL LUBRICATING OIL'
Length $3\frac{1}{2}$in.

32,030
D2 High-Sided Coal Wagon
Length $3\frac{1}{2}$in.

32,040
D1 Goods Van
Length $3\frac{1}{2}$in.

32,047
D1 Goods Brake Van B.R. (W.R.)
Length $4\frac{5}{16}$in.

The overall dimensions given above are measured over the Couplings

HORNBY-DUBLO TRACK

GAUGE OO ⅝ in. (16·5 mm.)

By adding more Rails, Points and Crossings to the contents of a Hornby-Dublo Train Set, a great variety of running schemes is possible. The present range of Hornby-Dublo track components is illustrated below. Strength and adaptability to all kinds of layouts are only two of the advantages of Hornby-Dublo track, with its metal base and solid running rails.

EDB1
Straight Rail
Length 11½in.

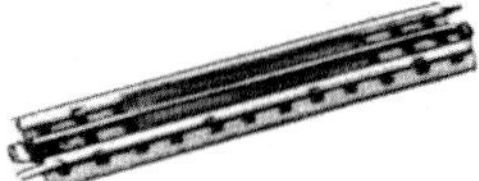

EDBX½
Straight Half Rail with Roadway
Length 5¾in.

EUBR
Electrically-Operated
Uncoupling Rail (with Switch)
Length 5¾in.

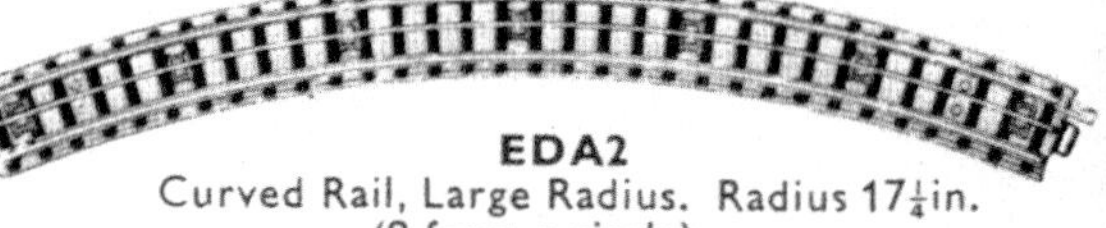

EDA2
Curved Rail, Large Radius. Radius 17¼in.
(8 form a circle)

EDB1½
Straight Half Rail
Length 5¾in.

EDB1¼
Straight Quarter Rail
Length 2⅞in.

ISPL
Isolating Switch Points, Left-hand
Length 5¾in.

ISPR
Isolating Switch Points, Right-hand
Length 5¾in.

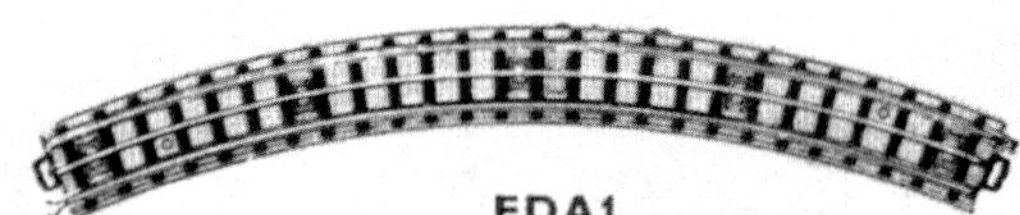

EDA1
Curved Rail. Radius 15in.
(8 form a circle)

EDBT1½
Straight Terminal
Half Rail
Length 5¾in.

IBR¼
Isolating Rail
Length 2⅞in.

EDCL
Diamond Crossing, Left-hand
Main line length 5¾in.

EDCR
Diamond Crossing, Right-hand
Main line length 5¾in.

EDA1¼
Curved Quarter Rail
Radius 15in.

EDA1½
Curved Half Rail
Radius 15in.

EDBS
Straight Short Rail
Length 1 5/16in.

UBR Uncoupling Rail
When the ramp is raised it disengages the couplings of vehicles passing over it.
Length 5¾in.

EODPL
Elec.-Operated Points, Left-hand
Length 5¾in.

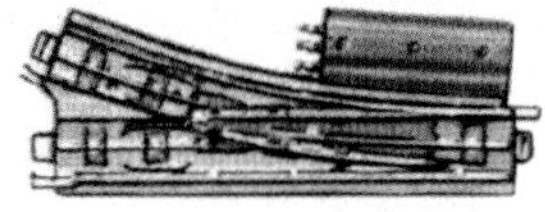

EODPR
Elec.-Operated Points, Right-hand
Length 5¾in.

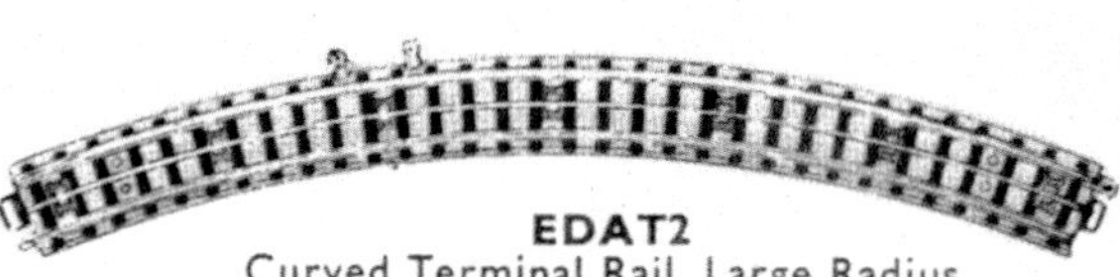

EDAT2
Curved Terminal Rail. Large Radius
Radius 17¼in.

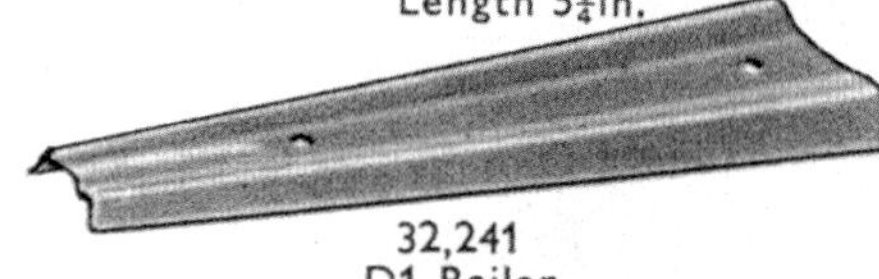

32,241
D1 Railer
Length 12in.

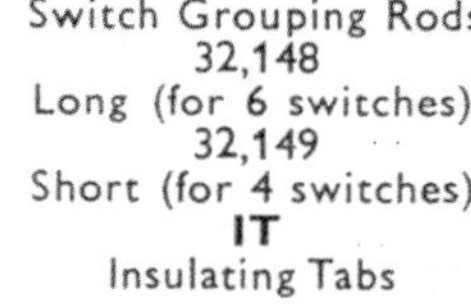

32,303
D2 Switch
(for Isolating
Rail **IBR¼**)

Switch Grouping Rods
32,148
Long (for 6 switches)
32,149
Short (for 4 switches)
IT
Insulating Tabs

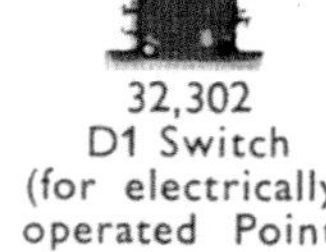

32,302
D1 Switch
(for electrically-operated Points and Signals)

EDAT1
Curved Terminal Rail
Radius 15in.

HORNBY-DUBLO SUNDRIES

32,171 Station Names to fit panels on Through Station and Signal Cabin (Packet of 5 pairs)
32,654 Hornby-Dublo Spanner
32,655 Vial of Oil
32,660 Transformer Fuse
32,911 Two Wheels with Axle (for rolling stock)
32,652 Brush for locomotives
32,653 Brush Spring for locomotives
32,657 Connecting Wire, 5-yard length
32,659 Connecting Wire, reel 50 yards
32,945 D1 Insulated Meat Container
32,946 D1 Furniture Container
32,947 D1 Cable Drum

32,099 HORNBY-DUBLO DI T.P.O MAIL VAN SET

With this magnificent set Hornby-Dublo owners can run trains that pick up mail and set it down without stopping, just as is done on real railways.

The Set comprises the Mail Van, the lineside apparatus, two mail bags, and a push button switch to operate the mechanism.

Current is supplied through a pick-up on the Mail Van from a contact rail on the outside of the track.

In the miniature, the delivery 'net' takes the form of a metal box, open at the approach end and at the side nearest the Mail Van. There is also a hut in which the postman on duty shelters while the exchange is taking place.

32,098 DI T.P.O Mail Van only (length $9\frac{1}{16}$in.), with 2 Mail Bags
32,198 DI T.P.O Lineside Apparatus (length $11\frac{1}{2}$in.), complete with switch

32,948 DI T.P.O Mail Bag

IMPORTANT

The source of the current supply for this component MUST be separate from that used to provide current for train driving. A separate 15 volt A.C. output of a power unit can be used, or a separate transformer, if available. Alternatively 12 volts D.C. from an accumulator, or even dry batteries, can be employed.

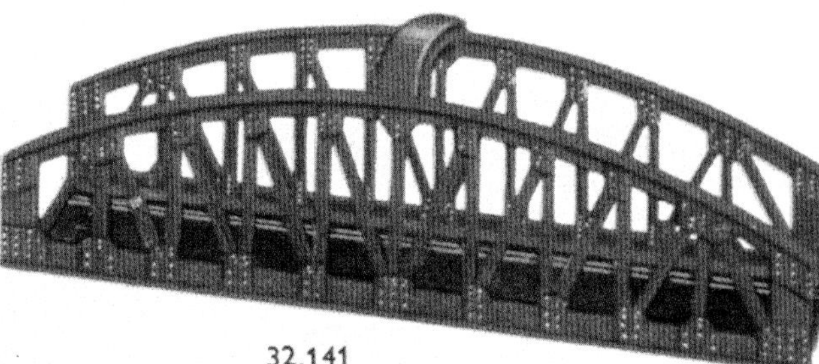

32,141
D1 Girder Bridge
Length $11\frac{1}{2}$in.

32,180
D1 Turntable
Diameter $14\frac{5}{8}$in.

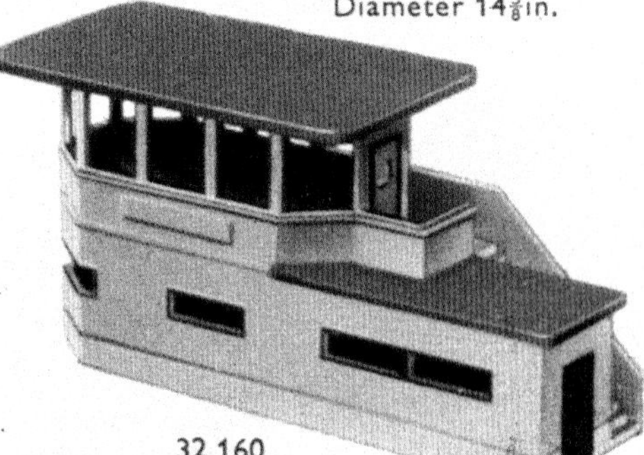

32,160
D1 Signal Cabin
Length $6\frac{3}{8}$in.

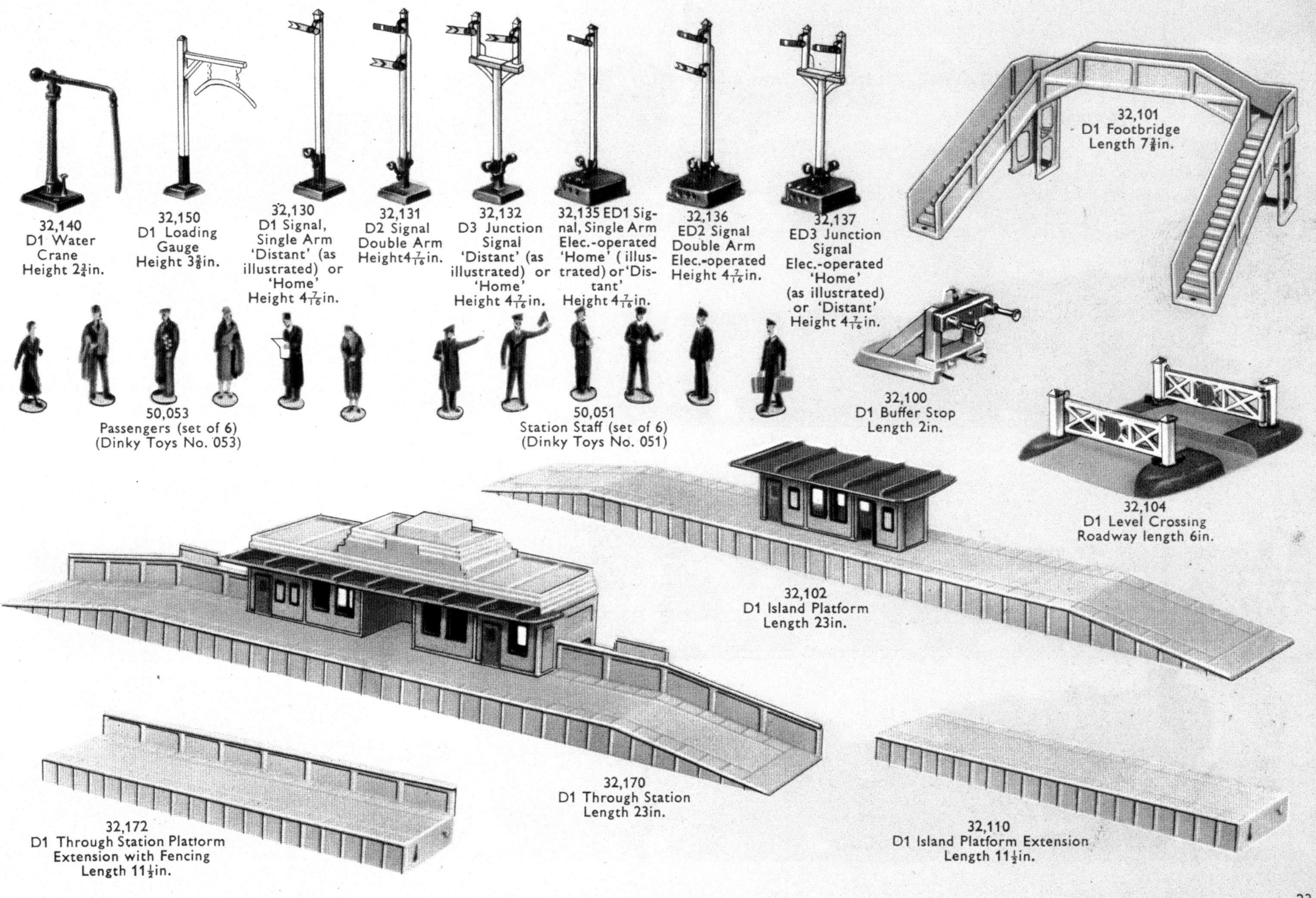

32,140
D1 Water Crane
Height $2\frac{3}{4}$in.

32,150
D1 Loading Gauge
Height $3\frac{3}{8}$in.

32,130
D1 Signal, Single Arm 'Distant' (as illustrated) or 'Home'
Height $4\frac{7}{16}$in.

32,131
D2 Signal Double Arm
Height $4\frac{7}{16}$in.

32,132
D3 Junction Signal 'Distant' (as illustrated) or 'Home'
Height $4\frac{7}{16}$in.

32,135 ED1 Signal, Single Arm Elec.-operated 'Home' (illustrated) or 'Distant'
Height $4\frac{7}{16}$in.

32,136
ED2 Signal Double Arm Elec.-operated
Height $4\frac{7}{16}$in.

32,137
ED3 Junction Signal Elec.-operated 'Home' (as illustrated) or 'Distant'
Height $4\frac{7}{16}$in.

32,101
D1 Footbridge
Length $7\frac{3}{8}$in.

50,053
Passengers (set of 6)
(Dinky Toys No. 053)

50,051
Station Staff (set of 6)
(Dinky Toys No. 051)

32,100
D1 Buffer Stop
Length 2in.

32,104
D1 Level Crossing
Roadway length 6in.

32,102
D1 Island Platform
Length 23in.

32,170
D1 Through Station
Length 23in.

32,172
D1 Through Station Platform Extension with Fencing
Length $11\frac{1}{2}$in.

32,110
D1 Island Platform Extension
Length $11\frac{1}{2}$in.

GAUGE O $1\frac{1}{4}$in. (32 mm.) CLOCKWORK

Hornby Trains are perfect models in O gauge, operated by reliable clockwork mechanisms, strong-pulling and long-running.

No. 20 GOODS TRAIN SET (above)
This set contains No. 20 Locomotive No. 20 Tender, two No. 20 Wagons and Rails.
The 1ft. radius rails supplied with this Train Set require a space measuring 3ft. 3in. by 2ft. 6in.

No. 21 PASSENGER TRAIN SET (left)
This set contains No. 20 Locomotive, No. 20 Tender, two No. 21 Coaches and Rails.
The 1ft. radius rails supplied with this Train Set require a space measuring 3ft. 3in. by 2ft. 6in.

No. 30 GOODS TRAIN SET (right)
This set contains No. 30 Locomotive, No. 30 Tender, No. 30 Wagon, No. 30 Goods Van and Rails.
The 1ft. radius rails supplied with this Train Set require a space measuring 3ft. 3in. by 2ft. 6in.

No. 31 PASSENGER TRAIN SET (left)
This set contains No. 30 Locomotive, No. 30 Tender, No. 31 Coach 1st/2nd, No. 31 Coach Brake/2nd and Rails.
The 1ft. radius rails supplied with this Train Set require a space measuring 3ft. 3in. by 2ft. 6in.

No. 45 TANK GOODS TRAIN SET *(right)*

Contains No. 40 Tank Locomotive (reversing), one No. 50 Wagon, one No. 50 Lumber Wagon, one No. 50 Tank Wagon and 2ft. radius rails requiring a space of 5ft. 4in. by 4ft. 6in.

No. 40 TANK GOODS TRAIN SET *(not illustrated)*

Contains Tank Locomotive No. 40 (reversing), one No. 1 Wagon, one Timber Wagon, one Tank Wagon No. 1.

No. 41 TANK PASSENGER TRAIN SET *(left)*

This set contains No. 40 Tank Locomotive (reversing), two No. 41 Coaches, one No. 41 Passenger Brake Van and 2ft. radius rails requiring a space of 5ft. 4in. by 4ft. 6in.

No. 55 GOODS TRAIN SET *(right)*

This set contains No. 50 Locomotive (reversible from track), No. 50 Tender, one No. 50 Low-sided Wagon, one No. 50 Wagon, one No. 50 Goods Brake Van and 2ft. radius rails requiring a space of 5ft. 4in. by 4ft. 6in.

No. 50 GOODS TRAIN SET *(not illustrated)*

Contains Locomotive No. 50 (reversible from track), Tender No. 50, one No. 1 Wagon, one Low-sided Wagon No. 1, one Goods Brake Van.

No. 51 PASSENGER TRAIN SET *(left)*

This set contains No. 51 Locomotive (reversible from track), No.51 Tender, two No. 51 Coaches, one No. 51 Passenger Brake Van and 2ft. radius rails requiring a space of 5ft. 4in. by 4ft. 6in.

Hornby Gauge O Clockwork Train Sets Nos. 20, 21, 30, 31 and M1 contain 1ft. radius rails, and additional Rails should be of the same radius. Although intended for 1ft. track, Locomotives Nos. 20, 30 and M1 will run on 2ft. radius track. Locomotives Nos. 40, 50 and 51 **MUST** have 2ft. radius rails: they will not run on 1ft. radius Curves or Points.

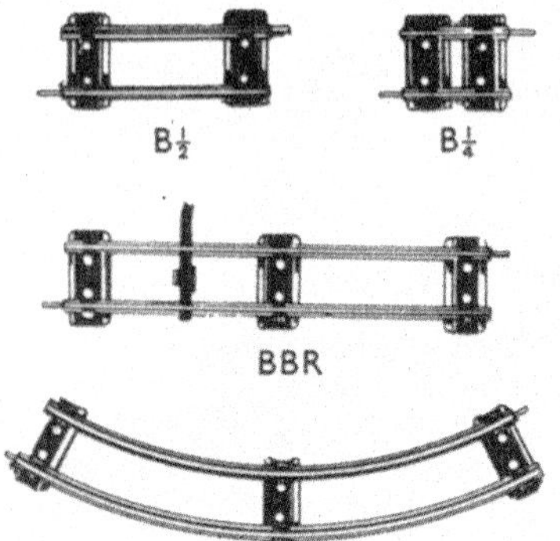

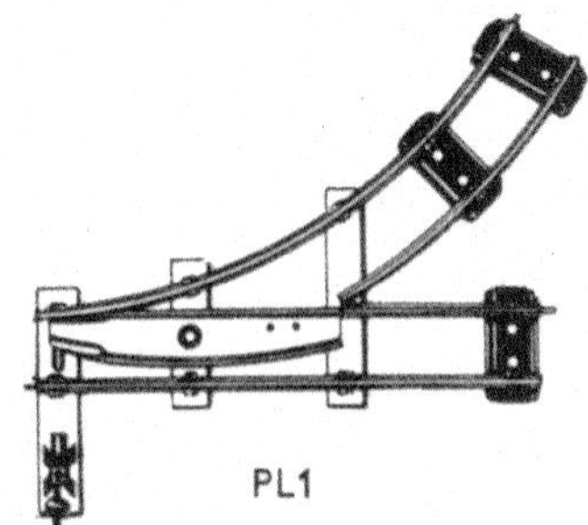

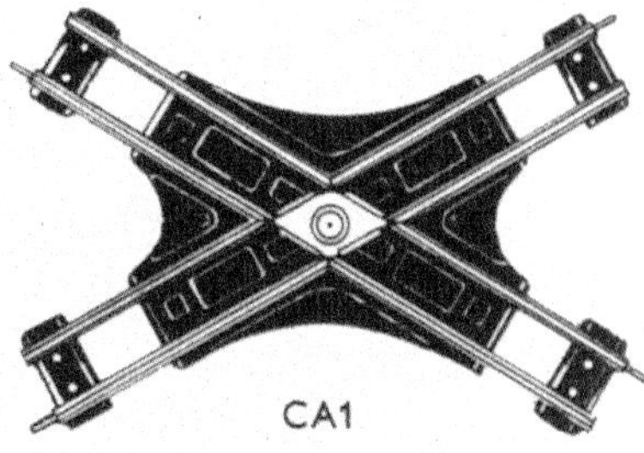

STRAIGHT RAILS

B1	Straight Rail (length 10$\frac{1}{4}$in.)
B$\frac{1}{2}$	Straight Half Rail (length 5$\frac{1}{8}$in.)
B$\frac{1}{4}$	Straight Quarter Rail (length 2$\frac{9}{16}$in.)
BBR	Straight Brake and Reverse Rail (length 10$\frac{1}{4}$in.)

The BBR Rail is not suitable for Locomotive No. 20

CURVED RAILS

A1	Curved Rail (1ft radius)
A1$\frac{1}{2}$	Curved Half Rail (1ft. radius)
A2	Curved Rail (2ft. radius)
A2$\frac{1}{2}$	Curved Half Rail (2ft. radius)
RCP	Rail Connecting Plate

CROSSINGS

CA1	Acute-angle Crossing (for 1ft. radius track)
CA2	Acute-angle Crossing (for 2ft. radius track)
CR1	Right-angle Crossing (for 1ft. radius track)
CR2	Right-angle Crossing (for 2ft. radius track)

POINTS

PR1	Right-hand Points (1ft. radius)
PL1	Left-hand Points (1ft. radius)
PR2	Right-hand Points (2ft. radius)
PL2	Left-hand Points (2ft. radius)
PCC	Points Connecting Clip

1ft. radius Curves, Points and Crossings cannot be used in the same layout with those of 2ft. radius.

GAUGE O
1$\frac{1}{4}$in. (32 mm.)
CLOCKWORK

No. 20 Locomotive (Non-reversing Locomotive, fitted for automatic braking from track.)
No. 20 Tender

No. 30 Locomotive (Reversing Locomotive, fitted for automatic braking from track.)
No. 30 Tender

No. 40 Tank Locomotive (Reversing, and fitted for automatic braking from track.)

No. 51 Locomotive (This Locomotive is fitted for automatic braking and reversing from track.)
No. 51 Tender

No. 50 Locomotive (This Locomotive is fitted for automatic braking and reversing from track.)
No. 50 Tender

42,340
No. 1 Platform Goods
Length 13in.
(not illustrated)

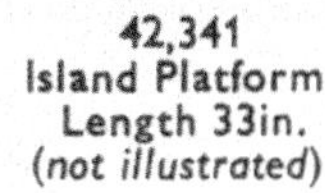

42,341
Island Platform
Length 33in.
(not illustrated)

42,370
No. 2 Signal Cabin
Length 6½in.
(not illustrated)

50,973
Goods Yard Crane
(No. 973 Dinky Supertoys)
Height 8in.

42,320
No. 1 Level Crossing
Roadway length 9¾in.

42,300
No. 1 Buffer
Stop
Length 3¼in.

42,360
No. 2 Signal, Single Arm
('Home' or 'distant')
Height 7¾in.

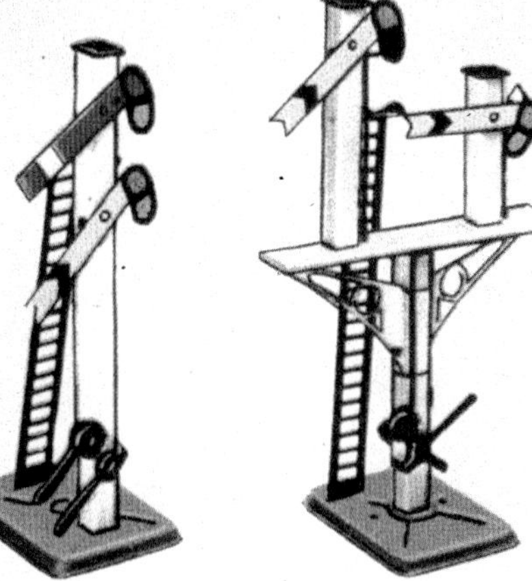

42,361
No. 2 Signal,
Double Arm
Height 8⅞in.

42,362
No. 2 Signal
Junction('Home'
or 'distant')
Height 9¾in.

42,390
No. 2 Turntable
Diameter 13⅝in

42,381
Station Hoarding
Length 3⅜in.

42,350
Posters

42,400
No. 1 Water Tank
Height 7in.

42,330
Platform Crane
Height 6⅝in.

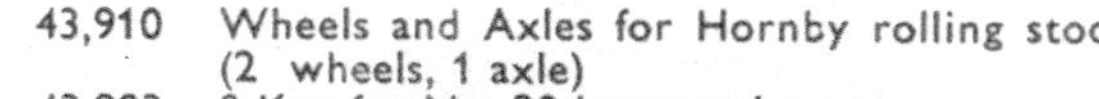

HORNBY O GAUGE SUNDRIES

43,910	Wheels and Axles for Hornby rolling stock (2 wheels, 1 axle)
43,903	S Key for No. 20 Locomotive
43,902	H Key for Nos. M1, 30, 40, 50 and 51 Locomotives
43,930	Head Lamp for Locomotives
43,931	Tail Lamp for Locomotives, or Goods or Passenger Brake Vans
43,932	Side Lamp for Goods Brake Van
43,916	No. 1 Furniture Container
43,917	No. 1 Insulated Meat Container
43,915	No. 1 Cable Drum
43,949	Milk Can

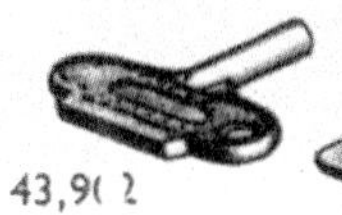

43,902

43,903

43,910

43,949

43,932

43,930

43,931

43,917

43,915

43,916

GAUGE O CLOCKWORK

Dimensions of Rolling Stock are measured over the couplings.

The Nos. 41, 50 and 51 vehicles illustrated in this section are fitted with automatic couplings and are not designed for use with components of Nos. 20, 21, 30 and 31 Train Sets.

42,140
No. 1 Low-Sided Wagon
Length 7in. (*not illustrated*)

42,141
No. 50 Low-Sided Wagon
Length 7in.

42,145
No. 1 Low-Sided Wagon
with Cable Drum
Length 7in. (*not illustrated*)

42,146
No. 50 Low-Sided Wagon with Cable Drum. Length 7in.

42,153
No. 50 Low-Sided Wagon with Insulated Meat Container
Length 7in. (*not illustrated*)

42,152
No. 50 Low-Sided Wagon with Furniture Container. Length 7in.

FOR Nos. 20 and 21 TRAIN SETS
(*May also be used with Nos. 30 and 31 rolling stock*).

42,238
No. 20 Wagon.
Length $4\frac{7}{8}$in.

42,206
No. 20 Tank Wagon
Length $4\frac{7}{8}$in.

42,186
No. 50 Lumber Wagon. Length 7in.

42,156
No. 50 Gas Cylinder Wagon
Length 7in.

42,224
No. 20 Side Tipping Wagon
Length $4\frac{7}{8}$in.

42,219
No. 20 Rotary Tipping Wagon
Length $4\frac{7}{8}$in.

42,181
No. 50 Hopper Wagon. Length 7in.

42,223
No. 50 'SAXA' Salt Wagon
(opening door in roof)
Length 7in.

42,134
No. 20 Crane Truck
Length $4\frac{7}{8}$in.

42,117
No. 21 Coach. Length $4\frac{5}{8}$in.

42,216
No. 50 Refrigerator Van
(opening doors) Length 7in.

42,106
No. 50 Cattle Truck
Length 7in.

42,240
Wagon No. 1
Length 7in. (*not illustrated*)

42,241
No. 50 Wagon
Length 7in.

42,136
No. 50 Crane Truck
Length 7in.

FOR Nos. 30 and 31 TRAIN SETS
(May also be used with Nos. 20 and 21 rolling stock)

42,239
No. 30 Wagon
Length $4\frac{7}{8}$in.

42,159
No. 30 Goods Van
Length $4\frac{7}{8}$in.

42,221
No. 50 Rotary Tipping Wagon
Length 7in.

42,226
No. 50 Side Tipping Wagon
Length 7in.

42,119
No. 31 Coach, Brake/2nd
Length $5\frac{3}{4}$in.

42,118
No. 31 Coach 1st/2nd
Length $5\frac{3}{4}$in.

42,208 No. 50 Tank Wagon
MANCHESTER OIL REFINERY
Length 7in.

42,207 No. 50 Tank Wagon
SHELL LUBRICATING OIL
Length 7in.

42,161
No. 50 Goods Van (opening doors)
Length 7in.

42,171
No. 50 Goods Brake Van
Length 7in.

42,123 No. 51 Coach 2nd Class
Length $7\frac{7}{8}$in.
42,122 No. 51 Coach 1st Class
Length $7\frac{7}{8}$in. (*not illustrated*)

42,202
No. 51 Passenger Brake Van
Length $7\frac{7}{8}$in.

42,121
No. 41 Coach 1st/2nd
Length $7\frac{7}{8}$in.

42,201
No. 41 Passenger Brake Van
Length $7\frac{7}{8}$in.

DINKY TOYS

Trade Mark Registered

Dinky Toys are unsurpassed for realism, wealth of detail, rich colouring and sturdy construction. All who delight in accurate miniatures will be thrilled by the splendid selection of Dinky Toys illustrated here; and it is **only a selection**, for the present range consists of more than 150 models—as listed—and new ones are being added regularly.

It's fun to be first with the latest Dinky Toys; keep your eye on your local dealer's window.

No. 340
Land-Rover
Length $3\frac{5}{8}$in.

No. 103
Austin-Healey 100 Sports
(Touring finish)
Length $3\frac{7}{8}$in.

No. 181
Volkswagen
Length $3\frac{9}{16}$in.

No. 157
Jaguar XK120 Coupé
Length $3\frac{7}{8}$in.

No.	
051	Station Staff (OO) (Set of 6)
053	Passengers (OO) (Set of 6)
101	Sunbeam Alpine Sports (Touring finish)
102	M.G. Midget Sports (Touring finish)
103	Austin-Healey 100 Sports (Touring finish)
104	Aston Martin DB3 S (Touring finish)
105	Triumph TR2 Sports (Touring finish)
106	Austin Atlantic Convertible
107	Sunbeam Alpine Sports (Racing finish)
108	M.G. Midget Sports (Racing finish)
109	Austin-Healey 100 Sports (Racing finish)
110	Aston Martin DB3 S (Racing finish)
111	Triumph TR2 Sports (Racing finish)
131	Cadillac Eldorado Tourer
132	Packard Convertible
133	Cunningham C-5R Road Racer
149	Gift Set, Sports Cars (Racing finish) (5 models)
151	Triumph 1800 Saloon
152	Austin Devon Saloon
153	Standard Vanguard Saloon
154	Hillman Minx Saloon
156	Rover 75 Saloon
157	Jaguar XK120 Coupé
158	Riley Saloon
159	Morris Oxford Saloon
161	Austin Somerset Saloon
162	Ford Zephyr Saloon
163	Bristol 450 Sports Coupé

No.	
164	Vauxhall Cresta Saloon
170	Ford Fordor Sedan
171	Hudson Commodore Sedan
172	Studebaker Land Cruiser
181	Volkswagen
190	Caravan
230	Talbot-Lago Racing Car
231	Maserati Racing Car
232	Alfa Romeo Racing Car
233	Cooper-Bristol Racing Car
234	Ferrari Racing Car
235	H.W.M. Racing Car
236	Connaught Racing Car
237	Mercedes Benz Racing Car
238	Jaguar Type D Racing Car
249	Gift Set, Racing Cars (5 models)
251	Aveling-Barford Diesel Roller
252	Refuse Wagon, Bedford chassis
253	Daimler Ambulance
254	Austin Taxi
255	Mersey Tunnel Police Van
260	Royal Mail Van
261	Telephone Service Van
281	Luxury Coach
282	Duple Roadmaster Coach
283	B.O.A.C. Coach
290	Double Deck Bus
299	Gift Set, Post Office Services
300	Massey-Harris Tractor
301	Field-Marshall Tractor
310	Farm Tractor and Hayrake
320	Halesowen Harvest Trailer
321	Massey-Harris Manure Spreader
322	Disc Harrow
323	Triple Gang Mower
324	Hayrake
340	Land-Rover
341	Land-Rover Trailer
342	Motocart

No. 132
Packard Convertible
Length $4\frac{1}{2}$in.

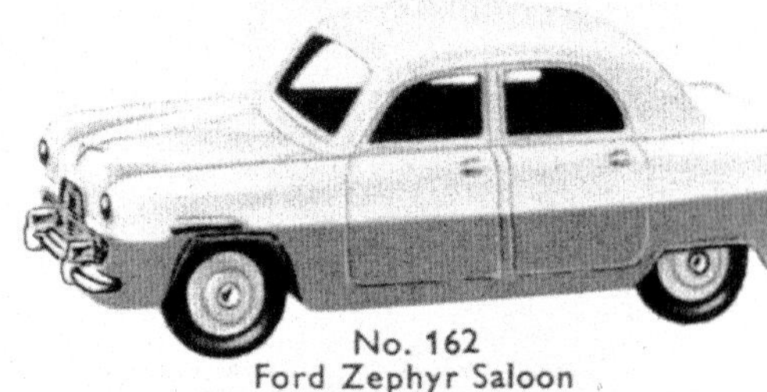

No. 162
Ford Zephyr Saloon
Length $3\frac{13}{16}$in.

No. 190
Caravan
Length $4\frac{3}{4}$in. (including towbar)

No. 716
Westland-Sikorsky Helicopter
Fuselage. Length $2\frac{3}{4}$in.

No. 735
Gloster Javelin
Delta Wing Fighter
Wing Span $3\frac{1}{4}$in.

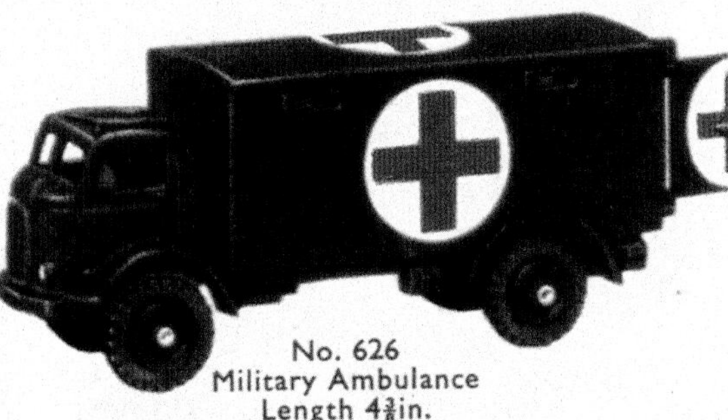

No. 626
Military Ambulance
Length $4\frac{3}{8}$in.

No. 300
Massey-Harris Tractor
Length $3\frac{1}{2}$in.

No.	
343	Farm Produce Wagon
344	Estate Car
381	Garden Roller
382	Wheelbarrow
383	4-wheel Hand Truck
384	Grass Cutter
385	Sack Truck
386	Lawn Mower
400	B.E.V. Electric Truck
401	Coventry Climax Fork Lift Truck
405	Universal Jeep
408	Big Bedford Lorry
409	Bedford Articulated Lorry
410	Bedford End Tipper
411	Bedford Truck
412	Austin Wagon
413	Austin Covered Wagon
414	Rear Tipping Wagon
415	Mechanical Horse and Open Wagon
417	Leyland Comet Lorry
418	Comet Wagon with hinged tailboard
419	Leyland Cement Wagon
420	Leyland Forward Control Lorry
421	Hindle-Smart Electric Articulated Lorry
422	Fordson Thames Flat Truck
428	Trailer, large
429	Trailer
430	Breakdown Lorry, Commer chassis
431	Guy 4-ton Lorry
432	Guy Flat Truck
433	Guy Flat Truck with tailboard
440	Tanker 'MOBILGAS'
441	Tanker 'CASTROL'
443	Tanker 'NATIONAL BENZOLE'
454	Trojan 15-cwt. Van 'CYDRAX'
455	Trojan 15-cwt. Van 'BROOKE BOND TEA'
465	Morris Commercial Van 'CAPSTAN'
471	Austin Van 'NESTLES'
472	Austin Van 'RALEIGH CYCLES'
482	Bedford 10-cwt. Van 'DINKY TOYS'
490	Electric Dairy Van 'EXPRESS'
603	Army Personnel — Private, seated
621	3-ton Army Wagon
623	Army Covered Wagon
626	Military Ambulance
641	Army 1-ton Cargo Truck

No.	
670	Armoured Car
673	Scout Car
674	Austin Champ Army Vehicle
676	Armoured Personnel Carrier
677	Armoured Command Vehicle
692	5·5 Medium Gun
697	25-pounder Field Gun Set
699	Gift Set, Military Vehicles (1) (4 models)
704	Avro York Airliner
705	Vickers Viking Airliner
706	Vickers Viscount Airliner 'AIR FRANCE'
708	Vickers Viscount Airliner 'B.E.A.'
715	Bristol 173 Helicopter
716	Westland-Sikorsky Helicopter
732	Meteor Twin Jet Fighter
733	Shooting Star Jet Fighter
734	Supermarine Swift Fighter
735	Gloster Javelin Delta Wing Fighter
736	Hawker Hunter Fighter
750	Telephone Call Box
751	Police Hut
771	International Road Signs (Set of 12)
773	Traffic Signal, 4-Face
777	Beacon
781	Petrol Pump Station 'ESSO'
794	Loading Ramp for Dinky Super-Toys No. 982
798	Express Passenger Train

TYRES

Spare tyres for Dinky Toys and Dinky Supertoys can be bought separately

6676	(094)	Tyre, $\frac{11}{16}$in. diam.
6677	(095)	Tyre, $\frac{11}{16}$in. diam. (engraved)
7067	(096)	Tyre, $\frac{19}{32}$in. diam.
10253	(099)	Tyre, $\frac{13}{16}$in. diam.
13978	(093)	Tyre, $1\frac{1}{16}$in. diam.

See the 'Meccano Magazine' every month for announcements of new models

No. 430
Breakdown Lorry, Commer chassis
Overall length $4\frac{7}{8}$in.

No. 443
Tanker 'NATIONAL BENZOLE'
Length $4\frac{3}{8}$in.

No. 283
B.O.A.C. Coach
Length $4\frac{3}{4}$in.

No. 290
Double Deck Bus
Length 4in.

DINKY SUPERTOYS

Trade Mark Registered

Dinky Supertoys are the 'big brothers' of Dinky Toys, being produced in the same superlative quality to a larger scale.

No.	
622	10-ton Army Truck
642	Pressure Refueller
651	Centurion Tank
660	Tank Transporter
661	Recovery Tractor
698	Gift Set, Tank Transporter with Tank
902	Foden Flat Truck
903	Foden Flat Truck with tailboard
905	Foden Flat Truck with chains
918	Guy Van 'EVER READY'
919	Guy Van 'GOLDEN SHRED'
923	Big Bedford Van 'HEINZ'
934	Leyland Octopus Wagon
942	Foden 14-ton Tanker 'REGENT'
943	Leyland Octopus Tanker 'ESSO'
955	Fire Engine with Extending Ladder
961	Blaw Knox Bulldozer
962	Muir-Hill Dumper Truck
963	Blaw Knox Heavy Tractor
964	Elevator Loader
965	Euclid Rear Dump Truck
971	Coles Mobile Crane
972	Coles 20-ton Lorry-mounted Crane
973	Goods Yard Crane
981	Horse Box
982	Pullmore Car Transporter
990	Gift Set, Pullmore Car Transporter with four cars
991	A.E.C. Tanker
999	D.H. Comet Airliner

No. 972
20-ton Lorry-mounted Crane COLES
Length 9⅝in.

No. 965
Euclid Rear Dump Truck
Length 5⅝in.

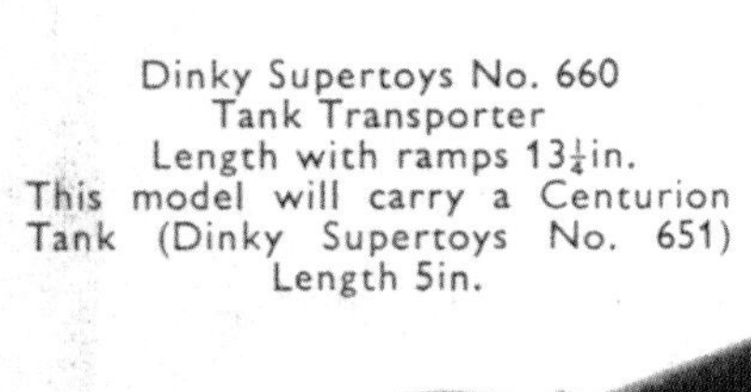

Dinky Supertoys No. 660
Tank Transporter
Length with ramps 13¼in.
This model will carry a Centurion Tank (Dinky Supertoys No. 651)
Length 5in.

No. 943
Leyland Octopus Tanker 'ESSO'
Length 7⅝in.

ALL GOODS LISTED IN THIS CATALOGUE ARE MADE IN ENGLAND BY MECCANO LTD, BINNS ROAD, LIVERPOOL 13

13/757/500
Printed in Engla

DINKY TOYS

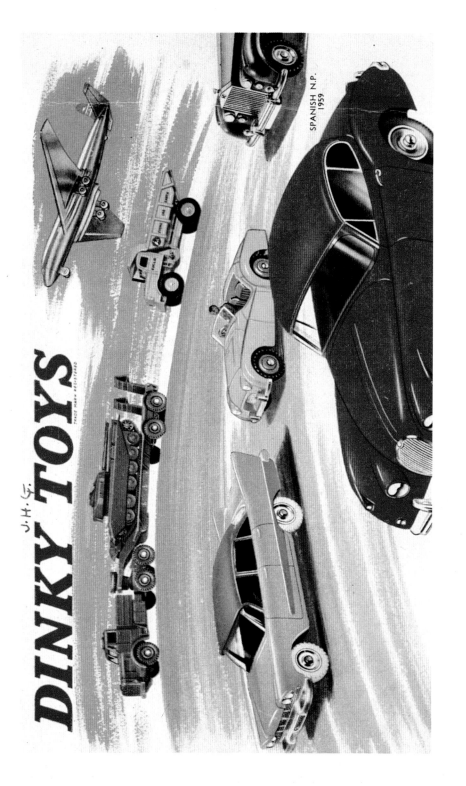

TRADE MARK REGISTERED

J. H. G.

SPANISH N.P.
1959

DUBLO *DINKY TOYS*

ESCALA "OO/HO"

He aqui seis atractivos modelos en la nueva serie de Dublo Dinky Toys fabricados á la escala de los trenes de trocha OO/HO. Estos añaden mucho realismo á la diversión de trabajar con trenes. Tambien son ideales en los tendidos de caminos—como asi para los jovencitos que aprecian y los coleccionan por su detalle y alto acabo. De vez en cuando aparecerán nuevos modelos.

061
Coche Salon Ford Prefect
Longitud 59 mm.

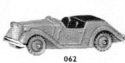

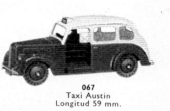

062
Coche de Turismo Singer
Longitud 51 mm.

063
Camioneta Commer
Longitud 54 mm.

064
Camión Austin
Longitud 64 mm.

065
Morris Pick-up
Longitud 54 mm.

066
Camión Plano Bedford
Longitud 108 mm.

067
Taxi Austin
Longitud 59 mm.

068
Auto de Correos
(con ventanas)
Longitud 47 mm.

072
Camión Articulado Bedford
(con ventanas)
Longitud 117 mm.

El Pasatiempo Favorito de Coleccionar

Qué es lo que tanto fascina en los Dinky Toys, y por qué llaman tanto la atención de los jóvenes de todas edades? La respuesta es, que estos atractivos modelos son insuperables en su realismo, detalle absoluto, perfección en color y fuerte construcción. A todos los interesados y entusiastas de miniaturas exactas, les causará un profundo deleite el conjunto ilustrado de Dinky Toys en este librito: la variedad actual excede de 180 modelos, y de vez en cuando se añaden otros nuevos. Es una gran diversión ser siempre el primero en conseguir el último modelo de Dinky Toys. No perdáis de vista los escaparates de vuestro vendedor local . . . y para tener noticias de los últimos modelos, no dejeís de adquirir la revista "Meccano Magazine".

101
Coche de Sports Sunbeam Alpine
Longitud 94 mm.

104
Coche de Sports Aston Martin DB3S
Longitud 87 mm.

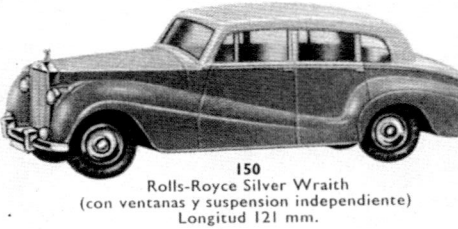

132
Automóvil Packard Convertible
Longitud 114 mm.

102
Coche de Sports M.G. Midget
Longitud 82 mm.

131
Coche de Turismo Cadillac
Longitud 119 mm.

133
Coche de Carreras Cunningham C-5R
Longitud 102 mm.

103
Coche de Sports Austin Healey 100
Longitud 86 mm.

105
Coche de Sports Triumph TR2
Longitud 86 mm.

150
Rolls-Royce Silver Wraith
(con ventanas y suspension independiente)
Longitud 121 mm.

COCHES DE PASAJEROS

157
Jaguar XK120 Coupé
Longitud 98 mm.

160
Coche Salon Austin A30
Longitud 78 mm.

162
Coche Salon Ford Zephyr
Longitud 97 mm.

164
Coche Salon Vauxhall Cresta
Longitud 97 mm.

189
Triumph Herald
(con ventanas y suspension independiente)
Longitud 86 mm.

166
Sunbeam Rapier (con ventanas)
Longitud 90 mm.

167
A.C. Coupé Aceca (con ventanas)
Longitud 89 mm.

168
Singer Gazelle (con ventanas)
Longitud 94 mm.

169
Studebaker Golden Hawk (con ventanas)
(Falcon de Oro)
Longitud 108 mm.

COCHES DE PASAJEROS

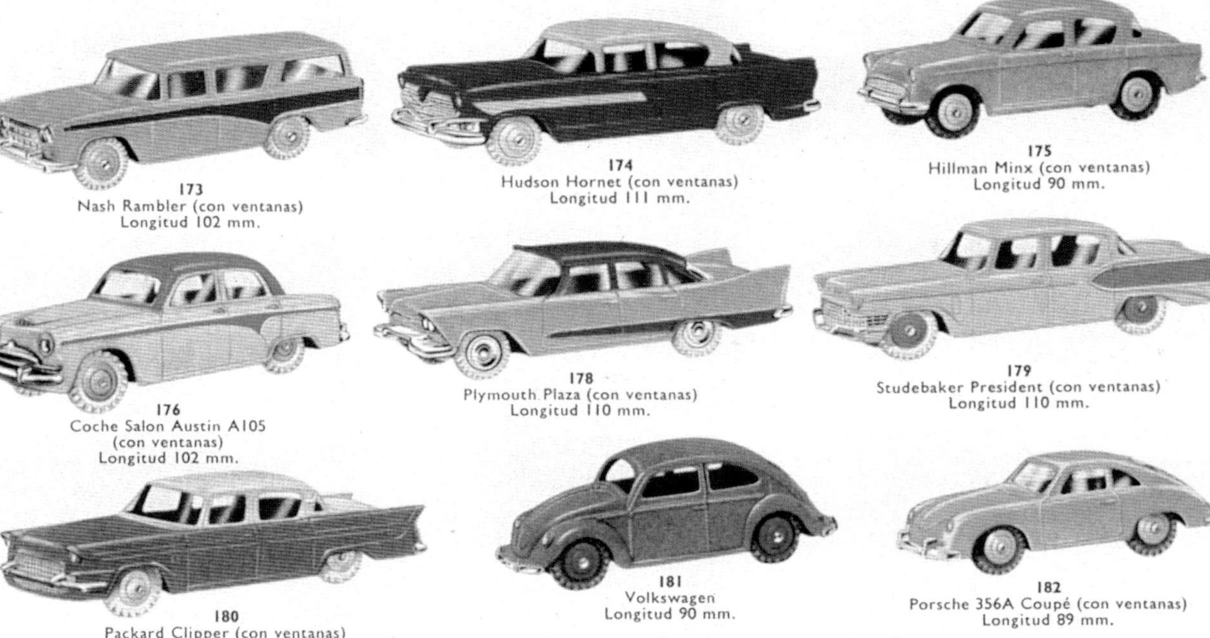

173
Nash Rambler (con ventanas)
Longitud 102 mm.

174
Hudson Hornet (con ventanas)
Longitud 111 mm.

175
Hillman Minx (con ventanas)
Longitud 90 mm.

176
Coche Salon Austin A105
(con ventanas)
Longitud 102 mm.

178
Plymouth Plaza (con ventanas)
Longitud 110 mm.

179
Studebaker President (con ventanas)
Longitud 110 mm.

180
Packard Clipper (con ventanas)
Longitud 113 mm.

181
Volkswagen
Longitud 90 mm.

182
Porsche 356A Coupé (con ventanas)
Longitud 89 mm.

183
Coche Salon Fiat 600
Longitud 71 mm.

165
Coche Salon "Humber Hawk"
(con ventanas y suspension independiente)
Longitud 102 mm.

190
Caravana
Longitud 121 mm.

191
Dodge Royal (con ventanas)
Longitud 113 mm.

232
Auto de Carreras Alfa-Romeo
Longitud 102 mm.

230
Auto de Carreras Talbot-Lago
Longitud 102 mm.

231
Auto de Carreras Maserati
Longitud 92 mm.

192
De Soto Fireflite (con ventanas)
Longitud 116 mm.

233
Auto de Carreras Cooper-Bristol
Longitud 89 mm.

234
Auto de Carreras Ferrari
Longitud 102 mm.

237
Auto de Carreras Mercedes-Benz
Longitud 98 mm.

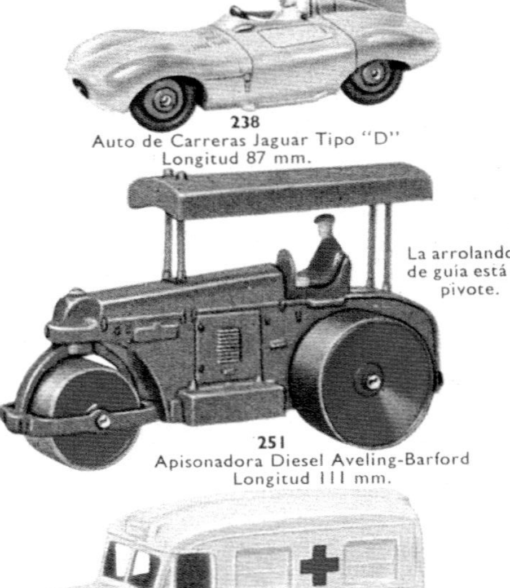

238
Auto de Carreras Jaguar Tipo "D"
Longitud 87 mm.

239
Auto de Carreras Vanwall
Longitud 95 mm.

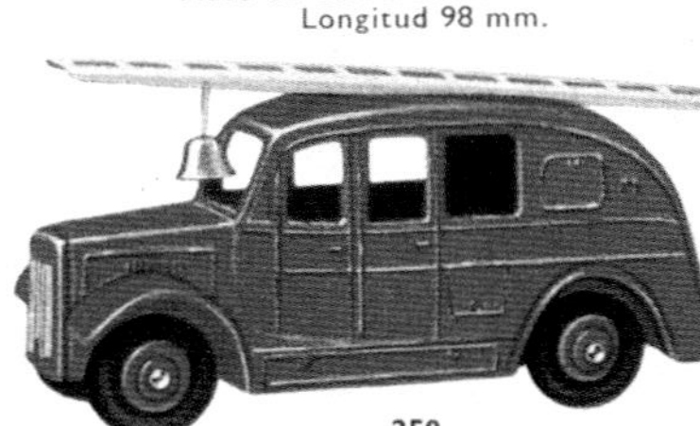

250
Bomba de Incendios Longitud 102 mm.

La arrolandora de guía está en pivote.

251
Apisonadora Diesel Aveling-Barford
Longitud 111 mm.

252
Carro de Basura Bedford
Longitud 108 mm.

Montado con cuerpo de volqueo, cubiertas corredizas y puerta abridera atrás.

253
Ambulancia Daimler
Longitud 95 mm.

VEHICULOS DE SERVICIO PUBLICO

254
Taxi Austin
Longitud 94 mm.

290
Autobus "Dunlop" Longitud 102 mm.

255
Camioneta de la Policia del Tunél Mersey
Longitud 73 mm.

261
Camioneta de Servicio Telefónico
Longitud 73 mm.

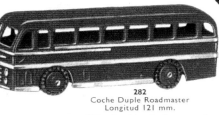

280
Coche Observatorio
Longitud 114 mm.

260
Auto de Correos
Longitud 79 mm.

282
Coche Duple Roadmaster
Longitud 121 mm.

270
Patrulla de Frontera
(motocicleta)
Longitud 47 mm.

283
Coche de B.O.A.C.
Longitud 121 mm.

299 Servicios de Correos Los siguientes modelos se incluyen en este atractivo equipo: Auto de Correos, Cabina Telefónica, Cartero y Ordenanza de Telégrafos, Camioneta de Servicio Telefónico.

EQUIPOS DE GRANJA

291
London Autobus "Exide"
Longitud 102 mm.

300
Tractor Agrícolo
Massey-Harris
Longitud 89 mm.

301
Tractor Agrícolo
Field Marshall
Longitud 76 mm.

Al mismo tiempo que giran las ruedas de camino los trilladores y distribuidores giran en rotación.

321
Repartidor de Abono Massey-Harris
Longitud 121 mm.

320
Remolque de Cosecha
Halesowen
Longitud 133 mm.

310
Tractor Agrícolo
con Rastro de Heno
Longitud 165 mm.

322
Arado a Discos
Longitud 86 mm.

323
Guadanero triple de Césped
Longitud 111 mm.

324
Rastro de Heno
Longitud 76 mm.

Todos los modelos ilustrados en esta página pueden usarse con los Dinky Toys Nos. 300, 301, y 340 los cuales tienen ganchos de remolque.

VEHICULES COMERCIALES

340
Explorador Land-Rover
Longitud 92 mm.

341
Remolque para
Explorador
Land-Rover
Longitud 79 mm.

342
Motocarrera
Longitud 111 mm.
Con plataforma de volqueo atrás.

343
Camión de Labrador
Longitud 108 mm.

400
Carro Eléctrico Longitud 86 mm.

405
Jeep (Universal)
Longitud 82 mm.
Tambor y cuchilla giratorios.

401
Vagoneta de Horquilla Coventry-Climax
Longitud 108 mm.
Dando vuelta a una manivela las horquillas suben y bajan.

344
Camioneta de Finca
Longitud 105 mm.

VEHICULOS COMERCIALES

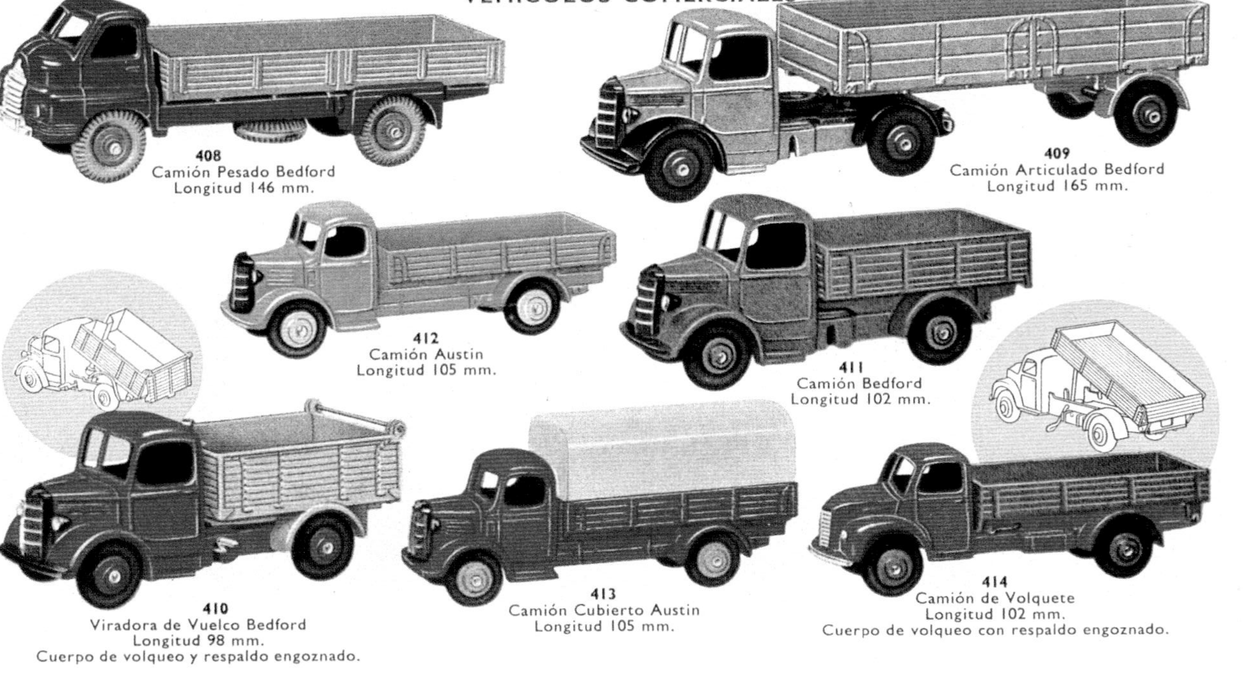

408
Camión Pesado Bedford
Longitud 146 mm.

409
Camión Articulado Bedford
Longitud 165 mm.

412
Camión Austin
Longitud 105 mm.

411
Camión Bedford
Longitud 102 mm.

410
Viradora de Vuelco Bedford
Longitud 98 mm.
Cuerpo de volqueo y respaldo engoznado.

413
Camión Cubierto Austin
Longitud 105 mm.

414
Camión de Volquete
Longitud 102 mm.
Cuerpo de volqueo con respaldo engoznado.

VEHICULOS COMERCIALES

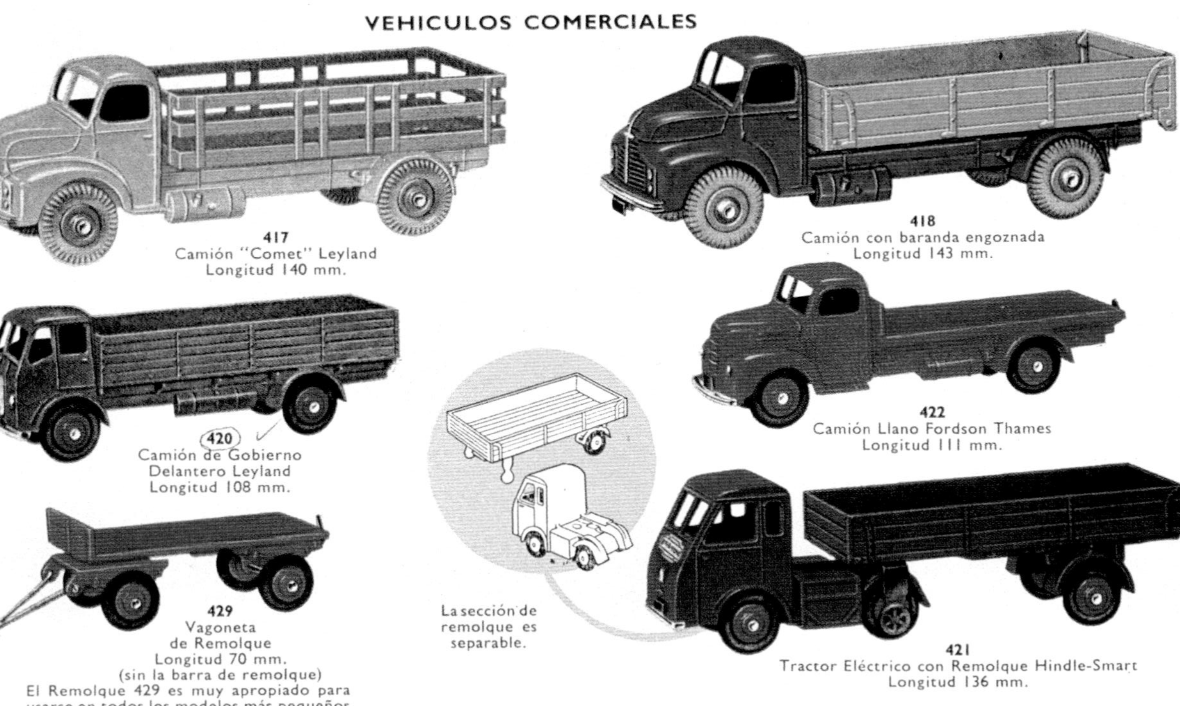

417
Camión "Comet" Leyland
Longitud 140 mm.

418
Camión con baranda engoznada
Longitud 143 mm.

420
Camión de Gobierno
Delantero Leyland
Longitud 108 mm.

422
Camión Llano Fordson Thames
Longitud 111 mm.

La sección de
remolque es
separable.

429
Vagoneta
de Remolque
Longitud 70 mm.
(sin la barra de remolque)
El Remolque 429 es muy apropiado para
usarse en todos los modelos más pequeños
que llevan ganchos de remolque.

421
Tractor Eléctrico con Remolque Hindle-Smart
Longitud 136 mm.

DINKY TOYS

VEHICULOS COMERCIALES

Este Remolque puede usarse con los Dinky Toys Nos. 251, 300, 301, 340, 408, 409, 417 y 431, también con Dinky Supertoys Nos. 902, 903, 905, 934, 961, 962, y 963, todos los cuales llevan montados ganchos de remolque.

428
Vagoneta de Remolque
Longitud del cuerpo 121 mm.

430
Auto Socorro
Longitud 124 mm.

431
Camión 4-toneladas, marca Guy Warrior
Longitud 133 mm.

432
Camión Llano, marca Guy Warrior
Longitud 133 mm.

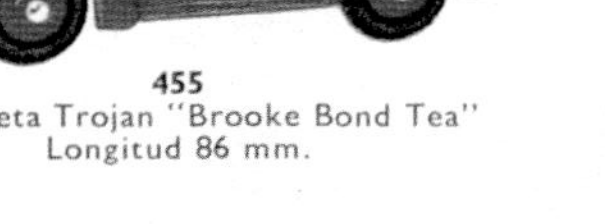

440
Tanque "Mobilgas"
Longitud 111 mm.

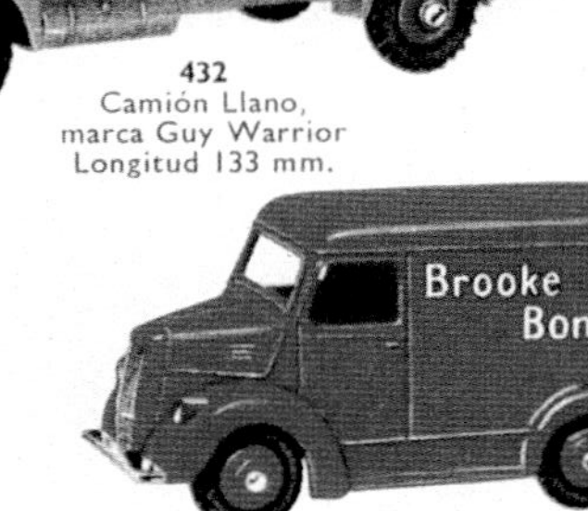
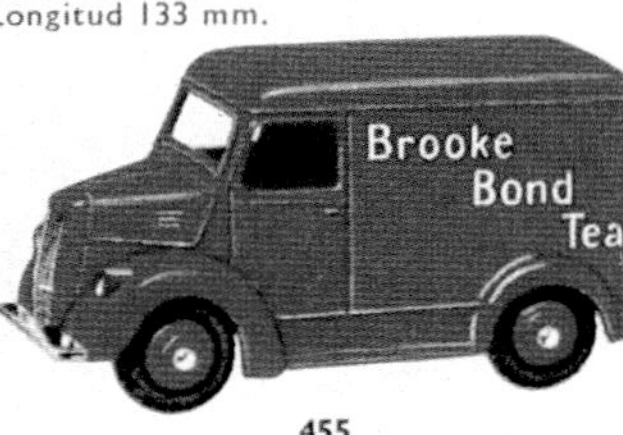

465
Camioneta Morris "Capstan"
Longitud 79 mm.

455
Camioneta Trojan "Brooke Bond Tea"
Longitud 86 mm.

VEHICULOS COMERCIALES—VEHICULOS MILITARES

472
Camioneta Austin "Raleigh Cycles"
Longitud 89 mm.

471
Camioneta Austin "Nestlé's"
Longitud 89 mm.

482
Camioneta Bedford "Dinky Toys"
Longitud 82 mm.

491
Camioneta Leche Eléctrica
Longitud 86 mm.

621
Camión de Ejército 3 toneladas
Longitud 114 mm.

623
Camión Militar Cubierto
Longitud 105 mm.

626
Ambulancia Militar
Longitud 111 mm.

641
Camión de Ejército
1 tonelada
Longitud 79 mm.

643
Cisterna de Ejército
Longitud 89 mm.

VEHICULOS MILITARES

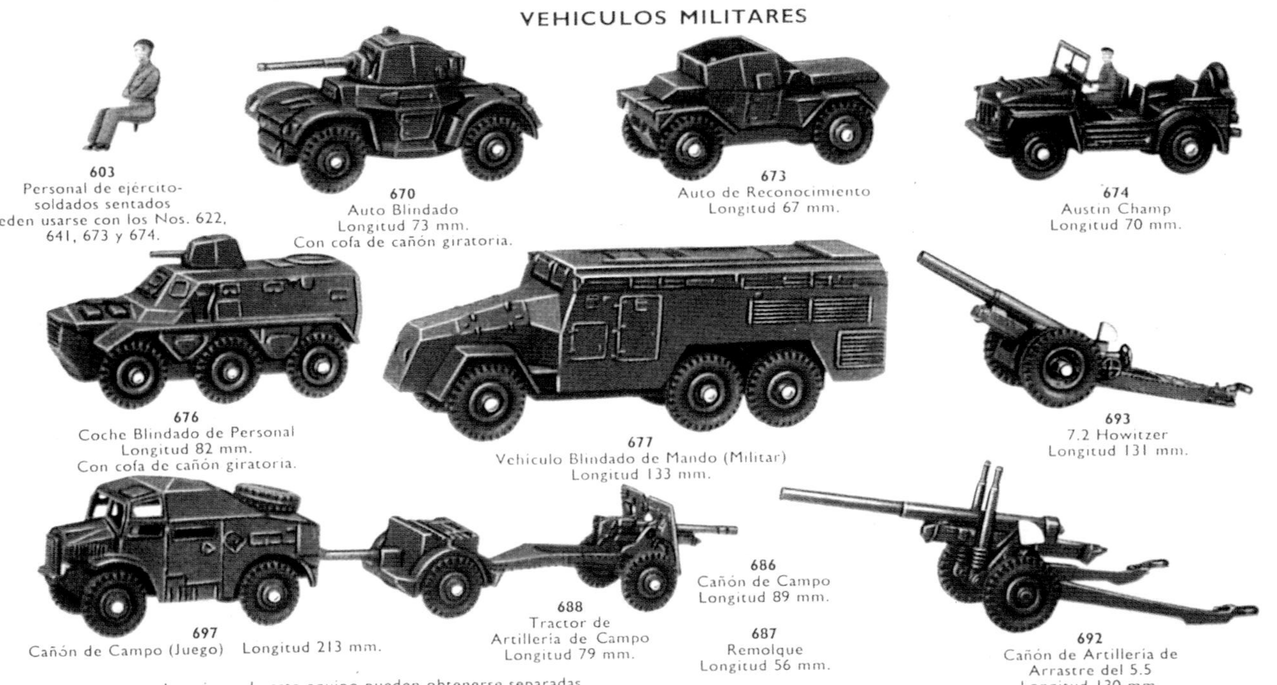

603
Personal de ejército-soldados sentados
Pueden usarse con los Nos. 622, 641, 673 y 674.

670
Auto Blindado
Longitud 73 mm.
Con cofa de cañón giratoria.

673
Auto de Reconocimiento
Longitud 67 mm.

674
Austin Champ
Longitud 70 mm.

676
Coche Blindado de Personal
Longitud 82 mm.
Con cofa de cañón giratoria.

677
Vehiculo Blindado de Mando (Militar)
Longitud 133 mm.

693
7.2 Howitzer
Longitud 131 mm.

686
Cañón de Campo
Longitud 89 mm.

688
Tractor de Artilleria de Campo
Longitud 79 mm.

697
Cañón de Campo (Juego) Longitud 213 mm.

687
Remolque
Longitud 56 mm.

692
Cañón de Artilleria de Arrastre del 5.5
Longitud 130 mm.

Las piezas de este equipo pueden obtenerse separadas.

704
Transaéreo Avro "York"
Extensión del Ala 159 mm.

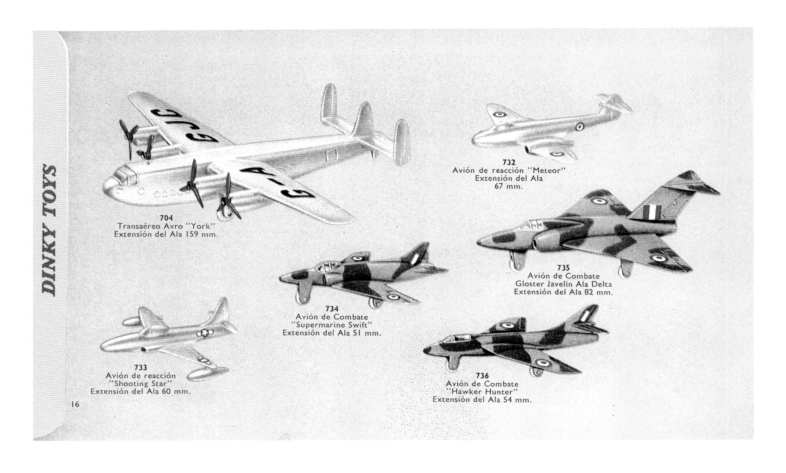

732
Avión de reacción "Meteor"
Extensión del Ala
67 mm.

735
Avión de Combate
Gloster Javelin Ala Delta
Extensión del Ala 82 mm.

734
Avión de Combate
"Supermarine Swift"
Extensión del Ala 51 mm.

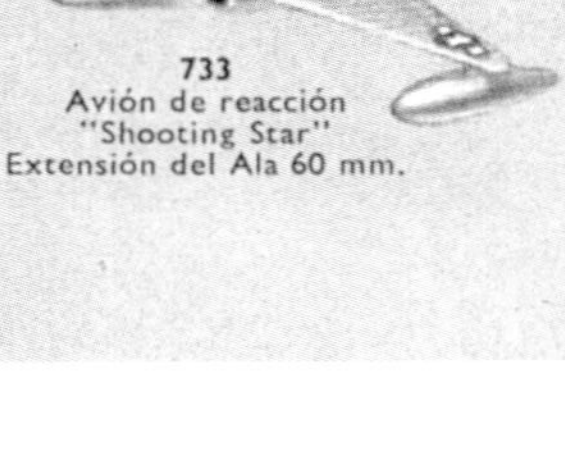

733
Avión de reacción
"Shooting Star"
Extensión del Ala 60 mm.

736
Avión de Combate
"Hawker Hunter"
Extensión del Ala 54 mm.

705
Transaéreo "Viking"
Extensión del Ala 140 mm.

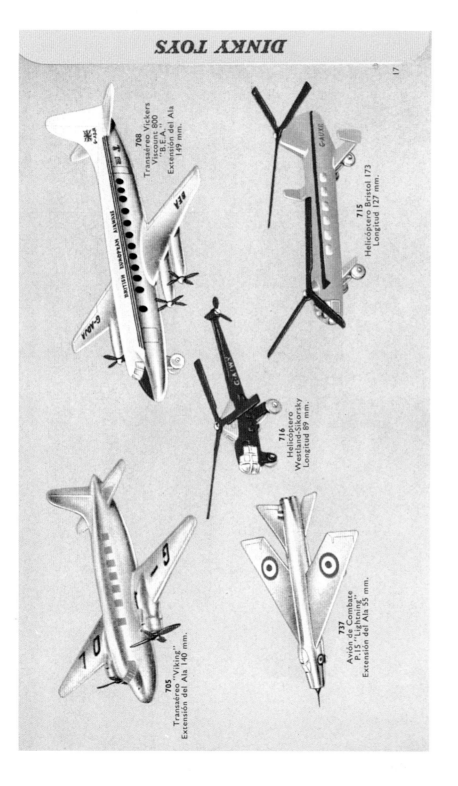

708
Transaéreo Vickers
Viscount 800
"B.E.A."
Extensión del Ala
149 mm.

716
Helicóptero
Westland-Sikorsky
Longitud 89 mm.

737
Avión de Combate
P.15 "Lightning"
Extensión del Ala 55 mm.

715
Helicóptero Bristol 173
Longitud 127 mm.

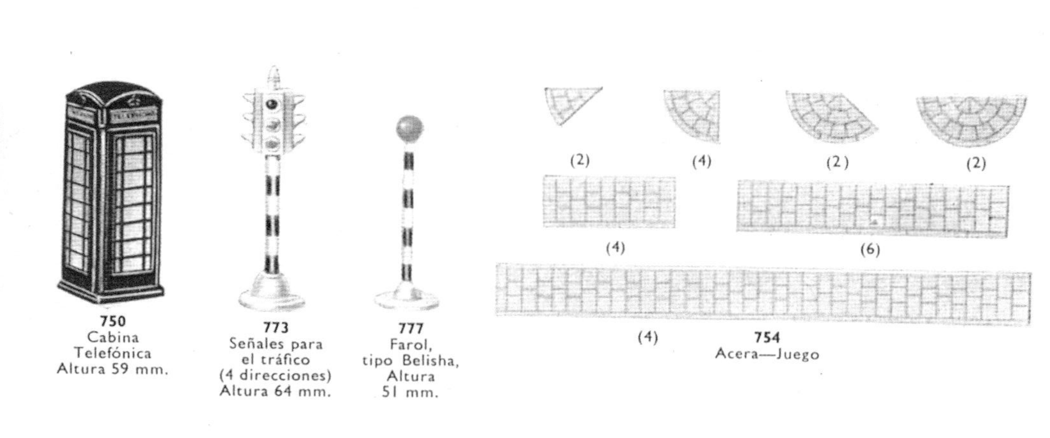

751
Caseta de Policia
Altura 67 mm.

750
Cabina
Telefónica
Altura 59 mm.

773
Señales para
el tráfico
(4 direcciones)
Altura 64 mm.

777
Farol,
tipo Belisha,
Altura
51 mm.

(2) (4) (2) (2)
(4) (6)
(4)

754
Acera—Juego

051 Personal de Estación (trocha OO), juego de 6 modelos
053 Pasajeros (trocha OO), juego de 6 modelos (no ilustrados)

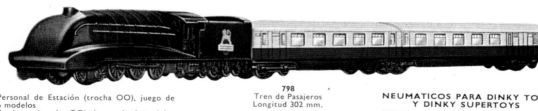

798
Tren de Pasajeros
Longitud 302 mm.

NEUMATICOS PARA DINKY TOYS
Y DINKY SUPERTOYS

6677 18 mm. diam.
10253 20 mm. diam.
14094 15 mm. diam.
14095 15 mm. diam.
13978 27 mm. diam.
60036 13 mm. diam.

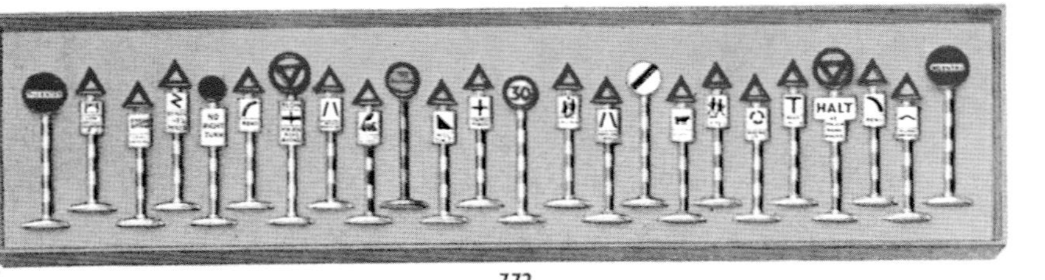

772
Señales de Vía Británicos
(juego de 24 piezas)

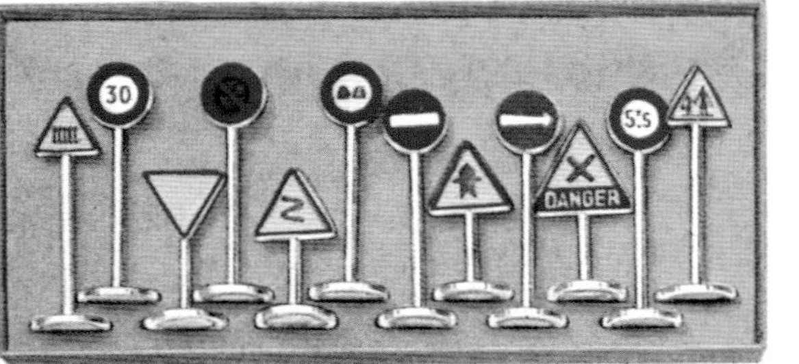

771
Señales de Vía Internacionales
(juego de 12 modelos)

781
Estación Gasolina "Esso"
Altura 114 mm.

DINKY SUPERTOYS

Los Dinky Supertoys—que son el "hermano mayor" de Dinky Toys—se hacen en la misma calidad superlativa, pero en tamaño mayor.

VEHICULOS MILITARES

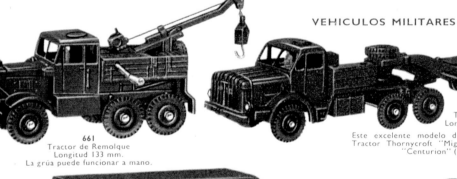

661
Tractor de Remolque
Longitud 133 mm.
La grúa puede funcionar a mano.

660
Transportador de Tanque
Longitud con rampas 337 mm.

Este excelente modelo de Transportador, remolcado por un Tractor Thornycroft "Mighty Antar", puede llevar el Tanque "Centurion" (Dinky Supertoys No. 651).

622
Camión de Ejército 10 toneladas
Longitud 136 mm.

698
Transportador de Tanque
con Tanque
Este excelente equipo consiste del Transportador de Tanque y Tanque "Centurion".

651
Tanque Militar "Centurion"
Longitud 146 mm.
La cofa de cañón gira en completo circulo. Rodaderas de caucho.

VEHICULOS COMERCIALES

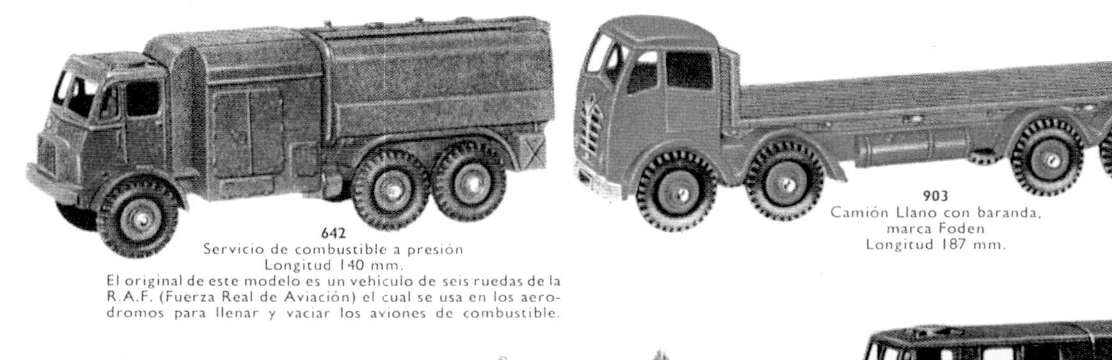

642
Servicio de combustible a presión
Longitud 140 mm.
El original de este modelo es un vehículo de seis ruedas de la R.A.F. (Fuerza Real de Aviación) el cual se usa en los aerodromos para llenar y vaciar los aviones de combustible.

903
Camión Llano con baranda, marca Foden
Longitud 187 mm.

902
Camión Llano, marca Foden
Longitud 187 mm.
(no ilustrado)

905
Camión Llano Foden con cadena
Longitud 187 mm.

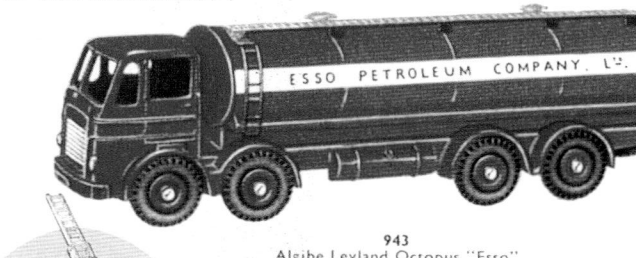

689
Tractor de Artilleria Media
Longitud 140 mm.
Este es un modelo excelente de un vehiculo de 6 ruedas de guia, usado para remolcar artilleria mediana y equipo sobre terreno malo.

VEHICULOS COMERCIALES

923
Gran Camioneta Bedford "Heinz"
Longitud 146 mm.
Puertas atrás.

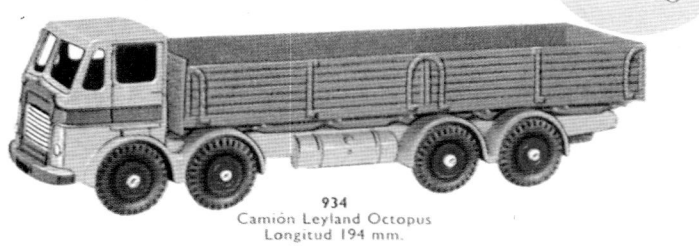

943
Algibe Leyland Octopus "Esso"
Longitud 194 mm.

934
Camión Leyland Octopus
Longitud 194 mm.

955
Bomba de Incendios con Escalera Extensible
Longitud 140 mm.
La base de la escalera gira en rotación, y la escalera pued: subir y extenderse.

VEHICULOS DE OBRAS PUBLICAS

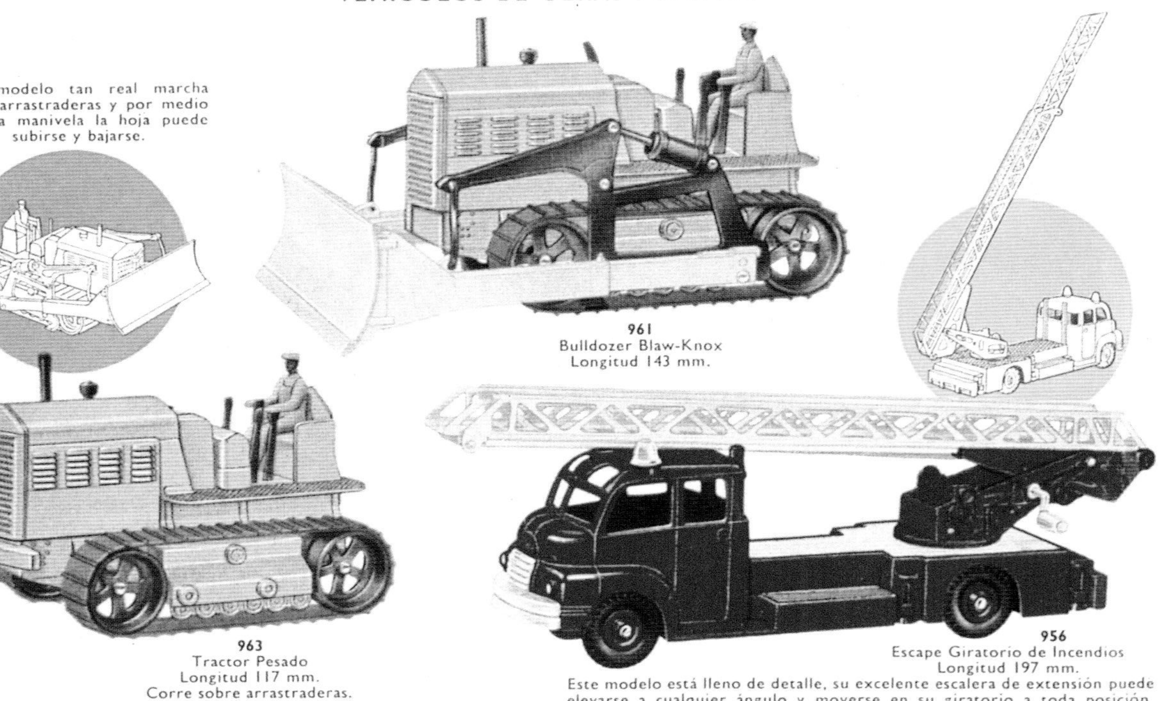

Este modelo tan real marcha sobre arrastraderas y por medio de una manivela la hoja puede subirse y bajarse.

961
Bulldozer Blaw-Knox
Longitud 143 mm.

963
Tractor Pesado
Longitud 117 mm.
Corre sobre arrastraderas.

956
Escape Giratorio de Incendios
Longitud 197 mm.
Este modelo está lleno de detalle, su excelente escalera de extensión puede elevarse a cualquier ángulo y moverse en su giratorio a toda posición.

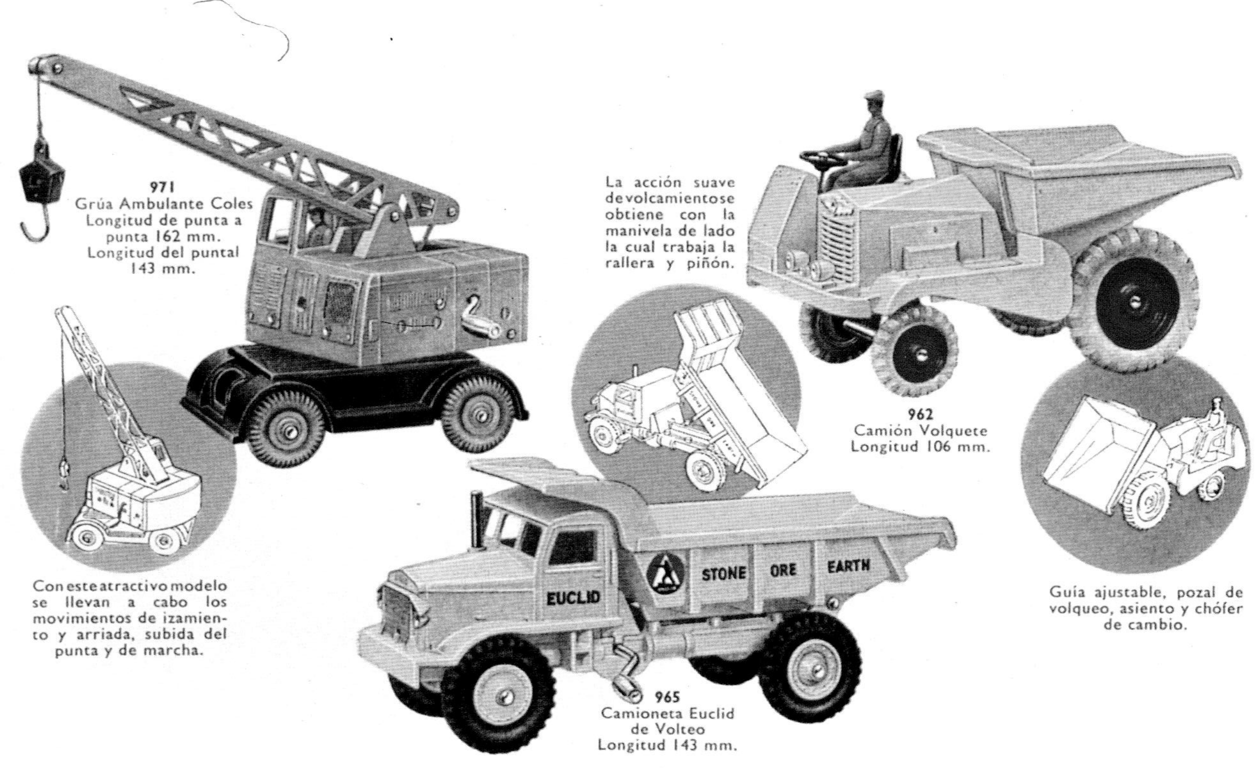

971
Grúa Ambulante Coles
Longitud de punta a punta 162 mm.
Longitud del puntal 143 mm.

Con este atractivo modelo se llevan a cabo los movimientos de izamiento y arriada, subida del punta y de marcha.

La acción suave devolcamientose obtiene con la manivela de lado la cual trabaja la rallera y piñón.

962
Camión Volquete
Longitud 106 mm.

Guía ajustable, pozal de volqueo, asiento y chófer de cambio.

965
Camioneta Euclid de Volteo
Longitud 143 mm.

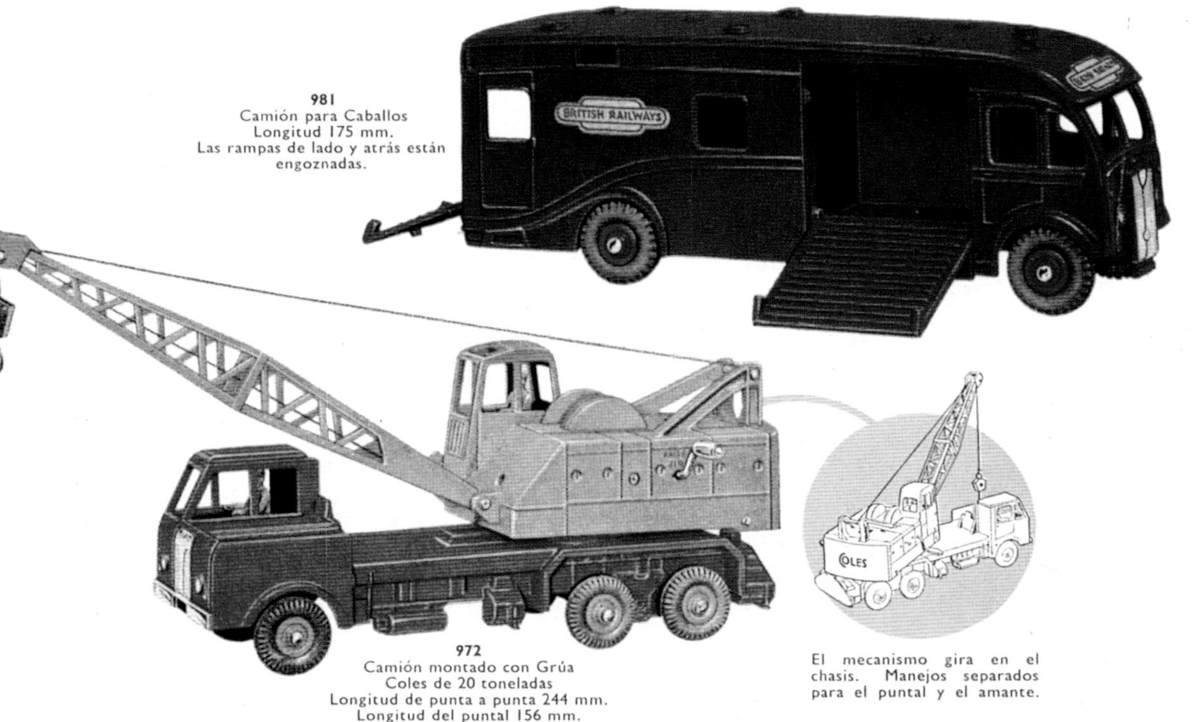

981
Camión para Caballos
Longitud 175 mm.
Las rampas de lado y atrás están engoznadas.

972
Camión montado con Grúa
Coles de 20 toneladas
Longitud de punta a punta 244 mm.
Longitud del puntal 156 mm.

El mecanismo gira en el chasis. Manejos separados para el puntal y el amante.

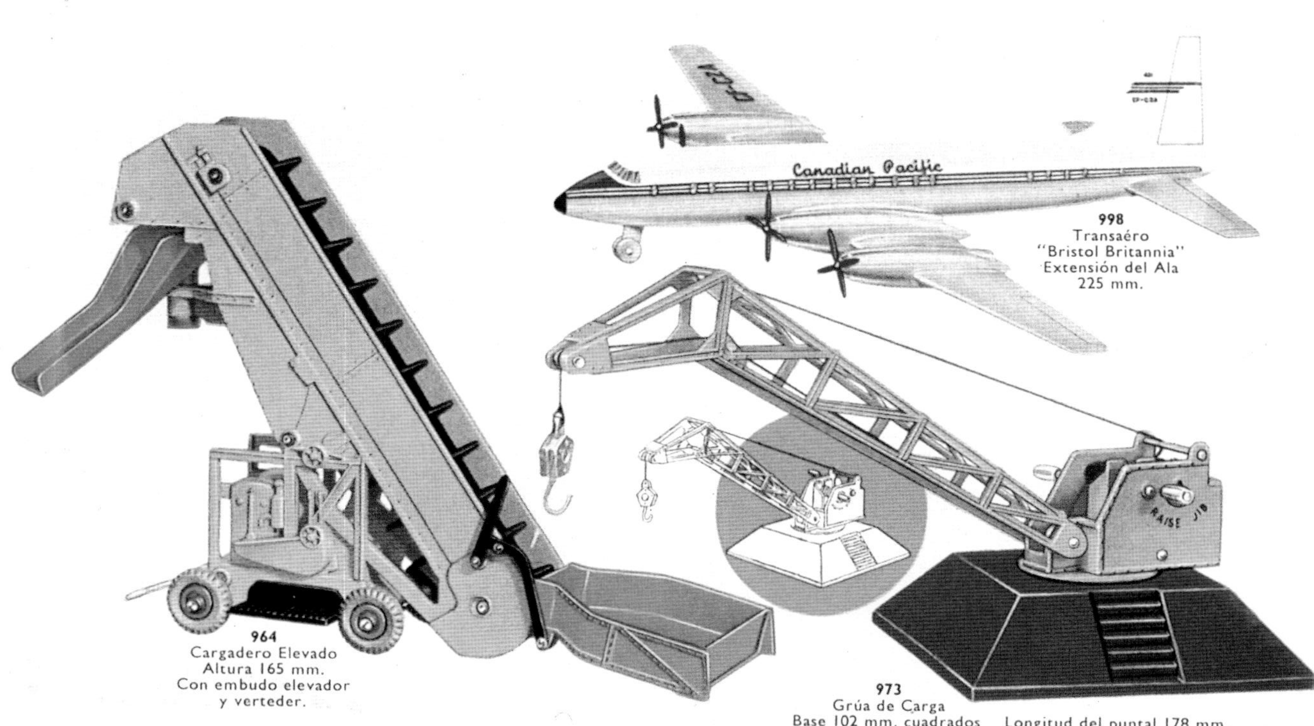

998
Transaéro
"Bristol Britannia"
Extensión del Ala
225 mm.

964
Cargadero Elevado
Altura 165 mm.
Con embudo elevador y verteder.

973
Grúa de Carga
Base 102 mm. cuadrados Longitud del puntal 178 mm.

794
Rampa de Carga para
Transportador Pullmore
Longitud 233 mm.
(no ilustrada)

982
Transportador de Coches Pullmore
Longitud con rampa 467 mm.
Este modelo lleva 4 Coches de Pasajeros Dinky Toys. La rampa alta de carga es separable y la baja es engoznada

968
Vehiculo "Ojo Explorádor" de televisión
de la BBC
Longitud 113 mm.

999
Transaé[illegible]o "Comet"
Extensión d[illegible] Ala 184 mm.

FRENCH SECTION

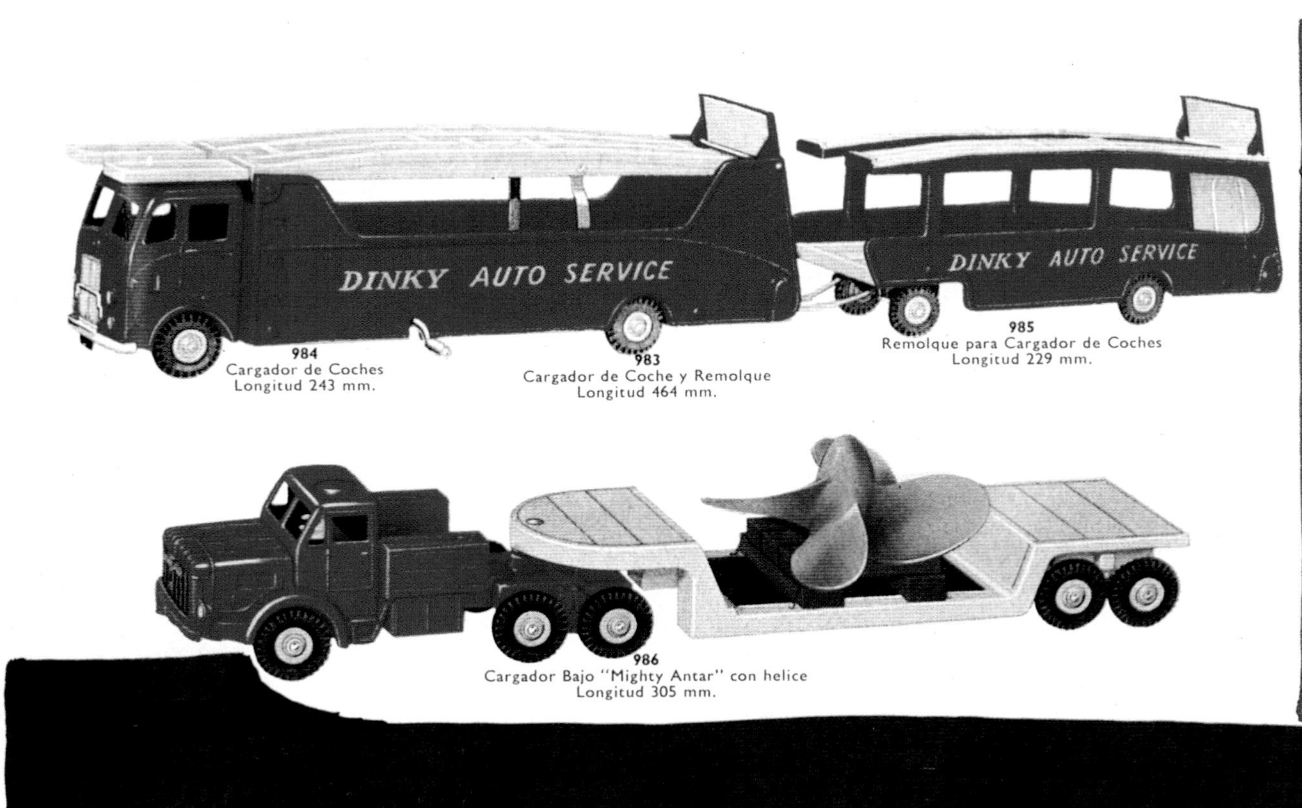

984
Cargador de Coches
Longitud 243 mm.

983
Cargador de Coche y Remolque
Longitud 464 mm.

985
Remolque para Cargador de Coches
Longitud 229 mm.

986
Cargador Bajo "Mighty Antar" con helice
Longitud 305 mm.

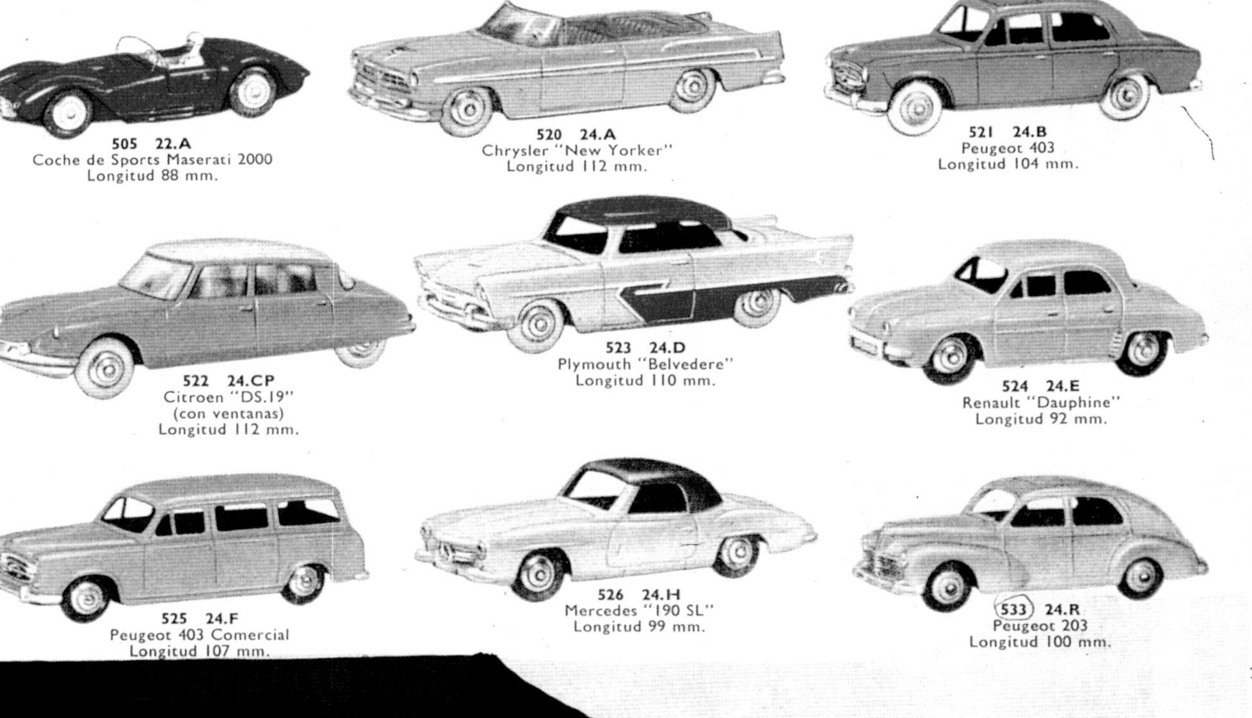

505 22.A
Coche de Sports Maserati 2000
Longitud 88 mm.

520 24.A
Chrysler "New Yorker"
Longitud 112 mm.

521 24.B
Peugeot 403
Longitud 104 mm.

522 24.CP
Citroen "DS.19"
(con ventanas)
Longitud 112 mm.

523 24.D
Plymouth "Belvedere"
Longitud 110 mm.

524 24.E
Renault "Dauphine"
Longitud 92 mm.

525 24.F
Peugeot 403 Comercial
Longitud 107 mm.

526 24.H
Mercedes "190 SL"
Longitud 99 mm.

533 24.R
Peugeot 203
Longitud 100 mm.

535 24.T
Citroen "2 C.V."
Longitud 88 mm.

536 24.U
Simca "Aronde"
Longitud 95 mm.

531 24.N
Fiat 1200
con ventanas
Longitud 91 mm.

539 24.XT
Taxi "Vedette 54"
Longitud 105 mm.

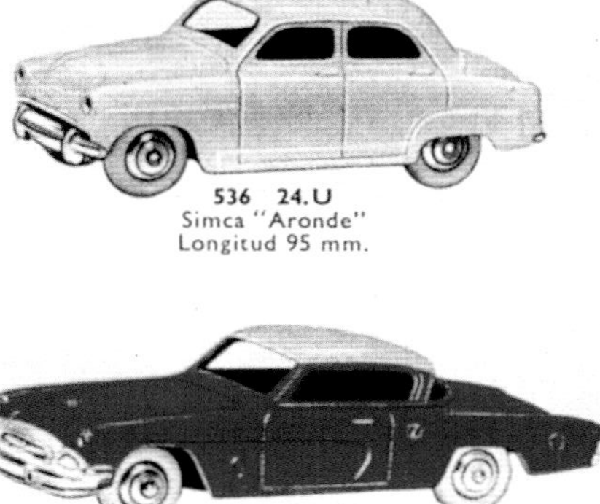

540 24.Y
Studebaker "Commander"
Longitud 109 mm.

527 24.J
Coche de Sports
Alfa Romeo 1900
con ventanas
Longitud 102 mm.

542 24.ZT
Taxi Simca "Ariane"
con ventanas
Longitud 105 mm.

528 24.K
Simca Vedette "Chambord"
con ventanas
Longitud 110 mm.

529 24.L
Vespa 400
con ventanas
Longitud 66 mm.

561 25.CG
Camión Citroen 1200 "Gervais"
Longitud 90 mm.

560 25.BV
Auto de Correos Peugeot
Longitud 90 mm.

562 25.D
Camión Citroen—Servicio de Incendios
Longitud 84 mm.

570 29.D
Autobus Parisiense
Longitud 143 mm.

571 29.F
Coche "Chausson"
Longitud 154 mm.

576 32.C
Tanque "Esso"
Longitud 178 mm.

575 32.AB
Tractor Panhard "SNCF"
Longitud 165 mm.

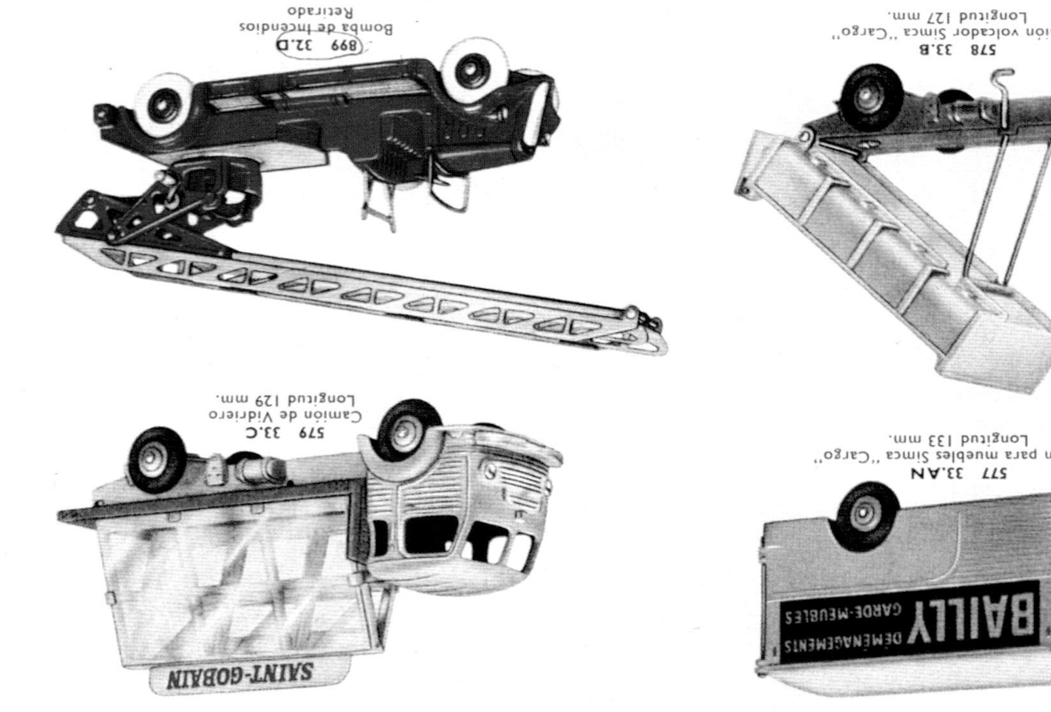

579 33.C
Camión de Vidriero
Longitud 129 mm.

899 32.D
Bomba de Incendios
Retirado

577 33.AN
Camión para muebles Simca "Cargo"
Longitud 133 mm.

578 33.B
Camión volcador Simca "Cargo"
Longitud 127 mm.

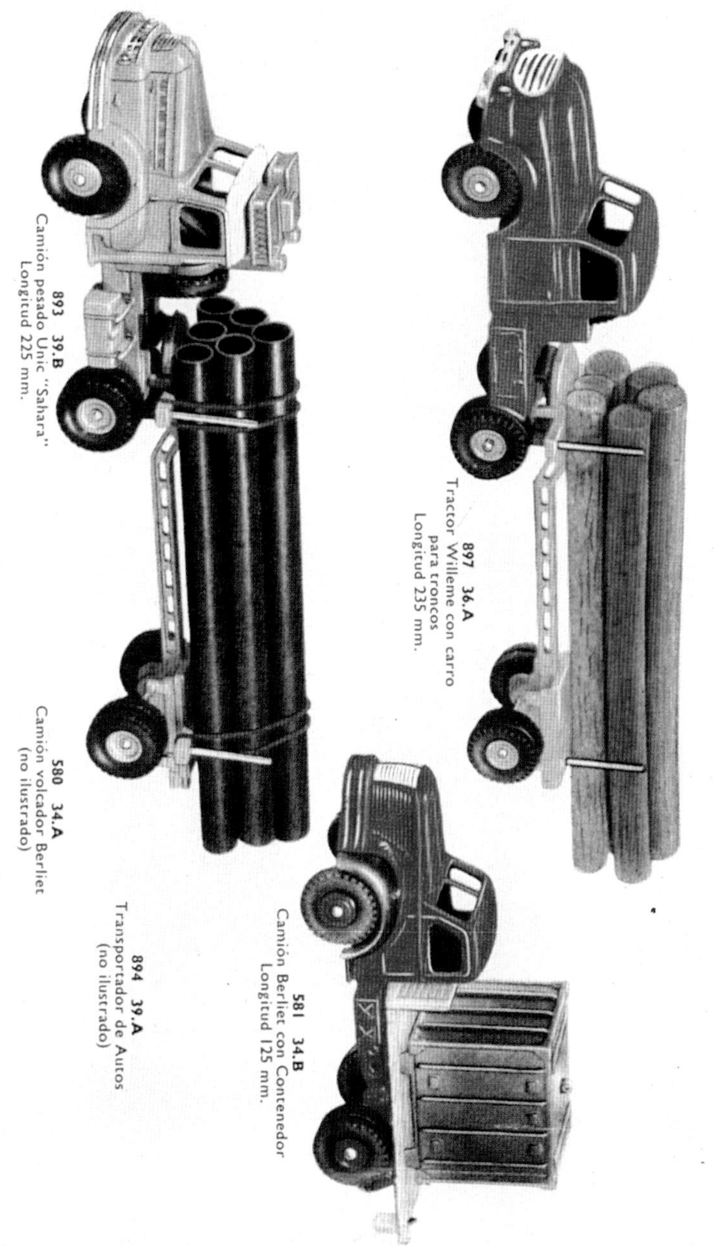

893 39.B
Camión pesado Unic "Sahara"
Longitud 225 mm.

580 34.A
Camión volcador Berliet
(no ilustrado)

894 39.A
Transportador de Autos
(no ilustrado)

897 36.A
Tractor Willeme con carro
para troncos
Longitud 235 mm.

581 34.B
Camión Berliet con Contenedor
Longitud 125 mm.

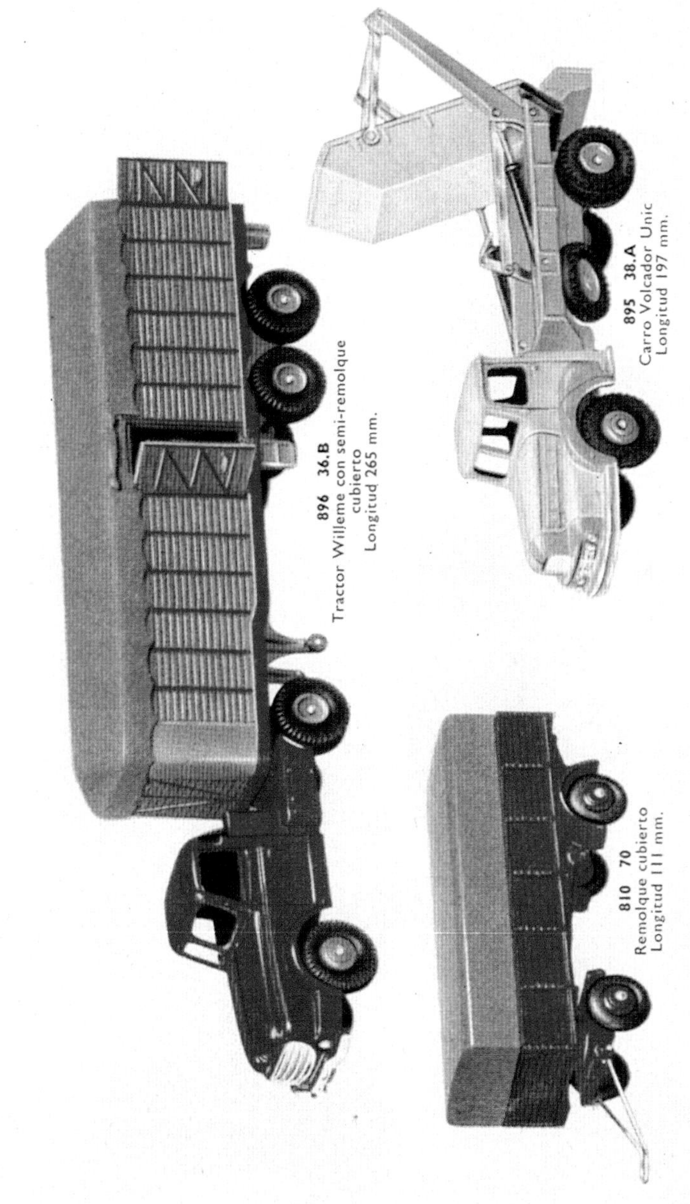

896 36.B
Tractor Willeme con semi-remolque
cubierto
Longitud 265 mm.

895 38.A
Carro Volcador Unic
Longitud 197 mm.

810 70
Remolque cubierto
Longitud 111 mm.

DINKY TOYS - DINKY SUPERTOYS

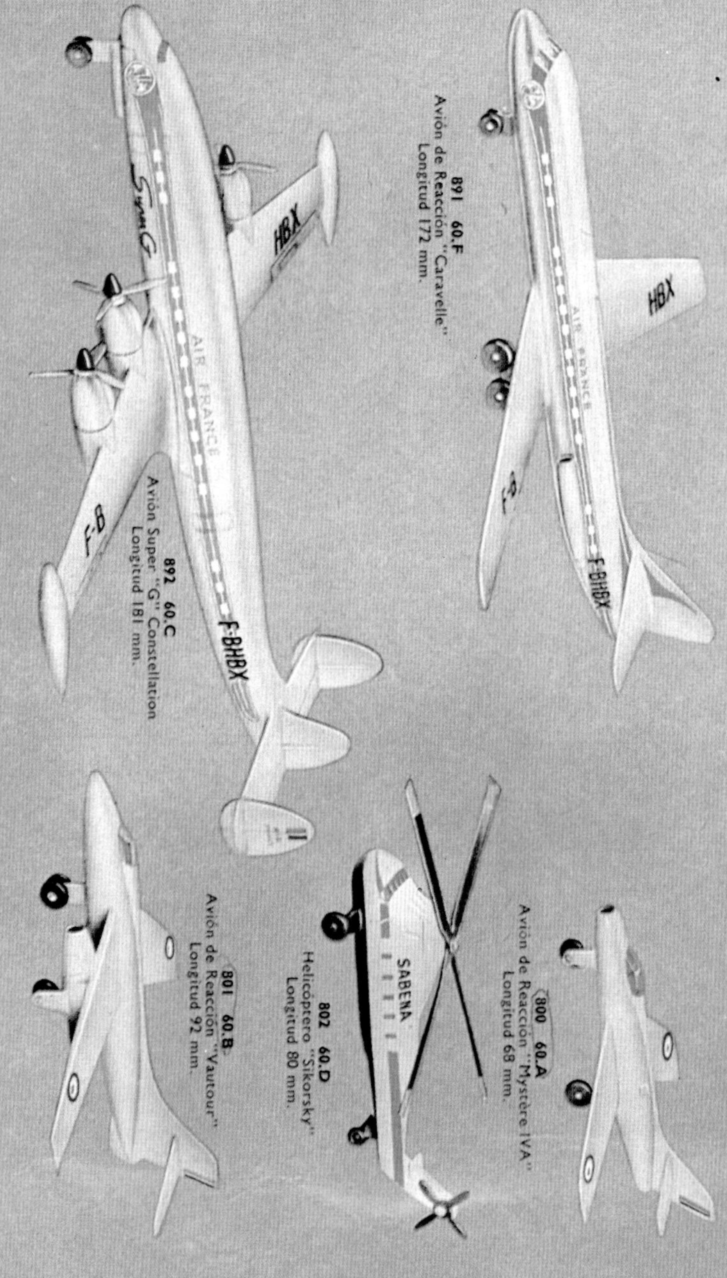

891 60.F
Avión de Reacción "Caravelle"
Longitud 172 mm.

892 60.C
Avión Super "G" Constellation
Longitud 181 mm.

800 60.A
Avión de Reacción "Mystère IVA"
Longitud 68 mm.

802 60.D
Helicóptero "Sikorsky"
Longitud 80 mm.

801 60.B
Avión de Reacción "Vautour"
Longitud 92 mm.

DINKY TOYS

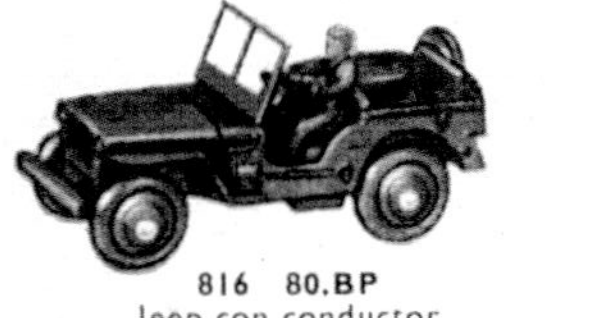

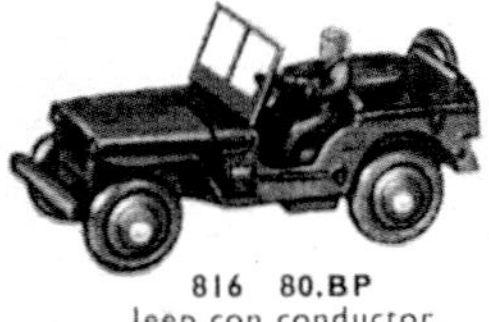

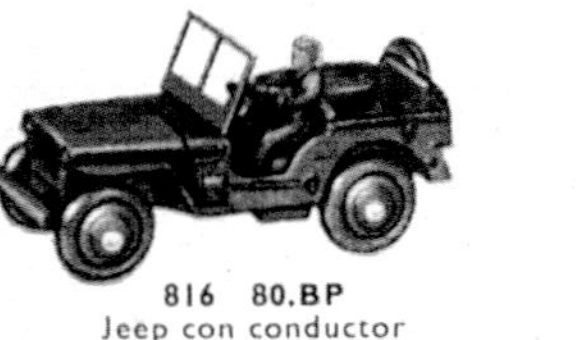

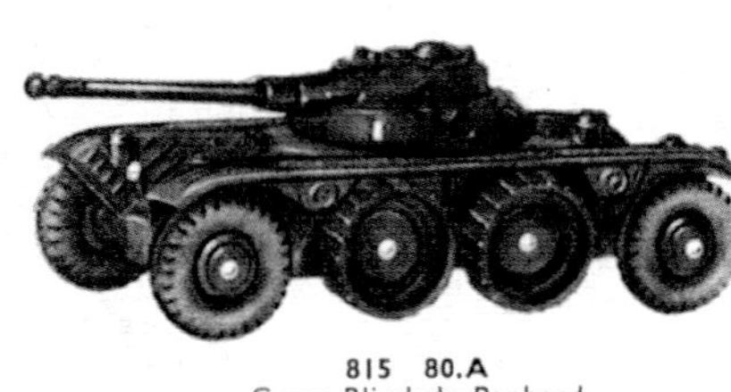

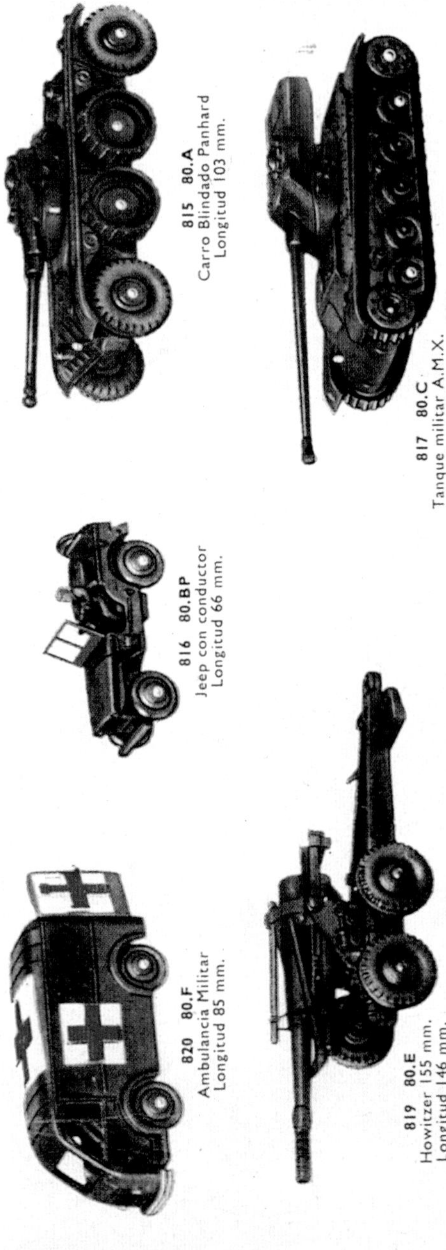

815 80.A
Carro Blindado Panhard
Longitud 103 mm.

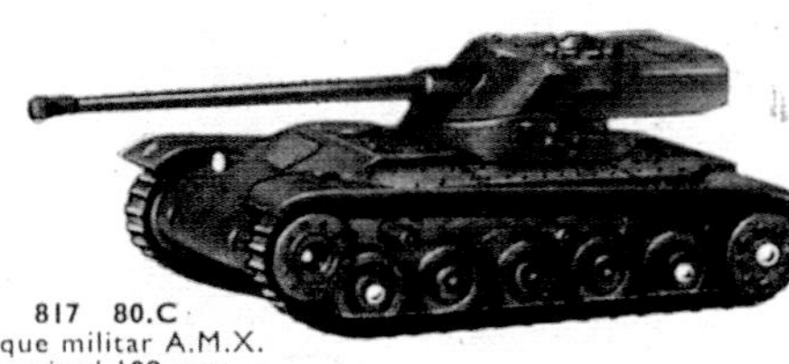

817 80.C
Tanque militar A.M.X.
Longitud 108 mm.

816 80.BP
Jeep con conductor
Longitud 66 mm.

820 80.F
Ambulancia Militar
Longitud 85 mm.

819 80.E
Howitzer 155 mm.
Longitud 146 mm.

Todo aficionado a Dinky Toys y Supertoys puede hacerse socio del Dinky Toys Club. Solicitad detalles a vuestro representante ó agente detallista.

FABRICADOS EN INGLATERRA POR MECCANO LTD.
Impreso en Inglaterra

7/559/15

Spanish N.P.

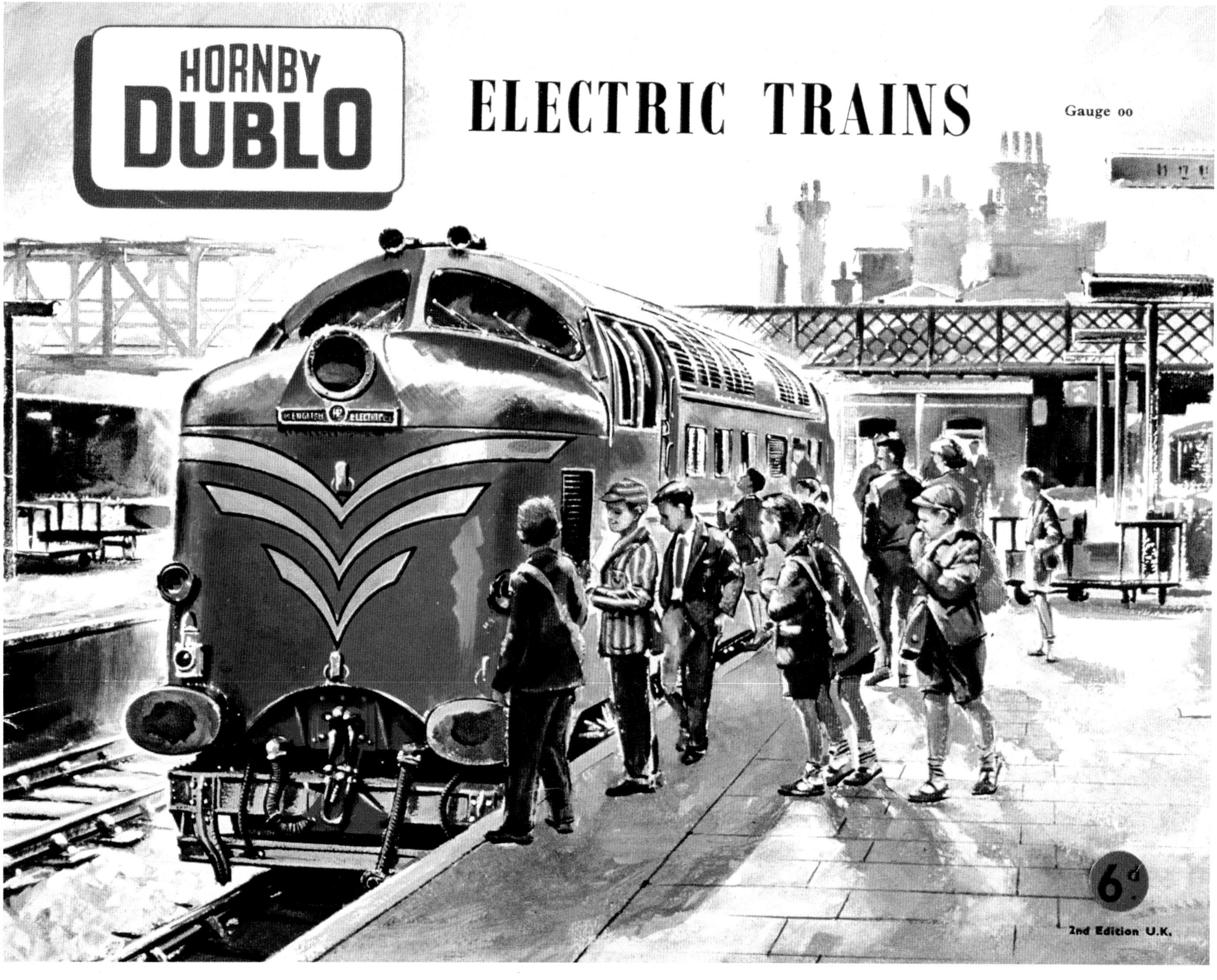

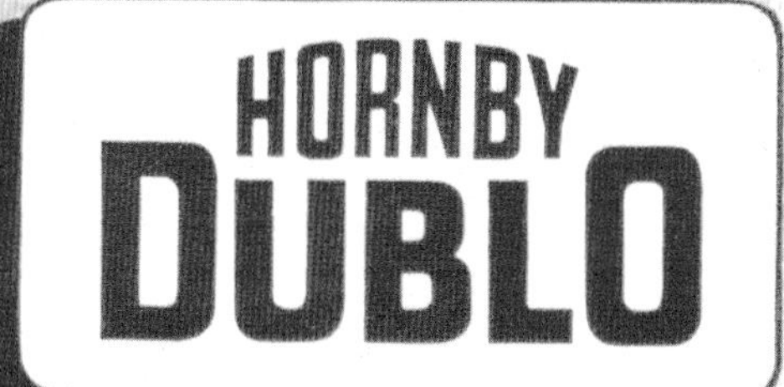

ELECTRIC TRAINS

Gauge OO

6d.

2nd Edition U.K.

Gauge 00—5/8 ins

HORNBY DUBLO

Owning a Hornby-Dublo railway, and running it by remote control, is something every boy longs to do. Hornby-Dublo models are 1/76th real size. The locomotives are scale proportioned, driven by powerful and efficient electric motors. The engineering precision which goes into every part ensures long life and unequalled performance.

This book primarily features the Hornby-Dublo 2-Rail system, introduced last year. It is important to note, that Hornby-Dublo 3-Rail equipment will continue to be produced for the benefit of those who already run layouts on this system.

Hornby-Dublo trains operate on direct current at 12 volts, and are, therefore, simple and absolutely safe for the youngest owners. All electrical equipment is designed and manufactured in strict accordance with the specifications of the British Standards Institute. The sturdiness of the motors is incredible. Hornby-Dublo locomotives in continuous operation at exhibitions have frequently travelled over 700 miles with no attention other than regular oiling and brush replacement.

Current can be obtained in any one of four different ways:—

1. **From A.C. mains through a suitable self-contained power unit.**
2. **From A.C. mains through a 15-volt transformer in conjunction with a suitable rectifier/controller.**
3. **From three 4-5-volt dry bell batteries, using a suitable battery control unit.**
4. **From a 12-volt accumulator using a suitable controller.**

Suppressors are fitted to all Hornby-Dublo Trains which effectively counter interference with Radio and T.V. reception.

MOTORS

The motor is the heart of a miniature electric locomotive and the motors of Hornby-Dublo Locomotives are scientifically designed and soundly constructed of best quality materials, to give long and reliable service.

LOCOMOTIVE MAINTENANCE

Little maintenance work is necessary to keep a Hornby-Dublo engine in good trim. Oiling should be carried out "little and often."

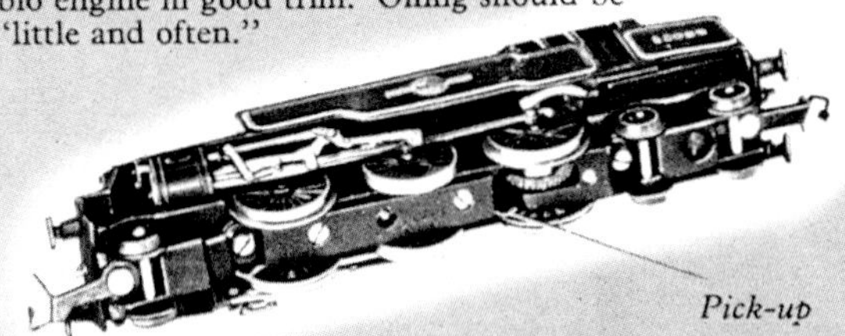

Pick-up

It is inadvisable to lay out the track on a carpet, or where fluff and foreign matter can be picked up by the motor. This seriously impairs the efficiency of the engine and will ultimately prevent its running.

2-Rail and 3-Rail TRACK

A railway is only as good as its track, and Hornby-Dublo track, either 2-Rail or 3-Rail, is of the highest quality. Running rails in 2-Rail track are of nickel silver, laid on base sections, incorporating individually moulded sleepers. The running rails of 3-Rail track are nickel plated brass, mounted on one-piece bases of stout metal.

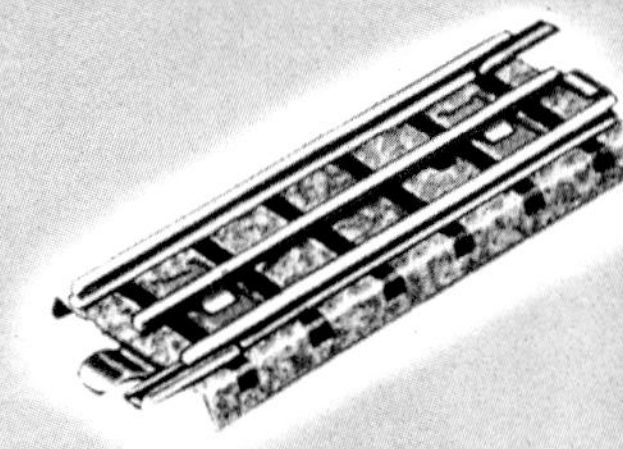

TRACK ASSEMBLY

Fishplates join the individual running rails in 2-Rail and 3-Rail. The rail ends are inserted into their opposite fishplates, while the rail sections are pushed together carefully *on a flat surface*. This method ensures the good sound rail joints essential for smooth running.

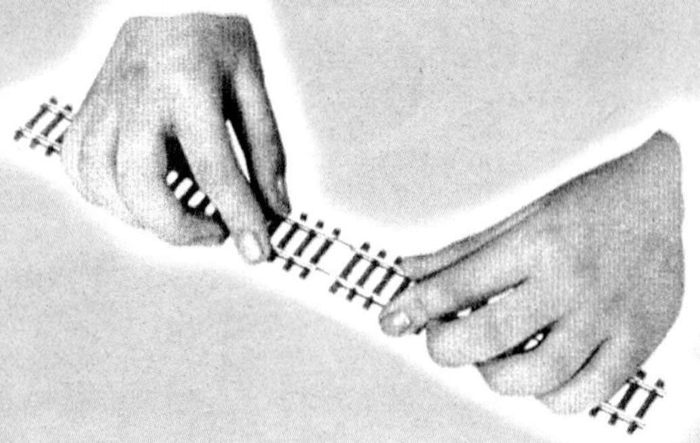

Gauge 00—⅝ in.

HORNBY
DUBLO

AUTOMATIC COUPLINGS

Couplings of ingenious and efficient design are fitted to all Hornby-Dublo Locomotives and Rolling Stock, and they engage automatically when an engine pushes the vehicles together. There is thus no need to touch the train.

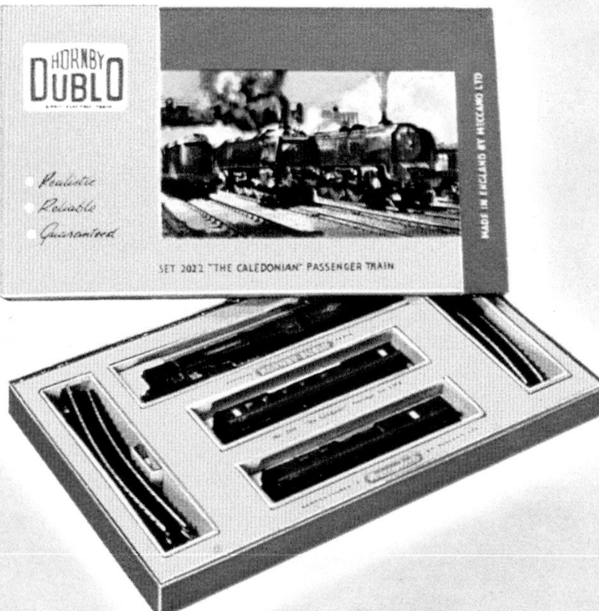

UNCOUPLING

As with coupling-up, so uncoupling operations in Hornby-Dublo can be carried out automatically. The track system includes Uncoupling Rails, both hand-operated and electrically-operated, incorporating a ramp of special shape that can be raised into the operating position and which then causes the couplings of vehicles passing over it to separate. Complete lineside control of ALL shunting and marshalling movements is thus provided.

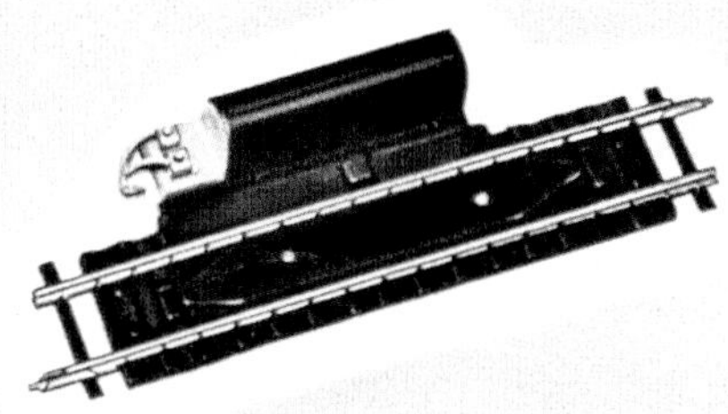

NYLON WHEELS

A feature of all Hornby-Dublo rolling stock nowadays is the use of moulded nylon wheels. Each pair of wheels, either spoked or disc is moulded complete on its axle, thus ensuring consistently steady and smooth running. These moulded wheels provide complete insulation for 2-Rail operation, and they are, of course, suitable for 3-Rail as well.

OPERATION FROM A.C. MAINS

Running a Hornby-Dublo railway from an A.C. mains supply is easily possible by the use of a power control unit, and your Dealer will be glad to advise the most suitable control equipment for your purpose. Where there is no A.C. mains supply available a Hornby-Dublo Train may be operated from suitable dry batteries using a suitable controller.

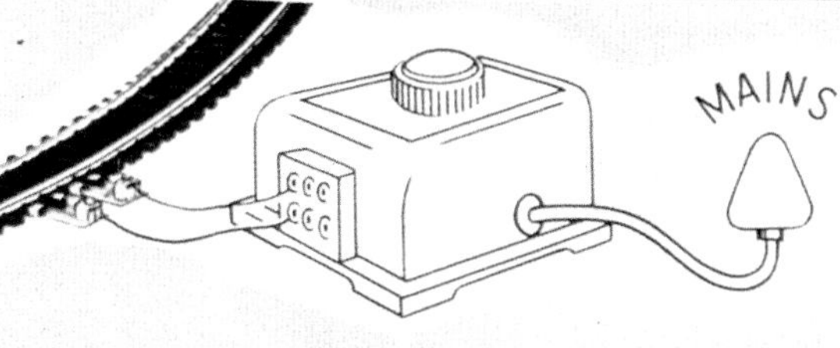

SIMPLE . . .
SAFE . . . . .
RELIABLE . .

Standard Class 4 2–6–4T Locomotive No. 80141 at Grove Junction. The signalman is handing out the staff for the single line to Tunbridge Wells West Station.

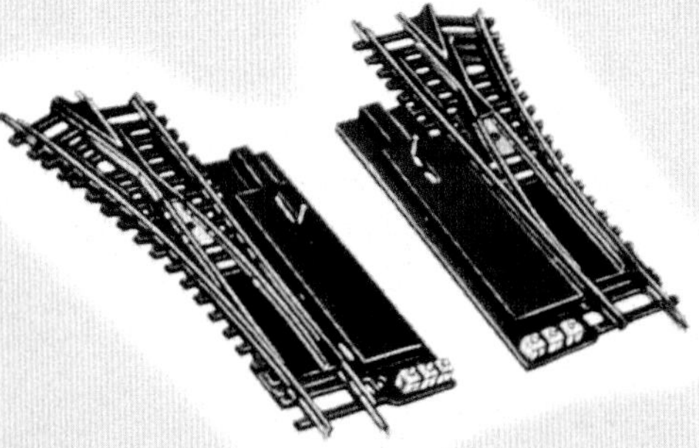

HORNBY - DUBLO 2 - RAIL HAND - OPERATED POINTS

The straight portion of each Point forms the "main" line, the branch curving to left or right, thus explaining the designation. The lever for operating the points blades is situated in the centre of the adjoining mechanism cover. The three terminals on the Points are for the purpose (1) of switching current into an isolating section, or (2) for wiring in a Colour Light-Signal to work in conjunction with the Points.

HORNBY - DUBLO 2 - RAIL ELECTRICALLY - OPERATED POINTS

These Points can be remotely operated from the control centre by means of the appropriate No. 1614 Switch (Maroon). They are fitted with two sets of terminals. Those at the "toe" serve the same function as those similarly situated on the hand points, but the terminals at the "heel" are for the purpose of wiring the Points to the operating Switch (and, if required, to an electrically-operated semaphore Signal working in conjunction with the Points).

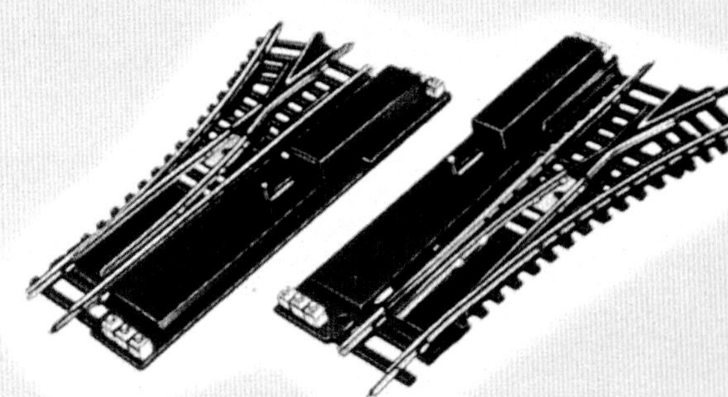

HORNBY - DUBLO 2 - RAIL ISOLATING RAILS

There are two types—Double and Single. The Double Isolating Rail is necessary with Points in most circumstances. In certain layouts, however, the Single Isolating Rail must be used in addition.

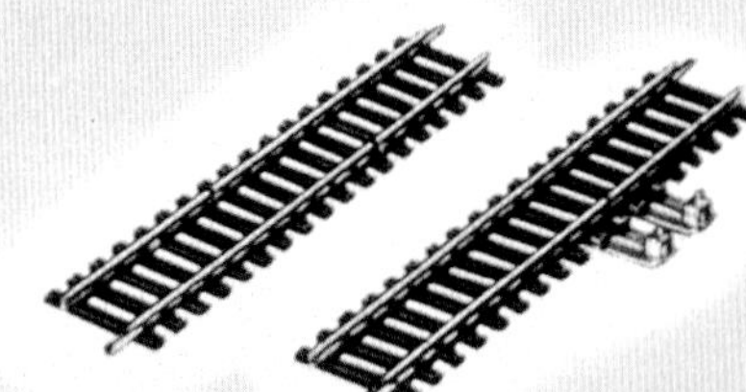

HORNBY-DUBLO SWITCHES

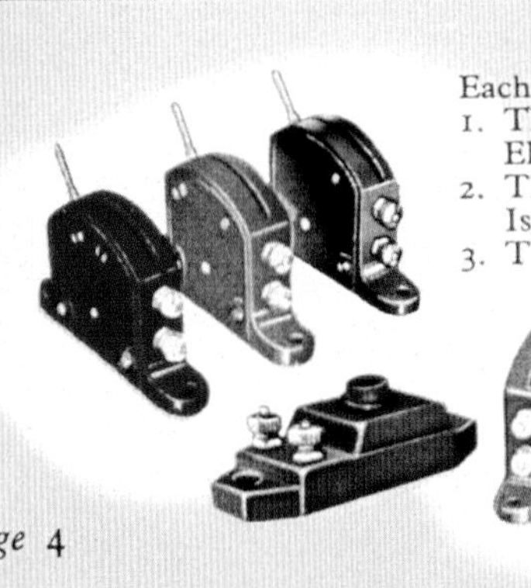

Each Switch is suitable for both 2-Rail and 3-Rail systems.

1. The maroon Switch, No. 1614, is for the operation of Electrically-Operated Points and Signals.
2. The black Switch No. 1616 D2 is for the operation of Isolating Rails.
3. The green Switch No. 1620 G3, is designed for operating Colour Light Signals only.

There are also "press button" Switches. That with the green button is for T.P.O. equipment, and that with the red button for controlling Electrically-Operated Uncoupling Rails.

ELECTRICALLY-OPERATED ACCESSORIES

The Hornby-Dublo System includes various Electrically-Operated Accessories. Among the most fascinating is the Travelling Post Office, which picks up and sets down mail automatically, while on the move, just like the real thing. Then there are the Signals, both Semaphore and Colour Light, which add so much to the realistic aspect of the track.

LIGHTING KIT

To provide illumination in the buildings such as the Engine Shed, Stations and so on that can be assembled from the standard Kits of parts, there is a Lighting Kit No. 1575 of simple but efficient design, together with a suitable Terminal Panel that makes the wiring of the lighting system easy and straightforward.

ACCESSORIES

A fine range of accessories enable the owner of a Hornby-Dublo layout to provide the right setting for his track. Stations, where the trains start or stop, Engine Sheds where the engines "live", a Goods Depot where freight is handled—all are available in easy-to-assemble kit form. There are other items too—Signal Cabin, Water Crane, Mile and Gradient Posts and so on that help to give the right atmosphere to the railway generally.

DUBLO DINKY TOYS

This attractive and growing series, is just right for use in and around the Stations, Goods Depots or on road systems connected with 'oo' gauge railways. Each model is made to the same scale as Hornby-Dublo Trains and a selection brings authenticity to model railway scenes. (See page 23 for details of the range now available).

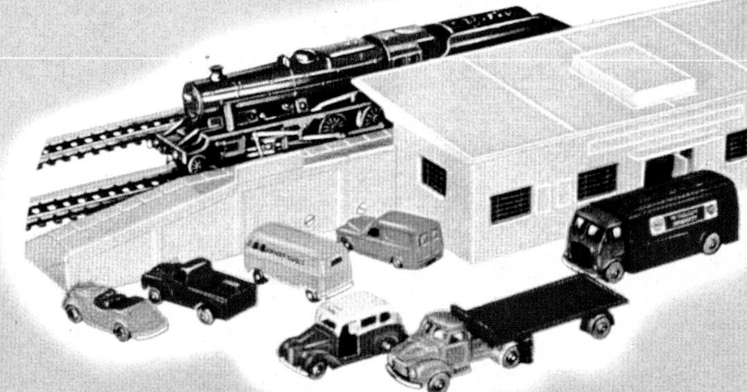

RAIL FORMATIONS

An endless variety of layouts is possible with the standard range of Hornby-Dublo Rails, both 2-Rail and 3-Rail. Below are 3 basic layout suggestions using 2-rail track.

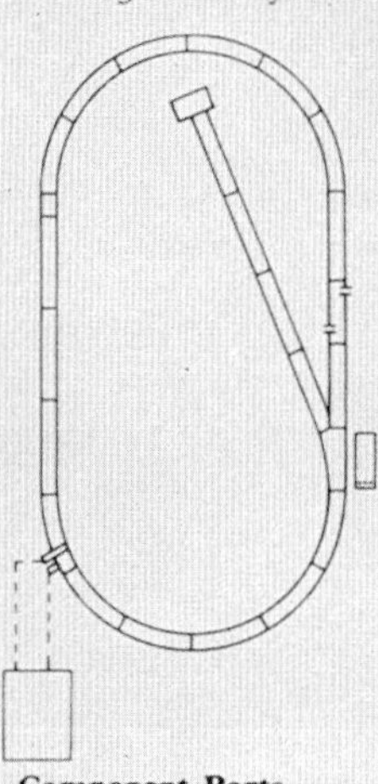

Component Parts
11 Curved Rails
1 Curved Terminal Rail
9 Straight Rails
1 Straight One-Third Rail
1 Straight Two-Third-Double Isolating Rail
1 Left Hand Point
1 Buffer Stop

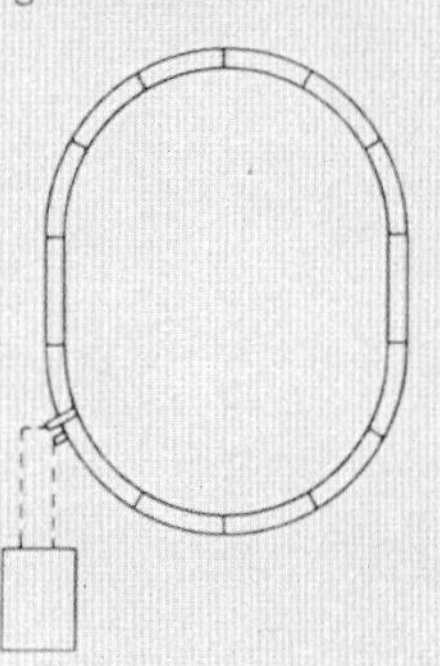

Component Parts
11 Curved Rails
1 Curved Terminal Rail
2 Straight Rails

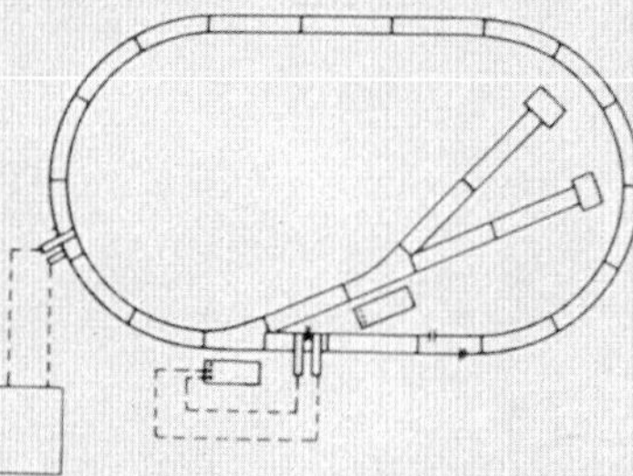

Component Parts
11 Curved Rails
1 Curved Terminal Rail
9 Straight Rails
1 Straight Two-Thirds Double Isolating Rail
1 Straight Two-Thirds Single Isolating Rail
2 Left Hand Points
2 Buffer Stops

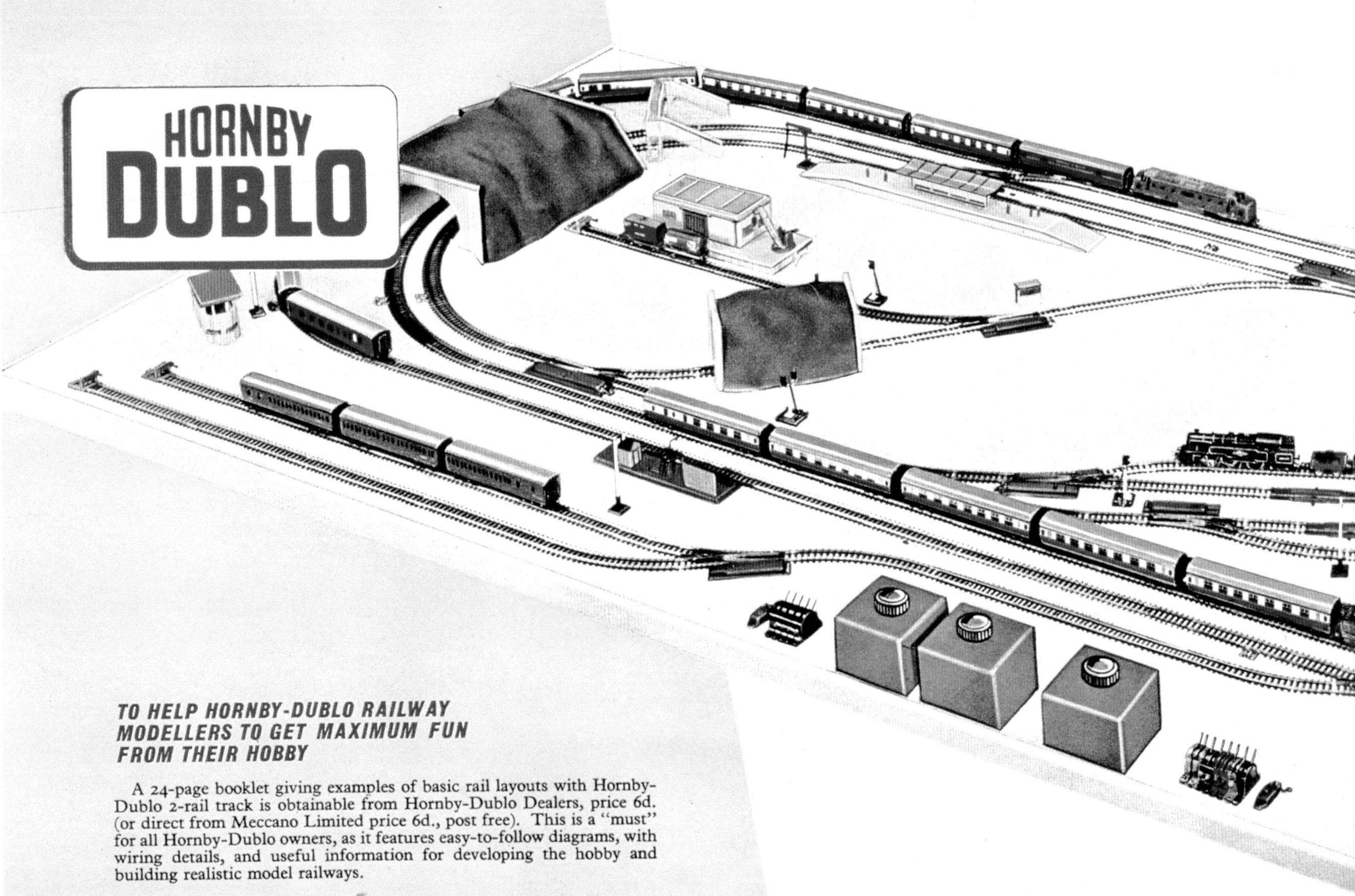

TO HELP HORNBY-DUBLO RAILWAY MODELLERS TO GET MAXIMUM FUN FROM THEIR HOBBY

A 24-page booklet giving examples of basic rail layouts with Hornby-Dublo 2-rail track is obtainable from Hornby-Dublo Dealers, price 6d. (or direct from Meccano Limited price 6d., post free). This is a "must" for all Hornby-Dublo owners, as it features easy-to-follow diagrams, with wiring details, and useful information for developing the hobby and building realistic model railways.

Power Control Units are NOT included in the Train Sets. Your dealer will be pleased to advise the most suitable power unit for your purpose.

REAL RAILWAY IN MINIATURE....

Here is an extensive Hornby-Dublo 2-Rail track layout, having three independently-controlled main lines, serving typical through Stations. There is a system of sidings for shunting and marshalling, with a Goods Depot and Engine Shed built up from standard Kits. In addition to the Hornby-Dublo locomotives already familiar to railway modellers, the equipment includes the new 0–6–0 Diesel Electric Shunting Locomotive and the Co–Co heavy main line Diesel-Electric of English Electric design.

Guarantee

All components of Hornby-Dublo Train Sets are thoroughly tested before despatch from the Meccano Works, and are guaranteed against mechanical and electrical defects. Meccano Ltd. will either repair free of charge or replace (at their option) any item that fails to operate satisfactory within 60 days from date of purchase.

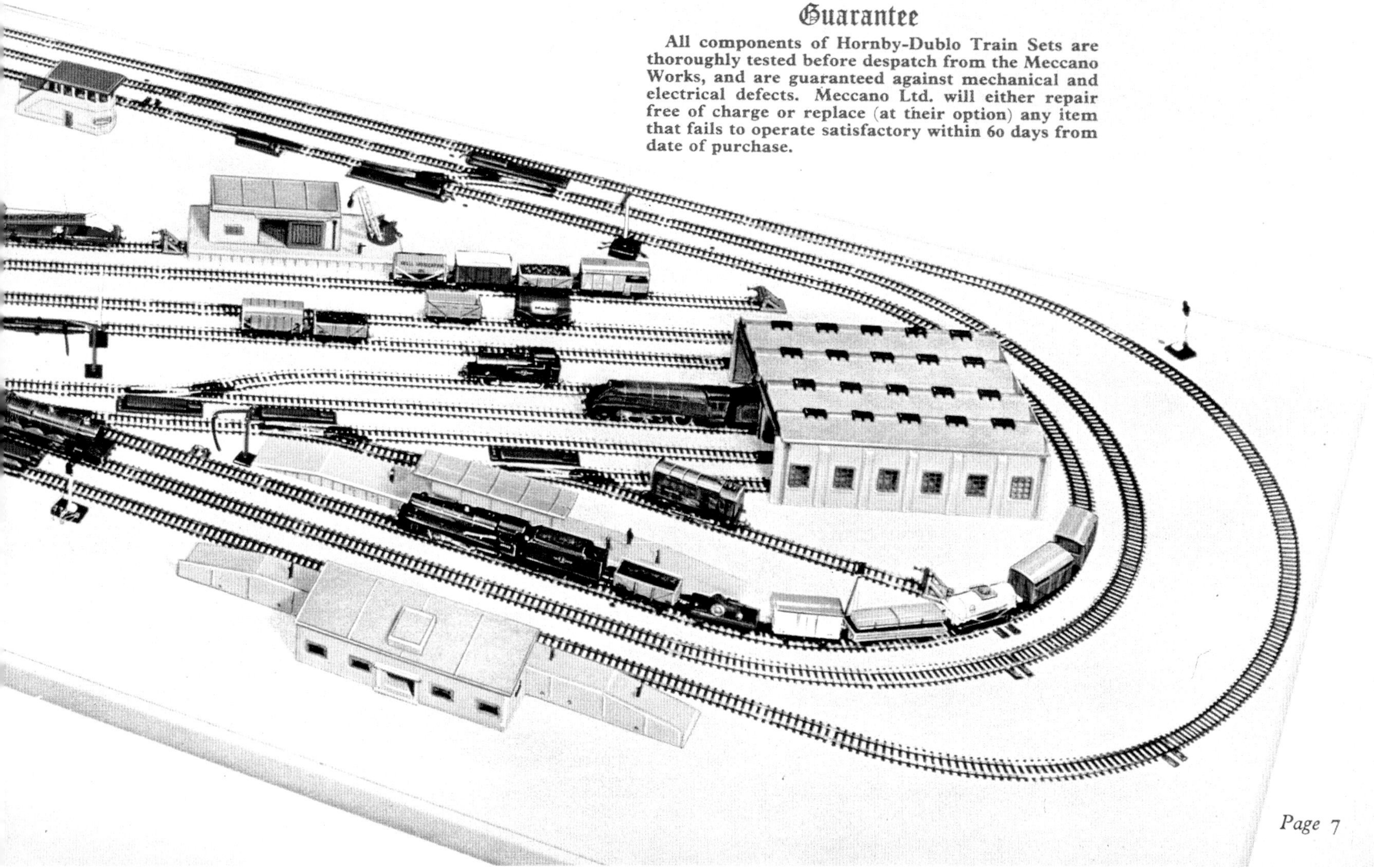

Gauge 00— $\frac{5}{8}$ in.

1

2

3

NEW

LOOK AT THESE FINELY-DETAILED HORNBY-DUBLO TRAINS!

Main line 'crack' British expresses . . . familiar suburban trains . . . goods trains with bustling, busy locomotives and varied rolling stock. These Hornby-Dublo Trains reproduce all the atmosphere of real railways and they are safe and simple to operate from a central control point. They're British made . . . they're reliable . . . they're guaranteed.

Beginning a Hornby-Dublo Railway is easy. After the purchase of a Train Set a suitable power unit is necessary. Any of the three simple, low-priced Hornby-Dublo Train Sets illustrated on this page forms a useful outfit for the beginner. Power units are NOT included in the Train Sets. Your local dealer will be pleased to advise the most suitable unit for your purpose.

Prices in this Catalogue include Purchase Tax where applicable.

OTHER TRAIN SETS — NOT ILLUSTRATED

Set No. 2006 0-6-0 TANK GOODS TRAIN. As Set No. 2008 but with green tank locomotive.

Price £3.3.6

Set No. 2009 0-6-0 TANK PASSENGER TRAIN. As set No. 2007 but with black tank locomotive and maroon coaches.

Price £3.15.0

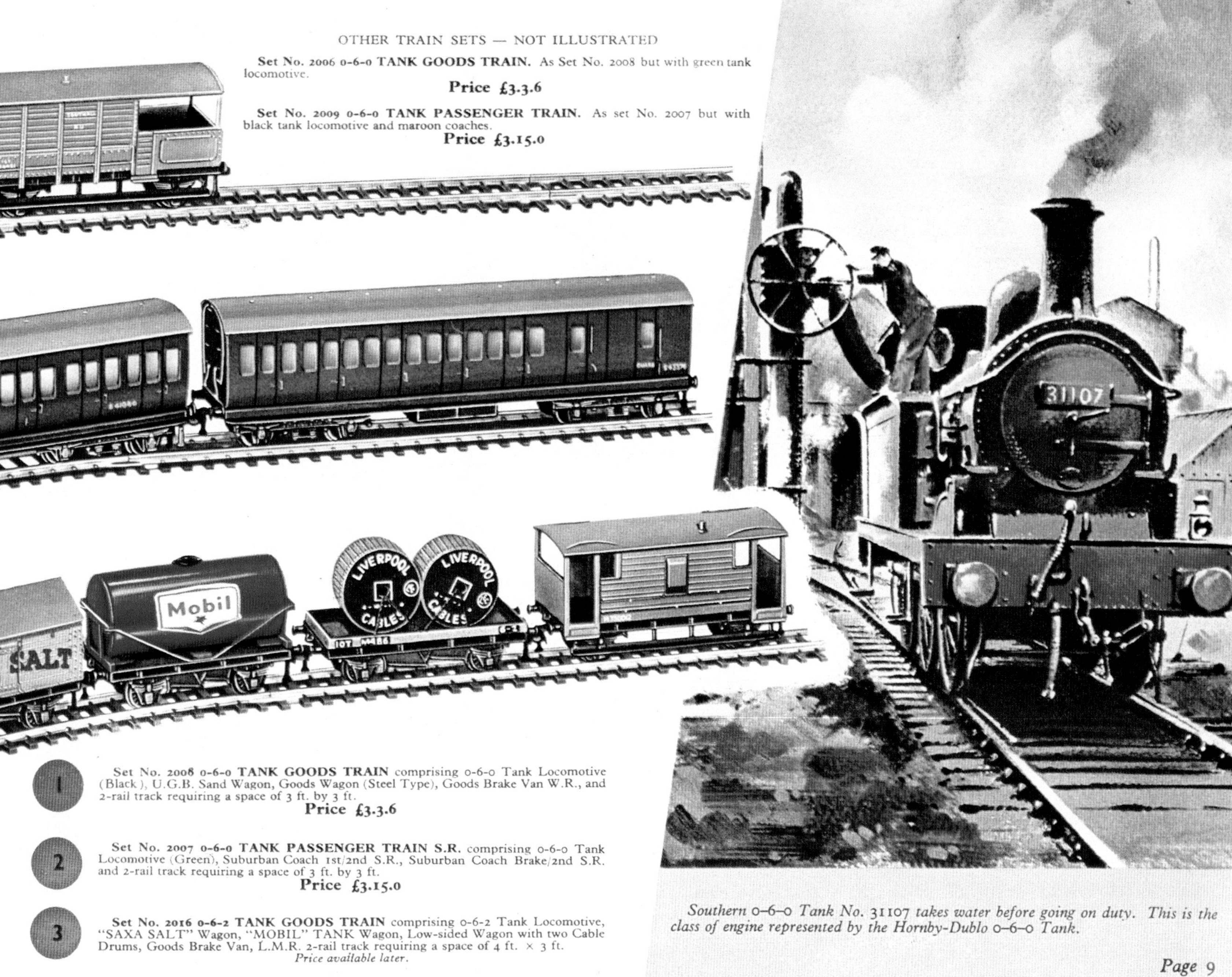

1 Set No. 2008 0-6-0 **TANK GOODS TRAIN** comprising 0-6-0 Tank Locomotive (Black), U.G.B. Sand Wagon, Goods Wagon (Steel Type), Goods Brake Van W.R., and 2-rail track requiring a space of 3 ft. by 3 ft.

Price £3.3.6

2 Set No. 2007 0-6-0 **TANK PASSENGER TRAIN S.R.** comprising 0-6-0 Tank Locomotive (Green), Suburban Coach 1st/2nd S.R., Suburban Coach Brake/2nd S.R. and 2-rail track requiring a space of 3 ft. by 3 ft.

Price £3.15.0

3 **Set No. 2016 0-6-2 TANK GOODS TRAIN** comprising 0-6-2 Tank Locomotive, "SAXA SALT" Wagon, "MOBIL" TANK Wagon, Low-sided Wagon with two Cable Drums, Goods Brake Van, L.M.R. 2-rail track requiring a space of 4 ft. × 3 ft.

Price available later.

Southern 0–6–0 Tank No. 31107 takes water before going on duty. This is the class of engine represented by the Hornby-Dublo 0–6–0 Tank.

THREE LOCOMOTIVES IN PROFILE. *An imposing engine shed scene showing three big steam locomotives side by side including, in the foreground, an A3 Pacific.*

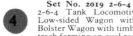

4 **Set No. 2019 2-6-4 TANK GOODS TRAIN** comprising 2-6-4 Tank Locomotive, Low-sided Wagon with Tractor, Low-sided Wagon with Insulated Meat Container, Double Bolster Wagon with timber load, Goods Brake Van B.R. and 2-rail track forming an oval requiring a space of 4 ft. by 3 ft.

£5.7.6

5 **Set No. 2030 1,000 b.h.p. DIESEL-ELECTRIC GOODS TRAIN** comprising 1,000 b.h.p. Bo-Bo Diesel-Electric Locomotive, 16-ton Mineral Wagon, 6-ton Refrigerator Van W.R., 20-ton Bulk Grain Wagon, 12-ton Ventilated Van, Goods Brake Van L.M.R., and 2-rail track forming an oval requiring a space of 4 ft. by 3 ft.

£5.12.6

6 **Set No. 2015 "THE TALISMAN" PASSENGER TRAIN E.R.** comprising "Golden Fleece" Locomotive and Tender E.R., Coach 1st/2nd B.R., Coach Brake/2nd B.R. and 2-rail track forming an oval requiring a space of 4 ft. by 3 ft.

£5.19.6

THE RIGHT ENGINE FOR EVERY PURPOSE—IN HORNBY-DUBLO

Illustration No. 4 is a goods train of more local type in charge of the Hornby-Dublo 2–6–4 Tank locomotive, a splendid representation of the B.R. Standard Class 4 Tank. The presence of the Insulated Meat Container on one of the Low-sided Wagons suggests a link-up with road transport at one of the stations.

A 'new look' in motive power is provided by the Hornby-Dublo Bo–Bo Diesel Electric locomotive at the head of a mixed goods train (No. 5). These modern and efficient locomotives are used on short distance freight work in certain districts, and on longer main line hauls where the work is suited to the power rating of this class of engine.

On through workings between London and Edinburgh are such well known trains as "The Talisman", and the popular Hornby-Dublo Set seen in illustration 6 is hauled by No. 60030 "Golden Fleece" of the A4 class.

Power Control Units are NOT included in the Train Sets. Your local dealer will be pleased to advise the most suitable unit for your purpose.

WHETHER A GOODS OR PASSENGER TRAIN IS REQUIRED, THERE IS A HORNBY - DUBLO TRAIN SET TO MEET YOUR NEEDS.

The first Train Set on this page is a fine example of a fast freight train headed by an L.M.R. 2–8–0 locomotive of class 8F. The vehicles making up the train have moulded bodies, incorporating a great deal of fine detail. A new and highly efficient Ring Field motor is fitted in this locomotive giving smooth and steady development of power.

A Set with special appeal to Western Region enthusiasts is "The Red Dragon", representing as it does one of the best-known expresses linking London with South Wales. Appropriately, No. 4075, "Cardiff Castle" is the engine, and this is fitted with the new Ring Field motor of very high efficiency.

A famous train on the London-Glasgow run is "The Caledonian" and the Hornby-Dublo model is hauled by the powerful "City of London" locomotive, in the maroon livery that distinguishes certain of the Stanier 4–6–2s regularly employed on this important train.

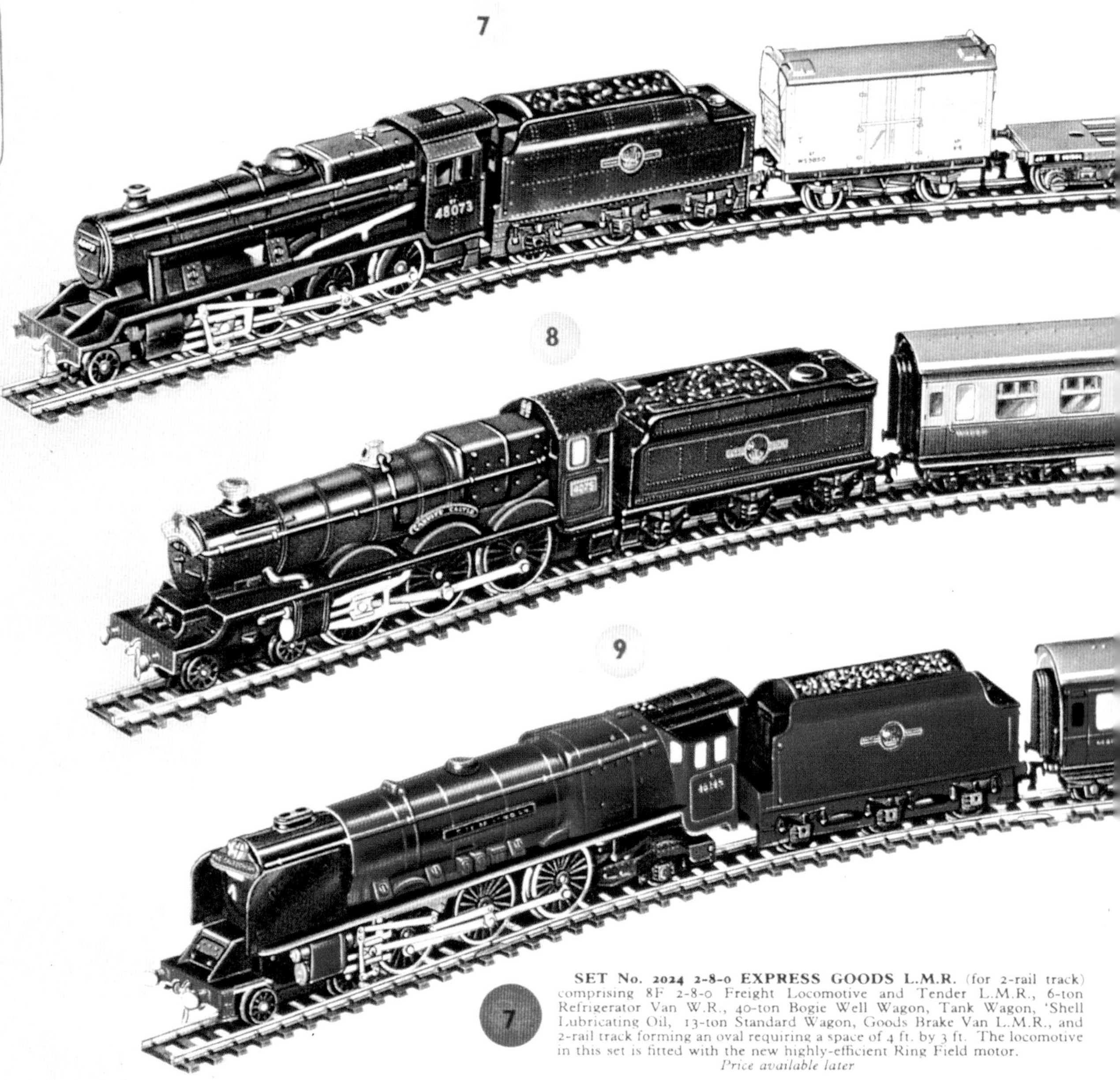

7

8

9

7 **SET No. 2024 2-8-0 EXPRESS GOODS L.M.R.** (for 2-rail track) comprising 8F 2-8-0 Freight Locomotive and Tender L.M.R., 6-ton Refrigerator Van W.R., 40-ton Bogie Well Wagon, Tank Wagon, 'Shell Lubricating Oil, 13-ton Standard Wagon, Goods Brake Van L.M.R., and 2-rail track forming an oval requiring a space of 4 ft. by 3 ft. The locomotive in this set is fitted with the new highly-efficient Ring Field motor.

Price available later

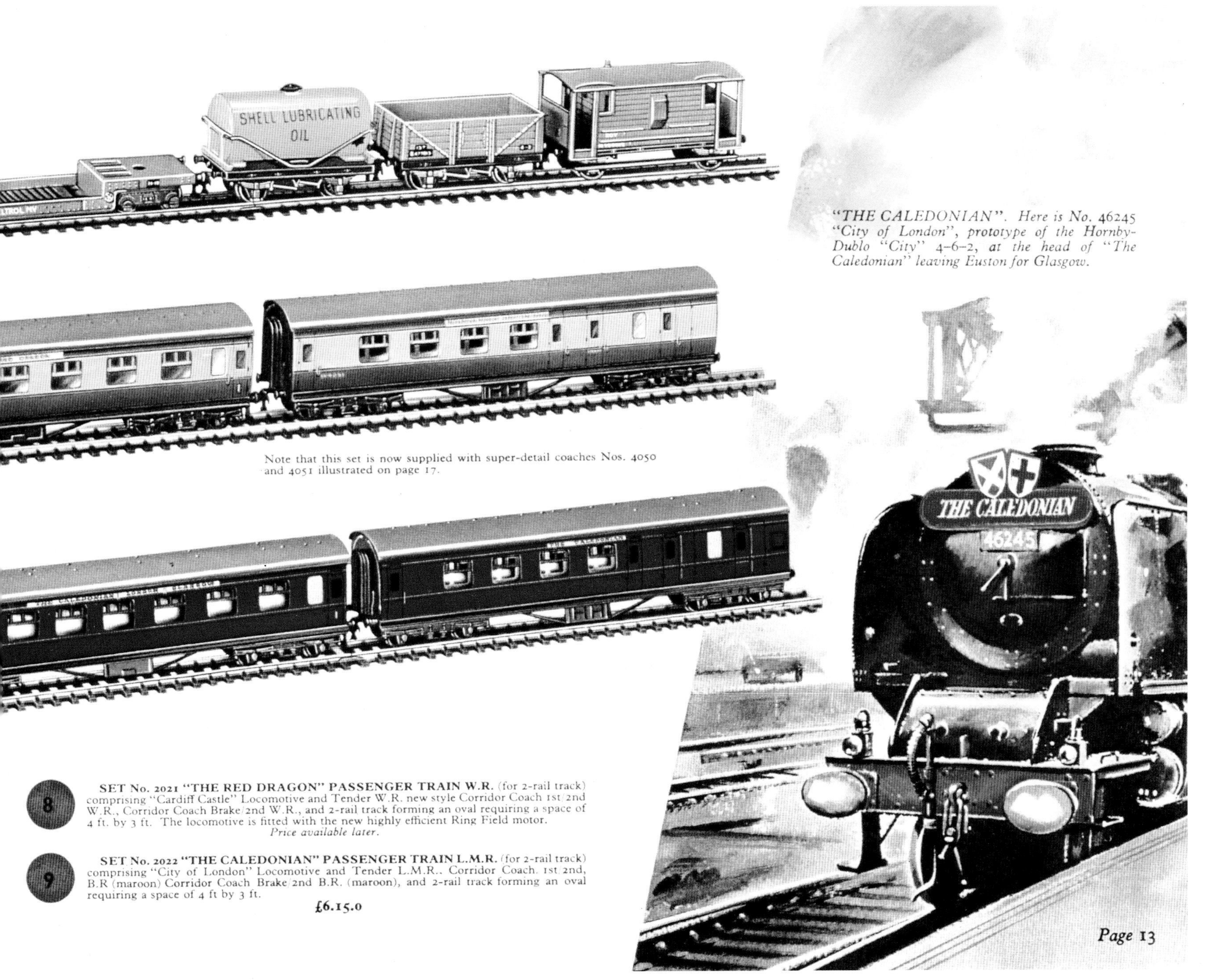

"THE CALEDONIAN". Here is No. 46245 "City of London", prototype of the Hornby-Dublo "City" 4–6–2, at the head of "The Caledonian" leaving Euston for Glasgow.

Note that this set is now supplied with super-detail coaches Nos. 4050 and 4051 illustrated on page 17.

8 **SET No. 2021 "THE RED DRAGON" PASSENGER TRAIN W.R.** (for 2-rail track) comprising "Cardiff Castle" Locomotive and Tender W.R. new style Corridor Coach 1st/2nd W.R., Corridor Coach Brake/2nd W.R., and 2-rail track forming an oval requiring a space of 4 ft. by 3 ft. The locomotive is fitted with the new highly efficient Ring Field motor.

Price available later.

9 **SET No. 2022 "THE CALEDONIAN" PASSENGER TRAIN L.M.R.** (for 2-rail track) comprising "City of London" Locomotive and Tender L.M.R.. Corridor Coach. 1st/2nd, B.R (maroon) Corridor Coach Brake/2nd B.R. (maroon), and 2-rail track forming an oval requiring a space of 4 ft by 3 ft.

£6.15.0

2-RAIL LOCOMOTIVES & TENDERS

No.	Description	Price
2206	0–6–0 Tank (Black)	£1 16 0
2207	0–6–0 Tank (Green)	£1 16 0
2211	" Golden Fleece " and Tender E.R.	£3 14 0
2217	0–6–2 Tank	*
2218	2–6–4 Tank B.R.	£3 8 0
2221	" Cardiff Castle " 4–6–0 and Tender	*
2224	2–8–0 8F Goods and Tender	*
2226	" City of London " and Tender L.M.R.	£4 1 6
2230	1,000 b.h.p. Bo-Bo Diesel-Electric B.R.	£3 1 0
2231	0–6–0 Diesel-Electric Shunting	*
2232	Co-Co Diesel Electric	*

3-RAIL LOCOMOTIVES & TENDERS

(Not illustrated)

No.	Description	Price
3211	" Mallard " with Tender (L11)	£3 14 0
3212	" Duchess of Montrose " with Tender (L12)	£3 18 6
3217	Tank 0–6–2 (L17)	£2 8 0
3218	Tank 2–6–4 (L18)	£3 8 0
3220	" Bristol Castle " and Tender (W.R.) (LT20)	£3 19 0
3225	L.M.R. 2–8–0 8F Freight and Tender (LT25)	£4 1 6
3230	1,000 b.h.p. Bo-Bo Diesel-Electric (L30)	£3 1 0
3231	0–6–0 Diesel-Electric Shunting	*
3232	Co-Co Diesel Electric	*

**Prices available later.*

Except for the 0-6-0 Tank and the "City of London", corresponding types of Three-Rail and Two-Rail Locomotives are obtainable.

A BUSY HORNBY - DUBLO MOTIVE POWER DEPOT

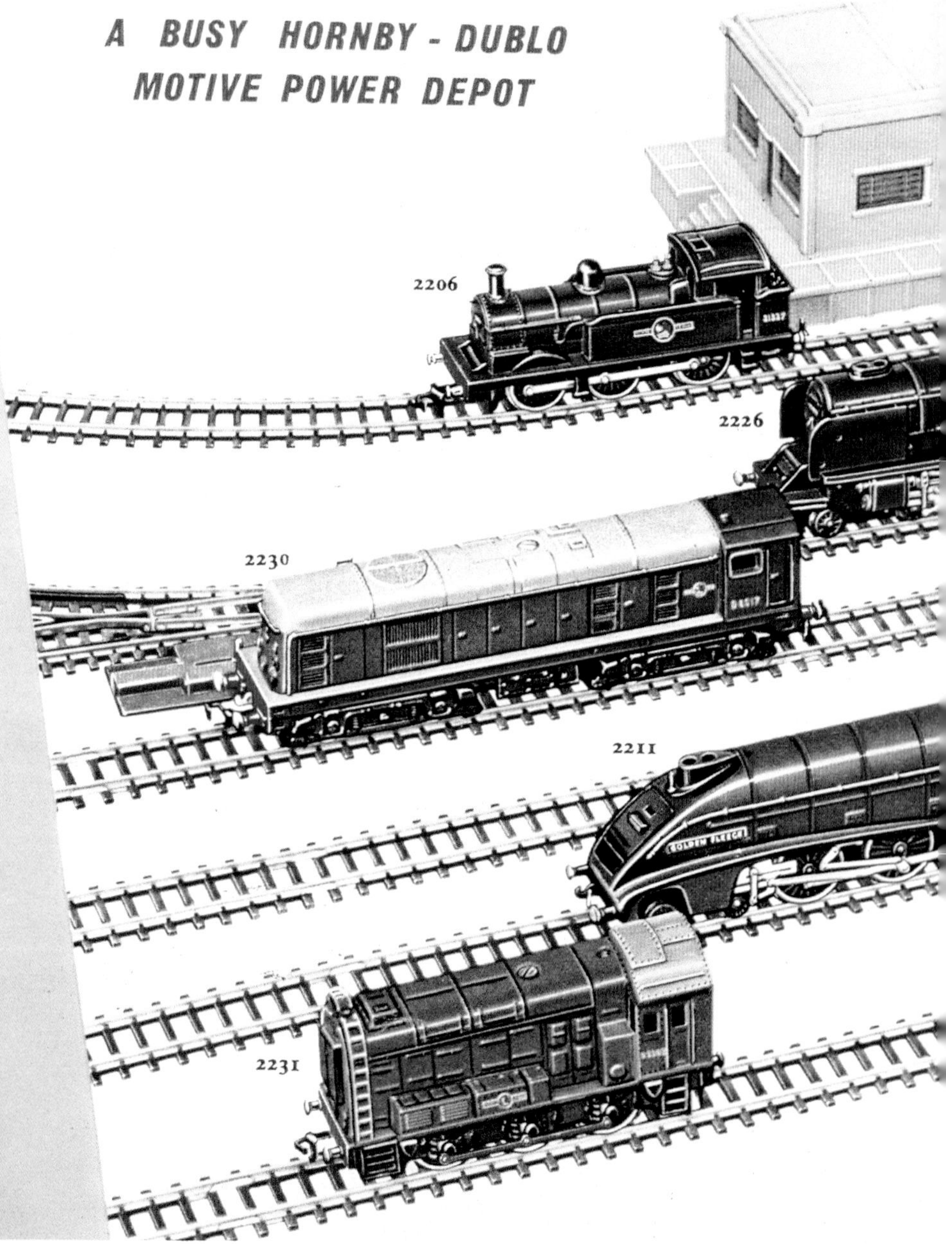

2206

2226

2230

2211

2231

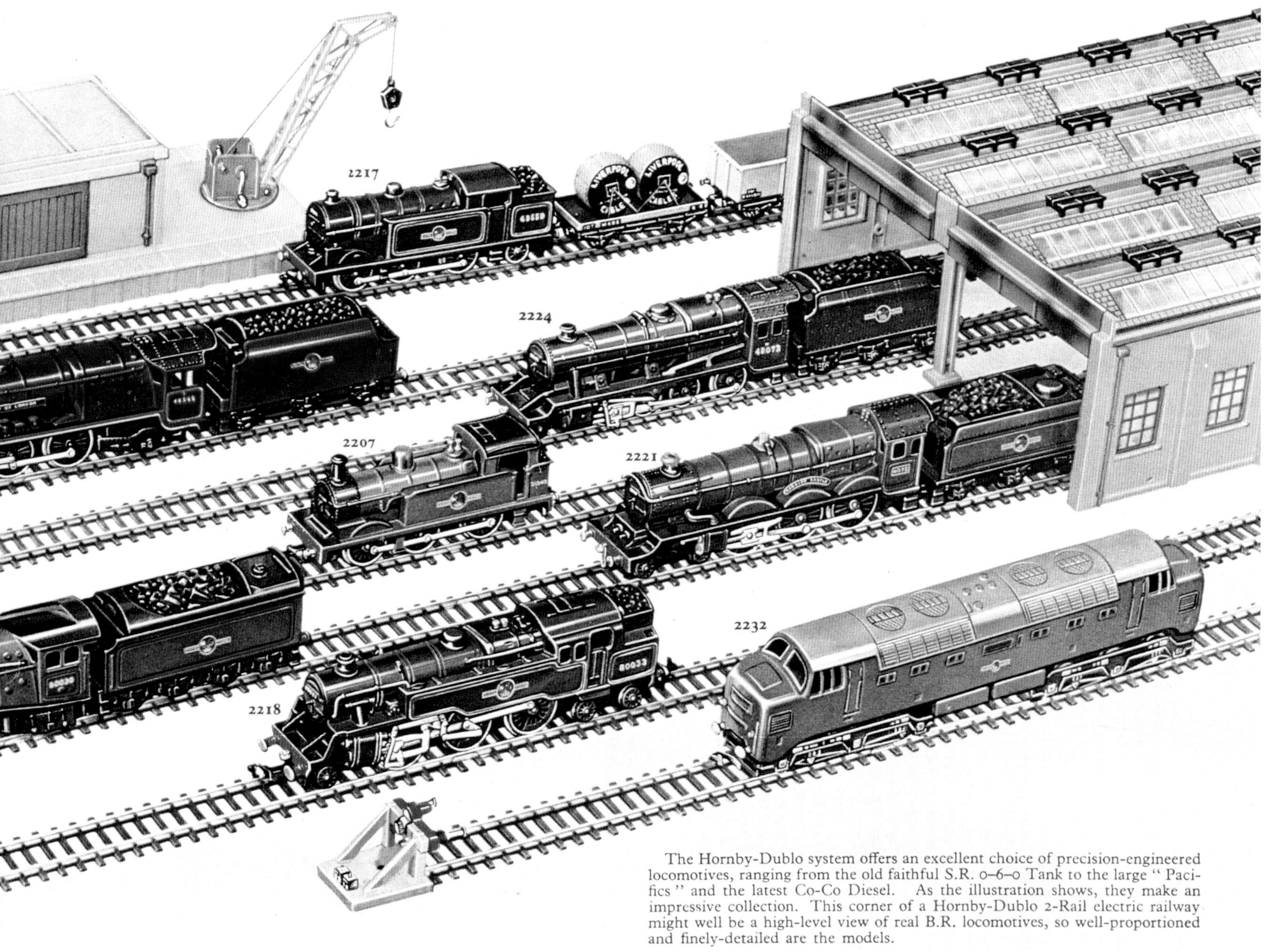

The Hornby-Dublo system offers an excellent choice of precision-engineered locomotives, ranging from the old faithful S.R. 0–6–0 Tank to the large "Pacifics" and the latest Co-Co Diesel. As the illustration shows, they make an impressive collection. This corner of a Hornby-Dublo 2-Rail electric railway might well be a high-level view of real B.R. locomotives, so well-proportioned and finely-detailed are the models.

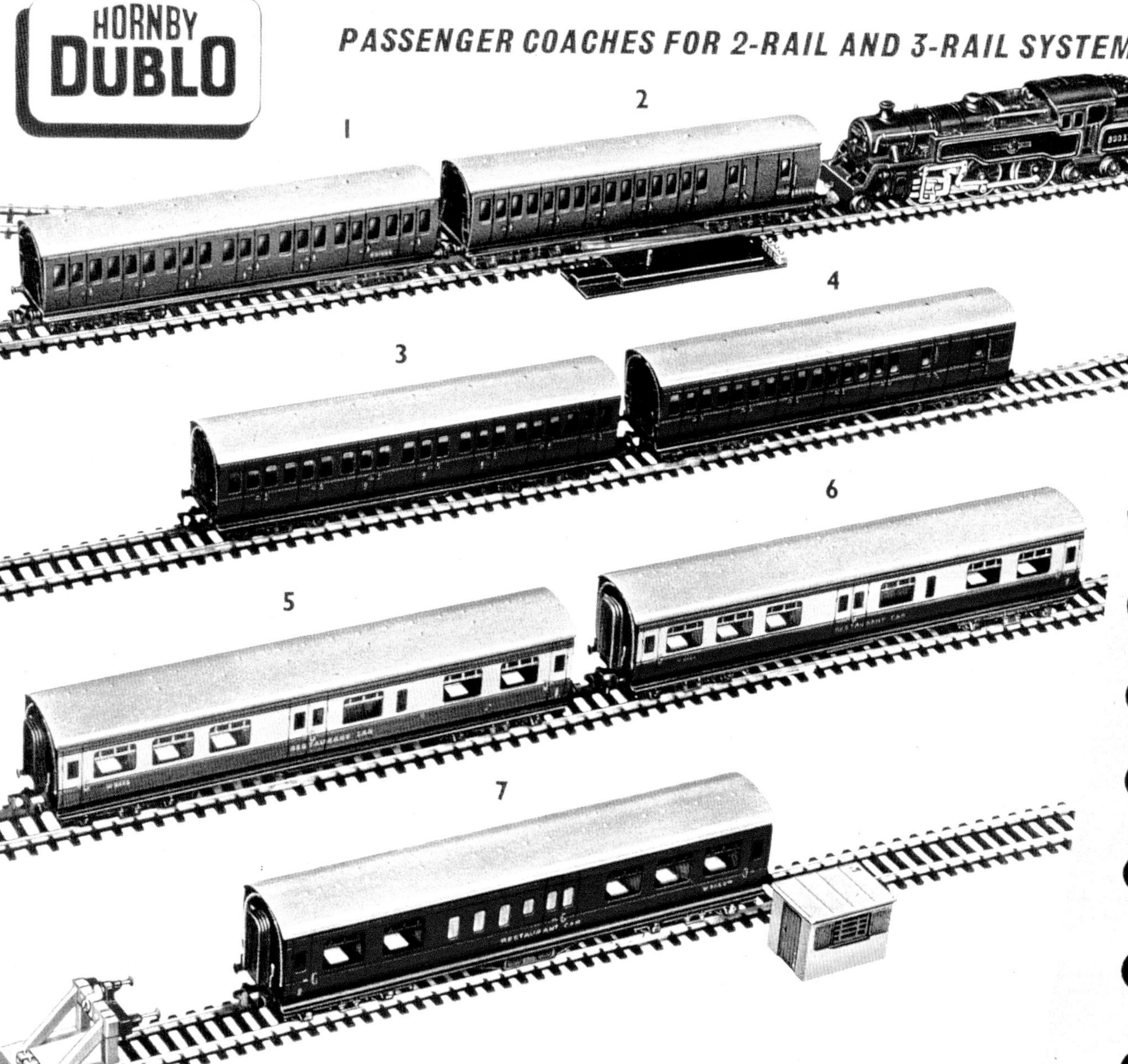

PASSENGER COACHES FOR 2-RAIL AND 3-RAIL SYSTEMS

Gauge 'oo'

These standard Coaches have tin-printed sides and die-cast underframes and are fitted with automatic couplings and Nylon wheels.

1 No. **4025**
Suburban Coach 1st/2nd (S.R.)
Length 7 $\frac{15}{16}$ in. 10/

2 No. **4026**
Suburban Coach Brake/2nd (S.R.)
Length 7 $\frac{15}{16}$ in. 10/

3 No. **4021**
Suburban Coach 1st/2nd B.R.
Length 7 $\frac{15}{16}$ in. 10/

4 No. **4022**
Suburban Coach Brake/2nd B.R.
Length 7 $\frac{15}{16}$ in. 10/

5 No. **4047**
Composite Restaurant Car (W.R.)
Length 9 $\frac{1}{16}$ in. 15/

6 No. **4048**
Composite Restaurant Car B.R. Crean
and Red.
Length 9 $\frac{1}{16}$ in. 15/

7 No. **4049**
Composite Restaurant Car B.R. Maroo
Length 9 $\frac{1}{16}$ in. 15/

PASSENGER COACHES FOR 2-RAIL AND 3-RAIL SYSTEMS

These new "super-detail" Corridor Coaches have Polystyrene ends, roofs and underframes, tin-printed sides and die-cast bogie sideframes. The Pullman Cars have moulded bodies and bases.

No. 4037
Pullman Car Brake/2nd with Interior Fittings
Overall length 9¾ in. **17/6**

No. 4051
Corridor Coach Brake/2nd W.R. with Interior Fittings
Overall length 9¾ in. **14/11**

No. 4053
Corridor Coach Brake/2nd B.R. with Interior Fittings
Overall length 9¾ in. **14/11**

No. 4035
Pullman Car 1st Class with Interior Fittings
Overall length 9¾ in. **17/6**

No. 4050
Corridor Coach 1st/2nd W.R. with Interior Fittings
Overall length 9¾ in. **14/11**

No. 4052
Corridor Coach 1st/2nd B.R. with Interior Fittings
Overall length 9¾ in. **14/11**

No. 4036
Pullman Car 2nd Class with Interior Fittings
Overall length 9¾ in. **17/6**

No. 4078
Corridor Composite Sleeping Car B.R.
Overall length 9¾ in. **14/11**

No. 4075
Passenger Brake Van B.R.
Overall length 9¾ in. **14/11**

Suitable for both 2-rail and 3-rail OO Gauge Track Automatic Couplings.

*No. **4312**
Goods Brake Van (W.R.)
Length $4\frac{5}{16}$ in.
5/11

No. **4605**
40-ton Bogie Well Wagon
Length $6\frac{3}{4}$ in.
7/6

*No. **4630**
8-ton Cattle Wagon
Length $3\frac{3}{4}$ in.
5/3

*No. **4305**
Passenger Fruit Van (W.R.)
Length $5\frac{5}{16}$ in.
6/8

*No. **4316**
Horse Box (S.R.), with Horse
Length $5\frac{5}{16}$ in.
Also available in (B.R.) Maroon
No. **4315**
9/6

No. **4610**
Bogie Bolster Wagon
Length $6\frac{3}{8}$ in.
8/3

*No. **4635**
Coal Wagon
Length $3\frac{1}{2}$ in.
5/3

* *Items marked with an asterisk have super-detail polystyrene bodywork.*

*No. **4310**
Goods Brake Van (L.M.R.)
Length $4\frac{5}{16}$ in.
5/11

*No. **4320**
6-ton Refrigerator Van (W.R.)
Length $3\frac{1}{2}$ in.
5/3

No. **4615**
Double Bolster Wagon with Timber Load
Length 5 in.
6/8

*No. **4640**
Goods Wagon, steel type
Length $3\frac{1}{2}$ in.
4/4

*No. **4311**
Goods Brake Van (B.R.)
Length $4\frac{5}{16}$ in.
5/11

*No. **4325**
12-ton Ventilated Van
Length $3\frac{1}{2}$ in.
4/8

*No. **4625**
20-ton Bulk Grain Wagon
Length $3\frac{3}{4}$ in.
6/8

No. **4646**
Low-sided Wagon with Cable Drums
Length $3\frac{7}{8}$ in.
5/11

No. **4647**
Low-sided Wagon with Furniture Container Length $3\frac{7}{8}$ in.
5/11
Also No. **4648**
Low-sided Wagon with Insulated Meat Container
5/11

No. **4649**
Low-sided Wagon with Tractor
Length $3\frac{7}{8}$ in.
5/10
Also No. **4645**
Low-sided Wagon
Length $3\frac{7}{8}$ in.
4/4

*No. **4655**
16-ton Mineral Wagon
Length $3\frac{1}{2}$ in.
5/3

*No. **4660**
U.G.B. Sand Wagon
Length $3\frac{1}{2}$ in.
4/8

*No. **4665**
SAXA SALT Wagon
Length $3\frac{1}{2}$ in.
5/6

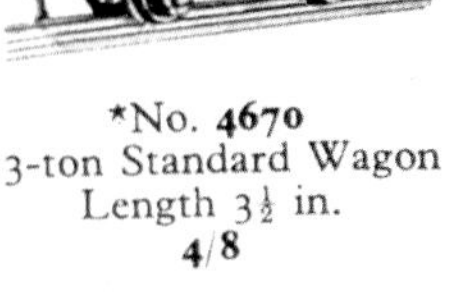

*No. **4670**
13-ton Standard Wagon
Length $3\frac{1}{2}$ in.
4/8

*No. **4675**
I.C.I. Chlorine Tank Wagon
Length $4\frac{1}{4}$ in.
9/-

No. **4676**
ESSO Tank Wagon
Length $3\frac{1}{2}$ in.
5/11

No. **4677**
MOBIL Tank Wagon
Length $3\frac{1}{2}$ in.
5/11

No. **4678**
SHELL Tank Wagon
Length $3\frac{1}{2}$ in.
5/11

*No. **4679**
TRAFFIC SERVICES LTD. Tank Wagon
Length $4\frac{5}{8}$ in.
9/6

No. **4680**
ESSO FUEL OIL Tank Wagon
Length $3\frac{1}{2}$ in.
5/11

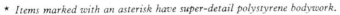

* *Items marked with an asterisk have super-detail polystyrene bodywork.*

*No. **4323**
S.R. 4-Wheeled Utility Van
Length $5\frac{7}{8}$ in.
11/-

*No. **4626**
PRESFLO Bulk Cement Wagon B.R.
Length $3\frac{1}{2}$ in.
6/8

*No. **4627**
I.C.I. 20-ton Bulk Salt Wagon
Length $3\frac{1}{2}$ in.
6/8

*No. **4652**
Machine Wagon LOWMAC
Length $5\frac{1}{2}$ in.
7/-

HORNBY DUBLO

2-RAIL TRACK

Solid drawn nickel silver rails for high conductivity and non-corrosion. Mounted on a moulded base incorporating individual sleepers, providing quiet running, perfect insulation and a remarkable degree of realism.

2701	Straight Rail Length 8⅝ in. ..	1/5
2702	Straight Two-thirds Rail Length 5¾ in.	1/3
2703	Straight One-third Rail Length 2⅞ in.	1/1
2704	Straight Terminal Rail Length 8⅝ in.	3/3
2705	Straight One-third Terminal Rail	2/11
2706	Straight Short Rail Length 1 1/16 in.	1/-
2710	Curved Rail (twelve to circle) Radius 15 in.	1/5
2711	Curved Half Rail, Radius 15 in. ..	1/3
2712	Curved Quarter Rail Radius 15 in.	1/1
2713	Curved Terminal Rail Radius 15 in.	3/3
2719	Curved Rail, Large radius 17¼ in.	1/7
2720	Curved Terminal Rail, Large radius 17¼ in.	3/6
2722	Curved Half Rail, large radius ..	*
2728	Switch Point Right-hand Length 5¾ in. (hand operated)	9/6
2729	Switch Point Left-hand Length 5¾ in. (hand operated)	9/6
2731	Elec.-Operated Point Right-hand	15/9
2732	Elec.-Operated Point Left-hand ..	15/9
2734	Diamond Crossing, Right-hand ..	*
2735	Diamond Crossing, Left-hand ..	*
2738	Straight Isolating Rail Two-thirds, Single, Length 5¾ in.	2/9
2739	Straight Isolating Rail Two-thirds, Double, Length 5¾ in.	1/11
2740	Curved Isolating Half Rail, Double	1/11
2741	Curved Isolating Half Rail, Single	*
2742	Straight Isolating One third Rail, Single	*
2743	Curved Isolating Half Rail, Double Large Radius	*
2745	Uncoupling Rail Length 5¾ in. (hand-operated)	5/6
2746	Elec.-Operated Uncoupling Rail (with Switch) Length 5¾ in. ..	13/11
1614	Switch for Electrically-Operated Points and Signals	4/4
1616	Switch for Isolating Rail, D2 ..	4/-
1620	Switch for Colour Light Signals, G3	4/4

**Prices available later.*

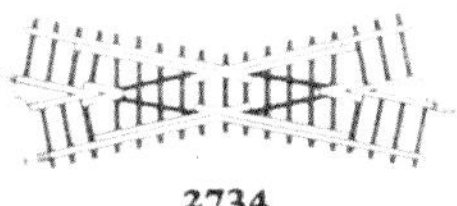
2734

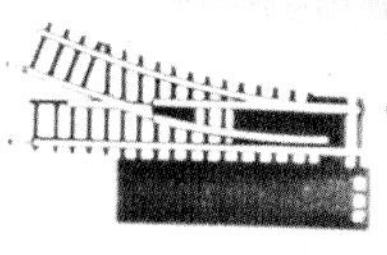
2728

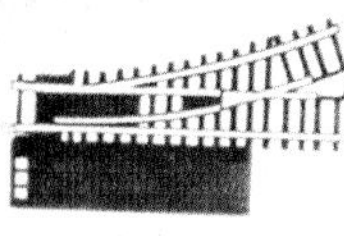
2729

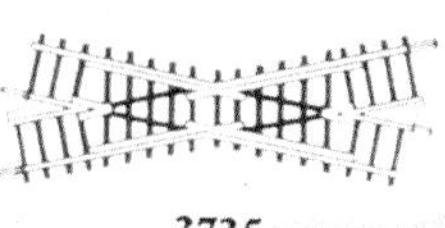
2735

2731

2732

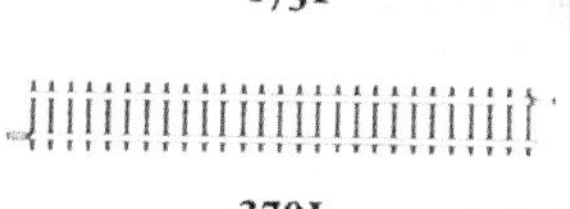
2701

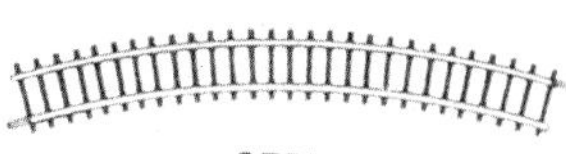
2719

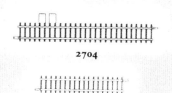

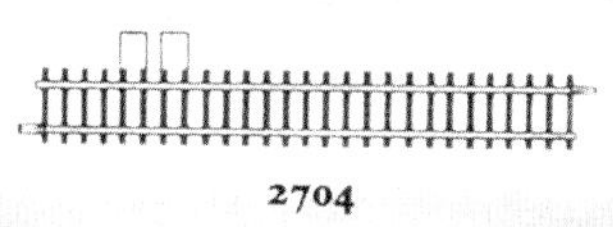
2704

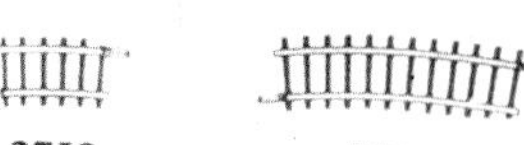
2712 2711

1614

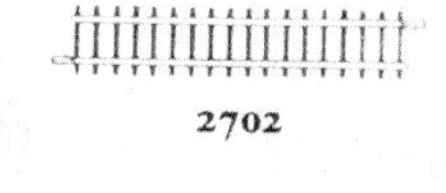
2702

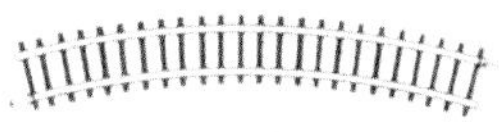
2710

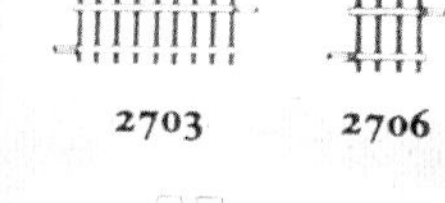
2703 2706

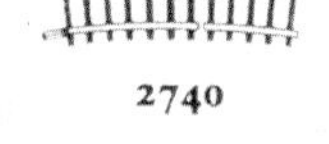
2740

1616

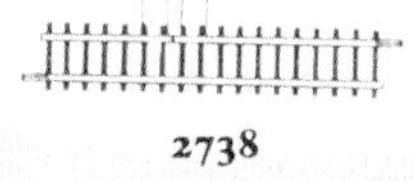
2738

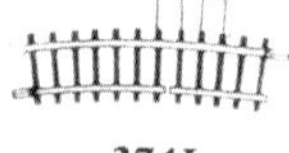
2741

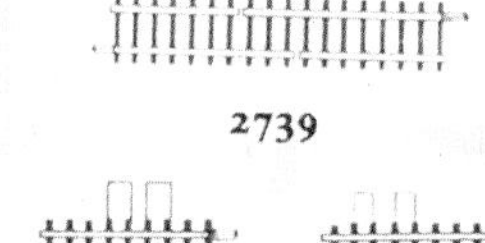
2739

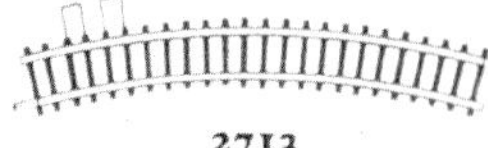
2713

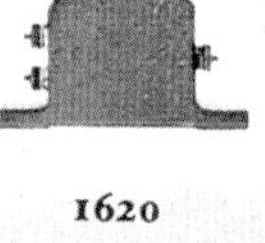
1620

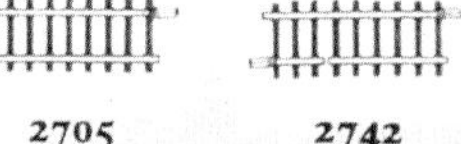
2705 2742

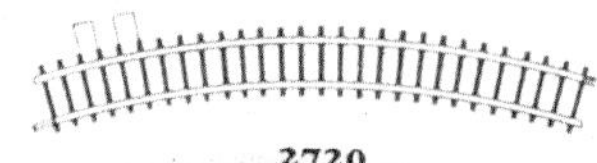
2720

2746

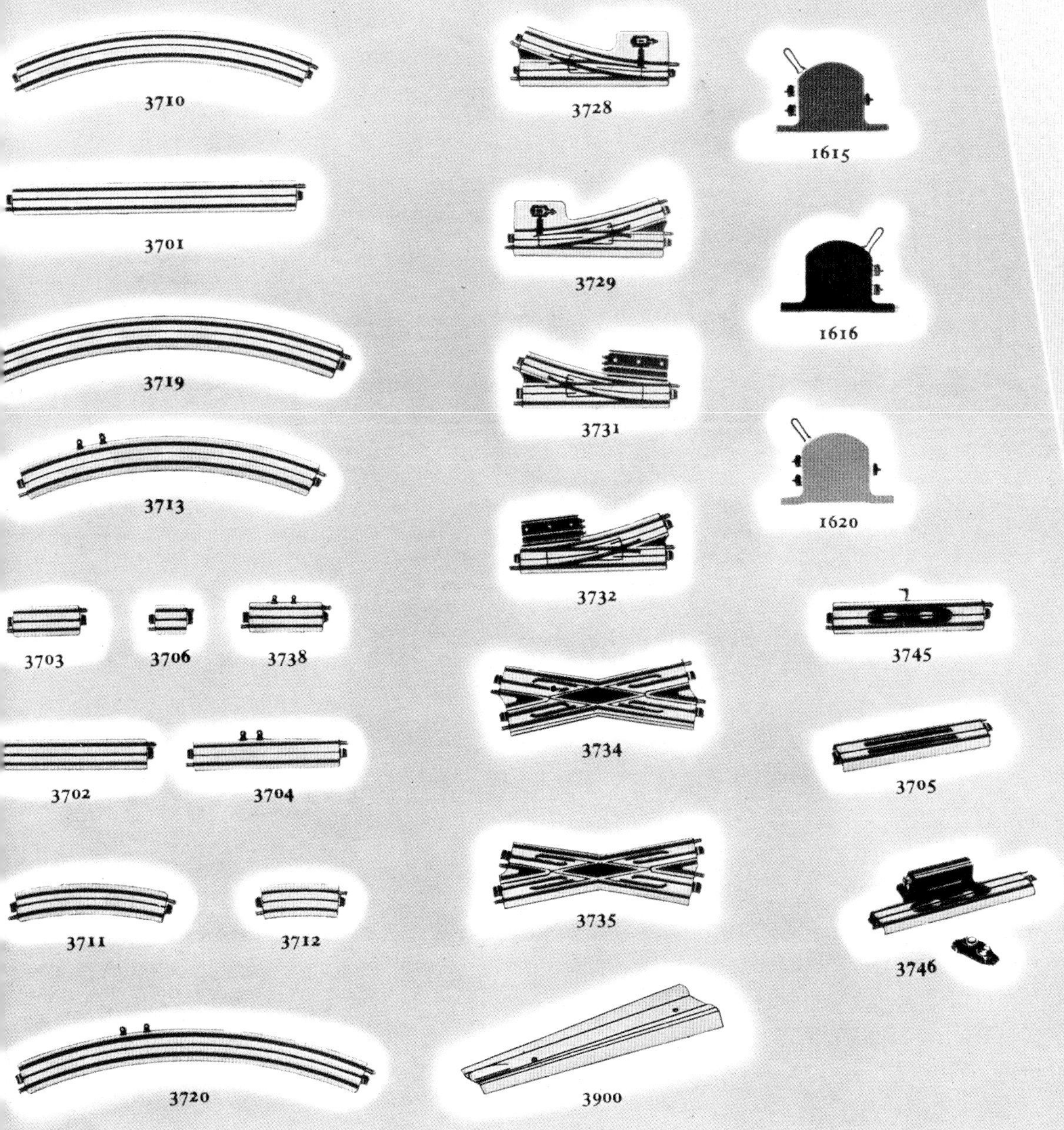

3710

3701

3719

3713

3703 3706 3738

3702 3704

3711 3712

3720

3728

3729

3731

3732

3734

3735

3900

1615

1616

1620

3745

3705

3746

3- RAIL TRACK

Nickel-plated solid brass running rails mounted on one-piece bases of strong metal.

3701	Straight Rail EDB1 Length $11\frac{1}{2}$ in.	**3/3**
3702	Straight Half Rail EDB1$\frac{1}{2}$ Length $5\frac{3}{4}$ in.	**2/5**
3703	Straight Quarter Rail EDB1$\frac{1}{4}$ Length $2\frac{7}{8}$ in.	**2/-**
3704	Straight Terminal Half Rail EDBT1$\frac{1}{2}$ Length $5\frac{3}{4}$ in. ..	**4/-**
3705	Straight Half Rail with Roadway EDBX$\frac{1}{2}$ Length $5\frac{3}{4}$ in. ..	**2/10**
3706	Straight Short Rail EDBS Length $1\frac{5}{16}$ in.	**2/-**
3710	Curved Rail EDA1 15 in. radius ..	**3/3**
3711	Curved Half Rail EDA1$\frac{1}{2}$ ..	**2/5**
3712	Curved Quarter Rail EDA1$\frac{1}{4}$ ..	**2/-**
3713	Curved Terminal Rail EDAT1 ..	**5/3**
3719	Curved Rail, large radius EDA2	**3/6**
3720	Curved Terminal Rail, large radius EDAT2	**5/3**
3728	Isolating Switch Point, right-hand ISPR Length $5\frac{3}{4}$ in.	**11/9**
3729	Isolating Switch Point, left-hand ISPL Length $5\frac{3}{4}$ in.	**11/9**
3731	Elec. Operated Point, right-hand EODPR Length $5\frac{3}{4}$ in. ..	**21/-**
3732	Elec. Operated Point, left-hand EODPL Length $5\frac{3}{4}$ in.	**21/-**
3734	Diamond Crossing, right-hand EDCR Length $5\frac{3}{4}$ in.	**8/6**
3735	Diamond Crossing, left-hand EDCL Length $5\frac{3}{4}$ in.	**8/6**
3738	Isolating Rail IBR$\frac{1}{4}$ Length $2\frac{7}{8}$ in.	**2/11**
3745	Uncoupling Rail UBR Length $5\frac{3}{4}$ in.	**5/6**
3746	Uncoupling Rail, Elec. Op. with Switch, EUBR Length $5\frac{3}{4}$ in. ..	**14/6**
3747	Insulating tabs .. .. **doz.**	**-/7**
3900	Railer Length 12 in.	**2/4**
1615	Switch for Electrically-operated Points and Signals D1	**4/4**
1616	Switch for Isolating Rail D2 ..	**4/-**
1620	Switch for Colour light Signals G3	**4/4**

Hornby - Dublo lineside accessories are getting a new look with these build-it-yourself kits of moulded polystyrene parts. They can be assembled in a few minutes, and dismantled even quicker.

A Castle speeds the "Torbay Express" through a wayside station.

No. **5006** Engine Shed Extension converts two road to four road
12/6

No. **1575** Lighting Kit
3/3

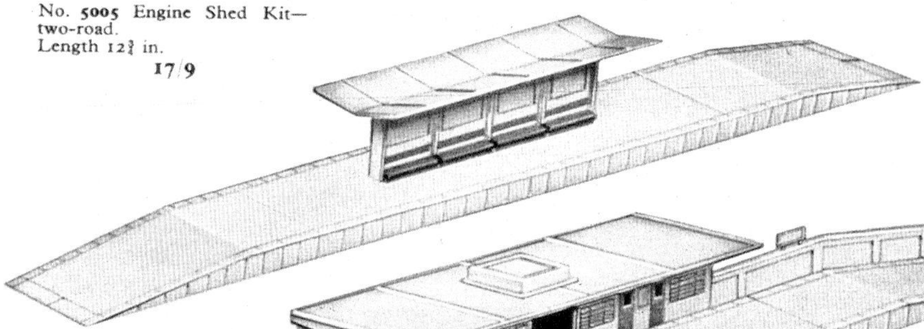

No. **5005** Engine Shed Kit—two-road.
Length 12¾ in.
17/9

No. **5030** Island Platform Kit
Length 23 in.
9/11

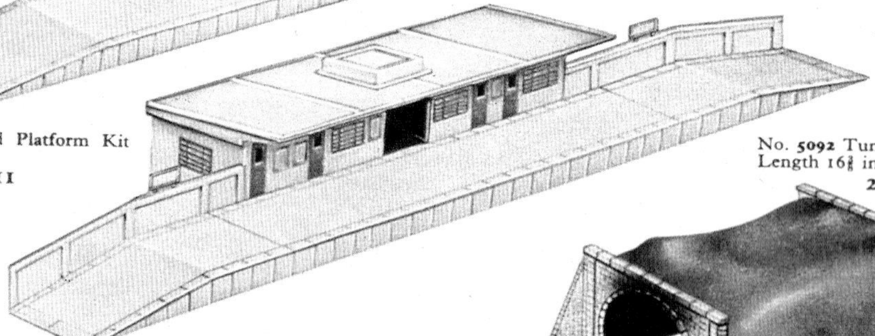

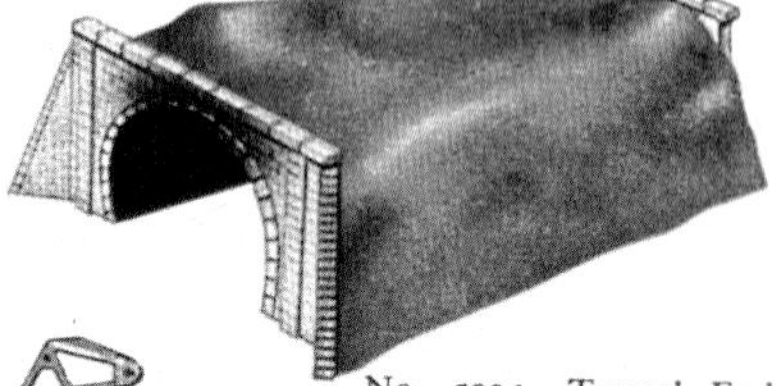

No. **5092** Tunnel—double track
Length 16⅜ in.
23/11

No. **5085** Suburban Station Kit.
Length 23 in.
22/6

No. **5094** Tunnel End only —Double track
2/9

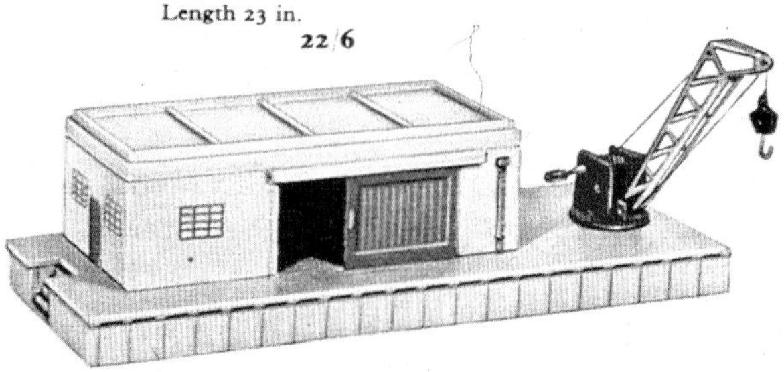

No. **5020** Goods Depot Kit
Length 11½ in.
25/-

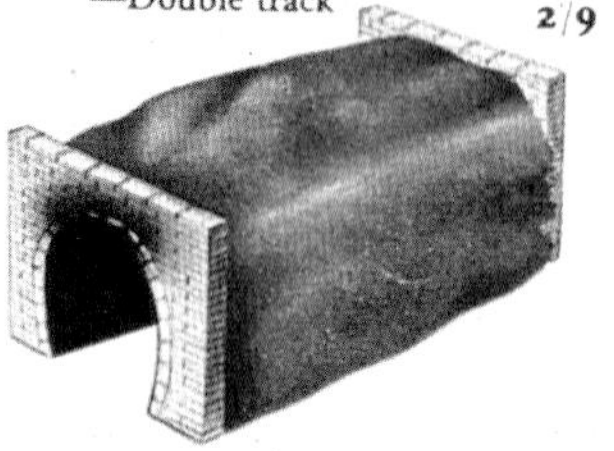

No. **5091** Tunnel—single track.
Length $8\frac{7}{16}$ in.
9/11

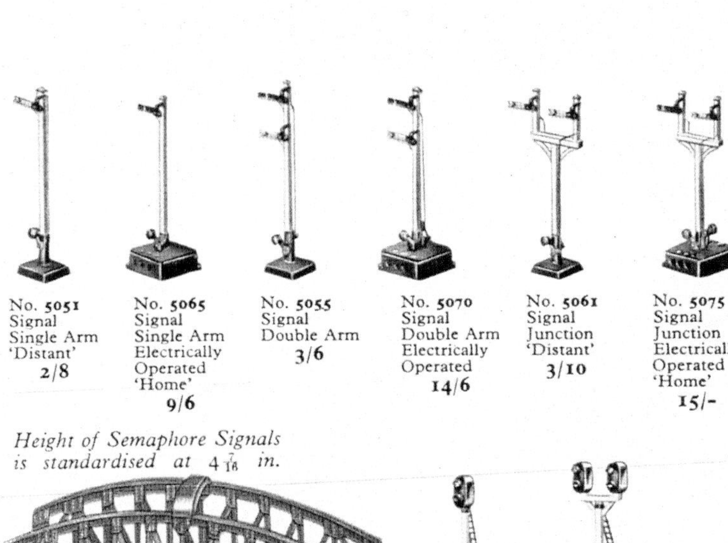

No. **5051**
Signal
Single Arm
'Distant'
2/8

No. **5065**
Signal
Single Arm
Electrically
Operated
'Home'
9/6

No. **5055**
Signal
Double Arm
3/6

No. **5070**
Signal
Double Arm
Electrically
Operated
14/6

No. **5061**
Signal
Junction
'Distant'
3/10

No. **5075**
Signal
Junction
Electrically
Operated
'Home'
15/-

No. **5090**
Telegraph
Pole
Height 3 13/16 in.
Pkt. of 6 **3/6**

Height of Semaphore Signals is standardised at 4 7/16 in.

No. **5015** Girder Bridge
Length 11½ in.
17/6

No. **5045**
Single Head
Colour Light
Signal
'Home'
Height 2¾ in.
10/3

No. **5047**
Junction Colour
Light Signal
'Home'
Height 2⅞ in.
16/11

No. **5035**
Loading
Gauge
Height 3⅜ in.
2/8

No. **5095**
Water Crane
Height 2¾ in.
1/9

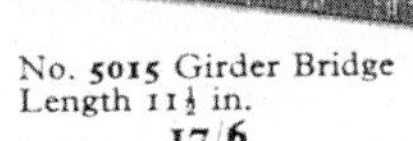

No. **3470** Turntable
For 3-rail systems only
Diameter 14⅜ in.
46/-

No. **3460**
Level Crossing
For 3-rail systems only
Length 6 in.
9/6

No. **5025**
Gradient and
Mile Posts
Height ⅝ in.
Box of 12 **2/11**

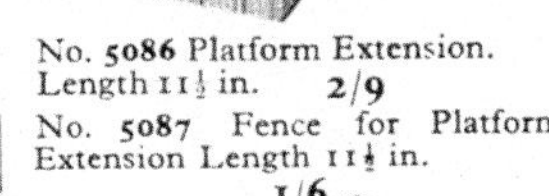

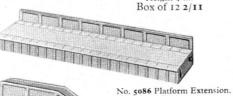

No. **5086** Platform Extension.
Length 11½ in. **2/9**

No. **5087** Fence for Platform
Extension Length 11½ in.
1/6

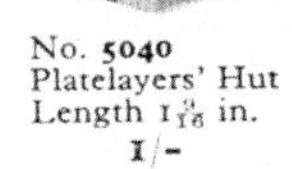

No. **5040**
Platelayers' Hut
Length 1 7/16 in.
1/-

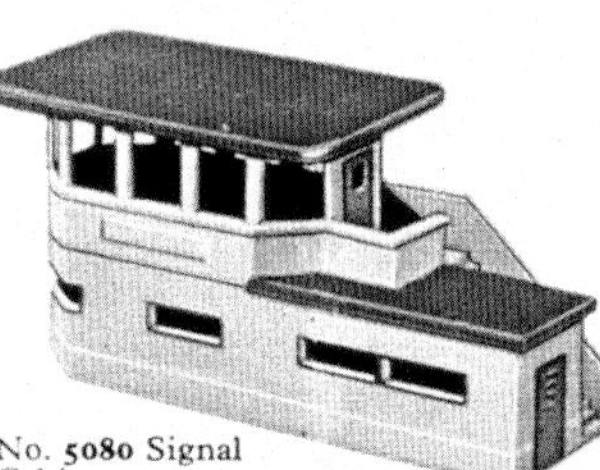

No. **5080** Signal
Cabin
Length 6⅜ in.
15/-

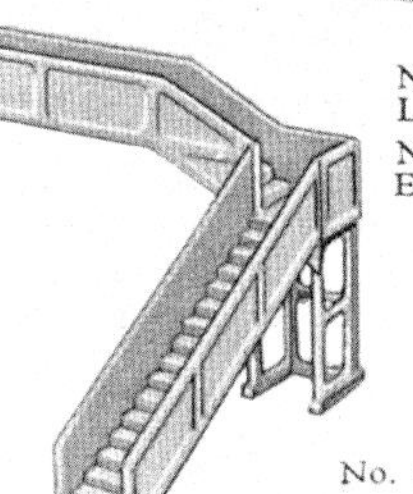

No. **5010**
Footbridge
Length 7⅜ in.
11/-

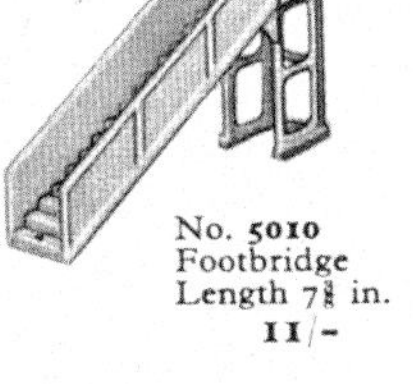

No. **2451** Buffer
Stop— Illuminated
For 2-rail systems
only. Length 2 in.
6/9

No. 2450 Buffer Stop 2/-

HORNBY DUBLO
ACCESSORIES

SUNDRIES

790	Granite Chippings (imitation) per bag	**9d**
791	Coal (imitation) per bag ..	**9d**
1505	Brush for Locomotive 2211, 2218, 2226, 3211, 3212, 3217, 3218 ..	**5d**
1506	Brush Spring for Locomotives 2211, 2218, 2226, 3211, 3212, 3217, 3218	**1d**
1510	Brush Arm Assembly for Locos 2206, 2207, 2220, 2225, 3220 and 3225	**7d**
1511	Brush Arm Assembly for 2230 and 3230 Locomotives	**9d**
1520	Cable Drum	**9d**
1525	Container (Insulated Meat) ..	**1/6**
1526	Container (Furniture)	**1/6**
1530	Connecting Wire, 5-yard length ..	**1/6**
1531	Connecting Wire, reel, 50-yards ..	**13/6**
1560	Lamp 15v, for Colour Light Signals	**2/2**
1561	Lamp 15v, for Colour Light Signals, mark 2T	**2/2**
1575	Lighting Kit	**3/3**
1576	Terminal Panel for 1575	**2/-**
1585	Lubricating Oil	**6d**
1605	Spanner	**2d**
1610	Station Names .. **5 pairs**	**3d**
1614	Switch for Electrically-operated Points and Signals	**4/4**
1615	Switch for Electrically-Operated Signals, Red D1	**4/4**
1616	Switch for Isolating Rail, Black D2	**4/-**
1620	Switch for Colour Light Signals, Green G3	**4/4**
1625	Switch Grouping Rods (long) ..	**2d**
1626	Switch Grouping Rods (short) ..	**2d**
1630	T.P.O. Mail Bag	**2d**
1635	Wheels on Axle, Nylon, Spoked ..	**3d**
1636	Wheels on Axle, Nylon, Disc ..	**3d**
	2-RAIL SYSTEM	
2905	Rail Connection Clip .. **Pkt 12**	**9d**
2910	Rail Securing Plate, with wood-screw .. .. .. **Pkt 12**	**1/2**
2915	Fishplate .. .. .. **Pkt 12**	**1/-**

DUBLO DINKY TOYS

Made to the scale of 'oo' gauge trains

062	Singer Roadster	**1/6**
063	Commer Van	**1/6**
064	Austin Lorry	**1/6**
066	Bedford Flat Truck	**1/9**
067	Austin Taxi	**2/5**
068	Royal Mail Van (with windows) ..	**2/2**
069	Massey-Harris Ferguson Tractor	**1/6**
070	A.E.C. Mercury Tanker Shell-BP (with windows)	**2/6**
071	Volkswagon Delivery Van ..	**2/-**
072	Bedford Articulated Flat Truck (with windows)	**2/6**
073	Land Rover & Horse Trailer (with horse)	*
076	Lansing Bagnall Tractor and Trailer	**2/9**

* *available later*

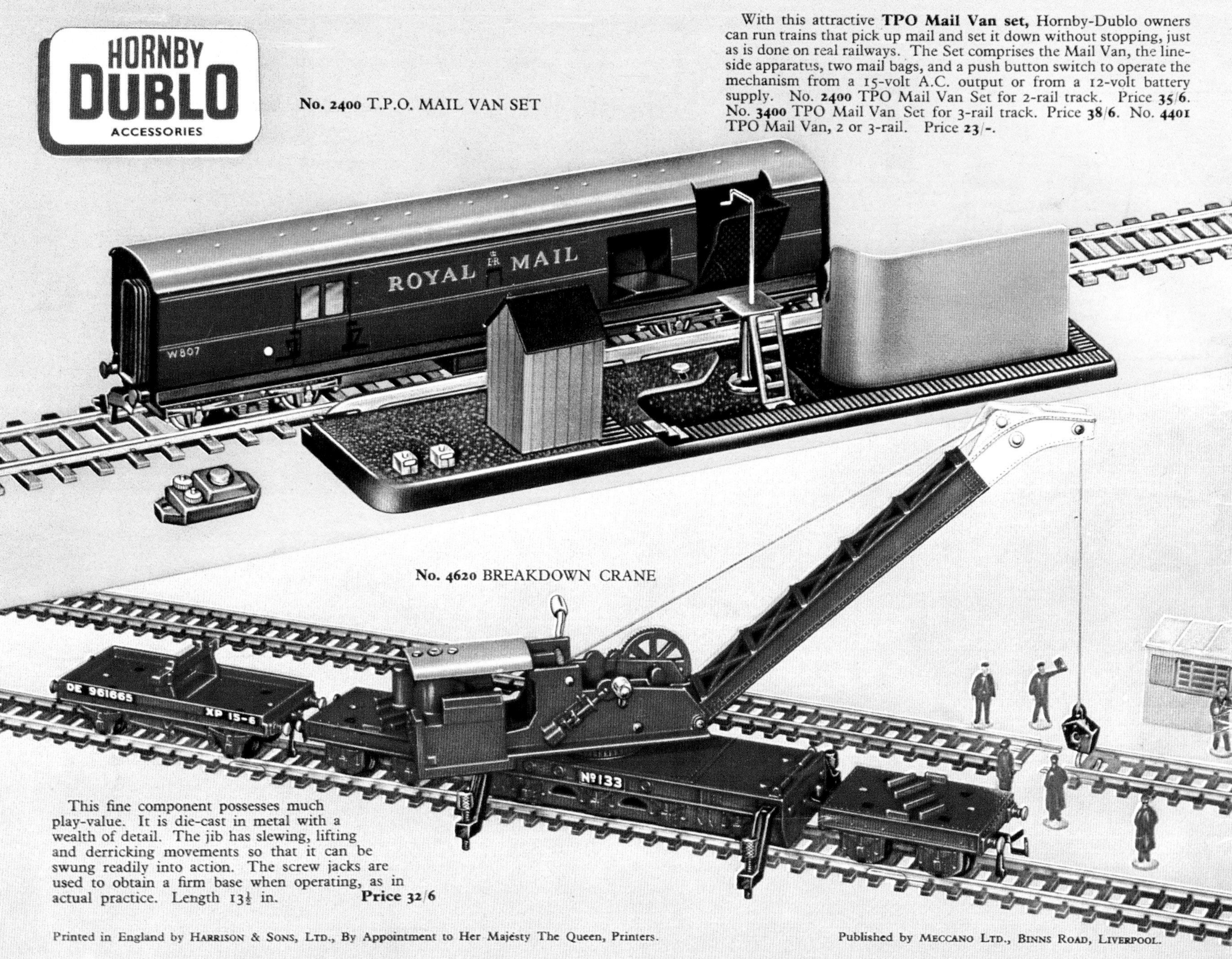

With this attractive **TPO Mail Van set,** Hornby-Dublo owners can run trains that pick up mail and set it down without stopping, just as is done on real railways. The Set comprises the Mail Van, the line-side apparatus, two mail bags, and a push button switch to operate the mechanism from a 15-volt A.C. output or from a 12-volt battery supply. No. **2400** TPO Mail Van Set for 2-rail track. Price **35/6**. No. **3400** TPO Mail Van Set for 3-rail track. Price **38/6**. No. **4401** TPO Mail Van, 2 or 3-rail. Price **23/-**.

No. 2400 T.P.O. MAIL VAN SET

No. 4620 BREAKDOWN CRANE

This fine component possesses much play-value. It is die-cast in metal with a wealth of detail. The jib has slewing, lifting and derricking movements so that it can be swung readily into action. The screw jacks are used to obtain a firm base when operating, as in actual practice. Length 13½ in. **Price 32/6**

Printed in England by Harrison & Sons, Ltd., By Appointment to Her Majesty The Queen, Printers.

Published by Meccano Ltd., Binns Road, Liverpool.

AN AMALGAMATION OF

AND HORNBY DUBLO

MAY 1965

Tri-ang RAILWAYS & HORNBY DUBLO

Following the incorporation of Meccano Limited, the manufacturers of Hornby Dublo trains, into the Lines Bros. Group (Tri-ang), a careful analysis was undertaken to study the advantages and disadvantages of maintaining production of two entirely separate Model Railway Systems. The evidence showed clearly that there was excessive duplication of products in all fields and that since both systems operated on the 2-rail 12 volt D.C. standard, there were no fundamental obstacles to amalgamation.

The two railways will, therefore, be progressively brought together under the name TRI-ANG HORNBY and will use Tri-ang Super 4 Track and Tri-ang Couplings.

Existing owners of Hornby Dublo will continue to be able to purchase Hornby Dublo components while stocks last and can then go on to Tri-ang Hornby track by means of the special converter rail. A converter wagon with mixed couplings is also now available, so that no Hornby Dublo system will become obsolete. It must be recognised, however, that running trains with mixed couplings does not permit full remote uncoupling operations.

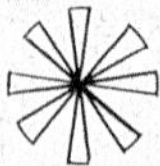

The cover picture 'Night Scene at Crewe' was specially painted for Tri-ang Hornby by Terence Cuneo

TRACK

Tri-ang Railways Super 4 Track and Hornby Dublo 2-rail Track are both ga OO/HO (16.5 mms.). There is a difference in the rail sections and fishplates that it is necessary to use special Converter Tracks when using the two syste together.

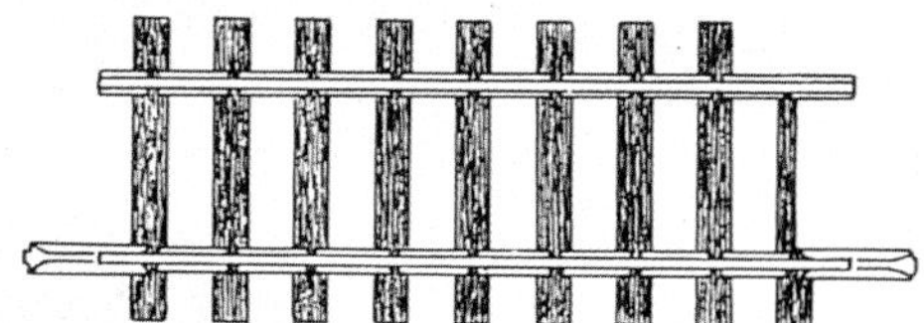

R.476 Tri-ang Hornby Converter Track. $2\frac{7}{8}''$ (7.2 cms.) long. U.K. Retail Price *1/-*.

How a Converter Track connects Tri-ang Railways Super 4 with Hornby Dublo Track.

Hornby Dublo 2-rail Locomotives and Rolling Stock will operate satisfactorily on Tri-ang Railways Super 4 Track and most modern Tri-ang Railways Locomotives and Rolling Stock will operate on Hornby Dublo 2-rail Track.

It is not possible to fit Tri-ang Railways Uncoup Ramps to Hornby Dublo Track, but if these exist o Tri-ang Railways layout they do not interfere with Hor Dublo couplings.

R.577 Tri-ang Hornby Converter Wagon. U.K. Retail Price *2/6*.

COUPLINGS

Tri-ang Railways Tension-Lock Couplings operate vertically wh Hornby Dublo Couplings operate horizontally. It is not, therefo possible for the two types to connect together directly. The Conver Wagon is now introduced to enable users of either system to opera mixed Freight Trains.

This Wagon is now supplied, automatically, with the five ex-Horn Dublo Locomotives listed under the name Tri-ang Hornby (see ov leaf).

A Passenger Converter Vehicle will be introduced when Hornby Dul Passenger Coaches cease to be available.

Tri-ang HORNBY

R.2235 4-6-2 West Country Class Locomotive 'Barnstaple' and Tender. U.K. Retail Price *£5.15.0.*

R.2233 Co-Bo Diesel-Electric Locomotive. U.K. Retail Price *£4.6.0.*

ach of these ex-Hornby Dublo Locomotives is now supplied complete with a Tri-ang Hornby Converter Wagon at) extra cost so that it can be used with Tri-ang Railways or ornby Dublo Rolling Stock.

ornby Dublo Locomotives have long been noted for their urdy construction and their 12 Volt D.C. electric motors e built to last a lifetime.

he station buildings below may be used equally well with ri-ang Railways and Hornby Dublo and the illustration verleaf shows what an exciting layout can now be created y the bringing together of these two marvellous Model ailways.

R.2217 0-6-2 Tank Locomotive. U.K. Retail Price *56/9.*

R.2207 0-6-0 Tank Locomotive. U.K. Retail Price *38/-.*

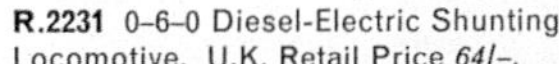

R.2231 0-6-0 Diesel-Electric Shunting Locomotive. U.K. Retail Price *64/-.*

.5083 Terminus and Through Station omposite Kit. U.K. Retail Price *59/11.*

.5084 Terminus Canopy xtension Kit ot illustrated). .K. Retail Price *22/-.*

Kit **R.5083** shown made up as a Terminus.

R.5005

R.5010

R.5020

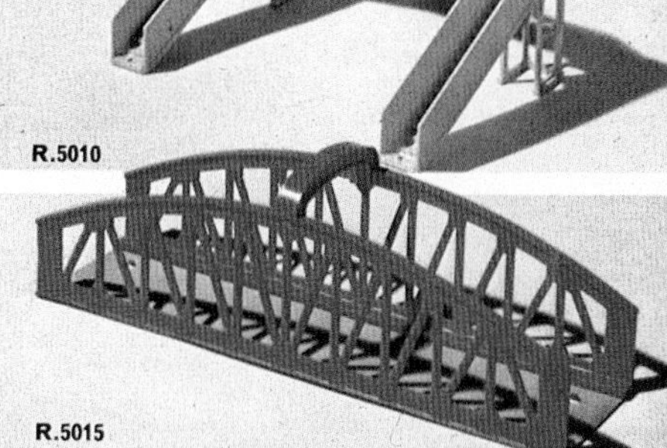

R.5015

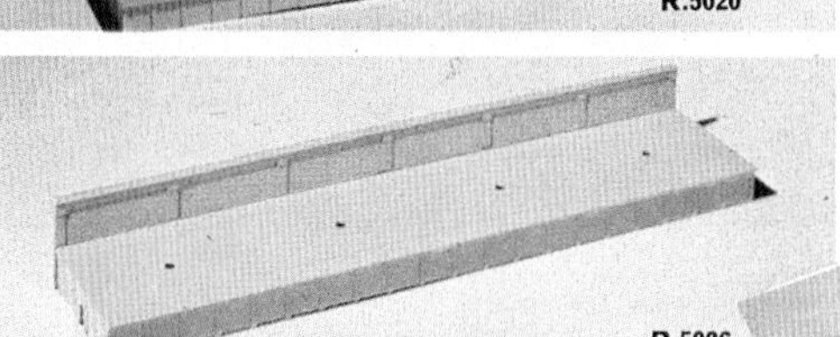

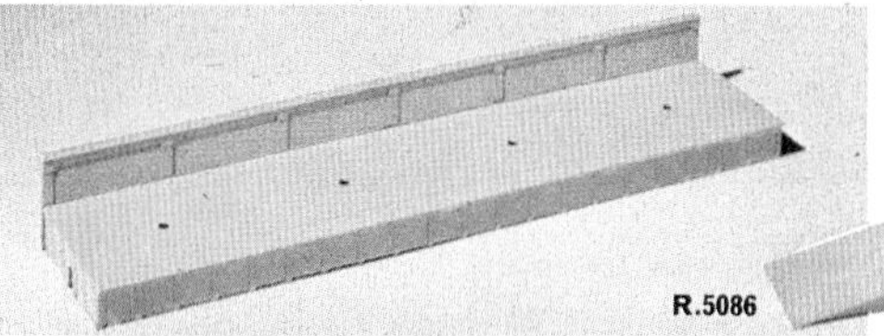

R.5086

R.5030

R.5092

R.5005 Two-road Engine Shed Kit. U.K. Retail Price *19/6.* **R.5006** (not illustrated). Engine Shed Extension Kit. Converts two-road shed into four-road. U.K. Retail Price *14/3.* **R.5010** Footbridge. U.K. Retail Price *12/6.* **R.5020** Goods Depot Kit with Working Crane. U.K. Retail Price *29/-.* **R.5015** Girder Bridge. U.K. Retail Price *11/9.* **R.5086** Platform Extension. U.K. Retail Price *2/11.* **R.5087** Platform Fence (illustrated fitted to **R.5086**). U.K. Retail Price *1/7.* **R.5089** Side Platform Extension (not illustrated). U.K. Retail Price *2/6.* **R.5030** Island Platform Kit. U.K. Retail Price *11/3* **R.5092** Double Track Tunnel. U.K. Retail Price *25/6.*

Here is how Tri-ang Railways and Hornby Dublo, now Tri-ang Hornby, can be used together to build a Model Railway unequalled by any other in the World. The electrical aspect is the ultra simple Tri-ang Railways system and the use of Hornby Dublo Locomotives, Rolling Stock and Stations provides a variety of style and architecture never before seen.

The activities of the Hornby Railway Company in helping users to get the best value from their trains, will be superseded by the Model Railway Operators section of Tri-ang Club. The Club issues a Bulletin at regular intervals and details of membership are published in the monthly Tri-ang Magazine.

SERVICING

ornby Dublo models requiring Servicing should be sent Meccano Limited, Binns oad, Liverpool 13. Tri-ang ornby models requiring ervicing should be sent to ovex Scale Models Ltd., Vestwood, Margate, Kent.

No. 2250 Electric Motor Coach with powered bogie. U.K. Retail Price *64/–*.

No. 4150 Electric Driving Trailer Coach (non-powered). U.K. Retail Price *10/6*.

No. 2245 E.3002 Electric Locomotive with Pantograph. U.K. Retail Price *75/–*.

These and many other Hornby Dublo Models which cannot be converted to Tri-ang Railways Couplings can, nevertheless, still operate on a Tri-ang Hornby layout. Consult your Dealer for details of availability of Hornby Dublo.

NEW MODELS

R.567 Radar Van with revolving scanner. U.K. Retail Price *15/6.*

R.566 Satellite Launching Car. U.K. Retail Price *16/6.*

THE SATELLITE R.397 All action Train with the excitement of computer radar control centre and flying satellite. The radar scanner on control car rotates as train moves into firing area and satellite is automatically launched. (Track not included). U.K. Retail Price **63/–.**

STRIKE FORCE 10 R.398 Train equipped for air and ground warfare with catapulting plane — flies up to 20 ft. — transporter with twin missile firing tank and smoke puffing Locomotive. (Track not included). U.K. Retail Price **79/6.**

R.568 Tank Transporter with twin missile firing tank. U.K. Retail Price *19/6.*

R.562 Plane Launching Car. U.K. Retail Price *18/6.*

MADE IN ENGLAND BY
ROVEX SCALE MODELS LIMITED
WESTWOOD MARGATE KENT

R.280S 1965 Printed in England

Index

Index of Original Source Material

Volume 4 - Dinky Toys and Modelled Miniatures

Volume 5 - The Hornby Gauge 0 System

Volume 6 - The Meccano System

Volume 7 - The Meccano Magazine 1916–1981

Contains every published cover of the Meccano Magazine

Volume 7a - The Meccano Magazine Anthology

Contains the full editorial text of the 1936 Meccano Magazine January to December in addition to selected articles from 1923–35 and 1937–63

On page 5, I acknowledged in particular the help received from Jim Gamble. Apart from the giving of his advice, knowledge and encouragement, he has also selflessly allowed me access to his unrivalled collection of Meccano Literature. Much of the rarest material especially from Chapter 9 comes from Jim and I am deeply indebted to him.

The following is a list of the illustrations his collection has provided. With a few exceptions, in particular the 1927/28 and 1933/4 Hornby Books of Trains and the Dinky and Hornby Dublo material, the remainder is from the author's own library.

ILLUSTRATIONS FROM THE JIM GAMBLE COLLECTION

Chapter 2. Figs. 5–29, 33, 39–53
Chapter 3. Figs. 1–18, 27–29, 37–46, 49–50
Chapter 4. Figs. 1, 9, 10
Chapter 5. Figs. 1–4
Chapter 6. Figs. 50
Chapter 7. Figs. 14–21, 31–35, 37–43, 60–72, plus various catalogue covers included on pages 284–288
Chapter 8. Figs. 1–9, 17
Chapter 9. Figs. 1–10 plus The 1925/6 Hornby Book of Trains.